STATE PROFILES

THE POPULATION AND ECONOMY OF EACH U.S. STATE

**Seventh Edition
2015**

Edited by Hannah M. Anderson

Bernan Press

Lanham, Maryland

Published in the United States of America
by Bernan Press, a wholly owned subsidiary of
The Rowman & Littlefield Publishing Group, Inc.
4501 Forbes Boulevard, Suite 200
Lanham, Maryland 20706

Bernan Press
800-865-3457
www.bernan.com

ISBN 13: 978-1-59888-801-0
E-ISBN: 978-1-59888-802-7

∞™ The paper used in this publication meets the minimum requirements of
American National Standard for Information Sciences—Permanence of
Paper for Printed Library Materials, ANSI/NISO Z39.48-1992.
Manufactured in the United States of America.

CONTENTS

LIST OF TABLES

The following tables are included for cach state and the District of Columbia:

PREFACE

Bernan Press is pleased to present the seventh edition of *State Profiles*, a publication that provides a state-by-state view of the United States. Topics covered include population composition by age, sex, race, and ethnicity; marital status; migration, origin, and language; households and housing; income and poverty; health insurance; employment; educational indicators; voting; crime; and other important aspects of the economy.

The publication's primary focus is on the 50 states and the District of Columbia, each of which possesses considerable differences in economic structure and demographics and has experienced various changes over time. Changes at the national level, including the diminished importance of agriculture and manufacturing and the growing influence of global trade, have resulted in today's information-based, service-providing economy. While national trends have laid the broad framework for change, each state has been affected differently. Cyclical fluctuations have also affected states in various ways during the nationwide recessions and the subsequent recovery periods. Recessions and recoveries spread unevenly among regions and states. Migration patterns have also reflected these changes, as states have experienced different influxes of workers from within the country and new residents from abroad.

Beyond the market forces, economic circumstances have been influenced by local and national government policies and expenditures on items such as education, health care, energy production and conservation, national defense, and homeland security.

The information provided in *State Profiles* aims to illuminate these trends. As such, the analysis and statistics are of interest not only to researchers and policy analysts but also to businesses seeking a broad basis for investments and expansion or relocation plans. The volume also profiles recent voting patterns, which will be of interest to political scientists.

DATA SELECTION

This edition of *State Profiles* generally continues the broad selection of information from previous editions. Most, but not all, of the data items have been updated through 2012, 2013, and even 2014, as demographic estimates from the U.S. Census Bureau became available.

As in the past, space constraints have influenced the amount of data presented for each state. The most meaningful and relevant data have thus been selected, analyzed, and highlighted. This edition expands upon the available information to include more detailed data on the demographics of each state, especially in regard to diversity of spoken languages and the foreign-born population. For most of the subjects addressed in this edition, further data are generally available from the source government agencies. Locations of sources information are listed in notes and definitions at the end of the volume.

Although the editor has taken care to present accurate data, all statistical data are subject to a degree of error, resulting from sampling variability, erroneous reporting, and other causes. Many of the data are subject to subsequent revision.

The data in this book meet the publication standards of the federal agencies from which they were obtained. The responsibilities of the editor and publisher of this volume are limited to reasonable care in the reproduction and presentation of the data from the established sources.

Hannah M. Anderson, editor of this edition of *State Profiles*, has worked as an assistant editor for Bernan Press since 2015. She previously worked as an editor and writer for several lifestyle and family magazines and for a weekly alternative newspaper. She studied magazine journalism at the University of Maryland.

USING THIS BOOK: ORGANIZATION AND CONTENTS

STATE PROFILES 2015 PROVIDES:

- Rankings of states for key demographic and economic indicators
- A chapter for each state, complete with tables and figures that summarize and illustrate common demographic and economic characteristics
- Notes and definitions to assist with interpreting the information contained in this volume

THE U.S. OVERVIEW. This short introduction to the demographics of the United States provides commentary on overall trends within the country.

THE STATE RANKINGS. The ranking tables that follow the national overview give state rankings by more than 30 characteristics, including population, demographic and age composition, income, per capita gross domestic product, homeownership, poverty, health indicators, education, and federal aid. These rankings provide the user with a quick analysis of the performance of each state in relation to the other states.

THE STATE CHAPTERS. The state chapters are the focus of this book. Each chapter follows a standard format and contains text highlighting the key features shown in the tables and figures. Some of these tables and figures contain references to the U.S. averages for the same characteristics.

Each of the state chapters is organized as follows:

Population: This table provides data on the state's total population and average annual population growth in comparison with the national average. It also shows the major population groups by sex, age, race, and ethnicity.

Marital status: The table shows the marital status for all men and women age 15 years and over.

Origin, migration, and language: This table provides statistics on residence one year ago, year of entry, place of origin, language spoken at home, and the native-born and foreign-born populations.

Housing: This table showcases data pertaining to housing, such as number of households, types of households, housing characteristics, and median gross rent, mortgage, and monthly owner cost amounts.

Income and poverty: Median household and family income and poverty rates by sex and age are contained in this table.

Health insurance coverage: This table provides information on health insurance, by type and coverage.

Employment: These tables illustrate each state's particular economic configuration. Employment status by detailed demographic group, labor force, participation rates, employment, unemployment, average wages and salaries by industry, and employment by family type.

Education: This section provides the user with details on educational attainment, elementary and secondary school enrollment, student/teacher ratios, per student expenditures, and higher education enrollments.

Voter participation: Information is given on voter registration and voter participation in the 2012 presidential election, categorized by sex and race and ethnicity.

Crime: This table include the number and rates of violent and property crime.

Government finance: These tables provide data on revenues and expenditures by source. In addition, tax information is included.

NOTES AND DEFINITIONS. Each chapter relies on the same standard set of federal data sources. Since the basic data sources are common to all chapters, the main body of the volume contains few footnotes. Basic data and corresponding definitions and sources are identified in the notes and definition section at the end of the volume. It provides brief descriptions, methodologies, data availability, information on calculations made by the editors, and references to additional sources of information.

UNITED STATES

Introduction

During the early 2000s, the United States experienced several economic fluctuations that greatly impacted the strength, size, and performance of its economy. The recession that began in March 2001 was concluded in a few months; however, the longer-lasting recession that began in December 2007 has had a more serious impact on the country. This edition of *State Profiles: The Population and Economy of Each U.S. State* creates a snapshot of the people and economy in each state and the District of Columbia. Each chapter (one per state/district) includes information on topics such as population, health, marital status, crime, government finance, housing, education, and language.

Summary

The U.S. population grew 3.3 percent between 2010 and 2014. North Dakota experienced the largest population growth in the nation at 9.9 percent. The states and areas with the largest population growth included the District of Columbia (9.5 percent), Texas (7.2 percent), Utah (6.5 percent), Colorado (6.5 percent), Florida (5.8 percent), Arizona (5.3 percent), Nevada (5.1 percent), Washington (5.0 percent), South Dakota (4.8 percent), South Carolina (4.5 percent), Hawaii (4.4 percent), and North Carolina (4.3 percent). States that grew in population by 0.5 percent or less included Ohio, Illinois, Michigan, Rhode Island, Vermont, and Maine. The population of West Virginia fell by 0.1 percent.

Vermont had the highest percentage of White alone residents in 2014, at 95.7 percent, followed by Maine at 95.6 percent. Hawaii had the lowest number of White alone residents, at 25.7 percent. The District of Columbia had the highest percentage of Black or African American alone residents at 51.6 percent, followed by Mississippi at 37.2 percent. At 0.4 percent, Montana had the lowest percentage of Black or African American alone residents.

Hispanic and Latino residents may be of any race, and New Mexico (46.3 percent) and West Virginia (1.2 percent) had the highest and lowest resident percentages, respectively.

In 2013, the median household income in the United States was $52,250. Maryland had the highest median household income at $72,483, followed by Alaska ($72,237), New Jersey ($70,165), Hawaii ($68,020), and the District of Columbia ($67,572). The states with the lowest median household incomes were Mississippi ($37,963), Arkansas ($40,511), West Virginia ($41,253), Alabama ($42,849), and Kentucky ($43,399). Some correlation to the percentage of residents with a bachelor's degree or more can be inferred, as Maryland and the District of Columbia rank in the top 5 states in this category. Mississippi, Arkansas, and West Virginia rank as the bottom 3 states in this category, with Alabama ranking 45th and Kentucky ranking 46th. The unemployment rate for the United States was 6.2 percent in 2014, which is down from 7.4 percent in 2013. The District of Columbia, Mississippi, and Nevada (7.8 percent each) had the highest percentage of unemployed residents in 2014, and North Dakota (2.8 percent) had the lowest percentage of unemployed residents.

In the United States in 2013, 15.8 percent of the population lived below the poverty level. Mississippi, which had the lowest median household income, also had the highest poverty rate, with 24.0 percent of its residents below the poverty level. New Hampshire had the lowest poverty rate, at 8.7 percent. Mississippi had the highest rate of persons under 18 years of age below the poverty level (34.0 percent), followed by New Mexico (31.2 percent), Arkansas (29.0 percent), Louisiana (27.7 percent), and South Carolina (27.5 percent). The states with the fewest residents under 18 years of age below the poverty level included New Hampshire (10.2 percent), North Dakota (12.0 percent), Alaska (12.1 percent), Wyoming (13.2 percent), and Hawaii (13.3 percent).

UNITED STATES RANKINGS

Population, 2014		
Rank	State	Population
	United States......................	318,857,056
1	California.............................	38,802,500
2	Texas.................................	26,956,958
3	Florida................................	19,893,297
4	New York.............................	19,746,227
5	Illinois................................	12,880,580
6	Pennsylvania........................	12,787,209
7	Ohio...................................	11,594,163
8	Georgia...............................	10,097,343
9	North Carolina......................	9,943,964
10	Michigan..............................	9,909,877
11	New Jersey	8,938,175
12	Virginia	8,326,289
13	Washington...........................	7,061,530
14	Massachusetts	6,745,408
15	Arizona................................	6,731,484
16	Indiana................................	6,596,855
17	Tennessee	6,549,352
18	Missouri...............................	6,063,589
19	Maryland..............................	5,976,407
20	Wisconsin	5,757,564
21	Minnesota	5,457,173
22	Colorado	5,355,866
23	Alabama...............................	4,849,377
24	South Carolina	4,832,482
25	Louisiana	4,649,676
26	Kentucky	4,413,457
27	Oregon.................................	3,970,239
28	Oklahoma.............................	3,878,051
29	Connecticut	3,596,677
30	Iowa....................................	3,107,126
31	Mississippi	2,994,079
32	Arkansas..............................	2,966,369
33	Utah....................................	2,942,902
34	Kansas	2,904,021
35	Nevada	2,839,099
36	New Mexico	2,085,572
37	Nebraska..............................	1,881,503
38	West Virginia.........................	1,850,326
39	Idaho...................................	1,634,464
40	Hawaii	1,419,561
41	Maine	1,330,089
42	New Hampshire......................	1,326,813
43	Rhode Island.........................	1,055,173
44	Montana...............................	1,023,579
45	Delaware..............................	935,614
46	South Dakota	853,175
47	North Dakota.........................	739,482
48	Alaska	736,732
49	District of Columbia	658,893
50	Vermont...............................	626,562
51	Wyoming	584,153

Population, Percent Change, 2010–2014		
Rank	State	Percent
	United States......................	3.3
1	North Dakota.........................	9.9
2	District of Columbia	9.5
3	Texas..................................	7.2
4	Colorado	6.5
4	Utah	6.5
6	Florida.................................	5.8
7	Arizona................................	5.3
8	Nevada	5.1
9	Washington...........................	5.0
10	South Dakota	4.8
11	South Carolina	4.5
12	Hawaii	4.4
13	Idaho...................................	4.3
13	North Carolina.......................	4.3
15	California..............................	4.2
15	Delaware..............................	4.2
15	Georgia................................	4.2
18	Virginia	4.1
19	Alaska	3.7
20	Oregon.................................	3.6
20	Wyoming	3.6
22	Maryland..............................	3.5
22	Montana...............................	3.5
24	Oklahoma.............................	3.4
25	Tennessee	3.2
26	Massachusetts	3.0
26	Nebraska..............................	3.0
28	Minnesota	2.9
29	Louisiana	2.6
30	Iowa....................................	2.0
31	New York..............................	1.9
32	Kansas	1.8
33	Arkansas..............................	1.7
33	Indiana................................	1.7
33	Kentucky	1.7
33	New Jersey	1.7
37	Alabama...............................	1.4
38	New Mexico	1.3
39	Missouri...............................	1.2
39	Wisconsin	1.2
41	Mississippi	0.9
42	New Hampshire......................	0.8
43	Pennsylvania........................	0.7
44	Connecticut	0.6
45	Ohio....................................	0.5
46	Illinois.................................	0.4
47	Michigan..............................	0.3
48	Rhode Island.........................	0.2
49	Maine	0.1
49	Vermont...............................	0.1
51	West Virginia.........................	-0.1

Population Under 18 Years Old, 2014		
Rank	State	Percent
	United States......................	23.1
1	Utah	30.7
2	Texas..................................	26.4
2	Idaho...................................	26.4
4	Alaska	25.3
5	Kansas	24.9
6	Nebraska..............................	24.8
7	Georgia................................	24.7
7	South Dakota	24.7
9	Oklahoma.............................	24.6
10	Mississippi	24.4
11	Arizona................................	24.1
11	New Mexico	24.1
13	Indiana................................	24.0
14	Louisiana	23.9
15	Arkansas..............................	23.8
16	Wyoming	23.7
17	California..............................	23.6
18	Minnesota	23.5
19	Iowa....................................	23.4
19	Nevada	23.4
21	Colorado	23.3
22	Illinois.................................	23.2
23	North Carolina.......................	23.0
23	Missouri...............................	23.0
25	Kentucky	22.9
26	Alabama...............................	22.8
26	Tennessee	22.8
26	North Dakota.........................	22.8
26	Ohio....................................	22.8
30	Washington...........................	22.7
31	Maryland..............................	22.6
31	Wisconsin	22.6
33	New Jersey	22.5
34	Virginia	22.4
34	South Carolina	22.4
34	Michigan..............................	22.4
37	Montana...............................	22.0
38	Delaware..............................	21.8
39	Hawaii	21.7
40	Oregon.................................	21.6
40	Connecticut	21.6
42	New York..............................	21.4
43	Pennsylvania........................	21.1
44	Massachusetts	20.6
45	West Virginia.........................	20.5
46	Florida.................................	20.4
47	Rhode Island.........................	20.2
48	New Hampshire......................	20.1
49	Maine	19.5
50	Vermont...............................	19.4
51	District of Columbia	17.5

	Population 65 Years and Over, 2014				Percent White Alone, 2014				Percent Black or African American Alone, 2014		
Rank	State	Percent		Rank	State	Percent		Rank	State	Percent
	United States......................	14.5			United States......................	78.4			United States......................	13.0
1	Florida..............................	19.1		1	Vermont............................	95.7		1	District of Columbia	51.6
2	Maine...............................	18.3		2	Maine...............................	95.6		2	Mississippi........................	37.2
3	West Virginia.....................	17.8		3	New Hampshire..................	94.8		3	Louisiana	32.3
4	Vermont............................	16.9		4	West Virginia.....................	94.3		4	Georgia	30.9
5	Montana............................	16.7		5	Idaho................................	94.2		5	Maryland...........................	30.0
5	Pennsylvania	16.7		6	Wyoming	93.9		6	South Carolina	28.2
7	Delaware	16.4		7	Iowa.................................	93.2		7	Alabama	26.3
8	Hawaii	16.1		8	Utah	92.2		8	North Carolina...................	21.9
9	Oregon	16.0		9	North Dakota	90.6		8	Delaware	21.9
10	New Hampshire..................	15.9		10	Nebraska...........................	90.3		10	Virginia.............................	19.7
10	Arizona.............................	15.9		11	Montana............................	90.1		11	New York...........................	17.4
12	Iowa.................................	15.8		12	Kentucky	89.0		12	Tennessee	16.8
12	South Carolina	15.8		13	Oregon	88.8		13	Florida..............................	16.4
14	Rhode Island......................	15.7		14	Wisconsin	88.6		14	Arkansas	15.6
14	Arkansas	15.7		15	Colorado	88.5		15	Illinois	14.8
16	Ohio.................................	15.5		16	Kansas..............................	87.7		16	New Jersey	14.6
16	Connecticut........................	15.5		17	Minnesota..........................	87.2		17	Michigan	14.3
18	Michigan	15.4		18	Indiana	87.0		18	Ohio.................................	12.4
18	Missouri............................	15.4		19	South Dakota	86.8		19	Texas................................	12.2
20	Alabama	15.3		20	Rhode Island......................	86.5		20	Missouri............................	11.7
20	New Mexico	15.3		21	Arizona.............................	84.8		21	Pennsylvania	11.3
20	South Dakota	15.3		22	Massachusetts	84.4		22	Connecticut........................	11.0
23	Wisconsin	15.2		23	Missouri............................	84.1		23	Indiana	9.3
24	Massachusetts	15.1		24	Pennsylvania	84.0		24	Nevada.............................	8.6
24	Tennessee	15.1		25	Ohio.................................	83.8		25	Kentucky	7.9
26	Kentucky	14.8		26	New Mexico	83.6		26	Massachusetts	7.7
27	North Carolina...................	14.7		27	Connecticut........................	82.6		27	Oklahoma..........................	7.6
27	New Jersey	14.7		28	Washington........................	82.3		28	Rhode Island......................	7.1
27	New York...........................	14.7		29	Texas................................	81.1		29	California...........................	6.7
30	Oklahoma..........................	14.5		30	Michigan	80.4		30	Wisconsin	6.5
31	Nebraska...........................	14.4		31	Arkansas	80.3		31	Kansas..............................	6.1
32	Mississippi........................	14.3		32	Tennessee	79.7		32	Minnesota..........................	5.3
32	Kansas..............................	14.3		33	Florida..............................	78.8		33	Nebraska...........................	4.7
32	Minnesota..........................	14.3		34	Illinois	78.2		34	Arizona.............................	4.4
32	Idaho................................	14.3		35	Nevada.............................	78.0		35	Colorado	4.3
32	Indiana	14.3		36	Oklahoma..........................	76.0		36	Washington........................	3.8
37	North Dakota	14.2		37	New Jersey	74.5		37	West Virginia.....................	3.4
37	Nevada.............................	14.2		38	California...........................	74.2		37	Alaska..............................	3.4
39	Washington........................	14.1		39	North Carolina...................	72.3		39	Iowa.................................	3.0
40	Wyoming	14.0		40	Delaware	71.9		40	New Mexico	2.4
41	Illinois	13.9		41	New York...........................	71.7		41	Oregon	1.9
42	Virginia.............................	13.8		42	Virginia.............................	71.6		42	Hawaii	1.7
42	Maryland...........................	13.8		43	Alabama	70.4		43	South Dakota	1.3
44	Louisiana	13.6		44	South Carolina	68.4		44	New Hampshire..................	1.2
45	California...........................	12.9		45	Alaska..............................	68.1		44	North Dakota	1.2
46	Colorado	12.7		46	Louisiana	64.0		44	Utah	1.2
47	Georgia	12.4		47	Georgia	63.4		44	Maine...............................	1.2
48	Texas................................	11.5		48	Maryland...........................	61.3		48	Vermont............................	1.0
49	District of Columbia	11.3		49	Mississippi........................	60.3		49	Wyoming	0.9
50	Utah	10.0		50	District of Columbia	41.8		50	Idaho................................	0.7
51	Alaska..............................	9.4		51	Hawaii	25.7		51	Montana............................	0.4

Percent American Indian and Alaska Native Alone, 2014

Rank	State	Percent
	United States	1.2
1	Alaska	15.0
2	New Mexico	10.1
3	Oklahoma	8.9
3	South Dakota	8.9
5	Montana	6.4
6	North Dakota	5.5
7	Arizona	5.2
8	Wyoming	2.6
9	Washington	1.8
10	Oregon	1.7
10	California	1.7
12	Idaho	1.6
12	Nevada	1.6
12	Colorado	1.6
15	North Carolina	1.5
15	Utah	1.5
17	Nebraska	1.3
17	Minnesota	1.3
19	Kansas	1.2
20	Wisconsin	1.1
21	Texas	1.0
22	New York	0.9
22	Arkansas	0.9
22	Rhode Island	0.9
25	Louisiana	0.7
25	Michigan	0.7
25	Alabama	0.7
25	Delaware	0.7
25	Maine	0.7
30	Illinois	0.6
30	New Jersey	0.6
30	Mississippi	0.6
33	District of Columbia	0.5
33	Maryland	0.5
33	South Carolina	0.5
33	Virginia	0.5
33	Missouri	0.5
33	Georgia	0.5
33	Florida	0.5
33	Connecticut	0.5
33	Massachusetts	0.5
42	Iowa	0.4
42	Tennessee	0.4
42	Indiana	0.4
42	Vermont	0.4
42	Hawaii	0.4
47	Pennsylvania	0.3
47	Kentucky	0.3
47	New Hampshire	0.3
47	Ohio	0.3
51	West Virginia	0.2

Percent Asian Alone, 2014

Rank	State	Percent
	United States	4.9
1	Hawaii	39.1
2	California	13.5
3	New Jersey	8.5
4	New York	7.6
5	Nevada	7.5
6	Washington	7.3
7	Maryland	5.7
8	Virginia	5.6
9	Massachusetts	5.5
9	Alaska	5.5
11	Illinois	4.7
12	Minnesota	4.1
13	Texas	4.0
14	Connecticut	3.9
15	Oregon	3.8
16	District of Columbia	3.6
17	Georgia	3.3
17	Delaware	3.3
19	Rhode Island	3.0
20	Arizona	2.9
20	Colorado	2.9
22	Pennsylvania	2.8
23	Florida	2.5
23	Michigan	2.5
25	Kansas	2.4
26	Wisconsin	2.3
26	North Carolina	2.3
28	New Hampshire	2.2
29	Utah	2.1
30	Nebraska	1.8
30	Oklahoma	1.8
30	Iowa	1.8
33	Ohio	1.7
33	Missouri	1.7
35	Indiana	1.6
35	Louisiana	1.6
37	New Mexico	1.5
37	Tennessee	1.5
39	South Carolina	1.3
39	Vermont	1.3
39	Arkansas	1.3
39	Idaho	1.3
43	Kentucky	1.2
43	Alabama	1.2
45	North Dakota	1.0
45	Maine	1.0
45	South Dakota	1.0
48	Mississippi	0.9
49	Wyoming	0.8
50	West Virginia	0.7
51	Montana	0.6

Percent Native Hawaiian and Other Pacific Islander Alone, 2014

Rank	State	Percent
	United States	0.2
1	Hawaii	10.2
2	Alaska	1.1
3	Utah	0.9
4	Nevada	0.7
5	Washington	0.6
6	California	0.5
7	Oregon	0.4
8	Arizona	0.3
9	Arkansas	0.2
9	Idaho	0.2
9	Colorado	0.2
9	Rhode Island	0.2
9	New Mexico	0.2
14	Oklahoma	0.1
14	District of Columbia	0.1
14	Texas	0.1
14	New York	0.1
14	Missouri	0.1
14	Nebraska	0.1
14	Alabama	0.1
14	North Carolina	0.1
14	Georgia	0.1
14	Virginia	0.1
14	Kansas	0.1
14	Florida	0.1
14	Connecticut	0.1
14	Maryland	0.1
14	Wyoming	0.1
14	Massachusetts	0.1
14	New Jersey	0.1
14	South Carolina	0.1
14	Tennessee	0.1
14	Iowa	0.1
14	Delaware	0.1
14	Montana	0.1
14	Kentucky	0.1
14	South Dakota	0.1
14	Illinois	0.1
14	Mississippi	0.1
14	Louisiana	0.1
14	Pennsylvania	0.1
14	Minnesota	0.1
14	Indiana	0.1
44	North Dakota	Z
44	Ohio	Z
44	Wisconsin	Z
44	New Hampshire	Z
44	Michigan	Z
44	Maine	Z
44	Vermont	Z
44	West Virginia	Z

Z = Value greater than zero but less than half of the unit shown.

Percent Two or More Races, 2014

Rank	State	Percent
	United States......................	2.3
1	Hawaii	23.1
2	Alaska	6.9
3	Oklahoma..........................	5.5
4	Washington........................	4.2
5	Nevada	3.6
6	California...........................	3.5
7	Oregon	3.3
8	Colorado	2.6
8	Kansas	2.6
10	Virginia.............................	2.5
11	Arizona.............................	2.4
11	Maryland	2.4
11	District of Columbia	2.4
14	Rhode Island.....................	2.3
14	Montana	2.3
16	New Mexico	2.2
16	Delaware	2.2
18	New York...........................	2.1
18	Utah	2.1
18	Minnesota	2.1
18	Michigan	2.1
22	Idaho................................	2.0
22	Connecticut.......................	2.0
22	South Dakota	2.0
25	Missouri............................	1.9
25	Massachusetts	1.9
27	Ohio	1.8
27	North Carolina....................	1.8
27	New Jersey	1.8
27	Nebraska	1.8
27	Florida..............................	1.8
32	Wyoming	1.7
32	Georgia	1.7
32	Arkansas	1.7
32	Indiana.............................	1.7
36	Illinois..............................	1.6
36	Vermont	1.6
36	North Dakota......................	1.6
36	Texas	1.6
36	Pennsylvania......................	1.6
36	Wisconsin	1.6
42	Kentucky	1.5
42	Tennessee	1.5
42	South Carolina	1.5
42	Iowa.................................	1.5
42	Maine...............................	1.5
47	New Hampshire...................	1.4
47	West Virginia......................	1.4
49	Alabama	1.3
49	Louisiana	1.3
51	Mississippi........................	1.0

Percent Hispanic or Latino,[1] 2014

Rank	State	Percent
	United States......................	16.3
1	New Mexico	46.3
2	Texas................................	37.6
2	California...........................	37.6
4	Arizona.............................	29.6
5	Nevada	26.5
6	Florida..............................	22.5
7	Colorado	20.7
8	New Jersey	17.7
9	New York...........................	17.6
10	Illinois..............................	15.8
11	Connecticut.......................	13.4
12	Utah	13.0
13	Rhode Island.....................	12.4
14	Oregon	11.7
15	Washington........................	11.2
15	Idaho................................	11.2
17	Kansas	10.5
18	Massachusetts	9.6
19	Nebraska	9.2
20	District of Columbia	9.1
21	Wyoming	8.9
21	Hawaii	8.9
21	Oklahoma..........................	8.9
24	Georgia	8.8
25	North Carolina....................	8.4
26	Delaware	8.2
26	Maryland	8.2
28	Virginia.............................	7.9
29	Arkansas	6.4
30	Indiana.............................	6.0
31	Wisconsin	5.9
32	Pennsylvania......................	5.7
33	Alaska	5.5
34	South Carolina	5.1
35	Iowa.................................	5.0
36	Minnesota	4.7
37	Tennessee	4.6
38	Michigan	4.4
39	Louisiana	4.2
40	Alabama	3.9
41	Missouri............................	3.5
42	Ohio	3.1
42	Kentucky	3.1
44	Montana	2.9
45	New Hampshire...................	2.8
46	Mississippi........................	2.7
46	South Dakota	2.7
48	North Dakota......................	2.0
49	Vermont	1.5
50	Maine...............................	1.3
51	West Virginia......................	1.2

[1]May be of any race.

Percent White Alone, Not Hispanic or Latino, 2014

Rank	State	Percent
	United States......................	63.9
1	Maine...............................	94.5
2	Vermont	94.4
3	West Virginia......................	93.2
4	New Hampshire...................	92.5
5	North Dakota......................	89.0
6	Iowa.................................	88.7
7	Montana	87.9
8	Kentucky	86.4
9	Wyoming	86.0
10	South Dakota	84.8
11	Idaho................................	84.1
12	Wisconsin	83.4
13	Minnesota	83.2
14	Nebraska	82.2
15	Indiana.............................	81.7
16	Ohio	81.2
17	Missouri............................	81.1
18	Utah	80.6
19	Pennsylvania......................	79.6
20	Oregon	78.6
21	Kansas	78.3
22	Rhode Island.....................	77.0
23	Massachusetts	76.9
24	Michigan	76.7
25	Tennessee	75.7
26	Arkansas	74.6
27	Washington........................	72.7
28	Connecticut.......................	71.5
29	Colorado	70.2
30	Oklahoma..........................	68.7
31	Alabama	67.1
32	Delaware	65.5
33	North Carolina....................	65.4
34	Virginia.............................	65.0
35	Alaska	64.3
36	South Carolina	64.2
37	Illinois..............................	63.8
38	Louisiana	60.5
39	New Jersey	59.6
40	New York...........................	58.5
41	Florida..............................	58.1
41	Mississippi........................	58.1
43	Arizona.............................	58.0
44	Georgia	56.0
45	Maryland	54.8
46	Nevada	54.3
47	Texas	45.4
48	New Mexico	40.7
49	California...........................	40.3
50	District of Columbia	35.0
51	Hawaii	22.8

Infant Mortality Rate, 2013

Rank	State	Rate per 1,000 live births (infants under 1 year old)
	United States......................	5.96
1	Mississippi.........................	9.65
2	Louisiana	8.65
3	Alabama	8.61
4	Arkansas	7.61
5	West Virginia.....................	7.59
6	Ohio	7.33
7	Indiana	7.22
8	Maine	7.04
8	Michigan	7.04
10	North Carolina.....................	6.99
11	Georgia	6.94
12	South Carolina	6.85
13	Oklahoma..........................	6.82
14	Tennessee	6.80
15	District of Columbia	6.78
16	Pennsylvania......................	6.66
17	Maryland............................	6.63
18	Hawaii	6.53
18	South Dakota	6.53
20	Missouri............................	6.52
21	Rhode Island......................	6.48
22	Kansas	6.44
23	Kentucky	6.38
24	Delaware	6.28
25	Wisconsin	6.24
26	Virginia.............................	6.21
27	Florida...............................	6.16
28	North Dakota......................	6.13
29	Illinois	6.00
30	Texas................................	5.84
31	Montana............................	5.66
32	New Hampshire...................	5.65
33	Idaho................................	5.63
34	Alaska	5.59
35	New Mexico	5.46
36	Nevada	5.45
37	Nebraska...........................	5.33
38	Arizona..............................	5.27
39	Utah	5.16
40	Colorado	5.09
41	Minnestoa	5.05
42	Oregon	4.96
43	New York...........................	4.92
44	California...........................	4.76
45	Connecticut........................	4.68
46	Wyoming	4.58
47	New Jersey	4.48
47	Washington........................	4.48
49	Vermont	4.35
50	Massachusetts	4.15
51	Iowa.................................	4.14

Birth Rate, 2013

Rank	State	Rate per 1,000 population
	United States......................	12.4
1	Utah	17.6
2	Alaska	15.6
3	North Dakota......................	14.7
4	Texas................................	14.6
5	South Dakota	14.5
6	District of Columbia	14.4
7	Nebraska...........................	14.0
8	Idaho................................	13.9
8	Oklahoma..........................	13.9
10	Louisiana	13.7
11	Hawaii	13.5
12	Kansas	13.4
13	Wyoming	13.1
14	Arizona..............................	12.9
14	California...........................	12.9
14	Georgia	12.9
14	Mississippi.........................	12.9
18	Arkansas	12.8
18	Minnesota	12.8
20	Kentucky	12.7
20	Iowa.................................	12.7
22	New Mexico	12.6
22	Indiana	12.6
22	Nevada	12.6
25	Missouri............................	12.5
26	Washington........................	12.4
26	Virginia.............................	12.4
28	Colorado	12.3
28	Tennessee	12.3
30	Illinois	12.2
30	Montana............................	12.2
32	Maryland............................	12.1
32	New York...........................	12.1
32	North Carolina....................	12.1
35	Alabama	12.0
35	Ohio	12.0
37	South Carolina	11.9
38	Delaware	11.7
39	Wisconsin	11.6
40	New Jersey	11.5
40	Oregon	11.5
40	Michigan	11.5
43	West Virginia......................	11.2
44	Pennsylvania......................	11.0
44	Florida...............................	11.0
46	Massachusetts	10.7
47	Rhode Island......................	10.3
48	Connecticut........................	10.0
49	Maine	9.6
50	Vermont	9.5
51	New Hampshire...................	9.4

Voting Population, 2012

Rank	State	Percent voted, total population
	United States......................	56.5
1	Mississippi.........................	73.3
2	Wisconsin	71.9
3	Minnesota	70.5
4	District of Columbia	67.7
5	Maine	67.2
6	New Hampshire...................	66.9
7	Iowa.................................	66.7
8	Colorado	65.4
8	Massachusetts	65.4
10	Louisiana	64.7
11	Michigan	64.5
11	Montana............................	64.5
13	North Carolina....................	63.7
14	Oregon	63.3
15	Missouri............................	62.3
16	Delaware	62.2
16	North Dakota......................	62.2
16	South Carolina	62.2
19	Vermont	62.1
20	Virginia.............................	62.0
21	Ohio	61.7
22	Washington........................	60.7
23	Idaho................................	60.2
24	South Dakota	60.1
25	Alabama	59.9
26	Pennsylvania......................	59.1
26	Rhode Island......................	59.1
28	Kansas	58.9
29	Maryland............................	58.7
30	Nebraska...........................	58.2
31	Georgia	58.1
32	Wyoming	57.8
33	Indiana	57.7
34	Kentucky	57.6
35	Connecticut........................	57.5
36	New Mexico	56.5
37	Illinois	56.2
38	Alaska	56.0
39	New Jersey	54.5
40	Florida...............................	53.9
41	Tennessee	53.7
42	Utah	53.3
43	Nevada	51.4
44	Arkansas	51.1
45	Oklahoma..........................	51.0
46	New York...........................	50.9
47	Arizona..............................	49.6
48	California...........................	47.5
48	West Virginia......................	47.5
50	Hawaii	47.4
51	Texas................................	46.4

Percent of Persons 25 Years and Over with a Bachelor's Degree or More, 2013

Rank	State	Percent
	United States......................	29.6
1	District of Columbia	55.1
2	Massachusetts....................	40.3
3	Colorado	37.8
4	Maryland	37.4
5	Connecticut.......................	37.2
6	New Jersey	36.6
7	Virginia	36.1
8	Vermont	35.7
9	New Hampshire..................	34.6
10	New York...........................	34.1
11	Minnesota	33.5
12	Washington.......................	32.7
13	Rhode Island.....................	32.4
14	Illinois	32.1
15	Utah	31.3
16	Hawaii	31.2
17	Kansas	31.1
18	California...........................	31.0
19	Oregon	30.7
20	Delaware	29.8
21	Nebraska	29.4
22	Montana	29.0
23	Pennsylvania	28.7
24	North Carolina...................	28.4
25	Georgia	28.3
26	Maine	28.2
27	Alaska	28.0
28	Wisconsin	27.7
29	Texas	27.5
30	Arizona	27.4
31	Florida..............................	27.2
32	North Dakota.....................	27.1
33	Missouri	27.0
34	Michigan	26.9
35	South Dakota	26.6
35	Wyoming	26.6
37	Iowa	26.4
37	New Mexico	26.4
39	Idaho	26.2
40	Ohio	26.1
40	South Carolina	26.1
42	Tennessee	24.8
43	Oklahoma..........................	23.8
43	Indiana	23.8
45	Alabama	23.5
46	Kentucky	22.6
47	Nevada	22.5
47	Louisiana	22.5
49	Arkansas	20.6
50	Mississippi........................	20.4
51	West Virginia.....................	18.9

Violent Crime, 2013

Rank	State	Rate per 100,000 population
	United States......................	367.9
1	District of Columbia[1,4]	1,300.3
2	Alaska[1]	640.4
3	New Mexico	613.0
4	Nevada	603.0
5	Tennessee[1]	590.6
6	Louisiana[2]	518.5
7	South Carolina[1]	508.5
8	Delaware[1]	491.4
9	Maryland	473.8
10	Florida[1]	470.4
11	Arkansas[1]	460.3
12	Michigan[1]	449.9
13	Oklahoma[2]........................	441.2
14	Missouri[1]	433.4
15	Alabama[1]	430.8
16	Arizona[2,3]	416.5
17	Massachusetts[2]	413.4
18	Texas[2]	408.3
19	California...........................	402.1
20	New York...........................	393.7
21	Illinois[2]	380.2
22	Georgia	365.7
23	Indiana[2]	357.4
24	North Carolina...................	342.2
25	Kansas2	339.9
26	Pennsylvania[1,3]	335.4
27	South Dakota[1]	316.5
28	Colorado[1]	308.0
29	West Virginia[1]	300.3
30	Washington[2,3]....................	289.1
31	New Jersey	288.5
32	Ohio[2]	286.2
33	Wisconsin[2,3]	277.9
34	Mississippi[2]......................	274.6
35	Iowa[1]	271.4
36	North Dakota[1]	270.1
37	Connecticut[2]	262.5
38	Nebraska[2]	262.1
39	Rhode Island[1]	257.2
40	Oregon[2]	254.0
41	Montana[1]	252.9
42	Hawaii	251.6
43	Minnesota[1]	234.4
44	Utah[2]	224.0
45	Idaho[1]	217.0
46	New Hampshire[1]	215.3
47	Kentucky[2]	209.8
48	Wyoming	205.1
49	Virginia[1]	196.2
50	Maine[2,3]	129.3
51	Vermont[1]	121.1

[1]This state's agencies submitted rape data according to the revised UCR definition of rape.
[2]Agencies within this state submitted rape data according to both the revised UCR definition of rape and the legacy UCR definition of rape.
[3]Because of changes in the state/local agency's reporting practices, figures are not comparable to previous years' data.
[4]Includes offenses reported by the Zoological Police and the Metro Transit Police.

Property Crime, 2013

Rank	State	Rate per 100,000 population
	United States......................	2,730.7
1	District of Columbia[1]	4,808.3
2	Washington.......................	3,710.3
3	New Mexico	3,704.8
4	South Carolina	3,624.2
5	Arkansas	3,602.6
6	Louisiana	3,582.0
7	Arizona	3,399.1
8	Alabama	3,351.3
9	Georgia	3,346.6
10	Oklahoma..........................	3,273.7
11	Texas	3,258.2
12	Tennessee	3,180.9
13	Oregon	3,173.9
14	Missouri	3,137.0
15	North Carolina...................	3,128.0
16	Florida..............................	3,105.3
17	Delaware	3,065.5
18	Hawaii	3,053.7
19	Utah	2,950.4
20	Kansas	2,946.8
21	Ohio	2,927.5
22	Alaska	2,885.2
23	Indiana	2,854.0
24	Nevada	2,837.7
25	Mississippi........................	2,724.7
26	Maryland	2,663.5
27	Colorado	2,658.5
28	California...........................	2,658.1
29	Nebraska	2,623.4
30	Montana	2,556.5
31	Rhode Island.....................	2,442.0
32	Minnesota	2,420.4
33	Kentucky	2,362.9
34	Michigan	2,327.6
35	Maine	2,292.2
36	Illinois	2,274.3
37	Vermont	2,214.2
38	Wyoming	2,198.4
39	New Hampshire..................	2,194.3
40	Iowa	2,193.9
41	Wisconsin	2,188.7
42	West Virginia.....................	2,103.9
43	North Dakota.....................	2,094.0
44	Virginia.............................	2,065.9
45	Pennsylvania	2,060.8
46	Massachusetts....................	2,051.2
47	Connecticut.......................	1,974.1
48	South Dakota	1,914.7
49	New Jersey	1,882.8
50	Idaho	1,864.3
51	New York...........................	1,824.8

[1]Includes offenses reported by the Zoological Police and the Metro Transit Police.

Rank	State	State employees per 1,000 residents
	State Government Employment, 2012 (Full-time equivalent employees)	
	United States......................	13.5
1	Hawaii	40.4
2	Alaska	37.0
3	Delaware	28.4
4	North Dakota......................	25.6
5	Vermont	24.0
6	Wyoming	23.4
7	West Virginia......................	21.7
7	New Mexico	21.7
9	Arkansas	21.4
10	Montana..............................	19.8
11	Mississippi	19.4
12	Kentucky	19.3
13	Utah	18.1
14	Rhode Island.......................	18.0
15	Alabama	17.9
16	South Dakota......................	17.5
17	Connecticut.........................	17.1
17	Louisiana	17.1
17	Nebraska.............................	17.1
20	Oklahoma............................	16.8
21	Kansas	16.7
22	Oregon	16.6
23	New Jersey	16.4
24	South Carolina	16.2
25	Washington.........................	15.8
25	Maine	15.8
27	Iowa	15.4
28	Virginia................................	15.2
29	North Carolina.....................	15.1
30	Michigan	14.7
31	Minnesota	14.6
31	Maryland	14.6
33	Massachusetts	14.3
34	Missouri..............................	14.2
35	New Hampshire....................	14.0
36	Colorado	13.7
37	Indiana	13.5
38	Idaho...................................	13.2
39	Tennessee	12.9
40	Georgia	12.7
41	Pennsylvania.......................	12.4
42	Wisconsin	12.3
42	New York.............................	12.3
44	Ohio....................................	11.7
45	Texas..................................	11.5
46	Arizona................................	10.3
47	California.............................	10.2
48	Illinois	10.1
49	Nevada................................	9.3
50	Florida.................................	9.1
51	District of Columbia	X

X = Not applicable.

Rank	State	Unemployment rate
	Unemployment Rate, 2014	
	United States......................	6.2
1	District of Columbia	7.8
1	Mississippi..........................	7.8
1	Nevada................................	7.8
4	Rhode Island.......................	7.7
5	California.............................	7.5
6	Michigan	7.3
7	Georgia	7.2
8	Illinois	7.1
9	Arizona................................	6.9
9	Oregon	6.9
11	Alabama	6.8
11	Alaska	6.8
13	Tennessee	6.7
14	Connecticut.........................	6.6
14	New Jersey	6.6
16	Kentucky	6.5
16	New Mexico	6.5
16	West Virginia.......................	6.5
19	Louisiana	6.4
19	South Carolina	6.4
21	Florida.................................	6.3
21	New York.............................	6.3
23	Washington.........................	6.2
24	Arkansas	6.1
24	Missouri..............................	6.1
24	North Carolina.....................	6.1
27	Indiana	6.0
28	Maryland	5.8
28	Massachusetts	5.8
28	Pennsylvania.......................	5.8
31	Delaware	5.7
31	Maine	5.7
31	Ohio....................................	5.7
34	Wisconsin	5.5
35	Virginia................................	5.2
36	Texas..................................	5.1
37	Colorado	5.0
38	Idaho...................................	4.8
39	Montana..............................	4.7
40	Kansas	4.5
40	Oklahoma............................	4.5
42	Hawaii	4.4
42	Iowa	4.4
44	New Hampshire....................	4.3
44	Wyoming	4.3
46	Minnesota	4.1
46	Vermont	4.1
48	Utah	3.8
49	South Dakota......................	3.4
50	Nebraska.............................	3.3
51	North Dakota......................	2.8

Rank	State	Percent
	Employees on Nonfarm Payrolls, Percent Change, 2013–2014	
	United States......................	1.9
1	North Dakota......................	3.8
2	Nevada................................	3.5
3	Colorado	3.3
4	Florida.................................	3.2
5	Texas..................................	3.1
6	California.............................	3.0
6	Georgia	3.0
8	Utah	2.9
9	Oregon	2.8
9	Washington.........................	2.8
11	Idaho...................................	2.7
12	South Carolina	2.5
13	Delaware	2.1
13	North Carolina.....................	2.1
13	Tennessee	2.1
16	Arizona................................	1.9
17	Michigan	1.7
18	Massachusetts	1.6
18	New York.............................	1.6
20	Indiana	1.5
20	Kansas	1.5
20	Kentucky	1.5
23	Louisiana	1.4
23	South Dakota......................	1.4
25	Iowa	1.3
25	Minnesota	1.3
25	Nebraska.............................	1.3
25	Ohio....................................	1.3
25	Wisconsin	1.3
30	Illinois	1.2
30	New Hampshire....................	1.2
30	Rhode Island.......................	1.2
33	Alabama	1.1
33	Arkansas	1.1
33	Hawaii	1.1
33	Oklahoma............................	1.1
33	Vermont	1.1
33	Wyoming	1.1
39	Montana..............................	1.0
40	Maryland	0.9
40	Missouri..............................	0.9
42	Connecticut.........................	0.8
42	New Mexico	0.8
42	Pennsylvania.......................	0.8
45	District of Columbia	0.7
45	Mississippi..........................	0.7
45	New Jersey	0.7
48	Alaska	0.4
48	Maine	0.4
48	Virginia................................	0.4
51	West Virginia.......................	-0.4

Per Capita Income in the Past 12 Months, 2013 (2013 Dollars)		
Rank	State	Dollars
	United States......................	28,184
1	District of Columbia	45,477
2	Connecticut.......................	37,726
3	Maryland...........................	36,177
4	Massachusetts....................	35,879
5	New Jersey	35,728
6	New Hampshire..................	33,269
7	Virginia.............................	33,145
8	New York...........................	32,514
9	Alaska	32,474
10	Colorado	31,421
11	Minnesota	31,358
12	North Dakota......................	30,855
13	Rhode Island......................	30,748
14	Washington........................	30,672
15	Illinois	29,856
16	Hawaii	29,577
17	California...........................	29,513
18	Delaware	29,484
19	Vermont	29,136
20	Wyoming	28,889
21	Pennsylvania......................	28,647
22	Alabama............................	28,184
23	Iowa	27,740
24	Wisconsin	27,448
25	Kansas	27,175
26	Nebraska	27,093
27	Oregon	27,048
28	Maine	26,630
29	Ohio	26,354
30	Texas	26,327
31	Montana............................	26,054
32	Michigan	25,918
32	Nevada	25,918
34	South Dakota	25,860
35	Florida	25,834
36	Missouri............................	25,384
37	North Carolina....................	25,377
38	Arizona.............................	25,164
39	Georgia	24,923
40	Indiana	24,796
41	Louisiana	24,695
42	Tennessee	24,678
43	Oklahoma..........................	24,284
44	Utah	24,250
45	South Carolina	23,687
46	Kentucky	23,668
47	New Mexico	23,334
48	West Virginia......................	23,159
49	Idaho	22,652
50	Arkansas	21,927
51	Mississippi........................	20,156

Real Gross Domestic Product in Chained (2009) Dollars, 2013		
Rank	State	Dollars (billions)
	United States......................	15,432
1	California...........................	2,055
2	Texas	1,395
3	New York...........................	1,248
4	Florida	749
5	Illinois	672
6	Pennsylvania......................	598
7	Ohio	521
8	New Jersey	502
9	North Carolina....................	434
10	Virginia.............................	427
11	Georgia	426
12	Massachusetts....................	415
13	Michigan	410
14	Washington........................	379
15	Maryland...........................	319
16	Indiana	288
17	Minnesota	284
18	Tennessee	271
19	Colorado	267
20	Wisconsin	266
21	Arizona.............................	257
21	Missouri............................	257
23	Connecticut.......................	231
24	Louisiana	212
25	Oregon	197
26	Alabama............................	181
27	South Carolina	171
28	Kentucky	170
29	Oklahoma..........................	158
30	Iowa	152
31	Kansas	131
32	Utah	124
33	Nevada	120
34	Arkansas	110
35	District of Columbia	103
36	Nebraska	98
37	Mississippi........................	96
38	New Mexico	83
39	Hawaii	70
40	New Hampshire..................	65
40	West Virginia......................	65
42	Delaware	56
42	Idaho	56
44	Maine	51
45	Rhode Island......................	50
46	Alaska	49
47	North Dakota......................	45
48	South Dakota	40
49	Montana............................	39
50	Wyoming	36
51	Vermont	27

Real Gross Domestic Product in Chained (2009) Dollars, Percent Change, 2012–2013		
Rank	State	Percent
	United States......................	1.9
1	Texas	5.5
2	Nebraska	3.9
3	Utah	3.7
4	Michigan	2.8
5	North Carolina....................	2.7
6	Idaho	2.6
7	Alabama............................	2.5
7	Florida	2.5
9	California...........................	2.3
9	Washington........................	2.3
11	Indiana	2.2
11	Iowa	2.2
11	Wisconsin	2.2
14	Colorado	2.1
14	Minnesota	2.1
14	Ohio	2.1
17	Georgia	2.0
18	Arkansas	1.9
18	Rhode Island......................	1.9
20	Missouri............................	1.8
20	Oklahoma..........................	1.8
22	Tennessee	1.6
23	Pennsylvania......................	1.5
24	Hawaii	1.4
24	New Hampshire..................	1.4
24	South Carolina	1.4
27	West Virginia......................	1.3
28	Kentucky	1.2
28	Massachusetts....................	1.2
30	Connecticut.......................	1.0
30	Montana............................	1.0
30	New Mexico	1.0
30	New York...........................	1.0
34	North Dakota......................	0.9
34	South Dakota	0.9
36	Arizona.............................	0.8
36	New Jersey	0.8
38	Delaware	0.7
38	Maryland...........................	0.7
38	Nevada	0.7
41	Maine	0.5
41	Wyoming	0.5
43	Virginia.............................	0.4
44	Illinois	0.2
45	Kansas	-0.3
45	Vermont	-0.3
47	District of Columbia	-0.6
48	Oregon	-1.0
49	Mississippi........................	-1.1
50	Louisiana	-2.5
51	Alaska	-4.0

Median Household Income, 2013		
Rank	State	Dollars
	United States......................	52,250
1	Maryland.............................	72,483
2	Alaska	72,237
3	New Jersey	70,165
4	Hawaii	68,020
5	District of Columbia	67,572
6	Connecticut........................	67,098
7	Massachusetts	66,768
8	New Hampshire...................	64,230
9	Virginia..............................	62,666
10	Minnesota	60,702
11	California............................	60,190
12	Utah	59,770
13	Colorado	58,823
14	Wyoming	58,752
15	Washington.........................	58,405
16	Delaware	57,846
17	New York............................	57,369
18	Illinois	56,210
19	Rhode Island.......................	55,902
20	North Dakota.......................	55,759
21	Vermont	52,578
22	Iowa	52,229
23	Pennsylvania.......................	52,007
24	Texas.................................	51,704
25	Wisconsin	51,467
26	Nebraska............................	51,440
27	Nevada...............................	51,230
28	Kansas	50,972
29	Oregon	50,251
30	South Dakota	48,947
31	Arizona...............................	48,510
32	Michigan	48,273
33	Ohio	48,081
34	Georgia	47,829
35	Indiana...............................	47,529
36	Maine	46,974
37	Montana	46,972
38	Missouri..............................	46,931
39	Idaho.................................	46,783
40	Florida	46,036
41	North Carolina.....................	45,906
42	Oklahoma............................	45,690
43	Tennessee	44,297
44	Louisiana	44,164
45	South Carolina	44,163
46	New Mexico	43,872
47	Kentucky.............................	43,399
48	Alabama..............................	42,849
49	West Virginia.......................	41,253
50	Arkansas	40,511
51	Mississippi..........................	37,963

Median Family Income, 2013		
Rank	State	Dollars
	United States......................	64,030
1	Maryland.............................	87,204
2	Connecticut........................	85,563
3	New Jersey	85,426
4	Alaska	85,385
5	Massachusetts	83,813
6	Hawaii	80,316
7	New Hampshire...................	77,646
8	Virginia..............................	75,524
9	Minnesota	75,112
10	North Dakota.......................	73,844
11	District of Columbia	72,337
12	Colorado	72,043
13	Rhode Island.......................	71,608
14	Wyoming	71,446
15	Washington.........................	71,371
16	New York............................	70,485
17	Illinois	69,557
18	Delaware	69,394
19	Vermont	68,382
20	California............................	68,222
21	Utah	67,231
22	Iowa	66,684
23	Pennsylvania.......................	66,522
24	Wisconsin	65,618
25	Kansas	64,969
26	Nebraska............................	64,763
27	Oregon	61,767
28	South Dakota	61,299
29	Texas.................................	61,208
30	Ohio	61,030
31	Michigan	60,846
32	Maine	60,141
33	Montana	60,122
34	Nevada...............................	59,462
35	Indiana...............................	59,428
36	Missouri..............................	58,754
37	Georgia	57,458
38	Arizona...............................	57,163
39	Oklahoma............................	56,655
40	Idaho.................................	56,176
41	North Carolina.....................	56,111
42	Louisiana	55,871
43	Florida	55,774
44	Tennessee	54,691
45	Kentucky.............................	54,690
46	South Carolina	54,686
47	New Mexico	54,565
48	Alabama..............................	54,045
49	West Virginia.......................	51,596
50	Arkansas	50,415
51	Mississippi..........................	47,615

Persons Below Poverty Level, 2013		
Rank	State	Percent
	United States......................	15.8
1	Mississippi..........................	24.0
2	New Mexico	21.9
3	Louisiana	19.8
4	Arkansas	19.7
5	Georgia	19.0
6	District of Columbia	18.9
7	Kentucky.............................	18.8
8	Alabama..............................	18.7
9	Arizona...............................	18.6
9	South Carolina	18.6
11	West Virginia.......................	18.5
12	North Carolina.....................	17.9
13	Tennessee	17.8
14	Texas.................................	17.5
15	Florida	17.0
15	Michigan	17.0
17	California............................	16.8
17	Oklahoma............................	16.8
19	Oregon	16.7
20	Montana	16.5
21	New York............................	16.0
21	Ohio	16.0
23	Indiana...............................	15.9
23	Missouri..............................	15.9
25	Nevada...............................	15.8
26	Idaho.................................	15.6
27	Illinois	14.7
27	Rhode Island.......................	14.3
29	South Dakota	14.2
30	Washington.........................	14.1
31	Kansas	14.0
31	Maine	14.0
33	Pennsylvania.......................	13.7
34	Wisconsin	13.5
35	Nebraska............................	13.2
36	Colorado	13.0
37	Iowa	12.7
37	Utah	12.7
39	Delaware	12.4
40	Vermont	12.3
41	Massachusetts	11.9
42	North Dakota.......................	11.8
43	Virginia..............................	11.7
44	New Jersey	11.4
45	Minnesota	11.2
46	Wyoming	10.9
47	Hawaii	10.8
48	Connecticut........................	10.7
49	Maryland.............................	10.1
50	Alaska	9.8
51	New Hampshire...................	8.7

	Persons Under 18 Years Old Below Poverty Level, 2013	
Rank	State	Percent
	United States......................	22.2
1	Mississippi.........................	34.0
2	New Mexico	31.2
3	Arkansas	29.0
4	Louisiana	27.7
5	South Carolina	27.5
6	Alabama	27.2
6	District of Columbia	27.2
8	West Virginia.....................	27.0
9	Arizona..............................	26.5
9	Georgia	26.5
9	Tennessee	26.5
12	Kentucky	25.3
13	North Carolina...................	25.2
14	Texas................................	25.0
15	Florida...............................	24.5
16	Oklahoma..........................	24.0
17	Michigan............................	23.8
18	California...........................	23.5
19	New York............................	22.8
20	Nevada..............................	22.7
20	Ohio..................................	22.7
22	Indiana..............................	22.2
22	Missouri............................	22.2
24	Oregon..............................	21.6
25	Rhode Island......................	21.5
26	Montana............................	21.3
27	Illinois...............................	20.7
28	Pennsylvania.....................	19.4
29	Idaho.................................	19.1
30	Washington........................	18.8
31	Kansas	18.7
32	South Dakota	18.6
33	Wisconsin	18.4
34	Delaware	18.0
35	Maine	17.7
35	Nebraska...........................	17.7
37	Colorado	16.9
38	New Jersey	16.7
39	Massachusetts...................	16.3
40	Iowa..................................	16.2
41	Virginia..............................	15.7
42	Vermont.............................	15.3
43	Utah..................................	14.8
44	Connecticut.......................	14.5
45	Minnesota	14.0
46	Maryland............................	13.6
47	Hawaii...............................	13.3
48	Wyoming	13.2
49	Alaska	12.1
50	North Dakota......................	12.0
51	New Hampshire..................	10.2

	Energy Consumption Per Capita, 2013	
Rank	State	Million Btu
	United States......................	306.9
1	Wyoming	918.1
2	Louisiana	828.4
3	Alaska	826.0
4	North Dakota......................	813.1
5	Iowa..................................	490.4
6	Texas................................	488.4
7	Nebraska...........................	466.5
8	South Dakota	461.7
9	Indiana..............................	441.4
10	Oklahoma..........................	421.2
11	Kentucky	414.3
12	Kansas	401.6
13	Alabama	399.5
14	West Virginia.....................	398.0
15	Montana............................	395.3
16	Mississippi.........................	381.6
17	Arkansas	369.4
18	Minnesota	343.0
19	South Carolina	333.5
20	New Mexico	329.9
21	Tennessee	328.7
22	Idaho.................................	328.3
23	Ohio..................................	323.7
24	Wisconsin	314.1
25	Illinois...............................	311.2
26	Missouri............................	307.2
27	Maine	306.4
28	Pennsylvania.....................	296.9
29	Delaware	296.6
30	Washington........................	292.4
31	Virginia..............................	291.5
32	Michigan............................	287.2
33	Utah..................................	286.2
34	Georgia	279.7
35	Colorado	279.2
36	District of Columbia	263.3
37	New Jersey	259.7
38	North Carolina...................	256.3
39	Oregon..............................	253.7
40	Maryland............................	236.4
41	Nevada..............................	235.4
42	New Hampshire..................	228.9
43	Massachusetts...................	215.0
44	Arizona..............................	213.2
45	Vermont.............................	213.2
46	Florida...............................	208.1
47	Connecticut.......................	207.8
48	California...........................	199.9
49	Hawaii...............................	196.7
50	New York............................	184.1
51	Rhode Island......................	183.8

	Homeownership Rate, 2013	
Rank	State	Percent
	United States......................	65.1
1	West Virginia.....................	76.8
2	Mississippi.........................	74.2
3	Delaware	74.1
3	New Hampshire..................	74.1
5	Michigan............................	73.9
6	Maine	73.5
7	Minnesota	73.4
8	Vermont.............................	73.0
9	Alabama	72.7
10	South Carolina	72.4
11	Indiana..............................	71.7
12	Idaho.................................	71.5
12	Pennsylvania.....................	71.5
14	Missouri............................	71.3
15	Utah..................................	70.9
16	Wyoming	70.5
17	Oklahoma..........................	69.9
18	Iowa..................................	69.8
19	Connecticut.......................	68.5
19	Wisconsin	68.5
21	Nebraska...........................	68.2
22	Virginia..............................	68.1
23	North Dakota......................	68.0
24	Ohio..................................	67.9
25	Louisiana	67.8
25	South Dakota	67.8
27	Kentucky	67.5
28	Montana............................	67.4
29	New Mexico	67.3
29	North Carolina...................	67.3
31	Illinois...............................	67.2
32	Maryland............................	66.9
33	Tennessee	66.8
34	Florida...............................	66.1
35	Arkansas	65.4
36	Massachusetts...................	65.3
37	Arizona..............................	65.1
38	New Jersey	64.9
39	Alaska	64.6
40	Colorado	64.4
41	Georgia	64.2
41	Oregon..............................	64.2
43	Kansas	63.5
44	Texas................................	63.3
45	Washington........................	62.7
46	Rhode Island......................	61.5
47	Hawaii...............................	57.3
48	Nevada..............................	56.0
49	California...........................	54.3
50	New York............................	53.0
51	District of Columbia	44.6

One-Unit Detached or Attached Housing Units, Percent of Total Occupied Units, 2013

Rank	State	Percent
	United States......................	68.7
1	Iowa.............................	78.9
2	Kansas.............................	78.2
3	Indiana.............................	77.7
3	Nebraska.............................	77.7
5	Idaho.............................	77.5
6	Michigan.............................	77.4
7	Utah.............................	76.8
8	Pennsylvania.............................	76.7
9	Oklahoma.............................	76.1
10	Delaware.............................	75.8
11	Missouri.............................	75.4
12	Minnesota.............................	74.9
13	Ohio.............................	74.8
14	West Virginia.............................	74.2
15	Maryland.............................	74.0
16	Virginia.............................	73.7
17	Tennessee.............................	73.4
18	Arkansas.............................	72.7
19	South Dakota.............................	72.3
20	Alabama.............................	72.2
21	Montana.............................	72.0
22	Kentucky.............................	71.9
22	Mississippi.............................	71.9
24	Wyoming.............................	71.8
25	Colorado.............................	71.6
26	Georgia.............................	71.4
27	Wisconsin.............................	71.2
28	Alaska.............................	70.7
29	Arizona.............................	70.5
30	North Carolina.............................	70.2
31	Vermont.............................	69.7
32	New Mexico.............................	69.6
33	Louisiana.............................	69.5
33	Maine.............................	69.5
35	Texas.............................	69.3
36	South Carolina.............................	68.2
37	New Hampshire.............................	68.0
38	Oregon.............................	67.9
39	Washington.............................	67.2
40	Nevada.............................	67.1
41	North Dakota.............................	66.9
42	Connecticut.............................	66.4
43	Illinois.............................	66.1
44	Hawaii.............................	65.7
45	California.............................	65.5
46	Florida.............................	64.8
47	New Jersey.............................	63.6
48	Rhode Island.............................	60.3
49	Massachusetts.............................	57.4
50	New York.............................	47.1
51	District of Columbia............	37.3

Mobile Homes, Percent of Total Housing Units, 2013

Rank	State	Percent
	United States......................	5.8
1	South Carolina.............................	16.5
2	New Mexico.............................	16.1
3	West Virginia.............................	14.6
4	Mississippi.............................	13.9
5	Wyoming.............................	13.4
6	Louisiana.............................	12.9
7	North Carolina.............................	12.8
8	Alabama.............................	12.6
9	Arkansas.............................	12.0
10	Kentucky.............................	10.7
10	Montana.............................	10.7
12	Arizona.............................	9.3
12	Maine.............................	9.3
14	Tennessee.............................	9.0
15	Idaho.............................	8.7
16	Georgia.............................	8.6
16	Oklahoma.............................	8.6
18	Oregon.............................	8.5
19	Florida.............................	8.3
20	South Dakota.............................	8.1
21	Delaware.............................	7.7
22	Vermont.............................	7.2
23	Washington.............................	7.1
24	North Dakota.............................	6.9
25	Texas.............................	6.8
26	Missouri.............................	5.9
27	New Hampshire.............................	5.6
28	Nevada.............................	5.3
29	Michigan.............................	4.9
30	Indiana.............................	4.7
30	Kansas.............................	4.7
30	Virginia.............................	4.7
33	Alaska.............................	4.3
34	Colorado.............................	4.0
35	Pennsylvania.............................	3.7
36	California.............................	3.6
37	Ohio.............................	3.5
38	Iowa.............................	3.2
39	Utah.............................	3.2
40	Nebraska.............................	3.1
41	Minnesota.............................	2.8
41	Wisconsin.............................	2.8
43	Illinois.............................	2.4
44	New York.............................	2.2
45	Maryland.............................	1.4
46	Rhode Island.............................	1.3
47	Connecticut.............................	0.8
47	Massachusetts.............................	0.8
47	New Jersey.............................	0.8
50	Hawaii.............................	0.1
51	District of Columbia............	-

- = Zero or rounds to zero.

Traffic Fatalities Per 100 Million Vehicle Miles, 2013

Rank	State	Rate
	United States......................	1.09
1	Montana.............................	1.90
2	West Virginia.............................	1.73
3	Mississippi.............................	1.58
4	South Carolina.............................	1.57
5	South Dakota.............................	1.48
6	Louisiana.............................	1.47
6	North Dakota.............................	1.47
8	Arkansas.............................	1.44
9	Oklahoma.............................	1.41
10	Arizona.............................	1.40
10	Tennessee.............................	1.40
12	Texas.............................	1.38
13	Kentucky.............................	1.36
14	Idaho.............................	1.34
15	Alabama.............................	1.31
16	Florida.............................	1.25
17	New Mexico.............................	1.24
18	North Carolina.............................	1.23
19	Pennsylvania.............................	1.22
20	Kansas.............................	1.16
21	Missouri.............................	1.09
21	Nebraska.............................	1.09
23	Georgia.............................	1.08
24	Delaware.............................	1.06
24	Nevada.............................	1.06
26	Alaska.............................	1.05
26	New Hampshire.............................	1.05
28	Maine.............................	1.03
29	Colorado.............................	1.02
30	Hawaii.............................	1.01
31	Indiana.............................	1.00
31	Iowa.............................	1.00
31	Michigan.............................	1.00
34	Vermont.............................	0.97
35	Illinois.............................	0.94
36	Oregon.............................	0.93
37	Wyoming.............................	0.93
38	New York.............................	0.92
39	Virginia.............................	0.92
40	California.............................	0.91
40	Wisconsin.............................	0.91
42	Connecticut.............................	0.89
43	Ohio.............................	0.88
44	Rhode Island.............................	0.84
45	Maryland.............................	0.82
46	Utah.............................	0.81
47	Washington.............................	0.76
48	New Jersey.............................	0.73
49	Minnesota.............................	0.68
50	Massachusetts.............................	0.58
51	District of Columbia............	0.57

ALABAMA

Facts and Figures

Location: Southeastern United States; bordered on the N by Tennessee, on the E by Georgia, on the S by Florida and the Gulf of Mexico, and on the W by Mississippi

Area: 52,420 sq. mi. (135,765 sq. km.); rank—30th

Population: 4,849,377 (2014 est.); rank—23rd

Principal Cities: capital—Montgomery; largest—Birmingham

Statehood: December 14, 1819; 22nd state

U.S. Congress: 2 senators, 7 representatives

State Motto: *Audemus jura nostra defendere* ("We dare defend our rights")

State Song: "Alabama"

State Nicknames: The Yellowhammer State; The Heart of Dixie; The Cotton State

Abbreviations: AL; Ala.

State Symbols: flower—camellia; tree—Southern longleaf pine; bird—yellowhammer

At a Glance

- With an increase in population of 1.4 percent, Alabama ranked 37th among the states in growth from 2010 to 2014.

- Alabama's per capita money income in 2013 was $28,184, ranking 22nd in the nation.

- With 8.61 deaths per 1,000 live births, Alabama's infant mortality rate ranked 3rd in the nation in 2013.

- In 2013, 18.7 percent of Alabama residents lived below the poverty level, a percentage that ranked 8th in the nation.

- Alabama's violent crime rate in 2013 was 430.8 per 100,000 residents, compared to 367.9 for the entire nation.

- Alabama's median household income of $42,849 ranked 48th in the nation.

Table AL-1. Population by Age, Sex, Race, and Hispanic Origin

(Number, percent, except where noted.)

Sex, age, race, and Hispanic origin	2000	2010	2014[1]	Average annual percent change, 2010–2014
Total Population	4,447,100	4,779,736	4,849,377	0.4
Percent of total U.S. population	1.6	1.5	1.5	X
Sex				
Male	2,146,504	2,320,188	2,349,967	0.3
Female	2,300,596	2,459,548	2,499,410	0.4
Age				
Under 5 years	295,992	304,957	294,705	-0.9
5 to 19 years	960,177	971,355	939,356	-0.8
20 to 64 years	2,611,133	2,845,632	2,871,384	0.2
65 years and over	579,798	657,792	743,932	3.1
Median age (years)	35.8	37.9	38.6	0.5
Race and Hispanic Origin				
One race				
White	3,162,808	3,362,877	3,377,605	0.1
Black	1,155,930	1,259,224	1,293,200	0.7
American Indian and Alaska Native	22,430	32,903	33,772	0.7
Asian	31,346	55,240	64,633	4.0
Native Hawaiian or Other Pacific Islander	1,409	5,208	5,089	-0.6
Two or more races	44,179	64,284	75,078	4.0
Hispanic (of any race)	75,830	192,498	200,664	1.0

X = Not applicable.
[1]Population figures for 2014 are July 1 estimates. The 2010 estimates are taken from the 2010 Census.

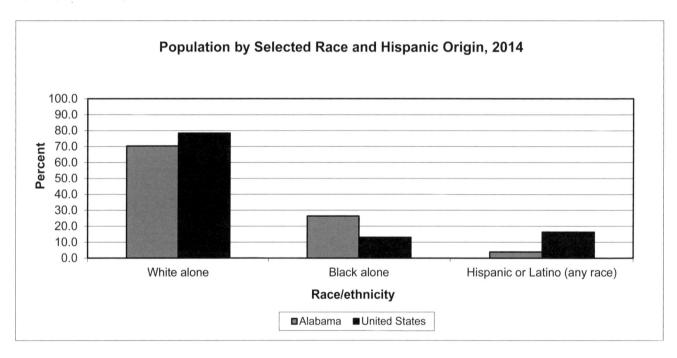

Population by Selected Race and Hispanic Origin, 2014

Table AL-2. Marital Status

(Number, percent distribution.)

Sex, age, and marital status	2000	2010	2013
Males, 15 Years and Over	1,666,798	1,844,661	1,870,698
Never married	26.7	32.5	33.4
Now married, except separated	59.0	50.6	49.7
Separated	1.8	2.5	2.2
Widowed	2.8	3.0	3.2
Divorced	9.8	11.4	11.5
Females, 15 Years and Over	1,847,401	2,004,450	2,040,300
Never married	21.4	26.1	27.5
Now married, except separated	52.5	45.9	45.0
Separated	2.5	3.1	2.9
Widowed	12.4	11.2	11.3
Divorced	11.2	13.6	13.4

Table AL-3. Households and Housing Characteristics

(Number, percent, dollars.)

Item	2000	2010	2013	Average annual percent change, 2000–2013
Total Households...	1,737,080	1,815,152	1,822,439	0.4
Family households	1,215,968	1,227,884	1,222,568	-
Married-couple family	906,916	868,946	857,865	-0.4
Other family	309,052	358,938	364,703	1.3
Male householder, no wife present..............	62,586	79,308	80,482	2.0
Female householder, no husband present...........	246,466	279,630	284,221	1.1
Nonfamily households	521,112	587,268	599,871	1.1
Householder living alone...............................	453,898	511,708	527,886	1.2
Householder not living alone........................	67,214	75,560	71,985	0.5
Housing Characteristics				
Total housing units..	1,963,711	2,174,428	2,190,027	0.8
Occupied housing units	1,737,080	1,815,152	1,822,439	0.3
Owner occupied	1,258,705	1,272,846	1,240,017	-0.1
Renter occupied	478,375	542,306	582,422	1.5
Average household size....................................	2.49	2.57	2.59	0.3
Financial Characteristics				
Median gross rent of renter-occupied housing	447	667	694	3.4
Median monthly owner costs for housing units with a mortgage	816	1,130	1,093	2.3
Median value of owner-occupied housing units........................	85,100	123,900	122,700	2.9

- = Zero or rounds to zero

Table AL-4. Migration, Origin, and Language

(Number, percent.)

Characteristic	State			U.S.		
	2012	2013	Percent change	2012	2013	Percent change
Residence 1 Year Ago						
Population 1 year and over	4,764,428	4,781,296	0.4	310,212,755	312,432,820	0.7
Same house	85.1	85.1	X	85.0	85.0	X
Different house in the U.S.	14.6	14.6	X	14.4	14.4	X
Same county	9.0	9.1	X	9.0	8.9	X
Different county	5.6	5.5	X	5.4	5.5	X
Same state	3.4	3.3	X	3.2	3.2	X
Different state	2.2	2.2	X	2.3	2.3	X
Abroad	0.3	0.3	X	0.6	0.6	X
Place of Birth						
Native born	4,658,344	4,671,496	0.3	273,089,382	274,780,773	0.6
Male	48.4	48.3	X	49.3	49.3	X
Female	51.6	51.7	X	50.7	50.7	X
Foreign born	163,679	162,226	-0.9	40,824,658	41,348,066	1.3
Male	50.1	51.8	X	48.7	48.8	X
Female	49.9	48.2	X	51.3	51.2	X
Foreign born; naturalized U.S. citizen................	56,167	59,782	6.4	18,686,237	19,294,710	3.3
Male	43.8	48.9	X	45.8	45.9	X
Female	56.2	51.1	X	54.2	54.1	X
Foreign born; not a U.S. citizen.....................	107,512	102,444	-4.7	22,138,421	22,053,356	-0.4
Male	53.3	53.5	X	51.1	51.3	X
Female	46.7	46.5	X	48.9	48.7	X
Entered 2010 or later	11.3	11.9	X	7.0	9.7	X
Entered 2000 to 2009	41.4	42.4	X	30.4	29.4	X
Entered before 2000..	47.2	45.7	X	62.7	61.0	X
World Region of Birth, Foreign						
Foreign-born population, excluding population born at sea	163,679	162,226	-0.9	40,824,553	41,347,945	1.3
Europe	10.9	10.7	X	11.8	11.6	X
Asia...	31.2	30.9	X	29.2	29.5	X
Africa..	4.3	4.6	X	4.2	4.4	X
Oceania	0.7	0.6	X	0.6	0.5	X
Latin America..	50.8	51.1	X	52.2	51.9	X
North America...	2.3	2.1	X	2.0	2.0	X
Language Spoken at Home and Ability to Speak English						
Population 5 years and over..............................	4,520,215	4,541,368	0.5	294,003,714	296,358,760	0.8
English only	94.9	94.9	X	79.0	79.2	X
Language other than English...........................	5.1	5.1	X	21.0	20.8	X
Speaks English less than "very well"..............	2.2	2.2	X	8.5	8.5	X

NA = Not available.
X = Not applicable.
- = Zero or rounds to zero.

Table AL-5. Median Income and Poverty Status, 2013

(Number, percent, except as noted.)

Characteristic	State Number	State Percent	U.S. Number	U.S. Percent
Median Income				
Households (dollars)..	42,849	X	52,250	X
Families (dollars)	54,045	X	64,030	X
Below Poverty Level (All People)...	883,371	18.7	48,810,868	15.8
Sex				
Male..	383,672	16.9	21,938,525	14.5
Female	499,699	20.5	26,872,343	17.1
Age				
Under 18 years..	297,591	27.2	16,086,960	22.2
Related children under 18 years...	293,936	27.0	15,769,921	21.9
18 to 64 years...	511,391	17.5	28,578,191	14.8
65 years and over	74,389	10.6	4,145,717	9.6

X = Not applicable.

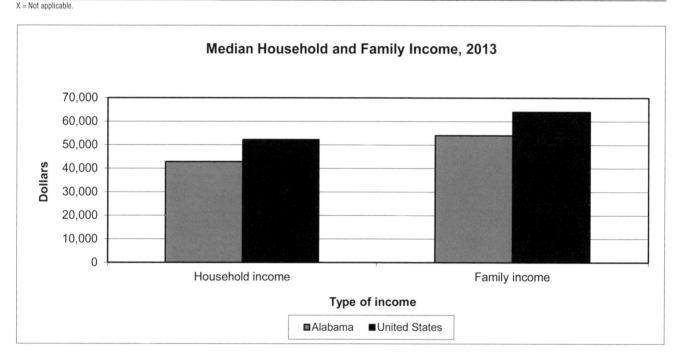

Median Household and Family Income, 2013

Table AL-6. Health Insurance Coverage Status for the Civilian Noninstitutionalized Population and Children Under 18 Years of Age

(Numbers in thousands, percent.)

Item	2005	2006	2007	2008	2009	2010	2011	2012	2013
Civilian Noninstitutionalized Population	4,524	4,532	4,570	4,574	4,616	4,703	4,720	4,742	4,755
Covered by Private or Public Insurance									
Number..	3,867	3,843	4,021	4,023	3,979	4,016	4,046	4,109	4,110
Percent...	85.5	84.8	88.0	88.0	86.2	85.4	85.7	86.7	86.4
Not Covered									
Number..	657	689	549	551	637	687	674	632	645
Percent...	14.5	15.2	12.0	12.0	13.8	14.6	14.3	13.3	13.6
Percent in the U.S. not covered...	15.3	15.8	15.3	15.1	15.1	15.5	15.1	14.8	14.5
Children Under 18 Years of Age...	1,083	1,114	1,083	1,120	1,124	1,134	1,122	1,123	1,108
Covered by Private or Public Insurance									
Number..	1,034	1,032	1,041	1,030	1,057	1,067	1,063	1,077	1,060
Percent...	95.5	92.6	92.7	92.0	94.1	94.1	94.7	95.9	95.7
Not Covered									
Number..	49	82	82	90	67	67	59	46	48
Percent...	4.5	7.4	7.3	8.0	5.9	5.9	5.3	4.1	4.3
Percent in the U.S. not covered...	10.9	11.7	11.0	9.7	8.6	8.0	7.5	7.2	7.1

Table AL-7. Employment Status by Demographic Group, 2014

(Numbers in thousands, percent.)

Characteristic	Civilian noninstitutional population	Civilian labor force		Employed		Unemployed	
		Number	Percent of population	Number	Percent of population	Number	Percent of population
Total..	3,786	2,164	57.2	2,011	53.1	153	7.1
Sex							
Male...	1,796	1,134	63.1	1,055	58.7	79	6.9
Female	1,990	1,031	51.8	956	48.0	75	7.2
Race, Sex, and Hispanic Origin							
White	2,714	1,563	57.6	1,481	54.6	82	5.2
Male	1,314	859	65.4	819	62.3	41	4.7
Female	1,400	703	50.2	662	47.3	41	5.9
Black or African American....................	963	539	55.9	473	49.1	66	12.2
Male	428	237	55.5	203	47.4	35	14.6
Female	536	301	56.3	270	50.5	31	10.3
Hispanic or Latino ethnicity[1]	129	90	70.1	81	63.1	9	10.0
Male	77	63	80.7	58	74.4	5	7.8
Female	NA	NA	NA	NA	NA	NA	NA
Age							
16 to 19 years......................................	241	62	25.7	44	18.1	18	29.7
20 to 24 years......................................	348	238	68.4	209	59.9	30	12.4
25 to 34 years......................................	572	455	79.6	409	71.5	46	10.1
35 to 44 years......................................	632	507	80.2	486	76.9	20	4.0
45 to 54 years......................................	641	469	73.1	446	69.6	22	4.8
55 to 64 years......................................	622	324	52.1	311	50.0	13	4.0
65 years and over	729	109	15.0	106	14.5	4	3.3

NOTE: Data in Table 7 are from the Current Population Survey (CPS) and do not match the estimates in Table 8. See notes and definitions for further information.
[1]May be of any race.
NA = Not available.

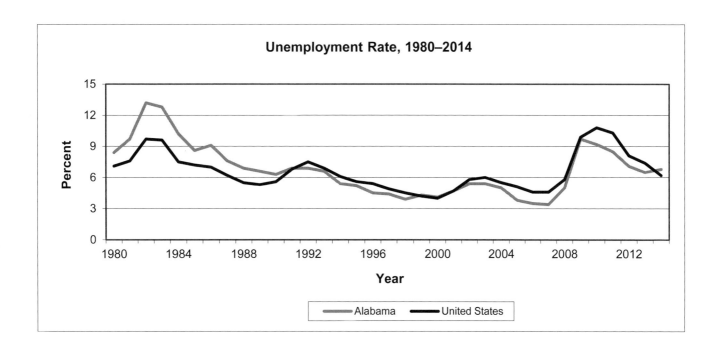

Table AL-8. Employment Status of the Civilian Noninstitutional Population Age 16 Years and Over

(Number, percent.)

Year	Civilian labor force	Civilian participation rate	Employed	Unemployed	Unemployment rate
2006	2,167,809	61.5	2,080,233	87,576	4.0
2007	2,175,612	61.1	2,089,127	86,485	4.0
2008	2,176,489	60.6	2,053,477	123,012	5.7
2009	2,162,999	59.7	1,924,747	238,252	11.0
2010	2,196,042	59.5	1,964,559	231,483	10.5
2011	2,201,473	59.1	1,988,753	212,720	9.7
2012	2,175,942	58.1	2,002,638	173,304	8.0
2013	2,168,594	57.6	2,011,596	156,998	7.2
2014	2,150,118	56.8	2,003,910	146,208	6.8

Table AL-9. Employment and Average Wages by Industry

(Estimates from 2007 through 2010 are based on the 2007 *North American Industry Classification System* [NAICS]. Estimates from 2011 onward are based on the 2012 NAICS.)

Industry	2007	2008	2009	2010	2011	2012	2013
				Number of jobs			
Wage and Salary Employment by Industry	2,101,829	2,082,617	1,978,414	1,960,904	1,962,049	1,967,479	1,983,624
Farm Wage and Salary Employment	7,648	7,750	9,482	7,957	8,074	8,015	8,597
Nonfarm Wage and Salary Employment	2,094,181	2,074,867	1,968,932	1,952,947	1,953,975	1,959,464	1,975,027
Private wage and salary employment	1,683,982	1,664,029	1,557,480	1,539,991	1,545,888	1,556,449	1,574,326
Forestry, fishing, and related activities	9,055	8,708	8,503	8,727	8,857	8,482	8,713
Mining	8,178	8,267	7,723	7,771	8,289	8,595	7,990
Utilities	13,350	13,971	13,865	14,093	14,262	14,248	14,377
Construction	116,957	112,693	95,983	91,361	85,262	82,318	82,463
Manufacturing	296,645	282,951	246,592	236,733	237,815	243,884	249,574
Durable goods manufacturing	186,669	178,501	152,566	146,428	148,023	154,486	159,866
Nondurable goods manufacturing	109,976	104,450	94,026	90,305	89,792	89,398	89,708
Wholesale trade	82,557	81,737	75,203	72,336	72,563	72,930	73,476
Retail trade	244,471	240,716	228,378	226,793	228,106	226,180	226,637
Transportation and warehousing	58,854	58,524	53,443	53,269	54,180	55,668	57,083
Information	28,042	27,380	25,325	24,016	23,098	22,709	22,607
Finance and insurance	73,486	73,664	71,718	70,355	71,988	72,218	73,265
Real estate and rental and leasing	26,393	25,659	24,041	22,753	21,878	21,800	22,415
Professional, scientific, and technical services	98,192	100,795	97,910	95,809	95,059	95,095	95,402
Management of companies and enterprises	14,705	14,439	15,190	15,496	15,982	16,878	15,952
Administrative and waste services	110,544	108,209	94,485	100,596	104,600	108,133	109,279
Educational services	25,698	25,905	27,042	28,053	28,817	29,491	29,078
Health care and social assistance	193,279	196,005	195,152	197,749	199,466	201,226	204,075
Arts, entertainment, and recreation	17,777	17,787	18,082	16,616	16,278	15,796	16,077
Accommodation and food services	158,106	158,467	153,918	153,104	155,098	159,136	163,951
Other services, except public administration	107,693	108,152	104,927	104,361	104,290	101,662	101,912
Government and government enterprises	410,199	410,838	411,452	412,956	408,087	403,015	400,701
				Dollars			
Average Wages and Salaries by Industry	36,846	38,085	38,701	39,607	40,461	41,288	41,579
Average Farm Wages and Salaries	25,831	23,102	18,923	22,692	20,050	22,475	21,643
Average Nonfarm Wages and Salaries	36,886	38,141	38,796	39,676	40,546	41,365	41,665
Average private wages and salaries	36,253	37,345	37,841	38,802	39,653	40,673	41,037
Forestry, fishing, and related activities	29,335	30,634	29,997	32,117	32,801	33,685	34,373
Mining	61,865	67,255	68,446	74,346	77,705	76,342	77,961
Utilities	83,860	81,835	80,520	78,785	85,859	88,189	88,407
Construction	39,197	40,970	41,761	43,398	43,496	45,255	45,524
Manufacturing	43,679	45,149	45,770	48,313	49,094	50,348	50,900
Durable goods manufacturing	45,898	47,563	48,039	51,079	51,728	52,901	53,251
Nondurable goods manufacturing	39,912	41,026	42,088	43,827	44,752	45,934	46,710
Wholesale trade	51,799	53,580	53,268	54,900	56,108	56,903	57,896
Retail trade	23,719	23,821	24,139	24,523	24,734	25,295	25,622
Transportation and warehousing	39,691	40,641	40,471	41,919	43,059	43,938	44,568
Information	47,982	48,804	47,929	48,328	50,897	51,274	51,562
Finance and insurance	58,404	58,570	58,364	58,243	62,143	64,393	65,097
Real estate and rental and leasing	33,138	33,444	32,982	35,275	36,598	38,746	38,450
Professional, scientific, and technical services	58,573	62,245	65,076	65,906	68,022	69,673	70,590
Management of companies and enterprises	70,037	70,406	69,189	74,595	78,602	80,746	83,380
Administrative and waste services	23,394	24,258	25,148	26,251	26,113	26,713	26,697
Educational services	23,811	23,660	24,069	24,045	24,536	24,627	25,296
Health care and social assistance	38,614	39,966	41,221	41,615	42,230	43,263	43,395
Arts, entertainment, and recreation	19,900	19,310	18,934	18,935	18,915	19,903	20,174
Accommodation and food services	14,125	14,346	14,700	15,353	15,715	15,964	15,952
Other services, except public administration	24,740	25,935	26,389	27,569	28,092	29,150	29,834
Government and government enterprises	39,484	41,366	42,412	42,937	43,929	44,035	44,133

Table AL-10. Employment Characteristics by Family Type

(Number, percent.)

Family type and labor force status	2011 Total	2011 Families with own children under 18 years	2012 Total	2012 Families with own children under 18 years	2013 Total	2013 Families with own children under 18 years
All Families...	1,227,884	511,392	1,233,937	502,537	1,222,568	492,554
FAMILY TYPE AND LABOR FORCE STATUS						
Married-Couple Families..................................	868,946	320,947	883,291	323,513	857,865	305,444
Both husband and wife in labor force.............	49.6	66.4	47.2	63.7	46.7	63.6
Husband in labor force, wife not in labor force	22.6	26.7	24.1	30.0	23.4	28.8
Wife in labor force, husband not in labor force	7.9	4.2	8.2	4.2	8.7	5.1
Both husband and wife not in labor force................	19.9	2.7	20.4	2.1	20.9	2.3
Other Families...................................	358,938	190,445	350,646	179,024	364,703	187,110
Female householder, no husband present..................	77.9	80.9	79.2	83.2	77.9	81.4
In labor force.................................	49.4	62.2	52	67.2	49.5	64.4
Not in labor force..............................	28.5	18.7	27.2	16.0	28.5	16.9
Male householder, no wife present..............	22.1	19.1	20.8	16.8	22.1	18.6
In labor force................................	15.9	16.9	14.3	14.2	16.1	16.7
Not in labor force.............................	6.1	2.2	6.5	2.6	6	2.0

Table AL-11. School Enrollment and Educational Attainment, 2013

(Number, percent.)

Item	State	U.S.
Enrollment		
Total population 3 years and over, enrolled in school	1,209,237	82,395,254
Enrolled in nursery school or preschool (percent).............................	5.9	6.0
Enrolled in kindergarten (percent).............................	5.2	5.2
Enrolled in elementary school, grades 1-8 (percent).........................	41.7	40.0
Enrolled in high school, grades 9-12 (percent).............................	21.1	20.6
Enrolled in college or graduate school (percent).............................	26.3	28.3
Attainment		
Total population 25 years and over	3,225,447	210,910,615
Less than ninth grade (percent).............................	4.9	5.8
9th to 12th grade, no diploma (percent).............................	10.6	7.6
High school graduate, including equivalency (percent).........................	31.0	27.8
Some college, no degree (percent).............................	22.0	21.1
Associate's degree (percent).............................	8.0	8.1
Bachelor's degree (percent).............................	14.8	18.4
Graduate or professional degree (percent).............................	8.7	11.2
High school graduate or higher (percent).............................	84.5	86.6
Bachelor's degree or higher (percent).............................	23.5	29.6

Table AL-12. Public School Characteristics and Educational Indicators

(Number, percent; data derived from National Center of Education Statistics.)

Item	State	U.S.
Public Schools, 2012–2013 (except where noted)		
Number of school districts.............................	173	18,093
Number of schools.............................	1,637	98,454
Number of students (in thousands)	745	49,771
Number of teachers (in thousands)	52	3,109
Student-teacher ratio.............................	14.4	16.0
Expenditures per student (dollars), FY 2012.............................	8,577	10,667
Four-year adjusted cohort graduation rate (ACGR)[1,2]	80.0	81.4
Students eligible for free or reduced-price lunch (in thousands)	430	25,188
English language learners (in thousands)	18	4,397
Students age 3 to 21 served under IDEA, part B (in thousands)	80	6,429

Public Schools by Type	Number	Percent of state public schools
Total number of schools.............................	1,637	100.0
Regular	1,402	85.6
Special education.............................	44	2.7
Vocational education.............................	72	4.4
Alternative education	119	7.3

NOTE: Every school is assigned only one school type based on its instructional emphasis.
[1]ACGR data represents a new method of calculating high-school completion rates and may not be comparable to previous years' data for Averaged Freshmen Graduation Rates (AFGR).
[2]The United States 4-year ACGRs were estimated using both the reported 4-year ACGR data from 49 states and the District of Columbia and using imputed data for Idaho. The estimate for American Indian/Alaska Native students also includes imputed data for Virginia.

Table AL-13. Reported Voting and Registration of the Voting-Age Population, November 2012

(Numbers in thousands, percent.)

Item	Total population	Total citizen population	Registered			Voted		
			Total registered	Percent registered (total population)	Percent registered (total citizen population)	Total voted	Percent voted (total population)	Percent voted (total citizen population)
U.S. Total	235,248	215,081	153,157	65.1	71.2	132,948	56.5	61.8
State Total	3,594	3,479	2,556	71.1	73.5	2,154	59.9	61.9
Sex	1,703	1,649	1,201	70.5	72.9	1,009	59.2	61.2
Male	1,891	1,831	1,354	71.6	74.0	1,145	60.6	62.6
Female								
Race								
White alone	2,580	2,502	1,878	72.8	75.1	1,530	59.3	61.2
White, non-Hispanic alone	2,473	2,467	1,866	75.5	75.6	1,530	61.9	62.0
Black alone	891	888	610	68.5	68.7	560	62.8	63.1
Asian alone	59	25	17	B	B	17	B	B
Hispanic (of any race)	107	35	12	11.5	35.1	-	B	B
White alone or in combination	2,605	2,527	1,904	73.1	75.3	1,556	59.7	61.6
Black alone or in combination	900	897	619	68.8	69.0	569	63.2	63.4
Asian alone or in combination	59	25	17	B	B	17	B	B
Age								
18 to 24 years	439	428	212	48.3	49.6	155	35.3	36.2
25 to 44 years	1,191	1,116	770	64.6	69.0	601	50.5	53.8
45 to 64 years	1,297	1,275	1,051	81.0	82.4	939	72.4	73.7
65 to 74 years	381	378	293	77.0	77.6	260	68.3	68.8
75 years and over	286	282	230	80.4	81.4	199	69.5	70.4

- = Zero or rounds to zero.
B = Base is less than 75,000 and therefore too small to show the derived measure.

Table AL-14. Crime

(Number, rate per 100,000. Data are derived from the FBI Uniform Crime Reports.)

Item	State			U.S.[1,2,3,4]		
	2012	2013	Percent change	2012	2013	Percent change
TOTAL POPULATION[5]........................	4,817,528	4,833,722	0.3	313,873,685	316,128,839	0.7
VIOLENT CRIME						
Number..................................	21,693	20,210	-6.8	1,217,067	1,163,146	-4.4
Rate	450.3	418.1	-7.1	387.8	367.9	-5.1
Murder and Nonnegligent Manslaughter						
Number..................................	342	347	1.5	14,866	14,196	-4.5
Rate	7.1	7.2	1.1	4.7	4.5	-5.2
Rape[6]						
Number..................................	X	2,044	X	X	108,612	X
Rate	X	42.3	X	X	34.4	X
Robbery						
Number..................................	5,020	4,648	-7.4	355,051	345,031	-2.8
Rate	104.2	96.2	-7.7	113.1	109.1	-3.5
Aggravated Assault						
Number..................................	15,035	13,787	-8.3	762,009	724,149	-5.0
Rate	312.1	285.2	-8.6	242.8	229.1	-5.6
PROPERTY CRIME						
Number..................................	168,878	161,993	-4.1	9,001,992	8,632,512	-4.1
Rate	3,505.5	3,351.3	-4.4	2,868.0	2,730.7	-4.8
Burglary						
Number..................................	47,481	42,429	-10.6	2,109,932	1,928,465	-8.6
Rate	985.6	877.8	-10.9	672.2	610.0	-9.3
Larceny-Theft						
Number..................................	111,523	108,993	-2.3	6,168,874	6,004,453	-2.7
Rate	2,314.9	2,254.8	-2.6	1,965.4	1,899.4	-3.4
Motor Vehicle Theft						
Number..................................	9,874	10,571	7.1	723,186	699,594	-3.3
Rate	205.0	218.7	6.7	230.4	221.3	-4.0

NOTE: Although arson data are included in the trend and clearance tables, sufficient data are not available to estimate totals for this offense. Therefore, no arson data are published in this table.
X = Not applicable.
- = Zero or rounds to zero.
[1]Because of changes in the state's reporting practices, figures are not comparable to previous years' data.
[2]The crime figures have been adjusted.
[3]The data collection methodology for the offense of forcible rape used by the Minnesota state Uniform Crime Reporting (UCR) Program (with the exception of Minneapolis and St. Paul, Minnesota) does not comply with national UCR Program guidelines. Consequently, its figures for forcible rape and violent crime (of which forcible rape is a part) are not published in this table.
[4]Includes offenses reported by the Zoological Police and the Metro Transit Police.
[5]Populations are U.S. Census Bureau provisional estimates as of July 1 of each year.
[6]The figures shown for the 2013 offense of rape were estimated using the revised Uniform Crime Reporting (UCR) definition of rape. Figures are not comparable to data from previous years.

Table AL-15. State Government Finances, 2013

(Dollar amounts in thousands, percent distribution.)

Item	Dollars	Percent distribution
Total Revenue	29,092,950	100.0
General revenue	22,759,645	78.2
Intergovernmental revenue	8,338,033	28.7
Taxes	9,267,567	31.9
General sales	2,331,676	8.0
Selective sales	2,376,842	8.2
License taxes	490,430	1.7
Individual income tax	3,202,520	11.0
Corporate income tax	382,202	1.3
Other taxes	483,897	1.7
Current charges	3,965,673	13.6
Miscellaneous general revenue	1,188,372	4.1
Utility revenue	0	-
Liquor stores revenue	278,248	1.0
Insurance trust revenue[1]	6,055,057	20.8
Total Expenditure	28,203,758	100.0
Intergovernmental expenditure	6,476,073	23.0
Direct expenditure	21,727,685	77.0
Current operation	15,061,164	53.4
Capital outlay	2,358,894	8.4
Insurance benefits and repayments	3,335,438	11.8
Assistance and subsidies	617,154	2.2
Interest on debt	355,035	1.3
Exhibit: Salaries and wages	4,511,760	16.0
Total Expenditure	28,203,758	100.0
General expenditure	24,601,701	87.2
Intergovernmental expenditure	6,476,073	23.0
Direct expenditure	18,125,628	64.3
General expenditure, by function:		
Education	10,616,535	37.6
Public welfare	6,386,764	22.6
Hospitals	2,132,163	7.6
Health	558,857	2.0
Highways	1,753,303	6.2
Police protection	160,779	0.6
Correction	533,083	1.9
Natural resources	276,034	1.0
Parks and recreation	20,371	0.1
Governmental administration	584,862	2.1
Interest on general debt	355,035	1.3
Other and unallocable	1,223,915	4.3
Utility expenditure	0	-
Liquor stores expenditure	266,619	0.9
Insurance trust expenditure	3,335,438	11.8
Debt at End of Fiscal Year	9,055,227	X
Cash and Security Holdings	41,204,130	X

X = Not applicable.
- = Zero or rounds to zero.
[1]Within insurance trust revenue, net earnings of state retirement systems is a calculated statistic (the item code in the data file is X08), and thus can be positive or negative. Net earnings is the sum of earnings on investments plus gains on investments minus losses on investments. The change made in 2002 for asset valuation from book to market value in accordance with Statement 34 of the Governmental Accounting Standards Board is reflected in the calculated statistics.

Table AL-16. State Government Tax Collections, 2014

(Dollars in thousands, percent.)

Item	Dollars	Percent distribution
Total Taxes	9,293,754	100.0
Property taxes	329,598	3.5
Sales and gross receipts	4,812,674	51.8
General sales and gross receipts	2,393,192	25.8
Selective sales and gross receipts	2,419,482	26.0
Alcoholic beverages	181,427	2.0
Amusements	70	-
Insurance premiums	304,441	3.3
Motor fuels	534,396	5.8
Pari-mutuels	1,547	0.0
Public utilities	734,105	7.9
Tobacco products	117,112	1.3
Other selective sales	546,384	5.9
Licenses	386,378	4.2
Alcoholic beverages	4,225	-
Amusements	0	-
Corporations in general	78,166	0.8
Hunting and fishing	21,311	0.2
Motor vehicle	189,345	2.0
Motor vehicle operators	20,920	0.2
Public utilities	14,233	0.2
Occupation and business, NEC	58,178	0.6
Other licenses	0	-
Income taxes	3,612,991	38.9
Individual income	3,206,583	34.5
Corporation net income	406,408	4.4
Other taxes	152,113	1.6
Death and gift	8	-
Documentary and stock transfer	36,668	0.4
Severance	115,437	1.2
Taxes, NEC	0	-

- = Zero or rounds to zero.

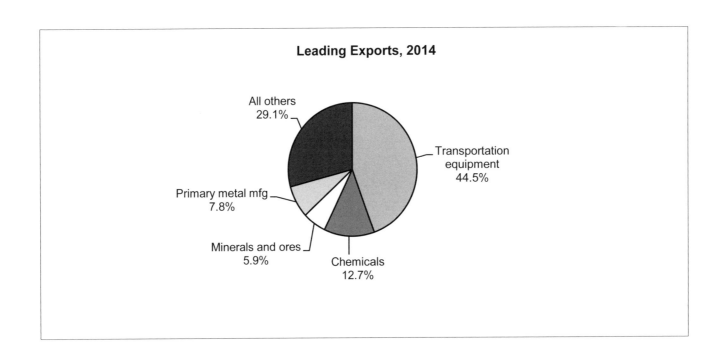

Leading Exports, 2014

All others 29.1%

Transportation equipment 44.5%

Primary metal mfg 7.8%

Minerals and ores 5.9%

Chemicals 12.7%

ALASKA

Facts and Figures

Location: Northwestern North America; bordered on the N by the Arctic Ocean, on the E by Canada, on the S by the Pacific Ocean and the Gulf of Alaska, and on the W by the Bering Sea

Area: 665,384 sq. mi. (1,717,854 sq. sq. km.); rank—1st

Population: 736,732 (2014 est.); rank—48th

Principal Cities: capital—Juneau; largest—Anchorage

Statehood: January 3, 1959; 49th state

U.S. Congress: 2 senators, 1 representative

State Motto: North to the Future

State Song: "Alaska's Flag"

State Nicknames: The Last Frontier; The Land of the Midnight Sun

Abbreviations: AK

State Symbols: flower—forget-me-not; tree—Sitka spruce; bird—willow ptarmigan

At a Glance

- With an increase in population of 3.7 percent, Alaska ranked 19th among the states for growth from 2010 to 2014.

- Alaska's 2013 violent crime rate ranked 2nd in the nation at 640.4 per 100,000 population, and the property crime rate (2,885.2 per 100,000 population) ranked 22nd.

- Alaska was the state with the second highest birth rate in 2013, at 17.6 births per 1,000 population.

- In 2013, 9.8 percent of Alaskans lived below the poverty level, a percentage that ranked 50th in the nation.

- Of all the states, Alaska had the 4th highest percentage of residents under 18 years old (25.3 percent) and the lowest percentage of residents age 65 and over (9.4 percent) in 2014.

Table AK-1. Population by Age, Sex, Race, and Hispanic Origin

(Number, percent, except where noted.)

Sex, age, race, and Hispanic origin	2000	2010	2014[1]	Average annual percent change, 2010–2014
Total Population	626,932	710,231	736,732	0.9
Percent of total U.S. population	0.2	0.2	0.2	X
Sex				
Male	324,112	369,628	387,296	1.2
Female	302,820	340,603	349,436	0.6
Age				
Under 5 years	47,591	53,996	54,708	0.3
5 to 19 years	160,526	153,844	150,885	-0.5
20 to 64 years	383,116	447,453	461,726	0.8
65 years and over	35,699	54,938	69,413	6.0
Median age (years)	32.4	33.8	33.3	-0.4
Race and Hispanic Origin				
One race				
White	434,534	483,873	492,522	0.4
Black	21,787	24,441	28,820	4.2
American Indian and Alaska Native	98,043	106,268	108,956	0.6
Asian	25,116	38,882	44,681	3.5
Native Hawaiian or Other Pacific Islander	3,309	7,622	9,296	5.1
Two or more races	34,146	49,105	52,457	1.7
Hispanic (of any race)	25,852	44,490	50,178	3.1

X = Not applicable.
[1] Population figures for 2014 are July 1 estimates. The 2010 estimates are taken from the 2010 Census.

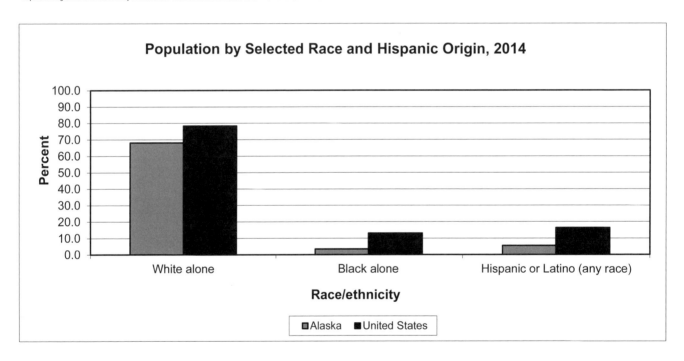

Table AK-2. Marital Status

(Number, percent distribution.)

Sex, age, and marital status	2000	2010	2013
Males, 15 Years and Over	243,024	290,598	304,721
Never married	32.5	35.5	39.2
Now married, except separated	53.6	49.7	47.5
Separated	1.7	1.7	1.5
Widowed	1.4	1.8	1.9
Divorced	10.8	11.4	9.9
Females, 15 Years and Over	225,837	267,563	271,658
Never married	24.1	27.3	30.2
Now married, except separated	55.6	50.2	49.9
Separated	2.3	2.6	1.9
Widowed	5.6	6.1	6.2
Divorced	12.5	13.7	11.8

Table AK-3. Households and Housing Characteristics

(Number, percent, dollars.)

Item	2000	2010	2013	Average annual percent change, 2000–2013
Total Households...	221,600	254,610	246,015	0.8
Family households	152,337	170,859	165,431	0.6
Married-couple family	116,318	127,969	126,502	0.6
Other family	36,019	42,890	38,929	0.6
Male householder, no wife present...........................	12,082	14,211	14,104	1.2
Female householder, no husband present	23,937	28,679	24,825	0.3
Nonfamily households	69,263	83,751	80,584	1.2
Householder living alone...	52,060	63,698	62,775	1.5
Householder not living alone....................................	17,203	20,053	17,809	0.3
Housing Characteristics				
Total housing units..	260,978	307,065	307,417	1.3
Occupied housing units	221,600	254,610	246,015	0.8
Owner occupied	138,509	162,785	156,107	0.9
Renter occupied	83,091	91,825	89,908	0.6
Average household size...	2.74	2.70	2.88	0.4
Financial Characteristics				
Median gross rent of renter-occupied housing	720	981	1,117	3.4
Median monthly owner costs for housing units with a mortgage	1,315	1,772	1,746	2.2
Median value of owner-occupied housing units.............	144,200	241,400	254,000	4.5

Table AK-4. Migration, Origin, and Language

(Number, percent.)

Characteristic	State			U.S.		
	2012	2013	Percent change	2012	2013	Percent change
Residence 1 Year Ago						
Population 1 year and over	721,186	725,193	0.6	310,212,755	312,432,820	0.7
Same house	82.2	80.5	X	85.0	85.0	X
Different house in the U.S.	17.2	18.5	X	14.4	14.4	X
Same county	10.2	11.2	X	9.0	8.9	X
Different county	7.0	7.4	X	5.4	5.5	X
Same state	2.4	2.6	X	3.2	3.2	X
Different state	4.6	4.7	X	2.3	2.3	X
Abroad	0.6	1.0	X	0.6	0.6	X
Place of Birth						
Native born	679,136	684,372	0.8	273,089,382	274,780,773	0.6
Male	52.5	53.0	X	49.3	49.3	X
Female	47.5	47.0	X	50.7	50.7	X
Foreign born	52,313	50,760	-3.0	40,824,658	41,348,066	1.3
Male	46.3	47.2	X	48.7	48.8	X
Female	53.7	52.8	X	51.3	51.2	X
Foreign born; naturalized U.S. citizen.........................	27,288	28,509	4.5	18,686,237	19,294,710	3.3
Male	42.3	46.9	X	45.8	45.9	X
Female	57.7	53.1	X	54.2	54.1	X
Foreign born; not a U.S. citizen.................................	25,025	22,251	-11.1	22,138,421	22,053,356	-0.4
Male	50.7	47.6	X	51.1	51.3	X
Female	49.3	52.4	X	48.9	48.7	X
Entered 2010 or later	11.7	10.7	X	7.0	9.7	X
Entered 2000 to 2009	30.2	27.7	X	30.4	29.4	X
Entered before 2000..	58.2	61.6	X	62.7	61.0	X
World Region of Birth, Foreign						
Foreign-born population, excluding population born at sea	52,313	50,760	-3.0	40,824,553	41,347,945	1.3
Europe	13.2	14.2	X	11.8	11.6	X
Asia...	58.5	56.4	X	29.2	29.5	X
Africa	3.5	3.1	X	4.2	4.4	X
Oceania	4.1	3.3	X	0.6	0.5	X
Latin America	17.0	17.2	X	52.2	51.9	X
North America	3.8	5.7	X	2.0	2.0	X
Language Spoken at Home and Ability to Speak English						
Population 5 years and over.......................................	677,515	680,427	0.4	294,003,714	296,358,760	0.8
English only	83.4	84.5	X	79.0	79.2	X
Language other than English.....................................	16.6	15.5	X	21.0	20.8	X
Speaks English less than "very well"..........................	4.8	4.8	X	8.5	8.5	X

NA = Not available.
X = Not applicable.
- = Zero or rounds to zero.

Table AK-5. Median Income and Poverty Status, 2013

(Number, percent, except as noted.)

Characteristic	State		U.S.	
	Number	Percent	Number	Percent
Median Income				
Households (dollars)..	72,237	X	52,250	X
Families (dollars)	54,045	X	64,030	X
Below Poverty Level (All People)	67,016	9.3	48,810,868	15.8
Sex				
Male...	32,287	8.6	21,938,525	14.5
Female	34,729	10.1	26,872,343	17.1
Age				
Under 18 years..	22,377	12.1	16,086,960	22.2
Related children under 18 years..........................	21,680	11.8	15,769,921	21.9
18 to 64 years..	41,288	8.8	28,578,191	14.8
65 years and over	3,351	5.2	4,145,717	9.6

X = Not applicable.

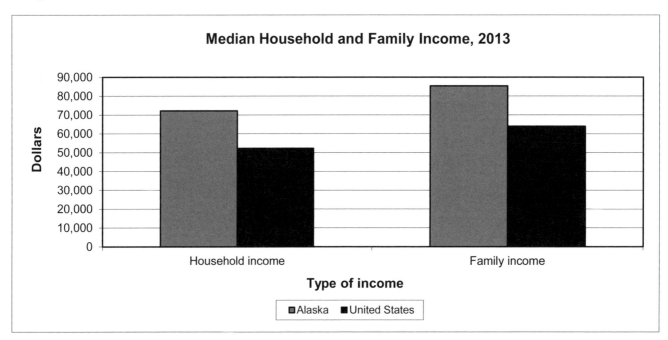

Table AK-6. Health Insurance Coverage Status for the Civilian Noninstitutionalized Population and Children Under 18 Years of Age

(Numbers in thousands, percent.)

Item	2005	2006	2007	2008	2009	2010	2011	2012	2013
Civilian Noninstitutionalized Population	659	659	675	659	678	689	699	709	712
Covered by Private or Public Insurance									
Number..	545	550	552	635	535	552	559	564	580
Percent..	82.8	83.5	81.8	96.4	78.9	80.1	79.9	79.5	81.5
Not Covered									
Number..	113	109	123	24	143	137	141	145	132
Percent..	17.2	16.5	18.2	3.6	21.1	19.9	20.1	20.5	18.5
Percent in the U.S. not covered..	15.3	15.8	15.3	15.1	15.1	15.5	15.1	14.8	14.5
Children Under 18 Years of Age..	187	181	185	180	183	188	188	187	188
Covered by Private or Public Insurance									
Number..	171	163	164	156	158	165	166	161	166
Percent..	91.6	89.7	88.6	86.7	86.4	87.8	88.2	86.1	88.4
Not Covered									
Number..	16	19	21	24	25	23	22	26	22
Percent..	8.4	10.3	11.4	13.3	13.6	12.2	11.8	13.9	11.6
Percent in the U.S. not covered..	10.9	11.7	11.0	9.7	8.6	8.0	7.5	7.2	7.1

Table AK-7. Employment Status by Demographic Group, 2014

(Numbers in thousands, percent.)

Characteristic	Civilian noninstitutional population	Civilian labor force		Employed		Unemployed	
		Number	Percent of population	Number	Percent of population	Number	Percent of population
Total...	541	368	68.0	342	63.2	26	7.1
Sex							
Male..	276	199	71.8	182	66.0	16	8.1
Female	264	169	64.0	159	60.2	10	5.9
Race, Sex, and Hispanic Origin							
White..	385	268	69.6	252	65.6	15	5.7
Male..	201	148	73.6	138	68.7	10	6.6
Female	184	120	65.2	115	62.3	5	4.5
Black or African American...................	19	12	67	11	61	1	9
Male..	NA	NA	NA	NA	NA	NA	NA
Female	NA	NA	NA	NA	NA	NA	NA
Hispanic or Latino ethnicity[1]	34	25	73.1	22	65.8	2	10.0
Male..	17	13	77.2	12	68.9	1	10.7
Female	NA	NA	NA	NA	NA	NA	NA
Age							
16 to 19 years...............................	41	17	40.8	13	32.8	3	19.5
20 to 24 years...............................	54	39	73.3	35	65.0	4	11.2
25 to 34 years...............................	108	86	80.0	80	74.2	6	7.3
35 to 44 years...............................	83	69	82.8	64	77.7	4	6.2
45 to 54 years...............................	94	78	83.2	75	79.6	3	4.4
55 to 64 years...............................	92	62	67.2	59	63.5	3	5.4
65 years and over	70	17	24.6	16	23.0	1	6.6

NOTE: Data in Table 7 are from the Current Population Survey (CPS) and do not match the estimates in Table 8. See notes and definitions for further information.
[1] May be of any race.
NA = Not available.

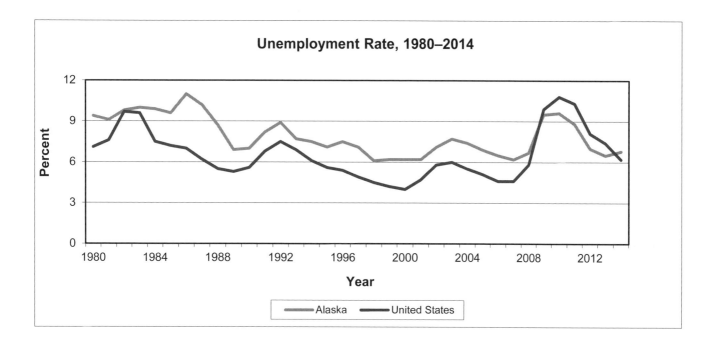

Unemployment Rate, 1980–2014

Table AK-8. Employment Status of the Civilian Noninstitutional Population Age 16 Years and Over

(Number, percent.)

Year	Civilian labor force	Civilian participation rate	Employed	Unemployed	Unemployment rate
2006	349,691	71.4	326,542	23,149	6.6
2007	350,785	70.7	328,579	22,206	6.3
2008	356,109	71.0	332,285	23,824	6.7
2009	359,647	70.3	331,792	27,855	7.7
2010	361,913	69.8	333,416	28,497	7.9
2011	366,003	69.2	338,268	27,735	7.6
2012	365,681	68.3	339,645	26,036	7.1
2013	365,537	67.8	340,332	25,205	6.9
2014	367,166	67.9	342,210	24,956	6.8

Table AK-9. Employment and Average Wages by Industry

(Estimates from 2007 through 2010 are based on the 2007 *North American Industry Classification System* [NAICS]. Estimates from 2011 onward are based on the 2012 NAICS.)

Industry	2007	2008	2009	2010	2011	2012	2013
	Number of jobs						
Wage and Salary Employment by Industry	347,537	351,532	351,192	353,467	359,669	365,031	366,027
Farm Wage and Salary Employment	195	179	175	187	210	188	244
Nonfarm Wage and Salary Employment	347,342	351,353	351,017	353,280	359,459	364,843	365,783
Private wage and salary employment	242,285	245,649	243,126	245,102	250,423	255,968	258,749
Forestry, fishing, and related activities	529	485	508	677	941	708	673
Mining	13,716	15,206	14,877	15,040	15,591	16,600	16,999
Utilities	1,843	1,895	1,982	2,142	2,107	2,120	2,136
Construction	18,196	17,945	17,050	16,812	16,673	16,997	17,189
Manufacturing	13,206	13,015	12,879	12,771	13,708	13,910	14,278
Durable goods manufacturing	2,119	2,186	2,042	1,891	1,865	2,015	2,079
Nondurable goods manufacturing	11,087	10,829	10,837	10,880	11,843	11,895	12,199
Wholesale trade	6,663	6,596	6,376	6,333	6,360	6,287	6,650
Retail trade	36,566	36,724	36,150	36,033	36,275	36,146	36,262
Transportation and warehousing	20,018	20,264	19,575	19,141	19,416	19,927	19,633
Information	6,934	7,000	6,607	6,458	6,316	6,205	6,161
Finance and insurance	9,112	9,145	8,955	9,085	9,047	8,730	7,416
Real estate and rental and leasing	4,988	4,801	4,899	5,073	5,013	4,891	4,992
Professional, scientific, and technical services	12,678	13,379	13,825	14,055	14,641	14,962	15,140
Management of companies and enterprises	1,187	1,206	1,247	1,156	1,240	1,822	3,056
Administrative and waste services	11,596	11,979	11,571	11,474	11,636	12,138	12,191
Educational services	3,054	3,048	3,023	3,128	3,236	3,277	3,300
Health care and social assistance	36,352	37,103	38,701	40,627	42,054	43,959	44,655
Arts, entertainment, and recreation	4,487	4,638	4,573	4,463	4,860	4,910	4,929
Accommodation and food services	27,978	27,979	26,908	27,379	28,039	28,607	29,038
Other services, except public administration	13,182	13,241	13,420	13,255	13,270	13,772	14,051
Government and government enterprises	105,057	105,704	107,891	108,178	109,036	108,875	107,034
	Dollars						
Average Wages and Salaries by Industry	45,208	47,088	48,401	49,543	50,806	53,579	54,523
Average Farm Wages and Salaries	26,528	28,430	28,320	28,487	29,324	19,867	33,156
Average Nonfarm Wages and Salaries	45,218	47,098	48,411	49,554	50,819	53,597	54,538
Average private wages and salaries	43,929	46,001	47,125	48,041	49,206	52,250	53,392
Forestry, fishing, and related activities	43,611	45,831	44,037	47,266	51,692	54,523	62,468
Mining	104,512	110,499	114,364	116,055	118,956	128,178	130,818
Utilities	66,598	70,620	74,032	73,526	78,613	85,671	88,125
Construction	63,032	66,902	69,498	71,000	70,793	74,703	77,367
Manufacturing	38,452	38,163	37,869	39,476	39,535	41,334	44,516
Durable goods manufacturing	45,862	47,471	49,774	49,620	49,568	53,282	55,315
Nondurable goods manufacturing	37,035	36,285	35,625	37,713	37,955	41,052	42,675
Wholesale trade	49,307	51,329	52,283	52,303	53,477	56,129	56,038
Retail trade	27,953	28,441	28,536	28,997	29,478	31,370	31,587
Transportation and warehousing	53,810	55,641	58,086	59,113	60,778	63,057	64,124
Information	52,803	55,511	56,738	56,105	59,742	62,106	63,397
Finance and insurance	55,339	56,815	57,805	59,910	61,358	66,115	63,502
Real estate and rental and leasing	33,020	35,354	37,045	38,255	38,912	41,665	42,450
Professional, scientific, and technical services	59,519	63,161	64,443	65,970	68,859	72,021	73,796
Management of companies and enterprises	76,695	77,402	77,772	81,629	79,747	78,980	81,459
Administrative and waste services	38,168	39,836	41,766	42,586	42,389	44,550	44,360
Educational services	28,261	28,340	28,229	28,092	27,795	28,567	29,553
Health care and social assistance	39,920	41,597	43,000	43,588	45,279	47,473	48,876
Arts, entertainment, and recreation	20,914	19,874	19,137	20,478	21,405	22,372	23,304
Accommodation and food services	22,318	22,199	21,907	22,619	23,430	24,579	24,901
Other services, except public administration	30,522	31,682	32,817	34,283	34,569	35,987	37,013
Government and government enterprises	48,192	49,647	51,309	52,980	54,522	56,762	57,308

Table AK-10. Employment Characteristics by Family Type

(Number, percent.)

Family type and labor force status	2011		2012		2013	
	Total	Families with own children under 18 years	Total	Families with own children under 18 years	Total	Families with own children under 18 years
All Families..	173,279	86,512	166,400	82,259	165,431	76,918
FAMILY TYPE AND LABOR FORCE STATUS						
Married-Couple Families..........................	127,277	56,973	123,248	54,673	126,502	54,850
Both husband and wife in labor force........................	58.4	64.0	56.7	62.6	58.1	64.2
Husband in labor force, wife not in labor force	21.9	29.4	22.2	29.3	22	28.5
Wife in labor force, husband not in labor force	8.7	4.5	9.5	5.9	8.8	5.2
Both husband and wife not in labor force.....................	11.0	2.1	11.6	2.2	10.9	2
Other Families....................................	46,002	29,539	43,152	27,586	38,929	22,068
Female householder, no husband present........................	65.8	65.0	68.6	73.4	63.8	64.4
In labor force.........................	50.9	54.0	49.7	57.6	47.6	54.6
Not in labor force......................	14.9	11.1	19	15.8	16.2	9.8
Male householder, no wife present...........................	34.2	35.0	31.4	26.6	36.2	35.6
In labor force.........................	26.5	28.3	26.2	23.7	30.5	32.4
Not in labor force......................	7.7	6.6	5.1	2.8	5.7	3.2

Table AK-11. School Enrollment and Educational Attainment, 2013

(Number, percent.)

Item	State	U.S.
Enrollment		
Total population 3 years and over, enrolled in school	200,784	82,395,254
Enrolled in nursery school or preschool (percent)..................	5.5	6.0
Enrolled in kindergarten (percent)................................	5.3	5.2
Enrolled in elementary school, grades 1-8 (percent)................	41.2	40.0
Enrolled in high school, grades 9-12 (percent)....................	21.9	20.6
Enrolled in college or graduate school (percent)..................	26.1	28.3
Attainment		
Total population 25 years and over	462,659	210,910,615
Less than ninth grade (percent).................................	3.1	5.8
9th to 12th grade, no diploma (percent)..........................	5.3	7.6
High school graduate, including equivalency (percent)..............	27.9	27.8
Some college, no degree (percent)...............................	27.5	21.1
Associate's degree (percent)....................................	8.3	8.1
Bachelor's degree (percent).....................................	18.2	18.4
Graduate or professional degree (percent)........................	9.8	11.2
High school graduate or higher (percent).........................	91.6	86.6
Bachelor's degree or higher (percent)............................	28.0	29.6

Table AK-12. Public School Characteristics and Educational Indicators

(Number, percent; data derived from National Center of Education Statistics.)

Item	State	U.S.
Public Schools, 2012–2013 (except where noted)		
Number of school districts.......................................	54	18,093
Number of schools..	509	98,454
Number of students (in thousands)	131	49,771
Number of teachers (in thousands)	8	3,109
Student-teacher ratio	17.1	16.0
Expenditures per student (dollars), FY 2012	17,475	10,667
Four-year adjusted cohort graduation rate (ACGR)[1,2]	71.8	81.4
Students eligible for free or reduced-price lunch (in thousands) ...	53	25,188
English language learners (in thousands)	15	4,397
Students age 3 to 21 served under IDEA, part B (in thousands)	18	6,429

Public Schools by Type	Number	Percent of state public schools
Total number of schools...	509	100.0
Regular	436	85.7
Special education..	3	0.6
Vocational education...	3	0.6
Alternative education..	67	13.2

NOTE: Every school is assigned only one school type based on its instructional emphasis.
[1]ACGR data represents a new method of calculating high-school completion rates and may not be comparable to previous years' data for Averaged Freshmen Graduation Rates (AFGR).
[2]The United States 4-year ACGRs were estimated using both the reported 4-year ACGR data from 49 states and the District of Columbia and using imputed data for Idaho. The estimate for American Indian/Alaska Native students also includes imputed data for Virginia.

Table AK-13. Reported Voting and Registration of the Voting-Age Population, November 2012

(Numbers in thousands, percent.)

Item	Total population	Total citizen population	Registered			Voted		
			Total registered	Percent registered (total population)	Percent registered (total citizen population)	Total voted	Percent voted (total population)	Percent voted (total citizen population)
U.S. Total	235,248	215,081	153,157	65.1	71.2	132,948	56.5	61.8
State Total	516	495	361	69.9	72.8	289	56.0	58.4
Sex								
Male	261	254	181	69.3	71.3	140	53.6	55.1
Female	255	241	180	70.5	74.4	149	58.6	61.8
Race								
White alone	373	365	283	75.7	77.4	232	62.1	63.4
White, non-Hispanic alone	355	352	273	76.8	77.5	225	63.3	63.9
Black alone.........................	21	20	10	B	B	6	B	B
Asian alone	30	21	13	B	B	10	B	B
Hispanic (of any race)	23	18	10	B	B	7	B	B
White alone or in combination	400	392	301	75.3	76.9	247	61.7	62.9
Black alone or in combination..........	23	22	12	B	B	7	B	B
Asian alone or in combination..........	35	25	14	B	B	11	B	B
Age								
18 to 24 years	63	61	31	B	B	20	B	B
25 to 44 years	195	183	130	66.8	71.0	97	49.6	52.8
45 to 64 years	186	182	144	77.6	79.3	122	65.7	67.1
65 to 74 years	46	45	35	B	77.1	32	B	70.5
75 years and over	26	24	20	B	B	19	B	B

B = Base is less than 75,000 and therefore too small to show the derived measure.

Table AK-14. Crime

(Number, rate per 100,000. Data are derived from the FBI Uniform Crime Reports.)

Item	State			U.S.[1,2,3,4]		
	2012	2013	Percent change	2012	2013	Percent change
TOTAL POPULATION[5]............................	730,307	735,132	0.7	313,873,685	316,128,839	0.7
VIOLENT CRIME						
Number............................	4,412	4,430	0.4	1,217,067	1,163,146	-4.4
Rate	604.1	602.6	-0.3	387.8	367.9	-5.1
Murder and Nonnegligent Manslaughter						
Number............................	30	34	13.3	14,866	14,196	-4.5
Rate	4.1	4.6	12.6	4.7	4.5	-5.2
Rape[6]						
Number............................	X	922	X	X	108,612	X
Rate	X	125.4	X	X	34.4	X
Robbery						
Number............................	630	624		355,051	345,031	-2.8
Rate	86.3	84.9	-1.6	113.1	109.1	-3.5
Aggravated Assault						
Number............................	3,169	3,128	-1.3	762,009	724,149	-5.0
Rate	433.9	425.5	-1.9	242.8	229.1	-5.6
PROPERTY CRIME						
Number............................	20,037	21,210	5.9	9,001,992	8,632,512	-4.1
Rate	2,743.6	2,885.2	5.2	2,868.0	2,730.7	-4.8
Burglary						
Number............................	2,950	2,916	-1.2	2,109,932	1,928,465	-8.6
Rate	403.9	396.7	-1.8	672.2	610.0	-9.3
Larceny-Theft						
Number............................	15,565	16,599	6.6	6,168,874	6,004,453	-2.7
Rate	2,131.3	2,258.0	5.9	1,965.4	1,899.4	-3.4
Motor Vehicle Theft						
Number............................	1,522	1,695	11.4	723,186	699,594	-3.3
Rate	208.4	230.6	10.6	230.4	221.3	-4.0

NOTE: Although arson data are included in the trend and clearance tables, sufficient data are not available to estimate totals for this offense. Therefore, no arson data are published in this table.

X = Not applicable.

- = Zero or rounds to zero.

[1]Because of changes in the state's reporting practices, figures are not comparable to previous years' data.

[2]The crime figures have been adjusted.

[3]The data collection methodology for the offense of forcible rape used by the Minnesota state Uniform Crime Reporting (UCR) Program (with the exception of Minneapolis and St. Paul, Minnesota) does not comply with national UCR Program guidelines. Consequently, its figures for forcible rape and violent crime (of which forcible rape is a part) are not published in this table.

[4]Includes offenses reported by the Zoological Police and the Metro Transit Police.

[5]Populations are U.S. Census Bureau provisional estimates as of July 1 of each year.

[6]The figures shown for the offense of rape were estimated using the revised Uniform Crime Reporting (UCR) definition of rape.

Table AK-15. State Government Finances, 2013

(Dollar amounts in thousands, percent distribution.)

Item	Dollars	Percent distribution
Total Revenue	14,018,474	100.0
General revenue	12,280,315	87.6
Intergovernmental revenue	2,754,412	19.6
Taxes	5,132,811	36.6
General sales	0	-
Selective sales	249,586	1.8
License taxes	135,720	1.0
Individual income tax	0	-
Corporate income tax	630,941	4.5
Other taxes	4,116,564	29.4
Current charges	623,797	4.4
Miscellaneous general revenue	3,769,295	26.9
Utility revenue	16,937	0.1
Liquor stores revenue	0	-
Insurance trust revenue[1]	1,721,222	12.3
Total Expenditure	12,214,598	100.0
Intergovernmental expenditure	2,032,061	16.6
Direct expenditure	10,182,537	83.4
Current operation	6,962,794	57.0
Capital outlay	1,460,784	12.0
Insurance benefits and repayments	1,298,440	10.6
Assistance and subsidies	192,835	1.6
Interest on debt	267,684	2.2
Exhibit: Salaries and wages	1,886,305	15.4
Total Expenditure	12,214,598	100.0
General expenditure	10,707,194	87.7
Intergovernmental expenditure	2,032,061	16.6
Direct expenditure	8,675,133	71.0
General expenditure, by function:		
Education	2,806,879	23.0
Public welfare	2,084,000	17.1
Hospitals	79,817	0.7
Health	348,730	2.9
Highways	1,152,768	9.4
Police protection	166,917	1.4
Correction	335,234	2.7
Natural resources	331,740	2.7
Parks and recreation	29,247	0.2
Governmental administration	663,166	5.4
Interest on general debt	263,066	2.2
Other and unallocable	2,445,630	20.0
Utility expenditure	208,964	1.7
Liquor stores expenditure	0	-
Insurance trust expenditure	1,298,440	10.6
Debt at End of Fiscal Year	6,218,363	X
Cash and Security Holdings	80,063,967	X

X = Not applicable.
- = Zero or rounds to zero.
[1]Within insurance trust revenue, net earnings of state retirement systems is a calculated statistic (the item code in the data file is X08), and thus can be positive or negative. Net earnings is the sum of earnings on investments plus gains on investments minus losses on investments. The change made in 2002 for asset valuation from book to market value in accordance with Statement 34 of the Governmental Accounting Standards Board is reflected in the calculated statistics.

Table AK-16. State Government Tax Collections, 2014

(Dollars in thousands, percent.)

Item	Dollars	Percent distribution
Total Taxes	3,392,869	100.0
Property taxes	128,076	3.8
Sales and gross receipts	257,696	7.6
General sales and gross receipts	X	X
Selective sales and gross receipts	257,696	7.6
Alcoholic beverages	39,078	1.2
Amusements	9,205	0.3
Insurance premiums	62,292	1.8
Motor fuels	42,467	1.3
Pari-mutuels	X	X
Public utilities	4,230	0.1
Tobacco products	72,004	2.1
Other selective sales	28,420	0.8
Licenses	141,947	4.2
Alcoholic beverages	1,905	0.1
Amusements	0	-
Corporations in general	0	-
Hunting and fishing	27,833	0.8
Motor vehicle	59,497	1.8
Motor vehicle operators	0	-
Public utilities	840	-
Occupation and business, NEC	43,060	1.3
Other licenses	8,812	0.3
Income taxes	408,938	12.1
Individual income	X	X
Corporation net income	408,938	12.1
Other taxes	2,456,212	72.4
Death and gift	0	-
Documentary and stock transfer	X	X
Severance	2,456,212	72.4
Taxes, NEC	0	-

X = Not applicable.
- = Zero or rounds to zero.

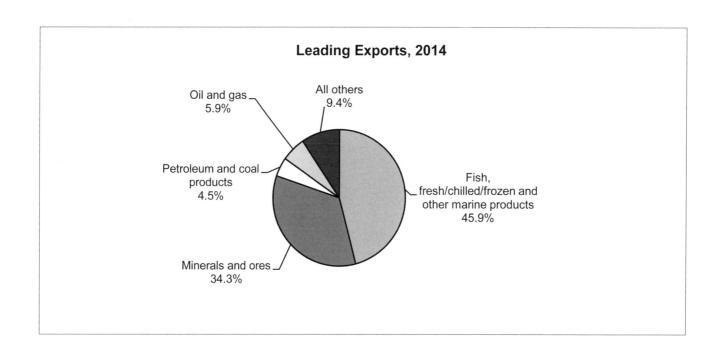

Leading Exports, 2014

Oil and gas 5.9%

All others 9.4%

Petroleum and coal products 4.5%

Fish, fresh/chilled/frozen and other marine products 45.9%

Minerals and ores 34.3%

ARIZONA

Facts and Figures

Location: Southwestern United States; bordered on the N by Utah, on the E by New Mexico, on the S by Mexico, and on the W by Nevada and California; Arizona is one of the Four Corner states—at its NE corner it touches Colorado, New Mexico, and Utah

Area: 113,990 sq, mi. (295,254 sq. km.); rank—6th

Population: 6,731,484 (2014 est.); rank—15th

Principal Cities: capital—Phoenix; largest—Phoenix

Statehood: February 14, 1912; 48th state

U.S. Congress: 2 senators, 9 representatives

State Motto: *Ditat Deus* ("God enriches")

State Song: "Arizona"

State Nickname: The Grand Canyon State

Abbreviations: AZ; Ariz.

State Symbols: flower—saguaro cactus blossom; tree—paloverde; bird—cactus wren

At a Glance

- With an increase in population of 5.3 percent, Arizona ranked 7th among the states in growth from 2010 to 2014.

- Arizonans consumed 213.2 million Btu of energy per capita in 2013, compared to the national average of 306.9 million Btu.

- Arizona's median household income in 2013 was $48,510, compared to the national median household income of $52,250.

- In 2013, 18.6 percent of Arizonans lived below the poverty level, a percentage that ranked 9th in the country.

- Arizona's violent crime rate in 2013 was 416.5 per 100,000 population, ranking 16th in the nation.

Table AZ-1. Population by Age, Sex, Race, and Hispanic Origin

(Number, percent, except where noted.)

Sex, age, race, and Hispanic origin	2000	2010	2014[1]	Average annual percent change, 2010–2014
Total Population	5,130,632	6,392,017	6,731,484	1.3
Percent of total U.S. population	1.8	2.1	2.1	X
Sex				
Male	2,561,057	3,175,823	3,343,847	1.3
Female	2,569,575	3,216,814	3,387,637	1.3
Age				
Under 5 years	382,386	455,715	430,888	-1.4
5 to 19 years	1,135,802	1,363,926	1,373,548	0.2
20 to 64 years	2,944,605	3,690,545	3,856,831	1.1
65 years and over	667,839	881,831	1,070,217	5.0
Median age (years)	34.2	35.9	37.1	0.8
Race and Hispanic Origin				
One race				
White	3,873,611	5,418,483	5,636,322	1.0
Black	158,873	280,905	318,202	3.2
American Indian and Alaska Native	255,879	335,278	357,672	1.6
Asian	92,236	188,456	221,347	4.1
Native Hawaiian or Other Pacific Islander	6,733	16,112	17,740	2.4
Two or more races	146,526	152,783	180,201	4.2
Hispanic (of any race)	1,295,617	1,943,466	2,056,455	1.4

X = Not applicable.
[1]Population figures for 2014 are July 1 estimates. The 2010 estimates are taken from the 2010 Census.

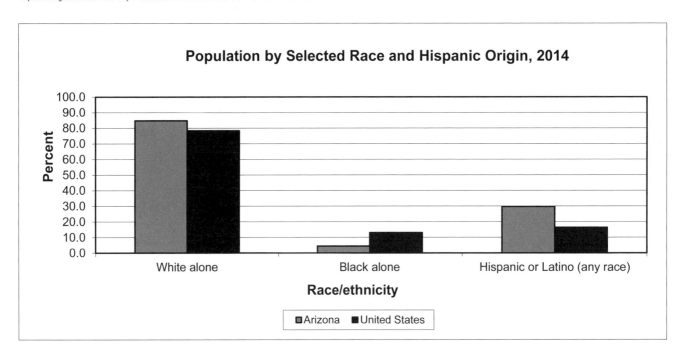

Table AZ-2. Marital Status

(Number, percent distribution.)

Sex, age, race, and Hispanic origin	2000	2010	2013
Males, 15 Years and Over	1,966,032	2,492,590	2,609,804
Never married	29.6	35.3	36.5
Now married, except separated	56.4	50.1	48.3
Separated	1.6	1.4	1.7
Widowed	2.6	2.5	2.5
Divorced	9.8	10.7	11.0
Females, 15 Years and Over	2,013,304	2,559,409	2,671,285
Never married	22.5	28.0	29.5
Now married, except separated	53.6	48.0	46.0
Separated	2.1	2.2	2.2
Widowed	9.4	8.3	8.4
Divorced	12.3	13.5	14.0

Table AZ-3. Households and Housing Characteristics

(Number, percent, dollars.)

Item	2000	2010	2013	Average annual percent change, 2000–2013
Total Households	1,901,327	2,334,050	2,400,809	1.8
Family households	1,287,367	1,548,428	1,572,310	1.5
Married-couple family	986,303	1,134,229	1,136,593	1.1
Other family	310,064	414,199	435,717	2.7
Male householder, no wife present	90,283	123,772	129,461	2.8
Female householder, no husband present	210,781	290,427	306,256	2.9
Nonfamily households	613,960	785,622	828,499	2.3
Householder living alone	472,006	621,291	661,142	2.6
Householder not living alone	141,954	164,331	167,357	1.3
Housing Characteristics				
Total housing units	2,189,189	2,846,738	2,892,359	2.2
Occupied housing units	1,901,327	2,334,050	2,400,809	1.8
Owner occupied	1,293,556	1,522,938	1,490,031	1.1
Renter occupied	607,771	811,112	910,778	3.2
Average household size	2.64	2.69	2.70	0.2
Financial Characteristics				
Median gross rent of renter-occupied housing	619	844	890	2.8
Median monthly owner costs for housing units with a mortgage	1,039	1,442	1,277	1.6
Median value of owner-occupied housing units	121,300	168,800	166,000	2.4

Table AZ-4. Migration, Origin, and Language

(Number, percent.)

Characteristic	State			U.S.		
	2012	2013	Percent change	2012	2013	Percent change
Residence 1 Year Ago						
Population 1 year and over	6,468,907	6,543,362	1.2	310,212,755	312,432,820	0.7
Same house	81.0	81.3	X	85.0	85.0	X
Different house in the U.S.	18.3	18.0	X	14.4	14.4	X
Same county	13.0	12.5	X	9.0	8.9	X
Different county	5.4	5.5	X	5.4	5.5	X
Same state	1.8	1.9	X	3.2	3.2	X
Different state	3.6	3.6	X	2.3	2.3	X
Abroad	0.6	0.7	X	0.6	0.6	X
Place of Birth						
Native born	5,677,328	5,730,314	0.9	273,089,382	274,780,773	0.6
Male	50.1	50.0	X	49.3	49.3	X
Female	49.9	50.0	X	50.7	50.7	X
Foreign born	875,927	896,310	2.3	40,824,658	41,348,066	1.3
Male	47.7	48.5	X	48.7	48.8	X
Female	52.3	51.5	X	51.3	51.2	X
Foreign born; naturalized U.S. citizen	344,372	342,265	-0.6	18,686,237	19,294,710	3.3
Male	44.8	45.5	X	45.8	45.9	X
Female	55.2	54.5	X	54.2	54.1	X
Foreign born; not a U.S. citizen	531,555	554,045	4.2	22,138,421	22,053,356	-0.4
Male	49.6	50.3	X	51.1	51.3	X
Female	50.4	49.7	X	48.9	48.7	X
Entered 2010 or later	6.7	9.4	X	7.0	9.7	X
Entered 2000 to 2009	27.7	26.9	X	30.4	29.4	X
Entered before 2000	65.6	63.7	X	62.7	61.0	X
World Region of Birth, Foreign						
Foreign-born population, excluding population born at sea	875,927	896,310	2.3	40,824,553	41,347,945	1.3
Europe	9.4	9.0	X	11.8	11.6	X
Asia	17.5	18.0	X	29.2	29.5	X
Africa	2.4	3.2	X	4.2	4.4	X
Oceania	0.6	0.5	X	0.6	0.5	X
Latin America	65.1	64.3	X	52.2	51.9	X
North America	5.1	5.0	X	2.0	2.0	X
Language Spoken at Home and Ability to Speak English						
Population 5 years and over	6,115,483	6,196,543	1.3	294,003,714	296,358,760	0.8
English only	72.9	73.2	X	79.0	79.2	X
Language other than English	27.1	26.8	X	21.0	20.8	X
Speaks English less than "very well"	9.2	9.1	X	8.5	8.5	X

NA = Not available.
X = Not applicable.
- = Zero or rounds to zero.

Table AZ-5. Median Income and Poverty Status, 2013

(Number, percent, except as noted.)

Characteristic	State		U.S.	
	Number	Percent	Number	Percent
Median Income				
Households (dollars)...	48,510	X	52,250	X
Families (dollars)	57,163	X	64,030	X
Below Poverty Level (All People).........................	1,206,460	18.6	48,810,868	15.8
Sex				
Male...	556,176	17.4	21,938,525	14.5
Female	650,284	19.8	26,872,343	17.1
Age				
Under 18 years...	421,100	26.5	16,086,960	22.2
Related children under 18 years............................	410,802	26.0	15,769,921	21.9
18 to 64 years...	695,810	17.9	28,578,191	14.8
65 years and over	89,550	8.9	4,145,717	9.6

X = Not applicable.

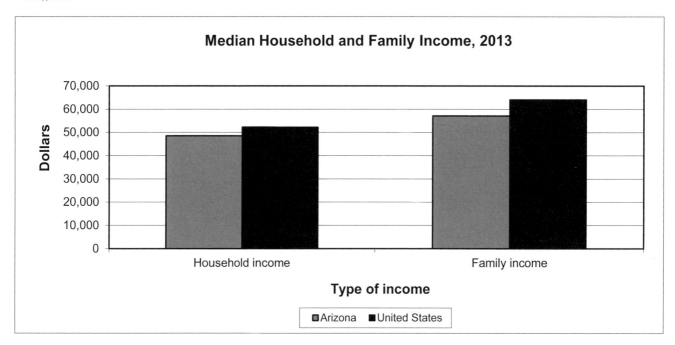

Table AZ-6. Health Insurance Coverage Status for the Civilian Noninstitutionalized Population and Children Under 18 Years of Age

(Numbers in thousands, percent.)

Item	2005	2006	2007	2008	2009	2010	2011	2012	2013
Civilian Noninstitutionalized Population.....................	6,047	6,269	6,368	6,403	6,502	6,310	6,378	6,444	6,521
Covered by Private or Public Insurance									
Number..	4,864	4,958	5,204	5,207	5,375	5,245	5,283	5,313	5,403
Percent..	80.4	79.1	81.7	81.3	82.7	83.1	82.8	82.4	82.9
Not Covered									
Number..	1,183	1,311	1,164	1,196	1,127	1,065	1,095	1,131	1,118
Percent..	19.6	20.9	18.3	18.7	17.3	16.9	17.2	17.6	17.1
Percent in the U.S. not covered.............................	15.3	15.8	15.3	15.1	15.1	15.5	15.1	14.8	14.5
Children Under 18 Years of Age.............................	1,627	1,662	1,697	1,706	1,730	1,630	1,622	1,617	1,614
Covered by Private or Public Insurance									
Number..	1,359	1,379	1,463	1,430	1,522	1,422	1,622	1,403	1,422
Percent..	83.6	83.0	86.2	83.8	88.0	87.2	87.1	86.8	88.1
Not Covered									
Number..	267	283	234	276	208	208	208	214	192
Percent..	16.4	17.0	13.8	16.2	12.0	12.8	12.9	13.2	11.9
Percent in the U.S. not covered.............................	10.9	11.7	11.0	9.7	8.6	8.0	7.5	7.2	7.1

Table AZ-7. Employment Status by Demographic Group, 2014

(Numbers in thousands, percent.)

Characteristic	Civilian noninstitutional population	Civilian labor force		Employed		Unemployed	
		Number	Percent of population	Number	Percent of population	Number	Percent of population
Total..	5,176	3,105	60.0	2,888	55.8	217	7.0
Sex							
Male...	2,519	1,673	66.4	1,557	61.8	116	6.9
Female	2,657	1,432	53.9	1,331	50.1	101	7.1
Race, Sex, and Hispanic Origin							
White...	4,388	2,634	60.0	2,464	56.2	170	6.4
Male...	2,134	1,427	66.9	1,334	62.5	93	6.5
Female	2,255	1,207	53.5	1,130	50.1	77	6.3
Black or African American...................	233	142	60.8	134	57.4	8	5.6
Male...	119	80	66.9	76	63.7	4	4.8
Female	115	62	54.4	58	50.8	4	6.5
Hispanic or Latino ethnicity[1]	1,716	1,062	61.9	974	56.8	88	8.3
Male...	838	602	71.8	551	65.8	51	8.4
Female	878	461	52.4	423	48.2	38	8.1
Age							
16 to 19 years.................................	389	133	34.1	102	26.1	31	23.3
20 to 24 years.................................	463	335	72.3	287	62.0	48	14.2
25 to 34 years.................................	837	654	78.1	616	73.6	37	5.7
35 to 44 years.................................	816	638	78.1	612	75.0	26	4.0
45 to 54 years.................................	899	709	78.9	676	75.2	33	4.7
55 to 64 years.................................	808	476	59.0	448	55.4	28	6.0
65 years and over	965	161	16.7	147	15.2	14	8.9

NOTE: Data in Table 7 are from the Current Population Survey (CPS) and do not match the estimates in Table 8. See notes and definitions for further information.
[1]May be of any race.
NA = Not available.

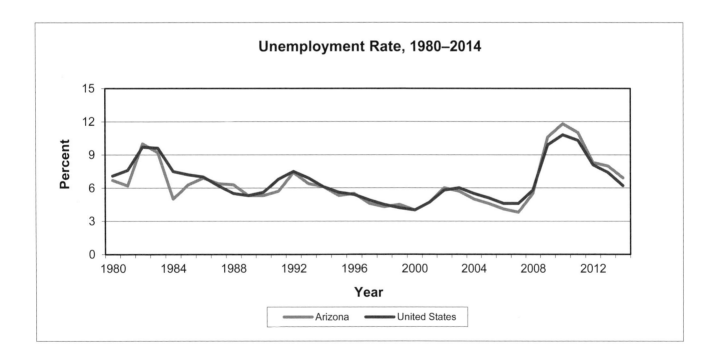

Unemployment Rate, 1980–2014

Table AZ-8. Employment Status of the Civilian Noninstitutional Population Age 16 Years and Over

(Number, percent.)

Year	Civilian labor force	Civilian participation rate	Employed	Unemployed	Unemployment rate
2006	2,990,441	64.6	2,864,385	126,056	4.2
2007	3,034,016	63.7	2,917,117	116,899	3.9
2008	3,104,863	63.8	2,913,903	190,960	6.2
2009	3,128,110	63.2	2,817,577	310,533	9.9
2010	3,089,705	63.1	2,769,454	320,251	10.4
2011	3,039,086	61.7	2,749,235	289,851	9.5
2012	3,034,050	60.6	2,779,187	254,863	8.4
2013	3,041,203	59.8	2,803,974	237,229	7.8
2014	3,090,628	59.7	2,877,643	212,985	6.9

Table AZ-9. Employment and Average Wages by Industry

(Estimates from 2007 through 2010 are based on the 2007 *North American Industry Classification System* [NAICS]. Estimates from 2011 onward are based on the 2012 NAICS.)

Industry	2007	2008	2009	2010	2011	2012	2013
	Number of jobs						
Wage and Salary Employment by Industry	2,779,312	2,713,899	2,524,521	2,483,674	2,510,358	2,558,795	2,619,055
Farm Wage and Salary Employment	13,272	11,632	12,134	11,583	11,342	12,000	13,751
Nonfarm Wage and Salary Employment	2,766,040	2,702,267	2,512,387	2,472,091	2,499,016	2,546,795	2,605,304
Private wage and salary employment	2,316,269	2,243,239	2,059,730	2,024,116	2,058,758	2,104,563	2,163,547
Forestry, fishing, and related activities	14,204	13,180	11,880	12,431	12,954	12,157	12,081
Mining	11,483	12,976	10,559	10,285	10,925	11,931	12,616
Utilities	12,745	12,738	12,435	12,079	11,975	12,290	11,932
Construction	233,245	193,649	134,757	116,705	117,015	120,118	128,145
Manufacturing	180,972	172,214	151,959	146,695	148,251	153,645	154,018
Durable goods manufacturing	146,899	139,141	121,379	116,492	117,601	121,694	121,388
Nondurable goods manufacturing	34,073	33,073	30,580	30,203	30,650	31,951	32,630
Wholesale trade	111,475	110,611	102,513	98,769	98,543	98,903	99,361
Retail trade	337,173	326,188	302,597	297,827	299,718	300,584	302,633
Transportation and warehousing	75,978	74,922	70,120	67,604	70,860	73,011	73,342
Information	42,056	40,878	38,185	36,733	36,683	38,284	41,847
Finance and insurance	134,236	127,573	123,284	121,948	125,932	129,752	135,954
Real estate and rental and leasing	54,989	53,938	49,042	47,092	46,332	46,947	48,424
Professional, scientific, and technical services	135,762	135,400	125,170	123,415	125,862	124,752	128,710
Management of companies and enterprises	26,938	27,646	26,577	25,422	25,216	26,735	28,748
Administrative and waste services	244,960	229,569	199,382	197,672	200,946	208,545	221,058
Educational services	41,829	45,006	47,281	51,291	53,767	56,000	56,587
Health care and social assistance	265,727	279,644	285,598	296,275	304,151	312,598	319,598
Arts, entertainment, and recreation	36,021	36,226	33,492	33,467	33,781	34,976	35,853
Accommodation and food services	240,783	236,949	225,280	223,334	228,368	233,536	241,850
Other services, except public administration	115,693	113,932	109,619	105,072	107,479	109,799	110,790
Government and government enterprises	449,771	459,028	452,657	447,975	440,258	442,232	441,757
	Dollars						
Average Wages and Salaries by Industry	42,367	43,309	43,580	44,145	45,396	46,417	46,797
Average Farm Wages and Salaries	32,451	35,735	38,035	34,616	36,679	29,631	38,734
Average Nonfarm Wages and Salaries	42,415	43,341	43,607	44,190	45,435	46,496	46,840
Average private wages and salaries	42,144	42,994	43,149	43,948	45,258	46,471	46,763
Forestry, fishing, and related activities	20,385	20,414	22,363	22,730	23,549	23,869	24,027
Mining	63,423	70,644	68,479	71,447	78,827	80,923	78,939
Utilities	83,264	87,512	91,045	92,192	95,114	95,384	97,378
Construction	43,123	45,101	44,867	45,018	45,931	47,964	48,426
Manufacturing	59,605	62,020	63,447	66,902	70,052	70,645	70,743
Durable goods manufacturing	64,079	67,051	69,137	73,482	77,173	77,819	78,007
Nondurable goods manufacturing	40,317	40,856	40,862	41,523	42,728	43,322	43,721
Wholesale trade	62,610	62,201	62,405	64,391	66,939	71,333	68,506
Retail trade	29,382	28,964	28,679	29,366	30,909	30,859	30,259
Transportation and warehousing	46,682	46,428	46,747	48,814	49,744	50,046	50,749
Information	54,718	55,738	57,476	57,915	59,814	61,620	62,888
Finance and insurance	61,382	60,329	58,925	61,003	63,500	67,007	69,577
Real estate and rental and leasing	43,007	43,606	42,085	42,624	44,623	46,810	46,491
Professional, scientific, and technical services	63,522	65,255	66,152	67,406	69,857	73,607	74,254
Management of companies and enterprises	77,033	76,555	75,094	74,940	77,325	82,548	85,637
Administrative and waste services	31,383	32,804	33,206	33,325	33,607	34,078	34,733
Educational services	35,475	37,183	39,065	39,625	40,119	40,700	40,585
Health care and social assistance	45,763	47,546	48,233	48,018	48,532	48,962	49,422
Arts, entertainment, and recreation	35,182	34,719	36,293	37,062	37,101	38,100	38,267
Accommodation and food services	20,334	19,778	19,475	20,005	20,467	20,873	20,892
Other services, except public administration	27,307	28,105	27,993	28,541	29,086	29,445	30,523
Government and government enterprises	43,810	45,037	45,691	45,281	46,265	46,616	47,217

Table AZ-10. Employment Characteristics by Family Type

(Number, percent.)

Family type and labor force status	2011		2012		2013	
	Total	Families with own children under 18 years	Total	Families with own children under 18 years	Total	Families with own children under 18 years
All Families..	1,543,923	674,157	1,560,687	674,358	1,572,310	671,500
FAMILY TYPE AND LABOR FORCE STATUS						
Married-Couple Families...................................	1,110,350	428,287	1,122,884	429,016	1,136,593	429,785
Both husband and wife in labor force..........................	46.9	59.8	45.6	60.3	43.3	57.6
Husband in labor force, wife not in labor force	23.0	34.1	23	33.7	23.8	35.3
Wife in labor force, husband not in labor force	7.5	4.1	7.5	4.0	7.8	4.4
Both husband and wife not in labor force....................	22.6	2.1	23.9	2.0	24.7	2.5
Other Families	433,573	245,870	437,803	245,342	435,717	241,715
Female householder, no husband present	70.6	71.7	70.5	71.5	70.3	73.2
In labor force..	51.0	58.9	50.7	58.4	49.9	59.6
Not in labor force	19.6	12.9	19.8	13.1	20.3	13.6
Male householder, no wife present...........................	29.4	28.3	29.5	28.5	29.7	26.8
In labor force..	23.2	25.1	23.1	25.7	23.1	24.0
Not in labor force	6.2	3.2	6.5	2.8	6.6	2.7

Table AZ-11. School Enrollment and Educational Attainment, 2013

(Number, percent.)

Item	State	U.S.
Enrollment		
Total population 3 years and over, enrolled in school	1,739,889	82,395,254
Enrolled in nursery school or preschool (percent)	4.8	6.0
Enrolled in kindergarten (percent)...	5.1	5.2
Enrolled in elementary school, grades 1-8 (percent)..	41.9	40.0
Enrolled in high school, grades 9-12 (percent)..	21.3	20.6
Enrolled in college or graduate school (percent)...	26.8	28.3
Attainment		
Total population 25 years and over	4,344,737	210,910,615
Less than ninth grade (percent)	6.4	5.8
9th to 12th grade, no diploma (percent)	7.7	7.6
High school graduate, including equivalency (percent).......................................	24.8	27.8
Some college, no degree (percent)	25.1	21.1
Associate's degree (percent)...	8.6	8.1
Bachelor's degree (percent)	17.1	18.4
Graduate or professional degree (percent)..	10.3	11.2
High school graduate or higher (percent)	85.9	86.6
Bachelor's degree or higher (percent)...	27.4	29.6

Table AZ-12. Public School Characteristics and Educational Indicators

(Number, percent; data derived from National Center of Education Statistics.)

Item	State	U.S.
Public Schools, 2012–2013 (except where noted)		
Number of school districts..	666	18,093
Number of schools..	2,267	98,454
Number of students (in thousands)	1,089	49,771
Number of teachers (in thousands)	49	3,109
Student-teacher ratio	22.3	16.0
Expenditures per student (dollars), FY 2012	7,382	10,667
Four-year adjusted cohort graduation rate (ACGR)[1,2]	75.1	81.4
Students eligible for free or reduced-price lunch (in thousands)	514	25,188
English language learners (in thousands)	59	4,397
Students age 3 to 21 served under IDEA, part B (in thousands)	128	6,429

Public Schools by Type	Number	Percent of state public schools
Total number of schools..	2,267	100.0
Regular	1,955	86.2
Special education..	22	1.0
Vocational education..	225	9.9
Alternative education...	65	2.9

NOTE: Every school is assigned only one school type based on its instructional emphasis.
[1]ACGR data represents a new method of calculating high-school completion rates and may not be comparable to previous years' data for Averaged Freshmen Graduation Rates (AFGR).
[2]The United States 4-year ACGRs were estimated using both the reported 4-year ACGR data from 49 states and the District of Columbia and using imputed data for Idaho. The estimate for American Indian/Alaska Native students also includes imputed data for Virginia.

Table AZ-13. Reported Voting and Registration of the Voting-Age Population, November 2012

(Numbers in thousands, percent.)

Item	Total population	Total citizen population	Registered			Voted		
			Total registered	Percent registered (total population)	Percent registered (total citizen population)	Total voted	Percent voted (total population)	Percent voted (total citizen population)
U.S. Total	2,35,248	2,15,081	1,53,157	65.1	71.2	1,32,948	56.5	61.8
State Total	4,863	4,314	2,812	57.8	65.2	2,412	49.6	55.9
Sex								
Male	2,361	2,110	1,398	59.2	66.2	1,193	50.5	56.6
Female	2,501	2,204	1,414	56.5	64.2	1,219	48.7	55.3
Race								
White alone	4,130	3,660	2,445	59.2	66.8	2,123	51.4	58.0
White, non-Hispanic alone	2,854	2,784	1,963	68.8	70.5	1,737	60.8	62.4
Black alone.................................	211	207	122	57.5	58.6	95	45.1	46.0
Asian alone	227	160	51	22.5	32.0	43	19.0	27.1
Hispanic (of any race)	1,396	989	516	37.0	52.2	400	28.7	40.4
Age								
18 to 24 years	586	545	301	51.4	55.3	234	40.0	43.0
25 to 44 years	1,729	1,422	837	48.4	58.8	671	38.8	47.2
45 to 64 years	1,656	1,502	1,015	61.3	67.6	901	54.4	60.0
65 to 74 years	504	474	368	73.0	77.6	351	69.5	73.9
75 years and over	388	371	291	75.1	78.5	255	65.8	68.8

Table AZ-14. Crime

(Number, rate per 100,000. Data are derived from the FBI Uniform Crime Reports.)

Item	State			U.S. 1,2,3,4		
	2012	2013	Percent change	2012	2013	Percent change
TOTAL POPULATION[5]	6,551,149	6,626,624	1.2	313,873,685	316,128,839	0.7
VIOLENT CRIME						
Number...	28,077	26,892	-4.2	1,217,067	1,163,146	-4.4
Rate...	428.6	405.8	-5.3	387.8	367.9	-5.1
Murder and Nonnegligent Manslaughter						
Number...	358	357	-0.3	14,866	14,196	-4.5
Rate	5.5	5.4	-1.4	4.7	4.5	-5.2
Rape[6]						
Number...	X	3,050	X	X	108,612	X
Rate	X	46.0	X	X	34.4	X
Robbery						
Number...	7,383	6,702	-9.2	355,051	345,031	-2.8
Rate	112.7	101.1	-10.3	113.1	109.1	-3.5
Aggravated Assault						
Number...	18,054	17,490	-3.1	762,009	724,149	-5.0
Rate	275.6	263.9	-4.2	242.8	229.1	-5.6
PROPERTY CRIME						
Number...	231,701	225,243	-2.8	9,001,992	8,632,512	-4.1
Rate	3,536.8	3,399.1	-3.9	2,868.0	2,730.7	-4.8
Burglary						
Number...	52,911	48,533	-8.3	2,109,932	1,928,465	-8.6
Rate	807.7	732.4	-9.3	672.2	610.0	-9.3
Larceny-Theft						
Number...	159,808	159,272	-0.3	6,168,874	6,004,453	-2.7
Rate	2,439.4	2,403.5	-1.5	1,965.4	1,899.4	-3.4
Motor Vehicle Theft						
Number...	18,982	17,438	-8.1	723,186	699,594	-3.3
Rate	289.8	263.2	-9.2	230.4	221.3	-4.0

NOTE: Although arson data are included in the trend and clearance tables, sufficient data are not available to estimate totals for this offense. Therefore, no arson data are published in this table.
X = Not applicable.
- = Zero or rounds to zero.
[1]Because of changes in the state's reporting practices, figures are not comparable to previous years' data.
[2]The data collection methodology for the offense of forcible rape used by the Minnesota state Uniform Crime Reporting (UCR) Program (with the exception of Minneapolis and St. Paul, Minnesota) does not comply with national UCR Program guidelines. Consequently, its figures for forcible rape and violent crime (of which forcible rape is a part) are not published in this table.
[3]Includes offenses reported by the Zoological Police and the Metro Transit Police.
[4]The crime figures have been adjusted.
[5]Populations are U.S. Census Bureau provisional estimates as of July 1 of each year.
[6]The figures shown for the offense of rape were estimated using the revised Uniform Crime Reporting (UCR) definition of rape.

Table AZ-15. State Government Finances, 2013

(Dollar amounts in thousands, percent distribution.)

Item	Dollars	Percent distribution
Total Revenue	36,947,686	100.0
General revenue	29,176,274	79.0
Intergovernmental revenue	10,580,523	28.6
Taxes	13,471,690	36.5
General sales	6,472,777	17.5
Selective sales	1,733,931	4.7
License taxes	412,769	1.1
Individual income tax	3,397,707	9.2
Corporate income tax	662,026	1.8
Other taxes	792,480	2.1
Current charges	3,381,853	9.2
Miscellaneous general revenue	1,742,208	4.7
Utility revenue	32,894	0.1
Liquor stores revenue	0	-
Insurance trust revenue[1]	7,738,518	20.9
Total Expenditure	31,968,081	100.0
Intergovernmental expenditure	8,209,708	25.7
Direct expenditure	23,758,373	74.3
Current operation	16,816,013	52.6
Capital outlay	1,568,048	4.9
Insurance benefits and repayments	4,182,959	13.1
Assistance and subsidies	691,319	2.2
Interest on debt	500,034	1.6
Exhibit: Salaries and wages	3,283,193	10.3
Total Expenditure	31,968,081	100.0
General expenditure	27,750,523	86.8
Intergovernmental expenditure	8,209,708	25.7
Direct expenditure	19,540,815	61.1
General expenditure, by function:		
Education	9,423,140	29.5
Public welfare	8,494,905	26.6
Hospitals	683,817	2.1
Health	1,924,080	6.0
Highways	1,971,558	6.2
Police protection	232,360	0.7
Correction	829,019	2.6
Natural resources	263,092	0.8
Parks and recreation	78,339	0.2
Governmental administration	649,188	2.0
Interest on general debt	498,304	1.6
Other and unallocable	2,702,721	8.5
Utility expenditure	34,599	0.1
Liquor stores expenditure	0	-
Insurance trust expenditure	4,182,959	13.1
Debt at End of Fiscal Year	13,723,166	X
Cash and Security Holdings	52,506,749	X

X = Not applicable.
- = Zero or rounds to zero.
[1]Within insurance trust revenue, net earnings of state retirement systems is a calculated statistic (the item code in the data file is X08), and thus can be positive or negative. Net earnings is the sum of earnings on investments plus gains on investments minus losses on investments. The change made in 2002 for asset valuation from book to market value in accordance with Statement 34 of the Governmental Accounting Standards Board is reflected in the calculated statistics.

Table AZ-16. State Government Tax Collections, 2014

(Dollars in thousands, percent.)

Item	Dollars	Percent distribution
Total Taxes	13,084,043	100.0
Property taxes	823,508	6.3
Sales and gross receipts	7,759,625	59.3
General sales and gross receipts	5,994,048	45.8
Selective sales and gross receipts	1,765,577	13.5
Alcoholic beverages	71,136	0.5
Amusements	533	-
Insurance premiums	448,115	3.4
Motor fuels	779,970	6.0
Pari-mutuels	216	-
Public utilities	21,760	0.2
Tobacco products	311,811	2.4
Other selective sales	132,036	1.0
Licenses	437,127	3.3
Alcoholic beverages	5,246	-
Amusements	0	-
Corporations in general	10,368	0.1
Hunting and fishing	32,787	0.3
Motor vehicle	198,227	1.5
Motor vehicle operators	30,215	0.2
Public utilities	25,986	0.2
Occupation and business, NEC	131,360	1.0
Other licenses	2,938	-
		-
Income taxes	4,037,593	30.9
Individual income	3,462,413	26.5
Corporation net income	575,180	4.4
Other taxes	26,190	0.2
Death and gift	0	-
Documentary and stock transfer	0	-
Severance	26,190	0.2
Taxes, NEC	0	-

- = Zero or rounds to zero.

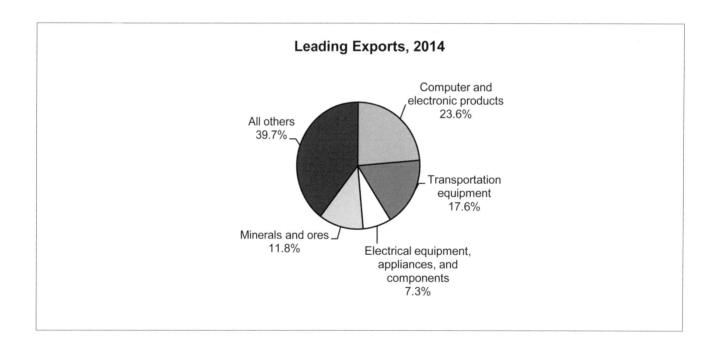

Leading Exports, 2014

Computer and electronic products 23.6%

Transportation equipment 17.6%

Electrical equipment, appliances, and components 7.3%

Minerals and ores 11.8%

All others 39.7%

ARKANSAS

Facts and Figures

Location: South central United States; bordered on the N by Missouri, on the E by Tennessee and Mississippi, on the S by Louisiana, and on the W by Oklahoma and Texas

Area: 53,178 sq. mi. (137,733 sq. km.); rank—29th

Population: 2,966,369 (2014 est.); rank—32nd

Principal Cities: capital—Little Rock; largest—Little Rock

Statehood: June 15, 1836; 25th state

U.S. Congress: 2 senators, 4 representatives

State Motto: *Regnat populus* ("The people rule")

State Song: "Arkansas"

State Nicknames: The Natural State; The Land of Opportunity

Abbreviations: AR; Ark.

State Symbols: flower—apple blossom; tree—pine; bird—mockingbird

At a Glance

- With an increase in population of 1.7 percent, Arkansas ranked 33rd among the states in growth from 2010 to 2014.

- The infant mortality rate in Arkansas was 7.61 per 1,000 live births, which ranked 4th in the nation.

- Arkansas's median household income in 2013 was $40,511, and 19.7 percent of its population lived below the poverty level.

- In 2013, 16.0 percent of Arkansans did not have health insurance, compared to 14.5 percent of the total U.S. population.

- Arkansas's property crime rate in 2013 was 3,602.6 per 100,000 population, which ranked 5th in the nation.

Table AR-1. Population by Age, Sex, Race, and Hispanic Origin

(Number, percent, except where noted.)

Sex, age, race, and Hispanic origin	2000	2010	2014[1]	Average annual percent change, 2010–2014
Total Population	2,673,400	2,915,918	2,966,369	0.4
Percent of total U.S. population	0.9	0.9	0.9	X
Sex				
Male	1,304,693	1,431,637	1,457,316	0.4
Female	1,368,707	1,484,281	1,509,053	0.4
Age				
Under 5 years	181,585	197,689	191,621	-0.8
5 to 19 years	578,924	598,241	592,181	-0.3
20 to 64 years	1,538,872	1,700,007	1,716,376	0.2
65 years and over	374,019	419,981	466,191	2.6
Median age (years)	36.0	37.4	37.8	0.3
Race and Hispanic Origin				
One race				
White	2,138,598	2,342,403	2,364,132	0.2
Black	418,950	454,021	463,360	0.5
American Indian and Alaska Native	17,808	26,134	28,689	2.4
Asian	20,220	37,537	44,193	4.2
Native Hawaiian or Other Pacific Islander	1,668	6,685	8,633	6.6
Two or more races	35,744	49,138	57,362	3.9
Hispanic (of any race)	86,866	191,535	208,821	2.2

X = Not applicable.
[1]Population figures for 2014 are July 1 estimates. The 2010 estimates are taken from the 2010 Census.

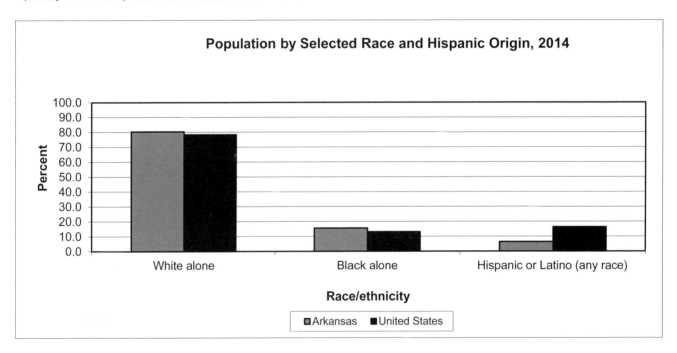

Population by Selected Race and Hispanic Origin, 2014

Table AR-2. Marital Status

(Number, percent distribution.)

Sex, age, race, and Hispanic origin	2000	2010	2013
Males, 15 Years and Over	1,015,594	1,128,804	1,151,058
Never married	24.2	29.5	31.1
Now married, except separated	61.0	53.3	51.8
Separated	1.6	2.2	2.0
Widowed	2.7	3.1	2.7
Divorced	10.4	12.0	12.4
Females, 15 Years and Over	1,096,069	1,200,974	1,212,821
Never married	18.4	23.5	24.6
Now married, except separated	55.7	48.8	48.0
Separated	2.2	2.9	2.6
Widowed	12.2	11.2	10.6
Divorced	11.6	13.6	14.2

Table AR-3. Households and Housing Characteristics

(Number, percent, dollars.)

Item	2000	2010	2013	Average annual percent change, 2000–2013
Total Households................................	1,042,696	1,114,902	1,125,899	0.6
Family households	732,261	761,361	751,124	0.2
Married-couple family...........................	566,401	554,946	548,537	-0.2
Other family	165,860	206,415	202,587	1.6
Male householder, no wife present...........	39,299	51,620	52,502	2.3
Female householder, no husband present........	126,561	154,795	150,085	1.3
Nonfamily households	310,435	353,541	374,775	1.5
Householder living alone........................	266,585	302,127	313,687	1.3
Householder not living alone..................	43,850	51,414	61,088	2.6
Housing Characteristics				
Total housing units....................................	1,173,043	1,317,818	1,329,777	1.0
Occupied housing units	1,042,696	1,114,902	1,125,899	0.6
Owner occupied	723,535	751,568	739,987	0.2
Renter occupied	319,161	363,334	385,912	1.5
Average household size..............................	2.49	2.55	2.56	0.2
Financial Characteristics				
Median gross rent of renter-occupied housing	453	638	659	2.9
Median monthly owner costs for housing units with a mortgage	737	987	979	2.2
Median value of owner-occupied housing units................	72,800	106,300	109,500	3.2

Table AR-4. Migration, Origin, and Language

(Number, percent.)

Characteristic	State			U.S.		
	2012	2013	Percent change	2012	2013	Percent change
Residence 1 Year Ago						
Population 1 year and over......................	2,912,680	2,923,642	0.4	310,212,755	312,432,820	0.7
Same house..	84.2	84.7	X	85.0	85.0	X
Different house in the U.S.............................	15.4	15.0	X	14.4	14.4	X
Same county..	9.4	9.1	X	9.0	8.9	X
Different county	6.1	5.9	X	5.4	5.5	X
Same state	3.4	3.5	X	3.2	3.2	X
Different state	2.6	2.4	X	2.3	2.3	X
Abroad	0.3	0.3	X	0.6	0.6	X
Place of Birth						
Native born	2,819,966	2,825,485	0.2	273,089,382	274,780,773	0.6
Male	49.0	49.3	X	49.3	49.3	X
Female	51.0	50.7	X	50.7	50.7	X
Foreign born	129,165	133,888	3.7	40,824,658	41,348,066	1.3
Male	51.9	50.4	X	48.7	48.8	X
Female	48.1	49.6	X	51.3	51.2	X
Foreign born; naturalized U.S. citizen...............	41,071	43,677	6.3	18,686,237	19,294,710	3.3
Male	50.9	46.4	X	45.8	45.9	X
Female	49.1	53.6	X	54.2	54.1	X
Foreign born; not a U.S. citizen.................	88,094	90,211	2.4	22,138,421	22,053,356	-0.4
Male	52.4	52.3	X	51.1	51.3	X
Female	47.6	47.7	X	48.9	48.7	X
Entered 2010 or later	8.8	13.6	X	7.0	9.7	X
Entered 2000 to 2009	35.6	34.4	X	30.4	29.4	X
Entered before 2000...................................	55.6	52.0	X	62.7	61.0	X
World Region of Birth, Foreign						
Foreign-born population, excluding population born at sea	129,165	133,888	3.7	40,824,553	41,347,945	1.3
Europe	8.1	7.2	X	11.8	11.6	X
Asia...	22.4	24.6	X	29.2	29.5	X
Africa	1.0	2.2	X	4.2	4.4	X
Oceania	2.4	0.7	X	0.6	0.5	X
Latin America	64.2	63.4	X	52.2	51.9	X
North America	2.0	2.0	X	2.0	2.0	X
Language Spoken at Home and Ability to Speak English						
Population 5 years and over.........................	2,757,475	2,769,171	0.4	294,003,714	296,358,760	0.8
English only	93.1	93.1	X	79.0	79.2	X
Language other than English......................	6.9	6.9	X	21.0	20.8	X
Speaks English less than "very well"..........	3.1	3.1	X	8.5	8.5	X

NA = Not available.
X = Not applicable.
- = Zero or rounds to zero.

Table AR-5. Median Income and Poverty Status, 2013

(Number, percent, except as noted.)

Characteristic	State		U.S.	
	Number	Percent	Number	Percent
Median Income				
Households (dollars)...	40,511	X	52,250	X
Families (dollars)	50,415	X	64,030	X
Below Poverty Level (All People)..	565,469	19.7	48,810,868	15.8
Sex				
Male..	260,201	18.4	21,938,525	14.5
Female	305,268	20.9	26,872,343	17.1
Age				
Under 18 years...	202,456	16.7	16,086,960	22.2
Related children under 18 years......................................	198,516	28.6	15,769,921	21.9
18 to 64 years..	316,939	18.2	28,578,191	14.8
65 years and over	46,074	10.5	4,145,717	9.6

X = Not applicable.

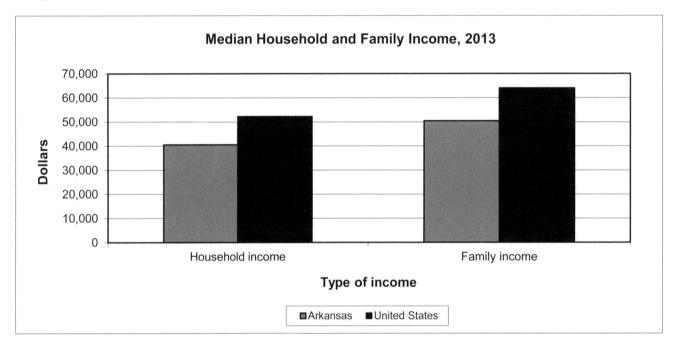

Table AR-6. Health Insurance Coverage Status for the Civilian Noninstitutionalized Population and Children Under 18 Years of Age

(Numbers in thousands, percent.)

Item	2005	2006	2007	2008	2009	2010	2011	2012	2013
Civilian Noninstitutionalized Population................................	2,760	2,758	2,805	2,802	2,833	2,868	2,885	2,896	2,907
Covered by Private or Public Insurance									
Number...	2,277	2,237	2,354	2,296	2,351	2,367	2,393	2,420	2,442
Percent..	82.5	81.1	83.9	81.9	83.0	82.5	82.9	83.6	84.0
Not Covered									
Number...	482	521	451	506	483	501	492	476	465
Percent..	17.5	18.9	16.1	18.1	17.0	17.5	17.1	16.4	16.0
Percent in the U.S. not covered..	15.3	15.8	15.3	15.1	15.1	15.5	15.1	14.8	14.5
Children Under 18 Years of Age.......................................	673	699	720	701	707	709	709	709	709
Covered by Private or Public Insurance									
Number...	600	634	679	640	663	663	669	667	670
Percent..	89.3	90.7	93.8	91.3	93.8	93.4	94.4	94.1	94.5
Not Covered									
Number...	72	65	44	61	44	46	40	42	39
Percent..	10.7	9.3	6.2	8.7	6.2	6.6	5.6	5.9	5.5
Percent in the U.S. not covered..	10.9	11.7	11.0	9.7	8.6	8.0	7.5	7.2	7.1

Table AR-7. Employment Status by Demographic Group, 2014

(Numbers in thousands, percent.)

Characteristic	Civilian noninstitutional population	Civilian labor force		Employed		Unemployed	
		Number	Percent of population	Number	Percent of population	Number	Percent of population
Total..	2,285	1,293	56.6	1,216	53.2	77	6.0
Sex							
Male..	1,099	676	61.6	640	58.2	37	5.4
Female..	1,186	617	52.0	576	48.5	41	6.6
Race, Sex, and Hispanic Origin							
White..	1,854	1,055	56.9	997	53.8	57	5.4
Male..	899	566	62.9	539	59.9	27	4.9
Female..	955	489	51.2	459	48.0	30	6.1
Black or African American..................	329	182	55.4	164	49.9	18	9.9
Male..	148	82	55.1	74	49.6	8	9.9
Female..	180	100	55.7	91	50.2	10	9.9
Hispanic or Latino ethnicity[1]............	160	109	68.2	103	64.8	5	5.0
Male..	87	66	76.1	63	72.5	3	4.7
Female..	73	43	58.8	40	55.5	2	5.5
Age							
16 to 19 years................................	156	52	33.4	45	29.0	7	13.1
20 to 24 years................................	202	139	68.8	124	61.3	15	10.9
25 to 34 years................................	374	296	79.2	281	75.0	16	5.3
35 to 44 years................................	350	273	78.1	262	74.7	12	4.4
45 to 54 years................................	390	275	70.5	260	66.6	15	5.5
55 to 64 years................................	355	194	54.5	184	51.9	9	4.9
65 years and over............................	458	64	13.9	61	13.2	3	5.0

NOTE: Data in Table 7 are from the Current Population Survey (CPS) and do not match the estimates in Table 8. See notes and definitions for further information.
[1] May be of any race.

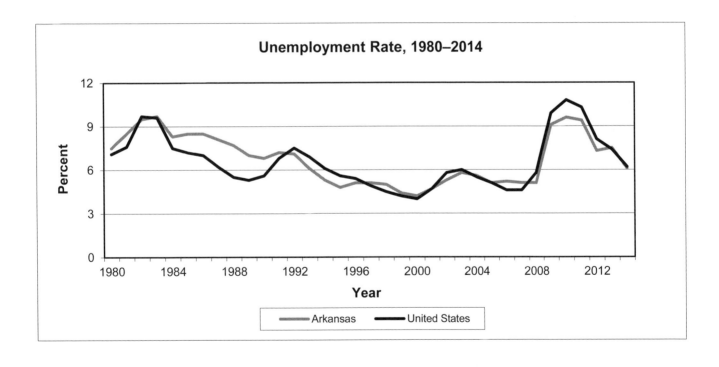

Unemployment Rate, 1980–2014

Table AR-8. Employment Status of the Civilian Noninstitutional Population Age 16 Years and Over

(Number, percent.)

Year	Civilian labor force	Civilian participation rate	Employed	Unemployed	Unemployment rate
2006	1,365,410	63.7	1,294,906	70,504	5.2
2007	1,369,284	63.2	1,296,572	72,712	5.3
2008	1,375,257	62.9	1,300,017	75,240	5.5
2009	1,358,911	61.7	1,252,399	106,512	7.8
2010	1,353,338	60.6	1,242,496	110,842	8.2
2011	1,361,789	60.5	1,248,726	113,063	8.3
2012	1,341,408	59.2	1,239,717	101,691	7.6
2013	1,307,465	57.5	1,211,317	96,148	7.4
2014	1,300,608	56.9	1,220,875	79,733	6.1

Table AR-9. Employment and Average Wages by Industry

(Estimates from 2007 through 2010 are based on the 2007 *North American Industry Classification System* [NAICS]. Estimates from 2011 onward are based on the 2012 NAICS.)

Industry	2007	2008	2009	2010	2011	2012	2013
	Number of jobs						
Wage and Salary Employment by Industry	1,262,522	1,263,298	1,227,077	1,226,354	1,229,913	1,231,172	1,234,941
Farm Wage and Salary Employment	10,700	12,453	12,493	13,208	11,972	8,820	11,397
Nonfarm Wage and Salary Employment	1,251,822	1,250,845	1,214,584	1,213,146	1,217,941	1,222,352	1,223,544
Private wage and salary employment	1,022,030	1,018,122	978,490	976,519	983,731	987,787	988,208
Forestry, fishing, and related activities	8,245	8,061	7,774	8,163	8,244	7,963	7,979
Mining	6,806	8,322	8,432	8,574	9,014	8,662	7,540
Utilities	6,956	6,971	7,028	7,315	7,170	7,700	8,088
Construction	58,651	58,642	54,361	51,129	49,824	49,041	47,155
Manufacturing	189,188	181,870	162,703	159,290	158,294	154,704	152,141
Durable goods manufacturing	100,214	94,796	80,067	77,864	78,484	76,862	75,449
Nondurable goods manufacturing	88,974	87,074	82,636	81,426	79,810	77,842	76,692
Wholesale trade	48,761	49,087	47,341	46,792	46,968	47,488	46,443
Retail trade	135,881	135,130	131,360	131,391	133,167	133,703	134,327
Transportation and warehousing	61,848	59,287	53,350	52,891	54,211	54,772	53,984
Information	19,617	18,518	17,437	16,545	16,077	15,594	15,362
Finance and insurance	38,551	37,616	36,472	36,135	36,797	36,850	37,091
Real estate and rental and leasing	14,849	14,754	14,334	14,074	13,719	13,543	13,534
Professional, scientific, and technical services	39,216	39,391	38,313	39,141	39,756	39,150	40,547
Management of companies and enterprises	24,998	26,130	26,357	25,904	26,048	30,901	31,442
Administrative and waste services	54,593	53,823	50,018	53,783	56,173	54,657	57,821
Educational services	13,857	14,170	14,454	14,841	15,224	15,855	15,756
Health care and social assistance	144,051	149,162	153,207	156,158	157,082	160,170	160,028
Arts, entertainment, and recreation	9,933	10,026	9,954	9,881	9,875	9,809	10,187
Accommodation and food services	90,756	91,945	90,991	90,288	91,548	93,708	95,552
Other services, except public administration	55,273	55,217	54,604	54,224	54,540	53,517	53,231
Government and government enterprises	229,792	232,723	236,094	236,627	234,210	234,565	235,336
	Dollars						
Average Wages and Salaries by Industry	34,611	35,321	36,032	36,686	37,787	38,897	39,532
Average Farm Wages and Salaries	23,814	22,276	18,839	19,023	19,145	24,550	27,352
Average Nonfarm Wages and Salaries	34,703	35,451	36,209	36,878	37,970	39,000	39,645
Average private wages and salaries	34,586	35,251	35,914	36,667	37,771	39,017	39,784
Forestry, fishing, and related activities	28,078	29,126	29,499	30,403	31,440	32,308	33,455
Mining	55,172	61,034	62,564	64,277	67,647	67,915	69,169
Utilities	67,942	72,220	72,644	71,533	74,513	76,612	79,103
Construction	36,691	39,321	40,284	40,169	40,709	42,307	41,704
Manufacturing	37,903	38,563	38,731	40,788	42,050	43,568	44,332
Durable goods manufacturing	39,237	40,064	40,397	42,621	44,068	45,640	46,665
Nondurable goods manufacturing	36,402	36,928	37,116	39,036	40,066	41,522	42,037
Wholesale trade	52,052	54,190	54,294	56,314	57,927	59,765	62,222
Retail trade	22,350	23,004	23,340	23,904	24,286	24,941	25,254
Transportation and warehousing	39,669	40,824	40,433	41,564	44,092	44,900	46,592
Information	77,610	50,957	65,601	48,243	50,025	49,713	50,659
Finance and insurance	48,536	50,838	51,213	52,920	55,027	57,740	57,983
Real estate and rental and leasing	29,162	30,007	30,480	31,376	32,788	34,354	34,651
Professional, scientific, and technical services	49,095	50,492	51,509	53,072	56,330	55,126	56,813
Management of companies and enterprises	73,220	77,734	81,263	90,405	91,222	96,145	103,349
Administrative and waste services	22,460	24,195	25,240	25,843	26,898	27,278	26,905
Educational services	23,091	24,105	25,937	26,232	26,894	26,441	27,263
Health care and social assistance	34,778	35,599	36,104	36,284	37,279	38,303	39,151
Arts, entertainment, and recreation	19,573	19,771	19,644	19,311	20,360	20,664	20,882
Accommodation and food services	13,800	13,826	14,097	14,688	15,144	15,511	15,501
Other services, except public administration	24,093	25,237	25,244	26,277	26,864	27,276	27,854
Government and government enterprises	35,223	36,323	37,431	37,749	38,808	38,927	39,064

Table AR-10. Employment Characteristics by Family Type

(Number, percent.)

Family type and labor force status	2011		2012		2013	
	Total	Families with own children under 18 years	Total	Families with own children under 18 years	Total	Families with own children under 18 years
All Families	757,205	320,053	758,601	315,273	751,124	313,438
FAMILY TYPE AND LABOR FORCE STATUS						
Married-Couple Families	556,108	205,856	557,982	206,752	548,537	204,825
Both husband and wife in labor force	47.7	64.2	48	63.4	46.4	63.5
Husband in labor force, wife not in labor force	21.8	27.7	22.6	28.8	22.9	28.7
Wife in labor force, husband not in labor force	9.3	4.9	9.5	5.2	9.3	5.2
Both husband and wife not in labor force	21.2	3.1	20	2.6	21.2	2.6
Other Families	201,097	114,197	200,619	108,521	202,587	108,613
Female householder, no husband present	76.1	78.5	74.9	77.0	74.1	75.7
In labor force	52.4	63.8	50.7	60.2	48.5	59.8
Not in labor force	23.8	14.7	24.2	16.7	25.6	15.8
Male householder, no wife present	23.9	21.5	25.1	23.0	25.9	24.3
In labor force	17.3	18.8	18.9	20.2	18.3	19.9
Not in labor force	6.6	2.7	6.2	2.9	7.6	4.4

Table AR-11. School Enrollment and Educational Attainment, 2013

(Number, percent.)

Item	State	U.S.
Enrollment		
Total population 3 years and over, enrolled in school	750,149	82,395,254
Enrolled in nursery school or preschool (percent)	6.9	6.0
Enrolled in kindergarten (percent)	6.0	5.2
Enrolled in elementary school, grades 1-8 (percent)	41.1	40.0
Enrolled in high school, grades 9-12 (percent)	20.1	20.6
Enrolled in college or graduate school (percent)	26.0	28.3
Attainment		
Total population 25 years and over	1,960,503	210,910,615
Less than ninth grade (percent)	5.6	5.8
9th to 12th grade, no diploma (percent)	10.0	7.6
High school graduate, including equivalency (percent)	35.3	27.8
Some college, no degree (percent)	22.4	21.1
Associate's degree (percent)	6.1	8.1
Bachelor's degree (percent)	13.4	18.4
Graduate or professional degree (percent)	7.2	11.2
High school graduate or higher (percent)	84.4	86.6
Bachelor's degree or higher (percent)	20.6	29.6

Table AR-12. Public School Characteristics and Educational Indicators

(Number, percent; data derived from National Center of Education Statistics.)

Item	State	U.S.
Public Schools, 2012–2013 (except where noted)		
Number of school districts	288	18,093
Number of schools	1,102	98,454
Number of students (in thousands)	486	49,771
Number of teachers (in thousands)	34	3,109
Student-teacher ratio	14.2	16.0
Expenditures per student (dollars), FY 2012	9,536	10,667
Four-year adjusted cohort graduation rate (ACGR)[1,2]	84.9	81.4
Students eligible for free or reduced-price lunch (in thousands)	299	25,188
English language learners (in thousands)	34	4,397
Students age 3 to 21 served under IDEA, part B (in thousands)	65	6,429

Public Schools by Type	Number	Percent of state public schools
Total number of schools	1,102	100.0
Regular	1,061	96.3
Special education	4	0.4
Vocational education	26	2.4
Alternative education	11	1.0

NOTE: Every school is assigned only one school type based on its instructional emphasis.
[1]ACGR data represents a new method of calculating high-school completion rates and may not be comparable to previous years' data for Averaged Freshmen Graduation Rates (AFGR).
[2]The United States 4-year ACGRs were estimated using both the reported 4-year ACGR data from 49 states and the District of Columbia and using imputed data for Idaho. The estimate for American Indian/Alaska Native students also includes imputed data for Virginia.

Table AR-13. Reported Voting and Registration of the Voting-Age Population, November 2012

(Numbers in thousands, percent.)

Item	Total population	Total citizen population	Registered			Voted		
			Total registered	Percent registered (total population)	Percent registered (total citizen population)	Total voted	Percent voted (total population)	Percent voted (total citizen population)
U.S. Total	235,248	215,081	153,157	65.1	71.2	132,948	56.5	61.8
State Total	2,198	2,109	1,376	62.6	65.3	1,124	51.1	53.3
Sex								
Male	1,044	1,006	637	61.0	63.4	531	50.9	52.8
Female	1,154	1,103	739	64.1	67.0	593	51.4	53.7
Race								
White alone	1,788	1,726	1,148	64.2	66.5	941	52.7	54.5
White, non-Hispanic alone	1,681	1,676	1,138	67.7	67.9	933	55.5	55.7
Black alone	313	313	192	61.3	61.3	155	49.4	49.4
Asian alone	33	21	9	B	B	9	B	B
Hispanic (of any race)	143	73	16	11.3	B	14	9.5	B
White alone or in combination	1,809	1,747	1,166	64.5	66.8	953	52.7	54.6
Black alone or in combination..........	319	319	195	61.1	61.1	155	48.5	48.5
Asian alone or in combination..........	33	21	9	B	B	9	B	B
Age								
18 to 24 years	288	281	126	43.8	44.8	70	24.3	24.8
25 to 44 years	719	676	428	59.6	63.3	345	48.0	51.0
45 to 64 years	742	704	498	67.1	70.8	442	59.6	62.8
65 to 74 years	301	299	212	70.6	71.0	185	61.7	62.0
75 years and over	149	149	111	75.0	75.0	81	54.7	54.7

B = Base is less than 75,000 and therefore too small to show the derived measure.

Table AR-14. Crime

(Number, rate per 100,000. Data are derived from the FBI Uniform Crime Reports.)

Item	State			U.S.[1,2,3,4]		
	2012	2013	Percent change	2012	2013	Percent change
TOTAL POPULATION[5]...........................	2,949,828	2,959,373	0.3	313,873,685	316,128,839	0.7
VIOLENT CRIME						
Number..................................	13,851	13,191	-4.8	1,217,067	1,163,146	-4.4
Rate	469.6	445.7	-5.1	387.8	367.9	-5.1
Murder and Nonnegligent Manslaughter						
Number..................................	174	159	-8.6	14,866	14,196	-4.5
Rate	5.9	5.4	-8.9	4.7	4.5	-5.2
Rape[6]						
Number..................................	X	1,423	X	X	108,612	X
Rate	X	48.1	X	X	34.4	X
Robbery						
Number..................................	2,310	2,258	-2.3	355,051	345,031	-2.8
Rate	78.3	76.3	-2.6	113.1	109.1	-3.5
Aggravated Assault						
Number..................................	10,134	9,781	-3.5	762,009	724,149	-5.0
Rate	343.5	330.5	-3.8	242.8	229.1	-5.6
PROPERTY CRIME						
Number..................................	109,389	106,613	-2.5	9,001,992	8,632,512	-4.1
Rate	3,708.3	3,602.6	-2.9	2,868.0	2,730.7	-4.8
Burglary						
Number..................................	32,673	30,485	-6.7	2,109,932	1,928,465	-8.6
Rate	1,107.6	1,030.1	-7.0	672.2	610.0	-9.3
Larceny-Theft						
Number..................................	70,982	70,450	-0.7	6,168,874	6,004,453	-2.7
Rate	2,406.3	2,380.6	-1.1	1,965.4	1,899.4	-3.4
Motor Vehicle Theft						
Number..................................	5,734	5,678		723,186	699,594	-3.3
Rate	194.4	191.9	-1.3	230.4	221.3	-4.0

NOTE: Although arson data are included in the trend and clearance tables, sufficient data are not available to estimate totals for this offense. Therefore, no arson data are published in this table.
X = Not applicable.
- = Zero or rounds to zero.
[1]The crime figures have been adjusted.
[2]The data collection methodology for the offense of forcible rape used by the Minnesota state Uniform Crime Reporting (UCR) Program (with the exception of Minneapolis and St. Paul, Minnesota) does not comply with national UCR Program guidelines. Consequently, its figures for forcible rape and violent crime (of which forcible rape is a part) are not published in this table.
[3]Includes offenses reported by the Zoological Police and the Metro Transit Police.
[4]Because of changes in the state's reporting practices, figures are not comparable to previous years' data.
[5]Populations are U.S. Census Bureau provisional estimates as of July 1 of each year.
[6]The figures shown for the offense of rape were estimated using the revised Uniform Crime Reporting (UCR) definition of rape.

Table AR-15. State Government Finances, 2013

(Dollar amounts in thousands, percent distribution.)

Item	Dollars	Percent distribution
Total Revenue	21,541,707	100.0
General revenue	17,310,068	80.4
Intergovernmental revenue	5,724,598	26.6
Taxes	8,586,407	39.9
General sales	2,837,788	13.2
Selective sales	1,181,415	5.5
License taxes	356,920	1.7
Individual income tax	2,649,577	12.3
Corporate income tax	402,874	1.9
Other taxes	1,157,833	5.4
Current charges	2,136,390	9.9
Miscellaneous general revenue	862,673	4.0
Utility revenue	0	-
Liquor stores revenue	0	-
Insurance trust revenue[1]	4,231,639	19.6
Total Expenditure	19,522,252	100.0
Intergovernmental expenditure	4,937,560	25.3
Direct expenditure	14,584,692	74.7
Current operation	10,892,041	55.8
Capital outlay	1,073,644	5.5
Insurance benefits and repayments	1,962,506	10.1
Assistance and subsidies	518,755	2.7
Interest on debt	137,746	0.7
Exhibit: Salaries and wages	2,981,327	15.3
Total Expenditure	19,522,252	100.0
General expenditure	17,559,746	89.9
Intergovernmental expenditure	4,937,560	25.3
Direct expenditure	12,622,186	64.7
General expenditure, by function:		
Education	7,518,389	38.5
Public welfare	5,139,921	26.3
Hospitals	936,138	4.8
Health	297,457	1.5
Highways	1,219,251	6.2
Police protection	109,098	0.6
Correction	403,821	2.1
Natural resources	248,511	1.3
Parks and recreation	58,214	0.3
Governmental administration	605,998	3.1
Interest on general debt	137,746	0.7
Other and unallocable	885,202	4.5
Utility expenditure	0	-
Liquor stores expenditure	0	-
Insurance trust expenditure	1,962,506	10.1
Debt at End of Fiscal Year	3,947,169	X
Cash and Security Holdings	27,941,835	X

X = Not applicable.
- = Zero or rounds to zero.
[1]Within insurance trust revenue, net earnings of state retirement systems is a calculated statistic (the item code in the data file is X08), and thus can be positive or negative. Net earnings is the sum of earnings on investments plus gains on investments minus losses on investments. The change made in 2002 for asset valuation from book to market value in accordance with Statement 34 of the Governmental Accounting Standards Board is reflected in the calculated statistics.

Table AR-16. State Government Tax Collections, 2014

(Dollars in thousands, percent.)

Item	Dollars	Percent distribution
Total Taxes	8,936,781	100.0
Property taxes	1,077,377	12.1
Sales and gross receipts	4,324,157	48.4
General sales and gross receipts	3,130,274	35.0
Selective sales and gross receipts	1,193,883	13.4
Alcoholic beverages	51,618	0.6
Amusements	39,660	0.4
Insurance premiums	182,092	2.0
Motor fuels	454,909	5.1
Pari-mutuels	3,090	0.0
Public utilities	0	-
Tobacco products	225,809	2.5
Other selective sales	236,705	2.6
Licenses	368,622	4.1
Alcoholic beverages	4,187	-
Amusements	426	-
Corporations in general	27,999	0.3
Hunting and fishing	23,533	0.3
Motor vehicle	153,445	1.7
Motor vehicle operators	17,657	0.2
Public utilities	9,985	0.1
Occupation and business, NEC	129,711	1.5
Other licenses	1,679	-
Income taxes	3,000,653	33.6
Individual income	2,602,160	29.1
Corporation net income	398,493	4.5
Other taxes	165,972	1.9
Death and gift	3	-
Documentary and stock transfer	32,715	0.4
Severance	108,511	1.2
Taxes, NEC	24,743	0.3

- = Zero or rounds to zero.

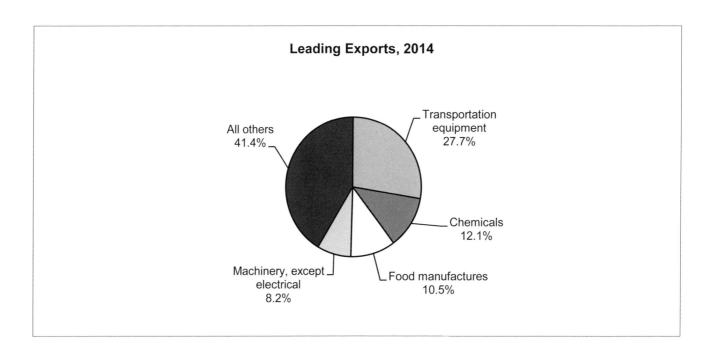

Leading Exports, 2014

Transportation equipment 27.7%
Chemicals 12.1%
Food manufactures 10.5%
Machinery, except electrical 8.2%
All others 41.4%

CALIFORNIA

Facts and Figures

Location: Western United States; bordered on the N by Oregon, on the E by Nevada and Arizona, on the S by Mexico, and on the W by the Pacific Ocean

Area: 163,694 sq. mi. (423,970 sq. km.); rank—3rd

Population: 38,802,500 (2014 est.); rank—1st

Principal Cities: capital—Sacramento; largest—Los Angeles

Statehood: September 9, 1850; 31st state

U.S. Congress: 2 senators, 53 representatives

State Motto: *Eureka* ("I have found it")

State Song: "I Love You, California"

State Nickname: The Golden State

Abbreviations: CA; Calif.

State Symbols: flower—California poppy; tree—redwood; bird—California valley quail

At a Glance

- With an increase in population of 4.2 percent, California ranked 15th among the states in growth from 2010 to 2014.

- In 2013, California's median household income was $60,190, and 16.8 percent of the population lived below the poverty level.

- California's violent crime rate in 2013 was 402.1 per 100,000 population, compared to 367.9 for the entire nation.

- In 2014, California's unemployment rate of 7.5 percent ranked 5th in the nation.

- Californians used 199.9 million Btu of energy in 2013, ranking 48th in the nation.

Table CA-1. Population by Age, Sex, Race, and Hispanic Origin

(Number, percent, except where noted.)

Sex, age, race, and Hispanic origin	2000	2010	2014¹	Average annual percent change, 2010–2014
Total Population	33,871,648	37,253,956	38,802,500	1.0
Percent of total U.S. population	12.0	12.1	12.2	X
Sex				
Male	16,874,892	18,517,830	19,268,904	1.0
Female	16,996,756	18,736,126	19,533,596	1.0
Age				
Under 5 years.................	2,486,981	2,531,333	2,515,727	-0.2
5 to 19 years.................	7,747,590	7,920,709	7,703,424	-0.7
20 to 64 years.................	20,041,419	22,555,400	23,590,302	1.1
65 years and over.................	3,595,658	4,246,514	4,993,047	4.1
Median age (years).................	33.3	35.2	36.0	0.6
Race and Hispanic Origin				
One race				
White	20,170,059	27,636,403	28,395,830	0.7
Black	2,263,882	2,486,549	2,541,367	0.5
American Indian and Alaska Native	333,346	622,107	645,309	0.9
Asian	3,697,513	5,038,123	5,586,184	2.6
Native Hawaiian or Other Pacific Islander	116,961	181,431	194,088	1.7
Two or more races	1,607,646	1,289,343	1,439,722	2.8
Hispanic (of any race)	10,966,556	14,440,187	14,988,768	0.9

X = Not applicable.
¹Population figures for 2014 are July 1 estimates. The 2010 estimates are taken from the 2010 Census.

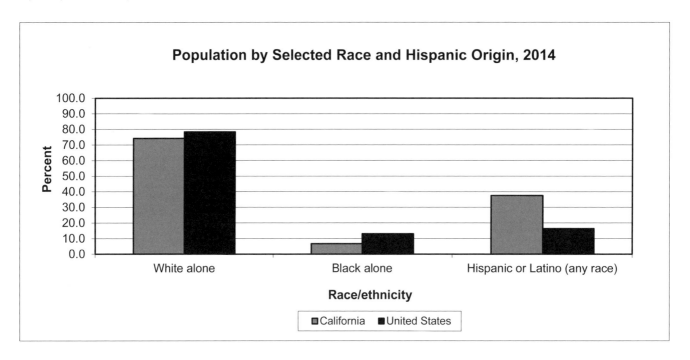

Table CA-2. Marital Status

(Number, percent distribution.)

Sex, age, race, and Hispanic origin	2000	2010	2013
Males, 15 Years and Over................	12,844,669	14,662,335	15,182,718
Never married	33.8	39.8	40.5
Now married, except separated.................	54.1	48.2	47.4
Separated.................	2.0	1.9	1.9
Widowed.................	2.2	2.1	2.2
Divorced.................	7.9	8.0	8.1
Females, 15 Years and Over................	13,231,494	15,043,190	15,550,134
Never married	26.5	32.3	33.2
Now married, except separated.................	50.7	45.7	45.0
Separated.................	2.9	2.7	2.8
Widowed.................	8.9	8.1	7.8
Divorced.................	11.0	11.2	11.2

Table CA-3. Households and Housing Characteristics

(Number, percent, dollars.)

Item	2000	2010	2013	Average annual percent change, 2000–2013
Total Households	11,502,870	12,406,475	12,650,592	0.7
Family households	7,920,049	8,507,856	8,645,970	0.7
Married-couple family	5,877,084	6,082,566	6,160,314	0.4
Other family	2,042,965	2,425,290	2,485,656	1.5
Male householder, no wife present	594,455	736,626	758,362	1.9
Female householder, no husband present	1,448,510	1,688,664	1,727,294	1.4
Nonfamily households	3,582,821	3,898,619	4,004,622	0.9
Householder living alone	2,708,308	3,001,307	3,071,545	1.0
Householder not living alone	874,513	897,312	933,077	0.5
Housing Characteristics				
Total housing units	12,214,549	13,682,976	13,791,262	0.9
Occupied housing units	11,502,870	12,406,475	12,650,592	0.7
Owner occupied	6,546,334	6,903,175	6,804,639	0.3
Renter occupied	4,956,536	5,503,300	5,845,953	1.3
Average household size	2.87	2.94	2.97	0.3
Financial Characteristics				
Median gross rent of renter-occupied housing	747	1,163	1,224	3.9
Median monthly owner costs for housing units with a mortgage	1,478	2,242	2,059	2.6
Median value of owner-occupied housing units	211,500	370,900	373,100	4.5

Table CA-4. Migration, Origin, and Language

(Number, percent.)

Characteristic	State			U.S.		
	2012	2013	Percent change	2012	2013	Percent change
Residence 1 Year Ago						
Population 1 year and over	37,572,738	37,873,189	0.8	310,212,755	312,432,820	0.7
Same house	84.6	85.0	X	85.0	85.0	X
Different house in the U.S.	14.7	14.2	X	14.4	14.4	X
Same county	10.6	10.1	X	9.0	8.9	X
Different county	4.1	4.1	X	5.4	5.5	X
Same state	2.8	2.8	X	3.2	3.2	X
Different state	1.3	1.3	X	2.3	2.3	X
Abroad	0.7	0.8	X	0.6	0.6	X
Place of Birth						
Native born	27,740,598	28,021,321	1.0	273,089,382	274,780,773	0.6
Male	50.2	50.2	X	49.3	49.3	X
Female	49.8	49.8	X	50.7	50.7	X
Foreign born	10,300,832	10,311,200	0.1	40,824,658	41,348,066	1.3
Male	48.4	48.5	X	48.7	48.8	X
Female	51.6	51.5	X	51.3	51.2	X
Foreign born; naturalized U.S. citizen	4,899,682	5,006,979	2.2	18,686,237	19,294,710	3.3
Male	46.0	46.1	X	45.8	45.9	X
Female	54.0	53.9	X	54.2	54.1	X
Foreign born; not a U.S. citizen	5,401,150	5,304,221	-1.8	22,138,421	22,053,356	-0.4
Male	50.5	50.7	X	51.1	51.3	X
Female	49.5	49.3	X	48.9	48.7	X
Entered 2010 or later	4.5	6.6	X	7.0	9.7	X
Entered 2000 to 2009	25.2	24.6	X	30.4	29.4	X
Entered before 2000	70.3	68.8	X	62.7	61.0	X
World Region of Birth, Foreign						
Foreign-born population, excluding population born at sea	10,300,832	10,311,079	0.1	40,824,553	41,347,945	1.3
Europe	6.5	6.5	X	11.8	11.6	X
Asia	36.9	37.2	X	29.2	29.5	X
Africa	1.6	1.7	X	4.2	4.4	X
Oceania	0.7	0.7	X	0.6	0.5	X
Latin America	52.9	52.6	X	52.2	51.9	X
North America	1.3	1.3	X	2.0	2.0	X
Language Spoken at Home and Ability to Speak English						
Population 5 years and over	35,504,620	35,831,956	0.9	294,003,714	296,358,760	0.8
English only	55.7	56.2	X	79.0	79.2	X
Language other than English	44.3	43.8	X	21.0	20.8	X
Speaks English less than "very well"	19.0	18.9	X	8.5	8.5	X

NA = Not available.
X = Not applicable.
- = Zero or rounds to zero.

Table CA-5. Median Income and Poverty Status, 2013

(Number, percent, except as noted.)

Characteristic	State		U.S.	
	Number	Percent	Number	Percent
Median Income				
Households (dollars)...............................	60,190	X	52,250	X
Families (dollars)	68,222	X	64,030	X
Below Poverty Level (All People)..........................	6,328,824	16.8	48,810,868	15.8
Sex				
Male..........................	2,917,397	15.7	21,938,525	14.5
Female	3,411,427	18.0	26,872,343	17.1
Age				
Under 18 years................................	2,121,351	23.5	16,086,960	22.2
Related children under 18 years........................	2,078,671	23.1	15,769,921	21.9
18 to 64 years..........................	3,719,280	15.6	28,578,191	14.8
65 years and over	488,193	10.4	4,145,717	9.6

X = Not applicable.

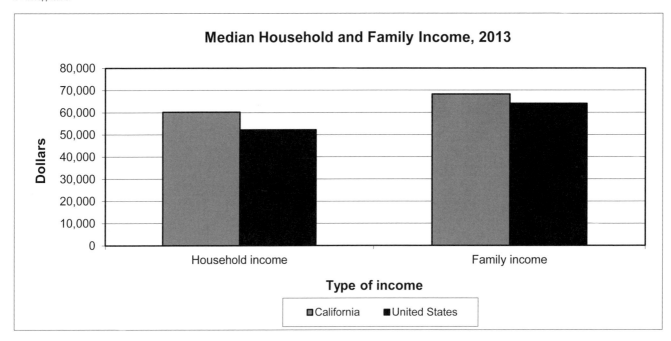

Median Household and Family Income, 2013

California   United States

Table CA-6. Health Insurance Coverage Status for the Civilian Noninstitutionalized Population and Children Under 18 Years of Age

(Numbers in thousands, percent.)

Item	2005	2006	2007	2008	2009	2010	2011	2012	2013
Civilian Noninstitutionalized Population...............................	35,940	36,208	36,295	36,161	36,377	36,816	37,162	37,524	37,832
Covered by Private or Public Insurance									
Number............................	29,182	29,417	29,682	29,730	29,818	29,990	30,436	30,815	31,331
Percent............................	81.2	81.2	81.8	82.2	82.0	81.5	81.9	82.1	82.8
Not Covered									
Number............................	6,757	6,791	6,613	6,431	6,559	6,835	6,726	6,709	6,500
Percent............................	18.8	18.8	18.2	17.8	18.0	18.5	18.1	17.9	17.2
Percent in the U.S. not covered.............	15.3	15.8	15.3	15.1	15.1	15.5	15.1	14.8	14.5
Children Under 18 Years of Age........................	9,738	9,571	9,423	9,348	9,423	9,289	9,252	9,223	9,158
Covered by Private or Public Insurance									
Number............................	8,429	8,346	8,410	8,337	8,532	8,456	8,507	8,503	8,485
Percent............................	86.6	87.2	89.3	89.2	90.5	91.0	92.0	92.1	92.6
Not Covered									
Number............................	1,309	1,225	1,013	1,011	891	833	745	720	673
Percent............................	13.4	12.8	10.7	10.8	9.5	9.0	8.0	7.9	7.4
Percent in the U.S. not covered.............	10.9	11.7	11.0	9.7	8.6	8.0	7.5	7.2	7.1

Table CA-7. Employment Status by Demographic Group, 2014

(Numbers in thousands, percent.)

Characteristic	Civilian noninstitutional population	Civilian labor force		Employed		Unemployed	
		Number	Percent of population	Number	Percent of population	Number	Percent of population
Total..	30,158	18,797	62.3	17,391	57.7	1,406	7.5
Sex							
Male..	14,739	10,232	69.4	9,484	64.4	748	7.3
Female	15,420	8,565	55.5	7,907	51.3	658	7.7
Race, Sex, and Hispanic Origin							
White...	22,378	13,998	62.6	13,008	58.1	990	7.1
Male..	11,059	7,773	70.3	7,242	65.5	530	6.8
Female	11,319	6,225	55.0	5,765	50.9	460	7.4
Black or African American....................	1,912	1,117	58.4	965	50.5	152	13.6
Male..	901	563	62.5	493	54.7	70	12.5
Female	1,011	555	54.8	473	46.7	82	14.8
Hispanic or Latino ethnicity[1]	10,553	6,863	65.0	6,280	59.5	583	8.5
Male..	5,297	3,959	74.7	3,649	68.9	311	7.8
Female	5,256	2,903	55.2	2,631	50.1	272	9.4
Age							
16 to 19 years..................................	2,146	528	24.6	391	18.2	137	25.9
20 to 24 years..................................	3,051	2,047	67.1	1,810	59.3	237	11.6
25 to 34 years..................................	5,354	4,230	79.0	3,903	72.9	327	7.7
35 to 44 years..................................	5,049	4,044	80.1	3,800	75.3	243	6.0
45 to 54 years..................................	5,168	4,056	78.5	3,822	74.0	234	5.8
55 to 64 years..................................	4,504	2,945	65.4	2,772	61.5	173	5.9
65 years and over	4,886	947	19.4	893	18.3	54	5.7

NOTE: Data in Table 7 are from the Current Population Survey (CPS) and do not match the estimates in Table 8. See notes and definitions for further information.
[1]May be of any race.

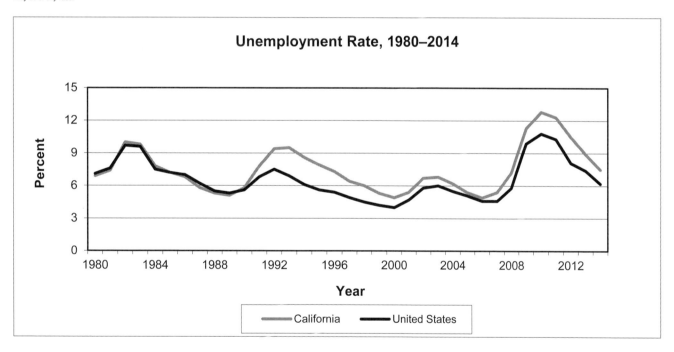

Table CA-8. Employment Status of the Civilian Noninstitutional Population Age 16 Years and Over

(Number, percent.)

Year	Civilian labor force	Civilian participation rate	Employed	Unemployed	Unemployment rate
2006	17,654,109	65.4	16,789,422	864,687	4.9
2007	17,893,080	65.6	16,931,590	961,490	5.4
2008	18,178,123	65.8	16,854,482	1,323,641	7.3
2009	18,215,140	65.2	16,182,572	2,032,568	11.2
2010	18,336,271	64.2	16,091,945	2,244,326	12.2
2011	18,419,494	63.5	16,260,099	2,159,395	11.7
2012	18,554,763	63.1	16,630,055	1,924,708	10.4
2013	18,671,637	62.7	17,002,894	1,668,743	8.9
2014	18,811,395	62.4	17,397,119	1,414,276	7.5

Table CA-9. Employment and Average Wages by Industry

(Estimates from 2007 through 2010 are based on the 2007 *North American Industry Classification System* [NAICS]. Estimates from 2011 onward are based on the 2012 NAICS.)

Industry	2007	2008	2009	2010	2011	2012	2013
	Number of jobs						
Wage and Salary Employment by Industry	16,289,089	16,110,889	15,233,396	15,047,583	15,204,435	15,443,410	16,225,103
Farm Wage and Salary Employment	167,671	156,022	161,058	169,614	160,906	152,310	165,882
Nonfarm Wage and Salary Employment	16,121,418	15,954,867	15,072,338	14,877,969	15,043,529	15,291,100	16,059,221
Private wage and salary employment	13,405,324	13,198,099	12,342,534	12,195,802	12,422,179	12,700,623	13,470,529
Forestry, fishing, and related activities	186,995	191,649	181,927	192,710	201,708	203,469	214,225
Mining	24,940	26,281	23,952	24,427	26,341	28,033	27,873
Utilities	58,048	58,774	60,033	57,126	58,304	59,382	58,937
Construction	925,124	818,256	650,724	585,150	590,831	609,226	659,968
Manufacturing	1,460,834	1,422,847	1,284,607	1,241,475	1,246,809	1,252,809	1,253,079
Durable goods manufacturing	925,445	898,963	800,113	770,103	777,998	781,436	780,445
Nondurable goods manufacturing	535,389	523,884	484,494	471,372	468,811	471,373	472,634
Wholesale trade	724,378	714,862	655,084	650,177	663,909	679,074	701,750
Retail trade	1,713,694	1,666,081	1,546,001	1,538,490	1,559,965	1,584,601	1,617,740
Transportation and warehousing	452,924	453,409	420,712	414,620	420,114	429,625	445,135
Information	475,159	464,230	435,783	427,352	429,627	434,780	448,765
Finance and insurance	636,275	591,900	558,634	536,180	544,545	555,424	552,710
Real estate and rental and leasing	291,708	286,684	267,267	261,542	258,009	258,077	267,333
Professional, scientific, and technical services	1,078,632	1,107,746	1,040,459	1,037,800	1,074,788	1,116,929	1,153,603
Management of companies and enterprises	208,041	206,764	198,742	192,985	199,149	203,448	218,826
Administrative and waste services	1,004,860	959,603	854,098	868,144	890,638	942,434	990,012
Educational services	312,605	326,221	335,608	338,629	349,487	358,825	367,262
Health care and social assistance	1,402,382	1,443,788	1,470,049	1,502,221	1,527,790	1,559,226	1,982,552
Arts, entertainment, and recreation	255,496	258,853	249,738	250,178	255,015	260,723	272,611
Accommodation and food services	1,320,487	1,329,333	1,270,556	1,272,004	1,301,337	1,347,228	1,414,682
Other services, except public administration	872,742	870,818	838,560	804,592	823,813	817,310	823,446
Government and government enterprises	2,716,094	2,756,768	2,729,804	2,682,167	2,621,350	2,590,477	2,588,692
	Dollars						
Average Wages and Salaries by Industry	51,411	52,474	52,641	54,355	56,097	58,259	57,608
Average Farm Wages and Salaries	26,134	32,196	33,633	31,788	29,768	25,973	38,119
Average Nonfarm Wages and Salaries	51,674	52,672	52,844	54,613	56,379	58,581	57,810
Average private wages and salaries	51,441	52,262	52,307	54,298	56,170	58,635	57,596
Forestry, fishing, and related activities	21,658	22,278	22,579	23,173	24,053	25,019	25,774
Mining	107,441	118,023	114,505	130,923	129,702	135,591	136,062
Utilities	95,311	96,972	100,935	103,261	108,002	111,080	117,409
Construction	52,267	55,127	55,846	55,814	57,238	59,070	59,152
Manufacturing	67,413	67,279	69,765	74,165	76,527	79,122	79,474
Durable goods manufacturing	76,717	75,953	77,579	85,553	88,777	90,699	90,291
Nondurable goods manufacturing	51,330	52,396	56,860	55,560	56,199	59,930	61,612
Wholesale trade	63,563	64,144	63,855	65,842	68,418	70,078	70,414
Retail trade	31,821	31,597	31,114	31,923	32,639	33,708	33,499
Transportation and warehousing	46,976	47,251	47,191	48,557	49,951	51,131	51,944
Information	92,317	92,922	92,646	101,563	107,712	114,823	133,886
Finance and insurance	93,779	93,323	89,206	93,938	97,258	103,042	103,372
Real estate and rental and leasing	50,812	50,237	48,526	49,852	52,639	55,728	57,039
Professional, scientific, and technical services	83,278	86,900	87,010	91,051	94,848	103,795	98,978
Management of companies and enterprises	93,262	92,037	90,436	97,434	103,817	108,749	112,989
Administrative and waste services	35,207	36,602	36,916	38,007	39,229	40,831	40,067
Educational services	36,592	37,941	39,081	41,151	42,187	42,778	43,653
Health care and social assistance	48,858	50,943	52,548	53,445	54,684	55,752	47,382
Arts, entertainment, and recreation	52,174	52,827	52,078	53,203	55,439	56,522	55,494
Accommodation and food services	21,333	21,205	20,815	21,455	22,154	22,558	22,455
Other services, except public administration	27,747	28,655	28,515	29,752	30,353	31,378	32,001
Government and government enterprises	52,826	54,632	55,274	56,041	57,366	58,318	58,922

Table CA-10. Employment Characteristics by Family Type

(Number, percent.)

Family type and labor force status	2011		2012		2013	
	Total	Families with own children under 18 years	Total	Families with own children under 18 years	Total	Families with own children under 18 years
All Families	8,518,518	4,064,364	8,585,787	4,046,765	8,645,970	3,984,574
FAMILY TYPE AND LABOR FORCE STATUS						
Married-Couple Families	6,059,185	2,793,349	6,104,099	2,787,943	6,160,314	2,753,934
Both husband and wife in labor force	52.2	61.5	51.3	60.7	50.5	60.2
Husband in labor force, wife not in labor force	25.3	32.7	25.9	33.3	25.8	33.8
Wife in labor force, husband not in labor force	7.3	3.7	7.3	4.0	7.4	3.8
Both husband and wife not in labor force	15.3	2.0	15.5	2.0	15.7	2.0
Other Families	2,459,333	1,271,015	2,481,688	1,258,822	2,485,656	1,230,640
Female householder, no husband present	69.6	72.2	69.4	72.2	69.5	72.4
In labor force	49.4	58.2	48.9	57.6	48.2	56.8
Not in labor force	20.2	14.0	20.5	14.6	21.3	15.6
Male householder, no wife present	30.4	27.8	30.6	27.8	30.5	27.6
In labor force	24.9	25.6	24.9	25.5	24.5	25.1
Not in labor force	5.6	2.2	5.7	2.3	6.0	2.5

Table CA-11. School Enrollment and Educational Attainment, 2013

(Number, percent.)

Item	State	U.S.
Enrollment		
Total population 3 years and over, enrolled in school	10,548,455	82,395,254
Enrolled in nursery school or preschool (percent)	5.5	6.0
Enrolled in kindergarten (percent)	4.9	5.2
Enrolled in elementary school, grades 1-8 (percent)	38.5	40.0
Enrolled in high school, grades 9-12 (percent)	21.0	20.6
Enrolled in college or graduate school (percent)	30.1	28.3
Attainment		
Total population 25 years and over	25,147,232	210,910,615
Less than ninth grade (percent)	10.1	5.8
9th to 12th grade, no diploma (percent)	8.2	7.6
High school graduate, including equivalency (percent)	20.8	27.8
Some college, no degree (percent)	22.0	21.1
Associate's degree (percent)	7.9	8.1
Bachelor's degree (percent)	19.5	18.4
Graduate or professional degree (percent)	11.5	11.2
High school graduate or higher (percent)	81.7	86.6
Bachelor's degree or higher (percent)	31.0	29.6

Table CA-12. Public School Characteristics and Educational Indicators

(Number, percent; data derived from National Center of Education Statistics.)

Item	State	U.S.
Public Schools, 2012–2013 (except where noted)		
Number of school districts	1,181	18,093
Number of schools	10,315	98,454
Number of students (in thousands)	6,299	49,771
Number of teachers (in thousands)	266	3,109
Student-teacher ratio	23.7	16.0
Expenditures per student (dollars), FY 2012	9,329	10,667
Four-year adjusted cohort graduation rate (ACGR)[1,2]	80.4	81.4
Students eligible for free or reduced-price lunch (in thousands)	3478	25,188
English language learners (in thousands)	1392	4,397
Students age 3 to 21 served under IDEA, part B (in thousands)	688	6,429

Public Schools by Type	Number	Percent of state public schools
Total number of schools	10,315	100.0
Regular	8,786	85.2
Special education	149	1.4
Vocational education	87	0.8
Alternative education	1,293	12.5

NOTE: Every school is assigned only one school type based on its instructional emphasis.
[1]ACGR data represents a new method of calculating high-school completion rates and may not be comparable to previous years' data for Averaged Freshmen Graduation Rates (AFGR).
[2]The United States 4-year ACGRs were estimated using both the reported 4-year ACGR data from 49 states and the District of Columbia and using imputed data for Idaho. The estimate for American Indian/Alaska Native students also includes imputed data for Virginia.

Table CA-13. Reported Voting and Registration of the Voting-Age Population, November 2012

(Numbers in thousands, percent.)

Item	Total population	Total citizen population	Registered			Voted		
			Total registered	Percent registered (total population)	Percent registered (total citizen population)	Total voted	Percent voted (total population)	Percent voted (total citizen population)
U.S. Total	235,248	215,081	153,157	65.1	71.2	132,948	56.5	61.8
State Total	28,357	23,419	15,356	54.2	65.6	13,462	47.5	57.5
Sex								
Male	13,887	11,374	7,245	52.2	63.7	6,326	45.6	55.6
Female	14,470	12,044	8,111	56.1	67.3	7,137	49.3	59.3
Race								
White alone	21,330	17,692	11,785	55.2	66.6	10,391	48.7	58.7
White, non-Hispanic alone	12,317	11,866	8,544	69.4	72.0	7,628	61.9	64.3
Black alone	1,810	1,740	1,192	65.8	68.5	1,063	58.7	61.1
Asian alone	3,915	2,839	1,645	42.0	57.9	1,380	35.2	48.6
Hispanic (of any race)	9,935	6,510	3,684	37.1	56.6	3,157	31.8	48.5
White alone or in combination	21,921	18,241	12,169	55.5	66.7	10,717	48.9	58.7
Black alone or in combination	2,003	1,924	1,314	65.6	68.3	1,172	58.5	60.9
Asian alone or in combination	4,122	3,029	1,790	43.4	59.1	1,499	36.4	49.5
Age								
18 to 24 years	3,962	3,479	1,787	45.1	51.4	1,447	36.5	41.6
25 to 44 years	10,386	7,828	5,026	48.4	64.2	4,188	40.3	53.5
45 to 64 years	9,356	7,827	5,459	58.3	69.7	4,926	52.6	62.9
65 to 74 years	2,591	2,358	1,696	65.5	71.9	1,612	62.2	68.3
75 years and over	2,062	1,926	1,388	67.3	72.1	1,290	62.6	67.0

Table CA-14. Crime

(Number, rate per 100,000. Data are derived from the FBI Uniform Crime Reports.)

Item	State			U.S.[1,2,3,4]		
	2012	2013	Percent change	2012	2013	Percent change
TOTAL POPULATION[5]	37,999,878	38,332,521	0.9	313,873,685	316,128,839	0.7
VIOLENT CRIME						
Number	160,944	151,879	-5.6	1,217,067	1,163,146	-4.4
Rate	423.5	396.2	-6.5	387.8	367.9	-5.1
Murder and Nonnegligent Manslaughter						
Number	1,884	1,746	-7.3	14,866	14,196	-4.5
Rate	5.0	4.6	-8.1	4.7	4.5	-5.2
Rape[6]						
Number	X	9,714	X	X	108,612	X
Rate	X	25.3	X	X	34.4	X
Robbery						
Number	56,521	53,640	-5.1	355,051	345,031	-2.8
Rate	148.7	139.9	-5.9	113.1	109.1	-3.5
Aggravated Assault						
Number	94,702	89,029	-6.0	762,009	724,149	-5.0
Rate	249.2	232.3	-6.8	242.8	229.1	-5.6
PROPERTY CRIME						
Number	1,049,465	1,018,907	-2.9	9,001,992	8,632,512	-4.1
Rate	2,761.8	2,658.1	-3.8	2,868.0	2,730.7	-4.8
Burglary						
Number	245,767	232,058	-5.6	2,109,932	1,928,465	-8.6
Rate	646.8	605.4	-6.4	672.2	610.0	-9.3
Larceny-Theft						
Number	635,090	621,557	-2.1	6,168,874	6,004,453	-2.7
Rate	1,671.3	1,621.5	-3.0	1,965.4	1,899.4	-3.4
Motor Vehicle Theft						
Number	168,608	165,292	-2.0	723,186	699,594	-3.3
Rate	443.7	431.2	-2.8	230.4	221.3	-4.0

NOTE: Although arson data are included in the trend and clearance tables, sufficient data are not available to estimate totals for this offense. Therefore, no arson data are published in this table.
X = Not applicable.
- = Zero or rounds to zero.
[1]The crime figures have been adjusted.
[2]The data collection methodology for the offense of forcible rape used by the Minnesota state Uniform Crime Reporting (UCR) Program (with the exception of Minneapolis and St. Paul, Minnesota) does not comply with national UCR Program guidelines. Consequently, its figures for forcible rape and violent crime (of which forcible rape is a part) are not published in this table.
[3]Includes offenses reported by the Zoological Police and the Metro Transit Police.
[4]Because of changes in the state's reporting practices, figures are not comparable to previous years' data.
[5]Populations are U.S. Census Bureau provisional estimates as of July 1 of each year.
[6]The figures shown for the offense of rape were estimated using the revised Uniform Crime Reporting (UCR) definition of rape.

Table CA-15. State Government Finances, 2013

(Dollar amounts in thousands, percent distribution.)

Item	Dollars	Percent distribution
Total Revenue	315,358,675	100.0
General revenue	219,692,720	69.7
Intergovernmental revenue	58,096,373	18.4
Taxes	133,184,246	42.2
General sales	33,915,885	10.8
Selective sales	14,158,695	4.5
License taxes	8,743,748	2.8
Individual income tax	66,809,000	21.2
Corporate income tax	7,462,000	2.4
Other taxes	2,094,918	0.7
Current charges	18,354,538	5.8
Miscellaneous general revenue	10,057,563	3.2
Utility revenue	1,021,277	0.3
Liquor stores revenue	0	-
Insurance trust revenue[1]	94,644,678	30.0
Total Expenditure	283,572,491	100.0
Intergovernmental expenditure	95,069,461	33.5
Direct expenditure	188,503,030	66.5
Current operation	118,110,030	41.7
Capital outlay	9,367,080	3.3
Insurance benefits and repayments	49,248,058	17.4
Assistance and subsidies	4,285,537	1.5
Interest on debt	7,492,325	2.6
Exhibit: Salaries and wages	28,083,907	9.9
Total Expenditure	283,572,491	100.0
General expenditure	233,454,218	82.3
Intergovernmental expenditure	95,069,461	33.5
Direct expenditure	138,384,757	48.8
General expenditure, by function:		
Education	80,195,847	28.3
Public welfare	80,014,405	28.2
Hospitals	9,107,869	3.2
Health	8,785,009	3.1
Highways	13,193,489	4.7
Police protection	1,600,910	0.6
Correction	7,844,627	2.8
Natural resources	4,102,500	1.4
Parks and recreation	523,095	0.2
Governmental administration	7,362,510	2.6
Interest on general debt	7,228,325	2.5
Other and unallocable	13,495,632	4.8
Utility expenditure	870,215	0.3
Liquor stores expenditure	0	-
Insurance trust expenditure	49,248,058	17.4
Debt at End of Fiscal Year	152,186,012	X
Cash and Security Holdings	559,096,417	X

X = Not applicable.
- = Zero or rounds to zero.
[1]Within insurance trust revenue, net earnings of state retirement systems is a calculated statistic (the item code in the data file is X08), and thus can be positive or negative. Net earnings is the sum of earnings on investments plus gains on investments minus losses on investments. The change made in 2002 for asset valuation from book to market value in accordance with Statement 34 of the Governmental Accounting Standards Board is reflected in the calculated statistics.

Table CA-16. State Government Tax Collections, 2014

(Dollars in thousands, percent.)

Item	Dollars	Percent distribution
Total Taxes	138,069,870	100.0
Property taxes	2,176,236	1.6
Sales and gross receipts	50,002,053	36.2
General sales and gross receipts	37,224,077	27.0
Selective sales and gross receipts	12,777,976	9.3
Alcoholic beverages	354,297	0.3
Amusements	0	-
Insurance premiums	2,362,738	1.7
Motor fuels	6,063,356	4.4
Pari-mutuels	13,899	-
Public utilities	663,448	0.5
Tobacco products	833,126	0.6
Other selective sales	2,487,112	1.8
Licenses	8,922,534	6.5
Alcoholic beverages	55,550	-
Amusements	15,457	-
Corporations in general	59,777	-
Hunting and fishing	101,237	0.1
Motor vehicle	3,745,377	2.7
Motor vehicle operators	280,038	0.2
Public utilities	388,443	0.3
Occupation and business, NEC	4,269,033	3.1
Other licenses	7,622	-
Income taxes	76,854,157	55.7
Individual income	67,995,659	49.2
Corporation net income	8,858,498	6.4
Other taxes	114,890	0.1
Death and gift	0	-
Documentary and stock transfer	0	-
Severance	38,686	-
Taxes, NEC	76,204	0.1

- = Zero or rounds to zero.

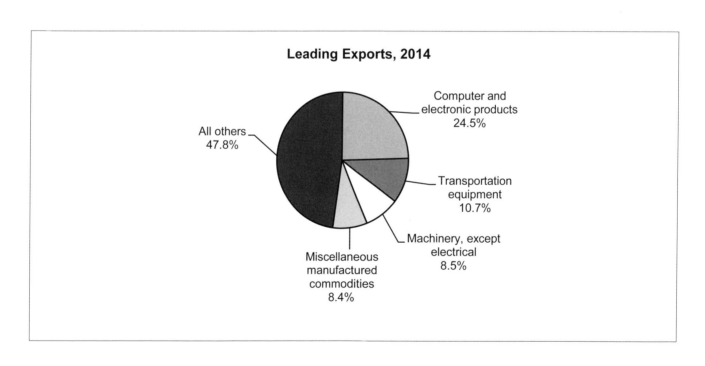

Leading Exports, 2014

All others 47.8%

Computer and electronic products 24.5%

Transportation equipment 10.7%

Machinery, except electrical 8.5%

Miscellaneous manufactured commodities 8.4%

COLORADO

Facts and Figures

Location: Western United States; bordered on the N by Wyoming and Nebraska, on the E by Nebraska and Kansas, on the S by Oklahoma and New Mexico, and on the W by Utah; Colorado is one of the Four Corner states—at its SW corner it touches Arizona, New Mexico, and Utah

Area: 104,093 sq. mi. (269,601 sq. km.); rank—8th

Population: 5,355,866 (2014 est.); rank—22nd

Principal Cities: capital—Denver; largest—Denver

Statehood: August 1, 1876; 38th state

U.S. Congress: 2 senators, 7 representatives

State Motto: *Nil sine numine* ("Nothing without providence")

State Songs: "Where the Columbines Grow"; "Rocky Mountain High"

State Nicknames: The Centennial State; Colorful Colorado

Abbreviations: CO; Colo.

State Symbols: flower—Rocky Mountain columbine; tree—Colorado blue spruce; bird—lark bunting

At a Glance

- With an increase in population of 6.5 percent, Colorado ranked 4th among the states in growth from 2010 to 2014.

- In 2013, 14.1 percent of Coloradans did not have health insurance, compared to 14.5 percent of the total U.S. population.

- Colorado's homeownership rate in 2013 was 64.4 percent, ranking 40th in the nation.

- The birth rate in Colorado in 2013 was 12.3 per 1,000 population, the same as the U.S. average.

- In Colorado, 13.0 percent of the total population and 16.9 percent of persons under 18 years old lived below the poverty level in 2013, compared to nationwide poverty levels of 15.8 percent and 22.2 percent, respectively.

Table CO-1. Population by Age, Sex, Race, and Hispanic Origin

(Number, percent, except where noted.)

Sex, age, race, and Hispanic origin	2000	2010	2014[1]	Average annual percent change, 2010–2014
Total Population	4,301,261	5,029,196	5,355,866	1.6
Percent of total U.S. population	1.5	1.6	1.7	X
Sex				
Male	2,165,983	2,520,662	2,691,159	1.6
Female	2,135,278	2,508,534	2,664,707	1.5
Age				
Under 5 years	297,505	343,960	334,931	-0.7
5 to 19 years	927,163	1,020,732	1,051,907	0.8
20 to 64 years	2,660,520	3,114,879	3,289,013	1.4
65 years and over	416,073	549,625	680,015	5.5
Median age (years)	34.3	36.1	36.5	0.3
Race and Hispanic Origin				
One race				
White	3,560,005	4,450,623	4,699,302	1.4
Black	165,063	214,919	238,720	2.7
American Indian and Alaska Native	44,241	78,144	84,946	2.1
Asian	95,213	144,819	168,460	3.9
Native Hawaiian or Other Pacific Islander	4,621	8,420	10,071	4.6
Two or more races	122,187	132,271	154,367	3.9
Hispanic (of any race)	735,601	1,078,225	1,135,109	1.3

X = Not applicable.
[1]Population figures for 2014 are July 1 estimates. The 2010 estimates are taken from the 2010 Census.

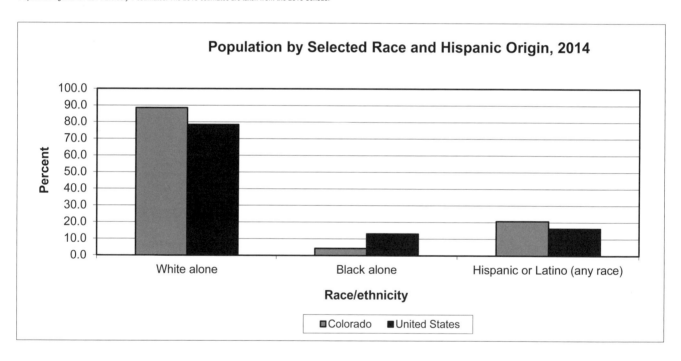

Population by Selected Race and Hispanic Origin, 2014

Legend: ▨ Colorado ■ United States

Table CO-2. Marital Status

(Number, percent distribution.)

Sex, age, race, and Hispanic origin	2000	2010	2013
Males, 15 Years and Over	1,694,635	2,004,303	2,110,584
Never married	30.5	34.4	35.3
Now married, except separated	56.6	51.7	50.7
Separated	1.4	1.6	1.3
Widowed	1.9	2.0	2.2
Divorced	9.6	10.3	10.5
Females, 15 Years and Over	1,690,734	2,017,425	2,114,093
Never married	23.4	26.9	27.5
Now married, except separated	54.7	50.8	50.0
Separated	1.8	2.0	1.8
Widowed	7.6	7.0	6.8
Divorced	12.5	13.3	13.9

Table CO-3. Households and Housing Characteristics

(Number, percent, dollars.)

Item	2000	2010	2013	Average annual percent change, 2000–2013
Total Households..	1,658,238	1,960,585	2,002,800	1.5
Family households	1,084,461	1,258,885	1,279,941	1.3
Married-couple family	858,671	959,624	982,202	1.0
Other family	225,790	299,261	297,739	2.2
Male householder, no wife present........................	66,811	90,518	88,386	2.2
Female householder, no husband present..............	158,979	208,743	209,353	2.1
Nonfamily households	573,777	701,700	722,859	1.8
Householder living alone......................................	435,778	555,080	529,856	1.5
Householder not living alone................................	137,999	146,620	193,003	2.6
Housing Characteristics				
Total housing units...	1,808,037	2,214,262	2,247,291	1.7
Occupied housing units	1,658,238	1,960,585	2,002,800	1.5
Owner occupied	1,116,173	1,292,792	1,291,945	1.1
Renter occupied	542,101	667,793	710,855	2.1
Average household size..	2.53	2.52	2.57	0.1
Financial Characteristics				
Median gross rent of renter-occupied housing	671	863	971	2.9
Median monthly owner costs for housing units with a mortgage	1,197	1,590	1,235	0.2
Median value of owner-occupied housing units.............	166,600	236,600	240,500	2.9

- = Zero or rounds to zero.

Table CO-4. Migration, Origin, and Language

(Number, percent.)

Characteristic	State			U.S.		
	2012	2013	Percent change	2012	2013	Percent change
Residence 1 Year Ago						
Population 1 year and over	5,123,944	5,206,012	1.6	310,212,755	312,432,820	0.7
Same house	80.6	80.4	X	85.0	85.0	X
Different house in the U.S.	18.7	18.9	X	14.4	14.4	X
Same county	9.6	10.1	X	9.0	8.9	X
Different county	9.1	8.9	X	5.4	5.5	X
Same state	5.1	4.9	X	3.2	3.2	X
Different state	4.0	4.0	X	2.3	2.3	X
Abroad	0.7	0.7	X	0.6	0.6	X
Place of Birth						
Native born	4,681,224	4,767,733	1.8	273,089,382	274,780,773	0.6
Male..	50.2	50.4	X	49.3	49.3	X
Female	49.8	49.6	X	50.7	50.7	X
Foreign born	506,358	500,634	-1.1	40,824,658	41,348,066	1.3
Male..	49.6	48.7	X	48.7	48.8	X
Female	50.4	51.3	X	51.3	51.2	X
Foreign born; naturalized U.S. citizen................	201,312	197,600	-1.8	18,686,237	19,294,710	3.3
Male..	45.8	45.7	X	45.8	45.9	X
Female	54.2	54.3	X	54.2	54.1	X
Foreign born; not a U.S. citizen........................	305,046	303,034	-0.7	22,138,421	22,053,356	-0.4
Male..	52.1	50.6	X	51.1	51.3	X
Female	47.9	49.4	X	48.9	48.7	X
Entered 2010 or later	7.4	9.4	X	7.0	9.7	X
Entered 2000 to 2009	33.2	32.1	X	30.4	29.4	X
Entered before 2000...................................	59.4	58.5	X	62.7	61.0	X
World Region of Birth, Foreign						
Foreign-born population, excluding population born at sea	506,358	500,634	-1.1	40,824,553	41,347,945	1.3
Europe	14.2	14.2	X	11.8	11.6	X
Asia..	22.1	22.7	X	29.2	29.5	X
Africa..	6.3	5.8	X	4.2	4.4	X
Oceania	1.0	0.6	X	0.6	0.5	X
Latin America	53.6	53.4	X	52.2	51.9	X
North America...	2.9	3.3	X	2.0	2.0	X
Language Spoken at Home and Ability to Speak English						
Population 5 years and over	4,850,587	4,934,794	1.7	294,003,714	296,358,760	0.8
English only	83.0	83.3	X	79.0	79.2	X
Language other than English.........................	17.0	16.7	X	21.0	20.8	X
Speaks English less than "very well"................	6.2	6.2	X	8.5	8.5	X

NA = Not available.
X = Not applicable.
- = Zero or rounds to zero.

Table CO-5. Median Income and Poverty Status, 2013

(Number, percent, except as noted.)

Characteristic	State		U.S.	
	Number	Percent	Number	Percent
Median Income				
Households (dollars)...	58,823	X	52,250	X
Families (dollars)	72,043	X	64,030	X
Below Poverty Level (All People)	667,446	13.0	48,810,868	15.8
Sex				
Male...	303,214	11.8	21,938,525	14.5
Female..	364,232	14.1	26,872,343	17.1
Age				
Under 18 years...	206,642	16.9	16,086,960	22.2
Related children under 18 years...	201,750	16.5	15,769,921	21.9
18 to 64 years...	414,460	12.6	28,578,191	14.8
65 years and over	46,344	7.4	4,145,717	9.6

X = Not applicable.

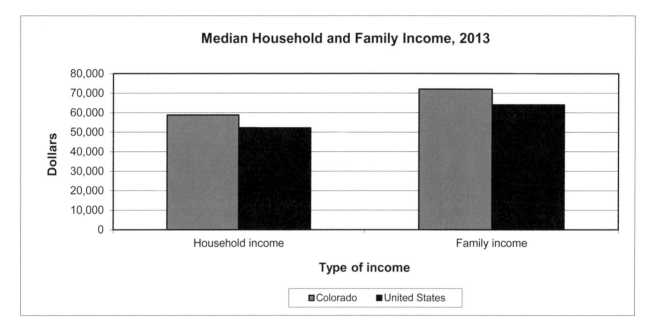

Median Household and Family Income, 2013

Colorado   United States

Table CO-6. Health Insurance Coverage Status for the Civilian Noninstitutionalized Population and Children Under 18 Years of Age

(Numbers in thousands, percent.)

Item	2005	2006	2007	2008	2009	2010	2011	2012	2013
Civilian Noninstitutionalized Population	4,641	4,803	4,877	4,853	4,930	4,957	5,025	5,095	5,173
Covered by Private or Public Insurance									
Number...	3,869	3,977	4,077	4,020	4,152	4,168	4,265	4,344	4,444
Percent...	83.4	82.8	83.6	82.8	84.2	84.1	84.9	85.3	85.9
Not Covered									
Number...	772	826	801	833	778	789	760	751	729
Percent...	16.6	17.2	16.4	17.2	15.8	15.9	15.1	14.7	14.1
Percent in the U.S. not covered...........................	15.3	15.8	15.3	15.1	15.1	15.5	15.1	14.8	14.5
Children Under 18 Years of Age...	1,187	1,209	1,208	1,204	1,225	1,226	1,227	1,229	1,239
Covered by Private or Public Insurance									
Number...	1,024	1,033	1,051	1,031	1,101	1,102	1,111	1,120	1,137
Percent...	86.3	85.4	87.0	85.6	89.8	89.9	90.6	91.2	91.8
Not Covered									
Number...	163	176	157	173	124	124	116	109	102
Percent...	13.7	14.6	13.0	14.4	10.2	10.1	9.4	8.8	8.2
Percent in the U.S. not covered...........................	10.9	11.7	11.0	9.7	8.6	8.0	7.5	7.2	7.1

Table CO-7. Employment Status by Demographic Group, 2014

(Numbers in thousands, percent.)

Characteristic	Civilian noninstitutional population	Civilian labor force		Employed		Unemployed	
		Number	Percent of population	Number	Percent of population	Number	Percent of population
Total..	4,145	2,822	68.1	2,683	64.7	139	4.9
Sex							
Male..	2,042	1,522	74.5	1,446	70.8	75	5.0
Female..	2,102	1,300	61.8	1,237	58.8	63	4.9
Race, Sex, and Hispanic Origin							
White...	3,729	2,553	68.5	2,436	65.3	117	4.6
Male..	1,837	1,372	74.7	1,308	71.2	65	4.7
Female..	1,892	1,181	62.4	1,129	59.7	52	4.4
Black or African American...................	163	107	65.9	96	58.8	12	10.8
Male..	83	56	67.7	51	60.8	6	10.2
Female..	79	51	64.1	45	56.7	6	11.6
Hispanic or Latino ethnicity[1].............	728	501	68.8	469	64.4	32	6.4
Male..	358	288	80.5	271	75.8	17	5.9
Female..	370	212	57.4	197	53.4	15	7.0
Age							
16 to 19 years....................................	270	106	39.4	87	32.2	19	18.3
20 to 24 years....................................	332	252	75.9	233	70.0	20	7.8
25 to 34 years....................................	764	641	83.9	611	80.0	30	4.7
35 to 44 years....................................	739	635	85.9	616	83.3	20	3.1
45 to 54 years....................................	717	595	83.1	573	80.0	22	3.7
55 to 64 years....................................	680	464	68.2	442	64.9	22	4.8
65 years and over...............................	642	128	19.9	122	19.0	5	4.3

NOTE: Data in Table 7 are from the Current Population Survey (CPS) and do not match the estimates in Table 8. See notes and definitions for further information.
[1]May be of any race.

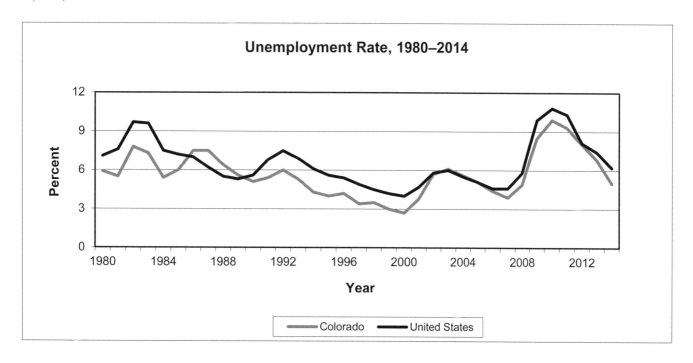

Table CO-8. Employment Status of the Civilian Noninstitutional Population Age 16 Years and Over

(Number, percent.)

Year	Civilian labor force	Civilian participation rate	Employed	Unemployed	Unemployment rate
2006	2,622,243	72.4	2,509,729	112,514	4.3
2007	2,664,677	72.2	2,565,218	99,459	3.7
2008	2,716,625	72.1	2,585,243	131,382	4.8
2009	2,722,982	70.9	2,524,443	198,539	7.3
2010	2,724,417	70.4	2,486,404	238,013	8.7
2011	2,734,416	69.7	2,507,786	226,630	8.3
2012	2,757,126	69.0	2,542,510	214,616	7.8
2013	2,779,631	68.3	2,590,608	189,023	6.8
2014	2,817,334	68.0	2,675,947	141,387	5.0

Table CO-9. Employment and Average Wages by Industry

(Estimates from 2007 through 2010 are based on the 2007 *North American Industry Classification System* [NAICS]. Estimates from 2011 onward are based on the 2012 NAICS.)

Industry	2007	2008	2009	2010	2011	2012	2013
				Number of jobs			
Wage and Salary Employment by Industry	2,451,987	2,478,747	2,373,917	2,355,555	2,393,084	2,441,958	2,514,654
Farm Wage and Salary Employment	11,903	12,505	12,051	12,775	11,691	11,605	12,833
Nonfarm Wage and Salary Employment	2,440,084	2,466,242	2,361,866	2,342,780	2,381,393	2,430,353	2,501,821
Private wage and salary employment	2,016,672	2,028,998	1,914,438	1,888,408	1,926,691	1,974,494	2,036,039
Forestry, fishing, and related activities	4,727	4,967	5,035	5,304	5,598	5,568	6,180
Mining	24,918	28,423	23,956	24,096	27,633	30,046	30,270
Utilities	7,958	8,142	8,313	8,181	8,140	8,045	7,839
Construction	174,101	168,329	137,237	120,670	118,361	119,773	132,446
Manufacturing	146,827	144,043	129,909	125,705	129,345	132,185	132,930
Durable goods manufacturing	98,670	95,828	84,535	81,247	84,053	86,451	86,113
Nondurable goods manufacturing	48,157	48,215	45,374	44,458	45,292	45,734	46,817
Wholesale trade	100,175	100,941	94,114	91,575	92,873	94,628	97,181
Retail trade	257,093	256,017	242,207	240,644	243,733	246,114	251,893
Transportation and warehousing	68,054	67,863	63,291	61,351	62,042	64,090	66,362
Information	76,943	77,101	74,824	71,864	72,033	69,990	70,008
Finance and insurance	110,499	107,554	103,408	101,846	102,542	104,620	107,681
Real estate and rental and leasing	49,231	48,596	44,742	43,415	42,920	42,997	44,251
Professional, scientific, and technical services	173,024	178,999	172,348	170,403	174,799	180,040	190,847
Management of companies and enterprises	28,600	29,026	28,556	28,823	29,921	31,802	34,648
Administrative and waste services	150,667	148,263	133,816	135,539	139,134	147,146	150,285
Educational services	37,154	39,631	39,930	40,984	42,344	43,819	44,570
Health care and social assistance	215,012	224,710	230,712	237,152	244,151	250,833	254,275
Arts, entertainment, and recreation	45,387	46,337	45,357	45,435	46,757	47,481	48,137
Accommodation and food services	228,146	229,772	220,157	220,787	228,234	234,287	243,670
Other services, except public administration	118,156	120,284	116,526	114,634	116,131	121,028	122,566
Government and government enterprises	423,412	437,244	447,428	454,372	454,702	455,859	465,782
				Dollars			
Average Wages and Salaries by Industry	46,070	47,201	47,427	48,477	49,788	51,211	51,537
Average Farm Wages and Salaries	37,147	34,126	39,317	32,222	36,532	31,456	42,611
Average Nonfarm Wages and Salaries	46,113	47,267	47,469	48,566	49,853	51,305	51,583
Average private wages and salaries	46,608	47,647	47,684	48,872	50,279	51,980	52,169
Forestry, fishing, and related activities	21,913	22,560	23,827	24,186	25,041	25,771	26,396
Mining	87,626	97,885	91,239	100,062	106,045	105,197	110,037
Utilities	80,115	82,256	82,187	87,106	91,672	100,640	90,921
Construction	46,201	48,488	48,650	48,775	49,866	51,226	52,030
Manufacturing	57,597	59,136	59,687	61,692	63,392	64,097	64,142
Durable goods manufacturing	62,688	63,279	64,868	67,783	69,996	70,928	71,036
Nondurable goods manufacturing	47,166	50,903	50,033	50,561	51,137	51,186	51,462
Wholesale trade	67,347	68,909	66,832	69,618	73,015	75,070	75,500
Retail trade	27,515	27,695	27,633	27,840	28,170	28,961	29,265
Transportation and warehousing	44,804	45,394	45,346	46,404	47,767	49,341	52,354
Information	78,618	78,235	79,114	83,528	85,778	90,319	91,880
Finance and insurance	70,679	72,428	70,751	73,396	76,280	79,786	81,450
Real estate and rental and leasing	44,200	42,676	41,997	43,100	45,260	48,429	50,438
Professional, scientific, and technical services	76,618	78,227	78,876	81,054	82,808	85,715	86,274
Management of companies and enterprises	116,961	112,467	119,266	127,683	133,814	155,824	126,899
Administrative and waste services	32,989	34,214	34,764	35,342	36,183	37,019	35,838
Educational services	31,819	32,160	32,943	34,003	34,312	35,006	35,118
Health care and social assistance	42,756	44,061	45,218	45,370	46,052	46,953	47,352
Arts, entertainment, and recreation	35,861	34,056	33,864	33,778	34,527	34,652	35,601
Accommodation and food services	19,546	19,501	19,261	19,882	20,598	21,018	21,250
Other services, except public administration	30,718	31,887	31,959	32,860	33,368	33,483	34,510
Government and government enterprises	43,756	45,504	46,549	47,295	48,050	48,380	49,021

Table CO-10. Employment Characteristics by Family Type

(Number, percent.)

Family type and labor force status	2011		2012		2013	
	Total	Families with own children under 18 years	Total	Families with own children under 18 years	Total	Families with own children under 18 years
All Families	1,256,471	587,062	1,278,264	589,021	1,279,941	584,086
FAMILY TYPE AND LABOR FORCE STATUS						
Married-Couple Families	970,556	420,122	975,070	411,938	982,202	411,595
Both husband and wife in labor force	56.7	66.0	55.7	65.0	54.1	64.9
Husband in labor force, wife not in labor force	22.5	29.2	23.2	30.0	23.6	30.4
Wife in labor force, husband not in labor force	6.8	3.4	6.6	3.5	7.0	3.3
Both husband and wife not in labor force	14.0	1.4	14.5	1.5	15.0	1.2
Other Families	285,915	166,940	303,194	177,083	297,739	172,491
Female householder, no husband present	69.3	69.6	69.6	72.4	70.3	72.9
In labor force	52.5	58.6	53.2	60.9	52.8	61.5
Not in labor force	16.8	11.0	16.3	11.5	17.5	11.4
Male householder, no wife present	30.7	30.4	30.4	27.6	29.7	27.1
In labor force	26.1	27.9	26.1	25.7	24.5	25.2
Not in labor force	4.6	2.4	4.4	1.9	5.2	1.9

Table CO-11. School Enrollment and Educational Attainment, 2013

(Number, percent.)

Item	State	U.S.
Enrollment		
Total population 3 years and over, enrolled in school	1,400,453	82,395,254
Enrolled in nursery school or preschool (percent)	6.2	6.0
Enrolled in kindergarten (percent)	5.0	5.2
Enrolled in elementary school, grades 1-8 (percent)	40.3	40.0
Enrolled in high school, grades 9-12 (percent)	19.8	20.6
Enrolled in college or graduate school (percent)	28.7	28.3
Attainment		
Total population 25 years and over	3,514,235	210,910,615
Less than ninth grade (percent)	3.7	5.8
9th to 12th grade, no diploma (percent)	5.8	7.6
High school graduate, including equivalency (percent)	21.7	27.8
Some college, no degree (percent)	22.8	21.1
Associate's degree (percent)	8.3	8.1
Bachelor's degree (percent)	23.8	18.4
Graduate or professional degree (percent)	14.0	11.2
High school graduate or higher (percent)	90.5	86.6
Bachelor's degree or higher (percent)	37.8	29.6

Table CO-12. Public School Characteristics and Educational Indicators

(Number, percent; data derived from National Center of Education Statistics.)

Item	State	U.S.
Public Schools, 2012–2013 (except where noted)		
Number of school districts	259	18,093
Number of schools	1,825	98,454
Number of students (in thousands)	864	49,771
Number of teachers (in thousands)	49	3,109
Student-teacher ratio	17.7	16.0
Expenditures per student (dollars), FY 2012	8,594	10,667
Four-year adjusted cohort graduation rate (ACGR)[1,2]	76.9	81.4
Students eligible for free or reduced-price lunch (in thousands)	359	25,188
English language learners (in thousands)	102	4,397
Students age 3 to 21 served under IDEA, part B (in thousands)	89	6,429

Public Schools by Type	Number	Percent of state public schools
Total number of schools	1,825	100.0
Regular	1,725	94.5
Special education	7	0.4
Vocational education	6	0.3
Alternative education	87	4.8

NOTE: Every school is assigned only one school type based on its instructional emphasis.
[1]ACGR data represents a new method of calculating high-school completion rates and may not be comparable to previous years' data for Averaged Freshmen Graduation Rates (AFGR).
[2]The United States 4-year ACGRs were estimated using both the reported 4-year ACGR data from 49 states and the District of Columbia and using imputed data for Idaho. The estimate for American Indian/Alaska Native students also includes imputed data for Virginia.

Table CO-13. Reported Voting and Registration of the Voting-Age Population, November 2012

(Numbers in thousands, percent.)

Item	Total population	Total citizen population	Registered			Voted		
			Total registered	Percent registered (total population)	Percent registered (total citizen population)	Total voted	Percent voted (total population)	Percent voted (total citizen population)
U.S. Total	235,248	215,081	153,157	65.1	71.2	132,948	56.5	61.8
State Total	3,817	3,544	2,635	69.0	74.4	2,495	65.4	70.4
Sex								
Male	1,882	1,725	1,251	66.5	72.5	1,179	62.7	68.4
Female	1,935	1,818	1,384	71.5	76.1	1,316	68.0	72.4
Race								
White alone........................	3,474	3,253	2,471	71.1	76.0	2,345	67.5	72.1
White, non-Hispanic alone	2,852	2,800	2,205	77.3	78.7	2,105	73.8	75.2
Black alone........................	140	125	75	53.6	60.1	69	49.6	55.6
Asian alone	119	98	39	32.9	40.0	31	26.0	31.6
Hispanic (any race)	681	497	284	41.7	57.2	259	38.0	52.1
White alone or in combination	3,529	3,304	2,510	71.1	76.0	2,385	67.6	72.2
Black alone or in combination..........	159	139	87	54.5	62.3	81	51.1	58.3
Asian alone or in combination..........	138	117	54	39.2	46.3	46	33.2	39.2
Age								
18 to 24 years.....................	493	461	278	56.5	60.3	259	52.5	56.1
25 to 44 years.....................	1,377	1,218	895	65.0	73.5	816	59.2	66.9
45 to 64 years.....................	1,354	1,287	1,025	75.7	79.7	989	73.0	76.9
65 to 74 years.....................	344	330	262	76.4	79.4	258	75.0	78.0
75 years and over	250	247	174	69.7	70.6	174	69.7	70.6

Table CO-14. Crime

(Number, rate per 100,000. Data are derived from the FBI Uniform Crime Reports.)

Item	State			U.S.[1,2,3,4]		
	2012	2013	Percent change	2012	2013	Percent change
TOTAL POPULATION[5]...........................	5,189,458	5,268,367	1.5	313,873,685	316,128,839	0.7
VIOLENT CRIME						
Number........................	15,951	15,342	-3.8	1,217,067	1,163,146	-4.4
Rate........................	307.4	291.2	-5.3	387.8	367.9	-5.1
Murder and Nonnegligent Manslaughter						
Number........................	152	178	17.1	14,866	14,196	-4.5
Rate........................	2.9	3.4	15.4	4.7	4.5	-5.2
Rape[6]						
Number........................	X	2,934	X	X	108,612	X
Rate........................	X	55.7	X	X	34.4	X
Robbery						
Number........................	3,392	3,151	-7.1	355,051	345,031	-2.8
Rate........................	65.4	59.8	-8.5	113.1	109.1	-3.5
Aggravated Assault						
Number........................	10,285	9,963	-3.1	762,009	724,149	-5.0
Rate........................	198.2	189.1	-4.6	242.8	229.1	-5.6
PROPERTY CRIME						
Number........................	139,355	140,057	0.5	9,001,992	8,632,512	-4.1
Rate........................	2,685.3	2,658.5		2,868.0	2,730.7	-4.8
Burglary						
Number........................	26,163	25,081	-4.1	2,109,932	1,928,465	-8.6
Rate........................	504.2	476.1	-5.6	672.2	610.0	-9.3
Larceny-Theft						
Number........................	101,091	102,443	1.3	6,168,874	6,004,453	-2.7
Rate........................	1,948.0	1,944.5	-0.2	1,965.4	1,899.4	-3.4
Motor Vehicle Theft						
Number........................	12,101	12,533	3.6	723,186	699,594	-3.3
Rate........................	233.2	237.9	2.0	230.4	221.3	-4.0

NOTE: Although arson data are included in the trend and clearance tables, sufficient data are not available to estimate totals for this offense. Therefore, no arson data are published in this table.

X = Not applicable.

- = Zero or rounds to zero.

[1]The crime figures have been adjusted.

[2]The data collection methodology for the offense of forcible rape used by the Minnesota state Uniform Crime Reporting (UCR) Program (with the exception of Minneapolis and St. Paul, Minnesota) does not comply with national UCR Program guidelines. Consequently, its figures for forcible rape and violent crime (of which forcible rape is a part) are not published in this table.

[3]Includes offenses reported by the Zoological Police and the Metro Transit Police.

[4]Because of changes in the state's reporting practices, figures are not comparable to previous years' data.

[5]Populations are U.S. Census Bureau provisional estimates as of July 1 of each year.

[6]The figures shown for the offense of rape were estimated using the revised Uniform Crime Reporting (UCR) definition of rape.

Table CO-15. State Government Finances, 2013

(Dollar amounts in thousands, percent distribution.)

Item	Dollars	Percent distribution
Total Revenue	30,986,766	100.0
General revenue	23,129,280	74.6
Intergovernmental revenue	6,508,932	21.0
Taxes	11,245,662	36.3
General sales	2,416,731	7.8
Selective sales	1,862,813	6.0
License taxes	637,707	2.1
Individual income tax	5,528,485	17.8
Corporate income tax	652,180	2.1
Other taxes	147,746	0.5
Current charges	3,196,792	10.3
Miscellaneous general revenue	2,177,894	7.0
Utility revenue	0	-
Liquor stores revenue	0	-
Insurance trust revenue[1]	7,857,486	25.4
Total Expenditure	28,743,913	100.0
Intergovernmental expenditure	6,291,390	21.9
Direct expenditure	22,452,523	78.1
Current operation	14,204,199	49.4
Capital outlay	1,485,834	5.2
Insurance benefits and repayments	5,539,020	19.3
Assistance and subsidies	362,907	1.3
Interest on debt	860,563	3.0
Exhibit: Salaries and wages	4,034,587	14.0
Total Expenditure	28,743,913	100.0
General expenditure	23,189,078	80.7
Intergovernmental expenditure	6,291,390	21.9
Direct expenditure	16,897,688	58.8
General expenditure, by function:		
Education	9,478,848	33.0
Public welfare	5,840,287	20.3
Hospitals	710,618	2.5
Health	1,055,306	3.7
Highways	1,448,635	5.0
Police protection	172,792	0.6
Correction	975,698	3.4
Natural resources	321,265	1.1
Parks and recreation	83,055	0.3
Governmental administration	806,029	2.8
Interest on general debt	846,807	2.9
Other and unallocable	1,449,738	5.0
Utility expenditure	15,815	0.1
Liquor stores expenditure	0	-
Insurance trust expenditure	5,539,020	19.3
Debt at End of Fiscal Year	16,309,217	X
Cash and Security Holdings	68,212,593	X

X = Not applicable.
- = Zero or rounds to zero.
[1]Within insurance trust revenue, net earnings of state retirement systems is a calculated statistic (the item code in the data file is X08), and thus can be positive or negative. Net earnings is the sum of earnings on investments plus gains on investments minus losses on investments. The change made in 2002 for asset valuation from book to market value in accordance with Statement 34 of the Governmental Accounting Standards Board is reflected in the calculated statistics.

Table CO-16. State Government Tax Collections, 2014

(Dollars in thousands, percent.)

Item	Dollars	Percent distribution
Total Taxes	11,755,394	100.0
Property taxes	X	X
Sales and gross receipts	4,474,294	38.1
General sales and gross receipts	2,615,601	22.3
Selective sales and gross receipts	1,858,693	15.8
Alcoholic beverages	40,886	0.3
Amusements	105,420	0.9
Insurance premiums	239,431	2.0
Motor fuels	647,104	5.5
Pari-mutuels	609	-
Public utilities	10,819	0.1
Tobacco products	194,192	1.7
Other selective sales	620,232	5.3
Licenses	659,616	5.6
Alcoholic beverages	7,212	0.1
Amusements	791	-
Corporations in general	17,569	0.1
Hunting and fishing	71,142	0.6
Motor vehicle	474,534	4.0
Motor vehicle operators	28,660	0.2
Public utilities	14,156	0.1
Occupation and business, NEC	44,577	0.4
Other licenses	975	-
Income taxes	6,375,963	54.2
Individual income	5,658,457	48.1
Corporation net income	717,506	6.1
Other taxes	245,521	2.1
Death and gift	434	-
Documentary and stock transfer	0	-
Severance	245,087	2.1
Taxes, NEC	0	-

X = Not applicable.
- = Zero or rounds to zero.

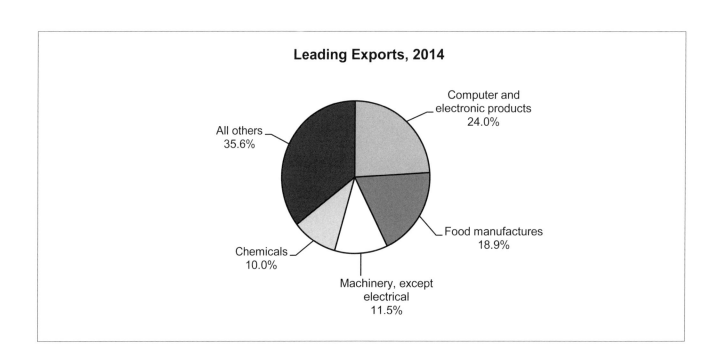

Leading Exports, 2014

Computer and electronic products 24.0%

All others 35.6%

Food manufactures 18.9%

Chemicals 10.0%

Machinery, except electrical 11.5%

CONNECTICUT

Facts and Figures

Location: Northeastern United States; bordered on the N by Massachusetts, on the E by Rhode Island, on the S by Long Island Sound, and on the W by New York

Area: 5,543 sq. mi. (14,357); rank—48th

Population: 3,596,677 (2014 est.); rank—29th

Principal Cities: capital—Hartford; largest—Bridgeport

Statehood: January 9, 1788; 5th state

U.S. Congress: 2 senators, 5 representatives

State Motto: *Qui transtulit sustinet* ("He who transplanted still sustains")

State Song: "Yankee Doodle"

State Nicknames: The Constitution State; The Nutmeg State

Abbreviations: CT; Conn.

State Symbols: flower—mountain laurel; tree—white oak; bird—American robin

At a Glance

- With an increase in population of 0.6 percent, Connecticut ranked 44th among the states in growth from 2010 to 2014.

- Connecticut's median household income in 2013 was $67,098, and 10.7 percent of its population lived below the poverty level.

- In 2013, Connecticut's unemployment rate was 6.6 percent, down from 7.8 percent in 2012.

- Connecticut's violent crime rate in 2013 was 262.5 per 100,000 population, compared to 367.9 for the entire nation.

- The property crime rate in Connecticut in 2013 ranked 47th in the nation, with 1,974.1 incidents per 100,000 population.

Table CT-1. Population by Age, Sex, Race, and Hispanic Origin

(Number, percent, except where noted.)

Sex, age, race, and Hispanic origin	2000	2010	2014[1]	Average annual percent change, 2010–2014
Total Population..................................	3,405,565	3,574,097	3,596,677	0.2
Percent of total U.S. population	1.2	1.2	1.1	X
Sex				
Male..................................	1,649,319	1,739,614	1,754,549	0.2
Female	1,756,246	1,834,483	1,842,128	0.1
Age				
Under 5 years..................................	233,344	202,106	189,437	-1.6
5 to 19 years..................................	702,358	713,670	692,259	-0.8
20 to 64 years..................................	2,009,680	2,151,762	2,159,058	0.1
65 years and over..................................	470,183	506,559	555,923	2.4
Median age (years)	37.4	40.0	40.6	0.4
Race and Hispanic Origin				
One race				
White..................................	2,780,355	2,950,820	2,919,746	-0.3
Black..................................	309,843	392,131	413,814	1.4
American Indian and Alaska Native	9,639	16,734	18,443	2.5
Asian..................................	82,313	140,516	161,770	3.6
Native Hawaiian or Other Pacific Islander	1,366	3,491	3,862	2.6
Two or more races	74,848	70,405	79,042	2.9
Hispanic (of any race)	320,323	498,638	541,152	2.1

X = Not applicable.
[1]Population figures for 2014 are July 1 estimates. The 2010 estimates are taken from the 2010 Census.

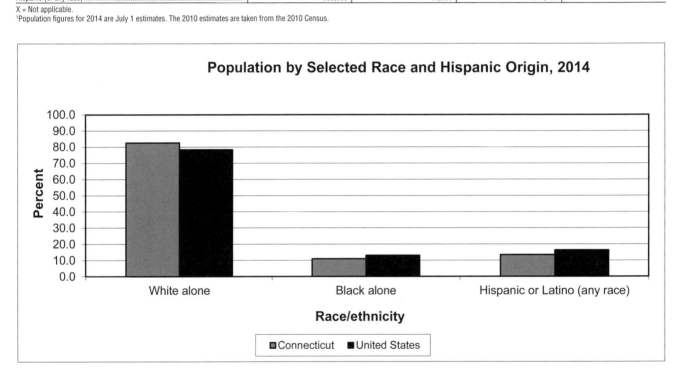

Table CT-2. Marital Status

(Number, percent distribution.)

Sex, age, race, and Hispanic origin	2000	2010	2013
Males, 15 Years and Over..................................	1,284,881	1,399,329	1,426,766
Never married	30.0	36.3	37.4
Now married, except separated..................................	58.0	50.6	49.9
Separated..................................	1.3	1.1	1.0
Widowed..................................	2.7	2.7	2.7
Divorced..................................	7.9	9.3	9.1
Females, 15 Years and Over..................................	1,411,369	1,512,492	1,528,565
Never married	24.5	29.9	30.9
Now married, except separated..................................	52.3	46.5	45.9
Separated..................................	1.8	1.8	1.7
Widowed..................................	10.8	9.3	9.1
Divorced..................................	10.5	12.5	12.3

Table CT-3. Households and Housing Characteristics

(Number, percent, dollars.)

Item	2000	2010	2013	Average annual percent change, 2000–2013
Total Households	1,301,670	1,358,809	1,339,860	0.2
Family households	881,170	890,770	890,293	0.1
Married-couple family	676,467	656,629	657,885	-0.2
Other family	204,703	234,141	232,408	1.0
Male householder, no wife present	47,292	58,325	57,268	1.5
Female householder, no husband present	157,411	175,816	175,140	0.8
Nonfamily households	420,500	468,039	449,567	0.5
Householder living alone	334,224	384,382	370,893	0.8
Householder not living alone	76,276	83,657	78,674	0.2
Housing Characteristics				
Total housing units	1,385,975	1,488,215	1,488,072	0.5
Occupied housing units	1,301,670	1,358,809	1,339,860	0.2
Owner occupied	869,729	923,617	888,478	0.2
Renter occupied	431,941	435,192	451,382	0.3
Average household size	2.53	2.55	2.60	0.2
Financial Characteristics				
Median gross rent of renter-occupied housing	681	992	1,040	3.3
Median monthly owner costs for housing units with a mortgage	1,426	2,068	1,986	2.6
Median value of owner-occupied housing units	166,900	288,800	267,000	3.7

Table CT-4. Migration, Origin, and Language

(Number, percent.)

Characteristic	State			U.S.		
	2012	2013	Percent change	2012	2013	Percent change
Residence 1 Year Ago						
Population 1 year and over	3,555,319	3,562,959	0.2	310,212,755	312,432,820	0.7
Same house	87.6	87.8	X	85.0	85.0	X
Different house in the U.S.	11.7	11.6	X	14.4	14.4	X
Same county	7.6	7.2	X	9.0	8.9	X
Different county	4.1	4.4	X	5.4	5.5	X
Same state	1.8	2.0	X	3.2	3.2	X
Different state	2.3	2.5	X	2.3	2.3	X
Abroad	0.7	0.6	X	0.6	0.6	X
Place of Birth						
Native born	3,094,926	3,096,437	-	273,089,382	274,780,773	0.6
Male	48.7	48.8	X	49.3	49.3	X
Female	51.3	51.2	X	50.7	50.7	X
Foreign born	495,421	499,643	0.9	40,824,658	41,348,066	1.3
Male	49.0	48.3	X	48.7	48.8	X
Female	51.0	51.7	X	51.3	51.2	X
Foreign born; naturalized U.S. citizen	233,804	244,730	4.7	18,686,237	19,294,710	3.3
Male	46.4	44.3	X	45.8	45.9	X
Female	53.6	55.7	X	54.2	54.1	X
Foreign born; not a U.S. citizen	261,617	254,913	-2.6	22,138,421	22,053,356	-0.4
Male	51.4	52.0	X	51.1	51.3	X
Female	48.6	48.0	X	48.9	48.7	X
Entered 2010 or later	8.9	10.3	X	7.0	9.7	X
Entered 2000 to 2009	31.6	29.9	X	30.4	29.4	X
Entered before 2000	59.5	59.7	X	62.7	61.0	X
World Region of Birth, Foreign						
Foreign-born population, excluding population born at sea	495,421	499,643	0.9	40,824,553	41,347,945	1.3
Europe	27.7	25.9	X	11.8	11.6	X
Asia	23.9	23.3	X	29.2	29.5	X
Africa	4.9	2.8	X	4.2	4.4	X
Oceania	0.3	0.2	X	0.6	0.5	X
Latin America	39.9	45.0	X	52.2	51.9	X
North America	3.2	2.7	X	2.0	2.0	X
Language Spoken at Home and Ability to Speak English						
Population 5 years and over	3,397,277	3,405,334	0.2	294,003,714	296,358,760	0.8
English only	77.8	78.5	X	79.0	79.2	X
Language other than English	22.2	21.5	X	21.0	20.8	X
Speaks English less than "very well"	8.5	8.2	X	8.5	8.5	X

NA = Not available.
X = Not applicable.
- = Zero or rounds to zero.

Table CT-5. Median Income and Poverty Status, 2013

(Number, percent, except as noted.)

Characteristic	State		U.S.	
	Number	Percent	Number	Percent
Median Income				
Households (dollars).............................	67,098	X	52,250	X
Families (dollars)	85,563	X	64,030	X
Below Poverty Level (All People)	373,900	10.7	48,810,868	15.8
Sex				
Male..	165,277	9.7	21,938,525	14.5
Female	208,623	11.7	26,872,343	17.1
Age				
Under 18 years....................................	112,723	14.5	16,086,960	22.2
Related children under 18 years.............	110,426	14.3	15,769,921	21.9
18 to 64 years....................................	222,573	10.2	28,578,191	14.8
65 years and over	38,604	7.4	4,145,717	9.6

X = Not applicable.

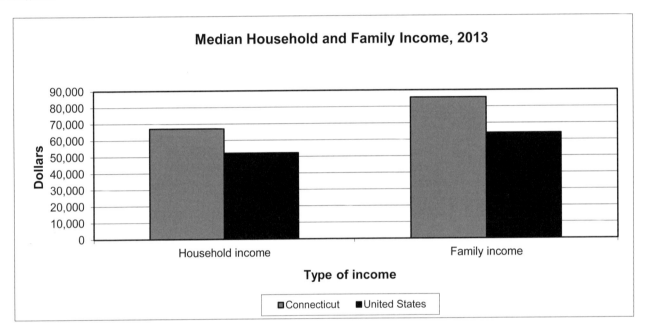

Table CT-6. Health Insurance Coverage Status for the Civilian Noninstitutionalized Population and Children Under 18 Years of Age

(Numbers in thousands, percent.)

Item	2005	2006	2007	2008	2009	2010	2011	2012	2013
Civilian Noninstitutionalized Population	3,487	3,462	3,476	3,441	3,457	3,520	3,523	3,535	3,541
Covered by Private or Public Insurance									
Number..	3,106	3,137	3,150	3,130	3,152	3,200	3,214	3,213	3,209
Percent...	89.1	90.6	90.6	91.0	91.2	90.9	91.2	90.9	90.6
Not Covered									
Number..	381	325	326	311	305	320	309	322	333
Percent...	10.9	9.4	9.4	9.0	8.8	9.1	8.8	9.1	9.4
Percent in the U.S. not covered................	15.3	15.8	15.3	15.1	15.1	15.5	15.1	14.8	14.5
Children Under 18 Years of Age	832	820	819	810	807	815	803	791	784
Covered by Private or Public Insurance									
Number..	768	771	776	770	777	791	780	761	751
Percent...	92.3	94.0	94.8	95.1	96.2	97.0	97.1	96.2	95.7
Not Covered									
Number..	64	49	43	40	30	24	23	30	34
Percent...	7.7	6.0	5.2	4.9	3.8	3.0	2.9	3.8	4.3
Percent in the U.S. not covered................	10.9	11.7	11.0	9.7	8.6	8.0	7.5	7.2	7.1

Table CT-7. Employment Status by Demographic Group, 2014

(Numbers in thousands, percent.)

Characteristic	Civilian noninstitutional population	Civilian labor force		Employed		Unemployed	
		Number	Percent of population	Number	Percent of population	Number	Percent of population
Total...	2,867	1,893	66.0	1,769	61.7	124	6.6
Sex							
Male..	1,375	979	71.2	910	66.2	68	7.0
Female	1,491	915	61.3	859	57.6	56	6.1
Race, Sex, and Hispanic Origin							
White	2,387	1,578	66.1	1,483	62.2	95	6.0
Male..	1,150	815	70.9	764	66.5	51	6.2
Female	1,237	763	61.7	719	58.1	44	5.8
Black or African American....................................	305	192	63.1	168	55.2	24	12.5
Male..	139	94	67.9	80	57.8	14	14.9
Female	166	98	59.0	88	53.0	10	10.2
Hispanic or Latino ethnicity[1]	323	221	68.5	197	61.0	24	10.9
Male..	150	117	78.1	103	68.7	14	12.0
Female	173	104	60.2	94	54.4	10	9.7
Age							
16 to 19 years...	196	64	32.8	53	27.3	11	16.9
20 to 24 years...	243	183	75.3	164	67.5	19	10.4
25 to 34 years...	426	358	84.1	328	77.1	30	8.3
35 to 44 years...	434	371	85.5	348	80.2	23	6.2
45 to 54 years...	567	472	83.3	451	79.5	21	4.5
55 to 64 years...	470	330	70.3	315	67.1	15	4.5
65 years and over	532	115	21.6	110	20.6	5	4.7

NOTE: Data in Table 7 are from the Current Population Survey (CPS) and do not match the estimates in Table 8. See notes and definitions for further information.
[1]May be of any race.

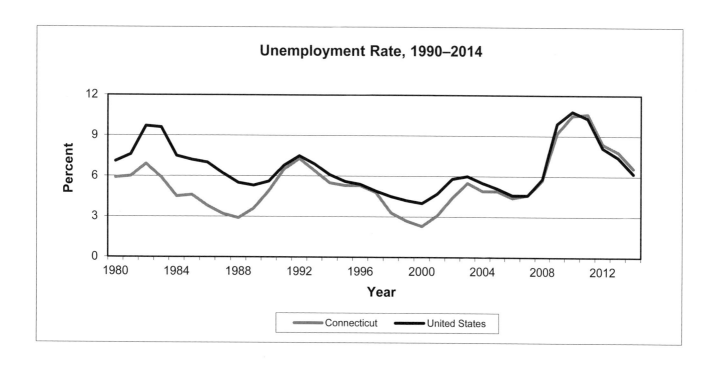

Unemployment Rate, 1990–2014

Table CT-8. Employment Status of the Civilian Noninstitutional Population Age 16 Years and Over

(Number, percent.)

Year	Civilian labor force	Civilian participation rate	Employed	Unemployed	Unemployment rate
2006	1,828,651	67.9	1,749,191	79,460	4.3
2007	1,856,209	68.5	1,773,159	83,050	4.5
2008	1,881,454	69.0	1,774,681	106,773	5.7
2009	1,891,077	68.8	1,740,971	150,106	7.9
2010	1,911,712	68.3	1,737,449	174,263	9.1
2011	1,913,447	67.6	1,744,929	168,518	8.8
2012	1,887,861	66.4	1,730,415	157,446	8.3
2013	1,869,069	65.4	1,724,489	144,580	7.7
2014	1,885,126	65.8	1,760,421	124,705	6.6

Table CT-9. Employment and Average Wages by Industry

(Estimates before 2007 are based on the 2002 *North American Industry Classification System* [NAICS]. Estimates from 2007 onward are based on the 2007 NAICS.)

Industry	2007	2008	2009	2010	2011	2012	2013
	Number of jobs						
Wage and Salary Employment by Industry	1,766,024	1,768,627	1,697,796	1,678,439	1,695,049	1,705,660	1,718,531
Farm Wage and Salary Employment	4,227	4,612	4,449	4,460	4,730	4,789	5,675
Nonfarm Wage and Salary Employment	1,761,797	1,764,015	1,693,347	1,673,979	1,690,319	1,700,871	1,712,856
Private wage and salary employment	1,493,426	1,491,508	1,424,167	1,407,694	1,428,832	1,441,703	1,452,960
Forestry, fishing, and related activities	811	815	800	830	906	921	656
Mining	715	737	629	571	542	554	543
Utilities	6,657	6,759	6,644	6,310	6,173	5,934	6,038
Construction	71,158	67,888	57,044	52,304	54,272	53,351	55,612
Manufacturing	191,381	187,230	171,479	165,835	166,442	165,431	164,043
Durable goods manufacturing	144,475	143,485	132,078	127,377	128,576	128,779	127,652
Nondurable goods manufacturing	46,906	43,745	39,401	38,458	37,866	36,652	36,391
Wholesale trade	68,612	69,891	65,526	63,209	63,914	63,527	63,465
Retail trade	194,127	191,035	181,585	181,490	183,247	184,098	185,592
Transportation and warehousing	43,539	43,337	40,829	40,274	41,375	41,920	42,519
Information	38,105	37,521	34,261	31,827	31,446	31,368	32,152
Finance and insurance	125,734	125,204	120,584	118,635	118,257	115,692	114,325
Real estate and rental and leasing	21,707	21,279	19,820	19,780	19,485	19,237	19,632
Professional, scientific, and technical services	93,691	93,970	88,629	87,408	89,298	90,365	91,273
Management of companies and enterprises	26,638	28,516	27,779	27,826	28,622	31,618	30,694
Administrative and waste services	90,627	87,546	77,461	78,853	81,765	84,818	85,852
Educational services	59,117	61,087	63,159	64,153	66,405	67,317	67,834
Health care and social assistance	236,470	243,264	248,409	251,509	255,468	258,687	261,472
Arts, entertainment, and recreation	24,155	24,211	23,964	23,873	24,538	3,886	26,299
Accommodation and food services	112,762	114,430	111,349	111,542	114,648	118,492	122,249
Other services, except public administration	87,420	86,788	84,216	81,465	82,029	83,159	82,710
Government and government enterprises	268,371	272,507	269,180	266,285	261,487	259,168	259,896
	Dollars						
Average Wages and Salaries by Industry	57,139	57,517	56,809	58,501	60,138	61,221	61,312
Average Farm Wages and Salaries	32,758	28,805	28,367	26,728	22,547	24,961	28,700
Average Nonfarm Wages and Salaries	57,198	57,592	56,884	58,585	60,243	61,323	61,420
Average private wages and salaries	58,490	58,670	57,627	59,713	61,357	62,602	62,585
Forestry, fishing, and related activities	21,705	22,004	23,028	22,981	23,056	23,811	25,942
Mining	61,070	64,171	64,526	67,965	68,950	64,549	64,164
Utilities	105,485	109,587	106,692	103,576	111,584	109,758	111,008
Construction	55,934	57,966	57,799	58,614	58,336	59,246	59,373
Manufacturing	69,254	70,484	70,207	73,403	76,894	78,934	81,100
Durable goods manufacturing	67,776	69,674	69,702	73,005	76,332	78,597	81,022
Nondurable goods manufacturing	73,806	73,142	71,900	74,724	78,801	80,117	81,374
Wholesale trade	80,003	79,758	79,147	81,467	83,383	85,392	85,925
Retail trade	30,207	30,356	30,636	30,909	31,211	31,496	31,572
Transportation and warehousing	47,411	47,040	46,145	46,410	47,499	47,870	46,867
Information	69,484	70,196	71,374	77,158	78,945	86,820	89,035
Finance and insurance	145,391	141,147	130,078	143,395	152,330	153,964	150,126
Real estate and rental and leasing	53,543	52,902	51,556	54,133	58,140	61,971	63,970
Professional, scientific, and technical services	83,165	85,411	85,225	88,164	89,592	91,723	92,541
Management of companies and enterprises	157,905	136,632	135,450	135,150	139,171	154,553	160,079
Administrative and waste services	36,770	38,188	38,583	40,063	40,837	41,257	40,800
Educational services	42,330	44,406	45,609	46,391	47,415	48,569	50,582
Health care and social assistance	44,072	45,815	46,433	46,972	47,523	48,405	48,594
Arts, entertainment, and recreation	31,101	29,742	29,230	29,054	29,259	189,738	29,010
Accommodation and food services	20,226	19,788	19,804	20,491	20,779	21,125	20,918
Other services, except public administration	29,273	30,166	30,344	31,253	31,708	32,015	32,623
Government and government enterprises	50,003	51,688	52,951	52,625	54,157	54,206	54,907

Table CT-10. Employment Characteristics by Family Type

(Number, percent.)

Family type and labor force status	2011		2012		2013	
	Total	Families with own children under 18 years	Total	Families with own children under 18 years	Total	Families with own children under 18 years
All Families.........	893,101	402,424	902,369	401,316	890,293	384,072
FAMILY TYPE AND LABOR FORCE STATUS						
Married-Couple Families....	660,299	275,446	660,876	272,625	657,885	262,395
Both husband and wife in labor force....	59.5	71.6	58.8	70.9	58.1	70.4
Husband in labor force, wife not in labor force ...	19.9	24.7	19.6	25.0	19.9	24.3
Wife in labor force, husband not in labor force ...	7.0	3.0	7.3	3.1	7.3	3.8
Both husband and wife not in labor force....	13.6	0.8	14.4	1.0	14.0	1.1
Other Families ...	232,802	126,978	241,493	128,691	232,408	121,677
Female householder, no husband present...	77.0	80.7	73.8	78.1	75.4	80.5
In labor force....	58.5	69.0	56.2	68.3	55.7	67.8
Not in labor force ...	18.5	11.7	17.6	9.8	19.6	12.7
Male householder, no wife present....	23.0	19.3	26.2	21.9	24.6	19.5
In labor force....	18.6	17.6	21.2	20.1	19.6	17.9
Not in labor force ...	4.4	1.8	5.0	1.9	5.1	1.6

Table CT-11. School Enrollment and Educational Attainment, 2013

(Number, percent.)

Item	State	U.S.
Enrollment		
Total population 3 years and over, enrolled in school ...	939,762	82,395,254
Enrolled in nursery school or preschool (percent)...	6.3	6.0
Enrolled in kindergarten (percent)...	4.6	5.2
Enrolled in elementary school, grades 1-8 (percent)...	38.6	40.0
Enrolled in high school, grades 9-12 (percent)...	21.6	20.6
Enrolled in college or graduate school (percent)...	28.9	28.3
Attainment		
Total population 25 years and over ...	2,465,315	210,910,615
Less than ninth grade (percent) ...	4.5	5.8
9th to 12th grade, no diploma (percent) ...	5.9	7.6
High school graduate, including equivalency (percent)...	27.3	27.8
Some college, no degree (percent) ...	17.7	21.1
Associate's degree (percent)...	7.5	8.1
Bachelor's degree (percent) ...	20.6	18.4
Graduate or professional degree (percent)...	16.6	11.2
High school graduate or higher (percent) ...	89.7	86.6
Bachelor's degree or higher (percent)...	37.2	29.6

Table CT-12. Public School Characteristics and Educational Indicators

(Number, percent; data derived from National Center of Education Statistics.)

Item	State	U.S.
Public Schools, 2012–2013 (except where noted)		
Number of school districts....	200	18,093
Number of schools....	1,148	98,454
Number of students (in thousands) ...	551	49,771
Number of teachers (in thousands) ...	44	3,109
Student-teacher ratio ...	12.5	16.0
Expenditures per student (dollars), FY 2012 ...	16,855	10,667
Four-year adjusted cohort graduation rate (ACGR)[1,2] ...	85.5	81.4
Students eligible for free or reduced-price lunch (in thousands) ...	201	25,188
English language learners (in thousands) ...	30	4,397
Students age 3 to 21 served under IDEA, part B (in thousands) ...	70	6,429

Public Schools by Type	Number	Percent of state public schools
Total number of schools....	1,148	100.0
Regular ...	1,035	90.2
Special education....	47	4.1
Vocational education....	16	1.4
Alternative education....	50	4.4

NOTE: Every school is assigned only one school type based on its instructional emphasis.
[1]ACGR data represents a new method of calculating high-school completion rates and may not be comparable to previous years' data for Averaged Freshmen Graduation Rates (AFGR).
[2]The United States 4-year ACGRs were estimated using both the reported 4-year ACGR data from 49 states and the District of Columbia and using imputed data for Idaho. The estimate for American Indian/Alaska Native students also includes imputed data for Virginia.

Table CT-13. Reported Voting and Registration of the Voting-Age Population, November 2012

(Numbers in thousands, percent.)

Item	Total population	Total citizen population	Registered			Voted		
			Total registered	Percent registered (total population)	Percent registered (total citizen population)	Total voted	Percent voted (total population)	Percent voted (total citizen population)
U.S. Total	235,248	215,081	153,157	65.1	71.2	132,948	56.5	61.8
State Total	2,726	2,499	1,760	64.6	70.4	1,568	57.5	62.7
Sex								
Male	1,297	1,188	811	62.6	68.3	712	54.9	59.9
Female	1,429	1,311	949	66.4	72.4	856	59.9	65.3
Race								
White alone.................................	2,238	2,115	1,520	67.9	71.8	1,352	60.4	63.9
White, non-Hispanic alone	2,004	1,931	1,420	70.9	73.5	1,271	63.4	65.8
Black alone.................................	279	256	164	58.7	64.0	159	57.1	62.2
Asian alone.................................	147	80	37	25.1	46.1	23	15.8	29.0
Hispanic (of any race)	292	220	127	43.5	57.7	103	35.4	47.0
White alone or in combination	2,280	2,152	1,551	68.0	72.1	1,379	60.5	64.1
Black alone or in combination..........	309	281	185	59.9	66.0	177	57.1	62.9
Asian alone or in combination..........	156	89	44	28.1	49.2	30	19.3	33.8
Age								
18 to 24 years	333	308	145	43.6	47.1	123	36.9	39.8
25 to 44 years	843	713	464	55.1	65.2	400	47.4	56.1
45 to 64 years	1,047	993	768	73.3	77.4	695	66.3	70.0
65 to 74 years	276	264	212	76.6	80.2	206	74.5	78.0
75 years and over	226	222	172	75.8	77.3	145	64.0	65.3

Table CT-14. Crime

(Number, rate per 100,000. Data are derived from the FBI Uniform Crime Reports.)

Item	State			U.S.[1,2,3,4]		
	2012	2013	Percent change	2012	2013	Percent change
TOTAL POPULATION[5]..........................	3,591,765	3,596,080	0.1	313,873,685	316,128,839	0.7
VIOLENT CRIME						
Number...............................	10,183	9,153	-10.1	1,217,067	1,163,146	-4.4
Rate	283.5	254.5	-10.2	387.8	367.9	-5.1
Murder and Nonnegligent Manslaughter						
Number...............................	117	86	-26.5	14,866	14,196	-4.5
Rate	3.3	2.4	-26.6	4.7	4.5	-5.2
Rape[6]						
Number...............................	X	955	X		108,612	
Rate	X	26.6	X		34.4	
Robbery						
Number...............................	3,709	3,530	-4.8	355,051	345,031	-2.8
Rate	103.3	98.2	-4.9	113.1	109.1	-3.5
Aggravated Assault						
Number...............................	5,424	4,869	-10.2	762,009	724,149	-5.0
Rate	151.0	135.4	-10.3	242.8	229.1	-5.6
PROPERTY CRIME						
Number...............................	77,169	70,990	-8.0	9,001,992	8,632,512	-4.1
Rate	2,148.5	1,974.1	-8.1	2,868.0	2,730.7	-4.8
Burglary						
Number...............................	14,787	12,892	-12.8	2,109,932	1,928,465	-8.6
Rate	411.7	358.5	-12.9	672.2	610.0	-9.3
Larceny-Theft						
Number...............................	55,904	51,876	-7.2	6,168,874	6,004,453	-2.7
Rate	1,556.4	1,442.6	-7.3	1,965.4	1,899.4	-3.4
Motor Vehicle Theft						
Number...............................	6,478	6,222	-4.0	723,186	699,594	-3.3
Rate	180.4	173.0	-4.1	230.4	221.3	-4.0

NOTE: Although arson data are included in the trend and clearance tables, sufficient data are not available to estimate totals for this offense. Therefore, no arson data are published in this table.

X = Not applicable.

- = Zero or rounds to zero.

[1]The crime figures have been adjusted.

[2]The data collection methodology for the offense of forcible rape used by the Minnesota state Uniform Crime Reporting (UCR) Program (with the exception of Minneapolis and St. Paul, Minnesota) does not comply with national UCR Program guidelines. Consequently, its figures for forcible rape and violent crime (of which forcible rape is a part) are not published in this table.

[3]Includes offenses reported by the Zoological Police and the Metro Transit Police.

[4]Because of changes in the state's reporting practices, figures are not comparable to previous years' data.

[5]Populations are U.S. Census Bureau provisional estimates as of July 1 of each year.

[6]The figures shown for the offense of rape were estimated using the revised Uniform Crime Reporting (UCR) definition of rape.

Table CT-15. State Government Finances, 2013

(Dollar amounts in thousands, percent distribution.)

Item	Dollars	Percent distribution
Total Revenue	31,851,296	100.0
General revenue	25,446,414	79.9
Intergovernmental revenue	5,962,699	18.7
Taxes	16,189,525	50.8
General sales	3,855,861	12.1
Selective sales	2,920,197	9.2
License taxes	453,112	1.4
Individual income tax	7,811,949	24.5
Corporate income tax	572,628	1.8
Other taxes	575,778	1.8
Current charges	1,797,331	5.6
Miscellaneous general revenue	1,496,859	4.7
Utility revenue	36,756	0.1
Liquor stores revenue	0	-
Insurance trust revenue[1]	6,368,126	20.0
Total Expenditure	29,302,715	100.0
Intergovernmental expenditure	4,908,546	16.8
Direct expenditure	24,394,169	83.2
Current operation	15,752,174	53.8
Capital outlay	1,827,444	6.2
Insurance benefits and repayments	4,831,889	16.5
Assistance and subsidies	547,167	1.9
Interest on debt	1,435,495	4.9
Exhibit: Salaries and wages	4,272,596	14.6
Total Expenditure	29,302,715	100.0
General expenditure	23,719,309	80.9
Intergovernmental expenditure	4,908,546	16.8
Direct expenditure	18,810,763	64.2
General expenditure, by function:		
Education	7,019,066	24.0
Public welfare	7,318,979	25.0
Hospitals	1,288,711	4.4
Health	950,351	3.2
Highways	1,056,211	3.6
Police protection	232,639	0.8
Correction	669,700	2.3
Natural resources	164,033	0.6
Parks and recreation	62,093	0.2
Governmental administration	1,189,621	4.1
Interest on general debt	1,435,495	4.9
Other and unallocable	2,332,410	8.0
Utility expenditure	751,517	2.6
Liquor stores expenditure	0	-
Insurance trust expenditure	4,831,889	16.5
Debt at End of Fiscal Year	32,356,807	X
Cash and Security Holdings	42,600,027	X

X = Not applicable.
- = Zero or rounds to zero.
[1]Within insurance trust revenue, net earnings of state retirement systems is a calculated statistic (the item code in the data file is X08), and thus can be positive or negative. Net earnings is the sum of earnings on investments plus gains on investments minus losses on investments. The change made in 2002 for asset valuation from book to market value in accordance with Statement 34 of the Governmental Accounting Standards Board is reflected in the calculated statistics.

Table CT-16. State Government Tax Collections, 2014

(Dollars in thousands, percent.)

Item	Dollars	Percent distribution
Total Taxes	15,937,742	100.0
Property taxes	X	X
Sales and gross receipts	6,782,404	42.6
General sales and gross receipts	3,981,362	25.0
Selective sales and gross receipts	2,801,042	17.6
Alcoholic beverages	60,686	0.4
Amusements	348,353	2.2
Insurance premiums	205,690	1.3
Motor fuels	503,252	3.2
Pari-mutuels	6,085	-
Public utilities	315,287	2.0
Tobacco products	376,489	2.4
Other selective sales	985,200	6.2
Licenses	433,024	2.7
Alcoholic beverages	9,265	0.1
Amusements	232	-
Corporations in general	27,828	0.2
Hunting and fishing	5,269	-
Motor vehicle	211,091	1.3
Motor vehicle operators	43,717	0.3
Public utilities	676	-
Occupation and business, NEC	132,703	0.8
Other licenses	2,243	-
Income taxes	8,399,960	52.7
Individual income	7,772,602	48.8
Corporation net income	627,358	3.9
Other taxes	322,354	2.0
Death and gift	147,737	0.9
Documentary and stock transfer	173,839	1.1
Severance	0	-
Taxes, NEC	778	-

- = Zero or rounds to zero.
X = Not applicable.

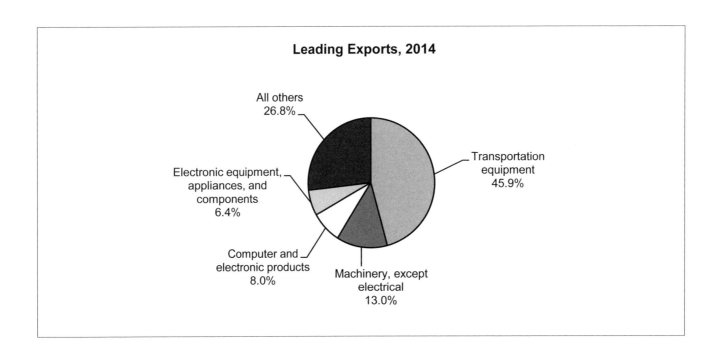

Leading Exports, 2014

All others 26.8%

Electronic equipment, appliances, and components 6.4%

Computer and electronic products 8.0%

Machinery, except electrical 13.0%

Transportation equipment 45.9%

DELAWARE

Facts and Figures

Location: Northeastern United States; bordered on the N by Pennsylvania, on the E by New Jersey, and on the S and W by Maryland

Area: 2,488 sq. mi. (6,447 sq. km.); rank—49th

Population: 935,614 (2014 est.); rank—45th

Principal Cities: capital—Dover; largest—Wilmington

Statehood: December 7, 1787; 1st state

U.S. Congress: 2 senators, 1 representative

State Motto: Liberty and Independence

State Song: "Our Delaware"

State Nickname: The First State

Abbreviations: DE; Del.

State Symbols: flower—peach blossom; tree—American holly; bird—blue hen chicken

At a Glance

- With an increase in population of 4.2 percent, Delaware ranked 15th among the states in growth from 2010 to 2014.

- In 2013, 9.1 percent of Delawareans did not have health insurance, compared to 14.5 percent of the total U.S. population.

- Delaware's violent crime rate in 2013 was 491.4 per 100,000 population, compared to 367.9 for the entire nation.

- Delaware's median household income was $57,846 in 2013, ranking 16th in the nation.

- In 2013, 12.4 percent of Delawareans lived below the poverty level, compared to 15.8 of the total U.S. population.

Table DE-1. Population by Age, Sex, Race, and Hispanic Origin

(Number, percent, except where noted.)

Sex, age, race, and Hispanic origin	2000	2010	2014[1]	Average annual percent change, 2010–2014
Total Population	783,600	897,934	935,614	1.0
Percent of total U.S. population	0.3	0.3	0.3	X
Sex				
Male	380,541	434,939	452,689	1.0
Female	403,059	462,995	482,925	1.1
Age				
Under 5 years	51,531	55,886	56,351	0.2
5 to 19 years	166,719	177,917	173,631	-0.6
20 to 64 years	463,624	648,387	551,725	-4.0
65 years and over	101,726	129,277	153,907	4.5
Median age (years)	36.0	38.8	39.7	0.6
Race and Hispanic Origin				
One race				
White	584,773	645,770	662,176	0.6
Black	150,666	196,281	208,081	1.5
American Indian and Alaska Native	2,731	5,929	6,188	1.1
Asian	16,259	29,342	35,093	4.6
Native Hawaiian or Other Pacific Islander	283	690	863	5.8
Two or more races	13,033	19,922	23,213	3.9
Hispanic (of any race)	37,277	76,137	83,325	2.3

X = Not applicable.

[1]Population figures for 2014 are July 1 estimates. The 2010 estimates are taken from the 2010 Census.

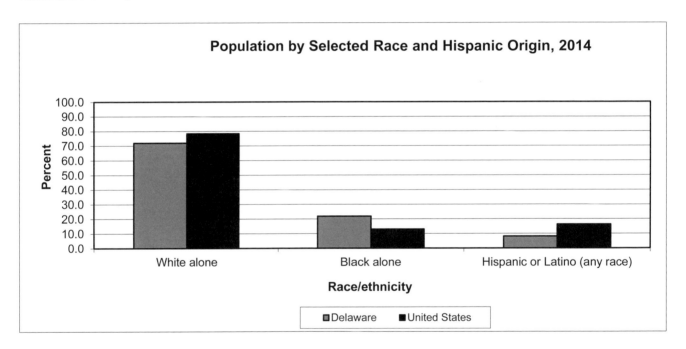

Table DE-2. Marital Status

(Number, percent distribution.)

Sex, age, race, and Hispanic origin	2000	2010	2013
Males, 15 Years and Over	296,619	350,025	361,111
Never married	29.4	35.3	36.1
Now married, except separated	57.4	50.4	50.0
Separated	1.8	1.9	1.6
Widowed	2.8	2.9	2.5
Divorced	8.7	9.4	9.9
Females, 15 Years and Over	324,042	380,618	393,701
Never married	25.3	30.8	31.1
Now married, except separated	50.9	45.3	44.7
Separated	2.2	2.0	2.0
Widowed	10.7	9.8	8.9
Divorced	10.9	12.1	13.3

Table DE-3. Households and Housing Characteristics

(Number, percent, dollars.)

Item	2000	2010	2013	Average annual percent change, 2000–2013
Total Households..................................	298,736	328,765	339,071	1.0
Family households	204,590	221,233	228,364	0.8
Married-couple family	153,136	161,575	164,733	0.6
Other family	51,454	59,658	63,631	1.6
Male householder, no wife present.................	12,468	14,124	14,648	1.2
Female householder, no husband present............	38,986	45,534	48,983	1.8
Nonfamily households	94,146	107,532	110,707	1.3
Householder living alone	74,639	86,990	89,894	1.4
Householder not living alone....................	19,507	20,542	20,813	0.5
Housing Characteristics				
Total housing units................................	343,072	406,489	412,015	1.4
Occupied housing units	298,736	328,765	339,071	1.0
Owner occupied	216,038	239,884	243,047	0.9
Renter occupied.................................	86,698	88,881	96,024	0.8
Average household size............................	2.54	2.66	2.66	0.4
Financial Characteristics				
Median gross rent of renter-occupied housing	639	952	999	3.5
Median monthly owner costs for housing units with a mortgage	1,101	1,569	1,504	2.4
Median value of owner-occupied housing units	130,400	243,600	226,200	4.3

Table DE-4. Migration, Origin, and Language

(Number, percent.)

Characteristic	State			U.S.		
	2012	2013	Percent change	2012	2013	Percent change
Residence 1 Year Ago						
Population 1 year and over	906,576	914,025	0.8	310,212,755	312,432,820	0.7
Same house	86.3	86.6	X	85.0	85.0	X
Different house in the U.S.	13.3	12.9	X	14.4	14.4	X
Same county	8.6	7.9	X	9.0	8.9	X
Different county	4.7	5.0	X	5.4	5.5	X
Same state	0.9	1.0	X	3.2	3.2	X
Different state	3.8	4.0	X	2.3	2.3	X
Abroad	0.4	0.5	X	0.6	0.6	X
Place of Birth						
Native born	839,595	848,981	1.1	273,089,382	274,780,773	0.6
Male	48.6	48.2	X	49.3	49.3	X
Female	51.4	51.8	X	50.7	50.7	X
Foreign born	77,497	76,768	-0.9	40,824,658	41,348,066	1.3
Male	47.3	50.7	X	48.7	48.8	X
Female	52.7	49.3	X	51.3	51.2	X
Foreign born; naturalized U.S. citizen...............	38,082	34,625	-9.1	18,686,237	19,294,710	3.3
Male	45.0	47.1	X	45.8	45.9	X
Female	55.0	52.9	X	54.2	54.1	X
Foreign born; not a U.S. citizen................	39,415	42,143	6.9	22,138,421	22,053,356	-0.4
Male	49.5	53.6	X	51.1	51.3	X
Female	50.5	46.4	X	48.9	48.7	X
Entered 2010 or later	7.5	13.0	X	7.0	9.7	X
Entered 2000 to 2009	36.2	33.7	X	30.4	29.4	X
Entered before 2000........................	56.3	53.3	X	62.7	61.0	X
World Region of Birth, Foreign						
Foreign-born population, excluding population born at sea	77,497	76,768	-0.9	40,824,553	41,347,945	1.3
Europe	13.0	15	X	11.8	11.6	X
Asia	31.5	32.2	X	29.2	29.5	X
Africa	11.3	11.1	X	4.2	4.4	X
Oceania	0.3	-	X	0.6	0.5	X
Latin America	43.2	40.0	X	52.2	51.9	X
North America.............................	0.7	1.8	X	2.0	2.0	X
Language Spoken at Home and Ability to Speak English						
Population 5 years and over......................	860,907	869,514	1.0	294,003,714	296,358,760	0.8
English only	87.1	87.9	X	79.0	79.2	X
Language other than English.................	12.9	12.1	X	21.0	20.8	X
Speaks English less than "very well".............	4.8	4.5	X	8.5	8.5	X

NA = Not available.
X = Not applicable.
- = Zero or rounds to zero.

Table DE-5. Median Income and Poverty Status, 2013

(Number, percent, except as noted.)

Characteristic	State		U.S.	
	Number	Percent	Number	Percent
Median Income				
Households (dollars)...	57,846	X	52,250	X
Families (dollars)	69,394	X	64,030	X
Below Poverty Level (All People)	111,327	12.4	48,810,868	15.8
Sex				
Male...	49,144	11.3	21,938,525	14.5
Female	62,183	13.3	26,872,343	17.1
Age				
Under 18 years..	36,060	18.0	16,086,960	22.2
Related children under 18 years......................	35,193	17.6	15,769,921	21.9
18 to 64 years...	64,934	11.7	28,578,191	14.8
65 years and over	10,333	7.2	4,145,717	9.6

X = Not applicable.

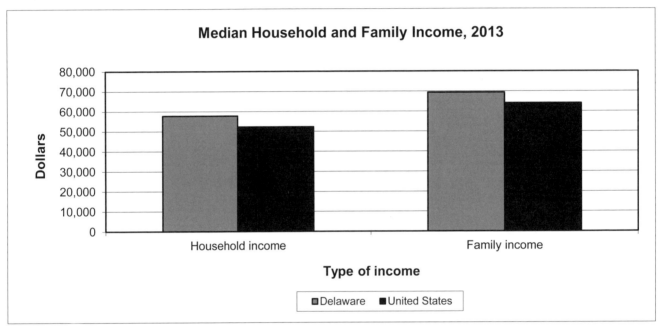

Median Household and Family Income, 2013

Legend: Delaware, United States. X-axis: Type of income (Household income, Family income). Y-axis: Dollars (0 to 80,000).

Table DE-6. Health Insurance Coverage Status for the Civilian Noninstitutionalized Population and Children Under 18 Years of Age

(Numbers in thousands, percent.)

Item	2005	2006	2007	2008	2009	2010	2011	2012	2013
Civilian Noninstitutionalized Population	844	862	863	856	869	885	892	903	912
Covered by Private or Public Insurance									
Number..	742	757	766	768	780	799	808	823	828
Percent..	87.8	87.9	88.8	89.7	89.8	90.3	90.6	91.2	90.9
Not Covered									
Number..	103	105	96	88	89	86	84	80	83
Percent..	12.2	12.1	11.2	10.3	10.2	9.7	9.4	8.8	9.1
Percent in the U.S. not covered................................	15.3	15.8	15.3	15.1	15.1	15.5	15.1	14.8	14.5
Children Under 18 Years of Age...............................	197	206	209	206	207	206	204	204	203
Covered by Private or Public Insurance									
Number..	173	182	194	190	196	195	110	197	194
Percent..	88.1	88.3	92.5	92.2	94.5	94.7	95.4	96.5	95.5
Not Covered									
Number..	23	24	16	16	11	11	9	7	9
Percent..	11.9	11.7	7.5	7.8	5.5	5.3	4.6	3.5	4.5
Percent in the U.S. not covered................................	10.9	11.7	11.0	9.7	8.6	8.0	7.5	7.2	7.1

Table DE-7. Employment Status by Demographic Group, 2014

(Numbers in thousands, percent.)

Characteristic	Civilian noninstitutional population	Civilian labor force		Employed		Unemployed	
		Number	Percent of population	Number	Percent of population	Number	Percent of population
Total..	738	453	61.4	427	57.9	26	5.8
Sex							
Male..	349	230	65.8	217	62.2	13	5.5
Female...	389	224	57.5	210	54.0	14	6.1
Race, Sex, and Hispanic Origin							
White...	541	329	60.8	313	57.9	16	4.8
Male..	260	171	65.6	162	62.4	8	4.9
Female.....................................	281	158	56.3	151	53.7	8	4.8
Black or African American....................	154	97	63.2	88	57.2	9	9.5
Male..	69	45	64.8	41	59.3	4	8.5
Female.....................................	85	52	61.8	47	55.5	5	10.3
Hispanic or Latino ethnicity[1]	51	36	69.3	32	62.9	3	9.3
Male..	27	21	78.1	20	74.6	1	4.5
Female.....................................	24	15	59.6	12	50.0	2	16.1
Age							
16 to 19 years................................	53	18	33.3	15	28.0	3	16.0
20 to 24 years................................	63	46	72.7	40	63.8	6	12.2
25 to 34 years................................	112	94	83.9	89	79.4	5	5.4
35 to 44 years................................	107	89	83.2	85	79.3	4	4.7
45 to 54 years................................	126	103	81.7	98	77.6	5	5.1
55 to 64 years................................	120	75	62.2	72	60.3	2	3.1
65 years and over	156	29	18.4	27	17.5	1	4.6

NOTE: Data in Table 7 are from the Current Population Survey (CPS) and do not match the estimates in Table 8. See notes and definitions for further information.
[1]May be of any race.

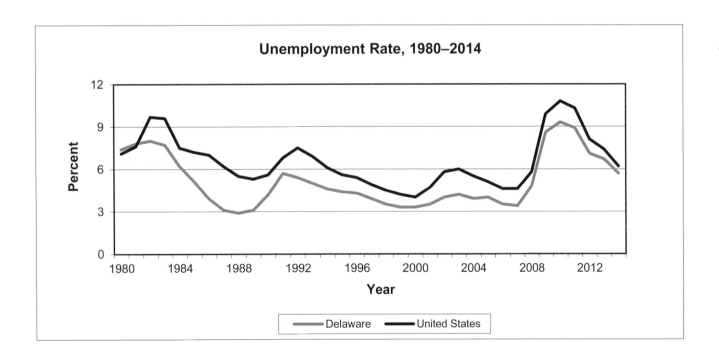

Unemployment Rate, 1980–2014

Table DE-8. Employment Status of the Civilian Noninstitutional Population Age 16 Years and Over

(Number, percent.)

Year	Civilian labor force	Civilian participation rate	Employed	Unemployed	Unemployment rate
2006	441,184	67.1	425,399	15,785	3.6
2007	443,573	66.4	428,312	15,261	3.4
2008	447,041	65.9	424,914	22,127	4.9
2009	437,500	63.8	401,312	36,188	8.3
2010	434,419	62.0	397,869	36,550	8.4
2011	443,220	62.3	409,949	33,271	7.5
2012	445,476	61.9	413,336	32,140	7.2
2013	442,490	60.8	412,788	29,702	6.7
2014	451,767	61.2	425,913	25,854	5.7

Table DE-9. Employment and Average Wages by Industry

(Estimates from 2007 through 2010 are based on the 2007 *North American Industry Classification System* [NAICS]. Estimates from 2011 onward are based on the 2012 NAICS.)

Industry	2007	2008	2009	2010	2011	2012	2013
	Number of jobs						
Wage and Salary Employment by Industry	452,042	451,791	430,104	428,089	432,161	433,304	442,726
Farm Wage and Salary Employment	1,200	1,069	1,036	1,161	1,126	1,459	1,396
Nonfarm Wage and Salary Employment	450,842	450,722	429,068	426,928	431,035	431,845	441,330
Private wage and salary employment	380,353	379,042	357,441	354,081	358,212	358,813	367,068
Forestry, fishing, and related activities	318	D	D	D	D	D	D
Mining	L	D	D	D	D	D	D
Utilities	2,127	2,204	2,129	2,090	1,961	2,014	2,086
Construction	27,837	25,636	20,959	20,265	20,318	19,158	20,291
Manufacturing	33,394	31,813	27,987	26,181	25,698	25,787	25,361
Durable goods manufacturing	13,937	12,968	10,211	9,737	9,691	9,649	9,424
Nondurable goods manufacturing	19,457	18,845	17,776	16,444	16,007	16,138	15,937
Wholesale trade	14,873	14,667	13,355	12,599	12,592	12,533	12,253
Retail trade	55,073	53,635	50,475	50,723	51,364	51,150	51,968
Transportation and warehousing	11,478	11,196	10,215	10,092	10,261	10,553	11,719
Information	6,941	7,072	6,502	5,985	5,661	5,461	5,257
Finance and insurance	39,207	39,591	38,507	37,764	37,845	38,056	39,263
Real estate and rental and leasing	6,843	6,708	6,164	5,894	5,732	5,568	5,667
Professional, scientific, and technical services	25,624	26,132	24,563	24,166	26,292	27,448	28,751
Management of companies and enterprises	11,403	10,745	9,933	9,409	8,048	7,490	5,966
Administrative and waste services	24,685	23,737	21,527	21,440	22,068	21,795	23,530
Educational services	7,006	6,981	6,865	6,974	7,179	6,991	6,745
Health care and social assistance	50,899	55,114	56,354	57,290	58,699	59,871	61,925
Arts, entertainment, and recreation	8,489	8,439	8,223	8,817	9,224	8,898	8,784
Accommodation and food services	32,966	33,497	33,233	34,064	34,748	35,308	36,391
Other services, except public administration	21,181	21,532	20,085	19,925	19,978	20,214	20,464
Government and government enterprises	70,489	71,680	71,627	72,847	72,823	73,032	74,262
	Dollars						
Average Wages and Salaries by Industry	46,570	46,831	47,075	47,961	49,661	50,860	51,093
Average Farm Wages and Salaries	29,762	32,054	31,419	26,482	24,429	21,132	30,092
Average Nonfarm Wages and Salaries	46,614	46,866	47,113	48,020	49,727	50,961	51,160
Average private wages and salaries	46,972	47,097	47,132	48,446	50,316	51,546	51,757
Forestry, fishing, and related activities	21,786	D	D	D	D	D	D
Mining	L	D	D	D	D	D	D
Utilities	83,612	88,640	94,420	94,430	96,294	95,593	98,759
Construction	47,432	49,628	48,641	49,049	52,483	50,990	53,079
Manufacturing	59,626	56,464	57,897	56,995	56,148	57,087	57,900
Durable goods manufacturing	72,649	64,317	69,954	65,811	67,990	67,241	68,246
Nondurable goods manufacturing	50,297	51,059	50,971	51,776	48,979	51,016	51,782
Wholesale trade	70,604	69,948	72,291	76,872	82,623	82,041	79,192
Retail trade	25,474	25,504	25,714	25,809	26,002	26,184	26,471
Transportation and warehousing	39,053	40,885	43,197	43,126	44,551	46,121	46,002
Information	54,653	55,013	55,492	56,439	57,380	59,118	61,039
Finance and insurance	80,783	76,765	74,028	79,068	84,043	86,353	89,511
Real estate and rental and leasing	39,771	40,138	39,671	40,745	41,443	41,997	42,630
Professional, scientific, and technical services	76,696	79,826	80,985	85,311	89,362	97,492	94,542
Management of companies and enterprises	80,450	90,221	88,304	105,373	127,272	130,107	143,164
Administrative and waste services	30,326	31,245	31,075	32,443	32,770	33,877	34,332
Educational services	32,808	34,012	35,465	35,617	36,172	36,858	38,458
Health care and social assistance	45,541	45,687	46,857	47,294	48,700	49,738	49,883
Arts, entertainment, and recreation	28,368	26,862	27,626	28,568	30,865	30,148	29,015
Accommodation and food services	19,056	18,840	18,364	18,853	18,637	18,635	18,507
Other services, except public administration	28,389	28,818	28,893	29,255	29,443	29,284	29,801
Government and government enterprises	45,541	45,687	47,015	45,948	46,827	48,086	48,207

D = Not shown to avoid disclosure of confidential information, but the estimates for this item are included in the total.
L = Less than 10 jobs, but the estimates for this item are included in the total.

Table DE-10. Employment Characteristics by Family Type

(Number, percent.)

Family type and labor force status	2011		2012		2013	
	Total	Families with own children under 18 years	Total	Families with own children under 18 years	Total	Families with own children under 18 years
All Families	227,101	94,229	225,593	92,860	228,364	88,214
FAMILY TYPE AND LABOR FORCE STATUS						
Married-Couple Families	161,755	59,348	163,460	59,809	164,733	55,941
Both husband and wife in labor force	53.5	70.1	53.3	70.7	49.9	72.5
Husband in labor force, wife not in labor force	19.4	24.7	19.3	24.1	20.4	22.6
Wife in labor force, husband not in labor force	7.8	3.5	8.3	3.7	8.2	3.2
Both husband and wife not in labor force	19.3	1.8	19.1	1.5	21.0	1.7
Other Families	65,346	34,881	62,133	33,051	63,631	32,273
Female householder, no husband present	71.4	71.6	73.8	74.1	77.0	77.2
In labor force	54.1	62.8	55.7	65.2	55.6	63.7
Not in labor force	17.3	8.8	18.1	8.8	21.4	13.5
Male householder, no wife present	28.6	28.4	26.2	25.9	23.0	22.8
In labor force	24.1	27.8	21.4	24.4	18.0	20.9
Not in labor force	4.5	0.6	4.8	1.5	5.1	2.0

Table DE-11. School Enrollment and Educational Attainment, 2013

(Number, percent.)

Item	State	U.S.
Enrollment		
Total population 3 years and over, enrolled in school	229,133	82,395,254
Enrolled in nursery school or preschool (percent)	5.7	6.0
Enrolled in kindergarten (percent)	4.8	5.2
Enrolled in elementary school, grades 1-8 (percent)	39.8	40.0
Enrolled in high school, grades 9-12 (percent)	19.7	20.6
Enrolled in college or graduate school (percent)	29.9	28.3
Attainment		
Total population 25 years and over	629,730	210,910,615
Less than ninth grade (percent)	3.9	5.8
9th to 12th grade, no diploma (percent)	7.7	7.6
High school graduate, including equivalency (percent)	31.2	27.8
Some college, no degree (percent)	19.7	21.1
Associate's degree (percent)	7.7	8.1
Bachelor's degree (percent)	17.2	18.4
Graduate or professional degree (percent)	12.6	11.2
High school graduate or higher (percent)	88.3	86.6
Bachelor's degree or higher (percent)	29.8	29.6

Table DE-12. Public School Characteristics and Educational Indicators

(Number, percent; data derived from National Center of Education Statistics.)

Item	State	U.S.
Public Schools, 2012–2013 (except where noted)		
Number of school districts	44	18,093
Number of schools	224	98,454
Number of students (in thousands)	129	49,771
Number of teachers (in thousands)	9	3,109
Student-teacher ratio	13.9	16.0
Expenditures per student (dollars), FY 2012	13,580	10,667
Four-year adjusted cohort graduation rate (ACGR)[1,2]	80.4	81.4
Students eligible for free or reduced-price lunch (in thousands)	66	25,188
English language learners (in thousands)	7	4,397
Students age 3 to 21 served under IDEA, part B (in thousands)	19	6,429

Public Schools by Type	Number	Percent of state public schools
Total number of schools	224	100.0
Regular	191	85.3
Special education	21	9.4
Vocational education	6	2.7
Alternative education	6	2.7

NOTE: Every school is assigned only one school type based on its instructional emphasis.
[1]ACGR data represents a new method of calculating high-school completion rates and may not be comparable to previous years' data for Averaged Freshmen Graduation Rates (AFGR).
[2]The United States 4-year ACGRs were estimated using both the reported 4-year ACGR data from 49 states and the District of Columbia and using imputed data for Idaho. The estimate for American Indian/Alaska Native students also includes imputed data for Virginia.

Table DE-13. Reported Voting and Registration of the Voting-Age Population, November 2012

(Numbers in thousands, percent.)

Item	Total population	Total citizen population	Registered			Voted		
			Total registered	Percent registered (total population)	Percent registered (total citizen population)	Total voted	Percent voted (total population)	Percent voted (total citizen population)
U.S. Total	235,248	215,081	153,157	65.1	71.2	132,948	56.5	61.8
State Total	693	641	470	67.8	73.3	431	62.2	67.3
Sex								
Male	329	302	218	66.1	72.1	196	59.6	65.0
Female	363	339	252	69.3	74.4	235	64.6	69.3
Race								
White alone.....................................	521	488	365	70.1	74.7	336	64.5	68.8
White, non-Hispanic alone	474	468	355	74.9	75.9	328	69.0	69.9
Black alone.....................................	142	134	91	64.0	67.5	86	60.5	63.7
Asian alone	26	15	12	B	B	8	B	B
Hispanic (of any race)	56	24	11	B	B	10	B	B
White alone or in combination	524	490	366	69.9	74.7	337	64.3	68.7
Black alone or in combination..........	144	136	92	63.5	67.5	86	59.5	63.3
Asian alone or in combination..........	26	15	12	B	B	8	B	B
Age								
18 to 24 years	82	77	38	46.1	49.4	33	40.5	43.4
25 to 44 years	225	187	131	58.2	70.1	117	51.8	62.3
45 to 64 years	240	232	182	75.9	78.6	168	69.9	72.3
65 to 74 years	83	82	66	80.0	80.4	63	76.7	77.1
75 years and over	63	63	52	B	B	50	B	B

B = Base is less than 75,000 and therefore too small to show the derived measure.

Table DE-14. Crime

(Number, rate per 100,000. Data are derived from the FBI Uniform Crime Reports.)

Item	State			U.S.[1,2,3,4]		
	2012	2013	Percent change	2012	2013	Percent change
TOTAL POPULATION[5]...........................	917,053	925,749	0.9	313,873,685	316,128,839	0.7
VIOLENT CRIME						
Number..	5,048	4,435	-12.1	1,217,067	1,163,146	-4.4
Rate	550.5	479.1	-13.0	387.8	367.9	-5.1
Murder and Nonnegligent Manslaughter						
Number..	56	39	-30.4	14,866	14,196	-4.5
Rate	6.1	4.2	-31.0	4.7	4.5	-5.2
Rape[6]						
Number..	X	380	X	X	108,612	X
Rate	X	41.0	X	X	34.4	X
Robbery						
Number..	1,498	1,226	-18.2	355,051	345,031	-2.8
Rate	163.3	132.4	-18.9	113.1	109.1	-3.5
Aggravated Assault						
Number..	3,245	2,904	-10.5	762,009	724,149	-5.0
Rate	353.9	313.7	-11.3	242.8	229.1	-5.6
PROPERTY CRIME						
Number..	30,707	28,379	-7.6	9,001,992	8,632,512	-4.1
Rate	3,348.4	3,065.5	-8.4	2,868.0	2,730.7	-4.8
Burglary						
Number..	7,389	6,131	-17.0	2,109,932	1,928,465	-8.6
Rate	805.7	662.3	-17.8	672.2	610.0	-9.3
Larceny-Theft						
Number..	21,880	20,916	-4.4	6,168,874	6,004,453	-2.7
Rate	2,385.9	2,259.4	-5.3	1,965.4	1,899.4	-3.4
Motor Vehicle Theft						
Number..	1,438	1,332	-7.4	723,186	699,594	-3.3
Rate	156.8	143.9	-8.2	230.4	221.3	-4.0

NOTE: Although arson data are included in the trend and clearance tables, sufficient data are not available to estimate totals for this offense. Therefore, no arson data are published in this table.
X = Not applicable.
- = Zero or rounds to zero.
[1]The crime figures have been adjusted.
[2]The data collection methodology for the offense of forcible rape used by the Minnesota state Uniform Crime Reporting (UCR) Program (with the exception of Minneapolis and St. Paul, Minnesota) does not comply with national UCR Program guidelines. Consequently, its figures for forcible rape and violent crime (of which forcible rape is a part) are not published in this table.
[3]Includes offenses reported by the Zoological Police and the Metro Transit Police.
[4]Because of changes in the state's reporting practices, figures are not comparable to previous years' data.
[5]Populations are U.S. Census Bureau provisional estimates as of July 1 of each year.
[6]The figures shown for the offense of rape were estimated using the revised Uniform Crime Reporting (UCR) definition of rape.

Table DE-15. State Government Finances, 2013

(Dollar amounts in thousands, percent distribution.)

Item	Dollars	Percent distribution
Total Revenue	8,908,038	100.0
General revenue	7,793,920	87.5
Intergovernmental revenue	1,996,011	22.4
Taxes	3,346,316	37.6
General sales	0	-
Selective sales	487,202	5.5
License taxes	1,259,277	14.1
Individual income tax	1,130,501	12.7
Corporate income tax	309,644	3.5
Other taxes	159,692	1.8
Current charges	1,134,009	12.7
Miscellaneous general revenue	1,317,584	14.8
Utility revenue	17,025	0.2
Liquor stores revenue	0	-
Insurance trust revenue[1]	1,097,093	12.3
Total Expenditure	8,648,250	100.0
Intergovernmental expenditure	1,271,359	14.7
Direct expenditure	7,376,891	85.3
Current operation	5,254,757	60.8
Capital outlay	780,520	9.0
Insurance benefits and repayments	730,646	8.4
Assistance and subsidies	257,805	3.0
Interest on debt	353,163	4.1
Exhibit: Salaries and wages	2,473,124	28.6
Total Expenditure	8,648,250	100.0
General expenditure	7,782,971	90.0
Intergovernmental expenditure	1,271,359	14.7
Direct expenditure	6,511,612	75.3
General expenditure, by function:		
Education	2,745,343	31.7
Public welfare	1,971,064	22.8
Hospitals	47,575	0.6
Health	449,699	5.2
Highways	595,377	6.9
Police protection	126,436	1.5
Correction	282,015	3.3
Natural resources	73,337	0.8
Parks and recreation	44,014	0.5
Governmental administration	483,713	5.6
Interest on general debt	353,163	4.1
Other and unallocable	611,235	7.1
Utility expenditure	134,633	1.6
Liquor stores expenditure	0	-
Insurance trust expenditure	730,646	8.4
Debt at End of Fiscal Year	5,754,587	X
Cash and Security Holdings	13,395,948	X

X = Not applicable.
- = Zero or rounds to zero.
[1]Within insurance trust revenue, net earnings of state retirement systems is a calculated statistic (the item code in the data file is X08), and thus can be positive or negative. Net earnings is the sum of earnings on investments plus gains on investments minus losses on investments. The change made in 2002 for asset valuation from book to market value in accordance with Statement 34 of the Governmental Accounting Standards Board is reflected in the calculated statistics.

Table DE-16. State Government Tax Collections, 2014

(Dollars in thousands, percent.)

Item	Dollars	Percent distribution
Total Taxes	3,176,169	100.0
Property taxes	X	X
Sales and gross receipts	480,352	15.1
General sales and gross receipts	X	X
Selective sales and gross receipts	480,352	15.1
Alcoholic beverages	19,616	0.6
Amusements	0	-
Insurance premiums	85,735	2.7
Motor fuels	113,326	3.6
Pari-mutuels	82	-
Public utilities	59,128	1.9
Tobacco products	114,659	3.6
Other selective sales	87,806	2.8
Licenses	1,301,737	41.0
Alcoholic beverages	1,547	-
Amusements	328	-
Corporations in general	1,002,576	31.6
Hunting and fishing	2,916	0.1
Motor vehicle	51,790	1.6
Motor vehicle operators	5,712	0.2
Public utilities	0	-
Occupation and business, NEC	231,407	7.3
Other licenses	5,461	0.2
Income taxes	1,319,213	41.5
Individual income	1,040,341	32.8
Corporation net income	278,872	8.8
Other taxes	74,867	2.4
Death and gift	1,434	-
Documentary and stock transfer	72,347	2.3
Severance	X	X
Taxes, NEC	1,086	-

X = Not applicable.
- = Zero or rounds to zero.

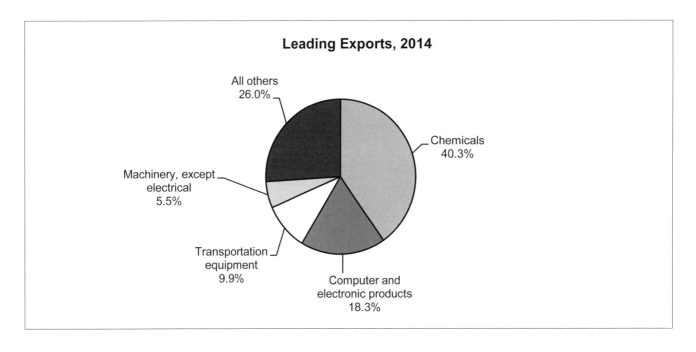

Leading Exports, 2014

All others 26.0%
Chemicals 40.3%
Machinery, except electrical 5.5%
Transportation equipment 9.9%
Computer and electronic products 18.3%

DISTRICT OF COLUMBIA

Facts and Figures

Location: South Atlantic United States; bordered on the SE, NE, and NW by Maryland and on the SW by Virginia

Area: 68 sq. mi.

Population: 658,893 (2014 est.); rank—49th

Official Motto: Justitia omnibus ("Justice for All")

U.S. Congress: 1 delegate

Abbreviation: D.C.

Symbols: flower—American beauty rose; tree—scarlet oak; bird—wood thrush

At a Glance

- From 2010 to 2014, the population of the District of Columbia increased by 9.5 percent, the second highest increase in the country.

- The violent crime rate in the District of Columbia was 1,300.3 per 100,000 population in 2013, compared to 367.9 for the U.S. as a whole.

- In 2013, The District of Columbia's property crime rate was 4,808.3 per 100,000 population, compared to 2,730.7 for the U.S. as a whole.

- Compared to the 50 states, the District of Columbia had the lowest percentage of people under 18 years of age (17.5 percent), and the second lowest percentage of people over age 65 (11.3 percent).

- In 2013, 18.9 percent of all District of Columbia residents lived in poverty, while 27.2 percent of children under 18 years of age lived in poverty.

Table DC-1. Population by Age, Sex, Race, and Hispanic Origin

(Number, percent, except where noted.)

Sex, age, race, and Hispanic origin	2000	2010	2014[1]	Average annual percent change, 2010–2014
Total Population	572,059	601,723	658,893	2.3
Percent of total U.S. population	0.2	0.2	0.2	X
Sex				
Male	269,366	284,222	312,600	2.4
Female	302,693	317,501	346,293	2.2
Age				
Under 5 years	32,536	32,613	42,894	7.1
5 to 19 years	103,270	91,107	94,443	0.9
20 to 64 years	366,355	409,194	446,802	2.2
65 years and over	69,898	68,809	74,754	2.1
Median age (years)	34.8	33.8	33.8	-
Race and Hispanic Origin				
One race				
White	176,101	251,265	287,441	3.4
Black	343,312	310,379	322,827	1.0
American Indian and Alaska Native	1,713	3,264	3,697	3.2
Asian	15,189	21,705	26,480	5.1
Native Hawaiian or Other Pacific Islander	348	770	989	6.5
Two or more races	13,446	14,340	17,459	5.0
Hispanic (of any race)	44,953	57,833	68,355	4.3

X = Not applicable.
- = Zero or rounds to zero.
[1]Population figures for 2014 are July 1 estimates. The 2010 estimates are taken from the 2010 Census.

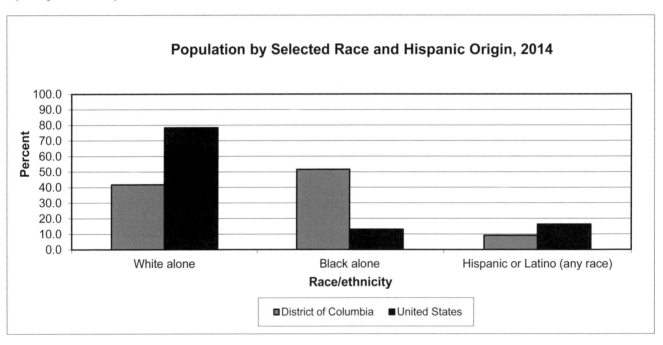

Table DC-2. Marital Status

(Number, percent distribution.)

Sex, age, race, and Hispanic origin	2000	2010	2013
Males, 15 Years and Over	219,706	243,152	257,524
Never married	51.2	58.9	56.4
Now married, except separated	32.8	28.2	30.2
Separated	3.9	2.4	2.5
Widowed	3.4	2.1	2.1
Divorced	8.7	8.4	8.8
Females, 15 Years and Over	254,711	277,203	292,586
Never married	46.0	55.8	55.6
Now married, except separated	27.5	22.8	24.7
Separated	4.4	3.1	2.4
Widowed	11.6	7.5	6.3
Divorced	10.6	10.8	11.0

Table DC-3. Households and Housing Characteristics

(Number, percent, dollars.)

Item	2000	2010	2013	Average annual percent change, 2000–2013
Total Households................................	248,338	252,388	271,651	0.7
Family households...............................	114,166	101,519	120,467	0.4
Married-couple family.......................	56,631	57,275	65,805	1.2
Other family.................................	57,535	44,244	54,662	-0.4
Male householder, no wife present............	10,503	8,740	11,769	0.9
Female householder, no husband present........	47,032	35,504	42,893	-0.7
Nonfamily households	134,172	150,869	151,184	0.9
Householder living alone....................	108,744	121,036	114,749	0.4
Householder not living alone................	25,428	29,833	36,435	2.8
Housing Characteristics				
Total housing units...........................	274,845	296,836	302,975	0.8
Occupied housing units	248,338	252,388	271,651	0.7
Owner occupied.............................	101,214	107,193	110,513	0.7
Renter occupied............................	147,124	145,195	161,138	0.7
Average household size........................	2.16	2.24	2.23	0.2
Financial Characteristics				
Median gross rent of renter-occupied housing	618	1,198	1,307	5.9
Median monthly owner costs for housing units with a mortgage	1,291	2,297	2,236	4.3
Median value of owner-occupied housing units...........	157,200	426,900	470,500	8.8

Table DC-4. Migration, Origin, and Language

(Number, percent.)

Characteristic	State 2012	State 2013	State Percent change	U.S. 2012	U.S. 2013	U.S. Percent change
Residence 1 Year Ago						
Population 1 year and over	624,847	636,535	1.9	310,212,755	312,432,820	0.7
Same house	80.1	80.1	X	85.0	85.0	X
Different house in the U.S.	18.5	18.1	X	14.4	14.4	X
Same county	9.9	10.8	X	9.0	8.9	X
Different county	8.6	7.3	X	5.4	5.5	X
Same state	0.0	0.0	X	3.2	3.2	X
Different state	8.6	7.3	X	2.3	2.3	X
Abroad..................................	1.4	1.7	X	0.6	0.6	X
Place of Birth						
Native born	542,000	553,630	2.1	273,089,382	274,780,773	0.6
Male....................................	47.0	47.1	X	49.3	49.3	X
Female..................................	53.0	52.9	X	50.7	50.7	X
Foreign born	90,323	92,819	2.8	40,824,658	41,348,066	1.3
Male....................................	49.2	48.9	X	48.7	48.8	X
Female..................................	50.8	51.1	X	51.3	51.2	X
Foreign born; naturalized U.S. citizen.......	36,348	38,038	4.6	18,686,237	19,294,710	3.3
Male....................................	47.9	48.0	X	45.8	45.9	X
Female..................................	52.1	52.0	X	54.2	54.1	X
Foreign born; not a U.S. citizen.............	53,975	54,781	1.5	22,138,421	22,053,356	-0.4
Male....................................	50.0	49.5	X	51.1	51.3	X
Female..................................	50.0	50.5	X	48.9	48.7	X
Entered 2010 or later	14.3	17.3	X	7.0	9.7	X
Entered 2000 to 2009	34.0	35.8	X	30.4	29.4	X
Entered before 2000.......................	51.8	46.9	X	62.7	61.0	X
World Region of Birth, Foreign						
Foreign-born population, excluding population born at sea	90,323	92,819	2.8	40,824,553	41,347,945	1.3
Europe	14.8	19.1	X	11.8	11.6	X
Asia	20.1	17.5	X	29.2	29.5	X
Africa	17.2	17.1	X	4.2	4.4	X
Oceania	1.2	1.0	X	0.6	0.5	X
Latin America	44.7	43.1	X	52.2	51.9	X
North America..........................	2.0	2.1	X	2.0	2.0	X
Language Spoken at Home and Ability to Speak English						
Population 5 years and over	593,321	605,388	2.0	294,003,714	296,358,760	0.8
English only	83.4	82.1	X	79.0	79.2	X
Language other than English................	16.6	17.9	X	21.0	20.8	X
Speaks English less than "very well".........	5.7	5.5	X	8.5	8.5	X

NA = Not available.
X = Not applicable.
- = Zero or rounds to zero.

Table DC-5. Median Income and Poverty Status, 2013

(Number, percent, except as noted.)

Characteristic	State		U.S.	
	Number	Percent	Number	Percent
Median Income				
Households (dollars)...	67,572	X	52,250	X
Families (dollars)	72,337	X	64,030	X
Below Poverty Level (All People)	115,551	18.9	48,810,868	15.8
Sex				
Male...	50,153	17.4	21,938,525	14.5
Female	65,398	20.2	26,872,343	17.1
Age				
Under 18 years..	29,705	27.2	16,086,960	22.2
Related children under 18 years..	29,020	26.7	15,769,921	21.9
18 to 64 years	73,367	17.0	28,578,191	14.8
65 years and over	12,479	17.5	4,145,717	9.6

X = Not applicable.

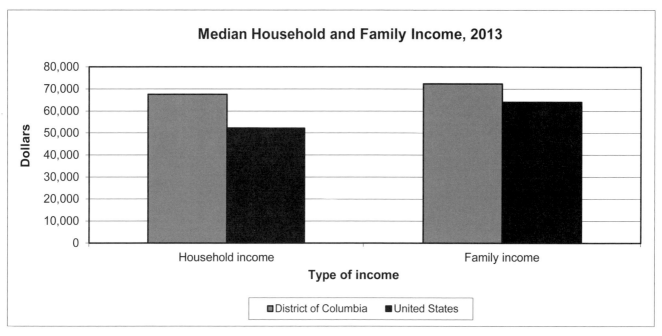

Median Household and Family Income, 2013

District of Columbia ■ United States

Table DC-6. Health Insurance Coverage Status for the Civilian Noninstitutionalized Population and Children Under 18 Years of Age

(Numbers in thousands, percent.)

Item	2005	2006	2007	2008	2009	2010	2011	2012	2013
Civilian Noninstitutionalized Population	540	569	582	580	589	594	608	621	636
Covered by Private or Public Insurance									
Number...	468	503	526	534	548	549	566	585	594
Percent..	86.8	88.5	90.5	92.1	93.0	92.4	93.1	94.1	93.3
Not Covered									
Number...	71	66	55	46	41	45	42	36	42
Percent..	13.2	11.6	9.5	7.9	7.0	7.6	6.9	5.9	6.7
Percent in the U.S. not covered....................................	15.3	15.8	15.3	15.1	15.1	15.5	15.1	14.8	14.5
Children Under 18 Years of Age...	112	115	112	111	114	101	105	109	111
Covered by Private or Public Insurance									
Number...	105	105	105	106	111	99	101	107	109
Percent..	93.7	91.3	93.8	95.5	97.2	97.7	96.1	98.3	97.6
Not Covered									
Number...	7	10	7	5	3	2	4	2	3
Percent..	6.3	8.7	6.2	4.5	2.8	2.3	3.9	1.7	2.4
Percent in the U.S. not covered....................................	10.9	11.7	11.0	9.7	8.6	8.0	7.5	7.2	7.1

Table DC-7. Employment Status by Demographic Group, 2014

(Numbers in thousands, percent.)

Characteristic	Civilian noninstitutional population	Civilian labor force		Employed		Unemployed	
		Number	Percent of population	Number	Percent of population	Number	Percent of population
Total...	543	378	69.5	348	64.0	30	7.8
Sex							
Male...	252	187	74.1	173	68.7	14	7.3
Female..	292	191	65.5	175	60.1	16	8.4
Race, Sex, and Hispanic Origin							
White..	251	206	82.0	200	79.6	6	2.9
Male...	127	108	85.6	105	82.7	4	3.4
Female..	124	98	78.4	95	76.5	2	2.4
Black or African American................................	256	144	56.4	122	47.8	22	15.4
Male...	112	67	59.9	57	51.5	9	14.1
Female..	144	78	53.7	65	44.9	13	16.4
Hispanic or Latino ethnicity[1]...........................	47	38	79.7	36	76.6	1	3.9
Male...	23	20	86.5	19	82.5	1	4.6
Female..	24	18	73.3	17	71.0	1	3.1
Age							
16 to 19 years...	22	3	15.4	3	12.3	1	20.2
20 to 24 years...	58	40	68.8	34	58.7	6	14.7
25 to 34 years...	157	135	86.1	127	80.7	8	6.3
35 to 44 years...	90	77	85.8	72	79.6	6	7.2
45 to 54 years...	75	61	80.5	56	75.0	4	6.8
55 to 64 years...	66	42	64.1	38	58.1	4	9.4
65 years and over	75	19	25.3	18	24.0	1	5.2

NOTE: Data in Table 7 are from the Current Population Survey (CPS) and do not match the estimates in Table 8. See notes and definitions for further information.
[1]May be of any race.

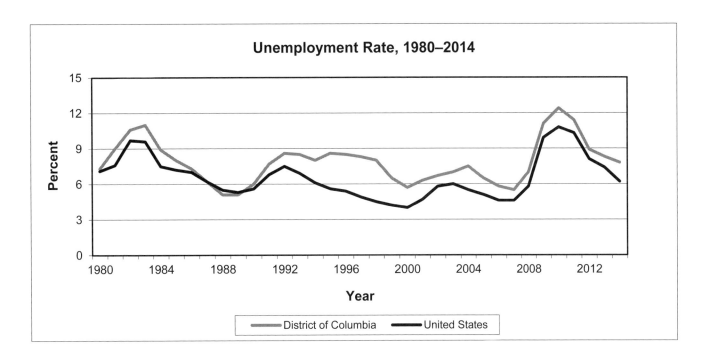

Table DC-8. Employment Status of the Civilian Noninstitutional Population Age 16 Years and Over

(Number, percent.)

Year	Civilian labor force	Civilian participation rate	Employed	Unemployed	Unemployment rate
2006............	316,083	67.2	297,786	18,297	5.8
2007............	322,237	68.1	304,426	17,811	5.5
2008............	330,544	69.2	309,192	21,352	6.5
2009............	335,672	69.1	304,500	31,172	9.3
2010............	346,065	68.8	313,508	32,557	9.4
2011............	350,842	67.9	315,159	35,683	10.2
2012............	365,025	69.2	332,013	33,012	9.0
2013............	373,495	69.6	341,753	31,742	8.5
2014............	377,448	69.4	348,049	29,399	7.8

Table DC-9. Employment and Average Wages by Industry

(Estimates from 2007 through 2010 are based on the 2007 *North American Industry Classification System* [NAICS]. Estimates from 2011 onward are based on the 2012 NAICS.)

Industry	2007	2008	2009	2010	2011	2012	2013
	Number of jobs						
Wage and Salary Employment by Industry........	729,092	733,517	733,350	744,878	757,818	748,009	757,897
Farm Wage and Salary Employment..............	0	0	0	0	0	0	0
Nonfarm Wage and Salary Employment............	729,092	733,517	733,350	744,878	757,818	748,009	757,897
Private wage and salary employment..............	478,923	481,877	474,925	476,224	489,895	493,348	506,757
Forestry, fishing, and related activities..........	0	0	0	0	0	0	0
Mining..................................	0	0	0	0	0	0	0
Utilities..................................	2,398	2,346	2,459	1,833	1,830	1,850	1,891
Construction..............................	13,306	13,598	12,281	11,251	12,828	14,121	14,535
Manufacturing............................	1,708	1,623	1,431	1,280	1,043	971	1,007
Durable goods manufacturing..............	566	579	528	476	424	423	441
Nondurable goods manufacturing..........	1,142	1,044	903	804	619	548	566
Wholesale trade..........................	5,012	4,852	4,673	4,819	4,651	4,980	4,899
Retail trade..............................	18,693	18,906	18,309	18,993	18,983	19,157	20,079
Transportation and warehousing..............	4,202	4,132	4,102	4,165	4,080	4,102	4,045
Information..............................	22,413	20,900	19,379	18,759	18,690	17,588	17,092
Finance and insurance....................	16,689	15,746	14,746	15,029	14,956	14,998	14,824
Real estate and rental and leasing............	10,562	10,481	10,563	10,456	10,641	10,940	11,057
Professional, scientific, and technical services..	103,754	105,097	102,924	102,220	104,222	107,473	108,794
Management of companies and enterprises......	1,366	1,422	1,294	2,020	2,018	2,011	2,045
Administrative and waste services............	45,373	44,695	42,286	42,712	45,578	45,879	46,454
Educational services......................	49,313	48,206	49,770	49,090	50,908	49,853	55,298
Health care and social assistance............	55,840	56,702	58,017	59,950	61,752	62,890	64,570
Arts, entertainment, and recreation..........	6,343	7,296	7,338	7,207	7,164	7,129	7,050
Accommodation and food services............	50,033	51,596	51,897	53,781	56,053	58,700	61,313
Other services, except public administration......	71,918	74,279	73,456	72,659	74,498	70,706	71,804
Government and government enterprises........	250,169	251,640	258,425	268,654	267,923	254,661	251,140
	Dollars						
Average Wages and Salaries by Industry........	72,022	74,759	75,910	78,560	79,851	81,663	81,902
Average Farm Wages and Salaries..............	0	0	0	0	0	0	0
Average Nonfarm Wages and Salaries............	72,022	74,759	75,910	78,560	79,851	81,663	81,902
Average private wages and salaries............	67,954	70,075	69,872	72,019	73,536	75,551	76,028
Forestry, fishing, and related activities..........	0	0	0	0	0	0	0
Mining..................................	0	0	0	0	0	0	0
Utilities..................................	124,907	134,725	130,292	125,669	138,570	126,814	98,345
Construction..............................	54,148	55,750	56,397	61,048	63,382	63,503	63,068
Manufacturing............................	76,138	77,417	80,783	84,192	104,606	106,494	109,981
Durable goods manufacturing..............	80,072	79,097	78,275	78,029	83,026	83,135	83,803
Nondurable goods manufacturing..........	74,187	76,486	82,250	87,841	119,388	124,526	130,378
Wholesale trade..........................	89,460	95,595	97,341	100,782	107,748	113,590	116,136
Retail trade..............................	29,318	29,003	29,420	30,688	31,739	33,848	33,396
Transportation and warehousing..............	58,770	67,129	65,654	66,085	69,395	71,749	75,390
Information..............................	97,249	103,994	102,813	103,198	106,842	112,165	122,414
Finance and insurance....................	138,096	133,784	120,567	128,361	137,434	143,100	148,721
Real estate and rental and leasing............	71,384	69,104	64,471	70,628	74,778	75,884	79,454
Professional, scientific, and technical services..	108,801	113,138	113,173	117,448	120,221	122,662	122,534
Management of companies and enterprises......	277,063	237,873	273,999	218,147	201,919	235,191	218,814
Administrative and waste services............	40,409	42,388	42,808	43,764	45,846	47,076	48,278
Educational services......................	39,687	43,550	44,413	45,190	45,369	47,327	46,513
Health care and social assistance............	52,686	54,254	55,691	56,786	57,529	58,054	58,121
Arts, entertainment, and recreation..........	55,746	60,157	61,914	63,999	55,361	50,225	54,597
Accommodation and food services............	32,025	30,918	30,575	31,751	32,479	32,417	32,934
Other services, except public administration......	64,572	67,754	69,914	72,831	75,100	78,616	81,388
Government and government enterprises........	79,811	83,727	87,005	90,156	91,399	93,505	93,756

D = Not shown to avoid disclosure of confidential information, but the estimates for this item are included in the total.

Table DC-10. Employment Characteristics by Family Type

(Number, percent.)

Family type and labor force status	2011		2012		2013	
	Total	Families with own children under 18 years	Total	Families with own children under 18 years	Total	Families with own children under 18 years
All Families..	114,045	46,540	112,493	46,568	120,467	51,277
FAMILY TYPE AND LABOR FORCE STATUS						
Married-Couple Families...............................	57,247	19,337	62,149	23,187	65,805	25,218
Both husband and wife in labor force.....................	64.2	77.3	62.2	76.1	58.9	71.3
Husband in labor force, wife not in labor force	15.2	17.0	16.9	19.6	18.5	22.3
Wife in labor force, husband not in labor force	7.7	4.0	8.3	3.2	6.9	3.5
Both husband and wife not in labor force................	12.9	1.7	12.6	1.2	13.2	1.3
Other Families	56,798	27,203	50,344	23,381	54,662	26,059
Female householder, no husband present................	80.4	82.4	81.4	85.8	78.5	79.1
In labor force	52.2	64.9	54.8	68.5	52.3	61.6
Not in labor force	28.2	17.5	26.5	17.3	26.1	17.5
Male householder, no wife present......................	19.6	17.6	18.6	14.2	21.5	20.9
In labor force	15.0	15.6	13.9	11.4	16.0	17.0
Not in labor force	4.6	2.0	4.7	2.9	5.5	4.0

Table DC-11. School Enrollment and Educational Attainment, 2013

(Number, percent.)

Item	State	U.S.
Enrollment		
Total population 3 years and over, enrolled in school	162,510	82,395,254
Enrolled in nursery school or preschool (percent)............................	8.2	6.0
Enrolled in kindergarten (percent)............................	5.0	5.2
Enrolled in elementary school, grades 1-8 (percent)............................	25.7	40.0
Enrolled in high school, grades 9-12 (percent)	13.8	20.6
Enrolled in college or graduate school (percent)............................	47.3	28.3
Attainment		
Total population 25 years and over	453,014	210,910,615
Less than ninth grade (percent)	3.8	5.8
9th to 12th grade, no diploma (percent)	6.1	7.6
High school graduate, including equivalency (percent)............................	18.6	27.8
Some college, no degree (percent)	13.4	21.1
Associate's degree (percent)	3.1	8.1
Bachelor's degree (percent)	22.7	18.4
Graduate or professional degree (percent)............................	32.4	11.2
High school graduate or higher (percent)	90.1	86.6
Bachelor's degree or higher (percent)............................	55.1	29.6

Table DC-12. Public School Characteristics and Educational Indicators

(Number, percent; data derived from National Center of Education Statistics.)

Item	District	U.S.
Public Schools, 2012–2013 (except where noted)		
Number of school districts............................	60	18,093
Number of schools............................	230	98,454
Number of students (in thousands)	76	49,771
Number of teachers (in thousands)	6	3,109
Student-teacher ratio	12.9	16.0
Expenditures per student (dollars), FY 2012............................	19,847	10,667
Four-year adjusted cohort graduation rate (ACGR)[1,2]	62.3	81.4
Students eligible for free or reduced-price lunch (in thousands)	46	25,188
English language learners (in thousands)	5	4,397
Students age 3 to 21 served under IDEA, part B (in thousands)	13	6,429

Public Schools by Type	Number	Percent of D.C. public schools
Total number of schools............................	230	100.0
Regular	208	90.4
Special education............................	7	3.0
Vocational education............................	3	1.3
Alternative education............................	12.0	5.2

NOTE: Every school is assigned only one school type based on its instructional emphasis.
[1]ACGR data represents a new method of calculating high-school completion rates and may not be comparable to previous years' data for Averaged Freshmen Graduation Rates (AFGR).
[2]The United States 4-year ACGRs were estimated using both the reported 4-year ACGR data from 49 states and the District of Columbia and using imputed data for Idaho. The estimate for American Indian/Alaska Native students also includes imputed data for Virginia.

Table DC-13. Reported Voting and Registration of the Voting-Age Population, November 2012

(Numbers in thousands, percent.)

Item	Total population	Total citizen population	Registered			Voted		
			Total registered	Percent registered (total population)	Percent registered (total citizen population)	Total voted	Percent voted (total population)	Percent voted (total citizen population)
U.S. Total	235,248	215,081	153,157	65.1	71.2	132,948	56.5	61.8
State Total	517	461	385	74.4	83.4	350	67.7	75.9
Sex								
Male	240	212	173	71.8	81.4	154	64.2	72.7
Female	277	249	212	76.6	85.0	196	70.8	78.6
Race								
White alone....................................	246	212	180	73.2	85.1	161	65.3	75.9
White, non-Hispanic alone	208	197	171	82.0	86.4	151	72.8	76.7
Black alone....................................	244	231	191	78.0	82.6	177	72.6	76.8
Asian alone....................................	20	13	10	B	B	9	B	B
Hispanic (of any race)	48	19	14	B	B	13	B	B
White alone or in combination	248	214	182	73.1	84.8	162	65.3	75.7
Black alone or in combination..........	248	233	193	77.7	82.7	179	72.2	76.9
Asian alone or in combination..........	21	15	10	B	B	9	B	B
Age								
18 to 24 years	71	61	43	B	B	38	B	B
25 to 44 years	233	200	173	74.2	86.3	156	67.2	78.1
45 to 64 years	140	129	109	77.7	84.4	99	70.9	77.0
65 to 74 years	40	38	34	B	B	33	B	B
75 years and over	34	33	26	B	B	24	B	B

B = Base is less than 75,000 and therefore too small to show the derived measure.

Table DC-14. Crime

(Number, rate per 100,000. Data are derived from the FBI Uniform Crime Reports.)

Item	State			U.S.[1,2,3,4]		
	2012	2013	Percent change	2012	2013	Percent change
TOTAL POPULATION[5]...	633,427	646,449	2.1	313,873,685	316,128,839	0.7
VIOLENT CRIME						
Number...................................	7,866	8,287	5.4	1,217,067	1,163,146	-4.4
Rate	1,241.8	1,281.9	3.2	387.8	367.9	-5.1
Murder and Nonnegligent Manslaughter						
Number...................................	88	103	17.0	14,866	14,196	-4.5
Rate	13.9	15.9	14.7	4.7	4.5	-5.2
Rape[6]						
Number...................................	X	395	X	X	108,612	X
Rate	X	61.1	X	X	34.4	X
Robbery						
Number...................................	4,037	4,078	1.0	355,051	345,031	-2.8
Rate	637.3	630.8		113.1	109.1	-3.5
Aggravated Assault						
Number...................................	3,505	3,830	9.3	762,009	724,149	-5.0
Rate	553.3	592.5	7.1	242.8	229.1	-5.6
PROPERTY CRIME						
Number...................................	30,757	31,083	1.1	9,001,992	8,632,512	-4.1
Rate	4,855.7	4,808.3		2,868.0	2,730.7	-4.8
Burglary						
Number...................................	3,519	3,316	-5.8	2,109,932	1,928,465	-8.6
Rate	555.5	513.0	-7.7	672.2	610.0	-9.3
Larceny-Theft						
Number...................................	23,575	24,533	4.1	6,168,874	6,004,453	-2.7
Rate	3,721.8	3,795.0	2.0	1,965.4	1,899.4	-3.4
Motor Vehicle Theft						
Number...................................	3,663	3,234	-11.7	723,186	699,594	-3.3
Rate	578.3	500.3	-13.5	230.4	221.3	-4.0

NOTE: Although arson data are included in the trend and clearance tables, sufficient data are not available to estimate totals for this offense. Therefore, no arson data are published in this table.

X = Not applicable.

- = Zero or rounds to zero.

[1]Includes offenses reported by the Zoological Police and the Metro Transit Police.

[2]The crime figures have been adjusted.

[3]The data collection methodology for the offense of forcible rape used by the Minnesota state Uniform Crime Reporting (UCR) Program (with the exception of Minneapolis and St. Paul, Minnesota) does not comply with national UCR Program guidelines. Consequently, its figures for forcible rape and violent crime (of which forcible rape is a part) are not published in this table.

[4]Because of changes in the state's reporting practices, figures are not comparable to previous years' data.

[5]Populations are U.S. Census Bureau provisional estimates as of July 1 of each year.

[6]The figures shown for the offense of rape were estimated using the revised Uniform Crime Reporting (UCR) definition of rape.

Table DC-15. Local Government Finances, 2012

(Dollar amounts in thousands, percent distribution.)

Item	Dollars	Percent distribution
Total Revenue	13,099,437	100.0
General revenue	11,142,142	85.1
Intergovernmental revenue	3,474,236	26.5
Taxes	5,933,779	45.3
General sales	1,111,044	8.5
Selective sales	427,989	3.3
License taxes	32,221	0.2
Individual income tax	1,490,694	11.4
Corporate income tax	465,896	3.6
Other taxes	528,187	4.0
Current charges	652,294	5.0
Miscellaneous general revenue	1,081,833	8.3
Utility revenue	1,041,455	8.0
Liquor stores revenue	0	-
Insurance trust revenue[1]	915,840	7.0
Total Expenditure	13,815,041	100.0
Intergovernmental expenditure	0	-
Direct expenditure	13,815,041	100.0
Current operation	10,313,468	74.7
Capital outlay	2,319,515	16.8
Insurance benefits and repayments	507,205	3.7
Assistance and subsidies	157,338	1.1
Interest on debt	517,515	3.7
Exhibit: Salaries and wages	3,443,560	24.9
Direct Expenditure	13,815,041	100.0
Direct expenditure by function:		
Direct general expenditure	10,765,049	77.9
Education services	4,808,807	34.8
Public welfare	2,864,003	20.7
Hospitals	230,300	1.7
Health	444,072	3.2
Highways	525,612	3.8
Police protection	563,763	4.1
Correction	240,658	1.7
Natural resources	44,753	0.3
Parks and recreation	203,455	1.5
Governmental administration	440,064	3.2
Interest on general debt	500,240	3.6
Other and unallocable	756,986	5.5
Utility expenditure	2,542,787	18.4
Liquor stores expenditure	0	-
Insurance trust expenditure	507,205	3.7
Debt at End of Fiscal Year	11,603,815	X
Cash and Security Holdings	11,925,672	X

NOTE: At the time of publication, the Census Bureau had not yet released 2013 finance data for the District of Columbia.

X = Not applicable.

- = Zero or rounds to zero.

[1]Within insurance trust revenue, net earnings of state retirement systems is a calculated statistic (the item code in the data file is X08), and thus can be positive or negative. Net earnings is the sum of earnings on investments plus gains on investments minus losses on investments. The change made in 2002 for asset valuation from book to market value in accordance with Statement 34 of the Governmental Accounting Standards Board is reflected in the calculated statistics.

NOTE: Since the Census Bureau does not provide detailed data for the District of Columbia there is no Table 16 for D. C.

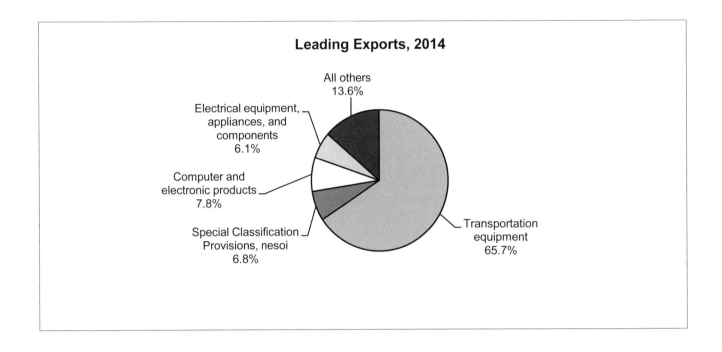

Leading Exports, 2014

All others
13.6%

Electrical equipment, appliances, and components
6.1%

Computer and electronic products
7.8%

Special Classification Provisions, nesoi
6.8%

Transportation equipment
65.7%

FLORIDA

Facts and Figures

Location: Southeastern United States; bordered on the N by Georgia and Alabama, on the E by the Atlantic Ocean, on the S by the Straits of Florida, and on the W by Alabama and the Gulf of Mexico

Area: 65,757 sq. mi. (170,304 sq. km.); rank—22nd

Population: 19,893,297 (2014 est.); rank—3rd

Principal Cities: capital—Tallahassee; largest—Jacksonville

Statehood: March 3, 1845; 27th state

U.S. Congress: 2 senators, 27 representatives

State Motto: In God We Trust

State Song: "The Swanee River (Old Folks at Home)"

State Nickname: The Sunshine State

Abbreviations: FL; Fla.

State Symbols: flower—orange blossom; tree—Sabal palm (cabbage palm); bird—mockingbird

At a Glance

- With an increase in population of 5.8 percent, Florida ranked 6th among the states in growth from 2010 to 2014.

- Florida's violent crime rate in 2013 was 470.4 incidents per 100,000 population, compared to 367.9 for the entire nation.

- In 2014, Florida was the state with the largest percentage of its population in the 65 and older age group (19.1 percent).

- The homeownership rate in Florida in 2013 was 66.1 percent, 34th in the nation.

- Florida had 1.25 traffic fatalities per million miles driven in 2013, compared to 1.09 for the U.S. as a whole.

Table FL-1. Population by Age, Sex, Race, and Hispanic Origin

(Number, percent, except where noted.)

Sex, age, race, and Hispanic origin	2000	2010	2014[1]	Average annual percent change, 2010–2014
Total Population	15,982,378	18,801,310	19,893,297	1.4
Percent of total U.S. population	5.7	6.1	6.2	X
Sex				
Male..	7,797,715	9,189,355	9,723,286	1.4
Female	8,184,663	9,611,955	10,170,011	1.4
Age				
Under 5 years..	945,823	1,073,506	1,084,349	0.3
5 to 19 years...	3,102,809	3,439,484	3,435,716	-0.0
20 to 64 years..	9,126,149	11,034,718	11,581,688	1.2
65 years and over......................................	2,807,597	3,259,602	3,791,544	3.9
Median age (years)	38.7	40.7	41.8	0.7
Race and Hispanic Origin				
One race				
White	12,465,029	14,808,867	15,485,874	1.1
Black	2,335,505	3,078,067	3,337,159	2.0
American Indian and Alaska Native	53,541	89,119	99,203	2.7
Asian..	266,256	474,199	553,820	4.0
Native Hawaiian or Other Pacific Islander	8,625	18,790	21,978	4.0
Two or more races...	376,315	332,268	395,263	4.4
Hispanic (of any race)....................................	2,682,715	4,301,853	4,788,869	2.7

X = Not applicable.
[1]Population figures for 2014 are July 1 estimates. The 2010 estimates are taken from the 2010 Census.

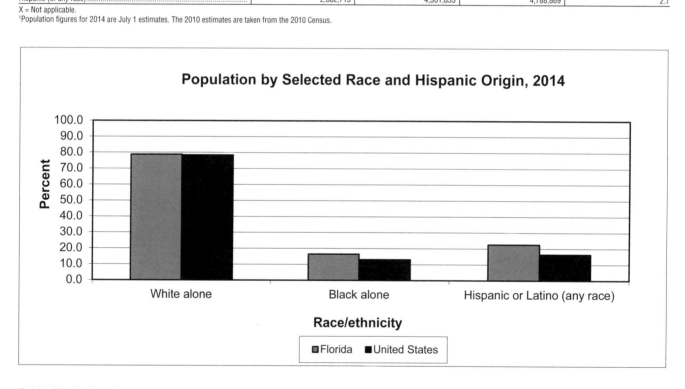

Table FL-2. Marital Status

(Number, percent distribution.)

Sex, age, race, and Hispanic origin	2000	2010	2013
Males, 15 Years and Over...	6,232,987	7,534,535	7,863,088
Never married	27.3	33.9	35.1
Now married, except separated..	56.9	49.3	48.1
Separated...	2.1	2.2	2.0
Widowed...	3.2	3.2	3.2
Divorced...	10.5	11.5	11.5
Females, 15 Years and Over..	6,714,003	8,021,290	8,363,408
Never married	20.5	26.6	27.9
Now married, except separated..	51.9	45.1	43.9
Separated...	2.7	3.0	2.9
Widowed...	12.3	10.8	10.7
Divorced...	12.7	14.5	14.6

Table FL-3. Households and Housing Characteristics

(Number, percent, dollars.)

Item	2000	2010	2013	Average annual percent change, 2000–2013
Total Households.............	6,337,929	7,035,068	7,211,584	1.0
Family households	4,210,760	4,556,930	4,626,388	0.7
Married-couple family	3,192,266	3,307,884	3,334,383	0.3
Other family	1,018,494	1,249,046	1,292,005	1.8
Male householder, no wife present........	259,924	313,305	335,618	2.0
Female householder, no husband present...........	759,000	935,741	956,387	1.8
Nonfamily households	2,127,169	2,478,138	2,585,196	1.5
Householder living alone............	1,687,303	2,013,028	2,114,690	1.8
Householder not living alone............	439,886	465,110	470,506	0.5
Housing Characteristics				
Total housing units.................	7,302,947	8,994,091	9,047,973	1.7
Occupied housing units	6,337,929	7,035,068	7,211,584	1.0
Owner occupied	4,441,799	4,794,130	4,672,482	0.4
Renter occupied	1,896,130	2,240,938	2,539,102	2.3
Average household size..............	2.46	2.62	2.65	0.6
Financial Characteristics				
Median gross rent of renter-occupied housing	641	947	972	3.3
Median monthly owner costs for housing units with a mortgage	1,004	1,505	1,368	2.4
Median value of owner-occupied housing units............	105,500	164,200	153,300	2.9

Table FL-4. Migration, Origin, and Language

(Number, percent.)

Characteristic	State			U.S.		
	2012	2013	Percent change	2012	2013	Percent change
Residence 1 Year Ago						
Population 1 year and over	19,114,620	19,345,059	1.2	310,212,755	312,432,820	0.7
Same house	83.9	83.7	X	85.0	85.0	X
Different house in the U.S.	15.3	15.4	X	14.4	14.4	X
Same county	9.5	9.5	X	9.0	8.9	X
Different county	5.8	5.8	X	5.4	5.5	X
Same state	3.0	3.1	X	3.2	3.2	X
Different state	2.8	2.7	X	2.3	2.3	X
Abroad	0.9	0.9	X	0.6	0.6	X
Place of Birth						
Native born	15,570,432	15,754,798	1.2	273,089,382	274,780,773	0.6
Male	49.3	49.4	X	49.3	49.3	X
Female	50.7	50.6	X	50.7	50.7	X
Foreign born	3,747,136	3,798,062	1.4	40,824,658	41,348,066	1.3
Male	47.1	47.1	X	48.7	48.8	X
Female	52.9	52.9	X	51.3	51.2	X
Foreign born; naturalized U.S. citizen............	1,933,280	2,028,738	4.9	18,686,237	19,294,710	3.3
Male	43.9	44.5	X	45.8	45.9	X
Female	56.1	55.5	X	54.2	54.1	X
Foreign born; not a U.S. citizen............	1,813,856	1,769,324	-2.5	22,138,421	22,053,356	-0.4
Male	50.6	50.1	X	51.1	51.3	X
Female	49.4	49.9	X	48.9	48.7	X
Entered 2010 or later	7.0	10.1	X	7.0	9.7	X
Entered 2000 to 2009	30.6	30.0	X	30.4	29.4	X
Entered before 2000.............	62.4	59.8	X	62.7	61.0	X
World Region of Birth, Foreign						
Foreign-born population, excluding population born at sea	3,747,136	3,798,062	1.4	40,824,553	41,347,945	1.3
Europe	10.0	9.8	X	11.8	11.6	X
Asia.............	10.5	10.7	X	29.2	29.5	X
Africa	1.7	1.5	X	4.2	4.4	X
Oceania	0.2	0.2	X	0.6	0.5	X
Latin America.............	74.8	74.8	X	52.2	51.9	X
North America	2.9	3.1	X	2.0	2.0	X
Language Spoken at Home and Ability to Speak English						
Population 5 years and over............	18,247,223	18,478,811	1.3	294,003,714	296,358,760	0.8
English only	72.1	72.6	X	79.0	79.2	X
Language other than English............	27.9	27.4	X	21.0	20.8	X
Speaks English less than "very well"	11.5	11.5	X	8.5	8.5	X

NA = Not available.
X = Not applicable.
- = Zero or rounds to zero.

Table FL-5. Median Income and Poverty Status, 2013

(Number, percent, except as noted.)

Characteristic	State		U.S.	
	Number	Percent	Number	Percent
Median Income				
Households (dollars)...	46,036	X	52,250	X
Families (dollars)	55,774	X	64,030	X
Below Poverty Level (All People)................................	3,253,333	17.0	48,810,868	15.8
Sex				
Male..	1,484,913	16.0	21,938,525	14.5
Female	1,768,420	18.0	26,872,343	17.1
Age				
Under 18 years..	968,765	24.5	16,086,960	22.2
Related children under 18 years.............................	951,379	24.2	15,769,921	21.9
18 to 64 years...	1,902,676	17.0	28,578,191	14.8
65 years and over	381,892	10.7	4,145,717	9.6

X = Not applicable.

Median Household and Family Income, 2013

Table FL-6. Health Insurance Coverage Status for the Civilian Noninstitutionalized Population and Children Under 18 Years of Age

(Numbers in thousands, percent.)

Item	2005	2006	2007	2008	2009	2010	2011	2012	2013
Civilian Noninstitutionalized Population...................	17,886	18,062	18,074	17,996	18,193	18,534	18,752	19,011	19,245
Covered by Private or Public Insurance									
Number..	14,270	14,233	14,426	14,247	14,397	14,593	14,841	15,195	15,392
Percent...	79.8	78.8	79.8	79.2	79.1	78.7	79.1	79.9	80.0
Not Covered									
Number..	3,616	3,828	3,648	3,749	3,795	3,941	3,911	3,816	3,853
Percent...	20.2	21.2	20.2	20.8	20.9	21.3	20.9	20.1	20.0
Percent in the U.S. not covered.............................	15.3	15.8	15.3	15.1	15.1	15.5	15.1	14.8	14.5
Children Under 18 Years of Age............................	4,038	4,076	4,084	3,996	4,051	3,990	3,987	3,991	4,020
Covered by Private or Public Insurance									
Number..	3,307	3,305	3,298	3,295	3,450	3,483	3,512	3,555	3,575
Percent...	81.9	81.1	80.8	82.5	85.2	87.3	88.1	89.1	88.9
Not Covered									
Number..	731	771	785	701	601	507	475	436	445
Percent...	18.1	18.9	19.2	17.5	14.8	12.7	11.9	10.9	11.1
Percent in the U.S. not covered.............................	10.9	11.7	11.0	9.7	8.6	8.0	7.5	7.2	7.1

Table FL-7. Employment Status by Demographic Group, 2014

(Numbers in thousands, percent.)

Characteristic	Civilian noninstitutional population	Civilian labor force		Employed		Unemployed	
		Number	Percent of population	Number	Percent of population	Number	Percent of population
Total..	15,978	9,680	60.6	9,073	56.8	606	6.3
Sex							
Male..	7,658	5,098	66.6	4,780	62.4	317	6.2
Female	8,320	4,582	55.1	4,293	51.6	289	6.3
Race, Sex, and Hispanic Origin							
White	12,853	7,689	59.8	7,275	56.6	414	5.4
Male..	6,250	4,145	66.3	3,925	62.8	220	5.3
Female	6,603	3,544	53.7	3,350	50.7	195	5.5
Black or African American...................................	2,430	1,541	63.4	1,374	56.5	167	10.8
Male..	1,112	726	65.3	642	57.7	84	11.6
Female	1,319	816	61.8	733	55.6	83	10.2
Hispanic or Latino ethnicity[1]	3,548	2,268	63.9	2,118	59.7	150	6.6
Male..	1,720	1,252	72.8	1,178	68.5	74	5.9
Female	1,828	1,016	55.6	940	51.4	77	7.5
Age							
16 to 19 years..	897	257	28.7	210	23.4	47	18.5
20 to 24 years..	1,158	807	69.7	705	60.8	102	12.7
25 to 34 years..	2,419	1,987	82.2	1,852	76.6	135	6.8
35 to 44 years..	2,533	2,076	82.0	1,967	77.6	109	5.3
45 to 54 years..	2,826	2,239	79.2	2,129	75.3	110	4.9
55 to 64 years..	2,684	1,696	63.2	1,619	60.3	77	4.5
65 years and over	3,460	618	17.8	592	17.1	26	4.2

NOTE: Data in Table 7 are from the Current Population Survey (CPS) and do not match the estimates in Table 8. See notes and definitions for further information.
[1]May be of any race.

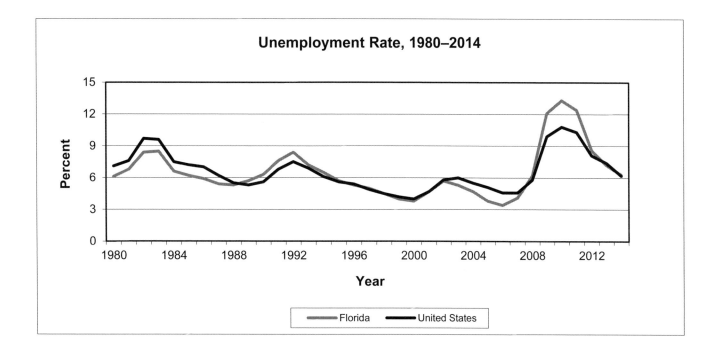

Unemployment Rate, 1980–2014

Table FL-8. Employment Status of the Civilian Noninstitutional Population Age 16 Years and Over

(Number, percent.)

Year	Civilian labor force	Civilian participation rate	Employed	Unemployed	Unemployment rate
2006	9,000,204	63.5	8,709,522	290,682	3.2
2007	9,157,124	63.9	8,789,770	367,354	4.0
2008	9,215,524	63.7	8,637,164	578,360	6.3
2009	9,094,825	62.3	8,148,123	946,702	10.4
2010	9,212,066	61.6	8,193,659	1,018,407	11.1
2011	9,302,491	61.0	8,372,024	930,467	10.0
2012	9,395,048	60.7	8,595,376	799,672	8.5
2013	9,472,960	60.3	8,782,803	690,157	7.3
2014	9,637,536	60.3	9,034,240	603,296	6.3

Table FL-9. Employment and Average Wages by Industry

(Estimates from 2007 through 2010 are based on the 2007 *North American Industry Classification System* [NAICS]. Estimates from 2011 onward are based on the 2012 NAICS.)

Industry	2007	2008	2009	2010	2011	2012	2013
	Number of jobs						
Wage and Salary Employment by Industry	8,401,090	8,125,945	7,630,376	7,563,323	7,649,469	7,779,074	7,948,084
Farm Wage and Salary Employment	46,988	45,006	40,631	43,823	43,610	46,283	44,696
Nonfarm Wage and Salary Employment	8,354,102	8,080,939	7,589,745	7,519,500	7,605,859	7,732,791	7,903,388
Private wage and salary employment	7,139,936	6,861,100	6,385,235	6,317,449	6,425,016	6,564,678	6,740,663
Forestry, fishing, and related activities	46,639	46,733	45,698	47,225	48,809	49,100	42,333
Mining	4,779	4,491	3,716	3,621	3,867	3,950	3,957
Utilities	23,966	23,899	23,635	22,536	22,449	22,654	22,296
Construction	628,439	533,034	411,498	363,731	352,460	353,977	379,181
Manufacturing	396,293	371,848	324,409	307,997	311,760	317,251	322,442
Durable goods manufacturing	267,971	250,147	214,229	202,824	205,712	209,521	215,080
Nondurable goods manufacturing	128,322	121,701	110,180	105,173	106,048	107,730	107,362
Wholesale trade	362,217	349,063	321,204	310,983	310,640	318,664	323,478
Retail trade	1,032,619	1,002,198	938,837	943,845	970,895	990,048	1,015,278
Transportation and warehousing	227,058	224,977	209,413	206,261	213,907	220,954	227,298
Information	162,786	156,989	143,058	136,033	134,453	134,280	134,400
Finance and insurance	376,700	360,662	334,599	331,483	340,393	351,288	356,304
Real estate and rental and leasing	182,644	177,961	161,689	158,406	157,696	164,977	171,122
Professional, scientific, and technical services	467,854	465,317	440,476	441,971	452,113	454,959	473,401
Management of companies and enterprises	79,498	82,146	79,963	78,138	81,001	83,737	91,048
Administrative and waste services	714,819	603,182	541,284	540,834	534,702	546,791	564,121
Educational services	128,587	135,985	139,499	146,429	151,325	149,307	148,992
Health care and social assistance	892,867	915,482	922,747	936,552	954,874	973,443	989,348
Arts, entertainment, and recreation	188,356	188,382	186,789	186,468	194,114	198,123	200,730
Accommodation and food services	770,630	770,528	735,030	745,657	773,615	807,546	844,460
Other services, except public administration	453,185	448,223	421,691	409,279	415,943	423,629	430,474
Government and government enterprises	1,214,166	1,219,839	1,204,510	1,202,051	1,180,843	1,168,113	1,162,725
	Dollars						
Average Wages and Salaries by Industry	41,029	41,818	42,146	42,871	43,660	44,556	45,064
Average Farm Wages and Salaries	24,790	28,713	30,381	28,183	25,536	17,416	30,306
Average Nonfarm Wages and Salaries	41,120	41,891	42,209	42,956	43,764	44,719	45,148
Average private wages and salaries	40,435	41,051	41,209	42,029	42,933	44,075	44,534
Forestry, fishing, and related activities	21,436	21,531	21,449	22,205	23,045	24,134	24,848
Mining	58,004	57,534	56,325	59,818	61,206	68,273	64,288
Utilities	70,306	76,318	80,133	80,142	84,153	86,106	88,031
Construction	42,272	42,914	42,484	42,173	42,044	42,774	43,242
Manufacturing	48,964	50,491	52,102	53,838	54,449	55,480	56,154
Durable goods manufacturing	51,278	52,660	54,854	56,778	57,454	58,657	59,262
Nondurable goods manufacturing	44,131	46,034	46,751	48,168	48,621	49,301	49,927
Wholesale trade	58,885	60,133	60,012	62,426	64,969	67,149	68,166
Retail trade	27,681	27,581	27,740	28,095	28,326	28,839	29,104
Transportation and warehousing	44,062	45,062	45,607	47,072	48,077	48,970	50,761
Information	58,681	60,097	60,896	63,321	66,495	68,969	70,525
Finance and insurance	66,790	66,651	65,488	68,184	70,986	73,616	75,621
Real estate and rental and leasing	40,986	39,866	39,360	40,310	41,834	43,164	44,195
Professional, scientific, and technical services	62,488	64,195	64,394	65,418	66,954	69,756	69,581
Management of companies and enterprises	92,335	86,320	85,668	91,656	95,799	106,503	101,676
Administrative and waste services	30,890	32,267	33,037	33,431	34,123	34,908	34,584
Educational services	34,432	35,264	35,821	36,176	37,532	37,304	37,887
Health care and social assistance	43,031	44,290	45,327	45,926	46,711	47,591	48,220
Arts, entertainment, and recreation	37,288	37,133	36,096	36,864	37,366	38,256	37,903
Accommodation and food services	21,457	20,810	20,434	21,174	21,844	22,285	22,559
Other services, except public administration	27,782	28,520	28,746	29,697	29,872	30,607	31,542
Government and government enterprises	45,151	46,613	47,508	47,829	48,285	48,333	48,706

Table FL-10. Employment Characteristics by Family Type

(Number, percent.)

Family type and labor force status	2011		2012		2013	
	Total	Families with own children under 18 years	Total	Families with own children under 18 years	Total	Families with own children under 18 years
All Families	4,559,858	1,788,705	4,598,222	1,781,769	4,626,388	1,753,872
FAMILY TYPE AND LABOR FORCE STATUS						
Married-Couple Families	3,293,055	1,126,757	3,319,620	1,121,347	3,334,383	1,109,448
Both husband and wife in labor force	47.0	66.8	46.3	66.1	45.3	65.3
Husband in labor force, wife not in labor force	20.1	26.5	20.3	27.6	20.5	28.4
Wife in labor force, husband not in labor force	8.3	4.7	8.2	4.3	8.3	4.3
Both husband and wife not in labor force	24.6	2.1	25.2	2.0	25.5	1.7
Other Families	1,266,803	661,948	1,278,602	660,422	1,292,005	644,424
Female householder, no husband present	74.4	77.0	74.7	77.3	74.0	77.4
In labor force	54.6	65.3	53.9	64.9	52.2	63.9
Not in labor force	19.8	11.7	20.8	12.5	21.8	13.4
Male householder, no wife present	25.6	23.0	25.3	22.7	26.0	22.6
In labor force	19.9	20.4	19.7	20.5	19.8	20.5
Not in labor force	5.7	2.6	5.7	2.2	6.2	2.1

Table FL-11. School Enrollment and Educational Attainment, 2013

(Number, percent.)

Item	State	U.S.
Enrollment		
Total population 3 years and over, enrolled in school	4,643,948	82,395,254
Enrolled in nursery school or preschool (percent)	6.2	6.0
Enrolled in kindergarten (percent)	4.9	5.2
Enrolled in elementary school, grades 1-8 (percent)	39.0	40.0
Enrolled in high school, grades 9-12 (percent)	20.6	20.6
Enrolled in college or graduate school (percent)	29.3	28.3
Attainment		
Total population 25 years and over	13,726,996	210,910,615
Less than ninth grade (percent)	5.3	5.8
9th to 12th grade, no diploma (percent)	7.9	7.6
High school graduate, including equivalency (percent)	29.5	27.8
Some college, no degree (percent)	20.7	21.1
Associate's degree (percent)	9.5	8.1
Bachelor's degree (percent)	17.6	18.4
Graduate or professional degree (percent)	9.7	11.2
High school graduate or higher (percent)	86.8	86.6
Bachelor's degree or higher (percent)	27.2	29.6

Table FL-12. Public School Characteristics and Educational Indicators

(Number, percent; data derived from National Center of Education Statistics.)

Item	State	U.S.
Public Schools, 2012–2013 (except where noted)		
Number of school districts	76	18,093
Number of schools	4,269	98,454
Number of students (in thousands)	2,692	49,771
Number of teachers (in thousands)	177	3,109
Student-teacher ratio	15.2	16.0
Expenditures per student (dollars), FY 2012	8,520	10,667
Four-year adjusted cohort graduation rate (ACGR)[1,2]	75.6	81.4
Students eligible for free or reduced-price lunch (in thousands)	1576	25,188
English language learners (in thousands)	242	4,397
Students age 3 to 21 served under IDEA, part B (in thousands)	354	6,429

Public Schools by Type	Number	Percent of state public schools
Total number of schools	4,269	100.0
Regular	3,609	84.5
Special education	185	4.3
Vocational education	51	1.2
Alternative education	424	9.9

NOTE: Every school is assigned only one school type based on its instructional emphasis.
[1]ACGR data represents a new method of calculating high-school completion rates and may not be comparable to previous years' data for Averaged Freshmen Graduation Rates (AFGR).
[2]The United States 4-year ACGRs were estimated using both the reported 4-year ACGR data from 49 states and the District of Columbia and using imputed data for Idaho. The estimate for American Indian/Alaska Native students also includes imputed data for Virginia.

Table FL-13. Reported Voting and Registration of the Voting-Age Population, November 2012

(Numbers in thousands, percent.)

Item	Total population	Total citizen population	Registered			Voted		
			Total registered	Percent registered (total population)	Percent registered (total citizen population)	Total voted	Percent voted (total population)	Percent voted (total citizen population)
U.S. Total	235,248	215,081	153,157	65.1	71.2	132,948	56.5	61.8
State Total	15,034	13,326	9,102	60.5	68.3	8,107	53.9	60.8
Sex								
Male	7,179	6,346	4,234	59.0	66.7	3,727	51.9	58.7
Female	7,855	6,980	4,869	62.0	69.8	4,379	55.8	62.7
Race								
White alone	12,054	10,834	7,515	62.3	69.4	6,712	55.7	62.0
White, non-Hispanic alone	9,024	8,771	6,039	66.9	68.9	5,430	60.2	61.9
Black alone	2,244	1,919	1,262	56.3	65.8	1,104	49.2	57.6
Asian alone	496	360	174	35.1	48.4	155	31.2	43.0
Hispanic (of any race)	3,349	2,250	1,622	48.4	72.1	1,399	41.8	62.2
White alone or in combination	12,172	10,941	7,591	62.4	69.4	6,783	55.7	62.0
Black alone or in combination	2,283	1,955	1,295	56.7	66.2	1,137	49.8	58.2
Asian alone or in combination	544	392	194	35.7	49.5	171	31.5	43.7
Age								
18 to 24 years	1,669	1,467	751	45.0	51.2	614	36.8	41.9
25 to 44 years	4,715	3,863	2,493	52.9	64.5	2,164	45.9	56.0
45 to 64 years	5,345	4,814	3,474	65.0	72.2	3,107	58.1	64.5
65 to 74 years	1,881	1,802	1,344	71.5	74.6	1,259	66.9	69.9
75 years and over	1,423	1,381	1,040	73.1	75.3	963	67.6	69.7

Table FL-14. Crime

(Number, rate per 100,000. Data are derived from the FBI Uniform Crime Reports.)

Item	State 2012	State 2013	State Percent change	U.S.[1,2,3,4] 2012	U.S. 2013	U.S. Percent change
TOTAL POPULATION[5]	19,320,749	19,552,860	1.2	313,873,685	316,128,839	0.7
VIOLENT CRIME						
Number	94,087	89,948	-4.4	1,217,067	1,163,146	-4.4
Rate	487.0	460.0	-5.5	387.8	367.9	-5.1
Murder and Nonnegligent Manslaughter						
Number	1,009	972	-3.7	14,866	14,196	-4.5
Rate	5.2	5.0	-4.8	4.7	4.5	-5.2
Rape[6]						
Number	X	6,760	X	X	108,612	X
Rate	X	34.6	X	X	34.4	X
Robbery						
Number	23,889	23,200	-2.9	355,051	345,031	-2.8
Rate	123.6	118.7	-4.0	113.1	109.1	-3.5
Aggravated Assault						
Number	63,929	61,054	-4.5	762,009	724,149	-5.0
Rate	330.9	312.3	-5.6	242.8	229.1	-5.6
PROPERTY CRIME						
Number	632,988	607,172	-4.1	9,001,992	8,632,512	-4.1
Rate	3,276.2	3,105.3	-5.2	2,868.0	2,730.7	-4.8
Burglary						
Number	153,563	138,916	-9.5	2,109,932	1,928,465	-8.6
Rate	794.8	710.5	-10.6	672.2	610.0	-9.3
Larceny-Theft						
Number	442,095	433,344	-2.0	6,168,874	6,004,453	-2.7
Rate	2,288.2	2,216.3	-3.1	1,965.4	1,899.4	-3.4
Motor Vehicle Theft						
Number	37,330	34,912	-6.5	723,186	699,594	-3.3
Rate	193.2	178.6	-7.6	230.4	221.3	-4.0

NOTE: Although arson data are included in the trend and clearance tables, sufficient data are not available to estimate totals for this offense. Therefore, no arson data are published in this table.
X = Not applicable.
- = Zero or rounds to zero.
[1]The crime figures have been adjusted.
[2]The data collection methodology for the offense of forcible rape used by the Minnesota state Uniform Crime Reporting (UCR) Program (with the exception of Minneapolis and St. Paul, Minnesota) does not comply with national UCR Program guidelines. Consequently, its figures for forcible rape and violent crime (of which forcible rape is a part) are not published in this table.
[3]Includes offenses reported by the Zoological Police and the Metro Transit Police.
[4]Because of changes in the state's reporting practices, figures are not comparable to previous years' data.
[5]Populations are U.S. Census Bureau provisional estimates as of July 1 of each year.
[6]The figures shown for the offense of rape were estimated using the revised Uniform Crime Reporting (UCR) definition of rape.

Table FL-15. State Government Finances, 2013

(Dollar amounts in thousands, percent distribution.)

Item	Dollars	Percent distribution
Total Revenue	95,693,798	100.0
General revenue	74,725,923	78.1
Intergovernmental revenue	23,880,229	25.0
Taxes	35,377,566	37.0
General sales	20,785,507	21.7
Selective sales	8,530,234	8.9
License taxes	1,993,965	2.1
Individual income tax	0	-
Corporate income tax	2,071,710	2.2
Other taxes	1,996,150	2.1
Current charges	9,018,813	9.4
Miscellaneous general revenue	6,449,315	6.7
Utility revenue	23,872	-
Liquor stores revenue	0	-
Insurance trust revenue[1]	20,944,003	21.9
Total Expenditure	80,436,036	100.0
Intergovernmental expenditure	17,809,542	22.1
Direct expenditure	62,626,494	77.9
Current operation	44,962,402	55.9
Capital outlay	5,190,234	6.5
Insurance benefits and repayments	9,196,389	11.4
Assistance and subsidies	1,963,673	2.4
Interest on debt	1,313,796	1.6
Exhibit: Salaries and wages	8,926,358	11.1
Total Expenditure	80,436,036	100.0
General expenditure	71,097,679	88.4
Intergovernmental expenditure	17,809,542	22.1
Direct expenditure	53,288,137	66.2
General expenditure, by function:		
Education	23,904,253	29.7
Public welfare	22,528,115	28.0
Hospitals	820,601	1.0
Health	3,763,817	4.7
Highways	5,869,267	7.3
Police protection	514,377	0.6
Correction	2,145,818	2.7
Natural resources	1,100,119	1.4
Parks and recreation	104,619	0.1
Governmental administration	2,564,023	3.2
Interest on general debt	1,313,796	1.6
Other and unallocable	6,468,874	8.0
Utility expenditure	141,968	0.2
Liquor stores expenditure	0	-
Insurance trust expenditure	9,196,389	11.4
Debt at End of Fiscal Year	37,892,165	X
Cash and Security Holdings	196,509,097	X

X = Not applicable.
- = Zero or rounds to zero.
[1]Within insurance trust revenue, net earnings of state retirement systems is a calculated statistic (the item code in the data file is X08), and thus can be positive or negative. Net earnings is the sum of earnings on investments plus gains on investments minus losses on investments. The change made in 2002 for asset valuation from book to market value in accordance with Statement 34 of the Governmental Accounting Standards Board is reflected in the calculated statistics.

Table FL-16. State Government Tax Collections, 2014

(Dollars in thousands, percent.)

Item	Dollars	Percent distribution
Total Taxes	35,384,350	100.0
Property taxes	250	-
Sales and gross receipts	29,046,930	82.1
General sales and gross receipts	21,480,910	60.7
Selective sales and gross receipts	7,566,020	21.4
Alcoholic beverages	452,370	1.3
Amusements	187,639	0.5
Insurance premiums	702,340	2.0
Motor fuels	2,422,718	6.8
Pari-mutuels	10,412	-
Public utilities	2,719,350	7.7
Tobacco products	370,993	1.0
Other selective sales	700,198	2.0
Licenses	2,133,240	6.0
Alcoholic beverages	8,663	-
Amusements	14,000	-
Corporations in general	298,604	0.8
Hunting and fishing	16,275	-
Motor vehicle	1,380,910	3.9
Motor vehicle operators	187,182	0.5
Public utilities	24,569	0.1
Occupation and business, NEC	198,483	0.6
Other licenses	4,554	-
Income taxes	2,043,750	5.8
Individual income	X	X
Corporation net income	2,043,750	5.8
Other taxes	2,160,180	6.1
Death and gift	1,710	-
Documentary and stock transfer	2,109,370	6.0
Severance	49,100	0.1
Taxes, NEC	0	-

X = Not applicable.
- = Zero or rounds to zero.

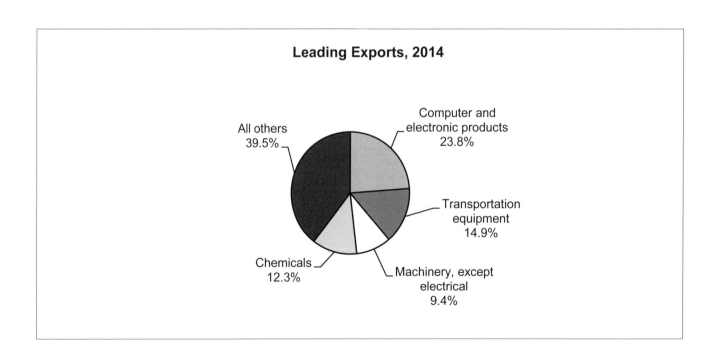

Leading Exports, 2014

- All others 39.5%
- Computer and electronic products 23.8%
- Transportation equipment 14.9%
- Machinery, except electrical 9.4%
- Chemicals 12.3%

GEORGIA

Facts and Figures

Location: Southeastern United States; bordered on the N by Tennessee and North Carolina, on the E by South Carolina and the Atlantic Ocean, on the S by Florida, and on the W by Florida and Alabama

Area: 59,425 sq. mi. (153,909 sq. km.); rank—21st

Population: 10,097,343 (2014 est.); rank—8th

Principal Cities: capital—Atlanta; largest—Atlanta

Statehood: January 2, 1788; 4th state

U.S. Congress: 2 senators, 14 representatives

State Motto: Wisdom, Justice, and Moderation

State Song: "Georgia on My Mind"

State Nicknames: The Empire State of the South; The Peach State

Abbreviations: GA; Ga.

State Symbols: flower—Cherokee rose; tree—live oak; bird—brown thrasher

At a Glance

- With an increase in population of 4.2 percent, Georgia ranked 15th among the states in growth from 2010 to 2014.

- Georgia's median household income in 2013 was $47,829, and 19.0 percent of the population lived below the poverty level.

- In 2013, 18.8 percent of Georgians did not have health insurance, compared to 14.5 percent of the total U.S. population.

- Georgia's violent crime rate was 365.7 per 100,000 population, compared to 367.9 for the U.S. as a whole.

- Approximately 8.6 percent of Georgians lived in mobile homes in 2013.

Table GA-1. Population by Age, Sex, Race, and Hispanic Origin

(Number, percent, except where noted.)

Sex, age, race, and Hispanic origin	2000	2010	2014[1]	Average annual percent change, 2010–2014
Total Population	8,186,453	9,687,653	10,097,343	1.0
Percent of total U.S. population	2.9	3.1	3.2	X
Sex				
Male	4,027,113	4,729,171	4,926,987	1.0
Female	4,159,340	4,958,482	5,170,356	1.1
Age				
Under 5 years	595,150	686,785	662,675	-0.9
5 to 19 years	1,819,620	2,094,844	2,110,421	0.2
20 to 64 years	4,986,408	5,873,989	6,072,709	0.8
65 years and over	785,275	1,032,035	1,251,538	4.9
Median age (years)	33.4	35.3	36.1	0.6
Race and Hispanic Origin				
One race				
White	5,327,281	6,144,931	6,266,166	0.5
Black	2,349,542	2,993,927	3,183,784	1.5
American Indian and Alaska Native	21,737	48,599	50,988	1.2
Asian	173,170	323,459	387,181	4.6
Native Hawaiian or Other Pacific Islander	4,246	10,454	11,895	3.3
Two or more races	114,188	166,283	197,329	4.4
Hispanic (of any race)	435,227	911,863	935,279	0.6

X = Not applicable.
[1]Population figures for 2014 are July 1 estimates. The 2010 estimates are taken from the 2010 Census.

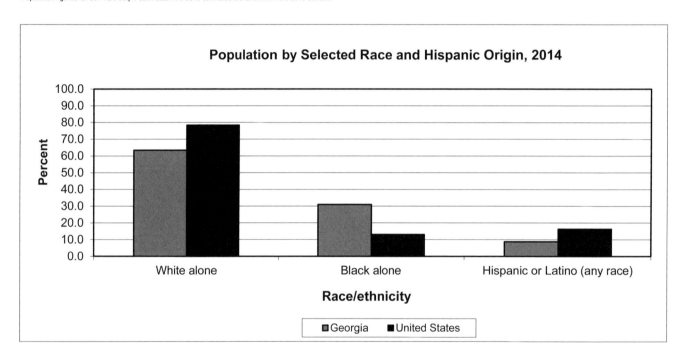

Table GA-2. Marital Status

(Number, percent distribution.)

Sex, age, race, and Hispanic origin	2000	2010	2013
Males, 15 Years and Over	3,092,736	3,683,258	3,819,234
Never married	30.4	35.4	36.9
Now married, except separated	56.5	50.5	48.6
Separated	2.0	2.1	2.2
Widowed	2.1	2.2	2.3
Divorced	9.0	9.9	10.1
Females, 15 Years and Over	3,273,889	3,954,542	4,097,149
Never married	24.4	29.7	31.1
Now married, except separated	51.5	46.1	44.4
Separated	2.7	2.9	2.7
Widowed	9.8	8.6	8.6
Divorced	11.6	12.7	13.2

Table GA-3. Households and Housing Characteristics

(Number, percent, dollars.)

Item	2000	2010	2013	Average annual percent change, 2000–2013
Total Households	3,006,369	3,482,420	3,546,965	1.3
Family households	2,111,647	2,385,969	2,389,803	1.0
Married-couple family	1,548,800	1,688,896	1,672,704	0.6
Other family	562,847	697,073	717,099	1.9
Male householder, no wife present	127,437	161,001	175,702	2.5
Female householder, no husband present	435,410	536,072	541,397	1.7
Nonfamily households	894,722	1,096,451	1,157,162	2.0
Householder living alone	710,523	921,005	959,287	2.3
Householder not living alone	184,199	175,446	197,875	0.6
Housing Characteristics				
Total housing units	3,281,737	4,091,482	4,110,162	1.7
Occupied housing units	3,006,369	3,482,420	3,546,965	1.3
Owner occupied	2,029,154	2,304,165	2,222,377	0.7
Renter occupied	977,215	1,178,255	1,324,588	2.4
Average household size	2.65	2.72	2.74	0.3
Financial Characteristics				
Median gross rent of renter-occupied housing	613	819	850	2.5
Median monthly owner costs for housing units with a mortgage	1,039	1,390	1,288	1.7
Median value of owner-occupied housing units	111,200	156,200	141,600	1.9

Table GA-4. Migration, Origin, and Language

(Number, percent.)

Characteristic	State 2012	State 2013	State Percent change	U.S. 2012	U.S. 2013	U.S. Percent change
Residence 1 Year Ago						
Population 1 year and over	9,796,547	9,870,319	0.8	310,212,755	312,432,820	0.7
Same house	84.0	83.6	X	85.0	85.0	X
Different house in the U.S.	15.5	15.8	X	14.4	14.4	X
Same county	7.9	8.7	X	9.0	8.9	X
Different county	7.5	7.1	X	5.4	5.5	X
Same state	4.7	4.2	X	3.2	3.2	X
Different state	2.8	2.8	X	2.3	2.3	X
Abroad	0.5	0.6	X	0.6	0.6	X
Place of Birth						
Native born	8,979,807	9,021,188	0.5	273,089,382	274,780,773	0.6
Male	48.7	48.6	X	49.3	49.3	X
Female	51.3	51.4	X	50.7	50.7	X
Foreign born	940,138	970,979	3.3	40,824,658	41,348,066	1.3
Male	50.6	51.2	X	48.7	48.8	X
Female	49.4	48.8	X	51.3	51.2	X
Foreign born; naturalized U.S. citizen	353,192	375,460	6.3	18,686,237	19,294,710	3.3
Male	47.2	47.0	X	45.8	45.9	X
Female	52.8	53.0	X	54.2	54.1	X
Foreign born; not a U.S. citizen	586,946	595,519	1.5	22,138,421	22,053,356	-0.4
Male	52.7	53.8	X	51.1	51.3	X
Female	47.3	46.2	X	48.9	48.7	X
Entered 2010 or later	7.0	10.5	X	7.0	9.7	X
Entered 2000 to 2009	37.0	35.9	X	30.4	29.4	X
Entered before 2000	56.0	53.6	X	62.7	61.0	X
World Region of Birth, Foreign						
Foreign-born population, excluding population born at sea	940,088	970,979	3.3	40,824,553	41,347,945	1.3
Europe	9.6	9.3	X	11.8	11.6	X
Asia	27.7	28.2	X	29.2	29.5	X
Africa	8.1	8.7	X	4.2	4.4	X
Oceania	0.3	0.2	X	0.6	0.5	X
Latin America	52.5	51.8	X	52.2	51.9	X
North America	1.9	1.8	X	2.0	2.0	X
Language Spoken at Home and Ability to Speak English						
Population 5 years and over	9,248,840	9,335,151	0.9	294,003,714	296,358,760	0.8
English only	86.6	86.4	X	79.0	79.2	X
Language other than English	13.4	13.6	X	21.0	20.8	X
Speaks English less than "very well"	5.6	5.7	X	8.5	8.5	X

NA = Not available.
X = Not applicable.
- = Zero or rounds to zero.

Table GA-5. Median Income and Poverty Status, 2013

(Number, percent, except as noted.)

Characteristic	State		U.S.	
	Number	Percent	Number	Percent
Median Income				
Households (dollars)..	47,829	X	52,250	X
Families (dollars)	57,458	X	64,030	X
Below Poverty Level (All People)	1,843,768	19.0	48,810,868	15.8
Sex				
Male...	815,981	17.3	21,938,525	14.5
Female	1,027,787	20.5	26,872,343	17.1
Age				
Under 18 years...	650,910	26.5	16,086,960	22.2
Related children under 18 years.....................................	642,195	26.2	15,769,921	21.9
18 to 64 years..	1,068,041	17.5	28,578,191	14.8
65 years and over	124,817	10.7	4,145,717	9.6

X = Not applicable.

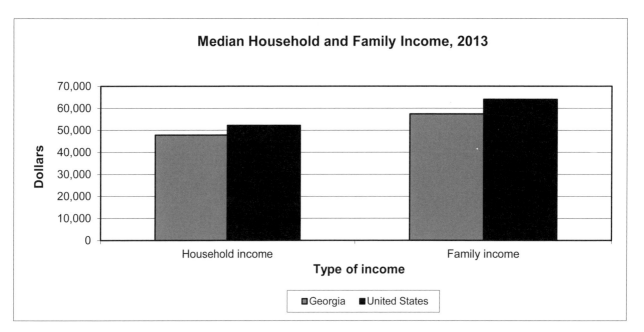

Table GA-6. Health Insurance Coverage Status for the Civilian Noninstitutionalized Population and Children Under 18 Years of Age

(Numbers in thousands, percent.)

Item	2005	2006	2007	2008	2009	2010	2011	2012	2013
Civilian Noninstitutionalized Population	9,045	9,347	9,493	9,473	9,594	9,520	9,620	9,719	9,801
Covered by Private or Public Insurance									
Number..	7,391	7,688	7,831	7,694	7,758	7,644	7,737	7,927	7,955
Percent..	81.7	82.3	82.5	81.2	80.9	80.3	80.4	81.6	81.2
Not Covered									
Number..	1,654	1,659	1,662	1,779	1,836	1,876	1,883	1,792	1,846
Percent..	18.3	17.7	17.5	18.8	19.1	19.7	19.6	18.4	18.8
Percent in the U.S. not covered...	15.3	15.8	15.3	15.1	15.1	15.5	15.1	14.8	14.5
Children Under 18 Years of Age...	2,371	2,455	2,517	2,536	2,576	2,492	2,485	2,492	2,487
Covered by Private or Public Insurance									
Number..	2,110	2,141	2,228	2,245	2,295	2,248	2,248	2,272	2,249
Percent..	89.0	87.2	88.5	88.5	89.1	90.2	90.5	91.2	90.4
Not Covered									
Number..	260	314	289	291	281	244	237	220	238
Percent..	11.0	12.8	11.5	11.5	10.9	9.8	9.5	8.8	9.6
Percent in the U.S. not covered...	10.9	11.7	11.0	9.7	8.6	8.0	7.5	7.2	7.1

Table GA-7. Employment Status by Demographic Group, 2014

(Numbers in thousands, percent.)

Characteristic	Civilian noninstitutional population	Civilian labor force		Employed		Unemployed	
		Number	Percent of population	Number	Percent of population	Number	Percent of population
Total..................................	7,669	4,735	61.7	4,392	57.3	343	7.2
Sex							
Male..	3,637	2,509	69.0	2,330	64.1	179	7.1
Female	4,032	2,225	55.2	2,061	51.1	164	7.4
Race, Sex, and Hispanic Origin							
White	4,835	2,948	61.0	2,812	58.2	136	4.6
Male..	2,366	1,663	70.3	1,591	67.3	72	4.3
Female	2,470	1,285	52.0	1,221	49.4	64	5.0
Black or African American...........................	2,327	1,480	63.6	1,297	55.7	184	12.4
Male..	1,033	689	66.7	593	57.4	96	13.9
Female	1,294	791	61.1	703	54.3	88	11.1
Hispanic or Latino ethnicity[1]	494	345	69.9	325	65.7	21	6.0
Male..	268	231	86.0	222	82.9	9	3.7
Female	226	115	50.7	102	45.3	12	10.6
Age							
16 to 19 years	513	151	29.3	113	22.0	38	25.0
20 to 24 years	668	439	65.8	379	56.7	61	13.8
25 to 34 years	1,332	1,032	77.5	930	69.9	102	9.9
35 to 44 years	1,392	1,156	83.0	1,110	79.7	46	4.0
45 to 54 years	1,388	1,073	77.3	1,024	73.8	49	4.6
55 to 64 years	1,121	668	59.6	636	56.7	32	4.8
65 years and over	1,254	215	17.2	200	15.9	16	7.3

NOTE: Data in Table 7 are from the Current Population Survey (CPS) and do not match the estimates in Table 8. See notes and definitions for further information.
[1]May be of any race.

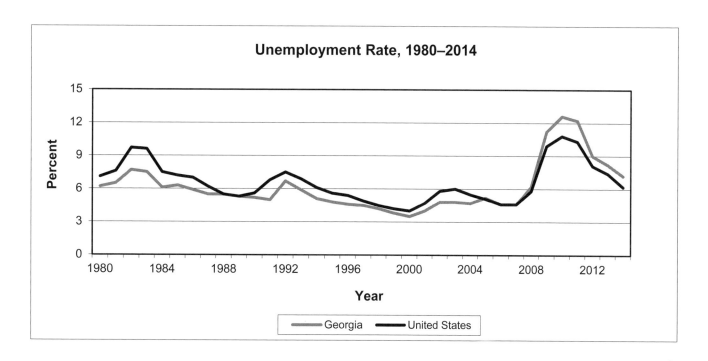

Unemployment Rate, 1980–2014

Table GA-8. Employment Status of the Civilian Noninstitutional Population Age 16 Years and Over

(Number, percent.)

Year	Civilian labor force	Civilian participation rate	Employed	Unemployed	Unemployment rate
2006	4,710,775	68.1	4,489,128	221,647	4.7
2007	4,815,818	68.1	4,597,640	218,178	4.5
2008	4,879,253	67.8	4,575,010	304,243	6.2
2009	4,787,749	65.6	4,311,854	475,895	9.9
2010	4,696,676	64.1	4,202,052	494,624	10.5
2011	4,748,579	64.3	4,262,403	486,176	10.2
2012	4,783,313	63.9	4,344,683	438,630	9.2
2013	4,758,725	62.8	4,367,926	390,799	8.2
2014	4,756,708	62.0	4,414,343	342,365	7.2

Table GA-9. Employment and Average Wages by Industry

(Estimates from 2007 through 2010 are based on the 2007 *North American Industry Classification System* [NAICS]. Estimates from 2011 onward are based on the 2012 NAICS.)

Industry	2007	2008	2009	2010	2011	2012	2013
	Number of jobs						
Wage and Salary Employment by Industry	4,364,184	4,326,738	4,092,799	4,050,847	4,089,152	4,125,128	4,200,830
Farm Wage and Salary Employment	15,603	17,301	16,401	13,804	14,578	14,650	15,025
Nonfarm Wage and Salary Employment	4,348,581	4,309,437	4,076,398	4,037,043	4,074,574	4,110,478	4,185,805
Private wage and salary employment	3,560,787	3,500,784	3,275,382	3,240,704	3,292,162	3,333,977	3,420,001
Forestry, fishing, and related activities	14,244	14,169	13,756	14,477	14,895	14,198	14,856
Mining	6,984	5,943	5,013	4,942	4,792	4,671	4,708
Utilities	20,681	20,625	20,437	19,738	20,011	19,850	19,858
Construction	230,627	213,709	174,419	157,079	154,046	146,376	151,500
Manufacturing	434,068	411,541	359,528	346,160	351,084	354,694	357,649
Durable goods manufacturing	202,291	190,194	161,496	155,681	161,698	166,741	171,342
Nondurable goods manufacturing	231,777	221,347	198,032	190,479	189,386	187,953	186,307
Wholesale trade	222,616	219,879	201,601	198,258	199,538	202,769	206,413
Retail trade	486,556	472,635	444,911	441,958	448,738	449,418	458,336
Transportation and warehousing	171,967	173,231	162,834	162,081	165,995	169,234	169,670
Information	112,649	110,244	101,744	97,935	98,631	100,074	102,835
Finance and insurance	169,227	164,341	160,226	156,825	159,145	163,398	166,470
Real estate and rental and leasing	66,779	64,997	59,978	58,451	58,078	57,531	58,908
Professional, scientific, and technical services	223,809	231,527	221,601	221,109	227,474	234,165	241,039
Management of companies and enterprises	52,860	54,251	52,583	52,879	54,026	57,410	60,052
Administrative and waste services	291,922	278,869	247,546	259,493	269,090	275,817	291,467
Educational services	73,722	75,806	77,301	79,567	81,954	81,601	81,492
Health care and social assistance	379,788	387,896	394,137	402,734	408,783	418,197	430,152
Arts, entertainment, and recreation	42,533	42,415	41,471	39,828	41,138	41,724	43,262
Accommodation and food services	359,069	357,622	342,524	339,751	345,699	355,174	371,494
Other services, except public administration	200,686	201,084	193,772	187,439	189,045	187,676	189,840
Government and government enterprises	787,794	808,653	801,016	796,339	782,412	776,501	765,804
	Dollars						
Average Wages and Salaries by Industry	42,916	43,568	43,873	44,924	46,170	47,419	47,823
Average Farm Wages and Salaries	25,789	23,731	18,790	23,004	20,178	22,255	22,925
Average Nonfarm Wages and Salaries	42,977	43,648	43,974	44,999	46,263	47,509	47,912
Average private wages and salaries	43,440	43,988	44,160	45,335	46,678	48,281	48,727
Forestry, fishing, and related activities	29,599	29,761	30,078	31,128	31,585	32,668	33,752
Mining	58,728	54,253	53,581	55,430	57,491	59,454	61,222
Utilities	75,808	78,570	81,539	76,775	84,511	84,932	85,496
Construction	44,224	45,449	45,940	46,524	47,134	48,898	49,873
Manufacturing	46,817	47,931	48,957	51,805	53,702	54,980	55,840
Durable goods manufacturing	49,012	50,599	52,057	54,755	56,989	57,182	58,298
Nondurable goods manufacturing	44,900	45,639	46,429	49,394	50,895	53,026	53,580
Wholesale trade	65,045	65,646	65,394	67,527	69,803	71,440	72,326
Retail trade	26,552	26,557	26,631	27,112	27,388	27,889	28,224
Transportation and warehousing	50,000	49,645	48,753	51,081	52,918	54,063	56,739
Information	75,337	74,449	73,878	76,733	79,875	85,779	85,858
Finance and insurance	71,496	72,191	70,080	72,883	76,669	80,087	81,890
Real estate and rental and leasing	48,352	46,902	45,213	45,955	48,695	50,958	51,857
Professional, scientific, and technical services	68,997	70,645	70,734	72,372	74,401	78,155	77,367
Management of companies and enterprises	91,384	83,871	85,454	89,287	94,652	100,560	98,874
Administrative and waste services	32,317	33,546	34,251	34,517	35,021	35,802	35,681
Educational services	37,625	39,002	39,754	40,262	41,022	42,047	43,012
Health care and social assistance	42,023	43,174	44,342	44,681	45,588	46,887	47,601
Arts, entertainment, and recreation	33,829	33,577	33,892	35,321	35,834	34,889	35,449
Accommodation and food services	17,937	17,731	17,778	18,519	19,027	19,413	19,253
Other services, except public administration	28,039	28,617	28,691	29,763	30,144	30,760	31,455
Government and government enterprises	40,887	42,174	43,213	43,633	44,514	44,193	44,273

Table GA-10. Employment Characteristics by Family Type

(Number, percent.)

Family type and labor force status	2011		2012		2013	
	Total	Families with own children under 18 years	Total	Families with own children under 18 years	Total	Families with own children under 18 years
All Families..	2,376,008	1,103,003	2,406,226	1,103,278	2,389,803	1,087,559
FAMILY TYPE AND LABOR FORCE STATUS						
Married-Couple Families................................	1,667,698	718,977	1,693,386	715,266	1,672,704	692,412
Both husband and wife in labor force..................	52.3	64.3	51.8	64.0	51.6	65.2
Husband in labor force, wife not in labor force	24.2	30.0	24.4	30.4	23.2	29.0
Wife in labor force, husband not in labor force	8.0	4.1	7.6	3.9	7.7	3.8
Both husband and wife not in labor force...............	15.5	1.6	16.2	1.7	17.0	1.8
Other Families	708,310	384,026	712,840	388,012	717,099	395,147
Female householder, no husband present................	76.7	80.4	76.7	80.1	75.5	78.1
In labor force..	54.3	65.8	54.3	66.0	53.8	64.7
Not in labor force	22.4	14.6	22.3	14.1	21.7	13.4
Male householder, no wife present.......................	23.3	19.6	23.3	19.9	24.5	21.9
In labor force..	18.4	17.4	17.8	17.9	19.3	19.9
Not in labor force	4.9	2.2	5.5	2.1	5.2	2.0

Table GA-11. School Enrollment and Educational Attainment, 2013

(Number, percent.)

Item	State	U.S.
Enrollment		
Total population 3 years and over, enrolled in school	2,784,646	82,395,254
Enrolled in nursery school or preschool (percent)...	6.5	6.0
Enrolled in kindergarten (percent)...	5.2	5.2
Enrolled in elementary school, grades 1-8 (percent).......................................	40.8	40.0
Enrolled in high school, grades 9-12 (percent)...	20.6	20.6
Enrolled in college or graduate school (percent)..	26.9	28.3
Attainment		
Total population 25 years and over	6,472,172	210,910,615
Less than ninth grade (percent)	5.6	5.8
9th to 12th grade, no diploma (percent)	9.0	7.6
High school graduate, including equivalency (percent).....................................	28.6	27.8
Some college, no degree (percent)	21.2	21.1
Associate's degree (percent)	7.4	8.1
Bachelor's degree (percent)	17.8	18.4
Graduate or professional degree (percent)...	10.6	11.2
High school graduate or higher (percent)	85.5	86.6
Bachelor's degree or higher (percent)...	28.3	29.6

Table GA-12. Public School Characteristics and Educational Indicators

(Number, percent; data derived from National Center of Education Statistics.)

Item	State	U.S.
Public Schools, 2012–2013 (except where noted)		
Number of school districts..	218	18,093
Number of schools..	2,387	98,454
Number of students (in thousands)	1,703	49,771
Number of teachers (in thousands)	109	3,109
Student-teacher ratio	15.6	16.0
Expenditures per student (dollars), FY 2012..	9,272	10,667
Four-year adjusted cohort graduation rate (ACGR)[1,2]	71.7	81.4
Students eligible for free or reduced-price lunch (in thousands)	1017	25,188
English language learners (in thousands)	87	4,397
Students age 3 to 21 served under IDEA, part B (in thousands)	185	6,429

Public Schools by Type	Number	Percent of state public schools
Total number of schools..	2,387	100.0
Regular	2,253	94.4
Special education...	59	2.5
Vocational education...	1	0.0
Alternative education..	74	3.1

NOTE: Every school is assigned only one school type based on its instructional emphasis.
[1]ACGR data represents a new method of calculating high-school completion rates and may not be comparable to previous years' data for Averaged Freshmen Graduation Rates (AFGR).
[2]The United States 4-year ACGRs were estimated using both the reported 4-year ACGR data from 49 states and the District of Columbia and using imputed data for Idaho. The estimate for American Indian/Alaska Native students also includes imputed data for Virginia.

Table GA-13. Reported Voting and Registration of the Voting-Age Population, November 2012

(Numbers in thousands, percent.)

Item	Total population	Total citizen population	Registered			Voted		
			Total registered	Percent registered (total population)	Percent registered (total citizen population)	Total voted	Percent voted (total population)	Percent voted (total citizen population)
U.S. Total	235,248	215,081	153,157	65.1	71.2	132,948	56.5	61.8
State Total	7,179	6,738	4,767	66.4	70.7	4,168	58.1	61.9
Sex								
Male	3,424	3,206	2,178	63.6	67.9	1,899	55.5	59.2
Female	3,755	3,532	2,589	68.9	73.3	2,269	60.4	64.2
Race								
White alone	4,659	4,388	3,121	67.0	71.1	2,683	57.6	61.1
White, non-Hispanic alone	4,227	4,176	3,006	71.1	72.0	2,590	61.3	62.0
Black alone	2,151	2,063	1,491	69.3	72.3	1,340	62.3	65.0
Asian alone	274	198	86	31.4	43.6	83	30.2	41.9
Hispanic (of any race)	489	238	140	28.7	59.0	114	23.3	47.8
White alone or in combination	4,697	4,424	3,148	67.0	71.2	2,706	57.6	61.2
Black alone or in combination	2,177	2,087	1,511	69.4	72.4	1,354	62.2	64.9
Asian alone or in combination	280	203	86	30.8	42.4	83	29.6	40.8
Age								
18 to 24 years	920	867	469	51.0	54.1	349	37.9	40.2
25 to 44 years	2,649	2,376	1,673	63.1	70.4	1,426	53.8	60.0
45 to 64 years	2,658	2,547	1,886	70.9	74.0	1,741	65.5	68.4
65 to 74 years	615	615	492	79.9	79.9	446	72.5	72.5
75 years and over	336	333	248	73.6	74.3	206	61.2	61.8

Table GA-14. Crime

(Number, rate per 100,000. Data are derived from the FBI Uniform Crime Reports.)

Item	State			U.S.[1,2,3,4]		
	2012	2013	Percent change	2012	2013	Percent change
TOTAL POPULATION[5]	9,915,646	9,992,167	0.8	313,873,685	316,128,839	0.7
VIOLENT CRIME						
Number............................	37,675	35,943	-4.6	1,217,067	1,163,146	-4.4
Rate	380.0	359.7	-5.3	387.8	367.9	-5.1
Murder and Nonnegligent Manslaughter						
Number............................	583	556	-4.6	14,866	14,196	-4.5
Rate	5.9	5.6	-5.4	4.7	4.5	-5.2
Rape[6]						
Number............................	X	2,582	X	X	108,612	X
Rate	X	25.8	X	X	34.4	X
Robbery						
Number............................	12,502	12,488	-0.1	355,051	345,031	-2.8
Rate	126.1	125.0	-0.9	113.1	109.1	-3.5
Aggravated Assault						
Number............................	22,447	20,915	-6.8	762,009	724,149	-5.0
Rate	226.4	209.3	-7.5	242.8	229.1	-5.6
PROPERTY CRIME						
Number............................	339,473	334,399	-1.5	9,001,992	8,632,512	-4.1
Rate	3,423.6	3,346.6	-2.2	2,868.0	2,730.7	-4.8
Burglary						
Number............................	86,992	82,258	-5.4	2,109,932	1,928,465	-8.6
Rate	877.3	823.2	-6.2	672.2	610.0	-9.3
Larceny-Theft						
Number............................	223,875	225,315	0.6	6,168,874	6,004,453	-2.7
Rate	2,257.8	2,254.9	-0.1	1,965.4	1,899.4	-3.4
Motor Vehicle Theft						
Number............................	28,606	26,826	-6.2	723,186	699,594	-3.3
Rate	288.5	268.5	-6.9	230.4	221.3	-4.0

NOTE: Although arson data are included in the trend and clearance tables, sufficient data are not available to estimate totals for this offense. Therefore, no arson data are published in this table.

X = Not applicable.

- = Zero or rounds to zero.

[1]The crime figures have been adjusted.

[2]The data collection methodology for the offense of forcible rape used by the Minnesota state Uniform Crime Reporting (UCR) Program (with the exception of Minneapolis and St. Paul, Minnesota) does not comply with national UCR Program guidelines. Consequently, its figures for forcible rape and violent crime (of which forcible rape is a part) are not published in this table.

[3]Includes offenses reported by the Zoological Police and the Metro Transit Police.

[4]Because of changes in the state's reporting practices, figures are not comparable to previous years' data.

[5]Populations are U.S. Census Bureau provisional estimates as of July 1 of each year.

[6]The figures shown for the offense of rape were estimated using the revised Uniform Crime Reporting (UCR) definition of rape.

Table GA-15. State Government Finances, 2013

(Dollar amounts in thousands, percent distribution.)

Item	Dollars	Percent distribution
Total Revenue	53,486,765	100.0
General revenue	38,391,794	71.8
Intergovernmental revenue	14,619,221	27.3
Taxes	17,794,152	33.3
General sales	5,277,211	9.9
Selective sales	2,131,211	4.0
License taxes	744,401	1.4
Individual income tax	8,772,227	16.4
Corporate income tax	797,255	1.5
Other taxes	71,847	0.1
Current charges	3,676,613	6.9
Miscellaneous general revenue	2,301,808	4.3
Utility revenue	7,118	-
Liquor stores revenue	0	-
Insurance trust revenue[1]	15,087,853	28.2
Total Expenditure	45,483,779	100.0
Intergovernmental expenditure	10,361,359	22.8
Direct expenditure	35,122,420	77.2
Current operation	24,073,754	52.9
Capital outlay	2,659,934	5.8
Insurance benefits and repayments	6,743,993	14.8
Assistance and subsidies	979,446	2.2
Interest on debt	665,293	1.5
Exhibit: Salaries and wages	5,931,608	13.0
Total Expenditure	45,483,779	100.0
General expenditure	38,702,490	85.1
Intergovernmental expenditure	10,361,359	22.8
Direct expenditure	28,341,131	62.3
General expenditure, by function:		
Education	17,337,702	38.1
Public welfare	11,518,235	25.3
Hospitals	948,316	2.1
Health	1,204,357	2.6
Highways	2,170,602	4.8
Police protection	319,687	0.7
Correction	1,487,452	3.3
Natural resources	454,830	1.0
Parks and recreation	196,605	0.4
Governmental administration	827,540	1.8
Interest on general debt	665,293	1.5
Other and unallocable	1,571,871	3.5
Utility expenditure	37,296	0.1
Liquor stores expenditure	0	-
Insurance trust expenditure	6,743,993	14.8
Debt at End of Fiscal Year	13,292,965	X
Cash and Security Holdings	86,022,569	X

X = Not applicable.
- = Zero or rounds to zero.
[1]Within insurance trust revenue, net earnings of state retirement systems is a calculated statistic (the item code in the data file is X08), and thus can be positive or negative. Net earnings is the sum of earnings on investments plus gains on investments minus losses on investments. The change made in 2002 for asset valuation from book to market value in accordance with Statement 34 of the Governmental Accounting Standards Board is reflected in the calculated statistics.

Table GA-16. State Government Tax Collections, 2014

(Dollars in thousands, percent.)

Item	Dollars	Percent distribution
Total Taxes	18,628,502	100.0
Property taxes	788,350	4.2
Sales and gross receipts	7,310,132	39.2
General sales and gross receipts	5,125,502	27.5
Selective sales and gross receipts	2,184,630	11.7
Alcoholic beverages	181,875	1.0
Amusements	0	-
Insurance premiums	372,122	2.0
Motor fuels	1,006,494	5.4
Pari-mutuels	0	-
Public utilities	0	-
Tobacco products	216,640	1.2
Other selective sales	407,499	2.2
Licenses	609,944	3.3
Alcoholic beverages	3,829	-
Amusements	148	-
Corporations in general	48,078	0.3
Hunting and fishing	24,899	0.1
Motor vehicle	337,456	1.8
Motor vehicle operators	91,117	0.5
Public utilities	0	-
Occupation and business, NEC	83,662	0.4
Other licenses	20,755	0.1
Income taxes	9,909,378	53.2
Individual income	8,965,572	48.1
Corporation net income	943,806	5.1
Other taxes	10,698	0.1
Death and gift	0	-
Documentary and stock transfer	10,698	0.1
Severance	X	X
Taxes, NEC	0	-

X = Not applicable.
- = Zero or rounds to zero.

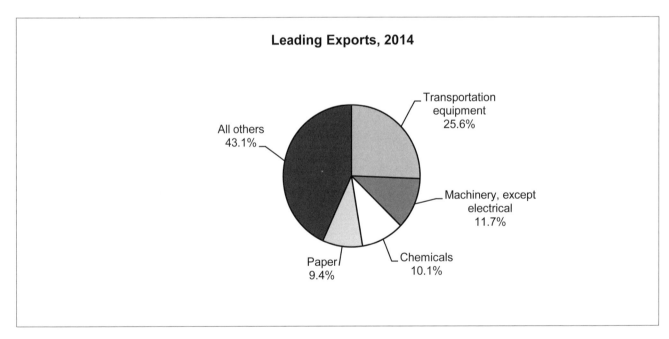

Leading Exports, 2014

Transportation equipment 25.6%

Machinery, except electrical 11.7%

Chemicals 10.1%

Paper 9.4%

All others 43.1%

HAWAII

Location: North Pacific Ocean

Area: 10,931 sq. mi. (28,311 sq. km.); rank—43rd

Population: 1,419,561 (2014 est.); rank—40th

Principal Cities: capital—Honolulu; largest—Honolulu

Statehood: August 21, 1959; 50th state

U.S. Congress: 2 senators, 2 representatives

State Motto: *Ua mau ke ea o ka'ina i ka pono* ("The life of the land is perpetuated in righteousness")

State Song: "Hawai'i Pono' (Hawaii's Own)"

State Nickname: The Aloha State

Abbreviations: HI

State Symbols: flower—native yellow hibiscus; tree—kukui (candlenut tree); bird—nene (Hawaiian goose)

At a Glance

- With an increase in population of 4.4 percent, Hawaii ranked 12th among the states in growth from 2010 to 2014.

- In 2013, 6.7 percent of Hawaiians did not have health insurance, compared to 14.5 percent of the total U.S. population.

- Hawaii's violent crime rate in 2013 was 251.6 per 100,000 population, compared to 367.9 for the entire nation.

- Hawaii had the highest proportion of state government employees to total residents in 2013, with 40.4 state employees per 1,000 residents, compared to the national average of 13.5 employees per 1,000 residents.

- Hawaiians used 196.7 million Btu of energy per capita in 2013, the third lowest energy consumption in the nation.

Table HI-1. Population by Age, Sex, Race, and Hispanic Origin

(Number, percent, except where noted.)

Sex, age, race, and Hispanic origin	2000	2010	2014[1]	Average annual percent change, 2010–2014
Total Population	1,211,537	1,360,301	1,419,561	1.1
Percent of total U.S. population	0.4	0.4	0.4	X
Sex				
Male	563,891	681,243	718,099	1.3
Female	544,338	679,058	701,462	0.8
Age				
Under 5 years	78,163	87,407	91,480	1.1
5 to 19 years	249,088	250,894	249,179	-0.2
20 to 64 years	723,685	826,868	850,748	0.7
65 years and over	160,601	195,138	228,154	4.0
Median age (years)	36.2	38.6	37.9	-0.5
Race and Hispanic Origin				
One race				
White	294,102	349,051	378,323	2.0
Black	22,003	22,473	34,864	11.6
American Indian and Alaska Native	3,535	4,960	6,356	6.4
Asian	503,868	531,633	532,371	0.0
Native Hawaiian or Other Pacific Islander	113,539	138,292	141,286	0.5
Two or more races	259,343	313,892	326,361	1.0
Hispanic (of any race)	87,699	133,342	143,239	1.8

X = Not applicable.
[1]Population figures for 2014 are July 1 estimates. The 2010 estimates are taken from the 2010 Census.

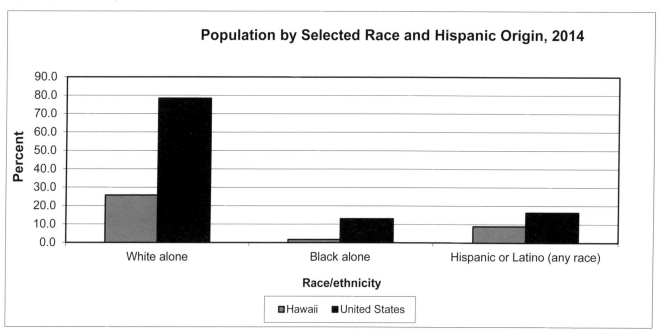

Population by Selected Race and Hispanic Origin, 2014

Table HI-2. Marital Status

(Number, percent distribution.)

Sex, age, race, and Hispanic origin	2000	2010	2013
Males, 15 Years and Over	481,768	554,154	576,976
Never married	34.6	37.8	37.5
Now married, except separated	53.7	49.1	50.5
Separated	1.4	1.2	1.3
Widowed	2.2	2.7	2.5
Divorced	8.1	9.2	8.2
Females, 15 Years and Over	484,107	556,915	568,322
Never married	25.9	28.7	28.9
Now married, except separated	52.5	48.5	49.7
Separated	1.7	1.8	1.6
Widowed	9.8	10.1	9.3
Divorced	10.0	11.0	10.5

Table HI-3. Households and Housing Characteristics

(Number, percent, dollars.)

Item	2000	2010	2013	Average annual percent change, 2000–2013
Total Households	403,240	445,812	450,120	0.8
Family households	287,068	303,075	311,203	0.6
Married-couple family	216,077	224,402	235,190	0.7
Other family	70,991	78,673	76,013	0.5
Male householder, no wife present	21,068	24,247	23,044	0.7
Female householder, no husband present	49,923	54,426	52,969	0.5
Nonfamily households	116,172	142,737	138,917	1.4
Householder living alone	88,153	108,872	109,633	1.7
Householder not living alone	28,019	33,865	30,284	0.6
Housing Characteristics				
Total housing units	460,542	519,992	526,305	1.0
Occupied housing units	403,240	445,812	450,120	0.8
Owner occupied	227,888	258,533	252,999	0.8
Renter occupied	175,352	187,279	197,121	0.9
Average household size	2.92	2.96	3.02	0.3
Financial Characteristics				
Median gross rent of renter-occupied housing	779	1,291	1,414	4.7
Median monthly owner costs for housing units with a mortgage	1,636	2,240	2,220	2.4
Median value of owner-occupied housing units	272,700	525,400	500,000	4.8

Table HI-4. Migration, Origin, and Language

(Number, percent.)

Characteristic	State			U.S.		
	2012	2013	Percent change	2012	2013	Percent change
Residence 1 Year Ago						
Population 1 year and over	1,374,852	1,387,361	0.9	310,212,755	312,432,820	0.7
Same house	84.7	84.9	X	85.0	85.0	X
Different house in the U.S.	13.8	14.0	X	14.4	14.4	X
Same county	9.3	9.3	X	9.0	8.9	X
Different county	4.5	4.7	X	5.4	5.5	X
Same state	0.5	0.5	X	3.2	3.2	X
Different state	4.0	4.2	X	2.3	2.3	X
Abroad	1.5	1.1	X	0.6	0.6	X
Place of Birth						
Native born	1,140,447	1,157,590	1.5	273,089,382	274,780,773	0.6
Male	52.2	52.1	X	49.3	49.3	X
Female	47.8	47.9	X	50.7	50.7	X
Foreign born	251,866	246,464	-2.1	40,824,658	41,348,066	1.3
Male	42.0	43.6	X	48.7	48.8	X
Female	58.0	56.4	X	51.3	51.2	X
Foreign born; naturalized U.S. citizen	140,194	139,732		18,686,237	19,294,710	3.3
Male	39.9	42.3	X	45.8	45.9	X
Female	60.1	57.7	X	54.2	54.1	X
Foreign born; not a U.S. citizen	111,672	106,732	-4.4	22,138,421	22,053,356	-0.4
Male	44.6	45.3	X	51.1	51.3	X
Female	55.4	54.7	X	48.9	48.7	X
Entered 2010 or later	8.0	9.4	X	7.0	9.7	X
Entered 2000 to 2009	27.4	27.5	X	30.4	29.4	X
Entered before 2000	64.7	63.1	X	62.7	61.0	X
World Region of Birth, Foreign						
Foreign-born population, excluding population born at sea	251,866	246,464	-2.1	40,824,553	41,347,945	1.3
Europe	4.6	4.5	X	11.8	11.6	X
Asia	77.7	79.2	X	29.2	29.5	X
Africa	0.7	0.8	X	4.2	4.4	X
Oceania	10.3	9.3	X	0.6	0.5	X
Latin America	4.8	4.1	X	52.2	51.9	X
North America	1.9	2.1	X	2.0	2.0	X
Language Spoken at Home and Ability to Speak English						
Population 5 years and over	1,303,300	1,313,348	0.8	294,003,714	296,358,760	0.8
English only	74.9	74.9	X	79.0	79.2	X
Language other than English	25.1	25.1	X	21.0	20.8	X
Speaks English less than "very well"	12.7	13.1	X	8.5	8.5	X

NA = Not available.
X = Not applicable.
- = Zero or rounds to zero.

Table HI-5. Median Income and Poverty Status, 2013

(Number, percent, except as noted.)

Characteristic	State		U.S.	
	Number	Percent	Number	Percent
Median Income				
Households (dollars)..	68,020	X	52,250	X
Families (dollars)	80,316	X	64,030	X
Below Poverty Level (All People).............................	148,368	10.8	48,810,868	15.8
Sex				
Male...	68,235	9.9	21,938,525	14.5
Female..	80,133	11.8	26,872,343	17.1
Age				
Under 18 years..	40,288	13.3	16,086,960	22.2
Related children under 18 years...........................	38,026	12.7	15,769,921	21.9
18 to 64 years...	92,621	10.9	28,578,191	14.8
65 years and over	15,459	7.2	4,145,717	9.6

X = Not applicable.

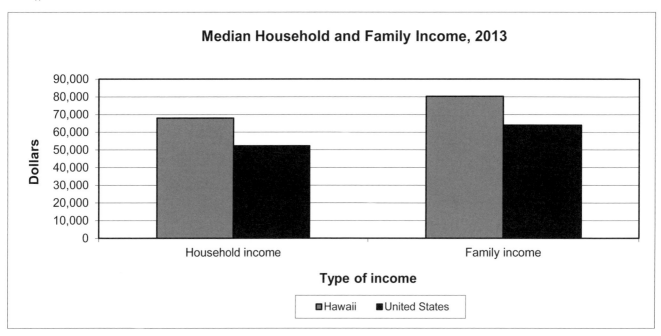

Median Household and Family Income, 2013

Legend: ▨ Hawaii   ■ United States

X-axis: Type of income (Household income, Family income)
Y-axis: Dollars (0 to 90,000)

Table HI-6. Health Insurance Coverage Status for the Civilian Noninstitutionalized Population and Children Under 18 Years of Age

(Numbers in thousands, percent.)

Item	2005	2006	2007	2008	2009	2010	2011	2012	2013
Civilian Noninstitutionalized Population........................	1,279	1,255	1,267	1,237	1,232	1,316	1,326	1,342	1,345
Covered by Private or Public Insurance									
Number...	1,169	1,144	1,172	1,154	1,146	1,212	1,232	1,249	1,254
Percent..	91.4	91.2	92.5	93.3	93.0	92.1	92.9	93.1	93.3
Not Covered									
Number...	110	110	96	83	86	104	94	93	91
Percent..	8.6	8.8	7.5	6.7	7.0	7.9	7.1	6.9	6.7
Percent in the U.S. not covered.................................	15.3	15.8	15.3	15.1	15.1	15.5	15.1	14.8	14.5
Children Under 18 Years of Age.................................	306	298	291	284	288	304	304	303	307
Covered by Private or Public Insurance									
Number...	290	279	277	274	281	293	293	293	298
Percent..	94.7	93.7	47.5	96.5	97.5	96.3	96.4	96.5	97.0
Not Covered									
Number...	16	19	14	10	7	11	11	10	9
Percent..	5.3	6.3	4.8	3.5	2.5	3.7	3.6	3.5	3.0
Percent in the U.S. not covered.................................	10.9	11.7	11.0	9.7	8.6	8.0	7.5	7.2	7.1

Table HI-7. Employment Status by Demographic Group, 2014

(Numbers in thousands, percent.)

Characteristic	Civilian noninstitutional population	Civilian labor force		Employed		Unemployed	
		Number	Percent of population	Number	Percent of population	Number	Percent of population
Total.........	1,084	671	61.9	642	59.2	29	4.4
Sex							
Male.........	528	354	67.1	338	63.9	16	4.7
Female	556	317	57.0	304	54.7	13	4.1
Race, Sex, and Hispanic Origin							
White	235	141	60.1	135	57.4	7	4.6
Male.........	123	83	67.0	79	64.0	4	4.5
Female	112	59	52.6	56	50.0	3	4.9
Black or African American.........	19	13	65.6	11	57.6	2	12.2
Male.........	NA	NA	NA	NA	NA	NA	NA
Female	NA	NA	NA	NA	NA	NA	NA
Hispanic or Latino ethnicity[1]	86	58	67.4	54	62.9	4	6.7
Male.........	41	30	73.4	28	69.4	2	5.5
Female	46	28	62.0	26	57.1	2	7.9
Age							
16 to 19 years.........	73	22	30.0	18	25.2	3	15.7
20 to 24 years.........	105	73	69.2	66	62.5	7	9.7
25 to 34 years.........	166	132	79.6	125	75.7	6	4.9
35 to 44 years.........	162	135	83.5	130	80.6	5	3.5
45 to 54 years.........	179	144	80.4	140	78.7	3	2.1
55 to 64 years.........	181	124	68.5	120	66.4	4	3.1
65 years and over	218	42	19.0	41	18.7	1	1.9

NOTE: Data in Table 7 are from the Current Population Survey (CPS) and do not match the estimates in Table 8. See notes and definitions for further information.
[1]May be of any race.
NA = Not available.

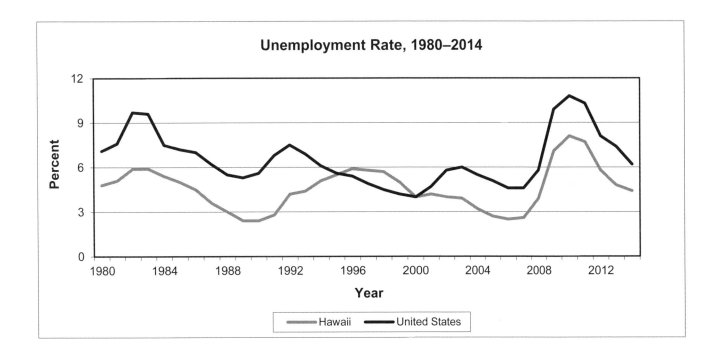

Table HI-8. Employment Status of the Civilian Noninstitutional Population Age 16 Years and Over

(Number, percent.)

Year	Civilian labor force	Civilian participation rate	Employed	Unemployed	Unemployment rate
2006	638,260	66.4	621,573	16,687	2.6
2007	638,395	65.9	620,535	17,860	2.8
2008	639,691	65.6	612,120	27,571	4.3
2009	631,690	64.3	586,522	45,168	7.2
2010	647,249	62.8	602,282	44,967	6.9
2011	660,131	62.6	615,117	45,014	6.8
2012	648,013	60.9	609,088	38,925	6.0
2013	651,080	60.6	619,528	31,552	4.8
2014	668,177	61.6	639,024	29,153	4.4

Table HI-9. Employment and Average Wages by Industry

(Estimates from 2007 through 2010 are based on the 2007 *North American Industry Classification System* [NAICS]. Estimates from 2011 onward are based on the 2012 NAICS.)

Industry	2007	2008	2009	2010	2011	2012	2013
	Number of jobs						
Wage and Salary Employment by Industry	700,378	695,721	668,418	665,430	674,452	681,963	695,044
Farm Wage and Salary Employment	6,331	5,822	5,699	6,087	6,808	6,106	6,359
Nonfarm Wage and Salary Employment	694,047	689,899	662,719	659,343	667,644	675,857	688,685
Private wage and salary employment	517,707	509,528	481,507	477,378	484,522	493,164	506,104
Forestry, fishing, and related activities	1,199	1,193	1,151	1,171	1,285	1,309	1,444
Mining	305	330	340	338	332	298	255
Utilities	3,020	3,086	3,193	3,215	3,329	3,568	3,769
Construction	40,264	39,066	32,516	29,925	29,882	30,114	31,832
Manufacturing	15,303	14,906	13,716	12,954	13,179	13,349	13,575
Durable goods manufacturing	4,625	4,607	4,154	3,793	3,881	3,619	3,633
Nondurable goods manufacturing	10,678	10,299	9,562	9,161	9,298	9,730	9,942
Wholesale trade	18,574	18,937	17,992	17,849	17,596	17,736	17,828
Retail trade	71,331	70,876	67,641	67,119	68,182	69,509	70,371
Transportation and warehousing	30,429	26,686	23,862	23,478	23,997	25,140	25,981
Information	10,721	10,083	9,095	9,931	8,510	8,470	8,811
Finance and insurance	17,386	17,206	16,725	16,154	16,016	16,046	15,771
Real estate and rental and leasing	13,519	13,126	11,864	11,888	11,775	11,811	12,121
Professional, scientific, and technical services	24,959	25,447	25,039	24,553	24,675	24,577	24,625
Management of companies and enterprises	7,620	7,442	7,001	6,649	6,926	7,508	8,252
Administrative and waste services	44,552	43,516	40,458	41,345	44,446	45,578	47,695
Educational services	14,939	15,664	15,778	15,790	16,072	16,502	16,125
Health care and social assistance	60,025	60,819	61,416	62,098	62,401	62,942	64,936
Arts, entertainment, and recreation	12,240	11,767	10,877	10,548	10,836	11,454	12,167
Accommodation and food services	98,788	96,394	90,989	90,918	93,410	96,476	99,698
Other services, except public administration	32,533	32,984	31,854	31,455	31,673	30,777	30,848
Government and government enterprises	176,340	180,371	181,212	181,965	183,122	182,693	182,581
	Dollars						
Average Wages and Salaries by Industry	40,893	42,012	42,708	43,202	44,085	44,885	45,302
Average Farm Wages and Salaries	26,512	28,365	28,219	28,395	29,353	19,847	31,649
Average Nonfarm Wages and Salaries	41,024	42,127	42,833	43,338	44,236	45,111	45,428
Average private wages and salaries	38,389	39,090	39,306	39,925	40,572	41,622	42,253
Forestry, fishing, and related activities	21,793	22,105	21,284	21,976	22,674	23,346	24,458
Mining	81,807	81,870	77,894	73,485	77,443	82,839	88,251
Utilities	75,765	78,450	80,427	83,879	88,489	90,370	92,368
Construction	59,313	62,052	62,750	62,573	63,604	64,809	65,104
Manufacturing	37,680	38,773	38,818	39,245	40,354	40,050	40,699
Durable goods manufacturing	45,647	47,183	47,850	48,272	50,996	49,964	50,807
Nondurable goods manufacturing	34,229	35,012	34,894	35,508	35,912	36,363	37,006
Wholesale trade	47,290	47,975	48,169	48,175	49,747	51,363	52,586
Retail trade	26,798	27,064	27,419	28,193	28,183	28,363	28,814
Transportation and warehousing	38,829	41,197	41,024	42,112	43,535	44,716	46,158
Information	53,494	54,887	55,815	55,593	57,663	58,627	58,561
Finance and insurance	56,595	56,764	56,897	58,145	60,284	63,148	64,483
Real estate and rental and leasing	41,570	40,717	40,386	41,368	42,542	44,025	46,202
Professional, scientific, and technical services	60,197	61,791	62,342	63,054	63,420	65,877	66,729
Management of companies and enterprises	71,907	71,675	71,200	76,806	79,812	83,741	82,599
Administrative and waste services	28,111	29,299	30,283	30,312	29,710	30,840	31,051
Educational services	30,494	31,430	32,337	33,386	34,416	33,477	34,514
Health care and social assistance	41,360	43,364	45,348	45,549	46,630	47,886	48,317
Arts, entertainment, and recreation	28,638	29,078	29,151	28,107	27,292	27,524	28,388
Accommodation and food services	30,276	28,777	27,819	29,329	30,557	31,771	32,209
Other services, except public administration	29,391	30,402	30,727	31,896	32,405	33,326	33,705
Government and government enterprises	48,760	50,707	52,204	52,294	53,929	54,531	54,229

Table HI-10. Employment Characteristics by Family Type

(Number, percent.)

Family type and labor force status	2011		2012		2013	
	Total	Families with own children under 18 years	Total	Families with own children under 18 years	Total	Families with own children under 18 years
All Families...	311,789	125,077	309,165	121,971	311,203	120,365
FAMILY TYPE AND LABOR FORCE STATUS						
Married-Couple Families..	229,641	89,648	229,027	89,864	235,190	91,038
Both husband and wife in labor force...................................	53.0	67.2	54.0	69.1	53.8	66.8
Husband in labor force, wife not in labor force	20.0	26.1	20.0	25.0	21.0	28.8
Wife in labor force, husband not in labor force	8.5	4.0	8.7	4.4	7.8	3.1
Both husband and wife not in labor force................................	18.5	2.8	17.4	1.5	17.1	1.1
Other Families...	82,148	35,429	80,138	32,107	76,013	29,327
Female householder, no husband present................................	68.6	70.0	70.6	76.0	69.7	70.0
In labor force..	41.5	54.9	42.4	59.0	44.3	57.1
Not in labor force	27.1	15.1	28.1	17.0	25.4	12.9
Male householder, no wife present...	31.4	30.0	29.4	24.0	30.3	30.0
In labor force..	23.8	27.8	22.5	22.5	21.7	26.3
Not in labor force	7.6	2.1	6.9	1.5	8.6	3.7

Table HI-11. School Enrollment and Educational Attainment, 2013

(Number, percent.)

Item	State	U.S.
Enrollment		
Total population 3 years and over, enrolled in school	338,688	82,395,254
Enrolled in nursery school or preschool (percent)	5.8	6.0
Enrolled in kindergarten (percent)..	5.7	5.2
Enrolled in elementary school, grades 1-8 (percent)..	38.3	40.0
Enrolled in high school, grades 9-12 (percent)	19.6	20.6
Enrolled in college or graduate school (percent)...	30.6	28.3
Attainment		
Total population 25 years and over	959,903	210,910,615
Less than ninth grade (percent)...	3.9	5.8
9th to 12th grade, no diploma (percent)	5.1	7.6
High school graduate, including equivalency (percent)...	27.4	27.8
Some college, no degree (percent)	22.0	21.1
Associate's degree (percent)..	10.4	8.1
Bachelor's degree (percent)...	20.8	18.4
Graduate or professional degree (percent)...	10.4	11.2
High school graduate or higher (percent)	91.0	86.6
Bachelor's degree or higher (percent)..	31.2	29.6

Table HI-12. Public School Characteristics and Educational Indicators

(Number, percent; data derived from National Center of Education Statistics.)

Item	State	U.S.
Public Schools, 2012–2013 (except where noted)		
Number of school districts...	1	18,093
Number of schools..	286	98,454
Number of students (in thousands)	185	49,771
Number of teachers (in thousands)	12	3,109
Student-teacher ratio...	15.9	16.0
Expenditures per student (dollars), FY 2012	11,973	10,667
Four-year adjusted cohort graduation rate (ACGR)[1,2]	82.4	81.4
Students eligible for free or reduced-price lunch (in thousands)	93	25,188
English language learners (in thousands)	16	4,397
Students age 3 to 21 served under IDEA, part B (in thousands)	20	6,429

Public Schools by Type	Number	Percent of state public schools
Total number of schools..	286	100.0
Regular	284	99.3
Special education...	1	0.3
Vocational education...	0	0.0
Alternative education..	1	0.3

NOTE: Every school is assigned only one school type based on its instructional emphasis.
[1]ACGR data represents a new method of calculating high-school completion rates and may not be comparable to previous years' data for Averaged Freshmen Graduation Rates (AFGR).
[2]The United States 4-year ACGRs were estimated using both the reported 4-year ACGR data from 49 states and the District of Columbia and using imputed data for Idaho. The estimate for American Indian/Alaska Native students also includes imputed data for Virginia.

Table HI-13. Reported Voting and Registration of the Voting-Age Population, November 2012

(Numbers in thousands, percent.)

Item	Total population	Total citizen population	Registered			Voted		
			Total registered	Percent registered (total population)	Percent registered (total citizen population)	Total voted	Percent voted (total population)	Percent voted (total citizen population)
U.S. Total	235,248	215,081	153,157	65.1	71.2	132,948	56.5	61.8
State Total	1,013	930	547	54.1	58.9	480	47.4	51.6
Sex								
Male	493	463	256	51.9	55.3	225	45.7	48.7
Female	520	467	292	56.1	62.4	255	49.1	54.6
Race								
White alone....................................	238	228	170	71.3	74.4	153	64.2	66.9
White, non-Hispanic alone	212	210	160	75.4	76.0	143	67.6	68.2
Black alone....................................	18	18	12	B	B	12	B	B
Asian alone	459	403	227	49.5	56.3	201	43.7	49.7
Hispanic (of any race).....................	81	73	33	41.0	B	25	31.4	B
White alone or in combination	362	350	236	65.3	67.5	208	57.4	59.3
Black alone or in combination..........	27	27	18	B	B	18	B	B
Asian alone or in combination..........	568	511	287	50.5	56.1	250	44.1	49.0
Age								
18 to 24 years...............................	107	91	33	30.6	36.0	24	22.1	26.0
25 to 44 years...............................	338	307	148	43.9	48.3	124	36.6	40.3
45 to 64 years...............................	343	317	217	63.2	68.4	196	57.0	61.8
65 to 74 years...............................	124	119	79	63.8	66.5	73	59.1	61.6
75 years and over	100	96	70	70.1	73.4	63	63.4	66.3

B = Base is less than 75,000 and therefore too small to show the derived measure.

Table HI-14. Crime

(Number, rate per 100,000. Data are derived from the FBI Uniform Crime Reports.)

Item	State			U.S.[1,2,3,4]		
	2012	2013	Percent change	2012	2013	Percent change
TOTAL POPULATION[5]...	1,390,090	1,404,054	1.0	313,873,685	316,128,839	0.7
VIOLENT CRIME						
Number..	3,378	3,444	2.0	1,217,067	1,163,146	-4.4
Rate	243.0	245.3	0.9	387.8	367.9	-5.1
Murder and Nonnegligent Manslaughter						
Number..	21	21	-	14,866	14,196	-4.5
Rate	1.5	1.5		4.7	4.5	-5.2
Rape[6]						
Number..	X	385	X	X	108,612	X
Rate	X	27.4	X	X	34.4	X
Robbery						
Number..	1,125	1,131	0.5	355,051	345,031	-2.8
Rate	80.9	80.6	-0.5	113.1	109.1	-3.5
Aggravated Assault						
Number..	1,953	1,996	2.2	762,009	724,149	-5.0
Rate	140.5	142.2	1.2	242.8	229.1	-5.6
PROPERTY CRIME						
Number..	43,419	42,875	-1.3	9,001,992	8,632,512	-4.1
Rate	3,123.5	3,053.7	-2.2	2,868.0	2,730.7	-4.8
Burglary						
Number..	7,653	7,533	-1.6	2,109,932	1,928,465	-8.6
Rate	550.5	536.5	-2.5	672.2	610.0	-9.3
Larceny-Theft						
Number..	31,901	31,658	-0.8	6,168,874	6,004,453	-2.7
Rate	2,294.9	2,254.8	-1.7	1,965.4	1,899.4	-3.4
Motor Vehicle Theft						
Number..	3,865	3,684	-4.7	723,186	699,594	-3.3
Rate	278.0	262.4	-5.6	230.4	221.3	-4.0

NOTE: Although arson data are included in the trend and clearance tables, sufficient data are not available to estimate totals for this offense. Therefore, no arson data are published in this table.
X = Not applicable.
- = Zero or rounds to zero.
[1]The crime figures have been adjusted.
[2]The data collection methodology for the offense of forcible rape used by the Minnesota state Uniform Crime Reporting (UCR) Program (with the exception of Minneapolis and St. Paul, Minnesota) does not comply with national UCR Program guidelines. Consequently, its figures for forcible rape and violent crime (of which forcible rape is a part) are not published in this table.
[3]Includes offenses reported by the Zoological Police and the Metro Transit Police.
[4]Because of changes in the state's reporting practices, figures are not comparable to previous years' data.
[5]Populations are U.S. Census Bureau provisional estimates as of July 1 of each year.
[6]The figures shown for the offense of rape were estimated using the revised Uniform Crime Reporting (UCR) definition of rape.

Table HI-15. State Government Finances, 2013

(Dollar amounts in thousands, percent distribution.)

Item	Dollars	Percent distribution
Total Revenue	12,944,952	100.0
General revenue	10,825,114	83.6
Intergovernmental revenue	2,331,449	18.0
Taxes	6,092,893	47.1
General sales	2,944,487	22.7
Selective sales	987,733	7.6
License taxes	230,189	1.8
Individual income tax	1,735,718	13.4
Corporate income tax	123,661	1.0
Other taxes	71,105	0.5
Current charges	1,626,827	12.6
Miscellaneous general revenue	773,945	6.0
Utility revenue	0	-
Liquor stores revenue	0	-
Insurance trust revenue[1]	2,119,838	16.4
Total Expenditure	11,477,711	100.0
Intergovernmental expenditure	220,844	1.9
Direct expenditure	11,256,867	98.1
Current operation	8,491,719	74.0
Capital outlay	897,975	7.8
Insurance benefits and repayments	1,374,043	12.0
Assistance and subsidies	144,068	1.3
Interest on debt	349,062	3.0
Exhibit: Salaries and wages	2,310,366	20.1
Total Expenditure	11,477,711	100.0
General expenditure	10,098,104	88.0
Intergovernmental expenditure	220,844	1.9
Direct expenditure	9,877,260	86.1
General expenditure, by function:		
Education	3,404,040	29.7
Public welfare	2,098,924	18.3
Hospitals	799,790	7.0
Health	494,927	4.3
Highways	409,269	3.6
Police protection	34,307	0.3
Correction	200,984	1.8
Natural resources	113,135	1.0
Parks and recreation	95,856	0.8
Governmental administration	413,238	3.6
Interest on general debt	349,062	3.0
Other and unallocable	1,684,572	14.7
Utility expenditure	5,564	-
Liquor stores expenditure	0	-
Insurance trust expenditure	1,374,043	12.0
Debt at End of Fiscal Year	8,318,403	X
Cash and Security Holdings	16,242,691	X

X = Not applicable.
- = Zero or rounds to zero.
[1]Within insurance trust revenue, net earnings of state retirement systems is a calculated statistic (the item code in the data file is X08), and thus can be positive or negative. Net earnings is the sum of earnings on investments plus gains on investments minus losses on investments. The change made in 2002 for asset valuation from book to market value in accordance with Statement 34 of the Governmental Accounting Standards Board is reflected in the calculated statistics.

Table HI-16. State Government Tax Collections, 2014

(Dollars in thousands, percent.)

Item	Dollars	Percent distribution
Total Taxes	6,033,331	100.0
Property taxes	X	X
Sales and gross receipts	3,847,662	63.8
General sales and gross receipts	2,825,041	46.8
Selective sales and gross receipts	1,022,621	16.9
Alcoholic beverages	48,305	0.8
Amusements	0	-
Insurance premiums	142,051	2.4
Motor fuels	93,598	1.6
Pari-mutuels	0	-
Public utilities	166,179	2.8
Tobacco products	107,685	1.8
Other selective sales	464,803	7.7
Licenses	223,543	3.7
Alcoholic beverages	0	-
Amusements	0	-
Corporations in general	1,691	-
Hunting and fishing	536	-
Motor vehicle	168,980	2.8
Motor vehicle operators	360	-
Public utilities	21,183	0.4
Occupation and business, NEC	29,480	0.5
Other licenses	1,313	-
Income taxes	1,871,506	31.0
Individual income	1,745,461	28.9
Corporation net income	126,045	2.1
Other taxes	90,620	1.5
Death and gift	14,789	0.2
Documentary and stock transfer	75,831	1.3
Severance	X	X
Taxes, NEC	0	-

X = Not applicable.
- = Zero or rounds to zero.

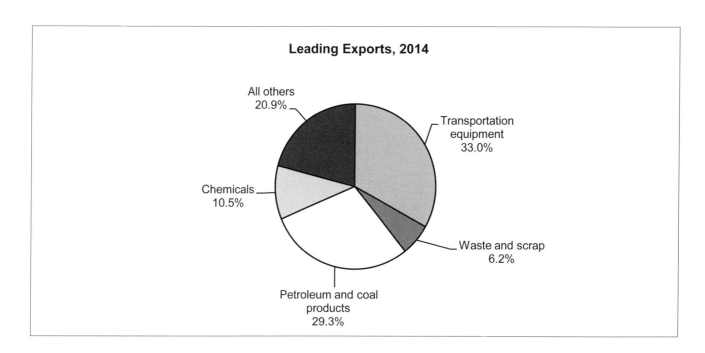

Leading Exports, 2014

All others 20.9%

Transportation equipment 33.0%

Chemicals 10.5%

Waste and scrap 6.2%

Petroleum and coal products 29.3%

Facts and Figures

Location: Northwestern United States; bordered on the N by Canada, on the E by Montana and Wyoming, on the S by Nevada and Utah, and on the W by Washington and Oregon

Area: 83,568 sq. mi. (216,446 sq. km.); rank—14th

Population: 1,634,464 (2014 est.); rank—39th

Principal Cities: capital—Boise; largest—Boise

Statehood: July 3, 1890; 43rd state

U.S. Congress: 2 senators, 2 representatives

State Motto: *Esto perpetua* ("Let it be perpetual")

State Song: "Here We Have Idaho"

State Nickname: The Gem State

Abbreviations: ID

State Symbols: flower—syringa (mock orange); tree—Western white pine; bird—mountain bluebird

At a Glance

- With an increase in population of 4.3 percent, Idaho ranked 13th among the states in growth from 2010 to 2014.

- With 1,864.3 incidents per 100,000 population, Idaho had the second lowest property crime rate in the country in 2013.

- Idaho's violent crime rate in 2013 was 217.0 per 100,000 population, compared to 367.9 for the entire nation.

- With 26.4 percent of its population under age 18, Idaho (tied with Texas) ranked 2nd among the states for the highest percent of children in 2014.

- In 2013, 77.5 percent of Idahoans lived in single-unit attached or detached housing, compared to 68.7 of the entire U.S. population.

Table ID-1. Population by Age, Sex, Race, and Hispanic Origin

(Number, percent, except where noted.)

Sex, age, race, and Hispanic origin	2000	2010	2014[1]	Average annual percent change, 2010–2014
Total Population	1,293,953	1,567,582	1,634,464	1.0
Percent of total U.S. population	0.5	0.5	0.5	X
Sex				
Male	648,660	785,324	818,496	1.0
Female	645,293	782,258	815,968	1.1
Age				
Under 5 years	97,643	121,772	113,832	-1.7
5 to 19 years	316,222	353,509	360,962	0.5
20 to 64 years	734,172	897,633	926,294	0.8
65 years and over	145,916	194,668	233,376	4.6
Median age (years)	33.2	34.6	35.7	0.8
Race and Hispanic Origin				
One race				
White	1,177,304	1,476,097	1,528,744	0.9
Black	5,456	10,950	13,507	5.4
American Indian and Alaska Native	17,645	25,782	28,152	2.2
Asian	11,889	20,034	23,180	3.7
Native Hawaiian or Other Pacific Islander	1,308	2,786	3,302	4.3
Two or more races	25,609	31,933	37,579	4.2
Hispanic (of any race)	101,690	182,424	196,502	1.9

X = Not applicable.
[1]Population figures for 2014 are July 1 estimates. The 2010 estimates are taken from the 2010 Census.

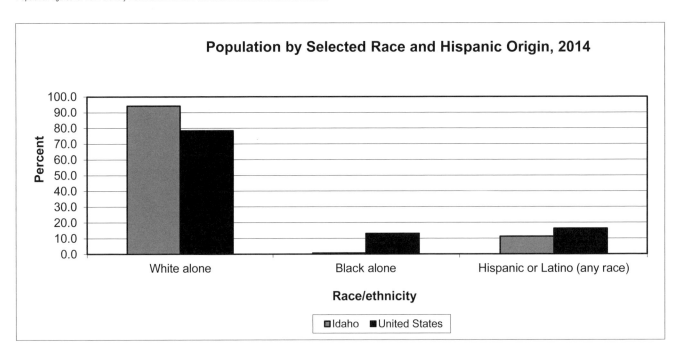

Table ID-2. Marital Status

(Number, percent distribution.)

Sex, age, race, and Hispanic origin	2000	2010	2013
Males, 15 Years and Over	493,045	602,308	626,569
Never married	26.1	28.3	59.8
Now married, except separated	61.0	57.0	55.7
Separated	1.0	1.4	0.8
Widowed	2.1	2.4	2.7
Divorced	9.9	10.9	11.1
Females, 15 Years and Over	498,579	608,900	628,790
Never married	19.6	22.4	22.3
Now married, except separated	59.0	55.3	54.6
Separated	1.3	1.6	1.5
Widowed	8.6	7.6	8.2
Divorced	11.4	13.1	13.4

Table ID-3. Households and Housing Characteristics

(Number, percent, dollars.)

Item	2000	2010	2013	Average annual percent change, 2000–2013
Total Households	469,645	576,709	588,489	1.8
Family households	333,588	401,806	410,061	1.6
Married-couple family	276,511	322,129	324,922	1.2
Other family	59,077	79,677	85,139	2.9
Male householder, no wife present	18,228	23,583	27,618	3.2
Female householder, no husband present	40,849	56,094	57,521	2.7
Nonfamily households	134,057	174,903	178,428	2.2
Householder living alone	105,175	139,909	141,672	2.3
Householder not living alone	28,882	34,994	36,756	1.9
Housing Characteristics				
Total housing units	527,824	668,634	676,192	1.9
Occupied housing units	469,645	576,709	588,489	1.8
Owner occupied	339,960	401,532	408,174	1.4
Renter occupied	129,685	175,177	180,315	2.6
Average household size	2.69	2.67	2.69	-
Financial Characteristics				
Median gross rent of renter-occupied housing	515	683	725	2.7
Median monthly owner costs for housing units with a mortgage	887	1,187	1,142	2.0
Median value of owner-occupied housing units	106,300	165,100	159,000	3.1

- = Zero or rounds to zero

Table ID-4. Migration, Origin, and Language

(Number, percent.)

Characteristic	State			U.S.		
	2012	2013	Percent change	2012	2013	Percent change
Residence 1 Year Ago						
Population 1 year and over	1,573,036	1,592,596	1.2	310,212,755	312,432,820	0.7
Same house	82.5	82.7	X	85.0	85.0	X
Different house in the U.S.	17.1	16.8	X	14.4	14.4	X
Same county	9.7	9.4	X	9.0	8.9	X
Different county	7.4	7.4	X	5.4	5.5	X
Same state	3.6	3.5	X	3.2	3.2	X
Different state	3.8	3.9	X	2.3	2.3	X
Abroad	0.4	0.5	X	0.6	0.6	X
Place of Birth						
Native born	1,499,160	1,516,611	1.2	273,089,382	274,780,773	0.6
Male	50.0	50.3	X	49.3	49.3	X
Female	50.0	49.7	X	50.7	50.7	X
Foreign born	96,568	95,525	-1.1	40,824,658	41,348,066	1.3
Male	50.3	51.1	X	48.7	48.8	X
Female	49.7	48.9	X	51.3	51.2	X
Foreign born; naturalized U.S. citizen	37,220	35,903	-3.5	18,686,237	19,294,710	3.3
Male	42.8	44.5	X	45.8	45.9	X
Female	57.2	55.5	X	54.2	54.1	X
Foreign born; not a U.S. citizen	59,348	59,622	0.5	22,138,421	22,053,356	-0.4
Male	55.0	55.0	X	51.1	51.3	X
Female	45.0	45.0	X	48.9	48.7	X
Entered 2010 or later	6.0	14.6	X	7.0	9.7	X
Entered 2000 to 2009	28.8	28.6	X	30.4	29.4	X
Entered before 2000	65.2	56.8	X	62.7	61.0	X
World Region of Birth, Foreign						
Foreign-born population, excluding population born at sea	96,568	95,525	-1.1	40,824,553	41,347,945	1.3
Europe	15.2	13.7	X	11.8	11.6	X
Asia	17.6	20.2	X	29.2	29.5	X
Africa	1.8	3.0	X	4.2	4.4	X
Oceania	1.0	1.2	X	0.6	0.5	X
Latin America	59.6	57.2	X	52.2	51.9	X
North America	4.9	4.7	X	2.0	2.0	X
Language Spoken at Home and Ability to Speak English						
Population 5 years and over	1,481,992	1,500,897	1.3	294,003,714	296,358,760	0.8
English only	89.6	89.1	X	79.0	79.2	X
Language other than English	10.4	10.9	X	21.0	20.8	X
Speaks English less than "very well"	3.9	4.1	X	8.5	8.5	X

NA = Not available.
X = Not applicable.
- = Zero or rounds to zero.

Table ID-5. Median Income and Poverty Status, 2013

(Number, percent, except as noted.)

Characteristic	State		U.S.	
	Number	Percent	Number	Percent
Median Income				
Households (dollars)........................	46,783	X	52,250	X
Families (dollars)	56,176	X	64,030	X
Below Poverty Level (All People)	246,550	15.6	48,810,868	15.8
Sex				
Male..	118,309	14.9	21,938,525	14.5
Female	128,241	16.2	26,872,343	17.1
Age				
Under 18 years..............................	80,676	19.1	16,086,960	22.2
Related children under 18 years..............	78,895	18.8	15,769,921	21.9
18 to 64 years	147,855	15.7	28,578,191	14.8
65 years and over	18,019	8.2	4,145,717	9.6

X = Not applicable.

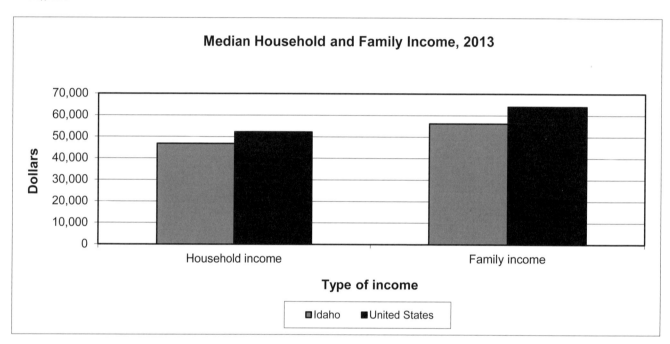

Table ID-6. Health Insurance Coverage Status for the Civilian Noninstitutionalized Population and Children Under 18 Years of Age

(Numbers in thousands, percent.)

Item	2005	2006	2007	2008	2009	2010	2011	2012	2013
Civilian Noninstitutionalized Population............................	1,442	1,475	1,501	1,499	1,521	1,552	1,566	1,576	1,592
Covered by Private or Public Insurance									
Number..	1,229	1,248	1,292	1,232	1,256	1,276	1,307	1,321	1,335
Percent..	85.2	84.6	86.1	82.2	82.6	82.3	83.5	83.8	83.8
Not Covered									
Number..	213	227	209	267	264	275	259	255	257
Percent..	14.8	15.4	13.9	17.8	17.4	17.7	16.5	16.2	16.2
Percent in the U.S. not covered........................	15.3	15.8	15.3	15.1	15.1	15.5	15.1	14.8	14.5
Children Under 18 Years of Age........................	394	420	415	413	418	428	427	424	426
Covered by Private or Public Insurance									
Number..	349	350	369	357	371	383	388	388	388
Percent..	88.6	87.0	89.0	86.4	88.8	89.5	90.9	91.5	91.1
Not Covered									
Number..	45	52	46	56	47	45	39	36	38
Percent..	11.4	13.0	11.0	13.6	11.2	10.5	9.1	8.5	8.9
Percent in the U.S. not covered........................	10.9	11.7	11.0	9.7	8.6	8.0	7.5	7.2	7.1

Table ID-7. Employment Status by Demographic Group, 2014

(Numbers in thousands, percent.)

Characteristic	Civilian noninstitutional population	Civilian labor force		Employed		Unemployed	
		Number	Percent of population	Number	Percent of population	Number	Percent of population
Total..	1,228	775	63.1	738	60.1	37	4.7
Sex							
Male...	605	426	70.5	405	67.0	21	5.0
Female	623	348	55.9	333	53.4	15	4.4
Race, Sex, and Hispanic Origin							
White...	1,163	734	63.1	700	60.2	34	4.6
Male...	574	403	70.2	384	66.8	20	4.8
Female	589	330	56.1	316	53.7	14	4.3
Black or African American.......................................	NA	NA	NA	NA	NA	NA	NA
Male...	NA	NA	NA	NA	NA	NA	NA
Female	NA	NA	NA	NA	NA	NA	NA
Hispanic or Latino ethnicity[1]	130	94	72.2	86	66.4	8	8.1
Male...	70	58	83.8	54	77.5	4	7.6
Female	60	35	58.7	32	53.5	3	8.9
Age							
16 to 19 years...	99	38	38.9	33	33.2	6	14.7
20 to 24 years...	116	84	72.9	76	65.9	8	9.7
25 to 34 years...	198	159	80.3	152	76.7	7	4.4
35 to 44 years...	191	157	81.8	151	78.9	6	3.5
45 to 54 years...	214	174	81.2	169	78.7	5	3.0
55 to 64 years...	189	123	65.1	120	63.5	3	2.5
65 years and over...	221	40	17.9	38	17.0	2	4.8

NOTE: Data in Table 7 are from the Current Population Survey (CPS) and do not match the estimates in Table 8. See notes and definitions for further information.
[1]May be of any race.
NA = Not available.

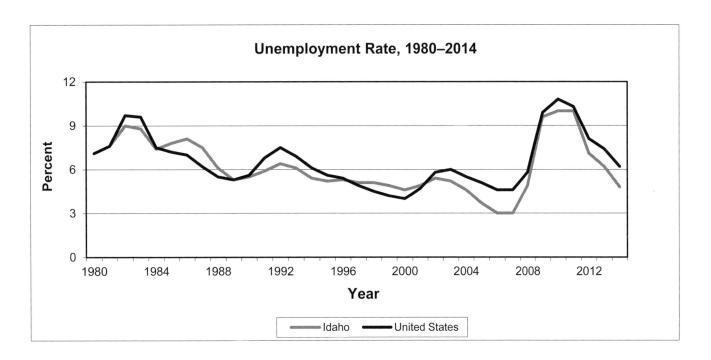

Unemployment Rate, 1980–2014

Table ID-8. Employment Status of the Civilian Noninstitutional Population Age 16 Years and Over

(Number, percent.)

Year	Civilian labor force	Civilian participation rate	Employed	Unemployed	Unemployment rate
2006	747,377	68.8	721,346	26,031	3.5
2007	754,438	67.8	731,235	23,203	3.1
2008	755,153	66.6	716,653	38,500	5.1
2009	757,131	65.8	690,722	66,409	8.8
2010	761,056	65.3	692,826	68,230	9.0
2011	764,890	64.9	701,645	63,245	8.3
2012	769,429	64.5	714,051	55,378	7.2
2013	771,154	63.7	724,121	47,033	6.1
2014	777,238	63.3	739,834	37,404	4.8

Table ID-9. Employment and Average Wages by Industry

(Estimates from 2007 through 2010 are based on the 2007 *North American Industry Classification System* [NAICS]. Estimates from 2011 onward are based on the 2012 NAICS.)

Industry	2007	2008	2009	2010	2011	2012	2013
				Number of jobs			
Wage and Salary Employment by Industry	701,608	694,229	653,408	646,725	649,999	654,214	670,896
Farm Wage and Salary Employment	14,490	15,287	14,323	14,700	16,442	17,023	17,526
Nonfarm Wage and Salary Employment	687,118	678,942	639,085	632,025	633,557	637,191	653,370
Private wage and salary employment	560,150	550,215	510,255	503,538	507,403	510,169	526,463
Forestry, fishing, and related activities	7,630	7,502	7,128	7,316	7,485	7,094	7,975
Mining	2,655	2,780	2,167	2,273	2,568	2,674	2,547
Utilities	2,069	2,161	2,098	2,729	2,798	2,826	2,805
Construction	54,383	47,063	36,067	32,693	31,140	30,563	32,942
Manufacturing	66,436	63,059	55,052	53,383	54,598	56,599	59,248
Durable goods manufacturing	42,473	38,378	31,182	29,954	31,309	32,653	34,072
Nondurable goods manufacturing	23,963	24,681	23,870	23,429	23,289	23,946	25,176
Wholesale trade	28,238	27,922	26,315	25,950	26,413	27,007	28,285
Retail trade	84,629	83,774	77,551	76,232	76,151	77,178	78,698
Transportation and warehousing	19,340	19,358	18,402	18,377	18,504	18,693	18,673
Information	10,920	11,075	10,077	9,702	9,424	9,312	9,256
Finance and insurance	22,248	21,997	21,063	20,980	21,343	21,359	21,768
Real estate and rental and leasing	9,081	8,615	7,515	7,168	6,924	6,726	6,889
Professional, scientific, and technical services	34,598	34,494	33,003	32,795	32,794	31,686	31,339
Management of companies and enterprises	7,846	7,250	6,719	5,863	5,874	5,916	5,435
Administrative and waste services	41,401	40,620	36,959	36,571	37,024	37,393	39,922
Educational services	9,677	9,890	10,043	10,295	10,585	11,009	11,176
Health care and social assistance	67,347	70,562	73,380	76,111	77,474	77,998	80,852
Arts, entertainment, and recreation	9,131	9,038	8,704	8,621	8,663	9,077	9,394
Accommodation and food services	54,675	54,748	50,606	50,047	51,144	52,081	53,763
Other services, except public administration	27,846	28,307	27,406	26,432	26,497	24,978	25,496
Government and government enterprises	126,968	128,727	128,830	128,487	126,154	127,022	126,907
				Dollars			
Average Wages and Salaries by Industry	34,391	34,651	35,066	35,781	36,452	36,911	37,800
Average Farm Wages and Salaries	39,021	35,696	42,301	35,808	33,216	27,421	39,897
Average Nonfarm Wages and Salaries	34,293	34,628	34,904	35,781	36,536	37,165	37,744
Average private wages and salaries	34,331	34,467	34,647	35,729	36,595	37,241	37,963
Forestry, fishing, and related activities	27,313	27,349	26,300	27,268	28,854	28,618	29,434
Mining	56,599	59,909	57,883	67,925	69,470	71,675	76,081
Utilities	59,417	62,911	65,184	73,834	75,159	77,161	79,131
Construction	37,952	38,167	37,942	39,040	39,436	40,207	39,915
Manufacturing	47,408	48,028	48,132	50,941	51,881	52,287	54,819
Durable goods manufacturing	53,096	54,184	54,423	58,795	58,355	58,267	62,185
Nondurable goods manufacturing	37,327	38,455	39,913	40,900	43,177	44,134	44,849
Wholesale trade	45,542	45,887	45,910	47,440	48,927	49,857	51,222
Retail trade	25,652	25,270	25,330	25,847	26,308	27,024	27,684
Transportation and warehousing	36,201	37,119	37,036	37,745	39,150	40,133	41,463
Information	39,759	41,268	41,888	42,599	44,478	47,257	46,788
Finance and insurance	47,936	47,440	47,444	48,734	49,575	52,832	54,124
Real estate and rental and leasing	29,602	28,616	28,478	28,465	28,854	30,455	32,061
Professional, scientific, and technical services	50,967	52,533	54,833	56,536	58,158	57,439	59,088
Management of companies and enterprises	83,910	77,648	78,219	81,421	87,177	90,193	87,420
Administrative and waste services	25,026	25,777	26,126	26,740	27,217	27,362	27,112
Educational services	23,988	24,594	25,495	26,243	26,993	27,204	27,177
Health care and social assistance	34,300	35,224	35,982	36,401	37,454	37,600	38,706
Arts, entertainment, and recreation	20,960	19,585	18,399	19,522	18,973	18,802	19,335
Accommodation and food services	14,484	14,306	14,482	15,110	15,442	15,835	15,730
Other services, except public administration	22,461	23,208	23,040	23,855	24,065	25,553	26,252
Government and government enterprises	34,127	35,315	35,921	35,983	36,296	36,859	36,835

Table ID-10. Employment Characteristics by Family Type

(Number, percent.)

Family type and labor force status	2011		2012		2013	
	Total	Families with own children under 18 years	Total	Families with own children under 18 years	Total	Families with own children under 18 years
All Families	398,682	180,257	405,908	184,148	410,061	190,524
FAMILY TYPE AND LABOR FORCE STATUS						
Married-Couple Families	319,270	132,413	322,225	133,177	324,922	137,775
Both husband and wife in labor force	50.8	60.3	49.7	62.6	48.9	60.1
Husband in labor force, wife not in labor force	23.4	34.1	24.1	31.9	25.1	34.6
Wife in labor force, husband not in labor force	7.2	3.9	7.6	3.8	7.5	3.2
Both husband and wife not in labor force	18.6	1.8	18.6	1.7	18.3	2.0
Other Families	79,412	47,844	83,683	50,971	85,139	52,749
Female householder, no husband present	68.3	70.2	70.9	70.8	67.6	67.1
In labor force	48.4	56.1	50.8	57.7	46.1	53.4
Not in labor force	19.9	14.2	20.1	13.1	21.4	13.7
Male householder, no wife present	31.7	29.8	29.1	29.2	32.4	32.9
In labor force	25.2	26.8	23.6	26.7	26.1	29.5
Not in labor force	6.5	3.0	5.5	2.4	6.4	3.3

Table ID-11. School Enrollment and Educational Attainment, 2013

(Number, percent.)

Item	State	U.S.
Enrollment		
Total population 3 years and over, enrolled in school	435,040	82,395,254
Enrolled in nursery school or preschool (percent)	4.9	6.0
Enrolled in kindergarten (percent)	5.3	5.2
Enrolled in elementary school, grades 1-8 (percent)	44.4	40.0
Enrolled in high school, grades 9-12 (percent)	21.4	20.6
Enrolled in college or graduate school (percent)	24.0	28.3
Attainment		
Total population 25 years and over	1,026,889	210,910,615
Less than ninth grade (percent)	4.3	5.8
9th to 12th grade, no diploma (percent)	6.3	7.6
High school graduate, including equivalency (percent)	27.4	27.8
Some college, no degree (percent)	26.7	21.1
Associate's degree (percent)	9.1	8.1
Bachelor's degree (percent)	18.0	18.4
Graduate or professional degree (percent)	8.2	11.2
High school graduate or higher (percent)	89.4	86.6
Bachelor's degree or higher (percent)	26.2	29.6

Table ID-12. Public School Characteristics and Educational Indicators

(Number, percent; data derived from National Center of Education Statistics.)

Item	State	U.S.
Public Schools, 2012–2013 (except where noted)		
Number of school districts	149	18,093
Number of schools	719	98,454
Number of students (in thousands)	285	49,771
Number of teachers (in thousands)	15	3,109
Student-teacher ratio	19.6	16.0
Expenditures per student (dollars), FY 2012	6,626	10,667
Four-year adjusted cohort graduation rate (ACGR)[1,2]	NA	81.4
Students eligible for free or reduced-price lunch (in thousands)	135	25,188
English language learners (in thousands)	17	4,397
Students age 3 to 21 served under IDEA, part B (in thousands)	27	6,429

Public Schools by Type	Number	Percent of state public schools
Total number of schools	719	100.0
Regular	629	87.5
Special education	11	1.5
Vocational education	10	1.4
Alternative education	69	9.6

NOTE: Every school is assigned only one school type based on its instructional emphasis.
[1]ACGR data represents a new method of calculating high-school completion rates and may not be comparable to previous years' data for Averaged Freshmen Graduation Rates (AFGR).
[2]The United States 4-year ACGRs were estimated using both the reported 4-year ACGR data from 49 states and the District of Columbia and using imputed data for Idaho. The estimate for American Indian/Alaska Native students also includes imputed data for Virginia.
NA = Not available.

Table ID-13. Reported Voting and Registration of the Voting-Age Population, November 2012

(Numbers in thousands, percent.)

Item	Total population	Total citizen population	Registered			Voted		
			Total registered	Percent registered (total population)	Percent registered (total citizen population)	Total voted	Percent voted (total population)	Percent voted (total citizen population)
U.S. Total	235,248	215,081	153,157	65.1	71.2	132,948	56.5	61.8
State Total	1,129	1,064	745	65.9	70.0	679	60.2	63.9
Sex								
Male	553	519	354	64.1	68.3	323	58.4	62.2
Female	577	545	390	67.7	71.6	357	61.8	65.4
Race								
White alone....................................	1,077	1,021	726	67.4	71.1	661	61.4	64.8
White, non-Hispanic alone	960	956	691	72.0	72.3	634	66.1	66.4
Black alone.....................................	7	7	-	B	B	-	B	B
Asian alone	15	6	2	B	B	2	B	B
Hispanic (of any race)......................	119	68	35	29.6	B	27	22.5	B
White alone or in combination	1,093	1,037	735	67.3	70.9	670	61.3	64.6
Black alone or in combination..........	9	9	1	B	B	1	B	B
Asian alone or in combination..........	19	9	5	B	B	5	B	B
Age								
18 to 24 years.................................	130	121	51	39.0	41.8	39	29.8	31.9
25 to 44 years.................................	397	359	256	64.4	71.1	231	58.1	64.2
45 to 64 years.................................	401	382	274	68.3	71.7	250	62.3	65.4
65 to 74 years.................................	112	112	90	80.7	80.7	86	77.1	77.1
75 years and over	89	89	74	82.6	82.6	74	82.6	82.6

- = Zero or rounds to zero.
B = Base is less than 75,000 and therefore too small to show the derived measure.

Table ID-14. Crime

(Number, rate per 100,000. Data are derived from the FBI Uniform Crime Reports.)

Item	State			U.S.[1,2,3,4]		
	2012	2013	Percent change	2012	2013	Percent change
TOTAL POPULATION[5]...........................	1,595,590	1,612,136	1.0	313,873,685	316,128,839	0.7
VIOLENT CRIME						
Number....................................	3,348	3,300	-1.4	1,217,067	1,163,146	-4.4
Rate	209.8	204.7	-2.4	387.8	367.9	-5.1
Murder and Nonnegligent Manslaughter						
Number....................................	30	27	-10.0	14,866	14,196	-4.5
Rate	1.9	1.7	-10.9	4.7	4.5	-5.2
Rape[6]						
Number....................................	X	655	X	X	108,612	X
Rate	X	40.6	X	X	34.4	X
Robbery						
Number....................................	243	220	-9.5	355,051	345,031	-2.8
Rate	15.2	13.6	-10.4	113.1	109.1	-3.5
Aggravated Assault						
Number....................................	2,580	2,596	0.6	762,009	724,149	-5.0
Rate	161.7	161.0	-0.4	242.8	229.1	-5.6
PROPERTY CRIME						
Number....................................	31,825	30,055	-5.6	9,001,992	8,632,512	-4.1
Rate	1,994.6	1,864.3	-6.5	2,868.0	2,730.7	-4.8
Burglary						
Number....................................	7,240	6,640	-8.3	2,109,932	1,928,465	-8.6
Rate	453.8	411.9	-9.2	672.2	610.0	-9.3
Larceny-Theft						
Number....................................	23,203	21,879	-5.7	6,168,874	6,004,453	-2.7
Rate	1,454.2	1,357.1	-6.7	1,965.4	1,899.4	-3.4
Motor Vehicle Theft						
Number....................................	1,382	1,536	11.1	723,186	699,594	-3.3
Rate	86.6	95.3	10.0	230.4	221.3	-4.0

NOTE: Although arson data are included in the trend and clearance tables, sufficient data are not available to estimate totals for this offense. Therefore, no arson data are published in this table.
X = Not applicable.
- = Zero or rounds to zero.
[1]The crime figures have been adjusted.
[2]The data collection methodology for the offense of forcible rape used by the Minnesota state Uniform Crime Reporting (UCR) Program (with the exception of Minneapolis and St. Paul, Minnesota) does not comply with national UCR Program guidelines. Consequently, its figures for forcible rape and violent crime (of which forcible rape is a part) are not published in this table.
[3]Includes offenses reported by the Zoological Police and the Metro Transit Police.
[4]Because of changes in the state's reporting practices, figures are not comparable to previous years' data.
[5]Populations are U.S. Census Bureau provisional estimates as of July 1 of each year.
[6]The figures shown for the offense of rape were estimated using the revised Uniform Crime Reporting (UCR) definition of rape.

Table ID-15. State Government Finances, 2013

(Dollar amounts in thousands, percent distribution.)

Item	Dollars	Percent distribution
Total Revenue	9,391,142	100.0
General revenue	7,340,263	78.2
Intergovernmental revenue	2,541,438	27.1
Taxes	3,579,093	38.1
General sales	1,324,182	14.1
Selective sales	449,088	4.8
License taxes	306,627	3.3
Individual income tax	1,292,562	13.8
Corporate income tax	200,340	2.1
Other taxes	6,294	0.1
Current charges	717,549	7.6
Miscellaneous general revenue	502,183	5.3
Utility revenue	0	-
Liquor stores revenue	136,717	1.5
Insurance trust revenue[1]	1,914,162	20.4
Total Expenditure	8,530,858	100.0
Intergovernmental expenditure	1,981,659	23.2
Direct expenditure	6,549,199	76.8
Current operation	4,653,245	54.5
Capital outlay	551,740	6.5
Insurance benefits and repayments	1,048,593	12.3
Assistance and subsidies	133,844	1.6
Interest on debt	161,777	1.9
Exhibit: Salaries and wages	1,090,045	12.8
Total Expenditure	8,530,858	100.0
General expenditure	7,378,235	86.5
Intergovernmental expenditure	1,981,659	23.2
Direct expenditure	5,396,576	63.3
General expenditure, by function:		
Education	2,658,667	31.2
Public welfare	2,190,795	25.7
Hospitals	52,453	0.6
Health	178,448	2.1
Highways	691,516	8.1
Police protection	54,577	0.6
Correction	251,160	2.9
Natural resources	217,916	2.6
Parks and recreation	38,477	0.5
Governmental administration	335,282	3.9
Interest on general debt	161,777	1.9
Other and unallocable	547,167	6.4
Utility expenditure	0	-
Liquor stores expenditure	104,030	1.2
Insurance trust expenditure	1,048,593	12.3
Debt at End of Fiscal Year	3,647,841	X
Cash and Security Holdings	20,043,910	X

X = Not applicable.
- = Zero or rounds to zero.
[1]Within insurance trust revenue, net earnings of state retirement systems is a calculated statistic (the item code in the data file is X08), and thus can be positive or negative. Net earnings is the sum of earnings on investments plus gains on investments minus losses on investments. The change made in 2002 for asset valuation from book to market value in accordance with Statement 34 of the Governmental Accounting Standards Board is reflected in the calculated statistics.

Table ID-16. State Government Tax Collections, 2014

(Dollars in thousands, percent.)

Item	Dollars	Percent distribution
Total Taxes	3,671,715	100.0
Property taxes	X	X
Sales and gross receipts	1,821,303	49.6
General sales and gross receipts	1,373,666	37.4
Selective sales and gross receipts	447,637	12.2
Alcoholic beverages	8,780	0.2
Amusements	0	
Insurance premiums	75,205	2.0
Motor fuels	248,454	6.8
Pari-mutuels	1,209	-
Public utilities	1,840	0.1
Tobacco products	47,816	1.3
Other selective sales	64,333	1.8
Licenses	316,331	8.6
Alcoholic beverages	1,617	-
Amusements	754	-
Corporations in general	2,203	0.1
Hunting and fishing	34,436	0.9
Motor vehicle	135,169	3.7
Motor vehicle operators	9,943	0.3
Public utilities	53,613	1.5
Occupation and business, NEC	74,790	2.0
Other licenses	3,806	0.1
Income taxes	1,528,077	41.6
Individual income	1,338,075	36.4
Corporation net income	190,002	5.2
Other taxes	6,004	0.2
Death and gift	0	-
Documentary and stock transfer	0	-
Severance	6,004	0.2
Taxes, NEC	0	-

X = Not applicable.
- = Zero or rounds to zero.

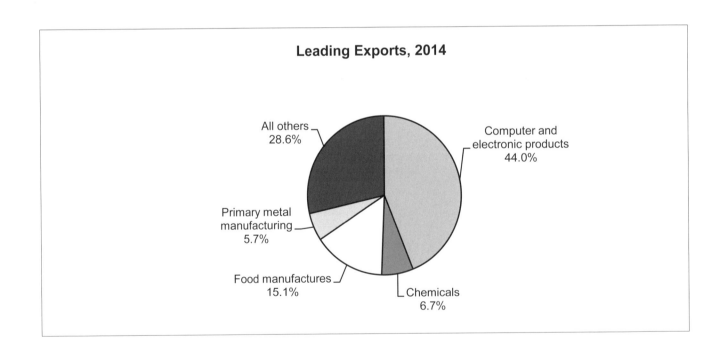

Leading Exports, 2014

All others 28.6%
Computer and electronic products 44.0%
Primary metal manufacturing 5.7%
Food manufactures 15.1%
Chemicals 6.7%

Facts and Figures

Location: North central United States; bordered on the N by Wisconsin, on the E by Lake Michigan and Indiana, on the S by Kentucky, and on the W by Iowa and Missouri

Area: 57,913 sq. mi. (149,998 sq. km.); rank—25th

Population: 12,880,580 (2014 est.); rank—5th

Principal Cities: capital—Springfield; largest—Chicago

Statehood: December 3, 1818; 21st state

U.S. Congress: 2 senators, 18 representatives

State Motto: State Sovereignty, National Union

State Song: "Illinois"

State Nicknames: The Prairie State; The Land of Lincoln

Abbreviations: IL; Ill.

State Symbols: flower—native violet; tree—white oak; bird—cardinal

At a Glance

- With an increase in population of 0.4 percent, Illinois ranked 46th among the states in growth from 2010 to 2014.

- Illinois's birth rate in 2013 was 12.2 per 1,000 population, slightly below the U.S. rate of 12.4 per 1,000 population.

- The violent crime rate in Illinois in 2013 was 380.2 per 100,000 population, compared to the U.S. rate of 367.9 per 100,000 population.

- Illinois ranked 18th for median household income in 2013, with an income of $56,210.

- In 2013, 12.7 percent of Illinois residents did not have health insurance, compared to 14.5 percent of the entire U.S. population.

Table IL-1. Population by Age, Sex, Race, and Hispanic Origin

(Number, percent, except where noted.)

Sex, age, race, and Hispanic origin	2000	2010	2014[1]	Average annual percent change, 2010–2014
Total Population	12,419,293	12,830,632	12,880,580	0.1
Percent of total U.S. population	4.4	4.2	4.0	X
Sex				
Male	6,080,336	6,292,276	6,320,886	0.1
Female	6,338,957	6,538,356	6,559,694	0.1
Age				
Under 5 years	876,549	835,557	790,685	-1.4
5 to 19 years	2,728,957	2,660,945	2,542,089	-1.1
20 to 64 years	7,313,762	7,724,917	7,759,273	0.1
65 years and over	1,500,025	1,609,213	1,788,533	2.7
Median age (years)	34.7	36.6	37.5	0.6
Race and Hispanic Origin				
One race				
White	9,125,471	10,030,587	9,984,775	-0.1
Black	1,878,875	1,903,458	1,892,255	-0.1
American Indian and Alaska Native	31,006	73,486	75,293	0.6
Asian	423,603	604,399	684,715	3.2
Native Hawaiian or Other Pacific Islander	4,610	7,436	8,193	2.5
Two or more races	235,016	210,906	235,349	2.8
Hispanic (of any race)	1,530,262	2,073,054	2,152,974	1.0

X = Not applicable.
[1]Population figures for 2014 are July 1 estimates. The 2010 estimates are taken from the 2010 Census.

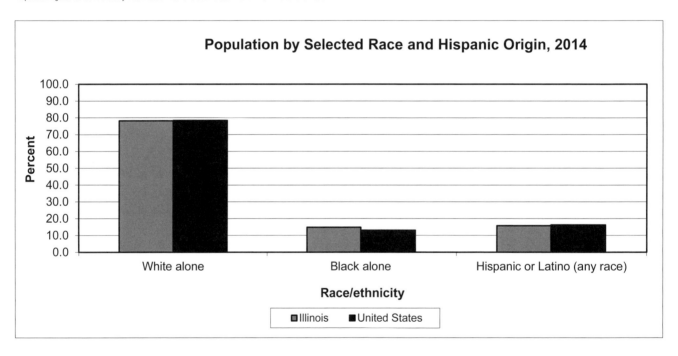

Population by Selected Race and Hispanic Origin, 2014

Illinois   United States

Table IL-2. Marital Status

(Number, percent distribution.)

Sex, age, race, and Hispanic origin	2000	2010	2013
Males, 15 Years and Over	4,685,982	4,977,964	5,049,119
Never married	31.9	37.2	38.1
Now married, except separated	56.1	50.0	49.7
Separated	1.6	1.4	1.4
Widowed	2.5	2.6	2.4
Divorced	7.9	8.8	8.4
Females, 15 Years and Over	5,021,855	5,289,803	5,335,165
Never married	26.1	31.1	31.8
Now married, except separated	51.3	46.3	46.1
Separated	2.0	2.1	2.0
Widowed	10.7	9.5	9.1
Divorced	9.9	11.0	10.9

Table IL-3. Households and Housing Characteristics

(Number, percent, dollars.)

Item	2000	2010	2013	Average annual percent change, 2000–2013
Total Households...	4,591,779	4,752,857	4,783,421	0.3
Family households	3,105,513	3,133,813	3,128,369	0.1
Married-couple family	2,353,892	2,301,009	2,299,644	-0.2
Other family	751,621	832,804	828,725	0.8
Male householder, no wife present.................	187,903	220,197	222,259	1.3
Female householder, no husband present.......	563,718	612,607	606,466	0.6
Nonfamily households	1,486,266	1,619,044	1,655,052	0.8
Householder living alone.................................	1,229,807	1,340,394	1,383,623	0.9
Householder not living alone...........................	256,459	278,650	271,429	0.4
Housing Characteristics				
Total housing units..	4,885,615	5,297,077	5,289,653	0.6
Occupied housing units	4,591,779	4,752,857	4,783,421	0.3
Owner occupied	3,088,884	3,219,338	3,154,027	0.2
Renter occupied	1,502,895	1,533,519	1,629,394	0.6
Average household size..	2.63	2.64	2.63	-
Financial Characteristics				
Median gross rent of renter-occupied housing	605	848	885	3.0
Median monthly owner costs for housing units with a mortgage	1,198	1,655	1,156	-0.3
Median value of owner-occupied housing units	130,800	191,800	169,600	2.0

- = Zero or rounds to zero.

Table IL-4. Migration, Origin, and Language

(Number, percent.)

Characteristic	State			U.S.		
	2012	2013	Percent change	2012	2013	Percent change
Residence 1 Year Ago						
Population 1 year and over	12,725,119	12,740,816	0.1	310,212,755	312,432,820	0.7
Same house	86.5	86.6	X	85.0	85.0	X
Different house in the U.S................................	13.0	12.8	X	14.4	14.4	X
Same county	8.7	8.6	X	9.0	8.9	X
Different county	4.2	4.2	X	5.4	5.5	X
Same state	2.6	2.5	X	3.2	3.2	X
Different state	1.6	1.8	X	2.3	2.3	X
Abroad	0.5	0.5	X	0.6	0.6	X
Place of Birth						
Native born	11,083,925	11,074,667	-0.1	273,089,382	274,780,773	0.6
Male	48.9	48.9	X	49.3	49.3	X
Female	51.1	51.1	X	50.7	50.7	X
Foreign born	1,791,330	1,807,468	0.9	40,824,658	41,348,066	1.3
Male	50.2	50.2	X	48.7	48.8	X
Female	49.8	49.8	X	51.3	51.2	X
Foreign born; naturalized U.S. citizen................	840,580	852,962	1.5	18,686,237	19,294,710	3.3
Male	47.8	47.6	X	45.8	45.9	X
Female	52.2	52.4	X	54.2	54.1	X
Foreign born; not a U.S. citizen........................	950,750	954,506	0.4	22,138,421	22,053,356	-0.4
Male	52.3	52.4	X	51.1	51.3	X
Female	47.7	47.6	X	48.9	48.7	X
Entered 2010 or later	6.1	8.2	X	7.0	9.7	X
Entered 2000 to 2009	28.3	28.4	X	30.4	29.4	X
Entered before 2000...	65.6	63.4	X	62.7	61.0	X
World Region of Birth, Foreign						
Foreign-born population, excluding population born at sea	1,791,330	1,807,468	0.9	40,824,553	41,347,945	1.3
Europe	21.6	21.4	X	11.8	11.6	X
Asia	27.6	28.3	X	29.2	29.5	X
Africa	3.0	3.6	X	4.2	4.4	X
Oceania	0.2	0.2	X	0.6	0.5	X
Latin America..	46.5	45.3	X	52.2	51.9	X
North America	1.0	1.2	X	2.0	2.0	X
Language Spoken at Home and Ability to Speak English						
Population 5 years and over.................................	12,061,228	12,085,046	0.2	294,003,714	296,358,760	0.8
English only	77.4	77.3	X	79.0	79.2	X
Language other than English..............................	22.6	22.7	X	21.0	20.8	X
Speaks English less than "very well"..............	9.2	9.2	X	8.5	8.5	X

NA = Not available.
X = Not applicable.
- = Zero or rounds to zero.

Table IL-5. Median Income and Poverty Status, 2013

(Number, percent, except as noted.)

Characteristic	State		U.S.	
	Number	Percent	Number	Percent
Median Income				
Households (dollars).............................	56,210	X	52,250	X
Families (dollars)	69,557	X	64,030	X
Below Poverty Level (All People)	1,845,393	14.7	48,810,868	15.8
Sex				
Male......................................	828,019	13.4	21,938,525	14.5
Female	1,017,374	15.9	26,872,343	17.1
Age				
Under 18 years.............................	616,060	20.7	16,086,960	22.2
Related children under 18 years.................	605,355	20.4	15,769,921	21.9
18 to 64 years	1,081,022	13.6	28,578,191	14.8
65 years and over	148,311	8.8	4,145,717	9.6

X = Not applicable.

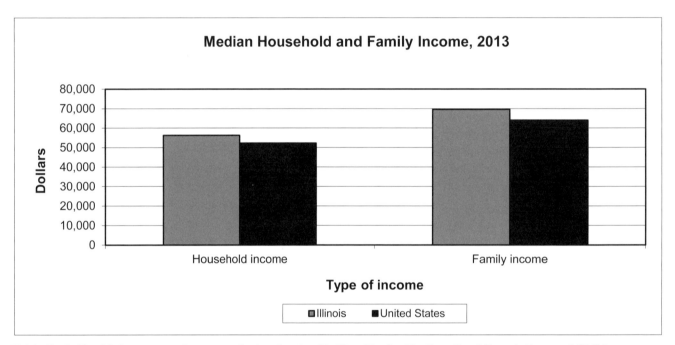

Table IL-6. Health Insurance Coverage Status for the Civilian Noninstitutionalized Population and Children Under 18 Years of Age

(Numbers in thousands, percent.)

Item	2005	2006	2007	2008	2009	2010	2011	2012	2013
Civilian Noninstitutionalized Population	12,608	12,644	12,688	12,709	12,720	12,673	12,689	12,698	12,705
Covered by Private or Public Insurance									
Number........................	10,878	10,867	10,988	11,086	11,025	10,928	11,029	11,076	11,086
Percent........................	86.3	86.0	86.6	87.2	86.7	86.2	86.9	87.2	87.3
Not Covered									
Number........................	1,730	1,776	1,700	1,623	1,694	1,746	1,659	1,622	1,618
Percent........................	13.7	14.0	13.4	12.8	13.3	13.8	13.1	12.8	12.7
Percent in the U.S. not covered....................	15.3	15.8	15.3	15.1	15.1	15.5	15.1	14.8	14.5
Children Under 18 Years of Age	3,276	3,188	3,180	3,176	3,168	3,122	3,092	3,059	3,018
Covered by Private or Public Insurance									
Number........................	2,947	2,886	2,970	2,997	3,026	2,982	2,979	2,958	2,893
Percent........................	89.9	90.5	93.4	94.4	95.5	95.5	96.3	96.7	95.8
Not Covered									
Number........................	329	302	210	179	142	140	113	101	125
Percent........................	10.1	9.5	6.6	5.6	4.5	4.5	3.7	3.3	4.2
Percent in the U.S. not covered....................	10.9	11.7	11.0	9.7	8.6	8.0	7.5	7.2	7.1

Table IL-7. Employment Status by Demographic Group, 2014

(Numbers in thousands, percent.)

Characteristic	Civilian noninstitutional population	Civilian labor force		Employed		Unemployed	
		Number	Percent of population	Number	Percent of population	Number	Percent of population
Total...	10,053	6,513	64.8	6,056	60.2	457	7.0
Sex							
Male...	4,857	3,402	70.1	3,154	64.9	249	7.3
Female...	5,196	3,110	59.9	2,903	55.9	208	6.7
Race, Sex, and Hispanic Origin							
White...	7,982	5,242	65.7	4,933	61.8	309	5.9
Male...	3,910	2,789	71.3	2,621	67.0	168	6.0
Female...	4,073	2,453	60.2	2,312	56.8	141	5.7
Black or African American....................	1,406	837	59.6	716	51.0	121	14.4
Male...	624	374	59.9	307	49.2	67	17.9
Female...	782	463	59.3	409	52.4	54	11.7
Hispanic or Latino ethnicity[1]	1,344	932	69.4	856	63.7	75	8.1
Male...	694	553	79.6	515	74.2	38	6.8
Female...	649	379	58.4	341	52.6	38	10.0
Age							
16 to 19 years...	687	251	36.6	196	28.5	55	22.1
20 to 24 years...	981	700	71.3	614	62.6	86	12.2
25 to 34 years...	1,712	1,435	83.8	1,348	78.7	88	6.1
35 to 44 years...	1,578	1,304	82.6	1,233	78.1	71	5.5
45 to 54 years...	1,752	1,441	82.3	1,365	77.9	76	5.3
55 to 64 years...	1,604	1,053	65.7	995	62.0	58	5.5
65 years and over	1,739	328	18.9	306	17.6	22	6.8

NOTE: Data in Table 7 are from the Current Population Survey (CPS) and do not match the estimates in Table 8. See notes and definitions for further information.
[1]May be of any race.

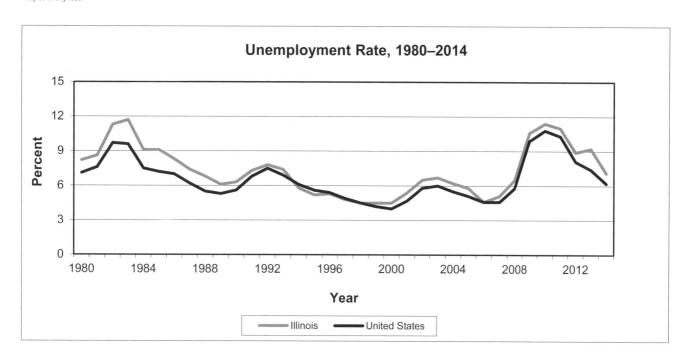

Table IL-8. Employment Status of the Civilian Noninstitutional Population Age 16 Years and Over

(Number, percent.)

Year	Civilian labor force	Civilian participation rate	Employed	Unemployed	Unemployment rate
2006	6,526,273	67.5	6,230,845	295,428	4.5
2007	6,665,601	68.4	6,334,010	331,591	5.0
2008	6,657,227	67.8	6,238,611	418,616	6.3
2009	6,618,658	67.0	5,943,229	675,429	10.2
2010	6,625,321	66.9	5,937,047	688,274	10.4
2011	6,586,045	66.2	5,949,053	636,992	9.7
2012	6,583,808	65.9	5,992,475	591,333	9.0
2013	6,554,978	65.4	5,960,851	594,127	9.1
2014	6,524,579	64.9	6,064,216	460,363	7.1

Table IL-9. Employment and Average Wages by Industry

(Estimates from 2007 through 2010 are based on the 2007 North American Industry Classification System [NAICS]. Estimates from 2011 onward are based on the 2012 NAICS.)

Industry	2007	2008	2009	2010	2011	2012	2013
				Number of jobs			
Wage and Salary Employment by Industry	6,181,343	6,153,026	5,869,095	5,821,234	5,882,915	5,932,144	5,974,045
Farm Wage and Salary Employment	17,831	16,207	15,271	18,237	17,069	16,174	12,222
Nonfarm Wage and Salary Employment	6,163,512	6,136,819	5,853,824	5,802,997	5,865,846	5,915,970	5,961,823
Private wage and salary employment	5,266,000	5,228,543	4,939,399	4,896,135	4,976,577	5,033,129	5,083,782
Forestry, fishing, and related activities	4,342	4,362	4,261	3,820	4,068	4,078	4,725
Mining	9,976	9,672	9,303	9,052	9,507	10,084	9,649
Utilities	23,063	23,520	23,716	23,189	23,528	23,857	23,788
Construction	281,896	269,100	229,839	208,243	206,472	195,541	198,343
Manufacturing	676,962	659,693	579,317	561,722	574,540	584,275	580,152
Durable goods manufacturing	416,173	403,843	340,047	329,461	343,356	354,586	350,932
Nondurable goods manufacturing	260,789	255,850	239,270	232,261	231,184	229,689	229,220
Wholesale trade	313,563	312,742	295,062	288,749	291,888	295,640	300,325
Retail trade	645,575	637,807	606,122	598,108	605,006	602,901	605,101
Transportation and warehousing	244,776	244,327	230,887	231,795	238,612	244,352	244,358
Information	117,018	115,305	106,957	101,883	100,183	100,561	99,051
Finance and insurance	320,786	313,174	298,307	293,720	291,833	294,661	293,926
Real estate and rental and leasing	86,906	83,548	77,976	75,984	74,436	73,855	76,024
Professional, scientific, and technical services	369,993	374,287	353,699	351,122	360,573	367,226	381,107
Management of companies and enterprises	96,939	97,693	95,264	96,365	98,340	102,697	103,652
Administrative and waste services	412,987	398,574	348,271	366,269	383,498	400,229	413,125
Educational services	142,874	148,711	155,293	160,381	165,620	166,775	166,810
Health care and social assistance	663,991	678,901	690,647	700,048	711,121	721,617	730,326
Arts, entertainment, and recreation	81,905	81,602	78,617	77,391	78,617	80,110	81,273
Accommodation and food services	457,989	458,044	445,269	444,352	450,849	459,981	469,209
Other services, except public administration	314,459	317,481	310,592	303,942	307,886	304,689	302,838
Government and government enterprises	897,512	908,276	914,425	906,862	889,269	882,841	878,041
				Dollars			
Average Wages and Salaries by Industry	48,330	49,415	49,012	50,271	51,711	53,078	53,541
Average Farm Wages and Salaries	28,313	32,632	31,157	24,440	34,006	24,929	35,420
Average Nonfarm Wages and Salaries	48,388	49,459	49,059	50,353	51,762	53,155	53,578
Average private wages and salaries	48,954	49,988	49,335	50,673	52,169	53,636	53,909
Forestry, fishing, and related activities	26,622	29,039	30,025	28,236	28,973	29,102	27,539
Mining	61,144	61,714	61,591	68,078	66,616	68,108	70,817
Utilities	98,659	102,320	98,866	98,417	104,422	107,901	106,768
Construction	57,679	61,204	60,378	59,921	60,768	61,376	62,921
Manufacturing	56,337	57,654	57,560	61,015	63,001	64,899	65,196
Durable goods manufacturing	57,153	58,749	58,578	61,613	64,517	65,803	65,489
Nondurable goods manufacturing	55,036	55,925	56,113	60,167	60,748	63,504	64,746
Wholesale trade	67,124	67,928	66,951	69,366	73,149	75,593	75,383
Retail trade	27,248	26,771	26,537	27,260	27,824	28,548	28,747
Transportation and warehousing	47,597	48,425	47,509	48,979	50,597	51,744	53,019
Information	66,952	68,607	67,216	68,704	72,819	74,964	77,244
Finance and insurance	91,732	94,533	89,628	91,361	97,120	101,123	99,750
Real estate and rental and leasing	54,018	51,702	49,771	51,723	53,603	56,535	58,298
Professional, scientific, and technical services	79,005	81,811	81,516	84,215	86,166	89,131	88,821
Management of companies and enterprises	112,118	108,889	107,457	114,816	117,501	121,268	123,360
Administrative and waste services	32,280	33,970	33,908	34,811	35,004	35,908	35,138
Educational services	37,772	39,346	40,063	40,989	42,103	42,655	43,945
Health care and social assistance	41,960	43,195	44,120	44,654	45,209	45,794	46,354
Arts, entertainment, and recreation	34,608	33,922	33,922	34,953	35,783	36,949	36,753
Accommodation and food services	19,066	18,906	18,807	19,510	20,189	20,693	20,710
Other services, except public administration	31,462	32,578	32,808	33,887	34,749	35,270	36,222
Government and government enterprises	45,064	46,412	47,565	48,623	49,487	50,413	51,664

Table IL-10. Employment Characteristics by Family Type

(Number, percent.)

Family type and labor force status	2011		2012		2013	
	Total	Families with own children under 18 years	Total	Families with own children under 18 years	Total	Families with own children under 18 years
All Families	3,098,864	1,405,017	3,121,020	1,398,372	3,128,369	1,383,676
FAMILY TYPE AND LABOR FORCE STATUS						
Married-Couple Families	2,269,243	966,588	2,289,429	958,861	2,299,644	950,188
Both husband and wife in labor force	55.7	66.5	55.8	68.1	55.1	67.4
Husband in labor force, wife not in labor force	21.7	28.8	21.3	27.7	21.2	27.2
Wife in labor force, husband not in labor force	7.3	3.2	7.6	3.1	7.8	3.8
Both husband and wife not in labor force	15.3	1.5	15.3	1.2	15.5	1.4
Other Families	829,621	438,429	831,591	439,511	828,725	433,488
Female householder, no husband present	74.4	77.2	73.5	77.0	73.2	76.4
In labor force	54.2	65.1	54.3	66.2	53.1	65.2
Not in labor force	20.3	12.1	19.2	10.8	20.1	11.1
Male householder, no wife present	25.6	22.8	26.5	23.0	26.8	23.6
In labor force	20.8	21.1	21.2	21.2	21.5	21.9
Not in labor force	4.8	1.7	5.3	1.8	5.3	1.7

Table IL-11. School Enrollment and Educational Attainment, 2013

(Number, percent.)

Item	State	U.S.
Enrollment		
Total population 3 years and over, enrolled in school	3,441,460	82,395,254
Enrolled in nursery school or preschool (percent)	6.5	6.0
Enrolled in kindergarten (percent)	5.0	5.2
Enrolled in elementary school, grades 1-8 (percent)	39.6	40.0
Enrolled in high school, grades 9-12 (percent)	20.9	20.6
Enrolled in college or graduate school (percent)	28.0	28.3
Attainment		
Total population 25 years and over	8,593,665	210,910,615
Less than ninth grade (percent)	5.5	5.8
9th to 12th grade, no diploma (percent)	6.6	7.6
High school graduate, including equivalency (percent)	27.0	27.8
Some college, no degree (percent)	21.1	21.1
Associate's degree (percent)	7.6	8.1
Bachelor's degree (percent)	19.8	18.4
Graduate or professional degree (percent)	12.4	11.2
High school graduate or higher (percent)	87.8	86.6
Bachelor's degree or higher (percent)	32.1	29.6

Table IL-12. Public School Characteristics and Educational Indicators

(Number, percent; data derived from National Center of Education Statistics.)

Item	State	U.S.
Public Schools, 2012–2013 (except where noted)		
Number of school districts	1,070	18,093
Number of schools	4,266	98,454
Number of students (in thousands)	2,073	49,771
Number of teachers (in thousands)	136	3,109
Student-teacher ratio	15.3	16.0
Expenditures per student (dollars), FY 2012	12,011	10,667
Four-year adjusted cohort graduation rate (ACGR)[1,2]	83.2	81.4
Students eligible for free or reduced-price lunch (in thousands)	1,027	25,188
English language learners (in thousands)	192	4,397
Students age 3 to 21 served under IDEA, part B (in thousands)	292	6,429

Public Schools by Type	Number	Percent of state public schools
Total number of schools	4,266	100.0
Regular	3,978	93.2
Special education	140	3.3
Vocational education	0	0.0
Alternative education	148	3.5

NOTE: Every school is assigned only one school type based on its instructional emphasis.
[1]ACGR data represents a new method of calculating high-school completion rates and may not be comparable to previous years' data for Averaged Freshmen Graduation Rates (AFGR).
[2]The United States 4-year ACGRs were estimated using both the reported 4-year ACGR data from 49 states and the District of Columbia and using imputed data for Idaho. The estimate for American Indian/Alaska Native students also includes imputed data for Virginia.

Table IL-13. Reported Voting and Registration of the Voting-Age Population, November 2012

(Numbers in thousands, percent.)

Item	Total population	Total citizen population	Registered			Voted		
			Total registered	Percent registered (total population)	Percent registered (total citizen population)	Total voted	Percent voted (total population)	Percent voted (total citizen population)
U.S. Total	235,248	215,081	153,157	65.1	71.2	132,948	56.5	61.8
State Total	9,651	8,831	6,425	66.6	72.7	5,428	56.2	61.5
Sex								
Male	4,638	4,244	3,010	64.9	70.9	2,517	54.3	59.3
Female	5,013	4,588	3,415	68.1	74.4	2,911	58.1	63.5
Race								
White alone	7,673	7,115	5,150	67.1	72.4	4,275	55.7	60.1
White, non-Hispanic alone	6,553	6,408	4,762	72.7	74.3	3,986	60.8	62.2
Black alone	1,322	1,278	987	74.7	77.2	918	69.5	71.8
Asian alone	557	356	228	40.9	64.0	198	35.5	55.4
Hispanic (of any race)	1,200	770	415	34.6	53.9	295	24.6	38.3
White alone or in combination	7,751	7,176	5,189	66.9	72.3	4,299	55.5	59.9
Black alone or in combination	1,372	1,312	1,009	73.5	76.9	934	68.0	71.1
Asian alone or in combination	579	378	243	41.9	64.1	204	35.3	54.1
Age								
18 to 24 years	1,228	1,122	608	49.5	54.2	396	32.2	35.3
25 to 44 years	3,396	2,961	2,086	61.4	70.5	1,719	50.6	58.0
45 to 64 years	3,407	3,182	2,471	72.5	77.7	2,206	64.7	69.3
65 to 74 years	946	920	763	80.7	82.9	688	72.7	74.7
75 years and over	674	646	495	73.5	76.7	420	62.4	65.1

Table IL-14. Crime

(Number, rate per 100,000. Data are derived from the FBI Uniform Crime Reports.)

Item	State			U.S.[1,2,3,4]		
	2012	2013	Percent change	2012	2013	Percent change
TOTAL POPULATION[5]	12,868,192	12,882,135	0.1	313,873,685	316,128,839	0.7
VIOLENT CRIME						
Number	53,556	47,987	-10.4	1,217,067	1,163,146	-4.4
Rate	416.2	372.5	-10.5	387.8	367.9	-5.1
Murder and Nonnegligent Manslaughter						
Number	770	706	-8.3	14,866	14,196	-4.5
Rate	6.0	5.5	-8.4	4.7	4.5	-5.2
Rape[6]						
Number	X	4,263	X	X	108,612	X
Rate	X	33.1	X	X	34.4	X
Robbery						
Number	19,480	17,722	-9.0	355,051	345,031	-2.8
Rate	151.4	137.6	-9.1	113.1	109.1	-3.5
Aggravated Assault						
Number	29,725	26,283	-11.6	762,009	724,149	-5.0
Rate	231.0	204.0	-11.7	242.8	229.1	-5.6
PROPERTY CRIME						
Number	332,706	292,983	-11.9	9,001,992	8,632,512	-4.1
Rate	2,585.5	2,274.3	-12.0	2,868.0	2,730.7	-4.8
Burglary						
Number	71,100	58,237	-18.1	2,109,932	1,928,465	-8.6
Rate	552.5	452.1	-18.2	672.2	610.0	-9.3
Larceny-Theft						
Number	235,314	213,813	-9.1	6,168,874	6,004,453	-2.7
Rate	1,828.6	1,659.8	-9.2	1,965.4	1,899.4	-3.4
Motor Vehicle Theft						
Number	26,292	20,933	-20.4	723,186	699,594	-3.3
Rate	204.3	162.5	-20.5	230.4	221.3	-4.0

NOTE: Although arson data are included in the trend and clearance tables, sufficient data are not available to estimate totals for this offense. Therefore, no arson data are published in this table.
X = Not applicable.
- = Zero or rounds to zero.
[1]The crime figures have been adjusted.
[2]The data collection methodology for the offense of forcible rape used by the Minnesota state Uniform Crime Reporting (UCR) Program (with the exception of Minneapolis and St. Paul, Minnesota) does not comply with national UCR Program guidelines. Consequently, its figures for forcible rape and violent crime (of which forcible rape is a part) are not published in this table.
[3]Includes offenses reported by the Zoological Police and the Metro Transit Police.
[4]Because of changes in the state's reporting practices, figures are not comparable to previous years' data.
[5]Populations are U.S. Census Bureau provisional estimates as of July 1 of each year.
[6]The figures shown for the offense of rape were estimated using the revised Uniform Crime Reporting (UCR) definition of rape.

Table IL-15. State Government Finances, 2013

(Dollar amounts in thousands, percent distribution.)

Item	Dollars	Percent distribution
Total Revenue	84,493,376	100.0
General revenue	65,561,519	77.6
Intergovernmental revenue	17,312,790	20.5
Taxes	38,729,322	45.8
General sales	8,159,003	9.7
Selective sales	6,560,738	7.8
License taxes	2,583,108	3.1
Individual income tax	16,538,662	19.6
Corporate income tax	4,462,627	5.3
Other taxes	425,184	0.5
Current charges	4,913,942	5.8
Miscellaneous general revenue	4,605,465	5.5
Utility revenue	0	-
Liquor stores revenue	0	-
Insurance trust revenue[1]	18,931,857	22.4
Total Expenditure	75,324,720	100.0
Intergovernmental expenditure	15,549,167	20.6
Direct expenditure	59,775,553	79.4
Current operation	36,944,818	49.0
Capital outlay	3,962,519	5.3
Insurance benefits and repayments	14,102,769	18.7
Assistance and subsidies	1,262,268	1.7
Interest on debt	3,503,179	4.7
Exhibit: Salaries and wages	8,904,708	11.8
Total Expenditure	75,324,720	100.0
General expenditure	61,221,951	81.3
Intergovernmental expenditure	15,549,167	20.6
Direct expenditure	45,672,784	60.6
General expenditure, by function:		
Education	17,272,058	22.9
Public welfare	20,424,637	27.1
Hospitals	1,345,563	1.8
Health	2,240,614	3.0
Highways	4,969,276	6.6
Police protection	467,598	0.6
Correction	1,327,176	1.8
Natural resources	237,443	0.3
Parks and recreation	262,417	0.3
Governmental administration	1,374,685	1.8
Interest on general debt	3,503,179	4.7
Other and unallocable	7,797,305	10.4
Utility expenditure	0	-
Liquor stores expenditure	0	-
Insurance trust expenditure	14,102,769	18.7
Debt at End of Fiscal Year	63,660,340	X
Cash and Security Holdings	128,340,625	X

X = Not applicable.
- = Zero or rounds to zero.
[1]Within insurance trust revenue, net earnings of state retirement systems is a calculated statistic (the item code in the data file is X08), and thus can be positive or negative. Net earnings is the sum of earnings on investments plus gains on investments minus losses on investments. The change made in 2002 for asset valuation from book to market value in accordance with Statement 34 of the Governmental Accounting Standards Board is reflected in the calculated statistics.

Table IL-16. State Government Tax Collections, 2014

(Dollars in thousands, percent.)

Item	Dollars	Percent distribution
Total Taxes	39,182,894	100.0
Property taxes	54,710	0.1
Sales and gross receipts	15,758,509	40.2
General sales and gross receipts	8,515,410	21.7
Selective sales and gross receipts	7,243,099	18.5
Alcoholic beverages	279,587	0.7
Amusements	662,592	1.7
Insurance premiums	359,240	0.9
Motor fuels	1,293,967	3.3
Pari-mutuels	6,534	-
Public utilities	1,651,211	4.2
Tobacco products	859,865	2.2
Other selective sales	2,130,103	5.4
Licenses	2,675,943	6.8
Alcoholic beverages	12,626	-
Amusements	14,972	-
Corporations in general	345,889	0.9
Hunting and fishing	42,936	0.1
Motor vehicle	1,623,571	4.1
Motor vehicle operators	116,206	0.3
Public utilities	16,217	-
Occupation and business, NEC	469,458	1.2
Other licenses	34,068	0.1
Income taxes	20,343,042	51.9
Individual income	16,058,396	41.0
Corporation net income	4,284,646	10.9
Other taxes	350,690	0.9
Death and gift	294,138	0.8
Documentary and stock transfer	56,552	0.1
Severance	X	X
Taxes, NEC	0	-

X = Not applicable.
- = Zero or rounds to zero.

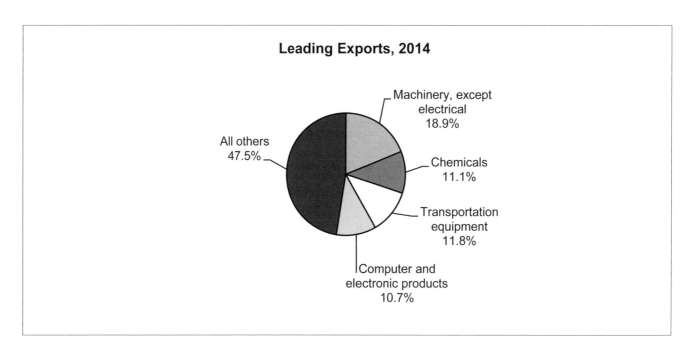

Leading Exports, 2014

Machinery, except electrical 18.9%
Chemicals 11.1%
Transportation equipment 11.8%
Computer and electronic products 10.7%
All others 47.5%

Facts and Figures

Location: East north central United States; bordered on the N by Michigan and Lake Michigan, on the E by Ohio, on the S by Kentucky, and on the W by Illinois

Area: 36,418 sq. mi. (94,321 sq. km.); rank—38th

Population: 6,596,855 (2014 est.); rank—16th

Principal Cities: capital—Indianapolis; largest—Indianapolis

Statehood: December 11, 1816; 19th state

U.S. Congress: 2 senators, 9 representatives

State Motto: The Crossroads of America

State Song: "On the Banks of the Wabash, Far Away"

State Nickname: The Hoosier State

Abbreviations: IN; Ind.

State Symbols: flower—peony; tree—tulip tree; bird—cardinal

At a Glance

- With an increase in population of 1.7 percent, Indiana ranked 33rd among the states in growth from 2010 to 2014.

- Indiana's violent crime rate in 2013 was 357.4 per 100,000 population, compared to 367.9 for the entire nation.

- The property crime rate in Indiana in 2013 was 2,854.0 per 100,000 population, ranking 23rd in the nation.

- The median household income in Indiana in 2013 was $47,529, compared to the nationwide median of $52,250.

- Approximately 15.9 percent of all Indianans lived in poverty in 2013; the percentage for children under 18 years of age was 22.2 percent.

Table IN-1. Population by Age, Sex, Race, and Hispanic Origin

(Number, percent, except where noted.)

Sex, age, race, and Hispanic origin	2000	2010	2014[1]	Average annual percent change, 2010–2014
Total Population	6,080,485	6,483,802	6,596,855	0.4
Percent of total U.S. population	2.2	2.1	2.1	X
Sex				
Male	2,982,474	3,189,737	3,249,444	0.5
Female	3,098,011	3,294,065	3,347,411	0.4
Age				
Under 5 years	423,215	434,075	419,487	-0.9
5 to 19 years	1,340,171	1,372,507	1,346,085	-0.5
20 to 64 years	3,564,268	3,836,112	3,889,839	0.3
65 years and over	752,831	841,108	941,444	2.9
Median age (years)	35.2	37.0	37.5	0.3
Race and Hispanic Origin				
One race				
White	5,320,022	5,638,833	5,678,447	0.2
Black	510,034	603,797	630,754	1.1
American Indian and Alaska Native	15,815	24,487	26,354	1.9
Asian	59,126	105,535	132,406	5.8
Native Hawaiian or Other Pacific Islander	2,005	3,532	4,093	3.8
Two or more races	75,672	107,618	124,801	3.8
Hispanic (of any race)	214,536	403,234	432,305	1.8

X = Not applicable.
[1]Population figures for 2014 are July 1 estimates. The 2010 estimates are taken from the 2010 Census.

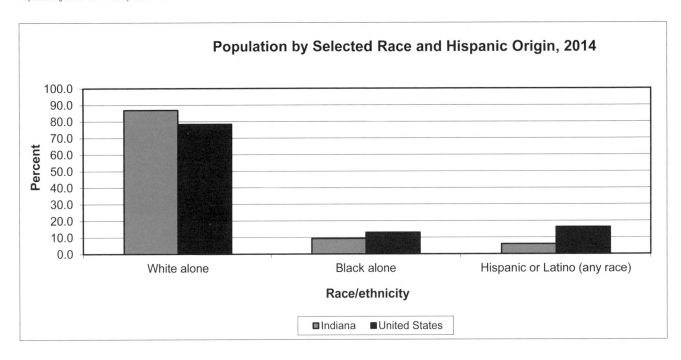

Table IN-2. Marital Status

(Number, percent distribution.)

Sex, age, race, and Hispanic origin	2000	2010	2013
Males, 15 Years and Over	2,308,917	2,513,953	2,552,856
Never married	27.9	32.6	33.0
Now married, except separated	58.5	52.3	51.2
Separated	1.3	1.1	1.3
Widowed	2.4	2.5	2.9
Divorced	10.0	11.4	11.6
Females, 15 Years and Over	2,462,123	2,644,068	2,698,738
Never married	22.0	26.7	27.5
Now married, except separated	54.3	49.1	47.8
Separated	1.5	1.8	1.7
Widowed	10.6	9.2	9.2
Divorced	11.6	13.2	13.8

Table IN-3. Households and Housing Characteristics

(Number, percent, dollars.)

Item	2000	2010	2013	Average annual percent change, 2000–2013
Total Households...	2,336,306	2,470,905	2,498,395	0.5
Family households	1,602,501	1,656,386	1,647,941	0.2
Married-couple family...	1,251,458	1,236,518	1,226,204	-0.2
Other family...	351,043	419,868	421,737	1.4
Male householder, no wife present...................	91,671	110,663	114,273	1.7
Female householder, no husband present..........	259,372	309,205	307,464	1.3
Nonfamily households	733,805	814,519	850,454	1.1
Householder living alone....................................	605,428	678,460	705,026	1.2
Householder not living alone..............................	128,377	136,059	145,428	1.0
Housing Characteristics				
Total housing units...	2,532,319	2,797,172	2,809,640	0.8
Occupied housing units	2,336,306	2,470,905	2,498,395	0.5
Owner occupied...	1,669,192	1,736,751	1,712,020	0.2
Renter occupied..	667,144	734,154	786,375	1.3
Average household size.......................................	2.53	2.55	2.55	0.1
Financial Characteristics				
Median gross rent of renter-occupied housing	521	683	730	2.6
Median monthly owner costs for housing units with a mortgage	869	1,090	1,062	1.6
Median value of owner-occupied housing units......	94,300	123,300	122,200	2.0

Table IN-4. Migration, Origin, and Language

(Number, percent.)

Characteristic	State 2012	State 2013	State Percent change	U.S. 2012	U.S. 2013	U.S. Percent change
Residence 1 Year Ago						
Population 1 year and over	6,457,067	6,492,306	0.5	310,212,755	312,432,820	0.7
Same house	85.1	84.7	X	85.0	85.0	X
Different house in the U.S.	14.5	14.9	X	14.4	14.4	X
Same county	8.9	9.2	X	9.0	8.9	X
Different county	5.6	5.7	X	5.4	5.5	X
Same state	3.5	3.6	X	3.2	3.2	X
Different state	2.1	2.1	X	2.3	2.3	X
Abroad	0.4	0.4	X	0.6	0.6	X
Place of Birth						
Native born	6,234,189	6,256,401	0.4	273,089,382	274,780,773	0.6
Male..	49.1	49.1	X	49.3	49.3	X
Female..	50.9	50.9	X	50.7	50.7	X
Foreign born	303,145	314,501	3.7	40,824,658	41,348,066	1.3
Male	51.7	50.6	X	48.7	48.8	X
Female..	48.3	49.4	X	51.3	51.2	X
Foreign born; naturalized U.S. citizen......	107,417	110,657	3.0	18,686,237	19,294,710	3.3
Male..	48.3	46.1	X	45.8	45.9	X
Female..	51.7	53.9	X	54.2	54.1	X
Foreign born; not a U.S. citizen................	195,728	203,844	4.1	22,138,421	22,053,356	-0.4
Male..	53.6	53.0	X	51.1	51.3	X
Female..	46.4	47.0	X	48.9	48.7	X
Entered 2010 or later	10.7	15.5	X	7.0	9.7	X
Entered 2000 to 2009	37.7	39.0	X	30.4	29.4	X
Entered before 2000...............................	51.6	45.5	X	62.7	61.0	X
World Region of Birth, Foreign						
Foreign-born population, excluding population born at sea	303,145	314,501	3.7	40,824,553	41,347,945	1.3
Europe..	14.1	13.5	X	11.8	11.6	X
Asia..	30.9	32.2	X	29.2	29.5	X
Africa..	5.6	6.9	X	4.2	4.4	X
Oceania	0.5	0.6	X	0.6	0.5	X
Latin America..	46.4	44.8	X	52.2	51.9	X
North America...	2.5	2.0	X	2.0	2.0	X
Language Spoken at Home and Ability to Speak English						
Population 5 years and over.....................	6,113,177	6,146,838	0.6	294,003,714	296,358,760	0.8
English only	91.5	91.8	X	79.0	79.2	X
Language other than English....................	8.5	8.2	X	21.0	20.8	X
Speaks English less than "very well".........	3.2	3.2	X	8.5	8.5	X

NA = Not available.
X = Not applicable.
- = Zero or rounds to zero.

Table IN-5. Median Income and Poverty Status, 2013

(Number, percent, except as noted.)

Characteristic	State		U.S.	
	Number	Percent	Number	Percent
Median Income				
Households (dollars)...	47,529	X	52,250	X
Families (dollars)	59,428	X	64,030	X
Below Poverty Level (All People)	1,015,127	15.9	48,810,868	15.8
Sex				
Male..	446,429	14.3	21,938,525	14.5
Female	568,698	17.5	26,872,343	17.1
Age				
Under 18 years...	345,056	22.2	16,086,960	22.2
Related children under 18 years........................	337,267	21.8	15,769,921	21.9
18 to 64 years..	600,853	15.3	28,578,191	14.8
65 years and over	69,218	7.9	4,145,717	9.6

X = Not applicable.

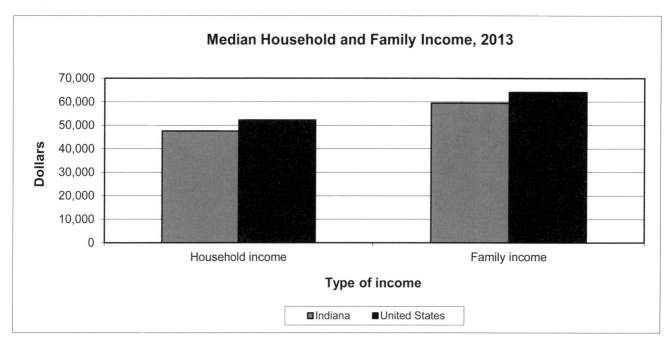

Table IN-6. Health Insurance Coverage Status for the Civilian Noninstitutionalized Population and Children Under 18 Years of Age

(Numbers in thousands, percent.)

Item	2005	2006	2007	2008	2009	2010	2011	2012	2013
Civilian Noninstitutionalized Population	6,141	6,337	6,263	6,271	6,316	6,391	6,418	6,437	6,472
Covered by Private or Public Insurance									
Number..	5,308	5,590	5,546	5,400	5,415	5,444	5,487	5,517	5,569
Percent..	86.4	88.2	88.6	86.1	85.7	85.2	85.5	85.7	86.0
Not Covered									
Number..	832	748	717	871	901	948	931	920	903
Percent..	13.6	11.8	11.4	13.9	14.3	14.8	14.5	14.3	14.0
Percent in the U.S. not covered..	15.3	15.8	15.3	15.1	15.1	15.5	15.1	14.8	14.5
Children Under 18 Years of Age...	1,614	1,582	1,593	1,580	1,583	1,602	1,594	1,585	1,584
Covered by Private or Public Insurance									
Number..	1,457	1,459	1,511	1,420	1,443	1,459	1,465	1,451	1,454
Percent..	90.2	92.2	94.8	89.9	91.2	91.1	91.9	91.5	91.8
Not Covered									
Number..	158	123	83	160	140	143	129	134	130
Percent..	9.8	7.8	5.2	10.1	8.8	8.9	8.1	8.5	8.2
Percent in the U.S. not covered..	10.9	11.7	11.0	9.7	8.6	8.0	7.5	7.2	7.1

Table IN-7. Employment Status by Demographic Group, 2014

(Numbers in thousands, percent.)

Characteristic	Civilian noninstitutional population	Civilian labor force		Employed		Unemployed	
		Number	Percent of population	Number	Percent of population	Number	Percent of population
Total..	5,097	3,237	63.5	3,041	59.7	196	6.1
Sex							
Male..	2,473	1,712	69.2	1,604	64.8	108	6.3
Female	2,624	1,525	58.1	1,438	54.8	88	5.7
Race, Sex, and Hispanic Origin							
White	4,507	2,894	64.2	2,736	60.7	158	5.5
Male..	2,211	1,560	70.5	1,469	66.4	91	5.8
Female	2,296	1,334	58.1	1,267	55.2	67	5.0
Black or African American..................	434	253	58.2	220	50.8	32	12.8
Male..	191	102	53.2	88	45.8	14	13.9
Female	243	151	62.2	133	54.7	18	12.2
Hispanic or Latino ethnicity[1]	299	213	71.2	195	65.1	18	8.6
Male..	169	141	83.4	132	78.0	9	6.5
Female	130	72	55.2	63	48.3	9	12.5
Age							
16 to 19 years...................................	368	140	37.9	113	30.7	26	19.0
20 to 24 years...................................	404	289	71.6	258	63.7	32	11.0
25 to 34 years...................................	871	710	81.5	663	76.1	47	6.6
35 to 44 years...................................	832	713	85.6	681	81.8	32	4.5
45 to 54 years...................................	881	704	79.9	672	76.3	31	4.5
55 to 64 years...................................	810	513	63.3	494	61.0	19	3.6
65 years and over	930	169	18.2	160	17.2	9	5.3

NOTE: Data in Table 7 are from the Current Population Survey (CPS) and do not match the estimates in Table 8. See notes and definitions for further information.
[1]May be of any race.

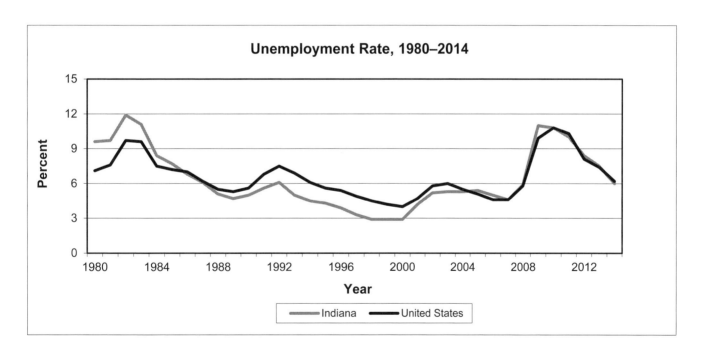

Unemployment Rate, 1980–2014

Table IN-8. Employment Status of the Civilian Noninstitutional Population Age 16 Years and Over

(Number, percent.)

Year	Civilian labor force	Civilian participation rate	Employed	Unemployed	Unemployment rate
2006	3,235,110	67.5	3,072,113	162,997	5.0
2007	3,207,687	66.3	3,061,042	146,645	4.6
2008	3,232,097	66.3	3,041,828	190,269	5.9
2009	3,193,989	65.1	2,864,985	329,004	10.3
2010	3,175,192	64.0	2,845,608	329,584	10.4
2011	3,182,463	63.6	2,892,327	290,136	9.1
2012	3,170,442	63.0	2,906,201	264,241	8.3
2013	3,191,866	63.0	2,947,114	244,752	7.7
2014	3,230,540	63.4	3,035,581	194,959	6.0

Table IN-9. Employment and Average Wages by Industry

(Estimates from 2007 through 2010 are based on the 2007 *North American Industry Classification System* [NAICS]. Estimates from 2011 onward are based on the 2012 NAICS.)

Industry	2007	2008	2009	2010	2011	2012	2013
	Number of jobs						
Wage and Salary Employment by Industry	3,075,446	3,042,659	2,877,302	2,886,635	2,930,409	2,982,649	3,016,449
Farm Wage and Salary Employment	12,146	9,368	10,488	13,576	10,314	13,535	12,721
Nonfarm Wage and Salary Employment	3,063,300	3,033,291	2,866,814	2,873,059	2,920,095	2,969,114	3,003,728
Private wage and salary employment	2,612,334	2,572,832	2,405,042	2,415,138	2,470,191	2,521,092	2,559,886
Forestry, fishing, and related activities	3,378	3,152	2,985	3,158	3,183	3,243	3,313
Mining	6,663	6,455	6,296	6,268	6,580	6,738	6,684
Utilities	14,748	14,996	15,291	14,952	14,729	14,349	14,172
Construction	157,062	150,313	126,089	121,231	126,627	129,260	127,819
Manufacturing	550,333	521,405	442,761	448,527	464,552	482,919	492,560
Durable goods manufacturing	401,509	377,451	309,284	314,026	330,610	346,630	352,396
Nondurable goods manufacturing	148,824	143,954	133,477	134,501	133,942	136,289	140,164
Wholesale trade	126,612	126,047	116,318	114,851	115,978	116,691	117,517
Retail trade	332,963	326,542	312,887	309,475	312,756	315,285	319,332
Transportation and warehousing	119,658	118,012	110,784	111,987	115,179	117,925	120,755
Information	40,345	39,759	37,772	35,811	34,274	35,829	35,826
Finance and insurance	103,035	101,823	98,256	97,609	98,073	98,138	97,815
Real estate and rental and leasing	37,006	35,920	34,329	33,286	33,249	33,162	33,488
Professional, scientific, and technical services	98,308	100,029	97,236	97,668	99,962	100,883	102,977
Management of companies and enterprises	28,535	29,218	27,518	26,995	28,043	29,106	31,082
Administrative and waste services	163,566	157,324	139,298	153,626	164,333	171,745	176,403
Educational services	59,673	61,830	61,146	62,728	64,520	65,737	66,620
Health care and social assistance	332,863	341,927	349,939	355,805	360,872	367,403	374,617
Arts, entertainment, and recreation	43,803	44,269	43,782	42,417	41,966	41,521	41,886
Accommodation and food services	243,587	243,915	236,425	234,685	239,687	245,647	250,846
Other services, except public administration	150,196	149,896	145,930	144,059	145,628	145,511	146,174
Government and government enterprises	450,966	460,459	461,772	457,921	449,904	448,022	443,842
	Dollars						
Average Wages and Salaries by Industry	38,066	38,950	38,869	39,885	40,970	41,830	42,328
Average Farm Wages and Salaries	27,880	33,586	32,706	25,400	33,141	24,449	34,539
Average Nonfarm Wages and Salaries	38,106	38,966	38,891	39,954	40,998	41,910	42,361
Average private wages and salaries	38,531	39,396	39,153	40,335	41,461	42,488	42,913
Forestry, fishing, and related activities	22,473	21,266	21,845	22,565	23,165	24,164	24,686
Mining	58,324	59,481	59,059	62,666	65,326	65,302	68,335
Utilities	70,756	75,360	76,469	79,645	82,447	84,740	88,413
Construction	45,347	47,883	47,845	50,401	52,444	55,052	54,484
Manufacturing	52,408	53,793	54,025	56,098	57,108	58,046	58,013
Durable goods manufacturing	52,754	53,426	53,484	55,455	56,727	57,978	57,340
Nondurable goods manufacturing	51,476	54,757	55,279	57,600	58,047	58,220	59,702
Wholesale trade	52,748	53,909	53,345	55,051	57,000	58,516	59,463
Retail trade	23,450	23,642	23,809	24,497	24,866	25,349	25,465
Transportation and warehousing	40,830	41,521	41,056	41,857	43,020	43,509	44,243
Information	47,724	49,087	49,371	50,488	52,277	54,146	55,344
Finance and insurance	54,536	54,888	54,304	56,496	59,275	62,108	63,277
Real estate and rental and leasing	33,552	34,066	34,024	35,267	36,779	38,082	38,979
Professional, scientific, and technical services	52,685	55,068	54,734	56,197	58,657	60,311	62,930
Management of companies and enterprises	75,849	75,634	74,953	79,612	84,796	86,569	88,180
Administrative and waste services	25,910	27,130	27,832	28,019	28,591	28,892	29,133
Educational services	26,998	27,890	29,731	30,030	30,984	30,997	31,182
Health care and social assistance	38,672	39,857	40,532	40,982	41,982	43,246	43,909
Arts, entertainment, and recreation	34,528	32,893	31,624	32,922	32,971	32,938	33,145
Accommodation and food services	14,464	14,374	14,553	15,157	15,576	15,881	15,839
Other services, except public administration	26,137	27,037	27,043	28,031	28,512	29,032	29,643
Government and government enterprises	35,644	36,564	37,526	37,946	38,455	38,654	39,182

Table IN-10. Employment Characteristics by Family Type

(Number, percent.)

Family type and labor force status	2011 Total	2011 Families with own children under 18 years	2012 Total	2012 Families with own children under 18 years	2013 Total	2013 Families with own children under 18 years
All Families	1,641,389	725,540	1,648,172	719,823	1,647,941	720,081
FAMILY TYPE AND LABOR FORCE STATUS						
Married-Couple Families	1,217,034	474,838	1,229,106	477,058	1,226,204	476,033
Both husband and wife in labor force	54.5	68.9	53.5	67.8	52.8	67.8
Husband in labor force, wife not in labor force	20.7	26.1	21.3	26.9	21.8	27.1
Wife in labor force, husband not in labor force	8.0	3.5	7.8	4.0	8.1	3.4
Both husband and wife not in labor force	16.8	1.5	17.4	1.4	17.1	1.5
Other Families	424,355	250,702	419,066	242,765	421,737	244,048
Female householder, no husband present	73.9	76.7	72.6	74.4	72.9	74.5
In labor force	53.7	63.1	52.5	62.4	51.4	61.0
Not in labor force	20.2	13.6	20.1	12.0	21.5	13.5
Male householder, no wife present	26.1	23.3	27.4	25.6	27.1	25.5
In labor force	20.8	21.2	22.3	23.3	21.3	22.6
Not in labor force	5.3	2.1	5.1	2.3	5.8	2.9

Table IN-11. School Enrollment and Educational Attainment, 2013

(Number, percent.)

Item	State	U.S.
Enrollment		
Total population 3 years and over, enrolled in school	1,726,742	82,395,254
Enrolled in nursery school or preschool (percent)	5.8	6.0
Enrolled in kindergarten (percent)	4.9	5.2
Enrolled in elementary school, grades 1-8 (percent)	41.7	40.0
Enrolled in high school, grades 9-12 (percent)	20.5	20.6
Enrolled in college or graduate school (percent)	27.1	28.3
Attainment		
Total population 25 years and over	4,312,892	210,910,615
Less than ninth grade (percent)	4.1	5.8
9th to 12th grade, no diploma (percent)	8.3	7.6
High school graduate, including equivalency (percent)	34.3	27.8
Some college, no degree (percent)	21.3	21.1
Associate's degree (percent)	8.2	8.1
Bachelor's degree (percent)	15.2	18.4
Graduate or professional degree (percent)	8.6	11.2
High school graduate or higher (percent)	87.6	86.6
Bachelor's degree or higher (percent)	23.8	29.6

Table IN-12. Public School Characteristics and Educational Indicators

(Number, percent; data derived from National Center of Education Statistics.)

Item	State	U.S.
Public Schools, 2012–2013 (except where noted)		
Number of school districts	407	18,093
Number of schools	1,925	98,454
Number of students (in thousands)	1,041	49,771
Number of teachers (in thousands)	60	3,109
Student-teacher ratio	17.4	16.0
Expenditures per student (dollars), FY 2012	9,588	10,667
Four-year adjusted cohort graduation rate (ACGR)[1,2]	87.0	81.4
Students eligible for free or reduced-price lunch (in thousands)	510	25,188
English language learners (in thousands)	51	4,397
Students age 3 to 21 served under IDEA, part B (in thousands)	169	6,429

Public Schools by Type	Number	Percent of state public schools
Total number of schools	1,925	100.0
Regular	1,860	96.6
Special education	29	1.5
Vocational education	27	1.4
Alternative education	9	0.5

NOTE: Every school is assigned only one school type based on its instructional emphasis.
[1]ACGR data represents a new method of calculating high-school completion rates and may not be comparable to previous years' data for Averaged Freshmen Graduation Rates (AFGR).
[2]The United States 4-year ACGRs were estimated using both the reported 4-year ACGR data from 49 states and the District of Columbia and using imputed data for Idaho. The estimate for American Indian/Alaska Native students also includes imputed data for Virginia.

Table IN-13. Reported Voting and Registration of the Voting-Age Population, November 2012

(Numbers in thousands, percent.)

Item	Total population	Total citizen population	Registered			Voted		
			Total registered	Percent registered (total population)	Percent registered (total citizen population)	Total voted	Percent voted (total population)	Percent voted (total citizen population)
U.S. Total	235,248	215,081	153,157	65.1	71.2	132,948	56.5	61.8
State Total	4,852	4,724	3,270	67.4	69.2	2,801	57.7	59.3
Sex								
Male	2,326	2,247	1,542	66.3	68.7	1,331	57.2	59.2
Female	2,526	2,478	1,727	68.4	69.7	1,470	58.2	59.3
Race								
White alone	4,349	4,255	2,926	67.3	68.8	2,509	57.7	59.0
White, non-Hispanic alone	4,179	4,151	2,861	68.4	68.9	2,460	58.9	59.3
Black alone	385	385	309	80.3	80.3	263	68.4	68.4
Asian alone	75	41	19	B	B	14	B	B
Hispanic (of any race)	184	118	71	38.5	59.7	49	26.5	41.1
White alone or in combination	4,373	4,279	2,938	67.2	68.7	2,521	57.7	58.9
Black alone or in combination	409	409	316	77.1	77.1	270	65.9	65.9
Asian alone or in combination	75	41	19	B	B	14	B	B
Age								
18 to 24 years	570	558	269	47.2	48.2	203	35.7	36.4
25 to 44 years	1,688	1,602	1,012	59.9	63.2	776	45.9	48.4
45 to 64 years	1,754	1,733	1,329	75.8	76.7	1,212	69.1	70.0
65 to 74 years	478	473	377	79.0	79.9	360	75.3	76.2
75 years and over	362	359	283	78.1	78.7	250	69.1	69.6

B = Base is less than 75,000 and therefore too small to show the derived measure.

Table IN-14. Crime

(Number, rate per 100,000. Data are derived from the FBI Uniform Crime Reports.)

Item	State			U.S. 1,2,3,4		
	2012	2013	Percent change	2012	2013	Percent change
TOTAL POPULATION[5]	6,537,782	6,570,902	0.5	313,873,685	316,128,839	0.7
VIOLENT CRIME						
Number	22,544	22,991	2.0	1,217,067	1,163,146	-4.4
Rate	344.8	349.9	1.5	387.8	367.9	-5.1
Murder and Nonnegligent Manslaughter						
Number	307	355	15.6	14,866	14,196	-4.5
Rate	4.7	5.4	15.1	4.7	4.5	-5.2
Rape[6]						
Number	X	2,142	X	X	108,612	X
Rate	X	32.6	X	X	34.4	X
Robbery						
Number	6,601	7,108	7.7	355,051	345,031	-2.8
Rate	101.0	108.2	7.1	113.1	109.1	-3.5
Aggravated Assault						
Number	13,975	13,882	-0.7	762,009	724,149	-5.0
Rate	213.8	211.3	-1.2	242.8	229.1	-5.6
PROPERTY CRIME						
Number	197,994	187,536	-5.3	9,001,992	8,632,512	-4.1
Rate	3,028.5	2,854.0	-5.8	2,868.0	2,730.7	-4.8
Burglary						
Number	47,689	42,909	-10.0	2,109,932	1,928,465	-8.6
Rate	729.4	653.0	-10.5	672.2	610.0	-9.3
Larceny-Theft						
Number	136,668	130,423	-4.6	6,168,874	6,004,453	-2.7
Rate	2,090.4	1,984.9	-5.1	1,965.4	1,899.4	-3.4
Motor Vehicle Theft						
Number	13,637	14,204	4.2	723,186	699,594	-3.3
Rate	208.6	216.2	3.6	230.4	221.3	-4.0

NOTE: Although arson data are included in the trend and clearance tables, sufficient data are not available to estimate totals for this offense. Therefore, no arson data are published in this table.
X = Not applicable.
- = Zero or rounds to zero.
[1]The crime figures have been adjusted.
[2]The data collection methodology for the offense of forcible rape used by the Minnesota state Uniform Crime Reporting (UCR) Program (with the exception of Minneapolis and St. Paul, Minnesota) does not comply with national UCR Program guidelines. Consequently, its figures for forcible rape and violent crime (of which forcible rape is a part) are not published in this table.
[3]Includes offenses reported by the Zoological Police and the Metro Transit Police.
[4]Because of changes in the state's reporting practices, figures are not comparable to previous years' data.
[5]Populations are U.S. Census Bureau provisional estimates as of July 1 of each year.
[6]The figures shown for the offense of rape were estimated using the revised Uniform Crime Reporting (UCR) definition of rape.

Table IN-15. State Government Finances, 2013

(Dollar amounts in thousands, percent distribution.)

Item	Dollars	Percent distribution
Total Revenue	38,141,709	100.0
General revenue	33,499,152	87.8
Intergovernmental revenue	11,267,810	29.5
Taxes	16,930,731	44.4
General sales	6,793,923	17.8
Selective sales	3,504,568	9.2
License taxes	699,373	1.8
Individual income tax	4,976,375	13.0
Corporate income tax	781,585	2.0
Other taxes	174,907	0.5
Current charges	3,429,363	9.0
Miscellaneous general revenue	1,871,248	4.9
Utility revenue	0	-
Liquor stores revenue	0	-
Insurance trust revenue[1]	4,642,557	12.2
Total Expenditure	36,793,639	100.0
Intergovernmental expenditure	9,292,344	25.3
Direct expenditure	27,501,295	74.7
Current operation	19,786,809	53.8
Capital outlay	2,427,613	6.6
Insurance benefits and repayments	3,343,517	9.1
Assistance and subsidies	981,692	2.7
Interest on debt	961,664	2.6
Exhibit: Salaries and wages	4,314,917	11.7
Total Expenditure	36,793,639	100.0
General expenditure	33,450,122	90.9
Intergovernmental expenditure	9,292,344	25.3
Direct expenditure	24,157,778	65.7
General expenditure, by function:		
Education	14,613,475	39.7
Public welfare	10,748,417	29.2
Hospitals	160,643	0.4
Health	495,892	1.3
Highways	2,530,006	6.9
Police protection	237,564	0.6
Correction	688,283	1.9
Natural resources	335,053	0.9
Parks and recreation	77,161	0.2
Governmental administration	560,115	1.5
Interest on general debt	961,664	2.6
Other and unallocable	2,041,849	5.5
Utility expenditure	0	-
Liquor stores expenditure	0	-
Insurance trust expenditure	3,343,517	9.1
Debt at End of Fiscal Year	22,564,017	X
Cash and Security Holdings	59,309,263	X

X = Not applicable.
- = Zero or rounds to zero.
[1]Within insurance trust revenue, net earnings of state retirement systems is a calculated statistic (the item code in the data file is X08), and thus can be positive or negative. Net earnings is the sum of earnings on investments plus gains on investments minus losses on investments. The change made in 2002 for asset valuation from book to market value in accordance with Statement 34 of the Governmental Accounting Standards Board is reflected in the calculated statistics.

Table IN-16. State Government Tax Collections, 2014

(Dollars in thousands, percent.)

Item	Dollars	Percent distribution
Total Taxes	16,846,961	100.0
Property taxes	8,052	-
Sales and gross receipts	10,395,150	61.7
General sales and gross receipts	7,003,426	41.6
Selective sales and gross receipts	3,391,724	20.1
Alcoholic beverages	45,955	0.3
Amusements	655,894	3.9
Insurance premiums	223,072	1.3
Motor fuels	814,549	4.8
Pari-mutuels	2,273	-
Public utilities	252,652	1.5
Tobacco products	447,561	2.7
Other selective sales	949,768	5.6
Licenses	590,483	3.5
Alcoholic beverages	13,073	0.1
Amusements	5,722	-
Corporations in general	7,045	-
Hunting and fishing	20,011	0.1
Motor vehicle	208,572	1.2
Motor vehicle operators	207,097	1.2
Public utilities	0	-
Occupation and business, NEC	46,157	0.3
Other licenses	82,806	0.5
Income taxes	5,763,064	34.2
Individual income	4,896,317	29.1
Corporation net income	866,747	5.1
Other taxes	90,212	0.5
Death and gift	87,712	0.5
Documentary and stock transfer	0	-
Severance	2,500	-
Taxes, NEC	0	-

- = Zero or rounds to zero.

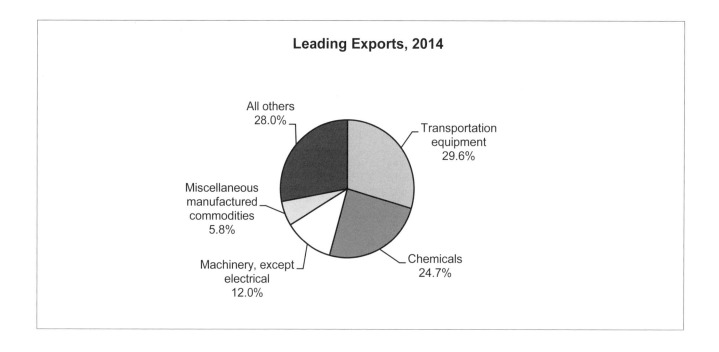

Leading Exports, 2014

All others 28.0%
Transportation equipment 29.6%
Miscellaneous manufactured commodities 5.8%
Machinery, except electrical 12.0%
Chemicals 24.7%

IOWA

Facts and Figures

Location: North central United States; bordered on the N by Minnesota, on the E by Wisconsin and Illinois, on the S by Missouri, and on the W by Nebraska and South Dakota

Area: 56,272 sq. mi. (145,743 sq. km.); rank—26th

Population: 3,107,126 (2014 est.); rank—30th

Principal Cities: capital—Des Moines; largest—Des Moines

Statehood: December 28, 1846; 29th state

U.S. Congress: 2 senators, 4 representatives

State Motto: Our Liberties We Prize and Our Rights We Will Maintain

State Song: "The Song of Iowa"

State Nickname: The Hawkeye State

Abbreviations: IA; Ia.

State Symbols: flower—wild prairie rose; tree—oak; bird—Eastern goldfinch

At a Glance

- With an increase in population of 2.0 percent, Iowa ranked 30th among the states in growth from 2010 to 2014.

- Iowa's median household income in 2013 was $52,229, and 12.7 percent of the population lived below the poverty level.

- In 2013, 8.1 percent of Iowans did not have health insurance, compared to 14.5 percent of the total U.S. population.

- Iowa's violent crime rate in 2013 was 271.4 per 100,000 population, compared to the rate of 367.9 for the United States as a whole.

- In 2013, Iowa had the lowest infant mortality rate in the country, at 4.14 deaths per 1,000 live births.

Table IA-1. Population by Age, Sex, Race, and Hispanic Origin

(Number, percent, except where noted.)

Sex, age, race, and Hispanic origin	2000	2010	2014[1]	Average annual percent change, 2010–2014
Total Population	2,926,324	3,046,355	3,107,126	0.5
Percent of total U.S. population	1.0	1.0	1.0	X
Sex				
Male	1,435,515	1,508,319	1,543,045	0.6
Female	1,490,809	1,538,036	1,564,081	0.4
Age				
Under 5 years	188,413	202,123	195,340	-0.8
5 to 19 years	639,570	618,387	621,061	0.1
20 to 64 years	1,662,128	1,772,957	1,799,376	0.4
65 years and over	436,213	452,888	491,349	2.1
Median age (years)	36.6	38.1	38.1	0.0
Race and Hispanic Origin				
One race				
White	2,748,640	2,839,615	2,860,661	0.2
Black	61,853	91,695	106,073	3.7
American Indian and Alaska Native	8,989	13,563	15,183	2.9
Asian	36,635	54,232	69,062	6.2
Native Hawaiian or Other Pacific Islander	1,009	2,419	2,953	5.1
Two or more races	31,778	44,831	53,194	4.4
Hispanic (of any race)	82,473	156,932	173,594	2.6

X = Not applicable.
- = Zero or rounds to zero.
[1]Population figures for 2014 are July 1 estimates. The 2010 estimates are taken from the 2010 Census.

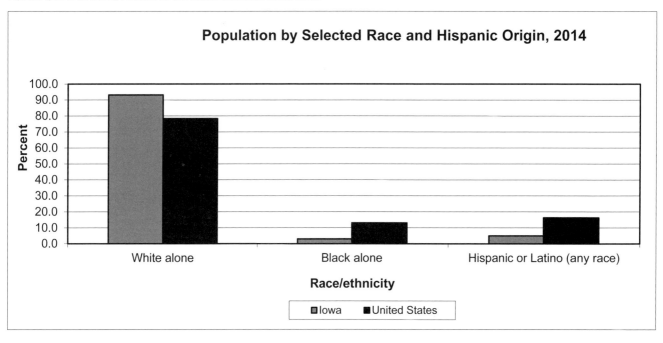

Table IA-2. Marital Status

(Number, percent distribution.)

Sex, age, race, and Hispanic origin	2000	2010	2013
Males, 15 Years and Over	1,126,566	1,199,509	1,221,528
Never married	28.2	31.3	32.6
Now married, except separated	59.8	55.2	53.5
Separated	0.9	1.1	1.2
Widowed	2.5	2.6	2.6
Divorced	8.5	9.7	10.2
Females, 15 Years and Over	1,198,297	1,250,612	1,269,964
Never married	21.8	24.7	25.9
Now married, except separated	55.8	52.4	51.5
Separated	1.1	1.5	1.6
Widowed	11.6	10.2	9.8
Divorced	9.6	11.2	11.1

Table IA-3. Households and Housing Characteristics

(Number, percent, dollars.)

Item	2000	2010	2013	Average annual percent change, 2000–2013
Total Households..	1,149,276	1,223,439	1,236,209	0.6
Family households	769,684	793,768	793,749	0.2
Married-couple family......................................	633,254	633,602	625,107	-0.1
Other family	136,430	160,166	168,642	1.6
Male householder, no wife present.....................	38,160	46,829	53,032	2.6
Female householder, no husband present............	98,270	113,337	115,610	1.3
Nonfamily households	379,592	429,671	442,460	1.2
Householder living alone.................................	313,083	349,736	358,393	1.0
Householder not living alone............................	66,509	79,935	84,067	1.8
Housing Characteristics				
Total housing units..	1,232,511	1,337,563	1,349,607	0.7
Occupied housing units	1,149,276	1,223,439	1,236,209	0.6
Owner occupied...	831,419	885,284	875,362	0.4
Renter occupied..	317,857	338,155	360,847	1.0
Average household size....................................	2.46	2.41	2.42	-0.1
Financial Characteristics				
Median gross rent of renter-occupied housing	470	629	679	2.9
Median monthly owner costs for housing units with a mortgage	829	1,140	1,118	2.3
Median value of owner-occupied housing units	82,500	123,400	126,900	3.4

Table IA-4. Migration, Origin, and Language

(Number, percent.)

Characteristic	State			U.S.		
	2012	2013	Percent change	2012	2013	Percent change
Residence 1 Year Ago						
Population 1 year and over	3,035,469	3,053,635	0.6	310,212,755	312,432,820	0.7
Same house..	85.2	84.7	X	85.0	85.0	X
Different house in the U.S...................................	14.5	14.9	X	14.4	14.4	X
Same county	8.6	8.8	X	9.0	8.9	X
Different county	5.8	6.1	X	5.4	5.5	X
Same state	3.3	3.7	X	3.2	3.2	X
Different state	2.5	2.5	X	2.3	2.3	X
Abroad	0.4	0.4	X	0.6	0.6	X
Place of Birth						
Native born	2,936,328	2,941,294	0.2	273,089,382	274,780,773	0.6
Male...	49.5	49.4	X	49.3	49.3	X
Female	50.5	50.6	X	50.7	50.7	X
Foreign born	137,858	149,122	8.2	40,824,658	41,348,066	1.3
Male...	51.8	50.8	X	48.7	48.8	X
Female	48.2	49.2	X	51.3	51.2	X
Foreign born; naturalized U.S. citizen.....................	53,175	55,195	3.8	18,686,237	19,294,710	3.3
Male...	48.8	48.9	X	45.8	45.9	X
Female	51.2	51.1	X	54.2	54.1	X
Foreign born; not a U.S. citizen..............................	84,683	93,927	10.9	22,138,421	22,053,356	-0.4
Male...	53.7	51.9	X	51.1	51.3	X
Female	46.3	48.1	X	48.9	48.7	X
Entered 2010 or later	11.9	17.6	X	7.0	9.7	X
Entered 2000 to 2009	35.0	36.1	X	30.4	29.4	X
Entered before 2000...	53.1	46.2	X	62.7	61.0	X
World Region of Birth, Foreign						
Foreign-born population, excluding population born at sea	137,858	149,122	8.2	40,824,553	41,347,945	1.3
Europe	14.6	15.5	X	11.8	11.6	X
Asia..	33.5	35.0	X	29.2	29.5	X
Africa	8.7	8.0	X	4.2	4.4	X
Oceania	0.9	0.3	X	0.6	0.5	X
Latin America..	39.1	38.4	X	52.2	51.9	X
North America	3.2	2.7	X	2.0	2.0	X
Language Spoken at Home and Ability to Speak English						
Population 5 years and over......................................	2,878,189	2,897,339	0.7	294,003,714	296,358,760	0.8
English only	92.8	92.8	X	79.0	79.2	X
Language other than English.................................	7.2	7.2	X	21.0	20.8	X
Speaks English less than "very well"...................	2.9	3.1	X	8.5	8.5	X

NA = Not available.
X = Not applicable.
- = Zero or rounds to zero.

Table IA-5. Median Income and Poverty Status, 2013

(Number, percent, except as noted.)

Characteristic	State		U.S.	
	Number	Percent	Number	Percent
Median Income				
Households (dollars)..	52,229	X	52,250	X
Families (dollars)	66,684	X	64,030	X
Below Poverty Level (All People).................................	379,127	12.7	48,810,868	15.8
Sex				
Male..	169,605	11.5	21,938,525	14.5
Female	209,522	13.8	26,872,343	17.1
Age				
Under 18 years..	115,194	16.2	16,086,960	22.2
Related children under 18 years................................	111,119	15.7	15,769,921	21.9
18 to 64 years...	228,205	12.5	28,578,191	14.8
65 years and over	35,728	7.8	4,145,717	9.6

X = Not applicable.

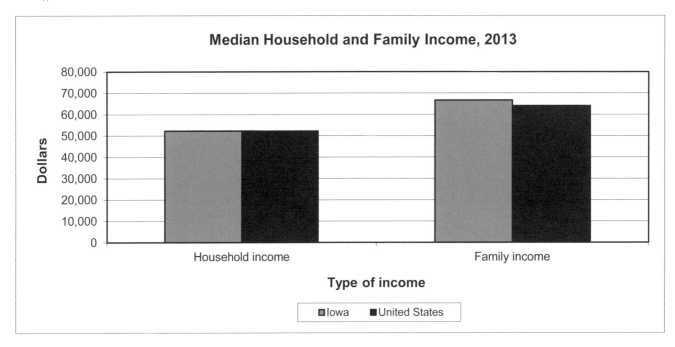

Table IA-6. Health Insurance Coverage Status for the Civilian Noninstitutionalized Population and Children Under 18 Years of Age

(Numbers in thousands, percent.)

Item	2005	2006	2007	2008	2009	2010	2011	2012	2013
Civilian Noninstitutionalized Population..........................	2,909	2,919	2,970	2,951	2,957	3,005	3,017	3,029	3,045
Covered by Private or Public Insurance									
Number..	2,639	2,612	2,695	2,683	2,702	2,725	2,748	2,775	2,798
Percent..	91.7	89.5	90.7	90.9	91.4	90.7	91.1	91.6	91.9
Not Covered									
Number..	241	307	275	268	255	280	269	254	248
Percent..	8.3	10.5	9.3	9.1	8.6	9.3	8.9	8.4	8.1
Percent in the U.S. not covered......................................	15.3	15.8	15.3	15.1	15.1	15.5	15.1	14.8	14.5
Children Under 18 Years of Age.......................................	683	708	709	708	707	722	722	720	721
Covered by Private or Public Insurance									
Number..	649	664	675	668	675	693	690	691	692
Percent..	95.0	93.7	95.2	94.4	95.4	96.0	95.6	96.0	95.9
Not Covered									
Number..	34	44	34	40	32	29	32	29	30
Percent..	5.0	6.3	4.8	5.6	4.6	4.0	4.4	4.0	4.1
Percent in the U.S. not covered......................................	10.9	11.7	11.0	9.7	8.6	8.0	7.5	7.2	7.1

Table IA-7. Employment Status by Demographic Group, 2014

(Numbers in thousands, percent.)

Characteristic	Civilian noninstitutional population	Civilian labor force		Employed		Unemployed	
		Number	Percent of population	Number	Percent of population	Number	Percent of population
Total..	2,420	1,709	70.6	1,630	67.3	79	4.6
Sex							
Male...	1,191	896	75.2	849	71.3	47	5.3
Female..	1,229	813	66.1	781	63.5	32	3.9
Race, Sex, and Hispanic Origin							
White...	2,242	1,582	70.6	1,513	67.5	69	4.4
Male...	1,100	828	75.2	786	71.4	42	5.1
Female..	1,141	754	66.1	727	63.7	27	3.6
Black or African American...................	66	45	68.5	39	58.8	6	14.1
Male...	32	22	69.6	18	57.9	4	16.9
Female..	35	23	67.5	21	59.7	3	11.5
Hispanic or Latino ethnicity[1]...............	102	77	75.6	70	69.2	7	8.5
Male...	53	44	82.4	40	75.6	4	8.2
Female..	48	33	68.1	30	62.1	3	8.8
Age							
16 to 19 years...............................	157	87	55.6	77	49.0	10	11.8
20 to 24 years...............................	224	188	84.0	178	79.1	11	5.8
25 to 34 years...............................	405	362	89.4	342	84.5	20	5.6
35 to 44 years...............................	353	316	89.5	302	85.5	14	4.5
45 to 54 years...............................	397	348	87.7	334	84.1	14	4.0
55 to 64 years...............................	442	321	72.5	314	71.1	6	2.0
65 years and over...........................	442	86	19.5	83	18.8	3	3.6

NOTE: Data in Table 7 are from the Current Population Survey (CPS) and do not match the estimates in Table 8. See notes and definitions for further information.
[1]May be of any race.

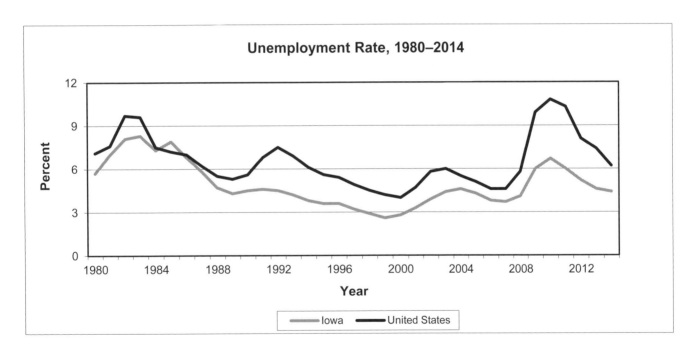

Unemployment Rate, 1980–2014

Table IA-8. Employment Status of the Civilian Noninstitutional Population Age 16 Years and Over

(Number, percent.)

Year	Civilian labor force	Civilian participation rate	Employed	Unemployed	Unemployment rate
2006	1,657,584	72.3	1,596,530	61,054	3.7
2007	1,660,677	72.0	1,599,332	61,345	3.7
2008	1,679,293	72.4	1,608,695	70,598	4.2
2009	1,687,411	72.3	1,579,248	108,163	6.4
2010	1,678,281	71.2	1,577,447	100,834	6.0
2011	1,662,881	70.0	1,570,433	92,448	5.6
2012	1,648,870	69.0	1,565,715	83,155	5.0
2013	1,673,590	69.6	1,593,835	79,755	4.8
2014	1,704,575	70.4	1,629,326	75,249	4.4

Table IA-9. Employment and Average Wages by Industry

(Estimates from 2007 through 2010 are based on the 2007 *North American Industry Classification System* [NAICS]. Estimates from 2011 onward are based on the 2012 NAICS.)

Industry	2007	2008	2009	2010	2011	2012	2013
				Number of jobs			
Wage and Salary Employment by Industry	1,582,832	1,590,045	1,546,421	1,541,196	1,556,200	1,574,044	1,595,727
Farm Wage and Salary Employment	15,557	18,140	16,360	18,966	18,011	15,276	19,266
Nonfarm Wage and Salary Employment	1,567,275	1,571,905	1,530,061	1,522,230	1,538,189	1,558,768	1,576,461
Private wage and salary employment	1,303,854	1,305,760	1,260,011	1,253,690	1,270,493	1,289,105	1,308,804
Forestry, fishing, and related activities	5,425	5,606	5,754	6,550	6,776	7,115	8,331
Mining	2,120	2,148	2,181	2,132	2,175	2,199	2,228
Utilities	6,997	7,103	7,007	6,785	6,605	6,499	6,451
Construction	75,445	75,946	67,998	64,513	65,729	66,772	70,333
Manufacturing	230,103	227,885	203,661	201,315	206,393	211,078	214,829
Durable goods manufacturing	142,141	139,276	117,787	116,664	122,271	126,667	129,046
Nondurable goods manufacturing	87,962	88,609	85,874	84,651	84,122	84,411	85,783
Wholesale trade	68,514	69,641	67,350	66,581	67,390	68,961	69,638
Retail trade	181,595	180,283	177,577	175,618	176,933	177,470	179,632
Transportation and warehousing	56,994	57,393	55,432	55,371	56,908	57,595	57,651
Information	32,451	31,944	30,269	28,786	28,192	27,047	26,164
Finance and insurance	91,640	92,084	91,221	92,004	92,320	92,991	94,108
Real estate and rental and leasing	14,332	14,278	14,489	14,089	13,531	13,372	13,854
Professional, scientific, and technical services	43,442	43,946	42,881	43,288	43,841	45,101	47,081
Management of companies and enterprises	13,020	12,934	13,152	13,208	14,902	16,083	16,532
Administrative and waste services	67,805	67,482	62,500	66,552	68,103	69,826	69,673
Educational services	35,823	36,887	37,938	38,091	38,752	40,686	40,568
Health care and social assistance	169,980	173,569	177,162	179,031	180,609	182,955	185,911
Arts, entertainment, and recreation	21,199	20,988	20,764	19,931	20,701	19,776	18,788
Accommodation and food services	117,553	115,983	113,441	111,486	112,472	115,113	118,585
Other services, except public administration	69,416	69,660	69,234	68,359	68,161	68,466	68,447
Government and government enterprises	263,421	266,145	270,050	268,540	267,696	269,663	267,657
				Dollars			
Average Wages and Salaries by Industry	35,210	36,259	36,413	37,323	38,386	39,468	40,213
Average Farm Wages and Salaries	40,135	30,211	33,470	29,462	30,892	38,063	33,629
Average Nonfarm Wages and Salaries	35,162	36,328	36,445	37,421	38,473	39,482	40,293
Average private wages and salaries	35,070	36,106	36,023	37,179	38,333	39,463	40,210
Forestry, fishing, and related activities	22,850	24,169	24,953	25,161	26,320	27,769	27,158
Mining	43,865	44,226	42,644	43,546	45,485	45,558	46,906
Utilities	74,234	75,231	75,802	76,433	80,037	82,985	80,974
Construction	42,158	44,009	43,507	43,749	45,122	47,068	48,502
Manufacturing	45,996	47,181	47,287	49,765	51,117	52,103	52,885
Durable goods manufacturing	48,515	49,249	49,696	52,516	54,519	55,169	55,972
Nondurable goods manufacturing	41,926	43,930	43,982	45,972	46,171	47,503	48,241
Wholesale trade	47,325	49,557	49,730	51,514	53,943	55,839	57,041
Retail trade	21,399	22,018	22,307	22,646	23,212	23,785	23,975
Transportation and warehousing	39,861	39,718	39,061	40,388	41,255	41,973	42,960
Information	42,387	43,267	43,600	45,192	46,745	47,014	48,938
Finance and insurance	55,943	56,584	55,622	59,010	61,219	63,398	65,911
Real estate and rental and leasing	32,063	33,576	36,264	37,415	39,330	41,057	41,065
Professional, scientific, and technical services	47,551	49,175	50,327	51,550	53,774	57,569	58,845
Management of companies and enterprises	71,094	71,217	69,756	70,069	71,396	76,921	75,678
Administrative and waste services	24,251	25,038	25,716	26,379	26,248	27,244	27,733
Educational services	22,421	23,429	23,553	24,048	24,540	24,016	24,623
Health care and social assistance	33,972	35,418	35,900	36,388	37,364	38,134	38,407
Arts, entertainment, and recreation	21,342	20,534	20,120	20,702	20,698	20,222	18,773
Accommodation and food services	13,141	13,533	13,444	13,875	14,426	15,061	15,336
Other services, except public administration	23,804	24,852	25,407	26,192	26,827	27,255	28,183
Government and government enterprises	35,616	37,418	38,409	38,553	39,141	39,572	40,701

Table IA-10. Employment Characteristics by Family Type

(Number, percent.)

Family type and labor force status	2011		2012		2013	
	Total	Families with own children under 18 years	Total	Families with own children under 18 years	Total	Families with own children under 18 years
All Families....................................	784,895	344,983	796,744	347,214	793,749	345,493
FAMILY TYPE AND LABOR FORCE STATUS						
Married-Couple Families..........................	625,231	241,863	625,952	239,520	625,107	238,739
Both husband and wife in labor force..................	60.5	77.9	59.5	77.5	59.2	78.5
Husband in labor force, wife not in labor force	15.8	17.6	16.2	18.5	16.1	17.5
Wife in labor force, husband not in labor force	7.4	3.1	7.4	3.2	7.3	2.9
Both husband and wife not in labor force..............	16.3	1.4	16.8	0.8	16.9	0.9
Other Families	159,664	103,120	170,792	107,694	168,642	106,754
Female householder, no husband present..............	70.4	73.6	70.9	71.8	68.6	70.3
In labor force..................................	52.6	62.9	54.3	62.1	51.5	60.4
Not in labor force	17.8	10.7	16.6	9.7	17.1	9.8
Male householder, no wife present...................	29.6	26.4	29.1	28.2	31.4	29.7
In labor force..................................	25.5	25.1	24.1	25.4	25.7	26.2
Not in labor force	4.1	1.3	5.1	2.7	5.7	3.5

Table IA-11. School Enrollment and Educational Attainment, 2013

(Number, percent.)

Item	State	U.S.
Enrollment		
Total population 3 years and over, enrolled in school	815,675	82,395,254
Enrolled in nursery school or preschool (percent)...	6.9	6.0
Enrolled in kindergarten (percent)...	5.5	5.2
Enrolled in elementary school, grades 1-8 (percent)...	39.1	40.0
Enrolled in high school, grades 9-12 (percent)	20.0	20.6
Enrolled in college or graduate school (percent)	28.5	28.3
Attainment		
Total population 25 years and over	2,048,270	210,910,615
Less than ninth grade (percent)	3.1	5.8
9th to 12th grade, no diploma (percent)	5.3	7.6
High school graduate, including equivalency (percent)...	32.7	27.8
Some college, no degree (percent)	21.4	21.1
Associate's degree (percent)	11.1	8.1
Bachelor's degree (percent)	18.1	18.4
Graduate or professional degree (percent)...	8.4	11.2
High school graduate or higher (percent)	91.6	86.6
Bachelor's degree or higher (percent)...	26.4	29.6

Table IA-12. Public School Characteristics and Educational Indicators

(Number, percent; data derived from National Center of Education Statistics.)

Item	State	U.S.
Public Schools, 2012–2013 (except where noted)		
Number of school districts...	357	18,093
Number of schools...	1,390	98,454
Number of students (in thousands)	500	49,771
Number of teachers (in thousands)	35	3,109
Student-teacher ratio	14.2	16.0
Expenditures per student (dollars), FY 2012...	10,027	10,667
Four-year adjusted cohort graduation rate (ACGR)[1,2]	89.7	81.4
Students eligible for free or reduced-price lunch (in thousands)	200	25,188
English language learners (in thousands)	22	4,397
Students age 3 to 21 served under IDEA, part B (in thousands)...	66	6,429

Public Schools by Type	Number	Percent of state public schools
Total number of schools...	1,390	100.0
Regular	1,354	97.4
Special education...	6	0.4
Vocational education...	0	-
Alternative education...	30	2.2

NOTE: Every school is assigned only one school type based on its instructional emphasis.
[1]ACGR data represents a new method of calculating high-school completion rates and may not be comparable to previous years' data for Averaged Freshmen Graduation Rates (AFGR).
[2]The United States 4-year ACGRs were estimated using both the reported 4-year ACGR data from 49 states and the District of Columbia and using imputed data for Idaho. The estimate for American Indian/Alaska Native students also includes imputed data for Virginia.
- = Zero or rounds to zero.

Table IA-13. Reported Voting and Registration of the Voting-Age Population, November 2012

(Numbers in thousands, percent.)

Item	Total population	Total citizen population	Registered			Voted		
			Total registered	Percent registered (total population)	Percent registered (total citizen population)	Total voted	Percent voted (total population)	Percent voted (total citizen population)
U.S. Total	235,248	215,081	153,157	65.1	71.2	132,948	56.5	61.8
State Total	2,320	2,232	1,745	75.2	78.2	1,548	66.7	69.4
Sex								
Male	1,135	1,084	838	73.9	77.3	733	64.6	67.6
Female	1,186	1,148	906	76.4	79.0	816	68.8	71.1
Race								
White alone......................	2,173	2,123	1,673	77.0	78.8	1,482	68.2	69.8
White, non-Hispanic alone	2,067	2,057	1,644	79.5	79.9	1,455	70.4	70.7
Black alone......................	54	51	35	B	B	33	B	B
Asian alone.....................	61	35	21	B	B	17	B	B
Hispanic (of any race)......................	120	71	32	26.8	B	30	25.1	B
White alone or in combination	2,197	2,138	1,685	76.7	78.8	1,494	68.0	69.9
Black alone or in combination..........	67	59	41	B	B	39	B	B
Asian alone or in combination.........	67	35	21	B	B	17	B	B
Age								
18 to 24 years.....................	260	243	150	57.7	61.8	121	46.6	49.9
25 to 44 years.....................	787	737	551	70.0	74.8	476	60.5	64.6
45 to 64 years.....................	828	812	652	78.7	80.3	586	70.8	72.2
65 to 74 years.....................	239	237	214	89.7	90.2	201	84.0	84.6
75 years and over	206	203	177	86.3	87.4	164	79.8	80.8

B = Base is less than 75,000 and therefore too small to show the derived measure.

Table IA-14. Crime

(Number, rate per 100,000. Data are derived from the FBI Uniform Crime Reports.)

Item	State			U.S.[1,2,3,4]		
	2012	2013	Percent change	2012	2013	Percent change
TOTAL POPULATION[5]...........................	3,075,039	3,090,416	0.5	313,873,685	316,128,839	0.7
VIOLENT CRIME						
Number	8,167	8,062	-1.3	1,217,067	1,163,146	-4.4
Rate	265.6	260.9	-1.8	387.8	367.9	-5.1
Murder and Nonnegligent Manslaughter						
Number	49	43	-12.2	14,866	14,196	-4.5
Rate	1.6	1.4	-12.7	4.7	4.5	-5.2
Rape[6]						
Number	X	1,083	X	X	108,612	X
Rate	X	35.0	X	X	34.4	X
Robbery						
Number	962	939	-2.4	355,051	345,031	-2.8
Rate	31.3	30.4	-2.9	113.1	109.1	-3.5
Aggravated Assault						
Number	6,255	6,323	1.1	762,009	724,149	-5.0
Rate	203.4	204.6	0.6	242.8	229.1	-5.6
PROPERTY CRIME						
Number	70,357	67,800	-3.6	9,001,992	8,632,512	-4.1
Rate	2,288.0	2,193.9	-4.1	2,868.0	2,730.7	-4.8
Burglary						
Number	17,201	15,868	-7.7	2,109,932	1,928,465	-8.6
Rate	559.4	513.5	-8.2	672.2	610.0	-9.3
Larceny-Theft						
Number	49,116	47,686	-2.9	6,168,874	6,004,453	-2.7
Rate	1,597.2	1,543.0	-3.4	1,965.4	1,899.4	-3.4
Motor Vehicle Theft						
Number.........................	4,040	4,246	5.1	723,186	699,594	-3.3
Rate	131.4	137.4	4.6	230.4	221.3	-4.0

NOTE: Although arson data are included in the trend and clearance tables, sufficient data are not available to estimate totals for this offense. Therefore, no arson data are published in this table.
- = Zero or rounds to zero.
X = Not applicable.
[1]The crime figures have been adjusted.
[2]The data collection methodology for the offense of forcible rape used by the Minnesota state Uniform Crime Reporting (UCR) Program (with the exception of Minneapolis and St. Paul, Minnesota) does not comply with national UCR Program guidelines. Consequently, its figures for forcible rape and violent crime (of which forcible rape is a part) are not published in this table.
[3]Includes offenses reported by the Zoological Police and the Metro Transit Police.
[4]Because of changes in the state's reporting practices, figures are not comparable to previous years' data.
[5]Populations are U.S. Census Bureau provisional estimates as of July 1 of each year.
[6]The figures shown for the offense of rape were estimated using the revised Uniform Crime Reporting (UCR) definition of rape.

Table IA-15. State Government Finances, 2013

(Dollar amounts in thousands, percent distribution.)

Item	Dollars	Percent distribution
Total Revenue	23,102,534	100.0
General revenue	18,533,679	80.2
Intergovernmental revenue	5,991,401	25.9
Taxes	8,374,376	36.2
General sales	2,520,072	10.9
Selective sales	1,088,919	4.7
License taxes	798,137	3.5
Individual income tax	3,436,758	14.9
Corporate income tax	428,554	1.9
Other taxes	101,936	0.4
Current charges	2,908,758	12.6
Miscellaneous general revenue	1,259,144	5.5
Utility revenue	0	-
Liquor stores revenue	258,676	1.1
Insurance trust revenue[1]	4,310,179	18.7
Total Expenditure	20,517,934	100.0
Intergovernmental expenditure	4,753,646	23.2
Direct expenditure	15,764,288	76.8
Current operation	10,900,406	53.1
Capital outlay	1,619,526	7.9
Insurance benefits and repayments	2,440,770	11.9
Assistance and subsidies	557,861	2.7
Interest on debt	245,725	1.2
Exhibit: Salaries and wages	2,682,143	13.1
Total Expenditure	20,517,934	100.0
General expenditure	17,901,551	87.2
Intergovernmental expenditure	4,753,646	23.2
Direct expenditure	13,147,905	64.1
General expenditure, by function:		
Education	6,469,134	31.5
Public welfare	5,265,106	25.7
Hospitals	1,519,773	7.4
Health	256,786	1.3
Highways	1,658,218	8.1
Police protection	96,322	0.5
Correction	334,893	1.6
Natural resources	295,335	1.4
Parks and recreation	31,074	0.2
Governmental administration	550,671	2.7
Interest on general debt	245,725	1.2
Other and unallocable	1,178,514	5.7
Utility expenditure	0	-
Liquor stores expenditure	175,613	0.9
Insurance trust expenditure	2,440,770	11.9
Debt at End of Fiscal Year	6,647,699	X
Cash and Security Holdings	40,606,486	X

X = Not applicable.
- = Zero or rounds to zero.
[1]Within insurance trust revenue, net earnings of state retirement systems is a calculated statistic (the item code in the data file is X08), and thus can be positive or negative. Net earnings is the sum of earnings on investments plus gains on investments minus losses on investments. The change made in 2002 for asset valuation from book to market value in accordance with Statement 34 of the Governmental Accounting Standards Board is reflected in the calculated statistics.

Table IA-16. State Government Tax Collections, 2014

(Dollars in thousands, percent.)

Item	Dollars	Percent distribution
Total Taxes	8,271,839	100.0
Property taxes	X	X
Sales and gross receipts	3,771,938	45.6
General sales and gross receipts	2,659,231	32.1
Selective sales and gross receipts	1,112,707	13.5
Alcoholic beverages	14,187	0.2
Amusements	282,713	3.4
Insurance premiums	105,532	1.3
Motor fuels	452,596	5.5
Pari-mutuels	3,962	-
Public utilities	0	-
Tobacco products	225,375	2.7
Other selective sales	28,342	0.3
Licenses	808,047	9.8
Alcoholic beverages	14,879	0.2
Amusements	22,703	0.3
Corporations in general	35,438	0.4
Hunting and fishing	28,262	0.3
Motor vehicle	548,670	6.6
Motor vehicle operators	21,867	0.3
Public utilities	17,590	0.2
Occupation and business, NEC	115,632	1.4
Other licenses	3,006	-
Income taxes	3,586,277	43.4
Individual income	3,197,578	38.7
Corporation net income	388,699	4.7
Other taxes	105,577	1.3
Death and gift	90,791	1.1
Documentary and stock transfer	14,786	0.2
Severance	X	X
Taxes, NEC	0	-

X = Not applicable.
- = Zero or rounds to zero.

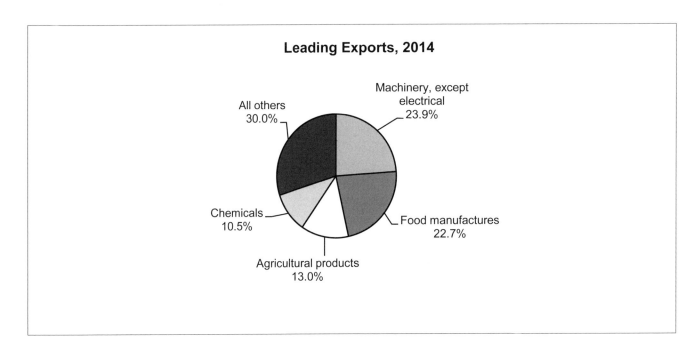

Leading Exports, 2014

Machinery, except electrical 23.9%

All others 30.0%

Chemicals 10.5%

Agricultural products 13.0%

Food manufactures 22.7%

Facts and Figures

Location: Central United States; bordered on the N by Nebraska, on the E by Missouri, on the S by Oklahoma, and on the W by Colorado

Area: 82,277 sq. mi. (213,096 sq. km.); rank—15th

Population: 2,904,021 (2014 est.); rank—34th

Principal Cities: capital—Topeka; largest—Wichita

Statehood: January 29, 1861; 34th state

U.S. Congress: 2 senators, 4 representatives

State Motto: *Ad astra per aspera* ("To the stars through difficulties")

State Song: "Home on the Range"

State Nicknames: The Sunflower State; The Jayhawk State

Abbreviations: KS; Kan.; Kans.

State Symbols: flower—wild native sunflower; tree—cottonwood; bird—Western meadowlark

At a Glance

- With an increase in population of 1.8 percent, Kansas ranked 32nd among the states in growth from 2010 to 2014.

- In 2013, 12.3 percent of Kansans did not have health insurance, compared to 14.5 percent of the total U.S. population.

- Kansas's homeownership rate in 2013, 63.5 percent, ranked 43rd in the nation.

- Approximately 24.9 percent of Kansans were under 18 years old in 2014, the 5th highest percentage in the United States.

- Kansas had an unemployment rate of 4.5 percent in 2014, compared to the national rate of 6.2 percent.

Table KS-1. Population by Age, Sex, Race, and Hispanic Origin

(Number, percent, except where noted.)

Sex, age, race, and Hispanic origin	2000	2010	2014[1]	Average annual percent change, 2010–2014
Total Population	2,688,418	2,853,118	2,904,021	0.4
Percent of total U.S. population	1.0	0.9	0.9	X
Sex				
Male	1,328,474	1,415,408	1,447,355	0.6
Female	1,359,944	1,437,710	1,456,666	0.3
Age				
Under 5 years	188,708	205,492	200,607	-0.6
5 to 19 years	609,710	605,152	604,018	-
20 to 64 years	1,533,771	1,666,358	1,683,937	0.3
65 years and over	356,229	376,116	415,459	2.5
Median age (years)	35.2	36.0	36.1	0.1
Race and Hispanic Origin				
One race				
White	2,313,944	2,501,057	2,521,932	0.2
Black	154,198	173,298	181,546	1.2
American Indian and Alaska Native	24,936	33,044	34,741	1.3
Asian	46,806	69,628	81,152	3.9
Native Hawaiian or Other Pacific Islander	1,313	2,864	3,228	3.0
Two or more races	56,496	73,227	81,422	2.7
Hispanic (of any race)	188,252	311,460	329,627	1.4

X = Not applicable.
- = Zero or rounds to zero.
[1]Population figures for 2014 are July 1 estimates. The 2010 estimates are taken from the 2010 Census.

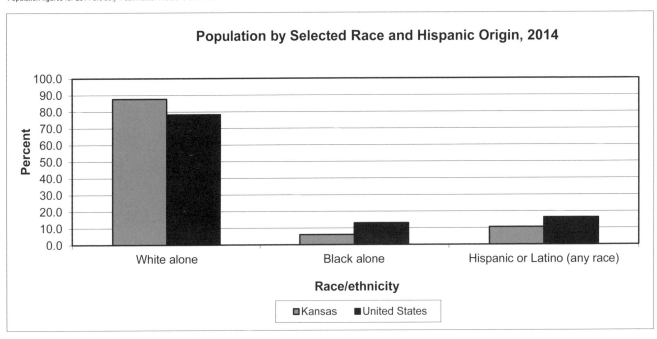

Table KS-2. Marital Status

(Number, percent distribution.)

Sex, age, race, and Hispanic origin	2000	2010	2013
Males, 15 Years and Over	1,025,114	1,106,102	1,130,809
Never married	27.4	31.6	31.8
Now married, except separated	59.9	53.9	53.8
Separated	1.1	1.4	1.3
Widowed	2.3	2.6	2.9
Divorced	9.2	10.5	10.2
Females, 15 Years and Over	1,075,542	1,145,453	1,160,119
Never married	20.8	25.1	25.5
Now married, except separated	56.4	51.4	51.2
Separated	1.3	1.7	1.5
Widowed	10.6	9.2	9.2
Divorced	10.9	12.6	12.6

Table KS-3. Households and Housing Characteristics

(Number, percent, dollars.)

Item	2000	2010	2013	Average annual percent change, 2000–2013
Total Households..	1,037,891	1,101,658	1,113,729	0.5
Family households..	701,547	721,592	735,596	0.4
Married-couple family.......................................	567,924	559,199	568,165	-
Other family..	133,623	162,393	167,431	1.8
Male householder, no wife present...................	36,962	46,692	48,344	2.1
Female householder, no husband present...........	96,661	115,701	119,087	1.6
Nonfamily households...	336,344	380,066	378,133	0.9
Householder living alone...................................	280,387	313,390	314,985	0.9
Householder not living alone..............................	55,957	66,676	63,148	0.9
Housing Characteristics				
Total housing units...	1,131,200	1,234,037	1,239,755	0.7
Occupied housing units	1,037,891	1,101,658	1,113,729	0.5
Owner occupied..	718,703	749,907	735,737	0.2
Renter occupied..	319,188	351,751	377,992	1.3
Average household size..	2.51	2.52	2.53	0.1
Financial Characteristics				
Median gross rent of renter-occupied housing	498	682	745	3.1
Median monthly owner costs for housing units with a mortgage	888	1,239	1,241	2.6
Median value of owner-occupied housing units..........	83,500	127,300	129,700	3.4

- = Zero or rounds to zero.

Table KS-4. Migration, Origin, and Language

(Number, percent.)

Characteristic	State			U.S.		
	2012	2013	Percent change	2012	2013	Percent change
Residence 1 Year Ago						
Population 1 year and over	2,848,708	2,854,869	0.2	310,212,755	312,432,820	0.7
Same house	82.9	2,386,028	X	85.0	85.0	X
Different house in the U.S.	16.5	453641.0	X	14.4	14.4	X
Same county	9.7	272,447	X	9.0	8.9	X
Different county	6.8	181194.0	X	5.4	5.5	X
Same state	3.7	91,459	X	3.2	3.2	X
Different state	3.1	89,735	X	2.3	2.3	X
Abroad	0.6	15,200	X	0.6	0.6	X
Place of Birth						
Native born	2,699,089	2,695,784	-0.1	273,089,382	274,780,773	0.6
Male	49.6	49.6	X	49.3	49.3	X
Female	50.4	50.4	X	50.7	50.7	X
Foreign born	186,816	198,173	6.1	40,824,658	41,348,066	1.3
Male	51.6	51.6	X	48.7	48.8	X
Female	48.4	48.4	X	51.3	51.2	X
Foreign born; naturalized U.S. citizen...................	67,937	66,850	-1.6	18,686,237	19,294,710	3.3
Male	50.2	49.0	X	45.8	45.9	X
Female	49.8	51.0	X	54.2	54.1	X
Foreign born; not a U.S. citizen...........................	118,879	131,323	10.5	22,138,421	22,053,356	-0.4
Male	52.4	52.9	X	51.1	51.3	X
Female	47.6	47.1	X	48.9	48.7	X
Entered 2010 or later	9.2	14.2	X	7.0	9.7	X
Entered 2000 to 2009	34.3	34.5	X	30.4	29.4	X
Entered before 2000..	56.4	51.3	X	62.7	61.0	X
World Region of Birth, Foreign						
Foreign-born population, excluding population born at sea	186,776	198,173	6.1	40,824,553	41,347,945	1.3
Europe..	7.0	7.2	X	11.8	11.6	X
Asia...	31.4	29.1	X	29.2	29.5	X
Africa...	4.4	5.8	X	4.2	4.4	X
Oceania..	0.4	0.6	X	0.6	0.5	X
Latin America...	55.3	56.0	X	52.2	51.9	X
North America..	1.4	1.3	X	2.0	2.0	X
Language Spoken at Home and Ability to Speak English						
Population 5 years and over....................................	2,684,487	2,694,653	0.4	294,003,714	296,358,760	0.8
English only...	88.8	89.1	X	79.0	79.2	X
Language other than English.................................	11.2	10.9	X	21.0	20.8	X
Speaks English less than "very well"..................	4.4	4.3	X	8.5	8.5	X

NA = Not available.
X = Not applicable.
- = Zero or rounds to zero.

Table KS-5. Median Income and Poverty Status, 2013

(Number, percent, except as noted.)

Characteristic	State		U.S.	
	Number	Percent	Number	Percent
Median Income				
Households (dollars)...	50,972	X	52,250	X
Families (dollars)	64,969	X	64,030	X
Below Poverty Level (All People)	393,358	14	48,810,868	15.8
Sex				
Male...	177,208	12.7	21,938,525	14.5
Female	216,150	15.2	26,872,343	17.1
Age				
Under 18 years..	132,460	18.7	16,086,960	22.2
Related children under 18 years......................................	129,113	18.3	15,769,921	21.9
18 to 64 years..	230,162	13.4	28,578,191	14.8
65 years and over	30,736	7.9	4,145,717	9.6

X = Not applicable.

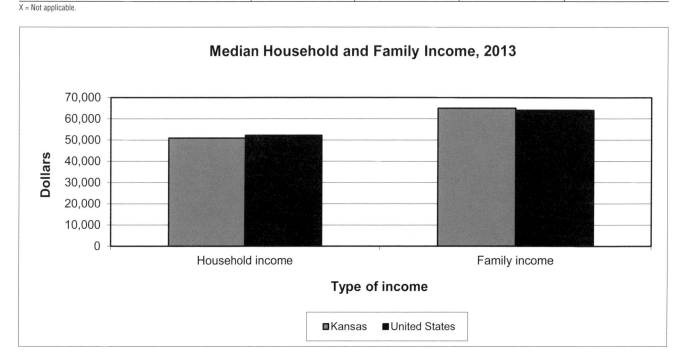

Table KS-6. Health Insurance Coverage Status for the Civilian Noninstitutionalized Population and Children Under 18 Years of Age

(Numbers in thousands, percent.)

Item	2005	2006	2007	2008	2009	2010	2011	2012	2013
Civilian Noninstitutionalized Population..	2,695	2,723	2,722	2,739	2,757	2,804	2,814	2,825	2,837
Covered by Private or Public Insurance									
Number...	2,417	2,387	2,376	2,405	2,394	2,415	2,459	2,470	2,489
Percent..	89.7	87.7	87.3	87.8	86.8	86.1	87.4	87.4	87.7
Not Covered									
Number...	278	335	345	334	363	389	355	355	348
Percent..	10.3	12.3	12.7	12.2	13.2	13.9	12.6	12.6	12.3
Percent in the U.S. not covered.......................................	15.3	15.8	15.3	15.1	15.1	15.5	15.1	14.8	14.5
Children Under 18 Years of Age	692	697	710	698	701	725	721	720	719
Covered by Private or Public Insurance									
Number...	648	646	655	640	643	665	675	672	675
Percent..	93.8	92.7	92.3	91.7	91.8	91.8	93.6	93.4	93.9
Not Covered									
Number...	43	51	54	58	58	60	46	48	44
Percent..	6.2	7.3	7.7	8.3	8.2	8.2	6.4	6.6	6.1
Percent in the U.S. not covered.......................................	10.9	11.7	11.0	9.7	8.6	8.0	7.5	7.2	7.1

Table KS-7. Employment Status by Demographic Group, 2014

(Numbers in thousands, percent.)

Characteristic	Civilian noninstitutional population	Civilian labor force		Employed		Unemployed	
		Number	Percent of population	Number	Percent of population	Number	Percent of population
Total	2,197	1,502	68.4	1,434	65.3	68	4.6
Sex							
Male	1,072	806	75.2	770	71.8	36	4.5
Female	1,125	696	61.9	664	59.0	32	4.6
Race, Sex, and Hispanic Origin							
White	1,896	1,300	68.5	1,245	65.7	55	4.2
Male	918	692	75.3	664	72.3	28	4.1
Female	978	608	62.2	582	59.5	26	4.3
Black or African American	117	79	67.1	73	62.0	6	7.6
Male	56	41	73.2	38	67.9	3	7.2
Female	62	38	61.6	35	56.7	3	8.0
Hispanic or Latino ethnicity[1]	191	145	75.8	137	71.7	8	5.5
Male	101	88	86.7	83	81.5	5	6.0
Female	90	57	63.6	54	60.6	3	4.8
Age							
16 to 19 years	156	75	48.0	66	42.3	9	12.0
20 to 24 years	217	172	79.4	159	73.3	13	7.6
25 to 34 years	391	332	84.8	317	81.1	14	4.3
35 to 44 years	308	261	84.6	249	80.8	12	4.6
45 to 54 years	364	303	83.2	294	80.6	10	3.1
55 to 64 years	366	264	72.0	256	69.9	8	2.9
65 years and over	394	96	24.4	93	23.6	3	3.2

NOTE: Data in Table 7 are from the Current Population Survey (CPS) and do not match the estimates in Table 8. See notes and definitions for further information.
[1]May be of any race.

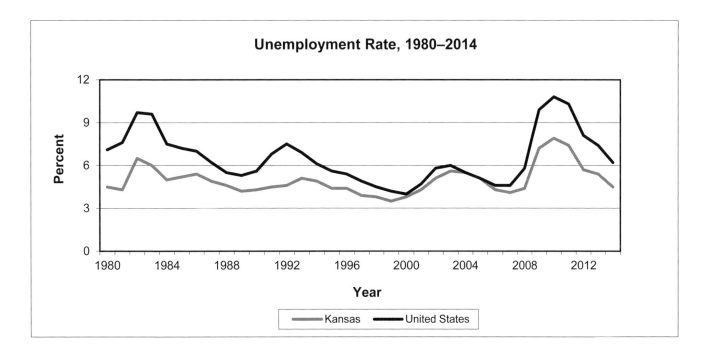

Unemployment Rate, 1980–2014

Table KS-8. Employment Status of the Civilian Noninstitutional Population Age 16 Years and Over

(Number, percent.)

Year	Civilian labor force	Civilian participation rate	Employed	Unemployed	Unemployment rate
2006	1,467,095	70.5	1,402,796	64,299	4.4
2007	1,483,458	70.8	1,420,449	63,009	4.2
2008	1,499,676	71.0	1,430,628	69,048	4.6
2009	1,518,207	71.3	1,413,873	104,334	6.9
2010	1,500,764	69.8	1,394,958	105,806	7.1
2011	1,491,258	69.0	1,394,230	97,028	6.5
2012	1,484,016	68.2	1,398,681	85,335	5.8
2013	1,486,764	68.0	1,407,562	79,202	5.3
2014	1,500,353	68.3	1,432,359	67,994	4.5

Table KS-9. Employment and Average Wages by Industry

(Estimates from 2007 through 2010 are based on the 2007 *North American Industry Classification System* [NAICS]. Estimates from 2011 onward are based on the 2012 NAICS.)

Industry	2007	2008	2009	2010	2011	2012	2013
				Number of jobs			
Wage and Salary Employment by Industry	1,468,721	1,478,020	1,428,586	1,414,533	1,425,056	1,434,672	1,449,149
Farm Wage and Salary Employment	10,680	9,499	8,833	10,270	11,830	10,207	9,475
Nonfarm Wage and Salary Employment	1,458,041	1,468,521	1,419,753	1,404,263	1,413,226	1,424,465	1,439,674
Private wage and salary employment	1,163,765	1,170,143	1,119,434	1,100,661	1,113,281	1,125,846	1,143,243
Forestry, fishing, and related activities	3,557	3,621	3,489	3,646	3,799	3,915	4,514
Mining	9,347	10,010	8,353	8,521	9,047	9,907	10,384
Utilities	7,339	7,565	7,726	7,808	8,049	7,978	7,750
Construction	68,283	67,786	60,872	56,968	55,810	56,895	59,000
Manufacturing	187,260	187,572	167,633	160,506	161,350	163,067	163,238
Durable goods manufacturing	118,999	121,515	104,021	97,481	98,111	100,029	100,607
Nondurable goods manufacturing	68,261	66,057	63,612	63,025	63,239	63,038	62,631
Wholesale trade	61,246	63,280	61,439	59,981	59,911	59,265	60,138
Retail trade	150,366	148,774	144,390	143,075	143,980	144,065	145,703
Transportation and warehousing	48,358	48,206	45,379	44,651	46,482	48,140	48,319
Information	41,009	38,908	34,741	29,403	27,945	27,847	27,579
Finance and insurance	59,851	59,734	58,356	58,366	60,274	61,033	61,437
Real estate and rental and leasing	15,829	15,576	15,078	15,078	15,029	14,127	14,365
Professional, scientific, and technical services	60,855	63,482	61,957	61,452	61,464	63,263	66,893
Management of companies and enterprises	12,507	13,739	13,452	15,182	13,984	13,636	15,193
Administrative and waste services	76,859	75,664	69,727	71,027	75,368	78,067	81,540
Educational services	17,982	18,904	18,879	19,343	19,929	20,082	20,546
Health care and social assistance	157,722	161,946	165,136	164,929	168,169	169,857	170,896
Arts, entertainment, and recreation	14,010	13,572	13,403	13,336	14,033	15,660	16,117
Accommodation and food services	103,670	103,860	102,165	101,445	102,518	104,878	106,165
Other services, except public administration	67,715	67,944	67,259	65,993	66,027	64,164	63,466
Government and government enterprises	294,276	298,378	300,319	303,602	299,945	298,619	296,431
				Dollars			
Average Wages and Salaries by Industry	37,851	39,091	39,046	39,824	40,958	42,215	42,713
Average Farm Wages and Salaries	44,878	50,280	44,140	35,828	39,315	41,878	43,442
Average Nonfarm Wages and Salaries	37,800	39,018	39,014	39,853	40,972	42,218	42,708
Average private wages and salaries	38,418	39,594	39,330	40,320	41,464	43,007	43,549
Forestry, fishing, and related activities	21,731	22,236	23,230	24,442	24,710	25,671	25,431
Mining	49,567	52,426	49,114	50,987	54,896	57,680	56,495
Utilities	73,143	75,535	78,281	79,209	87,794	84,981	88,282
Construction	41,731	44,119	43,977	45,580	45,925	48,251	48,817
Manufacturing	49,289	49,673	50,051	52,052	53,411	53,840	54,566
Durable goods manufacturing	53,161	52,920	53,844	56,405	58,084	58,510	58,674
Nondurable goods manufacturing	42,538	43,701	43,849	45,319	46,163	46,430	47,968
Wholesale trade	54,548	56,712	56,822	59,143	59,887	63,410	62,988
Retail trade	23,358	23,895	23,839	24,134	24,788	25,573	25,631
Transportation and warehousing	42,076	43,448	42,853	43,871	45,997	47,035	48,805
Information	64,511	65,252	62,395	64,040	64,533	67,241	69,621
Finance and insurance	54,442	56,062	55,670	57,718	61,059	66,263	66,905
Real estate and rental and leasing	31,718	33,176	32,981	33,767	35,296	36,280	36,989
Professional, scientific, and technical services	53,896	55,782	56,122	57,269	59,584	62,416	63,636
Management of companies and enterprises	83,516	85,476	79,859	81,323	87,707	95,254	93,145
Administrative and waste services	31,085	32,468	32,645	33,615	35,543	36,862	37,313
Educational services	25,360	26,876	27,528	27,481	28,249	29,003	28,897
Health care and social assistance	35,849	37,175	38,033	38,688	39,262	40,738	40,891
Arts, entertainment, and recreation	17,557	17,247	17,222	17,872	18,328	20,431	20,816
Accommodation and food services	14,210	14,175	14,277	14,779	15,186	15,588	15,738
Other services, except public administration	25,344	26,447	26,097	26,898	27,605	28,467	29,442
Government and government enterprises	35,354	36,759	37,836	38,162	39,147	39,243	39,466

Table KS-10. Employment Characteristics by Family Type

(Number, percent.)

Family type and labor force status	2011		2012		2013	
	Total	Families with own children under 18 years	Total	Families with own children under 18 years	Total	Families with own children under 18 years
All Families..	722,016	334,965	727,171	332,812	735,596	335,294
FAMILY TYPE AND LABOR FORCE STATUS						
Married-Couple Families..	557,419	233,734	563,407	232,015	568,165	236,490
Both husband and wife in labor force...................	59.3	71.3	56.6	69.6	56.5	70.1
Husband in labor force, wife not in labor force.........	20.1	24.8	21.9	26.6	21.2	25.4
Wife in labor force, husband not in labor force.........	6.8	3.0	6.6	3.0	7.4	3.5
Both husband and wife not in labor force..................	13.9	0.9	14.9	0.9	14.6	0.9
Other Families	164,597	101,231	163,764	100,797	167,431	98,804
Female householder, no husband present.....................	71.5	74.8	69.3	71.1	71.1	72.8
In labor force	55.8	63.7	52.7	61.1	51.7	60.6
Not in labor force	15.7	11.0	16.6	9.9	19.4	12.2
Male householder, no wife present.............................	28.5	25.2	30.7	28.9	28.9	27.2
In labor force..	23.8	23.6	25.6	26.6	24.3	25.8
Not in labor force	4.7	1.6	5.1	2.4	4.6	1.5

Table KS-11. School Enrollment and Educational Attainment, 2013

(Number, percent.)

Item	State	U.S.
Enrollment		
Total population 3 years and over, enrolled in school	797,058	82,395,254
Enrolled in nursery school or preschool (percent).................................	5.9	6.0
Enrolled in kindergarten (percent)..	5.7	5.2
Enrolled in elementary school, grades 1-8 (percent)..............................	39.8	40.0
Enrolled in high school, grades 9-12 (percent)	20.6	20.6
Enrolled in college or graduate school (percent)....................................	28.0	28.3
Attainment		
Total population 25 years and over	1,872,445	210,910,615
Less than ninth grade (percent)	4.0	5.8
9th to 12th grade, no diploma (percent)	5.9	7.6
High school graduate, including equivalency (percent)...........................	26.6	27.8
Some college, no degree (percent)	24.6	21.1
Associate's degree (percent)	7.8	8.1
Bachelor's degree (percent)	20.0	18.4
Graduate or professional degree (percent)..	11.1	11.2
High school graduate or higher (percent)	90.1	86.6
Bachelor's degree or higher (percent)...	31.1	29.6

Table KS-12. Public School Characteristics and Educational Indicators

(Number, percent; data derived from National Center of Education Statistics.)

Item	State	U.S.
Public Schools, 2012–2013 (except where noted)		
Number of school districts..	321	18,093
Number of schools...	1,351	98,454
Number of students (in thousands)	489	49,771
Number of teachers (in thousands)	41	3,109
Student-teacher ratio	11.9	16.0
Expenditures per student (dollars), FY 2012...	10,021	10,667
Four-year adjusted cohort graduation rate (ACGR)[1,2]	85.7	81.4
Students eligible for free or reduced-price lunch (in thousands)	233	25,188
English language learners (in thousands)	43	4,397
Students age 3 to 21 served under IDEA, part B (in thousands)	67	6,429

Public Schools by Type	Number	Percent of state public schools
Total number of schools..	1,351	100.0
Regular	1,338	99.0
Special education...	10	0.7
Vocational education..	1	0.1
Alternative education...	2	0.1

NOTE: Every school is assigned only one school type based on its instructional emphasis.
[1]ACGR data represents a new method of calculating high-school completion rates and may not be comparable to previous years' data for Averaged Freshmen Graduation Rates (AFGR).
[2]The United States 4-year ACGRs were estimated using both the reported 4-year ACGR data from 49 states and the District of Columbia and using imputed data for Idaho. The estimate for American Indian/Alaska Native students also includes imputed data for Virginia.

Table KS-13. Reported Voting and Registration of the Voting-Age Population, November 2012

(Numbers in thousands, percent.)

Item	Total population	Total citizen population	Registered			Voted		
			Total registered	Percent registered (total population)	Percent registered (total citizen population)	Total voted	Percent voted (total population)	Percent voted (total citizen population)
U.S. Total	235,248	215,081	153,157	65.1	71.2	132,948	56.5	61.8
State Total	2,120	1,973	1,467	69.2	74.4	1,249	58.9	63.3
Sex								
Male	1,029	953	671	65.2	70.4	567	55.1	59.5
Female	1,091	1,020	796	73.0	78.0	682	62.5	66.8
Race								
White alone...................................	1,851	1,759	1,342	72.5	76.3	1,148	62.0	65.3
White, non-Hispanic alone	1,675	1,664	1,294	77.2	77.8	1,115	66.6	67.0
Black alone..................................	105	103	64	61.3	62.5	54	51.4	52.4
Asian alone	66	27	9	B	B	6	B	B
Hispanic (of any race)	197	108	54	27.5	50.0	33	16.6	30.2
White alone or in combination	1,908	1,809	1,374	72.0	76.0	1,172	61.4	64.8
Black alone or in combination...........	126	124	74	58.5	59.4	63	50.2	51.0
Asian alone or in combination..........	80	33	15	18.9	B	8	10.6	B
Age								
18 to 24 years................................	294	262	127	43.2	48.4	88	30.1	33.7
25 to 44 years................................	706	627	439	62.2	70.0	341	48.3	54.4
45 to 64 years................................	757	721	583	77.0	80.9	535	70.7	74.2
65 to 74 years................................	188	188	162	86.4	86.4	147	78.5	78.5
75 years and over	176	176	156	88.9	88.9	137	78.2	78.2

B = Base is less than 75,000 and therefore too small to show the derived measure.

Table KS-14. Crime

(Number, rate per 100,000. Data are derived from the FBI Uniform Crime Reports.)

Item	State			U.S.[1,2,3,4]		
	2012	2013	Percent change	2012	2013	Percent change
TOTAL POPULATION[5]..	2,885,398	2,893,957	0.3	313,873,685	316,128,839	0.7
VIOLENT CRIME						
Number..	10,292	9,478	-7.9	1,217,067	1,163,146	-4.4
Rate	356.7	327.5	-8.2	387.8	367.9	-5.1
Murder and Nonnegligent Manslaughter						
Number..	85	112	31.8	14,866	14,196	-4.5
Rate	2.9	3.9	31.4	4.7	4.5	-5.2
Rape[6]						
Number..	X	1,195	X	X	108,612	X
Rate	X	41.3	X	X	34.4	X
Robbery						
Number..	1,493	1,350	-9.6	355,051	345,031	-2.8
Rate	51.7	46.6	-9.8	113.1	109.1	-3.5
Aggravated Assault						
Number..	7,609	7,181	-5.6	762,009	724,149	-5.0
Rate	263.7	248.1	-5.9	242.8	229.1	-5.6
PROPERTY CRIME						
Number..	91,066	85,280	-6.4	9,001,992	8,632,512	-4.1
Rate	3,156.1	2,946.8	-6.6	2,868.0	2,730.7	-4.8
Burglary						
Number..	18,874	17,375	-7.9	2,109,932	1,928,465	-8.6
Rate	654.1	600.4	-8.2	672.2	610.0	-9.3
Larceny-Theft						
Number..	65,413	61,264	-6.3	6,168,874	6,004,453	-2.7
Rate	2,267.0	2,117.0	-6.6	1,965.4	1,899.4	-3.4
Motor Vehicle Theft						
Number..	6,779	6,641	-2.0	723,186	699,594	-3.3
Rate	234.9	229.5	-2.3	230.4	221.3	-4.0

NOTE: Although arson data are included in the trend and clearance tables, sufficient data are not available to estimate totals for this offense. Therefore, no arson data are published in this table.
X = Not applicable.
- = Zero or rounds to zero.
[1]The crime figures have been adjusted.
[2]The data collection methodology for the offense of forcible rape used by the Minnesota state Uniform Crime Reporting (UCR) Program (with the exception of Minneapolis and St. Paul, Minnesota) does not comply with national UCR Program guidelines. Consequently, its figures for forcible rape and violent crime (of which forcible rape is a part) are not published in this table.
[3]Includes offenses reported by the Zoological Police and the Metro Transit Police.
[4]Because of changes in the state's reporting practices, figures are not comparable to previous years' data.
[5]Populations are U.S. Census Bureau provisional estimates as of July 1 of each year.
[6]The figures shown for the offense of rape were estimated using the revised Uniform Crime Reporting (UCR) definition of rape.

Table KS-15. State Government Finances, 2013

(Dollar amounts in thousands, percent distribution.)

Item	Dollars	Percent distribution
Total Revenue	18,013,265	100.0
General revenue	15,245,978	84.6
Intergovernmental revenue	3,845,073	21.3
Taxes	7,620,282	42.3
General sales	2,897,033	16.1
Selective sales	845,883	4.7
License taxes	382,944	2.1
Individual income tax	2,956,588	16.4
Corporate income tax	384,553	2.1
Other taxes	153,281	0.9
Current charges	2,781,722	15.4
Miscellaneous general revenue	998,901	5.5
Utility revenue	0	-
Liquor stores revenue	0	-
Insurance trust revenue[1]	2,767,287	15.4
Total Expenditure	16,436,706	100.0
Intergovernmental expenditure	4,057,504	24.7
Direct expenditure	12,379,202	75.3
Current operation	8,991,368	54.7
Capital outlay	1,089,440	6.6
Insurance benefits and repayments	1,920,842	11.7
Assistance and subsidies	162,307	1.0
Interest on debt	215,245	1.3
Exhibit: Salaries and wages	3,644,550	22.2
Total Expenditure	16,436,706	100.0
General expenditure	14,515,864	88.3
Intergovernmental expenditure	4,057,504	24.7
Direct expenditure	10,458,360	63.6
General expenditure, by function:		
Education	6,057,156	36.9
Public welfare	3,386,863	20.6
Hospitals	1,556,542	9.5
Health	356,630	2.2
Highways	1,181,586	7.2
Police protection	105,054	0.6
Correction	347,040	2.1
Natural resources	231,678	1.4
Parks and recreation	39,481	0.2
Governmental administration	411,604	2.5
Interest on general debt	215,245	1.3
Other and unallocable	626,985	3.8
Utility expenditure	0	-
Liquor stores expenditure	0	-
Insurance trust expenditure	1,920,842	11.7
Debt at End of Fiscal Year	6,825,293	X
Cash and Security Holdings	19,908,397	X

X = Not applicable.
- = Zero or rounds to zero.
[1]Within insurance trust revenue, net earnings of state retirement systems is a calculated statistic (the item code in the data file is X08), and thus can be positive or negative. Net earnings is the sum of earnings on investments plus gains on investments minus losses on investments. The change made in 2002 for asset valuation from book to market value in accordance with Statement 34 of the Governmental Accounting Standards Board is reflected in the calculated statistics.

Table KS-16. State Government Tax Collections, 2014

(Dollars in thousands, percent.)

Item	Dollars	Percent distribution
Total Taxes	7,334,481	100.0
Property taxes	81,267	1.1
Sales and gross receipts	3,890,900	53.0
General sales and gross receipts	2,983,664	40.7
Selective sales and gross receipts	907,236	12.4
Alcoholic beverages	126,861	1.7
Amusements	343	-
Insurance premiums	198,355	2.7
Motor fuels	441,843	6.0
Pari-mutuels	0	-
Public utilities	353	-
Tobacco products	97,813	1.3
Other selective sales	41,668	0.6
Licenses	395,454	5.4
Alcoholic beverages	3,575	-
Amusements	15	-
Corporations in general	63,582	0.9
Hunting and fishing	23,522	0.3
Motor vehicle	212,064	2.9
Motor vehicle operators	19,622	0.3
Public utilities	5,340	0.1
Occupation and business, NEC	65,516	0.9
Other licenses	2,218	-
Income taxes	2,841,841	38.7
Individual income	2,511,660	34.2
Corporation net income	330,181	4.5
Other taxes	125,019	1.7
Death and gift	136	-
Documentary and stock transfer	0	-
Severance	124,883	1.7
Taxes, NEC	0	-

- = Zero or rounds to zero.

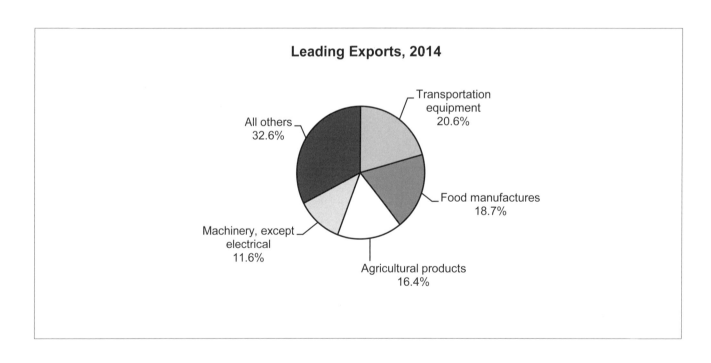

Leading Exports, 2014

- Transportation equipment 20.6%
- Food manufactures 18.7%
- Agricultural products 16.4%
- Machinery, except electrical 11.6%
- All others 32.6%

KENTUCKY

Facts and Figures

Location: East central United States; bordered on the N by Illinois, Indiana, and Ohio, on the E by West Virginia and Virginia, on the S by Tennessee, and on the W by Missouri and Illinois

Area: 40,409 sq. mi. (104,659 sq. km.); rank—37th

Population: 4,413,457 (2014 est.); rank—26th

Principal Cities: capital—Frankfort; largest—Lexington

Statehood: June 1, 1792; 15th state

U.S. Congress: 2 senators, 6 representatives

State Motto: United We Stand, Divided We Fall

State Song: "My Old Kentucky Home"

State Nickname: The Bluegrass State

Abbreviations: KY; Ky.

State Symbols: flower—goldenrod; tree—tulip poplar; bird—cardinal

At a Glance

- With an increase in population of 1.7 percent, Kentucky ranked 33rd among the states in growth from 2010 to 2014.

- In 2013, Kentucky's median household income was $43,399, the fourth lowest in the country, and 18.8 percent of the population lived below the poverty level.

- The property crime rate in Kentucky in 2013 was 2,362.9 per 100,000 population, compared to the U.S. rate of 2,730.7 per 100,000 population.

- In Kentucky in 2013, there were 1.36 traffic fatalities per 100 million miles driven, compared to the national average of 1.09 fatalities.

- In 2013, 14.3 percent of Kentucky residents did not have health insurance, which was slightly below the national rate of 14.5 percent.

Table KY-1. Population by Age, Sex, Race, and Hispanic Origin

(Number, percent, except where noted.)

Sex, age, race, and Hispanic origin	2000	2010	2014[1]	Average annual percent change, 2010–2014
Total Population	4,041,769	4,339,367	4,413,457	0.4
Percent of total U.S. population	1.4	1.4	1.4	X
Sex				
Male	1,975,368	2,134,952	2,173,158	0.4
Female	2,066,401	2,204,425	2,240,299	0.4
Age				
Under 5 years	265,901	282,367	276,233	-0.5
5 to 19 years	847,743	863,837	849,825	-0.4
20 to 64 years	2,423,332	2,614,936	2,632,885	0.2
65 years and over	504,793	578,227	654,514	3.1
Median age (years)	35.9	38.1	38.6	0.3
Race and Hispanic Origin				
One race				
White	3,640,889	3,864,193	3,895,463	0.2
Black	295,994	342,804	363,239	1.5
American Indian and Alaska Native	8,616	12,105	12,774	1.4
Asian	29,744	50,177	60,889	5.0
Native Hawaiian or Other Pacific Islander	1,460	3,199	3,693	3.7
Two or more races	42,443	66,889	77,399	3.7
Hispanic (of any race)	59,939	138,618	149,006	1.8

X = Not applicable.
[1]Population figures for 2014 are July 1 estimates. The 2010 estimates are taken from the 2010 Census.

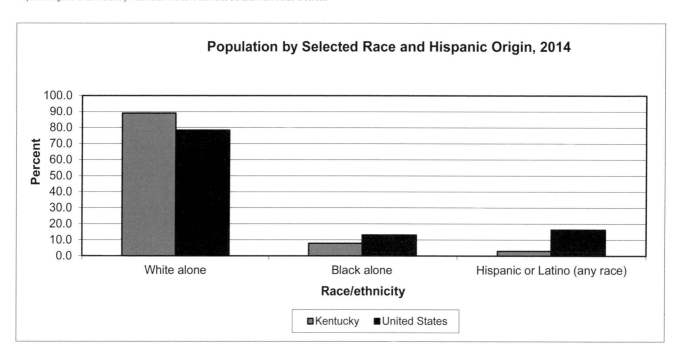

Table KY-2. Marital Status

(Number, percent distribution.)

Sex, age, race, and Hispanic origin	2000	2010	2013
Males, 15 Years and Over	1,551,174	1,702,020	1,729,330
Never married	25.9	30.8	31.7
Now married, except separated	59.9	52.0	51.7
Separated	1.5	2.1	1.9
Widowed	2.6	2.8	2.8
Divorced	10.2	12.3	11.9
Females, 15 Years and Over	1,665,993	1,794,164	1,819,135
Never married	19.7	24.2	24.5
Now married, except separated	55.0	48.9	48.6
Separated	2.1	2.6	2.6
Widowed	11.5	10.6	10.1
Divorced	11.8	13.7	14.2

Table KY-3. Households and Housing Characteristics

(Number, percent, dollars.)

Item	2000	2010	2013	Average annual percent change, 2000–2013
Total Households...	1,590,647	1,684,348	1,705,623	0.5
Family households	1,104,398	1,126,685	1,139,596	0.2
Married-couple family...	857,944	833,872	833,340	-0.2
Other family	246,454	292,813	306,256	1.7
Male householder, no wife present..	58,497	76,832	86,871	3.0
Female householder, no husband present..............................	187,957	215,981	219,385	1.2
Nonfamily households	486,249	557,663	566,027	1.2
Householder living alone...	414,095	470,103	472,633	1.0
Householder not living alone...	72,154	87,560	93,394	2.0
Housing Characteristics				
Total housing units..	1,750,927	1,928,617	1,936,634	0.8
Occupied housing units	1,590,647	1,684,348	1,705,623	0.5
Owner occupied	1,125,397	1,156,292	1,149,308	0.2
Renter occupied	465,250	528,056	556,315	1.4
Average household size..	2.47	2.51	2.5	0.1
Financial Characteristics				
Median gross rent of renter-occupied housing	445	613	668	3.2
Median monthly owner costs for housing units with a mortgage	816	1,072	1,074	2.1
Median value of owner-occupied housing units........................	86,700	121,600	120,900	2.6

Table KY-4. Migration, Origin, and Language

(Number, percent.)

Characteristic	State			U.S.		
	2012	2013	Percent change	2012	2013	Percent change
Residence 1 Year Ago						
Population 1 year and over	4,328,626	4,345,186	0.4	310,212,755	312,432,820	0.7
Same house	84.9	84.4	X	85.0	85.0	X
Different house in the U.S.	14.7	15.2	X	14.4	14.4	X
Same county	8.6	8.9	X	9.0	8.9	X
Different county	6.1	6.3	X	5.4	5.5	X
Same state	3.5	4.0	X	3.2	3.2	X
Different state	2.6	2.4	X	2.3	2.3	X
Abroad	0.4	0.4	X	0.6	0.6	X
Place of Birth						
Native born	4,243,004	4,246,279	0.1	273,089,382	274,780,773	0.6
Male	49.2	49.1	X	49.3	49.3	X
Female	50.8	50.9	X	50.7	50.7	X
Foreign born	137,411	149,016	8.4	40,824,658	41,348,066	1.3
Male	50.0	51.8	X	48.7	48.8	X
Female	50.0	48.2	X	51.3	51.2	X
Foreign born; naturalized U.S. citizen....................................	50,374	56,085	11.3	18,686,237	19,294,710	3.3
Male	43.8	44.2	X	45.8	45.9	X
Female	56.2	55.8	X	54.2	54.1	X
Foreign born; not a U.S. citizen...	87,037	92,931	6.8	22,138,421	22,053,356	-0.4
Male	53.5	56.4	X	51.1	51.3	X
Female	46.5	43.6	X	48.9	48.7	X
Entered 2010 or later	13.5	17.7	X	7.0	9.7	X
Entered 2000 to 2009	43.7	41.7	X	30.4	29.4	X
Entered before 2000..	42.8	40.5	X	62.7	61.0	X
World Region of Birth, Foreign						
Foreign-born population, excluding population born at sea	137,411	149,016	8.4	40,824,553	41,347,945	1.3
Europe	13.4	15.1	X	11.8	11.6	X
Asia	34.4	32.4	X	29.2	29.5	X
Africa	8.1	8.5	X	4.2	4.4	X
Oceania	0.7	0.1	X	0.6	0.5	X
Latin America	40.9	42.0	X	52.2	51.9	X
North America	2.5	1.9	X	2.0	2.0	X
Language Spoken at Home and Ability to Speak English						
Population 5 years and over...	4,103,742	4,123,458	0.5	294,003,714	296,358,760	0.8
English only	95.1	95.0	X	79.0	79.2	X
Language other than English..	4.9	5.0	X	21.0	20.8	X
Speaks English less than "very well".....................................	1.9	2.0	X	8.5	8.5	X

NA = Not available.
X = Not applicable.
- = Zero or rounds to zero.

Table KY-5. Median Income and Poverty Status, 2013

(Number, percent, except as noted.)

Characteristic	State		U.S.	
	Number	Percent	Number	Percent
Median Income				
Households (dollars)...	43,399	X	52,250	X
Families (dollars)	54,690	X	64,030	X
Below Poverty Level (All People)	800,635	18.8	48,810,868	15.8
Sex				
Male	353,981	17.0	21,938,525	14.5
Female	446,654	20.5	26,872,343	17.1
Age				
Under 18 years..	251,262	25.3	16,086,960	22.2
Related children under 18 years...	247,062	24.9	15,769,921	21.9
18 to 64 years...	480,593	18.1	28,578,191	14.8
65 years and over	68,780	11.2	4,145,717	9.6

X = Not applicable.

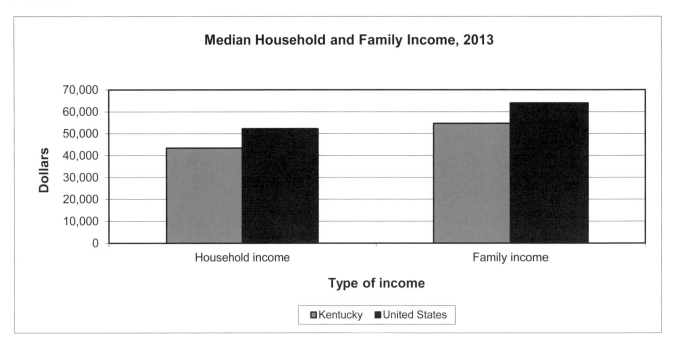

Table KY-6. Health Insurance Coverage Status for the Civilian Noninstitutionalized Population and Children Under 18 Years of Age

(Numbers in thousands, percent.)

Item	2005	2006	2007	2008	2009	2010	2011	2012	2013
Civilian Noninstitutionalized Population	4,052	4,106	4,207	4,188	4,225	4,243	4,284	4,293	4,312
Covered by Private or Public Insurance									
Number...	3,554	3,467	3,637	3,598	3,612	3,596	3,666	3,697	3,696
Percent..	87.7	84.4	86.4	85.9	85.5	84.7	85.6	86.1	85.7
Not Covered									
Number...	498	639	570	590	613	647	618	596	616
Percent..	12.3	15.6	13.6	14.1	14.5	15.3	14.4	13.9	14.3
Percent in the U.S. not covered..	15.3	15.8	15.3	15.1	15.1	15.5	15.1	14.8	14.5
Children Under 18 Years of Age..	991	1,006	1,026	1,004	1,015	1,018	1,023	1,016	1,012
Covered by Private or Public Insurance									
Number...	924	908	944	934	951	957	961	960	953
Percent..	93.3	90.3	92.0	93.0	93.7	94.0	93.9	94.5	94.1
Not Covered									
Number...	67	98	82	70	64	61	62	56	60
Percent..	6.7	9.7	8.0	7.0	6.3	6.0	6.1	5.5	5.9
Percent in the U.S. not covered..	10.9	11.7	11.0	9.7	8.6	8.0	7.5	7.2	7.1

Table KY-7. Employment Status by Demographic Group, 2014

(Numbers in thousands, percent.)

Characteristic	Civilian noninstitutional population	Civilian labor force		Employed		Unemployed	
		Number	Percent of population	Number	Percent of population	Number	Percent of population
Total...	3,425	2,007	58.6	1,877	54.8	130	6.5
Sex							
Male...	1,650	1,048	63.5	973	59.0	75	7.1
Female	1,775	959	54.0	903	50.9	55	5.8
Race, Sex, and Hispanic Origin							
White	3,050	1,776	58.2	1,666	54.6	109	6.2
Male...	1,479	932	63.0	870	58.8	62	6.7
Female	1,571	844	53.7	797	50.7	47	5.6
Black or African American...................	271	170	62.8	154	56.7	16	9.6
Male...	123	82	66.7	73	59.0	9	11.6
Female	148	88	59.5	81	54.8	7	7.8
Hispanic or Latino ethnicity[1]	97	66	68.4	61	63.2	5	7.6
Male...	54	43	79.3	40	73.9	3	6.8
Female	NA	NA	NA	NA	NA	NA	NA
Age							
16 to 19 years................................	202	76	37.7	58	28.8	18	23.5
20 to 24 years................................	331	239	72.3	210	63.5	29	12.1
25 to 34 years................................	553	436	78.8	408	73.8	27	6.3
35 to 44 years................................	528	404	76.6	380	72.0	24	5.9
45 to 54 years................................	601	429	71.4	413	68.6	16	3.8
55 to 64 years................................	584	321	54.9	309	53.0	11	3.5
65 years and over	626	102	16.3	98	15.6	4	4.1

NOTE: Data in Table 7 are from the Current Population Survey (CPS) and do not match the estimates in Table 8. See notes and definitions for further information.
[1]May be of any race.
NA = Not available.

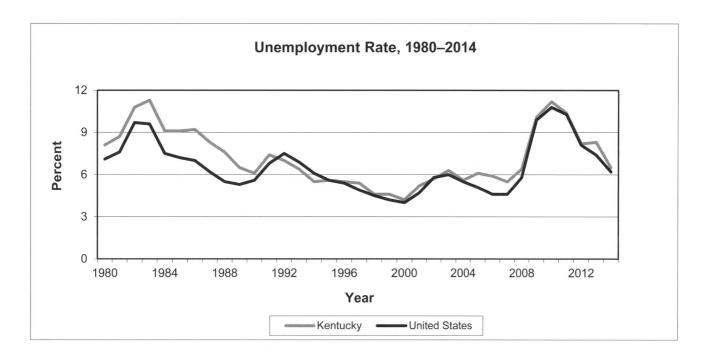

Unemployment Rate, 1980–2014

Table KY-8. Employment Status of the Civilian Noninstitutional Population Age 16 Years and Over

(Number, percent.)

Year	Civilian labor force	Civilian participation rate	Employed	Unemployed	Unemployment rate
2006	2,029,231	62.5	1,913,472	115,759	5.7
2007	2,032,082	62.1	1,922,220	109,862	5.4
2008	2,030,738	61.4	1,900,683	130,055	6.4
2009	2,060,162	61.9	1,847,126	213,036	10.3
2010	2,054,375	61.3	1,844,650	209,725	10.2
2011	2,055,500	61.0	1,862,691	192,809	9.4
2012	2,057,415	60.8	1,889,568	167,847	8.2
2013	2,057,370	60.4	1,892,108	165,262	8.0
2014	2,005,252	58.5	1,875,146	130,106	6.5

Table KY-9. Employment and Average Wages by Industry

(Estimates from 2007 through 2010 are based on the 2007 *North American Industry Classification System* [NAICS]. Estimates from 2011 onward are based on the 2012 NAICS.)

Industry	2007	2008	2009	2010	2011	2012	2013
	Number of jobs						
Wage and Salary Employment by Industry	1,956,992	1,950,323	1,871,120	1,876,202	1,900,942	1,913,171	1,928,456
Farm Wage and Salary Employment	14,655	14,146	12,629	12,847	13,783	14,407	13,793
Nonfarm Wage and Salary Employment	1,942,337	1,936,177	1,858,491	1,863,355	1,887,159	1,898,764	1,914,663
Private wage and salary employment	1,575,798	1,565,902	1,483,765	1,478,322	1,501,396	1,522,720	1,540,783
Forestry, fishing, and related activities	7,400	7,594	7,351	7,362	7,437	7,091	7,183
Mining	21,735	23,671	23,299	21,807	22,654	20,310	17,207
Utilities	6,590	6,453	6,501	6,424	6,522	6,566	6,509
Construction	88,493	88,033	77,487	71,126	71,270	69,642	70,565
Manufacturing	255,994	245,322	213,078	209,208	213,009	224,210	228,785
Durable goods manufacturing	162,385	153,729	127,339	124,800	128,920	139,540	143,023
Nondurable goods manufacturing	93,609	91,593	85,739	84,408	84,089	84,670	85,762
Wholesale trade	78,230	77,519	73,268	72,395	72,816	73,086	74,360
Retail trade	217,042	213,372	204,735	203,527	204,083	204,740	205,081
Transportation and warehousing	89,801	88,992	83,173	83,287	86,108	87,487	86,828
Information	29,477	29,192	27,206	26,277	26,849	26,617	26,314
Finance and insurance	72,467	73,261	71,045	69,826	70,243	72,232	73,931
Real estate and rental and leasing	19,957	20,166	19,164	18,978	18,465	18,284	18,752
Professional, scientific, and technical services	67,085	70,664	71,154	70,580	70,323	68,276	70,328
Management of companies and enterprises	19,487	19,582	19,700	19,454	19,563	20,081	20,513
Administrative and waste services	101,489	95,691	83,516	92,469	99,465	105,822	111,002
Educational services	29,011	29,125	29,794	30,613	31,673	32,396	32,281
Health care and social assistance	212,476	216,916	219,644	222,834	226,556	229,700	230,107
Arts, entertainment, and recreation	20,004	19,967	19,779	18,950	18,845	19,895	20,414
Accommodation and food services	155,009	154,499	150,416	150,872	152,893	156,429	160,411
Other services, except public administration	84,051	85,883	83,455	82,333	82,622	79,856	80,212
Government and government enterprises	366,539	370,275	374,726	385,033	385,763	376,044	373,880
	Dollars						
Average Wages and Salaries by Industry	36,182	37,207	37,783	38,532	39,538	40,279	40,674
Average Farm Wages and Salaries	21,534	21,403	22,775	20,748	17,634	18,910	26,912
Average Nonfarm Wages and Salaries	36,293	37,323	37,885	38,655	39,698	40,441	40,773
Average private wages and salaries	35,918	36,732	37,264	38,090	39,080	40,003	40,431
Forestry, fishing, and related activities	24,876	25,728	26,215	26,453	26,682	27,162	28,099
Mining	56,778	61,405	63,143	67,281	69,509	66,765	68,318
Utilities	64,176	67,238	70,540	70,655	72,214	74,125	76,467
Construction	39,560	42,062	43,479	43,597	44,021	45,908	47,396
Manufacturing	46,894	47,555	47,944	49,665	51,294	52,427	53,503
Durable goods manufacturing	48,362	48,853	49,507	51,125	53,250	54,012	55,177
Nondurable goods manufacturing	44,347	45,376	45,622	47,506	48,295	49,816	50,712
Wholesale trade	50,733	51,269	51,022	51,741	53,665	54,853	55,060
Retail trade	22,410	22,719	23,356	23,743	24,117	24,674	24,797
Transportation and warehousing	46,336	45,791	46,490	47,938	47,876	48,748	49,674
Information	40,380	41,598	42,749	43,463	44,510	45,906	46,321
Finance and insurance	52,479	53,410	53,825	56,627	58,941	60,342	60,921
Real estate and rental and leasing	31,906	32,268	32,233	33,474	35,370	36,413	35,396
Professional, scientific, and technical services	49,603	49,993	49,913	50,984	52,753	55,131	56,199
Management of companies and enterprises	83,863	82,602	81,553	86,292	92,016	95,382	91,305
Administrative and waste services	22,679	24,093	25,148	25,445	25,779	26,837	26,863
Educational services	21,596	22,346	23,467	24,318	24,649	24,362	24,580
Health care and social assistance	37,742	38,881	40,139	40,801	41,958	42,790	43,328
Arts, entertainment, and recreation	22,346	21,450	20,804	21,594	21,953	22,089	22,337
Accommodation and food services	14,389	14,358	14,775	15,294	15,635	15,974	15,842
Other services, except public administration	24,303	25,670	26,183	26,923	27,379	28,535	29,763
Government and government enterprises	37,905	39,821	40,344	40,825	42,105	42,215	42,183

Table KY-10. Employment Characteristics by Family Type

(Number, percent.)

Family type and labor force status	2011		2012		2013	
	Total	Families with own children under 18 years	Total	Families with own children under 18 years	Total	Families with own children under 18 years
All Families	1,119,880	475,828	1,140,771	475,764	1,139,596	469,000
FAMILY TYPE AND LABOR FORCE STATUS						
Married-Couple Families	827,519	312,461	834,642	308,124	833,340	305,408
Both husband and wife in labor force	49.7	66.6	50.2	66.5	48.4	66.3
Husband in labor force, wife not in labor force	20.9	25.7	20.0	24.7	21.0	25.8
Wife in labor force, husband not in labor force	8.9	4.7	9.1	5.3	8.9	4.3
Both husband and wife not in labor force	20.4	3.1	20.8	3.5	21.3	3.3
Other Families	292,361	163,367	306,129	167,640	306,256	163,592
Female householder, no husband present	74.3	76.1	73.5	75.9	71.6	75.5
In labor force	47.3	59.1	46.1	57.6	44.7	57.5
Not in labor force	27.0	17.0	27.4	18.3	27.0	18.0
Male householder, no wife present	25.7	23.9	26.5	24.1	28.4	24.5
In labor force	18.1	19.8	18.9	20.5	19.7	21.2
Not in labor force	7.6	4.0	7.6	3.6	8.7	3.3

Table KY-11. School Enrollment and Educational Attainment, 2013

(Number, percent.)

Item	State	U.S.
Enrollment		
Total population 3 years and over, enrolled in school	1,105,248	82,395,254
Enrolled in nursery school or preschool (percent)	5.7	6.0
Enrolled in kindergarten (percent)	5.2	5.2
Enrolled in elementary school, grades 1-8 (percent)	41.7	40.0
Enrolled in high school, grades 9-12 (percent)	20.4	20.6
Enrolled in college or graduate school (percent)	27.1	28.3
Attainment		
Total population 25 years and over	2,953,653	210,910,615
Less than ninth grade (percent)	6.6	5.8
9th to 12th grade, no diploma (percent)	9.3	7.6
High school graduate, including equivalency (percent)	33.1	27.8
Some college, no degree (percent)	20.8	21.1
Associate's degree (percent)	7.6	8.1
Bachelor's degree (percent)	13.3	18.4
Graduate or professional degree (percent)	9.3	11.2
High school graduate or higher (percent)	84.1	86.6
Bachelor's degree or higher (percent)	22.6	29.6

Table KY-12. Public School Characteristics and Educational Indicators

(Number, percent; data derived from National Center of Education Statistics.)

Item	State	U.S.
Public Schools, 2012–2013 (except where noted)		
Number of school districts	194	18,093
Number of schools	1,568	98,454
Number of students (in thousands)	685	49,771
Number of teachers (in thousands)	43	3,109
Student-teacher ratio	16.0	16.0
Expenditures per student (dollars), FY 2012	9,327	10,667
Four-year adjusted cohort graduation rate (ACGR)[1,2]	86.1	81.4
Students eligible for free or reduced-price lunch (in thousands)	374	25,188
English language learners (in thousands)	19	4,397
Students age 3 to 21 served under IDEA, part B (in thousands)	98	6,429

Public Schools by Type	Number	Percent of state public schools
Total number of schools	1,568	100.0
Regular	1,301	83.0
Special education	6	0.4
Vocational education	126	8.0
Alternative education	135	8.6

NOTE: Every school is assigned only one school type based on its instructional emphasis.
[1]ACGR data represents a new method of calculating high-school completion rates and may not be comparable to previous years' data for Averaged Freshmen Graduation Rates (AFGR).
[2]The United States 4-year ACGRs were estimated using both the reported 4-year ACGR data from 49 states and the District of Columbia and using imputed data for Idaho. The estimate for American Indian/Alaska Native students also includes imputed data for Virginia.

Table KY-13. Reported Voting and Registration of the Voting-Age Population, November 2012

(Numbers in thousands, percent.)

Item	Total population	Total citizen population	Registered			Voted		
			Total registered	Percent registered (total population)	Percent registered (total citizen population)	Total voted	Percent voted (total population)	Percent voted (total citizen population)
U.S. Total	235,248	215,081	153,157	65.1	71.2	132,948	56.5	61.8
State Total	3,291	3,194	2,303	70.0	72.1	1,895	57.6	59.3
Sex								
Male	1,581	1,531	1,041	65.8	68.0	843	53.3	55.1
Female	1,710	1,663	1,262	73.8	75.9	1,052	61.5	63.3
Race								
White alone	2,966	2,899	2,091	70.5	72.1	1,733	58.4	59.8
White, non-Hispanic alone	2,908	2,886	2,082	71.6	72.1	1,723	59.3	59.7
Black alone...................................	223	220	162	72.8	73.8	125	56.1	56.9
Asian alone	61	33	14	B	B	5	B	B
Hispanic (of any race)	82	34	20	24.0	B	13	15.5	B
White alone or in combination	3,001	2,935	2,120	70.6	72.2	1,758	58.6	59.9
Black alone or in combination	247	244	180	72.9	73.8	140	56.6	57.3
Asian alone or in combination..........	64	36	17	B	B	8	B	B
Age								
18 to 24 years	446	437	225	50.5	51.6	165	37.1	37.9
25 to 44 years	1,060	996	731	69.0	73.4	565	53.3	56.7
45 to 64 years	1,173	1,152	879	74.9	76.3	757	64.6	65.7
65 to 74 years	357	352	258	72.5	73.4	223	62.4	63.3
75 years and over	256	256	210	81.8	81.8	185	72.3	72.3

B = Base is less than 75,000 and therefore too small to show the derived measure.

Table KY-14. Crime

(Number, rate per 100,000. Data are derived from the FBI Uniform Crime Reports.)

Item	State			U.S.[1,2,3,4]		
	2012	2013	Percent change	2012	2013	Percent change
TOTAL POPULATION[5].....................................	4,379,730	4,395,295	0.4	313,873,685	316,128,839	0.7
VIOLENT CRIME						
Number..	9,852	8,737	-11.3	1,217,067	1,163,146	-4.4
Rate	224.9	198.8	-11.6	387.8	367.9	-5.1
Murder and Nonnegligent Manslaughter						
Number..	201	167	-16.9	14,866	14,196	-4.5
Rate	4.6	3.8	-17.2	4.7	4.5	-5.2
Rape[6]						
Number..	X	1,611	X	X	108,612	X
Rate	X	36.7	X	X	34.4	X
Robbery						
Number..	3,547	3,246	-8.5	355,051	345,031	-2.8
Rate	81.0	73.9	-8.8	113.1	109.1	-3.5
Aggravated Assault						
Number..	4,792	4,198	-12.4	762,009	724,149	-5.0
Rate	109.4	95.5	-12.7	242.8	229.1	-5.6
PROPERTY CRIME						
Number..	112,800	103,857	-7.9	9,001,992	8,632,512	-4.1
Rate	2,575.5	2,362.9	-8.3	2,868.0	2,730.7	-4.8
Burglary						
Number..	29,877	26,213	-12.3	2,109,932	1,928,465	-8.6
Rate	682.2	596.4	-12.6	672.2	610.0	-9.3
Larceny-Theft						
Number..	76,199	71,612	-6.0	6,168,874	6,004,453	-2.7
Rate	1,739.8	1,629.3	-6.4	1,965.4	1,899.4	-3.4
Motor Vehicle Theft						
Number..	6,724	6,032	-10.3	723,186	699,594	-3.3
Rate	153.5	137.2	-10.6	230.4	221.3	-4.0

NOTE: Although arson data are included in the trend and clearance tables, sufficient data are not available to estimate totals for this offense. Therefore, no arson data are published in this table.
X = Not applicable.
- = Zero or rounds to zero.
[1]The crime figures have been adjusted.
[2]The data collection methodology for the offense of forcible rape used by the Minnesota state Uniform Crime Reporting (UCR) Program (with the exception of Minneapolis and St. Paul, Minnesota) does not comply with national UCR Program guidelines. Consequently, its figures for forcible rape and violent crime (of which forcible rape is a part) are not published in this table.
[3]Includes offenses reported by the Zoological Police and the Metro Transit Police.
[4]Because of changes in the state's reporting practices, figures are not comparable to previous years' data.
[5]Populations are U.S. Census Bureau provisional estimates as of July 1 of each year.
[6]The figures shown for the offense of rape were estimated using the revised Uniform Crime Reporting (UCR) definition of rape.

Table KY-15. State Government Finances, 2013

(Dollar amounts in thousands, percent distribution.)

Item	Dollars	Percent distribution
Total Revenue	28,637,166	100.0
General revenue	22,926,606	80.1
Intergovernmental revenue	8,083,482	28.2
Taxes	10,815,954	37.8
General sales	3,021,794	10.6
Selective sales	2,088,662	7.3
License taxes	462,726	1.6
Individual income tax	3,722,964	13.0
Corporate income tax	646,875	2.3
Other taxes	872,933	3.0
Current charges	2,881,246	10.1
Miscellaneous general revenue	1,145,924	4.0
Utility revenue	0	-
Liquor stores revenue	0	-
Insurance trust revenue[1]	5,710,560	19.9
Total Expenditure	28,887,783	100.0
Intergovernmental expenditure	4,802,691	16.6
Direct expenditure	24,085,092	83.4
Current operation	16,123,500	55.8
Capital outlay	1,968,741	6.8
Insurance benefits and repayments	4,403,821	15.2
Assistance and subsidies	896,380	3.1
Interest on debt	692,650	2.4
Exhibit: Salaries and wages	3,969,946	13.7
Total Expenditure	28,887,783	100.0
General expenditure	24,457,976	84.7
Intergovernmental expenditure	4,802,691	16.6
Direct expenditure	19,655,285	68.0
General expenditure, by function:		
Education	9,453,475	32.7
Public welfare	7,083,731	24.5
Hospitals	1,132,362	3.9
Health	691,179	2.4
Highways	2,365,583	8.2
Police protection	197,374	0.7
Correction	532,134	1.8
Natural resources	333,797	1.2
Parks and recreation	99,115	0.3
Governmental administration	878,640	3.0
Interest on general debt	692,650	2.4
Other and unallocable	997,936	3.5
Utility expenditure	25,986	0.1
Liquor stores expenditure	0	-
Insurance trust expenditure	4,403,821	15.2
Debt at End of Fiscal Year	14,983,712	X
Cash and Security Holdings	38,512,998	X

X = Not applicable.
- = Zero or rounds to zero.

[1]Within insurance trust revenue, net earnings of state retirement systems is a calculated statistic (the item code in the data file is X08), and thus can be positive or negative. Net earnings is the sum of earnings on investments plus gains on investments minus losses on investments. The change made in 2002 for asset valuation from book to market value in accordance with Statement 34 of the Governmental Accounting Standards Board is reflected in the calculated statistics.

Table KY-16. State Government Tax Collections, 2014

(Dollars in thousands, percent.)

Item	Dollars	Percent distribution
Total Taxes	11,103,545	100.0
Property taxes	562,370	5.1
Sales and gross receipts	5,354,124	48.2
General sales and gross receipts	3,131,157	28.2
Selective sales and gross receipts	2,222,967	20.0
Alcoholic beverages	128,534	1.2
Amusements	214	-
Insurance premiums	141,639	1.3
Motor fuels	886,161	8.0
Pari-mutuels	2,421	-
Public utilities	63,898	0.6
Tobacco products	248,979	2.2
Other selective sales	751,121	6.8
Licenses	472,225	4.3
Alcoholic beverages	6,374	0.1
Amusements	291	-
Corporations in general	100,843	0.9
Hunting and fishing	26,536	0.2
Motor vehicle	190,370	1.7
Motor vehicle operators	16,600	0.1
Public utilities	0	-
Occupation and business, NEC	126,113	1.1
Other licenses	5,098	-
Income taxes	4,423,722	39.8
Individual income	3,749,258	33.8
Corporation net income	674,464	6.1
Other taxes	291,104	2.6
Death and gift	45,844	0.4
Documentary and stock transfer	3,271	-
Severance	241,989	2.2
Taxes, NEC	0	-

- = Zero or rounds to zero.

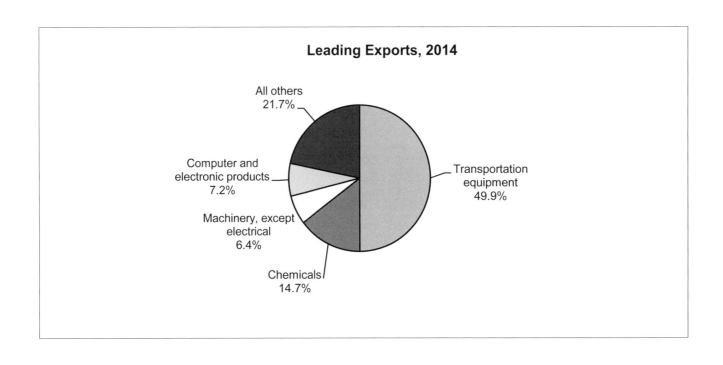

Leading Exports, 2014

All others 21.7%
Computer and electronic products 7.2%
Machinery, except electrical 6.4%
Chemicals 14.7%
Transportation equipment 49.9%

LOUISIANA

Location: South central United States; bordered on the N by Arkansas, on the E by Mississippi, on the S by the Gulf of Mexico, and on the W by Texas

Area: 51,840 sq. mi. (134,264 sq. km.); rank—31st

Population: 4,649,676 (2014 est.); rank—25th

Principal Cities: capital—Baton Rouge; largest—New Orleans

Statehood: April 30, 1812; 18th state

U.S. Congress: 2 senators, 6 representatives

State Motto: Union, Justice, Confidence

State Song: "Give Me Louisiana"

State Nicknames: The Pelican State; The Bayou State

Abbreviations: LA; La.

State Symbols: flower—magnolia; tree—bald cypress; bird—Eastern brown pelican

At a Glance

- With an increase in population of 2.6 percent, Louisiana ranked 29th in population growth from 2010 to 2014.

- Louisiana's median household income in 2013 was $44,164, and 19.8 percent of the population lived below the poverty level.

- Louisiana's violent crime rate in 2013 was 518.5 per 100,000 population, compared to 367.9 for the entire nation.

- In 2013, 16.6 percent of Louisiana's population did not have health insurance, compared to 14.5 percent of the entire U.S. population.

- With an infant mortality rate of 8.65 deaths per 1,000 live births, Louisiana ranked 2nd in the nation in 2013.

Table LA-1. Population by Age, Sex, Race, and Hispanic Origin

(Number, percent, except where noted.)

Sex, age, race, and Hispanic origin	2000	2010	2014[1]	Average annual percent change, 2010–2014
Total Population	4,468,976	4,533,372	4,649,676	0.6
Percent of total U.S. population	1.6	1.5	1.5	X
Sex				
Male	2,162,903	2,219,292	2,273,939	0.6
Female	2,306,073	2,314,080	2,375,737	0.7
Age				
Under 5 years	317,392	314,260	308,634	-0.5
5 to 19 years	1,050,637	939,977	921,654	-0.5
20 to 64 years	2,584,018	2,721,278	2,786,494	0.6
65 years and over	516,929	557,857	632,894	3.2
Median age (years)	34.0	35.8	36.3	0.3
Race and Hispanic Origin				
One race				
White	2,856,161	2,902,875	2,945,869	0.4
Black	1,451,944	1,462,969	1,510,676	0.8
American Indian and Alaska Native	25,477	33,037	35,276	1.7
Asian	54,758	71,829	83,181	3.7
Native Hawaiian or Other Pacific Islander	1,240	2,588	2,996	3.7
Two or more races	48,265	60,074	71,678	4.5
Hispanic (of any race)	107,738	200,653	224,867	2.9

X = Not applicable.
[1]Population figures for 2014 are July 1 estimates. The 2010 estimates are taken from the 2010 Census.

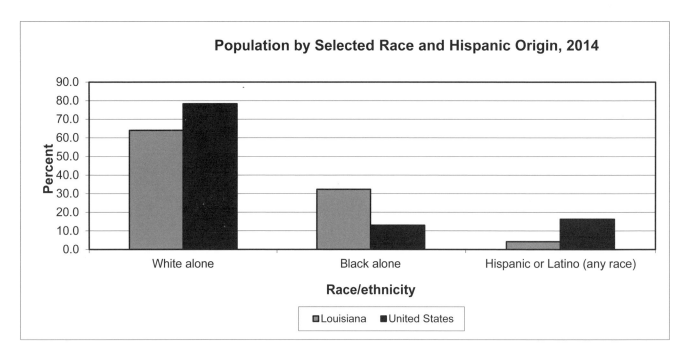

Table LA-2. Marital Status

(Number, percent distribution.)

Sex, age, race, and Hispanic origin	2000	2010	2013
Males, 15 Years and Over	1,648,133	1,751,556	1,786,865
Never married	31.2	37.0	37.5
Now married, except separated	54.5	47.2	45.9
Separated	2.2	2.2	2.3
Widowed	2.8	2.8	3.1
Divorced	9.2	10.8	11.2
Females, 15 Years and Over	1,828,247	1,861,490	1,904,535
Never married	26.3	30.8	31.7
Now married, except separated	48.2	42.6	41.9
Separated	2.9	3.2	3.2
Widowed	11.5	10.1	10.1
Divorced	11.1	13.3	13.1

Table LA-3. Households and Housing Characteristics

(Number, percent, dollars.)

Item	2000	2010	2013	Average annual percent change, 2000–2013
Total Households..	1,656,053	1,689,822	1,728,149	0.3
Family households	1,156,438	1,129,117	1,129,437	-0.2
Married-couple family..	809,498	753,423	745,632	-0.6
Other family	346,940	375,694	383,805	0.8
Male householder, no wife present........................	71,865	79,560	90,805	1.8
Female householder, no husband present.................	275,075	296,134	293,000	0.5
Nonfamily households	499,615	560,705	598,712	1.4
Householder living alone...	419,200	468,853	506,510	1.5
Householder not living alone....................................	80,415	91,852	92,202	1.1
Housing Characteristics				
Total housing units..	1,847,181	1,967,947	1,990,967	0.6
Occupied housing units	1,656,053	1,689,822	1,728,149	0.3
Owner occupied	1,125,135	1,141,504	1,140,052	0.1
Renter occupied	530,918	548,318	588,097	0.8
Average household size..	2.62	2.61	2.60	-0.1
Financial Characteristics				
Median gross rent of renter-occupied housing	466	736	763	3.9
Median monthly owner costs for housing units with a mortgage	816	1,163	1,166	2.8
Median value of owner-occupied housing units	85,000	137,500	140,300	3.9

Table LA-4. Migration, Origin, and Language

(Number, percent.)

Characteristic	State			U.S.		
	2012	2013	Percent change	2012	2013	Percent change
Residence 1 Year Ago						
Population 1 year and over	4,545,914	4,568,320	0.5	310,212,755	312,432,820	0.7
Same house	86.1	86.3	X	85.0	85.0	X
Different house in the U.S.	13.6	13.4	X	14.4	14.4	X
Same county	8.3	7.8	X	9.0	8.9	X
Different county	5.4	5.5	X	5.4	5.5	X
Same state	3.3	3.5	X	3.2	3.2	X
Different state	2.0	2.0	X	2.3	2.3	X
Abroad	0.3	0.4	X	0.6	0.6	X
Place of Birth						
Native born	4,433,741	4,442,911	0.2	273,089,382	274,780,773	0.6
Male...	48.7	48.5	X	49.3	49.3	X
Female	51.3	51.5	X	50.7	50.7	X
Foreign born	168,152	182,559	8.6	40,824,658	41,348,066	1.3
Male...	52.6	54.6	X	48.7	48.8	X
Female	47.4	45.4	X	51.3	51.2	X
Foreign born; naturalized U.S. citizen.................................	68,053	76,033	11.7	18,686,237	19,294,710	3.3
Male...	48.0	46.8	X	45.8	45.9	X
Female	52.0	53.2	X	54.2	54.1	X
Foreign born; not a U.S. citizen.................................	100,099	106,526	6.4	22,138,421	22,053,356	-0.4
Male...	55.7	60.2	X	51.1	51.3	X
Female	44.3	39.8	X	48.9	48.7	X
Entered 2010 or later	10.0	18.0	X	7.0	9.7	X
Entered 2000 to 2009	34.9	33.1	X	30.4	29.4	X
Entered before 2000...	55.2	48.9	X	62.7	61.0	X
World Region of Birth, Foreign						
Foreign-born population, excluding population born at sea	168,152	182,559	8.6	40,824,553	41,347,945	1.3
Europe	8.7	9.4	X	11.8	11.6	X
Asia...	31.7	32.8	X	29.2	29.5	X
Africa	3.2	3.2	X	4.2	4.4	X
Oceania	0.5	0.1	X	0.6	0.5	X
Latin America...	54.5	52.8	X	52.2	51.9	X
North America	1.4	1.7	X	2.0	2.0	X
Language Spoken at Home and Ability to Speak English						
Population 5 years and over...	4,292,613	4,320,472	0.6	294,003,714	296,358,760	0.8
English only	91.6	91.7	X	79.0	79.2	X
Language other than English...	8.4	8.3	X	21.0	20.8	X
Speaks English less than "very well".................................	2.7	2.8	X	8.5	8.5	X

NA = Not available.
X = Not applicable.
- = Zero or rounds to zero.

Table LA-5. Median Income and Poverty Status, 2013

(Number, percent, except as noted.)

Characteristic	State		U.S.	
	Number	Percent	Number	Percent
Median Income				
Households (dollars)..	44,164	X	52,250	X
Families (dollars)	55,871	X	64,030	X
Below Poverty Level (All People)	888,019	19.8	48,810,868	15.8
Sex				
Male...	378,072	17.4	21,938,525	14.5
Female	509,947	21.9	26,872,343	17.1
Age				
Under 18 years...	304,244	27.7	16,086,960	22.2
Related children under 18 years...	299,489	27.4	15,769,921	21.9
18 to 64 years..	509,189	18.1	28,578,191	14.8
65 years and over	74,586	12.7	4,145,717	9.6

X = Not applicable.

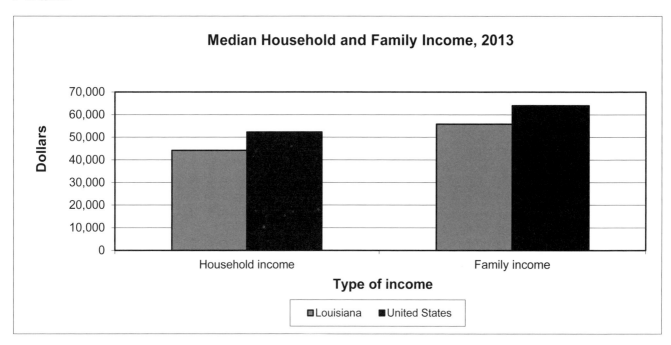

Table LA-6. Health Insurance Coverage Status for the Civilian Noninstitutionalized Population and Children Under 18 Years of Age

(Numbers in thousands, percent.)

Item	2005	2006	2007	2008	2009	2010	2011	2012	2013
Civilian Noninstitutionalized Population	4,088	4,212	4,197	4,313	4,392	4,440	4,473	4,499	4,523
Covered by Private or Public Insurance									
Number...	3,363	3,291	3,421	3,546	3,629	3,649	3,689	3,739	3,772
Percent...	82.3	78.1	81.5	82.2	82.6	82.2	82.5	83.1	83.4
Not Covered									
Number...	725	921	776	767	762	791	784	760	751
Percent...	17.7	21.9	18.5	17.8	17.4	17.8	17.5	16.9	16.6
Percent in the U.S. not covered..	15.3	15.8	15.3	15.1	15.1	15.5	15.1	14.8	14.5
Children Under 18 Years of Age..	1,064	1,067	1,097	1,106	1,120	1,113	1,117	1,117	1,111
Covered by Private or Public Insurance									
Number...	974	897	960	1,020	1,047	1,051	1,052	1,058	1,048
Percent...	91.6	84.1	87.5	92.2	93.5	94.5	94.2	94.7	94.3
Not Covered									
Number...	89	170	137	86	73	62	65	59	63
Percent...	8.4	15.9	12.5	7.8	6.5	5.5	5.8	5.3	5.7
Percent in the U.S. not covered..	10.9	11.7	11.0	9.7	8.6	8.0	7.5	7.2	7.1

Table LA-7. Employment Status by Demographic Group, 2014

(Numbers in thousands, percent.)

Characteristic	Civilian noninstitutional population	Civilian labor force		Employed		Unemployed	
		Number	Percent of population	Number	Percent of population	Number	Percent of population
Total...	3,551	2,159	60.8	2,021	56.9	138	6.4
Sex							
Male...	1,688	1,160	68.7	1,084	64.2	76	6.5
Female..	1,863	999	53.6	937	50.3	62	6.2
Race, Sex, and Hispanic Origin							
White..	2,336	1,459	62.5	1,393	59.6	67	4.6
Male..	1,139	822	72.2	784	68.9	38	4.6
Female...	1,197	637	53.2	608	50.8	29	4.5
Black or African American.............................	1,083	619	57.2	556	51.3	64	10.3
Male..	483	291	60.2	257	53.3	33	11.4
Female...	600	329	54.8	298	49.7	31	9.3
Hispanic or Latino ethnicity[1]	165	124	75.4	114	68.9	11	8.5
Male..	92	82	89.6	77	83.6	5	6.7
Female...	73	42	57.4	37	50.5	5	12.1
Age							
16 to 19 years...	227	73	32.1	57	25.3	15	21.2
20 to 24 years...	377	273	72.4	242	64.2	31	11.3
25 to 34 years...	621	500	80.5	462	74.3	38	7.7
35 to 44 years...	534	416	77.8	395	73.9	21	5.1
45 to 54 years...	607	452	74.5	437	72.1	15	3.3
55 to 64 years...	561	343	61.2	328	58.5	15	4.5
65 years and over	624	102	16.4	100	16.1	2	1.9

NOTE: Data in Table 7 are from the Current Population Survey (CPS) and do not match the estimates in Table 8. See notes and definitions for further information.
[1]May be of any race.

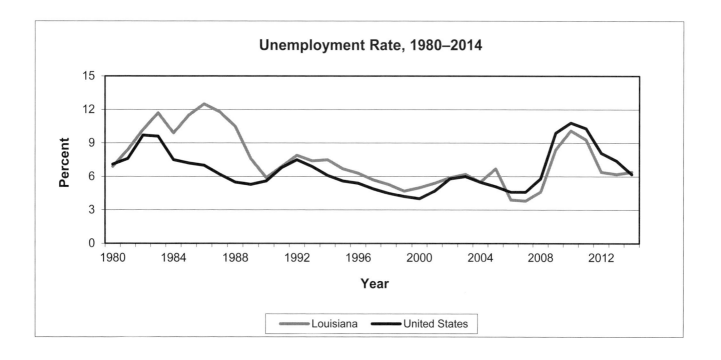

Table LA-8. Employment Status of the Civilian Noninstitutional Population Age 16 Years and Over

(Number, percent.)

Year	Civilian labor force	Civilian participation rate	Employed	Unemployed	Unemployment rate
2006	1,988,513	62.2	1,899,981	88,532	4.5
2007	2,030,434	61.7	1,944,038	86,396	4.3
2008	2,084,835	62.2	1,982,381	102,454	4.9
2009	2,064,768	60.9	1,923,884	140,884	6.8
2010	2,086,076	60.7	1,919,852	166,224	8.0
2011	2,073,353	59.6	1,910,703	162,650	7.8
2012	2,080,806	59.4	1,932,595	148,211	7.1
2013	2,106,621	59.7	1,964,932	141,689	6.7
2014	2,157,232	60.8	2,019,655	137,577	6.4

Table LA-9. Employment and Average Wages by Industry

(Estimates from 2007 through 2010 are based on the 2007 *North American Industry Classification System* [NAICS]. Estimates from 2011 onward are based on the 2012 NAICS.)

Industry	2007	2008	2009	2010	2011	2012	2013
	Number of jobs						
Wage and Salary Employment by Industry	2,014,645	2,040,323	2,003,169	1,990,201	2,005,804	2,022,998	2,042,221
Farm Wage and Salary Employment	7,904	7,734	8,817	8,969	8,089	6,958	6,285
Nonfarm Wage and Salary Employment	2,006,741	2,032,589	1,994,352	1,981,232	1,997,715	2,016,040	2,035,936
Private wage and salary employment	1,617,588	1,631,605	1,587,934	1,572,459	1,600,373	1,626,782	1,657,896
Forestry, fishing, and related activities	7,387	7,311	7,062	7,230	7,227	7,023	7,119
Mining	47,789	51,888	48,039	48,652	49,902	51,591	51,143
Utilities	9,314	9,328	9,523	9,482	9,348	9,158	9,151
Construction	141,411	140,889	136,972	126,709	127,925	130,758	136,086
Manufacturing	157,536	152,927	142,703	137,621	139,983	141,987	144,079
Durable goods manufacturing	86,731	82,805	74,529	69,661	71,156	73,079	74,662
Nondurable goods manufacturing	70,805	70,122	68,174	67,960	68,827	68,908	69,417
Wholesale trade	76,624	76,499	72,598	71,035	72,873	72,836	73,690
Retail trade	228,862	228,562	224,211	221,236	224,125	224,650	226,296
Transportation and warehousing	74,394	75,311	70,438	69,810	72,335	74,727	76,954
Information	27,829	28,606	24,778	24,628	23,709	24,810	26,537
Finance and insurance	60,891	60,294	58,857	60,615	62,178	61,045	60,602
Real estate and rental and leasing	34,753	33,580	31,397	31,349	32,022	32,314	33,565
Professional, scientific, and technical services	82,942	83,757	80,848	80,830	82,403	85,490	87,378
Management of companies and enterprises	22,098	23,512	24,189	23,860	24,368	25,126	25,274
Administrative and waste services	99,418	99,858	91,546	91,510	92,439	94,822	97,073
Educational services	34,499	36,063	36,795	37,716	39,051	40,988	41,905
Health care and social assistance	216,247	224,622	232,150	236,656	240,782	244,026	248,311
Arts, entertainment, and recreation	33,230	33,506	28,899	28,522	28,412	28,879	30,019
Accommodation and food services	162,934	165,158	168,102	168,568	174,942	179,632	184,927
Other services, except public administration	99,430	99,934	98,827	96,430	96,349	151,160	97,787
Government and government enterprises	389,153	400,984	406,418	408,773	397,342	389,258	378,040
	Dollars						
Average Wages and Salaries by Industry	39,029	41,097	41,216	42,181	43,154	44,047	44,828
Average Farm Wages and Salaries	23,039	21,339	18,758	18,557	18,447	23,864	27,288
Average Nonfarm Wages and Salaries	39,092	41,172	41,315	42,288	43,254	44,117	44,882
Average private wages and salaries	39,231	41,181	41,190	42,276	43,353	44,364	45,183
Forestry, fishing, and related activities	29,924	31,593	30,515	32,382	33,109	34,190	35,621
Mining	75,708	82,414	79,934	82,129	85,218	88,738	90,800
Utilities	66,426	73,578	73,572	72,406	76,596	78,489	80,446
Construction	45,957	50,192	51,721	51,220	51,894	52,501	53,554
Manufacturing	55,474	58,606	58,888	61,563	64,047	65,769	66,486
Durable goods manufacturing	49,074	51,827	51,561	54,313	56,764	57,912	58,443
Nondurable goods manufacturing	63,315	66,611	66,898	68,994	71,578	74,102	75,137
Wholesale trade	52,302	54,488	54,591	55,825	57,293	59,829	60,985
Retail trade	24,764	25,043	25,087	25,536	25,983	26,734	27,057
Transportation and warehousing	52,239	54,998	54,755	57,247	57,858	59,858	62,258
Information	44,885	45,494	48,121	49,770	51,482	52,217	50,038
Finance and insurance	52,328	53,342	52,520	55,110	58,855	60,207	62,225
Real estate and rental and leasing	42,174	43,294	42,759	45,710	48,216	48,411	49,040
Professional, scientific, and technical services	54,501	58,536	59,248	61,153	63,001	64,670	66,802
Management of companies and enterprises	64,741	67,830	65,151	67,592	71,194	73,448	79,506
Administrative and waste services	31,564	33,186	33,480	34,920	34,460	35,234	35,392
Educational services	29,038	30,973	32,485	33,256	33,857	34,167	34,055
Health care and social assistance	35,358	36,633	37,597	38,116	38,808	39,288	39,929
Arts, entertainment, and recreation	33,959	34,339	33,016	35,217	35,272	34,389	34,524
Accommodation and food services	17,556	17,572	18,089	18,898	19,152	19,433	19,482
Other services, except public administration	25,906	27,492	27,758	28,751	29,368	18,996	30,603
Government and government enterprises	38,512	41,139	41,803	42,333	42,855	43,087	43,559

Table LA-10. Employment Characteristics by Family Type

(Number, percent.)

Family type and labor force status	2011		2012		2013	
	Total	Families with own children under 18 years	Total	Families with own children under 18 years	Total	Families with own children under 18 years
All Families...	1,118,217	489,469	1,125,659	491,081	1,129,437	484,007
FAMILY TYPE AND LABOR FORCE STATUS						
Married-Couple Families...........................	743,138	286,474	744,806	280,552	745,632	282,943
Both husband and wife in labor force..............................	48.9	65.2	49.8	67.7	49.3	66.0
Husband in labor force, wife not in labor force	24.1	28.8	23.5	25.9	25.3	28.8
Wife in labor force, husband not in labor force	8.6	4.0	8.6	4.4	7.8	3.4
Both husband and wife not in labor force...............................	18.5	1.9	18.1	2.0	17.3	1.7
Other Families	375,079	202,995	380,853	210,529	383,805	201,064
Female householder, no husband present...........................	77.4	80.6	76.3	78.4	76.3	80.4
In labor force	52.6	64.5	53.3	64.3	51.0	64.2
Not in labor force	24.8	16.2	23.0	14.1	25.3	16.2
Male householder, no wife present...........................	22.6	19.4	23.7	21.6	23.7	19.6
In labor force	15.9	16.6	17.3	19.1	17.2	17.1
Not in labor force	6.6	2.7	6.4	2.5	6.5	2.5

Table LA-11. School Enrollment and Educational Attainment, 2013

(Number, percent.)

Item	State	U.S.
Enrollment		
Total population 3 years and over, enrolled in school	1,168,161	82,395,254
Enrolled in nursery school or preschool (percent)......................................	7.0	6.0
Enrolled in kindergarten (percent)...	5.7	5.2
Enrolled in elementary school, grades 1-8 (percent)...................................	43.8	40.0
Enrolled in high school, grades 9-12 (percent)...	19.7	20.6
Enrolled in college or graduate school (percent)...	23.8	28.3
Attainment		
Total population 25 years and over	3,034,973	210,910,615
Less than ninth grade (percent)...	5.8	5.8
9th to 12th grade, no diploma (percent)..	11.1	7.6
High school graduate, including equivalency (percent)................................	33.6	27.8
Some college, no degree (percent)	21.5	21.1
Associate's degree (percent)	5.4	8.1
Bachelor's degree (percent)	14.9	18.4
Graduate or professional degree (percent)..	7.6	11.2
High school graduate or higher (percent)	83.1	86.6
Bachelor's degree or higher (percent)	22.5	29.6

Table LA-12. Public School Characteristics and Educational Indicators

(Number, percent; data derived from National Center of Education Statistics.)

Item	State	U.S.
Public Schools, 2012–2013 (except where noted)		
Number of school districts..	131	18,093
Number of schools..	1,407	98,454
Number of students (in thousands)	711	49,771
Number of teachers (in thousands)	46	3,109
Student-teacher ratio	15.3	16.0
Expenditures per student (dollars), FY 2012...	10,726	10,667
Four-year adjusted cohort graduation rate (ACGR)[1,2]	73.5	81.4
Students eligible for free or reduced-price lunch (in thousands)	460	25,188
English language learners (in thousands)	13	4,397
Students age 3 to 21 served under IDEA, part B (in thousands)	81	6,429

Public Schools by Type	Number	Percent of state public schools
Total number of schools..	1,407	100.0
Regular	1,218	86.6
Special education..	28	2.0
Vocational education...	9	0.6
Alternative education	152	10.8

NOTE: Every school is assigned only one school type based on its instructional emphasis.

[1]ACGR data represents a new method of calculating high-school completion rates and may not be comparable to previous years' data for Averaged Freshmen Graduation Rates (AFGR).

[2]The United States 4-year ACGRs were estimated using both the reported 4-year ACGR data from 49 states and the District of Columbia and using imputed data for Idaho. The estimate for American Indian/Alaska Native students also includes imputed data for Virginia.

Table LA-13. Reported Voting and Registration of the Voting-Age Population, November 2012

(Numbers in thousands, percent.)

Item	Total population	Total citizen population	Registered			Voted		
			Total registered	Percent registered (total population)	Percent registered (total citizen population)	Total voted	Percent voted (total population)	Percent voted (total citizen population)
U.S. Total	235,248	215,081	153,157	65.1	71.2	132,948	56.5	61.8
State Total	3,321	3,239	2,498	75.2	77.1	2,148	64.7	66.3
Sex								
Male	1,554	1,494	1,102	70.9	73.7	931	59.9	62.4
Female	1,766	1,745	1,396	79.0	80.0	1,217	68.9	69.7
Race								
White alone.....................	2,242	2,174	1,681	75.0	77.3	1,421	63.4	65.4
White, non-Hispanic alone	2,141	2,128	1,644	76.8	77.3	1,389	64.9	65.2
Black alone.....................	996	996	768	77.1	77.1	692	69.5	69.5
Asian alone	37	23	6	B	B	6	B	B
Hispanic (of any race)	125	70	57	45.3	B	48	38.1	B
White alone or in combination	2,262	2,194	1,697	75.0	77.3	1,428	63.2	65.1
Black alone or in combination..........	1,013	1,013	786	77.5	77.5	700	69.1	69.1
Asian alone or in combination.........	41	27	6	B	B	6	B	B
Age								
18 to 24 years.................	431	415	226	52.5	54.6	174	40.4	42.0
25 to 44 years.................	1,122	1,078	821	73.1	76.1	709	63.2	65.8
45 to 64 years.................	1,199	1,184	968	80.7	81.7	846	70.5	71.4
65 to 74 years.................	335	332	294	87.7	88.4	258	77.1	77.8
75 years and over	233	230	189	80.9	82.2	161	69.1	70.2

B = Base is less than 75,000 and therefore too small to show the derived measure.

Table LA-14. Crime

(Number, rate per 100,000. Data are derived from the FBI Uniform Crime Reports.)

Item	State			U.S.[1,2,3,4]		
	2012	2013	Percent change	2012	2013	Percent change
TOTAL POPULATION[5]...........................	4,602,134	4,625,470	0.5	313,873,685	316,128,839	0.7
VIOLENT CRIME						
Number.............................	22,839	23,609	3.4	1,217,067	1,163,146	-4.4
Rate	496.3	510.4	2.8	387.8	367.9	-5.1
Murder and Nonnegligent Manslaughter						
Number.............................	489	498	1.8	14,866	14,196	-4.5
Rate	10.6	10.8	1.3	4.7	4.5	-5.2
Rape[6]						
Number.............................	X	1,619	X	X	108,612	X
Rate	X	35.0	X	X	34.4	X
Robbery						
Number.............................	5,458	5,548	1.6	355,051	345,031	-2.8
Rate	118.6	119.9	1.1	113.1	109.1	-3.5
Aggravated Assault						
Number.............................	15,737	16,319	3.7	762,009	724,149	-5.0
Rate	342.0	352.8	3.2	242.8	229.1	-5.6
PROPERTY CRIME						
Number.............................	162,673	165,686	1.9	9,001,992	8,632,512	-4.1
Rate	3,534.7	3,582.0	1.3	2,868.0	2,730.7	-4.8
Burglary						
Number.............................	42,037	41,184	-2.0	2,109,932	1,928,465	-8.6
Rate	913.4	890.4	-2.5	672.2	610.0	-9.3
Larceny-Theft						
Number.............................	112,764	115,342	2.3	6,168,874	6,004,453	-2.7
Rate	2,450.3	2,493.6	1.8	1,965.4	1,899.4	-3.4
Motor Vehicle Theft						
Number.............................	7,872	9,160	16.4	723,186	699,594	-3.3
Rate	171.1	198.0	15.8	230.4	221.3	-4.0

NOTE: Although arson data are included in the trend and clearance tables, sufficient data are not available to estimate totals for this offense. Therefore, no arson data are published in this table.
X = Not applicable.
- = Zero or rounds to zero.
[1]The crime figures have been adjusted.
[2]The data collection methodology for the offense of forcible rape used by the Minnesota state Uniform Crime Reporting (UCR) Program (with the exception of Minneapolis and St. Paul, Minnesota) does not comply with national UCR Program guidelines. Consequently, its figures for forcible rape and violent crime (of which forcible rape is a part) are not published in this table.
[3]Includes offenses reported by the Zoological Police and the Metro Transit Police.
[4]Because of changes in the state's reporting practices, figures are not comparable to previous years' data.
[5]Populations are U.S. Census Bureau provisional estimates as of July 1 of each year.
[6]The figures shown for the offense of rape were estimated using the revised Uniform Crime Reporting (UCR) definition of rape.

Table LA-15. State Government Finances, 2013

(Dollar amounts in thousands, percent distribution.)

Item	Dollars	Percent distribution
Total Revenue	31,238,181	100.0
General revenue	25,255,359	80.8
Intergovernmental revenue	10,660,261	34.1
Taxes	9,223,829	29.5
General sales	2,825,752	9.0
Selective sales	2,148,890	6.9
License taxes	369,930	1.2
Individual income tax	2,739,983	8.8
Corporate income tax	252,430	0.8
Other taxes	886,844	2.8
Current charges	2,967,466	9.5
Miscellaneous general revenue	2,403,803	7.7
Utility revenue	7,098	-
Liquor stores revenue	0	-
Insurance trust revenue[1]	5,975,724	19.1
Total Expenditure	32,037,578	100.0
Intergovernmental expenditure	6,241,308	19.5
Direct expenditure	25,796,270	80.5
Current operation	18,265,363	57.0
Capital outlay	1,998,074	6.2
Insurance benefits and repayments	4,232,506	13.2
Assistance and subsidies	451,268	1.4
Interest on debt	849,059	2.7
Exhibit: Salaries and wages	4,050,956	12.6
Total Expenditure	32,037,578	100.0
General expenditure	27,799,897	86.8
Intergovernmental expenditure	6,241,308	19.5
Direct expenditure	21,558,589	67.3
General expenditure, by function:		
Education	8,881,174	27.7
Public welfare	7,165,251	22.4
Hospitals	1,930,770	6.0
Health	523,905	1.6
Highways	1,716,072	5.4
Police protection	356,701	1.1
Correction	701,296	2.2
Natural resources	801,023	2.5
Parks and recreation	359,434	1.1
Governmental administration	944,961	2.9
Interest on general debt	849,059	2.7
Other and unallocable	3,570,251	11.1
Utility expenditure	5,175	-
Liquor stores expenditure	0	-
Insurance trust expenditure	4,232,506	13.2
Debt at End of Fiscal Year	18,589,438	X
Cash and Security Holdings	56,741,724	X

X = Not applicable.
- = Zero or rounds to zero.

[1]Within insurance trust revenue, net earnings of state retirement systems is a calculated statistic (the item code in the data file is X08), and thus can be positive or negative. Net earnings is the sum of earnings on investments plus gains on investments minus losses on investments. The change made in 2002 for asset valuation from book to market value in accordance with Statement 34 of the Governmental Accounting Standards Board is reflected in the calculated statistics.

Table LA-16. State Government Tax Collections, 2014

(Dollars in thousands, percent.)

Item	Dollars	Percent distribution
Total Taxes	9,695,281	100.0
Property taxes	55,363	0.6
Sales and gross receipts	5,115,636	52.8
General sales and gross receipts	2,923,336	30.2
Selective sales and gross receipts	2,192,300	22.6
Alcoholic beverages	56,967	0.6
Amusements	675,386	7.0
Insurance premiums	429,146	4.4
Motor fuels	588,860	6.1
Pari-mutuels	4,385	-
Public utilities	9,158	0.1
Tobacco products	130,045	1.3
Other selective sales	298,353	3.1
Licenses	427,090	4.4
Alcoholic beverages	0	-
Amusements	0	-
Corporations in general	188,197	1.9
Hunting and fishing	29,665	0.3
Motor vehicle	75,628	0.8
Motor vehicle operators	11,581	0.1
Public utilities	7,622	0.1
Occupation and business, NEC	110,176	1.1
Other licenses	4,221	-
Income taxes	3,234,892	33.4
Individual income	2,753,680	28.4
Corporation net income	481,212	5.0
Other taxes	862,300	8.9
Death and gift	150	-
Documentary and stock transfer	0	-
Severance	862,150	8.9
Taxes, NEC	0	0.0

- = Zero or rounds to zero.

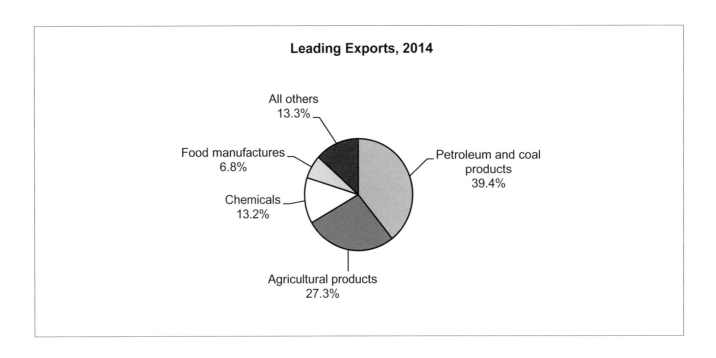

Leading Exports, 2014

All others 13.3%

Food manufactures 6.8%

Chemicals 13.2%

Agricultural products 27.3%

Petroleum and coal products 39.4%

MAINE

Facts and Figures

Location: Northeast corner of the United States; bordered on the N and E by New Brunswick, Canada; on the S by the Atlantic Ocean; on the W by New Hampshire; and on the NW by Quebec, Canada

Area: 35,385 sq. mi. (91,646 sq. km.); rank—39th

Population: 1,330,089 (2014 est.); rank—41st

Principal Cities: capital—Augusta; largest—Portland

Statehood: March 15, 1820; 23rd state

U.S. Congress: 2 senators, 2 representatives

State Motto: *Dirigo* ("I lead")

State Song: "State of Maine Song"

State Nickname: The Pine Tree State

Abbreviations: ME; Me.

State Symbols: flower—white pinecone and tassel; tree—Eastern white pine; bird—chickadee

At a Glance

- With a population that grew 0.1 percent, Maine ranked 49th among the states in growth from 2010 to 2014.

- In 2013, 11.2 percent of Mainers did not have health insurance, compared to 14.5 percent of the total U.S. population.

- Maine's violent crime rate was 129.3 per 100,000 population, the second lowest in the country in 2013.

- With 18.3 percent of its population in the 65 and older age group, Maine ranked second in this category in 2014.

- Maine's birth rate of 9.6 per 1,000 population was the third lowest in the country in 2013.

Table ME-1. Population by Age, Sex, Race, and Hispanic Origin

(Number, percent, except where noted.)

Sex, age, race, and Hispanic origin	2000	2010	2014¹	Average annual percent change, 2010–2014
Total Population	1,274,923	1,328,361	1,330,089	-
Percent of total U.S. population	0.5	0.4	0.4	X
Sex				
Male	620,309	650,056	651,271	-
Female	654,614	678,305	678,818	-
Age				
Under 5 years	70,726	69,520	64,779	-1.8
5 to 19 years	264,729	241,439	227,981	-1.4
20 to 64 years	756,036	806,322	793,822	-0.4
65 years and over	183,402	211,080	243,507	3.6
Median age (years)	38.6	42.7	44.2	0.9
Race and Hispanic Origin				
One race				
White	1,236,014	1,269,764	1,263,864	-0.1
Black	6,760	16,269	19,149	4.2
American Indian and Alaska Native	7,098	8,771	9,132	1.0
Asian	9,111	13,783	15,758	3.4
Native Hawaiian or Other Pacific Islander	382	377	469	5.6
Two or more races	12,647	19,397	21,717	2.9
Hispanic (of any race)	9,360	18,261	20,165	2.5

X = Not applicable.
- = Zero or rounds to zero.
¹Population figures for 2014 are July 1 estimates. The 2010 estimates are taken from the 2010 Census.

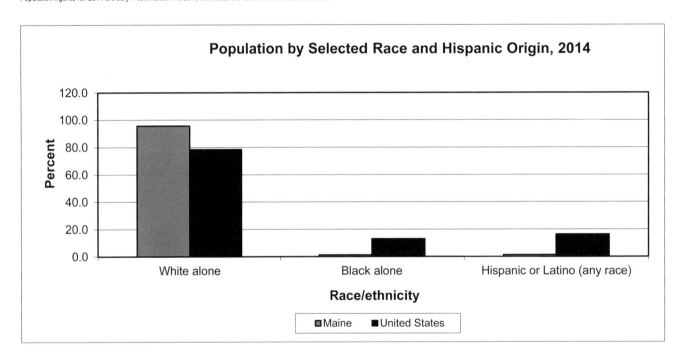

Table ME-2. Marital Status

(Number, percent distribution.)

Sex, age, race, and Hispanic origin	2000	2010	2013
Males, 15 Years and Over	494,217	534,474	541,865
Never married	26.8	31.0	31.8
Now married, except separated	58.8	52.5	51.3
Separated	1.1	1.2	0.8
Widowed	2.8	2.9	2.9
Divorced	10.5	12.5	13.1
Females, 15 Years and Over	534,606	570,281	575,253
Never married	21.2	24.2	25.4
Now married, except separated	54.1	49.3	48.3
Separated	1.3	1.6	1.1
Widowed	11.0	9.9	9.2
Divorced	12.4	15.0	16.0

Table ME-3. Households and Housing Characteristics

(Number, percent, dollars.)

Item	2000	2010	2013	Average annual percent change, 2000–2013
Total Households	518,200	545,417	547,686	0.4
Family households	340,685	345,328	338,609	-
Married-couple family	272,152	266,670	263,513	-0.2
Other family	68,533	78,658	75,096	0.7
Male householder, no wife present	19,511	23,620	23,711	1.5
Female householder, no husband present	49,022	55,038	51,385	0.4
Nonfamily households	177,515	200,089	209,077	1.3
Householder living alone	139,969	155,623	164,125	1.2
Householder not living alone	37,546	44,466	44,952	1.4
Housing Characteristics				
Total housing units	651,901	722,217	723,140	0.8
Occupied housing units	518,200	545,417	547,686	0.4
Owner occupied	370,905	396,395	384,237	0.3
Renter occupied	147,295	149,022	163,449	0.8
Average household size	2.39	2.37	2.36	-0.1
Financial Characteristics				
Median gross rent of renter-occupied housing	497	707	760	3.3
Median monthly owner costs for housing units with a mortgage	923	1,289	1,268	2.5
Median value of owner-occupied housing units	98,700	179,100	172,800	4.4

- = Zero or rounds to zero.

Table ME-4. Migration, Origin, and Language

(Number, percent.)

Characteristic	State 2012	State 2013	State Percent change	U.S. 2012	U.S. 2013	U.S. Percent change
Residence 1 Year Ago						
Population 1 year and over	1,315,586	1,315,753	-	310,212,755	312,432,820	0.7
Same house	86.1	85.8	X	85.0	85.0	X
Different house in the U.S.	13.6	13.9	X	14.4	14.4	X
Same county	8.7	8.5	X	9.0	8.9	X
Different county	4.9	5.5	X	5.4	5.5	X
Same state	2.8	2.7	X	3.2	3.2	X
Different state	2.1	2.8	X	2.3	2.3	X
Abroad	0.3	0.3	X	0.6	0.6	X
Place of Birth						
Native born	1,282,097	1,283,615	0.1	273,089,382	274,780,773	0.6
Male	49.1	49.2	X	49.3	49.3	X
Female	50.9	50.8	X	50.7	50.7	X
Foreign born	47,095	44,687	-5.1	40,824,658	41,348,066	1.3
Male	43.9	41.6	X	48.7	48.8	X
Female	56.1	58.4	X	51.3	51.2	X
Foreign born; naturalized U.S. citizen	25,188	25,351	0.6	18,686,237	19,294,710	3.3
Male	39.0	41.3	X	45.8	45.9	X
Female	61.0	58.7	X	54.2	54.1	X
Foreign born; not a U.S. citizen	21,907	19,336	-11.7	22,138,421	22,053,356	-0.4
Male	49.5	41.9	X	51.1	51.3	X
Female	50.5	58.1	X	48.9	48.7	X
Entered 2010 or later	8.8	13.6	X	7.0	9.7	X
Entered 2000 to 2009	29.4	25.8	X	30.4	29.4	X
Entered before 2000	61.7	60.6	X	62.7	61.0	X
World Region of Birth, Foreign						
Foreign-born population, excluding population born at sea	47,095	44,687	-5.1	40,824,553	41,347,945	1.3
Europe	24.9	23.1	X	11.8	11.6	X
Asia	30.7	28.9	X	29.2	29.5	X
Africa	11.9	12.2	X	4.2	4.4	X
Oceania	0.8	1.3	X	0.6	0.5	X
Latin America	8.5	9.8	X	52.2	51.9	X
North America	23.2	24.8	X	2.0	2.0	X
Language Spoken at Home and Ability to Speak English						
Population 5 years and over	1,263,002	1,264,125	0.1	294,003,714	296,358,760	0.8
English only	92.9	93.7	X	79.0	79.2	X
Language other than English	7.1	6.3	X	21.0	20.8	X
Speaks English less than "very well"	1.7	1.5	X	8.5	8.5	X

NA = Not available.
X = Not applicable.
- = Zero or rounds to zero.

Table ME-5. Median Income and Poverty Status, 2013

(Number, percent, except as noted.)

Characteristic	State		U.S.	
	Number	Percent	Number	Percent
Median Income				
Households (dollars)	46,974	X	52,250	X
Families (dollars)	60,141	X	64,030	X
Below Poverty Level (All People)	180,639	14.0	48,810,868	15.8
Sex				
Male	82,912	13.1	21,938,525	14.5
Female	97,727	14.7	26,872,343	17.1
Age				
Under 18 years	45,159	17.7	16,086,960	22.2
Related children under 18 years	43,014	17.0	15,769,921	21.9
18 to 64 years	114,763	14.2	28,578,191	14.8
65 years and over	20,717	9.1	4,145,717	9.6

X = Not applicable.

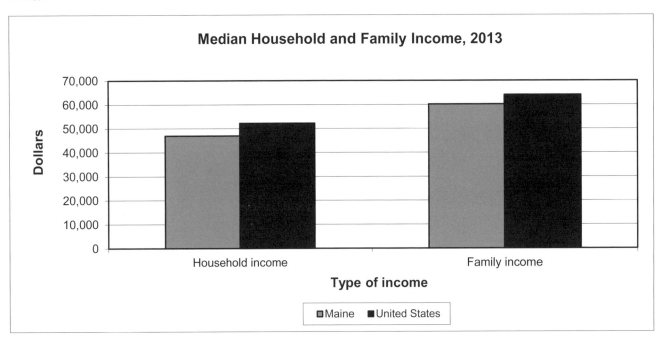

Table ME-6. Health Insurance Coverage Status for the Civilian Noninstitutionalized Population and Children Under 18 Years of Age

(Numbers in thousands, percent.)

Item	2005	2006	2007	2008	2009	2010	2011	2012	2013
Civilian Noninstitutionalized Population	1,320	1,315	1,313	1,299	1,301	1,313	1,314	1,316	1,314
Covered by Private or Public Insurance									
Number	1,185	1,192	1,197	1,157	1,164	1,180	1,174	1,181	1,167
Percent	89.7	90.7	91.2	89.1	89.5	89.8	89.3	89.8	88.8
Not Covered									
Number	136	122	115	142	137	133	140	135	147
Percent	10.3	9.3	8.8	10.9	10.5	10.1	10.7	10.2	11.2
Percent in the U.S. not covered	15.3	15.8	15.3	15.1	15.1	15.5	15.1	14.8	14.5
Children Under 18 Years of Age	279	286	281	275	270	273	270	265	260
Covered by Private or Public Insurance									
Number	272	258	268	255	255	262	256	253	244
Percent	92.3	93.6	94.9	92.7	94.4	96.0	94.8	95.4	94.1
Not Covered									
Number	21	18	14	20	15	11	14	12	15
Percent	7.7	6.4	5.1	7.3	5.6	4.0	5.2	4.6	5.9
Percent in the U.S. not covered	10.9	11.7	11.0	9.7	8.6	8.0	7.5	7.2	7.1

Table ME-7. Employment Status by Demographic Group, 2014

(Numbers in thousands, percent.)

Characteristic	Civilian noninstitutional population	Civilian labor force		Employed		Unemployed	
		Number	Percent of population	Number	Percent of population	Number	Percent of population
Total..	1,090	696	63.9	656	60.2	40	5.7
Sex							
Male..	528	360	68.2	335	63.5	25	6.9
Female...	562	336	59.8	321	57.2	15	4.4
Race, Sex, and Hispanic Origin							
White...	1,044	667	63.9	630	60.4	37	5.5
Male..	506	346	68.3	322	63.7	23	6.7
Female...	538	322	59.8	308	57.3	13	4.2
Black or African American.................	12	8	66.9	7	59.8	1	10.7
Male..	NA	NA	NA	NA	NA	NA	NA
Female...	NA	NA	NA	NA	NA	NA	NA
Hispanic or Latino ethnicity[1].............	NA	NA	NA	NA	NA	NA	NA
Male..	NA	NA	NA	NA	NA	NA	NA
Female...	NA	NA	NA	NA	NA	NA	NA
Age							
16 to 19 years...............................	56	26	47.3	22	39.0	5	17.6
20 to 24 years...............................	88	67	75.7	60	67.6	7	10.8
25 to 34 years...............................	148	122	82.3	112	75.8	10	7.8
35 to 44 years...............................	155	128	82.6	122	78.6	6	4.8
45 to 54 years...............................	190	153	80.8	146	77.2	7	4.5
55 to 64 years...............................	214	148	69.4	145	67.7	3	2.4
65 years and over...........................	238	51	21.4	49	20.6	2	3.5

NOTE: Data in Table 7 are from the Current Population Survey (CPS) and do not match the estimates in Table 8. See notes and definitions for further information.
[1]May be of any race.
NA = Not available.

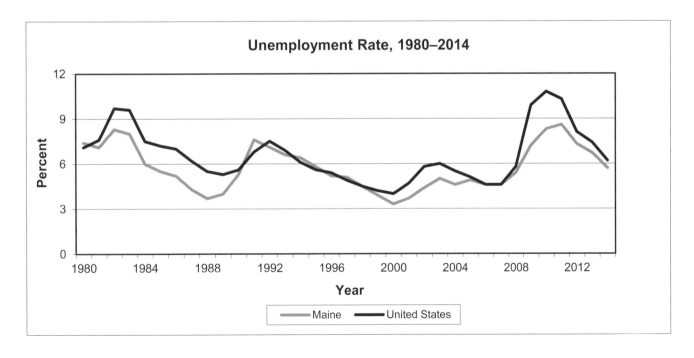

Table ME-8. Employment Status of the Civilian Noninstitutional Population Age 16 Years and Over

(Number, percent.)

Year	Civilian labor force	Civilian participation rate	Employed	Unemployed	Unemployment rate
2006	701,541	66.8	669,554	31,987	4.6
2007	700,468	66.3	667,781	32,687	4.7
2008	701,646	66.0	663,158	38,488	5.5
2009	696,219	65.4	639,954	56,265	8.1
2010	695,182	64.8	638,630	56,552	8.1
2011	699,171	64.8	644,091	55,080	7.9
2012	702,455	64.9	650,024	52,431	7.5
2013	707,188	65.1	660,259	46,929	6.6
2014	698,928	64.1	659,052	39,876	5.7

Table ME-9. Employment and Average Wages by Industry

(Estimates from 2007 through 2010 are based on the 2007 *North American Industry Classification System* [NAICS]. Estimates from 2011 onward are based on the 2012 NAICS.)

Industry	2007	2008	2009	2010	2011	2012	2013
	Number of jobs						
Wage and Salary Employment by Industry	637,508	637,589	616,379	611,786	613,325	613,326	616,647
Farm Wage and Salary Employment	2,701	2,946	2,843	2,849	3,023	3,060	3,626
Nonfarm Wage and Salary Employment	634,807	634,643	613,536	608,937	610,302	610,266	613,021
Private wage and salary employment	521,979	521,727	501,937	498,170	501,526	502,293	506,080
Forestry, fishing, and related activities	4,104	D	D	4,071	4,094	D	4,081
Mining	109	D	D	179	203	D	187
Utilities	1,936	1,895	1,862	1,817	1,609	1,630	1,619
Construction	32,000	30,502	26,371	25,484	26,588	26,443	26,446
Manufacturing	59,449	58,801	52,436	50,716	50,855	50,832	50,407
Durable goods manufacturing	31,548	31,337	27,643	26,974	27,219	27,101	27,266
Nondurable goods manufacturing	27,901	27,464	24,793	23,742	23,636	23,731	23,141
Wholesale trade	21,498	20,968	19,746	19,170	19,190	19,516	19,679
Retail trade	87,064	86,720	83,496	82,742	82,565	82,086	82,172
Transportation and warehousing	17,567	16,929	15,944	15,696	15,875	15,743	16,064
Information	10,666	10,146	9,239	9,159	8,289	7,920	7,651
Finance and insurance	25,682	25,369	24,841	24,775	25,288	24,965	25,014
Real estate and rental and leasing	7,330	7,260	6,931	6,749	6,510	6,497	6,654
Professional, scientific, and technical services	24,032	24,812	24,128	23,830	23,854	23,968	24,853
Management of companies and enterprises	6,470	7,025	6,899	6,990	7,113	7,565	7,425
Administrative and waste services	24,743	26,028	25,314	25,808	27,120	27,169	28,340
Educational services	13,242	13,613	13,536	14,228	14,480	14,853	14,990
Health care and social assistance	98,826	100,355	101,479	101,138	101,362	102,149	102,226
Arts, entertainment, and recreation	8,355	8,399	8,170	8,182	8,251	8,852	8,925
Accommodation and food services	52,600	52,345	51,679	52,319	52,713	53,236	54,253
Other services, except public administration	26,306	26,365	25,743	25,117	25,567	24,632	25,094
Government and government enterprises	112,828	112,916	111,599	110,767	108,776	107,973	106,941
	Dollars						
Average Wages and Salaries by Industry	36,258	37,374	37,539	38,329	39,055	39,716	40,295
Average Farm Wages and Salaries	32,756	28,813	28,365	26,735	22,542	24,961	28,700
Average Nonfarm Wages and Salaries	36,273	37,413	37,582	38,384	39,137	39,790	40,363
Average private wages and salaries	35,808	36,904	36,846	37,766	38,691	39,482	40,047
Forestry, fishing, and related activities	36,625	D	D	38,248	40,511	D	40,580
Mining	40,046	D	D	53,469	53,493	D	55,770
Utilities	63,514	67,348	66,236	71,138	75,606	77,785	79,755
Construction	39,441	41,160	41,016	41,257	42,576	43,605	44,616
Manufacturing	46,273	48,074	48,119	51,576	52,263	52,484	53,201
Durable goods manufacturing	46,485	48,695	48,590	51,619	52,725	52,480	53,197
Nondurable goods manufacturing	46,033	47,365	47,594	51,526	51,730	52,489	53,206
Wholesale trade	51,325	51,944	52,209	52,979	54,738	55,929	56,719
Retail trade	24,201	24,459	24,763	25,083	25,349	25,631	25,790
Transportation and warehousing	36,040	37,684	38,349	38,928	38,772	39,381	40,277
Information	43,355	44,094	44,847	46,823	45,622	46,161	47,315
Finance and insurance	55,814	56,826	56,432	58,670	61,847	64,086	66,279
Real estate and rental and leasing	32,010	32,873	33,077	33,825	35,659	37,191	37,551
Professional, scientific, and technical services	53,044	55,986	55,621	56,290	58,089	60,311	60,829
Management of companies and enterprises	70,032	75,339	65,920	68,478	71,534	75,537	75,206
Administrative and waste services	30,840	31,891	31,622	32,479	32,886	33,337	33,388
Educational services	32,133	32,078	33,148	32,939	34,510	34,576	35,202
Health care and social assistance	37,988	39,522	40,296	40,756	41,901	42,663	43,277
Arts, entertainment, and recreation	25,406	24,421	24,304	24,738	25,049	24,819	26,075
Accommodation and food services	17,657	17,457	17,310	18,038	18,486	18,931	19,259
Other services, except public administration	23,358	24,330	24,498	25,657	26,155	27,057	27,996
Government and government enterprises	38,427	39,766	40,891	41,162	41,194	41,220	41,858

D = Not shown to avoid disclosure of confidential information, but the estimates for this item are included in the total.

Table ME-10. Employment Characteristics by Family Type

(Number, percent.)

Family type and labor force status	2011		2012		2013	
	Total	Families with own children under 18 years	Total	Families with own children under 18 years	Total	Families with own children under 18 years
All Families	347,960	138,279	346,950	135,007	338,609	126,751
FAMILY TYPE AND LABOR FORCE STATUS						
Married-Couple Families	270,959	88,876	270,568	88,800	263,513	81,309
Both husband and wife in labor force	55.4	73.8	54.2	72.0	52.0	70.4
Husband in labor force, wife not in labor force	16.8	19.9	16.8	21.6	16.7	20.4
Wife in labor force, husband not in labor force	8.9	4.1	9.0	4.4	10.6	6.8
Both husband and wife not in labor force	19.0	2.2	19.9	2.0	20.1	2.0
Other Families	77,001	49,403	76,382	46,207	75,096	45,442
Female householder, no husband present	70.0	70.4	69.6	71.7	68.4	66.9
In labor force	50.1	56.2	47.2	53.3	47.7	54.1
Not in labor force	19.9	14.2	22.4	18.4	20.8	12.8
Male householder, no wife present	30.0	29.6	30.4	28.3	31.6	33.1
In labor force	24.0	26.1	22.9	24.1	23.8	27.3
Not in labor force	6.0	3.5	7.5	4.2	7.8	5.8

Table ME-11. School Enrollment and Educational Attainment, 2013

(Number, percent.)

Item	State	U.S.
Enrollment		
Total population 3 years and over, enrolled in school	300,221	82,395,254
Enrolled in nursery school or preschool (percent)	5.1	6.0
Enrolled in kindergarten (percent)	4.6	5.2
Enrolled in elementary school, grades 1-8 (percent)	39.9	40.0
Enrolled in high school, grades 9-12 (percent)	21.9	20.6
Enrolled in college or graduate school (percent)	28.4	28.3
Attainment		
Total population 25 years and over	953,962	210,910,615
Less than ninth grade (percent)	2.9	5.8
9th to 12th grade, no diploma (percent)	5.2	7.6
High school graduate, including equivalency (percent)	33.8	27.8
Some college, no degree (percent)	20.2	21.1
Associate's degree (percent)	9.6	8.1
Bachelor's degree (percent)	18.1	18.4
Graduate or professional degree (percent)	10.1	11.2
High school graduate or higher (percent)	91.8	86.6
Bachelor's degree or higher (percent)	28.2	29.6

Table ME-12. Public School Characteristics and Educational Indicators

(Number, percent; data derived from National Center of Education Statistics.)

Item	State	U.S.
Public Schools, 2012–2013 (except where noted)		
Number of school districts	255	18,093
Number of schools	617	98,454
Number of students (in thousands)	186	49,771
Number of teachers (in thousands)	15	3,109
Student-teacher ratio	12.2	16.0
Expenditures per student (dollars), FY 2012	12,335	10,667
Four-year adjusted cohort graduation rate (ACGR)[1,2]	86.4	81.4
Students eligible for free or reduced-price lunch (in thousands)	81	25,188
English language learners (in thousands)	5	4,397
Students age 3 to 21 served under IDEA, part B (in thousands)	32	6,429

Public Schools by Type	Number	Percent of state public schools
Total number of schools	617	100.0
Regular	587	95.1
Special education	3	0.5
Vocational education	27	4.4
Alternative education	0	-

NOTE: Every school is assigned only one school type based on its instructional emphasis.
[1]ACGR data represents a new method of calculating high-school completion rates and may not be comparable to previous years' data for Averaged Freshmen Graduation Rates (AFGR).
[2]The United States 4-year ACGRs were estimated using both the reported 4-year ACGR data from 49 states and the District of Columbia and using imputed data for Idaho. The estimate for American Indian/Alaska Native students also includes imputed data for Virginia.
- = Zero or rounds to zero.

Table ME-13. Reported Voting and Registration of the Voting-Age Population, November 2012

(Numbers in thousands, percent.)

Item	Total population	Total citizen population	Registered			Voted		
			Total registered	Percent registered (total population)	Percent registered (total citizen population)	Total voted	Percent voted (total population)	Percent voted (total citizen population)
U.S. Total	235,248	215,081	153,157	65.1	71.2	132,948	56.5	61.8
State Total	1,042	1,020	787	75.5	77.1	700	67.2	68.6
Sex								
Male	509	501	383	75.2	76.4	333	65.5	66.5
Female	533	519	404	75.8	77.9	367	68.8	70.7
Race								
White alone	1,001	986	766	76.5	77.7	682	68.1	69.1
White, non-Hispanic alone	993	981	762	76.8	77.7	678	68.3	69.1
Black alone	8	7	4	B	B	4	B	B
Asian alone	14	8	3	B	B	2	B	B
Hispanic (of any race)	10	7	4	B	B	4	B	B
White alone or in combination	1,015	1,000	776	76.4	77.6	691	68.0	69.0
Black alone or in combination	9	8	6	B	B	6	B	B
Asian alone or in combination	15	9	4	B	B	3	B	B
Age								
18 to 24 years	118	118	61	51.7	51.7	50	42.8	42.8
25 to 44 years	292	281	210	72.0	74.9	179	61.4	63.9
45 to 64 years	413	407	329	79.7	80.9	300	72.7	73.7
65 to 74 years	129	127	109	84.9	86.4	104	80.5	81.8
75 years and over	90	88	77	85.7	87.7	66	73.7	75.4

B = Base is less than 75,000 and therefore too small to show the derived measure.

Table ME-14. Crime

(Number, rate per 100,000. Data are derived from the FBI Uniform Crime Reports.)

Item	State			U.S.[1,2,3,4]		
	2012	2013	Percent change	2012	2013	Percent change
TOTAL POPULATION[5]	1,328,501	1,328,302	-	313,873,685	316,128,839	0.7
VIOLENT CRIME						
Number	1,626	1,615	-0.7	1,217,067	1,163,146	-4.4
Rate	122.4	121.6	-0.7	387.8	367.9	-5.1
Murder and Nonnegligent Manslaughter						
Number	26	24	-7.7	14,866	14,196	-4.5
Rate	2.0	1.8	-7.7	4.7	4.5	-5.2
Rape[6]						
Number	X	447	X	X	108,612	X
Rate	X	33.7	X	X	34.4	X
Robbery						
Number	420	335	-20.2	355,051	345,031	-2.8
Rate	31.6	25.2	-20.2	113.1	109.1	-3.5
Aggravated Assault						
Number	808	912	12.9	762,009	724,149	-5.0
Rate	60.8	68.7	12.9	242.8	229.1	-5.6
PROPERTY CRIME						
Number	33,398	30,447	-8.8	9,001,992	8,632,512	-4.1
Rate	2,514.0	2,292.2	-8.8	2,868.0	2,730.7	-4.8
Burglary						
Number	7,476	6,483	-13.3	2,109,932	1,928,465	-8.6
Rate	562.7	488.1	-13.3	672.2	610.0	-9.3
Larceny-Theft						
Number	24,931	23,050	-7.5	6,168,874	6,004,453	-2.7
Rate	1,876.6	1,735.3	-7.5	1,965.4	1,899.4	-3.4
Motor Vehicle Theft						
Number	991	914	-7.8	723,186	699,594	-3.3
Rate	74.6	68.8	-7.8	230.4	221.3	-4.0

NOTE: Although arson data are included in the trend and clearance tables, sufficient data are not available to estimate totals for this offense. Therefore, no arson data are published in this table.

X = Not applicable.

- = Zero or rounds to zero.

[1]The crime figures have been adjusted.

[2]The data collection methodology for the offense of forcible rape used by the Minnesota state Uniform Crime Reporting (UCR) Program (with the exception of Minneapolis and St. Paul, Minnesota) does not comply with national UCR Program guidelines. Consequently, its figures for forcible rape and violent crime (of which forcible rape is a part) are not published in this table.

[3]Includes offenses reported by the Zoological Police and the Metro Transit Police.

[4]Because of changes in the state's reporting practices, figures are not comparable to previous years' data.

[5]Populations are U.S. Census Bureau provisional estimates as of July 1 of each year.

[6]The figures shown for the offense of rape were estimated using the revised Uniform Crime Reporting (UCR) definition of rape.

Table ME-15. State Government Finances, 2013

(Dollar amounts in thousands, percent distribution.)

Item	Dollars	Percent distribution
Total Revenue	9,571,311	100.0
General revenue	7,990,979	83.5
Intergovernmental revenue	2,830,353	29.6
Taxes	3,884,450	40.6
General sales	1,071,886	11.2
Selective sales	707,987	7.4
License taxes	260,918	2.7
Individual income tax	1,531,504	16.0
Corporate income tax	171,987	1.8
Other taxes	140,168	1.5
Current charges	737,693	7.7
Miscellaneous general revenue	538,483	5.6
Utility revenue	9,129	0.1
Liquor stores revenue	33	-
Insurance trust revenue[1]	1,571,170	16.4
Total Expenditure	8,950,407	100.0
Intergovernmental expenditure	1,238,618	13.8
Direct expenditure	7,711,789	86.2
Current operation	5,852,116	65.4
Capital outlay	433,151	4.8
Insurance benefits and repayments	1,049,864	11.7
Assistance and subsidies	143,592	1.6
Interest on debt	233,066	2.6
Exhibit: Salaries and wages	756,435	8.5
Total Expenditure	8,950,407	100.0
General expenditure	7,876,981	88.0
Intergovernmental expenditure	1,238,618	13.8
Direct expenditure	6,638,363	74.2
General expenditure, by function:		
Education	2,019,094	22.6
Public welfare	2,892,491	32.3
Hospitals	111,922	1.3
Health	484,261	5.4
Highways	614,592	6.9
Police protection	75,602	0.8
Correction	136,811	1.5
Natural resources	171,924	1.9
Parks and recreation	24,992	0.3
Governmental administration	289,001	3.2
Interest on general debt	233,066	2.6
Other and unallocable	823,225	9.2
Utility expenditure	23,562	0.3
Liquor stores expenditure	0	-
Insurance trust expenditure	1,049,864	11.7
Debt at End of Fiscal Year	5,374,528	X
Cash and Security Holdings	17,672,368	X

X = Not applicable.
- = Zero or rounds to zero.
[1]Within insurance trust revenue, net earnings of state retirement systems is a calculated statistic (the item code in the data file is X08), and thus can be positive or negative. Net earnings is the sum of earnings on investments plus gains on investments minus losses on investments. The change made in 2002 for asset valuation from book to market value in accordance with Statement 34 of the Governmental Accounting Standards Board is reflected in the calculated statistics.

Table ME-16. State Government Tax Collections, 2014

(Dollars in thousands, percent.)

Item	Dollars	Percent distribution
Total Taxes	3,847,181	100.0
Property taxes	35,755	0.9
Sales and gross receipts	1,911,398	49.7
General sales and gross receipts	1,191,685	31.0
Selective sales and gross receipts	719,713	18.7
Alcoholic beverages	17,923	0.5
Amusements	50,854	1.3
Insurance premiums	106,372	2.8
Motor fuels	240,901	6.3
Pari-mutuels	1,816	-
Public utilities	32,432	0.8
Tobacco products	136,160	3.5
Other selective sales	133,255	3.5
Licenses	254,251	6.6
Alcoholic beverages	5,393	0.1
Amusements	654	-
Corporations in general	9,343	0.2
Hunting and fishing	16,282	0.4
Motor vehicle	102,306	2.7
Motor vehicle operators	10,064	0.3
Public utilities	0	-
Occupation and business, NEC	101,562	2.6
Other licenses	8,647	0.2
Income taxes	1,597,038	41.5
Individual income	1,414,110	36.8
Corporation net income	182,928	4.8
Other taxes	48,739	1.3
Death and gift	23,962	0.6
Documentary and stock transfer	24,777	0.6
Severance	X	X
Taxes, NEC	0	-

- = Zero or rounds to zero.

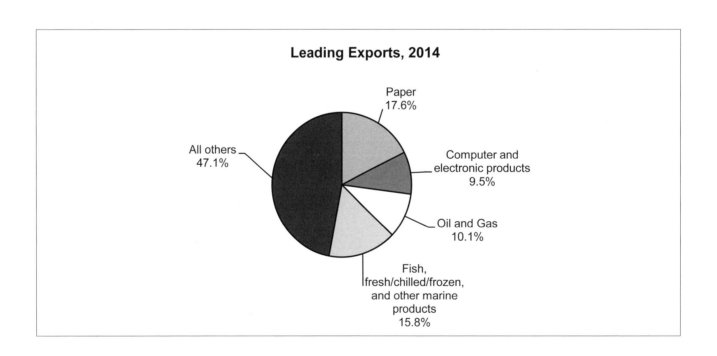

Leading Exports, 2014

- Paper 17.6%
- Computer and electronic products 9.5%
- Oil and Gas 10.1%
- Fish, fresh/chilled/frozen, and other marine products 15.8%
- All others 47.1%

MARYLAND

Facts and Figures

Location: Eastern United States; bordered on the N by Pennsylvania, on the E by Delaware and the Atlantic Ocean, and on the S and W by Virginia and West Virginia

Area: 12,407 sq. mi. (32,133 sq. km.); rank—42nd

Population: 5,976,407 (2014 est.); rank—19th

Principal Cities: capital—Annapolis; largest—Baltimore

Statehood: April 28, 1788; 7th state

U.S. Congress: 2 senators, 8 representatives

State Motto: *Fatti maschii parole femine* ("Manly deeds, womanly words")

State Song: "Maryland, My Maryland"

State Nicknames: The Old Line State; The Free State

Abbreviations: MD; Md.

State Symbols: flower—black-eyed susan; tree—white oak; bird—Baltimore oriole

At a Glance

- With an increase in population of 3.5 percent, Maryland ranked 22nd among the states in growth from 2010 to 2014.

- Maryland's median household income in 2013 was $72,483, the highest in the country, and 10.1 percent of the population lived below the poverty level.

- Maryland's violent crime rate in 2013 was 473.8 per 100,000 population, compared to 367.9 for the entire nation.

- The homeownership rate in Maryland in 2013 was 66.9 percent, ranking 32nd in the nation.

- Approximately 30.0 percent of Marylanders self-identified their race as "Black or African American alone" in 2014, the 5th highest percentage in the country.

Table MD-1. Population by Age, Sex, Race, and Hispanic Origin

(Number, percent, except where noted.)

Sex, age, race, and Hispanic origin	2000	2010	2014[1]	Average annual percent change, 2010–2014
Total Population	5,296,486	5,773,552	5,976,407	0.9
Percent of total U.S. population	1.9	1.9	1.9	X
Sex				
Male	2,557,794	2,791,762	2,896,418	0.9
Female	2,738,692	2,981,790	3,079,989	0.8
Age				
Under 5 years..	353,393	364,488	369,754	0.4
5 to 19 years...	1,139,572	1,152,138	1,138,672	-0.3
20 to 64 years...	3,204,214	3,549,284	3,645,721	0.7
65 years and over...	599,307	707,642	822,260	3.8
Median age (years)...	36.0	38.0	38.2	0.1
Race and Hispanic Origin				
One race				
White	3,391,308	3,542,379	3,589,555	0.3
Black	1,477,411	1,731,513	1,809,294	1.1
American Indian and Alaska Native	15,423	30,885	33,413	2.0
Asian...	210,929	326,655	380,168	3.9
Native Hawaiian or Other Pacific Islander	2,303	5,391	6,319	4.1
Two or more races..	103,587	137,729	157,658	3.4
Hispanic (of any race)...	227,916	493,811	557,371	3.1

X = Not applicable.
[1]Population figures for 2014 are July 1 estimates. The 2010 estimates are taken from the 2010 Census.

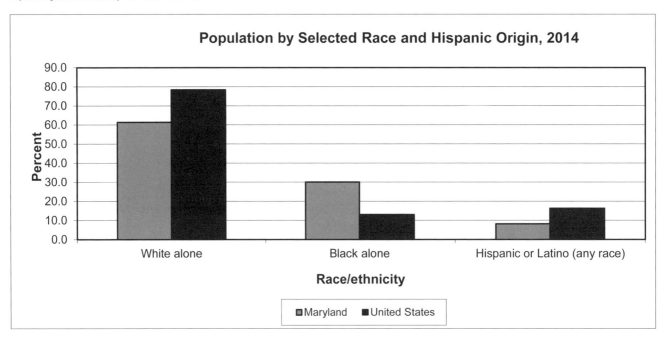

Table MD-2. Marital Status

(Number, percent distribution.)

Sex, age, race, and Hispanic origin	2000	2010	2013
Males, 15 Years and Over...	1,972,921	2,232,162	2,306,220
Never married	31.0	36.8	37.8
Now married, except separated...	56.3	50.2	49.3
Separated...	2.8	2.3	2.1
Widowed...	2.5	2.7	2.3
Divorced...	7.4	8.0	8.5
Females, 15 Years and Over...	2,186,715	2,442,021	2,507,986
Never married	26.8	32.2	33.1
Now married, except separated...	49.7	45.3	44.2
Separated...	3.4	2.9	2.7
Widowed...	10.1	9.0	8.7
Divorced...	10.1	10.7	11.3

Table MD-3. Households and Housing Characteristics

(Number, percent, dollars.)

Item	2000	2010	2013	Average annual percent change, 2000–2013
Total Households....................................	1,980,859	2,127,439	2,161,680	0.7
Family households	1,359,318	1,431,958	1,443,796	0.5
Married-couple family	994,549	1,022,613	1,022,394	0.2
Other family	364,789	409,345	421,402	1.1
Male householder, no wife present..........	84,893	104,112	102,135	1.4
Female householder, no husband present....	279,876	305,233	319,267	1.0
Nonfamily households	621,541	695,481	717,884	1.1
Householder living alone	495,459	570,388	587,947	1.3
Householder not living alone	126,082	125,093	129,937	0.2
Housing Characteristics				
Total housing units................................	2,145,283	2,380,605	2,404,177	0.9
Occupied housing units	1,980,859	2,127,439	2,161,680	0.7
Owner occupied	1,341,751	1,426,267	1,436,907	0.5
Renter occupied	639,108	701,172	724,773	1.0
Average household size..........................	2.61	2.65	2.68	0.2
Financial Characteristics				
Median gross rent of renter-occupied housing	689	1,131	1,210	4.4
Median monthly owner costs for housing units with a mortgage	1,296	2,016	1,867	2.8
Median value of owner-occupied housing units	146,000	301,400	280,200	5.1

Table MD-4. Migration, Origin, and Language

(Number, percent.)

Characteristic	State			U.S.		
	2012	2013	Percent change	2012	2013	Percent change
Residence 1 Year Ago						
Population 1 year and over	5,816,472	5,857,213	0.7	310,212,755	312,432,820	0.7
Same house	87.1	86.7	X	85.0	85.0	X
Different house in the U.S.	12.1	12.5	X	14.4	14.4	X
Same county	6.9	7.2	X	9.0	8.9	X
Different county	5.2	5.4	X	5.4	5.5	X
Same state	2.6	2.6	X	3.2	3.2	X
Different state	2.7	2.8	X	2.3	2.3	X
Abroad	0.7	0.8	X	0.6	0.6	X
Place of Birth						
Native born	5,045,227	5,086,564	0.8	273,089,382	274,780,773	0.6
Male	48.5	48.6	X	49.3	49.3	X
Female	51.5	51.4	X	50.7	50.7	X
Foreign born	839,336	842,250	0.3	40,824,658	41,348,066	1.3
Male	48.1	48.1	X	48.7	48.8	X
Female	51.9	51.9	X	51.3	51.2	X
Foreign born; naturalized U.S. citizen........	392,727	420,344	7.0	18,686,237	19,294,710	3.3
Male	45.2	45.3	X	45.8	45.9	X
Female	54.8	54.7	X	54.2	54.1	X
Foreign born; not a U.S. citizen................	446,609	421,906	-5.5	22,138,421	22,053,356	-0.4
Male	50.5	50.9	X	51.1	51.3	X
Female	49.5	49.1	X	48.9	48.7	X
Entered 2010 or later	8.6	10.8	X	7.0	9.7	X
Entered 2000 to 2009...........................	36.8	35.2	X	30.4	29.4	X
Entered before 2000.............................	54.6	54.0	X	62.7	61.0	X
World Region of Birth, Foreign						
Foreign-born population, excluding population born at sea	839,336	842,250	0.3	40,824,553	41,347,945	1.3
Europe	10.5	10.1	X	11.8	11.6	X
Asia...	32.5	33.3	X	29.2	29.5	X
Africa	15.4	16.4	X	4.2	4.4	X
Oceania	0.3	0.3	X	0.6	0.5	X
Latin America	40.1	39.0	X	52.2	51.9	X
North America	1.2	1.0	X	2.0	2.0	X
Language Spoken at Home and Ability to Speak English						
Population 5 years and over......................	5,519,938	5,562,102	0.8	294,003,714	296,358,760	0.8
English only	82.8	83.0	X	79.0	79.2	X
Language other than English.................	17.2	17.0	X	21.0	20.8	X
Speaks English less than "very well"........	6.4	6.3	X	8.5	8.5	X

NA = Not available.
X = Not applicable.
- = Zero or rounds to zero.

Table MD-5. Median Income and Poverty Status, 2013

(Number, percent, except as noted.)

Characteristic	State		U.S.	
	Number	Percent	Number	Percent
Median Income				
Households (dollars)...........................	72,483	X	52,250	X
Families (dollars)	87,204	X	64,030	X
Below Poverty Level (All People)...........................	585,571	10.1	48,810,868	15.8
Sex				
Male...........................	252,808	9.0	21,938,525	14.5
Female	332,763	11.1	26,872,343	17.1
Age				
Under 18 years...........................	180,351	13.6	16,086,960	22.2
Related children under 18 years...........................	175,540	13.3	15,769,921	21.9
18 to 64 years...........................	343,532	9.3	28,578,191	14.8
65 years and over...........................	61,688	8.0	4,145,717	9.6

X = Not applicable.

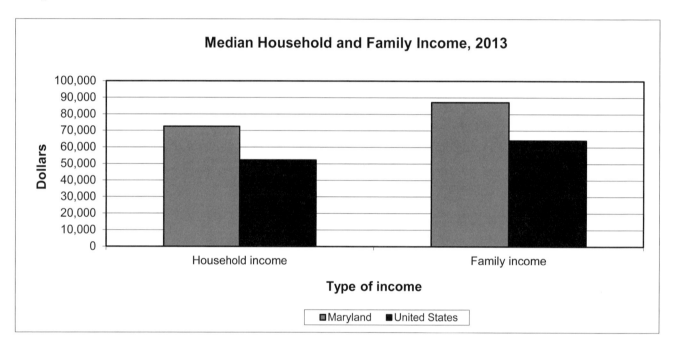

Median Household and Family Income, 2013

Table MD-6. Health Insurance Coverage Status for the Civilian Noninstitutionalized Population and Children Under 18 Years of Age

(Numbers in thousands, percent.)

Item	2005	2006	2007	2008	2009	2010	2011	2012	2013
Civilian Noninstitutionalized Population...........................	5,569	5,613	5,565	5,530	5,590	5,688	5,737	5,788	5,834
Covered by Private or Public Insurance									
Number...........................	4,823	4,836	4,804	4,919	4,969	5,047	5,138	5,191	5,241
Percent...........................	86.6	86.2	86.3	89.0	88.9	88.7	89.6	89.7	89.8
Not Covered									
Number...........................	746	776	762	611	621	641	598	597	593
Percent...........................	13.4	13.8	13.7	11.0	11.1	11.3	10.4	10.3	10.2
Percent in the U.S. not covered...........................	15.3	15.8	15.3	15.1	15.1	15.5	15.1	14.8	14.5
Children Under 18 Years of Age...........................	1,383	1,384	1,382	1,339	1,348	1,350	1,344	1,341	1,343
Covered by Private or Public Insurance									
Number...........................	1,268	1,247	1,237	1,269	1,283	1,286	1,283	1,290	1,284
Percent...........................	91.7	90.1	89.5	94.8	95.2	95.2	95.4	96.2	95.6
Not Covered									
Number...........................	115	137	146	70	65	64	61	51	59
Percent...........................	8.3	9.9	10.5	5.2	4.8	4.8	4.6	3.8	4.4
Percent in the U.S. not covered...........................	10.9	11.7	11.0	9.7	8.6	8.0	7.5	7.2	7.1

Table MD-7. Employment Status by Demographic Group, 2014

(Numbers in thousands, percent.)

Characteristic	Civilian noninstitutional population	Civilian labor force		Employed		Unemployed	
		Number	Percent of population	Number	Percent of population	Number	Percent of population
Total............................	4,684	3,097	66.1	2,918	62.3	179	5.8
Sex							
Male...............................	2,218	1,595	71.9	1,503	67.7	92	5.8
Female............................	2,465	1,502	60.9	1,415	57.4	87	5.8
Race, Sex, and Hispanic Origin							
White..............................	2,836	1,869	65.9	1,781	62.8	88	4.7
Male...............................	1,381	1,005	72.7	954	69.1	50	5.0
Female............................	1,455	864	59.4	826	56.8	38	4.4
Black or African American............	1,375	894	65.0	818	59.5	76	8.5
Male...............................	616	418	67.9	383	62.2	35	8.3
Female............................	759	476	62.7	435	57.3	41	8.7
Hispanic or Latino ethnicity[1]........	389	293	75.3	276	71.1	16	5.6
Male...............................	192	166	86.6	155	80.6	11	6.9
Female............................	197	126	64.3	122	61.7	5	3.9
Age							
16 to 19 years.....................	288	86	29.9	66	22.8	20	23.7
20 to 24 years.....................	421	296	70.3	263	62.4	33	11.3
25 to 34 years.....................	838	702	83.7	657	78.3	45	6.4
35 to 44 years.....................	708	606	85.6	579	81.7	28	4.6
45 to 54 years.....................	809	676	83.6	657	81.1	20	2.9
55 to 64 years.....................	775	548	70.7	527	68.0	21	3.9
65 years and over..................	844	182	21.6	170	20.2	12	6.6

NOTE: Data in Table 7 are from the Current Population Survey (CPS) and do not match the estimates in Table 8. See notes and definitions for further information.
[1]May be of any race.

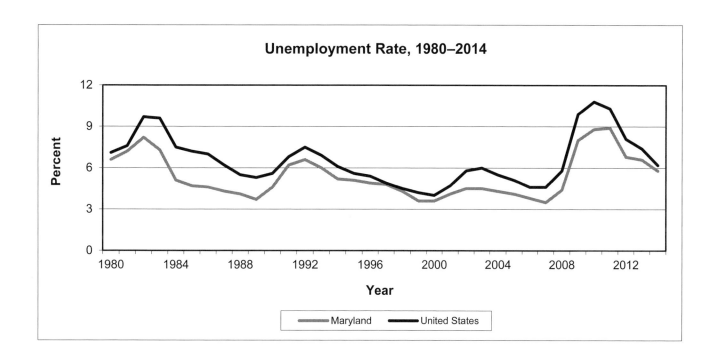

Unemployment Rate, 1980–2014

Table MD-8. Employment Status of the Civilian Noninstitutional Population Age 16 Years and Over

(Number, percent.)

Year	Civilian labor force	Civilian participation rate	Employed	Unemployed	Unemployment rate
2006	2,963,866	69.0	2,849,354	114,512	3.9
2007	2,970,094	68.7	2,867,348	102,746	3.5
2008	3,001,953	68.9	2,874,987	126,966	4.2
2009	3,032,700	69.0	2,820,245	212,455	7.0
2010	3,073,826	68.5	2,838,492	235,334	7.7
2011	3,095,984	68.0	2,871,965	224,019	7.2
2012	3,120,468	67.8	2,903,161	217,307	7.0
2013	3,124,102	67.2	2,917,212	206,890	6.6
2014	3,111,329	66.4	2,929,977	181,352	5.8

Table MD-9. Employment and Average Wages by Industry

(Estimates from 2007 through 2010 are based on the 2007 *North American Industry Classification System* [NAICS]. Estimates from 2011 onward are based on the 2012 NAICS.)

Industry	2007	2008	2009	2010	2011	2012	2013
	Number of jobs						
Wage and Salary Employment by Industry	2,731,261	2,721,297	2,643,648	2,636,857	2,664,514	2,691,293	2,709,290
Farm Wage and Salary Employment	4,975	4,436	4,298	4,816	4,670	6,052	5,790
Nonfarm Wage and Salary Employment	2,726,286	2,716,861	2,639,350	2,632,041	2,659,844	2,685,241	2,703,500
Private wage and salary employment	2,184,135	2,165,616	2,081,971	2,066,491	2,089,409	2,115,694	2,135,042
Forestry, fishing, and related activities	2,146	2,166	2,109	2,186	2,094	1,977	1,980
Mining	1,650	1,616	1,492	1,468	1,431	1,523	1,333
Utilities	9,928	10,274	10,104	9,719	10,071	10,103	9,776
Construction	195,062	185,201	160,300	149,522	150,948	148,037	151,472
Manufacturing	131,846	128,368	118,788	115,083	112,946	108,879	106,357
Durable goods manufacturing	70,986	69,424	63,902	61,503	60,185	57,882	56,329
Nondurable goods manufacturing	60,860	58,944	54,886	53,580	52,761	50,997	50,028
Wholesale trade	95,991	93,753	88,238	86,123	86,777	86,591	86,222
Retail trade	305,675	296,824	281,097	281,817	284,893	286,844	287,209
Transportation and warehousing	69,799	68,277	65,511	66,017	66,581	67,771	68,717
Information	51,107	49,955	46,319	43,949	41,019	39,950	39,578
Finance and insurance	109,978	105,486	101,598	99,412	98,965	99,367	99,412
Real estate and rental and leasing	48,974	48,013	44,864	44,307	43,659	43,708	44,421
Professional, scientific, and technical services	224,145	229,406	227,426	227,311	232,290	235,950	237,689
Management of companies and enterprises	20,469	20,997	19,877	19,532	22,148	24,685	25,873
Administrative and waste services	157,442	153,452	141,599	145,057	147,597	152,755	156,885
Educational services	66,768	68,717	69,358	70,351	73,095	73,114	71,788
Health care and social assistance	307,718	315,336	324,909	329,891	335,766	342,993	345,907
Arts, entertainment, and recreation	37,125	37,072	35,893	36,289	37,094	38,283	42,506
Accommodation and food services	199,704	201,902	197,244	196,821	199,636	207,455	213,744
Other services, except public administration	148,608	148,801	145,245	141,636	142,399	145,709	144,173
Government and government enterprises	542,151	551,245	557,379	565,550	570,435	569,547	568,458
	Dollars						
Average Wages and Salaries by Industry	49,323	50,629	51,705	52,945	54,281	55,493	55,446
Average Farm Wages and Salaries	29,777	32,039	31,414	26,481	24,431	21,131	30,094
Average Nonfarm Wages and Salaries	49,359	50,660	51,738	52,993	54,333	55,571	55,500
Average private wages and salaries	47,350	48,463	49,201	50,463	51,659	53,160	53,082
Forestry, fishing, and related activities	25,080	25,850	25,811	26,607	27,450	27,796	28,870
Mining	52,562	54,404	53,982	55,858	61,188	61,664	60,410
Utilities	101,234	101,535	96,608	107,058	109,583	119,093	115,148
Construction	51,310	53,314	54,431	54,972	55,910	57,143	57,191
Manufacturing	61,807	63,443	64,848	67,792	68,579	70,623	70,921
Durable goods manufacturing	67,273	69,976	72,442	75,905	75,857	77,664	78,255
Nondurable goods manufacturing	55,433	55,748	56,006	58,479	60,276	62,632	62,663
Wholesale trade	66,000	67,812	68,505	70,546	72,673	74,502	75,054
Retail trade	28,459	28,262	28,394	28,841	28,948	29,560	29,467
Transportation and warehousing	44,585	45,986	46,262	47,989	50,118	50,475	50,460
Information	66,250	68,618	70,584	74,037	78,331	80,562	82,945
Finance and insurance	80,216	79,960	78,522	82,242	85,075	93,791	93,408
Real estate and rental and leasing	52,056	52,211	51,876	55,258	56,471	58,194	57,983
Professional, scientific, and technical services	77,415	80,094	82,925	85,262	88,177	91,557	90,239
Management of companies and enterprises	97,366	94,427	97,673	107,580	106,464	105,754	107,573
Administrative and waste services	35,426	36,580	37,256	38,149	38,668	39,583	39,484
Educational services	40,361	41,290	42,967	43,527	45,390	46,788	47,063
Health care and social assistance	44,576	46,612	47,362	47,646	48,623	49,607	50,001
Arts, entertainment, and recreation	31,591	29,359	29,861	31,151	31,522	32,493	32,456
Accommodation and food services	19,707	19,610	19,498	20,084	20,594	20,881	20,841
Other services, except public administration	32,083	33,191	33,741	34,951	35,414	36,132	37,330
Government and government enterprises	57,454	59,290	61,217	62,239	64,128	64,527	64,582

Table MD-10. Employment Characteristics by Family Type

(Number, percent.)

Family type and labor force status	2011 Total	2011 Families with own children under 18 years	2012 Total	2012 Families with own children under 18 years	2013 Total	2013 Families with own children under 18 years
All Families	1,415,576	629,280	1,437,113	633,449	1,443,796	632,608
FAMILY TYPE AND LABOR FORCE STATUS						
Married-Couple Families	995,216	411,914	1,018,129	420,489	1,022,394	423,061
Both husband and wife in labor force	59.2	72.6	60.1	73.5	58.8	72.6
Husband in labor force, wife not in labor force	19.4	22.4	19.3	22.4	19.3	22.6
Wife in labor force, husband not in labor force	7.8	3.9	7.3	3.1	7.7	3.3
Both husband and wife not in labor force	13.7	1.1	13.3	1.0	13.4	1.0
Other Families	420,360	217,366	418,984	212,960	421,402	209,547
Female householder, no husband present	75.8	78.6	74.6	76.2	75.8	78.4
In labor force	59.1	70.0	57.0	66.3	57.8	67.0
Not in labor force	16.8	8.7	17.6	10.0	17.9	11.4
Male householder, no wife present	24.2	21.4	25.4	23.8	24.2	21.6
In labor force	19.8	20.2	21.1	22.2	20.1	20.5
Not in labor force	4.4	1.2	4.4	1.6	4.1	1.1

Table MD-11. School Enrollment and Educational Attainment, 2013

(Number, percent.)

Item	State	U.S.
Enrollment		
Total population 3 years and over, enrolled in school	1,562,663	82,395,254
Enrolled in nursery school or preschool (percent)	5.9	6.0
Enrolled in kindergarten (percent)	5.2	5.2
Enrolled in elementary school, grades 1-8 (percent)	37.1	40.0
Enrolled in high school, grades 9-12 (percent)	20.0	20.6
Enrolled in college or graduate school (percent)	31.8	28.3
Attainment		
Total population 25 years and over	4,018,701	210,910,615
Less than ninth grade (percent)	4.1	5.8
9th to 12th grade, no diploma (percent)	6.7	7.6
High school graduate, including equivalency (percent)	25.7	27.8
Some college, no degree (percent)	19.8	21.1
Associate's degree (percent)	6.3	8.1
Bachelor's degree (percent)	20.3	18.4
Graduate or professional degree (percent)	17.1	11.2
High school graduate or higher (percent)	89.1	86.6
Bachelor's degree or higher (percent)	37.4	29.6

Table MD-12. Public School Characteristics and Educational Indicators

(Number, percent; data derived from National Center of Education Statistics.)

Item	State	U.S.
Public Schools, 2012–2013 (except where noted)		
Number of school districts	25	18,093
Number of schools	1,449	98,454
Number of students (in thousands)	860	49,771
Number of teachers (in thousands)	58	3,109
Student-teacher ratio	14.9	16.0
Expenditures per student (dollars), FY 2012	13,871	10,667
Four-year adjusted cohort graduation rate (ACGR)[1,2]	85.0	81.4
Students eligible for free or reduced-price lunch (in thousands)	367	25,188
English language learners (in thousands)	55	4,397
Students age 3 to 21 served under IDEA, part B (in thousands)	103	6,429

Public Schools by Type	Number	Percent of state public schools
Total number of schools	1,449	100.0
Regular	1,327	91.6
Special education	39	2.7
Vocational education	26	1.8
Alternative education	57	3.9

NOTE: Every school is assigned only one school type based on its instructional emphasis.
[1]ACGR data represents a new method of calculating high-school completion rates and may not be comparable to previous years' data for Averaged Freshmen Graduation Rates (AFGR).
[2]The United States 4-year ACGRs were estimated using both the reported 4-year ACGR data from 49 states and the District of Columbia and using imputed data for Idaho. The estimate for American Indian/Alaska Native students also includes imputed data for Virginia.

Table MD-13. Reported Voting and Registration of the Voting-Age Population, November 2012

(Numbers in thousands, percent.)

Item	Total population	Total citizen population	Registered			Voted		
			Total registered	Percent registered (total population)	Percent registered (total citizen population)	Total voted	Percent voted (total population)	Percent voted (total citizen population)
U.S. Total	235,248	215,081	153,157	65.1	71.2	132,948	56.5	61.8
State Total	4,449	4,007	2,888	64.9	72.1	2,609	58.7	65.1
Sex								
Male	2,101	1,914	1,336	63.6	69.8	1,189	56.6	62.1
Female	2,348	2,093	1,552	66.1	74.2	1,421	60.5	67.9
Race								
White alone....................................	2,837	2,635	1,913	67.4	72.6	1,711	60.3	65.0
White, non-Hispanic alone	2,567	2,511	1,840	71.7	73.3	1,648	64.2	65.6
Black alone....................................	1,276	1,167	850	66.6	72.8	788	61.8	67.5
Asian alone	260	131	78	29.9	59.4	66	25.4	50.4
Hispanic (of any race).....................	342	176	115	33.7	65.6	103	30.2	58.7
White alone or in combination	2,886	2,681	1,940	67.2	72.4	1,735	60.1	64.7
Black alone or in combination..........	1,318	1,206	880	66.8	73.0	819	62.1	67.9
Asian alone or in combination..........	277	149	90	32.4	60.5	75	26.9	50.3
Age								
18 to 24 years.................................	585	558	301	51.5	54.0	246	42.1	44.1
25 to 44 years.................................	1,498	1,211	873	58.3	72.1	789	52.7	65.1
45 to 64 years.................................	1,557	1,450	1,107	71.1	76.3	1,025	65.8	70.7
65 to 74 years.................................	478	465	383	80.1	82.3	356	74.6	76.7
75 years and over	331	322	224	67.8	69.6	193	58.4	60.0

Table MD-14. Crime

(Number, rate per 100,000. Data are derived from the FBI Uniform Crime Reports.)

Item	State			U.S.[1,2,3,4]		
	2012	2013	Percent change	2012	2013	Percent change
TOTAL POPULATION[5]..	5,884,868	5,928,814	0.7	313,873,685	316,128,839	0.7
VIOLENT CRIME						
Number..	28,086	27,734	-1.3	1,217,067	1,163,146	-4.4
Rate	477.3	467.8	-2.0	387.8	367.9	-5.1
Murder and Nonnegligent Manslaughter						
Number..	373	381	2.1	14,866	14,196	-4.5
Rate	6.3	6.4	1.4	4.7	4.5	-5.2
Rape[6]						
Number..	X	1,532	X	X	108,612	X
Rate	X	25.8	X	X	34.4	X
Robbery						
Number..	10,173	10,048	-1.2	355,051	345,031	-2.8
Rate	172.9	169.5	-2.0	113.1	109.1	-3.5
Aggravated Assault						
Number..	16,303	16,128	-1.1	762,009	724,149	-5.0
Rate	277.0	272.0	-1.8	242.8	229.1	-5.6
PROPERTY CRIME						
Number..	162,309	157,913	-2.7	9,001,992	8,632,512	-4.1
Rate	2,758.1	2,663.5	-3.4	2,868.0	2,730.7	-4.8
Burglary						
Number..	33,803	31,949	-5.5	2,109,932	1,928,465	-8.6
Rate	574.4	538.9	-6.2	672.2	610.0	-9.3
Larceny-Theft						
Number..	113,550	112,546	-0.9	6,168,874	6,004,453	-2.7
Rate	1,929.5	1,898.3	-1.6	1,965.4	1,899.4	-3.4
Motor Vehicle Theft						
Number..	14,956	13,418	-10.3	723,186	699,594	-3.3
Rate	254.1	226.3	-10.9	230.4	221.3	-4.0

NOTE: Although arson data are included in the trend and clearance tables, sufficient data are not available to estimate totals for this offense. Therefore, no arson data are published in this table.

X = Not applicable.

- = Zero or rounds to zero.

[1]The crime figures have been adjusted.

[2]The data collection methodology for the offense of forcible rape used by the Minnesota state Uniform Crime Reporting (UCR) Program (with the exception of Minneapolis and St. Paul, Minnesota) does not comply with national UCR Program guidelines. Consequently, its figures for forcible rape and violent crime (of which forcible rape is a part) are not published in this table.

[3]Includes offenses reported by the Zoological Police and the Metro Transit Police.

[4]Because of changes in the state's reporting practices, figures are not comparable to previous years' data.

[5]Populations are U.S. Census Bureau provisional estimates as of July 1 of each year.

[6]The figures shown for the offense of rape were estimated using the revised Uniform Crime Reporting (UCR) definition of rape.

Table MD-15. State Government Finances, 2013

(Dollar amounts in thousands, percent distribution.)

Item	Dollars	Percent distribution
Total Revenue	41,802,233	100.0
General revenue	34,779,321	83.2
Intergovernmental revenue	10,325,181	24.7
Taxes	18,118,191	43.3
General sales	4,114,296	9.8
Selective sales	3,232,752	7.7
License taxes	805,292	1.9
Individual income tax	7,693,324	18.4
Corporate income tax	952,092	2.3
Other taxes	1,320,435	3.2
Current charges	3,428,410	8.2
Miscellaneous general revenue	2,907,539	7.0
Utility revenue	137,952	0.3
Liquor stores revenue	0	-
Insurance trust revenue[1]	6,884,960	16.5
Total Expenditure	39,556,993	100.0
Intergovernmental expenditure	8,641,281	21.8
Direct expenditure	30,915,712	78.2
Current operation	20,952,583	53.0
Capital outlay	2,493,037	6.3
Insurance benefits and repayments	4,453,735	11.3
Assistance and subsidies	1,914,736	4.8
Interest on debt	1,101,621	2.8
Exhibit: Salaries and wages	4,857,463	12.3
Total Expenditure	39,556,993	100.0
General expenditure	34,170,869	86.4
Intergovernmental expenditure	8,641,281	21.8
Direct expenditure	25,529,588	64.5
General expenditure, by function:		
Education	11,398,463	28.8
Public welfare	10,044,675	25.4
Hospitals	517,097	1.3
Health	2,149,504	5.4
Highways	1,949,117	4.9
Police protection	550,989	1.4
Correction	1,396,307	3.5
Natural resources	447,136	1.1
Parks and recreation	161,979	0.4
Governmental administration	1,644,697	4.2
Interest on general debt	1,101,621	2.8
Other and unallocable	2,809,284	7.1
Utility expenditure	932,389	2.4
Liquor stores expenditure	0	-
Insurance trust expenditure	4,453,735	11.3
Debt at End of Fiscal Year	26,066,617	X
Cash and Security Holdings	61,077,592	X

X = Not applicable.
- = Zero or rounds to zero.
[1]Within insurance trust revenue, net earnings of state retirement systems is a calculated statistic (the item code in the data file is X08), and thus can be positive or negative. Net earnings is the sum of earnings on investments plus gains on investments minus losses on investments. The change made in 2002 for asset valuation from book to market value in accordance with Statement 34 of the Governmental Accounting Standards Board is reflected in the calculated statistics.

Table MD-16. State Government Tax Collections, 2014

(Dollars in thousands, percent.)

Item	Dollars	Percent distribution
Total Taxes	18,929,069	100.0
Property taxes	725,694	3.8
Sales and gross receipts	8,022,537	42.4
General sales and gross receipts	4,195,996	22.2
Selective sales and gross receipts	3,826,541	20.2
Alcoholic beverages	30,808	0.2
Amusements	431,851	2.3
Insurance premiums	475,294	2.5
Motor fuels	812,739	4.3
Pari-mutuels	3,071	-
Public utilities	139,346	0.7
Tobacco products	402,403	2.1
Other selective sales	1,531,029	8.1
Licenses	853,851	4.5
Alcoholic beverages	1,358	-
Amusements	1,158	-
Corporations in general	106,658	0.6
Hunting and fishing	18,149	0.1
Motor vehicle	474,475	2.5
Motor vehicle operators	36,859	0.2
Public utilities	0	-
Occupation and business, NEC	213,324	1.1
Other licenses	1,870	-
Income taxes	8,756,557	46.3
Individual income	7,773,773	41.1
Corporation net income	982,784	5.2
Other taxes	570,430	3.0
Death and gift	213,780	1.1
Documentary and stock transfer	158,844	0.8
Severance	X	X
Taxes, NEC	197,806	1.0

X = Not applicable.
- = Zero or rounds to zero.

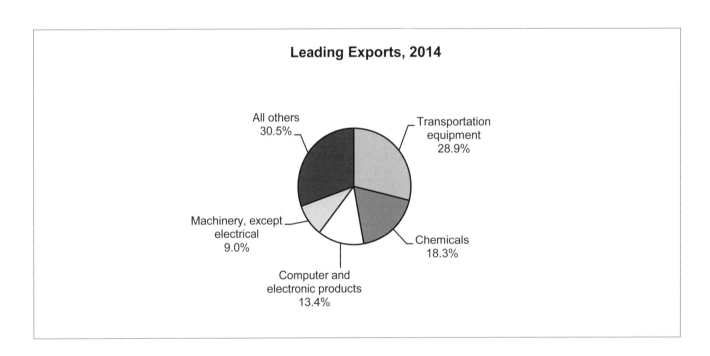

Leading Exports, 2014

All others 30.5%
Transportation equipment 28.9%
Machinery, except electrical 9.0%
Computer and electronic products 13.4%
Chemicals 18.3%

Facts and Figures

Location: Northeastern United States; bordered on the N by Vermont and New Hampshire, on the E by the Atlantic Ocean, on the S by Connecticut and Rhode Island, and on the W by New York

Area: 10,555 sq. mi. (27,336 sq. km.); rank—44th

Population: 6,745,408 (2014 est.); rank—14th

Principal Cities: capital—Boston; largest—Boston

Statehood: February 6, 1788; 6th state

U.S. Congress: 2 senators, 9 representatives

State Motto: *Ense petit placidam sub libertate quietem* ("By the sword we seek peace, but peace only under liberty")

State Song: "All Hail to Massachusetts"

State Nickname: The Bay State

Abbreviations: MA; Mass.

State Symbols: flower—mayflower; tree—American elm; bird—chickadee

At a Glance

- With an increase in population of 3.0 percent, Massachusetts ranked 26th among the states in growth from 2010 to 2014.

- Massachusetts's median household income in 2013 was $66,768, the 7th highest in the country.

- Approximately 11.9 percent of the state's population lived below the poverty level in 2013.

- Massachusetts's violent crime rate in 2013 was 413.4 per 100,000 population, compared to 367.9 for the entire nation.

- Massachusetts's infant mortality rate of 4.15 per 1,000 live births was the second lowest in the country in 2013.

Table MA-1. Population by Age, Sex, Race, and Hispanic Origin

(Number, percent, except where noted.)

Sex, age, race, and Hispanic origin	2000	2010	2014[1]	Average annual percent change, 2010–2014
Total Population	6,349,097	6,547,629	6,745,408	0.7
Percent of total U.S. population	2.3	2.1	2.1	X
Sex				
Male	3,058,816	3,166,628	3,270,824	0.8
Female	3,290,281	3,381,001	3,474,584	0.7
Age				
Under 5 years	397,268	367,087	366,055	-0.1
5 to 19 years	1,277,845	1,254,056	1,231,681	-0.4
20 to 64 years	3,813,822	4,023,762	4,131,435	0.7
65 years and over	860,162	902,724	1,016,237	3.0
Median age (years)	36.5	39.1	39.4	0.2
Race and Hispanic Origin				
One race				
White	5,367,286	5,524,937	5,574,178	0.2
Black	343,454	504,365	558,072	2.6
American Indian and Alaska Native	15,015	29,944	32,392	2.0
Asian	238,124	359,673	425,305	4.3
Native Hawaiian or Other Pacific Islander	2,489	5,971	6,679	2.8
Two or more races	146,005	122,739	148,782	4.9
Hispanic (of any race)	428,729	656,888	731,206	2.7

X = Not applicable.
[1]Population figures for 2014 are July 1 estimates. The 2010 estimates are taken from the 2010 Census.

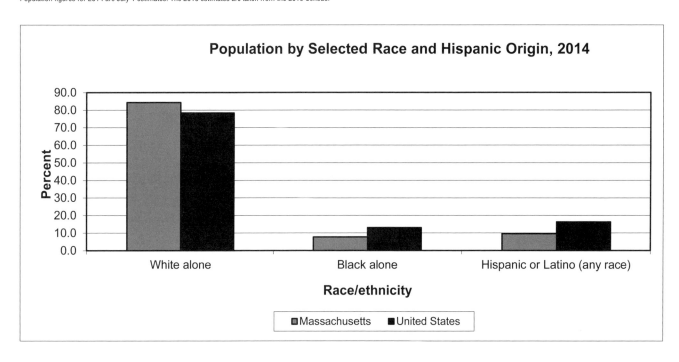

Table MA-2. Marital Status

(Number, percent distribution.)

Sex, age, race, and Hispanic origin	2000	2010	2013
Males, 15 Years and Over	2,412,349	2,579,221	2,659,685
Never married	33.9	38.7	39.3
Now married, except separated	54.7	49.1	48.8
Separated	1.6	1.6	1.5
Widowed	2.7	2.7	2.5
Divorced	7.0	8.0	7.9
Females, 15 Years and Over	2,679,020	2,819,768	2,890,105
Never married	28.5	33.2	33.7
Now married, except separated	48.9	44.1	44.5
Separated	2.3	2.4	2.2
Widowed	10.8	9.1	8.6
Divorced	9.5	11.1	11.0

Table MA-3. Households and Housing Characteristics

(Number, percent, dollars.)

Item	2000	2010	2013	Average annual percent change, 2000–2013
Total Households	2,443,580	2,520,419	2,536,321	0.3
Family households	1,576,696	1,590,257	1,620,802	0.2
Married-couple family	1,197,917	1,166,204	1,190,249	-
Other family	378,779	424,053	430,553	1.0
Male householder, no wife present	88,835	100,400	108,042	1.5
Female householder, no husband present	289,944	323,653	322,511	0.8
Nonfamily households	866,884	930,162	915,519	0.4
Householder living alone	684,345	736,320	721,429	0.4
Householder not living alone	182,539	193,842	194,090	0.5
Housing Characteristics				
Total housing units	2,621,989	2,808,727	2,813,641	0.5
Occupied housing units	2,443,580	2,520,419	2,161,680	-0.9
Owner occupied	1,508,052	1,568,382	1,560,809	0.3
Renter occupied	935,528	952,037	975,512	0.3
Average household size	2.51	2.51	2.54	0.1
Financial Characteristics				
Median gross rent of renter-occupied housing	684	1,009	1,077	3.6
Median monthly owner costs for housing units with a mortgage	1,353	2,036	1,976	3.0
Median value of owner-occupied housing units	185,700	334,100	327,200	4.5

- = Zero or rounds to zero

Table MA-4. Migration, Origin, and Language

(Number, percent.)

Characteristic	State			U.S.		
	2012	2013	Percent change	2012	2013	Percent change
Residence 1 Year Ago						
Population 1 year and over	6,580,641	6,619,999	0.6	310,212,755	312,432,820	0.7
Same house	87.4	86.5	X	85.0	85.0	X
Different house in the U.S.	11.7	12.6	X	14.4	14.4	X
Same county	7.1	7.7	X	9.0	8.9	X
Different county	4.6	4.9	X	5.4	5.5	X
Same state	2.4	2.9	X	3.2	3.2	X
Different state	2.2	2.0	X	2.3	2.3	X
Abroad	0.9	0.9	X	0.6	0.6	X
Place of Birth						
Native born	5,650,452	5,646,669	-0.1	273,089,382	274,780,773	0.6
Male	48.5	48.6	X	49.3	49.3	X
Female	51.5	51.4	X	50.7	50.7	X
Foreign born	995,692	1,046,155	5.1	40,824,658	41,348,066	1.3
Male	48.1	48.1	X	48.7	48.8	X
Female	51.9	51.9	X	51.3	51.2	X
Foreign born; naturalized U.S. citizen	510,210	549,009	7.6	18,686,237	19,294,710	3.3
Male	46.2	45.7	X	45.8	45.9	X
Female	53.8	54.3	X	54.2	54.1	X
Foreign born; not a U.S. citizen	485,482	497,146	2.4	22,138,421	22,053,356	-0.4
Male	50.1	50.7	X	51.1	51.3	X
Female	49.9	49.3	X	48.9	48.7	X
Entered 2010 or later	10.4	13.2	X	7.0	9.7	X
Entered 2000 to 2009	30.6	30.1	X	30.4	29.4	X
Entered before 2000	58.9	56.7	X	62.7	61.0	X
World Region of Birth, Foreign						
Foreign-born population, excluding population born at sea	995,692	1,046,155	5.1	40,824,553	41,347,945	1.3
Europe	23.3	22.9	X	11.8	11.6	X
Asia	29.5	29.2	X	29.2	29.5	X
Africa	8.2	8.7	X	4.2	4.4	X
Oceania	0.4	0.3	X	0.6	0.5	X
Latin America	35.6	35.8	X	52.2	51.9	X
North America	2.9	3.2	X	2.0	2.0	X
Language Spoken at Home and Ability to Speak English						
Population 5 years and over	6,282,285	6,328,899	0.7	294,003,714	296,358,760	0.8
English only	77.7	77.6	X	79.0	79.2	X
Language other than English	22.3	22.4	X	21.0	20.8	X
Speaks English less than "very well"	8.9	8.9	X	8.5	8.5	X

NA = Not available.
X = Not applicable.
- = Zero or rounds to zero.

Table MA-5. Median Income and Poverty Status, 2013

(Number, percent, except as noted.)

Characteristic	State		U.S.	
	Number	Percent	Number	Percent
Median Income				
Households (dollars)..	66,768	X	52,250	X
Families (dollars)	83,813	X	64,030	X
Below Poverty Level (All People)	770,513	11.9	48,810,868	15.8
Sex				
Male...	337,232	10.8	21,938,525	14.5
Female	433,281	13.0	26,872,343	17.1
Age				
Under 18 years...	223,480	16.3	16,086,960	22.2
Related children under 18 years.........................	217,747	16.0	15,769,921	21.9
18 to 64 years...	463,507	11.2	28,578,191	14.8
65 years and over	83,526	8.8	4,145,717	9.6

X = Not applicable.

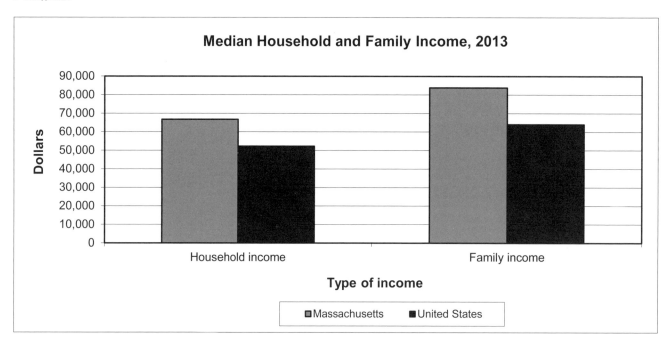

Median Household and Family Income, 2013

■ Massachusetts   ■ United States

Table MA-6. Health Insurance Coverage Status for the Civilian Noninstitutionalized Population and Children Under 18 Years of Age

(Numbers in thousands, percent.)

Item	2005	2006	2007	2008	2009	2010	2011	2012	2013
Civilian Noninstitutionalized Population	6,328	6,335	6,340	6,399	6,496	6,478	6,508	6,567	6,614
Covered by Private or Public Insurance									
Number...	5,745	5,678	6,000	6,135	6,225	6,192	6,231	6,313	6,367
Percent...	90.8	89.6	94.6	95.9	95.8	95.6	95.7	96.1	96.3
Not Covered									
Number...	583	657	340	264	271	286	277	254	247
Percent...	9.2	10.4	5.4	4.1	4.2	4.4	4.3	3.9	3.7
Percent in the U.S. not covered..	15.3	15.8	15.3	15.1	15.1	15.5	15.1	14.8	14.5
Children Under 18 Years of Age..	1,499	1,470	1,435	1,427	1,431	1,415	1,402	1,398	1,389
Covered by Private or Public Insurance									
Number...	1,436	1,367	1,392	1,397	1,411	1,393	1,378	1,378	1,368
Percent...	95.8	93.0	97.0	97.9	98.6	98.5	98.3	98.6	98.5
Not Covered									
Number...	63	103	43	30	20	22	24	20	21
Percent...	4.2	7.0	3.0	2.1	1.4	1.5	1.7	1.4	1.5
Percent in the U.S. not covered..	10.9	11.7	11.0	9.7	8.6	8.0	7.5	7.2	7.1

Table MA-7. Employment Status by Demographic Group, 2014

(Numbers in thousands, percent.)

Characteristic	Civilian noninstitutional population	Civilian labor force		Employed		Unemployed	
		Number	Percent of population	Number	Percent of population	Number	Percent of population
Total...	5,446	3,558	65.3	3,353	61.6	205	5.8
Sex							
Male...	2,603	1,835	70.5	1,720	66.1	114	6.2
Female..	2,843	1,723	60.6	1,632	57.4	91	5.3
Race, Sex, and Hispanic Origin							
White..	4,533	2,967	65.5	2,815	62.1	153	5.2
Male..	2,159	1,512	70.0	1,426	66.1	85	5.6
Female..	2,374	1,456	61.3	1,388	58.5	68	4.6
Black or African American............................	410	252	61.4	224	54.8	27	10.8
Male..	192	133	69.3	116	60.4	17	12.8
Female..	218	119	54.5	109	49.8	10	8.6
Hispanic or Latino ethnicity[1]......................	482	321	66.6	286	59.3	35	10.9
Male..	220	170	77.3	149	67.8	21	12.2
Female..	262	151	57.6	136	52.1	14	9.5
Age							
16 to 19 years..	383	145	37.9	119	31.2	26	17.7
20 to 24 years..	489	332	68.0	294	60.2	38	11.5
25 to 34 years..	927	776	83.7	740	79.8	37	4.7
35 to 44 years..	801	688	85.9	655	81.8	32	4.7
45 to 54 years..	936	769	82.1	734	78.4	35	4.5
55 to 64 years..	890	630	70.8	605	68.0	25	4.0
65 years and over....................................	1,020	217	21.3	205	20.1	12	5.5

NOTE: Data in Table 7 are from the Current Population Survey (CPS) and do not match the estimates in Table 8. See notes and definitions for further information.
[1]May be of any race.

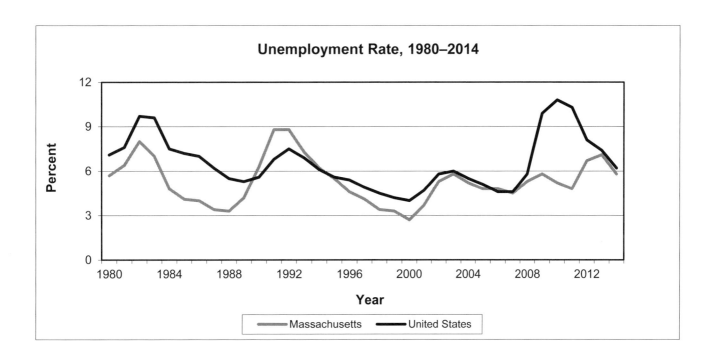

Table MA-8. Employment Status of the Civilian Noninstitutional Population Age 16 Years and Over

(Number, percent.)

Year	Civilian labor force	Civilian participation rate	Employed	Unemployed	Unemployment rate
2006	3,413,339	67.0	3,246,316	167,023	4.9
2007	3,426,009	66.7	3,268,096	157,913	4.6
2008	3,452,468	66.6	3,261,408	191,060	5.5
2009	3,470,382	66.3	3,189,010	281,372	8.1
2010	3,480,083	66.3	3,190,818	289,265	8.3
2011	3,469,585	65.5	3,218,116	251,469	7.2
2012	3,484,781	65.2	3,251,993	232,788	6.7
2013	3,508,542	65.0	3,272,002	236,540	6.7
2014	3,557,472	65.3	3,352,663	204,809	5.8

Table MA-9. Employment and Average Wages by Industry

(Estimates from 2007 through 2010 are based on the 2007 *North American Industry Classification System* [NAICS]. Estimates from 2011 onward are based on the 2012 NAICS.)

Industry	2007	2008	2009	2010	2011	2012	2013
	Number of jobs						
Wage and Salary Employment by Industry	3,404,202	3,410,858	3,300,521	3,311,859	3,350,292	3,396,978	3,480,691
Farm Wage and Salary Employment	3,535	3,858	3,721	3,730	3,956	4,005	4,746
Nonfarm Wage and Salary Employment	3,400,667	3,407,000	3,296,800	3,308,129	3,346,336	3,392,973	3,475,945
Private wage and salary employment	2,952,145	2,953,629	2,844,590	2,853,964	2,896,415	2,938,862	3,017,111
Forestry, fishing, and related activities	4,591	4,578	4,879	4,971	4,058	4,053	3,894
Mining	1,485	1,273	1,220	1,048	1,002	866	886
Utilities	9,867	10,026	10,209	10,432	10,453	10,250	10,052
Construction	142,803	137,785	116,521	112,186	116,555	119,310	126,675
Manufacturing	295,949	287,097	259,629	254,857	254,195	252,185	250,777
Durable goods manufacturing	195,806	190,450	170,461	166,166	167,191	165,397	163,595
Nondurable goods manufacturing	100,143	96,647	89,168	88,691	87,004	86,788	87,182
Wholesale trade	139,063	137,445	128,466	123,891	124,165	122,136	123,858
Retail trade	354,301	352,469	339,954	345,194	348,742	349,005	350,581
Transportation and warehousing	76,131	76,041	72,101	73,879	74,670	75,673	77,351
Information	88,070	89,450	84,864	85,363	84,355	87,170	86,274
Finance and insurance	185,195	182,975	176,477	173,524	173,682	171,932	170,560
Real estate and rental and leasing	44,916	43,947	42,062	41,765	41,714	42,051	43,288
Professional, scientific, and technical services	250,762	261,255	254,688	251,989	259,996	268,005	276,169
Management of companies and enterprises	61,356	61,351	59,060	57,436	58,604	63,326	64,260
Administrative and waste services	174,984	169,591	151,742	158,625	163,472	165,163	169,534
Educational services	181,131	180,664	183,512	182,461	186,329	190,356	192,938
Health care and social assistance	476,832	488,580	498,869	510,601	518,706	527,909	570,257
Arts, entertainment, and recreation	48,943	49,935	48,383	49,611	50,570	51,352	52,993
Accommodation and food services	257,160	259,566	255,091	261,794	268,399	276,792	283,713
Other services, except public administration	158,606	159,601	156,863	154,337	156,748	161,328	163,051
Government and government enterprises	448,522	453,371	452,210	454,165	449,921	454,111	458,834
	Dollars						
Average Wages and Salaries by Industry	54,234	55,737	55,235	56,808	58,620	59,859	60,307
Average Farm Wages and Salaries	32,760	28,799	28,366	26,728	22,546	24,963	28,701
Average Nonfarm Wages and Salaries	54,256	55,767	55,265	56,842	58,662	59,900	60,350
Average private wages and salaries	55,062	56,563	55,879	57,689	59,541	60,792	61,140
Forestry, fishing, and related activities	51,269	51,525	51,403	54,008	57,093	54,715	52,872
Mining	54,881	51,901	53,072	56,133	57,184	57,645	58,316
Utilities	94,037	99,517	102,825	104,102	109,970	107,949	107,780
Construction	59,050	62,174	61,845	62,162	63,266	65,123	66,463
Manufacturing	69,540	68,978	69,237	75,206	77,553	79,513	79,820
Durable goods manufacturing	75,789	75,487	75,716	83,905	86,712	89,034	88,657
Nondurable goods manufacturing	57,323	56,151	56,850	58,908	59,953	61,369	63,237
Wholesale trade	74,693	76,919	76,456	79,192	82,166	82,376	84,386
Retail trade	27,620	27,741	27,777	27,823	27,919	28,325	28,938
Transportation and warehousing	43,184	43,716	43,730	44,150	45,425	46,127	46,499
Information	83,415	86,277	84,680	91,985	95,875	97,033	97,270
Finance and insurance	115,345	118,230	110,406	114,391	119,299	124,439	126,337
Real estate and rental and leasing	56,657	56,632	55,582	60,295	63,205	66,408	69,763
Professional, scientific, and technical services	92,900	96,720	95,743	100,957	103,816	108,219	110,221
Management of companies and enterprises	99,816	100,424	101,498	104,263	123,065	115,671	118,633
Administrative and waste services	37,767	38,683	38,397	38,535	39,779	40,987	41,079
Educational services	39,078	41,583	42,058	44,404	45,969	46,037	47,200
Health care and social assistance	46,771	49,150	50,269	51,327	52,111	53,259	51,672
Arts, entertainment, and recreation	38,465	37,412	36,356	37,237	37,556	38,240	38,377
Accommodation and food services	21,495	21,316	21,000	21,409	21,976	22,340	22,653
Other services, except public administration	30,023	31,103	30,998	31,666	32,245	32,550	33,579
Government and government enterprises	48,950	50,586	51,400	51,519	53,008	54,130	55,158

Table MA-10. Employment Characteristics by Family Type

(Number, percent.)

Family type and labor force status	2011		2012		2013	
	Total	Families with own children under 18 years	Total	Families with own children under 18 years	Total	Families with own children under 18 years
All Families	1,597,920	718,136	1,598,867	698,945	1,620,802	701,258
FAMILY TYPE AND LABOR FORCE STATUS						
Married-Couple Families	1,174,019	495,852	1,173,287	479,890	1,190,249	482,070
Both husband and wife in labor force	60.9	72.9	60.1	73.5	58.5	72.1
Husband in labor force, wife not in labor force	18.2	22.3	17.7	21.7	18.4	22.1
Wife in labor force, husband not in labor force	6.9	3.4	7.7	3.5	7.7	3.7
Both husband and wife not in labor force	14.0	1.3	14.6	1.3	14.3	1.3
Other Families	423,901	222,284	425,580	219,055	430,553	219,188
Female householder, no husband present	76.4	81.5	75.6	80.4	74.9	79.3
In labor force	54.0	64.9	53.3	63.2	53.2	62.7
Not in labor force	22.5	16.6	22.3	17.1	21.7	16.6
Male householder, no wife present	23.6	18.5	24.4	19.6	25.1	20.7
In labor force	18.6	16.8	18.9	17.3	19.2	18.1
Not in labor force	5.0	1.7	5.5	2.4	5.9	2.6

Table MA-11. School Enrollment and Educational Attainment, 2013

(Number, percent.)

Item	State	U.S.
Enrollment		
Total population 3 years and over, enrolled in school	1,750,853	82,395,254
Enrolled in nursery school or preschool (percent)	6.4	6.0
Enrolled in kindergarten (percent)	4.5	5.2
Enrolled in elementary school, grades 1-8 (percent)	35.4	40.0
Enrolled in high school, grades 9-12 (percent)	19.7	20.6
Enrolled in college or graduate school (percent)	34.0	28.3
Attainment		
Total population 25 years and over	4,604,795	210,910,615
Less than ninth grade (percent)	4.9	5.8
9th to 12th grade, no diploma (percent)	5.2	7.6
High school graduate, including equivalency (percent)	25.9	27.8
Some college, no degree (percent)	16.0	21.1
Associate's degree (percent)	7.7	8.1
Bachelor's degree (percent)	22.5	18.4
Graduate or professional degree (percent)	17.8	11.2
High school graduate or higher (percent)	89.9	86.6
Bachelor's degree or higher (percent)	40.3	29.6

Table MA-12. Public School Characteristics and Educational Indicators

(Number, percent; data derived from National Center of Education Statistics.)

Item	State	U.S.
Public Schools, 2012–2013 (except where noted)		
Number of school districts	404	18,093
Number of schools	1,854	98,454
Number of students (in thousands)	955	49,771
Number of teachers (in thousands)	71	3,109
Student-teacher ratio	13.5	16.0
Expenditures per student (dollars), FY 2012	14,844	10,667
Four-year adjusted cohort graduation rate (ACGR)[1,2]	85.0	81.4
Students eligible for free or reduced-price lunch (in thousands)	353	25,188
English language learners (in thousands)	64	4,397
Students age 3 to 21 served under IDEA, part B (in thousands)	166	6,429

Public Schools by Type	Number	Percent of state public schools
Total number of schools	1,854	100.0
Regular	1,774	95.7
Special education	21	1.1
Vocational education	39	2.1
Alternative education	20	1.1

NOTE: Every school is assigned only one school type based on its instructional emphasis.
[1]ACGR data represents a new method of calculating high-school completion rates and may not be comparable to previous years' data for Averaged Freshmen Graduation Rates (AFGR).
[2]The United States 4-year ACGRs were estimated using both the reported 4-year ACGR data from 49 states and the District of Columbia and using imputed data for Idaho. The estimate for American Indian/Alaska Native students also includes imputed data for Virginia.

Table MA-13. Reported Voting and Registration of the Voting-Age Population, November 2012

(Numbers in thousands, percent.)

Item	Total population	Total citizen population	Registered			Voted		
			Total registered	Percent registered (total population)	Percent registered (total citizen population)	Total voted	Percent voted (total population)	Percent voted (total citizen population)
U.S. Total	235,248	215,081	153,157	65.1	71.2	132,948	56.5	61.8
State Total	5,170	4,774	3,759	72.7	78.7	3,382	65.4	70.8
Sex								
Male	2,452	2,238	1,750	71.4	78.2	1,576	64.3	70.4
Female	2,718	2,537	2,009	73.9	79.2	1,807	66.5	71.2
Race								
White alone	4,358	4,128	3,331	76.4	80.7	3,009	69.0	72.9
White, non-Hispanic alone	3,991	3,877	3,161	79.2	81.5	2,839	71.1	73.2
Black alone	385	321	228	59.2	70.9	211	54.7	65.6
Asian alone	317	219	119	37.6	54.3	98	30.8	44.5
Hispanic (of any race)	453	322	216	47.6	66.9	202	44.6	62.7
White alone or in combination	4,437	4,206	3,384	76.3	80.5	3,054	68.8	72.6
Black alone or in combination	451	387	275	61.1	71.2	248	55.1	64.2
Asian alone or in combination	333	235	131	39.4	55.9	102	30.6	43.3
Age								
18 to 24 years	694	633	395	56.9	62.4	316	45.6	49.9
25 to 44 years	1,697	1,489	1,107	65.2	74.3	980	57.7	65.8
45 to 64 years	1,784	1,677	1,424	79.8	84.9	1,327	74.4	79.2
65 to 74 years	584	573	494	84.6	86.1	465	79.7	81.2
75 years and over	411	402	339	82.5	84.3	294	71.5	73.1

Table MA-14. Crime

(Number, rate per 100,000. Data are derived from the FBI Uniform Crime Reports.)

Item	State			U.S.[1,2,3,4]		
	2012	2013	Percent change	2012	2013	Percent change
TOTAL POPULATION[5]	6,645,303	6,692,824	0.7	313,873,685	316,128,839	0.7
VIOLENT CRIME						
Number	27,047	27,038	-	1,217,067	1,163,146	-4.4
Rate	407.0	404.0	-0.7	387.8	367.9	-5.1
Murder and Nonnegligent Manslaughter						
Number	121	137	13.2	14,866	14,196	-4.5
Rate	1.8	2.0	12.4	4.7	4.5	-5.2
Rape[6]						
Number	X	2,718	X	X	108,612	X
Rate	X	40.6	X	X	34.4	X
Robbery						
Number	6,555	6,706	2.3	355,051	345,031	-2.8
Rate	98.6	100.2	1.6	113.1	109.1	-3.5
Aggravated Assault						
Number	18,721	18,106	-3.3	762,009	724,149	-5.0
Rate	281.7	270.5	-4.0	242.8	229.1	-5.6
PROPERTY CRIME						
Number	143,325	137,285	-4.2	9,001,992	8,632,512	-4.1
Rate	2,156.8	2,051.2	-4.9	2,868.0	2,730.7	-4.8
Burglary						
Number	34,635	30,735	-11.3	2,109,932	1,928,465	-8.6
Rate	521.2	459.2	-11.9	672.2	610.0	-9.3
Larceny-Theft						
Number	99,453	97,428	-2.0	6,168,874	6,004,453	-2.7
Rate	1,496.6	1,455.7	-2.7	1,965.4	1,899.4	-3.4
Motor Vehicle Theft						
Number	9,237	9,122	-1.2	723,186	699,594	-3.3
Rate	139.0	136.3	-1.9	230.4	221.3	-4.0

NOTE: Although arson data are included in the trend and clearance tables, sufficient data are not available to estimate totals for this offense. Therefore, no arson data are published in this table.
X = Not applicable.
- = Zero or rounds to zero.
[1]The crime figures have been adjusted.
[2]The data collection methodology for the offense of forcible rape used by the Minnesota state Uniform Crime Reporting (UCR) Program (with the exception of Minneapolis and St. Paul, Minnesota) does not comply with national UCR Program guidelines. Consequently, its figures for forcible rape and violent crime (of which forcible rape is a part) are not published in this table.
[3]Includes offenses reported by the Zoological Police and the Metro Transit Police.
[4]Because of changes in the state's reporting practices, figures are not comparable to previous years' data.
[5]Populations are U.S. Census Bureau provisional estimates as of July 1 of each year.
[6]The figures shown for the offense of rape were estimated using the revised Uniform Crime Reporting (UCR) definition of rape.

Table MA-15. State Government Finances, 2013

(Dollar amounts in thousands, percent distribution.)

Item	Dollars	Percent distribution
Total Revenue	55,437,787	100.0
General revenue	46,180,318	83.3
Intergovernmental revenue	13,706,498	24.7
Taxes	23,901,047	43.1
General sales	5,184,312	9.4
Selective sales	2,271,014	4.1
License taxes	945,922	1.7
Individual income tax	12,876,192	23.2
Corporate income tax	1,888,449	3.4
Other taxes	735,158	1.3
Current charges	4,606,589	8.3
Miscellaneous general revenue	3,966,184	7.2
Utility revenue	783,775	1.4
Liquor stores revenue	0	-
Insurance trust revenue[1]	8,473,694	15.3
Total Expenditure	56,772,774	100.0
Intergovernmental expenditure	9,401,248	16.6
Direct expenditure	47,371,526	83.4
Current operation	31,853,811	56.1
Capital outlay	3,290,261	5.8
Insurance benefits and repayments	8,123,132	14.3
Assistance and subsidies	840,410	1.5
Interest on debt	3,263,912	5.7
Exhibit: Salaries and wages	6,268,290	11.0
Total Expenditure	56,772,774	100.0
General expenditure	46,360,151	81.7
Intergovernmental expenditure	9,401,248	16.6
Direct expenditure	36,958,903	65.1
General expenditure, by function:		
Education	13,010,482	22.9
Public welfare	15,560,077	27.4
Hospitals	489,640	0.9
Health	1,151,865	2.0
Highways	2,005,325	3.5
Police protection	829,770	1.5
Correction	1,095,858	1.9
Natural resources	343,750	0.6
Parks and recreation	282,624	0.5
Governmental administration	1,725,580	3.0
Interest on general debt	2,899,752	5.1
Other and unallocable	6,965,428	12.3
Utility expenditure	2,289,491	4.0
Liquor stores expenditure	0	-
Insurance trust expenditure	8,123,132	14.3
Debt at End of Fiscal Year	76,160,503	X
Cash and Security Holdings	86,422,694	X

X = Not applicable.
- = Zero or rounds to zero.
[1]Within insurance trust revenue, net earnings of state retirement systems is a calculated statistic (the item code in the data file is X08), and thus can be positive or negative. Net earnings is the sum of earnings on investments plus gains on investments minus losses on investments. The change made in 2002 for asset valuation from book to market value in accordance with Statement 34 of the Governmental Accounting Standards Board is reflected in the calculated statistics.

Table MA-16. State Government Tax Collections, 2014

(Dollars in thousands, percent.)

Item	Dollars	Percent distribution
Total Taxes	25,235,726	100.0
Property taxes	3,433	-
Sales and gross receipts	7,933,030	31.4
General sales and gross receipts	5,518,580	21.9
Selective sales and gross receipts	2,414,450	9.6
Alcoholic beverages	78,817	0.3
Amusements	3,758	-
Insurance premiums	346,828	1.4
Motor fuels	732,207	2.9
Pari-mutuels	337	-
Public utilities	23,736	0.1
Tobacco products	660,029	2.6
Other selective sales	568,738	2.3
Licenses	1,012,557	4.0
Alcoholic beverages	3,056	-
Amusements	762	-
Corporations in general	25,972	0.1
Hunting and fishing	5,456	-
Motor vehicle	390,879	1.5
Motor vehicle operators	105,322	0.4
Public utilities	0	-
Occupation and business, NEC	317,250	1.3
Other licenses	163,860	0.6
Income taxes	15,440,841	61.2
Individual income	13,246,221	52.5
Corporation net income	2,194,620	8.7
Other taxes	845,865	3.4
Death and gift	401,512	1.6
Documentary and stock transfer	246,850	1.0
Severance	X	X
Taxes, NEC	197,503	0.8

X = Not applicable.
- = Zero or rounds to zero.

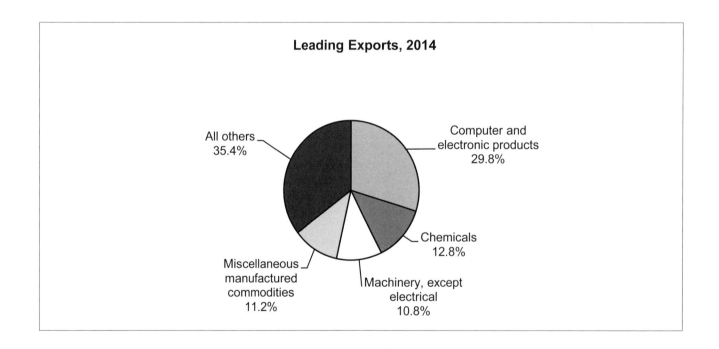

Leading Exports, 2014

All others 35.4%

Computer and electronic products 29.8%

Chemicals 12.8%

Machinery, except electrical 10.8%

Miscellaneous manufactured commodities 11.2%

MICHIGAN

Facts and Figures

Location: East north central United States; bordered on the N by Lake Superior, on the E by Ontario, Canada, and Lakes Huron and Erie, on the S by Indiana and Ohio, and on the W by Wisconsin and Lake Michigan

Area: 96,716 sq. mi. (250,494 sq. km.); rank—11th

Population: 9,909,877 (2014 est.); rank—10th

Principal Cities: capital—Lansing; largest—Detroit

Statehood: January 26, 1837; 26th state

U.S. Congress: 2 senators, 14 representatives

State Motto: *Si quaeris peninsulam amoenam, circumspice* ("If you seek a pleasant peninsula, look about you")

State Song: "Michigan, My Michigan"

State Nicknames: The Wolverine State; The Great Lakes State

Abbreviations: MI; Mich.

State Symbols: flower—apple blossom; tree—Eastern white pine; bird—robin

At a Glance

- With an increase in population of 0.3 percent, Michigan ranked 47th among the states in growth from 2010 to 2014.

- In 2013, 11.0 percent of Michiganders did not have health insurance, compared to 14.5 percent of the total U.S. population.

- Michigan's violent crime rate in 2013 was 449.9 per 100,000 population, compared to the U.S. rate of 367.9 per 100,000 population.

- Approximately 17.0 percent of Michiganders lived below the poverty level in 2013.

- Michigan's unemployment rate of 7.3 ranked 6th in the nation in 2014.

Table MI-1. Population by Age, Sex, Race, and Hispanic Origin

(Number, percent, except where noted.)

Sex, age, race, and Hispanic origin	2000	2010	2014[1]	Average annual percent change, 2010–2014
Total Population	9,938,444	9,883,640	9,909,877	0.1
Percent of total U.S. population	3.5	3.2	3.1	X
Sex				
Male	4,873,095	4,848,114	4,868,463	0.1
Female	5,065,349	5,035,526	5,041,414	-
Age				
Under 5 years	672,005	596,286	570,292	-1.1
5 to 19 years	2,212,060	2,052,599	1,926,411	-1.6
20 to 64 years	5,835,361	5,873,225	5,883,122	0.0
65 years and over	1,219,018	1,361,530	1,530,052	3.0
Median age (years)	35.5	38.9	39.6	0.4
Race and Hispanic Origin				
One race				
White	7,966,053	7,949,497	7,915,690	-0.1
Black	1,412,742	1,416,067	1,410,458	-0.1
American Indian and Alaska Native	58,479	68,396	71,030	0.9
Asian	176,510	243,062	283,968	4.0
Native Hawaiian or Other Pacific Islander	2,692	3,442	3,917	3.3
Two or more races	192,416	203,176	224,814	2.6
Hispanic (of any race)	323,877	459,751	476,285	0.9

X = Not applicable.
- = Zero or rounds to zero.
[1]Population figures for 2014 are July 1 estimates. The 2010 estimates are taken from the 2010 Census.

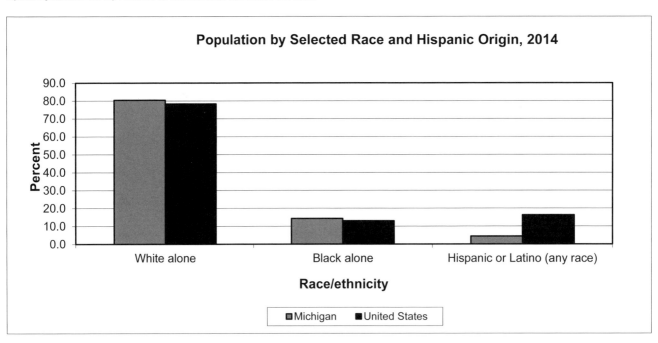

Table MI-2. Marital Status

(Number, percent distribution.)

Sex, age, race, and Hispanic origin	2000	2010	2013
Males, 15 Years and Over	3,761,881	3,875,107	3,916,804
Never married	30.8	34.9	36.0
Now married, except separated	56.1	50.5	49.1
Separated	1.3	1.3	1.3
Widowed	2.5	2.7	2.8
Divorced	9.3	10.6	10.9
Females, 15 Years and Over	4,013,722	4,099,384	4,142,912
Never married	25.0	29.0	30.0
Now married, except separated	51.8	47.2	46.2
Separated	1.6	1.6	1.8
Widowed	10.4	9.7	9.4
Divorced	11.2	12.5	12.7

Table MI-3. Households and Housing Characteristics

(Number, percent, dollars.)

Item	2000	2010	2013	Average annual percent change, 2000–2013
Total Households	3,785,661	3,806,621	3,832,466	0.1
Family households	2,575,699	2,508,780	2,484,558	-0.3
Married-couple family	1,947,610	1,845,094	1,809,823	-0.6
Other family	627,989	663,686	674,735	0.6
Male householder, no wife present	154,187	168,337	179,352	1.2
Female householder, no husband present	473,802	495,349	495,383	0.3
Nonfamily households	1,209,962	1,297,841	1,347,908	0.8
Householder living alone	993,607	1,090,126	1,110,676	0.9
Householder not living alone	216,335	207,715	237,232	0.7
Housing Characteristics				
Total housing units	4,234,279	4,531,231	4,525,266	0.5
Occupied housing units	3,785,661	3,806,621	3,832,466	0.1
Owner occupied	2,793,124	2,769,474	2,703,957	-0.2
Renter occupied	992,537	1,037,147	1,128,509	1.0
Average household size	2.56	2.53	2.52	-0.1
Financial Characteristics				
Median gross rent of renter-occupied housing	546	730	768	2.7
Median monthly owner costs for housing units with a mortgage	972	1,288	1,207	1.7
Median value of owner-occupied housing units	115,600	123,300	117,500	0.1

- = Zero or rounds to zero.

Table MI-4. Migration, Origin, and Language

(Number, percent.)

Characteristic	State			U.S.		
	2012	2013	Percent change	2012	2013	Percent change
Residence 1 Year Ago						
Population 1 year and over	9,778,980	9,784,094	0.1	310,212,755	312,432,820	0.7
Same house	85.2	84.8	X	85.0	85.0	X
Different house in the U.S.	14.3	14.7	X	14.4	14.4	X
Same county	9.3	9.2	X	9.0	8.9	X
Different county	5.0	5.5	X	5.4	5.5	X
Same state	3.7	4.0	X	3.2	3.2	X
Different state	1.4	1.5	X	2.3	2.3	X
Abroad	0.5	0.5	X	0.6	0.6	X
Place of Birth						
Native born	9,276,041	9,278,836	-	273,089,382	274,780,773	0.6
Male	49.1	49.1	X	49.3	49.3	X
Female	50.9	50.9	X	50.7	50.7	X
Foreign born	607,319	616,786	1.6	40,824,658	41,348,066	1.3
Male	49.1	48.8	X	48.7	48.8	X
Female	50.9	51.2	X	51.3	51.2	X
Foreign born; naturalized U.S. citizen	303,447	315,064	3.8	18,686,237	19,294,710	3.3
Male	48.6	47.5	X	45.8	45.9	X
Female	51.4	52.5	X	54.2	54.1	X
Foreign born; not a U.S. citizen	303,872	301,722	-0.7	22,138,421	22,053,356	-0.4
Male	49.5	50.2	X	51.1	51.3	X
Female	50.5	49.8	X	48.9	48.7	X
Entered 2010 or later	11.3	15.2	X	7.0	9.7	X
Entered 2000 to 2009	29.7	28.0	X	30.4	29.4	X
Entered before 2000	59.0	56.8	X	62.7	61.0	X
World Region of Birth, Foreign						
Foreign-born population, excluding population born at sea	607,319	616,786	1.6	40,824,553	41,347,945	1.3
Europe	23.4	20.9	X	11.8	11.6	X
Asia	46.3	49.1	X	29.2	29.5	X
Africa	3.9	4.1	X	4.2	4.4	X
Oceania	0.3	0.4	X	0.6	0.5	X
Latin America	19.4	18.4	X	52.2	51.9	X
North America	6.7	7.1	X	2.0	2.0	X
Language Spoken at Home and Ability to Speak English						
Population 5 years and over	9,311,715	9,325,319	0.1	294,003,714	296,358,760	0.8
English only	90.6	91.0	X	79.0	79.2	X
Language other than English	9.4	9.0	X	21.0	20.8	X
Speaks English less than "very well"	3.3	3.3	X	8.5	8.5	X

NA = Not available.
X = Not applicable.
- = Zero or rounds to zero.

Table MI-5. Median Income and Poverty Status, 2013

(Number, percent, except as noted.)

Characteristic	State		U.S.	
	Number	Percent	Number	Percent
Median Income				
Households (dollars)...............................	48,273	X	52,250	X
Families (dollars)	60,846	X	64,030	X
Below Poverty Level (All People)	1,648,436	17.0	48,810,868	15.8
Sex				
Male..	747,455	15.8	21,938,525	14.5
Female	900,981	18.2	26,872,343	17.1
Age				
Under 18 years.......................................	523,798	23.8	16,086,960	22.2
Related children under 18 years................	512,714	23.4	15,769,921	21.9
18 to 64 years..	1,004,638	16.7	28,578,191	14.8
65 years and over	120,000	8.3	4,145,717	9.6

X = Not applicable.

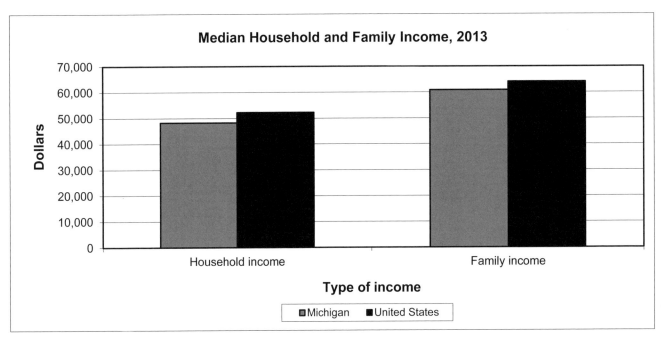

Table MI-6. Health Insurance Coverage Status for the Civilian Noninstitutionalized Population and Children Under 18 Years of Age

(Numbers in thousands, percent.)

Item	2005	2006	2007	2008	2009	2010	2011	2012	2013
Civilian Noninstitutionalized Population	9,982	9,970	9,927	9,866	9,835	9,764	9,762	9,773	9,784
Covered by Private or Public Insurance									
Number......................................	8,949	8,928	8,776	8,734	8,632	8,556	8,612	8,658	8,713
Percent......................................	89.7	89.5	88.4	88.5	87.8	87.6	88.2	88.6	89.0
Not Covered									
Number......................................	1,033	1,043	1,151	1,132	1,203	1,207	1,150	1,115	1,072
Percent......................................	10.3	10.5	11.6	11.5	12.2	12.4	11.8	11.4	11.0
Percent in the U.S. not covered................	15.3	15.8	15.3	15.1	15.1	15.5	15.1	14.8	14.5
Children Under 18 Years of Age..............	2,554	2,446	2,419	2,389	2,343	2,331	2,290	2,264	2,240
Covered by Private or Public Insurance									
Number......................................	2,427	2,330	2,270	2,265	2,236	2,236	2,196	2,174	2,150
Percent......................................	95.0	95.3	93.8	94.8	95.4	95.9	95.9	96.0	96.0
Not Covered									
Number......................................	128	116	149	124	107	95	94	90	90
Percent......................................	5.0	4.7	6.2	5.2	4.6	4.1	4.1	4.0	4.0
Percent in the U.S. not covered................	10.9	11.7	11.0	9.7	8.6	8.0	7.5	7.2	7.1

Table MI-7. Employment Status by Demographic Group, 2014

(Numbers in thousands, percent.)

Characteristic	Civilian noninstitutional population	Civilian labor force		Employed		Unemployed	
		Number	Percent of population	Number	Percent of population	Number	Percent of population
Total	7,846	4,749	60.5	4,406	56.2	343	7.2
Sex							
Male	3,792	2,469	65.1	2,294	60.5	175	7.1
Female	4,054	2,281	56.3	2,112	52.1	168	7.4
Race, Sex, and Hispanic Origin							
White	6,344	3,864	60.9	3,638	57.3	226	5.8
Male	3,107	2,052	66.1	1,937	62.3	115	5.6
Female	3,237	1,811	56.0	1,701	52.5	111	6.1
Black or African American	1,046	603	57.6	507	48.5	96	15.9
Male	473	266	56.2	219	46.2	47	17.7
Female	574	338	58.9	289	50.3	49	14.5
Hispanic or Latino ethnicity[1]	313	222	70.9	202	64.6	20	8.8
Male	165	124	75.3	116	70.5	8	6.4
Female	148	98	66.0	86	58.1	12	11.9
Age							
16 to 19 years	513	204	39.9	164	31.9	41	20.0
20 to 24 years	681	524	77.0	451	66.2	73	14.0
25 to 34 years	1,171	935	79.8	862	73.6	73	7.8
35 to 44 years	1,237	1,009	81.6	957	77.3	52	5.2
45 to 54 years	1,342	1,046	77.9	989	73.7	57	5.4
55 to 64 years	1,363	778	57.1	748	54.9	31	3.9
65 years and over	1,539	252	16.4	236	15.3	16	6.4

NOTE: Data in Table 7 are from the Current Population Survey (CPS) and do not match the estimates in Table 8. See notes and definitions for further information.
[1] May be of any race.

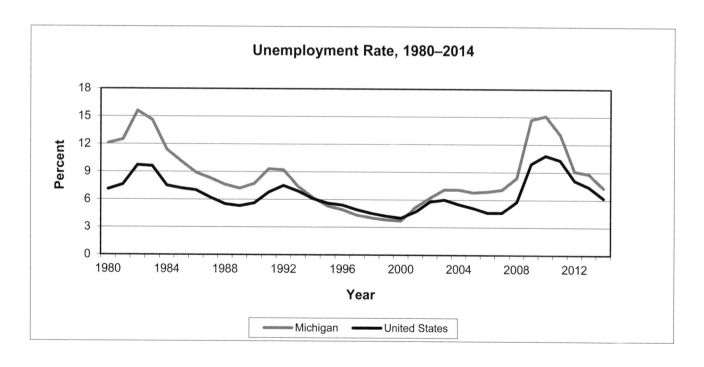

Table MI-8. Employment Status of the Civilian Noninstitutional Population Age 16 Years and Over

(Number, percent.)

Year	Civilian labor force	Civilian participation rate	Employed	Unemployed	Unemployment rate
2006	5,076,656	65.4	4,721,085	355,571	7.0
2007	5,011,120	64.4	4,658,939	352,181	7.0
2008	4,921,466	63.3	4,529,289	392,177	8.0
2009	4,903,544	63.1	4,233,803	669,741	13.7
2010	4,798,954	62.0	4,194,041	604,913	12.6
2011	4,686,948	60.5	4,198,276	488,672	10.4
2012	4,671,183	60.0	4,244,118	427,065	9.1
2013	4,728,376	60.5	4,306,448	421,928	8.9
2014	4,750,279	60.5	4,402,307	347,972	7.3

Table MI-9. Employment and Average Wages by Industry

(Estimates from 2007 through 2010 are based on the 2007 *North American Industry Classification System* [NAICS]. Estimates from 2011 onward are based on the 2012 NAICS.)

Industry	2007	2008	2009	2010	2011	2012	2013
				Number of jobs			
Wage and Salary Employment by Industry	4,372,840	4,257,567	3,960,939	3,955,898	4,049,195	4,108,945	4,186,832
Farm Wage and Salary Employment	20,793	17,600	18,072	16,719	22,521	19,054	22,198
Nonfarm Wage and Salary Employment	4,352,047	4,239,967	3,942,867	3,939,179	4,026,674	4,089,891	4,164,634
Private wage and salary employment	3,677,963	3,576,307	3,283,032	3,288,111	3,394,605	3,467,631	3,554,581
Forestry, fishing, and related activities	6,362	6,518	6,529	6,914	7,197	7,113	7,804
Mining	6,170	6,372	5,561	5,616	5,913	6,300	6,484
Utilities	20,393	20,784	20,269	19,480	19,337	19,210	19,359
Construction	169,621	156,768	131,059	126,044	131,659	132,531	138,379
Manufacturing	625,517	580,835	469,570	478,601	513,416	538,329	556,930
Durable goods manufacturing	481,738	441,778	345,961	352,953	383,282	405,915	421,523
Nondurable goods manufacturing	143,779	139,057	123,609	125,648	130,134	132,414	135,407
Wholesale trade	169,360	167,482	153,228	151,528	156,142	159,961	164,610
Retail trade	496,113	484,299	458,394	452,882	454,646	453,517	459,788
Transportation and warehousing	109,829	105,892	94,526	95,225	100,170	103,890	107,008
Information	64,567	62,210	58,739	57,287	55,819	56,222	58,003
Finance and insurance	156,399	150,208	139,717	137,114	139,336	143,824	147,468
Real estate and rental and leasing	57,108	55,028	52,015	51,539	51,930	49,396	50,966
Professional, scientific, and technical services	247,713	243,722	223,044	226,352	238,825	250,004	262,213
Management of companies and enterprises	57,270	54,259	48,686	48,132	50,858	52,119	54,679
Administrative and waste services	279,248	267,688	233,079	247,251	270,635	280,910	289,652
Educational services	73,636	74,388	74,690	76,157	77,917	77,407	78,952
Health care and social assistance	528,109	537,862	538,699	540,771	548,958	557,854	561,779
Arts, entertainment, and recreation	57,231	56,812	53,730	51,868	49,049	47,638	48,954
Accommodation and food services	351,354	344,926	330,301	328,629	334,721	344,073	352,455
Other services, except public administration	201,963	200,254	191,196	186,721	188,077	187,333	189,098
Government and government enterprises	674,084	663,660	659,835	651,068	632,069	622,260	610,053
				Dollars			
Average Wages and Salaries by Industry	42,846	43,674	43,076	43,865	45,194	46,153	46,623
Average Farm Wages and Salaries	33,130	34,099	33,837	28,444	25,937	31,325	35,726
Average Nonfarm Wages and Salaries	42,893	43,713	43,118	43,930	45,302	46,222	46,681
Average private wages and salaries	43,043	43,665	42,693	43,557	45,219	46,182	46,648
Forestry, fishing, and related activities	23,056	23,844	24,077	25,024	25,591	26,360	27,547
Mining	62,554	64,932	62,502	73,681	74,926	73,530	73,358
Utilities	87,176	84,167	89,233	93,787	98,236	102,234	104,152
Construction	48,943	50,543	49,648	50,564	52,013	53,231	53,631
Manufacturing	59,555	59,557	58,613	59,744	62,235	62,823	63,406
Durable goods manufacturing	62,640	62,368	61,167	62,268	65,352	65,346	66,018
Nondurable goods manufacturing	49,219	50,628	51,464	52,655	53,054	55,088	55,273
Wholesale trade	61,421	63,504	61,587	64,279	67,009	67,790	67,437
Retail trade	24,634	25,035	25,250	25,648	26,037	26,408	26,519
Transportation and warehousing	46,316	46,459	45,789	47,516	49,077	50,150	50,860
Information	55,990	57,452	57,371	58,548	62,044	62,067	64,237
Finance and insurance	58,668	60,081	60,305	62,076	63,967	66,392	68,195
Real estate and rental and leasing	31,994	32,892	33,255	34,119	36,048	37,625	38,226
Professional, scientific, and technical services	71,822	74,099	70,491	70,668	73,096	74,423	74,459
Management of companies and enterprises	100,070	104,241	99,959	103,246	113,268	116,195	110,606
Administrative and waste services	30,759	30,908	30,661	30,907	31,068	31,727	31,704
Educational services	27,582	28,132	28,107	28,602	28,637	29,414	29,855
Health care and social assistance	40,419	42,059	42,996	43,341	44,373	44,902	45,545
Arts, entertainment, and recreation	30,238	30,364	30,594	30,778	30,484	31,960	32,454
Accommodation and food services	15,342	15,136	15,186	15,790	16,551	16,770	16,717
Other services, except public administration	27,272	27,906	27,711	28,533	29,016	29,541	30,289
Government and government enterprises	42,073	43,972	45,232	45,813	45,748	46,446	46,874

Table MI-10. Employment Characteristics by Family Type

(Number, percent.)

Family type and labor force status	2011		2012		2013	
	Total	Families with own children under 18 years	Total	Families with own children under 18 years	Total	Families with own children under 18 years
All Families..	2,472,884	1,051,743	2,482,612	1,041,802	2,484,558	1,041,331
FAMILY TYPE AND LABOR FORCE STATUS						
Married-Couple Families................................	1,817,454	693,616	1,821,915	682,944	1,809,823	675,621
Both husband and wife in labor force.................	50.8	68.2	50.1	67.1	49.5	66.7
Husband in labor force, wife not in labor force	19.5	25.2	19.9	26.3	20.0	26.0
Wife in labor force, husband not in labor force	8.9	4.4	8.8	4.4	8.8	5.0
Both husband and wife not in labor force.................	20.8	2.2	21.2	2.2	21.4	2.1
Other Families..	655,430	358,127	660,697	358,858	674,735	365,710
Female householder, no husband present................	73.6	75.5	74.7	77.3	73.4	76.2
In labor force..	50.0	61.1	50.7	62.4	49.9	61.7
Not in labor force	23.6	14.4	24.0	14.9	23.5	14.5
Male householder, no wife present........................	26.4	24.5	25.3	22.7	26.6	23.8
In labor force..	19.2	21.3	19.0	19.9	19.9	21.0
Not in labor force	7.2	3.2	6.3	2.8	6.7	2.8

Table MI-11. School Enrollment and Educational Attainment, 2013

(Number, percent.)

Item	State	U.S.
Enrollment		
Total population 3 years and over, enrolled in school	2,594,352	82,395,254
Enrolled in nursery school or preschool (percent)	5.4	6.0
Enrolled in kindergarten (percent)...........................	4.9	5.2
Enrolled in elementary school, grades 1-8 (percent)..........	39.0	40.0
Enrolled in high school, grades 9-12 (percent)	21.1	20.6
Enrolled in college or graduate school (percent)..........	29.6	28.3
Attainment		
Total population 25 years and over	6,645,295	210,910,615
Less than ninth grade (percent)..........	3.3	5.8
9th to 12th grade, no diploma (percent)	7.3	7.6
High school graduate, including equivalency (percent)..........	29.7	27.8
Some college, no degree (percent)	23.9	21.1
Associate's degree (percent)	8.9	8.1
Bachelor's degree (percent)	16.4	18.4
Graduate or professional degree (percent)..........	10.5	11.2
High school graduate or higher (percent)	89.4	86.6
Bachelor's degree or higher (percent)..........	26.9	29.6

Table MI-12. Public School Characteristics and Educational Indicators

(Number, percent; data derived from National Center of Education Statistics.)

Item	State	U.S.
Public Schools, 2012–2013 (except where noted)		
Number of school districts...................	891	18,093
Number of schools...................	3,550	98,454
Number of students (in thousands)	1,555	49,771
Number of teachers (in thousands)	86	3,109
Student-teacher ratio	18.1	16.0
Expenditures per student (dollars), FY 2012...................	10,477	10,667
Four-year adjusted cohort graduation rate (ACGR)[1,2]	77.0	81.4
Students eligible for free or reduced-price lunch (in thousands)	724	25,188
English language learners (in thousands)	57	4,397
Students age 3 to 21 served under IDEA, part B (in thousands)	203	6,429

Public Schools by Type	Number	Percent of state public schools
Total number of schools...................	3,550	100.0
Regular	3,057	86.1
Special education...................	193	5.4
Vocational education...................	6	0.2
Alternative education...................	294	8.3

NOTE: Every school is assigned only one school type based on its instructional emphasis.
[1]ACGR data represents a new method of calculating high-school completion rates and may not be comparable to previous years' data for Averaged Freshmen Graduation Rates (AFGR).
[2]The United States 4-year ACGRs were estimated using both the reported 4-year ACGR data from 49 states and the District of Columbia and using imputed data for Idaho. The estimate for American Indian/Alaska Native students also includes imputed data for Virginia.

Table MI-13. Reported Voting and Registration of the Voting-Age Population, November 2012

(Numbers in thousands, percent.)

Item	Total population	Total citizen population	Registered			Voted		
			Total registered	Percent registered (total population)	Percent registered (total citizen population)	Total voted	Percent voted (total population)	Percent voted (total citizen population)
U.S. Total	235,248	215,081	153,157	65.1	71.2	132,948	56.5	61.8
State Total	7,496	7,228	5,620	75.0	77.8	4,832	64.5	66.8
Sex								
Male	3,601	3,458	2,663	73.9	77.0	2,273	63.1	65.7
Female	3,895	3,769	2,957	75.9	78.4	2,559	65.7	67.9
Race								
White alone	6,103	5,971	4,758	78.0	79.7	4,065	66.6	68.1
White, non-Hispanic alone	5,918	5,816	4,629	78.2	79.6	3,951	66.8	67.9
Black alone	1,028	991	687	66.8	69.3	627	61.0	63.3
Asian alone	240	141	84	34.9	59.3	73	30.4	51.6
Hispanic (of any race)	285	225	193	67.9	86.0	158	55.4	70.3
White alone or in combination	6,176	6,044	4,810	77.9	79.6	4,107	66.5	67.9
Black alone or in combination	1,062	1,024	716	67.4	69.9	653	61.6	63.8
Asian alone or in combination	255	157	97	37.8	61.7	75	29.5	48.1
Age								
18 to 24 years	905	894	536	59.2	59.9	394	43.5	44.0
25 to 44 years	2,403	2,242	1,729	72.0	77.1	1,397	58.1	62.3
45 to 64 years	2,676	2,611	2,141	80.0	82.0	1,906	71.2	73.0
65 to 74 years	871	855	703	80.6	82.1	670	77.0	78.4
75 years and over	641	624	512	79.8	82.0	464	72.4	74.3

Table MI-14. Crime

(Number, rate per 100,000. Data are derived from the FBI Uniform Crime Reports.)

Item	State			U.S.[1,2,3,4]		
	2012	2013	Percent change	2012	2013	Percent change
TOTAL POPULATION[5]	9,882,519	9,895,622	0.1	313,873,685	316,128,839	0.7
VIOLENT CRIME						
Number	44,962	42,536	-5.4	1,217,067	1,163,146	-4.4
Rate	455.0	429.8	-5.5	387.8	367.9	-5.1
Murder and Nonnegligent Manslaughter						
Number	701	631	-10.0	14,866	14,196	-4.5
Rate	7.1	6.4	-10.1	4.7	4.5	-5.2
Rape[6]						
Number	X	6,593	X	X	108,612	X
Rate	X	66.6	X	X	34.4	X
Robbery						
Number	10,423	10,105	-3.1	355,051	345,031	-2.8
Rate	105.5	102.1	-3.2	113.1	109.1	-3.5
Aggravated Assault						
Number	29,203	27,194	-6.9	762,009	724,149	-5.0
Rate	295.5	274.8	-7.0	242.8	229.1	-5.6
PROPERTY CRIME						
Number	249,249	230,334	-7.6	9,001,992	8,632,512	-4.1
Rate	2,522.1	2,327.6	-7.7	2,868.0	2,730.7	-4.8
Burglary						
Number	65,560	56,344	-14.1	2,109,932	1,928,465	-8.6
Rate	663.4	569.4	-14.2	672.2	610.0	-9.3
Larceny-Theft						
Number	158,609	149,423	-5.8	6,168,874	6,004,453	-2.7
Rate	1,604.9	1,510.0	-5.9	1,965.4	1,899.4	-3.4
Motor Vehicle Theft						
Number	25,080	24,567	-2.0	723,186	699,594	-3.3
Rate	253.8	248.3	-2.2	230.4	221.3	-4.0

NOTE: Although arson data are included in the trend and clearance tables, sufficient data are not available to estimate totals for this offense. Therefore, no arson data are published in this table.
X = Not applicable.
- = Zero or rounds to zero.
[1]The crime figures have been adjusted.
[2]The data collection methodology for the offense of forcible rape used by the Minnesota state Uniform Crime Reporting (UCR) Program (with the exception of Minneapolis and St. Paul, Minnesota) does not comply with national UCR Program guidelines. Consequently, its figures for forcible rape and violent crime (of which forcible rape is a part) are not published in this table.
[3]Includes offenses reported by the Zoological Police and the Metro Transit Police.
[4]Because of changes in the state's reporting practices, figures are not comparable to previous years' data.
[5]Populations are U.S. Census Bureau provisional estimates as of July 1 of each year.
[6]The figures shown for the offense of rape were estimated using the revised Uniform Crime Reporting (UCR) definition of rape.

Table MI-15. State Government Finances, 2013

(Dollar amounts in thousands, percent distribution.)

Item	Dollars	Percent distribution
Total Revenue	66,400,989	100.0
General revenue	54,343,294	81.8
Intergovernmental revenue	18,007,780	27.1
Taxes	24,936,087	37.6
General sales	8,465,895	12.7
Selective sales	3,832,174	5.8
License taxes	1,464,607	2.2
Individual income tax	8,126,352	12.2
Corporate income tax	895,183	1.3
Other taxes	2,151,876	3.2
Current charges	7,391,002	11.1
Miscellaneous general revenue	4,008,425	6.0
Utility revenue	0	-
Liquor stores revenue	912,112	1.4
Insurance trust revenue[1]	11,145,583	16.8
Total Expenditure	62,945,494	100.0
Intergovernmental expenditure	19,249,754	30.6
Direct expenditure	43,695,740	69.4
Current operation	30,360,266	48.2
Capital outlay	2,148,561	3.4
Insurance benefits and repayments	8,513,291	13.5
Assistance and subsidies	1,233,603	2.0
Interest on debt	1,440,019	2.3
Exhibit: Salaries and wages	7,727,625	12.3
Total Expenditure	62,945,494	100.0
General expenditure	53,549,642	85.1
Intergovernmental expenditure	19,249,754	30.6
Direct expenditure	34,299,888	54.5
General expenditure, by function:		
Education	22,972,166	36.5
Public welfare	14,985,940	23.8
Hospitals	3,080,402	4.9
Health	1,329,434	2.1
Highways	2,419,026	3.8
Police protection	401,026	0.6
Correction	1,857,508	3.0
Natural resources	318,918	0.5
Parks and recreation	113,369	0.2
Governmental administration	945,893	1.5
Interest on general debt	1,440,019	2.3
Other and unallocable	3,685,941	5.9
Utility expenditure	139,900	0.2
Liquor stores expenditure	742,661	1.2
Insurance trust expenditure	8,513,291	13.5
Debt at End of Fiscal Year	30,377,220	X
Cash and Security Holdings	70,534,543	X

X = Not applicable.
- = Zero or rounds to zero.
[1]Within insurance trust revenue, net earnings of state retirement systems is a calculated statistic (the item code in the data file is X08), and thus can be positive or negative. Net earnings is the sum of earnings on investments plus gains on investments minus losses on investments. The change made in 2002 for asset valuation from book to market value in accordance with Statement 34 of the Governmental Accounting Standards Board is reflected in the calculated statistics.

Table MI-16. State Government Tax Collections, 2014

(Dollars in thousands, percent.)

Item	Dollars	Percent distribution
Total Taxes	24,803,973	100.0
Property taxes	1,919,910	7.7
Sales and gross receipts	12,309,564	49.6
General sales and gross receipts	8,419,195	33.9
Selective sales and gross receipts	3,890,369	15.7
Alcoholic beverages	143,641	0.6
Amusements	106,903	0.4
Insurance premiums	362,397	1.5
Motor fuels	964,119	3.9
Pari-mutuels	4,252	-
Public utilities	28,412	0.1
Tobacco products	942,148	3.8
Other selective sales	1,338,497	5.4
Licenses	1,511,695	6.1
Alcoholic beverages	16,540	0.1
Amusements	0	-
Corporations in general	22,621	0.1
Hunting and fishing	58,440	0.2
Motor vehicle	979,061	3.9
Motor vehicle operators	54,695	0.2
Public utilities	27,357	0.1
Occupation and business, NEC	164,127	0.7
Other licenses	188,854	0.8
Income taxes	8,755,723	35.3
Individual income	7,874,712	31.7
Corporation net income	881,011	3.6
Other taxes	307,081	1.2
Death and gift	177	-
Documentary and stock transfer	233,416	0.9
Severance	73,488	0.3
Taxes, NEC	0	-

- = Zero or rounds to zero.

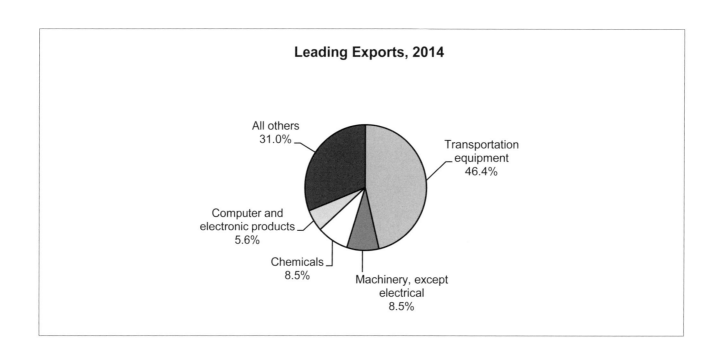

Leading Exports, 2014

All others 31.0%

Transportation equipment 46.4%

Computer and electronic products 5.6%

Chemicals 8.5%

Machinery, except electrical 8.5%

MINNESOTA

Facts and Figures

Location: North central United States; bordered on the N by Canada (Manitoba and Ontario), on the E by Lake Superior and Wisconsin, on the S by Iowa, and on the W by North Dakota and South Dakota

Area: 86,939 sq. mi. (225,171 sq. km.); rank—12th

Population: 5,457,173 (2014 est.); rank—21st

Principal Cities: capital—St. Paul; largest—Minneapolis

Statehood: May 11, 1858; 32nd state

U.S. Congress: 2 senators, 8 representatives

State Motto: *L'Etoile du Nord* ("The Star of the North")

State Song: "Hail! Minnesota"

State Nicknames: The North Star State; The Land of 10,000 Lakes; The Gopher State

Abbreviations: MN; Minn.

State Symbols: flower—showy (pink and white) lady's slipper; tree—red (Norway) pine; bird—loon

At a Glance

- With an increase in population of 2.9 percent, Minnesota ranked 28th among the states in growth from 2010 to 2014.

- Minnesota's violent crime rate in 2013 was 234.4 per 100,000 population, compared to 367.9 for the entire nation.

- With a property crime rate of 2,420.4 per 100,000 population in 2013, Minnesota ranked 32nd in the nation.

- Minnesota's median household income was $60,702 in 2013, the 10th highest in the country.

- In 2013, 11.2 percent of all Minnesotans and 14.0 percent of children in Minnesota lived below the poverty level, compared to 15.8 percent of the entire U.S. population and 22.2 percent of all U.S. children.

Table MN-1. Population by Age, Sex, Race, and Hispanic Origin

(Number, percent, except where noted.)

Sex, age, race, and Hispanic origin	2000	2010	2014[1]	Average annual percent change, 2010–2014
Total Population	4,919,479	5,303,925	5,457,173	0.7
Percent of total U.S. population	1.7	1.7	1.7	X
Sex				
Male	2,435,631	2,632,132	2,712,041	0.8
Female	2,483,848	2,671,793	2,745,132	0.7
Age				
Under 5 years	329,594	355,504	348,643	-0.5
5 to 19 years	1,105,251	1,075,707	1,076,352	-
20 to 64 years	2,890,368	3,189,593	3,252,036	0.5
65 years and over	594,266	683,121	780,142	3.4
Median age (years)	35.4	37.4	37.8	0.3
Race and Hispanic Origin				
One race				
White	4,400,282	4,623,461	4,677,716	0.3
Black	171,731	280,949	320,423	3.3
American Indian and Alaska Native	54,967	67,325	71,960	1.7
Asian	141,968	217,792	256,896	4.2
Native Hawaiian or Other Pacific Islander	1,979	2,958	3,391	3.5
Two or more races	82,742	111,440	126,787	3.3
Hispanic (of any race)	143,382	264,432	277,009	1.2

X = Not applicable.
- = Zero or rounds to zero.
[1]Population figures for 2014 are July 1 estimates. The 2010 estimates are taken from the 2010 Census.

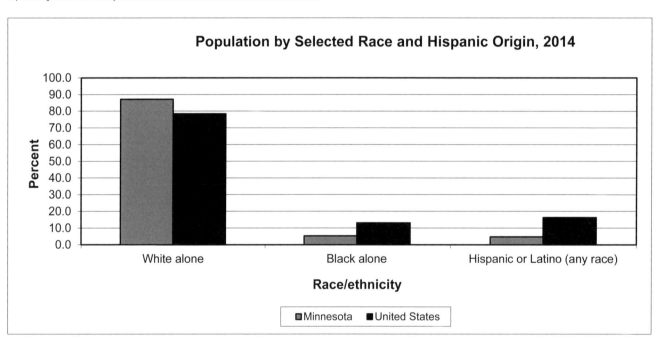

Population by Selected Race and Hispanic Origin, 2014

Table MN-2. Marital Status

(Number, percent distribution.)

Sex, age, race, and Hispanic origin	2000	2010	2013
Males, 15 Years and Over	1,889,936	2,090,940	2,145,450
Never married	31.3	34.6	34.8
Now married, except separated	57.7	53.5	52.8
Separated	0.9	0.9	1.0
Widowed	2.1	2.2	2.3
Divorced	8.0	8.7	9.1
Females, 15 Years and Over	1,967,819	2,155,042	2,205,248
Never married	25.0	28.2	28.3
Now married, except separated	55.0	51.5	51.1
Separated	1.2	1.2	1.4
Widowed	9.4	8.4	8.1
Divorced	9.5	10.7	11.1

Table MN-3. Households and Housing Characteristics

(Number, percent, dollars.)

Item	2000	2010	2013	Average annual percent change, 2000–2013
Total Households..	1,895,127	2,091,548	2,119,954	0.9
Family households	1,255,141	1,353,758	1,372,189	0.7
Married-couple family	1,018,245	1,069,000	1,077,897	0.4
Other family	236,986	284,758	294,292	1.7
Male householder, no wife present............................	68,114	87,757	85,975	1.8
Female householder, no husband present	168,782	197,001	208,317	1.6
Nonfamily households	639,986	737,790	747,765	1.2
Householder living alone......................................	509,468	591,124	599,708	1.3
Householder not living alone.................................	130,518	146,666	148,057	1.0
Housing Characteristics				
Total housing units..	2,065,946	2,348,242	2,368,754	1.1
Occupied housing units	1,895,127	2,091,548	2,119,954	0.9
Owner occupied	1,412,865	1,527,328	1,516,900	0.5
Renter occupied	482,262	564,220	603,054	1.7
Average household size...	2.52	2.47	2.49	-0.1
Financial Characteristics				
Median gross rent of renter-occupied housing	566	764	832	3.0
Median monthly owner costs for housing units with a mortgage	1,044	1,503	1,438	2.5
Median value of owner-occupied housing units	122,400	194,300	180,100	3.0

Table MN-4. Migration, Origin, and Language

(Number, percent.)

Characteristic	State			U.S.		
	2012	2013	Percent change	2012	2013	Percent change
Residence 1 Year Ago						
Population 1 year and over	5,315,228	5,353,441	0.7	310,212,755	312,432,820	0.7
Same house	85.3	85.6	X	85.0	85.0	X
Different house in the U.S.	14.2	13.8	X	14.4	14.4	X
Same county	7.9	7.3	X	9.0	8.9	X
Different county	6.3	6.5	X	5.4	5.5	X
Same state	4.4	4.6	X	3.2	3.2	X
Different state	1.9	2.0	X	2.3	2.3	X
Abroad	0.5	0.5	X	0.6	0.6	X
Place of Birth						
Native born	4,989,815	5,016,866	0.5	273,089,382	274,780,773	0.6
Male..	49.7	49.8	X	49.3	49.3	X
Female..	50.3	50.2	X	50.7	50.7	X
Foreign born	389,324	403,514	3.6	40,824,658	41,348,066	1.3
Male..	49.4	48.2	X	48.7	48.8	X
Female..	50.6	51.8	X	51.3	51.2	X
Foreign born; naturalized U.S. citizen....................	182,509	207,945	13.9	18,686,237	19,294,710	3.3
Male..	45.7	44.6	X	45.8	45.9	X
Female..	54.3	55.4	X	54.2	54.1	X
Foreign born; not a U.S. citizen............................	206,815	195,569	-5.4	22,138,421	22,053,356	-0.4
Male..	52.6	52.0	X	51.1	51.3	X
Female..	47.4	48.0	X	48.9	48.7	X
Entered 2010 or later	9.4	12.2	X	7.0	9.7	X
Entered 2000 to 2009	39.5	37.6	X	30.4	29.4	X
Entered before 2000..	51.1	50.1	X	62.7	61.0	X
World Region of Birth, Foreign						
Foreign-born population, excluding population born at sea	389,324	403,514	3.6	40,824,553	41,347,945	1.3
Europe..	11.7	10.9	X	11.8	11.6	X
Asia..	39.3	38.7	X	29.2	29.5	X
Africa	19.4	20.2	X	4.2	4.4	X
Oceania...	0.5	0.4	X	0.6	0.5	X
Latin America..	26.1	27.0	X	52.2	51.9	X
North America	3.0	2.7	X	2.0	2.0	X
Language Spoken at Home and Ability to Speak English						
Population 5 years and over..................................	5,031,558	5,074,032	0.8	294,003,714	296,358,760	0.8
English only	89.1	89.4	X	79.0	79.2	X
Language other than English.................................	10.9	10.6	X	21.0	20.8	X
Speaks English less than "very well"....................	4.2	4.2	X	8.5	8.5	X

NA = Not available.
X = Not applicable.
- = Zero or rounds to zero.

Table MN-5. Median Income and Poverty Status, 2013

(Number, percent, except as noted.)

Characteristic	State		U.S.	
	Number	Percent	Number	Percent
Median Income				
Households (dollars).................................	60,702	X	52,250	X
Families (dollars)	75,112	X	64,030	X
Below Poverty Level (All People)...................................	592,422	11.2	48,810,868	15.8
Sex				
Male...	272,959	10.4	21,938,525	14.5
Female	319,463	12	26,872,343	17.1
Age				
Under 18 years.......................................	176,719	14.0	16,086,960	22.2
Related children under 18 years......................	172,247	13.7	15,769,921	21.9
18 to 64 years	362,093	10.9	28,578,191	14.8
65 years and over	53,610	7.4	4,145,717	9.6

X = Not applicable.

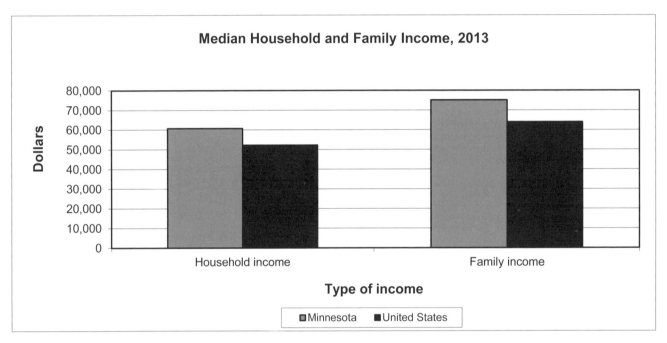

Table MN-6. Health Insurance Coverage Status for the Civilian Noninstitutionalized Population and Children Under 18 Years of Age

(Numbers in thousands, percent.)

Item	2005	2006	2007	2008	2009	2010	2011	2012	2013
Civilian Noninstitutionalized Population	5,129	5,149	5,190	5,151	5,197	5,252	5,287	5,320	5,363
Covered by Private or Public Insurance									
Number..	4,722	4,675	4,758	4,704	4,724	4,776	4,819	4,895	4,923
Percent..	92.1	90.8	91.7	91.3	90.9	90.9	91.2	92.0	91.8
Not Covered									
Number..	408	475	433	447	473	476	467	425	440
Percent..	7.9	9.2	8.3	8.7	9.1	9.1	8.8	8.0	8.2
Percent in the U.S. not covered................	15.3	15.8	15.3	15.1	15.1	15.5	15.1	14.8	14.5
Children Under 18 Years of Age...........................	1,230	1,256	1,246	1,248	1,256	1,281	1,276	1,276	1,280
Covered by Private or Public Insurance									
Number..	1,157	1,153	1,167	1,169	1,173	1,197	1,196	1,208	1,208
Percent..	94.1	91.7	93.6	93.7	93.4	93.4	93.7	94.6	94.4
Not Covered									
Number..	73	104	80	79	83	84	80	68	72
Percent..	5.9	8.3	6.4	6.3	6.6	6.6	6.3	5.4	5.6
Percent in the U.S. not covered................	10.9	11.7	11.0	9.7	8.6	8.0	7.5	7.2	7.1

Table MN-7. Employment Status by Demographic Group, 2014

(Numbers in thousands, percent.)

Characteristic	Civilian noninstitutional population	Civilian labor force		Employed		Unemployed	
		Number	Percent of population	Number	Percent of population	Number	Percent of population
Total.............................	4,259	2,971	69.8	2,853	67.0	119	4.0
Sex							
Male..............................	2,096	1,562	74.5	1,493	71.2	69	4.4
Female...........................	2,163	1,410	65.2	1,360	62.9	50	3.6
Race, Sex, and Hispanic Origin							
White.............................	3,777	2,640	69.9	2,552	67.6	88	3.3
Male..............................	1,859	1,382	74.4	1,330	71.6	52	3.8
Female...........................	1,918	1,258	65.6	1,222	63.7	36	2.9
Black or African American........	210	149	71.1	132	63.0	17	11.4
Male..............................	109	83	76.7	74	68.2	9	11.0
Female...........................	102	66	65.1	58	57.4	8	11.8
Hispanic or Latino ethnicity[1].....	175	134	76.6	125	71.3	9	7.0
Male..............................	89	73	82.7	69	78.0	4	5.6
Female...........................	86	61	70.3	56	64.3	5	8.6
Age							
16 to 19 years....................	284	138	48.5	122	42.9	16	11.4
20 to 24 years....................	381	304	79.7	283	74.3	20	6.7
25 to 34 years....................	740	660	89.1	636	85.9	23	3.5
35 to 44 years....................	636	565	88.9	548	86.1	18	3.1
45 to 54 years....................	766	670	87.4	648	84.6	21	3.2
55 to 64 years....................	675	493	73.0	477	70.6	17	3.4
65 years and over.................	775	143	18.4	139	17.9	4	2.7

NOTE: Data in Table 7 are from the Current Population Survey (CPS) and do not match the estimates in Table 8. See notes and definitions for further information.
[1]May be of any race.

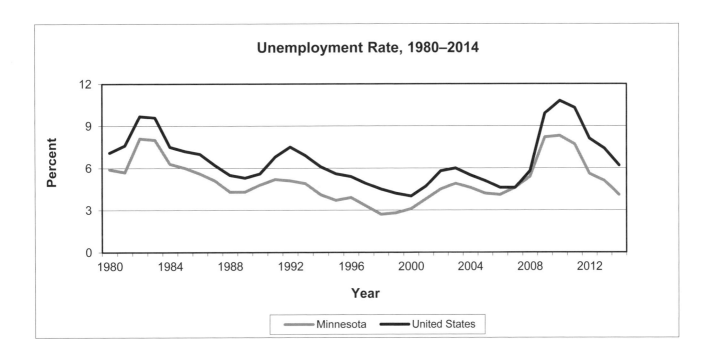

Unemployment Rate, 1980–2014

Table MN-8. Employment Status of the Civilian Noninstitutional Population Age 16 Years and Over

(Number, percent.)

Year	Civilian labor force	Civilian participation rate	Employed	Unemployed	Unemployment rate
2006	2,887,832	72.7	2,772,115	115,717	4.0
2007	2,906,390	72.4	2,773,704	132,686	4.6
2008	2,925,088	72.2	2,766,342	158,746	5.4
2009	2,941,976	72.0	2,713,426	228,550	7.8
2010	2,938,795	71.4	2,721,194	217,601	7.4
2011	2,944,331	70.9	2,753,540	190,791	6.5
2012	2,954,950	70.6	2,789,861	165,089	5.6
2013	2,965,675	70.2	2,819,252	146,423	4.9
2014	2,974,102	69.8	2,852,476	121,626	4.1

Table MN-9. Employment and Average Wages by Industry

(Estimates from 2007 through 2010 are based on the 2007 *North American Industry Classification System* [NAICS]. Estimates from 2011 onward are based on the 2012 NAICS.)

Industry	2007	2008	2009	2010	2011	2012	2013
	Number of jobs						
Wage and Salary Employment by Industry	2,841,732	2,828,921	2,725,314	2,718,113	2,759,615	2,797,535	2,838,575
Farm Wage and Salary Employment	15,530	13,424	18,409	19,372	16,349	18,940	15,758
Nonfarm Wage and Salary Employment	2,826,202	2,815,497	2,706,905	2,698,741	2,743,266	2,778,595	2,822,817
Private wage and salary employment	2,406,818	2,395,555	2,288,567	2,278,070	2,329,716	2,361,625	2,405,022
Forestry, fishing, and related activities	5,177	5,343	5,305	5,560	5,857	5,799	5,786
Mining	5,236	5,549	4,423	5,220	5,812	6,250	6,220
Utilities	12,065	12,515	12,726	12,691	12,807	12,716	13,007
Construction	124,792	114,760	97,786	91,776	96,726	98,137	104,390
Manufacturing	341,507	335,168	300,075	292,717	301,429	305,952	307,587
Durable goods manufacturing	220,192	215,463	188,537	183,413	190,285	194,517	195,392
Nondurable goods manufacturing	121,315	119,705	111,538	109,304	111,144	111,435	112,195
Wholesale trade	133,871	133,858	126,920	124,523	126,851	129,100	131,139
Retail trade	305,062	298,169	284,478	282,103	284,601	285,461	289,207
Transportation and warehousing	83,312	83,086	78,347	77,968	80,081	80,101	81,195
Information	58,892	58,384	55,751	54,322	53,743	53,838	53,360
Finance and insurance	141,720	140,441	137,888	138,560	141,436	141,797	144,335
Real estate and rental and leasing	40,332	39,018	37,533	37,602	37,220	39,964	40,860
Professional, scientific, and technical services	132,715	134,271	127,256	125,404	130,053	131,666	137,153
Management of companies and enterprises	67,191	71,126	69,812	70,657	72,693	74,843	77,002
Administrative and waste services	132,816	127,456	114,424	122,830	130,706	133,185	134,210
Educational services	61,538	64,442	66,222	68,249	70,521	70,617	70,742
Health care and social assistance	370,641	382,788	392,413	395,097	400,501	409,196	420,943
Arts, entertainment, and recreation	39,170	39,253	38,709	37,762	38,719	39,327	40,091
Accommodation and food services	211,561	209,464	202,402	200,927	204,507	208,027	211,984
Other services, except public administration	139,220	140,464	136,097	134,102	135,453	135,649	135,811
Government and government enterprises	419,384	419,942	418,338	420,671	413,550	416,970	417,795
	Dollars						
Average Wages and Salaries by Industry	43,656	45,091	44,585	45,910	46,990	48,412	49,222
Average Farm Wages and Salaries	34,381	36,202	35,677	29,421	27,805	33,022	37,300
Average Nonfarm Wages and Salaries	43,707	45,133	44,646	46,029	47,105	48,517	49,289
Average private wages and salaries	44,262	45,592	44,814	46,510	47,659	49,281	50,026
Forestry, fishing, and related activities	23,517	24,652	25,112	25,894	27,025	28,649	29,395
Mining	65,454	71,798	63,524	73,484	81,167	82,175	84,081
Utilities	79,812	82,755	81,799	86,375	90,413	92,783	97,296
Construction	50,577	52,759	52,270	51,887	53,447	55,572	57,321
Manufacturing	52,182	53,154	53,552	56,320	57,531	58,722	59,544
Durable goods manufacturing	55,503	56,620	57,398	60,764	61,822	63,087	64,204
Nondurable goods manufacturing	46,156	46,914	47,052	48,863	50,184	51,104	51,428
Wholesale trade	64,770	68,081	66,800	69,494	71,753	74,420	75,975
Retail trade	23,585	23,973	24,118	24,477	24,886	25,382	25,983
Transportation and warehousing	45,645	47,436	44,281	44,607	46,035	47,829	48,365
Information	59,578	60,148	60,124	62,098	66,119	65,000	66,675
Finance and insurance	78,509	76,451	74,681	77,746	82,075	89,515	88,627
Real estate and rental and leasing	41,945	44,610	43,831	44,962	46,859	51,826	53,617
Professional, scientific, and technical services	69,675	72,001	72,030	74,432	76,038	79,032	80,956
Management of companies and enterprises	103,565	114,802	94,856	110,451	109,296	112,103	112,757
Administrative and waste services	29,282	30,678	31,042	31,377	31,635	32,370	32,249
Educational services	27,393	28,353	29,225	29,137	29,660	29,926	29,910
Health care and social assistance	40,578	41,160	42,135	43,231	43,429	44,637	44,953
Arts, entertainment, and recreation	29,573	29,938	28,869	31,935	31,887	31,447	32,150
Accommodation and food services	15,586	15,545	15,533	16,044	16,682	17,016	17,131
Other services, except public administration	26,578	27,296	27,546	27,716	28,474	28,711	29,728
Government and government enterprises	40,521	42,513	43,726	43,424	43,980	44,189	45,046

Table MN-10. Employment Characteristics by Family Type

(Number, percent.)

Family type and labor force status	2011		2012		2013	
	Total	Families with own children under 18 years	Total	Families with own children under 18 years	Total	Families with own children under 18 years
All Families..................................	1,356,466	616,059	1,374,436	619,780	1,372,189	617,391
FAMILY TYPE AND LABOR FORCE STATUS						
Married-Couple Families.........................	1,066,483	437,819	1,079,809	437,066	1,077,897	436,434
Both husband and wife in labor force..................	62.1	77.3	62.0	78.1	61.0	75.7
Husband in labor force, wife not in labor force	15.7	18.8	15.5	18.4	15.7	19.4
Wife in labor force, husband not in labor force	7.2	2.9	6.8	2.5	7.3	3.7
Both husband and wife not in labor force..................	15.0	0.9	15.7	1.0	15.6	1.0
Other Families..	289,983	178,240	294,627	182,714	294,292	180,957
Female householder, no husband present.................	68.9	71.4	69.5	73.4	70.8	74.0
In labor force..	53.8	60.9	53.6	61.4	55.8	64.0
Not in labor force	15.1	10.5	15.9	12.0	15.0	10.0
Male householder, no wife present.........................	31.1	28.6	30.5	26.6	29.2	26.0
In labor force..	26.3	26.5	26.2	24.8	24.6	24.7
Not in labor force	4.8	2.1	4.3	1.8	4.6	1.3

Table MN-11. School Enrollment and Educational Attainment, 2013

(Number, percent.)

Item	State	U.S.
Enrollment		
Total population 3 years and over, enrolled in school	1,409,344	82,395,254
Enrolled in nursery school or preschool (percent)................................	6.4	6.0
Enrolled in kindergarten (percent)..	5.1	5.2
Enrolled in elementary school, grades 1-8 (percent).............................	40.6	40.0
Enrolled in high school, grades 9-12 (percent)	20.8	20.6
Enrolled in college or graduate school (percent)................................	27.1	28.3
Attainment		
Total population 25 years and over	3,629,333	210,910,615
Less than ninth grade (percent)...	3.1	5.8
9th to 12th grade, no diploma (percent)	4.5	7.6
High school graduate, including equivalency (percent)...........................	26.3	27.8
Some college, no degree (percent)..	21.9	21.1
Associate's degree (percent)	10.6	8.1
Bachelor's degree (percent)	22.4	18.4
Graduate or professional degree (percent)..	11.1	11.2
High school graduate or higher (percent)	92.4	86.6
Bachelor's degree or higher (percent)	33.5	29.6

Table MN-12. Public School Characteristics and Educational Indicators

(Number, percent; data derived from National Center of Education Statistics.)

Item	State	U.S.
Public Schools, 2012–2013 (except where noted)		
Number of school districts..	553	18,093
Number of schools...	2,403	98,454
Number of students (in thousands)	845	49,771
Number of teachers (in thousands)	54	3,109
Student-teacher ratio	15.8	16.0
Expenditures per student (dollars), FY 2012	10,781	10,667
Four-year adjusted cohort graduation rate (ACGR)[1,2]	79.8	81.4
Students eligible for free or reduced-price lunch (in thousands)	323	25,188
English language learners (in thousands)	51	4,397
Students age 3 to 21 served under IDEA, part B (in thousands)	124	6,429

Public Schools by Type	Number	Percent of state public schools
Total number of schools...	2,403	100.0
Regular	1,626	67.7
Special education..	279	11.6
Vocational education..	11	0.5
Alternative education..	487	20.3

NOTE: Every school is assigned only one school type based on its instructional emphasis.
[1]ACGR data represents a new method of calculating high-school completion rates and may not be comparable to previous years' data for Averaged Freshmen Graduation Rates (AFGR).
[2]The United States 4-year ACGRs were estimated using both the reported 4-year ACGR data from 49 states and the District of Columbia and using imputed data for Idaho. The estimate for American Indian/Alaska Native students also includes imputed data for Virginia.

Table MN-13. Reported Voting and Registration of the Voting-Age Population, November 2012

(Numbers in thousands, percent.)

Item	Total population	Total citizen population	Registered			Voted		
			Total registered	Percent registered (total population)	Percent registered (total citizen population)	Total voted	Percent voted (total population)	Percent voted (total citizen population)
U.S. Total	235,248	215,081	153,157	65.1	71.2	132,948	56.5	61.8
State Total	4,055	3,903	3,085	76.1	79.0	2,859	70.5	73.2
Sex								
Male	1,993	1,921	1,496	75.1	77.9	1,374	68.9	71.5
Female	2,062	1,981	1,589	77.0	80.2	1,485	72.0	75.0
Race								
White alone	3,639	3,576	2,846	78.2	79.6	2,646	72.7	74.0
White, non-Hispanic alone	3,532	3,508	2,808	79.5	80.1	2,615	74.0	74.5
Black alone	179	142	95	52.9	66.9	88	49.2	62.1
Asian alone	174	125	110	63.1	87.6	98	56.2	78.1
Hispanic (of any race)	136	96	54	39.9	56.1	44	32.5	45.7
White alone or in combination	3,680	3,616	2,868	77.9	79.3	2,664	72.4	73.7
Black alone or in combination	210	172	109	52.1	63.4	97	46.4	56.4
Asian alone or in combination..........	186	138	115	61.7	83.5	99	53.4	72.3
Age								
18 to 24 years	531	510	329	61.8	64.5	303	57.0	59.4
25 to 44 years	1,352	1,255	953	70.5	75.9	862	63.8	68.7
45 to 64 years	1,410	1,387	1,151	81.6	83.0	1,081	76.6	77.9
65 to 74 years	424	418	363	85.7	86.9	346	81.5	82.6
75 years and over	338	332	288	85.4	86.7	267	79.2	80.4

Table MN-14. Crime

(Number, rate per 100,000. Data are derived from the FBI Uniform Crime Reports.)

Item	State[1]			U.S.[1,2,3,4]		
	2012	2013	Percent change	2012	2013	Percent change
TOTAL POPULATION[5].............................	5,379,646	5,420,380	0.8	313,873,685	316,128,839	0.7
VIOLENT CRIME						
Number	12,419	12,100	-2.6	1,217,067	1,163,146	-4.4
Rate	230.9	223.2	-3.3	387.8	367.9	-5.1
Murder and Nonnegligent Manslaughter						
Number	99	114	15.2	14,866	14,196	-4.5
Rate	1.8	2.1	14.3	4.7	4.5	-5.2
Rape[6]						
Number	X	2,008	X	X	108,612	X
Rate	X	37.0	X	X	34.4	X
Robbery						
Number	3,475	3,674	5.7	355,051	345,031	-2.8
Rate	64.6	67.8	4.9	113.1	109.1	-3.5
Aggravated Assault						
Number	7,207	6,909	-4.1	762,009	724,149	-5.0
Rate	134.0	127.5	-4.9	242.8	229.1	-5.6
PROPERTY CRIME						
Number	138,152	131,195	-5.0	9,001,992	8,632,512	-4.1
Rate	2,568.1	2,420.4	-5.7	2,868.0	2,730.7	-4.8
Burglary						
Number	25,378	22,713	-10.5	2,109,932	1,928,465	-8.6
Rate	471.7	419.0	-11.2	672.2	610.0	-9.3
Larceny-Theft						
Number	104,316	100,516	-3.6	6,168,874	6,004,453	-2.7
Rate	1,939.1	1,854.4	-4.4	1,965.4	1,899.4	-3.4
Motor Vehicle Theft						
Number	8,458	7,966	-5.8	723,186	699,594	-3.3
Rate	157.2	147.0	-6.5	230.4	221.3	-4.0

NOTE: Although arson data are included in the trend and clearance tables, sufficient data are not available to estimate totals for this offense. Therefore, no arson data are published in this table.

X = Not applicable.

- = Zero or rounds to zero.

[1]The data collection methodology for the offense of forcible rape used by the Minnesota state Uniform Crime Reporting (UCR) Program (with the exception of Minneapolis and St. Paul, Minnesota) does not comply with national UCR Program guidelines. Consequently, its figures for forcible rape and violent crime (of which forcible rape is a part) are not published in this table.

[2]The crime figures have been adjusted.

[3]Includes offenses reported by the Zoological Police and the Metro Transit Police.

[4]Because of changes in the state's reporting practices, figures are not comparable to previous years' data.

[5]Populations are U.S. Census Bureau provisional estimates as of July 1 of each year.

[6]The figures shown for the offense of rape were estimated using the revised Uniform Crime Reporting (UCR) definition of rape.

8885585885888

8888888

Table MN-15. State Government Finances, 2013

(Dollar amounts in thousands, percent distribution.)

Item	Dollars	Percent distribution
Total Revenue	45,593,764	100.0
General revenue	34,651,478	76.0
Intergovernmental revenue	9,315,259	20.4
Taxes	21,031,809	46.1
General sales	5,009,508	11.0
Selective sales	3,280,272	7.2
License taxes	1,184,465	2.6
Individual income tax	8,950,755	19.6
Corporate income tax	1,363,128	3.0
Other taxes	1,243,681	2.7
Current charges	2,268,867	5.0
Miscellaneous general revenue	2,035,543	4.5
Utility revenue	0	-
Liquor stores revenue	0	-
Insurance trust revenue[1]	10,942,286	24.0
Total Expenditure	39,943,492	100.0
Intergovernmental expenditure	12,975,915	32.5
Direct expenditure	26,967,577	67.5
Current operation	18,908,308	47.3
Capital outlay	1,581,068	4.0
Insurance benefits and repayments	4,875,923	12.2
Assistance and subsidies	1,120,702	2.8
Interest on debt	481,576	1.2
Exhibit: Salaries and wages	5,209,914	13.0
Total Expenditure	39,943,492	100.0
General expenditure	35,058,976	87.8
Intergovernmental expenditure	12,975,915	32.5
Direct expenditure	22,083,061	55.3
General expenditure, by function:		
Education	15,026,229	37.6
Public welfare	11,323,904	28.3
Hospitals	265,135	0.7
Health	431,809	1.1
Highways	2,464,343	6.2
Police protection	382,588	1.0
Correction	514,959	1.3
Natural resources	607,961	1.5
Parks and recreation	249,254	0.6
Governmental administration	923,991	2.3
Interest on general debt	481,576	1.2
Other and unallocable	2,387,227	6.0
Utility expenditure	8,593	-
Liquor stores expenditure	0	-
Insurance trust expenditure	4,875,923	12.2
Debt at End of Fiscal Year	13,572,769	X
Cash and Security Holdings	66,050,563	X

X = Not applicable.
- = Zero or rounds to zero.
[1]Within insurance trust revenue, net earnings of state retirement systems is a calculated statistic (the item code in the data file is X08), and thus can be positive or negative. Net earnings is the sum of earnings on investments plus gains on investments minus losses on investments. The change made in 2002 for asset valuation from book to market value in accordance with Statement 34 of the Governmental Accounting Standards Board is reflected in the calculated statistics.

Table MN-16. State Government Tax Collections, 2014

(Dollars in thousands, percent.)

Item	Dollars	Percent distribution
Total Taxes	23,128,901	100.0
Property taxes	836,743	3.6
Sales and gross receipts	9,759,346	42.2
General sales and gross receipts	5,441,934	23.5
Selective sales and gross receipts	4,317,412	18.7
Alcoholic beverages	81,328	0.4
Amusements	44,705	0.2
Insurance premiums	403,280	1.7
Motor fuels	893,351	3.9
Pari-mutuels	492	-
Public utilities	51	-
Tobacco products	581,872	2.5
Other selective sales	2,312,333	10.0
Licenses	1,314,463	5.7
Alcoholic beverages	2,211	-
Amusements	1,211	-
Corporations in general	7,382	-
Hunting and fishing	59,156	0.3
Motor vehicle	695,796	3.0
Motor vehicle operators	43,544	0.2
Public utilities	284	-
Occupation and business, NEC	440,372	1.9
Other licenses	64,507	0.3
Income taxes	10,844,216	46.9
Individual income	9,528,454	41.2
Corporation net income	1,315,762	5.7
Other taxes	374,133	1.6
Death and gift	165,159	0.7
Documentary and stock transfer	166,912	0.7
Severance	42,062	0.2
Taxes, NEC	0	-

- = Zero or rounds to zero.

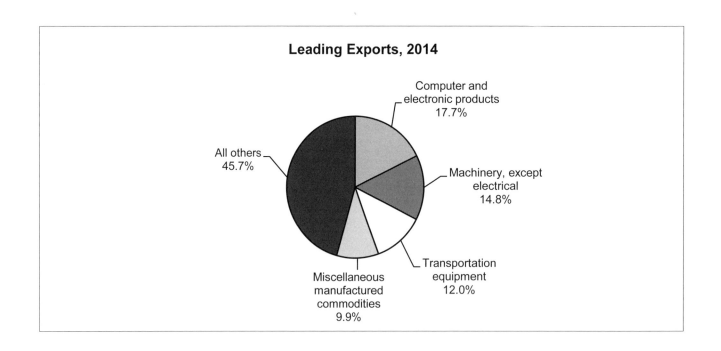

Leading Exports, 2014

Computer and electronic products 17.7%

Machinery, except electrical 14.8%

Transportation equipment 12.0%

Miscellaneous manufactured commodities 9.9%

All others 45.7%

Facts and Figures

Location: South central United States; bordered on the N by Tennessee, on the E by Alabama, on the S by Louisiana and the Gulf of Mexico, and on the W by Arkansas and Louisiana

Area: 48,430 sq. mi. (125,434 sq. km.); rank—32nd

Population: 2,994,079 (2014 est.); rank—31st

Principal Cities: capital—Jackson; largest—Jackson

Statehood: December 10, 1817; 20th state

U.S. Congress: 2 senators, 4 representatives

State Motto: *Virtute et armis* ("By valor and arms")

State Song: "Go, Mississippi"

State Nicknames: The Magnolia State; The Hospitality State

Abbreviations: MS; Miss.

State Symbols: flower—magnolia blossom; tree—Southern magnolia; bird—mockingbird

At a Glance

- With an increase in population of 0.9 percent, Mississippi ranked 41st among the states in growth from 2010 to 2014.

- Mississippi's median household income in 2013 was $37,963, the lowest in the country, and 24.0 percent of the population lived below the poverty level, the highest rate in the country.

- In 2013, 17.1 percent of Mississippians did not have health insurance, compared to 14.5 percent of the total U.S. population.

- Mississippi's infant mortality rate in 2013 was 9.65 deaths per 1,000 live births, the highest in the country.

- Approximately 13.9 percent of Mississippians lived in mobile homes in 2013, the 4th highest percentage in the country.

Table MS-1. Population by Age, Sex, Race, and Hispanic Origin

(Number, percent, except where noted.)

Sex, age, race, and Hispanic origin	2000	2010	2014¹	Average annual percent change, 2010–2014
Total Population	2,844,658	2,967,297	2,994,079	0.2
Percent of total U.S. population	1.0	1.0	0.9	X
Sex				
Male	1,373,554	1,441,240	1,454,556	0.2
Female	1,471,104	1,526,057	1,539,523	0.2
Age				
Under 5 years	204,364	210,956	194,108	-2.1
5 to 19 years	668,850	638,539	621,604	-0.7
20 to 64 years	1,627,921	1,737,395	1,749,984	0.2
65 years and over	343,523	380,407	428,383	3.0
Median age (years)	33.8	36.0	36.7	0.5
Race and Hispanic Origin				
One race				
White	1,746,099	1,789,391	1,786,028	-
Black	1,033,809	1,103,101	1,122,938	0.4
American Indian and Alaska Native	11,652	16,837	17,520	1.0
Asian	18,626	26,477	30,557	3.6
Native Hawaiian or Other Pacific Islander	667	1,700	1,811	1.6
Two or more races	20,021	29,791	35,225	4.3
Hispanic (of any race)	39,569	85,107	88,937	1.1

X = Not applicable.
- = Zero or rounds to zero.
¹Population figures for 2014 are July 1 estimates. The 2010 estimates are taken from the 2010 Census.

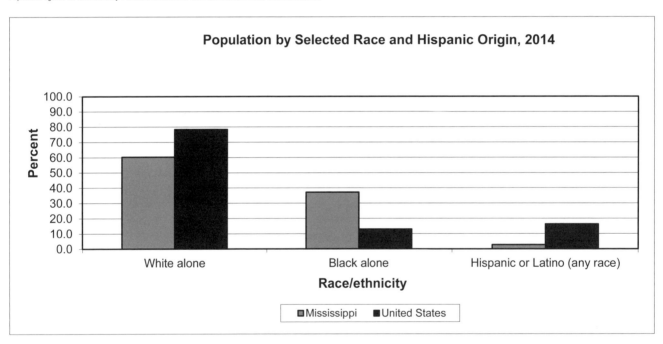

Table MS-2. Marital Status

(Number, percent distribution.)

Sex, age, race, and Hispanic origin	2000	2010	2013
Males, 15 Years and Over	1,046,252	1,121,265	1,139,779
Never married	30.6	34.9	36.7
Now married, except separated	54.6	48.3	46.9
Separated	2.4	2.5	2.7
Widowed	2.9	2.7	3.2
Divorced	9.5	11.7	10.6
Females, 15 Years and Over	1,157,363	1,224,423	1,235,775
Never married	25.1	29.8	30.5
Now married, except separated	48.6	43.8	42.6
Separated	3.2	3.4	3.5
Widowed	12.5	10.8	10.3
Divorced	10.6	12.3	13.1

Table MS-3. Households and Housing Characteristics

(Number, percent, dollars.)

Item	2000	2010	2013	Average annual percent change, 2000–2013
Total Households....................	1,046,434	1,079,999	1,091,002	0.3
Family households	747,159	746,115	745,079	-
Married-couple family	520,884	501,571	487,648	-0.5
Other family	226,315	244,544	257,431	1.0
Male householder, no wife present..............	45,610	51,400	53,641	1.3
Female householder, no husband present	180,705	193,144	203,790	0.9
Nonfamily households	299,275	333,884	345,923	1.1
Householder living alone................	257,708	293,185	296,802	1.1
Householder not living alone.............	41,567	40,699	49,121	1.3
Housing Characteristics				
Total housing units................	1,161,953	1,276,441	1,283,192	0.8
Occupied housing units	1,046,434	1,079,999	1,091,002	0.3
Owner occupied	756,967	753,374	733,101	-0.2
Renter occupied	289,467	326,625	357,901	1.6
Average household size...............	2.63	2.66	2.66	0.1
Financial Characteristics				
Median gross rent of renter-occupied housing	439	672	708	3.7
Median monthly owner costs for housing units with a mortgage	762	1,043	1,021	2.3
Median value of owner-occupied housing units.............	71,400	100,100	97,500	2.4

- = Zero or rounds to zero.

Table MS-4. Migration, Origin, and Language

(Number, percent.)

Characteristic	State			U.S.		
	2012	2013	Percent change	2012	2013	Percent change
Residence 1 Year Ago						
Population 1 year and over	2,947,696	2,957,797	0.3	310,212,755	312,432,820	0.7
Same house	85.8	85.6	X	85.0	85.0	X
Different house in the U.S.	14.0	14.2	X	14.4	14.4	X
Same county	7.7	8.1	X	9.0	8.9	X
Different county	6.3	6.1	X	5.4	5.5	X
Same state	3.8	3.7	X	3.2	3.2	X
Different state	2.5	2.3	X	2.3	2.3	X
Abroad	0.2	0.2	X	0.6	0.6	X
Place of Birth						
Native born	2,925,623	2,928,308	0.1	273,089,382	274,780,773	0.6
Male.................	48.2	48.5	X	49.3	49.3	X
Female.................	51.8	51.5	X	50.7	50.7	X
Foreign born	59,303	62,899	6.1	40,824,658	41,348,066	1.3
Male	54.2	51.6	X	48.7	48.8	X
Female	45.8	48.4	X	51.3	51.2	X
Foreign born; naturalized U.S. citizen.................	21,299	24,044	12.9	18,686,237	19,294,710	3.3
Male	45.3	42.2	X	45.8	45.9	X
Female	54.7	57.8	X	54.2	54.1	X
Foreign born; not a U.S. citizen.................	38,004	38,855	2.2	22,138,421	22,053,356	-0.4
Male	59.1	57.4	X	51.1	51.3	X
Female	40.9	42.6	X	48.9	48.7	X
Entered 2010 or later	8.5	15.9	X	7.0	9.7	X
Entered 2000 to 2009	42.2	34.6	X	30.4	29.4	X
Entered before 2000.................	49.4	49.5	X	62.7	61.0	X
World Region of Birth, Foreign						
Foreign-born population, excluding population born at sea	59,303	62,899	6.1	40,824,553	41,347,945	1.3
Europe	10.3	10.9	X	11.8	11.6	X
Asia.................	33.6	35.6	X	29.2	29.5	X
Africa	4.3	3.4	X	4.2	4.4	X
Oceania	0.5	0.2	X	0.6	0.5	X
Latin America.................	49.4	47.5	X	52.2	51.9	X
North America.................	1.8	2.4	X	2.0	2.0	X
Language Spoken at Home and Ability to Speak English						
Population 5 years and over.................	2,782,530	2,793,325	0.4	294,003,714	296,358,760	0.8
English only	96.4	96.3	X	79.0	79.2	X
Language other than English.................	3.6	3.7	X	21.0	20.8	X
Speaks English less than "very well".................	1.3	1.3	X	8.5	8.5	X

NA = Not available.
X = Not applicable.
- = Zero or rounds to zero.

Table MS-5. Median Income and Poverty Status, 2013

(Number, percent, except as noted.)

Characteristic	State		U.S.	
	Number	Percent	Number	Percent
Median Income				
Households (dollars)..	37,963	X	52,250	X
Families (dollars)	47,615	X	64,030	X
Below Poverty Level (All People)	695,915	24.0	48,810,868	15.8
Sex				
Male..	297,007	21.3	21,938,525	14.5
Female	398,908	26.6	26,872,343	17.1
Age				
Under 18 years...	246,298	34.0	16,086,960	22.2
Related children under 18 years........................	243,030	33.7	15,769,921	21.9
18 to 64 years...	390,895	22.1	28,578,191	14.8
65 years and over	58,722	14.7	4,145,717	9.6

X = Not applicable.

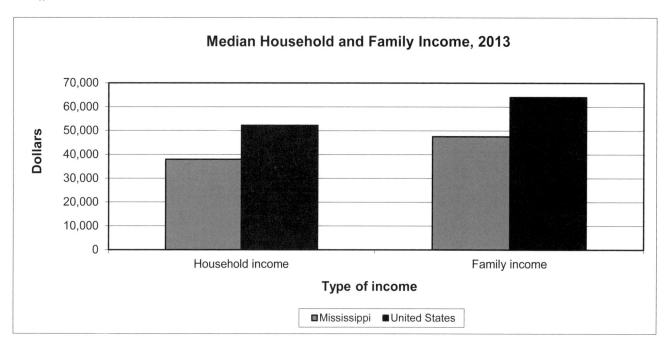

Median Household and Family Income, 2013

Table MS-6. Health Insurance Coverage Status for the Civilian Noninstitutionalized Population and Children Under 18 Years of Age

(Numbers in thousands, percent.)

Item	2005	2006	2007	2008	2009	2010	2011	2012	2013
Civilian Noninstitutionalized Population	2,854	2,892	2,903	2,868	2,880	2,903	2,912	2,918	2,925
Covered by Private or Public Insurance									
Number...	2,370	2,292	2,358	2,355	2,366	2,375	2,395	2,421	2,425
Percent..	83.1	79.2	81.2	82.1	82.1	81.8	82.3	83.0	82.9
Not Covered									
Number...	483	600	545	513	514	528	516	497	500
Percent..	16.9	20.8	18.8	17.9	17.9	18.2	17.7	17.0	17.1
Percent in the U.S. not covered..............................	15.3	15.8	15.3	15.1	15.1	15.5	15.1	14.8	14.5
Children Under 18 Years of Age..........................	754	774	778	763	764	752	750	746	734
Covered by Private or Public Insurance									
Number...	669	628	684	666	685	688	689	691	678
Percent..	88.7	81.1	87.9	87.3	89.7	91.6	91.9	92.7	92.4
Not Covered									
Number...	85	146	94	97	79	64	61	55	56
Percent..	11.3	18.9	12.1	12.7	10.3	8.4	8.1	7.3	7.6
Percent in the U.S. not covered..............................	10.9	11.7	11.0	9.7	8.6	8.0	7.5	7.2	7.1

Table MS-7. Employment Status by Demographic Group, 2014

(Numbers in thousands, percent.)

Characteristic	Civilian noninstitutional population	Civilian labor force		Employed		Unemployed	
		Number	Percent of population	Number	Percent of population	Number	Percent of population
Total..	2,274	1,231	54.1	1,137	50.0	94	7.7
Sex							
Male..	1,068	641	60.0	595	55.7	46	7.2
Female...	1,205	590	49.0	542	45.0	48	8.2
Race, Sex, and Hispanic Origin							
White...	1,408	780	55.4	739	52.5	42	5.3
Male..	677	427	63.1	407	60.2	20	4.7
Female...	731	353	48.3	331	45.3	22	6.1
Black or African American.....................	809	411	50.9	360	44.5	52	12.5
Male..	360	188	52.2	163	45.2	25	13.4
Female...	449	223	49.7	197	43.9	26	11.8
Hispanic or Latino ethnicity[1]..............	50	36	71.5	34	66.6	2	6.8
Male..	25	22	86.6	20	81.7	1	5.7
Female...	NA	NA	NA	NA	NA	NA	NA
Age							
16 to 19 years....................................	188	46	24.6	38	20.4	8	16.9
20 to 24 years....................................	209	123	58.8	99	47.5	24	19.3
25 to 34 years....................................	353	269	76.3	242	68.4	28	10.2
35 to 44 years....................................	355	269	76.0	255	72.0	14	5.2
45 to 54 years....................................	379	275	72.7	263	69.4	13	4.6
55 to 64 years....................................	370	190	51.4	184	49.8	6	3.1
65 years and over...............................	419	57	13.7	55	13.0	3	4.8

NOTE: Data in Table 7 are from the Current Population Survey (CPS) and do not match the estimates in Table 8. See notes and definitions for further information.
[1]May be of any race.
NA = Not available.

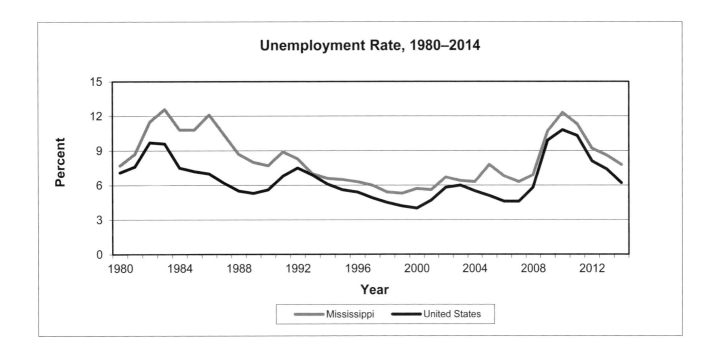

Table MS-8. Employment Status of the Civilian Noninstitutional Population Age 16 Years and Over

(Number, percent.)

Year	Civilian labor force	Civilian participation rate	Employed	Unemployed	Unemployment rate
2006...........	1,290,171	60.0	1,205,906	84,265	6.5
2007...........	1,303,514	60.0	1,224,059	79,455	6.1
2008...........	1,306,772	59.8	1,220,991	85,781	6.6
2009...........	1,269,219	57.7	1,148,930	120,289	9.5
2010...........	1,306,608	58.6	1,170,879	135,729	10.4
2011...........	1,344,904	59.9	1,209,971	134,933	10.0
2012...........	1,319,007	58.5	1,200,155	118,852	9.0
2013...........	1,273,643	56.2	1,162,756	110,887	8.7
2014...........	1,236,310	54.4	1,139,967	96,343	7.8

Table MS-9. Employment and Average Wages by Industry

(Estimates from 2007 through 2010 are based on the 2007 *North American Industry Classification System* [NAICS]. Estimates from 2011 onward are based on the 2012 NAICS.)

Industry	2007	2008	2009	2010	2011	2012	2013
				Number of jobs			
Wage and Salary Employment by Industry......................	1,232,917	1,230,068	1,179,833	1,172,459	1,173,633	1,177,334	1,182,655
Farm Wage and Salary Employment................................	8,806	8,617	9,824	9,993	9,012	7,752	7,003
Nonfarm Wage and Salary Employment..........................	1,224,111	1,221,451	1,170,009	1,162,466	1,164,621	1,169,582	1,175,652
Private wage and salary employment..............................	944,704	937,690	885,322	880,596	885,304	890,508	898,417
Forestry, fishing, and related activities..........................	8,591	8,183	7,591	7,994	8,230	7,903	7,726
Mining..	6,140	6,513	5,667	5,700	6,126	6,311	6,175
Utilities..	7,567	7,626	7,714	7,733	7,733	7,723	7,871
Construction	61,310	63,234	53,950	52,070	51,468	50,029	53,114
Manufacturing..	169,416	159,641	141,508	136,188	135,493	137,267	136,976
Durable goods manufacturing..................................	112,710	105,221	90,678	87,373	88,112	90,931	90,681
Nondurable goods manufacturing............................	56,706	54,420	50,830	48,815	47,381	46,336	46,295
Wholesale trade	37,243	36,773	35,103	34,521	34,561	34,380	34,294
Retail trade..	143,575	141,108	135,253	134,361	134,996	134,785	134,794
Transportation and warehousing....................................	41,381	41,408	39,490	39,545	40,037	40,299	41,033
Information	13,397	13,482	12,815	12,315	11,886	12,597	12,811
Finance and insurance	35,172	34,983	34,143	33,974	34,093	34,181	33,523
Real estate and rental and leasing.................................	12,656	12,733	12,382	11,911	11,801	11,726	11,819
Professional, scientific, and technical services	33,192	33,876	32,219	32,138	32,161	31,539	30,948
Management of companies and enterprises.....................	9,789	9,890	9,816	9,749	10,139	10,153	10,773
Administrative and waste services	51,972	52,431	46,671	51,490	52,749	55,697	58,113
Educational services	17,981	18,841	18,642	19,134	19,720	20,074	20,022
Health care and social assistance..................................	114,565	116,457	118,460	120,870	122,437	122,973	123,667
Arts, entertainment, and recreation...............................	13,319	12,895	12,260	12,074	11,021	11,290	11,639
Accommodation and food services	113,499	113,635	108,839	107,503	109,490	111,085	113,210
Other services, except public administration..................	53,939	53,981	52,799	51,326	51,163	50,086	49,909
Government and government enterprises........................	279,407	283,761	284,687	281,870	279,317	279,484	277,235
				Dollars			
Average Wages and Salaries by Industry........................	33,012	34,240	34,559	35,274	35,951	36,990	37,571
Average Farm Wages and Salaries	23,039	21,338	18,757	18,556	18,447	23,865	27,285
Average Nonfarm Wages and Salaries...........................	33,083	34,331	34,692	35,418	36,086	37,077	37,633
Average private wages and salaries...............................	32,686	33,839	34,004	34,699	35,486	36,719	37,433
Forestry, fishing, and related activities..........................	27,601	28,441	28,466	29,121	29,948	30,896	33,133
Mining..	61,486	67,919	64,256	65,743	70,024	75,344	76,009
Utilities..	63,963	66,823	66,225	67,384	68,006	71,420	72,381
Construction	38,028	42,339	41,392	41,424	42,437	44,885	46,901
Manufacturing..	38,624	40,150	41,196	42,220	43,610	45,233	46,085
Durable goods manufacturing..................................	39,549	41,460	42,837	43,813	45,175	46,585	47,494
Nondurable goods manufacturing............................	36,785	37,618	38,267	39,368	40,699	42,580	43,325
Wholesale trade	47,793	48,838	48,284	48,893	50,327	52,124	53,192
Retail trade..	22,500	22,854	23,062	23,691	24,012	24,809	25,166
Transportation and warehousing....................................	38,991	40,173	39,800	40,843	41,834	43,302	44,287
Information	39,810	40,676	40,359	42,190	44,033	45,106	46,571
Finance and insurance	46,179	47,229	47,250	48,978	50,007	52,639	55,269
Real estate and rental and leasing.................................	28,571	29,801	29,536	30,689	31,823	33,698	33,686
Professional, scientific, and technical services	48,220	50,764	52,024	52,203	53,074	55,122	55,991
Management of companies and enterprises.....................	69,779	70,716	70,928	73,586	77,992	82,498	80,868
Administrative and waste services	23,771	24,452	25,108	25,816	25,596	26,701	27,805
Educational services	22,510	23,653	24,664	25,469	26,816	27,450	28,440
Health care and social assistance..................................	36,283	37,562	38,602	38,853	39,568	40,680	40,904
Arts, entertainment, and recreation...............................	26,569	24,819	24,332	24,800	24,240	23,827	23,774
Accommodation and food services	18,193	17,785	17,340	18,057	18,495	18,590	18,557
Other services, except public administration..................	23,402	24,684	24,744	26,043	26,362	27,528	28,554
Government and government enterprises........................	34,428	35,957	36,831	37,662	37,988	38,162	38,281

Table MS-10. Employment Characteristics by Family Type

(Number, percent.)

Family type and labor force status	2011		2012		2013	
	Total	Families with own children under 18 years	Total	Families with own children under 18 years	Total	Families with own children under 18 years
All Families..	740,958	321,953	747,620	322,759	745,079	310,168
FAMILY TYPE AND LABOR FORCE STATUS						
Married-Couple Families...	487,509	186,686	481,032	180,872	487,648	176,292
Both husband and wife in labor force.............................	49.5	67.3	49.1	65.7	47.4	67.9
Husband in labor force, wife not in labor force	22.5	26.1	22.6	26.0	21.1	23.4
Wife in labor force, husband not in labor force	9.0	4.6	8.8	5.6	10.7	6.0
Both husband and wife not in labor force........................	18.9	2.0	19.6	2.7	20.5	2.5
Other Families ....:	253,449	135,267	266,588	141,887	257,431	133,876
Female householder, no husband present.........................	80.3	83.8	78.6	81.6	79.2	84.2
In labor force...	52.0	67.0	50.9	63.6	51.9	67.5
Not in labor force	28.3	16.8	27.7	18.0	27.3	16.7
Male householder, no wife present.................................	19.7	16.2	21.4	18.4	20.8	15.8
In labor force...	13.6	14.4	15.1	16.7	13.5	13.7
Not in labor force	6.1	1.8	6.3	1.7	7.3	2.1

Table MS-11. School Enrollment and Educational Attainment, 2013

(Number, percent.)

Item	State	U.S.
Enrollment		
Total population 3 years and over, enrolled in school	810,969	82,395,254
Enrolled in nursery school or preschool (percent)	6.3	6.0
Enrolled in kindergarten (percent)..	6.0	5.2
Enrolled in elementary school, grades 1-8 (percent)...............................	41.0	40.0
Enrolled in high school, grades 9-12 (percent)	20.0	20.6
Enrolled in college or graduate school (percent).....................................	26.7	28.3
Attainment		
Total population 25 years and over	1,931,054	210,910,615
Less than ninth grade (percent)	6.3	5.8
9th to 12th grade, no diploma (percent)	11.3	7.6
High school graduate, including equivalency (percent).............................	30.6	27.8
Some college, no degree (percent)...	23.0	21.1
Associate's degree (percent)	8.4	8.1
Bachelor's degree (percent)	12.9	18.4
Graduate or professional degree (percent)..	7.5	11.2
High school graduate or higher (percent)	82.4	86.6
Bachelor's degree or higher (percent)..	20.4	29.6

Table MS-12. Public School Characteristics and Educational Indicators

(Number, percent; data derived from National Center of Education Statistics.)

Item	State	U.S.
Public Schools, 2012–2013 (except where noted)		
Number of school districts..	162	18,093
Number of schools...	1,063	98,454
Number of students (in thousands)	494	49,771
Number of teachers (in thousands)	33	3,109
Student-teacher ratio...	15	16.0
Expenditures per student (dollars), FY 2012..	8,097	10,667
Four-year adjusted cohort graduation rate (ACGR)[1,2]	75.5	81.4
Students eligible for free or reduced-price lunch (in thousands)	352.1	25,188
English language learners (in thousands)	8	4,397
Students age 3 to 21 served under IDEA, part B (in thousands)	65	6,429

Public Schools by Type	Number	Percent of state public schools
Total number of schools..	1,063	100.0
Regular	908	85.4
Special education...	4	0.4
Vocational education...	90	8.5
Alternative education..	61	5.7

NOTE: Every school is assigned only one school type based on its instructional emphasis.
[1]ACGR data represents a new method of calculating high-school completion rates and may not be comparable to previous years' data for Averaged Freshmen Graduation Rates (AFGR).
[2]The United States 4-year ACGRs were estimated using both the reported 4-year ACGR data from 49 states and the District of Columbia and using imputed data for Idaho. The estimate for American Indian/Alaska Native students also includes imputed data for Virginia.

Table MS-13. Reported Voting and Registration of the Voting-Age Population, November 2012

(Numbers in thousands, percent.)

Item	Total population	Total citizen population	Registered			Voted		
			Total registered	Percent registered (total population)	Percent registered (total citizen population)	Total voted	Percent voted (total population)	Percent voted (total citizen population)
U.S. Total	235,248	215,081	153,157	65.1	71.2	132,948	56.5	61.8
State Total	2,166	2,130	1,794	82.8	84.2	1,588	73.3	74.5
Sex								
Male	1,019	995	824	80.9	82.8	710	69.7	71.4
Female	1,147	1,135	971	84.6	85.5	877	76.4	77.3
Race								
White alone......................................	1,355	1,338	1,094	80.7	81.8	951	70.2	71.1
White, non-Hispanic alone	1,321	1,321	1,089	82.4	82.4	949	71.8	71.8
Black alone.......................................	748	744	674	90.2	90.6	613	82.0	82.4
Asian alone......................................	26	10	5	B	B	2	B	B
Hispanic (of any race)......................	35	17	5	B	B	2	B	B
White alone or in combination	1,372	1,354	1,104	80.5	81.5	962	70.1	71.0
Black alone or in combination..........	758	755	685	90.4	90.8	624	82.3	82.7
Asian alone or in combination..........	26	10	5	B	B	2	B	B
Age								
18 to 24 years..................................	300	294	222	73.9	75.5	187	62.4	63.8
25 to 44 years..................................	716	700	587	81.9	83.9	500	69.8	71.5
45 to 64 years..................................	734	727	614	83.7	84.5	563	76.7	77.4
65 to 74 years..................................	258	252	227	87.9	90.1	204	79.1	81.1
75 years and over	158	158	145	91.3	91.3	133	83.8	83.8

B = Base is less than 75,000 and therefore too small to show the derived measure.

Table MS-14. Crime

(Number, rate per 100,000. Data are derived from the FBI Uniform Crime Reports.)

Item	State			U.S.[1,2,3,4]		
	2012	2013	Percent change	2012	2013	Percent change
TOTAL POPULATION[5]......................................	2,986,450	2,991,207	0.2	313,873,685	316,128,839	0.7
VIOLENT CRIME						
Number..	7,769	7,999	3.0	1,217,067	1,163,146	-4.4
Rate	260.1	267.4	2.8	387.8	367.9	-5.1
Murder and Nonnegligent Manslaughter						
Number..	213	195	-8.5	14,866	14,196	-4.5
Rate	7.1	6.5	-8.6	4.7	4.5	-5.2
Rape[6]						
Number..	X	930	X	X	108,612	X
Rate	X	31.1	X	X	34.4	X
Robbery						
Number..	2,277	2,409	5.8	355,051	345,031	-2.8
Rate	76.2	80.5	5.6	113.1	109.1	-3.5
Aggravated Assault						
Number..	4,460	4,680	4.9	762,009	724,149	-5.0
Rate	149.3	156.5	4.8	242.8	229.1	-5.6
PROPERTY CRIME						
Number..	83,933	81,500	-2.9	9,001,992	8,632,512	-4.1
Rate	2,810.5	2,724.7	-3.1	2,868.0	2,730.7	-4.8
Burglary						
Number..	28,084	24,995	-11.0	2,109,932	1,928,465	-8.6
Rate	940.4	835.6	-11.1	672.2	610.0	-9.3
Larceny-Theft						
Number..	51,520	52,117	1.2	6,168,874	6,004,453	-2.7
Rate	1,725.1	1,742.3	1.0	1,965.4	1,899.4	-3.4
Motor Vehicle Theft						
Number..	4,329	4,388	1.4	723,186	699,594	-3.3
Rate	145.0	146.7	1.2	230.4	221.3	-4.0

NOTE: Although arson data are included in the trend and clearance tables, sufficient data are not available to estimate totals for this offense. Therefore, no arson data are published in this table.

X = Not applicable.

- = Zero or rounds to zero.

[1]The crime figures have been adjusted.

[2]The data collection methodology for the offense of forcible rape used by the Minnesota state Uniform Crime Reporting (UCR) Program (with the exception of Minneapolis and St. Paul, Minnesota) does not comply with national UCR Program guidelines. Consequently, its figures for forcible rape and violent crime (of which forcible rape is a part) are not published in this table.

[3]Includes offenses reported by the Zoological Police and the Metro Transit Police.

[4]Because of changes in the state's reporting practices, figures are not comparable to previous years' data.

[5]Populations are U.S. Census Bureau provisional estimates as of July 1 of each year.

[6]The figures shown for the offense of rape were estimated using the revised Uniform Crime Reporting (UCR) definition of rape.

Table MS-15. State Government Finances, 2013

(Dollar amounts in thousands, percent distribution.)

Item	Dollars	Percent distribution
Total Revenue	21,865,219	100.0
General revenue	17,510,532	80.1
Intergovernmental revenue	7,649,292	35.0
Taxes	7,402,725	33.9
General sales	3,191,683	14.6
Selective sales	1,379,611	6.3
License taxes	530,010	2.4
Individual income tax	1,755,424	8.0
Corporate income tax	415,980	1.9
Other taxes	130,017	0.6
Current charges	1,830,894	8.4
Miscellaneous general revenue	627,621	2.9
Utility revenue	0	-
Liquor stores revenue	282,183	1.3
Insurance trust revenue[1]	4,072,504	18.6
Total Expenditure	20,101,926	100.0
Intergovernmental expenditure	5,053,070	25.1
Direct expenditure	15,048,856	74.9
Current operation	10,814,367	53.8
Capital outlay	1,190,761	5.9
Insurance benefits and repayments	2,488,249	12.4
Assistance and subsidies	280,220	1.4
Interest on debt	275,259	1.4
Exhibit: Salaries and wages	2,518,296	12.5
Total Expenditure	20,101,926	100.0
General expenditure	17,386,707	86.5
Intergovernmental expenditure	5,053,070	25.1
Direct expenditure	12,333,637	61.4
General expenditure, by function:		
Education	5,456,159	27.1
Public welfare	5,816,559	28.9
Hospitals	1,131,700	5.6
Health	403,671	2.0
Highways	1,376,640	6.8
Police protection	112,169	0.6
Correction	376,455	1.9
Natural resources	291,359	1.4
Parks and recreation	89,791	0.4
Governmental administration	448,806	2.2
Interest on general debt	275,259	1.4
Other and unallocable	1,608,139	8.0
Utility expenditure	0	-
Liquor stores expenditure	226,970	1.1
Insurance trust expenditure	2,488,249	12.4
Debt at End of Fiscal Year	7,112,560	X
Cash and Security Holdings	28,226,936	X

X = Not applicable.
- = Zero or rounds to zero.
[1]Within insurance trust revenue, net earnings of state retirement systems is a calculated statistic (the item code in the data file is X08), and thus can be positive or negative. Net earnings is the sum of earnings on investments plus gains on investments minus losses on investments. The change made in 2002 for asset valuation from book to market value in accordance with Statement 34 of the Governmental Accounting Standards Board is reflected in the calculated statistics.

Table MS-16. State Government Tax Collections, 2014

(Dollars in thousands, percent.)

Item	Dollars	Percent distribution
Total Taxes	7,574,515	100.0
Property taxes	25,103	0.3
Sales and gross receipts	4,704,955	62.1
General sales and gross receipts	3,304,632	43.6
Selective sales and gross receipts	1,400,323	18.5
Alcoholic beverages	42,402	0.6
Amusements	127,777	1.7
Insurance premiums	263,809	3.5
Motor fuels	409,836	5.4
Pari-mutuels	0	-
Public utilities	4,384	0.1
Tobacco products	146,050	1.9
Other selective sales	406,065	5.4
Licenses	559,218	7.4
Alcoholic beverages	2,945	-
Amusements	18,619	0.2
Corporations in general	182,624	2.4
Hunting and fishing	17,862	0.2
Motor vehicle	154,677	2.0
Motor vehicle operators	40,086	0.5
Public utilities	3,212	0.0
Occupation and business, NEC	100,025	1.3
Other licenses	39,168	0.5
Income taxes	2,193,646	29.0
Individual income	1,667,344	22.0
Corporation net income	526,302	6.9
Other taxes	91,593	1.2
Death and gift	9	-
Documentary and stock transfer	0	-
Severance	91,059	1.2
Taxes, NEC	525	-

- = Zero or rounds to zero.

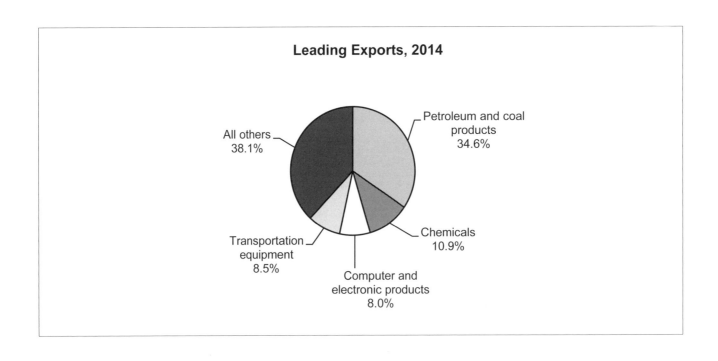

Leading Exports, 2014

- Petroleum and coal products 34.6%
- Chemicals 10.9%
- Computer and electronic products 8.0%
- Transportation equipment 8.5%
- All others 38.1%

Facts and Figures

Location: Central United States; bordered on the N by Iowa, on the E by Illinois, Kentucky, and Tennessee, on the S by Arkansas, and on the W by Oklahoma, Kansas, and Nebraska

Area: 69,704 sq. mi. (180,533 sq. km.); rank—21st

Population: 6,063,589 (2014 est.); rank—18th

Principal Cities: capital—Jefferson City; largest—Kansas City

Statehood: August 10, 1821; 24th state

U.S. Congress: 2 senators, 8 representatives

State Motto: *Salus populi suprema lex esto* ("The welfare of the people shall be the supreme law")

State Song: "Missouri Waltz"

State Nickname: The Show Me State

Abbreviations: MO; Mo

State Symbols: flower—hawthorn; tree—flowering dogwood; bird—Eastern bluebird

At a Glance

- With an increase in population of 1.2 percent, Missouri ranked 39th among the states in growth from 2010 to 2014.

- In 2013, 13.0 percent of Missourians did not have health insurance, compared to 14.5 percent of the total U.S. population.

- Missouri's violent crime rate was 433.4 per 100,000 population in 2013, compared to the U.S. rate of 367.9 per 100,000 population.

- Missouri's median household income of $46,931 ranked 38th in the country in 2013.

- In Missouri in 2013, 15.9 percent of residents lived below the poverty level, just one-tenth a percentage point higher than the national average of 15.8 percent; 22.2 percent of Missouri children lived in poverty, which was the same as the national average.

Table MO-1. Population by Age, Sex, Race, and Hispanic Origin

(Number, percent, except where noted.)

Sex, age, race, and Hispanic origin	2000	2010	2014[1]	Average annual percent change, 2010–2014
Total Population	5,595,211	5,988,927	6,063,589	0.3
Percent of total U.S. population	2.0	1.9	1.9	X
Sex				
Male	2,720,177	2,933,477	2,974,222	0.3
Female	2,875,034	3,055,450	3,089,367	0.3
Age				
Under 5 years	269,898	390,237	374,318	-1.0
5 to 19 years	1,224,274	1,211,174	1,176,911	-0.7
20 to 64 years	3,245,660	3,549,222	3,580,145	0.2
65 years and over	755,379	838,294	932,215	2.7
Median age (years)	36.1	37.9	38.3	0.3
Race and Hispanic Origin				
One race				
White	4,748,083	5,038,407	5,063,452	0.1
Black	629,391	700,178	714,595	0.5
American Indian and Alaska Native	25,076	30,595	32,828	1.8
Asian	61,595	100,213	116,213	3.8
Native Hawaiian or Other Pacific Islander	3,178	7,178	8,527	4.4
Two or more races	82,061	112,356	127,974	3.3
Hispanic (of any race)	118,592	223,421	240,222	1.8

X = Not applicable.
[1]Population figures for 2014 are July 1 estimates. The 2010 estimates are taken from the 2010 Census.

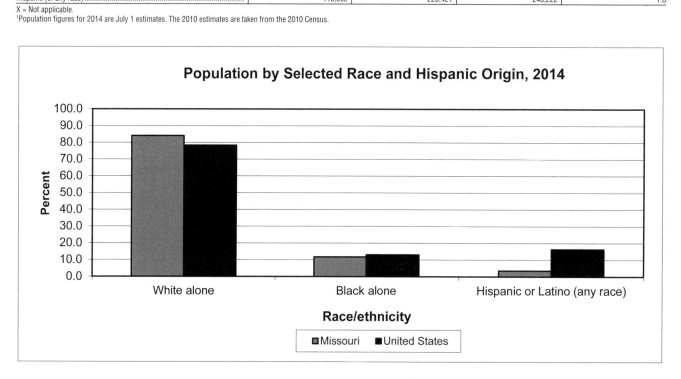

Table MO-2. Marital Status

(Number, percent distribution.)

Sex, age, race, and Hispanic origin	2000	2010	2013
Males, 15 Years and Over	2,114,280	2,332,888	2,366,221
Never married	27.8	32.1	33.1
Now married, except separated	58.0	52.5	51.1
Separated	1.6	1.7	1.6
Widowed	2.6	2.6	2.9
Divorced	10.0	11.0	11.3
Females, 15 Years and Over	2,300,111	2,492,198	2,514,264
Never married	22.1	26.8	27.5
Now married, except separated	53.1	48.2	47.9
Separated	2.0	2.2	2.0
Widowed	11.3	10.0	9.6
Divorced	11.5	12.8	13.0

Table MO-3. Households and Housing Characteristics

(Number, percent, dollars.)

Item	2000	2010	2013	Average annual percent change, 2000–2013
Total Households..	2,194,594	2,350,628	2,362,853	0.6
Family households..	1,476,516	1,524,078	1,523,085	0.2
Married-couple family	1,140,866	1,146,501	1,133,983	-
Other family	335,650	377,577	389,102	1.1
Male householder, no wife present...................	81,890	99,807	100,783	1.6
Female householder, no husband present..........	253,760	277,770	288,319	1.0
Nonfamily households	718,078	826,550	839,768	1.2
Householder living alone....................................	599,808	689,361	692,809	1.1
Householder not living alone..............................	118,270	137,189	146,959	1.7
Housing Characteristics				
Total housing units...	2,442,017	2,714,017	2,719,109	0.8
Occupied housing units	2,194,594	2,350,628	2,362,853	0.6
Owner occupied	1,542,149	1,621,371	1,582,412	0.2
Renter occupied	652,445	729,257	780,441	1.4
Average household size...	2.48	2.48	2.48	-
Financial Characteristics				
Median gross rent of renter-occupied housing	484	682	734	3.3
Median monthly owner costs for housing units with a mortgage	861	1,182	1,162	2.3
Median value of owner-occupied housing units.....	89,900	139,000	133,200	3.1

- = Zero or rounds to zero.

Table MO-4. Migration, Origin, and Language

(Number, percent.)

Characteristic	State			U.S.		
	2012	2013	Percent change	2012	2013	Percent change
Residence 1 Year Ago						
Population 1 year and over	5,951,913	5,973,448	0.4	310,212,755	312,432,820	0.7
Same house	83.4	84.0	X	85.0	85.0	X
Different house in the U.S.	16.2	15.7	X	14.4	14.4	X
Same county	9.3	8.7	X	9.0	8.9	X
Different county	6.9	7.0	X	5.4	5.5	X
Same state	4.2	4.4	X	3.2	3.2	X
Different state	2.7	2.7	X	2.3	2.3	X
Abroad	0.4	0.3	X	0.6	0.6	X
Place of Birth						
Native born	5,793,912	5,810,910	0.3	273,089,382	274,780,773	0.6
Male	49.1	49.0	X	49.3	49.3	X
Female	50.9	51.0	X	50.7	50.7	X
Foreign born	228,076	233,261	2.3	40,824,658	41,348,066	1.3
Male	48.6	48.6	X	48.7	48.8	X
Female	51.4	51.4	X	51.3	51.2	X
Foreign born; naturalized U.S. citizen..............	98,935	105,387	6.5	18,686,237	19,294,710	3.3
Male	43.7	44.2	X	45.8	45.9	X
Female	56.3	55.8	X	54.2	54.1	X
Foreign born; not a U.S. citizen........................	129,141	127,874	-0.4	22,138,421	22,053,356	-0.4
Male	52.3	52.1	X	51.1	51.3	X
Female	47.7	47.9	X	48.9	48.7	X
Entered 2010 or later	12.3	15.1	X	7.0	9.7	X
Entered 2000 to 2009	37.3	33.0	X	30.4	29.4	X
Entered before 2000..	50.4	51.8	X	62.7	61.0	X
World Region of Birth, Foreign						
Foreign-born population, excluding population born at sea	228,076	233,261	2.3	40,824,553	41,347,945	1.3
Europe	20.4	21.3	X	11.8	11.6	X
Asia...	37.3	37.6	X	29.2	29.5	X
Africa..	9.8	7.3	X	4.2	4.4	X
Oceania...	1.5	1.2	X	0.6	0.5	X
Latin America	28.4	30.0	X	52.2	51.9	X
North America	2.7	2.6	X	2.0	2.0	X
Language Spoken at Home and Ability to Speak English						
Population 5 years and over.................................	5,647,397	5,669,938	0.4	294,003,714	296,358,760	0.8
English only	94.0	94.2	X	79.0	79.2	X
Language other than English.............................	6.0	5.8	X	21.0	20.8	X
Speaks English less than "very well".............	2.2	2.1	X	8.5	8.5	X

NA = Not available.
X = Not applicable.
- = Zero or rounds to zero.

Table MO-5. Median Income and Poverty Status, 2013

(Number, percent, except as noted.)

Characteristic	State		U.S.	
	Number	Percent	Number	Percent
Median Income				
Households (dollars)	46,931	X	52,250	X
Families (dollars)	58,754	X	64,030	X
Below Poverty Level (All People)	931,066	15.9	48,810,868	15.8
Sex				
Male	420,110	14.7	21,938,525	14.5
Female	510,956	17.0	26,872,343	17.1
Age				
Under 18 years	304,178	22.2	16,086,960	22.2
Related children under 18 years	296,877	21.8	15,769,921	21.9
18 to 64 years	545,324	15.1	28,578,191	14.8
65 years and over	81,564	9.4	4,145,717	9.6

X = Not applicable.

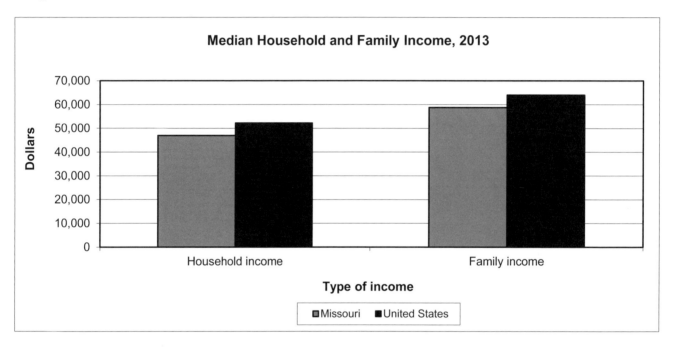

Table MO-6. Health Insurance Coverage Status for the Civilian Noninstitutionalized Population and Children Under 18 Years of Age

(Numbers in thousands, percent.)

Item	2005	2006	2007	2008	2009	2010	2011	2012	2013
Civilian Noninstitutionalized Population	5,710	5,800	5,791	5,795	5,871	5,880	5,899	5,909	5,931
Covered by Private or Public Insurance									
Number	5,041	5,028	5,062	5,040	5,098	5,106	5,092	5,108	5,158
Percent	88.3	86.7	87.4	87.0	86.8	86.8	86.3	86.4	87.0
Not Covered									
Number	668	772	729	755	773	774	807	801	773
Percent	11.7	13.3	12.6	13.0	13.2	13.2	13.7	13.6	13.0
Percent in the U.S. not covered	15.3	15.8	15.3	15.1	15.1	15.5	15.1	14.8	14.5
Children Under 18 Years of Age	1,384	1,398	1,442	1,418	1,427	1,414	1,409	1,400	1,395
Covered by Private or Public Insurance									
Number	1,281	1,271	1,291	1,317	1,329	1,326	1,314	1,302	1,297
Percent	92.5	90.9	89.6	92.9	93.1	93.8	93.3	93.0	93.0
Not Covered									
Number	104	127	150	101	98	88	95	98	98
Percent	7.5	9.1	10.4	7.1	6.9	6.2	6.7	7.0	7.0
Percent in the U.S. not covered	10.9	11.7	11.0	9.7	8.6	8.0	7.5	7.2	7.1

Table MO-7. Employment Status by Demographic Group, 2014

(Numbers in thousands, percent.)

Characteristic	Civilian noninstitutional opulation	Civilian labor force		Employed		Unemployed	
		Number	Percent of population	Number	Percent of population	Number	Percent of population
Total...	4,719	3,049	64.6	2,855	60.5	194	6.4
Sex							
Male...	2,272	1,582	69.6	1,473	64.8	109	6.9
Female...	2,447	1,467	59.9	1,382	56.5	84	5.8
Race, Sex, and Hispanic Origin							
White...	4,018	2,584	64.3	2,453	61.0	131	5.1
Male...	1,956	1,366	69.8	1,295	66.2	72	5.2
Female...	2,062	1,218	59.1	1,158	56.2	59	4.9
Black or African American..................	515	333	64.8	286	55.4	48	14.4
Male...	231	150	64.7	122	52.9	27	18.2
Female...	284	184	64.8	163	57.5	21	11.2
Hispanic or Latino ethnicity[1].............	120	85	70.7	78	64.9	7	8.2
Male...	61	46	75.4	42	69.4	4	8.0
Female...	60	39	65.9	36	60.4	3	8.4
Age							
16 to 19 years...............................	316	132	41.7	111	35.2	21	15.6
20 to 24 years...............................	373	298	79.9	266	71.2	32	10.8
25 to 34 years...............................	761	653	85.7	610	80.1	43	6.6
35 to 44 years...............................	776	649	83.7	617	79.6	32	5.0
45 to 54 years...............................	790	642	81.3	608	76.9	35	5.4
55 to 64 years...............................	752	498	66.2	475	63.2	23	4.5
65 years and over...........................	950	176	18.6	168	17.7	8	4.8

NOTE: Data in Table 7 are from the Current Population Survey (CPS) and do not match the estimates in Table 8. See notes and definitions for further information.
[1]May be of any race.

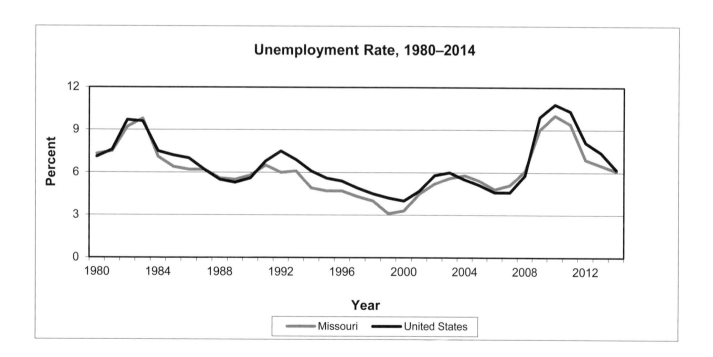

Unemployment Rate, 1980–2014

Table MO-8. Employment Status of the Civilian Noninstitutional Population Age 16 Years and Over

(Number, percent.)

Year	Civilian labor force	Civilian participation rate	Employed	Unemployed	Unemployment rate
2006	3,029,689	67.5	2,882,757	146,932	4.8
2007	3,034,579	66.9	2,879,647	154,932	5.1
2008	3,028,857	66.2	2,842,845	186,012	6.1
2009	3,049,563	66.1	2,766,711	282,852	9.3
2010	3,056,484	66.0	2,763,535	292,949	9.6
2011	3,049,016	65.6	2,790,271	258,745	8.5
2012	3,018,211	64.6	2,807,796	210,415	7.0
2013	3,015,888	64.3	2,813,839	202,049	6.7
2014	3,058,118	64.8	2,871,217	186,901	6.1

Table MO-9. Employment and Average Wages by Industry

(Estimates from 2007 through 2010 are based on the 2007 *North American Industry Classification System* [NAICS]. Estimates from 2011 onward are based on the 2012 NAICS.)

Industry	2007	2008	2009	2010	2011	2012	2013
	Number of jobs						
Wage and Salary Employment by Industry	2,908,875	2,896,954	2,788,974	2,750,304	2,760,024	2,772,488	2,816,639
Farm Wage and Salary Employment	7,836	8,863	8,116	8,921	8,557	8,931	8,669
Nonfarm Wage and Salary Employment	2,901,039	2,888,091	2,780,858	2,741,383	2,751,467	2,763,557	2,807,970
Private wage and salary employment	2,415,088	2,394,176	2,281,338	2,250,632	2,268,829	2,286,856	2,332,258
Forestry, fishing, and related activities	4,262	4,264	4,226	4,495	4,814	4,631	5,254
Mining	5,033	4,941	4,134	4,092	4,018	3,977	3,947
Utilities	12,273	12,331	12,658	12,601	12,345	12,177	12,115
Construction	152,906	145,995	124,519	111,287	108,890	107,958	111,594
Manufacturing	301,245	289,656	255,609	243,699	246,939	248,935	252,934
Durable goods manufacturing	184,559	173,322	146,730	140,234	143,541	144,143	147,842
Nondurable goods manufacturing	116,686	116,334	108,879	103,465	103,398	104,792	105,092
Wholesale trade	125,564	126,199	119,174	117,277	117,049	117,921	119,171
Retail trade	321,041	315,917	305,987	303,854	306,198	305,245	304,891
Transportation and warehousing	99,348	97,805	91,795	87,770	88,187	90,187	92,208
Information	63,613	64,172	62,346	58,375	55,695	52,833	52,591
Finance and insurance	123,031	122,837	122,059	124,107	124,873	129,249	128,006
Real estate and rental and leasing	41,147	40,926	38,664	37,860	36,335	35,649	35,354
Professional, scientific, and technical services	129,326	132,081	126,273	123,375	125,928	131,626	134,023
Management of companies and enterprises	67,405	66,282	59,953	59,560	61,213	60,987	63,836
Administrative and waste services	144,762	147,292	134,528	141,668	147,755	147,754	152,249
Educational services	68,668	59,990	61,553	61,765	63,569	66,301	66,084
Health care and social assistance	330,508	337,906	344,115	348,782	355,202	360,767	381,230
Arts, entertainment, and recreation	44,068	45,422	43,689	43,236	42,394	42,281	43,566
Accommodation and food services	240,134	238,855	233,016	232,403	232,098	234,424	239,449
Other services, except public administration	140,754	141,305	137,040	134,426	135,327	133,954	133,756
Government and government enterprises	485,951	493,915	499,520	490,751	482,638	476,701	475,712
	Dollars						
Average Wages and Salaries by Industry	39,500	41,191	40,925	41,677	42,579	43,873	44,094
Average Farm Wages and Salaries	40,054	29,405	33,948	29,826	32,897	38,605	33,341
Average Nonfarm Wages and Salaries	39,498	41,227	40,945	41,716	42,609	43,890	44,128
Average private wages and salaries	40,000	41,772	41,259	42,051	43,052	44,565	44,747
Forestry, fishing, and related activities	26,482	29,364	29,782	27,610	25,881	26,999	27,024
Mining	64,035	70,036	61,185	59,665	70,043	70,457	68,346
Utilities	72,327	77,624	77,419	79,424	82,797	83,476	86,206
Construction	46,154	48,995	50,078	49,247	49,676	51,289	51,609
Manufacturing	48,111	51,072	50,285	50,976	52,163	54,162	54,785
Durable goods manufacturing	50,087	50,902	52,483	52,524	54,397	55,576	57,416
Nondurable goods manufacturing	44,987	51,325	47,324	48,878	49,060	52,217	51,083
Wholesale trade	55,996	57,906	57,634	58,917	60,403	62,279	62,168
Retail trade	24,114	24,823	25,070	25,389	25,698	26,313	26,482
Transportation and warehousing	42,674	44,092	43,071	44,087	44,978	45,827	47,746
Information	57,543	59,461	62,345	66,726	70,135	72,496	70,489
Finance and insurance	57,484	58,612	59,036	61,974	65,176	69,687	69,718
Real estate and rental and leasing	33,863	34,335	34,683	35,407	36,681	38,934	39,206
Professional, scientific, and technical services	64,239	66,875	67,871	67,950	68,890	71,569	71,165
Management of companies and enterprises	84,369	101,489	79,290	88,952	90,430	96,495	98,008
Administrative and waste services	28,476	29,889	30,634	31,365	32,092	32,572	32,995
Educational services	34,256	30,857	31,757	32,327	32,851	33,764	34,907
Health care and social assistance	38,856	40,261	41,288	41,649	42,546	43,665	42,878
Arts, entertainment, and recreation	36,247	34,415	35,426	35,997	38,107	38,116	39,998
Accommodation and food services	16,128	15,996	16,069	16,686	17,049	17,188	17,226
Other services, except public administration	27,073	27,957	28,106	28,755	29,192	29,768	30,265
Government and government enterprises	37,005	38,583	39,510	40,181	40,528	40,655	41,091

Table MO-10. Employment Characteristics by Family Type

(Number, percent.)

Family type and labor force status	2011		2012		2013	
	Total	Families with own children under18 years	Total	Families with own children under 18 years	Total	Families with own children under 18 years
All Families	1,534,831	665,667	1,517,231	641,438	1,523,085	645,682
FAMILY TYPE AND LABOR FORCE STATUS						
Married-Couple Families	1,144,804	436,692	1,124,203	417,452	1,133,983	426,596
Both husband and wife in labor force	54.0	71.2	53.7	70.9	52.1	68.6
Husband in labor force, wife not in labor force	19.0	23.5	19.1	23.2	19.9	25.0
Wife in labor force, husband not in labor force	8.4	3.6	8.4	3.9	8.8	3.9
Both husband and wife not in labor force	18.7	1.7	18.8	2.0	18.9	2.2
Other Families	390,027	228,975	393,028	223,986	389,102	219,086
Female householder, no husband present	74.5	76.4	74.4	76.2	74.1	76.4
In labor force	53.7	63.4	53.2	62.0	53.9	64.6
Not in labor force	20.8	13.0	21.2	14.2	20.2	11.7
Male householder, no wife present	25.5	23.6	25.6	23.8	25.9	23.6
In labor force	20.5	21.5	19.6	21.4	19.7	21.4
Not in labor force	4.9	2.1	6.0	2.3	6.2	2.2

Table MO-11. School Enrollment and Educational Attainment, 2013

(Number, percent.)

Item	State	U.S.
Enrollment		
Total population 3 years and over, enrolled in school	1,549,456	82,395,254
Enrolled in nursery school or preschool (percent)	6.6	6.0
Enrolled in kindergarten (percent)	5.2	5.2
Enrolled in elementary school, grades 1-8 (percent)	40.4	40.0
Enrolled in high school, grades 9-12 (percent)	20.0	20.6
Enrolled in college or graduate school (percent)	27.8	28.3
Attainment		
Total population 25 years and over	4,047,283	210,910,615
Less than ninth grade (percent)	3.7	5.8
9th to 12th grade, no diploma (percent)	7.6	7.6
High school graduate, including equivalency (percent)	31.5	27.8
Some college, no degree (percent)	22.6	21.1
Associate's degree (percent)	7.6	8.1
Bachelor's degree (percent)	16.9	18.4
Graduate or professional degree (percent)	10.0	11.2
High school graduate or higher (percent)	88.7	86.6
Bachelor's degree or higher (percent)	27.0	29.6

Table MO-12. Public School Characteristics and Educational Indicators

(Number, percent; data derived from National Center of Education Statistics.)

Item	State	U.S.
Public Schools, 2012–2013 (except where noted)		
Number of school districts	567	18,093
Number of schools	2,406	98,454
Number of students (in thousands)	918	49,771
Number of teachers (in thousands)	66	3,109
Student-teacher ratio	13.9	16.0
Expenditures per student (dollars), FY 2012	9,514	10,667
Four-year adjusted cohort graduation rate (ACGR)[1,2]	85.7	81.4
Students eligible for free or reduced-price lunch (in thousands)	409	25,188
English language learners (in thousands)	24	4,397
Students age 3 to 21 served under IDEA, part B (in thousands)	124	6,429

Public Schools by Type	Number	Percent of state public schools
Total number of schools	2,406	100.0
Regular	2,173	90.3
Special education	64	2.7
Vocational education	64	2.7
Alternative education	105	4.4

NOTE: Every school is assigned only one school type based on its instructional emphasis.
[1]ACGR data represents a new method of calculating high-school completion rates and may not be comparable to previous years' data for Averaged Freshmen Graduation Rates (AFGR).
[2]The United States 4-year ACGRs were estimated using both the reported 4-year ACGR data from 49 states and the District of Columbia and using imputed data for Idaho. The estimate for American Indian/Alaska Native students also includes imputed data for Virginia.

Table MO-13. Reported Voting and Registration of the Voting-Age Population, November 2012

(Numbers in thousands, percent.)

Item	Total population	Total citizen population	Registered			Voted		
			Total registered	Percent registered (total population)	Percent registered (total citizen population)	Total voted	Percent voted (total population)	Percent voted (total citizen population)
U.S. Total	235,248	215,081	153,157	65.1	71.2	132,948	56.5	61.8
State Total	4,521	4,409	3,384	74.8	76.7	2,818	62.3	63.9
Sex								
Male	2,169	2,114	1,608	74.1	76.1	1,321	60.9	62.5
Female	2,352	2,295	1,776	75.5	77.4	1,497	63.7	65.2
Race								
White alone	3,887	3,830	2,923	75.2	76.3	2,452	63.1	64.0
White, non-Hispanic alone	3,765	3,732	2,857	75.9	76.6	2,395	63.6	64.2
Black alone	484	465	374	77.2	80.3	313	64.7	67.3
Asian alone	67	30	23	B	B	20	B	B
Hispanic (of any race)	140	104	71	50.9	68.6	63	45.0	60.7
White alone or in combination	3,965	3,908	2,987	75.3	76.4	2,485	62.7	63.6
Black alone or in combination	501	482	388	77.4	80.4	318	63.6	66.0
Asian alone or in combination	72	35	26	B	B	23	B	B
Age								
18 to 24 years	525	520	332	63.3	64.0	223	42.5	42.9
25 to 44 years	1,526	1,460	1,083	71.0	74.2	875	57.4	60.0
45 to 64 years	1,714	1,684	1,344	78.4	79.8	1,175	68.5	69.8
65 to 74 years	425	425	358	84.2	84.2	308	72.4	72.4
75 years and over	330	320	266	80.7	83.2	237	71.9	74.0

B = Base is less than 75,000 and therefore too small to show the derived measure.

Table MO-14. Crime

(Number, rate per 100,000. Data are derived from the FBI Uniform Crime Reports.)

Item	State			U.S.[1,2,3,4]		
	2012	2013	Percent Change	2012	2013	Percent change
TOTAL POPULATION[5]	6,024,522	6,044,171	0.3	313,873,685	316,128,839	0.7
VIOLENT CRIME						
Number	27,189	25,509	-6.2	1,217,067	1,163,146	-4.4
Rate	451.3	422.0	-6.5	387.8	367.9	-5.1
Murder and Nonnegligent Manslaughter						
Number	390	371	-4.9	14,866	14,196	-4.5
Rate	6.5	6.1	-5.2	4.7	4.5	-5.2
Rape[6]						
Number	X	2,287	X	X	108,612	X
Rate	X	37.8	X	X	34.4	X
Robbery						
Number	5,782	5,484	-5.2	355,051	345,031	-2.8
Rate	96.0	90.7	-5.5	113.1	109.1	-3.5
Aggravated Assault						
Number	19,490	18,055	-7.4	762,009	724,149	-5.0
Rate	323.5	298.7	-7.7	242.8	229.1	-5.6
PROPERTY CRIME						
Number	199,813	189,606	-5.1	9,001,992	8,632,512	-4.1
Rate	3,316.7	3,137.0	-5.4	2,868.0	2,730.7	-4.8
Burglary						
Number	42,510	38,865	-8.6	2,109,932	1,928,465	-8.6
Rate	705.6	643.0	-8.9	672.2	610.0	-9.3
Larceny-Theft						
Number	140,971	134,416	-4.6	6,168,874	6,004,453	-2.7
Rate	2,340.0	2,223.9	-5.0	1,965.4	1,899.4	-3.4
Motor Vehicle Theft						
Number	16,332	16,325	*	723,186	699,594	-3.3
Rate	271.1	270.1	-0.4	230.4	221.3	-4.0

NOTE: Although arson data are included in the trend and clearance tables, sufficient data are not available to estimate totals for this offense. Therefore, no arson data are published in this table.
X = Not applicable.
- = Zero or rounds to zero.
[1] The crime figures have been adjusted.
[2] The data collection methodology for the offense of forcible rape used by the Minnesota state Uniform Crime Reporting (UCR) Program (with the exception of Minneapolis and St. Paul, Minnesota) does not comply with national UCR Program guidelines. Consequently, its figures for forcible rape and violent crime (of which forcible rape is a part) are not published in this table.
[3] Includes offenses reported by the Zoological Police and the Metro Transit Police.
[4] Because of changes in the state's reporting practices, figures are not comparable to previous years' data.
[5] Populations are U.S. Census Bureau provisional estimates as of July 1 of each year.
[6] The figures shown for the offense of rape were estimated using the revised Uniform Crime Reporting (UCR) definition of rape.

Table MO-15. State Government Finances, 2013

(Dollar amounts in thousands, percent distribution.)

Item	Dollars	Percent distribution
Total Revenue	37,529,136	100.0
General revenue	26,662,036	71.0
Intergovernmental revenue	10,497,449	28.0
Taxes	11,139,394	29.7
General sales	3,154,531	8.4
Selective sales	1,636,512	4.4
License taxes	549,473	1.5
Individual income tax	5,380,651	14.3
Corporate income tax	377,258	1.0
Other taxes	40,969	0.1
Current charges	2,715,431	7.2
Miscellaneous general revenue	2,309,762	6.2
Utility revenue	0	-
Liquor stores revenue	0	-
Insurance trust revenue[1]	10,867,100	29.0
Total Expenditure	30,451,378	100.0
Intergovernmental expenditure	5,771,802	19.0
Direct expenditure	24,679,576	81.0
Current operation	17,463,592	57.3
Capital outlay	1,457,994	4.8
Insurance benefits and repayments	4,412,372	14.5
Assistance and subsidies	554,905	1.8
Interest on debt	790,713	2.6
Exhibit: Salaries and wages	3,794,857	12.5
Total Expenditure	30,451,378	100.0
General expenditure	26,039,006	85.5
Intergovernmental expenditure	5,771,802	19.0
Direct expenditure	20,267,204	66.6
General expenditure, by function:		
Education	8,952,460	29.4
Public welfare	7,988,161	26.2
Hospitals	1,683,129	5.5
Health	1,585,857	5.2
Highways	1,595,271	5.2
Police protection	214,524	0.7
Correction	736,445	2.4
Natural resources	339,286	1.1
Parks and recreation	41,386	0.1
Governmental administration	523,093	1.7
Interest on general debt	790,713	2.6
Other and unallocable	1,588,681	5.2
Utility expenditure	0	-
Liquor stores expenditure	0	-
Insurance trust expenditure	4,412,372	14.5
Debt at End of Fiscal Year	19,307,770	X
Cash and Security Holdings	62,864,144	X

X = Not applicable.
- = Zero or rounds to zero.
[1]Within insurance trust revenue, net earnings of state retirement systems is a calculated statistic (the item code in the data file is X08), and thus can be positive or negative. Net earnings is the sum of earnings on investments plus gains on investments minus losses on investments. The change made in 2002 for asset valuation from book to market value in accordance with Statement 34 of the Governmental Accounting Standards Board is reflected in the calculated statistics.

Table MO-16. State Government Tax Collections, 2014

(Dollars in thousands, percent.)

Item	Dollars	Percent distribution
Total Taxes	11,240,657	100.0
Property taxes	29,725	0.3
Sales and gross receipts	4,915,210	43.7
General sales and gross receipts	3,285,563	29.2
Selective sales and gross receipts	1,629,647	14.5
Alcoholic beverages	35,760	0.3
Amusements	361,046	3.2
Insurance premiums	302,166	2.7
Motor fuels	696,458	6.2
Pari-mutuels	0	-
Public utilities	0	-
Tobacco products	99,527	0.9
Other selective sales	134,690	1.2
Licenses	564,474	5.0
Alcoholic beverages	5,308	-
Amusements	1,980	-
Corporations in general	59,421	0.5
Hunting and fishing	32,740	0.3
Motor vehicle	272,542	2.4
Motor vehicle operators	15,829	0.1
Public utilities	20,118	0.2
Occupation and business, NEC	134,644	1.2
Other licenses	21,892	0.2
Income taxes	5,719,700	50.9
Individual income	5,361,976	47.7
Corporation net income	357,724	3.2
Other taxes	11,548	0.1
Death and gift	129	-
Documentary and stock transfer	11,340	0.1
Severance	5	-
Taxes, NEC	74	-

- = Zero or rounds to zero.

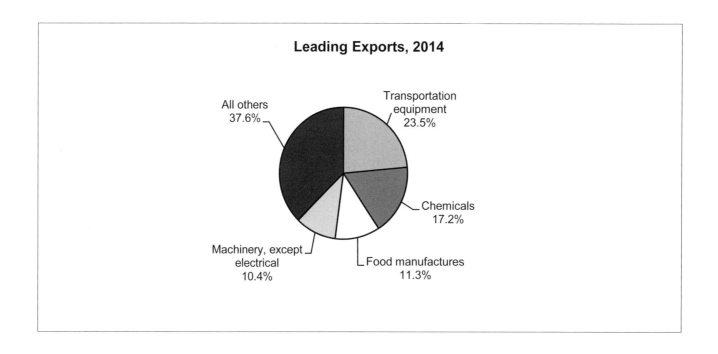

Leading Exports, 2014

All others 37.6%

Transportation equipment 23.5%

Chemicals 17.2%

Food manufactures 11.3%

Machinery, except electrical 10.4%

Facts and Figures

Location: Northwestern United States; bordered on the N by Canada (British Columbia, Alberta, and Saskatchewan), on the E by North Dakota and South Dakota, on the S by Idaho and Wyoming, and on the W by Idaho

Area: 147,042 sq. mi. (380,838 sq. km.); rank—4th

Population: 1,023,579 (2014 est.); rank—44th

Principal Cities: capital—Helena; largest—Billings

Statehood: November 8, 1889; 41st state

U.S. Congress: 2 senators, 1 representative

State Motto: *Oro y plata* ("Gold and silver")

State Song: "Montana"

State Nicknames: The Treasure State; Big Sky Country

Abbreviations: MT; Mont.

State Symbols: flower—bitterroot; tree—ponderosa pine; bird—Western meadowlark

At a Glance

- With an increase in population of 3.5 percent, Montana ranked 22nd among the states in growth from 2010 to 2014.

- Montana's violent crime rate in 2013 was 252.9 per 100,000 population, compared to 367.9 for the entire nation.

- Montana ranked first for traffic fatalities in 2013, with 1.90 deaths per 100 million miles driven, compared to the national average of 1.09 deaths per 100 million miles.

- In 2014, 16.7 percent of Montana residents were in the 65 and older age group, a percentage that ranked 5th in the country.

- Montanans used 395.3 million Btu per capita in energy in 2013, the 15th highest rate in the nation.

Table MT-1. Population by Age, Sex, Race, and Hispanic Origin

(Number, percent, except where noted.)

Sex, age, race, and Hispanic origin	2000	2010	2014[1]	Average annual percent change, 2010–2014
Total Population	902,195	989,415	1,023,579	0.9
Percent of total U.S. population	0.3	0.3	0.3	X
Sex				
Male	449,480	496,667	514,123	0.9
Female	452,715	492,748	509,456	0.8
Age				
Under 5 years	54,869	62,423	61,194	-0.5
5 to 19 years	202,571	188,613	190,005	0.2
20 to 64 years	523,806	591,637	601,225	0.4
65 years and over	120,949	146,742	171,155	3.9
Median age (years)	37.5	39.8	39.8	0.0
Race and Hispanic Origin				
One race				
White	817,229	891,529	914,674	0.6
Black	2,692	4,215	6,108	9.7
American Indian and Alaska Native	56,068	63,495	67,065	1.4
Asian	4,691	6,379	8,256	6.7
Native Hawaiian or Other Pacific Islander	470	734	897	5.1
Two or more races	15,730	23,063	26,579	3.6
Hispanic (of any race)	18,081	31,018	35,362	3.3

X = Not applicable.
[1]Population figures for 2014 are July 1 estimates. The 2010 estimates are taken from the 2010 Census.

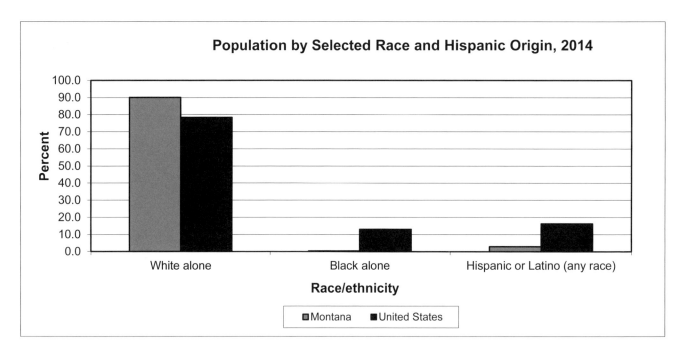

Table MT-2. Marital Status

(Number, percent distribution.)

Sex, age, race, and Hispanic origin	2000	2010	2013
Males, 15 Years and Over	353,801	404,179	412,935
Never married	27.7	30.5	31.1
Now married, except separated	58.3	53.4	52.2
Separated	1.2	1.5	1.5
Widowed	2.6	2.3	3.1
Divorced	10.2	12.4	12.1
Females, 15 Years and Over	362,114	403,766	416,254
Never married	20.4	23.5	25.4
Now married, except separated	56.3	52.9	50.1
Separated	1.3	1.6	1.5
Widowed	10.4	9.7	9.2
Divorced	11.6	12.3	13.8

Table MT-3. Households and Housing Characteristics

(Number, percent, dollars.)

Item	2000	2010	2013	Average annual percent change, 2000–2013
Total Households	358,667	402,747	406,288	1.0
Family households	237,407	255,199	256,091	0.6
Married-couple family	192,067	203,500	199,251	0.3
Other family	45,340	51,699	56,840	1.8
Male householder, no wife present	13,324	16,926	18,977	2.8
Female householder, no husband present	32,016	34,773	37,863	1.3
Nonfamily households	121,260	147,548	150,197	1.7
Householder living alone	98,422	119,762	123,011	1.7
Householder not living alone	22,838	27,786	27,186	1.3
Housing Characteristics				
Total housing units	412,633	483,006	485,767	1.3
Occupied housing units	358,667	402,747	406,288	1.0
Owner occupied	247,723	280,633	271,719	0.7
Renter occupied	110,944	122,114	134,569	1.5
Average household size	2.45	2.39	2.43	-0.1
Financial Characteristics				
Median gross rent of renter-occupied housing	447	642	690	3.4
Median monthly owner costs for housing units with a mortgage	863	1,217	1,259	2.9
Median value of owner-occupied housing units	99,500	181,200	190,100	5.1

Table MT-4. Migration, Origin, and Language

(Number, percent.)

Characteristic	State			U.S.		
	2012	2013	Percent change	2012	2013	Percent change
Residence 1 Year Ago						
Population 1 year and over	995,544	1,003,013	0.8	310,212,755	312,432,820	0.7
Same house	83.3	82.5	X	85.0	85.0	X
Different house in the U.S.	16.5	17.0	X	14.4	14.4	X
Same county	9.2	9.4	X	9.0	8.9	X
Different county	7.3	7.6	X	5.4	5.5	X
Same state	3.5	3.6	X	3.2	3.2	X
Different state	3.8	4.0	X	2.3	2.3	X
Abroad	0.2	0.5	X	0.6	0.6	X
Place of Birth						
Native born	986,797	995,700	0.9	273,089,382	274,780,773	0.6
Male	50.3	50.1	X	49.3	49.3	X
Female	49.7	49.9	X	50.7	50.7	X
Foreign born	18,344	19,465	6.1	40,824,658	41,348,066	1.3
Male	40.4	43.6	X	48.7	48.8	X
Female	59.6	56.4	X	51.3	51.2	X
Foreign born; naturalized U.S. citizen	10,413	11,127	6.9	18,686,237	19,294,710	3.3
Male	36.3	37.9	X	45.8	45.9	X
Female	63.7	62.1	X	54.2	54.1	X
Foreign born; not a U.S. citizen	7,931	8,338	5.1	22,138,421	22,053,356	-0.4
Male	45.8	51.2	X	51.1	51.3	X
Female	54.2	48.8	X	48.9	48.7	X
Entered 2010 or later	8.6	15.7	X	7.0	9.7	X
Entered 2000 to 2009	25.6	19.7	X	30.4	29.4	X
Entered before 2000	65.8	64.7	X	62.7	61.0	X
World Region of Birth, Foreign						
Foreign-born population, excluding population born at sea	18,344	19,465	6.1	40,824,553	41,347,945	1.3
Europe	31.8	36.1	X	11.8	11.6	X
Asia	28.5	26.5	X	29.2	29.5	X
Africa	1.3	0.4	X	4.2	4.4	X
Oceania	2.8	2.5	X	0.6	0.5	X
Latin America	15.6	17.1	X	52.2	51.9	X
North America	20.0	17.5	X	2.0	2.0	X
Language Spoken at Home and Ability to Speak English						
Population 5 years and over	946,302	954,022	0.8	294,003,714	296,358,760	0.8
English only	95.7	96.3	X	79.0	79.2	X
Language other than English	4.3	3.7	X	21.0	20.8	X
Speaks English less than "very well"	1.1	0.7	X	8.5	8.5	X

NA = Not available.
X = Not applicable.
- = Zero or rounds to zero.

Table MT-5. Median Income and Poverty Status, 2013

(Number, percent, except as noted.)

Characteristic	State Number	State Percent	U.S. Number	U.S. Percent
Median Income				
Households (dollars)...	46,972	X	52,250	X
Families (dollars)	60,122	X	64,030	X
Below Poverty Level (All People)..................................	163,637	16.5	48,810,868	15.8
Sex				
Male..	75,596	15.3	21,938,525	14.5
Female	88,041	17.7	26,872,343	17.1
Age				
Under 18 years..	46,806	21.3	16,086,960	22.2
Related children under 18 years....................................	45,829	21.0	15,769,921	21.9
18 to 64 years...	102,028	16.7	28,578,191	14.8
65 years and over	14,803	9.2	4,145,717	9.6

X = Not applicable.

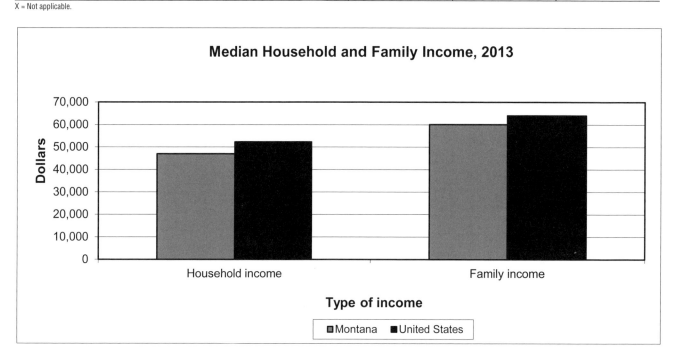

Median Household and Family Income, 2013

(Bar chart showing Dollars on y-axis from 0 to 70,000 and Type of income on x-axis: Household income and Family income. Legend: Montana, United States.)

Table MT-6. Health Insurance Coverage Status for the Civilian Noninstitutionalized Population and Children Under 18 Years of Age

(Numbers in thousands, percent.)

Item	2005	2006	2007	2008	2009	2010	2011	2012	2013
Civilian Noninstitutionalized Population............................	928	931	939	950	958	976	983	990	999
Covered by Private or Public Insurance									
Number..	746	783	772	775	783	807	804	811	835
Percent..	84.4	82.9	84.4	81.6	81.8	82.7	81.7	82.0	83.5
Not Covered									
Number..	145	160	146	175	174	169	180	179	165
Percent..	15.6	17.1	15.6	18.4	18.2	17.3	18.3	18.0	16.5
Percent in the U.S. not covered...................................	15.3	15.8	15.3	15.1	15.1	15.5	15.1	14.8	14.5
Children Under 18 Years of Age..................................	215	212	219	222	220	221	222	219	223
Covered by Private or Public Insurance									
Number..	184	181	191	190	192	193	196	195	201
Percent..	86.1	85.8	85.5	85.6	87.1	87.6	88.5	88.9	89.9
Not Covered									
Number..	30	31	28	32	28	28	26	24	22
Percent..	14.2	14.5	12.6	14.4	12.9	12.4	11.5	11.1	10.1
Percent in the U.S. not covered...................................	10.9	11.7	11.0	9.7	8.6	8.0	7.5	7.2	7.1

Table MT-7. Employment Status by Demographic Group, 2014

(Numbers in thousands, percent.)

Characteristic	Civilian noninstitutional population	Civilian labor force		Employed		Unemployed	
		Number	Percent of population	Number	Percent of population	Number	Percent of population
Total..	808	524	64.8	500	61.8	24	4.6
Sex							
Male..	402	277	68.9	262	65.2	15	5.4
Female	407	247	60.8	238	58.6	9	3.7
Race, Sex, and Hispanic Origin							
White	749	489	65.2	468	62.4	21	4.3
Male..	374	259	69.4	246	65.8	13	5.1
Female	376	230	61.2	222	59.1	8	3.4
Black or African American...............................	NA	NA	NA	NA	NA	NA	NA
Male..	NA	NA	NA	NA	NA	NA	NA
Female	NA	NA	NA	NA	NA	NA	NA
Hispanic or Latino ethnicity[1]	18	13	68.9	11	62.5	1	9.4
Male..	NA	NA	NA	NA	NA	NA	NA
Female	NA	NA	NA	NA	NA	NA	NA
Age							
16 to 19 years..	49	22	45.3	20	42.0	2	7.3
20 to 24 years..	73	56	77.0	52	71.1	4	7.6
25 to 34 years..	131	110	83.9	105	80.1	5	4.5
35 to 44 years..	110	98	88.5	94	85.2	4	3.7
45 to 54 years..	122	101	82.2	97	78.8	4	4.0
55 to 64 years..	153	101	66.1	97	63.2	5	4.5
65 years and over	170	37	21.7	36	21.0	1	3.1

NOTE: Data in Table 7 are from the Current Population Survey (CPS) and do not match the estimates in Table 8. See notes and definitions for further information.

[1]May be of any race.

NA = Not available.

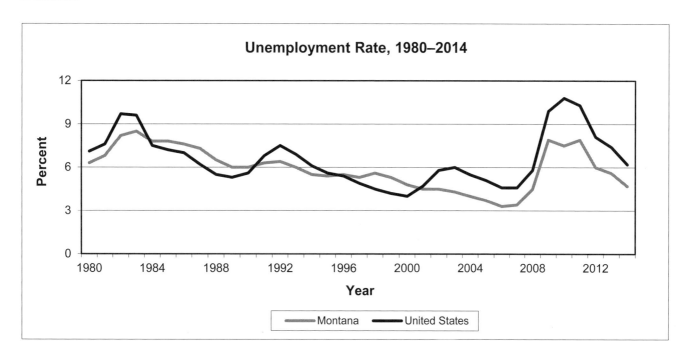

Table MT-8. Employment Status of the Civilian Noninstitutional Population Age 16 Years and Over

(Number, percent.)

Year	Civilian labor force	Civilian participation rate	Employed	Unemployed	Unemployment rate
2006	493,614	66.7	476,377	17,237	3.5
2007	502,070	66.9	484,189	17,881	3.6
2008	509,163	67.0	483,347	25,816	5.1
2009	501,014	65.3	466,713	34,301	6.8
2010	500,525	64.4	463,998	36,527	7.3
2011	501,328	63.9	466,448	34,880	7.0
2012	506,479	63.9	476,052	30,427	6.0
2013	513,768	64.2	485,854	27,914	5.4
2014	516,437	63.9	492,091	24,346	4.7

Table MT-9. Employment and Average Wages by Industry

(Estimates from 2007 through 2010 are based on the 2007 *North American Industry Classification System* [NAICS]. Estimates from 2011 onward are based on the 2012 NAICS.)

Industry	2007	2008	2009	2010	2011	2012	2013
				Number of jobs			
Wage and Salary Employment by Industry	467,731	468,540	452,213	449,797	454,484	460,085	466,710
Farm Wage and Salary Employment	4,761	5,023	4,705	4,830	5,402	5,593	5,758
Nonfarm Wage and Salary Employment	462,970	463,517	447,508	444,967	449,082	454,492	460,952
Private wage and salary employment	369,433	369,354	351,490	347,936	352,843	358,944	366,154
Forestry, fishing, and related activities	2,864	2,771	2,444	2,616	2,742	2,808	3,428
Mining	7,466	7,541	6,489	6,835	7,561	8,730	8,825
Utilities	3,027	3,084	3,067	3,047	3,117	3,196	3,178
Construction	33,573	30,887	25,114	23,796	23,960	23,892	24,983
Manufacturing	20,430	19,939	17,331	16,352	16,864	17,537	18,365
Durable goods manufacturing	12,930	12,309	10,018	9,405	9,758	10,578	11,127
Nondurable goods manufacturing	7,500	7,630	7,313	6,947	7,106	6,959	7,238
Wholesale trade	17,052	16,887	16,118	15,788	15,770	16,334	17,139
Retail trade	59,395	59,660	56,579	55,568	55,609	55,826	56,545
Transportation and warehousing	14,115	13,803	13,334	13,371	13,848	14,531	15,036
Information	7,665	7,667	7,475	7,413	7,214	6,949	6,916
Finance and insurance	16,688	16,930	16,571	16,244	16,257	15,707	15,961
Real estate and rental and leasing	6,189	6,046	5,619	5,414	5,301	5,262	5,433
Professional, scientific, and technical services	19,289	19,607	18,842	18,945	19,341	19,706	20,261
Management of companies and enterprises	1,283	1,439	1,570	1,695	2,006	2,057	1,973
Administrative and waste services	19,844	19,210	18,019	18,458	19,283	19,727	17,780
Educational services	5,118	5,246	5,310	5,459	5,732	5,672	5,924
Health care and social assistance	55,475	57,541	59,202	59,969	60,186	62,185	63,355
Arts, entertainment, and recreation	11,619	11,759	11,415	10,894	10,965	10,885	11,332
Accommodation and food services	47,223	47,908	45,962	45,361	46,157	47,467	49,077
Other services, except public administration	21,118	21,429	21,029	20,711	20,930	20,473	20,643
Government and government enterprises	93,537	94,163	96,018	97,031	96,239	95,548	94,798
				Dollars			
Average Wages and Salaries by Industry	32,363	33,379	33,880	34,679	35,814	37,033	37,707
Average Farm Wages and Salaries	39,020	35,694	42,310	35,807	33,217	27,422	39,900
Average Nonfarm Wages and Salaries	32,294	33,354	33,791	34,667	35,846	37,151	37,679
Average private wages and salaries	31,404	32,316	32,605	33,637	34,986	36,469	37,026
Forestry, fishing, and related activities	27,734	28,327	28,029	27,305	28,833	30,654	30,101
Mining	67,500	72,383	70,377	74,599	80,502	81,885	83,430
Utilities	66,512	69,686	73,969	74,994	78,167	76,683	78,702
Construction	38,091	38,937	39,870	40,854	42,713	43,891	44,781
Manufacturing	39,781	40,594	41,224	42,588	42,588	43,411	43,670
Durable goods manufacturing	38,075	38,533	38,163	39,393	39,934	41,673	42,872
Nondurable goods manufacturing	42,722	43,920	45,417	46,914	46,232	46,053	44,897
Wholesale trade	43,246	45,040	44,642	45,187	47,891	49,846	50,792
Retail trade	23,099	23,475	23,613	24,217	24,685	25,340	25,856
Transportation and warehousing	40,537	42,222	42,125	44,085	47,294	47,750	49,599
Information	38,506	39,673	40,048	41,624	41,931	43,011	43,991
Finance and insurance	45,997	46,655	47,123	48,886	49,884	53,670	55,558
Real estate and rental and leasing	27,869	27,336	25,656	26,554	28,413	30,567	30,432
Professional, scientific, and technical services	45,330	47,435	48,237	49,575	51,672	57,590	54,362
Management of companies and enterprises	58,102	63,205	59,889	58,055	59,589	68,618	73,024
Administrative and waste services	23,601	24,981	25,690	27,130	27,858	29,301	28,761
Educational services	19,473	20,014	20,566	20,476	21,467	21,358	21,712
Health care and social assistance	34,184	35,745	36,876	37,713	39,103	39,929	41,071
Arts, entertainment, and recreation	19,857	18,767	19,194	19,567	20,341	20,289	20,887
Accommodation and food services	14,577	14,475	14,654	15,381	16,149	16,726	16,996
Other services, except public administration	22,555	23,544	23,789	24,511	25,008	26,173	26,835
Government and government enterprises	35,809	37,427	38,130	38,360	38,999	39,717	40,201

Table MT-10. Employment Characteristics by Family Type

(Number, percent.)

Family type and labor force status	2011		2012		2013	
	Total	Families with own children under 18 years	Total	Families with own children under 18 years	Total	Families with own children under 18 years
All Families	253,131	98,821	259,650	105,017	256,091	104,971
FAMILY TYPE AND LABOR FORCE STATUS						
Married-Couple Families	199,556	68,083	205,584	73,268	199,251	70,607
Both husband and wife in labor force	54.1	70.2	53.7	69.4	51.6	67.2
Husband in labor force, wife not in labor force	18.4	24.6	19.1	24.6	20.2	27.1
Wife in labor force, husband not in labor force	8.2	3.2	8.2	4.7	8.6	3.5
Both husband and wife not in labor force	19.2	1.9	19.0	1.3	19.4	2.0
Other Families	53,575	30,738	54,066	31,749	56,840	34,364
Female householder, no husband present	69.9	69.5	64.2	65.5	66.6	69.5
In labor force	54.1	60.4	48.0	57.6	50.9	56.6
Not in labor force	15.8	9.1	16.2	7.9	15.7	12.9
Male householder, no wife present	30.1	30.5	35.8	34.5	33.4	30.5
In labor force	25.2	27.4	30.4	32.0	26.3	27.3
Not in labor force	4.9	3.1	5.5	2.5	7.0	3.2

Table MT-11. School Enrollment and Educational Attainment, 2013

(Number, percent.)

Item	State	U.S.
Enrollment		
Total population 3 years and over, enrolled in school	238,510	82,395,254
Enrolled in nursery school or preschool (percent)	5.4	6.0
Enrolled in kindergarten (percent)	6.3	5.2
Enrolled in elementary school, grades 1-8 (percent)	40.5	40.0
Enrolled in high school, grades 9-12 (percent)	20.4	20.6
Enrolled in college or graduate school (percent)	27.4	28.3
Attainment		
Total population 25 years and over	689,169	210,910,615
Less than ninth grade (percent)	2.2	5.8
9th to 12th grade, no diploma (percent)	5.1	7.6
High school graduate, including equivalency (percent)	29.1	27.8
Some college, no degree (percent)	26.2	21.1
Associate's degree (percent)	8.5	8.1
Bachelor's degree (percent)	19.7	18.4
Graduate or professional degree (percent)	9.3	11.2
High school graduate or higher (percent)	92.7	86.6
Bachelor's degree or higher (percent)	29.0	29.6

Table MT-12. Public School Characteristics and Educational Indicators

(Number, percent; data derived from National Center of Education Statistics.)

Item	State	U.S.
Public Schools, 2012–2013 (except where noted)		
Number of school districts	496	18,093
Number of schools	824	98,454
Number of students (in thousands)	143	49,771
Number of teachers (in thousands)	10	3,109
Student-teacher ratio	14.0	16.0
Expenditures per student (dollars), FY 2012	10,569	10,667
Four-year adjusted cohort graduation rate (ACGR)[1,2]	84.4	81.4
Students eligible for free or reduced-price lunch (in thousands)	60	25,188
English language learners (in thousands)	4	4,397
Students age 3 to 21 served under IDEA, part B (in thousands)	16	6,429

Public Schools by Type	Number	Percent of state public schools
Total number of schools	824	100.0
Regular	818	99.3
Special education	2	0.2
Vocational education	0	-
Alternative education	4	0.5

NOTE: Every school is assigned only one school type based on its instructional emphasis.

[1]ACGR data represents a new method of calculating high-school completion rates and may not be comparable to previous years' data for Averaged Freshmen Graduation Rates (AFGR).

[2]The United States 4-year ACGRs were estimated using both the reported 4-year ACGR data from 49 states and the District of Columbia and using imputed data for Idaho. The estimate for American Indian/Alaska Native students also includes imputed data for Virginia.

Table MT-13. Reported Voting and Registration of the Voting-Age Population, November 2012

(Numbers in thousands, percent.)

Item	Total population	Total citizen population	Registered			Voted		
			Total registered	Percent registered (total population)	Percent registered (total citizen population)	Total voted	Percent voted (total population)	Percent voted (total citizen population)
U.S. Total	235,248	215,081	153,157	65.1	71.2	132,948	56.5	61.8
State Total	768	754	553	72.0	73.3	495	64.5	65.7
Sex								
Male	379	375	263	69.3	70.1	238	62.7	63.4
Female	389	380	290	74.5	76.3	258	66.2	67.9
Race								
White alone............................	698	689	506	72.5	73.5	461	66.1	67.0
White, non-Hispanic alone	688	680	500	72.7	73.6	457	66.4	67.2
Black alone............................	2	-	-	B	B	-	B	B
Asian alone	2	-	-	B	B	-	B	B
Hispanic (of any race)	15	13	8	B	B	7	B	B
White alone or in combination	712	702	514	72.2	73.2	466	65.4	66.3
Black alone or in combination..........	2	-	-	B	B	-	B	B
Asian alone or in combination...........	2	-	-	B	B	-	B	B
Age								
18 to 24 years.....................	82	79	53	65.0	66.9	33	40.7	41.9
25 to 44 years.....................	247	242	146	59.2	60.3	127	51.7	52.7
45 to 64 years.....................	254	249	201	79.1	80.5	189	74.3	75.6
65 to 74 years.....................	115	114	95	82.3	83.2	90	78.1	79.0
75 years and over	71	70	58	B	B	56	B	B

- = Zero or rounds to zero.
B = Base is less than 75,000 and therefore too small to show the derived measure.

Table MT-14. Crime

(Number, rate per 100,000. Data are derived from the FBI Uniform Crime Reports.)

Item	State			U.S.[1,2,3,4]		
	2012	2013	Percent change	2012	2013	Percent change
TOTAL POPULATION[5]..	1,005,494	1,015,165	1.0	313,873,685	316,128,839	0.7
VIOLENT CRIME						
Number..	2,803	2,444	-12.8	1,217,067	1,163,146	-4.4
Rate	278.8	240.7	-13.6	387.8	367.9	-5.1
Murder and Nonnegligent Manslaughter						
Number..	29	22	-24.1	14,866	14,196	-4.5
Rate	2.9	2.2	-24.9	4.7	4.5	-5.2
Rape[6]						
Number..	X	410	X	X	108,612	X
Rate	X	40.4	X	X	34.4	X
Robbery						
Number..	202	204	1.0	355,051	345,031	-2.8
Rate	20.1	20.1	-	113.1	109.1	-3.5
Aggravated Assault						
Number..	2,180	1,931	-11.4	762,009	724,149	-5.0
Rate	216.8	190.2	-12.3	242.8	229.1	-5.6
PROPERTY CRIME						
Number..	26,102	25,953	-0.6	9,001,992	8,632,512	-4.1
Rate	2,595.9	2,556.5	-1.5	2,868.0	2,730.7	-4.8
Burglary						
Number..	3,920	4,064	3.7	2,109,932	1,928,465	-8.6
Rate	389.9	400.3	2.7	672.2	610.0	-9.3
Larceny-Theft						
Number..	20,484	20,039	-2.2	6,168,874	6,004,453	-2.7
Rate	2,037.2	1,974.0	-3.1	1,965.4	1,899.4	-3.4
Motor Vehicle Theft						
Number..	1,698	1,850	9.0	723,186	699,594	-3.3
Rate	168.9	182.2	7.9	230.4	221.3	-4.0

NOTE: Although arson data are included in the trend and clearance tables, sufficient data are not available to estimate totals for this offense. Therefore, no arson data are published in this table.
X = Not applicable.
- = Zero or rounds to zero.
[1]Because of changes in the state's reporting practices, figures are not comparable to previous years' data.
[2]The crime figures have been adjusted.
[3]The data collection methodology for the offense of forcible rape used by the Minnesota state Uniform Crime Reporting (UCR) Program (with the exception of Minneapolis and St. Paul, Minnesota) does not comply with national UCR Program guidelines. Consequently, its figures for forcible rape and violent crime (of which forcible rape is a part) are not published in this table.
[4]Includes offenses reported by the Zoological Police and the Metro Transit Police.
[5]Populations are U.S. Census Bureau provisional estimates as of July 1 of each year.
[6]The figures shown for the offense of rape were estimated using the revised Uniform Crime Reporting (UCR) definition of rape.

Table MT-15. State Government Finances, 2013

(Dollar amounts in thousands, percent distribution.)

Item	Dollars	Percent distribution
Total Revenue	7,982,053	100.0
General revenue	5,767,554	72.3
Intergovernmental revenue	2,161,997	27.1
Taxes	2,644,610	33.1
General sales	0	-
Selective sales	558,961	7.0
License taxes	320,858	4.0
Individual income tax	1,045,500	13.1
Corporate income tax	170,999	2.1
Other taxes	548,292	6.9
Current charges	540,793	6.8
Miscellaneous general revenue	420,154	5.3
Utility revenue	0	-
Liquor stores revenue	82,147	1.0
Insurance trust revenue[1]	2,132,352	26.7
Total Expenditure	7,075,417	100.0
Intergovernmental expenditure	1,373,069	19.4
Direct expenditure	5,702,348	80.6
Current operation	3,883,434	54.9
Capital outlay	630,469	8.9
Insurance benefits and repayments	931,996	13.2
Assistance and subsidies	115,506	1.6
Interest on debt	140,943	2.0
Exhibit: Salaries and wages	1,026,453	14.5
Total Expenditure	7,075,417	100.0
General expenditure	6,060,601	85.7
Intergovernmental expenditure	1,373,069	19.4
Direct expenditure	4,687,532	66.3
General expenditure, by function:		
Education	1,856,783	26.2
Public welfare	1,421,146	20.1
Hospitals	49,673	0.7
Health	175,007	2.5
Highways	683,224	9.7
Police protection	51,138	0.7
Correction	191,150	2.7
Natural resources	322,807	4.6
Parks and recreation	17,486	0.2
Governmental administration	380,054	5.4
Interest on general debt	140,943	2.0
Other and unallocable	771,190	10.9
Utility expenditure	11,934	0.2
Liquor stores expenditure	70,886	1.0
Insurance trust expenditure	931,996	13.2
Debt at End of Fiscal Year	3,558,343	X
Cash and Security Holdings	17,769,784	X

X = Not applicable.
- = Zero or rounds to zero.
[1]Within insurance trust revenue, net earnings of state retirement systems is a calculated statistic (the item code in the data file is X08), and thus can be positive or negative. Net earnings is the sum of earnings on investments plus gains on investments minus losses on investments. The change made in 2002 for asset valuation from book to market value in accordance with Statement 34 of the Governmental Accounting Standards Board is reflected in the calculated statistics.

Table MT-16. State Government Tax Collections, 2014

(Dollars in thousands, percent.)

Item	Dollars	Percent distribution
Total Taxes	2,655,553	100.0
Property taxes	268,508	10.1
Sales and gross receipts	550,254	20.7
General sales and gross receipts	X	X
Selective sales and gross receipts	550,254	20.7
Alcoholic beverages	30,053	1.1
Amusements	56,900	2.1
Insurance premiums	88,106	3.3
Motor fuels	196,965	7.4
Pari-mutuels	21	-
Public utilities	47,390	1.8
Tobacco products	85,404	3.2
Other selective sales	45,415	1.7
Licenses	314,271	11.8
Alcoholic beverages	3,215	0.1
Amusements	8,512	0.3
Corporations in general	3,311	0.1
Hunting and fishing	45,606	1.7
Motor vehicle	136,787	5.2
Motor vehicle operators	8,042	0.3
Public utilities	12	-
Occupation and business, NEC	98,851	3.7
Other licenses	9,935	0.4
Income taxes	1,213,400	45.7
Individual income	1,063,261	40.0
Corporation net income	150,139	5.7
Other taxes	309,120	11.6
Death and gift	4	-
Documentary and stock transfer	0	-
Severance	305,614	11.5
Taxes, NEC	3,502	0.1

X = Not applicable.
- = Zero or rounds to zero.

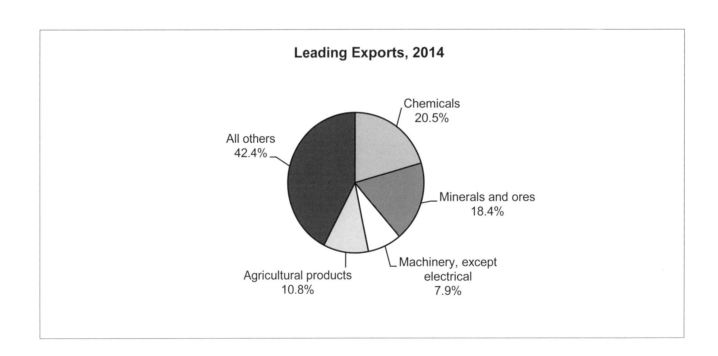

Leading Exports, 2014

Chemicals 20.5%
Minerals and ores 18.4%
Machinery, except electrical 7.9%
Agricultural products 10.8%
All others 42.4%

NEBRASKA

Facts and Figures

Location: Central United States; bordered on the N by South Dakota, on the E by Iowa and Missouri, on the S by Kansas and Colorado, and on the W by Wyoming

Area: 77,354 sq. mi. (200,345 sq. km.); rank — 16th

Population: 1,881,503 (2014 est.); rank — 37th

Principal Cities: capital — Lincoln; largest — Omaha

Statehood: March 1, 1867; 37th state

U.S. Congress: 2 senators, 3 representatives

State Motto: Equality Before the Law

State Song: "Beautiful Nebraska"

State Nickname: The Cornhusker State

Abbreviations: NE; Nebr.; Neb.

State Symbols: flower — goldenrod; tree — cottonwood; bird — Western meadowlark

At a Glance

- With an increase in population of 3.0 percent, Nebraska ranked 26th among the states in growth from 2010 to 2014.

- In 2013, 11.3 percent of Nebraskans did not have health insurance, compared to 14.5 percent of the total U.S. population.

- Nebraska's unemployment rate, 3.3 percent, was the second lowest in the country in 2014. The unemployment rate in the entire U.S. was 6.2 percent.

- Nebraska had the 10th highest percentage of residents self-reporting their race as "White alone" in 2014 (90.3 percent).

- The state's violent crime rate in 2013 was 262.1 per 100,000 population, compared to the national rate of 367.9 per 100,000 population.

Table NE-1. Population by Age, Sex, Race, and Hispanic Origin

(Number, percent, except where noted.)

Sex, age, race, and Hispanic origin	2000	2010	2014[1]	Average annual percent change, 2010–2014
Total Population	1,711,263	1,826,341	1,881,503	0.7
Percent of total U.S. population	0.6	0.6	0.6	X
Sex				
Male	843,351	906,296	936,863	0.8
Female	867,912	920,045	944,640	0.7
Age				
Under 5 years	117,048	131,908	130,178	-0.3
5 to 19 years	387,288	380,564	389,683	0.6
20 to 64 years	974,732	1,067,192	1,090,653	0.5
65 years and over	232,195	246,677	270,989	2.4
Median age (years)	35.3	36.2	36.2	-
Race and Hispanic Origin				
One race				
White	1,533,261	1,649,264	1,682,074	0.5
Black	68,541	85,971	92,289	1.8
American Indian and Alaska Native	14,896	23,418	25,690	2.3
Asian	21,931	33,322	41,216	5.5
Native Hawaiian or Other Pacific Islander	836	2,061	2,235	2.0
Two or more races	23,953	32,305	37,999	4.1
Hispanic (of any race)	94,425	173,058	191,325	2.5

X = Not applicable.
- = Zero or rounds to zero.
[1]Population figures for 2014 are July 1 estimates. The 2010 estimates are taken from the 2010 Census.

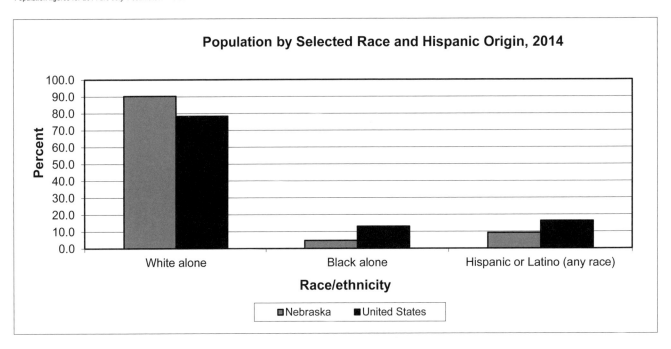

Population by Selected Race and Hispanic Origin, 2014

Table NE-2. Marital Status

(Number, percent distribution.)

Sex, age, race, and Hispanic origin	2000	2010	2013
Males, 15 Years and Over	654,559	708,783	728,713
Never married	29.2	32.4	32.3
Now married, except separated	59.1	54.0	54.7
Separated	1.0	1.4	1.3
Widowed	2.4	2.3	2.2
Divorced	8.3	9.9	9.5
Females, 15 Years and Over	687,863	735,744	750,206
Never married	22.5	25.3	26.8
Now married, except separated	55.7	52.7	51.7
Separated	1.3	1.5	1.5
Widowed	10.8	9.5	8.7
Divorced	9.7	10.9	11.3

Table NE-3. Households and Housing Characteristics

(Number, percent, dollars.)

Item	2000	2010	2013	Average annual percent change, 2000–2013
Total Households................	666,184	719,304	730,579	0.7
Family households	443,411	468,407	475,000	0.5
Married-couple family	360,996	368,023	372,805	0.2
Other family	82,415	100,384	102,195	1.7
Male householder, no wife present........	22,072	31,177	30,769	2.6
Female householder, no husband present......	60,343	69,207	71,426	1.3
Nonfamily households	222,773	250,897	255,579	1.1
Householder living alone................	183,550	205,263	210,853	1.1
Householder not living alone................	39,223	45,634	44,726	1.0
Housing Characteristics				
Total housing units................	722,668	797,677	806,888	0.9
Occupied housing units	666,184	719,304	730,579	0.7
Owner occupied	449,317	484,649	482,452	0.5
Renter occupied	216,867	234,655	248,127	1.0
Average household size................	2.49	2.47	2.49	-
Financial Characteristics				
Median gross rent of renter-occupied housing	491	669	714	2.9
Median monthly owner costs for housing units with a mortgage	895	1,218	1,226	2.5
Median value of owner-occupied housing units........	88,000	127,600	132,700	3.2

- = Zero or rounds to zero

Table NE-4. Migration, Origin, and Language

(Number, percent.)

Characteristic	State 2012	State 2013	State Percent change	U.S. 2012	U.S. 2013	U.S. Percent change
Residence 1 Year Ago						
Population 1 year and over	1,829,420	1,842,900	0.7	310,212,755	312,432,820	0.7
Same house	84.2	83.9	X	85.0	85.0	X
Different house in the U.S.	15.4	15.6	X	14.4	14.4	X
Same county	9.7	9.2	X	9.0	8.9	X
Different county	5.7	6.4	X	5.4	5.5	X
Same state	3.3	3.9	X	3.2	3.2	X
Different state	2.4	2.5	X	2.3	2.3	X
Abroad	0.4	0.5	X	0.6	0.6	X
Place of Birth						
Native born	1,737,003	1,745,334	0.5	273,089,382	274,780,773	0.6
Male	49.6	49.4	X	49.3	49.3	X
Female	50.4	50.6	X	50.7	50.7	X
Foreign born	118,522	123,182	3.9	40,824,658	41,348,066	1.3
Male	51.5	51.4	X	48.7	48.8	X
Female	48.5	48.6	X	51.3	51.2	X
Foreign born; naturalized U.S. citizen................	42,684	41,774	-2.1	18,686,237	19,294,710	3.3
Male	48.7	47.7	X	45.8	45.9	X
Female	51.3	52.3	X	54.2	54.1	X
Foreign born; not a U.S. citizen................	75,838	81,408	7.3	22,138,421	22,053,356	-0.4
Male	53.1	53.3	X	51.1	51.3	X
Female	46.9	46.7	X	48.9	48.7	X
Entered 2010 or later	9.1	14.6	X	7.0	9.7	X
Entered 2000 to 2009	41.1	38.5	X	30.4	29.4	X
Entered before 2000................	49.8	46.9	X	62.7	61.0	X
World Region of Birth, Foreign						
Foreign-born population, excluding population born at sea	118,522	123,182	3.9	40,824,553	41,347,945	1.3
Europe	7.4	7.3	X	11.8	11.6	X
Asia................	26.9	25.7	X	29.2	29.5	X
Africa................	7.8	7.3	X	4.2	4.4	X
Oceania................	0.4	0.7	X	0.6	0.5	X
Latin America................	56.5	57.4	X	52.2	51.9	X
North America................	1.0	1.5	X	2.0	2.0	X
Language Spoken at Home and Ability to Speak English						
Population 5 years and over	1,723,524	1,739,686	0.9	294,003,714	296,358,760	0.8
English only	88.8	89.5	X	79.0	79.2	X
Language other than English................	11.2	10.5	X	21.0	20.8	X
Speaks English less than "very well"................	5.1	4.7	X	8.5	8.5	X

NA = Not available.
X = Not applicable.
- = Zero or rounds to zero.

Table NE-5. Median Income and Poverty Status, 2013

(Number, percent, except as noted.)

Characteristic	State		U.S.	
	Number	Percent	Number	Percent
Median Income				
Households (dollars)...	51,440	X	52,250	X
Families (dollars)	64,763	X	64,030	X
Below Poverty Level (All People)...............................	239,433	13.2	48,810,868	15.8
Sex				
Male...	105,492	11.7	21,938,525	14.5
Female	133,941	14.6	26,872,343	17.1
Age				
Under 18 years..	80,653	17.7	16,086,960	22.2
Related children under 18 years............................	78,551	17.3	15,769,921	21.9
18 to 64 years...	137,514	12.4	28,578,191	14.8
65 years and over	21,266	8.4	4,145,717	9.6

X = Not applicable.

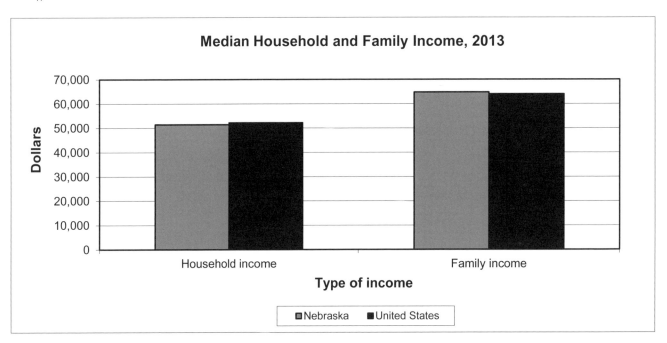

Table NE-6. Health Insurance Coverage Status for the Civilian Noninstitutionalized Population and Children Under 18 Years of Age

(Numbers in thousands, percent.)

Item	2005	2006	2007	2008	2009	2010	2011	2012	2013
Civilian Noninstitutionalized Population............................	1,766	1,767	1,753	1,750	1,763	1,802	1,814	1,827	1,841
Covered by Private or Public Insurance									
Number..	1,581	1,549	1,522	1,555	1,553	1,594	1,607	1,621	1,632
Percent..	89.6	87.7	86.8	88.9	88.1	88.5	88.6	88.7	88.7
Not Covered...									
Number..	185	217	232	195	210	208	207	206	209
Percent..	10.5	12.3	13.2	11.1	11.9	11.5	11.4	11.3	11.3
Percent in the U.S. not covered..	15.3	15.8	15.3	15.1	15.1	15.5	15.1	14.8	14.5
Children Under 18 Years of Age.......................................	439	444	452	445	445	459	459	461	463
Covered by Private or Public Insurance									
Number..	416	399	407	414	417	433	432	433	437
Percent..	94.7	89.9	90.0	93.0	93.7	94.4	94.1	94.0	94.5
Not Covered...									
Number..	23	45	45	31	28	26	27	28	25
Percent..	5.3	10.1	10.0	7.0	6.3	5.6	5.9	6.0	5.5
Percent in the U.S. not covered..	10.9	11.7	11.0	9.7	8.6	8.0	7.5	7.2	7.1

Table NE-7. Employment Status by Demographic Group, 2014

(Numbers in thousands, percent.)

Characteristic	Civilian noninstitutional population	Civilian labor force		Employed		Unemployed	
		Number	Percent of population	Number	Percent of population	Number	Percent of population
Total..................................	1,434	1,016	70.8	983	68.5	33	3.3
Sex							
Male.................................	705	535	75.9	516	73.3	19	3.5
Female	730	481	65.9	466	63.9	15	3.1
Race, Sex, and Hispanic Origin							
White	1,309	927	70.8	900	68.8	27	2.9
Male.................................	642	487	75.8	472	73.5	15	3.1
Female	667	440	66.0	428	64.2	12	2.8
Black or African American....................	58	43	74.4	39	68.2	4	8.3
Male.................................	NA	NA	NA	NA	NA	NA	NA
Female	NA	NA	NA	NA	NA	NA	NA
Hispanic or Latino ethnicity[1]	135	102	75.6	97	71.3	6	5.7
Male.................................	69	59	86.0	56	80.5	4	6.4
Female	66	43	64.8	41	61.7	2	4.8
Age							
16 to 19 years....................	90	47	51.8	42	46.0	5	11.3
20 to 24 years....................	139	113	81.0	107	76.9	6	5.0
25 to 34 years....................	265	228	86.2	221	83.3	8	3.4
35 to 44 years....................	209	184	88.1	179	86.0	4	2.3
45 to 54 years....................	239	210	87.8	206	86.1	4	2.0
55 to 64 years....................	225	168	74.8	165	73.4	3	1.9
65 years and over	267	66	24.6	63	23.5	3	4.4

NOTE: Data in Table 7 are from the Current Population Survey (CPS) and do not match the estimates in Table 8. See notes and definitions for further information.
[1]May be of any race.
NA = Not available.

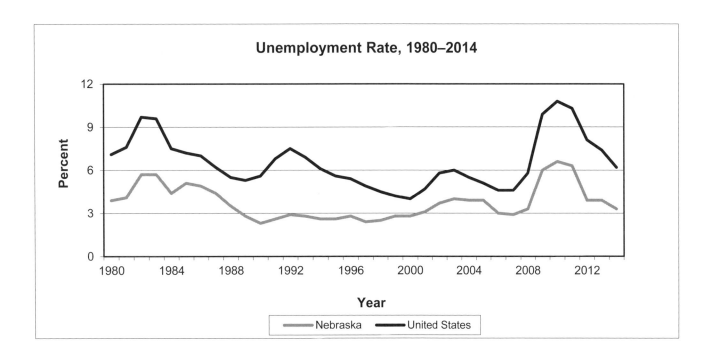

Table NE-8. Employment Status of the Civilian Noninstitutional Population Age 16 Years and Over

(Number, percent.)

Year	Civilian labor force	Civilian participation rate	Employed	Unemployed	Unemployment rate
2006	970,052	72.7	939,874	30,178	3.1
2007	978,763	72.9	949,494	29,269	3.0
2008	989,757	73.2	956,759	32,998	3.3
2009	991,583	72.7	945,648	45,935	4.6
2010	993,398	71.6	947,360	46,038	4.6
2011	1,003,437	71.6	959,345	44,092	4.4
2012	1,016,459	71.9	975,974	40,485	4.0
2013	1,022,062	71.8	983,491	38,571	3.8
2014	1,022,152	71.3	988,249	33,903	3.3

Table NE-9. Employment and Average Wages by Industry

(Estimates from 2007 through 2010 are based on the 2007 *North American Industry Classification System* [NAICS]. Estimates from 2011 onward are based on the 2012 NAICS.)

Industry	2007	2008	2009	2010	2011	2012	2013
	Number of jobs						
Wage and Salary Employment by Industry	989,419	994,614	974,841	972,094	977,551	982,608	1,002,080
Farm Wage and Salary Employment	11,026	10,149	11,549	13,017	13,457	10,154	12,271
Nonfarm Wage and Salary Employment	978,393	984,465	963,292	959,077	964,094	972,454	989,809
Private wage and salary employment	806,706	811,170	787,107	782,045	789,051	798,253	816,370
Forestry, fishing, and related activities	4,268	4,156	4,398	4,634	4,958	5,015	5,896
Mining	961	982	938	940	1,022	1,125	1,043
Utilities	1,660	1,850	1,918	1,656	1,627	1,605	1,290
Construction	51,252	51,148	48,453	43,653	42,634	43,637	45,825
Manufacturing	101,695	101,599	93,466	91,740	93,723	95,232	96,568
Durable goods manufacturing	50,036	49,371	42,697	41,435	42,786	44,013	44,994
Nondurable goods manufacturing	51,659	52,228	50,769	50,305	50,937	51,219	51,574
Wholesale trade	41,296	42,354	41,593	40,945	41,178	41,529	42,158
Retail trade	109,277	109,204	106,159	106,114	106,433	106,547	107,458
Transportation and warehousing	55,302	54,573	51,764	51,086	51,873	52,481	52,627
Information	19,686	18,847	17,520	16,984	17,190	17,217	17,208
Finance and insurance	55,662	56,076	55,107	55,283	55,227	55,545	55,754
Real estate and rental and leasing	9,856	9,648	9,434	9,398	9,309	9,067	9,287
Professional, scientific, and technical services	41,595	43,687	43,063	43,570	43,950	45,152	44,494
Management of companies and enterprises	17,380	16,948	17,164	17,150	16,678	16,702	19,335
Administrative and waste services	46,325	46,263	41,816	41,965	43,251	45,432	46,813
Educational services	17,481	17,625	18,087	18,292	18,621	18,636	18,176
Health care and social assistance	105,713	108,710	109,967	111,811	113,518	115,202	122,047
Arts, entertainment, and recreation	12,371	12,822	12,906	12,413	12,583	13,017	13,454
Accommodation and food services	70,953	70,762	69,637	69,497	70,316	71,758	73,015
Other services, except public administration	43,973	43,916	43,717	44,914	44,960	43,354	43,922
Government and government enterprises	171,687	173,295	176,185	177,032	175,043	174,201	173,439
	Dollars						
Average Wages and Salaries by Industry	36,789	37,942	38,153	38,782	39,869	41,268	41,662
Average Farm Wages and Salaries	44,482	50,981	44,552	35,511	39,151	41,227	44,493
Average Nonfarm Wages and Salaries	36,703	37,808	38,076	38,826	39,879	41,268	41,627
Average private wages and salaries	36,495	37,546	37,643	38,325	39,359	40,901	41,194
Forestry, fishing, and related activities	18,648	21,497	20,949	20,996	23,706	24,749	25,631
Mining	42,287	44,410	43,762	45,790	48,119	52,144	52,407
Utilities	116,528	125,026	96,752	88,457	90,972	92,103	86,304
Construction	40,122	41,048	41,802	41,735	42,097	43,808	44,266
Manufacturing	40,765	42,117	41,983	43,695	44,641	45,593	45,727
Durable goods manufacturing	42,538	44,108	44,151	46,140	48,043	48,525	48,861
Nondurable goods manufacturing	39,048	40,235	40,160	41,681	41,783	43,073	42,993
Wholesale trade	47,905	50,131	49,940	51,243	52,832	55,539	56,209
Retail trade	22,557	23,069	23,133	23,859	24,064	25,064	25,173
Transportation and warehousing	47,507	48,770	47,360	48,605	51,136	51,825	54,305
Information	57,936	51,032	50,677	51,205	54,084	55,238	56,400
Finance and insurance	51,061	52,598	52,848	54,850	57,359	59,873	61,511
Real estate and rental and leasing	31,744	32,267	32,310	32,817	34,225	36,216	37,398
Professional, scientific, and technical services	53,350	56,601	57,806	58,533	59,706	62,565	60,892
Management of companies and enterprises	77,178	79,706	78,977	78,708	80,953	90,716	92,417
Administrative and waste services	27,635	28,341	29,233	29,039	30,080	31,654	32,422
Educational services	28,611	29,585	29,820	30,312	30,479	31,172	30,316
Health care and social assistance	37,808	39,140	39,857	40,084	41,068	42,173	41,060
Arts, entertainment, and recreation	17,552	16,663	16,825	17,683	18,106	18,437	18,761
Accommodation and food services	13,378	13,516	13,628	14,152	14,607	15,154	15,181
Other services, except public administration	24,001	25,181	25,518	26,120	26,637	28,102	28,476
Government and government enterprises	37,677	39,033	40,012	41,041	42,225	42,952	43,666

Table NE-10. Employment Characteristics by Family Type

(Number, percent.)

Family type and labor force status	2011		2012		2013	
	Total	Families with own children under 18 years	Total	Families with own children under 18 years	Total	Families with own children under 18 years
All Families...	470,445	215,933	474,564	216,935	475,000	212,719
FAMILY TYPE AND LABOR FORCE STATUS						
Married-Couple Families.................................	369,983	152,305	369,338	150,038	372,805	149,660
Both husband and wife in labor force...................	63.1	76.3	61.9	76.2	59.7	73.1
Husband in labor force, wife not in labor force	17.3	20.1	17.7	20.3	18.6	23.0
Wife in labor force, husband not in labor force	6.1	2.6	6.6	2.5	6.9	2.6
Both husband and wife not in labor force................	13.5	1.0	13.8	1.1	14.4	1.1
Other Families...	100,462	63,628	105,226	66,897	102,195	63,059
Female householder, no husband present.................	69.9	71.7	69.8	71.3	69.9	72.8
In labor force...	56.7	64.0	55.6	62.5	53.7	63.2
Not in labor force	13.1	7.7	14.2	8.8	16.2	9.7
Male householder, no wife present.........................	30.1	28.3	30.2	28.7	30.1	27.2
In labor force...	24.9	26.0	26.7	27.7	25.9	25.9
Not in labor force	5.3	2.3	3.4	1.0	4.2	1.3

Table NE-11. School Enrollment and Educational Attainment, 2013

(Number, percent.)

Item	State	U.S.
Enrollment		
Total population 3 years and over, enrolled in school	517,420	82,395,254
Enrolled in nursery school or preschool (percent)	6.2	6.0
Enrolled in kindergarten (percent)...................................	5.2	5.2
Enrolled in elementary school, grades 1-8 (percent).................	39.7	40.0
Enrolled in high school, grades 9-12 (percent)	19.6	20.6
Enrolled in college or graduate school (percent)	29.3	28.3
Attainment		
Total population 25 years and over	1,215,208	210,910,615
Less than ninth grade (percent)	4.4	5.8
9th to 12th grade, no diploma (percent)	5.4	7.6
High school graduate, including equivalency (percent)...............	27.1	27.8
Some college, no degree (percent)	23.9	21.1
Associate's degree (percent)	9.8	8.1
Bachelor's degree (percent)	19.6	18.4
Graduate or professional degree (percent)...........................	9.8	11.2
High school graduate or higher (percent)	90.2	86.6
Bachelor's degree or higher (percent)...............................	29.4	29.6

Table NE-12. Public School Characteristics and Educational Indicators

(Number, percent; data derived from National Center of Education Statistics.)

Item	State	U.S.
Public Schools, 2012–2013 (except where noted)		
Number of school districts...	286	18,093
Number of schools...	1,090	98,454
Number of students (in thousands)	304	49,771
Number of teachers (in thousands)	22	3,109
Student-teacher ratio	13.7	16.0
Expenditures per student (dollars), FY 2012	11,640	10,667
Four-year adjusted cohort graduation rate (ACGR)[1,2]	88.5	81.4
Students eligible for free or reduced-price lunch (in thousands) ...	134	25,188
English language learners (in thousands)	17	4,397
Students age 3 to 21 served under IDEA, part B (in thousands)	46	6,429

Public Schools by Type	Number	Percent of state public schools
Total number of schools..	1,090	100.0
Regular	1,011	92.8
Special education..	26	2.4
Vocational education...	0	0.0
Alternative education..	53	4.9

NOTE: Every school is assigned only one school type based on its instructional emphasis.
[1]ACGR data represents a new method of calculating high-school completion rates and may not be comparable to previous years' data for Averaged Freshmen Graduation Rates (AFGR).
[2]The United States 4-year ACGRs were estimated using both the reported 4-year ACGR data from 49 states and the District of Columbia and using imputed data for Idaho. The estimate for American Indian/Alaska Native students also includes imputed data for Virginia.

Table NE-13. Reported Voting and Registration of the Voting-Age Population, November 2012

(Numbers in thousands, percent.)

Item	Total population	Total citizen population	Registered			Voted		
			Total registered	Percent registered (total population)	Percent registered (total citizen population)	Total voted	Percent voted (total population)	Percent voted (total citizen population)
U.S. Total	235,248	215,081	153,157	65.1	71.2	132,948	56.5	61.8
State Total	1,371	1,296	901	65.7	69.5	798	58.2	61.6
Sex								
Male	677	639	441	65.1	69.0	386	57.1	60.4
Female	694	657	460	66.3	70.0	412	59.4	62.7
Race								
White alone	1,265	1,210	846	66.8	69.9	750	59.3	62.0
White, non-Hispanic alone	1,161	1,150	824	70.9	71.6	731	63.0	63.6
Black alone	51	45	32	B	B	29	B	B
Asian alone	31	18	7	B	B	5	B	B
Hispanic (of any race)	110	64	27	25.0	B	21	19.4	B
White alone or in combination	1,283	1,227	857	66.8	69.9	762	59.4	62.0
Black alone or in combination	55	50	37	B	B	33	B	B
Asian alone or in combination	32	18	8	B	B	6	B	B
Age								
18 to 24 years	168	151	71	42.2	47.0	61	36.2	40.3
25 to 44 years	477	442	282	59.1	63.8	238	49.8	53.8
45 to 64 years	462	445	331	71.7	74.5	300	64.9	67.4
65 to 74 years	143	139	119	83.4	85.8	112	78.2	80.5
75 years and over	121	120	98	80.7	81.4	88	72.8	73.5

B = Base is less than 75,000 and therefore too small to show the derived measure.

Table NE-14. Crime

(Number, rate per 100,000. Data are derived from the FBI Uniform Crime Reports.)

Item	State			U.S.[1,2,3,4]		
	2012	2013	Percent change	2012	2013	Percent change
TOTAL POPULATION[5]	1,855,350	1,868,516	0.7	313,873,685	316,128,839	0.7
VIOLENT CRIME						
Number..................................	4,802	4,712	-1.9	1,217,067	1,163,146	-4.4
Rate	258.8	252.2	-2.6	387.8	367.9	-5.1
Murder and Nonnegligent Manslaughter						
Number..................................	52	57	9.6	14,866	14,196	-4.5
Rate	2.8	3.1	8.8	4.7	4.5	-5.2
Rape[6]						
Number..................................	X	801	X	X	108,612	X
Rate	X	42.9	X	X	34.4	X
Robbery						
Number..................................	1,128	1,040	-7.8	355,051	345,031	-2.8
Rate	60.8	55.7	-8.5	113.1	109.1	-3.5
Aggravated Assault						
Number..................................	2,912	2,999	3.0	762,009	724,149	-5.0
Rate	157.0	160.5	2.3	242.8	229.1	-5.6
PROPERTY CRIME						
Number..................................	51,203	49,018	-4.3	9,001,992	8,632,512	-4.1
Rate	2,759.7	2,623.4	-4.9	2,868.0	2,730.7	-4.8
Burglary						
Number..................................	8,745	8,900	1.8	2,109,932	1,928,465	-8.6
Rate	471.3	476.3	1.1	672.2	610.0	-9.3
Larceny-Theft						
Number..................................	38,301	35,655	-6.9	6,168,874	6,004,453	-2.7
Rate	2,064.4	1,908.2	-7.6	1,965.4	1,899.4	-3.4
Motor Vehicle Theft						
Number..................................	4,157	4,463	7.4	723,186	699,594	-3.3
Rate	224.1	238.9	6.6	230.4	221.3	-4.0

NOTE: Although arson data are included in the trend and clearance tables, sufficient data are not available to estimate totals for this offense. Therefore, no arson data are published in this table.
X = Not applicable.
- = Zero or rounds to zero.
[1]The crime figures have been adjusted.
[2]The data collection methodology for the offense of forcible rape used by the Minnesota state Uniform Crime Reporting (UCR) Program (with the exception of Minneapolis and St. Paul, Minnesota) does not comply with national UCR Program guidelines. Consequently, its figures for forcible rape and violent crime (of which forcible rape is a part) are not published in this table.
[3]Includes offenses reported by the Zoological Police and the Metro Transit Police.
[4]Because of changes in the state's reporting practices, figures are not comparable to previous years' data.
[5]Populations are U.S. Census Bureau provisional estimates as of July 1 of each year.
[6]The figures shown for the offense of rape were estimated using the revised Uniform Crime Reporting (UCR) definition of rape.

Table NE-15. State Government Finances, 2013

(Dollar amounts in thousands, percent distribution.)

Item	Dollars	Percent distribution
Total Revenue	11,484,492	100.0
General revenue	9,819,327	85.5
Intergovernmental revenue	3,212,304	28.0
Taxes	4,718,944	41.1
General sales	1,669,380	14.5
Selective sales	528,608	4.6
License taxes	130,762	1.1
Individual income tax	2,101,694	18.3
Corporate income tax	275,563	2.4
Other taxes	12,937	0.1
Current charges	1,028,061	9.0
Miscellaneous general revenue	860,018	7.5
Utility revenue	0	-
Liquor stores revenue	0	-
Insurance trust revenue[1]	1,665,165	14.5
Total Expenditure	9,880,837	100.0
Intergovernmental expenditure	2,170,630	22.0
Direct expenditure	7,710,207	78.0
Current operation	5,891,144	59.6
Capital outlay	879,194	8.9
Insurance benefits and repayments	696,384	7.0
Assistance and subsidies	173,474	1.8
Interest on debt	70,011	0.7
Exhibit: Salaries and wages	2,372,694	24.0
Total Expenditure	9,880,837	100.0
General expenditure	9,184,453	93.0
Intergovernmental expenditure	2,170,630	22.0
Direct expenditure	7,013,823	71.0
General expenditure, by function:		
Education	3,367,219	34.1
Public welfare	2,517,272	25.5
Hospitals	261,809	2.6
Health	476,668	4.8
Highways	754,226	7.6
Police protection	86,623	0.9
Correction	246,519	2.5
Natural resources	251,065	2.5
Parks and recreation	45,105	0.5
Governmental administration	196,763	2.0
Interest on general debt	70,011	0.7
Other and unallocable	911,173	9.2
Utility expenditure	0	-
Liquor stores expenditure	0	-
Insurance trust expenditure	696,384	7.0
Debt at End of Fiscal Year	1,846,583	X
Cash and Security Holdings	15,788,836	X

X = Not applicable.
- = Zero or rounds to zero.

[1]Within insurance trust revenue, net earnings of state retirement systems is a calculated statistic (the item code in the data file is X08), and thus can be positive or negative. Net earnings is the sum of earnings on investments plus gains on investments minus losses on investments. The change made in 2002 for asset valuation from book to market value in accordance with Statement 34 of the Governmental Accounting Standards Board is reflected in the calculated statistics.

Table NE-16. State Government Tax Collections, 2014

(Dollars in thousands, percent.)

Item	Dollars	Percent distribution
Total Taxes	4,877,401	100.0
Property taxes	143	-
Sales and gross receipts	2,303,952	47.2
General sales and gross receipts	1,763,695	36.2
Selective sales and gross receipts	540,257	11.1
Alcoholic beverages	30,258	0.6
Amusements	5,342	0.1
Insurance premiums	42,746	0.9
Motor fuels	335,153	6.9
Pari-mutuels	143	-
Public utilities	53,009	1.1
Tobacco products	63,425	1.3
Other selective sales	10,181	0.2
Licenses	126,745	2.6
Alcoholic beverages	1,475	-
Amusements	1,290	-
Corporations in general	2,123	-
Hunting and fishing	13,576	0.3
Motor vehicle	92,600	1.9
Motor vehicle operators	6,062	0.1
Public utilities	0	-
Occupation and business, NEC	9,619	0.2
Other licenses	0	-
Income taxes	2,430,755	49.8
Individual income	2,124,164	43.6
Corporation net income	306,591	6.3
Other taxes	15,806	0.3
Death and gift	0	-
Documentary and stock transfer	9,044	0.2
Severance	6,762	0.1
Taxes, NEC	0	-

- = Zero or rounds to zero.

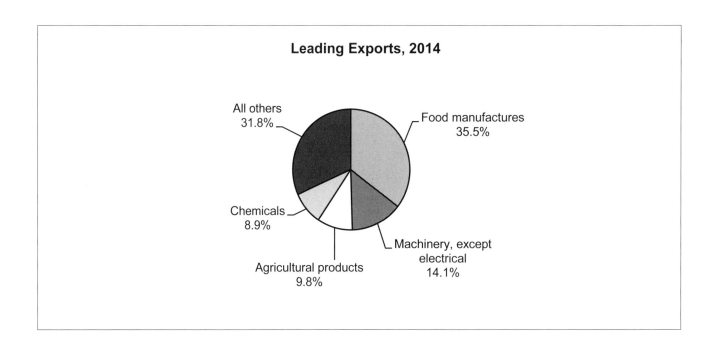

Leading Exports, 2014

All others 31.8%

Food manufactures 35.5%

Chemicals 8.9%

Agricultural products 9.8%

Machinery, except electrical 14.1%

NEVADA

Facts and Figures

Location: Western United States; bordered on the N by Oregon and Idaho, on the E by Utah and Arizona, on the S by Arizona and California, and on the W by California

Area: 110,561 sq. mi. (286,351 sq. km.); rank—7th

Population: 2,839,099 (2014 est.); rank—35th

Principal Cities: capital—Carson City; largest—Las Vegas

Statehood: October 31, 1864; 36th state

U.S. Congress: 2 senators, 4 representatives

State Motto: All for Our Country

State Song: "Home Means Nevada"

State Nicknames: The Silver State; The Sagebrush State

Abbreviations: NV; Nev.

State Symbols: flower—sagebrush; tree—single-leaf piñon and bristlecone pine; bird—mountain bluebird

At a Glance

- With an increase in population of 5.1 percent, Nevada ranked 8th among the states in growth from 2010 to 2014.

- In 2014, 7.8 percent of Nevadans were unemployed, compared to 6.2 percent of the total U.S. population.

- Nevada's violent crime rate in 2013 was 603.0 per 100,000 population, which ranked 4th among the states. The national violent crime rate was 367.9 per 100,000 population.

- Approximately 26.5 percent of Nevadans self-identified their ethnicity as "Hispanic or Latino" in 2014, the 5th highest percentage in the country.

Table NV-1. Population by Age, Sex, Race, and Hispanic Origin

(Number, percent, except where noted.)

Sex, age, race, and Hispanic origin	2000	2010	2014[1]	Average annual percent change, 2010–2014
Total Population	1,998,257	2,700,551	2,839,099	1.3
Percent of total U.S. population	0.7	0.9	0.9	X
Sex				
Male	1,018,051	1,363,616	1,426,793	1.1
Female	980,206	1,336,935	1,412,306	1.4
Age				
Under 5 years	145,817	187,478	176,397	-1.5
5 to 19 years	415,684	548,850	552,449	0.2
20 to 64 years	1,217,827	1,639,864	1,708,406	1.0
65 years and over	218,929	324,359	401,847	5.5
Median age (years)	35.0	36.3	37.5	0.8
Race and Hispanic Origin				
One race				
White	1,501,886	2,106,494	2,163,454	0.7
Black	135,477	231,224	258,492	2.8
American Indian and Alaska Native	26,420	42,965	46,535	2.0
Asian	90,266	203,478	236,304	3.8
Native Hawaiian or Other Pacific Islander	8,426	19,307	21,140	2.3
Two or more races	76,428	97,083	113,174	3.9
Hispanic (of any race)	393,970	741,200	790,034	1.6

X = Not applicable.
[1]Population figures for 2014 are July 1 estimates. The 2010 estimates are taken from the 2010 Census.

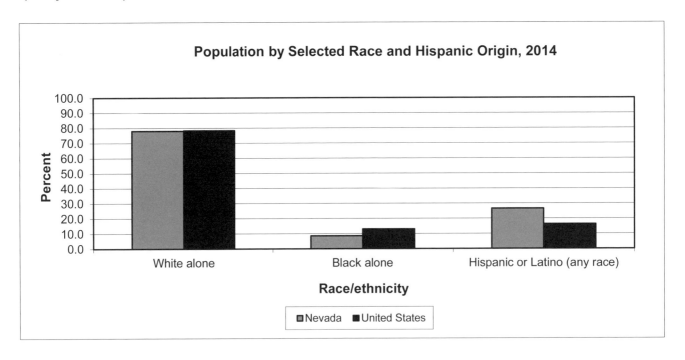

Population by Selected Race and Hispanic Origin, 2014

Legend: Nevada, United States

Table NV-2. Marital Status

(Number, percent distribution.)

Sex, age, race, and Hispanic origin	2000	2010	2013
Males, 15 Years and Over	792,317	1,081,514	1,122,350
Never married	28.8	35.0	36.2
Now married, except separated	53.8	47.6	46.3
Separated	2.0	2.0	1.8
Widowed	2.5	2.9	2.8
Divorced	12.9	12.5	12.9
Females, 15 Years and Over	771,263	1,069,123	1,117,233
Never married	20.9	27.2	28.8
Now married, except separated	53.1	47.2	45.4
Separated	2.7	2.8	3.2
Widowed	8.6	8.0	8.1
Divorced	14.7	14.8	14.4

Table NV-3. Households and Housing Characteristics

(Number, percent, dollars.)

Item	2000	2010	2013	Average annual percent change, 2000–2013
Total Households	751,165	989,811	1,002,571	2.2
Family households	498,333	639,686	639,825	1.9
Married-couple family	373,201	452,361	456,219	1.6
Other family	125,132	187,325	183,606	3.0
Male householder, no wife present	41,650	63,327	56,409	2.4
Female householder, no husband present	83,482	123,998	127,197	3.3
Nonfamily households	252,832	350,125	362,746	2.8
Householder living alone	186,745	266,232	286,932	3.4
Householder not living alone	66,087	83,893	75,814	1.1
Housing Characteristics				
Total housing units	827,457	1,175,070	1,186,936	2.8
Occupied housing units	751,165	989,811	1,002,571	2.2
Owner occupied	457,247	565,869	544,455	1.4
Renter occupied	293,918	423,942	458,116	3.5
Average household size	2.62	2.70	2.75	0.4
Financial Characteristics				
Median gross rent of renter-occupied housing	699	952	952	2.4
Median monthly owner costs for housing units with a mortgage	1,190	1,638	1,361	1.0
Median value of owner-occupied housing units	142,000	174,800	165,300	1.2

Table NV-4. Migration, Origin, and Language

(Number, percent.)

Characteristic	State 2012	State 2013	State Percent change	U.S. 2012	U.S. 2013	U.S. Percent change
Residence 1 Year Ago						
Population 1 year and over	2,725,280	2,757,365	1.2	310,212,755	312,432,820	0.7
Same house	77.2	78.6	X	85.0	85.0	X
Different house in the U.S.	22.2	20.8	X	14.4	14.4	X
Same county	16.7	15.2	X	9.0	8.9	X
Different county	5.5	5.6	X	5.4	5.5	X
Same state	0.9	1.0	X	3.2	3.2	X
Different state	4.6	4.6	X	2.3	2.3	X
Abroad	0.5	0.6	X	0.6	0.6	X
Place of Birth						
Native born	2,228,341	2,260,972	1.5	273,089,382	274,780,773	0.6
Male	50.9	50.8	X	49.3	49.3	X
Female	49.1	49.2	X	50.7	50.7	X
Foreign born	530,590	529,164	-0.3	40,824,658	41,348,066	1.3
Male	48.5	47.9	X	48.7	48.8	X
Female	51.5	52.1	X	51.3	51.2	X
Foreign born; naturalized U.S. citizen	228,471	250,949	9.8	18,686,237	19,294,710	3.3
Male	45.5	46.2	X	45.8	45.9	X
Female	54.5	53.8	X	54.2	54.1	X
Foreign born; not a U.S. citizen	302,119	278,215	-7.9	22,138,421	22,053,356	-0.4
Male	50.7	49.5	X	51.1	51.3	X
Female	49.3	50.5	X	48.9	48.7	X
Entered 2010 or later	4.8	5.8	X	7.0	9.7	X
Entered 2000 to 2009	31.9	28.8	X	30.4	29.4	X
Entered before 2000	63.3	65.4	X	62.7	61.0	X
World Region of Birth, Foreign						
Foreign-born population, excluding population born at sea	530,590	529,164	-0.3	40,824,553	41,347,945	1.3
Europe	7.9	8.0	X	11.8	11.6	X
Asia	29.1	30.6	X	29.2	29.5	X
Africa	2.3	3.0	X	4.2	4.4	X
Oceania	0.6	0.4	X	0.6	0.5	X
Latin America	58.2	56.0	X	52.2	51.9	X
North America	1.8	2.0	X	2.0	2.0	X
Language Spoken at Home and Ability to Speak English						
Population 5 years and over	2,576,019	2,612,849	1.4	294,003,714	296,358,760	0.8
English only	69.8	69.7	X	79.0	79.2	X
Language other than English	30.2	30.3	X	21.0	20.8	X
Speaks English less than "very well"	12.1	11.6	X	8.5	8.5	X

NA = Not available.
X = Not applicable.
- = Zero or rounds to zero.

Table NV-5. Median Income and Poverty Status, 2013

(Number, percent, except as noted.)

Characteristic	State		U.S.	
	Number	Percent	Number	Percent
Median Income				
Households (dollars)..	51,230	X	52,250	X
Families (dollars)	59,462	X	64,030	X
Below Poverty Level (All People)	433,576	15.8	48,810,868	15.8
Sex				
Male..	203,112	14.8	21,938,525	14.5
Female	230,464	16.8	26,872,343	17.1
Age				
Under 18 years..	147,696	22.7	16,086,960	22.2
Related children under 18 years..	143,976	22.2	15,769,921	21.9
18 to 64 years	253,138	14.7	28,578,191	14.8
65 years and over	32,742	8.7	4,145,717	9.6

X = Not applicable.

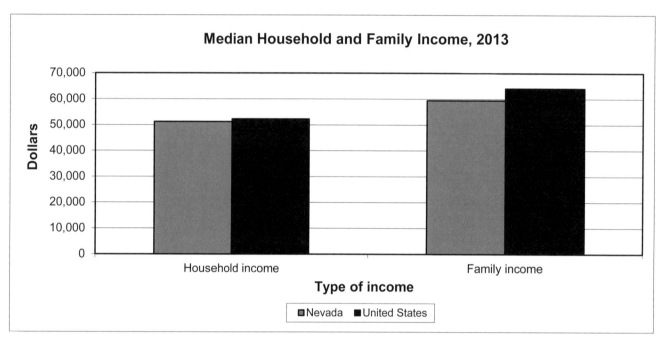

Table NV-6. Health Insurance Coverage Status for the Civilian Noninstitutionalized Population and Children Under 18 Years of Age

(Numbers in thousands, percent.)

Item	2005	2006	2007	2008	2009	2010	2011	2012	2013
Civilian Noninstitutionalized Population	2,448	2,535	2,568	2,568	2,610	2,669	2,687	2,724	2,757
Covered by Private or Public Insurance									
Number..	2,030	2,039	2,126	2,020	2,038	2,065	2,098	2,121	2,187
Percent...	82.9	80.4	82.8	78.7	78.1	77.4	78.1	77.8	79.3
Not Covered									
Number..	418	496	441	548	572	604	589	603	570
Percent...	17.1	19.6	17.2	21.3	21.9	22.6	21.9	22.2	20.7
Percent in the U.S. not covered...	15.3	15.8	15.3	15.1	15.1	15.5	15.1	14.8	14.5
Children Under 18 Years of Age	648	649	660	667	682	664	662	663	661
Covered by Private or Public Insurance									
Number..	555	527	566	532	561	549	155	553	563
Percent...	85.7	81.2	85.7	79.8	82.2	82.6	83.8	83.4	85.1
Not Covered									
Number..	93	122	94	135	121	115	107	110	99
Percent...	14.3	18.8	14.3	20.2	17.8	17.4	16.2	16.6	14.9
Percent in the U.S. not covered...	10.9	11.7	11.0	9.7	8.6	8.0	7.5	7.2	7.1

Table NV-7. Employment Status by Demographic Group, 2014

(Numbers in thousands, percent.)

Characteristic	Civilian noninstitutional population	Civilian labor force		Employed		Unemployed	
		Number	Percent of population	Number	Percent of population	Number	Percent of population
Total...	2,210	1,396	63.2	1,288	58.3	108	7.7
Sex							
Male...	1,097	768	70.0	712	64.9	56	7.3
Female..	1,112	628	56.5	576	51.8	52	8.3
Race, Sex, and Hispanic Origin							
White..	1,679	1,061	63.2	984	58.6	77	7.3
Male...	848	595	70.2	554	65.3	41	6.9
Female..	831	466	56.2	430	51.8	36	7.8
Black or African American...............................	187	114	61.0	96	51.6	18	15.4
Male...	87	53	61.0	46	52.3	8	14.3
Female..	99	61	61.0	51	51.0	10	16.4
Hispanic or Latino ethnicity[1]	522	373	71.5	345	66.1	28	7.5
Male...	264	215	81.3	200	75.7	15	6.8
Female..	258	159	61.4	145	56.3	13	8.4
Age							
16 to 19 years...	144	47	32.6	35	24.2	12	25.7
20 to 24 years...	190	145	76.5	129	68.0	16	11.1
25 to 34 years...	379	312	82.4	291	76.8	21	6.7
35 to 44 years...	383	316	82.6	294	76.7	23	7.1
45 to 54 years...	383	302	78.9	284	74.2	18	5.9
55 to 64 years...	327	198	60.6	188	57.4	11	5.3
65 years and over..	405	75	18.6	67	16.7	8	10.5

NOTE: Data in Table 7 are from the Current Population Survey (CPS) and do not match the estimates in Table 8. See notes and definitions for further information.
[1]May be of any race.

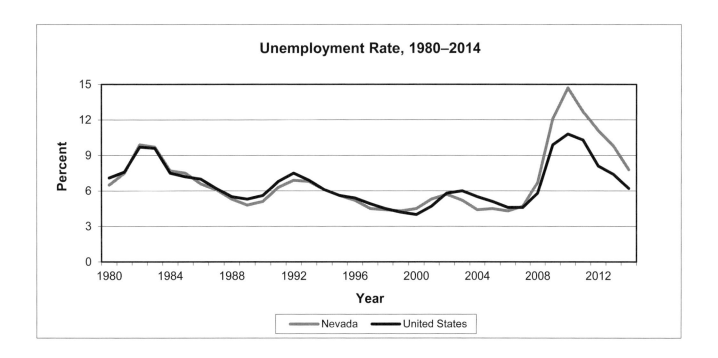

Table NV-8. Employment Status of the Civilian Noninstitutional Population Age 16 Years and Over

(Number, percent.)

Year	Civilian labor force	Civilian participation rate	Employed	Unemployed	Unemployment rate
2006	1,285,318	68.2	1,233,287	52,031	4.0
2007	1,330,396	68.6	1,270,572	59,824	4.5
2008	1,363,574	69.0	1,272,187	91,387	6.7
2009	1,349,299	67.5	1,196,758	152,541	11.3
2010	1,358,578	65.9	1,174,774	183,804	13.5
2011	1,373,663	65.5	1,194,061	179,602	13.1
2012	1,378,361	64.6	1,224,415	153,946	11.2
2013	1,384,463	63.8	1,252,326	132,137	9.5
2014	1,394,599	63.1	1,286,474	108,125	7.8

Table NV-9. Employment and Average Wages by Industry

(Estimates from 2007 through 2010 are based on the 2007 *North American Industry Classification System* [NAICS]. Estimates from 2011 onward are based on the 2012 NAICS.)

Industry	2007	2008	2009	2010	2011	2012	2013
	Number of jobs						
Wage and Salary Employment by Industry	1,332,830	1,305,162	1,188,773	1,158,863	1,166,183	1,181,659	1,209,426
Farm Wage and Salary Employment	1,985	2,085	2,009	2,130	1,949	1,935	2,140
Nonfarm Wage and Salary Employment	1,330,845	1,303,077	1,186,764	1,156,733	1,164,234	1,179,724	1,207,286
Private wage and salary employment	1,161,947	1,128,518	1,015,497	987,759	998,170	1,013,156	1,040,308
Forestry, fishing, and related activities	482	532	524	566	591	595	669
Mining	12,025	12,292	11,630	12,200	13,884	15,428	15,314
Utilities	4,520	4,585	4,571	4,325	4,188	4,037	3,965
Construction	138,923	121,218	84,657	62,103	54,921	53,620	58,944
Manufacturing	50,487	48,260	40,303	38,004	38,259	39,288	40,634
Durable goods manufacturing	34,505	33,001	26,805	24,810	24,693	25,121	25,683
Nondurable goods manufacturing	15,982	15,259	13,498	13,194	13,566	14,167	14,951
Wholesale trade	39,878	39,389	35,343	33,281	33,009	32,785	33,093
Retail trade	141,945	140,500	130,421	129,415	131,017	133,607	136,628
Transportation and warehousing	50,027	50,686	47,125	46,689	47,965	49,925	50,582
Information	15,904	15,097	13,208	12,549	12,560	12,838	12,859
Finance and insurance	38,418	36,495	33,728	32,258	31,754	32,266	33,073
Real estate and rental and leasing	28,233	27,062	23,748	22,627	22,547	22,359	23,400
Professional, scientific, and technical services	55,797	54,667	49,649	48,141	47,896	48,154	49,567
Management of companies and enterprises	16,677	18,246	17,895	18,267	18,086	19,582	20,216
Administrative and waste services	88,554	81,042	69,953	71,705	75,552	78,437	81,525
Educational services	7,952	8,560	8,950	9,652	9,928	9,856	9,702
Health care and social assistance	86,919	90,841	92,172	94,135	96,043	98,034	100,418
Arts, entertainment, and recreation	31,175	29,294	26,540	25,786	27,388	27,142	27,578
Accommodation and food services	310,726	306,354	283,937	285,722	291,193	291,642	298,154
Other services, except public administration	43,305	43,398	41,143	40,334	41,389	43,561	43,987
Government and government enterprises	168,898	174,559	171,267	168,974	166,064	166,568	166,978
	Dollars						
Average Wages and Salaries by Industry	43,760	44,019	43,596	43,637	44,375	44,915	45,356
Average Farm Wages and Salaries	37,142	34,128	39,325	32,224	36,539	31,457	42,606
Average Nonfarm Wages and Salaries	43,769	44,035	43,603	43,658	44,388	44,937	45,360
Average private wages and salaries	43,089	43,119	42,265	42,328	43,227	43,977	44,450
Forestry, fishing, and related activities	28,602	32,778	34,977	34,133	36,203	36,886	35,876
Mining	74,839	77,126	78,537	82,914	84,536	83,065	87,041
Utilities	84,671	87,670	87,856	89,942	94,683	96,358	107,144
Construction	52,390	57,676	58,683	55,475	53,130	52,114	51,443
Manufacturing	47,794	49,764	49,928	50,384	51,753	53,008	53,721
Durable goods manufacturing	51,344	53,895	54,173	54,952	56,747	58,730	60,372
Nondurable goods manufacturing	40,128	40,829	41,499	41,795	42,663	42,861	42,297
Wholesale trade	58,034	59,277	59,428	60,609	62,925	65,697	65,571
Retail trade	28,415	28,015	27,488	27,711	28,220	28,739	29,172
Transportation and warehousing	41,504	44,431	46,410	48,525	50,346	49,658	49,840
Information	51,987	53,834	55,084	55,526	56,871	58,115	58,421
Finance and insurance	55,983	56,266	55,461	57,152	59,342	62,172	65,327
Real estate and rental and leasing	41,014	39,693	38,795	39,244	40,159	40,823	42,027
Professional, scientific, and technical services	65,005	66,208	65,794	66,306	68,210	69,918	70,248
Management of companies and enterprises	148,699	116,522	99,353	102,450	110,820	116,696	121,122
Administrative and waste services	27,886	29,497	29,904	29,739	30,023	29,832	29,657
Educational services	33,308	34,912	35,875	36,122	35,797	35,398	37,344
Health care and social assistance	46,889	47,976	48,944	48,533	49,399	50,203	50,568
Arts, entertainment, and recreation	34,074	33,225	32,949	32,806	34,671	34,228	34,066
Accommodation and food services	36,245	33,805	32,123	33,345	34,616	35,144	35,206
Other services, except public administration	29,537	30,282	30,384	30,909	31,324	32,325	32,922
Government and government enterprises	48,449	49,959	51,540	51,433	51,365	50,772	51,031

Table NV-10. Employment Characteristics by Family Type

(Number, percent.)

Family type and labor force status	2011		2012		2013	
	Total	Families with own children under 18 years	Total	Families with own children under 18 years	Total	Families with own children under 18 years
All Families..	636,981	296,472	650,833	298,464	639,825	286,895
FAMILY TYPE AND LABOR FORCE STATUS						
Married-Couple Families....................................	450,072	191,500	445,312	182,637	456,219	185,645
Both husband and wife in labor force.......................	50.9	62.3	50.1	63.1	49.7	63.1
Husband in labor force, wife not in labor force	23.7	32.2	23.3	31.2	23.7	30.6
Wife in labor force, husband not in labor force	7.9	3.8	8.7	4.1	8.3	4.1
Both husband and wife not in labor force..................	17.6	1.6	17.9	1.5	17.8	2.0
Other Families...	186,909	104,972	205,521	115,827	183,606	101,250
Female householder, no husband present...................	67.1	71.6	68.1	72.2	69.3	72.9
In labor force	50.8	62.0	51.1	59.6	52.1	61.5
Not in labor force	16.3	9.6	17.0	12.6	17.2	11.4
Male householder, no wife present...........................	32.9	28.4	31.9	27.8	30.7	27.1
In labor force	27.0	26.6	26.9	25.6	25.9	25.5
Not in labor force	5.9	1.7	5.0	2.2	4.9	1.6

Table NV-11. School Enrollment and Educational Attainment, 2013

(Number, percent.)

Item	State	U.S.
Enrollment		
Total population 3 years and over, enrolled in school	682,666	82,395,254
Enrolled in nursery school or preschool (percent)..	4.4	6.0
Enrolled in kindergarten (percent)..	5.3	5.2
Enrolled in elementary school, grades 1-8 (percent)...	43.8	40.0
Enrolled in high school, grades 9-12 (percent)...	22.5	20.6
Enrolled in college or graduate school (percent)...	24.0	28.3
Attainment		
Total population 25 years and over	1,872,884	210,910,615
Less than ninth grade (percent)	6.0	5.8
9th to 12th grade, no diploma (percent)	8.8	7.6
High school graduate, including equivalency (percent)	28.4	27.8
Some college, no degree (percent)	26.0	21.1
Associate's degree (percent)...	8.1	8.1
Bachelor's degree (percent)	15.1	18.4
Graduate or professional degree (percent)..	7.5	11.2
High school graduate or higher (percent)	85.2	86.6
Bachelor's degree or higher (percent)..	22.5	29.6

Table NV-12. Public School Characteristics and Educational Indicators

(Number, percent; data derived from National Center of Education Statistics.)

Item	State	U.S.
Public Schools, 2012–2013 (except where noted)		
Number of school districts...	18	18,093
Number of schools...	664	98,454
Number of students (in thousands)	446	49,771
Number of teachers (in thousands)	21	3,109
Student-teacher ratio	21.5	16.0
Expenditures per student (dollars), FY 2012...	8,130	10,667
Four-year adjusted cohort graduation rate (ACGR)[1,2]	70.7	81.4
Students eligible for free or reduced-price lunch (in thousands)	229	25,188
English language learners (in thousands)	68	4,397
Students age 3 to 21 served under IDEA, part B (in thousands)	50	6,429

Public Schools by Type	Number	Percent of state public schools
Total number of schools..	664	100.0
Regular	599	90.2
Special education..	12	1.8
Vocational education...	1	0.2
Alternative education	52	7.8

NOTE: Every school is assigned only one school type based on its instructional emphasis.
[1]ACGR data represents a new method of calculating high-school completion rates and may not be comparable to previous years' data for Averaged Freshmen Graduation Rates (AFGR).
[2]The United States 4-year ACGRs were estimated using both the reported 4-year ACGR data from 49 states and the District of Columbia and using imputed data for Idaho. The estimate for American Indian/Alaska Native students also includes imputed data for Virginia.

Table NV-13. Reported Voting and Registration of the Voting-Age Population, November 2012

(Numbers in thousands, percent.)

Item	Total population	Total citizen population	Registered			Voted		
			Total registered	Percent registered (total population)	Percent registered (total citizen population)	Total voted	Percent voted (total population)	Percent voted (total citizen population)
U.S. Total	235,248	215,081	153,157	65.1	71.2	132,948	56.5	61.8
State Total	2,039	1,808	1,176	57.7	65.0	1,048	51.4	57.9
Sex								
Male	1,015	910	574	56.5	63.1	511	50.3	56.2
Female	1,024	898	602	58.8	67.0	536	52.4	59.7
Race								
White alone	1,627	1,439	947	58.2	65.8	845	51.9	58.7
White, non-Hispanic alone	1,194	1,167	785	65.7	67.2	704	58.9	60.3
Black alone	169	164	107	63.3	65.1	101	60.2	61.8
Asian alone	152	115	82	54.4	71.9	67	44.5	58.8
Hispanic (of any race)	464	302	181	38.9	59.9	157	33.7	52.0
White alone or in combination	1,674	1,484	966	57.7	65.1	860	51.4	57.9
Black alone or in combination	185	181	112	60.6	62.1	107	57.7	59.2
Asian alone or in combination	164	127	90	54.8	70.8	73	44.7	57.7
Age								
18 to 24 years	320	295	145	45.4	49.1	122	38.2	41.4
25 to 44 years	671	557	348	51.9	62.5	304	45.3	54.5
45 to 64 years	680	606	413	60.7	68.1	376	55.2	61.9
65 to 74 years	220	206	159	72.2	77.0	147	67.1	71.5
75 years and over	149	144	112	75.0	77.9	99	66.4	68.9

Table NV-14. Crime

(Number, rate per 100,000. Data are derived from the FBI Uniform Crime Reports.)

Item	State			U.S.[1,2,3,4]		
	2012	2013	Percent change	2012	2013	Percent change
TOTAL POPULATION[5]	2,754,354	2,790,136	1.3	313,873,685	316,128,839	0.7
VIOLENT CRIME						
Number	16,763	16,496	-1.6	1,217,067	1,163,146	-4.4
Rate	608.6	591.2	-2.9	387.8	367.9	-5.1
Murder and Nonnegligent Manslaughter						
Number	124	163	31.5	14,866	14,196	-4.5
Rate	4.5	5.8	29.8	4.7	4.5	-5.2
Rape[6]						
Number	X	1,418	X	X	108,612	X
Rate	X	50.8	X	X	34.4	X
Robbery						
Number	4,918	5,183	5.4	355,051	345,031	-2.8
Rate	178.6	185.8	4.0	113.1	109.1	-3.5
Aggravated Assault						
Number	10,790	10,060	-6.8	762,009	724,149	-5.0
Rate	391.7	360.6	-8.0	242.8	229.1	-5.6
PROPERTY CRIME						
Number	77,510	79,177	2.2	9,001,992	8,632,512	-4.1
Rate	2,814.1	2,837.7	0.8	2,868.0	2,730.7	-4.8
Burglary						
Number	22,120	23,047	4.2	2,109,932	1,928,465	-8.6
Rate	803.1	826.0	2.9	672.2	610.0	-9.3
Larceny-Theft						
Number	45,372	46,132	1.7	6,168,874	6,004,453	-2.7
Rate	1,647.3	1,653.4	0.4	1,965.4	1,899.4	-3.4
Motor Vehicle Theft						
Number	10,018	9,998	-0.2	723,186	699,594	-3.3
Rate	363.7	358.3	-1.5	230.4	221.3	-4.0

NOTE: Although arson data are included in the trend and clearance tables, sufficient data are not available to estimate totals for this offense. Therefore, no arson data are published in this table.
X = Not applicable.
- = Zero or rounds to zero.
[1]The crime figures have been adjusted.
[2]The data collection methodology for the offense of forcible rape used by the Minnesota state Uniform Crime Reporting (UCR) Program (with the exception of Minneapolis and St. Paul, Minnesota) does not comply with national UCR Program guidelines. Consequently, its figures for forcible rape and violent crime (of which forcible rape is a part) are not published in this table.
[3]Includes offenses reported by the Zoological Police and the Metro Transit Police.
[4]Because of changes in the state's reporting practices, figures are not comparable to previous years' data.
[5]Populations are U.S. Census Bureau provisional estimates as of July 1 of each year.
[6]The figures shown for the offense of rape were estimated using the revised Uniform Crime Reporting (UCR) definition of rape.

Table NV-15. State Government Finances, 2013

(Dollar amounts in thousands, percent distribution.)

Item	Dollars	Percent distribution
Total Revenue	17,040,569	100.0
General revenue	11,402,396	66.9
Intergovernmental revenue	3,080,240	18.1
Taxes	7,026,626	41.2
General sales	3,637,356	21.3
Selective sales	1,831,007	10.7
License taxes	586,801	3.4
Individual income tax	0	-
Corporate income tax	0	-
Other taxes	971,462	5.7
Current charges	673,634	4.0
Miscellaneous general revenue	621,896	3.6
Utility revenue	79,165	0.5
Liquor stores revenue	0	-
Insurance trust revenue[1]	5,559,008	32.6
Total Expenditure	13,273,807	100.0
Intergovernmental expenditure	4,214,581	31.8
Direct expenditure	9,059,226	68.2
Current operation	5,368,958	40.4
Capital outlay	632,219	4.8
Insurance benefits and repayments	2,550,727	19.2
Assistance and subsidies	315,805	2.4
Interest on debt	191,517	1.4
Exhibit: Salaries and wages	1,563,233	11.8
Total Expenditure	13,273,807	100.0
General expenditure	10,639,400	80.2
Intergovernmental expenditure	4,214,581	31.8
Direct expenditure	6,424,819	48.4
General expenditure, by function:		
Education	4,365,150	32.9
Public welfare	2,400,389	18.1
Hospitals	265,446	2.0
Health	275,542	2.1
Highways	721,780	5.4
Police protection	101,604	0.8
Correction	283,918	2.1
Natural resources	116,153	0.9
Parks and recreation	19,216	0.1
Governmental administration	296,341	2.2
Interest on general debt	189,309	1.4
Other and unallocable	1,604,552	12.1
Utility expenditure	83,680	0.6
Liquor stores expenditure	0	-
Insurance trust expenditure	2,550,727	19.2
Debt at End of Fiscal Year	3,609,752	X
Cash and Security Holdings	31,311,152	X

X = Not applicable.
- = Zero or rounds to zero.

[1]Within insurance trust revenue, net earnings of state retirement systems is a calculated statistic (the item code in the data file is X08), and thus can be positive or negative. Net earnings is the sum of earnings on investments plus gains on investments minus losses on investments. The change made in 2002 for asset valuation from book to market value in accordance with Statement 34 of the Governmental Accounting Standards Board is reflected in the calculated statistics.

Table NV-16. State Government Tax Collections, 2014

(Dollars in thousands, percent.)

Item	Dollars	Percent distribution
Total Taxes	7,143,169	100.0
Property taxes	258,600	3.6
Sales and gross receipts	5,714,197	80.0
General sales and gross receipts	3,828,869	53.6
Selective sales and gross receipts	1,885,328	26.4
Alcoholic beverages	42,917	0.6
Amusements	947,290	13.3
Insurance premiums	264,522	3.7
Motor fuels	296,649	4.2
Pari-mutuels	0	-
Public utilities	22,636	0.3
Tobacco products	102,116	1.4
Other selective sales	209,198	2.9
Licenses	608,375	8.5
Alcoholic beverages	0	-
Amusements	95,717	1.3
Corporations in general	66,665	0.9
Hunting and fishing	10,496	0.1
Motor vehicle	166,067	2.3
Motor vehicle operators	26,517	0.4
Public utilities	0	-
Occupation and business, NEC	239,476	3.4
Other licenses	3,437	-
Income taxes	0	-
Individual income	X	X
Corporation net income	X	X
Other taxes	561,997	7.9
Death and gift	50	-
Documentary and stock transfer	64,712	0.9
Severance	111,395	1.6
Taxes, NEC	385,840	5.4

X = Not applicable.
- = Zero or rounds to zero.

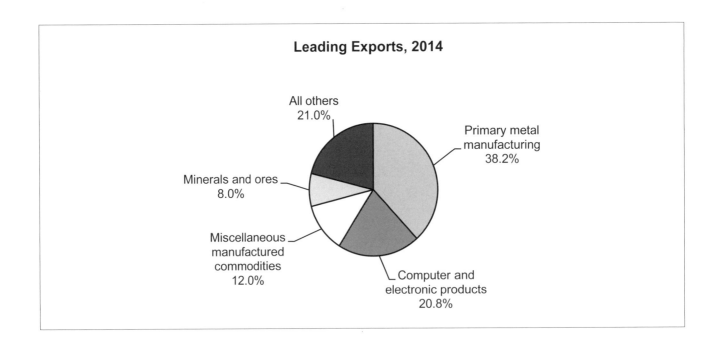

Leading Exports, 2014

All others 21.0%

Primary metal manufacturing 38.2%

Minerals and ores 8.0%

Miscellaneous manufactured commodities 12.0%

Computer and electronic products 20.8%

Facts and Figures

Location: Northeastern United States; bordered on the N by Canada (Quebec), on the E by Maine, on the SE by the Atlantic Ocean, on the S by Massachusetts, and on the W by Vermont

Area: 9,350 sq. mi. (24,216 sq. km.); rank—46th

Population: 1,326,813 (2014 est.); rank—42nd

Principal Cities: capital—Concord; largest—Manchester

Statehood: June 21, 1788; 9th state

U.S. Congress: 2 senators, 2 representatives

State Motto: Live Free or Die

State Song: "Old New Hampshire"

State Nickname: The Granite State

Abbreviations: NH; N.H.

State Symbols: flower—purple lilac; tree—white birch; bird—purple finch

At a Glance

- With an increase in population of 0.8 percent, New Hampshire ranked 42nd among the states in growth from 2010 to 2014.

- New Hampshire's violent crime rate in 2013 was 215.3 per 100,000 population, the 6th lowest in the country, compared to a rate of 367.9 for the entire nation.

- The state's property crime rate, 2,194.3 per 100,000 population, ranked 39th in the country in 2013.

- In 2013, 10.7 percent of New Hampshirites did not have health insurance, compared to 14.5 percent of the entire U.S. populace.

- New Hampshire's unemployment rate of 4.3 percent in 2014 ranked 44th nationwide.

- New Hampshire had the lowest birth rate in the country in 2013, with 9.4 births per 1,000 population.

Table NH-1. Population by Age, Sex, Race, and Hispanic Origin

(Number, percent, except where noted.)

Sex, age, race, and Hispanic origin	2000	2010	2014[1]	Average annual percent change, 2010–2014
Total Population	1,235,786	1,316,470	1,326,813	0.2
Percent of total U.S. population	0.4	0.4	0.4	X
Sex				
Male	607,687	649,394	655,469	0.2
Female	628,099	667,076	671,344	0.2
Age				
Under 5 years	75,685	69,806	64,545	-1.9
5 to 19 years	268,480	255,996	240,847	-1.5
20 to 64 years	743,651	812,400	810,358	-0.1
65 years and over	147,970	178,268	211,063	4.3
Median age (years)	37.1	41.1	42.6	0.9
Race and Hispanic Origin				
One race				
White	1,186,851	1,248,321	1,247,714	-
Black	9,035	16,365	19,686	4.7
American Indian and Alaska Native	2,964	3,530	3,849	2.2
Asian	15,931	28,933	33,742	3.9
Native Hawaiian or Other Pacific Islander	371	532	636	4.6
Two or more races	13,214	18,789	21,186	3.0
Hispanic (of any race)	20,489	38,688	43,544	3.0

X = Not applicable.
- = Zero or rounds to zero.
[1]Population figures for 2014 are July 1 estimates. The 2010 estimates are taken from the 2010 Census.

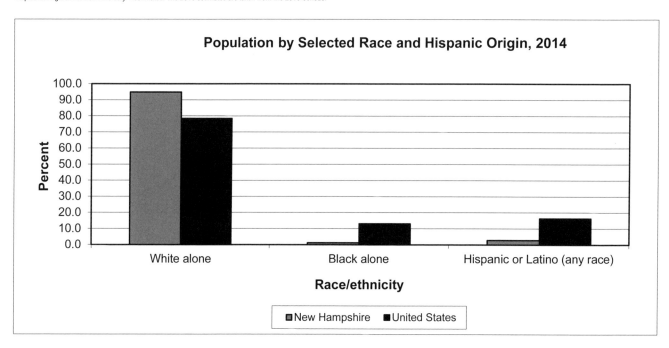

Table NH-2. Marital Status

(Number, percent distribution.)

Sex, age, race, and Hispanic origin	2000	2010	2013
Males, 15 Years and Over	476,409	529,439	541,785
Never married	27.7	30.5	31.9
Now married, except separated	59.1	54.7	53.7
Separated	1.2	1.3	1.2
Widowed	2.4	2.6	2.3
Divorced	9.6	10.9	10.8
Females, 15 Years and Over	502,232	555,698	561,936
Never married	22.3	25.4	26.7
Now married, except separated	55.7	51.4	50.0
Separated	1.5	1.3	1.6
Widowed	9.2	8.6	8.4
Divorced	11.3	13.4	13.3

Table NH-3. Households and Housing Characteristics

(Number, percent, dollars.)

Item	2000	2010	2013	Average annual percent change, 2000–2013
Total Households...	474,606	515,431	519,246	0.7
Family households	323,651	344,057	347,272	0.5
Married-couple family	262,438	274,195	272,206	0.3
Other family	61,213	69,862	75,066	1.6
Male householder, no wife present............................	18,261	22,205	22,694	1.7
Female householder, no husband present....................	42,952	47,657	52,372	1.5
Nonfamily households	150,955	171,374	171,974	1.0
Householder living alone	116,014	130,327	132,592	1.0
Householder not living alone.................................	34,941	41,047	39,382	0.9
Housing Characteristics				
Total housing units..	547,024	614,996	616,496	0.9
Occupied housing units	474,606	515,431	519,246	0.7
Owner occupied	330,700	369,448	364,255	0.7
Renter occupied	143,906	145,983	154,991	0.6
Average household size..	2.53	2.48	2.47	-0.2
Financial Characteristics				
Median gross rent of renter-occupied housing	646	951	995	3.4
Median monthly owner costs for housing units with a mortgage	1,226	1,853	1,778	2.9
Median value of owner-occupied housing units.............	133,300	243,000	233,300	4.4

Table NH-4. Migration, Origin, and Language

(Number, percent.)

Characteristic	State			U.S.		
	2012	2013	Percent change	2012	2013	Percent change
Residence 1 Year Ago						
Population 1 year and over	1,309,203	1,310,978	0.1	310,212,755	312,432,820	0.7
Same house	86.1	86.1	X	85.0	85.0	X
Different house in the U.S.	13.4	13.4	X	14.4	14.4	X
Same county	7.1	7.7	X	9.0	8.9	X
Different county	6.3	5.7	X	5.4	5.5	X
Same state	2.4	2.3	X	3.2	3.2	X
Different state	3.9	3.4	X	2.3	2.3	X
Abroad	0.5	0.5	X	0.6	0.6	X
Place of Birth						
Native born	1,249,349	1,248,284	-0.1	273,089,382	274,780,773	0.6
Male	49.3	49.5	X	49.3	49.3	X
Female	50.7	50.5	X	50.7	50.7	X
Foreign born	71,369	75,175	5.3	40,824,658	41,348,066	1.3
Male	45.7	46.4	X	48.7	48.8	X
Female	54.3	53.6	X	51.3	51.2	X
Foreign born; naturalized U.S. citizen............................	34,864	40,448	16.0	18,686,237	19,294,710	3.3
Male	42.4	45.6	X	45.8	45.9	X
Female	57.6	54.4	X	54.2	54.1	X
Foreign born; not a U.S. citizen...................................	36,505	34,727	-4.9	22,138,421	22,053,356	-0.4
Male	48.8	47.3	X	51.1	51.3	X
Female	51.2	52.7	X	48.9	48.7	X
Entered 2010 or later	10.3	11.7	X	7.0	9.7	X
Entered 2000 to 2009	28.9	27.2	X	30.4	29.4	X
Entered before 2000..	60.8	61.1	X	62.7	61.0	X
World Region of Birth, Foreign						
Foreign-born population, excluding population born at sea	71,354	75,175	5.4	40,824,553	41,347,945	1.3
Europe	25.6	25.6	X	11.8	11.6	X
Asia..	37.3	35.3	X	29.2	29.5	X
Africa	4.2	4.3	X	4.2	4.4	X
Oceania	0.9	0.3	X	0.6	0.5	X
Latin America	18.8	21.3	X	52.2	51.9	X
North America	13.3	13.3	X	2.0	2.0	X
Language Spoken at Home and Ability to Speak English						
Population 5 years and over..	1,255,212	1,257,652	0.2	294,003,714	296,358,760	0.8
English only	92.1	91.6	X	79.0	79.2	X
Language other than English.......................................	7.9	8.4	X	21.0	20.8	X
Speaks English less than "very well"............................	2.4	2.5	X	8.5	8.5	X

NA = Not available.
X = Not applicable.
- = Zero or rounds to zero.

Table NH-5. Median Income and Poverty Status, 2013

(Number, percent, except as noted.)

Characteristic	State		U.S.	
	Number	Percent	Number	Percent
Median Income				
Households (dollars)..	64,230	X	52,250	X
Families (dollars)	77,646	X	64,030	X
Below Poverty Level (All People)	111,495	8.7	48,810,868	15.8
Sex				
Male...	49,727	7.9	21,938,525	14.5
Female	61,768	9.5	26,872,343	17.1
Age				
Under 18 years...	27,122	10.2	16,086,960	22.2
Related children under 18 years..	25,586	9.7	15,769,921	21.9
18 to 64 years..	73,431	8.9	28,578,191	14.8
65 years and over	10,942	5.6	4,145,717	9.6

X = Not applicable.

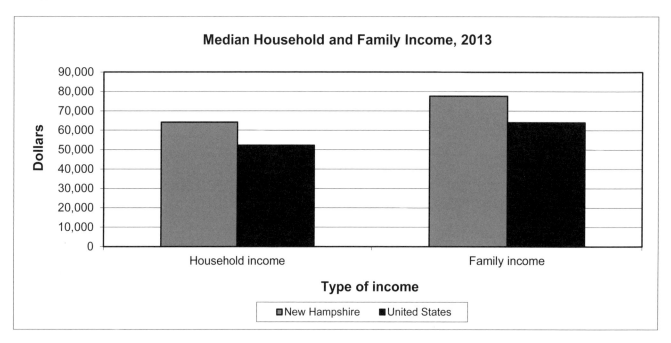

Table NH-6. Health Insurance Coverage Status for the Civilian Noninstitutionalized Population and Children Under 18 Years of Age

(Numbers in thousands, percent.)

Item	2005	2006	2007	2008	2009	2010	2011	2012	2013
Civilian Noninstitutionalized Population	1,301	1,309	1,314	1,299	1,309	1,303	1,304	1,306	1,309
Covered by Private or Public Insurance									
Number	1,175	119	1,177	1,159	1,175	1,157	1,167	1,167	1,168
Percent..	90.3	88.5	89.5	89.2	89.8	88.9	89.5	89.4	89.3
Not Covered									
Number	126	150	137	140	134	145	137	139	140
Percent..	9.7	11.5	10.5	10.8	10.2	11.1	10.5	10.6	10.7
Percent in the U.S. not covered...	15.3	15.8	15.3	15.1	15.1	15.5	15.1	14.8	14.5
Children Under 18 Years of Age...	298	301	296	293	289	286	279	275	271
Covered by Private or Public Insurance									
Number	282	278	277	278	276	272	269	264	260
Percent..	94.7	92.5	93.5	94.9	95.3	95.2	96.3	96.0	96.2
Not Covered									
Number	16	22	19	15	13	14	10	11	10
Percent..	5.3	7.5	6.5	5.1	4.7	4.8	3.7	4.0	3.8
Percent in the U.S. not covered...	10.9	11.7	11.0	9.7	8.6	8.0	7.5	7.2	7.1

Table NH-7. Employment Status by Demographic Group, 2014

(Numbers in thousands, percent.)

Characteristic	Civilian noninstitutional population	Civilian labor force		Employed		Unemployed	
		Number	Percent of population	Number	Percent of population	Number	Percent of population
Total..	1,079	739	68.5	708	65.6	31	4.2
Sex							
Male..	529	384	72.6	367	69.4	17	4.4
Female	550	355	64.5	341	61.9	14	4.0
Race, Sex, and Hispanic Origin							
White..	1,025	703	68.5	673	65.6	30	4.2
Male..	503	365	72.5	348	69.2	16	4.5
Female	523	338	64.7	325	62.1	13	4.0
Black or African American......................	14	10	69.8	9	64.9	1	7.0
Male..	NA	NA	NA	NA	NA	NA	NA
Female	NA	NA	NA	NA	NA	NA	NA
Hispanic or Latino ethnicity[1]	27	22	80.0	20	71.9	2	10.0
Male..	14	12	86.4	11	77.0	1	10.9
Female	13	10	73.0	9	66.5	1	8.9
Age							
16 to 19 years...................................	63	30	47.5	26	41.2	4	13.3
20 to 24 years...................................	92	71	76.7	65	71.0	5	7.5
25 to 34 years...................................	158	135	85.9	130	82.2	6	4.3
35 to 44 years...................................	157	136	87.0	133	84.6	4	2.7
45 to 54 years...................................	204	176	86.2	171	83.6	5	3.0
55 to 64 years...................................	198	145	73.4	140	70.9	5	3.3
65 years and over	207	45	21.9	43	20.8	2	5.0

NOTE: Data in Table 7 are from the Current Population Survey (CPS) and do not match the estimates in Table 8. See notes and definitions for further information.
[1]May be of any race.
NA = Not available.

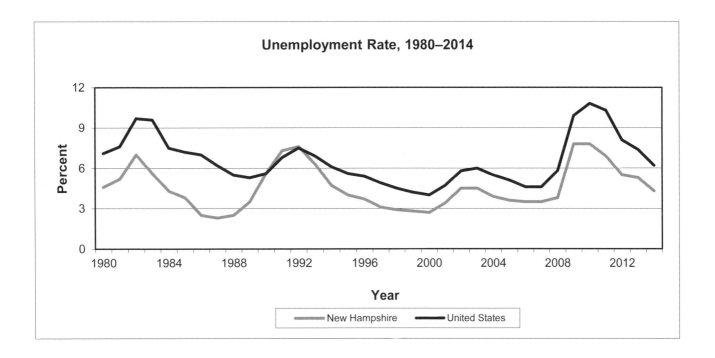

Table NH-8. Employment Status of the Civilian Noninstitutional Population Age 16 Years and Over

(Number, percent.)

Year	Civilian labor force	Civilian participation rate	Employed	Unemployed	Unemployment rate
2006	731,854	70.9	706,777	25,077	3.4
2007	737,942	70.8	712,008	25,934	3.5
2008	742,781	70.7	714,104	28,677	3.9
2009	744,227	70.4	697,802	46,425	6.2
2010	738,257	69.9	695,135	43,122	5.8
2011	736,077	69.5	696,326	39,751	5.4
2012	740,323	69.4	699,589	40,734	5.5
2013	742,017	69.2	704,294	37,723	5.1
2014	741,178	68.7	709,219	31,959	4.3

Table NH-9. Employment and Average Wages by Industry

(Estimates from 2007 through 2010 are based on the 2007 *North American Industry Classification System* [NAICS]. Estimates from 2011 onward are based on the 2012 NAICS.)

Industry	2007	2008	2009	2010	2011	2012	2013
	Number of jobs						
Wage and Salary Employment by Industry	660,712	659,277	636,169	633,655	638,856	642,126	648,182
Farm Wage and Salary Employment	1,081	1,180	1,139	1,141	1,210	1,225	1,452
Nonfarm Wage and Salary Employment	659,631	658,097	635,030	632,514	637,646	640,901	646,730
Private wage and salary employment	564,948	562,461	538,792	534,869	541,705	545,847	552,254
Forestry, fishing, and related activities	805	810	785	775	778	764	776
Mining	682	607	510	490	493	501	531
Utilities	2,521	2,454	2,532	2,513	2,474	2,454	2,480
Construction	28,568	27,161	23,700	22,437	23,338	22,918	23,361
Manufacturing	77,974	76,095	68,115	65,821	66,667	66,075	66,082
Durable goods manufacturing	59,763	58,096	51,982	50,313	51,168	50,230	49,916
Nondurable goods manufacturing	18,211	17,999	16,133	15,508	15,499	15,845	16,166
Wholesale trade	28,574	28,289	26,649	26,093	26,383	26,727	26,882
Retail trade	99,293	98,298	94,565	94,033	94,604	95,347	95,761
Transportation and warehousing	13,139	12,930	12,383	12,346	12,524	12,602	12,614
Information	12,377	12,547	12,181	11,220	11,151	12,103	11,936
Finance and insurance	29,610	29,201	27,870	27,525	28,173	28,889	29,184
Real estate and rental and leasing	8,111	7,850	7,354	7,044	7,051	6,728	6,979
Professional, scientific, and technical services	30,525	31,433	29,948	29,686	30,345	30,696	32,063
Management of companies and enterprises	7,889	8,170	7,968	8,013	8,098	8,155	8,184
Administrative and waste services	27,815	27,753	25,864	27,661	28,856	30,011	30,756
Educational services	22,034	22,160	22,229	22,043	22,280	22,583	22,932
Health care and social assistance	80,862	82,900	84,749	85,391	85,739	86,097	86,737
Arts, entertainment, and recreation	10,969	11,099	11,081	11,199	11,479	11,364	11,447
Accommodation and food services	53,712	53,355	51,513	52,061	52,651	53,654	55,313
Other services, except public administration	29,488	29,349	28,796	28,518	28,621	28,179	28,236
Government and government enterprises	94,683	95,636	96,238	97,645	95,941	95,054	94,476
	Dollars						
Average Wages and Salaries by Industry	43,278	44,249	44,197	45,150	46,380	47,491	48,201
Average Farm Wages and Salaries	32,781	28,812	28,356	26,736	22,556	24,973	28,706
Average Nonfarm Wages and Salaries	43,295	44,277	44,225	45,183	46,425	47,534	48,244
Average private wages and salaries	44,066	44,918	44,684	45,896	47,183	48,441	49,139
Forestry, fishing, and related activities	37,652	34,717	34,851	36,034	37,478	43,800	41,473
Mining	50,419	50,936	52,245	55,849	55,507	56,655	53,305
Utilities	77,457	91,296	87,771	87,860	96,418	94,523	94,702
Construction	48,389	49,942	49,068	49,392	50,144	51,485	52,979
Manufacturing	57,843	58,738	58,299	61,926	63,219	63,337	64,602
Durable goods manufacturing	61,193	62,066	61,533	65,486	66,697	66,557	67,946
Nondurable goods manufacturing	46,849	47,995	47,876	50,376	51,735	53,131	54,276
Wholesale trade	71,292	72,268	70,957	74,646	77,793	80,535	82,132
Retail trade	26,490	26,502	26,350	26,760	27,406	27,935	28,497
Transportation and warehousing	36,016	36,684	36,602	37,434	38,705	39,332	40,299
Information	67,251	71,344	69,375	75,172	74,503	75,499	78,854
Finance and insurance	71,078	73,916	74,362	78,080	81,346	84,450	85,902
Real estate and rental and leasing	37,958	43,846	43,993	40,820	47,017	44,889	46,082
Professional, scientific, and technical services	69,018	73,296	72,500	74,270	76,812	79,566	80,125
Management of companies and enterprises	105,067	77,627	76,944	80,829	82,361	97,872	89,710
Administrative and waste services	38,534	38,712	40,207	40,031	40,296	42,659	42,393
Educational services	37,046	38,585	39,360	40,020	40,638	41,424	42,643
Health care and social assistance	42,406	44,568	45,709	46,500	47,829	48,486	49,120
Arts, entertainment, and recreation	25,338	21,981	21,073	21,263	21,597	22,036	22,969
Accommodation and food services	18,597	18,151	18,462	18,880	19,339	19,612	19,730
Other services, except public administration	28,060	29,282	28,856	29,739	30,126	31,304	32,600
Government and government enterprises	38,696	40,505	41,653	41,277	42,148	42,328	43,016

Table NH-10. Employment Characteristics by Family Type

(Number, percent.)

Family type and labor force status	2011		2012		2013	
	Total	Families with own children under 18 years	Total	Families with own children under 18 years	Total	Families with own children under 18 years
All Families...	349,501	145,570	341,718	139,546	347,272	145,235
FAMILY TYPE AND LABOR FORCE STATUS						
Married-Couple Families......................	276,775	103,769	269,048	97,873	272,206	102,397
Both husband and wife in labor force..................	60.1	72.8	59.3	72.1	56.3	71.7
Husband in labor force, wife not in labor force	17.1	22.6	17.5	23.3	19.9	23.5
Wife in labor force, husband not in labor force	8.0	3.3	7.3	3.1	7.6	3.0
Both husband and wife not in labor force................	14.8	1.3	15.9	1.5	15.4	1.3
Other Families	72,726	41,801	72,670	41,673	75,066	42,838
Female householder, no husband present................	70.5	72.5	70.2	71.9	69.8	70.0
In labor force....................................	50.4	59.0	53.8	59.2	53.0	59.7
Not in labor force	20.0	13.5	16.3	12.7	16.8	10.3
Male householder, no wife present........................	29.5	27.5	29.8	28.1	30.2	30.0
In labor force....................................	23.9	24.9	24.6	24.9	24.2	26.5
Not in labor force	5.7	2.6	5.2	3.1	6.0	3.5

Table NH-11. School Enrollment and Educational Attainment, 2013

(Number, percent.)

Item	State	U.S.
Enrollment		
Total population 3 years and over, enrolled in school	318,912	82,395,254
Enrolled in nursery school or preschool (percent)......................	5.9	6.0
Enrolled in kindergarten (percent)..	4.4	5.2
Enrolled in elementary school, grades 1-8 (percent)...................	39.1	40.0
Enrolled in high school, grades 9-12 (percent).........................	21.5	20.6
Enrolled in college or graduate school (percent).......................	29.1	28.3
Attainment		
Total population 25 years and over	924,568	210,910,615
Less than ninth grade (percent)...	2.9	5.8
9th to 12th grade, no diploma (percent)	4.4	7.6
High school graduate, including equivalency (percent)................	29.3	27.8
Some college, no degree (percent)..	19.4	21.1
Associate's degree (percent)	9.5	8.1
Bachelor's degree (percent)..	21.9	18.4
Graduate or professional degree (percent)...............................	12.6	11.2
High school graduate or higher (percent)	92.8	86.6
Bachelor's degree or higher (percent)	34.6	29.6

Table NH-12. Public School Characteristics and Educational Indicators

(Number, percent; data derived from National Center of Education Statistics.)

Item	State	U.S.
Public Schools, 2012–2013 (except where noted)		
Number of school districts..	288	18,093
Number of schools..	481	98,454
Number of students (in thousands)	189	49,771
Number of teachers (in thousands)	15	3,109
Student-teacher ratio	12.7	16.0
Expenditures per student (dollars), FY 2012	13,774	10,667
Four-year adjusted cohort graduation rate (ACGR)[1,2]	87.3	81.4
Students eligible for free or reduced-price lunch (in thousands)	51	25,188
English language learners (in thousands)	4	4,397
Students age 3 to 21 served under IDEA, part B (in thousands)	29	6,429

Public Schools by Type	Number	Percent of state public schools
Total number of schools...	481	100.0
Regular	481	100.0
Special education...	0	-
Vocational education..	0	-
Alternative education	0	-

NOTE: Every school is assigned only one school type based on its instructional emphasis.
[1]ACGR data represents a new method of calculating high-school completion rates and may not be comparable to previous years' data for Averaged Freshmen Graduation Rates (AFGR).
[2]The United States 4-year ACGRs were estimated using both the reported 4-year ACGR data from 49 states and the District of Columbia and using imputed data for Idaho. The estimate for American Indian/Alaska Native students also includes imputed data for Virginia.
- = Zero or rounds to zero.

Table NH-13. Reported Voting and Registration of the Voting-Age Population, November 2012

(Numbers in thousands, percent.)

Item	Total population	Total citizen population	Registered			Voted		
			Total registered	Percent registered (total population)	Percent registered (total citizen population)	Total voted	Percent voted (total population)	Percent voted (total citizen population)
U.S. Total	235,248	215,081	153,157	65.1	71.2	132,948	56.5	61.8
State Total	1,028	991	752	73.1	75.9	688	66.9	69.4
Sex								
Male	503	482	353	70.3	73.4	322	64.0	66.8
Female	525	509	398	75.8	78.2	366	69.7	71.9
Race								
White alone......................................	980	958	730	74.5	76.1	670	68.4	69.9
White, non-Hispanic alone	952	935	715	75.1	76.4	655	68.8	70.0
Black alone.......................................	12	10	7	B	B	6	B	B
Asian alone	20	9	5	B	B	4	B	B
Hispanic (of any race)	29	23	15	B	B	15	B	B
White alone or in combination	993	970	738	74.3	76.1	677	68.2	69.8
Black alone or in combination...........	14	11	8	B	B	7	B	B
Asian alone or in combination..........	23	10	6	B	B	4	B	B
Age								
18 to 24 years.................................	123	119	71	57.5	59.6	61	50.0	51.9
25 to 44 years.................................	309	290	199	64.3	68.6	180	58.3	62.2
45 to 64 years.................................	425	414	337	79.4	81.5	312	73.4	75.4
65 to 74 years.................................	97	96	84	87.0	87.4	79	81.6	82.0
75 years and over	74	72	61	B	B	55	B	B

B = Base is less than 75,000 and therefore too small to show the derived measure.

Table NH-14. Crime

(Number, rate per 100,000. Data are derived from the FBI Uniform Crime Reports.)

Item	State			U.S.[1,2,3,4]		
	2012	2013	Percent change	2012	2013	Percent change
TOTAL POPULATION[5]..	1,321,617	1,323,459	0.1	313,873,685	316,128,839	0.7
VIOLENT CRIME						
Number...	2,841	2,642	-7.0	1,217,067	1,163,146	-4.4
Rate	215.0	199.6	-7.1	387.8	367.9	-5.1
Murder and Nonnegligent Manslaughter						
Number...	15	22	46.7	14,866	14,196	-4.5
Rate	1.1	1.7	46.5	4.7	4.5	-5.2
Rape[6]						
Number...	X	686	X	X	108,612	X
Rate	X	51.8	X	X	34.4	X
Robbery						
Number...	471	649	37.8	355,051	345,031	-2.8
Rate	35.6	49.0	37.6	113.1	109.1	-3.5
Aggravated Assault						
Number...	1,869	1,492	-20.2	762,009	724,149	-5.0
Rate	141.4	112.7	-20.3	242.8	229.1	-5.6
PROPERTY CRIME						
Number...	32,074	29,040	-9.5	9,001,992	8,632,512	-4.1
Rate	2,426.9	2,194.3	-9.6	2,868.0	2,730.7	-4.8
Burglary						
Number...	5,988	4,936	-17.6	2,109,932	1,928,465	-8.6
Rate	453.1	373.0	-17.7	672.2	610.0	-9.3
Larceny-Theft						
Number...	25,024	23,164	-7.4	6,168,874	6,004,453	-2.7
Rate	1,893.4	1,750.3	-7.6	1,965.4	1,899.4	-3.4
Motor Vehicle Theft						
Number...	1,062	940	-11.5	723,186	699,594	-3.3
Rate	80.4	71.0	-11.6	230.4	221.3	-4.0

NOTE: Although arson data are included in the trend and clearance tables, sufficient data are not available to estimate totals for this offense. Therefore, no arson data are published in this table.
X = Not applicable.
- = Zero or rounds to zero.
[1]The crime figures have been adjusted.
[2]The data collection methodology for the offense of forcible rape used by the Minnesota state Uniform Crime Reporting (UCR) Program (with the exception of Minneapolis and St. Paul, Minnesota) does not comply with national UCR Program guidelines. Consequently, its figures for forcible rape and violent crime (of which forcible rape is a part) are not published in this table.
[3]Includes offenses reported by the Zoological Police and the Metro Transit Police.
[4]Because of changes in the state's reporting practices, figures are not comparable to previous years' data.
[5]Populations are U.S. Census Bureau provisional estimates as of July 1 of each year.
[6]The figures shown for the offense of rape were estimated using the revised Uniform Crime Reporting (UCR) definition of rape.

Table NH-15. State Government Finances, 2013

(Dollar amounts in thousands, percent distribution.)

Item	Dollars	Percent distribution
Total Revenue	8,163,713	100.0
General revenue	6,132,439	75.1
Intergovernmental revenue	1,883,424	23.1
Taxes	2,349,693	28.8
General sales	0	-
Selective sales	945,290	11.6
License taxes	252,442	3.1
Individual income tax	99,027	1.2
Corporate income tax	553,197	6.8
Other taxes	499,737	6.1
Current charges	933,371	11.4
Miscellaneous general revenue	965,951	11.8
Utility revenue	0	-
Liquor stores revenue	588,729	7.2
Insurance trust revenue[1]	1,442,545	17.7
Total Expenditure	7,420,420	100.0
Intergovernmental expenditure	1,300,770	17.5
Direct expenditure	6,119,650	82.5
Current operation	4,385,046	59.1
Capital outlay	484,826	6.5
Insurance benefits and repayments	744,130	10.0
Assistance and subsidies	148,436	2.0
Interest on debt	357,212	4.8
Exhibit: Salaries and wages	900,538	12.1
Total Expenditure	7,420,420	100.0
General expenditure	6,207,431	83.7
Intergovernmental expenditure	1,300,770	17.5
Direct expenditure	4,906,661	66.1
General expenditure, by function:		
Education	2,068,121	27.9
Public welfare	1,682,499	22.7
Hospitals	49,410	0.7
Health	140,321	1.9
Highways	557,978	7.5
Police protection	56,132	0.8
Correction	112,422	1.5
Natural resources	76,860	1.0
Parks and recreation	22,998	0.3
Governmental administration	254,442	3.4
Interest on general debt	357,212	4.8
Other and unallocable	829,036	11.2
Utility expenditure	6,301	0.1
Liquor stores expenditure	462,558	6.2
Insurance trust expenditure	744,130	10.0
Debt at End of Fiscal Year	8,763,339	X
Cash and Security Holdings	13,888,712	X

X = Not applicable.
- = Zero or rounds to zero.
[1]Within insurance trust revenue, net earnings of state retirement systems is a calculated statistic (the item code in the data file is X08), and thus can be positive or negative. Net earnings is the sum of earnings on investments plus gains on investments minus losses on investments. The change made in 2002 for asset valuation from book to market value in accordance with Statement 34 of the Governmental Accounting Standards Board is reflected in the calculated statistics.

Table NH-16. State Government Tax Collections, 2014

(Dollars in thousands, percent.)

Item	Dollars	Percent distribution
Total Taxes	2,282,507	100.0
Property taxes	383,126	16.8
Sales and gross receipts	877,035	38.4
General sales and gross receipts	X	
Selective sales and gross receipts	877,035	38.4
Alcoholic beverages	9,545	0.4
Amusements	444	-
Insurance premiums	84,518	3.7
Motor fuels	146,101	6.4
Pari-mutuels	827	-
Public utilities	69,877	3.1
Tobacco products	215,012	9.4
Other selective sales	350,711	15.4
Licenses	280,011	12.3
Alcoholic beverages	4,306	0.2
Amusements	244	-
Corporations in general	50,783	2.2
Hunting and fishing	9,804	0.4
Motor vehicle	94,395	4.1
Motor vehicle operators	12,125	0.5
Public utilities	9,081	0.4
Occupation and business, NEC	91,654	4.0
Other licenses	7,619	0.3
Income taxes	635,590	27.8
Individual income	92,743	4.1
Corporation net income	542,847	23.8
Other taxes	106,745	4.7
Death and gift	0	-
Documentary and stock transfer	106,745	4.7
Severance	X	X
Taxes, NEC	0	-

X = Not applicable.
- = Zero or rounds to zero.

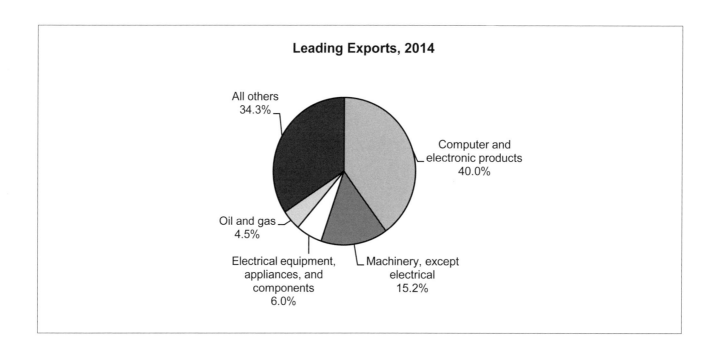

Leading Exports, 2014

All others 34.3%
Computer and electronic products 40.0%
Oil and gas 4.5%
Electrical equipment, appliances, and components 6.0%
Machinery, except electrical 15.2%

NEW JERSEY

Facts and Figures

Location: Middle Atlantic region of the United States; bordered on the N and NE by New York, on the E by the Atlantic Ocean, on the S by Delaware Bay, and on the W by Delaware and Pennsylvania

Area: 8,721 sq. mi. (22,588 sq. km.); rank—47th

Population: 8,938,175 (2014 est.); rank—11th

Principal Cities: capital—Trenton; largest—Newark

Statehood: December 18, 1787; 3rd state

U.S. Congress: 2 senators, 12 representatives

State Motto: Liberty and Prosperity

State Song: None

State Nickname: The Garden State

Abbreviations: NJ; N.J.

State Symbols: flower—common meadow violet; tree—red oak; bird—Eastern goldfinch

At a Glance

- With an increase in population of 1.7 percent, New Jersey ranked 33rd among the states in growth from 2010 to 2014.

- New Jersey's median household income was $70,165 in 2013, which ranked 3rd in the country.

- In 2013, 11.4 percent of the New Jersey's population lived below the poverty level, compared to 15.8 percent of the entire U.S. population.

- New Jersey's property crime rate of 1,882.8 incidents per 100,000 population, was the third lowest rate in the country in 2013.

- Approximately 36.6 percent of New Jersey residents had a bachelor's degree or more in 2013, the 6th highest percentage in the country.

Table NJ-1. Population by Age, Sex, Race, and Hispanic Origin

(Number, percent, except where noted.)

Sex, age, race, and Hispanic origin	2000	2010	2014[1]	Average annual percent change, 2010–2014
Total Population	8,414,350	8,791,894	8,938,175	0.4
Percent of total U.S. population	3.0	2.8	2.8	X
Sex				
Male	4,082,813	4,279,600	4,361,952	0.5
Female	4,331,357	4,512,294	4,576,223	0.4
Age				
Under 5 years	563,785	541,020	532,519	-0.4
5 to 19 years	1,720,332	1,750,184	1,701,514	-0.7
20 to 64 years	5,017,107	5,314,697	5,390,639	0.4
65 years and over	1,113,136	1,185,993	1,313,503	2.6
Median age (years)	36.7	39.0	39.5	0.3
Race and Hispanic Origin				
One race				
White	6,104,705	6,546,498	6,526,416	-0.1
Black	1,141,821	1,282,005	1,321,105	0.8
American Indian and Alaska Native	19,492	49,907	53,223	1.6
Asian	480,276	746,212	844,324	3.1
Native Hawaiian or Other Pacific Islander	3,329	7,731	8,917	3.6
Two or more races	13,755	159,541	184,190	3.7
Hispanic (of any race)	1,117,191	1,606,006	1,729,172	1.9

X = Not applicable.
[1] Population figures for 2014 are July 1 estimates. The 2010 estimates are taken from the 2010 Census.

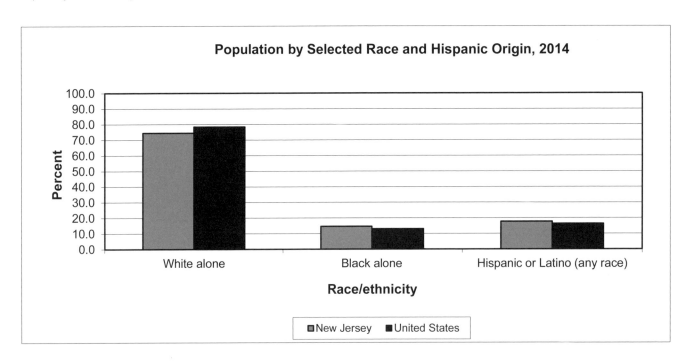

Population by Selected Race and Hispanic Origin, 2014

□ New Jersey   ■ United States

Table NJ-2. Marital Status

(Number, percent distribution.)

Sex, age, race, and Hispanic origin	2000	2010	2013
Males, 15 Years and Over	3,176,413	3,419,050	3,492,050
Never married	31.1	36.4	37.3
Now married, except separated	57.7	52.1	51.4
Separated	2.0	1.8	1.7
Widowed	2.9	2.6	2.6
Divorced	6.2	7.1	6.9
Females, 15 Years and Over	3,478,920	3,690,673	3,740,853
Never married	25.3	30.2	31.3
Now married, except separated	51.8	47.6	46.5
Separated	2.7	2.2	2.3
Widowed	11.5	10.2	9.6
Divorced	8.7	9.8	10.3

Table NJ-3. Households and Housing Characteristics

(Number, percent, dollars.)

Item	2000	2010	2013	Average annual percent change, 2000–2013
Total Households	3,064,645	3,172,421	3,176,139	0.3
Family households	2,154,539	2,185,732	2,207,108	0.2
Married-couple family	1,638,322	1,614,230	1,609,473	-0.1
Other family	516,217	571,502	597,635	1.1
Male householder, no wife present	129,205	154,036	160,268	0.9
Female householder, no husband present	387,012	417,466	437,367	
Nonfamily households	910,106	986,689	969,031	0.5
Householder living alone	751,287	827,294	809,141	0.6
Householder not living alone	158,819	159,395	159,890	0.1
Housing Characteristics				
Total housing units	3,310,275	3,554,909	3,578,260	0.6
Occupied housing units	3,064,645	3,172,421	3,176,139	0.3
Owner occupied	2,012,473	2,106,728	2,034,223	0.1
Renter occupied	1,053,172	1,065,693	1,141,916	0.6
Average household size	2.68	2.72	2.74	0.2
Financial Characteristics				
Median gross rent of renter-occupied housing	751	1,114	1,171	3.5
Median monthly owner costs for housing units with a mortgage	1,560	2,370	2,296	3.0
Median value of owner-occupied housing units	170,800	339,200	307,700	4.6

Table NJ-4. Migration, Origin, and Language

(Number, percent.)

Characteristic	State			U.S.		
	2012	2013	Percent change	2012	2013	Percent change
Residence 1 Year Ago						
Population 1 year and over	8,772,744	8,803,679	0.4	310,212,755	312,432,820	0.7
Same house	90.4	90.2	X	85.0	85.0	X
Different house in the U.S.	9.0	9.1	X	14.4	14.4	X
Same county	5.4	5.3	X	9.0	8.9	X
Different county	3.5	3.8	X	5.4	5.5	X
Same state	2.0	2.3	X	3.2	3.2	X
Different state	1.5	1.6	X	2.3	2.3	X
Abroad	0.7	0.7	X	0.6	0.6	X
Place of Birth						
Native born	6,981,291	6,973,566	-0.1	273,089,382	274,780,773	0.6
Male	48.8	48.8	X	49.3	49.3	X
Female	51.2	51.2	X	50.7	50.7	X
Foreign born	1,883,299	1,925,773	2.3	40,824,658	41,348,066	1.3
Male	48.6	48.8	X	48.7	48.8	X
Female	51.4	51.2	X	51.3	51.2	X
Foreign born; naturalized U.S. citizen	974,020	1,021,084	4.8	18,686,237	19,294,710	3.3
Male	46.5	46.9	X	45.8	45.9	X
Female	53.5	53.1	X	54.2	54.1	X
Foreign born; not a U.S. citizen	909,279	904,689	-0.5	22,138,421	22,053,356	-0.4
Male	50.9	51.0	X	51.1	51.3	X
Female	49.1	49.0	X	48.9	48.7	X
Entered 2010 or later	6.8	9.3	X	7.0	9.7	X
Entered 2000 to 2009	31.0	30.5	X	30.4	29.4	X
Entered before 2000	62.2	60.2	X	62.7	61.0	X
World Region of Birth, Foreign						
Foreign-born population, excluding population born at sea	1,883,299	1,925,773	2.3	40,824,553	41,347,945	1.3
Europe	15.9	16.3	X	11.8	11.6	X
Asia	32.1	32.2	X	29.2	29.5	X
Africa	5.4	5.2	X	4.2	4.4	X
Oceania	0.2	0.2	X	0.6	0.5	X
Latin America	45.7	45.3	X	52.2	51.9	X
North America	0.8	0.8	X	2.0	2.0	X
Language Spoken at Home and Ability to Speak English						
Population 5 years and over	8,338,003	8,368,158	0.4	294,003,714	296,358,760	0.8
English only	69.6	69.6	X	79.0	79.2	X
Language other than English	30.4	30.4	X	21.0	20.8	X
Speaks English less than "very well"	12.3	12.0	X	8.5	8.5	X

NA = Not available.
X = Not applicable.
- = Zero or rounds to zero.

Table NJ-5. Median Income and Poverty Status, 2013

(Number, percent, except as noted.)

Characteristic	State		U.S.	
	Number	Percent	Number	Percent
Median Income				
Households (dollars)..	70,165	X	52,250	X
Families (dollars)	85,426	X	64,030	X
Below Poverty Level (All People)............................	998,549	11.4	48,810,868	15.8
Sex				
Male..	445,849	10.5	21,938,525	14.5
Female	552,700	12.3	26,872,343	17.1
Age				
Under 18 years..	333,375	16.7	16,086,960	22.2
Related children under 18 years.............................	326,859	16.4	15,769,921	21.9
18 to 64 years	563,642	10.3	28,578,191	14.8
65 years and over	101,532	8.2	4,145,717	9.6

X = Not applicable.

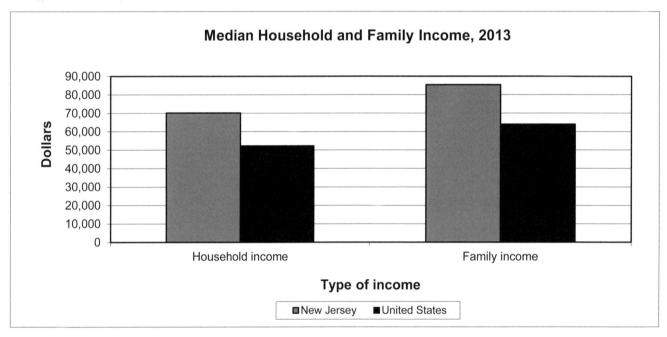

Table NJ-6. Health Insurance Coverage Status for the Civilian Noninstitutionalized Population and Children Under 18 Years of Age

(Numbers in thousands, percent.)

Item	2005	2006	2007	2008	2009	2010	2011	2012	2013
Civilian Noninstitutionalized Population.......................	8,725	8,660	8,556	8,557	8,583	8,694	8,713	8,757	8,792
Covered by Private or Public Insurance									
Number..	7,461	7,319	7,208	7,499	7,499	7,542	7,574	7,644	7,631
Percent..	85.5	84.5	84.2	87.6	87.4	86.8	86.9	87.3	86.8
Not Covered									
Number..	1,265	1,341	1,348	1,058	1,084	1,151	1,139	1,113	1,160
Percent..	14.5	15.5	15.8	12.4	12.6	13.2	13.1	12.7	13.2
Percent in the U.S. not covered.............................	15.3	15.8	15.3	15.1	15.1	15.5	15.1	14.8	14.5
Children Under 18 Years of Age...............................	2,172	2,088	2,091	2,045	2,044	2,057	2,038	2,024	2,017
Covered by Private or Public Insurance									
Number..	1,944	1,810	1,821	1,897	1,914	1,934	1,933	1,921	1,906
Percent..	89.5	86.7	87.1	92.8	93.6	94.0	94.8	94.9	94.4
Not Covered									
Number..	228	277	270	148	130	123	105	103	112
Percent..	10.5	13.3	12.9	7.2	6.4	6.0	5.2	5.1	5.6
Percent in the U.S. not covered.............................	10.9	11.7	11.0	9.7	8.6	8.0	7.5	7.2	7.1

Table NJ-7. Employment Status by Demographic Group, 2014

(Numbers in thousands, percent.)

Characteristic	Civilian noninstitutional population	Civilian labor force		Employed		Unemployed	
		Number	Percent of population	Number	Percent of population	Number	Percent of population
Total.................................	7,057	4,523	64.1	4,221	59.8	302	6.7
Sex							
Male...............	3,388	2,431	71.8	2,262	66.8	169	6.9
Female	3,670	2,092	57.0	1,959	53.4	133	6.4
Race, Sex, and Hispanic Origin							
White	5,336	3,390	63.5	3,188	59.7	202	6.0
Male................	2,585	1,832	70.9	1,718	66.5	114	6.2
Female	2,751	1,557	56.6	1,470	53.4	88	5.6
Black or African American.................	982	633	64.4	560	57.0	73	11.5
Male................	438	306	70.0	270	61.7	36	11.8
Female	545	327	60.0	290	53.3	36	11.1
Hispanic or Latino ethnicity[1]	1,259	859	68.2	795	63.1	65	7.5
Male................	626	494	78.9	463	73.9	31	6.3
Female	633	366	57.7	332	52.4	33	9.2
Age							
16 to 19 years.................	496	155	31.3	130	26.1	26	16.6
20 to 24 years.................	580	403	69.5	352	60.7	51	12.5
25 to 34 years.................	1,123	918	81.7	856	76.2	62	6.7
35 to 44 years.................	1,105	911	82.5	865	78.3	46	5.0
45 to 54 years.................	1,266	1,017	80.3	964	76.1	53	5.2
55 to 64 years.................	1,173	827	70.5	778	66.3	49	5.9
65 years and over	1,314	291	22.2	274	20.9	17	5.7

NOTE: Data in Table 7 are from the Current Population Survey (CPS) and do not match the estimates in Table 8. See notes and definitions for further information.
[1] May be of any race.

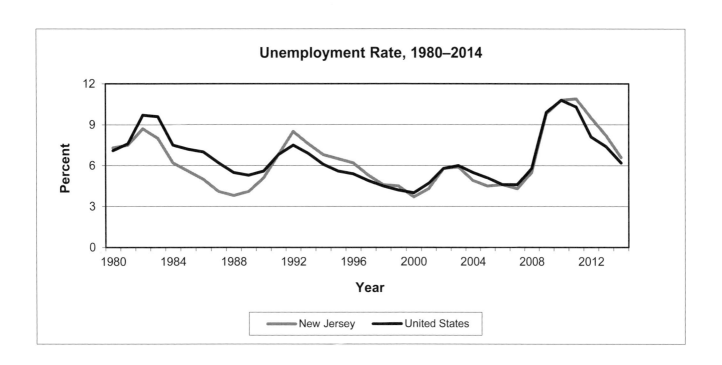

Table NJ-8. Employment Status of the Civilian Noninstitutional Population Age 16 Years and Over

(Number, percent.)

Year	Civilian labor force	Civilian participation rate	Employed	Unemployed	Unemployment rate
2006	4,445,879	66.8	4,236,485	209,394	4.7
2007	4,441,797	66.4	4,251,815	189,982	4.3
2008	4,504,432	67.0	4,263,965	240,467	5.3
2009	4,550,645	67.3	4,138,570	412,075	9.1
2010	4,555,330	66.4	4,121,455	433,875	9.5
2011	4,565,727	65.9	4,140,464	425,263	9.3
2012	4,588,106	65.8	4,162,068	426,038	9.3
2013	4,534,402	64.6	4,164,444	369,958	8.2
2014	4,518,712	64.0	4,218,435	300,277	6.6

Table NJ-9. Employment and Average Wages by Industry

(Estimates from 2007 through 2010 are based on the 2007 *North American Industry Classification System* [NAICS]. Estimates from 2011 onward are based on the 2012 NAICS.)

Industry	2007	2008	2009	2010	2011	2012	2013
	Number of jobs						
Wage and Salary Employment by Industry	4,146,632	4,118,820	3,960,283	3,922,946	3,923,939	3,951,205	3,989,089
Farm Wage and Salary Employment	7,819	6,971	6,755	7,570	7,339	9,511	9,099
Nonfarm Wage and Salary Employment	4,138,813	4,111,849	3,953,528	3,915,376	3,916,600	3,941,694	3,979,990
Private wage and salary employment	3,481,911	3,452,565	3,293,683	3,267,478	3,290,968	3,320,739	3,359,773
Forestry, fishing, and related activities	2,842	2,945	3,078	3,677	3,811	3,890	2,870
Mining	1,604	1,605	1,492	1,371	1,305	1,251	1,317
Utilities	13,367	11,939	11,776	14,345	13,596	13,805	13,668
Construction	178,554	170,499	145,200	136,019	136,803	134,904	142,821
Manufacturing	308,113	298,064	266,926	257,696	253,333	245,520	243,022
Durable goods manufacturing	139,218	135,115	118,946	114,308	114,628	112,106	110,998
Nondurable goods manufacturing	168,895	162,949	147,980	143,388	138,705	133,414	132,024
Wholesale trade	236,155	234,458	218,250	212,135	211,455	213,869	214,116
Retail trade	473,982	464,036	443,251	444,675	448,211	448,461	453,082
Transportation and warehousing	164,622	163,582	153,789	151,198	152,332	151,671	150,777
Information	97,722	92,278	84,171	79,458	75,774	77,882	75,339
Finance and insurance	210,260	205,875	195,473	193,181	192,542	191,736	191,347
Real estate and rental and leasing	61,371	61,663	57,963	56,975	55,182	54,272	56,048
Professional, scientific, and technical services	290,167	293,729	281,110	276,511	281,203	281,409	286,136
Management of companies and enterprises	71,800	74,702	75,743	72,785	77,400	79,573	83,312
Administrative and waste services	260,041	252,539	235,034	241,793	250,969	261,602	267,697
Educational services	89,714	91,383	92,550	93,419	96,108	94,821	95,353
Health care and social assistance	481,320	490,545	497,698	505,292	509,745	519,172	527,688
Arts, entertainment, and recreation	52,621	54,877	53,763	53,664	54,897	56,869	58,238
Accommodation and food services	290,780	290,812	283,892	285,282	285,593	291,880	297,865
Other services, except public administration	196,876	197,034	192,524	188,002	190,709	198,152	199,077
Government and government enterprises	656,902	659,284	659,845	647,898	625,632	620,955	620,217
	Dollars						
Average Wages and Salaries by Industry	53,170	54,523	54,370	55,587	56,722	57,784	58,712
Average Farm Wages and Salaries	29,776	32,043	31,414	26,478	24,434	21,133	30,097
Average Nonfarm Wages and Salaries	53,215	54,561	54,409	55,643	56,783	57,873	58,778
Average private wages and salaries	53,160	54,412	53,986	55,228	56,377	57,556	58,548
Forestry, fishing, and related activities	22,755	23,952	24,754	23,878	24,140	24,155	27,852
Mining	60,415	62,782	64,157	67,177	66,959	70,261	72,102
Utilities	88,880	96,909	95,359	99,507	106,182	108,470	107,170
Construction	57,403	60,266	60,519	60,678	61,676	62,269	63,766
Manufacturing	68,313	70,564	71,230	74,016	74,981	75,929	77,224
Durable goods manufacturing	61,490	63,105	63,700	65,867	68,023	68,931	69,603
Nondurable goods manufacturing	73,937	76,748	77,283	80,512	80,732	81,809	83,630
Wholesale trade	72,320	73,633	74,077	76,696	79,469	81,011	82,326
Retail trade	29,880	29,742	29,686	30,003	30,390	30,578	30,969
Transportation and warehousing	46,696	47,455	47,215	48,360	49,321	50,206	51,643
Information	80,403	82,775	83,274	86,114	89,636	92,730	96,140
Finance and insurance	98,635	101,375	97,256	104,128	106,852	108,681	110,930
Real estate and rental and leasing	54,182	52,884	51,637	54,032	54,103	58,945	58,512
Professional, scientific, and technical services	82,957	85,411	85,976	88,091	90,889	95,576	97,568
Management of companies and enterprises	124,099	124,500	124,666	132,582	136,761	146,350	150,391
Administrative and waste services	35,630	37,284	36,723	37,264	38,182	38,560	39,149
Educational services	34,386	35,196	36,281	37,226	37,976	38,313	39,670
Health care and social assistance	44,691	46,364	46,792	46,802	47,448	48,267	48,632
Arts, entertainment, and recreation	34,648	35,863	35,868	36,633	35,269	36,753	36,910
Accommodation and food services	23,697	22,987	22,057	22,536	22,779	22,985	23,287
Other services, except public administration	30,699	31,519	31,359	32,027	32,429	32,161	32,866
Government and government enterprises	53,506	55,343	56,525	57,740	58,919	59,570	60,021

Table NJ-10. Employment Characteristics by Family Type

(Number, percent.)

Family type and labor force status	2011		2012		2013	
	Total	Families with own children under 18 years	Total	Families with own children under 18 years	Total	Families with own children under 18 years
All Families..	2,191,404	1,003,032	2,211,642	1,009,713	2,207,108	985,032
FAMILY TYPE AND LABOR FORCE STATUS						
Married-Couple Families..................................	1,607,317	708,322	1,626,018	720,912	1,609,473	703,827
Both husband and wife in labor force............................	56.8	67.6	56.4	67.9	55.1	67.4
Husband in labor force, wife not in labor force	22.3	27.7	22.3	27.6	22.9	27.8
Wife in labor force, husband not in labor force	7.1	3.6	7.4	3.4	7.4	3.6
Both husband and wife not in labor force.........................	13.8	1.2	13.9	1.1	14.2	0.9
Other Families	584,087	294,710	585,624	288,801	597,635	281,205
Female householder, no husband present...........................	73.8	77.6	73.7	78.2	73.2	76.2
In labor force...	54.8	65.6	53.4	64.8	52.7	63.2
Not in labor force	19.1	12.0	20.3	13.4	20.5	13.0
Male householder, no wife present................................	26.2	22.4	26.3	21.8	26.8	23.8
In labor force...	21.7	21.2	21.2	20.4	21.0	21.4
Not in labor force	4.5	1.2	5.1	1.4	5.8	2.4

Table NJ-11. School Enrollment and Educational Attainment, 2013

(Number, percent.)

Item	State	U.S.
Enrollment		
Total population 3 years and over, enrolled in school	2,265,632	82,395,254
Enrolled in nursery school or preschool (percent)	7.4	6.0
Enrolled in kindergarten (percent)......................................	5.3	5.2
Enrolled in elementary school, grades 1-8 (percent).....................	39.8	40.0
Enrolled in high school, grades 9-12 (percent)...........................	21.3	20.6
Enrolled in college or graduate school (percent).........................	26.2	28.3
Attainment		
Total population 25 years and over	6,086,705	210,910,615
Less than ninth grade (percent)	5.5	5.8
9th to 12th grade, no diploma (percent)	6.0	7.6
High school graduate, including equivalency (percent)	28.8	27.8
Some college, no degree (percent)	16.8	21.1
Associate's degree (percent)	6.4	8.1
Bachelor's degree (percent)	22.6	18.4
Graduate or professional degree (percent)...............................	14.0	11.2
High school graduate or higher (percent)	88.5	86.6
Bachelor's degree or higher (percent)...................................	36.6	29.6

Table NJ-12. Public School Characteristics and Educational Indicators

(Number, percent; data derived from National Center of Education Statistics.)

Item	State	U.S.
Public Schools, 2012–2013 (except where noted)		
Number of school districts..	691	18,093
Number of schools...	2,598	98,454
Number of students (in thousands)	1,372	49,771
Number of teachers (in thousands)	111	3,109
Student-teacher ratio...	12.4	16.0
Expenditures per student (dollars), FY 2012.............................	17,982	10,667
Four-year adjusted cohort graduation rate (ACGR)1,2	87.5	81.4
Students eligible for free or reduced-price lunch (in thousands)	502	25,188
English language learners (in thousands)	58	4,397
Students age 3 to 21 served under IDEA, part B (in thousands)	232	6,429

Public Schools by Type	Number	Percent of state public schools
Total number of schools..	2,598	100.0
Regular	2,360	90.8
Special education..	59	2.3
Vocational education...	62	2.4
Alternative education	117	4.5

NOTE: Every school is assigned only one school type based on its instructional emphasis.
[1] ACGR data represents a new method of calculating high-school completion rates and may not be comparable to previous years' data for Averaged Freshmen Graduation Rates (AFGR).
[2] The United States 4-year ACGRs were estimated using both the reported 4-year ACGR data from 49 states and the District of Columbia and using imputed data for Idaho. The estimate for American Indian/Alaska Native students also includes imputed data for Virginia.

Table NJ-13. Reported Voting and Registration of the Voting-Age Population, November 2012

(Numbers in thousands, percent.)

Item	Total population	Total citizen population	Registered			Voted		
			Total registered	Percent registered (total population)	Percent registered (total citizen population)	Total voted	Percent voted (total population)	Percent voted (total citizen population)
U.S. Total	235,248	215,081	153,157	65.1	71.2	132,948	56.5	61.8
State Total	6,730	5,929	4,326	64.3	73.0	3,670	54.5	61.9
Sex								
Male	3,215	2,795	1,982	61.6	70.9	1,676	52.1	60.0
Female	3,514	3,134	2,344	66.7	74.8	1,994	56.7	63.6
Race								
White alone..	5,173	4,695	3,448	66.6	73.4	2,907	56.2	61.9
White, non-Hispanic alone	4,145	4,030	3,037	73.3	75.3	2,556	61.7	63.4
Black alone..	907	789	586	64.7	74.3	540	59.6	68.5
Asian alone	566	373	243	43.0	65.2	179	31.7	48.1
Hispanic (of any race)	1,170	773	468	40.0	60.6	395	33.8	51.1
White alone or in combination	5,197	4,719	3,466	66.7	73.5	2,926	56.3	62.0
Black alone or in combination..........	922	804	602	65.3	74.8	549	59.6	68.3
Asian alone or in combination..........	577	384	250	43.3	65.0	186	32.2	48.4
Age								
18 to 24 years.....................................	792	707	379	47.8	53.6	276	34.9	39.1
25 to 44 years.....................................	2,255	1,781	1,211	53.7	68.0	1,011	44.8	56.8
45 to 64 years.....................................	2,424	2,217	1,732	71.4	78.1	1,545	63.7	69.7
65 to 74 years.....................................	644	631	504	78.3	80.0	434	67.4	68.8
75 years and over	615	593	499	81.2	84.2	404	65.7	68.1

Table NJ-14. Crime

(Number, rate per 100,000. Data are derived from the FBI Uniform Crime Reports.)

Item	State			U.S.[1,2,3,4]		
	2012	2013	Percent change	2012	2013	Percent change
TOTAL POPULATION[5]...........................	8,867,749	8,899,339	0.4	313,873,685	316,128,839	0.7
VIOLENT CRIME						
Number..	25,727	25,415	-1.2	1,217,067	1,163,146	-4.4
Rate	290.1	285.6	-1.6	387.8	367.9	-5.1
Murder and Nonnegligent Manslaughter						
Number..	388	401	3.4	14,866	14,196	-4.5
Rate	4.4	4.5	3.0	4.7	4.5	-5.2
Rape[6]						
Number..	X	1,120	X	X	108,612	X
Rate	X	12.6	X	X	34.4	X
Robbery						
Number..	11,385	12,082	6.1	355,051	345,031	-2.8
Rate	128.4	135.8	5.7	113.1	109.1	-3.5
Aggravated Assault						
Number..	12,919	12,071	-6.6	762,009	724,149	-5.0
Rate	145.7	135.6	-6.9	242.8	229.1	-5.6
PROPERTY CRIME						
Number..	181,481	167,556	-7.7	9,001,992	8,632,512	-4.1
Rate	2,046.5	1,882.8	-8.0	2,868.0	2,730.7	-4.8
Burglary						
Number..	42,338	35,873	-15.3	2,109,932	1,928,465	-8.6
Rate	477.4	403.1	-15.6	672.2	610.0	-9.3
Larceny-Theft						
Number..	122,662	117,936	-3.9	6,168,874	6,004,453	-2.7
Rate	1,383.2	1,325.2	-4.2	1,965.4	1,899.4	-3.4
Motor Vehicle Theft						
Number..	16,481	13,747	-16.6	723,186	699,594	-3.3
Rate	185.9	154.5	-16.9	230.4	221.3	-4.0

NOTE: Although arson data are included in the trend and clearance tables, sufficient data are not available to estimate totals for this offense. Therefore, no arson data are published in this table.

X = Not applicable.

- = Zero or rounds to zero.

[1] The crime figures have been adjusted.

[2] The data collection methodology for the offense of forcible rape used by the Minnesota state Uniform Crime Reporting (UCR) Program (with the exception of Minneapolis and St. Paul, Minnesota) does not comply with national UCR Program guidelines. Consequently, its figures for forcible rape and violent crime (of which forcible rape is a part) are not published in this table.

[3] Includes offenses reported by the Zoological Police and the Metro Transit Police.

[4] Because of changes in the state's reporting practices, figures are not comparable to previous years' data.

[5] Populations are U.S. Census Bureau provisional estimates as of July 1 of each year.

[6] The figures shown for the offense of rape were estimated using the revised Uniform Crime Reporting (UCR) definition of rape.

Table NJ-15. State Government Finances, 2013

(Dollar amounts in thousands, percent distribution.)

Item	Dollars	Percent distribution
Total Revenue	67,918,016	100.0
General revenue	53,863,834	79.3
Intergovernmental revenue	14,471,986	21.3
Taxes	29,076,881	42.8
General sales	8,454,788	12.4
Selective sales	3,743,345	5.5
License taxes	1,516,432	2.2
Individual income tax	12,108,615	17.8
Corporate income tax	2,282,055	3.4
Other taxes	971,646	1.4
Current charges	5,900,251	8.7
Miscellaneous general revenue	4,414,716	6.5
Utility revenue	988,882	1.5
Liquor stores revenue	0	-
Insurance trust revenue[1]	13,065,300	19.2
Total Expenditure	67,362,610	100.0
Intergovernmental expenditure	11,102,269	16.5
Direct expenditure	56,260,341	83.5
Current operation	34,168,935	50.7
Capital outlay	4,102,039	6.1
Insurance benefits and repayments	14,532,854	21.6
Assistance and subsidies	1,292,133	1.9
Interest on debt	2,164,380	3.2
Exhibit: Salaries and wages	10,349,020	15.4
Total Expenditure	67,362,610	100.0
General expenditure	50,052,284	74.3
Intergovernmental expenditure	11,102,269	16.5
Direct expenditure	38,950,015	57.8
General expenditure, by function:		
Education	16,426,314	24.4
Public welfare	14,701,447	21.8
Hospitals	2,106,102	3.1
Health	1,260,358	1.9
Highways	3,192,396	4.7
Police protection	818,347	1.2
Correction	1,436,484	2.1
Natural resources	581,243	0.9
Parks and recreation	190,647	0.3
Governmental administration	1,691,288	2.5
Interest on general debt	2,161,780	3.2
Other and unallocable	5,485,878	8.1
Utility expenditure	2,777,472	4.1
Liquor stores expenditure	0	-
Insurance trust expenditure	14,532,854	21.6
Debt at End of Fiscal Year	64,264,050	X
Cash and Security Holdings	113,530,613	X

X = Not applicable.
- = Zero or rounds to zero.

[1] Within insurance trust revenue, net earnings of state retirement systems is a calculated statistic (the item code in the data file is X08), and thus can be positive or negative. Net earnings is the sum of earnings on investments plus gains on investments minus losses on investments. The change made in 2002 for asset valuation from book to market value in accordance with Statement 34 of the Governmental Accounting Standards Board is reflected in the calculated statistics.

Table NJ-16. State Government Tax Collections, 2014

(Dollars in thousands, percent.)

Item	Dollars	Percent distribution
Total Taxes	29,679,226	100.0
Property taxes	6,705	-
Sales and gross receipts	12,751,851	43.0
General sales and gross receipts	8,885,847	29.9
Selective sales and gross receipts	3,866,004	13.0
Alcoholic beverages	139,438	0.5
Amusements	219,000	0.7
Insurance premiums	599,169	2.0
Motor fuels	539,155	1.8
Pari-mutuels	0	-
Public utilities	1,012,028	3.4
Tobacco products	740,605	2.5
Other selective sales	616,609	2.1
Licenses	1,516,698	5.1
Alcoholic beverages	3,965	-
Amusements	49,618	0.2
Corporations in general	275,705	0.9
Hunting and fishing	13,206	-
Motor vehicle	617,428	2.1
Motor vehicle operators	53,016	0.2
Public utilities	6,765	-
Occupation and business, NEC	495,599	1.7
Other licenses	1,396	-
Income taxes	14,341,741	48.3
Individual income	11,973,673	40.3
Corporation net income	2,368,068	8.0
Other taxes	1,062,231	3.6
Death and gift	685,459	2.3
Documentary and stock transfer	376,772	1.3
Severance	X	X
Taxes, NEC	0	-

X = Not applicable.
- = Zero or rounds to zero.

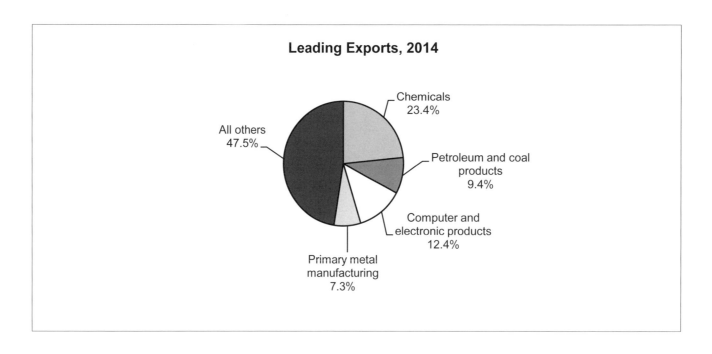

Leading Exports, 2014

Chemicals 23.4%
Petroleum and coal products 9.4%
Computer and electronic products 12.4%
Primary metal manufacturing 7.3%
All others 47.5%

NEW MEXICO

Facts and Figures

Location: Southwestern United States; bordered on the N by Colorado, on the E by Oklahoma and Texas, on the S by Texas and Mexico, and on the W by Arizona; New Mexico is one of the Four Corner states—at its NW corner it touches Arizona, Colorado, and Utah

Area: 121,590 sq. mi. (314,915 sq. km.); rank—5th

Population: 2,085,572 (2014 est.); rank—36th

Principal Cities: capital—Santa Fe; largest—Albuquerque

Statehood: January 6, 1912; 47th state

U.S. Congress: 2 senators, 3 representatives

State Motto: *Crescit eundo* ("It grows as it goes")

State Song: "O, Fair New Mexico"

State Nickname: The Land of Enchantment

Abbreviations: NM; N. Mex.

State Symbols: flower—yucca; tree—piñon; bird—roadrunner

At a Glance

- With an increase in population of 1.3 percent, New Mexico ranked 38th among the states in growth from 2010 to 2014.

- In 2013, New Mexico's violent crime rate of 613.0 per 100,000 population was the 3rd highest rate in the country, and its property crime rate of 3,704.8 per 100,000 population, was the 5th highest in the country.

- With approximately 46.3 percent of its residents self-identifying as "Hispanic or Latino," New Mexico was the state with the highest percentage of this population in 2014.

- New Mexico had the 2nd highest percentage of residents living below the poverty line in 2013 (21.9 percent).

- In 2014, 18.6 percent of New Mexico residents were unemployed, compared to 14.5 percent of the entire U.S. population.

Table NM-1. Population by Age, Sex, Race, and Hispanic Origin

(Number, percent, except where noted.)

Sex, age, race, and Hispanic origin	2000	2010	2014[1]	Average annual percent change, 2010–2014
Total Population	1,819,046	2,059,179	2,085,572	0.3
Percent of total U.S. population	0.6	0.7	0.7	X
Sex				
Male	894,317	1,017,421	1,032,882	0.4
Female	924,729	1,041,758	1,052,690	0.3
Age				
Under 5 years	130,628	144,981	137,133	-1.4
5 to 19 years	434,231	434,860	420,462	-0.8
20 to 64 years	1,041,962	1,207,083	1,209,122	-
65 years and over	212,225	272,255	318,855	4.0
Median age (years)	34.6	36.7	37.1	0.3
Race and Hispanic Origin				
One race				
White	1,214,253	1,720,992	1,726,182	0.1
Black	34,343	49,006	52,666	1.8
American Indian and Alaska Native	173,483	208,890	217,262	1.0
Asian	19,255	31,253	34,848	2.8
Native Hawaiian or Other Pacific Islander	1,503	3,132	3,472	2.6
Two or more races	66,327	45,906	51,142	2.7
Hispanic (of any race)	765,386	973,088	994,151	0.5

X = Not applicable.
- = Zero or rounds to zero.
[1]Population figures for 2014 are July 1 estimates. The 2010 estimates are taken from the 2010 Census.

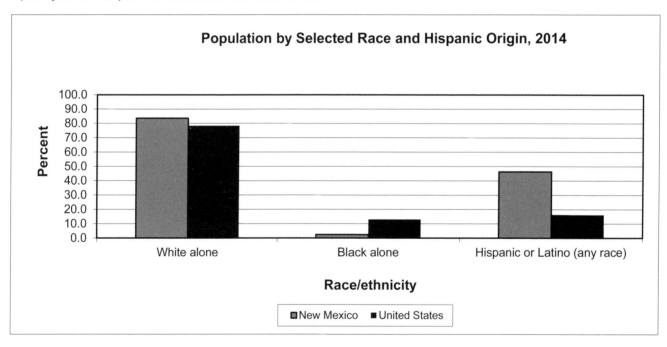

Table NM-2. Marital Status

(Number, percent distribution.)

Sex, age, race, and Hispanic origin	2000	2010	2013
Males, 15 Years and Over	677,967	801,901	816,904
Never married	30.5	35.4	38.3
Now married, except separated	55.0	48.4	46.4
Separated	1.6	1.6	1.6
Widowed	2.6	2.6	3.1
Divorced	10.4	11.9	10.6
Females, 15 Years and Over	720,529	833,357	843,627
Never married	24.7	29.9	31.6
Now married, except separated	51.2	45.0	42.8
Separated	2.0	2.6	2.5
Widowed	9.4	8.5	9.0
Divorced	12.8	14.1	14.2

Table NM-3. Households and Housing Characteristics

(Number, percent, dollars.)

Item	2000	2010	2013	Average annual percent change, 2000–2013
Total Households	677,971	765,183	753,507	0.8
Family households	466,515	501,092	482,570	0.3
Married-couple family	341,818	349,344	336,560	-0.1
Other family	124,697	151,748	146,010	1.2
Male householder, no wife present..	35,075	49,041	39,017	0.8
Female householder, no husband present..................................	89,622	102,707	106,993	1.4
Nonfamily households	211,456	264,091	270,937	1.9
Householder living alone...	172,181	216,704	223,252	2.0
Householder not living alone...	39,275	47,387	47,685	1.5
Housing Characteristics				
Total housing units...	780,579	902,242	905,134	1.1
Occupied housing units	677,971	765,183	753,507	0.8
Owner occupied	474,445	519,864	511,693	0.6
Renter occupied	203,526	245,319	241,814	1.3
Average household size...	2.63	2.64	2.71	0.2
Financial Characteristics				
Median gross rent of renter-occupied housing	503	699	772	3.4
Median monthly owner costs for housing units with a mortgage	929	1,202	1,193	1.9
Median value of owner-occupied housing units	108,100	161,200	159,200	3

Table NM-4. Migration, Origin, and Language

(Number, percent.)

Characteristic	State			U.S.		
	2012	2013	Percent change	2012	2013	Percent change
Residence 1 Year Ago						
Population 1 year and over	2,060,595	2,059,689	-	310,212,755	312,432,820	0.7
Same house	85.9	85.7	X	85.0	85.0	X
Different house in the U.S.	13.6	13.7	X	14.4	14.4	X
Same county	8.7	8.6	X	9.0	8.9	X
Different county	4.9	5.1	X	5.4	5.5	X
Same state	2.3	2.3	X	3.2	3.2	X
Different state	2.7	2.8	X	2.3	2.3	X
Abroad	0.5	0.7	X	0.6	0.6	X
Place of Birth						
Native born	1,893,350	1,874,038		273,089,382	274,780,773	0.6
Male	49.5	49.6	X	49.3	49.3	X
Female	50.5	50.4	X	50.7	50.7	X
Foreign born	192,188	211,249	9.9	40,824,658	41,348,066	1.3
Male	51.3	49.1	X	48.7	48.8	X
Female	48.7	50.9	X	51.3	51.2	X
Foreign born; naturalized U.S. citizen.........................	66,010	72,651	10.1	18,686,237	19,294,710	3.3
Male	46.8	43.4	X	45.8	45.9	X
Female	53.2	56.6	X	54.2	54.1	X
Foreign born; not a U.S. citizen.................................	126,178	138,598	9.8	22,138,421	22,053,356	-0.4
Male	53.6	52.1	X	51.1	51.3	X
Female	46.4	47.9	X	48.9	48.7	X
Entered 2010 or later	6.4	8.1	X	7.0	9.7	X
Entered 2000 to 2009	29.5	28.5	X	30.4	29.4	X
Entered before 2000..	64.1	63.4	X	62.7	61.0	X
World Region of Birth, Foreign						
Foreign-born population, excluding population born at sea	192,188	211,249	9.9	40,824,553	41,347,945	1.3
Europe	7.3	8.3	X	11.8	11.6	X
Asia..	12.5	10.6	X	29.2	29.5	X
Africa	1.4	1.0	X	4.2	4.4	X
Oceania	0.2	0.3	X	0.6	0.5	X
Latin America	76.8	78.6	X	52.2	51.9	X
North America	1.9	1.2	X	2.0	2.0	X
Language Spoken at Home and Ability to Speak English						
Population 5 years and over...	1,942,502	1,946,891	0.2	294,003,714	296,358,760	0.8
English only	64.6	64.0	X	79.0	79.2	X
Language other than English....................................	35.4	36.0	X	21.0	20.8	X
Speaks English less than "very well"......................	8.8	9.8	X	8.5	8.5	X

NA = Not available.
X = Not applicable.
- = Zero or rounds to zero.

Table NM-5. Median Income and Poverty Status, 2013

(Number, percent, except as noted.)

Characteristic	State		U.S.	
	Number	Percent	Number	Percent
Median Income				
Households (dollars)................................	43,872	X	52,250	X
Families (dollars)	54,565	X	64,030	X
Below Poverty Level (All People)................................	448,461	21.9	48,810,868	15.8
Sex				
Male...................................	205,252	20.4	21,938,525	14.5
Female	243,209	23.4	26,872,343	17.1
Age				
Under 18 years...................................	156,610	31.2	16,086,960	22.2
Related children under 18 years........................	154,970	30.9	15,769,921	21.9
18 to 64 years...................................	256,495	20.7	28,578,191	14.8
65 years and over	35,356	11.7	4,145,717	9.6

X = Not applicable.

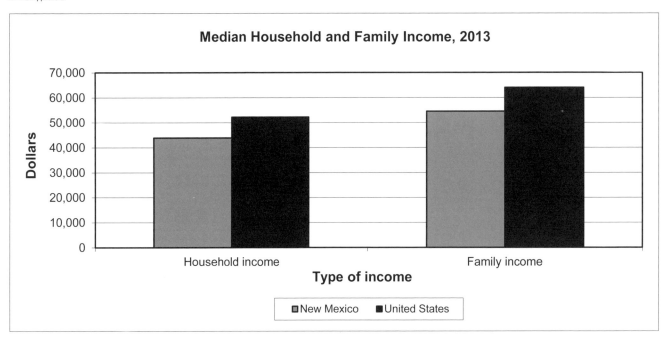

Median Household and Family Income, 2013

Table NM-6. Health Insurance Coverage Status for the Civilian Noninstitutionalized Population and Children Under 18 Years of Age

(Numbers in thousands, percent.)

Item	2005	2006	2007	2008	2009	2010	2011	2012	2013
Civilian Noninstitutionalized Population................................	1,938	1,943	1,946	1,952	1,976	2,033	2,047	2,052	2,052
Covered by Private or Public Insurance									
Number................................	1,545	1,498	1,509	1,533	1,586	1,634	1,641	1,674	1,669
Percent................................	79.7	77.1	77.5	78.5	80.3	80.4	80.2	81.6	81.4
Not Covered									
Number................................	393	445	437	419	390	399	406	378	382
Percent................................	20.3	22.9	22.5	21.5	19.7	19.6	19.8	18.4	18.6
Percent in the U.S. not covered................	15.3	15.8	15.3	15.1	15.1	15.5	15.1	14.8	14.5
Children Under 18 Years of Age................	493	520	495	501	514	518	517	515	507
Covered by Private or Public Insurance									
Number................................	394	428	419	432	455	465	470	474	464
Percent................................	80.0	82.1	84.5	86.2	88.6	89.8	90.8	92.0	91.5
Not Covered									
Number................................	99	93	77	69	59	53	47	41	43
Percent................................	20.0	17.9	15.5	13.8	11.4	10.2	9.2	8.0	8.5
Percent in the U.S. not covered................	10.9	11.7	11.0	9.7	8.6	8.0	7.5	7.2	7.1

Table NM-7. Employment Status by Demographic Group, 2014

(Numbers in thousands, percent.)

Characteristic	Civilian noninstitutional population	Civilian labor force		Employed		Unemployed	
		Number	Percent of population	Number	Percent of population	Number	Percent of population
Total...	1,601	917	57.3	852	53.2	64	7.0
Sex							
Male..	777	491	63.2	461	59.3	30	6.1
Female.....................................	824	426	51.7	392	47.5	34	8.0
Race, Sex, and Hispanic Origin							
White	1,337	772	57.8	728	54.5	44	5.7
Male..	648	418	64.6	397	61.3	21	5.1
Female.....................................	689	354	51.4	331	48.0	23	6.5
Black or African American................	42	26	62.6	23	54.7	3	12.5
Male..	NA	NA	NA	NA	NA	NA	NA
Female.....................................	NA	NA	NA	NA	NA	NA	NA
Hispanic or Latino ethnicity[1]	688	409	59.4	378	55.0	30	7.4
Male..	331	219	66.2	206	62.1	13	6.1
Female.....................................	357	190	53.1	173	48.4	17	9.0
Age							
16 to 19 years.............................	109	33	30.2	25	23.1	8	23.7
20 to 24 years.............................	143	90	62.8	78	54.5	12	13.2
25 to 34 years.............................	269	197	73.1	178	66.4	18	9.2
35 to 44 years.............................	238	189	79.4	179	75.5	9	4.8
45 to 54 years.............................	252	189	74.8	181	71.6	8	4.3
55 to 64 years.............................	257	156	60.7	149	58.1	7	4.3
65 years and over	332	64	19.2	61	18.4	3	4.1

NOTE: Data in Table 7 are from the Current Population Survey (CPS) and do not match the estimates in Table 8. See notes and definitions for further information.
[1]May be of any race.
NA = Not available.

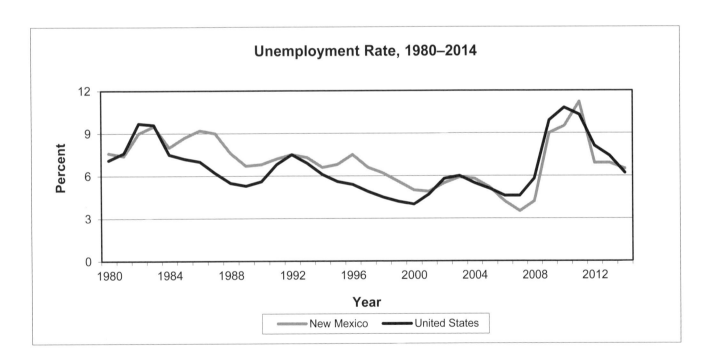

Table NM-8. Employment Status of the Civilian Noninstitutional Population Age 16 Years and Over

(Number, percent.)

Year	Civilian labor force	Civilian participation rate	Employed	Unemployed	Unemployment rate
2006	928,094	63.5	889,448	38,646	4.2
2007	934,027	63.0	898,998	35,029	3.8
2008	944,548	63.0	902,411	42,137	4.5
2009	940,352	62.0	869,491	70,861	7.5
2010	936,088	60.0	860,154	75,934	8.1
2011	929,862	58.8	859,603	70,259	7.6
2012	928,050	58.3	861,829	66,221	7.1
2013	922,960	57.8	859,270	63,690	6.9
2014	918,206	57.4	858,149	60,057	6.5

Table NM-9. Employment and Average Wages by Industry

(Estimates from 2007 through 2010 are based on the 2007 *North American Industry Classification System* [NAICS]. Estimates from 2011 onward are based on the 2012 NAICS.)

Industry	2007	2008	2009	2010	2011	2012	2013
				Number of jobs			
Wage and Salary Employment by Industry	878,205	881,357	848,403	840,219	840,690	842,939	849,701
Farm Wage and Salary Employment	7,611	6,671	6,958	6,643	6,503	6,881	7,886
Nonfarm Wage and Salary Employment	870,594	874,686	841,445	833,576	834,187	836,058	841,815
Private wage and salary employment	660,727	661,461	625,304	616,320	620,357	623,788	630,455
Forestry, fishing, and related activities	2,792	2,858	2,753	2,923	3,034	3,028	2,899
Mining	19,616	21,111	17,511	18,284	21,096	23,795	25,805
Utilities	4,259	4,327	4,614	4,374	4,367	4,386	4,445
Construction	61,380	59,690	50,030	45,973	44,534	42,641	43,739
Manufacturing	36,818	35,080	30,075	29,064	29,602	29,706	29,111
Durable goods manufacturing	25,548	24,052	19,761	19,040	19,346	19,082	18,299
Nondurable goods manufacturing	11,270	11,028	10,314	10,024	10,256	10,624	10,812
Wholesale trade	23,714	23,777	21,870	22,074	21,162	21,521	21,684
Retail trade	97,317	97,673	93,059	91,272	91,545	91,866	92,853
Transportation and warehousing	20,942	20,632	18,301	17,812	18,475	19,264	19,201
Information	16,025	16,000	14,737	14,329	13,470	13,644	13,115
Finance and insurance	23,291	23,069	22,736	22,323	22,167	22,136	22,293
Real estate and rental and leasing	11,568	11,376	10,361	10,167	10,012	9,896	10,205
Professional, scientific, and technical services	56,698	56,951	55,923	54,422	54,174	52,831	52,654
Management of companies and enterprises	5,779	5,372	5,079	4,954	5,071	4,989	5,072
Administrative and waste services	47,395	47,419	42,544	41,722	42,179	40,888	41,895
Educational services	10,120	10,069	10,042	10,319	10,652	10,679	10,351
Health care and social assistance	95,131	98,316	101,908	103,733	105,592	107,232	108,183
Arts, entertainment, and recreation	8,692	8,763	8,779	8,648	8,668	9,021	9,135
Accommodation and food services	79,949	78,725	76,361	76,134	76,763	77,789	79,846
Other services, except public administration	39,241	40,253	38,621	37,793	37,794	38,476	37,969
Government and government enterprises	209,867	213,225	216,141	217,256	213,830	212,270	211,360
				Dollars			
Average Wages and Salaries by Industry	37,147	38,686	39,301	40,069	40,905	41,603	41,800
Average Farm Wages and Salaries	32,450	35,732	38,036	34,612	36,685	29,633	38,732
Average Nonfarm Wages and Salaries	37,188	38,709	39,312	40,112	40,938	41,702	41,829
Average private wages and salaries	36,158	37,663	37,998	38,919	39,741	40,751	40,855
Forestry, fishing, and related activities	20,447	21,006	21,433	21,521	22,348	23,077	23,794
Mining	62,802	68,956	66,837	75,764	72,876	74,377	74,348
Utilities	67,684	73,015	72,143	72,919	73,908	76,180	77,145
Construction	37,348	41,149	41,603	41,389	41,880	42,618	42,373
Manufacturing	48,557	48,893	50,838	53,528	55,293	57,181	57,160
Durable goods manufacturing	53,406	53,800	55,871	59,412	61,778	64,214	64,152
Nondurable goods manufacturing	37,564	38,189	41,197	42,351	43,062	44,549	45,326
Wholesale trade	47,766	49,257	49,111	50,051	50,329	51,553	51,534
Retail trade	25,406	25,684	25,631	26,042	26,471	27,101	27,197
Transportation and warehousing	43,791	45,026	44,328	45,490	48,050	49,851	50,213
Information	39,928	42,896	43,859	43,071	45,768	47,375	47,465
Finance and insurance	49,384	49,503	50,511	52,482	54,856	57,515	58,911
Real estate and rental and leasing	32,631	32,602	32,264	33,893	36,108	36,511	36,846
Professional, scientific, and technical services	65,149	67,105	68,167	70,507	71,223	72,976	72,439
Management of companies and enterprises	55,519	56,736	60,495	62,340	63,530	68,018	66,629
Administrative and waste services	30,033	31,433	32,809	32,980	34,530	35,245	34,740
Educational services	27,959	30,616	31,175	31,699	32,179	31,535	32,505
Health care and social assistance	35,613	37,295	38,311	38,503	39,074	39,863	40,268
Arts, entertainment, and recreation	22,341	22,225	21,554	21,532	21,844	22,091	22,580
Accommodation and food services	16,077	16,397	16,746	17,224	17,548	17,871	17,980
Other services, except public administration	24,326	25,444	25,567	26,325	26,768	27,381	27,615
Government and government enterprises	40,434	41,952	43,114	43,497	44,412	44,496	44,735

Table NM-10. Employment Characteristics by Family Type

(Number, percent.)

Family type and labor force status	2011		2012		2013	
	Total	Families with own children under 18 years	Total	Families with own children under 18 years	Total	Families with own children under 18 years
All Families............................	502,498	214,387	501,421	213,058	482,570	210,516
FAMILY TYPE AND LABOR FORCE STATUS						
Married-Couple Families....................	349,608	129,102	347,070	125,725	336,560	125,487
Both husband and wife in labor force................	46.0	58.9	46.5	62.6	44.1	58.5
Husband in labor force, wife not in labor force..........	24.7	34.0	22.9	29.4	25.0	34.5
Wife in labor force, husband not in labor force..........	8.6	4.6	8.9	4.9	9.3	5.0
Both husband and wife not in labor force................	20.7	2.5	21.7	3.1	21.2	1.8
Other Families	152,890	85,285	154,351	87,333	146,010	85,029
Female householder, no husband present................	71.2	75.3	71.7	73.2	73.3	73.4
In labor force.................	51.3	61.9	49.2	57.5	50.7	58.3
Not in labor force..................	19.9	13.4	22.5	15.6	22.6	15.1
Male householder, no wife present................	28.8	24.7	28.3	26.8	26.7	26.6
In labor force...................	22.2	21.8	22.0	24.1	18.9	22.8
Not in labor force..................	6.6	3.0	6.3	2.8	7.8	3.8

Table NM-11. School Enrollment and Educational Attainment, 2013

(Number, percent.)

Item	State	U.S.
Enrollment		
Total population 3 years and over, enrolled in school	565,242	82,395,254
Enrolled in nursery school or preschool (percent)	5.1	6.0
Enrolled in kindergarten (percent)	5.3	5.2
Enrolled in elementary school, grades 1-8 (percent)...	40.7	40.0
Enrolled in high school, grades 9-12 (percent)	20.8	20.6
Enrolled in college or graduate school (percent)...	28.1	28.3
Attainment		
Total population 25 years and over	1,361,846	210,910,615
Less than ninth grade (percent)	7.4	5.8
9th to 12th grade, no diploma (percent)	8.4	7.6
High school graduate, including equivalency (percent)...	26.5	27.8
Some college, no degree (percent)	23.5	21.1
Associate's degree (percent)	7.8	8.1
Bachelor's degree (percent)	15.0	18.4
Graduate or professional degree (percent)...	11.4	11.2
High school graduate or higher (percent)	84.3	86.6
Bachelor's degree or higher (percent)...	26.4	29.6

Table NM-12. Public School Characteristics and Educational Indicators

(Number, percent; data derived from National Center of Education Statistics.)

Item	State	U.S.
Public Schools, 2012–2013 (except where noted)		
Number of school districts...	146	18,093
Number of schools...	877	98,454
Number of students (in thousands)	338	49,771
Number of teachers (in thousands)	22	3,109
Student-teacher ratio	15.2	16.0
Expenditures per student (dollars), FY 2012...	9,013	10,667
Four-year adjusted cohort graduation rate (ACGR)[1,2]	70.3	81.4
Students eligible for free or reduced-price lunch (in thousands)	229	25,188
English language learners (in thousands)	52	4,397
Students age 3 to 21 served under IDEA, part B (in thousands)	46	6,429

Public Schools by Type	Number	Percent of state public schools
Total number of schools...	877	100.0
Regular	829	94.5
Special education...	8	0.9
Vocational education...	1	0.1
Alternative education...	39	4.4

NOTE: Every school is assigned only one school type based on its instructional emphasis.
[1]ACGR data represents a new method of calculating high-school completion rates and may not be comparable to previous years' data for Averaged Freshmen Graduation Rates (AFGR).
[2]The United States 4-year ACGRs were estimated using both the reported 4-year ACGR data from 49 states and the District of Columbia and using imputed data for Idaho. The estimate for American Indian/Alaska Native students also includes imputed data for Virginia.

Table NM-13. Reported Voting and Registration of the Voting-Age Population, November 2012

(Numbers in thousands, percent.)

Item	Total population	Total citizen population	Registered			Voted		
			Total registered	Percent registered (total population)	Percent registered (total citizen population)	Total voted	Percent voted (total population)	Percent voted (total citizen population)
U.S. Total	235,248	215,081	153,157	65.1	71.2	132,948	56.5	61.8
State Total	1,553	1,426	978	63.0	68.6	878	56.5	61.6
Sex								
Male	754	684	450	59.7	65.8	404	53.6	59.1
Female	799	742	528	66.1	71.2	474	59.3	63.9
Race								
White alone......................................	1,310	1,215	875	66.8	72.0	789	60.2	64.9
White, non-Hispanic alone	729	713	545	74.8	76.4	503	69.0	70.5
Black alone......................................	43	39	24	B	B	24	B	B
Asian alone	39	12	3	B	B	3	B	B
Hispanic (of any race)	624	544	349	55.9	64.1	306	49.0	56.2
White alone or in combination	1,318	1,223	879	66.7	71.9	793	60.2	64.9
Black alone or in combination..........	43	39	24	B	B	24	B	B
Asian alone or in combination..........	43	16	3	B	B	3	B	B
Age								
18 to 24 years	177	163	84	47.4	51.3	66	37.1	40.2
25 to 44 years	542	471	296	54.5	62.7	253	46.7	53.7
45 to 64 years	588	551	414	70.4	75.1	390	66.3	70.8
65 to 74 years	129	124	87	67.3	70.0	82	63.7	66.3
75 years and over	118	116	99	83.9	85.0	87	74.3	75.2

B = Base is less than 75,000 and therefore too small to show the derived measure.

Table NM-14. Crime

(Number, rate per 100,000. Data are derived from the FBI Uniform Crime Reports.)

Item	State			U.S.[1,2,3,4]		
	2012	2013	Percent change	2012	2013	Percent change
TOTAL POPULATION[5]...........................	2,083,540	2,085,287	0.1	313,873,685	316,128,839	0.7
VIOLENT CRIME						
Number..........	11,660	12,443	6.7	1,217,067	1,163,146	-4.4
Rate	559.6	596.7	6.6	387.8	367.9	-5.1
Murder and Nonnegligent Manslaughter						
Number..........	116	125	7.8	14,866	14,196	-4.5
Rate	5.6	6.0	7.7	4.7	4.5	-5.2
Rape[6]						
Number..........	X	1,465	X	X	108,612	X
Rate	X	70.3	X	X	34.4	X
Robbery						
Number..........	1,847	1,810	-2.0	355,051	345,031	-2.8
Rate	88.6	86.8	-2.1	113.1	109.1	-3.5
Aggravated Assault						
Number..........	8,740	9,382	7.3	762,009	724,149	-5.0
Rate	419.5	449.9	7.3	242.8	229.1	-5.6
PROPERTY CRIME						
Number..........	75,094	77,256	2.9	9,001,992	8,632,512	-4.1
Rate	3,604.2	3,704.8	2.8	2,868.0	2,730.7	-4.8
Burglary						
Number..........	21,384	21,476	0.4	2,109,932	1,928,465	-8.6
Rate	1,026.3	1,029.9	0.3	672.2	610.0	-9.3
Larceny-Theft						
Number..........	48,247	49,875	3.4	6,168,874	6,004,453	-2.7
Rate	2,315.6	2,391.8	3.3	1,965.4	1,899.4	-3.4
Motor Vehicle Theft						
Number..........	5,463	5,905	8.1	723,186	699,594	-3.3
Rate	262.2	283.2	8.0	230.4	221.3	-4.0

NOTE: Although arson data are included in the trend and clearance tables, sufficient data are not available to estimate totals for this offense. Therefore, no arson data are published in this table.
X = Not applicable.
- = Zero or rounds to zero.
[1]The crime figures have been adjusted.
[2]The data collection methodology for the offense of forcible rape used by the Minnesota state Uniform Crime Reporting (UCR) Program (with the exception of Minneapolis and St. Paul, Minnesota) does not comply with national UCR Program guidelines. Consequently, its figures for forcible rape and violent crime (of which forcible rape is a part) are not published in this table.
[3]Includes offenses reported by the Zoological Police and the Metro Transit Police.
[4]Because of changes in the state's reporting practices, figures are not comparable to previous years' data.
[5]Populations are U.S. Census Bureau provisional estimates as of July 1 of each year.
[6]The figures shown for the offense of rape were estimated using the revised Uniform Crime Reporting (UCR) definition of rape.

Table NM-15. State Government Finances, 2013

(Dollar amounts in thousands, percent distribution.)

Item	Dollars	Percent distribution
Total Revenue	17,808,300	100.0
General revenue	14,295,361	80.3
Intergovernmental revenue	5,416,068	30.4
Taxes	5,201,576	29.2
General sales	1,968,571	11.1
Selective sales	683,054	3.8
License taxes	255,968	1.4
Individual income tax	1,240,945	7.0
Corporate income tax	267,457	1.5
Other taxes	785,581	4.4
Current charges	1,370,093	7.7
Miscellaneous general revenue	2,307,624	13.0
Utility revenue	0	-
Liquor stores revenue	0	-
Insurance trust revenue[1]	3,512,939	19.7
Total Expenditure	17,200,474	100.0
Intergovernmental expenditure	4,500,634	26.2
Direct expenditure	12,699,840	73.8
Current operation	9,093,983	52.9
Capital outlay	872,853	5.1
Insurance benefits and repayments	2,185,230	12.7
Assistance and subsidies	259,745	1.5
Interest on debt	288,029	1.7
Exhibit: Salaries and wages	2,662,738	15.5
Total Expenditure	17,200,474	100.0
General expenditure	15,015,244	87.3
Intergovernmental expenditure	4,500,634	26.2
Direct expenditure	10,514,610	61.1
General expenditure, by function:		
Education	5,406,138	31.4
Public welfare	3,946,347	22.9
Hospitals	953,684	5.5
Health	491,298	2.9
Highways	756,210	4.4
Police protection	134,511	0.8
Correction	400,947	2.3
Natural resources	182,694	1.1
Parks and recreation	50,999	0.3
Governmental administration	597,546	3.5
Interest on general debt	288,029	1.7
Other and unallocable	1,806,841	10.5
Utility expenditure	0	-
Liquor stores expenditure	0	-
Insurance trust expenditure	2,185,230	12.7
Debt at End of Fiscal Year	7,232,938	X
Cash and Security Holdings	46,720,845	X

X = Not applicable.

- = Zero or rounds to zero.

[1]Within insurance trust revenue, net earnings of state retirement systems is a calculated statistic (the item code in the data file is X08), and thus can be positive or negative. Net earnings is the sum of earnings on investments plus gains on investments minus losses on investments. The change made in 2002 for asset valuation from book to market value in accordance with Statement 34 of the Governmental Accounting Standards Board is reflected in the calculated statistics.

Table NM-16. State Government Tax Collections, 2014

(Dollars in thousands, percent.)

Item	Dollars	Percent distribution
Total Taxes	5,757,432	100.0
Property taxes	105,637	1.8
Sales and gross receipts	2,799,875	48.6
General sales and gross receipts	2,098,676	36.5
Selective sales and gross receipts	701,199	12.2
Alcoholic beverages	44,968	0.8
Amusements	70,226	1.2
Insurance premiums	99,832	1.7
Motor fuels	234,881	4.1
Pari-mutuels	596	-
Public utilities	29,894	0.5
Tobacco products	81,272	1.4
Other selective sales	139,530	2.4
Licenses	282,382	4.9
Alcoholic beverages	0	-
Amusements	373	-
Corporations in general	24,464	0.4
Hunting and fishing	24,655	0.4
Motor vehicle	188,156	3.3
Motor vehicle operators	3,671	0.1
Public utilities	1,151	-
Occupation and business, NEC	39,912	0.7
Other licenses	0	-
Income taxes	1,503,195	26.1
Individual income	1,297,493	22.5
Corporation net income	205,702	3.6
Other taxes	1,066,343	18.5
Death and gift	0	-
Documentary and stock transfer	0	-
Severance	1,066,343	18.5
Taxes, NEC	0	-

- = Zero or rounds to zero.

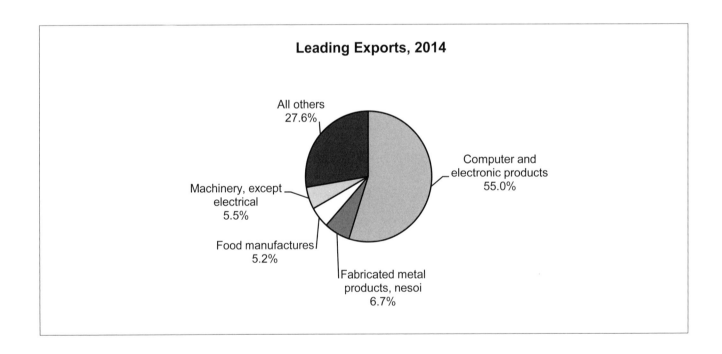

Leading Exports, 2014

All others 27.6%

Computer and electronic products 55.0%

Machinery, except electrical 5.5%

Food manufactures 5.2%

Fabricated metal products, nesoi 6.7%

NEW YORK

Facts and Figures

Location: Northeastern United States; bordered on the N by Canada (Ontario and Quebec) and Lake Ontario; on the E by Vermont, Massachusetts, and Connecticut; on the S by New Jersey and Pennsylvania; and on the W by Pennsylvania, Lake Erie, Canada (Ontario), and Lake Ontario

Area: 54,556 sq. mi. (141,299 sq. km.); rank—27th

Population: 19,746,227 (2014 est.); rank—4th

Principal Cities: capital—Albany; largest—New York City

Statehood: July 26, 1788; 11th state

U.S. Congress: 2 senators, 27 representatives

State Motto: *Excelsior* ("Ever upward")

State Song: "I Love New York"

State Nickname: The Empire State

Abbreviations: NY; N.Y.

State Symbols: flower—rose; tree—sugar maple; bird—bluebird

At a Glance

- With an increase in population of 1.9 percent, New York ranked 31st among the states in growth from 2010 to 2014.

- In 2013, 10.7 percent of New Yorkers did not have health insurance, compared to 14.5 percent of the total U.S. population.

- New York had the 2nd lowest rate of homeownership in the country in 2013 at 53.0 percent.

- The state's infant mortality rate of 4.92 per 1,000 live births ranked 43rd in the nation in 2013.

- New York had the lowest property crime rate in the country in 2013, at 1,824.8 incidents per 100,000 population.

Table NY-1. Population by Age, Sex, Race, and Hispanic Origin

(Number, percent, except where noted.)

Sex, age, race, and Hispanic origin	2000	2010	2014[1]	Average annual percent change, 2010–2014
Total Population	18,976,457	19,378,102	19,746,227	0.5
Percent of total U.S. population	6.7	6.3	6.2	X
Sex				
Male	9,146,748	9,377,147	9,581,261	0.5
Female	9,829,709	10,000,955	10,164,966	0.4
Age				
Under 5 years	1,239,417	1,155,822	1,184,591	0.6
5 to 19 years	3,971,834	3,741,689	3,576,630	-1.1
20 to 64 years	11,316,854	11,862,648	12,086,912	0.5
65 years and over	2,448,352	2,617,943	2,898,094	2.6
Median age (years)	35.9	38.0	38.3	0.2
Race and Hispanic Origin				
One race				
White	12,893,689	13,901,661	13,906,584	0.0
Black	3,014,385	3,378,047	3,479,242	0.7
American Indian and Alaska Native	82,461	183,046	189,764	0.9
Asian	1,044,976	1,481,555	1,677,323	3.2
Native Hawaiian or Other Pacific Islander	8,818	24,000	26,223	2.2
Two or more races	590,182	409,793	467,091	3.3
Hispanic (of any race)	2,867,583	3,564,228	3,672,791	0.8

X = Not applicable.
[1]Population figures for 2014 are July 1 estimates. The 2010 estimates are taken from the 2010 Census.

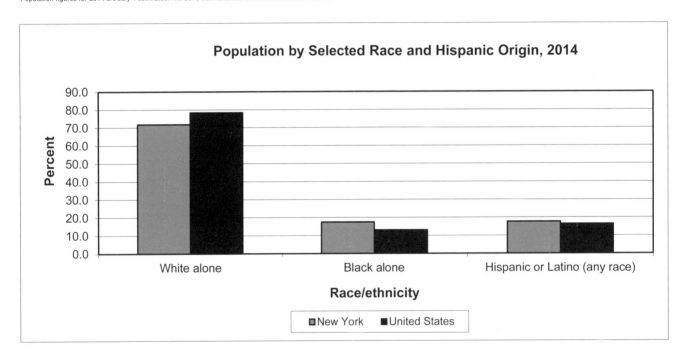

Population by Selected Race and Hispanic Origin, 2014

Legend: New York   United States

Table NY-2. Marital Status

(Number, percent distribution.)

Sex, age, race, and Hispanic origin	2000	2010	2013
Males, 15 Years and Over	7,125,715	7,586,733	7,743,068
Never married	34.7	40.5	41.3
Now married, except separated	53.3	47.6	46.7
Separated	2.7	2.2	2.1
Widowed	2.8	2.6	2.6
Divorced	6.5	7.2	7.3
Females, 15 Years and Over	7,932,161	8,283,542	8,404,705
Never married	29.0	34.8	35.5
Now married, except separated	47.1	42.8	42.0
Separated	3.7	3.1	3.2
Widowed	11.2	9.6	9.3
Divorced	8.9	9.7	10.0

Table NY-3. Households and Housing Characteristics

(Number, percent, dollars.)

Item	2000	2010	2013	Average annual percent change, 2000–2013
Total Households	7,056,860	7,196,427	7,219,356	0.2
Family households	4,639,387	4,632,676	4,584,095	-0.1
Married-couple family	3,289,514	3,210,895	3,158,468	-0.3
Other family	1,349,873	1,421,781	1,425,627	0.4
Male householder, no wife present	311,697	355,236	363,987	1.2
Female householder, no husband present	1,038,176	1,066,545	1,061,640	0.5
Nonfamily households	2,417,473	2,563,751	2,635,261	0.7
Householder living alone	1,982,742	2,089,816	2,160,914	0.7
Householder not living alone	434,731	473,935	474,347	0.7
Housing Characteristics				
Total housing units	7,679,301	8,108,211	8,126,399	0.4
Occupied housing units	7,056,860	7,196,427	7,219,356	0.2
Owner occupied	3,739,166	3,904,123	3,873,299	0.3
Renter occupied	3,317,694	3,292,304	3,346,057	0.1
Average household size	2.61	2.61	2.64	0.1
Financial Characteristics				
Median gross rent of renter-occupied housing	627	1,020	1,109	4.5
Median monthly owner costs for housing units with a mortgage	1,357	1,963	1,956	2.9
Median value of owner-occupied housing units	148,700	296,500	277,600	4.9

- = Zero or rounds to zero.

Table NY-4. Migration, Origin, and Language

(Number, percent.)

Characteristic	State			U.S.		
	2012	2013	Percent change	2012	2013	Percent change
Residence 1 Year Ago						
Population 1 year and over	19,352,153	19,431,954	0.4	310,212,755	312,432,820	0.7
Same house	88.9	89.0	X	85.0	85.0	X
Different house in the U.S.	10.3	10.2	X	14.4	14.4	X
Same county	6.5	6.3	X	9.0	8.9	X
Different county	3.8	3.9	X	5.4	5.5	X
Same state	2.4	2.5	X	3.2	3.2	X
Different state	1.4	1.4	X	2.3	2.3	X
Abroad	0.8	0.8	X	0.6	0.6	X
Place of Birth						
Native born	15,145,891	15,267,816	0.8	273,089,382	274,780,773	0.6
Male	48.8	48.9	X	49.3	49.3	X
Female	51.2	51.1	X	50.7	50.7	X
Foreign born	4,424,370	4,383,311	-0.9	40,824,658	41,348,066	1.3
Male	47.2	47.2	X	48.7	48.8	X
Female	52.8	52.8	X	51.3	51.2	X
Foreign born; naturalized U.S. citizen	2,340,833	2,359,247	0.8	18,686,237	19,294,710	3.3
Male	45.0	44.7	X	45.8	45.9	X
Female	55.0	55.3	X	54.2	54.1	X
Foreign born; not a U.S. citizen	2,083,537	2,024,064	-2.9	22,138,421	22,053,356	-0.4
Male	49.8	50.1	X	51.1	51.3	X
Female	50.2	49.9	X	48.9	48.7	X
Entered 2010 or later	7.1	9.5	X	7.0	9.7	X
Entered 2000 to 2009	27.7	26.8	X	30.4	29.4	X
Entered before 2000	65.2	63.7	X	62.7	61.0	X
World Region of Birth, Foreign						
Foreign-born population, excluding population born at sea	4,424,370	4,383,311	-0.9	40,824,553	41,347,945	1.3
Europe	17.2	17.1	X	11.8	11.6	X
Asia	27.4	27.6	X	29.2	29.5	X
Africa	3.9	4.2	X	4.2	4.4	X
Oceania	0.4	0.3	X	0.6	0.5	X
Latin America	50.0	49.4	X	52.2	51.9	X
North America	1.2	1.4	X	2.0	2.0	X
Language Spoken at Home and Ability to Speak English						
Population 5 years and over	18,405,939	18,480,702	0.4	294,003,714	296,358,760	0.8
English only	69.6	69.9	X	79.0	79.2	X
Language other than English	30.4	30.1	X	21.0	20.8	X
Speaks English less than "very well"	13.4	13.4	X	8.5	8.5	X

NA = Not available.
X = Not applicable.
- = Zero or rounds to zero.

Table NY-5. Median Income and Poverty Status, 2013

(Number, percent, except as noted.)

Characteristic	State		U.S.	
	Number	Percent	Number	Percent
Median Income				
Households (dollars)..	57,369	X	52,250	X
Families (dollars)	70,485	X	64,030	X
Below Poverty Level (All People)	3,055,645	16.0	48,810,868	15.8
Sex				
Male..	1,357,487	14.7	21,938,525	14.5
Female	1,698,158	17.2	26,872,343	17.1
Age				
Under 18 years...	950,077	22.8	16,086,960	22.2
Related children under 18 years...........................	934,576	22.5	15,769,921	21.9
18 to 64 years	1,789,322	14.6	28,578,191	14.8
65 years and over	316,246	11.6	4,145,717	9.6

X = Not applicable.

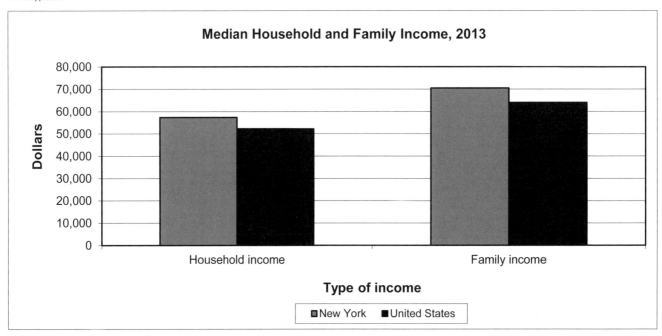

Table NY-6. Health Insurance Coverage Status for the Civilian Noninstitutionalized Population and Children Under 18 Years of Age

(Numbers in thousands, percent.)

Item	2005	2006	2007	2008	2009	2010	2011	2012	2013
Civilian Noninstitutionalized Population	19,022	19,040	19,062	19,207	19,264	19,134	19,208	19,317	19,400
Covered by Private or Public Insurance									
Number...	16,548	16,378	16,543	16,949	17,070	16,857	17,013	17,214	17,331
Percent...	87.0	86.0	86.8	88.2	88.6	88.1	88.6	89.1	89.3
Not Covered									
Number...	2,474	2,662	2,519	2,258	2,195	2,277	2,195	2,103	2,070
Percent...	13.0	14.0	13.2	11.8	11.4	11.9	11.4	10.9	10.7
Percent in the U.S. not covered............................	15.3	15.8	15.3	15.1	15.1	15.5	15.1	14.8	14.5
Children Under 18 Years of Age............................	4,534	4,547	4,437	4,402	4,414	4,302	4,270	4,253	4,231
Covered by Private or Public Insurance									
Number...	4,187	4,167	4,042	4,147	4,209	4,094	4,089	4,085	4,060
Percent...	92.3	91.6	91.1	94.2	95.4	95.2	95.8	96.1	96.0
Not Covered									
Number...	347	380	395	255	205	208	181	168	171
Percent...	7.7	8.4	8.9	5.8	4.6	4.8	4.2	3.9	4.0
Percent in the U.S. not covered............................	10.9	11.7	11.0	9.7	8.6	8.0	7.5	7.2	7.1

Table NY-7. Employment Status by Demographic Group, 2014

(Numbers in thousands, percent.)

Characteristic	Civilian noninstitutional population	Civilian labor force		Employed		Unemployed	
		Number	Percent of population	Number	Percent of population	Number	Percent of population
Total.........	15,765	9,554	60.6	8,946	56.7	608	6.4
Sex							
Male............	7,516	5,030	66.9	4,687	62.4	344	6.8
Female	8,249	4,524	54.8	4,259	51.6	265	5.9
Race, Sex, and Hispanic Origin							
White	11,324	6,897	60.9	6,533	57.7	364	5.3
Male............	5,485	3,687	67.2	3,483	63.5	204	5.5
Female	5,839	3,210	55.0	3,050	52.2	160	5.0
Black or African American....................	2,641	1,592	60.3	1,421	53.8	170	10.7
Male............	1,173	741	63.2	652	55.6	89	12.0
Female	1,468	850	57.9	769	52.4	82	9.6
Hispanic or Latino ethnicity[1]	2,597	1,539	59.3	1,408	54.2	130	8.5
Male............	1,258	844	67.1	769	61.2	75	8.9
Female	1,339	694	51.9	639	47.7	55	8.0
Age							
16 to 19 years.............	1,032	263	25.5	209	20.2	55	20.8
20 to 24 years.............	1,432	888	62.0	790	55.1	98	11.0
25 to 34 years.............	2,833	2,243	79.2	2,069	73.0	174	7.8
35 to 44 years.............	2,396	1,923	80.3	1,837	76.7	86	4.4
45 to 54 years.............	2,719	2,113	77.7	2,013	74.0	100	4.7
55 to 64 years.............	2,485	1,608	64.7	1,534	61.7	74	4.6
65 years and over	2,868	516	18.0	494	17.2	22	4.3

NOTE: Data in Table 7 are from the Current Population Survey (CPS) and do not match the estimates in Table 8. See notes and definitions for further information.
[1]May be of any race.

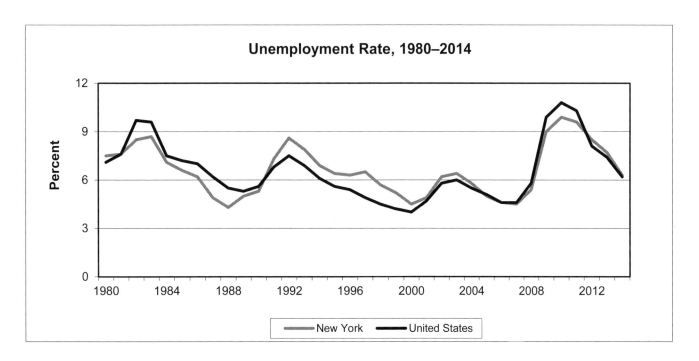

Unemployment Rate, 1980–2014

Table NY-8. Employment Status of the Civilian Noninstitutional Population Age 16 Years and Over

(Number, percent.)

Year	Civilian labor force	Civilian participation rate	Employed	Unemployed	Unemployment rate
2006	9,508,149	63.0	9,077,529	430,620	4.5
2007	9,522,056	62.7	9,088,207	433,849	4.6
2008	9,664,773	63.3	9,139,080	525,693	5.4
2009	9,647,485	62.8	8,844,486	802,999	8.3
2010	9,595,362	62.4	8,769,723	825,639	8.6
2011	9,517,788	61.4	8,727,961	789,827	8.3
2012	9,615,035	61.7	8,796,100	818,935	8.5
2013	9,631,802	61.4	8,890,997	740,805	7.7
2014	9,569,062	60.7	8,964,021	605,041	6.3

Table NY-9. Employment and Average Wages by Industry

(Estimates from 2007 through 2010 are based on the 2007 *North American Industry Classification System* [NAICS]. Estimates from 2011 onward are based on the 2012 NAICS.)

Industry	2007	2008	2009	2010	2011	2012	2013
				Number of jobs			
Wage and Salary Employment by Industry	8,939,191	9,003,322	8,735,423	8,732,197	8,837,168	8,935,624	9,066,866
Farm Wage and Salary Employment	17,437	19,023	18,351	18,392	19,509	19,751	23,408
Nonfarm Wage and Salary Employment	8,921,754	8,984,299	8,717,072	8,713,805	8,817,659	8,915,873	9,043,458
Private wage and salary employment	7,410,505	7,455,737	7,191,241	7,195,895	7,339,851	7,458,722	7,584,862
Forestry, fishing, and related activities	4,814	5,029	5,045	5,158	5,446	4,988	5,194
Mining	5,493	5,635	4,777	4,634	4,681	4,678	4,405
Utilities	38,719	38,886	39,359	38,327	37,278	36,043	36,355
Construction	366,885	375,382	340,039	321,327	324,855	325,097	338,963
Manufacturing	554,240	534,317	477,631	458,109	459,252	459,568	456,471
Durable goods manufacturing	326,557	317,602	281,194	268,367	271,254	269,657	266,892
Nondurable goods manufacturing	227,683	216,715	196,437	189,742	187,998	189,911	189,579
Wholesale trade	360,553	354,528	332,696	328,545	334,142	336,350	337,993
Retail trade	909,619	910,003	878,238	891,411	907,655	922,498	936,377
Transportation and warehousing	240,727	242,217	230,532	226,846	230,202	231,718	231,997
Information	267,120	265,147	253,295	253,220	256,473	261,625	262,108
Finance and insurance	556,515	547,195	509,996	503,703	517,938	517,035	511,941
Real estate and rental and leasing	192,092	194,552	188,380	187,147	185,901	184,649	188,926
Professional, scientific, and technical services	584,206	597,315	571,505	564,281	584,824	604,447	620,320
Management of companies and enterprises	128,824	131,576	130,725	132,092	133,230	134,734	138,666
Administrative and waste services	441,932	443,118	410,762	420,108	432,763	443,111	455,797
Educational services	344,028	353,266	353,666	359,334	366,831	374,891	378,982
Health care and social assistance	1,249,795	1,271,880	1,293,921	1,318,983	1,331,403	1,344,308	1,365,381
Arts, entertainment, and recreation	140,971	146,531	143,117	143,118	145,968	150,564	158,222
Accommodation and food services	570,411	580,974	579,229	603,010	632,911	659,140	688,203
Other services, except public administration	453,561	458,186	448,328	436,542	448,098	463,278	468,561
Government and government enterprises	1,511,249	1,528,562	1,525,831	1,517,910	1,477,808	1,457,151	1,458,596
				Dollars			
Average Wages and Salaries by Industry	58,616	59,418	57,004	59,511	61,042	61,863	62,327
Average Farm Wages and Salaries	32,541	28,804	27,627	26,371	22,547	24,963	28,400
Average Nonfarm Wages and Salaries	58,667	59,483	57,066	59,581	61,127	61,945	62,415
Average private wages and salaries	60,602	61,252	58,106	60,831	62,437	63,333	63,655
Forestry, fishing, and related activities	26,542	27,844	28,753	28,865	29,137	29,420	30,011
Mining	54,095	60,086	55,486	58,210	67,444	63,460	60,295
Utilities	92,446	93,933	92,583	97,932	103,008	108,849	106,014
Construction	55,778	58,868	59,674	60,281	61,489	62,343	63,448
Manufacturing	55,679	57,040	57,052	59,391	59,979	60,917	61,160
Durable goods manufacturing	58,850	60,327	60,591	62,768	64,386	65,990	66,322
Nondurable goods manufacturing	51,132	52,223	51,987	54,614	53,620	53,713	53,893
Wholesale trade	69,067	68,900	68,769	71,633	73,738	77,718	76,862
Retail trade	29,169	29,469	29,215	29,626	30,299	30,725	31,485
Transportation and warehousing	43,664	44,356	44,025	45,460	46,132	47,038	48,197
Information	87,294	89,110	89,193	90,840	95,814	100,128	102,414
Finance and insurance	205,524	204,962	171,837	191,436	198,094	197,340	197,220
Real estate and rental and leasing	55,542	54,783	52,242	54,584	56,582	59,437	60,014
Professional, scientific, and technical services	84,184	87,363	86,296	90,752	93,826	96,078	97,881
Management of companies and enterprises	141,151	133,419	119,634	140,138	142,451	144,017	142,725
Administrative and waste services	39,383	40,668	40,503	42,540	41,922	43,713	43,900
Educational services	37,480	39,096	40,537	41,077	42,297	43,178	44,548
Health care and social assistance	41,038	42,536	43,733	44,359	45,135	45,775	46,602
Arts, entertainment, and recreation	47,769	47,315	46,484	47,111	48,224	48,865	48,565
Accommodation and food services	24,097	24,269	23,693	24,573	25,483	26,121	26,116
Other services, except public administration	30,919	32,397	32,576	33,582	33,971	34,578	35,503
Government and government enterprises	49,175	50,850	52,168	53,654	54,618	54,841	55,969

Table NY-10. Employment Characteristics by Family Type

(Number, percent.)

Family type and labor force status	2011		2012		2013	
	Total	Families with own children under 18 years	Total	Families with own children under 18 years	Total	Families with own children under 18 years
All Families..	4,607,636	2,042,822	4,587,857	2,015,419	4,584,095	1,980,127
FAMILY TYPE AND LABOR FORCE STATUS						
Married-Couple Families..................................	3,166,722	1,330,561	3,147,912	1,307,147	3,158,468	1,303,725
Both husband and wife in labor force........................	53.4	64.9	53.5	65.4	52.6	64.6
Husband in labor force, wife not in labor force............	21.9	28.7	21.6	28.2	21.7	28.3
Wife in labor force, husband not in labor force............	8.2	4.5	8.5	4.6	8.7	4.8
Both husband and wife not in labor force...................	16.5	1.9	16.4	1.8	16.2	1.7
Other Families	1,440,914	712,261	1,439,945	708,272	1,425,627	676,402
Female householder, no husband present...................	75.4	79.7	74.3	78.1	74.5	78.9
In labor force...	51.5	63.4	51.8	63.0	51.0	62.2
Not in labor force.......................................	23.9	16.3	22.5	15.1	23.5	16.7
Male householder, no wife present..........................	24.6	20.3	25.7	21.9	25.5	21.1
In labor force...	18.9	18.1	19.9	19.6	19.7	18.7
Not in labor force.......................................	5.8	2.2	5.8	2.3	5.9	2.4

Table NY-11. School Enrollment and Educational Attainment, 2013

(Number, percent.)

Item	State	U.S.
Enrollment		
Total population 3 years and over, enrolled in school	4,957,486	82,395,254
Enrolled in nursery school or preschool (percent).................	6.0	6.0
Enrolled in kindergarten (percent)................................	4.8	5.2
Enrolled in elementary school, grades 1-8 (percent)..............	37.9	40.0
Enrolled in high school, grades 9-12 (percent)...................	20.3	20.6
Enrolled in college or graduate school (percent).................	31.2	28.3
Attainment		
Total population 25 years and over	13,419,310	210,910,615
Less than ninth grade (percent)..................................	6.8	5.8
9th to 12th grade, no diploma (percent)..........................	7.6	7.6
High school graduate, including equivalency (percent)............	26.8	27.8
Some college, no degree (percent)................................	16.1	21.1
Associate's degree (percent).....................................	8.6	8.1
Bachelor's degree (percent)......................................	19.3	18.4
Graduate or professional degree (percent)........................	14.8	11.2
High school graduate or higher (percent)	85.6	86.6
Bachelor's degree or higher (percent)............................	34.1	29.6

Table NY-12. Public School Characteristics and Educational Indicators

(Number, percent; data derived from National Center of Education Statistics.)

Item	State	U.S.
Public Schools, 2012–2013 (except where noted)		
Number of school districts.......................................	950	18,093
Number of schools..	4,822	98,454
Number of students (in thousands)................................	2,711	49,771
Number of teachers (in thousands)	207	3,109
Student-teacher ratio	13.1	16.0
Expenditures per student (dollars), FY 2012......................	19,396	10,667
Four-year adjusted cohort graduation rate (ACGR)[1,2]	76.8	81.4
Students eligible for free or reduced-price lunch (in thousands) ..	1297	25,188
English language learners (in thousands)	198	4,397
Students age 3 to 21 served under IDEA, part B (in thousands)	451	6,429

Public Schools by Type	Number	Percent of state public schools
Total number of schools..	4,822	100.0
Regular	4,644	96.3
Special education...	123	2.6
Vocational education..	29	0.6
Alternative education...	26	0.5

NOTE: Every school is assigned only one school type based on its instructional emphasis.

[1]ACGR data represents a new method of calculating high-school completion rates and may not be comparable to previous years' data for Averaged Freshmen Graduation Rates (AFGR).

[2]The United States 4-year ACGRs were estimated using both the reported 4-year ACGR data from 49 states and the District of Columbia and using imputed data for Idaho. The estimate for American Indian/Alaska Native students also includes imputed data for Virginia.

Table NY-13. Reported Voting and Registration of the Voting-Age Population, November 2012

(Numbers in thousands, percent.)

Item	Total population	Total citizen population	Registered			Voted		
			Total registered	Percent registered (total population)	Percent registered (total citizen population)	Total voted	Percent voted (total population)	Percent voted (total citizen population)
U.S. Total	235,248	215,081	153,157	65.1	71.2	132,948	56.5	61.8
State Total	15,066	13,082	8,887	59.0	67.9	7,675	50.9	58.7
Sex								
Male	7,151	6,194	4,084	57.1	65.9	3,503	49.0	56.5
Female	7,916	6,887	4,803	60.7	69.7	4,172	52.7	60.6
Race								
White alone..................................	10,925	9,929	6,837	62.6	68.9	5,781	52.9	58.2
White, non-Hispanic alone	8,992	8,672	6,075	67.6	70.1	5,152	57.3	59.4
Black alone..................................	2,482	2,103	1,542	62.1	73.3	1,456	58.7	69.2
Asian alone	1,442	848	384	26.6	45.3	333	23.1	39.2
Hispanic (of any race)	2,363	1,548	983	41.6	63.5	835	35.3	53.9
White alone or in combination	11,077	10,074	6,920	62.5	68.7	5,847	52.8	58.0
Black alone or in combination..........	2,562	2,177	1,594	62.2	73.2	1,503	58.7	69.0
Asian alone or in combination..........	1,476	882	414	28.1	47.0	354	24.0	40.2
Age								
18 to 24 years................................	2,028	1,790	926	45.7	51.8	710	35.0	39.6
25 to 44 years................................	5,109	4,042	2,676	52.4	66.2	2,278	44.6	56.3
45 to 64 years................................	5,217	4,706	3,381	64.8	71.8	3,046	58.4	64.7
65 to 74 years................................	1,558	1,467	1,094	70.2	74.6	976	62.7	66.6
75 years and over	1,154	1,077	810	70.2	75.3	665	57.7	61.8

Table NY-14. Crime

(Number, rate per 100,000. Data are derived from the FBI Uniform Crime Reports.)

Item	State			U.S.[1,2,3,4]		
	2012	2013	Percent change	2012	2013	Percent change
TOTAL POPULATION[5].....................................	19,576,125	19,651,127	0.4	313,873,685	316,128,839	0.7
VIOLENT CRIME						
Number..........	79,535	76,596	-3.7	1,217,067	1,163,146	-4.4
Rate	406.3	389.8	-4.1	387.8	367.9	-5.1
Murder and Nonnegligent Manslaughter						
Number..........	683	648	-5.1	14,866	14,196	-4.5
Rate	3.5	3.3	-5.5	4.7	4.5	-5.2
Rape[6]						
Number..........	X	3,353	X		108,612	
Rate	X	17.1	X		34.4	
Robbery						
Number..........	28,633	27,241	-4.9	355,051	345,031	-2.8
Rate	146.3	138.6	-5.2	113.1	109.1	-3.5
Aggravated Assault						
Number..........	47,382	46,130	-2.6	762,009	724,149	-5.0
Rate	242.0	234.7	-3.0	242.8	229.1	-5.6
PROPERTY CRIME						
Number..........	375,268	358,598	-4.4	9,001,992	8,632,512	-4.1
Rate	1,917.0	1,824.8	-4.8	2,868.0	2,730.7	-4.8
Burglary						
Number..........	64,389	56,442	-12.3	2,109,932	1,928,465	-8.6
Rate	328.9	287.2	-12.7	672.2	610.0	-9.3
Larceny-Theft						
Number..........	293,562	286,674	-2.3	6,168,874	6,004,453	-2.7
Rate	1,499.6	1,458.8	-2.7	1,965.4	1,899.4	-3.4
Motor Vehicle Theft						
Number..........	17,317	15,482	-10.6	723,186	699,594	-3.3
Rate	88.5	78.8	-10.9	230.4	221.3	-4.0

NOTE: Although arson data are included in the trend and clearance tables, sufficient data are not available to estimate totals for this offense. Therefore, no arson data are published in this table.

X = Not applicable.

- = Zero or rounds to zero.

[1]The crime figures have been adjusted.

[2]The data collection methodology for the offense of forcible rape used by the Minnesota state Uniform Crime Reporting (UCR) Program (with the exception of Minneapolis and St. Paul, Minnesota) does not comply with national UCR Program guidelines. Consequently, its figures for forcible rape and violent crime (of which forcible rape is a part) are not published in this table.

[3]Includes offenses reported by the Zoological Police and the Metro Transit Police.

[4]Because of changes in the state's reporting practices, figures are not comparable to previous years' data.

[5]Populations are U.S. Census Bureau provisional estimates as of July 1 of each year.

[6]The figures shown for the offense of rape were estimated using the revised Uniform Crime Reporting (UCR) definition of rape.

Table NY-15. State Government Finances, 2013

(Dollar amounts in thousands, percent distribution.)

Item	Dollars	Percent distribution
Total Revenue	212,858,793	100.0
General revenue	165,200,561	77.6
Intergovernmental revenue	71,682,137	33.7
Taxes	73,667,171	34.6
General sales	12,117,579	5.7
Selective sales	11,099,912	5.2
License taxes	1,952,367	0.9
Individual income tax	40,230,379	18.9
Corporate income tax	4,920,605	2.3
Other taxes	3,346,329	1.6
Current charges	8,510,037	4.0
Miscellaneous general revenue	11,341,216	5.3
Utility revenue	7,900,199	3.7
Liquor stores revenue	0	-
Insurance trust revenue[1]	39,758,033	18.7
Total Expenditure	184,040,200	100.0
Intergovernmental expenditure	56,236,537	30.6
Direct expenditure	127,803,663	69.4
Current operation	86,853,934	47.2
Capital outlay	9,493,079	5.2
Insurance benefits and repayments	24,088,890	13.1
Assistance and subsidies	1,636,851	0.9
Interest on debt	5,730,909	3.1
Exhibit: Salaries and wages	22,974,180	12.5
Total Expenditure	184,040,200	100.0
General expenditure	147,156,113	80.0
Intergovernmental expenditure	56,236,537	30.6
Direct expenditure	90,919,576	49.4
General expenditure, by function:		
Education	41,151,716	22.4
Public welfare	58,009,518	31.5
Hospitals	4,750,662	2.6
Health	9,215,195	5.0
Highways	4,238,973	2.3
Police protection	995,306	0.5
Correction	3,438,227	1.9
Natural resources	423,976	0.2
Parks and recreation	550,477	0.3
Governmental administration	5,524,280	3.0
Interest on general debt	4,291,315	2.3
Other and unallocable	14,566,468	7.9
Utility expenditure	12,795,197	7.0
Liquor stores expenditure	0	-
Insurance trust expenditure	24,088,890	13.1
Debt at End of Fiscal Year	136,014,460	X
Cash and Security Holdings	318,155,785	X

X = Not applicable.
- = Zero or rounds to zero.
[1]Within insurance trust revenue, net earnings of state retirement systems is a calculated statistic (the item code in the data file is X08), and thus can be positive or negative. Net earnings is the sum of earnings on investments plus gains on investments minus losses on investments. The change made in 2002 for asset valuation from book to market value in accordance with Statement 34 of the Governmental Accounting Standards Board is reflected in the calculated statistics.

Table NY-16. State Government Tax Collections, 2014

(Dollars in thousands, percent.)

Item	Dollars	Percent distribution
Total Taxes	76,978,982	100.0
Property taxes	X	X
Sales and gross receipts	23,544,789	30.6
General sales and gross receipts	12,668,587	16.5
Selective sales and gross receipts	10,876,202	14.1
Alcoholic beverages	250,926	0.3
Amusements	996	-
Insurance premiums	1,345,394	1.7
Motor fuels	1,630,358	2.1
Pari-mutuels	21,420	-
Public utilities	929,929	1.2
Tobacco products	1,446,184	1.9
Other selective sales	5,250,995	6.8
Licenses	1,884,841	2.4
Alcoholic beverages	64,576	0.1
Amusements	50	-
Corporations in general	63,488	0.1
Hunting and fishing	51,775	0.1
Motor vehicle	1,357,553	1.8
Motor vehicle operators	145,500	0.2
Public utilities	24,165	-
Occupation and business, NEC	176,275	0.2
Other licenses	1,459	-
Income taxes	47,826,461	62.1
Individual income	42,964,774	55.8
Corporation net income	4,861,687	6.3
Other taxes	3,722,891	4.8
Death and gift	1,238,320	1.6
Documentary and stock transfer	1,037,341	1.3
Severance	X	X
Taxes, NEC	1,447,230	1.9

X = Not applicable.
- = Zero or rounds to zero.

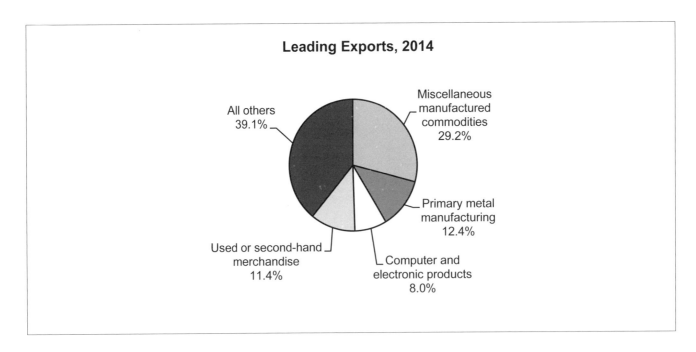

Leading Exports, 2014

- All others 39.1%
- Miscellaneous manufactured commodities 29.2%
- Primary metal manufacturing 12.4%
- Computer and electronic products 8.0%
- Used or second-hand merchandise 11.4%

NORTH CAROLINA

Facts and Figures

Location: Southeastern United States; bordered on the N by Virginia, on the E by the Atlantic Ocean, on the S by South Carolina and Georgia, and on the W by Tennessee

Area: 53,819 sq. mi. (139,389 sq. km.); rank—28th

Population: 9,943,964 (2014 est.); rank—9th

Principal Cities: capital—Raleigh; largest—Charlotte

Statehood: November 21, 1789; 12th state

U.S. Congress: 2 senators, 13 representatives

State Motto: *Esse quam videri* ("To be rather than to seem")

State Song: "The Old North State"

State Nicknames: The Tar Heel State; The Old North State

Abbreviations: NC; N.C.

State Symbols: flower—flowering dogwood; tree—pine; bird—cardinal

At a Glance

- With an increase in population of 4.3 percent, North Carolina ranked 13th among the states in growth from 2010 to 2014.

- North Carolina's median household income in 2013 was $45,906, and 17.9 percent of the population lived below the poverty level.

- North Carolina's violent crime rate in 2013 was 342.2 per 100,000 population, compared to 367.9 for the entire nation.

- In 2013, 15.6 percent of North Carolinians did not have health insurance, compared to 14.5 percent of the entire U.S. population.

- With 12.8 percent of its residents living in mobile homes in 2011, North Carolina ranked 7th in the nation in this category.

Table NC-1. Population by Age, Sex, Race, and Hispanic Origin

(Number, percent, except where noted.)

Sex, age, race, and Hispanic origin	2000	2010	2014[1]	Average annual percent change, 2010–2014
Total Population	8,049,313	9,535,483	9,943,964	1.1
Percent of total U.S. population	2.9	3.1	3.1	X
Sex				
Male	3,942,695	4,645,492	4,844,593	1.1
Female	4,106,618	4,889,991	5,099,371	1.1
Age				
Under 5 years	539,509	632,040	607,476	-1.0
5 to 19 years	1,653,851	1,926,640	1,949,700	0.3
20 to 64 years	4,886,905	5,742,724	5,923,426	0.8
65 years and over	969,048	1,234,079	1,463,362	4.4
Median age (years)	35.3	37.4	38.2	0.5
Race and Hispanic Origin				
One race				
White	5,804,656	6,898,296	7,108,057	0.8
Black	1,737,545	2,088,362	2,196,390	1.3
American Indian and Alaska Native	99,551	147,566	154,735	1.2
Asian	113,689	215,952	267,385	5.5
Native Hawaiian or Other Pacific Islander	3,983	10,309	11,930	3.7
Two or more races	103,260	174,998	205,467	4.1
Hispanic (of any race)	378,963	830,172	894,276	1.9

X = Not applicable.
[1]Population figures for 2014 are July 1 estimates. The 2010 estimates are taken from the 2010 Census.

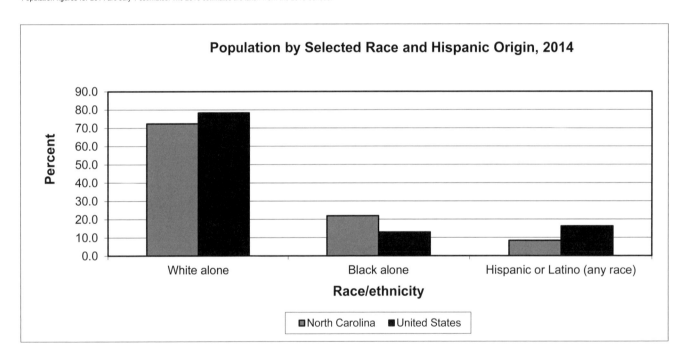

Table NC-2. Marital Status

(Number, percent distribution.)

Sex, age, race, and Hispanic origin	2000	2010	2013
Males, 15 Years and Over	3,092,380	3,678,950	3,823,442
Never married	28.2	33.3	34.7
Now married, except separated	58.7	51.8	50.7
Separated	2.7	2.9	2.6
Widowed	2.4	2.5	2.5
Divorced	8.1	9.6	9.5
Females, 15 Years and Over	3,301,327	3,975,748	4,115,182
Never married	22.0	27.3	28.8
Now married, except separated	53.9	47.3	46.1
Separated	3.3	3.5	3.4
Widowed	10.9	9.8	9.5
Divorced	9.9	12.1	12.1

Table NC-3. Households and Housing Characteristics

(Number, percent, dollars.)

Item	2000	2010	2013	Average annual percent change, 2000–2013
Total Households	3,132,012	3,670,859	3,757,480	1.4
Family households	2,158,869	2,441,916	2,474,802	1.1
Married-couple family	1,645,346	1,770,863	1,786,356	0.6
Other family	513,523	671,053	688,446	2.3
Male householder, no wife present	123,526	159,752	168,512	2.4
Female householder, no husband present	389,997	511,301	519,934	2.2
Nonfamily households	973,144	1,228,943	1,282,678	2.1
Householder living alone	795,271	1,022,017	1,055,644	2.2
Householder not living alone	177,873	206,926	227,034	1.9
Housing Characteristics				
Total housing units	3,523,944	4,333,479	4,394,515	1.7
Occupied housing units	3,132,012	3,670,859	3,757,480	1.4
Owner occupied	2,172,355	2,465,551	2,414,717	0.8
Renter occupied	959,658	1,205,308	1,342,763	2.6
Average household size	2.49	2.53	2.55	0.2
Financial Characteristics				
Median gross rent of renter-occupied housing	548	731	778	2.7
Median monthly owner costs for housing units with a mortgage	985	1,250	1,205	1.6
Median value of owner-occupied housing units	108,300	154,200	154,300	2.8

Table NC-4. Migration, Origin, and Language

(Number, percent.)

Characteristic	State			U.S.		
	2012	2013	Percent change	2012	2013	Percent change
Residence 1 Year Ago						
Population 1 year and over	9,640,490	9,737,365	1.0	310,212,755	312,432,820	0.7
Same house	84.7	84.6	X	85.0	85.0	X
Different house in the U.S.	14.8	14.9	X	14.4	14.4	X
Same county	8.4	8.4	X	9.0	8.9	X
Different county	6.3	6.5	X	5.4	5.5	X
Same state	3.5	3.7	X	3.2	3.2	X
Different state	2.8	2.8	X	2.3	2.3	X
Abroad	0.5	0.5	X	0.6	0.6	X
Place of Birth						
Native born	9,004,001	9,098,634	1.1	273,089,382	274,780,773	0.6
Male	48.5	48.4	X	49.3	49.3	X
Female	51.5	51.6	X	50.7	50.7	X
Foreign born	748,072	749,426	0.2	40,824,658	41,348,066	1.3
Male	51.3	52.2	X	48.7	48.8	X
Female	48.7	47.8	X	51.3	51.2	X
Foreign born; naturalized U.S. citizen	239,280	239,232	-	18,686,237	19,294,710	3.3
Male	46.5	47.1	X	45.8	45.9	X
Female	53.5	52.9	X	54.2	54.1	X
Foreign born; not a U.S. citizen	508,792	510,194	0.3	22,138,421	22,053,356	-0.4
Male	53.6	54.6	X	51.1	51.3	X
Female	46.4	45.4	X	48.9	48.7	X
Entered 2010 or later	8.2	11.4	X	7.0	9.7	X
Entered 2000 to 2009	40.3	37.5	X	30.4	29.4	X
Entered before 2000	51.4	51.1	X	62.7	61.0	X
World Region of Birth, Foreign						
Foreign-born population, excluding population born at sea	748,072	749,426	0.2	40,824,553	41,347,945	1.3
Europe	11.0	10.5	X	11.8	11.6	X
Asia	23.9	24.4	X	29.2	29.5	X
Africa	6.2	5.9	X	4.2	4.4	X
Oceania	0.5	0.5	X	0.6	0.5	X
Latin America	56.3	56.4	X	52.2	51.9	X
North America	2.1	2.3	X	2.0	2.0	X
Language Spoken at Home and Ability to Speak English						
Population 5 years and over	9,140,321	9,240,578	1.1	294,003,714	296,358,760	0.8
English only	88.9	89.0	X	79.0	79.2	X
Language other than English	11.1	11.0	X	21.0	20.8	X
Speaks English less than "very well"	4.9	4.8	X	8.5	8.5	X

NA = Not available.
X = Not applicable.
- = Zero or rounds to zero.

Table NC-5. Median Income and Poverty Status, 2013

(Number, percent, except as noted.)

Characteristic	State		U.S.	
	Number	Percent	Number	Percent
Median Income				
Households (dollars)...............	45,906	X	52,250	X
Families (dollars)	56,111	X	64,030	X
Below Poverty Level (All People)	1,715,397	17.9	48,810,868	15.8
Sex				
Male...............	761,677	16.4	21,938,525	14.5
Female	953,720	19.3	26,872,343	17.1
Age				
Under 18 years...............	565,996	25.2	16,086,960	22.2
Related children under 18 years...............	555,621	24.9	15,769,921	21.9
18 to 64 years...............	1,012,788	16.9	28,578,191	14.8
65 years and over...............	136,613	10.0	4,145,717	9.6

X = Not applicable.

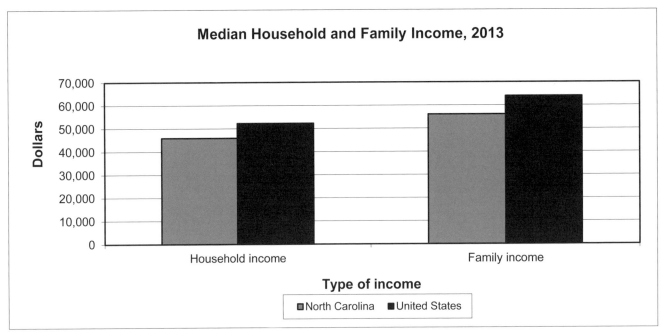

Median Household and Family Income, 2013

Table NC-6. Health Insurance Coverage Status for the Civilian Noninstitutionalized Population and Children Under 18 Years of Age

(Numbers in thousands, percent.)

Item	2005	2006	2007	2008	2009	2010	2011	2012	2013
Civilian Noninstitutionalized Population	8,561	8,851	9,183	9,004	9,149	9,361	9,461	9,553	9,645
Covered by Private or Public Insurance									
Number...............	7,249	7,266	7,673	7,570	7,679	7,791	7,916	7,970	8,136
Percent...............	84.7	82.1	83.6	84.1	83.9	83.2	83.7	83.4	84.4
Not Covered									
Number...............	1,312	1,585	1,510	1,434	1,471	1,570	1,545	1,583	1,509
Percent...............	15.3	17.9	16.4	15.9	16.1	16.8	16.3	16.6	15.6
Percent in the U.S. not covered...............	15.3	15.8	15.3	15.1	15.1	15.5	15.1	14.8	14.5
Children Under 18 Years of Age...............	2,205	2,198	2,247	2,237	2,271	2,281	2,287	2,282	2,281
Covered by Private or Public Insurance									
Number...............	1,946	1,891	1,975	2,018	2,085	2,104	2,112	2,109	2,136
Percent...............	88.3	86.0	87.9	90.2	91.8	92.3	92.4	92.4	93.7
Not Covered									
Number...............	259	307	272	219	186	177	175	173	144
Percent...............	11.7	14.0	12.1	9.8	8.2	7.7	7.6	7.6	6.3
Percent in the U.S. not covered...............	10.9	11.7	11.0	9.7	8.6	8.0	7.5	7.2	7.1

Table NC-7. Employment Status by Demographic Group, 2014

(Numbers in thousands, percent.)

Characteristic	Civilian noninstitutional population	Civilian labor force		Employed		Unemployed	
		Number	Percent of population	Number	Percent of population	Number	Percent of population
Total..	7,690	4,648	60.4	4,360	56.7	287	6.2
Sex							
Male..	3,640	2,437	66.9	2,289	62.9	148	6.1
Female..	4,050	2,210	54.6	2,071	51.2	139	6.3
Race, Sex, and Hispanic Origin							
White	5,501	3,325	60.4	3,157	57.4	168	5.0
Male..	2,655	1,818	68.5	1,731	65.2	87	4.8
Female..	2,845	1,507	53.0	1,426	50.1	81	5.4
Black or African American...................	1,644	988	60.1	885	53.9	102	10.4
Male..	732	445	60.8	393	53.8	52	11.6
Female..	911	543	59.5	492	54.0	51	9.4
Hispanic or Latino ethnicity[1]	633	456	72.1	427	67.4	30	6.5
Male..	356	307	86.3	291	81.8	16	5.2
Female..	277	149	53.8	135	48.9	14	9.2
Age							
16 to 19 years...............................	531	177	33.4	135	25.5	42	23.6
20 to 24 years...............................	694	466	67.1	406	58.5	60	12.9
25 to 34 years...............................	1,227	967	78.8	897	73.1	70	7.2
35 to 44 years...............................	1,235	1,010	81.8	972	78.8	37	3.7
45 to 54 years...............................	1,278	1,021	79.9	981	76.8	41	4.0
55 to 64 years...............................	1,281	784	61.2	756	59.0	28	3.5
65 years and over	1,445	223	15.4	212	14.7	10	4.5

NOTE: Data in Table 7 are from the Current Population Survey (CPS) and do not match the estimates in Table 8. See notes and definitions for further information.
[1]May be of any race.

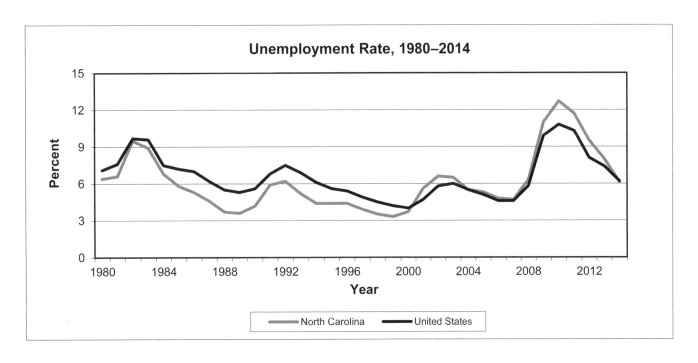

Table NC-8. Employment Status of the Civilian Noninstitutional Population Age 16 Years and Over

(Number, percent.)

Year	Civilian labor force	Civilian participation rate	Employed	Unemployed	Unemployment rate
2006	4,444,967	66.1	4,234,095	210,872	4.7
2007	4,512,856	65.6	4,300,304	212,552	4.7
2008	4,560,059	65.0	4,281,713	278,346	6.1
2009	4,570,789	64.2	4,087,105	483,684	10.6
2010	4,616,691	63.4	4,115,629	501,062	10.9
2011	4,634,470	62.6	4,160,613	473,857	10.2
2012	4,682,671	62.4	4,251,021	431,650	9.2
2013	4,680,748	61.6	4,310,422	370,326	7.9
2014	4,656,194	60.5	4,370,379	285,815	6.1

Table NC-9. Employment and Average Wages by Industry

(Estimates from 2007 through 2010 are based on the 2007 *North American Industry Classification System* [NAICS]. Estimates from 2011 onward are based on the 2012 NAICS.)

Industry	2007	2008	2009	2010	2011	2012	2013
				Number of jobs			
Wage and Salary Employment by Industry	4,389,750	4,380,014	4,170,430	4,142,475	4,194,673	4,245,620	4,316,789
Farm Wage and Salary Employment	22,318	21,240	19,787	20,537	22,498	18,969	22,756
Nonfarm Wage and Salary Employment	4,367,432	4,358,774	4,150,643	4,121,938	4,172,175	4,226,651	4,294,033
Private wage and salary employment	3,543,270	3,509,755	3,291,218	3,255,024	3,311,094	3,366,353	3,432,840
Forestry, fishing, and related activities	13,434	13,276	13,184	13,756	14,185	13,932	13,897
Mining	3,977	3,857	3,421	3,017	3,041	3,004	2,934
Utilities	12,598	12,696	12,655	12,151	12,142	12,278	12,456
Construction	265,582	246,443	201,912	185,010	183,076	178,009	180,023
Manufacturing	544,235	520,425	450,378	432,671	435,641	440,116	443,237
Durable goods manufacturing	291,893	278,378	233,187	222,044	226,553	234,356	236,402
Nondurable goods manufacturing	252,342	242,047	217,191	210,627	209,088	205,760	206,835
Wholesale trade	182,479	180,249	168,500	166,187	169,313	172,309	174,725
Retail trade	475,162	470,147	445,199	441,978	447,766	455,304	464,821
Transportation and warehousing	119,826	116,205	106,853	104,879	108,408	110,500	111,506
Information	73,291	72,418	69,904	68,391	68,765	69,307	69,831
Finance and insurance	157,187	158,175	151,690	152,281	154,409	155,364	157,089
Real estate and rental and leasing	55,814	54,845	51,271	49,619	49,191	49,388	51,550
Professional, scientific, and technical services	186,384	190,501	182,479	183,673	191,014	196,984	201,933
Management of companies and enterprises	71,447	76,037	73,366	73,211	77,301	80,558	77,921
Administrative and waste services	249,721	243,984	217,521	234,201	251,092	261,258	273,328
Educational services	78,817	82,677	86,226	87,362	89,348	89,503	90,662
Health care and social assistance	455,994	464,786	470,835	465,393	465,269	471,261	480,533
Arts, entertainment, and recreation	52,701	53,965	57,441	56,560	58,051	58,972	61,181
Accommodation and food services	347,628	351,085	340,522	340,644	346,828	359,188	372,840
Other services, except public administration	196,993	197,984	187,861	184,040	186,254	189,118	192,373
Government and government enterprises	824,162	849,019	859,425	866,914	861,081	860,298	861,193
				Dollars			
Average Wages and Salaries by Industry	39,748	40,708	40,802	42,039	43,107	44,217	44,656
Average Farm Wages and Salaries	30,476	29,361	25,702	18,438	21,834	23,650	28,625
Average Nonfarm Wages and Salaries	39,795	40,763	40,874	42,157	43,221	44,309	44,741
Average private wages and salaries	39,480	40,274	40,185	41,689	42,827	44,159	44,696
Forestry, fishing, and related activities	25,360	25,890	26,470	27,046	27,915	28,973	30,810
Mining	64,642	53,137	51,558	43,772	46,996	47,266	48,091
Utilities	76,378	78,538	76,185	80,911	82,200	86,571	93,305
Construction	39,567	40,517	40,246	41,015	42,240	44,164	44,779
Manufacturing	48,429	49,177	50,468	52,809	54,176	54,906	56,201
Durable goods manufacturing	51,202	51,999	53,639	56,441	58,112	59,327	61,063
Nondurable goods manufacturing	45,222	45,931	47,064	48,980	49,910	49,870	50,644
Wholesale trade	57,069	58,029	57,951	60,561	62,665	64,539	65,755
Retail trade	25,204	25,175	24,984	25,594	25,625	26,398	26,788
Transportation and warehousing	40,164	42,174	42,055	42,980	43,845	44,226	45,668
Information	57,582	60,284	60,354	63,009	65,922	69,672	72,017
Finance and insurance	74,459	72,619	68,467	73,822	76,784	79,594	82,886
Real estate and rental and leasing	37,957	37,566	36,701	37,924	39,752	42,764	43,541
Professional, scientific, and technical services	60,420	62,622	63,425	66,463	68,258	71,579	71,219
Management of companies and enterprises	84,902	86,643	81,911	88,227	91,823	95,573	97,287
Administrative and waste services	27,784	29,370	30,103	30,982	31,550	33,544	32,656
Educational services	32,349	33,695	33,923	34,997	36,130	36,255	37,172
Health care and social assistance	37,458	38,926	39,811	40,599	41,688	42,909	43,626
Arts, entertainment, and recreation	32,885	32,648	30,330	30,474	31,388	31,749	31,811
Accommodation and food services	15,870	15,791	15,875	16,630	16,965	17,379	17,234
Other services, except public administration	25,752	26,532	27,128	28,223	28,798	29,314	30,202
Government and government enterprises	41,150	42,784	43,513	43,914	44,736	44,895	44,923

Table NC-10. Employment Characteristics by Family Type

(Number, percent.)

Family type and labor force status	2011		2012		2013	
	Total	Families with own children under 18 years	Total	Families with own children under 18 years	Total	Families with own children under 18 years
All Families.............................	2,455,564	1,060,465	2,472,230	1,077,533	2,474,802	1,048,744
FAMILY TYPE AND LABOR FORCE STATUS						
Married-Couple Families................	1,788,142	675,851	1,795,932	697,959	1,786,356	674,065
Both husband and wife in labor force....................	52.2	66.8	51.5	65.8	50.7	65.9
Husband in labor force, wife not in labor force	21.7	27.7	22.0	28.2	21.7	27.4
Wife in labor force, husband not in labor force	8.2	4.1	8.4	4.3	8.4	4.5
Both husband and wife not in labor force.................	17.9	1.4	18.1	1.7	18.9	2.0
Other Families...............................	667,422	384,614	676,298	379,574	688,446	374,679
Female householder, no husband present...................	76.7	78.7	74.7	76.9	75.5	77.6
In labor force...........................	54.9	64.8	52.8	63.2	53.6	64.3
Not in labor force	21.9	13.9	21.9	13.7	21.9	13.3
Male householder, no wife present...........	23.3	21.3	25.3	23.1	24.5	22.4
In labor force............................	18.3	19.4	19.3	20.7	18.7	20.4
Not in labor force	4.9	1.9	6.0	2.4	5.8	2.0

Table NC-11. School Enrollment and Educational Attainment, 2013

(Number, percent.)

Item	State	U.S.
Enrollment		
Total population 3 years and over, enrolled in school	2,560,742	82,395,254
Enrolled in nursery school or preschool (percent)......................	5.7	6.0
Enrolled in kindergarten (percent)........................	5.5	5.2
Enrolled in elementary school, grades 1-8 (percent)................	40.0	40.0
Enrolled in high school, grades 9-12 (percent)................	20.3	20.6
Enrolled in college or graduate school (percent)................	28.6	28.3
Attainment		
Total population 25 years and over	6,568,110	210,910,615
Less than ninth grade (percent)...........................	5.4	5.8
9th to 12th grade, no diploma (percent).................	8.8	7.6
High school graduate, including equivalency (percent).........	26.5	27.8
Some college, no degree (percent)	22.0	21.1
Associate's degree (percent)...........................	8.8	8.1
Bachelor's degree (percent)..............................	18.4	18.4
Graduate or professional degree (percent)........................	9.9	11.2
High school graduate or higher (percent)...............	85.7	86.6
Bachelor's degree or higher (percent).................	28.4	29.6

Table NC-12. Public School Characteristics and Educational Indicators

(Number, percent; data derived from National Center of Education Statistics.)

Item	State	U.S.
Public Schools, 2012–2013 (except where noted)		
Number of school districts....................................	244	18,093
Number of schools..	2,557	98,454
Number of students (in thousands)	1,518	49,771
Number of teachers (in thousands)	99	3,109
Student-teacher ratio	15.4	16.0
Expenditures per student (dollars), FY 2012	8,160	10,667
Four-year adjusted cohort graduation rate (ACGR)[1,2]	82.5	81.4
Students eligible for free or reduced-price lunch (in thousands)	810	25,188
English language learners (in thousands)	97	4,397
Students age 3 to 21 served under IDEA, part B (in thousands)	190	6,429

Public Schools by Type	Number	Percent of state public schools
Total number of schools...	2,557	100.0
Regular	2,444	95.6
Special education...	25	1.0
Vocational education..	7	0.3
Alternative education	81	3.2

NOTE: Every school is assigned only one school type based on its instructional emphasis.
[1]ACGR data represents a new method of calculating high-school completion rates and may not be comparable to previous years' data for Averaged Freshmen Graduation Rates (AFGR).
[2]The United States 4-year ACGRs were estimated using both the reported 4-year ACGR data from 49 states and the District of Columbia and using imputed data for Idaho. The estimate for American Indian/Alaska Native students also includes imputed data for Virginia.

Table NC-13. Reported Voting and Registration of the Voting-Age Population, November 2012

(Numbers in thousands, percent.)

Item	Total population	Total citizen population	Registered			Voted		
			Total registered	Percent registered (total population)	Percent registered (total citizen population)	Total voted	Percent voted (total population)	Percent voted (total citizen population)
U.S. Total	235,248	215,081	153,157	65.1	71.2	132,948	56.5	61.8
State Total	7,265	6,712	5,295	72.9	78.9	4,624	63.7	68.9
Sex								
Male	3,439	3,125	2,401	69.8	76.8	2,103	61.2	67.3
Female	3,826	3,587	2,894	75.7	80.7	2,521	65.9	70.3
Race								
White alone	5,453	4,966	3,848	70.6	77.5	3,276	60.1	66.0
White, non-Hispanic alone	4,898	4,820	3,755	76.7	77.9	3,194	65.2	66.3
Black alone	1,529	1,501	1,279	83.7	85.3	1,203	78.7	80.2
Asian alone	95	57	34	35.4	B	34	35.4	B
Hispanic (of any race)	603	169	115	19.1	68.0	95	15.7	56.0
White alone or in combination	5,520	5,033	3,905	70.8	77.6	3,325	60.2	66.1
Black alone or in combination	1,557	1,529	1,303	83.7	85.2	1,227	78.8	80.2
Asian alone or in combination	103	65	42	40.4	B	42	40.4	B
Age								
18 to 24 years	863	779	496	57.5	63.7	389	45.1	50.0
25 to 44 years	2,541	2,194	1,735	68.3	79.1	1,468	57.8	66.9
45 to 64 years	2,470	2,373	1,925	77.9	81.1	1,710	69.2	72.1
65 to 74 years	741	727	620	83.7	85.4	577	77.9	79.4
75 years and over	649	640	518	79.8	81.0	480	73.9	75.0

B = Base is less than 75,000 and therefore too small to show the derived measure.

Table NC-14. Crime

(Number, rate per 100,000. Data are derived from the FBI Uniform Crime Reports.)

Item	State			U.S.[1,2,3,4]		
	2012	2013	Percent change	2012	2013	Percent change
TOTAL POPULATION[5]	9,748,364	9,848,060	1.0	313,873,685	316,128,839	0.7
VIOLENT CRIME						
Number	34,464	33,152	-3.8	1,217,067	1,163,146	-4.4
Rate	353.5	336.6	-4.8	387.8	367.9	-5.1
Murder and Nonnegligent Manslaughter						
Number	479	469	-2.1	14,866	14,196	-4.5
Rate	4.9	4.8	-3.1	4.7	4.5	-5.2
Rape[6]						
Number	X	2,369	X	X	108,612	X
Rate	X	24.1	X	X	34.4	X
Robbery						
Number	9,392	9,349	-0.5	355,051	345,031	-2.8
Rate	96.3	94.9	-1.5	113.1	109.1	-3.5
Aggravated Assault						
Number	22,609	21,513	-4.8	762,009	724,149	-5.0
Rate	231.9	218.4	-5.8	242.8	229.1	-5.6
PROPERTY CRIME						
Number	328,594	308,049	-6.3	9,001,992	8,632,512	-4.1
Rate	3,370.8	3,128.0	-7.2	2,868.0	2,730.7	-4.8
Burglary						
Number	99,323	90,702	-8.7	2,109,932	1,928,465	-8.6
Rate	1,018.9	921.0	-9.6	672.2	610.0	-9.3
Larceny-Theft						
Number	213,151	202,741	-4.9	6,168,874	6,004,453	-2.7
Rate	2,186.5	2,058.7	-5.8	1,965.4	1,899.4	-3.4
Motor Vehicle Theft						
Number	16,120	14,606	-9.4	723,186	699,594	-3.3
Rate	165.4	148.3	-10.3	230.4	221.3	-4.0

NOTE: Although arson data are included in the trend and clearance tables, sufficient data are not available to estimate totals for this offense. Therefore, no arson data are published in this table.
X = Not applicable.
- = Zero or rounds to zero.
[1]The crime figures have been adjusted.
[2]The data collection methodology for the offense of forcible rape used by the Minnesota state Uniform Crime Reporting (UCR) Program (with the exception of Minneapolis and St. Paul, Minnesota) does not comply with national UCR Program guidelines. Consequently, its figures for forcible rape and violent crime (of which forcible rape is a part) are not published in this table.
[3]Includes offenses reported by the Zoological Police and the Metro Transit Police.
[4]Because of changes in the state's reporting practices, figures are not comparable to previous years' data.
[5]Populations are U.S. Census Bureau provisional estimates as of July 1 of each year.
[6]The figures shown for the offense of rape were estimated using the revised Uniform Crime Reporting (UCR) definition of rape.

Table NC-15. State Government Finances, 2013

(Dollar amounts in thousands, percent distribution.)

Item	Dollars	Percent distribution
Total Revenue	60,004,493	100.0
General revenue	47,574,530	79.3
Intergovernmental revenue	15,769,950	26.3
Taxes	23,768,578	39.6
General sales	5,592,560	9.3
Selective sales	4,121,657	6.9
License taxes	1,543,201	2.6
Individual income tax	11,068,166	18.4
Corporate income tax	1,285,907	2.1
Other taxes	157,087	0.3
Current charges	5,149,449	8.6
Miscellaneous general revenue	2,886,553	4.8
Utility revenue	2	-
Liquor stores revenue	0	-
Insurance trust revenue[1]	12,429,961	20.7
Total Expenditure	53,625,862	100.0
Intergovernmental expenditure	13,172,640	24.6
Direct expenditure	40,453,222	75.4
Current operation	28,260,807	52.7
Capital outlay	3,466,699	6.5
Insurance benefits and repayments	7,450,937	13.9
Assistance and subsidies	655,108	1.2
Interest on debt	619,671	1.2
Exhibit: Salaries and wages	9,281,523	17.3
Total Expenditure	53,625,862	100.0
General expenditure	46,102,728	86.0
Intergovernmental expenditure	13,172,640	24.6
Direct expenditure	32,930,088	61.4
General expenditure, by function:		
Education	19,250,605	35.9
Public welfare	12,977,012	24.2
Hospitals	2,020,269	3.8
Health	1,368,833	2.6
Highways	3,688,451	6.9
Police protection	703,083	1.3
Correction	1,210,318	2.3
Natural resources	511,455	1.0
Parks and recreation	171,930	0.3
Governmental administration	1,296,416	2.4
Interest on general debt	619,671	1.2
Other and unallocable	2,284,685	4.3
Utility expenditure	72,197	0.1
Liquor stores expenditure	0	-
Insurance trust expenditure	7,450,937	13.9
Debt at End of Fiscal Year	19,054,585	X
Cash and Security Holdings	101,336,221	X

X = Not applicable.
- = Zero or rounds to zero.
[1]Within insurance trust revenue, net earnings of state retirement systems is a calculated statistic (the item code in the data file is X08), and thus can be positive or negative. Net earnings is the sum of earnings on investments plus gains on investments minus losses on investments. The change made in 2002 for asset valuation from book to market value in accordance with Statement 34 of the Governmental Accounting Standards Board is reflected in the calculated statistics.

Table NC-16. State Government Tax Collections, 2014

(Dollars in thousands, percent.)

Item	Dollars	Percent distribution
Total Taxes	23,396,751	100.0
Property taxes	X	X
Sales and gross receipts	9,978,484	42.6
General sales and gross receipts	5,842,182	25.0
Selective sales and gross receipts	4,136,302	17.7
Alcoholic beverages	343,344	1.5
Amusements	14,157	0.1
Insurance premiums	476,376	2.0
Motor fuels	1,915,670	8.2
Pari-mutuels	X	X
Public utilities	403,194	1.7
Tobacco products	281,773	1.2
Other selective sales	701,788	3.0
Licenses	1,600,058	6.8
Alcoholic beverages	15,916	0.1
Amusements	X	X
Corporations in general	617,408	2.6
Hunting and fishing	17,488	0.1
Motor vehicle	591,457	2.5
Motor vehicle operators	111,132	0.5
Public utilities	X	X
Occupation and business, NEC	233,463	1.0
Other licenses	13,194	0.1
Income taxes	11,751,148	50.2
Individual income	10,390,520	44.4
Corporation net income	1,360,628	5.8
Other taxes	67,061	0.3
Death and gift	19,932	0.1
Documentary and stock transfer	45,353	0.2
Severance	1,776	-
Taxes, NEC	0	-

X = Not applicable.
- = Zero or rounds to zero.

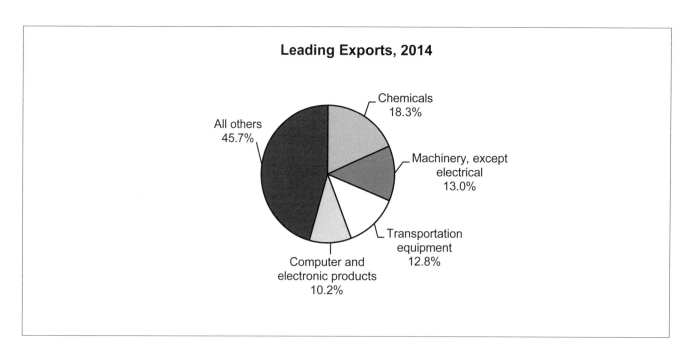

Leading Exports, 2014

Chemicals 18.3%
Machinery, except electrical 13.0%
Transportation equipment 12.8%
Computer and electronic products 10.2%
All others 45.7%

NORTH DAKOTA

Facts and Figures

Location: North central United States; bordered on the N by Canada (Manitoba and Saskatchewan), on the E by Minnesota, on the S by South Dakota, and on the W by Montana

Area: 70,700 sq. mi. (183,112 sq. km.); rank—19th

Population: 739,482 (2014 est.); rank—47th

Principal Cities: capital—Bismarck; largest—Fargo

Statehood: November 2, 1889; 39th state

U.S. Congress: 2 senators, 1 representative

State Motto: Liberty and Union, Now and Forever, One and Inseparable

State Song: "North Dakota Hymn"

State Nicknames: The Peace Garden State; The Flickertail State; The Rough Rider State

Abbreviations: ND; N.D.; N. Dak.

State Symbols: flower—wild prairie rose; tree—American elm; bird—Western meadowlark

At a Glance

- With an increase in population of 9.9 percent, North Dakota ranked 1st for population growth between 2010 and 2014.

- In 2013, 10.4 percent of North Dakotans did not have health insurance, compared to 14.5 percent of the total U.S. population.

- North Dakota had the 3rd highest birth rate in the country in 2013 (14.7 births per 1,000 population).

- In 2014, 2.8 percent of North Dakotans were unemployed, which was the lowest unemployment rate in the country.

- With 12.0 percent of children under 18 years old living below the poverty level, North Dakota had the second lowest childhood poverty rate in the country in 2013.

Table ND-1. Population by Age, Sex, Race, and Hispanic Origin

(Number, percent, except where noted.)

Sex, age, race, and Hispanic origin	2000	2010	2014[1]	Average annual percent change, 2010–2014
Total Population	642,200	672,591	739,482	2.4
Percent of total U.S. population	0.2	0.2	0.2	X
Sex				
Male	320,524	339,864	379,019	2.8
Female	321,676	332,727	360,463	2.0
Age				
Under 5 years	39,400	44,595	51,016	3.4
5 to 19 years	144,064	127,340	140,555	2.5
20 to 64 years	364,258	403,179	442,913	2.4
65 years and over	94,478	97,477	104,998	1.9
Median age (years)	36.2	37.0	34.9	-1.5
Race and Hispanic Origin				
One race				
White	593,181	609,136	659,128	2.0
Black	3,916	8,248	15,555	17.2
American Indian and Alaska Native	31,329	36,948	40,277	2.2
Asian	3,606	7,032	9,412	7.6
Native Hawaiian or Other Pacific Islander	230	334	545	13.0
Two or more races	7,398	10,893	14,565	7.5
Hispanic (of any race)	7,786	14,407	23,439	12.9

X = Not applicable.

[1]Population figures for 2014 are July 1 estimates. The 2010 estimates are taken from the 2010 Census.

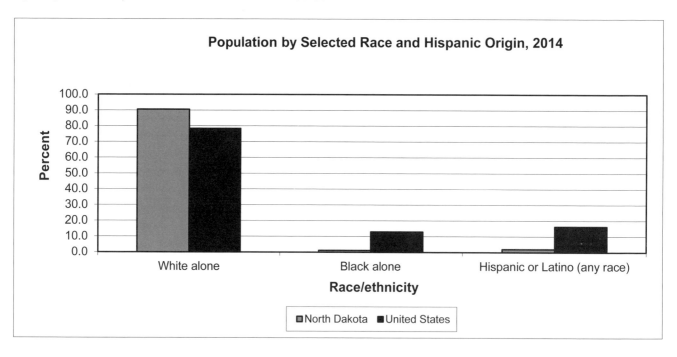

Table ND-2. Marital Status

(Number, percent distribution.)

Sex, age, race, and Hispanic origin	2000	2010	2013
Males, 15 Years and Over	253,900	278,276	299,510
Never married	32.0	35.8	36.7
Now married, except separated	57.5	53.1	51.2
Separated	0.6	0.6	0.9
Widowed	2.5	2.1	2.2
Divorced	7.3	8.4	9.0
Females, 15 Years and Over	258,381	271,462	287,969
Never married	23.2	26.6	27.5
Now married, except separated	56.0	52.5	52.3
Separated	0.8	0.7	1.0
Widowed	11.7	10.1	9.4
Divorced	8.2	10.2	9.8

Table ND-3. Households and Housing Characteristics

(Number, percent, dollars.)

Item	2000	2010	2013	Average annual percent change, 2000–2013
Total Households..	257,252	280,412	298,298	1.1
Family households	166,150	171,945	180,213	0.6
Married-couple family...	137,433	140,277	145,079	0.4
Other family	28,717	31,668	35,134	1.6
Male householder, no wife present.................................	8,569	8,846	12,969	3.2
Female householder, no husband present.......................	20,148	22,822	22,165	0.7
Nonfamily households	91,002	108,467	118,085	2.0
Householder living alone...	75,420	87,883	91,044	1.5
Householder not living alone......................................	15,582	20,584	27,041	4.3
Housing Characteristics				
Total housing units...	289,677	318,099	339,293	1.2
Occupied housing units	257,252	280,412	298,298	1.1
Owner occupied	171,299	187,673	193,389	0.9
Renter occupied...	85,853	92,739	104,909	1.6
Average household size..	2.41	2.32	2.33	-0.3
Financial Characteristics				
Median gross rent of renter-occupied housing	412	583	690	4.0
Median monthly owner costs for housing units with a mortgage	818	1,133	1,207	3.0
Median value of owner-occupied housing units	74,400	123,000	155,400	5.8

Table ND-4. Migration, Origin, and Language

(Number, percent.)

Characteristic	State			U.S.		
	2012	2013	Percent change	2012	2013	Percent change
Residence 1 Year Ago						
Population 1 year and over	689,838	714,804	3.6	310,212,755	312,432,820	0.7
Same house	81.8	83.1	X	85.0	85.0	X
Different house in the U.S.	17.8	16.5	X	14.4	14.4	X
Same county	8.4	7.7	X	9.0	8.9	X
Different county	9.4	8.8	X	5.4	5.5	X
Same state	3.8	3.4	X	3.2	3.2	X
Different state	5.5	5.4	X	2.3	2.3	X
Abroad	0.5	0.5	X	0.6	0.6	X
Place of Birth						
Native born	680,248	702,286	3.2	273,089,382	274,780,773	0.6
Male	51.1	51.1	X	49.3	49.3	X
Female	48.9	48.9	X	50.7	50.7	X
Foreign born	19,380	21,107	8.9	40,824,658	41,348,066	1.3
Male	51.8	48.1	X	48.7	48.8	X
Female	48.2	51.9	X	51.3	51.2	X
Foreign born; naturalized U.S. citizen........................	8,232	6,548	-20.5	18,686,237	19,294,710	3.3
Male	46.0	41.5	X	45.8	45.9	X
Female	54.0	58.5	X	54.2	54.1	X
Foreign born; not a U.S. citizen...............................	11,148	14,559	30.6	22,138,421	22,053,356	-0.4
Male	56.1	51.1	X	51.1	51.3	X
Female	43.9	48.9	X	48.9	48.7	X
Entered 2010 or later	14.4	35.5	X	7.0	9.7	X
Entered 2000 to 2009	42.2	33.2	X	30.4	29.4	X
Entered before 2000	43.4	31.3	X	62.7	61.0	X
World Region of Birth, Foreign						
Foreign-born population, excluding population born at sea	19,380	21,107	8.9	40,824,553	41,347,945	1.3
Europe	21.4	13.1	X	11.8	11.6	X
Asia...	29.5	44.3	X	29.2	29.5	X
Africa...	22.3	14.8	X	4.2	4.4	X
Oceania	0.2	2.0	X	0.6	0.5	X
Latin America	15.8	12.0	X	52.2	51.9	X
North America	10.8	13.8	X	2.0	2.0	X
Language Spoken at Home and Ability to Speak English						
Population 5 years and over..	654,508	675,918	3.3	294,003,714	296,358,760	0.8
English only	94.2	94.7	X	79.0	79.2	X
Language other than English..................................	5.8	5.3	X	21.0	20.8	X
Speaks English less than "very well".......................	1.7	1.5	X	8.5	8.5	X

NA = Not available.
X = Not applicable.
- = Zero or rounds to zero.

Table ND-5. Median Income and Poverty Status, 2013

(Number, percent, except as noted.)

Characteristic	State		U.S.	
	Number	Percent	Number	Percent
Median Income				
Households (dollars)..	55,759	X	52,250	X
Families (dollars)	73,844	X	64,030	X
Below Poverty Level (All People)	20,076	7.2	48,810,868	15.8
Sex				
Male..	38,688	10.9	21,938,525	14.5
Female	43,710	12.8	26,872,343	17.1
Age				
Under 18 years..	19,070	12	16,086,960	22.2
Related children under 18 years...	18,621	11.8	15,769,921	21.9
18 to 64 years...	54,230	12.2	28,578,191	14.8
65 years and over	9,098	9.4	4,145,717	9.6

X = Not applicable.

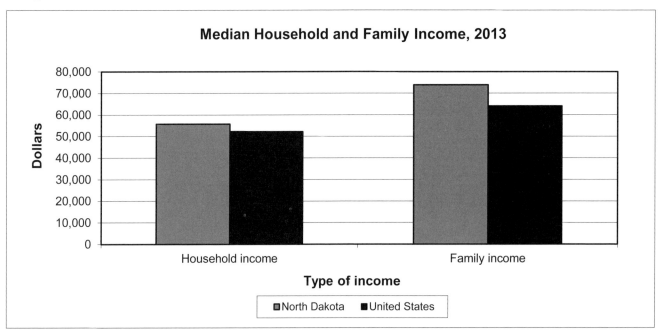

Table ND-6. Health Insurance Coverage Status for the Civilian Noninstitutionalized Population and Children Under 18 Years of Age

(Numbers in thousands, percent.)

Item	2005	2006	2007	2008	2009	2010	2011	2012	2013
Civilian Noninstitutionalized Population......................................	626	617	615	624	630	661	669	685	708
Covered by Private or Public Insurance									
Number...	558	541	553	558	569	596	604	616	635
Percent..	89.0	87.8	90.0	89.4	90.3	90.2	90.2	90.0	89.6
Not Covered									
Number...	69	75	61	66	61	65	65	69	73
Percent..	11.0	12.2	10.0	10.6	9.7	9.8	9.8	10.0	10.4
Percent in the U.S. not covered..............................	15.3	15.8	15.3	15.1	15.1	15.5	15.1	14.8	14.5
Children Under 18 Years of Age............................	142	144	146	141	141	150	151	154	160
Covered by Private or Public Insurance									
Number...	129	130	135	130	133	140	141	143	148
Percent..	91.1	89.7	92.1	92.2	94.4	93.5	93.6	93.1	92.1
Not Covered									
Number...	13	15	11	11	8	10	10	11	13
Percent..	8.9	10.3	7.9	7.8	5.6	6.5	6.4	6.9	7.9
Percent in the U.S. not covered..............................	10.9	11.7	11.0	9.7	8.6	8.0	7.5	7.2	7.1

Table ND-7. Employment Status by Demographic Group, 2014

(Numbers in thousands, percent.)

Characteristic	Civilian noninstitutional population	Civilian labor force		Employed		Unemployed	
		Number	Percent of population	Number	Percent of population	Number	Percent of population
Total...	572	417	72.9	405	70.9	12	2.8
Sex							
Male...	291	229	78.6	222	76.4	6	2.8
Female...	281	188	67.1	183	65.2	5	2.8
Race, Sex, and Hispanic Origin							
White...	519	382	73.5	374	71.9	8	2.2
Male...	265	210	78.9	205	77.2	5	2.2
Female...	254	172	67.9	169	66.4	4	2.3
Black or African American...............	NA	NA	NA	NA	NA	NA	NA
Male...	NA	NA	NA	NA	NA	NA	NA
Female...	NA	NA	NA	NA	NA	NA	NA
Hispanic or Latino ethnicity[1]...........	15	12	82	12	77	1	6
Male...	NA	NA	NA	NA	NA	NA	NA
Female...	NA	NA	NA	NA	NA	NA	NA
Age							
16 to 19 years...............................	33	16	49.6	15	44.2	2	11.0
20 to 24 years...............................	60	50	82.0	47	78.2	2	4.6
25 to 34 years...............................	116	102	88.4	99	85.8	3	2.9
35 to 44 years...............................	82	74	89.4	72	87.5	2	2.1
45 to 54 years...............................	91	80	87.5	78	85.7	2	2.1
55 to 64 years...............................	97	72	74.5	71	73.4	1	1.5
65 years and over..........................	92	23	25.0	23	24.5	...	1.8

NOTE: Data in Table 7 are from the Current Population Survey (CPS) and do not match the estimates in Table 8. See notes and definitions for further information.
[1]May be of any race.
NA = Not available.
... = Fewer than 500 persons.

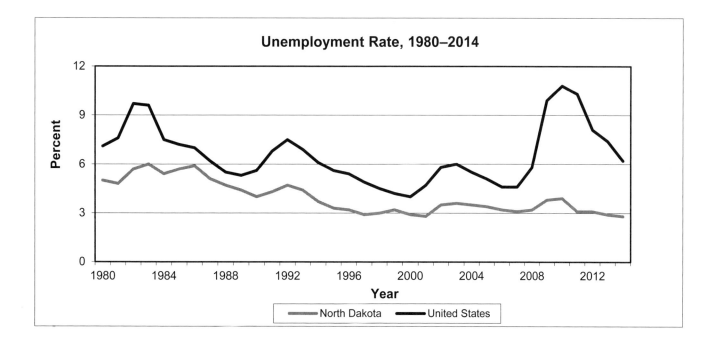

Unemployment Rate, 1980–2014

Table ND-8. Employment Status of the Civilian Noninstitutional Population Age 16 Years and Over

(Number, percent.)

Year	Civilian labor force	Civilian participation rate	Employed	Unemployed	Unemployment rate
2006	361,459	73.2	349,821	11,638	3.2
2007	367,234	74.1	355,766	11,468	3.1
2008	371,025	74.4	359,333	11,692	3.2
2009	368,665	73.2	353,455	15,210	4.1
2010	378,342	72.6	364,053	14,289	3.8
2011	388,502	72.9	375,034	13,468	3.5
2012	397,892	73.1	385,718	12,174	3.1
2013	406,759	72.7	394,891	11,868	2.9
2014	416,367	72.8	404,864	11,503	2.8

Table ND-9. Employment and Average Wages by Industry

(Estimates from 2007 through 2010 are based on the 2007 *North American Industry Classification System* [NAICS]. Estimates from 2011 onward are based on the 2012 NAICS.)

Industry	2007	2008	2009	2010	2011	2012	2013
	Number of jobs						
Wage and Salary Employment by Industry	375,856	384,084	383,488	393,623	415,288	447,570	464,077
Farm Wage and Salary Employment	4,998	5,210	4,395	4,829	5,282	7,088	6,254
Nonfarm Wage and Salary Employment	370,858	378,874	379,093	388,794	410,006	440,482	457,823
Private wage and salary employment	289,663	298,381	296,084	304,071	325,678	355,787	371,593
Forestry, fishing, and related activities	1,538	1,630	1,639	1,713	1,790	1,757	2,472
Mining	5,075	6,791	6,906	10,523	16,580	24,122	25,916
Utilities	3,288	3,415	3,384	3,418	3,419	3,506	3,592
Construction	19,809	21,428	21,560	22,271	25,607	30,437	33,552
Manufacturing	26,099	26,362	23,607	22,591	23,792	25,190	25,432
Durable goods manufacturing	17,695	18,002	15,494	14,626	15,850	16,955	17,241
Nondurable goods manufacturing	8,404	8,360	8,113	7,965	7,942	8,235	8,191
Wholesale trade	19,498	20,045	20,377	21,252	22,885	25,223	26,545
Retail trade	43,691	43,692	43,438	44,221	45,418	47,500	49,488
Transportation and warehousing	11,048	11,854	12,038	12,965	16,287	21,222	22,455
Information	7,615	7,453	7,510	7,325	7,122	6,966	6,827
Finance and insurance	16,337	16,821	16,750	17,061	17,397	17,456	17,940
Real estate and rental and leasing	3,485	3,580	3,563	3,735	4,161	4,735	5,237
Professional, scientific, and technical services	12,332	13,115	12,661	12,657	12,869	14,456	15,717
Management of companies and enterprises	4,169	4,288	4,298	4,329	4,470	4,764	5,132
Administrative and waste services	13,264	13,216	12,420	11,752	12,852	13,564	13,601
Educational services	3,551	3,734	3,744	3,808	3,862	4,065	4,121
Health care and social assistance	48,103	49,289	50,325	52,031	53,345	54,651	55,777
Arts, entertainment, and recreation	3,619	3,765	3,760	3,863	3,829	4,016	4,200
Accommodation and food services	29,624	30,177	30,572	30,865	32,043	34,298	35,272
Other services, except public administration	17,518	17,726	17,532	17,691	17,950	17,859	18,317
Government and government enterprises	81,195	80,493	83,009	84,723	84,328	84,695	86,230
	Dollars						
Average Wages and Salaries by Industry	32,981	35,002	35,695	37,653	41,122	45,083	46,775
Average Farm Wages and Salaries	43,384	48,556	43,162	36,388	39,453	40,236	42,118
Average Nonfarm Wages and Salaries	32,841	34,815	35,609	37,668	41,143	45,161	46,838
Average private wages and salaries	32,845	34,861	35,599	37,915	41,952	46,633	48,462
Forestry, fishing, and related activities	22,540	23,642	25,836	26,684	27,991	29,367	27,722
Mining	69,506	74,767	72,801	79,246	89,204	95,806	97,160
Utilities	71,868	73,221	76,940	78,508	81,965	82,099	86,489
Construction	40,481	44,039	45,341	46,471	51,110	56,396	60,148
Manufacturing	40,149	41,725	41,559	43,376	44,736	46,673	48,056
Durable goods manufacturing	41,734	43,347	42,539	44,151	45,410	47,348	48,594
Nondurable goods manufacturing	36,812	38,233	39,687	41,953	43,390	45,283	46,924
Wholesale trade	44,389	48,136	48,743	51,324	57,530	51,773	65,249
Retail trade	21,718	22,883	23,268	24,198	25,689	6,261	28,355
Transportation and warehousing	42,654	46,134	46,621	50,095	56,400	62,114	63,858
Information	47,359	46,629	47,571	49,015	50,884	54,434	55,689
Finance and insurance	42,339	44,360	45,374	46,704	49,865	52,942	54,118
Real estate and rental and leasing	25,679	29,290	30,980	34,482	44,079	50,393	53,306
Professional, scientific, and technical services	42,993	44,349	46,514	51,424	55,841	63,242	67,230
Management of companies and enterprises	59,622	58,812	59,976	63,720	65,945	69,354	69,897
Administrative and waste services	21,630	22,135	23,060	25,166	27,901	31,639	31,947
Educational services	20,364	20,605	21,310	21,678	22,096	21,756	22,606
Health care and social assistance	34,839	36,783	37,922	39,366	41,243	43,406	44,573
Arts, entertainment, and recreation	15,145	14,667	15,121	15,562	16,327	16,809	17,191
Accommodation and food services	12,616	12,907	13,232	14,119	15,422	17,245	18,138
Other services, except public administration	21,166	22,051	22,856	23,847	25,122	27,123	28,943
Government and government enterprises	32,826	34,644	35,642	36,785	38,021	38,979	39,841

Table ND-10. Employment Characteristics by Family Type

(Number, percent.)

Family type and labor force status	2011		2012		2013	
	Total	Families with own children under 18 years	Total	Families with own children under 18 years	Total	Families with own children under 18 years
All Families..	175,219	77,838	175,380	74,751	180,213	78,738
FAMILY TYPE AND LABOR FORCE STATUS						
Married-Couple Families............................	142,172	56,394	139,907	52,133	145,079	57,092
Both husband and wife in labor force..................	62.5	77.8	61.4	77.3	59.9	72.3
Husband in labor force, wife not in labor force	16.8	19.3	17.5	20.4	18.2	23.4
Wife in labor force, husband not in labor force	6.6	2.2	6.8	1.9	7.0	2.9
Both husband and wife not in labor force................	14.1	0.7	14.3	0.4	14.5	1.3
Other Families	33,047	21,444	35,473	22,618	35,134	21,646
Female householder, no husband present................	67.8	72.6	66.1	70.5	63.1	63.8
In labor force...	51.7	61.2	51.6	60.0	47.6	50.8
Not in labor force	16.1	11.4	14.6	10.5	15.4	13.0
Male householder, no wife present........................	32.2	27.4	33.9	29.5	36.9	36.2
In labor force...	28.7	26.5	30.7	28.6	31.7	34.2
Not in labor force	3.5	1.0	3.2	0.9	5.2	2.0

Table ND-11. School Enrollment and Educational Attainment, 2013

(Number, percent.)

Item	State	U.S.
Enrollment		
Total population 3 years and over, enrolled in school	180,316	82,395,254
Enrolled in nursery school or preschool (percent)...	6.5	6.0
Enrolled in kindergarten (percent)...	5.3	5.2
Enrolled in elementary school, grades 1-8 (percent)...	37.9	40.0
Enrolled in high school, grades 9-12 (percent)..	17.2	20.6
Enrolled in college or graduate school (percent)..	33.1	28.3
Attainment		
Total population 25 years and over	467,815	210,910,615
Less than ninth grade (percent)	4.1	5.8
9th to 12th grade, no diploma (percent)	4.4	7.6
High school graduate, including equivalency (percent)...	27.5	27.8
Some college, no degree (percent)	23.1	21.1
Associate's degree (percent)	13.8	8.1
Bachelor's degree (percent)	20.0	18.4
Graduate or professional degree (percent)...	7.2	11.2
High school graduate or higher (percent)	91.5	86.6
Bachelor's degree or higher (percent)...	27.1	29.6

Table ND-12. Public School Characteristics and Educational Indicators

(Number, percent; data derived from National Center of Education Statistics.)

Item	State	U.S.
Public Schools, 2012–2013 (except where noted)		
Number of school districts...	227	18,093
Number of schools..	517	98,454
Number of students (in thousands)	101	49,771
Number of teachers (in thousands)	9	3,109
Student-teacher ratio	11.7	16.0
Expenditures per student (dollars), FY 2012...	11,246	10,667
Four-year adjusted cohort graduation rate (ACGR)[1,2]	87.5	81.4
Students eligible for free or reduced-price lunch (in thousands)	30	25,188
English language learners (in thousands)	3	4,397
Students age 3 to 21 served under IDEA, part B (in thousands).................................	13	6,429

Public Schools by Type	Number	Percent of state public schools
Total number of schools..	517	100.0
Regular	472	91.3
Special education...	33	6.4
Vocational education..	12	2.3
Alternative education	0	-

NOTE: Every school is assigned only one school type based on its instructional emphasis.
[1]ACGR data represents a new method of calculating high-school completion rates and may not be comparable to previous years' data for Averaged Freshmen Graduation Rates (AFGR).
[2]The United States 4-year ACGRs were estimated using both the reported 4-year ACGR data from 49 states and the District of Columbia and using imputed data for Idaho. The estimate for American Indian/Alaska Native students also includes imputed data for Virginia.
- = Zero or rounds to zero.

Table ND-13. Reported Voting and Registration of the Voting-Age Population, November 2012

(Numbers in thousands, percent.)

Item	Total population	Total citizen population	Registered			Voted		
			Total registered	Percent registered (total population)	Percent registered (total citizen population)	Total voted	Percent voted (total population)	Percent voted (total citizen population)
U.S. Total	235,248	215,081	153,157	65.1	71.2	132,948	56.5	61.8
State Total	528	514	383	72.5	74.5	328	62.2	63.9
Sex								
Male	263	256	192	73.0	74.9	165	62.8	64.5
Female	265	258	191	72.1	74.1	163	61.6	63.3
Race								
White alone	471	466	354	75.1	75.9	305	64.8	65.5
White, non-Hispanic alone	457	454	347	75.8	76.4	299	65.4	66.0
Black alone	6	4	2	B	B	2	B	B
Asian alone	7	1	-	B	B	-	B	B
Hispanic (of any race)	16	14	7	B	B	6	B	B
White alone or in combination	475	469	357	75.2	76.0	308	64.8	65.5
Black alone or in combination..........	6	4	3	B	B	3	B	B
Asian alone or in combination..........	7	1	-	B	B	-	B	B
Age								
18 to 24 years	67	66	43	B	B	32	B	B
25 to 44 years.................................	183	175	128	70.4	73.6	106	58.1	60.7
45 to 64 years.................................	194	190	148	76.3	77.8	129	66.9	68.2
65 to 74 years.................................	43	42	33	B	B	33	B	B
75 years and over	42	42	31	B	B	28	B	B

- = Zero or rounds to zero.
B = Base is less than 75,000 and therefore too small to show the derived measure.

Table ND-14. Crime

(Number, rate per 100,000. Data are derived from the FBI Uniform Crime Reports.)

Item	State			U.S.[1,2,3,4]		
	2012	2013	Percent change	2012	2013	Percent change
TOTAL POPULATION[5]..	701,345	723,393	3.1	313,873,685	316,128,839	0.7
VIOLENT CRIME						
Number...	1,723	1,854	7.6	1,217,067	1,163,146	-4.4
Rate	245.7	256.3	4.3	387.8	367.9	-5.1
Murder and Nonnegligent Manslaughter						
Number...	25	16	-36.0	14,866	14,196	-4.5
Rate	3.6	2.2	-38.0	4.7	4.5	-5.2
Rape[6]						
Number...	X	330	X	X	108,612	X
Rate	X	45.6	X	X	34.4	X
Robbery						
Number...	127	162	27.6	355,051	345,031	-2.8
Rate	18.1	22.4	23.7	113.1	109.1	-3.5
Aggravated Assault						
Number...	1,292	1,446	11.9	762,009	724,149	-5.0
Rate	184.2	199.9	8.5	242.8	229.1	-5.6
PROPERTY CRIME						
Number...	14,297	15,148	6.0	9,001,992	8,632,512	-4.1
Rate	2,038.5	2,094.0	2.7	2,868.0	2,730.7	-4.8
Burglary						
Number...	2,429	2,934	20.8	2,109,932	1,928,465	-8.6
Rate	346.3	405.6	17.1	672.2	610.0	-9.3
Larceny-Theft						
Number...	10,687	10,798	1.0	6,168,874	6,004,453	-2.7
Rate	1,523.8	1,492.7	-2.0	1,965.4	1,899.4	-3.4
Motor Vehicle Theft						
Number...	1,181	1,416	19.9	723,186	699,594	-3.3
Rate	168.4	195.7	16.2	230.4	221.3	-4.0

NOTE: Although arson data are included in the trend and clearance tables, sufficient data are not available to estimate totals for this offense. Therefore, no arson data are published in this table.
X = Not applicable.
- = Zero or rounds to zero.
[1]The crime figures have been adjusted.
[2]The data collection methodology for the offense of forcible rape used by the Minnesota state Uniform Crime Reporting (UCR) Program (with the exception of Minneapolis and St. Paul, Minnesota) does not comply with national UCR Program guidelines. Consequently, its figures for forcible rape and violent crime (of which forcible rape is a part) are not published in this table.
[3]Includes offenses reported by the Zoological Police and the Metro Transit Police.
[4]Because of changes in the state's reporting practices, figures are not comparable to previous years' data.
[5]Populations are U.S. Census Bureau provisional estimates as of July 1 of each year.
[6]The figures shown for the offense of rape were estimated using the revised Uniform Crime Reporting (UCR) definition of rape.

Table ND-15. State Government Finances, 2013

(Dollar amounts in thousands, percent distribution.)

Item	Dollars	Percent distribution
Total Revenue	8,830,465	100.0
General revenue	8,059,929	91.3
Intergovernmental revenue	1,572,480	17.8
Taxes	5,298,770	60.0
General sales	1,268,695	14.4
Selective sales	494,742	5.6
License taxes	207,482	2.3
Individual income tax	641,766	7.3
Corporate income tax	225,719	2.6
Other taxes	2,460,366	27.9
Current charges	764,567	8.7
Miscellaneous general revenue	424,112	4.8
Utility revenue	0	-
Liquor stores revenue	0	-
Insurance trust revenue[1]	770,536	8.7
Total Expenditure	6,410,161	100.0
Intergovernmental expenditure	1,632,316	25.5
Direct expenditure	4,777,845	74.5
Current operation	3,055,372	47.7
Capital outlay	841,567	13.1
Insurance benefits and repayments	623,759	9.7
Assistance and subsidies	159,841	2.5
Interest on debt	97,306	1.5
Exhibit: Salaries and wages	1,108,571	17.3
Total Expenditure	6,410,161	100.0
General expenditure	5,786,402	90.3
Intergovernmental expenditure	1,632,316	25.5
Direct expenditure	4,154,086	64.8
General expenditure, by function:		
Education	1,931,216	30.1
Public welfare	943,371	14.7
Hospitals	53,709	0.8
Health	161,118	2.5
Highways	1,051,899	16.4
Police protection	35,210	0.5
Correction	96,683	1.5
Natural resources	329,500	5.1
Parks and recreation	39,872	0.6
Governmental administration	157,626	2.5
Interest on general debt	97,306	1.5
Other and unallocable	888,892	13.9
Utility expenditure	0	-
Liquor stores expenditure	0	-
Insurance trust expenditure	623,759	9.7
Debt at End of Fiscal Year	1,834,319	X
Cash and Security Holdings	20,325,841	X

X = Not applicable.
- = Zero or rounds to zero.
[1]Within insurance trust revenue, net earnings of state retirement systems is a calculated statistic (the item code in the data file is X08), and thus can be positive or negative. Net earnings is the sum of earnings on investments plus gains on investments minus losses on investments. The change made in 2002 for asset valuation from book to market value in accordance with Statement 34 of the Governmental Accounting Standards Board is reflected in the calculated statistics.

Table ND-16. State Government Tax Collections, 2014

(Dollars in thousands, percent.)

Item	Dollars	Percent distribution
Total Taxes	6,120,435	100.0
Property taxes	3,026	-
Sales and gross receipts	1,848,130	30.2
General sales and gross receipts	1,320,196	21.6
Selective sales and gross receipts	527,934	8.6
Alcoholic beverages	9,220	0.2
Amusements	3,620	0.1
Insurance premiums	51,047	0.8
Motor fuels	228,022	3.7
Pari-mutuels	1,159	-
Public utilities	40,411	0.7
Tobacco products	31,262	0.5
Other selective sales	163,193	2.7
Licenses	227,245	3.7
Alcoholic beverages	367	-
Amusements	801	-
Corporations in general	0	-
Hunting and fishing	14,814	0.2
Motor vehicle	119,312	1.9
Motor vehicle operators	5,289	0.1
Public utilities	6	-
Occupation and business, NEC	86,656	1.4
Other licenses	0	-
Income taxes	748,966	12.2
Individual income	498,528	8.1
Corporation net income	250,438	4.1
Other taxes	3,293,068	53.8
Death and gift	15	-
Documentary and stock transfer	0	-
Severance	3,293,053	53.8
Taxes, NEC	0	-

- = Zero or rounds to zero.

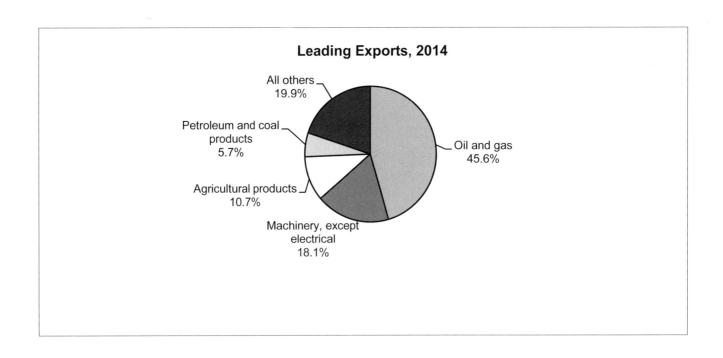

Leading Exports, 2014

All others 19.9%

Petroleum and coal products 5.7%

Agricultural products 10.7%

Machinery, except electrical 18.1%

Oil and gas 45.6%

Facts and Figures

Location: East north central United States; bordered on the N by Michigan and Lake Erie, on the E by Pennsylvania and West Virginia, on the S by West Virginia and Kentucky, and on the W by Indiana

Area: 44,825 sq. mi. (116,096 sq. km.); rank—34th

Population: 11,594,163 (2014 est.); rank—7th

Principal Cities: capital—Columbus; largest—Columbus

Statehood: March 1, 1803; 17th state

U.S. Congress: 2 senators, 16 representatives

State Motto: With God, All Things Are Possible

State Song: "Beautiful Ohio"

State Nickname: The Buckeye State

Abbreviations: OH

State Symbols: flower—scarlet carnation; tree—Ohio buckeye; bird—cardinal

At a Glance

- With an increase in population of 0.5 percent, Ohio ranked 45th among the states in growth from 2010 to 2014.

- Ohio's violent crime rate in 2013 was 286.2 per 100,000 population, compared to 367.9 for the entire nation.

- In 2013, 11.0 percent of Ohioans did not have health insurance, compared to 14.5 percent of the entire U.S. population.

- Ohio had the 6th highest infant mortality rate in 2013, with a rate of 7.33 deaths per 1,000 live births.

- Approximately 26.1 percent of Ohioans had a bachelor's degree or more in 2013, compared to 29.6 percent of residents nationwide.

Table OH-1. Population by Age, Sex, Race, and Hispanic Origin

(Number, percent, except where noted.)

Sex, age, race, and Hispanic origin	2000	2010	2014[1]	Average annual percent change, 2010–2014
Total Population	11,353,140	11,536,504	11,594,163	0.1
Percent of total U.S. population	4.0	3.7	3.6	X
Sex				
Male	5,512,262	5,632,156	5,674,772	0.2
Female	5,840,878	5,904,348	5,919,391	0.1
Age				
Under 5 years	754,930	720,856	690,576	-1.1
5 to 19 years	2,461,025	2,346,270	2,256,759	-1.0
20 to 64 years	6,629,428	6,847,363	6,847,659	-
65 years and over	1,507,757	1,622,015	1,799,169	2.6
Median age (years)	36.2	38.8	39.3	0.3
Race and Hispanic Origin				
One race				
White	9,645,453	9,664,524	9,618,404	-0.1
Black	1,301,307	1,426,861	1,463,594	0.6
American Indian and Alaska Native	24,486	29,674	31,585	1.6
Asian	132,633	196,693	233,379	4.4
Native Hawaiian or Other Pacific Islander	2,749	5,336	5,846	2.3
Two or more races	157,885	213,416	241,355	3.1
Hispanic (of any race)	217,123	375,004	403,190	1.8

X = Not applicable.
- = Zero or rounds to zero.
[1]Population figures for 2014 are July 1 estimates. The 2010 estimates are taken from the 2010 Census.

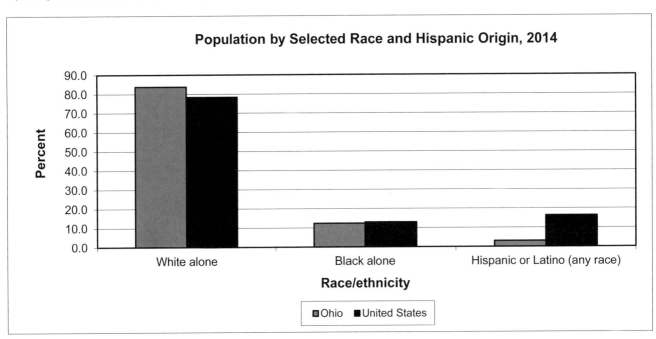

Table OH-2. Marital Status

(Number, percent distribution.)

Sex, age, race, and Hispanic origin	2000	2010	2013
Males, 15 Years and Over	4,281,736	4,487,900	4,540,388
Never married	29.2	33.5	34.8
Now married, except separated	57.0	51.2	49.6
Separated	1.4	1.7	1.7
Widowed	2.7	2.9	3.0
Divorced	9.7	10.8	10.9
Females, 15 Years and Over	4,670,985	4,809,613	4,845,965
Never married	23.5	27.9	29.0
Now married, except separated	52.1	46.9	46.2
Separated	1.7	2.1	2.0
Widowed	11.1	10.1	9.7
Divorced	11.5	12.9	13.1

Table OH-3. Households and Housing Characteristics

(Number, percent, dollars.)

Item	2000	2010	2013	Average annual percent change, 2000–2013
Total Households..	4,445,773	4,525,066	4,564,745	0.2
Family households..	2,993,023	2,960,107	2,923,404	-0.2
Married-couple family..	2,285,798	2,169,003	2,118,209	-0.6
Other family..	707,225	791,104	805,195	1.0
Male householder, no wife present......................	170,347	196,130	212,537	1.7
Female householder, no husband present..............	536,878	594,974	592,658	0.8
Nonfamily households	1,452,750	1,564,959	1,641,341	0.9
Householder living alone......................................	1,215,614	1,315,321	1,363,954	0.9
Householder not living alone.................................	237,136	249,638	277,387	1.2
Housing Characteristics				
Total housing units..	4,783,051	5,128,113	5,124,126	0.5
Occupied housing units	4,445,773	4,525,066	4,564,745	0.2
Owner occupied..	3,072,522	3,095,197	3,015,795	-0.1
Renter occupied..	1,373,251	1,429,869	1,548,950	0.9
Average household size...	2.49	2.48	2.47	-0.1
Financial Characteristics				
Median gross rent of renter-occupied housing	515	685	709	2.5
Median monthly owner costs for housing units with a mortgage	983	1,246	1,209	1.6
Median value of owner-occupied housing units..........	103,700	134,400	127,000	1.6

Table OH-4. Migration, Origin, and Language

(Number, percent.)

Characteristic	State			U.S.		
	2012	2013	Percent change	2012	2013	Percent change
Residence 1 Year Ago						
Population 1 year and over	11,414,635	11,439,593	0.2	310,212,755	312,432,820	0.7
Same house	85.3	85.2	X	85.0	85.0	X
Different house in the U.S.	14.3	14.4	X	14.4	14.4	X
Same county	9.4	9.4	X	9.0	8.9	X
Different county	5.0	4.9	X	5.4	5.5	X
Same state	3.3	3.3	X	3.2	3.2	X
Different state	1.7	1.6	X	2.3	2.3	X
Abroad	0.4	0.4	X	0.6	0.6	X
Place of Birth						
Native born	11,092,895	11,093,471	-	273,089,382	274,780,773	0.6
Male	48.8	48.9	X	49.3	49.3	X
Female	51.2	51.1	X	50.7	50.7	X
Foreign born	451,330	477,337	5.8	40,824,658	41,348,066	1.3
Male	49.8	49.7	X	48.7	48.8	X
Female	50.2	50.3	X	51.3	51.2	X
Foreign born; naturalized U.S. citizen..................	231,207	237,404	2.7	18,686,237	19,294,710	3.3
Male	46.0	47.6	X	45.8	45.9	X
Female	54.0	52.4	X	54.2	54.1	X
Foreign born; not a U.S. citizen.........................	220,123	239,933	9.0	22,138,421	22,053,356	-0.4
Male	53.9	51.9	X	51.1	51.3	X
Female	46.1	48.1	X	48.9	48.7	X
Entered 2010 or later	11.2	15.4	X	7.0	9.7	X
Entered 2000 to 2009	34.2	31.7	X	30.4	29.4	X
Entered before 2000..	54.6	53.0	X	62.7	61.0	X
World Region of Birth, Foreign						
Foreign-born population, excluding population born at sea	451,330	477,337	5.8	40,824,553	41,347,945	1.3
Europe	24.6	23.3	X	11.8	11.6	X
Asia..	39.5	40.1	X	29.2	29.5	X
Africa..	12.8	12.5	X	4.2	4.4	X
Oceania..	0.4	0.4	X	0.6	0.5	X
Latin America..	19.8	20.2	X	52.2	51.9	X
North America..	2.9	3.3	X	2.0	2.0	X
Language Spoken at Home and Ability to Speak English						
Population 5 years and over................................	10,854,170	10,879,145	0.2	294,003,714	296,358,760	0.8
English only	93.3	93.4	X	79.0	79.2	X
Language other than English............................	6.7	6.6	X	21.0	20.8	X
Speaks English less than "very well"..................	2.3	2.4	X	8.5	8.5	X

NA = Not available.
X = Not applicable.
- = Zero or rounds to zero.

Table OH-5. Median Income and Poverty Status, 2013

(Number, percent, except as noted.)

Characteristic	State		U.S.	
	Number	Percent	Number	Percent
Median Income				
Households (dollars)	48,081	X	52,250	X
Families (dollars)	61,030	X	64,030	X
Below Poverty Level (All People)	1,796,942	16.0	48,810,868	15.8
Sex				
Male	808,056	14.8	21,938,525	14.5
Female	988,886	17.1	26,872,343	17.1
Age				
Under 18 years	591,328	22.7	16,086,960	22.2
Related children under 18 years	579,687	22.4	15,769,921	21.9
18 to 64 years	1,064,327	15.3	28,578,191	14.8
65 years and over	141,287	8.4	4,145,717	9.6

X = Not applicable.

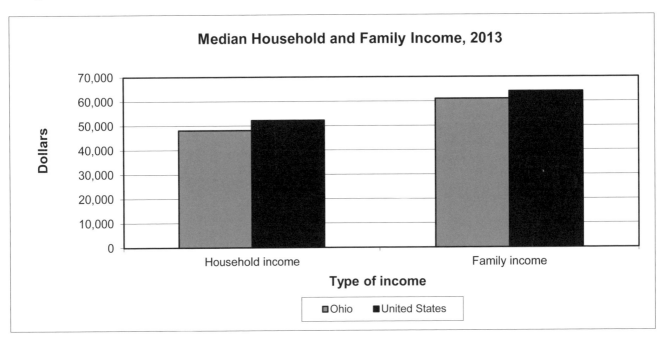

Table OH-6. Health Insurance Coverage Status for the Civilian Noninstitutionalized Population and Children Under 18 Years of Age

(Numbers in thousands, percent.)

Item	2005	2006	2007	2008	2009	2010	2011	2012	2013
Civilian Noninstitutionalized Population	11,334	11,319	11,300	11,296	11,352	11,359	11,369	11,372	11,398
Covered by Private or Public Insurance									
Number	10,046	10,181	9,979	9,966	9,969	9,960	10,015	10,068	10,141
Percent	88.6	89.9	88.3	88.2	87.8	87.7	88.1	88.5	89.0
Not Covered									
Number	1,288	1,138	1,322	1,330	1,383	1,399	1,354	1,304	1,258
Percent	11.4	10.1	11.7	11.8	12.2	12.3	11.9	11.5	11.0
Percent in the U.S. not covered	15.3	15.8	15.3	15.1	15.1	15.5	15.1	14.8	14.5
Children Under 18 Years of Age	2,724	2,784	2,790	2,728	2,710	2,715	2,688	2,657	2,645
Covered by Private or Public Insurance									
Number	2,517	2,626	2,551	2,531	2,538	2,553	2,531	2,516	2,504
Percent	92.4	94.3	91.4	92.8	93.6	94.0	94.2	94.7	94.7
Not Covered									
Number	207	157	239	197	172	162	157	141	141
Percent	7.6	5.7	8.6	7.2	6.4	6.0	5.8	5.3	5.3
Percent in the U.S. not covered	10.9	11.7	11.0	9.7	8.6	8.0	7.5	7.2	7.1

Table OH-7. Employment Status by Demographic Group, 2014

(Numbers in thousands, percent.)

Characteristic	Civilian noninstitutional population	Civilian labor force		Employed		Unemployed	
		Number	Percent of population	Number	Percent of population	Number	Percent of population
Total.........................	9,092	5,708	62.8	5,390	59.3	318	5.6
Sex							
Male..............................	4,377	2,957	67.6	2,782	63.6	175	5.9
Female	4,715	2,751	58.3	2,608	55.3	143	5.2
Race, Sex, and Hispanic Origin							
White	7,720	4,892	63.4	4,659	60.3	233	4.8
Male..............................	3,763	2,572	68.3	2,445	65.0	127	4.9
Female	3,957	2,321	58.6	2,214	56.0	106	4.6
Black or African American...........	1,056	615	58.2	543	51.5	71	11.6
Male..............................	478	288	60.2	246	51.4	42	14.6
Female	578	327	56.5	297	51.5	29	9.0
Hispanic or Latino ethnicity[1]	249	167	67.2	157	63.3	10	5.9
Male..............................	125	92	73.5	87	69.8	5	5.0
Female	124	76	61.0	70	56.7	5	7.0
Age							
16 to 19 years.....................	617	266	43.0	211	34.2	54	20.5
20 to 24 years.....................	739	567	76.7	522	70.7	45	7.9
25 to 34 years.....................	1,460	1,220	83.6	1,156	79.2	63	5.2
35 to 44 years.....................	1,386	1,133	81.7	1,077	77.7	56	4.9
45 to 54 years.....................	1,541	1,223	79.4	1,175	76.3	48	3.9
55 to 64 years.....................	1,567	965	61.6	928	59.2	37	3.8
65 years and over	1,782	334	18.8	320	17.9	14	4.3

NOTE: Data in Table 7 are from the Current Population Survey (CPS) and do not match the estimates in Table 8. See notes and definitions for further information.
[1]May be of any race.

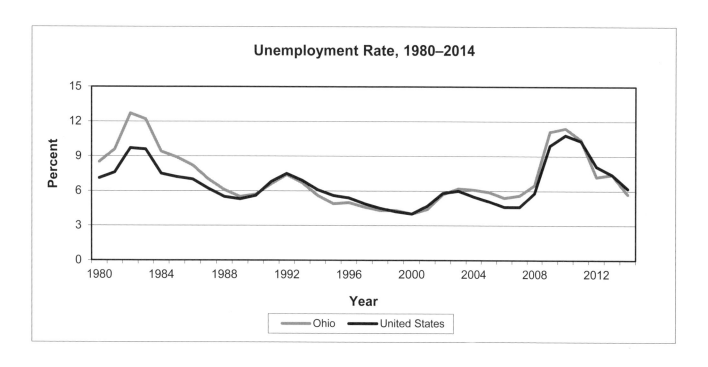

Unemployment Rate, 1980–2014

Table OH-8. Employment Status of the Civilian Noninstitutional Population Age 16 Years and Over

(Number, percent.)

Year	Civilian labor force	Civilian participation rate	Employed	Unemployed	Unemployment rate
2006	5,945,482	67.1	5,624,435	321,047	5.4
2007	5,990,292	67.3	5,657,718	332,574	5.6
2008	5,965,166	66.8	5,580,843	384,323	6.4
2009	5,906,768	66.0	5,297,098	609,670	10.3
2010	5,846,886	65.2	5,247,050	599,836	10.3
2011	5,772,420	64.2	5,261,833	510,587	8.8
2012	5,710,010	63.3	5,288,262	421,748	7.4
2013	5,725,509	63.2	5,298,591	426,918	7.5
2014	5,719,472	62.9	5,391,503	327,969	5.7

Table OH-9. Employment and Average Wages by Industry

(Estimates from 2007 through 2010 are based on the 2007 *North American Industry Classification System* [NAICS]. Estimates from 2011 onward are based on the 2012 NAICS.)

Industry	2007	2008	2009	2010	2011	2012	2013
	Number of jobs						
Wage and Salary Employment by Industry	5,598,268	5,526,611	5,234,992	5,201,963	5,262,063	5,316,040	5,378,863
Farm Wage and Salary Employment	16,710	12,730	13,697	13,802	12,718	17,737	16,197
Nonfarm Wage and Salary Employment	5,581,558	5,513,881	5,221,295	5,188,161	5,249,345	5,298,303	5,362,666
Private wage and salary employment	4,737,170	4,670,242	4,382,490	4,352,940	4,431,887	4,503,667	4,568,746
Forestry, fishing, and related activities	4,176	4,247	4,166	4,392	4,529	4,665	4,922
Mining	11,304	11,681	11,450	10,914	11,393	12,199	12,099
Utilities	21,098	21,718	21,320	19,957	19,307	19,107	18,792
Construction	233,257	219,940	189,639	177,091	185,850	187,070	192,778
Manufacturing	773,857	740,114	630,843	621,438	638,984	657,648	663,478
Durable goods manufacturing	531,463	506,735	419,584	411,775	429,018	444,988	449,513
Nondurable goods manufacturing	242,394	233,379	211,259	209,663	209,966	212,660	213,965
Wholesale trade	241,645	239,183	223,515	218,849	220,413	225,326	228,855
Retail trade	610,473	597,304	569,535	561,431	564,106	565,357	568,665
Transportation and warehousing	193,984	191,370	169,014	164,862	168,885	172,871	175,385
Information	87,503	86,190	80,895	77,731	76,034	74,843	75,500
Finance and insurance	231,822	223,876	216,850	215,875	217,771	219,832	220,500
Real estate and rental and leasing	68,513	65,570	62,618	60,735	60,051	59,373	61,271
Professional, scientific, and technical services	250,537	254,371	243,084	242,733	249,760	244,314	246,986
Management of companies and enterprises	104,548	108,567	107,929	107,288	112,869	127,187	132,331
Administrative and waste services	317,496	310,400	271,613	282,344	295,856	306,404	314,699
Educational services	108,372	111,091	112,079	114,689	116,556	116,759	114,635
Health care and social assistance	703,795	721,396	731,134	741,362	750,158	760,675	769,853
Arts, entertainment, and recreation	67,086	65,933	64,222	63,308	64,865	68,823	74,657
Accommodation and food services	439,628	433,322	419,071	418,689	425,014	435,342	447,431
Other services, except public administration	268,076	263,969	253,513	249,252	249,486	245,872	245,909
Government and government enterprises	844,388	843,639	838,805	835,221	817,458	794,636	793,920
	Dollars						
Average Wages and Salaries by Industry	40,309	41,144	41,283	42,218	43,455	44,988	45,435
Average Farm Wages and Salaries	27,991	31,963	30,403	23,394	31,184	23,067	33,244
Average Nonfarm Wages and Salaries	40,346	41,165	41,312	42,268	43,485	45,062	45,472
Average private wages and salaries	40,284	41,039	40,988	41,986	43,270	44,835	45,298
Forestry, fishing, and related activities	22,930	23,940	24,931	25,591	26,626	27,411	28,195
Mining	59,670	61,679	62,894	66,664	71,352	73,067	65,277
Utilities	77,752	80,870	82,809	84,143	86,348	88,796	90,502
Construction	45,013	46,799	47,900	47,887	49,572	51,660	52,958
Manufacturing	52,684	53,103	52,790	54,852	56,921	57,440	57,525
Durable goods manufacturing	54,621	54,876	53,831	56,038	58,076	58,521	58,590
Nondurable goods manufacturing	48,435	49,254	50,723	52,523	54,562	55,179	55,285
Wholesale trade	56,959	58,427	57,871	60,005	62,244	64,097	64,471
Retail trade	24,203	24,445	24,501	25,095	25,698	26,481	26,593
Transportation and warehousing	43,034	44,342	45,055	45,019	46,216	47,415	47,989
Information	54,688	56,190	56,249	58,293	60,119	62,031	63,392
Finance and insurance	60,523	60,327	60,818	62,884	64,817	66,865	69,420
Real estate and rental and leasing	35,067	35,689	35,974	37,253	39,013	40,722	42,323
Professional, scientific, and technical services	60,094	61,854	62,153	63,559	65,853	67,618	68,603
Management of companies and enterprises	92,539	91,845	86,569	93,856	96,377	108,260	104,941
Administrative and waste services	28,176	29,099	29,782	29,943	30,547	31,844	32,202
Educational services	27,579	28,585	29,347	29,686	30,562	30,352	30,757
Health care and social assistance	38,353	39,538	40,411	40,701	41,351	42,780	43,607
Arts, entertainment, and recreation	30,355	30,293	29,997	31,335	30,675	32,019	31,918
Accommodation and food services	14,906	14,847	14,869	15,343	15,806	16,275	16,336
Other services, except public administration	25,369	26,024	26,134	26,991	27,575	28,371	29,348
Government and government enterprises	40,691	41,868	43,004	43,734	44,648	46,347	46,472

Table OH-10. Employment Characteristics by Family Type

(Number, percent.)

Family type and labor force status	2011		2012		2013	
	Total	Families with own children under 18 years	Total	Families with own children under 18 years	Total	Families with own children under 18 years
All Families..	2,915,927	1,244,537	2,913,312	1,230,760	2,923,404	1,232,209
FAMILY TYPE AND LABOR FORCE STATUS						
Married-Couple Families	2,137,964	796,948	2,131,425	787,247	2,118,209	781,239
Both husband and wife in labor force...........................	53.5	70.0	53.0	69.5	52.3	69.7
Husband in labor force, wife not in labor force	20.1	24.4	20.0	24.9	20.3	24.3
Wife in labor force, husband not in labor force	8.2	4.0	8.4	4.0	8.6	3.8
Both husband and wife not in labor force...................	18.2	1.6	18.7	1.7	18.5	2.1
Other Families..	777,963	447,589	781,887	443,513	805,195	450,970
Female householder, no husband present.................	75.4	78.6	74.0	76.5	73.6	76.2
In labor force...	53.4	64.4	51.8	61.5	51.7	62.9
Not in labor force	22.0	14.2	22.3	14.9	21.9	13.3
Male householder, no wife present........................	24.6	21.4	26.0	23.5	26.4	23.8
In labor force...	18.6	18.5	19.8	21.2	20.0	21.2
Not in labor force	5.9	2.9	6.1	2.4	6.4	2.6

Table OH-11. School Enrollment and Educational Attainment, 2013

(Number, percent.)

Item	State	U.S.
Enrollment		
Total population 3 years and over, enrolled in school	2,952,357	82,395,254
Enrolled in nursery school or preschool (percent)	6.3	6.0
Enrolled in kindergarten (percent)	4.9	5.2
Enrolled in elementary school, grades 1-8 (percent)......................	40.4	40.0
Enrolled in high school, grades 9-12 (percent)............................	21.0	20.6
Enrolled in college or graduate school (percent).........................	27.4	28.3
Attainment		
Total population 25 years and over	7,805,254	210,910,615
Less than ninth grade (percent)...	3.2	5.8
9th to 12th grade, no diploma (percent)....................................	7.8	7.6
High school graduate, including equivalency (percent)....................	34.2	27.8
Some college, no degree (percent)	20.5	21.1
Associate's degree (percent)...	8.2	8.1
Bachelor's degree (percent)	16.4	18.4
Graduate or professional degree (percent)................................	9.7	11.2
High school graduate or higher (percent)	89.0	86.6
Bachelor's degree or higher (percent)......................................	26.1	29.6

Table OH-12. Public School Characteristics and Educational Indicators

(Number, percent; data derived from National Center of Education Statistics.)

Item	State	U.S.
Public Schools, 2012–2013 (except where noted)		
Number of school districts..	1,093	18,093
Number of schools...	3,685	98,454
Number of students (in thousands)	1,730	49,771
Number of teachers (in thousands)	106	3,109
Student-teacher ratio	16.3	16.0
Expenditures per student (dollars), FY 2012..............................	11,323	10,667
Four-year adjusted cohort graduation rate (ACGR)[1,2]	82.2	81.4
Students eligible for free or reduced-price lunch (in thousands)	674	25,188
English language learners (in thousands)	37	4,397
Students age 3 to 21 served under IDEA, part B (in thousands)	256	6,429

Public Schools by Type	Number	Percent of state public schools
Total number of schools..	3,685	100.0
Regular	3,555	96.5
Special education..	54	1.5
Vocational education..	70	1.9
Alternative education...	6	0.2

NOTE: Every school is assigned only one school type based on its instructional emphasis.
[1]ACGR data represents a new method of calculating high-school completion rates and may not be comparable to previous years' data for Averaged Freshmen Graduation Rates (AFGR).
[2]The United States 4-year ACGRs were estimated using both the reported 4-year ACGR data from 49 states and the District of Columbia and using imputed data for Idaho. The estimate for American Indian/Alaska Native students also includes imputed data for Virginia.

Table OH-13. Reported Voting and Registration of the Voting-Age Population, November 2012

(Numbers in thousands, percent.)

Item	Total population	Total citizen population	Registered			Voted		
			Total registered	Percent registered (total population)	Percent registered (total citizen population)	Total voted	Percent voted (total population)	Percent voted (total citizen population)
U.S. Total	235,248	215,081	153,157	65.1	71.2	132,948	56.5	61.8
State Total	8,750	8,550	6,076	69.4	71.1	5,395	61.7	63.1
Sex								
Male	4,175	4,074	2,798	67.0	68.7	2,463	59.0	60.4
Female	4,576	4,476	3,278	71.6	73.2	2,932	64.1	65.5
Race								
White alone	7,291	7,262	5,120	70.2	70.5	4,498	61.7	61.9
White, non-Hispanic alone	1,028	975	723	70.3	74.2	699	68.0	71.7
Black alone	104	60	41	40.0	B	38	36.4	B
Asian alone	252	173	116	45.9	67.0	98	39.0	56.9
Hispanic (of any race)								
White alone or in combination	7,590	7,486	5,291	69.7	70.7	4,640	61.1	62.0
Black alone or in combination	1,088	1,035	773	71.1	74.7	742	68.2	71.7
Asian alone or in combination	126	83	48	37.7	57.5	44	34.7	53.0
Age								
18 to 24 years	1,145	1,105	629	55.0	57.0	511	44.7	46.3
25 to 44 years	2,753	2,626	1,820	66.1	69.3	1,544	56.1	58.8
45 to 64 years	3,213	3,179	2,325	72.4	73.1	2,159	67.2	67.9
65 to 74 years	859	859	667	77.7	77.7	605	70.4	70.4
75 years and over	781	781	635	81.3	81.3	576	73.7	73.7

B = Base is less than 75,000 and therefore too small to show the derived measure.

Table OH-14. Crime

(Number, rate per 100,000. Data are derived from the FBI Uniform Crime Reports.)

Item	State			U.S. [1,2,3,4]		
	2012	2013	Percent change	2012	2013	Percent change
TOTAL POPULATION[5]	11,553,031	11,570,808	0.2	313,873,685	316,128,839	0.7
VIOLENT CRIME						
Number	34,827	31,904	-8.4	1,217,067	1,163,146	-4.4
Rate	301.5	275.7	-8.5	387.8	367.9	-5.1
Murder and Nonnegligent Manslaughter						
Number	478	455	-4.8	14,866	14,196	-4.5
Rate	4.1	3.9	-5.0	4.7	4.5	-5.2
Rape[6]						
Number	X	4,041	X	X	108,612	X
Rate	X	34.9	X	X	34.4	X
Robbery						
Number	15,396	14,368	-6.7	355,051	345,031	-2.8
Rate	133.3	124.2	-6.8	113.1	109.1	-3.5
Aggravated Assault						
Number	15,140	14,257	-5.8	762,009	724,149	-5.0
Rate	131.0	123.2	-6.0	242.8	229.1	-5.6
PROPERTY CRIME						
Number	370,435	338,731	-8.6	9,001,992	8,632,512	-4.1
Rate	3,206.4	2,927.5	-8.7	2,868.0	2,730.7	-4.8
Burglary						
Number	105,312	91,433	-13.2	2,109,932	1,928,465	-8.6
Rate	911.6	790.2	-13.3	672.2	610.0	-9.3
Larceny-Theft						
Number	245,372	227,766	-7.2	6,168,874	6,004,453	-2.7
Rate	2,123.9	1,968.5	-7.3	1,965.4	1,899.4	-3.4
Motor Vehicle Theft						
Number	19,751	19,532	-1.1	723,186	699,594	-3.3
Rate	171.0	168.8	-1.3	230.4	221.3	-4.0

NOTE: Although arson data are included in the trend and clearance tables, sufficient data are not available to estimate totals for this offense. Therefore, no arson data are published in this table.

X = Not applicable.

- = Zero or rounds to zero.

[1]The crime figures have been adjusted.

[2]The data collection methodology for the offense of forcible rape used by the Minnesota state Uniform Crime Reporting (UCR) Program (with the exception of Minneapolis and St. Paul, Minnesota) does not comply with national UCR Program guidelines. Consequently, its figures for forcible rape and violent crime (of which forcible rape is a part) are not published in this table.

[3]Includes offenses reported by the Zoological Police and the Metro Transit Police.

[4]Because of changes in the state's reporting practices, figures are not comparable to previous years' data.

[5]Populations are U.S. Census Bureau provisional estimates as of July 1 of each year.

[6]The figures shown for the offense of rape were estimated using the revised Uniform Crime Reporting (UCR) definition of rape.

Table OH-15. State Government Finances, 2013

(Dollar amounts in thousands, percent distribution.)

Item	Dollars	Percent distribution
Total Revenue	90,343,990	100.0
General revenue	60,945,518	67.5
Intergovernmental revenue	21,113,847	23.4
Taxes	27,516,947	30.5
General sales	8,626,426	9.5
Selective sales	5,195,619	5.8
License taxes	3,445,620	3.8
Individual income tax	9,869,545	10.9
Corporate income tax	262,226	0.3
Other taxes	117,511	0.1
Current charges	7,950,754	8.8
Miscellaneous general revenue	4,363,970	4.8
Utility revenue	0	-
Liquor stores revenue	928,987	1.0
Insurance trust revenue[1]	28,469,485	31.5
Total Expenditure	76,291,671	100.0
Intergovernmental expenditure	16,517,064	21.6
Direct expenditure	59,774,607	78.4
Current operation	35,493,425	46.5
Capital outlay	4,611,905	6.0
Insurance benefits and repayments	16,434,097	21.5
Assistance and subsidies	2,003,369	2.6
Interest on debt	1,231,811	1.6
Exhibit: Salaries and wages	9,396,073	12.3
Total Expenditure	76,291,671	100.0
General expenditure	59,501,507	78.0
Intergovernmental expenditure	16,517,064	21.6
Direct expenditure	42,984,443	56.3
General expenditure, by function:		
Education	21,606,929	28.3
Public welfare	19,186,691	25.1
Hospitals	3,125,123	4.1
Health	2,493,472	3.3
Highways	3,678,390	4.8
Police protection	318,780	0.4
Correction	1,543,631	2.0
Natural resources	390,327	0.5
Parks and recreation	83,384	0.1
Governmental administration	1,796,127	2.4
Interest on general debt	1,231,811	1.6
Other and unallocable	4,046,842	5.3
Utility expenditure	0	-
Liquor stores expenditure	356,067	0.5
Insurance trust expenditure	16,434,097	21.5
Debt at End of Fiscal Year	33,132,906	X
Cash and Security Holdings	220,914,699	X

X = Not applicable.
- = Zero or rounds to zero.
[1]Within insurance trust revenue, net earnings of state retirement systems is a calculated statistic (the item code in the data file is X08), and thus can be positive or negative. Net earnings is the sum of earnings on investments plus gains on investments minus losses on investments. The change made in 2002 for asset valuation from book to market value in accordance with Statement 34 of the Governmental Accounting Standards Board is reflected in the calculated statistics.

Table OH-16. State Government Tax Collections, 2014

(Dollars in thousands, percent.)

Item	Dollars	Percent distribution
Total Taxes	27,020,625	100.0
Property taxes	X	X
Sales and gross receipts	15,617,920	57.8
General sales and gross receipts	10,217,826	37.8
Selective sales and gross receipts	5,400,094	20.0
Alcoholic beverages	98,397	0.4
Amusements	273,393	1.0
Insurance premiums	510,345	1.9
Motor fuels	1,839,594	6.8
Pari-mutuels	5,024	-
Public utilities	1,125,461	4.2
Tobacco products	815,532	3.0
Other selective sales	732,348	2.7
Licenses	2,928,276	10.8
Alcoholic beverages	41,327	0.2
Amusements	16,209	0.1
Corporations in general	1,026,121	3.8
Hunting and fishing	38,428	0.1
Motor vehicle	725,263	2.7
Motor vehicle operators	82,388	0.3
Public utilities	29,523	0.1
Occupation and business, NEC	940,646	3.5
Other licenses	28,371	0.1
Income taxes	8,424,843	31.2
Individual income	8,424,843	31.2
Corporation net income	0	-
Other taxes	49,586	0.2
Death and gift	39,392	0.1
Documentary and stock transfer	X	X
Severance	10,194	-
Taxes, NEC	0	-

X = Not applicable.
- = Zero or rounds to zero.

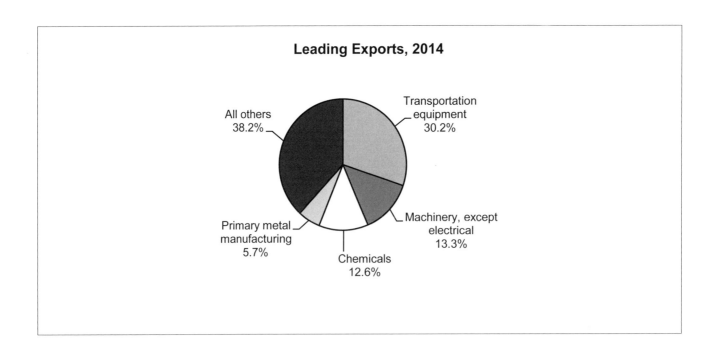

Leading Exports, 2014

All others 38.2%
Transportation equipment 30.2%
Machinery, except electrical 13.3%
Chemicals 12.6%
Primary metal manufacturing 5.7%

OKLAHOMA

Facts and Figures

Location: West south central United States; bordered on the N by Colorado and Kansas, on the E by Missouri and Arkansas, on the S by Texas, and on the W by Texas and New Mexico

Area: 69,898 sq. mi. (181,036 sq. km.); rank—20th

Population: 3,878,051 (2014 est.); rank—28th

Principal Cities: capital—Oklahoma City; largest—Oklahoma City

Statehood: November 16, 1907; 46th state

U.S. Congress: 2 senators, 5 representatives

State Motto: *Labor omnia vincit* ("Labor conquers all things")

State Song: "Oklahoma!"

State Nickname: The Sooner State

Abbreviations: OK; Okla.

State Symbols: flower—mistletoe; tree—redbud; bird—scissor-tailed flycatcher

At a Glance

- With an increase in population of 3.4 percent, Oklahoma ranked 24th among the states in growth from 2010 to 2014.

- Oklahoma's median household income in 2013 was $45,690, and 16.8 percent of the population lived below the poverty level.

- In 2013, 17.7 percent of Oklahomans did not have health insurance, compared to 14.5 percent of the total U.S. population.

- Oklahoma's violent crime rate in 2013 was 441.2 per 100,000 population, compared to 367.9 for the entire nation.

- The state ranked 10th for property crime rate in 2013, with a rate of 3,273.7 incidents per 100,000 population.

Table OK-1. Population by Age, Sex, Race, and Hispanic Origin

(Number, percent, except where noted.)

Sex, age, race, and Hispanic origin	2000	2010	2014[1]	Average annual percent change, 2010–2014
Total Population	3,450,654	3,751,351	3,878,051	0.8
Percent of total U.S. population	1.2	1.2	1.2	X
Sex				
Male	1,695,895	1,856,977	1,920,148	0.8
Female	1,754,759	1,894,374	1,957,903	0.8
Age				
Under 5 years	236,353	264,126	265,474	0.1
5 to 19 years	765,927	777,484	789,882	0.4
20 to 64 years	1,992,424	2,203,027	2,260,164	0.6
65 years and over	455,950	506,714	562,531	2.6
Median age (years)	35.5	36.2	36.2	-
Race and Hispanic Origin				
One race				
White	2,628,434	2,851,510	2,910,952	0.5
Black	260,968	284,332	299,574	1.3
American Indian and Alaska Native	273,230	335,664	350,892	1.1
Asian	46,767	67,126	81,394	4.9
Native Hawaiian or Other Pacific Islander	2,372	5,354	6,393	4.5
Two or more races	155,985	207,365	228,846	2.5
Hispanic (of any race)	179,304	351,542	381,531	2.1

X = Not applicable.
- = Zero or rounds to zero.
[1]Population figures for 2014 are July 1 estimates. The 2010 estimates are taken from the 2010 Census.

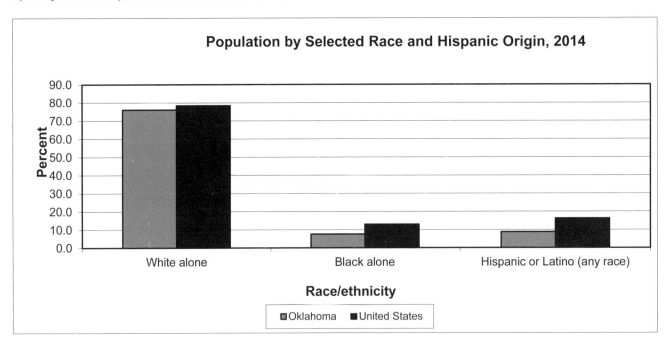

Table OK-2. Marital Status

(Number, percent distribution.)

Sex, age, race, and Hispanic origin	2000	2010	2013
Males, 15 Years and Over	1,318,729	1,457,860	1,497,900
Never married	25.8	30.7	31.4
Now married, except separated	59.5	52.2	51.4
Separated	1.6	1.8	1.7
Widowed	2.5	3.0	3.0
Divorced	10.6	12.3	12.5
Females, 15 Years and Over	1,398,823	1,521,546	1,555,600
Never married	19.1	23.8	24.6
Now married, except separated	55.3	49.7	48.7
Separated	1.9	2.7	2.5
Widowed	11.1	10.1	9.9
Divorced	12.5	13.7	14.3

Table OK-3. Households and Housing Characteristics

(Number, percent, dollars.)

Item	2000	2010	2013	Average annual percent change, 2000–2013
Total Households	1,342,293	1,432,959	1,447,277	0.6
Family households	921,750	954,622	956,517	0.3
Married-couple family	717,611	709,256	702,897	-0.2
Other family	204,139	245,366	253,620	1.7
Male householder, no wife present	51,564	62,855	72,977	2.7
Female householder, no husband present	152,575	182,511	180,643	1.3
Nonfamily households	420,543	478,337	490,760	1.2
Householder living alone	358,560	400,840	413,711	1.1
Householder not living alone	61,983	77,497	77,049	1.7
Housing Characteristics				
Total housing units	1,514,400	1,666,205	1,682,358	0.8
Occupied housing units	1,342,293	1,432,959	1,447,277	0.6
Owner occupied	918,259	971,378	948,540	0.2
Renter occupied	424,034	461,581	498,737	1.3
Average household size	2.49	2.55	2.58	0.3
Financial Characteristics				
Median gross rent of renter-occupied housing	456	659	705	3.4
Median monthly owner costs for housing units with a mortgage	764	1,089	1,094	2.8
Median value of owner-occupied housing units	70,700	111,400	116,500	3.9

Table OK-4. Migration, Origin, and Language

(Number, percent.)

Characteristic	State			U.S.		
	2012	2013	Percent change	2012	2013	Percent change
Residence 1 Year Ago						
Population 1 year and over	3,762,311	3,801,521	1.0	310,212,755	312,432,820	0.7
Same house	82.6	82.4	X	85.0	85.0	X
Different house in the U.S.	17.0	17.2	X	14.4	14.4	X
Same county	9.8	9.9	X	9.0	8.9	X
Different county	7.2	7.3	X	5.4	5.5	X
Same state	4.3	4.4	X	3.2	3.2	X
Different state	2.9	2.9	X	2.3	2.3	X
Abroad	0.4	0.4	X	0.6	0.6	X
Place of Birth						
Native born	3,601,536	3,632,136	0.8	273,089,382	274,780,773	0.6
Male	49.5	49.4	X	49.3	49.3	X
Female	50.5	50.6	X	50.7	50.7	X
Foreign born	213,284	218,432	2.4	40,824,658	41,348,066	1.3
Male	50.6	52.1	X	48.7	48.8	X
Female	49.4	47.9	X	51.3	51.2	X
Foreign born; naturalized U.S. citizen	68,357	76,353	11.7	18,686,237	19,294,710	3.3
Male	46.1	48.2	X	45.8	45.9	X
Female	53.9	51.8	X	54.2	54.1	X
Foreign born; not a U.S. citizen	144,927	142,079	-2.0	22,138,421	22,053,356	-0.4
Male	52.7	54.2	X	51.1	51.3	X
Female	47.3	45.8	X	48.9	48.7	X
Entered 2010 or later	10.7	14.4	X	7.0	9.7	X
Entered 2000 to 2009	36.2	36.9	X	30.4	29.4	X
Entered before 2000	53.1	48.7	X	62.7	61.0	X
World Region of Birth, Foreign						
Foreign-born population, excluding population born at sea	213,284	218,432	2.4	40,824,553	41,347,945	1.3
Europe	8.7	6.4	X	11.8	11.6	X
Asia	26.4	25.3	X	29.2	29.5	X
Africa	2.8	4.6	X	4.2	4.4	X
Oceania	0.8	1.3	X	0.6	0.5	X
Latin America	59.1	61.0	X	52.2	51.9	X
North America	2.2	1.5	X	2.0	2.0	X
Language Spoken at Home and Ability to Speak English						
Population 5 years and over	3,552,659	3,587,881	1.0	294,003,714	296,358,760	0.8
English only	90.3	90.2	X	79.0	79.2	X
Language other than English	9.7	9.8	X	21.0	20.8	X
Speaks English less than "very well"	4.0	4.0	X	8.5	8.5	X

NA = Not available.
X = Not applicable.
- = Zero or rounds to zero.

Table OK-5. Median Income and Poverty Status, 2013

(Number, percent, except as noted.)

Characteristic	State		U.S.	
	Number	Percent	Number	Percent
Median Income				
Households (dollars)...	45,690	X	52,250	X
Families (dollars)	56,655	X	64,030	X
Below Poverty Level (All People)	626,906	16.8	48,810,868	15.8
Sex				
Male..	271,216	14.8	21,938,525	14.5
Female	355,690	18.7	26,872,343	17.1
Age				
Under 18 years..	223,114	24	16,086,960	22.2
Related children under 18 years.......................	217,522	23.5	15,769,921	21.9
18 to 64 years...	353,810	15.5	28,578,191	14.8
65 years and over	49,982	9.5	4,145,717	9.6

X = Not applicable.

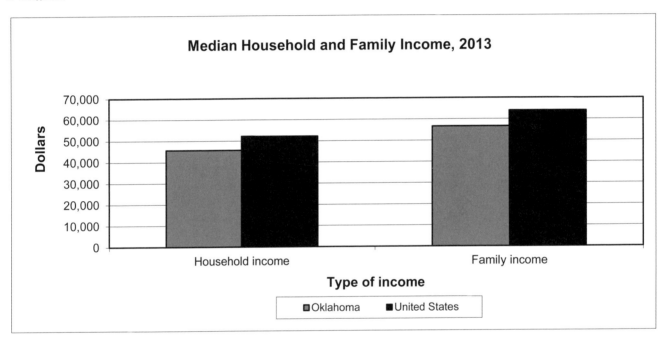

Table OK-6. Health Insurance Coverage Status for the Civilian Noninstitutionalized Population and Children Under 18 Years of Age

(Numbers in thousands, percent.)

Item	2005	2006	2007	2008	2009	2010	2011	2012	2013
Civilian Noninstitutionalized Population	3,505	3,492	3,551	3,550	3,590	3,677	3,710	3,733	3,770
Covered by Private or Public Insurance									
Number...	2,878	2,831	2,920	2,858	2,919	2,984	3,017	3,048	3,104
Percent..	82.1	81.1	82.2	80.5	81.3	81.1	81.3	81.6	82.3
Not Covered									
Number...	627	661	631	692	672	694	694	685	666
Percent..	17.9	18.9	17.8	19.5	18.7	18.9	18.7	18.4	17.7
Percent in the U.S. not covered..........................	15.3	15.8	15.3	15.1	15.1	15.5	15.1	14.8	14.5
Children Under 18 Years of Age..........................	867	913	920	903	919	929	934	935	946
Covered by Private or Public Insurance									
Number...	772	799	804	786	816	836	834	841	851
Percent..	89.0	87.5	87.4	87.0	88.8	90.0	89.4	89.9	90.0
Not Covered									
Number...	95	114	116	117	103	93	100	94	95
Percent..	11.0	12.5	12.6	13.0	11.2	10.0	10.6	10.1	10.0
Percent in the U.S. not covered..........................	10.9	11.7	11.0	9.7	8.6	8.0	7.5	7.2	7.1

Table OK-7. Employment Status by Demographic Group, 2014

(Numbers in thousands, percent.)

Characteristic	Civilian noninstitutional population	Civilian labor force		Employed		Unemployed	
		Number	Percent of population	Number	Percent of population	Number	Percent of population
Total...	2,946	1,768	60.0	1,688	57.3	80	4.5
Sex							
Male..	1,424	962	67.6	916	64.3	46	4.8
Female	1,522	806	53.0	772	50.7	34	4.2
Race, Sex, and Hispanic Origin							
White..	2,288	1,365	59.7	1,313	57.4	53	3.9
Male...	1,119	753	67.3	723	64.6	30	4.0
Female	1,169	612	52.4	590	50.4	22	3.7
Black or African American...................	200	117	58.6	109	54.5	8	7.0
Male...	91	58	62.9	53	58.3	4	7.3
Female	108	60	55.0	56	51.3	4	6.7
Hispanic or Latino ethnicity[1]	251	172	68.5	161	64.3	10	6.0
Male...	136	110	81.0	105	76.8	6	5.1
Female	114	61	53.5	57	49.5	5	7.6
Age							
16 to 19 years...................................	215	64	29.6	53	24.5	11	17.0
20 to 24 years...................................	268	184	68.8	169	63.3	15	8.1
25 to 34 years...................................	532	422	79.4	402	75.5	21	4.9
35 to 44 years...................................	428	344	80.3	328	76.6	16	4.6
45 to 54 years...................................	476	370	77.6	359	75.3	11	3.0
55 to 64 years...................................	459	271	59.1	265	57.8	6	2.1
65 years and over	569	114	20.0	113	19.8	1	1.2

NOTE: Data in Table 7 are from the Current Population Survey (CPS) and do not match the estimates in Table 8. See notes and definitions for further information.
[1]May be of any race.

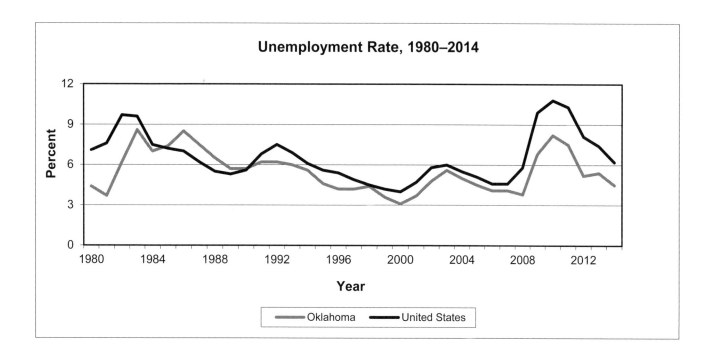

Table OK-8. Employment Status of the Civilian Noninstitutional Population Age 16 Years and Over

(Number, percent.)

Year	Civilian labor force	Civilian participation rate	Employed	Unemployed	Unemployment rate
2006	1,715,794	63.8	1,647,098	68,696	4.0
2007	1,726,259	63.5	1,655,490	70,769	4.1
2008	1,746,466	63.7	1,681,081	65,385	3.7
2009	1,764,432	63.6	1,652,023	112,409	6.4
2010	1,768,284	62.4	1,648,138	120,146	6.8
2011	1,773,880	61.9	1,669,281	104,599	5.9
2012	1,799,898	62.2	1,705,123	94,775	5.3
2013	1,803,215	61.7	1,706,785	96,430	5.3
2014	1,784,035	60.6	1,703,832	80,203	4.5

Table OK-9. Employment and Average Wages by Industry

(Estimates from 2007 through 2010 are based on the 2007 *North American Industry Classification System* [NAICS]. Estimates from 2011 onward are based on the 2012 NAICS.)

Industry	2007	2008	2009	2010	2011	2012	2013
	Number of jobs						
Wage and Salary Employment by Industry	1,649,403	1,678,945	1,626,342	1,614,647	1,633,708	1,663,796	1,683,711
Farm Wage and Salary Employment	11,616	12,605	11,244	9,532	8,599	13,525	13,731
Nonfarm Wage and Salary Employment	1,637,787	1,666,340	1,615,098	1,605,115	1,625,109	1,650,271	1,669,980
Private wage and salary employment	1,275,458	1,298,032	1,236,244	1,225,337	1,253,214	1,279,746	1,300,479
Forestry, fishing, and related activities	4,131	4,189	3,949	4,128	4,111	4,138	4,082
Mining	46,344	50,710	42,591	43,229	50,925	57,564	59,043
Utilities	10,514	10,966	11,445	11,234	11,195	11,726	11,712
Construction	74,370	78,639	72,381	70,769	71,827	72,563	77,309
Manufacturing	150,496	150,338	132,008	125,385	132,255	137,752	138,817
Durable goods manufacturing	103,070	103,772	87,553	81,836	87,858	94,374	95,750
Nondurable goods manufacturing	47,426	46,566	44,455	43,549	44,397	43,378	43,067
Wholesale trade	60,256	60,227	56,970	56,037	58,651	60,695	62,417
Retail trade	173,596	175,088	172,028	171,161	172,829	174,873	176,510
Transportation and warehousing	47,737	46,540	44,482	42,453	43,280	45,225	46,520
Information	27,986	28,036	26,504	25,036	24,103	22,696	21,850
Finance and insurance	58,252	59,186	58,452	57,958	57,990	59,226	58,847
Real estate and rental and leasing	24,635	24,303	22,981	22,460	22,250	21,991	22,730
Professional, scientific, and technical services	65,267	66,899	64,137	63,806	65,688	66,519	67,637
Management of companies and enterprises	13,286	15,231	14,536	15,159	14,928	15,980	16,564
Administrative and waste services	106,144	107,178	92,240	93,926	94,967	96,659	97,596
Educational services	19,325	19,188	19,603	19,843	20,339	20,942	21,181
Health care and social assistance	173,659	178,613	181,094	183,915	185,043	186,423	187,968
Arts, entertainment, and recreation	14,637	14,905	14,561	14,477	14,976	14,484	14,892
Accommodation and food services	124,459	126,748	127,327	126,311	129,910	133,457	137,660
Other services, except public administration	80,364	81,048	78,955	78,050	77,947	76,833	77,144
Government and government enterprises	362,329	368,308	378,854	379,778	371,895	370,525	369,501
	Dollars						
Average Wages and Salaries by Industry	36,250	37,829	37,764	38,854	40,747	42,110	43,047
Average Farm Wages and Salaries	28,010	30,116	25,316	27,917	35,963	31,642	29,223
Average Nonfarm Wages and Salaries	36,308	37,887	37,851	38,919	40,772	42,196	43,161
Average private wages and salaries	36,174	37,860	37,596	38,745	40,918	42,628	43,554
Forestry, fishing, and related activities	22,183	22,223	22,178	22,920	23,605	24,361	25,129
Mining	79,401	86,657	81,300	84,802	95,092	92,564	95,308
Utilities	78,858	77,270	80,310	79,789	82,744	92,066	96,204
Construction	37,007	39,847	40,073	41,572	42,402	44,727	46,927
Manufacturing	43,969	45,600	45,737	47,704	49,460	51,913	53,128
Durable goods manufacturing	45,269	47,280	47,470	49,546	51,535	53,845	55,092
Nondurable goods manufacturing	41,144	41,857	42,325	44,244	45,353	47,708	48,763
Wholesale trade	49,257	52,032	50,717	50,318	52,424	54,855	55,514
Retail trade	23,679	24,304	24,436	25,234	25,957	26,986	27,310
Transportation and warehousing	45,944	47,540	47,528	50,334	53,017	54,181	55,644
Information	46,299	48,045	47,102	47,954	51,776	53,130	54,900
Finance and insurance	46,665	48,050	48,557	50,266	52,328	55,175	56,894
Real estate and rental and leasing	36,822	36,005	34,460	36,293	39,347	42,519	41,968
Professional, scientific, and technical services	49,713	51,206	52,315	54,200	55,811	59,325	60,907
Management of companies and enterprises	72,217	71,882	71,789	75,324	96,022	88,331	88,988
Administrative and waste services	27,667	29,639	30,517	30,975	31,846	33,273	33,487
Educational services	27,186	28,828	29,604	30,274	30,788	30,408	31,055
Health care and social assistance	35,710	37,031	37,965	38,640	39,954	41,177	42,000
Arts, entertainment, and recreation	25,313	23,067	27,201	28,064	28,805	31,121	31,143
Accommodation and food services	14,383	14,711	14,887	15,691	16,127	16,601	16,607
Other services, except public administration	24,238	25,653	25,637	26,721	27,496	28,466	29,064
Government and government enterprises	36,779	37,983	38,680	39,480	40,280	40,704	41,777

Table OK-10. Employment Characteristics by Family Type

(Number, percent.)

Family type and labor force status	2011		2012		2013	
	Total	Families with own children under 18 years	Total	Families with own children under 18 years	Total	Families with own children under 18 years
All Families	957,855	424,367	957,067	416,517	956,517	415,825
FAMILY TYPE AND LABOR FORCE STATUS						
Married-Couple Families	715,154	281,099	702,265	272,752	702,897	271,793
Both husband and wife in labor force	50.2	64.0	49.4	64.2	48.7	62.4
Husband in labor force, wife not in labor force	24.1	30.3	24.4	29.3	24.9	30.9
Wife in labor force, husband not in labor force	7.9	3.7	7.6	4.4	8.0	4.2
Both husband and wife not in labor force	17.8	2.0	18.5	2.2	18.2	2.3
Other Families	242,701	143,268	254,802	143,765	253,620	144,032
Female householder, no husband present	72.2	74.0	71.1	73.7	71.2	73.8
In labor force	49.6	57.8	48.3	58.9	48.4	57.5
Not in labor force	22.6	16.2	22.8	14.7	22.8	16.3
Male householder, no wife present	27.8	26.0	28.9	26.3	28.8	26.2
In labor force	22.3	24.1	22.5	23.9	22.2	23.1
Not in labor force	5.5	1.9	6.3	2.4	6.6	3.1

Table OK-11. School Enrollment and Educational Attainment, 2013

(Number, percent.)

Item	State	U.S.
Enrollment		
Total population 3 years and over, enrolled in school	994,407	82,395,254
Enrolled in nursery school or preschool (percent)	6.7	6.0
Enrolled in kindergarten (percent)	6.1	5.2
Enrolled in elementary school, grades 1-8 (percent)	42.7	40.0
Enrolled in high school, grades 9-12 (percent)	20.0	20.6
Enrolled in college or graduate school (percent)	24.5	28.3
Attainment		
Total population 25 years and over	2,506,437	210,910,615
Less than ninth grade (percent)	4.4	5.8
9th to 12th grade, no diploma (percent)	8.9	7.6
High school graduate, including equivalency (percent)	32.3	27.8
Some college, no degree (percent)	23.5	21.1
Associate's degree (percent)	7.2	8.1
Bachelor's degree (percent)	16.1	18.4
Graduate or professional degree (percent)	7.7	11.2
High school graduate or higher (percent)	86.7	86.6
Bachelor's degree or higher (percent)	23.8	29.6

Table OK-12. Public School Characteristics and Educational Indicators

(Number, percent; data derived from National Center of Education Statistics.)

Item	State	U.S.
Public Schools, 2012–2013 (except where noted)		
Number of school districts	584	18,093
Number of schools	1,784	98,454
Number of students (in thousands)	673	49,771
Number of teachers (in thousands)	42	3,109
Student-teacher ratio	16.1	16.0
Expenditures per student (dollars), FY 2012	7,763	10,667
Four-year adjusted cohort graduation rate (ACGR)[1,2]	84.8	81.4
Students eligible for free or reduced-price lunch (in thousands)	410	25,188
English language learners (in thousands)	46	4,397
Students age 3 to 21 served under IDEA, part B (in thousands)	101	6,429

Public Schools by Type	Number	Percent of state public schools
Total number of schools	1,784	100.0
Regular	1,776	99.6
Special education	4	0.2
Vocational education	0	-
Alternative education	4	0.2

NOTE: Every school is assigned only one school type based on its instructional emphasis.
[1]ACGR data represents a new method of calculating high-school completion rates and may not be comparable to previous years' data for Averaged Freshmen Graduation Rates (AFGR).
[2]The United States 4-year ACGRs were estimated using both the reported 4-year ACGR data from 49 states and the District of Columbia and using imputed data for Idaho. The estimate for American Indian/Alaska Native students also includes imputed data for Virginia.
- = Zero or rounds to zero.

Table OK-13. Reported Voting and Registration of the Voting-Age Population, November 2012

(Numbers in thousands, percent.)

Item	Total population	Total citizen population	Registered			Voted		
			Total registered	Percent registered (total population)	Percent registered (total citizen population)	Total voted	Percent voted (total population)	Percent voted (total citizen population)
U.S. Total	235,248	215,081	153,157	65.1	71.2	132,948	56.5	61.8
State Total	2,808	2,733	1,806	64.3	66.1	1,431	51.0	52.4
Sex								
Male	1,358	1,319	835	61.5	63.3	656	48.3	49.8
Female	1,449	1,414	970	66.9	68.6	775	53.5	54.8
Race								
White alone	2,072	2,018	1,364	65.8	67.6	1,101	53.1	54.6
White, non-Hispanic alone	1,931	1,925	1,331	68.9	69.2	1,076	55.7	55.9
Black alone...................................	191	187	116	61.1	62.2	102	53.6	54.6
Asian alone	58	41	25	B	B	22	B	B
Hispanic (of any race)	174	127	53	30.4	41.8	36	20.9	28.7
White alone or in combination	2,285	2,231	1,501	65.7	67.3	1,199	52.5	53.7
Black alone or in combination..........	223	220	139	62.1	63.1	121	54.2	55.0
Asian alone or in combination..........	72	55	32	B	B	25	B	B
Age								
18 to 24 years.................................	325	323	130	40.1	40.3	88	27.2	27.3
25 to 44 years.................................	1,000	958	577	57.7	60.2	396	39.6	41.4
45 to 64 years.................................	1,001	980	720	72.0	73.5	602	60.1	61.4
65 to 74 years.................................	275	269	240	87.4	89.2	217	79.1	80.7
75 years and over	208	204	138	66.5	67.9	128	61.4	62.8

B = Base is less than 75,000 and therefore too small to show the derived measure.

Table OK-14. Crime

(Number, rate per 100,000. Data are derived from the FBI Uniform Crime Reports.)

Item	State			U.S.[1,2,3,4]		
	2012	2013	Percent change	2012	2013	Percent change
TOTAL POPULATION[5]...	3,815,780	3,850,568	0.9	313,873,685	316,128,839	0.7
VIOLENT CRIME						
Number.......................................	18,102	16,484	-8.9	1,217,067	1,163,146	-4.4
Rate	474.4	428.1	-9.8	387.8	367.9	-5.1
Murder and Nonnegligent Manslaughter						
Number.......................................	220	195	-11.4	14,866	14,196	-4.5
Rate	5.8	5.1	-12.2	4.7	4.5	-5.2
Rape[6]						
Number.......................................	X	2,180	X	X	108,612	X
Rate	X	56.6	X	X	34.4	X
Robbery						
Number.......................................	3,248	3,031	-6.7	355,051	345,031	-2.8
Rate	85.1	78.7	-7.5	113.1	109.1	-3.5
Aggravated Assault						
Number.......................................	13,012	11,583	-11.0	762,009	724,149	-5.0
Rate	341.0	300.8	-11.8	242.8	229.1	-5.6
PROPERTY CRIME						
Number.......................................	130,969	126,057	-3.8	9,001,992	8,632,512	-4.1
Rate	3,432.3	3,273.7	-4.6	2,868.0	2,730.7	-4.8
Burglary						
Number.......................................	36,094	33,348	-7.6	2,109,932	1,928,465	-8.6
Rate	945.9	866.1	-8.4	672.2	610.0	-9.3
Larceny-Theft						
Number.......................................	83,131	81,495	-2.0	6,168,874	6,004,453	-2.7
Rate	2,178.6	2,116.4	-2.9	1,965.4	1,899.4	-3.4
Motor Vehicle Theft						
Number.......................................	11,744	11,214	-4.5	723,186	699,594	-3.3
Rate	307.8	291.2	-5.4	230.4	221.3	-4.0

NOTE: Although arson data are included in the trend and clearance tables, sufficient data are not available to estimate totals for this offense. Therefore, no arson data are published in this table.

X = Not applicable.

- = Zero or rounds to zero.

[1]The crime figures have been adjusted.

[2]The data collection methodology for the offense of forcible rape used by the Minnesota state Uniform Crime Reporting (UCR) Program (with the exception of Minneapolis and St. Paul, Minnesota) does not comply with national UCR Program guidelines. Consequently, its figures for forcible rape and violent crime (of which forcible rape is a part) are not published in this table.

[3]Includes offenses reported by the Zoological Police and the Metro Transit Police.

[4]Because of changes in the state's reporting practices, figures are not comparable to previous years' data.

[5]Populations are U.S. Census Bureau provisional estimates as of July 1 of each year.

[6]The figures shown for the offense of rape were estimated using the revised Uniform Crime Reporting (UCR) definition of rape.

Table OK-15. State Government Finances, 2013

(Dollar amounts in thousands, percent distribution.)

Item	Dollars	Percent distribution
Total Revenue	26,344,587	100.0
General revenue	20,799,702	79.0
Intergovernmental revenue	7,159,511	27.2
Taxes	8,892,503	33.8
General sales	2,518,598	9.6
Selective sales	1,329,853	5.0
License taxes	1,010,430	3.8
Individual income tax	2,916,615	11.1
Corporate income tax	585,146	2.2
Other taxes	531,861	2.0
Current charges	2,491,130	9.5
Miscellaneous general revenue	2,256,558	8.6
Utility revenue	601,877	2.3
Liquor stores revenue	0	-
Insurance trust revenue[1]	4,943,008	18.8
Total Expenditure	22,920,374	100.0
Intergovernmental expenditure	4,213,211	18.4
Direct expenditure	18,707,163	81.6
Current operation	13,302,644	58.0
Capital outlay	1,883,892	8.2
Insurance benefits and repayments	2,527,396	11.0
Assistance and subsidies	453,666	2.0
Interest on debt	539,565	2.4
Exhibit: Salaries and wages	3,162,736	13.8
Total Expenditure	22,920,374	100.0
General expenditure	19,579,099	85.4
Intergovernmental expenditure	4,213,211	18.4
Direct expenditure	15,365,888	67.0
General expenditure, by function:		
Education	7,321,724	31.9
Public welfare	6,258,083	27.3
Hospitals	258,175	1.1
Health	861,552	3.8
Highways	1,802,547	7.9
Police protection	233,623	1.0
Correction	569,140	2.5
Natural resources	231,332	1.0
Parks and recreation	81,657	0.4
Governmental administration	747,200	3.3
Interest on general debt	460,984	2.0
Other and unallocable	753,082	3.3
Utility expenditure	813,879	3.6
Liquor stores expenditure	0	-
Insurance trust expenditure	2,527,396	11.0
Debt at End of Fiscal Year	9,514,281	X
Cash and Security Holdings	40,244,056	X

X = Not applicable.
- = Zero or rounds to zero.
[1]Within insurance trust revenue, net earnings of state retirement systems is a calculated statistic (the item code in the data file is X08), and thus can be positive or negative. Net earnings is the sum of earnings on investments plus gains on investments minus losses on investments. The change made in 2002 for asset valuation from book to market value in accordance with Statement 34 of the Governmental Accounting Standards Board is reflected in the calculated statistics.

Table OK-16. State Government Tax Collections, 2014

(Dollars in thousands, percent.)

Item	Dollars	Percent distribution
Total Taxes	9,103,302	100.0
Property taxes	X	X
Sales and gross receipts	3,989,358	43.8
General sales and gross receipts	2,599,203	28.6
Selective sales and gross receipts	1,390,155	15.3
Alcoholic beverages	110,941	1.2
Amusements	20,823	0.2
Insurance premiums	294,762	3.2
Motor fuels	450,807	5.0
Pari-mutuels	1,113	-
Public utilities	46,306	0.5
Tobacco products	292,752	3.2
Other selective sales	172,651	1.9
Licenses	1,057,768	11.6
Alcoholic beverages	1,326	-
Amusements	146,857	1.6
Corporations in general	35,351	0.4
Hunting and fishing	19,910	0.2
Motor vehicle	754,435	8.3
Motor vehicle operators	20,109	0.2
Public utilities	947	-
Occupation and business, NEC	78,572	0.9
Other licenses	261	-
Income taxes	3,359,418	36.9
Individual income	2,962,128	32.5
Corporation net income	397,290	4.4
Other taxes	696,758	7.7
Death and gift	1,056	-
Documentary and stock transfer	16,296	0.2
Severance	679,406	7.5
Taxes, NEC	0	-

X = Not applicable.
- = Zero or rounds to zero.

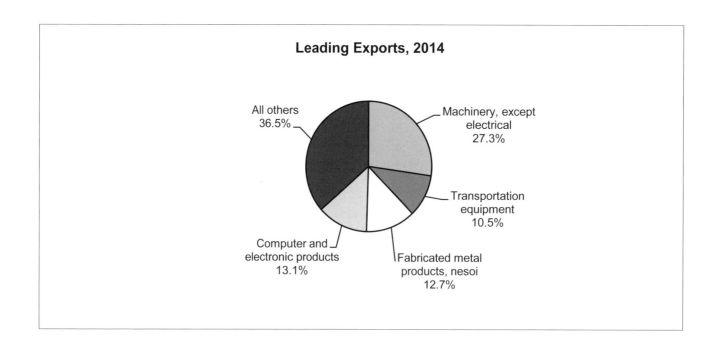

Leading Exports, 2014

All others 36.5%

Machinery, except electrical 27.3%

Transportation equipment 10.5%

Fabricated metal products, nesoi 12.7%

Computer and electronic products 13.1%

OREGON

Facts and Figures

Location: Northwestern United States; bordered on the N by Washington, on the E by Idaho, on the S by Nevada and California, and on the W by the Pacific Ocean

Area: 98,381 sq. mi. (254,805 sq. km.); rank—9th

Population: 3,970,239 (2014 est.); rank—27th

Principal Cities: capital—Salem; largest—Portland

Statehood: February 14, 1859; 33rd state

U.S. Congress: 2 senators, 5 representatives

State Motto: She Flies With Her Own Wings

State Song: "Oregon, My Oregon"

State Nickname: The Beaver State

Abbreviations: OR; Oreg.

State Symbols: flower—Oregon grape; tree—Douglas fir; bird—Western meadowlark

At a Glance

- With an increase in population of 3.6 percent, Oregon ranked 20th among the states in growth from 2010 to 2014.

- In 2013, 14.7 percent of Oregonians did not have health insurance, which was close to the rate of 14.5 percent among the total U.S. population.

- Oregon's violent crime rate in 2013 was 254.0 per 100,000 population, compared to 367.9 for the entire nation.

- Oregon's median income in 2013 was $50,251, and 16.7 percent of its residents lived below the poverty level.

- The state's homeownership rate of 64.2 percent ranked 41st in the nation in 2013.

Table OR-1. Population by Age, Sex, Race, and Hispanic Origin

(Number, percent, except where noted.)

Sex, age, race, and Hispanic origin	2000	2010	2014[1]	Average annual percent change, 2010–2014
Total Population	3,421,399	3,831,074	3,970,239	0.9
Percent of total U.S. population	1.2	1.2	1.2	X
Sex				
Male	1,696,550	1,896,002	1,964,100	0.9
Female	1,724,849	1,935,072	2,006,139	0.9
Age				
Under 5 years	223,005	237,556	229,463	-0.9
5 to 19 years	720,999	734,627	725,593	-0.3
20 to 64 years	2,039,218	2,325,358	2,381,296	0.6
65 years and over	438,177	533,533	633,887	4.4
Median age (years)	36.3	38.4	39.2	0.5
Race and Hispanic Origin				
One race				
White	2,961,623	3,403,252	3,488,798	0.6
Black	55,662	74,414	80,962	2.1
American Indian and Alaska Native	45,211	66,784	70,842	1.5
Asian	101,350	145,009	169,517	4.0
Native Hawaiian or Other Pacific Islander	7,976	14,649	16,861	3.6
Two or more races	104,745	126,966	143,259	3.1
Hispanic (of any race)	275,314	467,030	496,789	1.6

X = Not applicable.
[1]Population figures for 2014 are July 1 estimates. The 2010 estimates are taken from the 2010 Census.

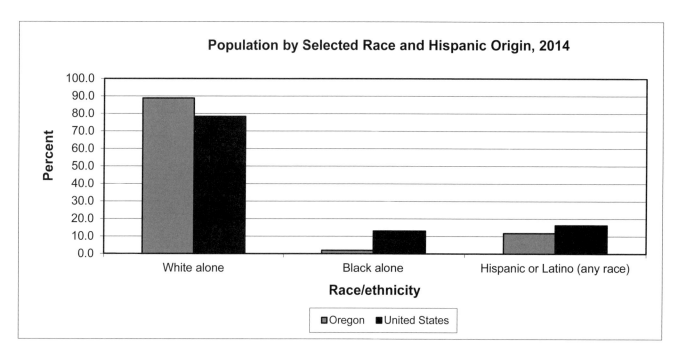

Table OR-2. Marital Status

(Number, percent distribution.)

Sex, age, race, and Hispanic origin	2000	2010	2013
Males, 15 Years and Over	1,336,805	1,533,177	1,581,553
Never married	28.5	32.6	33.8
Now married, except separated	57.1	51.4	50.5
Separated	1.5	1.6	1.5
Widowed	2.4	2.7	2.6
Divorced	10.6	11.8	11.6
Females, 15 Years and Over	1,385,329	1,588,428	1,637,606
Never married	21.9	25.8	26.8
Now married, except separated	53.9	48.9	48.0
Separated	1.9	1.9	2.3
Widowed	9.6	8.5	8.4
Divorced	12.7	14.9	14.6

Table OR-3. Households and Housing Characteristics

(Number, percent, dollars.)

Item	2000	2010	2013	Average annual percent change, 2000–2013
Total Households.............................	1,333,723	1,507,137	1,523,799	1.0
Family households	877,671	963,362	961,197	0.7
Married-couple family	692,532	733,095	731,763	0.4
Other family	185,139	230,267	229,434	1.7
Male householder, no wife present............	54,357	65,972	66,409	1.6
Female householder, no husband present........	130,782	164,295	163,025	1.7
Nonfamily households	456,032	543,775	562,602	1.6
Householder living alone................	347,624	416,500	430,953	1.7
Householder not living alone............	108,428	127,275	131,649	1.5
Housing Characteristics				
Total housing units........................	1,452,709	1,676,476	1,684,107	1.1
Occupied housing units	1,333,723	1,507,137	1,523,799	1.0
Owner occupied	856,951	942,674	926,930	0.6
Renter occupied	476,772	564,463	596,869	1.7
Average household size....................	2.51	2.49	2.52	-
Financial Characteristics				
Median gross rent of renter-occupied housing	620	816	887	2.8
Median monthly owner costs for housing units with a mortgage	1,125	1,577	1,502	2.2
Median value of owner-occupied housing units............	152,100	244,500	229,700	3.2

- = Zero or rounds to zero.

Table OR-4. Migration, Origin, and Language

(Number, percent.)

Characteristic	State			U.S.		
	2012	2013	Percent change	2012	2013	Percent change
Residence 1 Year Ago						
Population 1 year and over	3,857,465	3,888,216	0.8	310,212,755	312,432,820	0.7
Same house	81.9	81.1	X	85.0	85.0	X
Different house in the U.S.	17.6	18.4	X	14.4	14.4	X
Same county	11.1	10.7	X	9.0	8.9	X
Different county	6.5	7.7	X	5.4	5.5	X
Same state	3.5	4.0	X	3.2	3.2	X
Different state	3.1	3.7	X	2.3	2.3	X
Abroad	0.5	0.5	X	0.6	0.6	X
Place of Birth						
Native born	3,526,586	3,538,859	0.3	273,089,382	274,780,773	0.6
Male	49.6	49.5	X	49.3	49.3	X
Female	50.4	50.5	X	50.7	50.7	X
Foreign born	372,767	391,206	4.9	40,824,658	41,348,066	1.3
Male	49.6	49.4	X	48.7	48.8	X
Female	50.4	50.6	X	51.3	51.2	X
Foreign born; naturalized U.S. citizen....................	151,720	155,415	2.4	18,686,237	19,294,710	3.3
Male	44.2	45.9	X	45.8	45.9	X
Female	55.8	54.1	X	54.2	54.1	X
Foreign born; not a U.S. citizen.......................	221,047	235,791	6.7	22,138,421	22,053,356	-0.4
Male	53.3	51.7	X	51.1	51.3	X
Female	46.7	48.3	X	48.9	48.7	X
Entered 2010 or later	5.6	9.3	X	7.0	9.7	X
Entered 2000 to 2009	32.5	28.3	X	30.4	29.4	X
Entered before 2000..................................	61.8	62.4	X	62.7	61.0	X
World Region of Birth, Foreign						
Foreign-born population, excluding population born at sea	372,767	391,206	4.9	40,824,553	41,347,945	1.3
Europe	15.2	16.7	X	11.8	11.6	X
Asia...	29.8	28.5	X	29.2	29.5	X
Africa	2.5	3.1	X	4.2	4.4	X
Oceania	2.4	1.7	X	0.6	0.5	X
Latin America	45.5	46.4	X	52.2	51.9	X
North America	4.6	3.6	X	2.0	2.0	X
Language Spoken at Home and Ability to Speak English						
Population 5 years and over..............................	3,667,240	3,701,662	0.9	294,003,714	296,358,760	0.8
English only	85.3	85.1	X	79.0	79.2	X
Language other than English.........................	14.7	14.9	X	21.0	20.8	X
Speaks English less than "very well"...........	6.0	5.9	X	8.5	8.5	X

NA = Not available.
X = Not applicable.
- = Zero or rounds to zero.

Table OR-5. Median Income and Poverty Status, 2013

(Number, percent, except as noted.)

Characteristic	State		U.S.	
	Number	Percent	Number	Percent
Median Income				
Households (dollars)............................	50,251	X	52,250	X
Families (dollars)	61,767	X	64,030	X
Below Poverty Level (All People)...............	642,138	16.7	48,810,868	15.8
Sex				
Male...	299,227	15.7	21,938,525	14.5
Female	342,911	17.6	26,872,343	17.1
Age				
Under 18 years................................	182,088	21.6	16,086,960	22.2
Related children under 18 years..........	175,916	21.0	15,769,921	21.9
18 to 64 years................................	406,806	16.8	28,578,191	14.8
65 years and over	53,244	9.0	4,145,717	9.6

X = Not applicable.

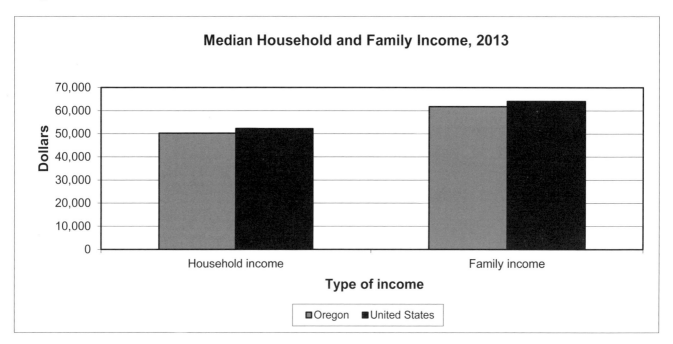

Median Household and Family Income, 2013

Table OR-6. Health Insurance Coverage Status for the Civilian Noninstitutionalized Population and Children Under 18 Years of Age

(Numbers in thousands, percent.)

Item	2005	2006	2007	2008	2009	2010	2011	2012	2013
Civilian Noninstitutionalized Population....................	3,627	3,715	3,762	3,746	3,780	3,799	3,833	3,860	3,893
Covered by Private or Public Insurance									
Number...	3,062	3,051	3,130	3,132	3,137	3,148	3,230	3,284	3,322
Percent...	84.4	82.1	83.2	83.6	83.0	82.9	84.3	85.1	85.3
Not Covered									
Number...	566	665	632	614	643	652	602	576	571
Percent...	15.6	17.9	16.8	16.4	17.0	17.1	15.7	14.9	14.7
Percent in the U.S. not covered.................	15.3	15.8	15.3	15.1	15.1	15.5	15.1	14.8	14.5
Children Under 18 Years of Age...................	881	870	864	865	871	865	861	860	858
Covered by Private or Public Insurance									
Number...	790	755	772	755	781	789	798	805	808
Percent...	89.6	86.9	89.4	87.3	89.6	91.2	92.7	93.6	94.2
Not Covered									
Number...	91	114	92	110	90	76	63	55	50
Percent...	10.4	13.1	10.6	12.7	10.4	8.8	7.3	6.4	5.8
Percent in the U.S. not covered.................	10.9	11.7	11.0	9.7	8.6	8.0	7.5	7.2	7.1

Table OR-7. Employment Status by Demographic Group, 2014

(Numbers in thousands, percent.)

Characteristic	Civilian noninstitutional population	Civilian labor force		Employed		Unemployed	
		Number	Percent of population	Number	Percent of population	Number	Percent of population
Total..	3,171	1,945	61.4	1,807	57.0	138	7.1
Sex							
Male..	1,547	1,031	66.7	954	61.7	77	7.5
Female	1,624	914	56.3	854	52.6	61	6.6
Race, Sex, and Hispanic Origin							
White..	2,822	1,726	61.2	1,608	57.0	118	6.8
Male..	1,380	919	66.6	856	62.0	64	6.9
Female	1,442	806	55.9	752	52.2	54	6.7
Black or African American........................	54	34	62.8	29	54.3	5	13.6
Male..	NA	NA	NA	NA	NA	NA	NA
Female	NA	NA	NA	NA	NA	NA	NA
Hispanic or Latino ethnicity[1]	298	202	67.8	182	61.3	19	9.6
Male..	170	126	74.1	115	67.8	11	8.4
Female	128	76	59.6	67	52.7	9	11.6
Age							
16 to 19 years......................................	197	72	36.4	52	26.2	20	28.0
20 to 24 years......................................	241	174	72.0	152	62.8	22	12.7
25 to 34 years......................................	525	434	82.8	407	77.6	27	6.2
35 to 44 years......................................	539	437	81.1	415	76.9	23	5.2
45 to 54 years......................................	480	373	77.9	353	73.6	21	5.5
55 to 64 years......................................	549	343	62.5	325	59.3	18	5.1
65 years and over	641	112	17.5	104	16.3	8	7.1

NOTE: Data in Table 7 are from the Current Population Survey (CPS) and do not match the estimates in Table 8. See notes and definitions for further information.
[1]May be of any race.
NA = Not available.

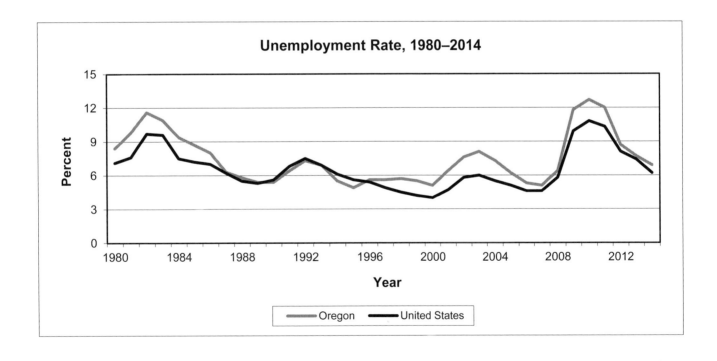

Table OR-8. Employment Status of the Civilian Noninstitutional Population Age 16 Years and Over

(Number, percent.)

Year	Civilian labor force	Civilian participation rate	Employed	Unemployed	Unemployment rate
2006	1,885,385	65.5	1,785,044	100,341	5.3
2007	1,921,766	65.7	1,822,772	98,994	5.2
2008	1,955,121	65.8	1,827,352	127,769	6.5
2009	1,976,638	65.7	1,753,682	222,956	11.3
2010	1,984,039	65.4	1,773,076	210,963	10.6
2011	1,991,325	65.0	1,802,477	188,848	9.5
2012	1,953,631	63.0	1,781,391	172,240	8.8
2013	1,911,207	61.0	1,761,021	150,186	7.9
2014	1,942,025	61.3	1,807,069	134,956	6.9

Table OR-9. Employment and Average Wages by Industry

(Estimates from 2007 through 2010 are based on the 2007 *North American Industry Classification System* [NAICS]. Estimates from 2011 onward are based on the 2012 NAICS.)

Industry	2007	2008	2009	2010	2011	2012	2013
	Number of jobs						
Wage and Salary Employment by Industry	1,823,312	1,810,443	1,707,674	1,701,494	1,720,379	1,719,728	1,756,815
Farm Wage and Salary Employment	30,621	30,351	30,942	33,578	33,358	30,302	32,834
Nonfarm Wage and Salary Employment	1,792,691	1,780,092	1,676,732	1,667,916	1,687,021	1,689,426	1,723,981
Private wage and salary employment	1,503,391	1,484,093	1,378,007	1,367,286	1,392,299	1,409,680	1,447,306
Forestry, fishing, and related activities	20,614	20,701	18,818	19,157	19,894	19,685	21,908
Mining	2,153	1,989	1,676	1,575	1,600	1,592	1,527
Utilities	4,675	4,757	4,713	4,548	4,493	4,561	4,497
Construction	107,068	96,526	75,992	69,366	70,932	71,394	76,074
Manufacturing	203,829	195,054	166,964	163,545	167,984	171,712	174,944
Durable goods manufacturing	150,761	142,762	117,683	114,793	118,572	121,582	123,272
Nondurable goods manufacturing	53,068	52,292	49,281	48,752	49,412	50,130	51,672
Wholesale trade	81,469	80,878	75,856	73,576	74,573	75,492	71,731
Retail trade	203,498	199,067	185,856	185,643	187,109	188,621	193,095
Transportation and warehousing	55,093	54,585	49,670	48,640	49,738	50,303	50,864
Information	35,648	35,546	33,114	32,262	32,081	32,697	32,451
Finance and insurance	62,821	61,199	58,711	57,793	58,489	58,552	58,972
Real estate and rental and leasing	28,637	27,617	26,058	25,241	24,317	23,950	24,478
Professional, scientific, and technical services	71,838	73,537	70,752	71,233	74,713	77,324	80,723
Management of companies and enterprises	31,103	32,306	30,737	30,529	30,417	30,490	37,908
Administrative and waste services	97,028	92,256	80,225	81,936	84,103	88,476	91,418
Educational services	38,548	40,274	41,272	42,398	43,746	43,805	44,607
Health care and social assistance	196,930	203,894	207,421	212,172	215,966	218,727	222,947
Arts, entertainment, and recreation	23,352	23,489	22,212	21,827	22,402	21,978	22,734
Accommodation and food services	150,326	150,923	142,293	142,362	145,034	149,010	154,779
Other services, except public administration	88,761	89,495	85,667	83,483	84,708	81,311	81,649
Government and government enterprises	289,300	295,999	298,725	300,630	294,722	279,746	276,675
	Dollars						
Average Wages and Salaries by Industry	40,086	40,993	41,087	42,014	43,464	45,021	45,783
Average Farm Wages and Salaries	29,141	30,087	29,122	25,649	26,787	25,205	34,844
Average Nonfarm Wages and Salaries	40,272	41,179	41,308	42,343	43,794	45,377	45,991
Average private wages and salaries	40,154	40,930	40,842	41,985	43,486	44,981	45,513
Forestry, fishing, and related activities	31,782	32,026	30,616	30,165	32,435	34,131	34,901
Mining	49,182	47,813	45,646	45,480	48,768	48,648	50,654
Utilities	81,016	81,550	84,565	84,415	87,030	89,150	89,681
Construction	44,723	46,849	47,701	48,104	50,135	51,755	52,513
Manufacturing	53,180	54,743	55,243	59,172	62,062	64,224	63,496
Durable goods manufacturing	57,630	59,582	60,969	66,380	70,223	72,736	71,763
Nondurable goods manufacturing	40,540	41,532	41,567	42,200	42,479	43,582	43,772
Wholesale trade	62,791	63,628	63,188	66,367	69,594	71,719	63,023
Retail trade	26,671	26,521	26,556	26,970	27,377	28,050	28,262
Transportation and warehousing	41,791	42,335	42,123	43,417	44,345	44,945	45,462
Information	62,262	64,256	63,423	64,691	67,921	68,035	68,882
Finance and insurance	61,510	61,237	60,791	62,564	64,080	67,832	69,827
Real estate and rental and leasing	33,151	32,757	32,283	33,180	34,391	35,830	36,249
Professional, scientific, and technical services	57,738	59,581	59,170	61,348	63,638	66,854	67,672
Management of companies and enterprises	77,936	77,415	75,014	76,861	81,449	85,024	107,240
Administrative and waste services	28,136	29,578	30,308	30,294	30,931	32,037	32,073
Educational services	21,971	22,868	23,281	23,864	24,737	25,048	25,677
Health care and social assistance	40,227	41,870	42,419	42,924	44,224	45,295	46,001
Arts, entertainment, and recreation	25,723	24,917	24,686	26,357	25,509	28,090	27,112
Accommodation and food services	17,718	17,498	17,598	18,175	18,737	19,290	19,419
Other services, except public administration	26,883	27,148	27,009	27,986	28,489	29,736	30,726
Government and government enterprises	40,888	42,429	43,459	43,970	45,247	47,368	48,494

Table OR-10. Employment Characteristics by Family Type

(Number, percent.)

Family type and labor force status	2011		2012		2013	
	Total	Families with own children under 18 years	Total	Families with own children under 18 years	Total	Families with own children under 18 years
All Families..	956,746	406,586	964,892	406,243	961,197	405,368
FAMILY TYPE AND LABOR FORCE STATUS						
Married-Couple Families................................	734,223	278,537	729,381	270,464	731,763	276,074
Both husband and wife in labor force................................	50.7	64.2	50.1	64.2	49.2	65.1
Husband in labor force, wife not in labor force	21.0	29.8	21.4	29.8	20.7	28.3
Wife in labor force, husband not in labor force	8.3	4.2	8.2	4.0	8.6	4.3
Both husband and wife not in labor force..................	20.0	1.8	20.4	2.0	21.1	2.0
Other Families	222,523	128,049	235,511	135,779	229,434	129,294
Female householder, no husband present............................	68.3	68.6	70.7	72.1	71.1	73.7
In labor force..	45.8	52.5	49.3	57.1	48.9	59.7
Not in labor force	22.5	16.1	21.4	15.0	22.1	14.0
Male householder, no wife present............................	31.7	31.4	29.3	27.9	28.9	26.3
In labor force..	24.8	27.6	23.2	25.2	22.5	23.5
Not in labor force	6.9	3.8	6.1	2.8	6.5	2.8

Table OR-11. School Enrollment and Educational Attainment, 2013

(Number, percent.)

Item	State	U.S.
Enrollment		
Total population 3 years and over, enrolled in school	961,860	82,395,254
Enrolled in nursery school or preschool (percent)	5.5	6.0
Enrolled in kindergarten (percent)	5.1	5.2
Enrolled in elementary school, grades 1-8 (percent)..	39.4	40.0
Enrolled in high school, grades 9-12 (percent)	20.3	20.6
Enrolled in college or graduate school (percent)..	29.8	28.3
Attainment		
Total population 25 years and over	2,704,043	210,910,615
Less than ninth grade (percent)	4.1	5.8
9th to 12th grade, no diploma (percent)	6.1	7.6
High school graduate, including equivalency (percent)..	24.3	27.8
Some college, no degree (percent)	26.3	21.1
Associate's degree (percent)	8.4	8.1
Bachelor's degree (percent)	19.3	18.4
Graduate or professional degree (percent)..	11.5	11.2
High school graduate or higher (percent)	89.7	86.6
Bachelor's degree or higher (percent)	30.7	29.6

Table OR-12. Public School Characteristics and Educational Indicators

(Number, percent; data derived from National Center of Education Statistics.)

Item	State	U.S.
Public Schools, 2012–2013 (except where noted)		
Number of school districts..	220	18,093
Number of schools..	1,251	98,454
Number of students (in thousands)	588	49,771
Number of teachers (in thousands)	26	3,109
Student-teacher ratio	22.2	16.0
Expenditures per student (dollars), FY 2012..	9,485	10,667
Four-year adjusted cohort graduation rate (ACGR)[1,2]	68.7	81.4
Students eligible for free or reduced-price lunch (in thousands)	287	25,188
English language learners (in thousands)	50	4,397
Students age 3 to 21 served under IDEA, part B (in thousands)	82	6,429

Public Schools by Type	Number	Percent of state public schools
Total number of schools..	1,251	100.0
Regular	1,211	96.8
Special education..	2	0.2
Vocational education..	0	-
Alternative education..	38	3.0

NOTE: Every school is assigned only one school type based on its instructional emphasis.
[1]ACGR data represents a new method of calculating high-school completion rates and may not be comparable to previous years' data for Averaged Freshmen Graduation Rates (AFGR).
[2]The United States 4-year ACGRs were estimated using both the reported 4-year ACGR data from 49 states and the District of Columbia and using imputed data for Idaho. The estimate for American Indian/Alaska Native students also includes imputed data for Virginia.
- = Zero or rounds to zero.

Table OR-13. Reported Voting and Registration of the Voting-Age Population, November 2012

(Numbers in thousands, percent.)

Item	Total population	Total citizen population	Registered			Voted		
			Total registered	Percent registered (total population)	Percent registered (total citizen population)	Total voted	Percent voted (total population)	Percent voted (total citizen population)
U.S. Total	235,248	215,081	153,157	65.1	71.2	132,948	56.5	61.8
State Total	2,998	2,806	2,086	69.6	74.3	1,897	63.3	67.6
Sex								
Male	1,480	1,377	990	66.9	71.9	893	60.3	64.8
Female	1,518	1,429	1,095	72.2	76.6	1,004	66.1	70.2
Race								
White alone	2,633	2,505	1,903	72.3	76.0	1,733	65.8	69.2
White, non-Hispanic alone	2,438	2,405	1,849	75.9	76.9	1,688	69.2	70.2
Black alone...............................	57	40	32	B	B	26	B	B
Asian alone	101	71	23	22.5	B	23	22.5	B
Hispanic (of any race).................	226	121	69	30.6	57.2	60	26.7	50.0
White alone or in combination	2,728	2,594	1,965	72.0	75.7	1,786	65.5	68.9
Black alone or in combination..........	76	55	36	47.5	B	28	36.9	B
Asian alone or in combination..........	136	98	39	28.4	39.4	39	28.4	39.4
Age								
18 to 24 years	391	364	216	55.3	59.4	186	47.6	51.1
25 to 44 years	987	878	600	60.8	68.4	511	51.8	58.2
45 to 64 years	1,004	961	756	75.3	78.7	709	70.6	73.7
65 to 74 years	322	320	272	84.6	85.1	270	84.0	84.5
75 years and over	294	284	241	81.9	84.8	221	75.0	77.7

B = Base is less than 75,000 and therefore too small to show the derived measure.

Table OR-14. Crime

(Number, rate per 100,000. Data are derived from the FBI Uniform Crime Reports.)

Item	State			U.S [1,2,3,4]		
	2012	2013	Percent change	2012	2013	Percent change
TOTAL POPULATION[5].................................	3,899,801	3,930,065	0.8	313,873,685	316,128,839	0.7
VIOLENT CRIME						
Number...	9,638	9,546		1,217,067	1,163,146	-4.4
Rate..	247.1	242.9	-1.7	387.8	367.9	-5.1
Murder and Nonnegligent Manslaughter						
Number...	91	80	-12.1	14,866	14,196	-4.5
Rate..	2.3	2.0	-12.8	4.7	4.5	-5.2
Rape[6]						
Number...	X	1,897	X	X	108,612	X
Rate..	X	48.3	X	X	34.4	X
Robbery						
Number...	2,419	2,397	-0.9	355,051	345,031	-2.8
Rate..	62.0	61.0	-1.7	113.1	109.1	-3.5
Aggravated Assault						
Number...	5,969	5,610	-6.0	762,009	724,149	-5.0
Rate..	153.1	142.7	-6.7	242.8	229.1	-5.6
PROPERTY CRIME						
Number...	126,417	124,737	-1.3	9,001,992	8,632,512	-4.1
Rate..	3,241.6	3,173.9	-2.1	2,868.0	2,730.7	-4.8
Burglary						
Number...	22,051	20,769	-5.8	2,109,932	1,928,465	-8.6
Rate..	565.4	528.5	-6.5	672.2	610.0	-9.3
Larceny-Theft						
Number...	94,114	94,106	*	6,168,874	6,004,453	-2.7
Rate..	2,413.3	2,394.5	-0.8	1,965.4	1,899.4	-3.4
Motor Vehicle Theft						
Number...	10,252	9,862	-3.8	723,186	699,594	-3.3
Rate..	262.9	250.9	-4.5	230.4	221.3	-4.0

NOTE: Although arson data are included in the trend and clearance tables, sufficient data are not available to estimate totals for this offense. Therefore, no arson data are published in this table.
X = Not applicable.
- = Zero or rounds to zero.
[1]The crime figures have been adjusted.
[2]The data collection methodology for the offense of forcible rape used by the Minnesota state Uniform Crime Reporting (UCR) Program (with the exception of Minneapolis and St. Paul, Minnesota) does not comply with national UCR Program guidelines. Consequently, its figures for forcible rape and violent crime (of which forcible rape is a part) are not published in this table.
[3]Includes offenses reported by the Zoological Police and the Metro Transit Police.
[4]Because of changes in the state's reporting practices, figures are not comparable to previous years' data.
[5]Populations are U.S. Census Bureau provisional estimates as of July 1 of each year.
[6]The figures shown for the offense of rape were estimated using the revised Uniform Crime Reporting (UCR) definition of rape.

Table OR-15. State Government Finances, 2013

(Dollar amounts in thousands, percent distribution.)

Item	Dollars	Percent distribution
Total Revenue	32,914,634	100.0
General revenue	22,833,016	69.4
Intergovernmental revenue	8,003,252	24.3
Taxes	9,160,887	27.8
General sales	0	-
Selective sales	1,369,266	4.2
License taxes	923,123	2.8
Individual income tax	6,260,161	19.0
Corporate income tax	459,744	1.4
Other taxes	148,593	0.5
Current charges	3,720,003	11.3
Miscellaneous general revenue	1,948,874	5.9
Utility revenue	13	-
Liquor stores revenue	497,674	1.5
Insurance trust revenue[1]	9,583,931	29.1
Total Expenditure	26,850,084	100.0
Intergovernmental expenditure	5,495,337	20.5
Direct expenditure	21,354,747	79.5
Current operation	14,100,769	52.5
Capital outlay	1,138,779	4.2
Insurance benefits and repayments	5,113,960	19.0
Assistance and subsidies	577,064	2.1
Interest on debt	424,175	1.6
Exhibit: Salaries and wages	4,797,424	17.9
Total Expenditure	26,850,084	100.0
General expenditure	21,465,429	79.9
Intergovernmental expenditure	5,495,337	20.5
Direct expenditure	15,970,092	59.5
General expenditure, by function:		
Education	7,172,341	26.7
Public welfare	6,575,475	24.5
Hospitals	1,548,755	5.8
Health	792,133	3.0
Highways	1,312,821	4.9
Police protection	183,495	0.7
Correction	730,873	2.7
Natural resources	449,716	1.7
Parks and recreation	81,087	0.3
Governmental administration	1,109,197	4.1
Interest on general debt	424,175	1.6
Other and unallocable	1,085,361	4.0
Utility expenditure	27,393	0.1
Liquor stores expenditure	243,302	0.9
Insurance trust expenditure	5,113,960	19.0
Debt at End of Fiscal Year	13,598,468	X
Cash and Security Holdings	69,418,893	X

X = Not applicable.
- = Zero or rounds to zero.
[1]Within insurance trust revenue, net earnings of state retirement systems is a calculated statistic (the item code in the data file is X08), and thus can be positive or negative. Net earnings is the sum of earnings on investments plus gains on investments minus losses on investments. The change made in 2002 for asset valuation from book to market value in accordance with Statement 34 of the Governmental Accounting Standards Board is reflected in the calculated statistics.

Table OR-16. State Government Tax Collections, 2014

(Dollars in thousands, percent.)

Item	Dollars	Percent distribution
Total Taxes	9,683,640	100.0
Property taxes	21,740	0.2
Sales and gross receipts	1,444,542	14.9
General sales and gross receipts	X	X
Selective sales and gross receipts	1,444,542	14.9
Alcoholic beverages	17,627	0.2
Amusements	0	-
Insurance premiums	85,196	0.9
Motor fuels	512,342	5.3
Pari-mutuels	2,253	-
Public utilities	85,401	0.9
Tobacco products	257,583	2.7
Other selective sales	484,140	5.0
Licenses	960,777	9.9
Alcoholic beverages	4,609	-
Amusements	812	-
Corporations in general	29,471	0.3
Hunting and fishing	54,100	0.6
Motor vehicle	514,003	5.3
Motor vehicle operators	41,484	0.4
Public utilities	14,061	0.1
Occupation and business, NEC	295,379	3.1
Other licenses	6,858	0.1
Income taxes	7,144,552	73.8
Individual income	6,649,418	68.7
Corporation net income	495,134	5.1
Other taxes	112,029	1.2
Death and gift	85,491	0.9
Documentary and stock transfer	3,114	-
Severance	23,424	0.2
Taxes, NEC	0	-

X = Not applicable.
- = Zero or rounds to zero.

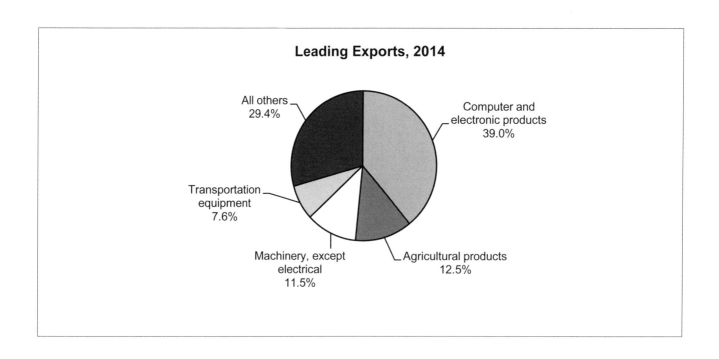

Leading Exports, 2014

All others 29.4%

Computer and electronic products 39.0%

Transportation equipment 7.6%

Machinery, except electrical 11.5%

Agricultural products 12.5%

PENNSYLVANIA

Facts and Figures

Location: Northeastern United States; bordered on the N by Lake Erie and New York, on the E by New York and New Jersey, on the S by Delaware, Maryland, and West Virginia, and on the W by West Virginia and Ohio

Area: 46,055 sq. mi. (119,283 sq. km.); rank—33rd

Population: 12,787,209 (2014 est.); rank—6th

Principal Cities: capital—Harrisburg; largest—Philadelphia

Statehood: December 12, 1787; 2nd state

U.S. Congress: 2 senators, 18 representatives

State Motto: Virtue, Liberty, and Independence

State Song: "Pennsylvania"

State Nicknames: The Keystone State; The Quaker State

Abbreviations: PA; Penn.

State Symbols: flower—mountain laurel; tree—Eastern hemlock; bird—ruffed grouse

At a Glance

- With an increase in population of 0.7 percent, Pennsylvania ranked 43rd among the states in growth from 2010 to 2014.

- Pennsylvania's median household income in 2013 was $52,007, and 13.7 percent of the population lived below the poverty level.

- Approximately 9.7 percent of Pennsylvanians did not have health insurance in 2013, compared to the national rate of 14.5 percent.

- Pennsylvania's violent crime rate in 2013 was 335.4 per 100,000 population, compared to 367.9 for the entire nation.

- The unemployment rate in Pennsylvania was 5.8 percent in 2014, compared to the national unemployment rate of 6.2 percent

Table PA-1. Population by Age, Sex, Race, and Hispanic Origin

(Number, percent, except where noted.)

Sex, age, race, and Hispanic origin	2000	2010	2014[1]	Average annual percent change, 2010–2014
Total Population	12,281,054	12,702,379	12,787,209	0.2
Percent of total U.S. population	4.4	4.1	4.0	X
Sex				
Male	5,929,663	6,190,363	6,253,817	0.3
Female	6,351,391	6,512,016	6,533,392	0.1
Age				
Under 5 years	727,804	729,538	715,084	-0.5
5 to 19 years	2,542,780	2,449,852	2,343,415	-1.1
20 to 64 years	7,091,305	7,563,682	7,594,189	0.1
65 years and over	1,919,165	1,959,307	2,134,521	2.2
Median age (years)	38.0	40.1	40.7	0.4
Race and Hispanic Origin				
One race				
White	10,484,203	10,663,774	10,598,587	-0.2
Black	1,224,612	1,431,826	1,484,746	0.9
American Indian and Alaska Native	18,348	39,735	44,142	2.7
Asian	219,813	358,195	417,607	3.9
Native Hawaiian or Other Pacific Islander	3,417	7,115	8,516	4.6
Two or more races	142,224	201,734	233,611	3.7
Hispanic (of any race)	394,088	758,058	838,823	2.6

X = Not applicable.
[1]Population figures for 2014 are July 1 estimates. The 2010 estimates are taken from the 2010 Census.

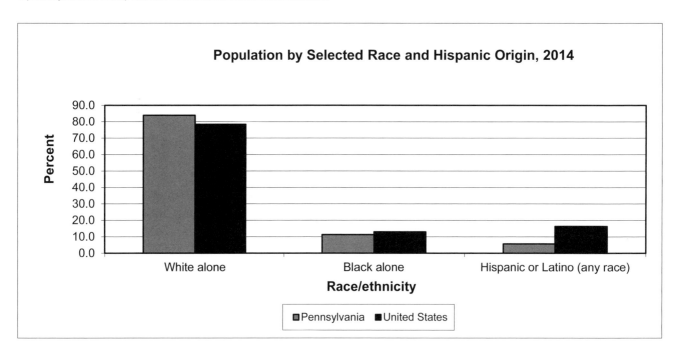

Population by Selected Race and Hispanic Origin, 2014

■ Pennsylvania   ■ United States

Table PA-2. Marital Status

(Number, percent distribution.)

Sex, age, race, and Hispanic origin	2000	2010	2013
Males, 15 Years and Over	4,686,277	5,031,761	5,101,281
Never married	30.1	35.9	36.6
Now married, except separated	57.4	50.6	49.7
Separated	1.9	2.0	2.0
Widowed	3.3	3.1	3.1
Divorced	7.3	8.5	8.7
Females, 15 Years and Over	5,175,436	5,406,494	5,438,424
Never married	24.6	29.8	30.8
Now married, except separated	51.5	46.2	45.6
Separated	2.4	2.7	2.4
Widowed	12.7	11.2	10.6
Divorced	8.8	10.2	10.7

Table PA-3. Households and Housing Characteristics

(Number, percent, dollars.)

Item	2000	2010	2013	Average annual percent change, 2000–2013
Total Households	4,777,003	4,936,030	4,938,894	0.3
Family households	3,208,388	3,197,710	3,152,234	-0.1
Married-couple family	2,467,673	2,381,094	2,354,778	-0.4
Other family	740,715	816,616	797,456	0.6
Male householder, no wife present	186,022	215,082	208,921	0.9
Female householder, no husband present	554,693	601,534	588,535	0.5
Nonfamily households	1,568,615	1,738,320	1,786,660	1.0
Householder living alone	1,320,941	1,458,055	1,486,501	0.9
Householder not living alone	247,674	280,265	300,159	1.5
Housing Characteristics				
Total housing units	5,249,750	5,568,820	5,565,354	0.5
Occupied housing units	4,777,003	4,936,030	4,938,894	0.3
Owner occupied	3,406,337	3,461,678	3,405,170	-
Renter occupied	1,370,666	1,474,352	1,533,724	0.9
Average household size	2.48	2.49	2.50	0.1
Financial Characteristics				
Median gross rent of renter-occupied housing	531	763	828	3.5
Median monthly owner costs for housing units with a mortgage	1,010	1,390	1,373	2.4
Median value of owner-occupied housing units	97,000	165,500	164,200	4.1

- = Zero or rounds to zero.

Table PA-4. Migration, Origin, and Language

(Number, percent.)

Characteristic	State 2012	State 2013	Percent change	U.S. 2012	U.S. 2013	Percent change
Residence 1 Year Ago						
Population 1 year and over	12,630,082	12,639,493	0.1	310,212,755	312,432,820	0.7
Same house	87.9	87.9	X	85.0	85.0	X
Different house in the U.S.	11.6	11.6	X	14.4	14.4	X
Same county	7.3	7.2	X	9.0	8.9	X
Different county	4.3	4.3	X	5.4	5.5	X
Same state	2.6	2.6	X	3.2	3.2	X
Different state	1.7	1.8	X	2.3	2.3	X
Abroad	0.4	0.5	X	0.6	0.6	X
Place of Birth						
Native born	11,994,272	11,977,642	-0.1	273,089,382	274,780,773	0.6
Male	48.8	48.9	X	49.3	49.3	X
Female	51.2	51.1	X	50.7	50.7	X
Foreign born	769,264	796,159	3.5	40,824,658	41,348,066	1.3
Male	48.7	48.8	X	48.7	48.8	X
Female	51.3	51.2	X	51.3	51.2	X
Foreign born; naturalized U.S. citizen	398,495	410,524	3.0	18,686,237	19,294,710	3.3
Male	45.2	46.9	X	45.8	45.9	X
Female	54.8	53.1	X	54.2	54.1	X
Foreign born; not a U.S. citizen	370,769	385,635	4.0	22,138,421	22,053,356	-0.4
Male	52.5	50.7	X	51.1	51.3	X
Female	47.5	49.3	X	48.9	48.7	X
Entered 2010 or later	9.9	14.1	X	7.0	9.7	X
Entered 2000 to 2009	32.6	31.4	X	30.4	29.4	X
Entered before 2000	57.5	54.5	X	62.7	61.0	X
World Region of Birth, Foreign						
Foreign-born population, excluding population born at sea	769,264	796,159	3.5	40,824,553	41,347,945	1.3
Europe	22.0	21.2	X	11.8	11.6	X
Asia	38.5	39.1	X	29.2	29.5	X
Africa	7.3	8.2	X	4.2	4.4	X
Oceania	0.4	0.4	X	0.6	0.5	X
Latin America	29.9	29.2	X	52.2	51.9	X
North America	1.9	1.9	X	2.0	2.0	X
Language Spoken at Home and Ability to Speak English						
Population 5 years and over	12,045,220	12,059,233	0.1	294,003,714	296,358,760	0.8
English only	89.4	89.4	X	79.0	79.2	X
Language other than English	10.6	10.6	X	21.0	20.8	X
Speaks English less than "very well"	4.1	4.1	X	8.5	8.5	X

NA = Not available.
X = Not applicable.
- = Zero or rounds to zero.

Table PA-5. Median Income and Poverty Status, 2013

(Number, percent, except as noted.)

Characteristic	State		U.S.	
	Number	Percent	Number	Percent
Median Income				
Households (dollars)...............	52,007	X	52,250	X
Families (dollars)	66,522	X	64,030	X
Below Poverty Level (All People)...............	1,690,405	13.7	48,810,868	15.8
Sex				
Male...............	752,936	12.5	21,938,525	14.5
Female	937,469	14.8	26,872,343	17.1
Age				
Under 18 years...............	516,390	19.4	16,086,960	22.2
Related children under 18 years...............	503,395	19.0	15,769,921	21.9
18 to 64 years...............	1,002,905	13.1	28,578,191	14.8
65 years and over	171,110	8.5	4,145,717	9.6

X = Not applicable.

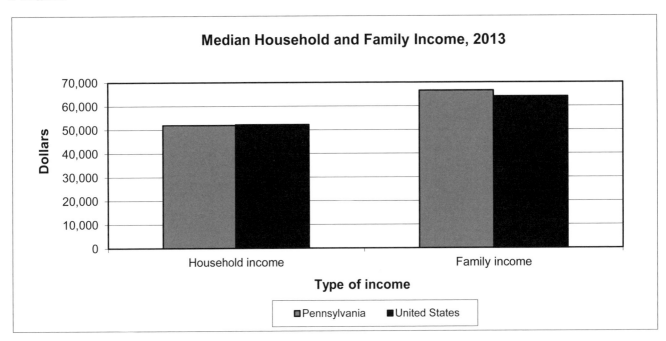

Median Household and Family Income, 2013

Table PA-6. Health Insurance Coverage Status for the Civilian Noninstitutionalized Population and Children Under 18 Years of Age

(Numbers in thousands, percent.)

Item	2005	2006	2007	2008	2009	2010	2011	2012	2013
Civilian Noninstitutionalized Population	12,281	12,345	12,313	12,209	12,366	12,506	12,540	12,559	12,569
Covered by Private or Public Insurance									
Number...............	11,085	11,108	11,138	11,058	11,146	11,235	11,275	11,335	11,347
Percent...............	90.3	90.0	90.5	90.6	90.1	89.8	89.9	90.2	90.3
Not Covered									
Number...............	1,196	1,237	1,176	1,151	1,220	1,271	1,265	1,224	1,222
Percent...............	9.7	10.0	9.5	9.4	9.9	10.2	10.1	9.8	9.7
Percent in the U.S. not covered...............	15.3	15.8	15.3	15.1	15.1	15.5	15.1	14.8	14.5
Children Under 18 Years of Age...............	2,830	2,778	2,775	2,757	2,766	2,778	2,755	2,731	2,709
Covered by Private or Public Insurance									
Number...............	2,621	2,575	2,568	2,588	2,619	2,634	2,606	2,592	2,562
Percent...............	92.6	92.7	92.6	93.9	94.7	94.8	94.6	94.9	94.6
Not Covered									
Number...............	209	203	207	169	147	144	149	139	147
Percent...............	7.4	7.3	7.4	6.1	5.3	5.2	5.4	5.1	5.4
Percent in the U.S. not covered...............	10.9	11.7	11.0	9.7	8.6	8.0	7.5	7.2	7.1

Table PA-7. Employment Status by Demographic Group, 2014

(Numbers in thousands, percent.)

Characteristic	Civilian noninstitutional population	Civilian labor force		Employed		Unemployed	
		Number	Percent of population	Number	Percent of population	Number	Percent of population
Total..	10,205	6,368	62.4	6,005	58.8	364	5.7
Sex							
Male..	4,905	3,349	68.3	3,132	63.9	217	6.5
Female	5,301	3,019	57.0	2,873	54.2	146	4.8
Race, Sex, and Hispanic Origin							
White	8,611	5,445	63.2	5,172	60.1	274	5.0
Male..	4,177	2,893	69.3	2,727	65.3	166	5.7
Female	4,434	2,552	57.6	2,445	55.1	108	4.2
Black or African American................................	1,075	616	57.3	549	51.1	67	10.9
Male..	485	290	59.8	250	51.6	40	13.8
Female	590	326	55.3	299	50.7	27	8.3
Hispanic or Latino ethnicity[1]	639	391	61.2	354	55.4	37	9.5
Male..	291	206	70.6	186	63.8	20	9.6
Female	348	185	53.4	168	48.3	18	9.5
Age							
16 to 19 years..	631	258	40.9	214	33.8	44	17.2
20 to 24 years..	877	613	69.9	543	61.9	70	11.5
25 to 34 years..	1,622	1,327	81.8	1,255	77.3	72	5.5
35 to 44 years..	1,460	1,217	83.4	1,155	79.1	62	5.1
45 to 54 years..	1,815	1,440	79.3	1,381	76.1	59	4.1
55 to 64 years..	1,730	1,164	67.3	1,119	64.7	45	3.9
65 years and over	2,070	349	16.9	339	16.4	11	3.0

NOTE: Data in Table 7 are from the Current Population Survey (CPS) and do not match the estimates in Table 8. See notes and definitions for further information.
[1]May be of any race.

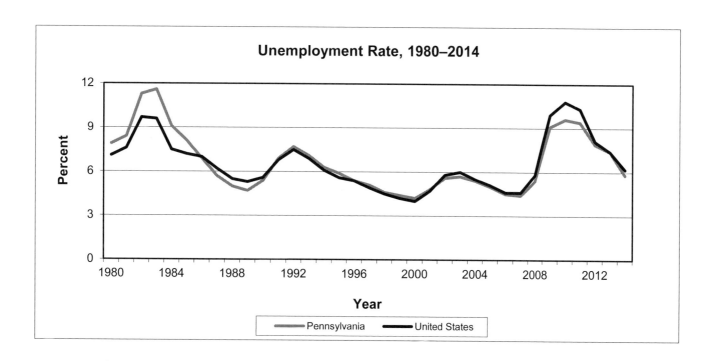

Unemployment Rate, 1980–2014

Table PA-8. Employment Status of the Civilian Noninstitutional Population Age 16 Years and Over

(Number, percent.)

Year	Civilian labor force	Civilian participation rate	Employed	Unemployed	Unemployment rate
2006	6,294,504	64.4	6,006,634	287,870	4.6
2007	6,342,997	64.5	6,064,063	278,934	4.4
2008	6,451,535	65.2	6,109,645	341,890	5.3
2009	6,400,263	64.4	5,885,351	514,912	8.0
2010	6,380,949	63.5	5,840,887	540,062	8.5
2011	6,395,026	63.2	5,887,860	507,166	7.9
2012	6,464,605	63.6	5,956,662	507,943	7.9
2013	6,441,752	63.3	5,963,909	477,843	7.4
2014	6,378,495	62.5	6,008,533	369,962	5.8

Table PA-9. Employment and Average Wages by Industry

(Estimates from 2007 through 2010 are based on the 2007 *North American Industry Classification System* [NAICS]. Estimates from 2011 onward are based on the 2012 NAICS.)

Industry	2007	2008	2009	2010	2011	2012	2013
				Number of jobs			
Wage and Salary Employment by Industry	5,994,123	5,999,422	5,812,006	5,821,316	5,882,592	5,920,251	5,945,600
Farm Wage and Salary Employment	19,440	17,328	16,794	18,821	18,245	23,646	22,621
Nonfarm Wage and Salary Employment	5,974,683	5,982,094	5,795,212	5,802,495	5,864,347	5,896,605	5,922,979
Private wage and salary employment	5,163,874	5,165,218	4,972,955	4,978,951	5,061,393	5,108,422	5,135,279
Forestry, fishing, and related activities	7,391	7,711	7,699	8,047	8,442	8,452	7,816
Mining	20,546	21,573	21,563	25,871	32,359	35,913	34,982
Utilities	21,051	21,711	21,757	21,789	22,307	22,310	22,001
Construction	272,623	264,504	235,072	226,635	234,753	233,627	234,094
Manufacturing	656,542	643,396	576,265	561,421	565,523	567,871	564,472
Durable goods manufacturing	405,324	398,373	346,316	334,818	342,113	347,985	346,811
Nondurable goods manufacturing	251,218	245,023	229,949	226,603	223,410	219,886	217,661
Wholesale trade	242,427	241,597	227,853	225,618	229,466	228,893	226,626
Retail trade	665,740	657,690	635,555	636,332	639,415	640,009	639,012
Transportation and warehousing	221,211	220,879	212,539	212,878	219,226	221,640	224,279
Information	108,495	106,479	99,971	93,374	91,157	90,700	88,662
Finance and insurance	271,150	269,922	263,622	261,039	261,035	262,634	263,606
Real estate and rental and leasing	68,235	67,550	63,329	61,569	60,481	59,956	60,706
Professional, scientific, and technical services	315,371	321,572	310,690	307,556	312,866	319,652	327,656
Management of companies and enterprises	111,332	113,669	113,124	117,387	123,164	129,633	133,428
Administrative and waste services	288,872	282,632	256,985	272,269	286,829	288,284	294,869
Educational services	226,098	231,463	236,232	238,936	242,115	244,154	244,396
Health care and social assistance	860,627	882,144	895,324	907,540	919,745	933,110	936,747
Arts, entertainment, and recreation	85,615	88,252	88,277	90,597	94,463	94,667	93,933
Accommodation and food services	420,845	421,383	411,940	416,964	422,777	432,461	442,794
Other services, except public administration	299,703	301,091	295,158	293,129	295,270	294,456	295,200
Government and government enterprises	810,809	816,876	822,257	823,544	802,954	788,183	787,700
				Dollars			
Average Wages and Salaries by Industry	42,413	43,502	43,920	44,805	46,100	47,334	48,035
Average Farm Wages and Salaries	29,579	32,047	30,538	26,133	24,434	21,132	29,743
Average Nonfarm Wages and Salaries	42,455	43,535	43,959	44,865	46,168	47,439	48,105
Average private wages and salaries	42,497	43,592	43,851	44,795	46,160	47,596	48,239
Forestry, fishing, and related activities	23,265	23,902	24,674	25,283	25,795	26,597	28,500
Mining	56,497	59,901	61,585	67,930	72,635	75,604	77,752
Utilities	95,939	96,558	92,745	94,549	100,402	101,798	103,374
Construction	49,834	51,852	52,439	53,080	54,636	56,024	56,801
Manufacturing	49,904	51,203	51,527	53,646	55,211	56,367	56,701
Durable goods manufacturing	50,055	51,584	51,590	54,131	56,158	56,867	57,288
Nondurable goods manufacturing	49,662	50,583	51,432	52,928	53,761	55,575	55,765
Wholesale trade	61,775	63,407	63,607	65,473	68,682	70,827	72,399
Retail trade	24,125	24,438	24,676	25,028	25,347	25,693	25,806
Transportation and warehousing	39,128	39,813	39,795	40,556	41,626	42,230	43,154
Information	57,805	59,566	60,666	63,432	65,779	67,445	68,999
Finance and insurance	70,667	71,680	69,934	71,965	74,930	78,947	80,529
Real estate and rental and leasing	43,702	44,949	44,338	46,437	48,655	51,160	51,170
Professional, scientific, and technical services	71,653	73,643	75,651	77,352	78,901	82,312	82,720
Management of companies and enterprises	98,030	98,287	98,095	101,145	106,922	114,405	114,849
Administrative and waste services	29,881	30,914	31,024	31,168	31,316	31,981	32,316
Educational services	35,730	37,330	38,527	39,373	40,340	40,946	42,185
Health care and social assistance	39,518	40,937	41,838	42,260	43,178	44,151	44,916
Arts, entertainment, and recreation	28,639	28,790	29,414	30,550	32,233	32,254	32,416
Accommodation and food services	16,682	16,388	16,260	16,773	17,292	17,646	17,891
Other services, except public administration	26,472	27,319	27,588	28,299	28,828	29,391	30,022
Government and government enterprises	42,190	43,178	44,610	45,288	46,218	46,423	47,233

Table PA-10. Employment Characteristics by Family Type

(Number, percent.)

Family type and labor force status	2011		2012		2013	
	Total	Families with own children under 18 years	Total	Families with own children under 18 years	Total	Families with own children under 18 years
All Families..	3,193,701	1,319,563	3,202,089	1,285,713	3,152,234	1,253,201
FAMILY TYPE AND LABOR FORCE STATUS						
Married-Couple Families..............................	2,374,705	887,711	2,386,165	864,021	2,354,778	845,149
Both husband and wife in labor force...............	54.6	70.2	54.1	70.2	53.1	69.3
Husband in labor force, wife not in labor force	19.4	24.1	20.1	24.7	20.0	24.9
Wife in labor force, husband not in labor force	7.8	4.0	7.8	3.5	8.3	3.7
Both husband and wife not in labor force..............	18.2	1.6	18.0	1.6	18.3	1.8
Other Families...................................	818,996	431,852	815,924	421,692	797,456	408,052
Female householder, no husband present................	73.0	75.2	73.6	75.7	73.8	76.0
In labor force......................................	49.1	58.9	49.8	59.9	51.2	62.6
Not in labor force	23.9	16.3	23.8	15.8	22.6	13.4
Male householder, no wife present..................	27.0	24.8	26.4	24.3	26.2	24.0
In labor force......................................	20.6	22.1	19.7	21.3	19.6	21.3
Not in labor force	6.4	2.7	6.7	3.0	6.6	2.8

Table PA-11. School Enrollment and Educational Attainment, 2013

(Number, percent.)

Item	State	U.S.
Enrollment		
Total population 3 years and over, enrolled in school	3,053,479	82,395,254
Enrolled in nursery school or preschool (percent)...................................	6.1	6.0
Enrolled in kindergarten (percent)..	4.8	5.2
Enrolled in elementary school, grades 1-8 (percent)..........................	39.4	40.0
Enrolled in high school, grades 9-12 (percent).................................	21.1	20.6
Enrolled in college or graduate school (percent)..............................	28.5	28.3
Attainment		
Total population 25 years and over	8,809,510	210,910,615
Less than ninth grade (percent)	3.6	5.8
9th to 12th grade, no diploma (percent)	7.2	7.6
High school graduate, including equivalency (percent).......................	36.4	27.8
Some college, no degree (percent)	16.2	21.1
Associate's degree (percent)	7.9	8.1
Bachelor's degree (percent)	17.5	18.4
Graduate or professional degree (percent)......................................	11.2	11.2
High school graduate or higher (percent)	89.2	86.6
Bachelor's degree or higher (percent)..	28.7	29.6

Table PA-12. Public School Characteristics and Educational Indicators

(Number, percent; data derived from National Center of Education Statistics.)

Item	State	U.S.
Public Schools, 2012–2013 (except where noted)		
Number of school districts..	799	18,093
Number of schools...	3,127	98,454
Number of students (in thousands)	1,764	49,771
Number of teachers (in thousands)	123	3,109
Student-teacher ratio	14.3	16.0
Expenditures per student (dollars), FY 2012...................................	13,091	10,667
Four-year adjusted cohort graduation rate (ACGR)[1,2]	85.5	81.4
Students eligible for free or reduced-price lunch (in thousands)	713	25,188
English language learners (in thousands)	44	4,397
Students age 3 to 21 served under IDEA, part B (in thousands)	296	6,429

Public Schools by Type	Number	Percent of state public schools
Total number of schools...	3,127	100.0
Regular	3,021	96.6
Special education...	8	0.3
Vocational education...	87	2.8
Alternative education..	11	0.4

NOTE: Every school is assigned only one school type based on its instructional emphasis.
[1]ACGR data represents a new method of calculating high-school completion rates and may not be comparable to previous years' data for Averaged Freshmen Graduation Rates (AFGR).
[2]The United States 4-year ACGRs were estimated using both the reported 4-year ACGR data from 49 states and the District of Columbia and using imputed data for Idaho. The estimate for American Indian/Alaska Native students also includes imputed data for Virginia.

Table PA-13. Reported Voting and Registration of the Voting-Age Population, November 2012

(Numbers in thousands, percent.)

Item	Total population	Total citizen population	Registered			Voted		
			Total registered	Percent registered (total population)	Percent registered (total citizen population)	Total voted	Percent voted (total population)	Percent voted (total citizen population)
U.S. Total	235,248	215,081	153,157	65.1	71.2	132,948	56.5	61.8
State Total	9,847	9,452	6,795	69.0	71.9	5,824	59.1	61.6
Sex								
Male	4,727	4,532	3,217	68.0	71.0	2,740	58.0	60.4
Female	5,120	4,919	3,578	69.9	72.7	3,084	60.2	62.7
Race								
White alone......................	8,382	8,228	5,951	71.0	72.3	5,074	60.5	61.7
White, non-Hispanic alone	7,994	7,901	5,779	72.3	73.1	4,937	61.8	62.5
Black alone......................	1,006	940	675	67.0	71.8	614	61.0	65.2
Asian alone	272	110	68	25.0	61.7	53	19.3	47.6
Hispanic (of any race)......................	501	407	225	45.0	55.3	184	36.7	45.1
White alone or in combination	8,482	8,327	6,002	70.8	72.1	5,118	60.3	61.5
Black alone or in combination..........	1,078	1,012	725	67.2	71.6	653	60.6	64.5
Asian alone or in combination..........	295	133	74	25.1	55.7	58	19.9	44.0
Age								
18 to 24 years	1,198	1,137	645	53.8	56.7	478	39.9	42.1
25 to 44 years......................	3,063	2,884	2,038	66.5	70.7	1,718	56.1	59.6
45 to 64 years......................	3,674	3,547	2,648	72.1	74.6	2,331	63.4	65.7
65 to 74 years......................	998	978	740	74.2	75.7	673	67.5	68.8
75 years and over	915	905	723	79.0	79.9	624	68.1	68.9

Table PA-14. Crime

(Number, rate per 100,000. Data are derived from the FBI Uniform Crime Reports.)

Item	State			U.S.[1,2,3,4]		
	2012	2013	Percent change	2012	2013	Percent change
TOTAL POPULATION[5]...	12,764,475	12,773,801	0.1	313,873,685	316,128,839	0.7
VIOLENT CRIME						
Number..	45,384	41,713	-8.1	1,217,067	1,163,146	-4.4
Rate	355.5	326.6	-8.2	387.8	367.9	-5.1
Murder and Nonnegligent Manslaughter						
Number..	707	594	-16.0	14,866	14,196	-4.5
Rate	5.5	4.7	-16.0	4.7	4.5	-5.2
Rape[6]						
Number..	X	3,774	X	X	108,612	X
Rate	X	29.5	X	X	34.4	X
Robbery						
Number..	15,735	14,762	-6.2	355,051	345,031	-2.8
Rate	123.3	115.6	-6.3	113.1	109.1	-3.5
Aggravated Assault						
Number..	25,571	23,719	-7.2	762,009	724,149	-5.0
Rate	200.3	185.7	-7.3	242.8	229.1	-5.6
PROPERTY CRIME						
Number..	276,562	263,240	-4.8	9,001,992	8,632,512	-4.1
Rate	2,166.7	2,060.8	-4.9	2,868.0	2,730.7	-4.8
Burglary						
Number..	57,040	52,034	-8.8	2,109,932	1,928,465	-8.6
Rate	446.9	407.3	-8.8	672.2	610.0	-9.3
Larceny-Theft						
Number..	204,409	197,436	-3.4	6,168,874	6,004,453	-2.7
Rate	1,601.4	1,545.6	-3.5	1,965.4	1,899.4	-3.4
Motor Vehicle Theft						
Number..	15,113	13,770	-8.9	723,186	699,594	-3.3
Rate	118.4	107.8	-9.0	230.4	221.3	-4.0

NOTE: Although arson data are included in the trend and clearance tables, sufficient data are not available to estimate totals for this offense. Therefore, no arson data are published in this table.

X = Not applicable.

- = Zero or rounds to zero.

[1]The crime figures have been adjusted.

[2]The data collection methodology for the offense of forcible rape used by the Minnesota state Uniform Crime Reporting (UCR) Program (with the exception of Minneapolis and St. Paul, Minnesota) does not comply with national UCR Program guidelines. Consequently, its figures for forcible rape and violent crime (of which forcible rape is a part) are not published in this table.

[3]Includes offenses reported by the Zoological Police and the Metro Transit Police.

[4]Because of changes in the state's reporting practices, figures are not comparable to previous years' data.

[5]Populations are U.S. Census Bureau provisional estimates as of July 1 of each year.

[6]The figures shown for the offense of rape were estimated using the revised Uniform Crime Reporting (UCR) definition of rape.

Table PA-15. State Government Finances, 2013

(Dollar amounts in thousands, percent distribution.)

Item	Dollars	Percent distribution
Total Revenue	87,910,876	100.0
General revenue	69,755,731	79.3
Intergovernmental revenue	21,412,638	24.4
Taxes	33,965,626	38.6
General sales	9,243,355	10.5
Selective sales	7,862,945	8.9
License taxes	2,585,202	2.9
Individual income tax	10,777,334	12.3
Corporate income tax	2,208,163	2.5
Other taxes	1,288,627	1.5
Current charges	9,691,460	11.0
Miscellaneous general revenue	4,686,007	5.3
Utility revenue	0	-
Liquor stores revenue	1,731,463	2.0
Insurance trust revenue[1]	16,423,682	18.7
Total Expenditure	87,532,654	100.0
Intergovernmental expenditure	18,834,325	21.5
Direct expenditure	68,698,329	78.5
Current operation	44,347,538	50.7
Capital outlay	7,054,683	8.1
Insurance benefits and repayments	13,702,203	15.7
Assistance and subsidies	2,147,773	2.5
Interest on debt	1,446,132	1.7
Exhibit: Salaries and wages	8,090,451	9.2
Total Expenditure	87,532,654	100.0
General expenditure	72,244,141	82.5
Intergovernmental expenditure	18,834,325	21.5
Direct expenditure	53,409,816	61.0
General expenditure, by function:		
Education	22,628,667	25.9
Public welfare	23,078,652	26.4
Hospitals	3,789,791	4.3
Health	3,080,531	3.5
Highways	7,601,344	8.7
Police protection	911,672	1.0
Correction	2,119,602	2.4
Natural resources	642,051	0.7
Parks and recreation	327,664	0.4
Governmental administration	2,958,712	3.4
Interest on general debt	1,446,132	1.7
Other and unallocable	3,659,323	4.2
Utility expenditure	10	-
Liquor stores expenditure	1,586,300	1.8
Insurance trust expenditure	13,702,203	15.7
Debt at End of Fiscal Year	47,020,552	X
Cash and Security Holdings	124,835,296	X

X = Not applicable.
- = Zero or rounds to zero.
[1]Within insurance trust revenue, net earnings of state retirement systems is a calculated statistic (the item code in the data file is X08), and thus can be positive or negative. Net earnings is the sum of earnings on investments plus gains on investments minus losses on investments. The change made in 2002 for asset valuation from book to market value in accordance with Statement 34 of the Governmental Accounting Standards Board is reflected in the calculated statistics.

Table PA-16. State Government Tax Collections, 2014

(Dollars in thousands, percent.)

Item	Dollars	Percent distribution
Total Taxes	34,192,869	100.0
Property taxes	45,017	0.1
Sales and gross receipts	17,419,429	50.9
General sales and gross receipts	9,497,906	27.8
Selective sales and gross receipts	7,921,523	23.2
Alcoholic beverages	346,008	1.0
Amusements	1,400,232	4.1
Insurance premiums	773,462	2.3
Motor fuels	2,231,348	6.5
Pari-mutuels	11,758	-
Public utilities	1,284,892	3.8
Tobacco products	1,028,006	3.0
Other selective sales	845,817	2.5
Licenses	2,302,934	6.7
Alcoholic beverages	16,952	-
Amusements	12,157	-
Corporations in general	229,686	0.7
Hunting and fishing	74,679	0.2
Motor vehicle	837,823	2.5
Motor vehicle operators	54,847	0.2
Public utilities	75,269	0.2
Occupation and business, NEC	981,965	2.9
Other licenses	19,556	0.1
Income taxes	13,111,325	38.3
Individual income	10,809,736	31.6
Corporation net income	2,301,589	6.7
Other taxes	1,314,164	3.8
Death and gift	849,194	2.5
Documentary and stock transfer	438,984	1.3
Severance	X	X
Taxes, NEC	25,986	0.1

X = Not applicable.
- = Zero or rounds to zero.

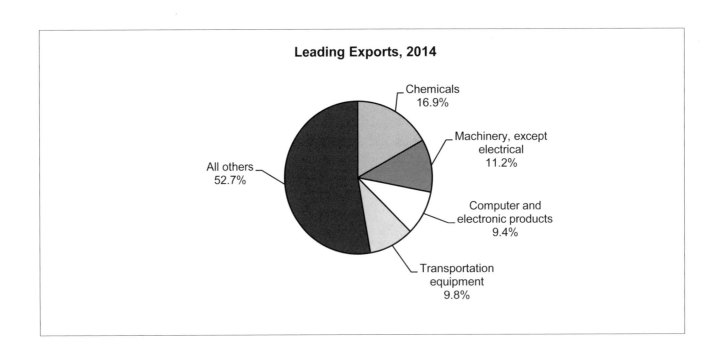

Leading Exports, 2014

Chemicals 16.9%
Machinery, except electrical 11.2%
Computer and electronic products 9.4%
Transportation equipment 9.8%
All others 52.7%

RHODE ISLAND

Facts and Figures

Location: Eastern United States; bordered on the N by Massachusetts, on the E by Massachusetts and the Atlantic Ocean, on the S by Block Island Sound and the Atlantic Ocean, and on the W by Connecticut

Area: 1,545 sq. mi. (4,002 sq. km.); rank—50th

Population: 1,055,173 (2014 est.); rank—43rd

Principal Cities: capital—Providence; largest—Providence

Statehood: May 29, 1790; 13th state

U.S. Congress: 2 senators, 2 representatives

State Motto: Hope

State Song: "Rhode Island"

State Nickname: The Ocean State

Abbreviations: RI; R.I.

State Symbols: flower—violet; tree—red maple; bird—Rhode Island red

At a Glance

- With an increase in population of 0.2 percent, Rhode Island ranked 48th among the states in growth from 2010 to 2014.

- In 2013, 11.6 percent of Rhode Islanders did not have health insurance, compared to 14.5 percent of the total U.S. population.

- Rhode Island's violent crime rate in 2013 was 257.2 per 100,000 population, compared to 367.9 for the entire nation.

- The state's median income in 2013 was $55,902, and 14.3 percent of its residents lived below the poverty level.

- Rhode Island had the lowest per capita energy consumption in 2013, with a rate of 183.8 million Btu.

Table RI-1. Population by Age, Sex, Race, and Hispanic Origin

(Number, percent, except where noted.)

Sex, age, race, and Hispanic origin	2000	2010	2014[1]	Average annual percent change, 2010–2014
Total Population	1,048,319	1,052,567	1,055,173	0.1
Percent of total U.S. population	0.4	0.3	0.3	X
Sex				
Male	503,635	508,400	511,363	0.1
Female	544,684	544,167	543,810	-
Age				
Under 5 years	63,896	57,448	54,896	-1.1
5 to 19 years	218,720	204,310	193,588	-1.3
20 to 64 years	613,301	638,928	640,542	0.1
65 years and over	152,402	151,881	166,147	2.3
Median age (years)	36.7	39.4	39.9	0.3
Race and Hispanic Origin				
One race				
White	891,191	910,253	898,297	-0.3
Black	46,908	75,073	81,149	2.0
American Indian and Alaska Native	5,121	9,173	9,965	2.1
Asian	23,665	31,768	36,785	3.7
Native Hawaiian or Other Pacific Islander	567	1,602	1,800	3.0
Two or more races	28,251	24,698	27,177	2.4
Hispanic (of any race)	90,820	137,169	148,095	1.9

X = Not applicable.
- = Zero or rounds to zero.
[1]Population figures for 2014 are July 1 estimates. The 2010 estimates are taken from the 2010 Census.

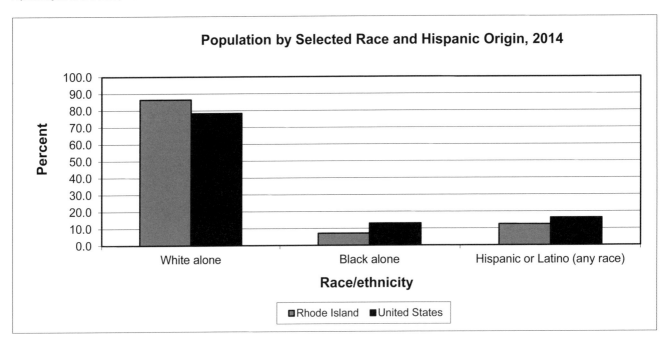

Table RI-2. Marital Status

(Number, percent distribution.)

Sex, age, race, and Hispanic origin	2000	2010	2013
Males, 15 Years and Over	396,396	414,628	422,789
Never married	32.5	39.8	39.0
Now married, except separated	54.9	45.2	47.2
Separated	1.5	1.6	1.4
Widowed	3.0	3.1	2.7
Divorced	8.0	10.3	9.7
Females, 15 Years and Over	445,107	456,425	454,403
Never married	27.1	32.4	33.0
Now married, except separated	48.5	41.8	42.1
Separated	2.3	2.4	2.3
Widowed	11.5	10.4	10.2
Divorced	10.7	13.0	12.4

Table RI-3. Households and Housing Characteristics

(Number, percent, dollars.)

Item	2000	2010	2013	Average annual percent change, 2000–2013
Total Households..	408,424	402,295	406,366	-
Family households	265,398	246,028	259,863	-0.2
Married-couple family	196,757	173,848	180,930	-0.6
Other family	68,641	72,180	78,933	1.1
Male householder, no wife present................	16,032	17,525	21,210	2.2
Female householder, no husband present	52,609	54,655	57,723	0.7
Nonfamily households	143,026	156,267	146,503	0.2
Householder living alone.............................	116,678	125,371	121,158	0.3
Householder not living alone.........................	26,348	30,896	25,345	-0.3
Housing Characteristics				
Total housing units..	439,837	463,416	461,658	0.4
Occupied housing units	408,424	402,295	406,366	-
Owner occupied	245,156	244,516	245,409	-
Renter occupied..	163,268	157,779	160,957	-0.1
Average household size..................................	2.47	2.51	2.49	0.1
Financial Characteristics				
Median gross rent of renter-occupied housing	553	868	918	4.0
Median monthly owner costs for housing units with a mortgage	1,205	1,837	1,751	2.9
Median value of owner-occupied housing units........................	133,000	254,500	232,300	4.4

- = Zero or rounds to zero.

Table RI-4. Migration, Origin, and Language

(Number, percent.)

Characteristic	State			U.S.		
	2012	2013	Percent change	2012	2013	Percent change
Residence 1 Year Ago						
Population 1 year and over	1,040,527	1,040,986	-	310,212,755	312,432,820	0.7
Same house	86.5	86.9	X	85.0	85.0	X
Different house in the U.S.	12.9	12.3	X	14.4	14.4	X
Same county	7.7	7.3	X	9.0	8.9	X
Different county	5.2	5.0	X	5.4	5.5	X
Same state	2.0	1.7	X	3.2	3.2	X
Different state	3.2	3.3	X	2.3	2.3	X
Abroad	0.6	0.7	X	0.6	0.6	X
Place of Birth						
Native born	910,167	915,539	0.6	273,089,382	274,780,773	0.6
Male..	48.6	48.9	X	49.3	49.3	X
Female...	51.4	51.1	X	50.7	50.7	X
Foreign born	140,125	135,972	-3.0	40,824,658	41,348,066	1.3
Male..	46.1	48.0	X	48.7	48.8	X
Female...	53.9	52.0	X	51.3	51.2	X
Foreign born; naturalized U.S. citizen................	71,278	69,709	-2.2	18,686,237	19,294,710	3.3
Male..	44.0	45.6	X	45.8	45.9	X
Female...	56.0	54.4	X	54.2	54.1	X
Foreign born; not a U.S. citizen......................	68,847	66,263	-3.8	22,138,421	22,053,356	-0.4
Male..	48.2	50.5	X	51.1	51.3	X
Female...	51.8	49.5	X	48.9	48.7	X
Entered 2010 or later	9.8	10.2	X	7.0	9.7	X
Entered 2000 to 2009	28.9	26.3	X	30.4	29.4	X
Entered before 2000.....................................	61.3	63.5	X	62.7	61.0	X
World Region of Birth, Foreign						
Foreign-born population, excluding population born at sea	140,125	135,972	-3.0	40,824,553	41,347,945	1.3
Europe	23.0	21.3	X	11.8	11.6	X
Asia	19.0	18.6	X	29.2	29.5	X
Africa	12.3	12.5	X	4.2	4.4	X
Oceania	0.3	0.3	X	0.6	0.5	X
Latin America	43.4	45.6	X	52.2	51.9	X
North America..	2.0	1.6	X	2.0	2.0	X
Language Spoken at Home and Ability to Speak English						
Population 5 years and over..........................	994,145	997,310	0.3	294,003,714	296,358,760	0.8
English only	79.1	78.7	X	79.0	79.2	X
Language other than English.........................	20.9	21.3	X	21.0	20.8	X
Speaks English less than "very well"................	8.5	7.7	X	8.5	8.5	X

NA = Not available.
X = Not applicable.
- = Zero or rounds to zero.

Table RI-5. Median Income and Poverty Status, 2013

(Number, percent, except as noted.)

Characteristic	State		U.S.	
	Number	Percent	Number	Percent
Median Income				
Households (dollars)..	55,902	X	52,250	X
Families (dollars)	71,608	X	64,030	X
Below Poverty Level (All People)	144,446	14.3	48,810,868	15.8
Sex				
Male..	66,108	13.4	21,938,525	14.5
Female	78,338	15.2	26,872,343	17.1
Age				
Under 18 years..	44,923	21.5	16,086,960	22.2
Related children under 18 years...	44,183	21.3	15,769,921	21.9
18 to 64 years	86,376	13.4	28,578,191	14.8
65 years and over	13,147	8.5	4,145,717	9.6

X = Not applicable.

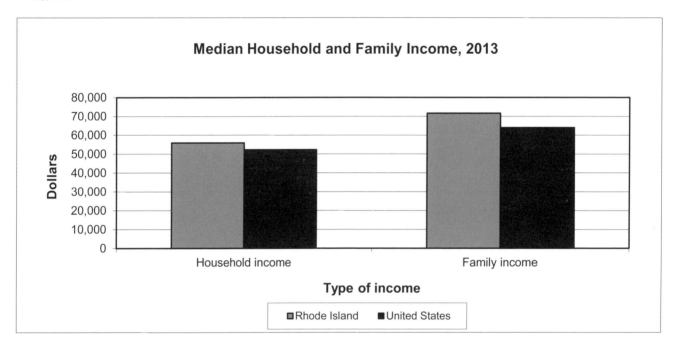

Median Household and Family Income, 2013

Rhode Island   United States

Table RI-6. Health Insurance Coverage Status for the Civilian Noninstitutionalized Population and Children Under 18 Years of Age

(Numbers in thousands, percent.)

Item	2005	2006	2007	2008	2009	2010	2011	2012	2013
Civilian Noninstitutionalized Population	1,054	1,054	1,044	1,030	1,035	1,037	1,035	1,035	1,036
Covered by Private or Public Insurance									
Number..	932	963	931	922	919	911	923	920	916
Percent..	88.5	91.4	89.2	89.5	88.7	87.8	89.2	88.9	88.4
Not Covered									
Number..	122	91	113	108	117	126	112	115	120
Percent..	11.5	8.6	10.8	10.5	11.3	12.2	10.8	11.1	11.6
Percent in the U.S. not covered..	15.3	15.8	15.3	15.1	15.1	15.5	15.1	14.8	14.5
Children Under 18 Years of Age..	251	237	238	228	227	224	219	217	212
Covered by Private or Public Insurance									
Number..	232	227	217	215	215	212	211	207	201
Percent..	92.4	95.8	91.2	94.3	94.6	94.4	96.0	95.5	94.6
Not Covered									
Number..	19	10	21	13	12	12	8	10	12
Percent..	7.6	4.1	8.8	5.7	5.4	5.6	4.0	4.5	5.4
Percent in the U.S. not covered..	10.9	11.7	11.0	9.7	8.6	8.0	7.5	7.2	7.1

Table RI-7. Employment Status by Demographic Group, 2014

(Numbers in thousands, percent.)

Characteristic	Civilian noninstitutional population	Civilian labor force		Employed		Unemployed	
		Number	Percent of population	Number	Percent of population	Number	Percent of population
Total..........	852	554	65.0	511	60.0	43	7.7
Sex							
Male..........	406	286	70.5	261	64.4	25	8.6
Female..........	447	268	60.0	250	56.0	18	6.7
Race, Sex, and Hispanic Origin							
White..........	735	478	65.1	445	60.5	33	7.0
Male..........	350	247	70.6	229	65.3	18	7.5
Female..........	384	231	60.0	216	56.2	15	6.5
Black or African American..........	56	36	63.5	30	54.1	5	14.8
Male..........	27	19	68.6	15	56.1	3	18.2
Female..........	29	17	58.6	15	52.1	2	11.1
Hispanic or Latino ethnicity[1]..........	98	64	65.3	54	54.8	10	16.1
Male..........	47	34	72.2	28	59.4	6	17.7
Female..........	51	30	59.0	26	50.6	4	14.3
Age							
16 to 19 years..........	59	24	40.8	19	32.4	5	20.6
20 to 24 years..........	79	59	74.8	52	65.5	7	12.5
25 to 34 years..........	131	107	82.2	99	75.8	8	7.8
35 to 44 years..........	129	109	84.6	103	79.7	6	5.8
45 to 54 years..........	147	120	82.1	113	76.8	8	6.5
55 to 64 years..........	138	100	72.0	93	67.3	6	6.4
65 years and over..........	169	34	20.1	33	19.3	1	4.0

NOTE: Data in Table 7 are from the Current Population Survey (CPS) and do not match the estimates in Table 8. See notes and definitions for further information.
[1]May be of any race.

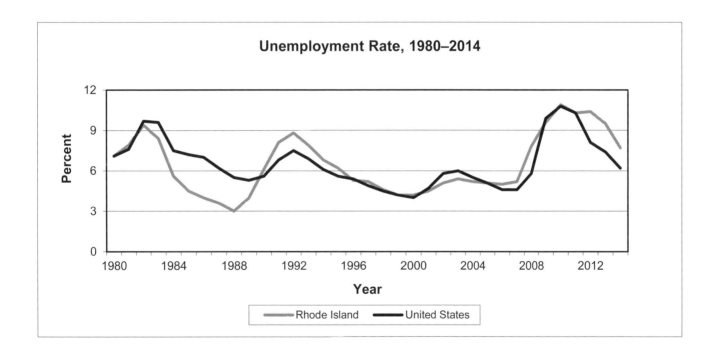

Table RI-8. Employment Status of the Civilian Noninstitutional Population Age 16 Years and Over

(Number, percent.)

Year	Civilian labor force	Civilian participation rate	Employed	Unemployed	Unemployment rate
2006................................	572,601	68.4	544,357	28,244	4.9
2007................................	573,173	68.4	543,401	29,772	5.2
2008................................	570,328	68.0	525,941	44,387	7.8
2009................................	567,280	67.4	504,951	62,329	11.0
2010................................	566,704	67.3	503,216	63,488	11.2
2011................................	560,455	66.5	498,250	62,205	11.1
2012................................	558,089	66.0	500,283	57,806	10.4
2013................................	556,910	65.6	505,370	51,540	9.3
2014................................	553,332	64.9	510,902	42,430	7.7

Table RI-9. Employment and Average Wages by Industry

(Estimates from 2007 through 2010 are based on the 2007 *North American Industry Classification System* [NAICS]. Estimates from 2011 onward are based on the 2012 NAICS.)

Industry	2007	2008	2009	2010	2011	2012	2013
				Number of jobs			
Wage and Salary Employment by Industry........................	509,447	499,308	477,886	476,805	478,046	478,698	485,026
Farm Wage and Salary Employment	483	527	509	510	541	548	649
Nonfarm Wage and Salary Employment...........................	508,964	498,781	477,377	476,295	477,505	478,150	484,377
Private wage and salary employment...................................	433,561	424,126	403,989	403,247	405,394	406,575	412,600
Forestry, fishing, and related activities	530	514	558	D	D	600	D
Mining..	279	246	194	D	D	188	D
Utilities..	1,113	1,111	1,119	1,130	1,077	1,056	1,059
Construction	22,957	21,182	17,990	16,719	16,523	16,548	16,705
Manufacturing..	50,920	48,034	41,841	40,431	40,416	39,701	40,121
Durable goods manufacturing.................................	33,009	31,219	26,904	25,828	25,863	25,352	25,619
Nondurable goods manufacturing............................	17,911	16,815	14,937	14,603	14,553	14,349	14,502
Wholesale trade	17,325	16,957	16,226	15,935	16,278	16,896	16,767
Retail trade..	52,221	50,320	47,840	47,701	47,640	47,373	47,030
Transportation and warehousing................................	10,017	9,883	9,186	9,247	9,693	9,815	9,761
Information	10,495	10,757	10,158	10,033	10,172	9,600	9,088
Finance and insurance	27,020	25,603	24,136	24,148	23,919	24,226	24,735
Real estate and rental and leasing...............................	6,943	6,699	6,229	5,931	5,887	5,934	6,091
Professional, scientific, and technical services	22,141	21,967	21,470	21,248	21,287	21,677	22,213
Management of companies and enterprises....................	9,447	9,302	9,207	9,326	9,856	10,524	11,342
Administrative and waste services..............................	25,203	24,211	22,483	23,554	23,702	24,351	25,608
Educational services	23,556	24,403	24,847	25,068	25,340	24,329	24,121
Health care and social assistance..............................	77,501	78,004	78,388	79,691	79,534	79,742	81,394
Arts, entertainment, and recreation............................	8,286	8,166	7,768	7,679	7,703	7,739	8,525
Accommodation and food services.............................	43,636	43,387	41,803	42,533	43,064	44,403	45,494
Other services, except public administration..................	23,971	23,380	22,546	22,127	22,554	21,873	21,801
Government and government enterprises	75,403	74,655	73,388	73,048	72,111	71,575	71,777
				Dollars			
Average Wages and Salaries by Industry........................	42,180	43,525	43,930	45,275	46,375	47,510	48,305
Average Farm Wages and Salaries	32,783	28,825	28,354	26,727	22,543	24,943	28,696
Average Nonfarm Wages and Salaries...........................	42,189	43,541	43,947	45,295	46,402	47,536	48,332
Average private wages and salaries................................	40,847	42,069	42,271	43,650	44,760	46,018	46,946
Forestry, fishing, and related activities	38,649	39,484	37,618	D	D	38,045	D
Mining..	48,229	48,297	48,582	D	D	51,580	D
Utilities..	75,501	81,681	85,218	86,633	93,909	86,992	96,837
Construction	49,313	51,431	53,037	52,520	53,841	54,691	55,247
Manufacturing..	47,457	47,975	48,872	50,989	52,722	53,956	55,263
Durable goods manufacturing.................................	48,055	48,842	49,863	52,470	54,322	55,482	56,865
Nondurable goods manufacturing............................	46,355	46,365	47,087	48,371	49,877	51,261	52,434
Wholesale trade	60,364	61,469	61,378	64,751	65,451	67,262	69,237
Retail trade..	27,572	27,456	27,294	28,154	27,821	28,412	28,603
Transportation and warehousing................................	36,491	37,934	38,992	39,861	40,949	41,488	41,893
Information	59,034	59,222	61,392	62,900	65,816	69,087	67,584
Finance and insurance	62,878	69,842	69,956	75,543	80,261	84,493	86,698
Real estate and rental and leasing...............................	38,033	37,713	37,323	38,914	40,170	41,909	42,592
Professional, scientific, and technical services	60,714	63,007	63,211	65,446	66,555	67,827	69,273
Management of companies and enterprises....................	99,392	107,131	95,224	104,620	106,642	115,243	116,768
Administrative and waste services..............................	29,526	30,903	31,200	31,606	32,403	33,564	34,493
Educational services	37,178	38,160	38,554	39,520	40,155	40,132	42,158
Health care and social assistance..............................	39,227	40,384	41,708	42,311	43,169	43,679	44,120
Arts, entertainment, and recreation............................	28,031	26,444	26,487	27,149	28,115	28,769	29,196
Accommodation and food services.............................	18,006	17,756	17,832	18,360	18,946	19,309	19,547
Other services, except public administration..................	27,025	27,915	28,124	28,941	29,190	29,713	30,680
Government and government enterprises	49,906	51,902	53,171	54,370	55,634	56,158	56,294

D = Not shown to avoid disclosure of confidential information, but the estimates for this item are included in the total.

Table RI-10. Employment Characteristics by Family Type

(Number, percent.)

Family type and labor force status	2011 Total	2011 Families with own children under 18 years	2012 Total	2012 Families with own children under 18 years	2013 Total	2013 Families with own children under 18 years
All Families	256,181	111,314	257,419	106,858	259,863	108,073
FAMILY TYPE AND LABOR FORCE STATUS						
Married-Couple Families	181,495	70,306	180,454	66,254	180,930	66,807
Both husband and wife in labor force	58.5	74.3	58.5	77.1	56.3	71.6
Husband in labor force, wife not in labor force	17.8	21.0	17.3	18.3	18.6	22.6
Wife in labor force, husband not in labor force	8.3	3.6	8.0	3.8	8.8	4.4
Both husband and wife not in labor force	15.4	1.1	16.2	0.9	15.5	0.9
Other Families	74,686	41,008	76,965	40,604	78,933	41,266
Female householder, no husband present	74.0	79.2	75.4	80.0	73.1	78.1
In labor force	54.0	65.1	55.0	65.9	52.7	61.9
Not in labor force	20.0	14.1	20.4	14.1	20.4	16.2
Male householder, no wife present	26.0	20.8	24.6	20.0	26.9	21.9
In labor force	19.7	18.4	19.3	18.8	20.1	19.8
Not in labor force	6.3	2.4	5.3	1.3	6.8	2.1

Table RI-11. School Enrollment and Educational Attainment, 2013

(Number, percent.)

Item	State	U.S.
Enrollment		
Total population 3 years and over, enrolled in school	263,971	82,395,254
Enrolled in nursery school or preschool (percent)	4.9	6.0
Enrolled in kindergarten (percent)	4.0	5.2
Enrolled in elementary school, grades 1-8 (percent)	35.7	40.0
Enrolled in high school, grades 9-12 (percent)	20.1	20.6
Enrolled in college or graduate school (percent)	35.3	28.3
Attainment		
Total population 25 years and over	719,956	210,910,615
Less than ninth grade (percent)	6.1	5.8
9th to 12th grade, no diploma (percent)	8.0	7.6
High school graduate, including equivalency (percent)	26.6	27.8
Some college, no degree (percent)	18.5	21.1
Associate's degree (percent)	8.3	8.1
Bachelor's degree (percent)	19.8	18.4
Graduate or professional degree (percent)	12.6	11.2
High school graduate or higher (percent)	85.9	86.6
Bachelor's degree or higher (percent)	32.4	29.6

Table RI-12. Public School Characteristics and Educational Indicators

(Number, percent; data derived from National Center of Education Statistics.)

Item	State	U.S.
Public Schools, 2012–2013 (except where noted)		
Number of school districts	54	18,093
Number of schools	304	98,454
Number of students (in thousands)	142	49,771
Number of teachers (in thousands)	10	3,109
Student-teacher ratio	14.4	16.0
Expenditures per student (dollars), FY 2012	15,172	10,667
Four-year adjusted cohort graduation rate (ACGR)[1,2]	79.7	81.4
Students eligible for free or reduced-price lunch (in thousands)	65	25,188
English language learners (in thousands)	8	4,397
Students age 3 to 21 served under IDEA, part B (in thousands)	24	6,429

Public Schools by Type	Number	Percent of state public schools
Total number of schools	304	100.0
Regular	285	93.8
Special education	2	0.7
Vocational education	12	3.9
Alternative education	5	1.6

NOTE: Every school is assigned only one school type based on its instructional emphasis.
[1]ACGR data represents a new method of calculating high-school completion rates and may not be comparable to previous years' data for Averaged Freshmen Graduation Rates (AFGR).
[2]The United States 4-year ACGRs were estimated using both the reported 4-year ACGR data from 49 states and the District of Columbia and using imputed data for Idaho. The estimate for American Indian/Alaska Native students also includes imputed data for Virginia.

Table RI-13. Reported Voting and Registration of the Voting-Age Population, November 2012

(Numbers in thousands, percent.)

Item	Total population	Total citizen population	Registered			Voted		
			Total registered	Percent registered (total population)	Percent registered (total citizen population)	Total voted	Percent voted (total population)	Percent voted (total citizen population)
U.S. Total	235,248	215,081	153,157	65.1	71.2	132,948	56.5	61.8
State Total	9,847	9,452	6,795	69.0	71.9	5,824	59.1	61.6
Sex								
Male	384	352	254	66.1	72.0	212	55.3	60.2
Female	434	399	298	68.8	74.8	257	59.3	64.5
Race								
White alone..	713	673	497	69.7	74.0	420	58.9	62.5
White, non-Hispanic alone	646	632	472	73.0	74.7	400	61.9	63.3
Black alone..	50	43	33	B	B	30	B	B
Asian alone	25	16	6	B	B	5	B	B
Hispanic (of any race)	95	57	37	39.1	B	32	33.6	B
White alone or in combination	734	686	508	69.2	74.1	430	58.5	62.6
Black alone or in combination..........	65	54	41	B	B	37	B	B
Asian alone or in combination..........	31	21	10	B	B	9	B	B
Age								
18 to 24 years...................................	99	89	61	61.8	68.9	45	45.2	50.3
25 to 44 years...................................	271	235	159	58.7	67.6	134	49.4	56.9
45 to 64 years...................................	290	272	213	73.4	78.3	185	64.0	68.3
65 to 74 years...................................	84	82	64	76.3	78.1	59	70.5	72.2
75 years and over	74	74	55	B	B	46	B	B

B = Base is less than 75,000 and therefore too small to show the derived measure.

Table RI-14. Crime

(Number, rate per 100,000. Data are derived from the FBI Uniform Crime Reports.)

Item	State			U.S.[1,2,3,4]		
	2012	2013	Percent change	2012	2013	Percent change
TOTAL POPULATION[5]..	1,050,304	1,051,511	0.1	313,873,685	316,128,839	0.7
VIOLENT CRIME						
Number..	2,657	2,572	-3.2	1,217,067	1,163,146	-4.4
Rate	253.0	244.6	-3.3	387.8	367.9	-5.1
Murder and Nonnegligent Manslaughter						
Number..	36	31	-13.9	14,866	14,196	-4.5
Rate	3.4	2.9	-14.0	4.7	4.5	-5.2
Rape[6]						
Number..	X	440	X	X	108,612	X
Rate	X	41.8	X	X	34.4	X
Robbery						
Number..	715	684	-4.3	355,051	345,031	-2.8
Rate	68.1	65.0	-4.4	113.1	109.1	-3.5
Aggravated Assault						
Number..	1,614	1,550	-4.0	762,009	724,149	-5.0
Rate	153.7	147.4	-4.1	242.8	229.1	-5.6
PROPERTY CRIME						
Number..	27,039	25,678	-5.0	9,001,992	8,632,512	-4.1
Rate	2,574.4	2,442.0	-5.1	2,868.0	2,730.7	-4.8
Burglary						
Number..	5,929	5,607	-5.4	2,109,932	1,928,465	-8.6
Rate	564.5	533.2	-5.5	672.2	610.0	-9.3
Larceny-Theft						
Number..	18,478	17,838	-3.5	6,168,874	6,004,453	-2.7
Rate	1,759.3	1,696.4	-3.6	1,965.4	1,899.4	-3.4
Motor Vehicle Theft						
Number..	2,632	2,233	-15.2	723,186	699,594	-3.3
Rate	250.6	212.4	-15.3	230.4	221.3	-4.0

NOTE: Although arson data are included in the trend and clearance tables, sufficient data are not available to estimate totals for this offense. Therefore, no arson data are published in this table.
X = Not applicable.
- = Zero or rounds to zero.
[1]The crime figures have been adjusted.
[2]The data collection methodology for the offense of forcible rape used by the Minnesota state Uniform Crime Reporting (UCR) Program (with the exception of Minneapolis and St. Paul, Minnesota) does not comply with national UCR Program guidelines. Consequently, its figures for forcible rape and violent crime (of which forcible rape is a part) are not published in this table.
[3]Includes offenses reported by the Zoological Police and the Metro Transit Police.
[4]Because of changes in the state's reporting practices, figures are not comparable to previous years' data.
[5]Populations are U.S. Census Bureau provisional estimates as of July 1 of each year.
[6]The figures shown for the offense of rape were estimated using the revised Uniform Crime Reporting (UCR) definition of rape.

Table RI-15. State Government Finances, 2013

(Dollar amounts in thousands, percent distribution.)

Item	Dollars	Percent distribution
Total Revenue	8,681,540	100.0
General revenue	6,933,496	79.9
Intergovernmental revenue	2,369,822	27.3
Taxes	2,940,433	33.9
General sales	881,458	10.2
Selective sales	634,965	7.3
License taxes	138,518	1.6
Individual income tax	1,088,992	12.5
Corporate income tax	144,310	1.7
Other taxes	52,190	0.6
Current charges	744,765	8.6
Miscellaneous general revenue	878,476	10.1
Utility revenue	33,239	0.4
Liquor stores revenue	0	-
Insurance trust revenue[1]	1,714,805	19.8
Total Expenditure	8,189,015	100.0
Intergovernmental expenditure	1,170,440	14.3
Direct expenditure	7,018,575	85.7
Current operation	4,518,481	55.2
Capital outlay	404,000	4.9
Insurance benefits and repayments	1,471,624	18.0
Assistance and subsidies	150,354	1.8
Interest on debt	474,116	5.8
Exhibit: Salaries and wages	1,176,761	14.4
Total Expenditure	8,189,015	100.0
General expenditure	6,562,768	80.1
Intergovernmental expenditure	1,170,440	14.3
Direct expenditure	5,392,328	65.8
General expenditure, by function:		
Education	1,986,630	24.3
Public welfare	2,394,541	29.2
Hospitals	66,449	0.8
Health	158,767	1.9
Highways	318,630	3.9
Police protection	71,704	0.9
Correction	182,888	2.2
Natural resources	59,205	0.7
Parks and recreation	29,055	0.4
Governmental administration	351,759	4.3
Interest on general debt	474,116	5.8
Other and unallocable	469,024	5.7
Utility expenditure	154,623	1.9
Liquor stores expenditure	0	-
Insurance trust expenditure	1,471,624	18.0
Debt at End of Fiscal Year	9,568,297	X
Cash and Security Holdings	15,099,812	X

X = Not applicable.
- = Zero or rounds to zero.

[1]Within insurance trust revenue, net earnings of state retirement systems is a calculated statistic (the item code in the data file is X08), and thus can be positive or negative. Net earnings is the sum of earnings on investments plus gains on investments minus losses on investments. The change made in 2002 for asset valuation from book to market value in accordance with Statement 34 of the Governmental Accounting Standards Board is reflected in the calculated statistics.

Table RI-16. State Government Tax Collections, 2014

(Dollars in thousands, percent.)

Item	Dollars	Percent distribution
Total Taxes	2,965,975	100.0
Property taxes	2,591	0.1
Sales and gross receipts	1,566,191	52.8
General sales and gross receipts	915,468	30.9
Selective sales and gross receipts	650,723	21.9
Alcoholic beverages	16,803	0.6
Amusements	0	-
Insurance premiums	85,801	2.9
Motor fuels	95,828	3.2
Pari-mutuels	1,147	-
Public utilities	105,296	3.6
Tobacco products	134,805	4.5
Other selective sales	211,043	7.1
Licenses	132,146	4.5
Alcoholic beverages	174	-
Amusements	223	-
Corporations in general	4,875	0.2
Hunting and fishing	1,748	0.1
Motor vehicle	69,349	2.3
Motor vehicle operators	4,988	0.2
Public utilities	0	-
Occupation and business, NEC	46,827	1.6
Other licenses	3,962	0.1
Income taxes	1,208,517	40.7
Individual income	1,088,405	36.7
Corporation net income	120,112	4.0
Other taxes	56,530	1.9
Death and gift	38,899	1.3
Documentary and stock transfer	17,631	0.6
Severance	X	X
Taxes, NEC	0	-

X = Not applicable.
- = Zero or rounds to zero.

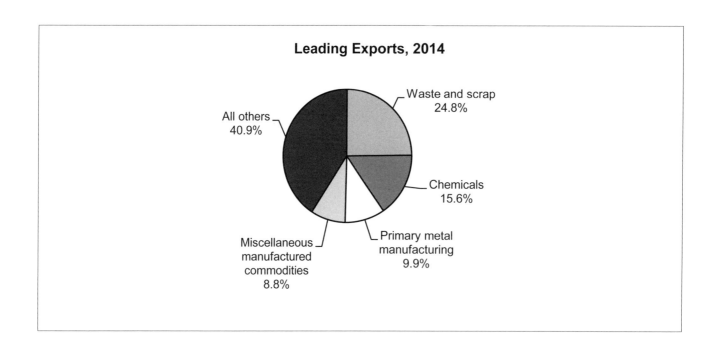

Leading Exports, 2014

Waste and scrap 24.8%
Chemicals 15.6%
Primary metal manufacturing 9.9%
Miscellaneous manufactured commodities 8.8%
All others 40.9%

SOUTH CAROLINA

Facts and Figures

Location: Southeastern United States; bordered on the N by North Carolina, on the E by the Atlantic Ocean, on the S by the Atlantic Ocean and Georgia, and on the W by Georgia

Area: 32,020 sq. mi. (82,932 sq. km.); rank—40th

Population: 4,832,482 (2014 est.); rank—24th

Principal Cities: capital—Columbia; largest—Columbia

Statehood: May 23, 1788; 8th state

U.S. Congress: 2 senators, 7 representatives

State Mottoes: *Animis opibusque parati* ("Prepared in mind and resources"); *Dum spiro, spero* ("While I breathe, I hope")

State Songs: "Carolina"; "South Carolina on My Mind"

State Nickname: The Palmetto State

Abbreviations: SC; S.C.

State Symbols: flower—yellow jessamine; tree—cabbage palmetto; bird—Carolina wren

At a Glance

- With an increase in population of 4.5 percent, South Carolina ranked 11th among the states in growth from 2010 to 2014.

- South Carolina's median household income in 2013 was $44,163, and 18.6 percent of the population lived below the poverty level.

- South Carolina's violent crime rate in 2013 was 508.5 per 100,000 population, compared to 367.9 for the entire nation.

- South Carolina had the highest proportion of residents in mobile homes in 2013, with 16.5 percent of its residents in these types of dwellings.

- In 2013, 15.8 percent of South Carolinians did not have health insurance, compared to 14.5 percent of the total U.S. population.

Table SC-1. Population by Age, Sex, Race, and Hispanic Origin

(Number, percent, except where noted.)

Sex, age, race, and Hispanic origin	2000	2010	2014[1]	Average annual percent change, 2010–2014
Total Population	4,012,013	4,625,364	4,832,482	1.1
Percent of total U.S. population	1.4	1.5	1.5	X
Sex				
Male	1,948,929	2,250,101	2,349,394	1.1
Female	2,063,083	2,375,263	2,483,088	1.1
Age				
Under 5 years	264,679	302,297	290,519	-1.0
5 to 19 years	871,099	922,128	923,500	-
20 to 64 years	2,390,901	2,769,065	2,856,598	0.8
65 years and over	485,333	631,874	761,865	4.8
Median age (years)	35.4	37.9	38.8	0.6
Race and Hispanic Origin				
One race				
White	2,695,560	3,164,143	3,302,736	1.1
Black	1,185,216	1,302,865	1,342,308	0.7
American Indian and Alaska Native	13,718	24,665	25,961	1.3
Asian	36,014	61,247	74,319	5.0
Native Hawaiian or Other Pacific Islander	1,628	3,957	4,520	3.4
Two or more races	39,950	68,487	82,638	4.8
Hispanic (of any race)	95,076	243,923	261,752	1.8

X = Not applicable.
- = Zero or rounds to zero.
[1]Population figures for 2014 are July 1 estimates. The 2010 estimates are taken from the 2010 Census.

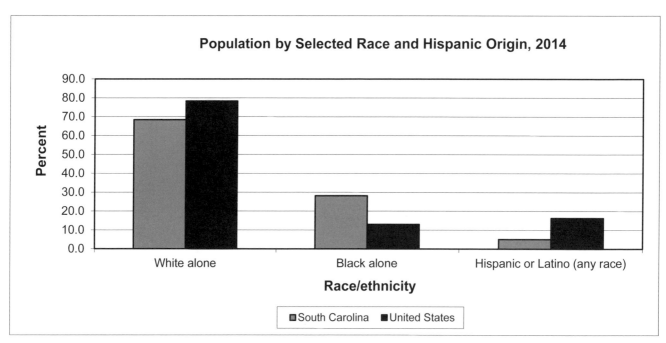

Table SC-2. Marital Status

(Number, percent distribution.)

Sex, age, race, and Hispanic origin	2000	2010	2013
Males, 15 Years and Over	1,516,125	1,797,441	1,862,523
Never married	28.8	35.2	35.2
Now married, except separated	57.3	49.4	48.8
Separated	2.8	3.0	2.9
Widowed	2.7	2.8	3.2
Divorced	8.3	9.5	9.8
Females, 15 Years and Over	1,652,793	1,939,054	2,010,225
Never married	23.4	29.1	29.4
Now married, except separated	51.4	45.2	44.7
Separated	3.8	3.9	2.8
Widowed	11.5	10.6	10.3
Divorced	9.9	11.2	11.7

Table SC-3. Households and Housing Characteristics

(Number, percent, dollars.)

Item	2000	2010	2013	Average annual percent change, 2000–2013
Total Households..	1,533,854	1,761,393	1,794,989	1.2
Family households	1,072,822	1,180,687	1,195,104	0.8
Married-couple family	783,142	827,387	840,762	0.5
Other family	289,680	353,300	354,342	1.6
Male householder, no wife present..	62,722	77,062	81,127	2.0
Female householder, no husband present..................................	226,958	276,238	273,215	1.4
Nonfamily households	461,032	580,706	599,885	2.0
Householder living alone..	383,142	489,995	502,704	2.1
Householder not living alone..	77,890	90,711	97,181	1.7
Housing Characteristics				
Total housing units..	1,753,670	2,140,337	2,158,784	1.6
Occupied housing units	1,533,854	1,761,393	1,794,989	1.2
Owner occupied..	1,107,617	1,210,160	1,223,614	0.8
Renter occupied...	426,237	551,233	571,375	2.3
Average household size...	2.53	2.55	2.58	0.2
Financial Characteristics				
Median gross rent of renter-occupied housing	510	728	766	3.2
Median monthly owner costs for housing units with a mortgage	894	1,177	1,144	1.9
Median value of owner-occupied housing units............................	94,900	138,100	139,200	3.0

Table SC-4. Migration, Origin, and Language

(Number, percent.)

Characteristic	State			U.S.		
	2012	2013	Percent change	2012	2013	Percent change
Residence 1 Year Ago						
Population 1 year and over	4,624,180	4,720,602	2.1	310,212,755	312,432,820	0.7
Same house	84.3	84.7	X	85.0	85.0	X
Different house in the U.S.	15.2	14.9	X	14.4	14.4	X
Same county	8.8	8.3	X	9.0	8.9	X
Different county	6.4	6.6	X	5.4	5.5	X
Same state	3.0	3.1	X	3.2	3.2	X
Different state	3.4	3.5	X	2.3	2.3	X
Abroad	0.4	0.4	X	0.6	0.6	X
Place of Birth						
Native born	4,457,297	4,543,561	1.9	273,089,382	274,780,773	0.6
Male	48.4	48.5	X	49.3	49.3	X
Female	51.6	51.5	X	50.7	50.7	X
Foreign born	221,933	231,278	4.2	40,824,658	41,348,066	1.3
Male	52.0	51.2	X	48.7	48.8	X
Female	48.0	48.8	X	51.3	51.2	X
Foreign born; naturalized U.S. citizen..	74,818	89,661	19.8	18,686,237	19,294,710	3.3
Male	46.5	46.9	X	45.8	45.9	X
Female	53.5	53.1	X	54.2	54.1	X
Foreign born; not a U.S. citizen...	147,115	141,617	-3.7	22,138,421	22,053,356	-0.4
Male	54.8	53.9	X	51.1	51.3	X
Female	45.2	46.1	X	48.9	48.7	X
Entered 2010 or later	45.6	8.9	X	7.0	9.7	X
Entered 2000 to 2009	24.6	38.8	X	30.4	29.4	X
Entered before 2000...	29.8	52.3	X	62.7	61.0	X
World Region of Birth, Foreign						
Foreign-born population, excluding population born at sea	221,933	231,278	4.2	40,824,553	41,347,945	1.3
Europe	18.3	15.6	X	11.8	11.6	X
Asia...	22.2	21.3	X	29.2	29.5	X
Africa	1.8	3.8	X	4.2	4.4	X
Oceania	0.2	0.7	X	0.6	0.5	X
Latin America	53.7	54.4	X	52.2	51.9	X
North America	3.8	4.1	X	2.0	2.0	X
Language Spoken at Home and Ability to Speak English						
Population 5 years and over...	4,376,509	4,481,196	2.4	294,003,714	296,358,760	0.8
English only	93.4	93.1	X	79.0	79.2	X
Language other than English..	6.6	6.9	X	21.0	20.8	X
Speaks English less than "very well"..	2.7	2.8	X	8.5	8.5	X

NA = Not available.
X = Not applicable.
- = Zero or rounds to zero.

Table SC-5. Median Income and Poverty Status, 2013

(Number, percent, except as noted.)

Characteristic	State		U.S.	
	Number	Percent	Number	Percent
Median Income				
Households (dollars).............................	44,163	X	52,250	X
Families (dollars)	54,686	X	64,030	X
Below Poverty Level (All People)	860,380	18.6	48,810,868	15.8
Sex				
Male...	375,090	16.8	21,938,525	14.5
Female	485,290	20.2	26,872,343	17.1
Age				
Under 18 years................................	291,832	27.5	16,086,960	22.2
Related children under 18 years................	288,705	27.3	15,769,921	21.9
18 to 64 years................................	496,555	17.4	28,578,191	14.8
65 years and over	71,993	10.2	4,145,717	9.6

X = Not applicable.

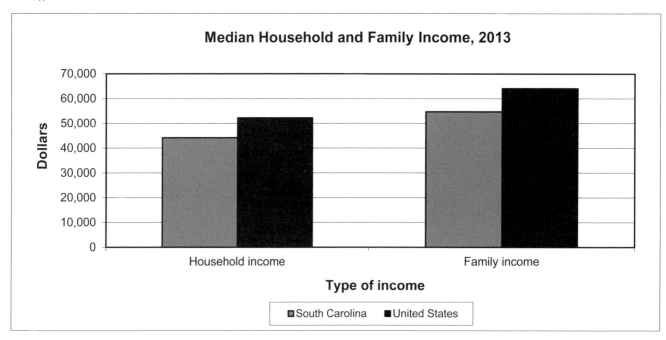

Table SC-6. Health Insurance Coverage Status for the Civilian Noninstitutionalized Population and Children Under 18 Years of Age

(Numbers in thousands, percent.)

Item	2005	2006	2007	2008	2009	2010	2011	2012	2013
Civilian Noninstitutionalized Population	4,181	4,226	4,384	4,373	4,454	4,537	4,579	4,623	4,678
Covered by Private or Public Insurance									
Number..	3,459	3,553	3,664	3,612	3,705	3,742	3,813	3,845	3,939
Percent..	82.7	84.1	83.6	82.6	83.2	82.5	83.3	83.2	84.2
Not Covered									
Number..	721	672	721	761	750	795	766	778	739
Percent..	17.3	15.9	16.4	17.4	16.8	17.5	16.7	16.8	15.8
Percent in the U.S. not covered........................	15.3	15.8	15.3	15.1	15.1	15.5	15.1	14.8	14.5
Children Under 18 Years of Age.........................	1,016	1,042	1,070	1,064	1,078	1,078	1,079	1,078	1,077
Covered by Private or Public Insurance									
Number..	912	930	918	930	971	976	988	989	1,004
Percent..	89.8	89.3	85.8	87.4	90.0	90.6	91.6	91.7	93.3
Not Covered									
Number..	104	112	152	134	107	102	91	89	73
Percent..	10.2	10.7	14.2	12.6	10.0	9.4	8.4	8.3	6.7
Percent in the U.S. not covered........................	10.9	11.7	11.0	9.7	8.6	8.0	7.5	7.2	7.1

Table SC-7. Employment Status by Demographic Group, 2014

(Numbers in thousands, percent.)

Characteristic	Civilian noninstitutional population	Civilian labor force		Employed		Unemployed	
		Number	Percent of population	Number	Percent of population	Number	Percent of population
Total...	3,762	2,212	58.8	2,070	55.0	142	6.4
Sex							
Male...	1,778	1,145	64.4	1,076	60.6	69	6.0
Female..	1,984	1,066	53.7	993	50.1	73	6.9
Race, Sex, and Hispanic Origin							
White..	2,664	1,567	58.8	1,484	55.7	83	5.3
Male...	1,283	840	65.4	794	61.9	45	5.4
Female...	1,381	728	52.7	690	49.9	38	5.2
Black or African American..................	994	574	57.8	517	52.0	57	9.9
Male...	442	265	60.0	242	54.8	23	8.7
Female...	552	308	55.9	275	49.8	34	10.9
Hispanic or Latino ethnicity[1]............	157	104	66.1	94	60.1	9	9.0
Male...	85	66	77.9	60	70.6	6	9.3
Female...	72	37	52.0	34	47.6	3	8.6
Age							
16 to 19 years.................................	209	75	36.0	55	26.1	21	27.4
20 to 24 years.................................	338	227	67.2	202	59.7	25	11.1
25 to 34 years.................................	617	487	78.9	451	73.0	36	7.5
35 to 44 years.................................	588	487	82.8	465	79.2	21	4.4
45 to 54 years.................................	631	479	75.8	457	72.4	22	4.5
55 to 64 years.................................	630	348	55.2	335	53.2	13	3.7
65 years and over............................	748	108	14.5	104	14.0	4	3.5

NOTE: Data in Table 7 are from the Current Population Survey (CPS) and do not match the estimates in Table 8. See notes and definitions for further information.
[1]May be of any race.

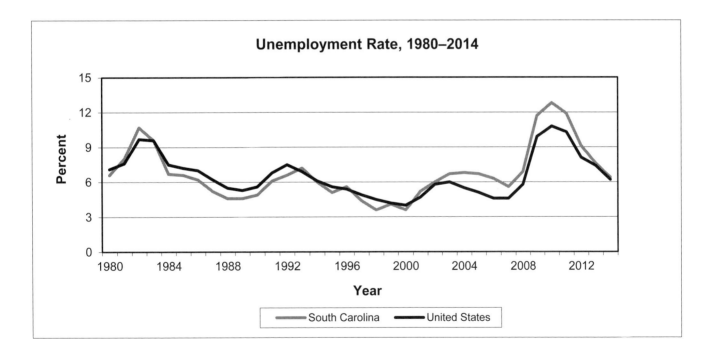

Unemployment Rate, 1980–2014

Table SC-8. Employment Status of the Civilian Noninstitutional Population Age 16 Years and Over

(Number, percent.)

Year	Civilian labor force	Civilian participation rate	Employed	Unemployed	Unemployment rate
2006	2,109,097	63.8	1,973,337	135,760	6.4
2007	2,125,891	63.0	2,005,686	120,205	5.7
2008	2,142,232	62.3	1,996,409	145,823	6.8
2009	2,152,745	61.7	1,910,670	242,075	11.2
2010	2,155,668	60.5	1,915,045	240,623	11.2
2011	2,171,046	60.1	1,942,109	228,937	10.5
2012	2,178,158	59.5	1,978,328	199,830	9.2
2013	2,180,093	58.8	2,013,452	166,641	7.6
2014	2,197,587	58.4	2,056,136	141,451	6.4

Table SC-9. Employment and Average Wages by Industry

(Estimates from 2007 through 2010 are based on the 2007 *North American Industry Classification System* [NAICS]. Estimates from 2011 onward are based on the 2012 NAICS.)

Industry	2007	2008	2009	2010	2011	2012	2013
				Number of jobs			
Wage and Salary Employment by Industry	2,033,893	2,020,732	1,912,435	1,903,467	1,926,026	1,946,432	1,985,162
Farm Wage and Salary Employment	6,367	6,453	7,894	6,624	6,722	6,673	7,157
Nonfarm Wage and Salary Employment	2,027,526	2,014,279	1,904,541	1,896,843	1,919,304	1,939,759	1,978,005
Private wage and salary employment	1,636,554	1,613,489	1,502,296	1,498,976	1,526,368	1,544,812	1,578,825
Forestry, fishing, and related activities	6,740	6,635	6,468	6,697	6,905	6,305	6,867
Mining	1,453	1,482	1,340	1,244	1,232	1,195	1,141
Utilities	12,063	12,363	12,435	12,048	11,922	12,134	12,207
Construction	129,711	115,006	92,463	83,731	80,892	80,209	82,871
Manufacturing	250,677	243,301	214,821	208,203	216,381	221,444	225,092
Durable goods manufacturing	139,041	136,638	118,293	114,174	121,111	126,085	129,606
Nondurable goods manufacturing	111,636	106,663	96,528	94,029	95,270	95,359	95,486
Wholesale trade	71,870	71,671	65,668	64,222	65,039	65,974	66,757
Retail trade	243,762	239,826	227,174	226,866	228,832	228,443	233,103
Transportation and warehousing	54,730	52,830	47,673	47,205	48,312	50,280	52,667
Information	28,378	28,573	27,229	25,893	25,858	25,801	26,455
Finance and insurance	72,056	72,084	70,386	68,999	68,948	69,762	70,634
Real estate and rental and leasing	31,399	30,955	28,586	27,141	26,660	26,021	26,980
Professional, scientific, and technical services	74,048	77,270	74,138	75,713	80,155	80,284	82,667
Management of companies and enterprises	15,621	15,659	14,516	14,290	15,053	16,414	17,238
Administrative and waste services	138,265	131,288	115,370	129,873	136,527	141,475	144,335
Educational services	26,939	28,069	28,271	29,289	29,922	30,679	30,451
Health care and social assistance	161,332	166,737	168,480	172,707	175,238	178,057	180,993
Arts, entertainment, and recreation	27,249	28,779	27,029	26,044	26,805	26,975	27,585
Accommodation and food services	192,398	191,371	183,894	183,777	186,392	191,290	196,943
Other services, except public administration	97,863	99,590	96,355	95,034	95,295	92,070	93,839
Government and government enterprises	390,972	400,790	402,245	397,867	392,936	394,947	399,180
				Dollars			
Average Wages and Salaries by Industry	36,428	37,330	37,832	38,715	39,627	40,646	41,021
Average Farm Wages and Salaries	25,833	23,101	18,925	22,695	20,051	22,476	21,645
Average Nonfarm Wages and Salaries	36,461	37,375	37,910	38,771	39,696	40,709	41,092
Average private wages and salaries	35,764	36,469	36,798	37,836	38,842	39,967	40,361
Forestry, fishing, and related activities	29,978	29,913	29,906	31,148	31,518	33,322	33,858
Mining	47,912	46,090	43,035	48,012	50,545	53,413	55,358
Utilities	68,704	72,803	73,936	78,446	80,316	81,491	85,000
Construction	39,740	41,013	40,979	41,924	42,903	44,787	45,501
Manufacturing	46,341	47,851	48,779	51,196	52,793	54,208	54,985
Durable goods manufacturing	47,189	48,930	50,369	53,280	55,232	56,511	57,285
Nondurable goods manufacturing	45,284	46,468	46,832	48,666	49,693	51,164	51,865
Wholesale trade	54,112	55,336	54,676	55,975	58,095	60,513	61,173
Retail trade	24,668	24,850	24,928	25,432	25,518	26,023	26,245
Transportation and warehousing	38,521	38,908	39,240	40,449	41,243	41,900	42,156
Information	49,041	50,236	50,835	52,112	52,169	53,915	55,440
Finance and insurance	54,599	52,945	53,973	55,028	57,235	59,551	60,736
Real estate and rental and leasing	34,327	33,909	33,906	34,536	36,297	37,934	39,132
Professional, scientific, and technical services	56,492	57,089	57,937	59,901	61,272	64,002	64,109
Management of companies and enterprises	63,281	64,102	65,759	67,177	70,185	72,381	71,074
Administrative and waste services	29,084	30,739	32,200	32,930	33,796	33,615	32,835
Educational services	25,658	26,651	27,675	27,824	28,457	28,983	29,658
Health care and social assistance	38,125	39,183	40,059	41,319	42,089	43,108	43,776
Arts, entertainment, and recreation	21,769	20,390	20,026	20,396	21,023	21,143	20,890
Accommodation and food services	16,412	16,294	16,312	17,036	17,494	17,918	17,935
Other services, except public administration	25,120	26,071	26,257	27,246	27,792	28,898	29,939
Government and government enterprises	39,380	41,025	42,062	42,296	43,015	43,612	43,980

Table SC-10. Employment Characteristics by Family Type

(Number, percent.)

Family type and labor force status	2011 Total	2011 Families with own children under 18 years	2012 Total	2012 Families with own children under 18 years	2013 Total	2013 Families with own children under 18 years
All Families	1,201,688	499,036	1,204,041	491,485	1,195,104	479,885
FAMILY TYPE AND LABOR FORCE STATUS						
Married-Couple Families	855,034	313,733	839,168	298,889	840,762	298,898
Both husband and wife in labor force	48.6	65.0	48.2	66.7	47.8	66.4
Husband in labor force, wife not in labor force	22.6	28.7	21.2	26.7	21.3	26.1
Wife in labor force, husband not in labor force	8.7	3.9	9.0	4.3	9.4	4.8
Both husband and wife not in labor force	20.1	2.4	21.6	2.2	21.2	2.5
Other Families	346,654	185,303	364,873	192,596	354,342	180,987
Female householder, no husband present	77.0	78.7	76.3	80.6	77.1	80.1
In labor force	52.2	64.6	52.3	66.5	52.2	65.8
Not in labor force	24.8	14.1	24.0	14.1	24.9	14.2
Male householder, no wife present	23.0	21.3	23.7	19.4	22.9	19.9
In labor force	17.5	18.7	17.5	17.8	16.7	17.9
Not in labor force	5.5	2.6	6.2	1.5	6.2	2.0

Table SC-11. School Enrollment and Educational Attainment, 2013

(Number, percent.)

Item	State	U.S.
Enrollment		
Total population 3 years and over, enrolled in school	1,210,706	82,395,254
Enrolled in nursery school or preschool (percent)	5.2	6.0
Enrolled in kindergarten (percent)	6.0	5.2
Enrolled in elementary school, grades 1-8 (percent)	39.9	40.0
Enrolled in high school, grades 9-12 (percent)	20.7	20.6
Enrolled in college or graduate school (percent)	28.3	28.3
Attainment		
Total population 25 years and over	3,198,816	210,910,615
Less than ninth grade (percent)	5.0	5.8
9th to 12th grade, no diploma (percent)	9.3	7.6
High school graduate, including equivalency (percent)	29.4	27.8
Some college, no degree (percent)	21.3	21.1
Associate's degree (percent)	8.9	8.1
Bachelor's degree (percent)	16.6	18.4
Graduate or professional degree (percent)	9.5	11.2
High school graduate or higher (percent)	85.6	86.6
Bachelor's degree or higher (percent)	26.1	29.6

Table SC-12. Public School Characteristics and Educational Indicators

(Number, percent; data derived from National Center of Education Statistics.)

Item	State	U.S.
Public Schools, 2012–2013 (except where noted)		
Number of school districts	103	18,093
Number of schools	1,239	98,454
Number of students (in thousands)	736	49,771
Number of teachers (in thousands)	48	3,109
Student-teacher ratio	15.3	16.0
Expenditures per student (dollars), FY 2012	9,077	10,667
Four-year adjusted cohort graduation rate (ACGR)[1,2]	77.6	81.4
Students eligible for free or reduced-price lunch (in thousands)	427	25,188
English language learners (in thousands)	41	4,397
Students age 3 to 21 served under IDEA, part B (in thousands)	100	6,429

Public Schools by Type	Number	Percent of state public schools
Total number of schools	1,239	100.0
Regular	1,166	94.1
Special education	10	0.8
Vocational education	42	3.4
Alternative education	21	1.7

NOTE: Every school is assigned only one school type based on its instructional emphasis.
[1]ACGR data represents a new method of calculating high-school completion rates and may not be comparable to previous years' data for Averaged Freshmen Graduation Rates (AFGR).
[2]The United States 4-year ACGRs were estimated using both the reported 4-year ACGR data from 49 states and the District of Columbia and using imputed data for Idaho. The estimate for American Indian/Alaska Native students also includes imputed data for Virginia.

Table SC-13. Reported Voting and Registration of the Voting-Age Population, November 2012

(Numbers in thousands, percent.)

Item	Total population	Total citizen population	Registered			Voted		
			Total registered	Percent registered (total population)	Percent registered (total citizen population)	Total voted	Percent voted (total population)	Percent voted (total citizen population)
U.S. Total	235,248	215,081	153,157	65.1	71.2	132,948	56.5	61.8
State Total	3,516	3,380	2,479	70.5	73.3	2,187	62.2	64.7
Sex								
Male	1,660	1,580	1,096	66.1	69.4	940	56.6	59.5
Female	1,856	1,801	1,382	74.5	76.8	1,247	67.2	69.3
Race								
White alone...........................	2,508	2,400	1,745	69.6	72.7	1,515	60.4	63.1
White, non-Hispanic alone...........	2,403	2,363	1,724	71.7	73.0	1,500	62.4	63.5
Black alone............................	919	911	691	75.1	75.8	631	68.7	69.3
Asian alone............................	48	30	17	B	B	17	B	B
Hispanic (of any race)................	114	37	21	18.7	B	16	13.6	B
White alone or in combination	2,538	2,429	1,760	69.4	72.5	1,529	60.2	62.9
Black alone or in combination..........	935	927	703	75.2	75.9	644	68.8	69.5
Asian alone or in combination..........	48	30	17	B	B	17	B	B
Age								
18 to 24 years............................	474	451	265	55.9	58.8	243	51.3	54.0
25 to 44 years............................	1,111	1,037	769	69.2	74.1	636	57.2	61.3
45 to 64 years............................	1,319	1,289	956	72.4	74.2	866	65.7	67.2
65 to 74 years............................	366	366	301	82.3	82.3	277	75.7	75.7
75 years and over	245	238	188	76.6	79.0	165	67.2	69.2

B = Base is less than 75,000 and therefore too small to show the derived measure.

Table SC-14. Crime

(Number, rate per 100,000. Data are derived from the FBI Uniform Crime Reports.)

Item	State			U.S.[1,2,3,4]		
	2012	2013	Percent change	2012	2013	Percent change
TOTAL POPULATION[5]...........................	4,723,417	4,774,839	1.1	313,873,685	316,128,839	0.7
VIOLENT CRIME						
Number..	26,474	23,625	-10.8	1,217,067	1,163,146	-4.4
Rate	560.5	494.8	-11.7	387.8	367.9	-5.1
Murder and Nonnegligent Manslaughter						
Number..	332	297	-10.5	14,866	14,196	-4.5
Rate	7.0	6.2	-11.5	4.7	4.5	-5.2
Rape[6]						
Number..	X	2,171	X	X	108,612	X
Rate	X	45.5	X	X	34.4	X
Robbery						
Number..	4,511	3,972	-11.9	355,051	345,031	-2.8
Rate	95.5	83.2	-12.9	113.1	109.1	-3.5
Aggravated Assault						
Number..	19,919	17,838	-10.4	762,009	724,149	-5.0
Rate	421.7	373.6	-11.4	242.8	229.1	-5.6
PROPERTY CRIME						
Number..	181,049	173,049	-4.4	9,001,992	8,632,512	-4.1
Rate	3,833.0	3,624.2	-5.4	2,868.0	2,730.7	-4.8
Burglary						
Number..	45,222	40,958	-9.4	2,109,932	1,928,465	-8.6
Rate	957.4	857.8	-10.4	672.2	610.0	-9.3
Larceny-Theft						
Number..	122,340	119,511	-2.3	6,168,874	6,004,453	-2.7
Rate	2,590.1	2,502.9	-3.4	1,965.4	1,899.4	-3.4
Motor Vehicle Theft						
Number..	13,487	12,580	-6.7	723,186	699,594	-3.3
Rate	285.5	263.5	-7.7	230.4	221.3	-4.0

NOTE: Although arson data are included in the trend and clearance tables, sufficient data are not available to estimate totals for this offense. Therefore, no arson data are published in this table.
X = Not applicable.
- = Zero or rounds to zero.
[1]The crime figures have been adjusted.
[2]The data collection methodology for the offense of forcible rape used by the Minnesota state Uniform Crime Reporting (UCR) Program (with the exception of Minneapolis and St. Paul, Minnesota) does not comply with national UCR Program guidelines. Consequently, its figures for forcible rape and violent crime (of which forcible rape is a part) are not published in this table.
[3]Includes offenses reported by the Zoological Police and the Metro Transit Police.
[4]Because of changes in the state's reporting practices, figures are not comparable to previous years' data.
[5]Populations are U.S. Census Bureau provisional estimates as of July 1 of each year.
[6]The figures shown for the offense of rape were estimated using the revised Uniform Crime Reporting (UCR) definition of rape.

Table SC-15. State Government Finances, 2013

(Dollar amounts in thousands, percent distribution.)

Item	Dollars	Percent distribution
Total Revenue	29,638,637	100.0
General revenue	22,160,859	74.8
Intergovernmental revenue	7,202,824	24.3
Taxes	8,721,305	29.4
General sales	3,199,752	10.8
Selective sales	1,277,230	4.3
License taxes	439,843	1.5
Individual income tax	3,357,518	11.3
Corporate income tax	386,669	1.3
Other taxes	60,293	0.2
Current charges	4,193,046	14.1
Miscellaneous general revenue	2,043,684	6.9
Utility revenue	1,874,959	6.3
Liquor stores revenue	0	-
Insurance trust revenue[1]	5,602,819	18.9
Total Expenditure	28,245,704	100.0
Intergovernmental expenditure	5,454,008	19.3
Direct expenditure	22,791,696	80.7
Current operation	15,772,341	55.8
Capital outlay	1,663,802	5.9
Insurance benefits and repayments	3,687,516	13.1
Assistance and subsidies	1,017,174	3.6
Interest on debt	650,863	2.3
Exhibit: Salaries and wages	3,596,657	12.7
Total Expenditure	28,245,704	100.0
General expenditure	22,331,442	79.1
Intergovernmental expenditure	5,454,008	19.3
Direct expenditure	16,877,434	59.8
General expenditure, by function:		
Education	8,352,080	29.6
Public welfare	6,050,877	21.4
Hospitals	1,444,046	5.1
Health	1,011,767	3.6
Highways	923,605	3.3
Police protection	183,055	0.6
Correction	490,627	1.7
Natural resources	196,531	0.7
Parks and recreation	86,910	0.3
Governmental administration	551,247	2.0
Interest on general debt	432,314	1.5
Other and unallocable	2,608,383	9.2
Utility expenditure	2,226,746	7.9
Liquor stores expenditure	0	-
Insurance trust expenditure	3,687,516	13.1
Debt at End of Fiscal Year	14,723,546	X
Cash and Security Holdings	41,024,628	X

X = Not applicable.
- = Zero or rounds to zero.
[1]Within insurance trust revenue, net earnings of state retirement systems is a calculated statistic (the item code in the data file is X08), and thus can be positive or negative. Net earnings is the sum of earnings on investments plus gains on investments minus losses on investments. The change made in 2002 for asset valuation from book to market value in accordance with Statement 34 of the Governmental Accounting Standards Board is reflected in the calculated statistics.

Table SC-16. State Government Tax Collections, 2014

(Dollars in thousands, percent.)

Item	Dollars	Percent distribution
Total Taxes	8,932,564	100.0
Property taxes	21,664	0.2
Sales and gross receipts	4,628,363	51.8
General sales and gross receipts	3,370,643	37.7
Selective sales and gross receipts	1,257,720	14.1
Alcoholic beverages	162,313	1.8
Amusements	38,481	0.4
Insurance premiums	214,600	2.4
Motor fuels	529,655	5.9
Pari-mutuels	0	-
Public utilities	28,450	0.3
Tobacco products	25,632	0.3
Other selective sales	258,589	2.9
Licenses	471,862	5.3
Alcoholic beverages	11,382	0.1
Amusements	1,371	-
Corporations in general	95,139	1.1
Hunting and fishing	17,541	0.2
Motor vehicle	214,192	2.4
Motor vehicle operators	8,813	0.1
Public utilities	10,144	0.1
Occupation and business, NEC	96,472	1.1
Other licenses	16,808	0.2
Income taxes	3,750,341	42.0
Individual income	3,422,532	38.3
Corporation net income	327,809	3.7
Other taxes	60,334	0.7
Death and gift	0	-
Documentary and stock transfer	60,334	0.7
Severance	X	X
Taxes, NEC	0	-

X = Not applicable.
- = Zero or rounds to zero.

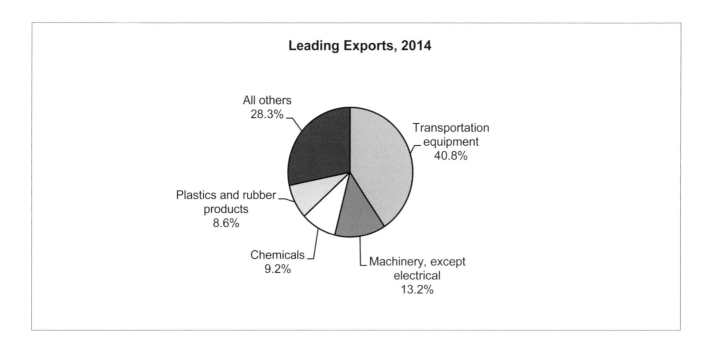

Leading Exports, 2014

All others 28.3%
Transportation equipment 40.8%
Plastics and rubber products 8.6%
Chemicals 9.2%
Machinery, except electrical 13.2%

SOUTH DAKOTA

Facts and Figures

Location: North central United States; bordered on the N by North Dakota, on the E by Minnesota and Iowa, on the S by Nebraska, and on the W by Wyoming and Montana

Area: 77,117 sq. mi. (199,731 sq. km.); rank—17th

Population: 853,175 (2014 est.); rank—46th

Principal Cities: capital—Pierre; largest—Sioux Falls

Statehood: November 2, 1889; 40th state

U.S. Congress: 2 senators, 1 representative

State Motto: Under God the People Rule

State Song: "Hail, South Dakota"

State Nickname: The Mount Rushmore State

Abbreviations: SD; S.D.; S. Dak.

State Symbols: flower—pasqueflower; tree—Black Hills spruce; bird—ring-necked pheasant

At a Glance

- With an increase in population of 4.8 percent, South Dakota ranked 10th among the states in growth from 2010 to 2014.

- In 2013, 11.3 percent of South Dakotans did not have health insurance, compared to 14.5 percent of the total U.S. population.

- South Dakota's violent crime rate in 2013 was 316.5 per 100,000 population, compared to 367.9 for the entire nation.

- South Dakota's median income in 2013 was $48,947, and 14.2 percent of its residents lived below the poverty level.

- In 2014, 3.4 percent of South Dakotans were unemployed, compared to 6.2 percent of the entire U.S. population.

Table SD-1. Population by Age, Sex, Race, and Hispanic Origin

(Number, percent, except where noted.)

Sex, age, race, and Hispanic origin	2000	2010	2014[1]	Average annual percent change, 2010–2014
Total Population	754,844	814,180	853,175	1.2
Percent of total U.S. population	0.4	0.3	0.3	X
Sex				
Male	374,558	407,381	429,313	1.3
Female	380,286	406,799	423,862	1.0
Age				
Under 5 years	51,069	59,621	60,610	0.4
5 to 19 years	176,412	167,119	173,778	1.0
20 to 64 years	419,232	470,859	488,564	0.9
65 years and over	108,131	116,581	130,223	2.8
Median age (years)	35.6	36.9	36.8	-0.1
Race and Hispanic Origin				
One race				
White	669,404	706,690	731,359	0.9
Black	4,685	10,533	15,971	11.0
American Indian and Alaska Native	62,283	72,782	75,879	1.0
Asian	4,378	7,775	10,739	8.4
Native Hawaiian or Other Pacific Islander	261	517	625	4.9
Two or more races	10,156	15,883	18,602	4.0
Hispanic (of any race)	10,903	23,699	30,537	6.5

X = Not applicable.

[1]Population figures for 2014 are July 1 estimates. The 2010 estimates are taken from the 2010 Census.

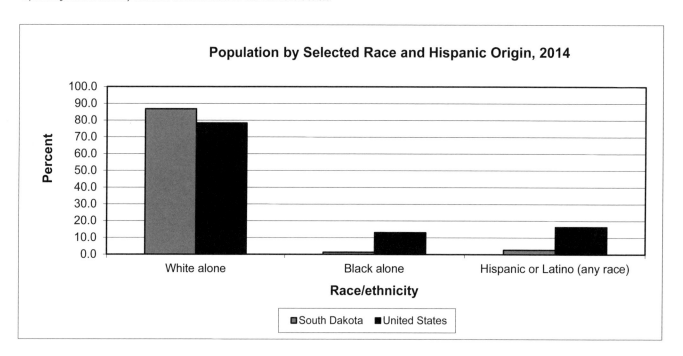

Population by Selected Race and Hispanic Origin, 2014

Table SD-2. Marital Status

(Number, percent distribution.)

Sex, age, race, and Hispanic origin	2000	2010	2013
Males, 15 Years and Over	289,858	322,689	333,069
Never married	29.8	33.5	33.2
Now married, except separated	58.2	52.5	53.3
Separated	1.0	0.9	0.7
Widowed	2.4	2.8	2.2
Divorced	8.5	10.3	10.6
Females, 15 Years and Over	299,754	325,640	335,742
Never married	22.5	26.0	26.5
Now married, except separated	55.9	52.1	51.6
Separated	1.1	1.0	1.3
Widowed	11.4	9.5	9.0
Divorced	9.0	11.4	11.6

Table SD-3. Households and Housing Characteristics

(Number, percent, dollars.)

Item	2000	2010	2013	Average annual percent change, 2000–2013
Total Households...	290,245	318,955	331,406	1.0
Family households	194,330	204,029	213,838	0.7
Married-couple family	157,391	161,534	166,793	0.4
Other family	36,939	42,495	47,045	1.9
Male householder, no wife present...................	10,734	12,526	15,340	2.8
Female householder, no husband present	26,205	29,969	31,705	1.5
Nonfamily households	95,915	114,926	117,568	1.6
Householder living alone	80,040	95,610	96,641	1.5
Householder not living alone.............................	15,875	19,316	20,927	2.1
Housing Characteristics				
Total housing units...	323,208	364,031	370,207	1.0
Occupied housing units	290,245	318,955	331,406	1.0
Owner occupied	197,940	216,821	222,809	0.9
Renter occupied	92,305	102,134	108,597	1.3
Average household size...	2.50	2.45	2.45	-0.2
Financial Characteristics				
Median gross rent of renter-occupied housing	426	591	637	3.1
Median monthly owner costs for housing units with a mortgage	828	1,151	1,150	2.6
Median value of owner-occupied housing units	79,600	129,700	138,400	4.3

Table SD-4. Migration, Origin, and Language

(Number, percent.)

Characteristic	State			U.S.		
	2012	2013	Percent change	2012	2013	Percent change
Residence 1 Year Ago						
Population 1 year and over	821,669	832,703	1.3	310,212,755	312,432,820	0.7
Same house	82.3	83.1	X	85.0	85.0	X
Different house in the U.S.	17.2	16.7	X	14.4	14.4	X
Same county	9.1	8.7	X	9.0	8.9	X
Different county	8.1	8.0	X	5.4	5.5	X
Same state	4.9	4.4	X	3.2	3.2	X
Different state	3.2	3.6	X	2.3	2.3	X
Abroad	0.5	0.3	X	0.6	0.6	X
Place of Birth						
Native born	810,497	820,418	1.2	273,089,382	274,780,773	0.6
Male	50.0	50.2	X	49.3	49.3	X
Female	50.0	49.8	X	50.7	50.7	X
Foreign born	22,857	24,459	7.0	40,824,658	41,348,066	1.3
Male	53.2	49.0	X	48.7	48.8	X
Female	46.8	51.0	X	51.3	51.2	X
Foreign born; naturalized U.S. citizen....................	8,804	8,035	-8.7	18,686,237	19,294,710	3.3
Male	45.9	49.5	X	45.8	45.9	X
Female	54.1	50.5	X	54.2	54.1	X
Foreign born; not a U.S. citizen	14,053	16,424	16.9	22,138,421	22,053,356	-0.4
Male	57.7	48.8	X	51.1	51.3	X
Female	42.3	51.2	X	48.9	48.7	X
Entered 2010 or later	21.8	20.6	X	7.0	9.7	X
Entered 2000 to 2009	39.8	39.9	X	30.4	29.4	X
Entered before 2000..	38.4	39.4	X	62.7	61.0	X
World Region of Birth, Foreign						
Foreign-born population, excluding population born at sea	22,857	24,459	7.0	40,824,553	41,347,945	1.3
Europe	16.3	15.6	X	11.8	11.6	X
Asia..	34.5	31.8	X	29.2	29.5	X
Africa	18.1	23.9	X	4.2	4.4	X
Oceania	0.6	0.6	X	0.6	0.5	X
Latin America...	26.7	23.9	X	52.2	51.9	X
North America..	3.9	4.2	X	2.0	2.0	X
Language Spoken at Home and Ability to Speak English						
Population 5 years and over....................................	774,671	786,260	1.5	294,003,714	296,358,760	0.8
English only	93.7	93.5	X	79.0	79.2	X
Language other than English..................................	6.3	6.5	X	21.0	20.8	X
Speaks English less than "very well"...................	2.3	1.9	X	8.5	8.5	X

NA = Not available.
X = Not applicable.
- = Zero or rounds to zero.

Table SD-5. Median Income and Poverty Status, 2013

(Number, percent, except as noted.)

Characteristic	State		U.S.	
	Number	Percent	Number	Percent
Median Income				
Households (dollars)..	48,947	X	52,250	X
Families (dollars)	61,299	X	64,030	X
Below Poverty Level (All People)...	115,454	14.2	48,810,868	15.8
Sex				
Male..	52,278	12.8	21,938,525	14.5
Female..	63,176	15.5	26,872,343	17.1
Age				
Under 18 years..	37,739	18.6	16,086,960	22.2
Related children under 18 years...	36,817	18.2	15,769,921	21.9
18 to 64 years...	65,802	13.3	28,578,191	14.8
65 years and over	11,913	10.1	4,145,717	9.6

X = Not applicable.

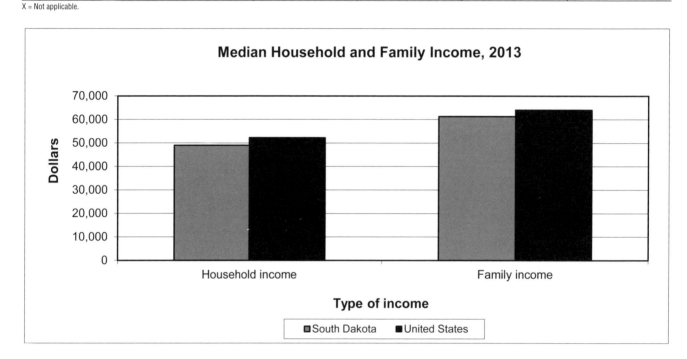

Table SD-6. Health Insurance Coverage Status for the Civilian Noninstitutionalized Population and Children Under 18 Years of Age

(Numbers in thousands, percent.)

Item	2005	2006	2007	2008	2009	2010	2011	2012	2013
Civilian Noninstitutionalized Population..................................	768	770	788	784	793	798	806	816	827
Covered by Private or Public Insurance									
Number...	679	679	708	692	689	699	710	722	734
Percent...	88.3	88.2	89.9	88.3	86.9	87.6	88.1	88.5	88.7
Not Covered									
Number...	90	91	80	92	104	99	96	94	93
Percent...	11.7	11.8	10.1	11.7	13.1	12.4	11.9	11.5	11.3
Percent in the U.S. not covered...	15.3	15.8	15.3	15.1	15.1	15.5	15.1	14.8	14.5
Children Under 18 Years of Age..	188	193	198	196	195	201	201	203	207
Covered by Private or Public Insurance									
Number...	173	175	183	179	180	184	189	191	194
Percent...	91.9	90.8	92.0	91.3	92.4	91.7	94.0	94.2	93.7
Not Covered									
Number...	15	18	16	17	15	17	12	12	13
Percent...	8.1	9.2	8.0	8.7	7.6	8.3	6.0	5.8	6.3
Percent in the U.S. not covered...	10.9	11.7	11.0	9.7	8.6	8.0	7.5	7.2	7.1

Table SD-7. Employment Status by Demographic Group, 2014

(Numbers in thousands, percent.)

Characteristic	Civilian noninstitutional population	Civilian labor force		Employed		Unemployed	
		Number	Percent of population	Number	Percent of population	Number	Percent of population
Total..	647	449	69.3	433	66.9	16	3.5
Sex							
Male..	320	238	74.3	230	71.8	8	3.3
Female	327	211	64.5	203	62.1	8	3.7
Race, Sex, and Hispanic Origin							
White	588	413	70.1	401	68.2	11	2.8
Male..	291	218	75.1	212	72.9	6	2.8
Female	298	194	65.3	189	63.5	5	2.7
Black or African American............................	NA	NA	NA	NA	NA	NA	NA
Male..	NA	NA	NA	NA	NA	NA	NA
Female	NA	NA	NA	NA	NA	NA	NA
Hispanic or Latino ethnicity[1]	15	12	82.5	12	77.4	1	6.1
Male..	NA	NA	NA	NA	NA	NA	NA
Female	NA	NA	NA	NA	NA	NA	NA
Age							
16 to 19 years...	41	21	50.0	18	44.4	2	11.1
20 to 24 years...	58	44	76.1	41	71.3	3	6.4
25 to 34 years...	116	104	89.3	101	86.5	3	3.2
35 to 44 years...	91	80	87.8	78	85.3	2	2.8
45 to 54 years...	104	89	85.9	87	83.7	2	2.5
55 to 64 years...	107	81	75.2	78	73.2	2	2.6
65 years and over	130	31	23.6	30	23.2	1	1.9

NOTE: Data in Table 7 are from the Current Population Survey (CPS) and do not match the estimates in Table 8. See notes and definitions for further information.
[1]May be of any race.
NA = Not available.

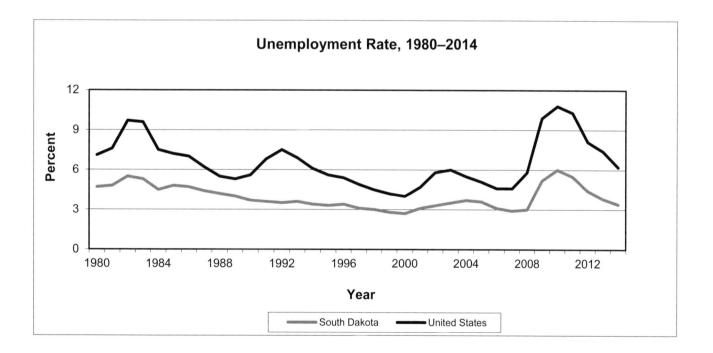

Table SD-8. Employment Status of the Civilian Noninstitutional Population Age 16 Years and Over

(Number, percent.)

Year	Civilian labor force	Civilian participation rate	Employed	Unemployed	Unemployment rate
2006	435,007	72.8	421,483	13,524	3.1
2007	442,499	73.2	430,011	12,488	2.8
2008	446,618	73.0	432,925	13,693	3.1
2009	446,010	72.2	423,993	22,017	4.9
2010	441,339	71.3	419,355	21,984	5.0
2011	440,865	70.6	419,998	20,867	4.7
2012	442,551	69.9	423,644	18,907	4.3
2013	444,975	69.4	428,162	16,813	3.8
2014	448,201	69.2	432,973	15,228	3.4

Table SD-9. Employment and Average Wages by Industry

(Estimates from 2007 through 2010 are based on the 2007 *North American Industry Classification System* [NAICS]. Estimates from 2011 onward are based on the 2012 NAICS.)

Industry	2007	2008	2009	2010	2011	2012	2013
	Number of jobs						
Wage and Salary Employment by Industry	424,522	431,600	423,697	425,114	430,256	436,165	439,202
Farm Wage and Salary Employment	5,224	5,446	4,595	5,049	5,522	7,410	6,538
Nonfarm Wage and Salary Employment	419,298	426,154	419,102	420,065	424,734	428,755	432,664
Private wage and salary employment	338,828	344,190	334,741	334,353	339,612	344,489	348,757
Forestry, fishing, and related activities	1,653	1,685	1,659	1,750	1,887	1,888	2,336
Mining	849	932	836	818	832	849	846
Utilities	2,229	2,073	2,112	2,092	2,071	1,968	1,950
Construction	23,052	23,157	21,842	21,086	21,234	20,833	21,249
Manufacturing	42,105	42,789	37,806	37,044	39,291	41,244	41,582
Durable goods manufacturing	28,882	29,331	24,780	24,033	25,909	27,225	27,535
Nondurable goods manufacturing	13,223	13,458	13,026	13,011	13,382	14,019	14,047
Wholesale trade	18,502	18,854	18,474	18,741	19,138	19,596	19,988
Retail trade	50,641	50,829	50,351	50,354	50,958	51,535	51,742
Transportation and warehousing	10,923	11,012	10,617	10,484	10,576	10,547	10,563
Information	7,170	6,967	6,709	6,556	6,388	6,213	6,034
Finance and insurance	27,562	27,632	27,150	26,098	25,537	26,149	27,155
Real estate and rental and leasing	3,770	3,815	3,700	3,540	3,561	3,552	3,649
Professional, scientific, and technical services	10,630	11,167	11,210	11,363	11,353	11,662	12,569
Management of companies and enterprises	3,039	3,500	3,474	3,624	3,768	4,145	4,234
Administrative and waste services	14,155	13,925	12,568	12,965	13,850	13,645	13,125
Educational services	7,307	7,562	7,547	7,755	7,995	8,257	8,104
Health care and social assistance	53,089	55,047	56,043	57,046	57,726	59,188	59,915
Arts, entertainment, and recreation	6,828	6,694	6,564	6,492	6,494	6,355	6,218
Accommodation and food services	36,704	37,003	36,822	37,067	37,497	38,265	38,738
Other services, except public administration	18,620	19,547	19,257	19,478	19,456	18,598	18,760
Government and government enterprises	80,470	81,964	84,361	85,712	85,122	84,266	83,907
	Dollars						
Average Wages and Salaries by Industry	31,585	32,681	33,063	33,922	34,997	36,143	36,818
Average Farm Wages and Salaries	43,389	48,558	43,156	36,547	39,449	40,233	42,115
Average Nonfarm Wages and Salaries	31,438	32,478	32,952	33,890	34,939	36,072	36,738
Average private wages and salaries	31,205	32,238	32,635	33,664	34,871	36,137	36,880
Forestry, fishing, and related activities	22,878	23,228	23,896	25,166	26,424	26,815	27,262
Mining	46,789	51,013	46,606	49,559	55,826	57,390	55,916
Utilities	61,702	62,172	61,671	64,919	67,087	69,488	73,263
Construction	35,825	36,834	38,064	38,086	38,975	39,916	40,944
Manufacturing	37,078	37,766	38,331	39,905	41,470	42,169	42,441
Durable goods manufacturing	37,049	38,057	38,738	40,479	42,408	42,827	43,521
Nondurable goods manufacturing	37,140	37,130	37,556	38,844	39,653	40,891	40,324
Wholesale trade	43,183	45,108	45,552	46,634	48,900	51,348	52,936
Retail trade	21,489	21,951	22,174	23,106	23,737	24,553	25,175
Transportation and warehousing	37,116	38,531	38,151	39,442	41,362	42,678	42,658
Information	38,499	39,198	39,258	39,883	41,852	42,761	43,315
Finance and insurance	42,571	43,764	44,097	45,798	48,146	49,779	50,341
Real estate and rental and leasing	24,689	25,308	25,806	26,736	28,099	29,592	30,629
Professional, scientific, and technical services	43,329	45,148	44,612	46,400	49,024	51,611	49,892
Management of companies and enterprises	72,121	78,377	74,858	88,748	88,044	89,097	91,512
Administrative and waste services	24,236	23,904	24,478	25,336	25,528	26,948	27,162
Educational services	21,688	22,972	23,579	24,613	24,618	23,821	24,751
Health care and social assistance	36,510	38,257	39,496	40,093	41,580	43,084	44,302
Arts, entertainment, and recreation	17,867	17,459	17,863	17,795	18,001	17,939	18,142
Accommodation and food services	13,119	13,271	13,390	14,050	14,494	14,922	15,243
Other services, except public administration	22,182	22,661	23,171	23,623	24,220	25,654	26,270
Government and government enterprises	32,417	33,486	34,210	34,770	35,210	35,806	36,147

Table SD-10. Employment Characteristics by Family Type

(Number, percent.)

Family type and labor force status	2011		2012		2013	
	Total	Families with own children under 18 years	Total	Families with own children under 18 years	Total	Families with own children under 18 years
All Families	210,679	91,614	206,668	88,894	213,838	94,183
FAMILY TYPE AND LABOR FORCE STATUS						
Married-Couple Families	163,103	61,158	159,567	58,663	166,793	62,905
Both husband and wife in labor force	63.0	78.5	61.6	79.2	62.3	79.6
Husband in labor force, wife not in labor force	15.0	18.0	16.0	17.0	15.5	15.6
Wife in labor force, husband not in labor force	6.3	2.2	7.3	3.0	6.9	3.1
Both husband and wife not in labor force	15.8	1.2	15.1	0.8	14.9	1.4
Other Families	47,576	30,456	47,101	30,231	47,045	31,278
Female householder, no husband present	66.1	70.3	70.4	73.9	67.4	69.9
In labor force	53.0	62.9	54.9	65.9	51.0	58.5
Not in labor force	13.1	7.4	15.5	8.0	16.4	11.4
Male householder, no wife present	33.9	29.7	29.6	26.1	32.6	30.1
In labor force	26.9	26.9	23.9	23.4	25.6	26.9
Not in labor force	6.9	2.8	5.6	2.7	7.0	3.2

Table SD-11. School Enrollment and Educational Attainment, 2013

(Number, percent.)

Item	State	U.S.
Enrollment		
Total population 3 years and over, enrolled in school	219,960	82,395,254
Enrolled in nursery school or preschool (percent)	5.9	6.0
Enrolled in kindergarten (percent)	6.4	5.2
Enrolled in elementary school, grades 1-8 (percent)	41.2	40.0
Enrolled in high school, grades 9-12 (percent)	20.1	20.6
Enrolled in college or graduate school (percent)	26.4	28.3
Attainment		
Total population 25 years and over	550,959	210,910,615
Less than ninth grade (percent)	3.5	5.8
9th to 12th grade, no diploma (percent)	4.9	7.6
High school graduate, including equivalency (percent)	31.3	27.8
Some college, no degree (percent)	22.3	21.1
Associate's degree (percent)	11.4	8.1
Bachelor's degree (percent)	18.9	18.4
Graduate or professional degree (percent)	7.6	11.2
High school graduate or higher (percent)	91.6	86.6
Bachelor's degree or higher (percent)	26.6	29.6

Table SD-12. Public School Characteristics and Educational Indicators

(Number, percent; data derived from National Center of Education Statistics.)

Item	State	U.S.
Public Schools, 2012–2013 (except where noted)		
Number of school districts	170	18,093
Number of schools	697	98,454
Number of students (in thousands)	130	49,771
Number of teachers (in thousands)	9	3,109
Student-teacher ratio	14.0	16.0
Expenditures per student (dollars), FY 2012	8,593	10,667
Four-year adjusted cohort graduation rate (ACGR)[1,2]	82.7	81.4
Students eligible for free or reduced-price lunch (in thousands)	52	25,188
English language learners (in thousands)	5	4,397
Students age 3 to 21 served under IDEA, part B (in thousands)	18	6,429

Public Schools by Type	Number	Percent of state public schools
Total number of schools	697	100.0
Regular	651	93.4
Special education	9	1.3
Vocational education	3	0.4
Alternative education	34	4.9

NOTE: Every school is assigned only one school type based on its instructional emphasis.
[1]ACGR data represents a new method of calculating high-school completion rates and may not be comparable to previous years' data for Averaged Freshmen Graduation Rates (AFGR).
[2]The United States 4-year ACGRs were estimated using both the reported 4-year ACGR data from 49 states and the District of Columbia and using imputed data for Idaho. The estimate for American Indian/Alaska Native students also includes imputed data for Virginia.

Table SD-13. Reported Voting and Registration of the Voting-Age Population, November 2012

(Numbers in thousands, percent.)

Item	Total population	Total citizen population	Registered			Voted		
			Total registered	Percent registered (total population)	Percent registered (total citizen population)	Total voted	Percent voted (total population)	Percent voted (total citizen population)
U.S. Total	235,248	215,081	153,157	65.1	71.2	132,948	56.5	61.8
State Total	616	607	454	73.7	74.8	370	60.1	61.0
Sex								
Male	304	300	220	72.3	73.3	180	59.1	59.9
Female	312	307	235	75.1	76.3	191	61.1	62.0
Race								
White alone	541	536	405	74.9	75.6	341	63.0	63.5
White, non-Hispanic alone	527	526	400	75.9	76.1	338	64.2	64.3
Black alone	6	5	3	B	B	-	B	B
Asian alone	4	1	1	B	B	-	B	B
Hispanic (of any race)	16	13	6	B	B	3	B	B
White alone or in combination	550	545	411	74.7	75.4	343	62.5	63.0
Black alone or in combination	9	8	4	B	B	2	B	B
Asian alone or in combination	4	1	1	B	B	-	B	B
Age								
18 to 24 years	95	94	52	54.4	54.7	31	32.7	32.9
25 to 44 years	186	180	130	69.8	71.9	99	53.2	54.7
45 to 64 years	204	202	167	82.0	82.7	145	70.9	71.5
65 to 74 years	77	76	61	79.7	80.9	56	73.4	74.4
75 years and over	55	55	45	B	B	40	B	B

- = Zero or rounds to zero.
B = Base is less than 75,000 and therefore too small to show the derived measure.

Table SD-14. Crime

(Number, rate per 100,000. Data are derived from the FBI Uniform Crime Reports.)

Item	State			U.S.[1,2,3,4]		
	2012	2013	Percent change	2012	2013	Percent change
TOTAL POPULATION[5]	834,047	844,877	1.3	313,873,685	316,128,839	0.7
VIOLENT CRIME						
Number	2,701	2,524	-6.6	1,217,067	1,163,146	-4.4
Rate	323.8	298.7	-7.8	387.8	367.9	-5.1
Murder and Nonnegligent Manslaughter						
Number	23	20	-13.0	14,866	14,196	-4.5
Rate	2.8	2.4	-14.2	4.7	4.5	-5.2
Rape[6]						
Number	X	499	X	X	108,612	X
Rate	X	59.1	X	X	34.4	X
Robbery						
Number	157	159	1.3	355,051	345,031	-2.8
Rate	18.8	18.8	-	113.1	109.1	-3.5
Aggravated Assault						
Number	1,921	1,996	3.9	762,009	724,149	-5.0
Rate	230.3	236.2	2.6	242.8	229.1	-5.6
PROPERTY CRIME						
Number	17,326	16,177	-6.6	9,001,992	8,632,512	-4.1
Rate	2,077.3	1,914.7	-7.8	2,868.0	2,730.7	-4.8
Burglary						
Number	3,280	3,372	2.8	2,109,932	1,928,465	-8.6
Rate	393.3	399.1	1.5	672.2	610.0	-9.3
Larceny-Theft						
Number	12,973	11,867	-8.5	6,168,874	6,004,453	-2.7
Rate	1,555.4	1,404.6	-9.7	1,965.4	1,899.4	-3.4
Motor Vehicle Theft						
Number	1,073	938	-12.6	723,186	699,594	-3.3
Rate	128.6	111.0	-13.7	230.4	221.3	-4.0

NOTE: Although arson data are included in the trend and clearance tables, sufficient data are not available to estimate totals for this offense. Therefore, no arson data are published in this table.
X = Not applicable.
- = Zero or rounds to zero.
[1]The crime figures have been adjusted.
[2]The data collection methodology for the offense of forcible rape used by the Minnesota state Uniform Crime Reporting (UCR) Program (with the exception of Minneapolis and St. Paul, Minnesota) does not comply with national UCR Program guidelines. Consequently, its figures for forcible rape and violent crime (of which forcible rape is a part) are not published in this table.
[3]Includes offenses reported by the Zoological Police and the Metro Transit Police.
[4]Because of changes in the state's reporting practices, figures are not comparable to previous years' data.
[5]Populations are U.S. Census Bureau provisional estimates as of July 1 of each year.
[6]The figures shown for the offense of rape were estimated using the revised Uniform Crime Reporting (UCR) definition of rape.

Table SD-15. State Government Finances, 2013

(Dollar amounts in thousands, percent distribution.)

Item	Dollars	Percent distribution
Total Revenue	5,759,268	100.0
General revenue	4,035,680	70.1
Intergovernmental revenue	1,605,537	27.9
Taxes	1,533,663	26.6
General sales	853,570	14.8
Selective sales	374,692	6.5
License taxes	257,220	4.5
Individual income tax	0	-
Corporate income tax	37,172	0.6
Other taxes	11,009	0.2
Current charges	344,499	6.0
Miscellaneous general revenue	551,981	9.6
Utility revenue	0	-
Liquor stores revenue	0	-
Insurance trust revenue[1]	1,723,588	29.9
Total Expenditure	4,476,725	100.0
Intergovernmental expenditure	740,104	16.5
Direct expenditure	3,736,621	83.5
Current operation	2,433,676	54.4
Capital outlay	639,183	14.3
Insurance benefits and repayments	465,639	10.4
Assistance and subsidies	83,929	1.9
Interest on debt	114,194	2.6
Exhibit: Salaries and wages	956,329	21.4
Total Expenditure	4,476,725	100.0
General expenditure	4,011,086	89.6
Intergovernmental expenditure	740,104	16.5
Direct expenditure	3,270,982	73.1
General expenditure, by function:		
Education	1,266,106	28.3
Public welfare	971,649	21.7
Hospitals	21,930	0.5
Health	178,414	4.0
Highways	653,007	14.6
Police protection	38,321	0.9
Correction	116,535	2.6
Natural resources	178,255	4.0
Parks and recreation	46,133	1.0
Governmental administration	166,448	3.7
Interest on general debt	114,194	2.6
Other and unallocable	260,094	5.8
Utility expenditure	0	-
Liquor stores expenditure	0	-
Insurance trust expenditure	465,639	10.4
Debt at End of Fiscal Year	3,425,424	X
Cash and Security Holdings	14,201,763	X

X = Not applicable.
- = Zero or rounds to zero.
[1]Within insurance trust revenue, net earnings of state retirement systems is a calculated statistic (the item code in the data file is X08), and thus can be positive or negative. Net earnings is the sum of earnings on investments plus gains on investments minus losses on investments. The change made in 2002 for asset valuation from book to market value in accordance with Statement 34 of the Governmental Accounting Standards Board is reflected in the calculated statistics.

Table SD-16. State Government Tax Collections, 2014

(Dollars in thousands, percent.)

Item	Dollars	Percent distribution
Total Taxes	1,608,496	100.0
Property taxes	X	X
Sales and gross receipts	1,296,748	80.6
General sales and gross receipts	914,979	56.9
Selective sales and gross receipts	381,769	23.7
Alcoholic beverages	16,205	1.0
Amusements	8,885	0.6
Insurance premiums	77,374	4.8
Motor fuels	138,087	8.6
Pari-mutuels	461	-
Public utilities	3,709	0.2
Tobacco products	61,811	3.8
Other selective sales	75,237	4.7
Licenses	277,787	17.3
Alcoholic beverages	840	0.1
Amusements	6,980	0.4
Corporations in general	4,688	0.3
Hunting and fishing	27,781	1.7
Motor vehicle	76,143	4.7
Motor vehicle operators	3,773	0.2
Public utilities	0	-
Occupation and business, NEC	135,841	8.4
Other licenses	21,741	1.4
Income taxes	24,819	1.5
Individual income	X	X
Corporation net income	24,819	1.5
Other taxes	9,142	0.6
Death and gift	0	-
Documentary and stock transfer	192	-
Severance	8,950	0.6
Taxes, NEC	0	-

X = Not applicable.
- = Zero or rounds to zero.

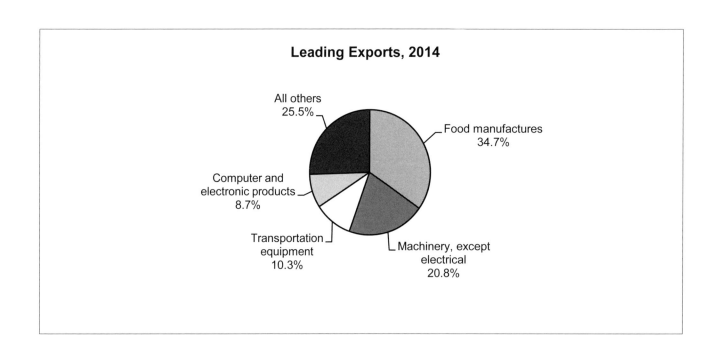

Leading Exports, 2014

- All others 25.5%
- Food manufactures 34.7%
- Computer and electronic products 8.7%
- Transportation equipment 10.3%
- Machinery, except electrical 20.8%

TENNESSEE

Facts and Figures

Location: South central United States; bordered on the N by Kentucky and Virginia, on the E by North Carolina, on the S by Georgia, Alabama, and Mississippi, and on the W by Arkansas and Missouri

Area: 42,143 sq. mi. (109,151 sq. km.); rank—36th

Population: 6,549,352 (2014 est.); rank—17th

Principal Cities: capital—Nashville; largest—Memphis

Statehood: June 1, 1796; 16th state

U.S. Congress: 2 senators, 9 representatives

State Motto: Agriculture and Commerce

State Song: "The Tennessee Waltz"

State Nickname: The Volunteer State

Abbreviations: TN; Tenn.

State Symbols: flower—iris; tree—yellow poplar (tulip poplar); bird—mockingbird

At a Glance

- With an increase in population of 3.2 percent, Tennessee ranked 25th among the states in growth from 2010 to 2014.

- Tennessee's median household income in 2013 was $44,297, and 17.8 percent of the population lived below the poverty level.

- In 2013, 13.9 percent of Tennesseans did not have health insurance, compared to 14.5 percent of the total U.S. population.

- Tennessee's violent crime rate in 2013 was 590.6 per 100,000 population, compared to 367.9 for the entire nation; this was the 5th highest rate in the country.

- The traffic fatality rate in Tennessee ranked 10th in the country in 2013, with 1.40 deaths per 100 million miles driven, compared to the national average of 1.09 deaths per 100 million miles driven.

Table TN-1. Population by Age, Sex, Race, and Hispanic Origin

(Number, percent, except where noted.)

Sex, age, race, and Hispanic origin	2000	2010	2014[1]	Average annual percent change, 2010–2014
Total Population	5,689,283	6,346,105	6,549,352	0.8
Percent of total U.S. population	2.0	2.1	2.1	X
Sex				
Male	2,770,275	3,093,504	3,192,180	0.8
Female	2,919,008	3,252,601	3,357,172	0.8
Age				
Under 5 years	374,880	407,813	400,431	-0.5
5 to 19 years	1,186,152	1,268,308	1,259,424	-0.2
20 to 64 years	3,424,940	3,816,522	3,903,797	0.6
65 years and over	703,311	853,462	985,700	3.7
Median age (years)	35.9	38.0	38.6	0.4
Race and Hispanic Origin				
One race				
White	4,563,310	5,056,311	5,169,234	0.6
Black	932,809	1,068,010	1,119,119	1.2
American Indian and Alaska Native	15,152	26,256	28,845	2.4
Asian	56,662	93,897	112,524	4.6
Native Hawaiian or Other Pacific Islander	2,205	5,426	6,192	3.4
Two or more races	63,109	96,205	113,438	4.2
Hispanic (of any race)	123,838	301,090	328,979	2.2

X = Not applicable.
[1]Population figures for 2014 are July 1 estimates. The 2010 estimates are taken from the 2010 Census.

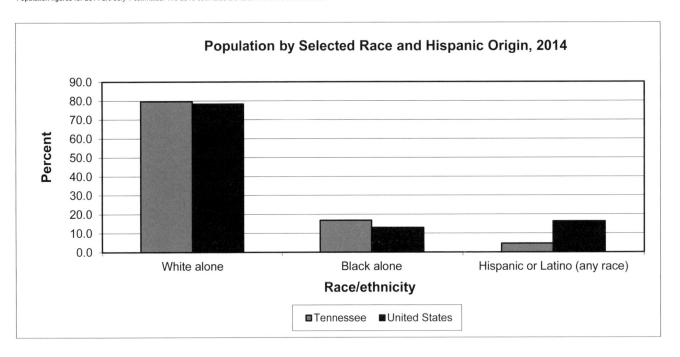

Table TN-2. Marital Status

(Number, percent distribution.)

Sex, age, race, and Hispanic origin	2000	2010	2013
Males, 15 Years and Over	2,169,327	2,461,573	2,537,029
Never married	26.6	31.4	32.1
Now married, except separated	58.9	52.2	51.3
Separated	1.7	2.1	1.9
Widowed	2.5	2.7	2.7
Divorced	10.4	11.7	12.0
Females, 15 Years and Over	2,353,303	2,652,823	2,718,099
Never married	20.7	25.3	26.6
Now married, except separated	53.6	47.9	47.4
Separated	2.3	2.7	2.6
Widowed	11.2	10.3	10.0
Divorced	12.2	13.7	13.3

Table TN-3. Households and Housing Characteristics

(Number, percent, dollars.)

Item	2000	2010	2013	Average annual percent change, 2000–2013
Total Households............................	2,232,905	2,440,663	2,490,249	0.8
Family households	1,547,835	1,644,896	1,658,071	0.5
Married-couple family	1,173,960	1,195,406	1,208,430	0.2
Other family	373,875	449,490	449,641	1.4
Male householder, no wife present............	85,976	106,616	116,605	2.4
Female householder, no husband present........	287,899	342,874	333,036	1.1
Nonfamily households	685,070	795,767	832,178	1.5
Householder living alone............................	576,401	675,565	700,694	1.5
Householder not living alone........................	108,669	120,202	131,484	1.5
Housing Characteristics				
Total housing units............................	2,439,443	2,815,087	2,840,998	1.2
Occupied housing units	2,232,905	2,440,663	2,490,249	0.8
Owner occupied	1,561,363	1,662,768	1,652,976	0.4
Renter occupied	671,542	777,895	837,273	1.7
Average household size............................	2.48	2.54	2.55	0.2
Financial Characteristics				
Median gross rent of renter-occupied housing	505	697	748	3.1
Median monthly owner costs for housing units with a mortgage	882	1,161	1,138	2.0
Median value of owner-occupied housing units............	93,000	139,000	140,300	3.2

Table TN-4. Migration, Origin, and Language

(Number, percent.)

Characteristic	State 2012	State 2013	State Percent change	U.S. 2012	U.S. 2013	U.S. Percent change
Residence 1 Year Ago						
Population 1 year and over	6,378,278	6,419,226	0.6	310,212,755	312,432,820	0.7
Same house	84.6	84.6	X	85.0	85.0	X
Different house in the U.S.	15.1	15.0	X	14.4	14.4	X
Same county	9.1	9.2	X	9.0	8.9	X
Different county	5.9	5.9	X	5.4	5.5	X
Same state	3.1	3.0	X	3.2	3.2	X
Different state	2.8	2.9	X	2.3	2.3	X
Abroad	0.3	0.4	X	0.6	0.6	X
Place of Birth						
Native born	6,164,602	6,191,177	0.4	273,089,382	274,780,773	0.6
Male	48.6	48.7	X	49.3	49.3	X
Female	51.4	51.3	X	50.7	50.7	X
Foreign born	291,641	304,801	4.5	40,824,658	41,348,066	1.3
Male	52.0	53.2	X	48.7	48.8	X
Female	48.0	46.8	X	51.3	51.2	X
Foreign born; naturalized U.S. citizen............	105,025	114,362	8.9	18,686,237	19,294,710	3.3
Male............	47.2	48.8	X	45.8	45.9	X
Female............	52.8	51.2	X	54.2	54.1	X
Foreign born; not a U.S. citizen............	186,616	190,439	2.0	22,138,421	22,053,356	-0.4
Male............	54.8	55.8	X	51.1	51.3	X
Female............	45.2	44.2	X	48.9	48.7	X
Entered 2010 or later	9.4	12.8	X	7.0	9.7	X
Entered 2000 to 2009	41.2	41.8	X	30.4	29.4	X
Entered before 2000............................	49.4	45.4	X	62.7	61.0	X
World Region of Birth, Foreign						
Foreign-born population, excluding population born at sea	291,641	304,801	4.5	40,824,553	41,347,945	1.3
Europe	11.3	9.6	X	11.8	11.6	X
Asia............................	29.6	29.9	X	29.2	29.5	X
Africa............................	8.1	10.7	X	4.2	4.4	X
Oceania............................	0.6	0.4	X	0.6	0.5	X
Latin America	46.9	46.8	X	52.2	51.9	X
North America............................	3.5	2.6	X	2.0	2.0	X
Language Spoken at Home and Ability to Speak English						
Population 5 years and over............................	6,056,220	6,098,770	0.7	294,003,714	296,358,760	0.8
English only	93.3	93.5	X	79.0	79.2	X
Language other than English............................	6.7	6.5	X	21.0	20.8	X
Speaks English less than "very well"............	2.6	2.7	X	8.5	8.5	X

NA = Not available.
X = Not applicable.
- = Zero or rounds to zero.

Table TN-5. Median Income and Poverty Status, 2013

(Number, percent, except as noted.)

Characteristic	State		U.S.	
	Number	Percent	Number	Percent
Median Income				
Households (dollars)....................................	44,297	X	52,250	X
Families (dollars)	54,691	X	64,030	X
Below Poverty Level (All People)...................	1,126,772	17.8	48,810,868	15.8
Sex				
Male..	509,172	16.5	21,938,525	14.5
Female	617,600	19.0	26,872,343	17.1
Age				
Under 18 years...	389,536	26.5	16,086,960	22.2
Related children under 18 years......................	383,703	26.2	15,769,921	21.9
18 to 64 years...	647,870	16.4	28,578,191	14.8
65 years and over	89,366	9.7	4,145,717	9.6

X = Not applicable.

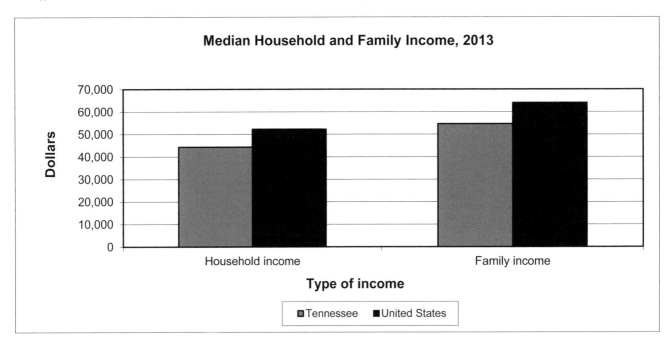

Table TN-6. Health Insurance Coverage Status for the Civilian Noninstitutionalized Population and Children Under 18 Years of Age

(Numbers in thousands, percent.)

Item	2005	2006	2007	2008	2009	2010	2011	2012	2013
Civilian Noninstitutionalized Population...............................	5,867	5,920	6,150	6,113	6,188	6,260	6,302	6,355	6,395
Covered by Private or Public Insurance									
Number..	5,069	5,111	5,268	5,279	5,305	5,361	5,380	5,473	5,508
Percent..	86.4	86.3	85.6	86.4	85.7	85.6	85.4	86.1	86.1
Not Covered									
Number..	798	809	883	834	883	899	923	882	887
Percent..	13.6	13.7	14.4	13.6	14.3	14.4	14.6	13.9	13.9
Percent in the U.S. not covered..	15.3	15.8	15.3	15.1	15.1	15.5	15.1	14.8	14.5
Children Under 18 Years of Age...	1,403	1,468	1,479	1,476	1,488	1,493	1,488	1,490	1,490
Covered by Private or Public Insurance									
Number..	1,276	1,376	1,344	1,370	1,401	1,414	1,403	1,405	1,404
Percent..	90.9	93.6	90.9	92.8	94.1	94.7	94.3	94.3	94.3
Not Covered									
Number..	127	94	135	106	87	79	85	85	85
Percent..	9.1	6.4	9.1	7.2	5.9	5.3	5.7	5.7	5.7
Percent in the U.S. not covered..	10.9	11.7	11.0	9.7	8.6	8.0	7.5	7.2	7.1

Table TN-7. Employment Status by Demographic Group, 2014

(Numbers in thousands, percent.)

Characteristic	Civilian noninstitutional population	Civilian labor force		Employed		Unemployed	
		Number	Percent of population	Number	Percent of population	Number	Percent of population
Total...	5,117	3,025	59.1	2,826	55.2	199	6.6
Sex							
Male..	2,441	1,613	66.1	1,513	62.0	100	6.2
Female	2,676	1,412	52.8	1,313	49.1	99	7.0
Race, Sex, and Hispanic Origin							
White	4,148	2,421	58.4	2,287	55.1	134	5.5
Male	2,009	1,329	66.2	1,260	62.7	69	5.2
Female	2,139	1,092	51.1	1,027	48.0	65	6.0
Black or African American........................	815	513	63.0	454	55.7	59	11.5
Male	368	244	66.2	215	58.3	29	11.9
Female	447	270	60.3	239	53.6	30	11.2
Hispanic or Latino ethnicity[1]	247	175	70.8	167	67.7	8	4.4
Male	131	113	86.0	108	82.7	4	3.9
Female	116	62	53.6	59	50.8	3	5.3
Age							
16 to 19 years.................................	391	137	35.0	111	28.2	26	19.3
20 to 24 years.................................	400	292	73.0	255	63.8	37	12.6
25 to 34 years.................................	791	620	78.4	572	72.3	48	7.7
35 to 44 years.................................	845	682	80.7	649	76.8	33	4.8
45 to 54 years.................................	879	654	74.4	624	71.0	30	4.7
55 to 64 years.................................	827	480	58.1	459	55.5	21	4.5
65 years and over	984	160	16.3	157	15.9	3	2.1

NOTE: Data in Table 7 are from the Current Population Survey (CPS) and do not match the estimates in Table 8. See notes and definitions for further information.
[1]May be of any race.

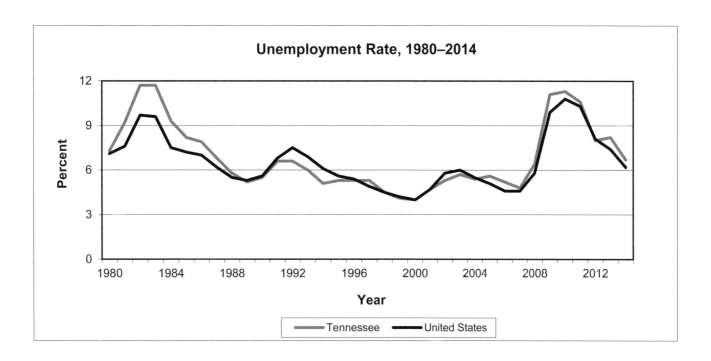

Table TN-8. Employment Status of the Civilian Noninstitutional Population Age 16 Years and Over

(Number, percent.)

Year	Civilian labor force	Civilian participation rate	Employed	Unemployed	Unemployment rate
2006	3,036,029	64.7	2,878,455	157,574	5.2
2007	3,063,669	64.4	2,920,352	143,317	4.7
2008	3,054,785	63.4	2,853,746	201,039	6.6
2009	3,052,678	62.7	2,733,113	319,565	10.5
2010	3,090,795	62.7	2,792,063	298,732	9.7
2011	3,130,116	62.9	2,849,677	280,439	9.0
2012	3,110,571	61.9	2,868,057	242,514	7.8
2013	3,081,528	60.8	2,842,200	239,328	7.8
2014	3,011,495	58.9	2,810,862	200,633	6.7

Table TN-9. Employment and Average Wages by Industry

(Estimates from 2007 through 2010 are based on the 2007 *North American Industry Classification System* [NAICS]. Estimates from 2011 onward are based on the 2012 NAICS.)

Industry	2007	2008	2009	2010	2011	2012	2013
	Number of jobs						
Wage and Salary Employment by Industry	2,910,068	2,888,909	2,728,711	2,724,777	2,769,845	2,812,441	2,849,940
Farm Wage and Salary Employment	9,757	9,417	8,408	8,553	9,176	9,592	9,183
Nonfarm Wage and Salary Employment	2,900,311	2,879,492	2,720,303	2,716,224	2,760,669	2,802,849	2,840,757
Private wage and salary employment	2,453,858	2,425,718	2,267,069	2,258,202	2,306,093	2,353,034	2,394,111
Forestry, fishing, and related activities	4,500	4,435	4,364	4,640	4,946	5,061	4,672
Mining	3,878	3,921	3,228	3,549	3,595	3,429	3,424
Utilities	3,576	3,502	3,557	3,358	3,318	3,375	3,341
Construction	138,403	133,007	110,843	105,805	110,330	108,364	107,599
Manufacturing	383,093	361,391	310,581	300,054	304,462	314,069	319,023
Durable goods manufacturing	239,260	220,844	183,414	177,658	183,824	194,495	199,166
Nondurable goods manufacturing	143,833	140,547	127,167	122,396	120,638	119,574	119,857
Wholesale trade	133,539	133,097	121,872	117,878	118,463	121,131	122,885
Retail trade	335,739	330,882	311,720	312,020	314,622	315,881	318,240
Transportation and warehousing	147,527	142,618	132,539	131,704	135,709	141,067	144,189
Information	49,312	49,457	46,328	44,465	43,166	42,858	43,563
Finance and insurance	109,967	110,908	108,330	108,748	107,450	108,597	106,915
Real estate and rental and leasing	37,045	37,054	34,418	33,566	32,197	32,483	33,816
Professional, scientific, and technical services	110,464	113,057	109,270	108,798	111,188	112,012	115,315
Management of companies and enterprises	23,623	25,011	25,384	26,049	28,981	31,555	35,187
Administrative and waste services	191,668	186,666	162,171	172,034	186,512	195,911	205,247
Educational services	47,201	50,179	51,646	52,859	54,018	55,506	55,925
Health care and social assistance	312,185	319,706	324,095	329,625	337,410	344,253	347,840
Arts, entertainment, and recreation	31,102	31,678	30,643	30,098	30,688	30,776	31,888
Accommodation and food services	248,741	245,713	236,137	235,798	240,228	248,324	256,544
Other services, except public administration	142,295	143,436	139,943	137,154	138,810	138,382	138,498
Government and government enterprises	446,453	453,774	453,234	458,022	454,576	449,815	446,646
	Dollars						
Average Wages and Salaries by Industry	38,606	39,445	39,703	41,014	41,876	43,328	43,516
Average Farm Wages and Salaries	21,533	21,405	22,775	21,148	17,635	18,909	26,911
Average Nonfarm Wages and Salaries	38,664	39,504	39,755	41,076	41,957	43,411	43,570
Average private wages and salaries	38,933	39,735	39,966	41,469	42,371	43,971	44,032
Forestry, fishing, and related activities	21,635	21,564	21,791	22,823	23,723	24,422	25,446
Mining	54,177	58,717	56,977	63,525	61,540	64,397	63,443
Utilities	55,732	58,384	60,849	61,574	63,018	63,663	65,546
Construction	42,673	43,717	43,063	44,294	45,565	47,108	47,568
Manufacturing	46,235	48,142	48,676	51,869	52,883	54,726	54,654
Durable goods manufacturing	45,300	47,416	47,799	50,763	51,775	54,256	53,186
Nondurable goods manufacturing	47,791	49,282	49,942	53,474	54,572	55,490	57,093
Wholesale trade	55,362	55,927	55,571	57,503	59,658	62,080	61,569
Retail trade	26,105	26,000	26,140	27,034	27,726	28,105	27,871
Transportation and warehousing	46,120	46,866	46,212	48,116	49,590	50,007	50,847
Information	51,833	52,288	52,156	54,018	57,046	59,006	58,898
Finance and insurance	62,742	62,796	62,915	66,006	68,066	72,406	72,240
Real estate and rental and leasing	38,003	37,351	37,077	38,103	39,862	42,098	42,620
Professional, scientific, and technical services	58,272	60,904	61,699	64,532	65,860	70,896	70,483
Management of companies and enterprises	75,943	77,906	73,568	82,160	83,175	99,429	98,288
Administrative and waste services	28,624	29,674	30,985	31,425	31,174	32,651	33,174
Educational services	32,705	32,786	33,462	33,653	34,218	34,605	35,561
Health care and social assistance	41,624	42,791	44,015	44,835	45,500	46,352	46,680
Arts, entertainment, and recreation	39,156	38,710	37,798	40,385	41,880	44,209	44,020
Accommodation and food services	17,620	16,981	17,059	17,829	18,186	18,365	17,957
Other services, except public administration	26,217	27,052	27,517	28,455	29,204	29,825	30,171
Government and government enterprises	37,182	38,271	38,701	39,142	39,856	40,485	41,093

Table TN-10. Employment Characteristics by Family Type

(Number, percent.)

Family type and labor force status	2011		2012		2013	
	Total	Families with own children under 18 years	Total	Families with own children under 18 years	Total	Families with own children under 18 years
All Families...........................	1,625,686	674,287	1,641,665	681,582	1,658,071	677,544
FAMILY TYPE AND LABOR FORCE STATUS						
Married-Couple Families...............	1,189,542	445,519	1,200,647	446,140	1,208,430	439,638
Both husband and wife in labor force..................	50.6	65.9	48.4	63.5	48.6	64.3
Husband in labor force, wife not in labor force	21.8	27.1	23.3	30.0	22.4	28.6
Wife in labor force, husband not in labor force	8.4	4.4	8.8	4.2	9.1	4.7
Both husband and wife not in labor force................	19.2	2.6	19.5	2.3	19.8	2.2
Other Families	436,144	228,768	441,018	235,442	449,641	237,906
Female householder, no husband present..............	75.4	79.1	74.9	76.0	74.1	75.6
In labor force	51.1	63.6	50.8	60.8	50.5	60.9
Not in labor force	24.3	15.5	24.1	15.2	23.6	14.7
Male householder, no wife present...................	24.6	20.9	25.1	24.0	25.9	24.4
In labor force..	18.1	18.4	19.1	21.3	19.8	21.9
Not in labor force	6.6	2.5	6.0	2.7	6.1	2.6

Table TN-11. School Enrollment and Educational Attainment, 2013

(Number, percent.)

Item	State	U.S.
Enrollment		
Total population 3 years and over, enrolled in school	1,597,851	82,395,254
Enrolled in nursery school or preschool (percent)	5.4	6.0
Enrolled in kindergarten (percent).................................	5.5	5.2
Enrolled in elementary school, grades 1-8 (percent)...................	41.8	40.0
Enrolled in high school, grades 9-12 (percent)	21.2	20.6
Enrolled in college or graduate school (percent).....................	26.1	28.3
Attainment		
Total population 25 years and over	4,370,035	210,910,615
Less than ninth grade (percent)...................................	5.6	5.8
9th to 12th grade, no diploma (percent)	8.8	7.6
High school graduate, including equivalency (percent).................	32.9	27.8
Some college, no degree (percent)	21.2	21.1
Associate's degree (percent)	6.7	8.1
Bachelor's degree (percent)	15.6	18.4
Graduate or professional degree (percent)..........................	9.2	11.2
High school graduate or higher (percent)	85.6	86.6
Bachelor's degree or higher (percent)..............................	24.8	29.6

Table TN-12. Public School Characteristics and Educational Indicators

(Number, percent; data derived from National Center of Education Statistics.)

Item	State	U.S.
Public Schools, 2012–2013 (except where noted)		
Number of school districts..	141	18,093
Number of schools...	1,817	98,454
Number of students (in thousands)	993	49,771
Number of teachers (in thousands)	66	3,109
Student-teacher ratio	15.0	16.0
Expenditures per student (dollars), FY 2012.........................	8,354	10,667
Four-year adjusted cohort graduation rate (ACGR)[1,2]	86.3	81.4
Students eligible for free or reduced-price lunch (in thousands)	576	25,188
English language learners (in thousands)	32	4,397
Students age 3 to 21 served under IDEA, part B (in thousands)	127	6,429

Public Schools by Type	Number	Percent of state public schools
Total number of schools..	1,817	100.0
Regular	1,764	97.1
Special education..	16	0.9
Vocational education...	16	0.9
Alternative education	21	1.2

NOTE: Every school is assigned only one school type based on its instructional emphasis.
[1]ACGR data represents a new method of calculating high-school completion rates and may not be comparable to previous years' data for Averaged Freshmen Graduation Rates (AFGR).
[2]The United States 4-year ACGRs were estimated using both the reported 4-year ACGR data from 49 states and the District of Columbia and using imputed data for Idaho. The estimate for American Indian/Alaska Native students also includes imputed data for Virginia.

Table TN-13. Reported Voting and Registration of the Voting-Age Population, November 2012

(Numbers in thousands, percent.)

Item	Total population	Total citizen population	Registered			Voted		
			Total registered	Percent registered (total population)	Percent registered (total citizen population)	Total voted	Percent voted (total population)	Percent voted (total citizen population)
U.S. Total	235,248	215,081	153,157	65.1	71.2	132,948	56.5	61.8
State Total	4,849	4,678	3,210	66.2	68.6	2,606	53.7	55.7
Sex								
Male	2,300	2,203	1,432	62.3	65.0	1,172	50.9	53.2
Female	2,548	2,475	1,778	69.8	71.8	1,434	56.3	57.9
Race								
White alone..........................	3,925	3,836	2,621	66.8	68.3	2,098	53.4	54.7
White, non-Hispanic alone	3,768	3,746	2,559	67.9	68.3	2,052	54.5	54.8
Black alone..........................	768	722	513	66.8	71.1	441	57.4	61.1
Asian alone	50	20	13	B	B	13	B	B
Hispanic (of any race)	241	134	107	44.4	79.7	84	34.7	62.3
White alone or in combination	3,996	3,907	2,669	66.8	68.3	2,136	53.5	54.7
Black alone or in combination	782	735	527	67.4	71.6	450	57.6	61.3
Asian alone or in combination..........	70	41	33	B	B	33	B	B
Age								
18 to 24 years	610	590	306	50.2	51.9	207	34.0	35.2
25 to 44 years	1,615	1,513	1,030	63.8	68.1	796	49.3	52.6
45 to 64 years	1,607	1,563	1,081	67.2	69.1	904	56.3	57.9
65 to 74 years	631	628	503	79.7	80.1	457	72.3	72.7
75 years and over	385	385	290	75.4	75.4	241	62.7	62.7

B = Base is less than 75,000 and therefore too small to show the derived measure.

Table TN-14. Crime

(Number, rate per 100,000. Data are derived from the FBI Uniform Crime Reports.)

Item	State			U.S.[1,2,3,4]		
	2012	2013	Percent change	2012	2013	Percent change
TOTAL POPULATION[5]..	6,454,914	6,495,978	0.6	313,873,685	316,128,839	0.7
VIOLENT CRIME						
Number..............................	41,213	37,655	-8.6	1,217,067	1,163,146	-4.4
Rate	638.5	579.7	-9.2	387.8	367.9	-5.1
Murder and Nonnegligent Manslaughter						
Number..............................	400	328	-18.0	14,866	14,196	-4.5
Rate	6.2	5.0	-18.5	4.7	4.5	-5.2
Rape[6]						
Number..............................	X	2,351	X	X	108,612	X
Rate	X	36.2	X	X	34.4	X
Robbery						
Number..............................	8,151	7,307	-10.4	355,051	345,031	-2.8
Rate	126.3	112.5	-10.9	113.1	109.1	-3.5
Aggravated Assault						
Number..............................	30,615	28,378	-7.3	762,009	724,149	-5.0
Rate	474.3	436.9	-7.9	242.8	229.1	-5.6
PROPERTY CRIME						
Number..............................	217,925	206,629	-5.2	9,001,992	8,632,512	-4.1
Rate	3,376.1	3,180.9	-5.8	2,868.0	2,730.7	-4.8
Burglary						
Number..............................	56,231	50,999	-9.3	2,109,932	1,928,465	-8.6
Rate	871.1	785.1	-9.9	672.2	610.0	-9.3
Larceny-Theft						
Number..............................	148,731	143,802	-3.3	6,168,874	6,004,453	-2.7
Rate	2,304.2	2,213.7	-3.9	1,965.4	1,899.4	-3.4
Motor Vehicle Theft						
Number..............................	12,963	11,828	-8.8	723,186	699,594	-3.3
Rate	200.8	182.1	-9.3	230.4	221.3	-4.0

NOTE: Although arson data are included in the trend and clearance tables, sufficient data are not available to estimate totals for this offense. Therefore, no arson data are published in this table.

X = Not applicable.

- = Zero or rounds to zero.

[1]The crime figures have been adjusted.

[2]The data collection methodology for the offense of forcible rape used by the Minnesota state Uniform Crime Reporting (UCR) Program (with the exception of Minneapolis and St. Paul, Minnesota) does not comply with national UCR Program guidelines. Consequently, its figures for forcible rape and violent crime (of which forcible rape is a part) are not published in this table.

[3]Includes offenses reported by the Zoological Police and the Metro Transit Police.

[4]Because of changes in the state's reporting practices, figures are not comparable to previous years' data.

[5]Populations are U.S. Census Bureau provisional estimates as of July 1 of each year.

[6]The figures shown for the offense of rape were estimated using the revised Uniform Crime Reporting (UCR) definition of rape.

Table TN-15. State Government Finances, 2013

(Dollar amounts in thousands, percent distribution.)

Item	Dollars	Percent distribution
Total Revenue	32,356,348	100.0
General revenue	27,401,810	84.7
Intergovernmental revenue	10,900,626	33.7
Taxes	12,366,891	38.2
General sales	6,629,923	20.5
Selective sales	2,498,252	7.7
License taxes	1,421,174	4.4
Individual income tax	262,842	0.8
Corporate income tax	1,256,173	3.9
Other taxes	298,527	0.9
Current charges	2,016,428	6.2
Miscellaneous general revenue	2,117,865	6.5
Utility revenue	0	-
Liquor stores revenue	0	-
Insurance trust revenue[1]	4,954,538	15.3
Total Expenditure	30,586,320	100.0
Intergovernmental expenditure	7,074,682	23.1
Direct expenditure	23,511,638	76.9
Current operation	17,700,839	57.9
Capital outlay	1,618,748	5.3
Insurance benefits and repayments	2,755,113	9.0
Assistance and subsidies	1,172,474	3.8
Interest on debt	264,464	0.9
Exhibit: Salaries and wages	3,766,072	12.3
Total Expenditure	30,586,320	100.0
General expenditure	27,831,207	91.0
Intergovernmental expenditure	7,074,682	23.1
Direct expenditure	20,756,525	67.9
General expenditure, by function:		
Education	9,810,510	32.1
Public welfare	10,959,849	35.8
Hospitals	404,978	1.3
Health	672,883	2.2
Highways	1,752,119	5.7
Police protection	232,868	0.8
Correction	889,870	2.9
Natural resources	291,223	1.0
Parks and recreation	85,428	0.3
Governmental administration	868,161	2.8
Interest on general debt	264,464	0.9
Other and unallocable	1,598,854	5.2
Utility expenditure	0	-
Liquor stores expenditure	0	-
Insurance trust expenditure	2,755,113	9.0
Debt at End of Fiscal Year	6,191,955	X
Cash and Security Holdings	47,293,346	X

X = Not applicable.
- = Zero or rounds to zero.
[1]Within insurance trust revenue, net earnings of state retirement systems is a calculated statistic (the item code in the data file is X08), and thus can be positive or negative. Net earnings is the sum of earnings on investments plus gains on investments minus losses on investments. The change made in 2002 for asset valuation from book to market value in accordance with Statement 34 of the Governmental Accounting Standards Board is reflected in the calculated statistics.

Table TN-16. State Government Tax Collections, 2014

(Dollars in thousands, percent.)

Item	Dollars	Percent distribution
Total Taxes	11,806,329	100.0
Property taxes	X	X
Sales and gross receipts	8,758,085	74.2
General sales and gross receipts	6,192,281	52.4
Selective sales and gross receipts	2,565,804	21.7
Alcoholic beverages	147,812	1.3
Amusements	0	-
Insurance premiums	749,470	6.3
Motor fuels	845,395	7.2
Pari-mutuels	0	-
Public utilities	6,840	0.1
Tobacco products	261,101	2.2
Other selective sales	555,186	4.7
Licenses	1,335,392	11.3
Alcoholic beverages	1,317	-
Amusements	376	-
Corporations in general	676,478	5.7
Hunting and fishing	32,959	0.3
Motor vehicle	269,317	2.3
Motor vehicle operators	47,194	0.4
Public utilities	5,840	-
Occupation and business, NEC	293,122	2.5
Other licenses	8,789	0.1
Income taxes	1,416,190	12.0
Individual income	239,219	2.0
Corporation net income	1,176,971	10.0
Other taxes	296,662	2.5
Death and gift	107,341	0.9
Documentary and stock transfer	167,055	1.4
Severance	2,487	-
Taxes, NEC	19,779	0.2

X = Not applicable.
- = Zero or rounds to zero.

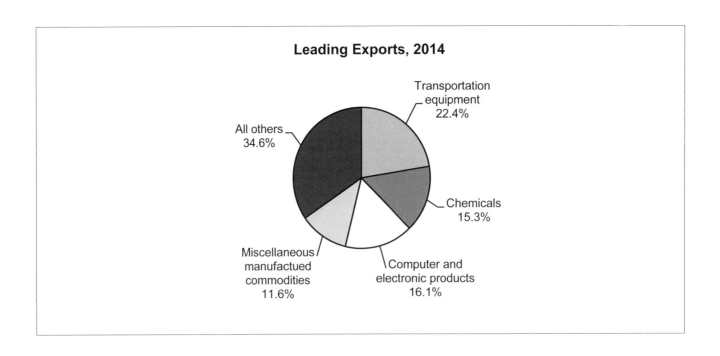

Leading Exports, 2014

Transportation equipment 22.4%

Chemicals 15.3%

Computer and electronic products 16.1%

Miscellaneous manufactued commodities 11.6%

All others 34.6%

TEXAS

Facts and Figures

Location: West south central United States; bordered on the N by Oklahoma, on the E by Arkansas and Louisiana, on the S by Mexico and the Gulf of Mexico, and on the W by Mexico and New Mexico

Area: 268,581 sq. mi. (695,621 sq. km.); rank—2nd

Population: 26,956,958 (2014 est.); rank—2nd

Principal Cities: capital—Austin; largest—Houston

Statehood: December 29, 1845; 28th state

U.S. Congress: 2 senators, 36 representatives

State Motto: Friendship

State Song: "Texas, Our Texas"

State Nickname: The Lone Star State

Abbreviations: TX; Tex.

State Symbols: flower—bluebonnet; tree—pecan; bird—mockingbird

At a Glance

- With an increase in population of 7.2 percent, Texas ranked 3rd among the states in growth from 2010 to 2014.

- Texas's median household income in 2013 was $51,704, and 17.5 percent of the population lived below the poverty level.

- In 2013, 22.1 percent of Texans did not have health insurance, compared to 14.5 percent of the total U.S. population.

- Texas's violent crime rate in 2013 was 408.3 per 100,000 population, compared to 367.9 for the entire nation.

- The property crime rate in Texas in 2013, 3,258.2 per 100,000 population, ranked 11th in the United States.

Table TX-1. Population by Age, Sex, Race, and Hispanic Origin

(Number, percent, except where noted.)

Sex, age, race, and Hispanic origin	2000	2010	2014[1]	Average annual percent change, 2010–2014
Total Population	20,851,820	25,145,561	26,956,958	1.8
Percent of total U.S. population	7.4	8.1	8.5	X
Sex				
Male	10,352,910	12,472,280	13,382,386	1.8
Female	10,498,910	12,673,281	13,574,572	1.7
Age				
Under 5 years	1,625,628	1,928,473	1,956,213	0.4
5 to 19 years	4,291,608	5,693,241	5,906,521	0.9
20 to 64 years	12,233,052	14,921,961	15,995,143	1.8
65 years and over	2,072,532	2,601,886	3,099,081	4.5
Median age (years)	32.3	33.6	34.2	0.4
Race and Hispanic Origin				
One race				
White	14,799,505	20,389,793	21,565,643	1.4
Black	2,404,566	3,070,440	3,364,416	2.3
American Indian and Alaska Native	118,362	251,209	274,452	2.2
Asian	562,319	1,000,473	1,223,865	5.2
Native Hawaiian or Other Pacific Islander	14,434	31,242	36,632	4.1
Two or more races	514,633	402,404	491,950	5.2
Hispanic (of any race)	6,699,666	9,578,505	10,411,340	2.1

X = Not applicable.
[1]Population figures for 2014 are July 1 estimates. The 2010 estimates are taken from the 2010 Census.

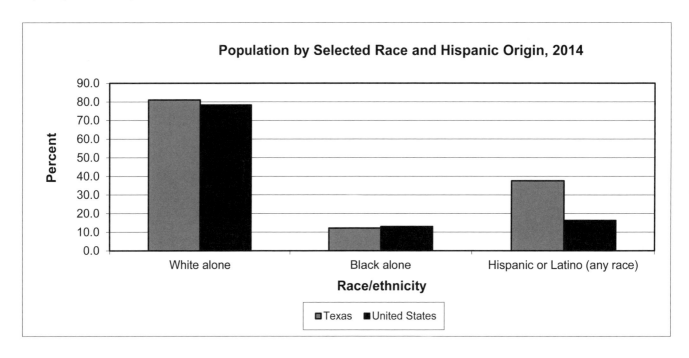

Table TX-2. Marital Status

(Number, percent distribution.)

Sex, age, race, and Hispanic origin	2000	2010	2013
Males, 15 Years and Over	7,820,248	9,587,343	10,130,288
Never married	28.6	34.6	35.3
Now married, except separated	58.8	51.6	51.0
Separated	2.0	2.3	2.1
Widowed	2.1	2.2	2.3
Divorced	8.5	9.4	9.3
Females, 15 Years and Over	8,117,395	9,903,147	10,416,977
Never married	22.6	27.6	29.1
Now married, except separated	54.3	48.5	47.4
Separated	2.9	3.3	3.2
Widowed	9.1	8.1	8.0
Divorced	11.0	12.5	12.3

Table TX-3. Households and Housing Characteristics

(Number, percent, dollars.)

Item	2000	2010	2013	Average annual percent change, 2000–2013
Total Households..	7,393,354	8,738,664	9,110,853	1.6
Family households	5,247,794	6,091,590	6,322,542	1.4
Married-couple family	3,989,741	4,386,996	4,552,753	1.0
Other family	1,258,053	1,704,594	1,769,789	2.7
Male householder, no wife present..............	320,464	436,727	460,617	2.8
Female householder, no husband present...........	937,489	1,267,867	1,309,172	2.6
Nonfamily households	2,145,560	2,647,074	2,788,311	2.0
Householder living alone....................................	1,752,141	2,166,469	2,280,838	2.0
Householder not living alone.............................	393,419	480,605	507,473	2.0
Housing Characteristics				
Total housing units..	8,157,575	9,996,209	10,256,203	1.8
Occupied housing units	7,393,354	8,738,664	9,110,853	1.6
Owner occupied	4,716,959	5,555,903	5,634,317	1.4
Renter occupied	2,676,395	3,182,761	3,476,536	2.0
Average household size...	2.74	2.82	2.84	0.3
Financial Characteristics				
Median gross rent of renter-occupied housing	574	801	857	3.1
Median monthly owner costs for housing units with a mortgage	986	1,402	1,375	2.6
Median value of owner-occupied housing units........................	82,500	128,100	132,000	3.7

Table TX-4. Migration, Origin, and Language

(Number, percent.)

Characteristic	State			U.S.		
	2012	2013	Percent change	2012	2013	Percent change
Residence 1 Year Ago						
Population 1 year and over	25,711,791	26,087,349	1.5	310,212,755	312,432,820	0.7
Same house	83.1	83.0	X	85.0	85.0	X
Different house in the U.S.	16.2	16.3	X	14.4	14.4	X
Same county	10.3	10.0	X	9.0	8.9	X
Different county	5.9	6.2	X	5.4	5.5	X
Same state	3.9	4.1	X	3.2	3.2	X
Different state	2.0	2.1	X	2.3	2.3	X
Abroad	0.8	0.7	X	0.6	0.6	X
Place of Birth						
Native born	21,789,510	22,078,922	1.3	273,089,382	274,780,773	0.6
Male	49.6	49.5	X	49.3	49.3	X
Female	50.4	50.5	X	50.7	50.7	X
Foreign born	4,269,693	4,369,271	2.3	40,824,658	41,348,066	1.3
Male	49.9	50.6	X	48.7	48.8	X
Female	50.1	49.4	X	51.3	51.2	X
Foreign born; naturalized U.S. citizen..................	1,436,948	1,491,058	3.8	18,686,237	19,294,710	3.3
Male	46.9	47.4	X	45.8	45.9	X
Female	53.1	52.6	X	54.2	54.1	X
Foreign born; not a U.S. citizen...........................	2,832,745	2,878,213	1.6	22,138,421	22,053,356	-0.4
Male	51.4	52.3	X	51.1	51.3	X
Female	48.6	47.7	X	48.9	48.7	X
Entered 2010 or later	7.1	9.6	X	7.0	9.7	X
Entered 2000 to 2009	32.5	31.2	X	30.4	29.4	X
Entered before 2000..	60.4	59.2	X	62.7	61.0	X
World Region of Birth, Foreign						
Foreign-born population, excluding population born at sea	4,269,693	4,369,271	2.3	40,824,553	41,347,945	1.3
Europe	4.2	4.3	X	11.8	11.6	X
Asia..	19.4	19.5	X	29.2	29.5	X
Africa...	3.7	3.8	X	4.2	4.4	X
Oceania...	0.2	0.2	X	0.6	0.5	X
Latin America	71.5	71.1	X	52.2	51.9	X
North America...	1.0	1.2	X	2.0	2.0	X
Language Spoken at Home and Ability to Speak English						
Population 5 years and over....................................	24,126,355	24,521,695	1.6	294,003,714	296,358,760	0.8
English only	64.8	65.3	X	79.0	79.2	X
Language other than English...............................	35.2	34.7	X	21.0	20.8	X
Speaks English less than "very well".................	14.0	14.0	X	8.5	8.5	X

NA = Not available.
X = Not applicable.
- = Zero or rounds to zero.

Table TX-5. Median Income and Poverty Status, 2013

(Number, percent, except as noted.)

Characteristic	State		U.S.	
	Number	Percent	Number	Percent
Median Income				
Households (dollars)...	51,704	X	52,250	X
Families (dollars)	61,208	X	64,030	X
Below Poverty Level (All People)	4,530,039	17.5	48,810,868	15.8
Sex				
Male...	2,022,852	15.9	21,938,525	14.5
Female	2,507,187	19.1	26,872,343	17.1
Age				
Under 18 years...	1,740,560	25.0	16,086,960	22.2
Related children under 18 years...........................	1,719,957	24.8	15,769,921	21.9
18 to 64 years..	2,472,655	15.5	28,578,191	14.8
65 years and over..	316,824	11.0	4,145,717	9.6

X = Not applicable.

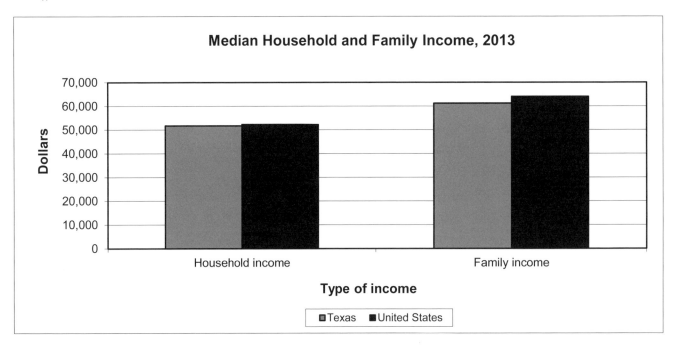

Median Household and Family Income, 2013

Table TX-6. Health Insurance Coverage Status for the Civilian Noninstitutionalized Population and Children Under 18 Years of Age

(Numbers in thousands, percent.)

Item	2005	2006	2007	2008	2009	2010	2011	2012	2013
Civilian Noninstitutionalized Population	22,819	23,236	23,704	23,827	24,292	24,779	25,197	25,584	25,977
Covered by Private or Public Insurance									
Number...	17,426	17,533	17,742	18,082	18,508	18,904	19,408	19,822	20,228
Percent..	76.4	75.5	74.8	75.9	76.2	76.3	77.0	77.5	77.9
Not Covered									
Number...	5,394	5,704	5,962	5,745	5,783	5,875	5,790	5,762	5,748
Percent..	23.6	24.5	25.2	24.1	23.8	23.7	23.0	22.5	22.1
Percent in the U.S. not covered............................	15.3	15.8	15.3	15.1	15.1	15.5	15.1	14.8	14.5
Children Under 18 Years of Age...	6,477	6,556	6,720	6,714	6,878	6,876	6,947	6,972	7,029
Covered by Private or Public Insurance									
Number...	5,253	5,164	5,285	5,518	5,758	5,880	6,030	6,109	6,140
Percent..	81.1	78.8	78.6	82.2	83.7	85.5	86.8	87.6	87.4
Not Covered									
Number...	1,224	1,392	1,435	1,196	1,120	996	917	863	888
Percent..	18.9	21.2	21.4	17.8	16.3	14.5	13.2	12.4	12.6
Percent in the U.S. not covered............................	10.9	11.7	11.0	9.7	8.6	8.0	7.5	7.2	7.1

Table TX-7. Employment Status by Demographic Group, 2014

(Numbers in thousands, percent.)

Characteristic	Civilian noninstitutional population	Civilian labor force		Employed		Unemployed	
		Number	Percent of population	Number	Percent of population	Number	Percent of population
Total...	20,095	13,115	65.3	12,453	62.0	662	5.0
Sex							
Male......................................	9,779	7,246	74.1	6,910	70.7	336	4.6
Female	10,317	5,869	56.9	5,543	53.7	326	5.6
Race, Sex, and Hispanic Origin							
White	16,264	10,551	64.9	10,097	62.1	454	4.3
Male......................................	7,990	5,940	74.3	5,707	71.4	232	3.9
Female	8,274	4,612	55.7	4,390	53.1	222	4.8
Black or African American..................	2,433	1,618	66.5	1,465	60.2	153	9.5
Male......................................	1,116	772	69.2	694	62.2	79	10.2
Female	1,316	845	64.2	771	58.6	75	8.8
Hispanic or Latino ethnicity[1]	7,436	4,928	66.3	4,665	62.7	263	5.3
Male......................................	3,698	2,866	77.5	2,729	73.8	137	4.8
Female	3,738	2,063	55.2	1,937	51.8	126	6.1
Age							
16 to 19 years...........................	1,469	485	33.0	408	27.8	78	16.0
20 to 24 years...........................	1,924	1,403	72.9	1,269	66.0	134	9.6
25 to 34 years...........................	3,889	3,120	80.2	2,959	76.1	161	5.2
35 to 44 years...........................	3,460	2,830	81.8	2,723	78.7	107	3.8
45 to 54 years...........................	3,580	2,872	80.2	2,778	77.6	94	3.3
55 to 64 years...........................	2,870	1,799	62.7	1,730	60.3	69	3.8
65 years and over	2,903	604	20.8	586	20.2	19	3.1

NOTE: Data in Table 7 are from the Current Population Survey (CPS) and do not match the estimates in Table 8. See notes and definitions for further information.
[1]May be of any race.

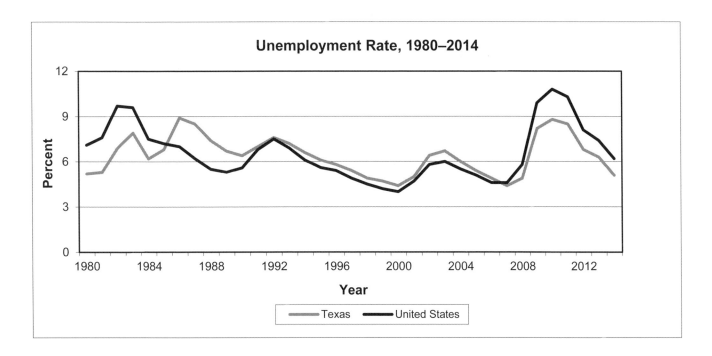

Unemployment Rate, 1980–2014

Table TX-8. Employment Status of the Civilian Noninstitutional Population Age 16 Years and Over

(Number, percent.)

Year	Civilian labor force	Civilian participation rate	Employed	Unemployed	Unemployment rate
2006	11,327,995	66.6	10,774,490	553,505	4.9
2007	11,431,631	65.7	10,941,413	490,218	4.3
2008	11,664,390	65.8	11,104,115	560,275	4.8
2009	11,910,799	65.8	11,008,903	901,896	7.6
2010	12,241,970	65.9	11,244,632	997,338	8.1
2011	12,495,726	65.8	11,527,028	968,698	7.8
2012	12,678,890	65.6	11,827,485	851,405	6.7
2013	12,904,629	65.5	12,104,092	800,537	6.2
2014	13,111,548	65.2	12,447,551	663,997	5.1

Table TX-9. Employment and Average Wages by Industry

(Estimates from 2007 through 2010 are based on the 2007 *North American Industry Classification System* [NAICS]. Estimates from 2011 onward are based on the 2012 NAICS.)

Industry	2007	2008	2009	2010	2011	2012	2013
	Number of jobs						
Wage and Salary Employment by Industry	10,858,772	11,096,319	10,808,235	10,828,653	11,072,783	11,354,264	11,679,288
Farm Wage and Salary Employment	43,404	42,703	48,479	44,051	41,328	38,762	45,186
Nonfarm Wage and Salary Employment	10,815,368	11,053,616	10,759,756	10,784,602	11,031,455	11,315,502	11,634,102
Private wage and salary employment	8,929,873	9,116,924	8,776,668	8,771,530	9,046,768	9,347,629	9,660,191
Forestry, fishing, and related activities	28,504	28,127	27,127	28,302	28,775	27,464	31,184
Mining	204,434	230,088	203,229	203,461	234,092	267,802	287,554
Utilities	45,605	47,516	48,042	48,316	49,026	48,682	48,928
Construction	673,014	700,532	626,586	592,472	595,688	605,212	636,359
Manufacturing	934,915	924,271	838,653	811,550	837,471	864,944	874,683
Durable goods manufacturing	615,008	608,562	537,342	515,868	543,706	569,709	579,102
Nondurable goods manufacturing	319,907	315,709	301,311	295,682	293,765	295,235	295,581
Wholesale trade	523,444	533,936	502,987	501,522	519,424	543,048	563,205
Retail trade	1,179,228	1,190,978	1,159,288	1,155,041	1,178,723	1,199,113	1,232,635
Transportation and warehousing	393,727	398,766	376,704	377,833	391,232	408,016	416,353
Information	222,003	217,408	205,464	196,069	195,523	197,153	201,393
Finance and insurance	465,602	467,810	458,773	464,849	477,157	493,384	507,422
Real estate and rental and leasing	187,041	192,012	182,340	179,127	180,900	184,237	193,518
Professional, scientific, and technical services	566,421	595,415	570,446	577,632	596,946	627,178	653,131
Management of companies and enterprises	67,858	74,981	77,042	79,307	83,489	87,586	90,106
Administrative and waste services	679,395	683,145	622,713	637,018	676,759	708,116	731,265
Educational services	138,053	143,269	148,431	153,919	158,713	165,372	166,484
Health care and social assistance	1,073,888	1,108,291	1,155,375	1,196,470	1,228,565	1,257,684	1,296,295
Arts, entertainment, and recreation	108,673	110,219	111,675	111,881	112,998	113,287	119,044
Accommodation and food services	884,080	908,255	905,928	909,188	942,578	979,898	1,028,949
Other services, except public administration	553,988	561,905	555,865	547,573	558,709	569,453	581,683
Government and government enterprises	1,885,495	1,936,692	1,983,088	2,013,072	1,984,687	1,967,873	1,973,911
	Dollars						
Average Wages and Salaries by Industry	44,272	45,526	45,255	46,542	48,351	50,087	50,643
Average Farm Wages and Salaries	27,864	31,452	25,333	27,486	35,284	30,938	29,150
Average Nonfarm Wages and Salaries	44,338	45,580	45,345	46,619	48,400	50,153	50,726
Average private wages and salaries	45,065	46,247	45,703	47,146	49,079	51,111	51,652
Forestry, fishing, and related activities	23,092	24,408	24,805	25,451	25,907	27,055	26,577
Mining	107,182	113,073	111,559	117,244	122,085	120,842	119,782
Utilities	93,955	88,718	88,531	90,004	90,239	98,792	97,694
Construction	46,599	48,950	48,943	49,195	50,908	54,188	55,707
Manufacturing	59,903	60,462	60,239	63,181	65,897	68,333	68,729
Durable goods manufacturing	60,927	61,921	62,256	65,452	68,327	70,252	70,533
Nondurable goods manufacturing	57,934	57,648	56,641	59,220	61,401	64,630	65,196
Wholesale trade	64,610	65,786	65,020	67,874	71,415	74,561	74,164
Retail trade	26,633	26,668	26,511	27,165	27,902	28,838	29,124
Transportation and warehousing	50,457	51,143	50,639	53,376	55,373	58,444	58,845
Information	64,618	67,122	66,835	67,330	70,722	73,374	75,405
Finance and insurance	66,544	67,795	65,364	68,514	71,569	74,610	75,777
Real estate and rental and leasing	45,050	45,620	44,045	45,764	49,099	52,594	53,918
Professional, scientific, and technical services	71,659	73,749	73,877	76,448	79,425	81,796	83,760
Management of companies and enterprises	102,335	96,622	94,096	100,017	106,866	113,626	114,060
Administrative and waste services	33,788	34,895	35,198	36,084	36,965	38,382	38,891
Educational services	32,197	34,008	35,127	35,508	36,131	36,912	38,350
Health care and social assistance	38,106	39,377	40,482	40,945	41,719	42,649	42,708
Arts, entertainment, and recreation	32,072	31,476	31,916	31,827	32,702	33,899	32,824
Accommodation and food services	17,765	17,625	17,679	18,429	18,982	19,424	19,480
Other services, except public administration	25,839	27,049	27,341	28,346	29,197	29,883	30,922
Government and government enterprises	40,891	42,445	43,757	44,323	45,306	45,603	46,195

Table TX-10. Employment Characteristics by Family Type

(Number, percent.)

Family type and labor force status	2011 Total	2011 Families with own children under 18 years	2012 Total	2012 Families with own children under 18 years	2013 Total	2013 Families with own children under 18 years
All Families	6,171,317	2,990,780	6,239,195	3,027,703	6,322,542	3,033,950
FAMILY TYPE AND LABOR FORCE STATUS						
Married-Couple Families	4,429,883	2,017,757	4,492,603	2,051,269	4,552,753	2,049,461
Both husband and wife in labor force	51.6	59.9	51.2	60.3	50.4	59.2
Husband in labor force, wife not in labor force	27.8	35.2	28.1	34.8	28.4	35.6
Wife in labor force, husband not in labor force	6.7	3.3	6.5	3.3	6.9	3.4
Both husband and wife not in labor force	13.9	1.7	14.1	1.6	14.0	1.6
Other Families	1,741,434	973,023	1,746,592	976,434	1,769,789	984,489
Female householder, no husband present	73.8	78.4	73.3	77.4	74.0	77.9
In labor force	53.3	64.1	52.9	63.3	54.2	64.9
Not in labor force	20.4	14.3	20.5	14.1	19.7	13.0
Male householder, no wife present	26.2	21.6	26.7	22.6	26.0	22.1
In labor force	21.3	19.8	21.8	20.9	21.0	20.1
Not in labor force	4.9	1.8	4.9	1.7	5.1	2.0

Table TX-11. School Enrollment and Educational Attainment, 2013

(Number, percent.)

Item	State	U.S.
Enrollment		
Total population 3 years and over, enrolled in school	7,416,105	82,395,254
Enrolled in nursery school or preschool (percent)	6.2	6.0
Enrolled in kindergarten (percent)	5.7	5.2
Enrolled in elementary school, grades 1-8 (percent)	43.2	40.0
Enrolled in high school, grades 9-12 (percent)	20.4	20.6
Enrolled in college or graduate school (percent)	24.5	28.3
Attainment		
Total population 25 years and over	16,673,656	210,910,615
Less than ninth grade (percent)	9.1	5.8
9th to 12th grade, no diploma (percent)	9.0	7.6
High school graduate, including equivalency (percent)	25.2	27.8
Some college, no degree (percent)	22.6	21.1
Associate's degree (percent)	6.5	8.1
Bachelor's degree (percent)	18.3	18.4
Graduate or professional degree (percent)	9.3	11.2
High school graduate or higher (percent)	81.9	86.6
Bachelor's degree or higher (percent)	27.5	29.6

Table TX-12. Public School Characteristics and Educational Indicators

(Number, percent; data derived from National Center of Education Statistics.)

Item	State	U.S.
Public Schools, 2012–2013 (except where noted)		
Number of school districts	1,254	18,093
Number of schools	8,731	98,454
Number of students (in thousands)	5,078	49,771
Number of teachers (in thousands)	327	3,109
Student-teacher ratio	15.5	16.0
Expenditures per student (dollars), FY 2012	8,213	10,667
Four-year adjusted cohort graduation rate (ACGR)[1,2]	88.0	81.4
Students eligible for free or reduced-price lunch (in thousands)	3060	25,188
English language learners (in thousands)	740	4,397
Students age 3 to 21 served under IDEA, part B (in thousands)	440	6,429

Public Schools by Type	Number	Percent of state public schools
Total number of schools	8,731	100.0
Regular	7,710	88.3
Special education	22	0.3
Vocational education	0	-
Alternative education	999	11.4

NOTE: Every school is assigned only one school type based on its instructional emphasis.
[1]ACGR data represents a new method of calculating high-school completion rates and may not be comparable to previous years' data for Averaged Freshmen Graduation Rates (AFGR).
[2]The United States 4-year ACGRs were estimated using both the reported 4-year ACGR data from 49 states and the District of Columbia and using imputed data for Idaho. The estimate for American Indian/Alaska Native students also includes imputed data for Virginia.
- = Zero or rounds to zero.

Table TX-13. Reported Voting and Registration of the Voting-Age Population, November 2012

(Numbers in thousands, percent.)

Item	Total population	Total citizen population	Registered			Voted		
			Total registered	Percent registered (total population)	Percent registered (total citizen population)	Total voted	Percent voted (total population)	Percent voted (total citizen population)
U.S. Total	235,248	215,081	153,157	65.1	71.2	132,948	56.5	61.8
State Total	18,642	16,062	10,749	57.7	66.9	8,643	46.4	53.8
Sex								
Male	9,046	7,719	4,977	55.0	64.5	3,925	43.4	50.8
Female	9,596	8,344	5,772	60.1	69.2	4,719	49.2	56.6
Race								
White alone........................	15,029	12,989	8,643	57.5	66.5	6,900	45.9	53.1
White, non-Hispanic alone	8,512	8,360	6,101	71.7	73.0	5,087	59.8	60.9
Black alone........................	2,213	2,144	1,569	70.9	73.2	1,352	61.1	63.1
Asian alone	900	506	299	33.2	59.1	214	23.8	42.4
Hispanic (of any race)	6,831	4,867	2,652	38.8	54.5	1,890	27.7	38.8
White alone or in combination	15,200	13,144	8,749	57.6	66.6	6,968	45.8	53.0
Black alone or in combination..........	2,293	2,207	1,606	70.0	72.8	1,380	60.2	62.5
Asian alone or in combination..........	909	515	305	33.5	59.2	220	24.2	42.8
Age								
18 to 24 years...................	2,538	2,249	971	38.2	43.1	572	22.5	25.4
25 to 44 years...................	7,140	5,713	3,573	50.0	62.5	2,701	37.8	47.3
45 to 64 years...................	6,115	5,429	3,981	65.1	73.3	3,399	55.6	62.6
65 to 74 years...................	1,719	1,610	1,329	77.4	82.6	1,201	69.9	74.6
75 years and over	1,131	1,061	895	79.2	84.4	770	68.1	72.6

Table TX-14. Crime

(Number, rate per 100,000. Data are derived from the FBI Uniform Crime Reports.)

Item	State			U.S.[1,2,3,4]		
	2012	2013	Percent change	2012	2013	Percent change
TOTAL POPULATION[5]...............................	26,060,796	26,448,193	1.5	313,873,685	316,128,839	0.7
VIOLENT CRIME						
Number..................................	106,475	105,736	-0.7	1,217,067	1,163,146	-4.4
Rate.......................................	408.6	399.8	-2.1	387.8	367.9	-5.1
Murder and Nonnegligent Manslaughter						
Number..................................	1,148	1,139	-0.8	14,866	14,196	-4.5
Rate	4.4	4.3	-2.2	4.7	4.5	-5.2
Rape[6]						
Number..................................	X	9,766	X	X	108,612	X
Rate.......................................	X	36.9	X	X	34.4	X
Robbery						
Number..................................	30,385	31,801	4.7	355,051	345,031	-2.8
Rate.......................................	116.6	120.2	3.1	113.1	109.1	-3.5
Aggravated Assault						
Number..................................	67,227	65,292	-2.9	762,009	724,149	-5.0
Rate.......................................	258.0	246.9	-4.3	242.8	229.1	-5.6
PROPERTY CRIME						
Number..................................	876,459	861,734	-1.7	9,001,992	8,632,512	-4.1
Rate.......................................	3,363.1	3,258.2	-3.1	2,868.0	2,730.7	-4.8
Burglary						
Number..................................	205,002	190,898	-6.9	2,109,932	1,928,465	-8.6
Rate.......................................	786.6	721.8	-8.2	672.2	610.0	-9.3
Larceny-Theft						
Number..................................	606,425	605,091	-0.2	6,168,874	6,004,453	-2.7
Rate.......................................	2,327.0	2,287.8	-1.7	1,965.4	1,899.4	-3.4
Motor Vehicle Theft						
Number..................................	65,032	65,745	1.1	723,186	699,594	-3.3
Rate.......................................	249.5	248.6	-0.4	230.4	221.3	-4.0

NOTE: Although arson data are included in the trend and clearance tables, sufficient data are not available to estimate totals for this offense. Therefore, no arson data are published in this table.

X = Not applicable.

- = Zero or rounds to zero.

[1]The crime figures have been adjusted.

[2]The data collection methodology for the offense of forcible rape used by the Minnesota state Uniform Crime Reporting (UCR) Program (with the exception of Minneapolis and St. Paul, Minnesota) does not comply with national UCR Program guidelines. Consequently, its figures for forcible rape and violent crime (of which forcible rape is a part) are not published in this table.

[3]Includes offenses reported by the Zoological Police and the Metro Transit Police.

[4]Because of changes in the state's reporting practices, figures are not comparable to previous years' data.

[5]Populations are U.S. Census Bureau provisional estimates as of July 1 of each year.

[6]The figures shown for the offense of rape were estimated using the revised Uniform Crime Reporting (UCR) definition of rape.

Table TX-15. State Government Finances, 2013

(Dollar amounts in thousands, percent distribution.)

Item	Dollars	Percent distribution
Total Revenue	136,486,968	100.0
General revenue	112,935,910	82.7
Intergovernmental revenue	37,580,061	27.5
Taxes	51,714,295	37.9
General sales	26,127,421	19.1
Selective sales	13,150,162	9.6
License taxes	7,788,864	5.7
Individual income tax	0	-
Corporate income tax	0	-
Other taxes	4,647,848	3.4
Current charges	12,641,609	9.3
Miscellaneous general revenue	10,999,945	8.1
Utility revenue	0	-
Liquor stores revenue	0	-
Insurance trust revenue[1]	23,551,058	17.3
Total Expenditure	124,929,538	100.0
Intergovernmental expenditure	27,590,295	22.1
Direct expenditure	97,339,243	77.9
Current operation	68,361,537	54.7
Capital outlay	8,045,756	6.4
Insurance benefits and repayments	16,904,612	13.5
Assistance and subsidies	2,297,935	1.8
Interest on debt	1,729,403	1.4
Exhibit: Salaries and wages	16,384,939	13.1
Total Expenditure	124,929,538	100.0
General expenditure	108,024,926	86.5
Intergovernmental expenditure	27,590,295	22.1
Direct expenditure	80,434,631	64.4
General expenditure, by function:		
Education	47,479,191	38.0
Public welfare	30,780,705	24.6
Hospitals	5,237,650	4.2
Health	2,774,086	2.2
Highways	7,536,463	6.0
Police protection	799,712	0.6
Correction	3,701,789	3.0
Natural resources	1,040,736	0.8
Parks and recreation	166,995	0.1
Governmental administration	1,818,589	1.5
Interest on general debt	1,729,403	1.4
Other and unallocable	4,959,607	4.0
Utility expenditure	0	-
Liquor stores expenditure	0	-
Insurance trust expenditure	16,904,612	13.5
Debt at End of Fiscal Year	39,624,672	X
Cash and Security Holdings	303,265,809	X

X = Not applicable.
- = Zero or rounds to zero.
[1]Within insurance trust revenue, net earnings of state retirement systems is a calculated statistic (the item code in the data file is X08), and thus can be positive or negative. Net earnings is the sum of earnings on investments plus gains on investments minus losses on investments. The change made in 2002 for asset valuation from book to market value in accordance with Statement 34 of the Governmental Accounting Standards Board is reflected in the calculated statistics.

Table TX-16. State Government Tax Collections, 2014

(Dollars in thousands, percent.)

Item	Dollars	Percent distribution
Total Taxes	55,260,850	100.0
Property taxes	X	X
Sales and gross receipts	45,746,598	82.8
General sales and gross receipts	32,336,032	58.5
Selective sales and gross receipts	13,410,566	24.3
Alcoholic beverages	1,066,512	1.9
Amusements	29,659	0.1
Insurance premiums	1,886,289	3.4
Motor fuels	3,325,916	6.0
Pari-mutuels	7,356	-
Public utilities	768,000	1.4
Tobacco products	1,446,144	2.6
Other selective sales	4,880,690	8.8
Licenses	3,499,902	6.3
Alcoholic beverages	71,661	0.1
Amusements	20,664	0.0
Corporations in general	124,996	0.2
Hunting and fishing	104,390	0.2
Motor vehicle	2,177,571	3.9
Motor vehicle operators	139,337	0.3
Public utilities	28,080	0.1
Occupation and business, NEC	668,807	1.2
Other licenses	164,396	0.3
Income taxes	0	-
Individual income	X	X
Corporation net income	X	X
Other taxes	6,014,350	10.9
Death and gift	X	X
Documentary and stock transfer	0	-
Severance	6,014,350	10.9
Taxes, NEC	0	-

X = Not applicable.
- = Zero or rounds to zero.

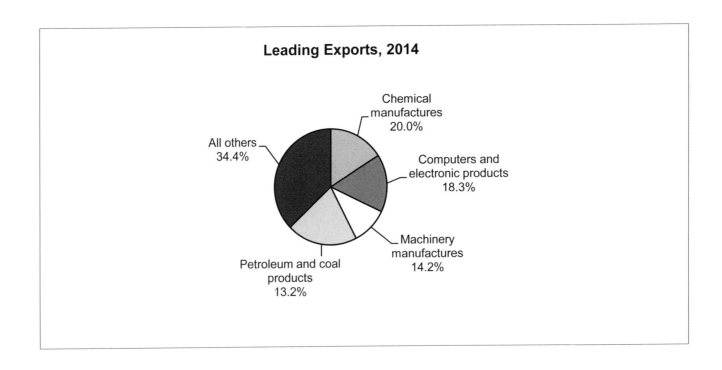

Leading Exports, 2014

Chemical manufactures 20.0%

Computers and electronic products 18.3%

Machinery manufactures 14.2%

Petroleum and coal products 13.2%

All others 34.4%

Facts and Figures

Location: Western United States; bordered on the N by Idaho and Wyoming, on the E by Colorado, on the S by Arizona, and on the W by Nevada; Utah is one of the Four Corner states—at its SE corner it touches Arizona, Colorado, and New Mexico

Area: 84,899 sq. mi. (219,887 sq. km.); rank—13th

Population: 2,942,902 (2014 est.); rank—33rd

Principal Cities: capital—Salt Lake City; largest—Salt Lake City

Statehood: January 4, 1896; 45th state

U.S. Congress: 2 senators, 4 representatives

State Motto: Industry

State Song: "Utah, We Love Thee"

State Nickname: The Beehive State

Abbreviations: UT

State Symbols: flower—sego lily; tree—blue spruce; bird—California seagull

At a Glance

- With an increase in population of 6.5 percent, Utah ranked 4th among the states in growth from 2010 to 2014.

- Utah's violent crime rate in 2013 was 224.0 per 100,000 population, compared to 367.9 for the entire nation.

- Of all the states, Utah had the highest percent of children in 2014, with 30.7 percent of its population under age 18.

- Utah's median household income in 2013 was $59,770, and 12.7 percent of the population lived below the poverty level.

- In 2013, 14.0 percent of Utahns did not have health insurance, compared to 14.5 percent of the total U.S. population.

Table UT-1. Population by Age, Sex, Race, and Hispanic Origin

(Number, percent, except where noted.)

Sex, age, race, and Hispanic origin	2000	2010	2014[1]	Average annual percent change, 2010–2014
Total Population	2,233,169	2,763,885	2,942,902	1.6
Percent of total U.S. population	0.8	0.9	0.9	X
Sex				
Male	1,119,031	1,388,317	1,479,750	1.6
Female	1,114,138	1,375,568	1,463,152	1.6
Age				
Under 5 years	209,378	263,924	252,131	-1.1
5 to 19 years	601,599	698,613	737,775	1.4
20 to 64 years	1,231,970	1,551,886	1,657,736	1.7
65 years and over	190,222	249,462	295,260	4.3
Median age (years)	27.1	29.2	30.5	1.1
Race and Hispanic Origin				
One race				
White	1,992,975	2,547,328	2,689,846	1.4
Black	17,657	33,864	39,655	4.0
American Indian and Alaska Native	29,684	40,729	44,551	2.3
Asian	37,108	57,800	70,407	5.1
Native Hawaiian or Other Pacific Islander	15,145	26,049	29,046	2.8
Two or more races	47,185	58,114	69,397	4.5
Hispanic (of any race)	201,559	370,870	398,760	1.8

X = Not applicable.

[1]Population figures for 2014 are July 1 estimates. The 2010 estimates are taken from the 2010 Census.

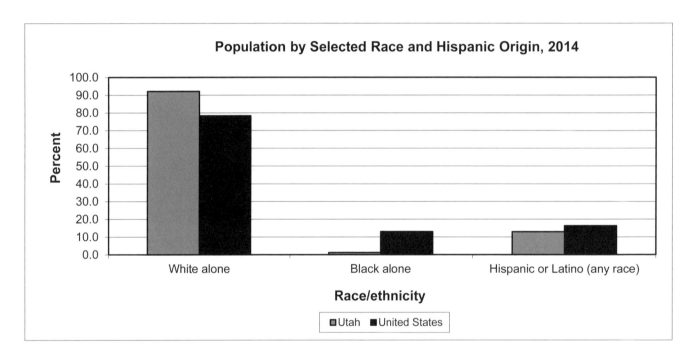

Table UT-2. Marital Status

(Number, percent distribution.)

Sex, age, race, and Hispanic origin	2000	2010	2013
Males, 15 Years and Over	813,693	1,014,706	1,067,533
Never married	30.6	31.3	32.2
Now married, except separated	59.5	58.0	56.6
Separated	1.1	1.3	1.3
Widowed	1.6	1.8	1.6
Divorced	7.3	7.6	8.4
Females, 15 Years and Over	852,995	1,019,010	1,074,003
Never married	25.2	25.8	26.6
Now married, except separated	58.0	56.6	55.1
Separated	1.4	1.6	1.9
Widowed	6.6	5.8	6.0
Divorced	8.8	10.1	10.4

Table UT-3. Households and Housing Characteristics

(Number, percent, dollars.)

Item	2000	2010	2013	Average annual percent change, 2000–2013
Total Households...............	701,281	880,025	899,475	1.9
Family households	535,294	665,964	677,332	1.8
Married-couple family	442,931	543,212	551,975	1.7
Other family	92,363	122,752	125,357	2.4
Male householder, no wife present.....	26,422	37,258	38,848	3.0
Female householder, no husband present........	65,941	85,494	86,509	2.1
Nonfamily households	165,987	214,061	222,143	2.3
Householder living alone.............	124,756	164,863	172,161	2.5
Householder not living alone.........	41,231	49,198	49,982	1.5
Housing Characteristics				
Total housing units..................	768,594	981,821	1,006,164	2.1
Occupied housing units	701,281	880,025	899,475	1.9
Owner occupied	501,547	615,142	622,572	1.7
Renter occupied	188,734	264,883	276,903	3.0
Average household size...............	3.13	3.10	3.17	0.1
Financial Characteristics				
Median gross rent of renter-occupied housing	597	796	881	3.0
Median monthly owner costs for housing units with a mortgage	1,102	1,433	1,377	1.7
Median value of owner-occupied housing units	146,100	217,200	211,400	2.9

- = Zero or rounds to zero.

Table UT-4. Migration, Origin, and Language

(Number, percent.)

Characteristic	State			U.S.		
	2012	2013	Percent change	2012	2013	Percent change
Residence 1 Year Ago						
Population 1 year and over	2,805,440	2,854,667	1.8	310,212,755	312,432,820	0.7
Same house...............	82.8	82.7	X	85.0	85.0	X
Different house in the U.S.............	16.5	16.7	X	14.4	14.4	X
Same county...............	10.3	10.2	X	9.0	8.9	X
Different county	6.2	6.5	X	5.4	5.5	X
Same state	3.1	3.0	X	3.2	3.2	X
Different state	3.1	3.4	X	2.3	2.3	X
Abroad	0.7	0.6	X	0.6	0.6	X
Place of Birth						
Native born	2,614,415	2,663,918	1.9	273,089,382	274,780,773	0.6
Male	50.4	50.4	X	49.3	49.3	X
Female	49.6	49.6	X	50.7	50.7	X
Foreign born	240,872	236,954	-1.6	40,824,658	41,348,066	1.3
Male	48.6	48.9	X	48.7	48.8	X
Female	51.4	51.1	X	51.3	51.2	X
Foreign born; naturalized U.S. citizen..........	83,880	88,045	5.0	18,686,237	19,294,710	3.3
Male	46.5	45.6	X	45.8	45.9	X
Female	53.5	54.4	X	54.2	54.1	X
Foreign born; not a U.S. citizen..........	156,992	148,909	-5.1	22,138,421	22,053,356	-0.4
Male	49.8	50.9	X	51.1	51.3	X
Female	50.2	49.1	X	48.9	48.7	X
Entered 2010 or later	7.1	11.3	X	7.0	9.7	X
Entered 2000 to 2009	38.1	33.9	X	30.4	29.4	X
Entered before 2000.........	54.9	54.8	X	62.7	61.0	X
World Region of Birth, Foreign						
Foreign-born population, excluding population born at sea	240,872	236,954	-1.6	40,824,553	41,347,945	1.3
Europe	10.4	12.1	X	11.8	11.6	X
Asia......................	20.4	19.5	X	29.2	29.5	X
Africa	2.6	3.0	X	4.2	4.4	X
Oceania	3.9	3.3	X	0.6	0.5	X
Latin America	59.6	57.9	X	52.2	51.9	X
North America	3.1	4.1	X	2.0	2.0	X
Language Spoken at Home and Ability to Speak English						
Population 5 years and over.........	2,597,358	2,647,463	1.9	294,003,714	296,358,760	0.8
English only	85.3	85.9	X	79.0	79.2	X
Language other than English.........	14.7	14.1	X	21.0	20.8	X
Speaks English less than "very well".........	5.3	4.8	X	8.5	8.5	X

NA = Not available.
X = Not applicable.
- = Zero or rounds to zero.

Table UT-5. Median Income and Poverty Status, 2013

(Number, percent, except as noted.)

Characteristic	State		U.S.	
	Number	Percent	Number	Percent
Median Income				
Households (dollars)...	59,770	X	52,250	X
Families (dollars)	67,231	X	64,030	X
Below Poverty Level (All People)	361,181	12.7	48,810,868	15.8
Sex				
Male..	168,386	11.8	21,938,525	14.5
Female...	192,795	13.6	26,872,343	17.1
Age				
Under 18 years..	130,345	14.8	16,086,960	22.2
Related children under 18 years.......................	127,079	14.4	15,769,921	21.9
18 to 64 years	210,760	12.5	28,578,191	14.8
65 years and over	20,076	7.2	4,145,717	9.6

X = Not applicable.

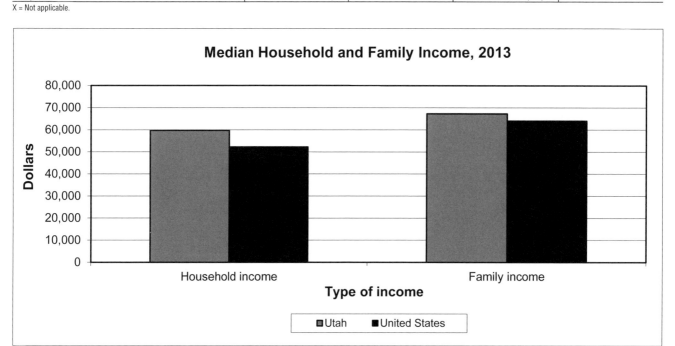

Table UT-6. Health Insurance Coverage Status for the Civilian Noninstitutionalized Population and Children Under 18 Years of Age

(Numbers in thousands, percent.)

Item	2005	2006	2007	2008	2009	2010	2011	2012	2013
Civilian Noninstitutionalized Population	2,524	2,537	2,657	2,705	2,755	2,750	2,790	2,829	2,874
Covered by Private or Public Insurance									
Number..	2,110	2,094	2,317	2,286	2,354	2,328	2,364	2,420	2,472
Percent..	83.6	82.6	87.2	84.5	85.4	84.7	84.7	85.5	86.0
Not Covered									
Number..	414	442	340	419	401	422	426	409	402
Percent..	16.4	17.4	12.8	15.5	14.6	15.3	15.3	14.5	14.0
Percent in the U.S. not covered..	15.3	15.8	15.3	15.1	15.1	15.5	15.1	14.8	14.5
Children Under 18 Years of Age...	762	801	832	849	869	870	878	884	894
Covered by Private or Public Insurance									
Number..	668	681	746	738	780	775	781	794	809
Percent..	87.7	85.0	89.6	86.9	89.7	89.1	88.9	89.9	90.5
Not Covered									
Number..	94	120	87	111	89	95	97	90	85
Percent..	12.3	15.0	10.4	13.1	10.3	10.9	11.1	10.1	9.5
Percent in the U.S. not covered..	10.9	11.7	11.0	9.7	8.6	8.0	7.5	7.2	7.1

Table UT-7. Employment Status by Demographic Group, 2014

(Numbers in thousands, percent.)

Characteristic	Civilian noninstitutional population	Civilian labor force		Employed		Unemployed	
		Number	Percent of population	Number	Percent of population	Number	Percent of population
Total...	2,104	1,428	67.9	1,372	65.2	55	3.9
Sex							
Male...	1,047	825	78.9	792	75.7	33	4.0
Female	1,057	602	56.9	580	54.8	22	3.7
Race, Sex, and Hispanic Origin							
White...	1,978	1,342	67.9	1,292	65.3	51	3.8
Male...	982	775	78.9	744	75.8	30	3.9
Female	996	568	57.0	547	54.9	20	3.6
Black or African American....................................	NA	NA	NA	NA	NA	NA	NA
Male...	NA	NA	NA	NA	NA	NA	NA
Female	NA	NA	NA	NA	NA	NA	NA
Hispanic or Latino ethnicity[1]	251	186	73.9	177	70.6	8	4.5
Male...	135	115	85.1	109	80.8	6	5.1
Female	116	71	61.0	68	58.8	3	3.5
Age							
16 to 19 years..	153	71	46.5	64	41.6	8	10.5
20 to 24 years..	213	164	77.1	153	71.9	11	6.7
25 to 34 years..	462	371	80.4	360	78.0	11	3.1
35 to 44 years..	411	328	79.9	316	77.0	12	3.6
45 to 54 years..	310	250	80.7	243	78.3	7	2.9
55 to 64 years..	273	186	68.2	181	66.4	5	2.7
65 years and over	283	57	20.1	55	19.6	2	2.8

NOTE: Data in Table 7 are from the Current Population Survey (CPS) and do not match the estimates in Table 8. See notes and definitions for further information.
[1]May be of any race.
NA = Not available.

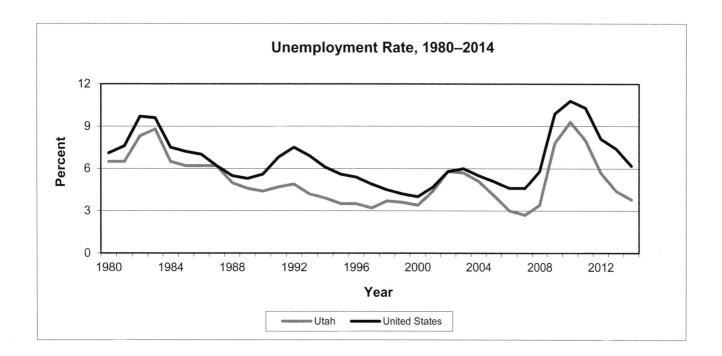

Table UT-8. Employment Status of the Civilian Noninstitutional Population Age 16 Years and Over

(Number, percent.)

Year	Civilian labor force	Civilian participation rate	Employed	Unemployed	Unemployment rate
2006	1,318,450	71.8	1,279,328	39,122	3.0
2007	1,359,129	71.9	1,324,060	35,069	2.6
2008	1,371,201	70.9	1,322,089	49,112	3.6
2009	1,365,850	69.2	1,266,009	99,841	7.3
2010	1,356,097	68.8	1,249,814	106,283	7.8
2011	1,351,420	67.8	1,260,104	91,316	6.8
2012	1,374,622	67.8	1,299,910	74,712	5.4
2013	1,409,607	68.2	1,343,885	65,722	4.7
2014	1,431,104	68.0	1,376,946	54,158	3.8

Table UT-9. Employment and Average Wages by Industry

(Estimates from 2007 through 2010 are based on the 2007 *North American Industry Classification System* [NAICS]. Estimates from 2011 onward are based on the 2012 NAICS.)

Industry	2007	2008	2009	2010	2011	2012	2013
				Number of jobs			
Wage and Salary Employment by Industry	1,310,226	1,311,608	1,247,606	1,241,818	1,268,399	1,305,665	1,346,365
Farm Wage and Salary Employment	4,486	4,713	4,542	4,814	4,406	4,373	4,836
Nonfarm Wage and Salary Employment	1,305,740	1,306,895	1,243,064	1,237,004	1,263,993	1,301,292	1,341,529
Private wage and salary employment	1,080,328	1,078,399	1,011,524	1,002,726	1,026,412	1,060,080	1,098,297
Forestry, fishing, and related activities	1,330	1,382	1,345	1,416	1,520	1,516	1,419
Mining	11,147	12,538	10,661	10,377	11,594	12,493	12,043
Utilities	4,116	4,152	4,138	4,063	4,020	4,019	3,905
Construction	107,457	94,065	73,808	68,344	68,728	71,628	76,148
Manufacturing	127,071	125,310	112,322	110,493	113,063	116,022	118,140
Durable goods manufacturing	87,208	84,643	73,484	71,763	74,057	76,652	77,925
Nondurable goods manufacturing	39,863	40,667	38,838	38,730	39,006	39,370	40,215
Wholesale trade	47,549	48,489	45,518	44,329	46,413	48,009	48,520
Retail trade	149,607	150,693	143,176	140,395	140,822	145,085	149,257
Transportation and warehousing	47,108	47,263	44,387	43,566	45,111	46,662	47,139
Information	29,143	29,633	28,441	28,184	28,366	30,274	31,344
Finance and insurance	57,591	57,218	55,562	53,534	54,128	55,260	57,687
Real estate and rental and leasing	19,004	18,706	17,314	17,051	17,247	17,196	18,170
Professional, scientific, and technical services	65,664	69,048	66,306	66,276	69,200	73,072	79,214
Management of companies and enterprises	18,459	18,575	17,631	16,747	16,759	17,363	17,410
Administrative and waste services	78,741	74,471	65,477	69,473	73,645	76,581	80,522
Educational services	34,865	36,706	37,869	39,440	40,781	42,207	42,909
Health care and social assistance	108,005	113,600	116,693	119,358	121,951	124,463	130,117
Arts, entertainment, and recreation	18,333	17,880	17,726	17,724	18,363	19,377	19,785
Accommodation and food services	95,730	98,236	94,413	94,375	96,696	100,053	104,719
Other services, except public administration	59,408	60,434	58,737	57,581	58,005	58,800	59,849
Government and government enterprises	225,412	228,496	231,540	234,278	237,581	241,212	243,232
				Dollars			
Average Wages and Salaries by Industry	37,697	38,692	39,319	40,174	41,105	42,220	42,693
Average Farm Wages and Salaries	37,146	34,123	39,314	32,225	36,531	31,459	42,613
Average Nonfarm Wages and Salaries	37,699	38,708	39,319	40,205	41,121	42,256	42,693
Average private wages and salaries	37,748	38,652	39,162	40,273	41,292	42,729	43,188
Forestry, fishing, and related activities	25,381	25,229	25,462	26,348	26,901	27,600	30,378
Mining	68,266	70,405	66,927	70,788	74,076	77,188	77,857
Utilities	80,223	81,494	83,143	87,092	87,564	86,843	89,133
Construction	38,204	39,977	41,563	42,876	43,528	45,044	44,350
Manufacturing	45,274	47,864	49,081	50,872	51,558	52,795	53,191
Durable goods manufacturing	47,679	50,955	52,739	54,604	55,385	56,122	56,264
Nondurable goods manufacturing	40,012	41,429	42,159	43,958	44,293	46,319	47,235
Wholesale trade	54,101	54,896	54,677	55,743	58,575	60,147	62,269
Retail trade	26,710	26,213	26,129	26,850	27,280	28,480	28,771
Transportation and warehousing	45,031	42,733	42,455	43,839	44,729	45,091	46,736
Information	48,899	49,037	50,251	53,670	57,933	60,721	61,302
Finance and insurance	52,386	52,538	53,399	55,963	58,425	63,047	63,627
Real estate and rental and leasing	36,183	35,780	35,628	36,662	38,749	40,374	40,684
Professional, scientific, and technical services	57,318	59,646	60,220	60,855	62,758	63,937	63,434
Management of companies and enterprises	66,759	68,704	70,365	80,746	78,792	86,277	85,448
Administrative and waste services	26,586	27,890	28,582	28,863	29,656	30,629	31,372
Educational services	25,777	26,326	26,558	27,559	28,441	28,510	29,067
Health care and social assistance	36,222	37,112	38,548	38,536	39,100	40,067	40,593
Arts, entertainment, and recreation	25,158	24,260	24,477	25,277	25,180	24,973	26,383
Accommodation and food services	16,266	16,298	15,971	16,567	17,056	17,529	17,420
Other services, except public administration	34,661	36,713	38,518	40,508	40,876	42,603	44,771
Government and government enterprises	37,464	38,977	40,005	39,914	40,384	40,181	40,459

Table UT-10. Employment Characteristics by Family Type

(Number, percent.)

Family type and labor force status	2011		2012		2013	
	Total	Families with own children under 18 years	Total	Families with own children under 18 years	Total	Families with own children under 18 years
All Families	662,478	339,646	666,661	345,172	677,332	352,191
FAMILY TYPE AND LABOR FORCE STATUS						
Married-Couple Families	534,006	267,353	542,587	274,021	551,975	283,134
Both husband and wife in labor force	51.3	55.0	52.4	57.7	49.9	54.1
Husband in labor force, wife not in labor force	29.7	41.4	29.2	39.0	31.2	41.1
Wife in labor force, husband not in labor force	5.5	2.6	5.4	2.2	5.9	3.5
Both husband and wife not in labor force	13.4	1.1	13.0	1.1	12.6	1.1
Other Families	128,472	72,293	124,074	71,151	125,357	69,057
Female householder, no husband present	70.3	74.7	69.4	71.4	69.0	70.6
In labor force	52.4	63.5	50.4	60.0	51.1	58.7
Not in labor force	17.9	11.2	18.9	11.4	17.9	11.9
Male householder, no wife present	29.7	25.3	30.6	28.6	31.0	29.4
In labor force	24.8	24.0	25.3	26.2	25.0	28.3
Not in labor force	4.9	1.3	5.3	2.3	5.9	1.2

Table UT-11. School Enrollment and Educational Attainment, 2013

(Number, percent.)

Item	State	U.S.
Enrollment		
Total population 3 years and over, enrolled in school	945,104	82,395,254
Enrolled in nursery school or preschool (percent)	6.1	6.0
Enrolled in kindergarten (percent)	5.6	5.2
Enrolled in elementary school, grades 1-8 (percent)	41.4	40.0
Enrolled in high school, grades 9-12 (percent)	20.1	20.6
Enrolled in college or graduate school (percent)	26.7	28.3
Attainment		
Total population 25 years and over	1,670,449	210,910,615
Less than ninth grade (percent)	2.9	5.8
9th to 12th grade, no diploma (percent)	5.5	7.6
High school graduate, including equivalency (percent)	22.9	27.8
Some college, no degree (percent)	27.8	21.1
Associate's degree (percent)	9.5	8.1
Bachelor's degree (percent)	20.9	18.4
Graduate or professional degree (percent)	10.5	11.2
High school graduate or higher (percent)	91.5	86.6
Bachelor's degree or higher (percent)	31.3	29.6

Table UT-12. Public School Characteristics and Educational Indicators

(Number, percent; data derived from National Center of Education Statistics.)

Item	State	U.S.
Public Schools, 2012–2013 (except where noted)		
Number of school districts	132	18,093
Number of schools	995	98,454
Number of students (in thousands)	613	49,771
Number of teachers (in thousands)	27	3,109
Student-teacher ratio	23.0	16.0
Expenditures per student (dollars), FY 2012	6,441	10,667
Four-year adjusted cohort graduation rate (ACGR)[1,2]	83.0	81.4
Students eligible for free or reduced-price lunch (in thousands)	363	25,188
English language learners (in thousands)	32	4,397
Students age 3 to 21 served under IDEA, part B (in thousands)	78	6,429

Public Schools by Type	Number	Percent of state public schools
Total number of schools	995	100.0
Regular	897	90.2
Special education	69	6.9
Vocational education	3	0.3
Alternative education	26	2.6

NOTE: Every school is assigned only one school type based on its instructional emphasis.
[1]ACGR data represents a new method of calculating high-school completion rates and may not be comparable to previous years' data for Averaged Freshmen Graduation Rates (AFGR).
[2]The United States 4-year ACGRs were estimated using both the reported 4-year ACGR data from 49 states and the District of Columbia and using imputed data for Idaho. The estimate for American Indian/Alaska Native students also includes imputed data for Virginia.

Table UT-13. Reported Voting and Registration of the Voting-Age Population, November 2012

(Numbers in thousands, percent.)

			Registered			Voted		
Item	Total population	Total citizen population	Total registered	Percent registered (total population)	Percent registered (total citizen population)	Total voted	Percent voted (total population)	Percent voted (total citizen population)
U.S. Total	235,248	215,081	153,157	65.1	71.2	132,948	56.5	61.8
State Total	1,917	1,793	1,138	59.4	63.5	1,022	53.3	57.0
Sex								
Male	940	869	543	57.8	62.4	494	52.6	56.9
Female	977	924	595	60.9	64.4	528	54.0	57.1
Race								
White alone.............................	1,780	1,683	1,089	61.2	64.7	989	55.6	58.8
White, non-Hispanic alone	1,561	1,546	1,030	66.0	66.6	943	60.4	61.0
Black alone.............................	23	18	9	B	B	9	B	B
Asian alone	57	37	20	B	B	12	B	B
Hispanic (of any race)	233	151	61	26.1	40.1	49	20.9	32.1
White alone or in combination	1,808	1,712	1,097	60.7	64.1	997	55.1	58.2
Black alone or in combination..........	34	28	11	B	B	11	B	B
Asian alone or in combination..........	59	40	22	B	B	14	B	B
Age								
18 to 24 years	279	263	115	41.2	43.7	97	34.8	36.9
25 to 44 years	803	714	418	52.1	58.5	355	44.2	49.7
45 to 64 years	592	576	396	67.0	68.8	375	63.4	65.1
65 to 74 years	141	138	118	83.8	85.5	111	78.9	80.5
75 years and over	101	101	90	88.9	88.9	84	82.5	82.5

B = Base is less than 75,000 and therefore too small to show the derived measure.

Table UT-14. Crime

(Number, rate per 100,000. Data are derived from the FBI Uniform Crime Reports.)

	State			U.S.[1,2,3,4]		
Item	2012	2013	Percent change	2012	2013	Percent change
TOTAL POPULATION[5]..	2,854,871	2,900,872	1.6	313,873,685	316,128,839	0.7
VIOLENT CRIME						
Number.............................	5,939	6,070	2.2	1,217,067	1,163,146	-4.4
Rate.................................	208.0	209.2	0.6	387.8	367.9	-5.1
Murder and Nonnegligent Manslaughter						
Number.............................	52	49	-5.8	14,866	14,196	-4.5
Rate.................................	1.8	1.7	-7.3	4.7	4.5	-5.2
Rape[6]						
Number.............................	X	1,422	X	X	108,612	X
Rate.................................	X	49.0	X	X	34.4	X
Robbery						
Number.............................	1,105	1,243	12.5	355,051	345,031	-2.8
Rate.................................	38.7	42.8	10.7	113.1	109.1	-3.5
Aggravated Assault						
Number.............................	3,807	3,784	-0.6	762,009	724,149	-5.0
Rate.................................	133.4	130.4	-2.2	242.8	229.1	-5.6
PROPERTY CRIME						
Number.............................	86,284	85,586	-0.8	9,001,992	8,632,512	-4.1
Rate.................................	3,022.3	2,950.4	-2.4	2,868.0	2,730.7	-4.8
Burglary						
Number.............................	13,095	13,333	1.8	2,109,932	1,928,465	-8.6
Rate.................................	458.7	459.6	0.2	672.2	610.0	-9.3
Larceny-Theft						
Number.............................	67,157	64,788	-3.5	6,168,874	6,004,453	-2.7
Rate.................................	2,352.4	2,233.4	-5.1	1,965.4	1,899.4	-3.4
Motor Vehicle Theft						
Number.............................	6,032	7,465	23.8	723,186	699,594	-3.3
Rate.................................	211.3	257.3	21.8	230.4	221.3	-4.0

NOTE: Although arson data are included in the trend and clearance tables, sufficient data are not available to estimate totals for this offense. Therefore, no arson data are published in this table.
X = Not applicable.
- = Zero or rounds to zero.
[1]The crime figures have been adjusted.
[2]The data collection methodology for the offense of forcible rape used by the Minnesota state Uniform Crime Reporting (UCR) Program (with the exception of Minneapolis and St. Paul, Minnesota) does not comply with national UCR Program guidelines. Consequently, its figures for forcible rape and violent crime (of which forcible rape is a part) are not published in this table.
[3]Includes offenses reported by the Zoological Police and the Metro Transit Police.
[4]Because of changes in the state's reporting practices, figures are not comparable to previous years' data.
[5]Populations are U.S. Census Bureau provisional estimates as of July 1 of each year.
[6]The figures shown for the offense of rape were estimated using the revised Uniform Crime Reporting (UCR) definition of rape.

Table UT-15. State Government Finances, 2013

(Dollar amounts in thousands, percent distribution.)

Item	Dollars	Percent distribution
Total Revenue	18,442,207	100.0
General revenue	14,810,655	80.3
Intergovernmental revenue	4,304,061	23.3
Taxes	6,325,126	34.3
General sales	1,884,170	10.2
Selective sales	855,746	4.6
License taxes	290,388	1.6
Individual income tax	2,852,088	15.5
Corporate income tax	330,684	1.8
Other taxes	112,050	0.6
Current charges	3,181,111	17.2
Miscellaneous general revenue	1,000,357	5.4
Utility revenue	0	-
Liquor stores revenue	290,757	1.6
Insurance trust revenue[1]	3,340,795	18.1
Total Expenditure	16,822,502	100.0
Intergovernmental expenditure	3,069,082	18.2
Direct expenditure	13,753,420	81.8
Current operation	9,766,636	58.1
Capital outlay	1,324,378	7.9
Insurance benefits and repayments	1,659,853	9.9
Assistance and subsidies	731,866	4.4
Interest on debt	270,687	1.6
Exhibit: Salaries and wages	2,925,621	17.4
Total Expenditure	16,822,502	100.0
General expenditure	14,956,224	88.9
Intergovernmental expenditure	3,069,082	18.2
Direct expenditure	11,887,142	70.7
General expenditure, by function:		
Education	6,874,554	40.9
Public welfare	3,017,968	17.9
Hospitals	1,180,848	7.0
Health	390,835	2.3
Highways	961,772	5.7
Police protection	143,594	0.9
Correction	310,560	1.8
Natural resources	172,571	1.0
Parks and recreation	37,823	0.2
Governmental administration	650,991	3.9
Interest on general debt	270,687	1.6
Other and unallocable	944,021	5.6
Utility expenditure	0	-
Liquor stores expenditure	206,425	1.2
Insurance trust expenditure	1,659,853	9.9
Debt at End of Fiscal Year	7,049,552	X
Cash and Security Holdings	29,360,710	X

X = Not applicable.
- = Zero or rounds to zero.
[1]Within insurance trust revenue, net earnings of state retirement systems is a calculated statistic (the item code in the data file is X08), and thus can be positive or negative. Net earnings is the sum of earnings on investments plus gains on investments minus losses on investments. The change made in 2002 for asset valuation from book to market value in accordance with Statement 34 of the Governmental Accounting Standards Board is reflected in the calculated statistics.

Table UT-16. State Government Tax Collections, 2014

(Dollars in thousands, percent.)

Item	Dollars	Percent distribution
Total Taxes	6,312,489	100.0
Property taxes	X	X
Sales and gross receipts	2,682,100	42.5
General sales and gross receipts	1,823,355	28.9
Selective sales and gross receipts	858,745	13.6
Alcoholic beverages	48,413	0.8
Amusements	0	-
Insurance premiums	113,316	1.8
Motor fuels	372,935	5.9
Pari-mutuels	0	-
Public utilities	24,319	0.4
Tobacco products	113,184	1.8
Other selective sales	186,578	3.0
Licenses	276,824	4.4
Alcoholic beverages	1,936	0.0
Amusements	0	-
Corporations in general	484	0.0
Hunting and fishing	28,720	0.5
Motor vehicle	175,679	2.8
Motor vehicle operators	15,733	0.2
Public utilities	0	-
Occupation and business, NEC	53,264	0.8
Other licenses	1,008	-
Income taxes	3,197,822	50.7
Individual income	2,889,912	45.8
Corporation net income	307,910	4.9
Other taxes	155,743	2.5
Death and gift	0	-
Documentary and stock transfer	0	-
Severance	155,743	2.5
Taxes, NEC	0	-

X = Not applicable.
- = Zero or rounds to zero.

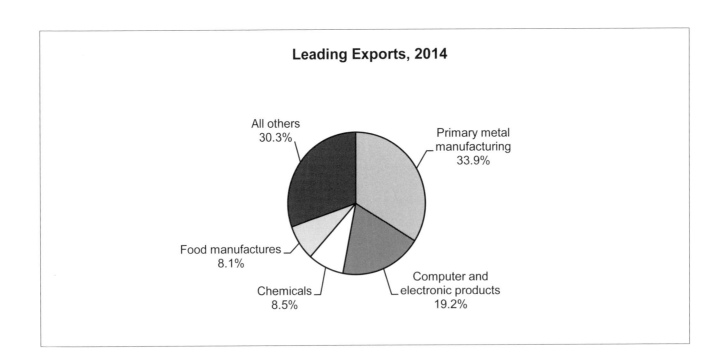

Leading Exports, 2014

All others 30.3%
Primary metal manufacturing 33.9%
Food manufactures 8.1%
Chemicals 8.5%
Computer and electronic products 19.2%

VERMONT

Facts and Figures

Location: Northeastern United States; bordered on the N by Canada (Quebec), on the E by New Hampshire, on the S by Massachusetts, and on the W by New York

Area: 9,614 sq. mi. (24,901 sq. km.); rank—45th

Population: 626,562 (2014 est.); rank—50th

Principal Cities: capital—Montpelier; largest—Burlington

Statehood: March 4, 1791; the 14th state

U.S. Congress: 2 senators, 1 representative

State Motto: Freedom and Unity

State Song: "These Green Mountains"

State Nickname: The Green Mountain State

Abbreviations: VT; Vt.

State Symbols: flower—red clover; tree—sugar maple; bird—hermit thrush

At a Glance

- With an increase in population of 0.1 percent, Vermont ranked 49th among the states in growth from 2010 to 2014.

- Vermont's median household income in 2013 was $52,578, and 12.3 percent of the population lived below the poverty level.

- Vermont's violent crime rate in 2013 was the lowest in the nation at 121.1 incidents per 100,000 population.

- In 2013, 7.2 percent of Vermonters did not have health insurance, compared to 14.5 percent of the total U.S. population.

- Vermont had the third lowest infant mortality rate in the country in 2013, with 4.35 deaths per 1,000 live births.

Table VT-1. Population by Age, Sex, Race, and Hispanic Origin

(Number, percent, except where noted.)

Sex, age, race, and Hispanic origin	2000	2010	2014[1]	Average annual percent change, 2010–2014
Total Population	608,827	625,741	626,562	-
Percent of total U.S. population	0.2	0.2	0.2	X
Sex				
Male	298,337	308,206	308,849	0.1
Female	310,490	317,535	317,713	-
Age				
Under 5 years	33,989	31,952	30,417	-1.2
5 to 19 years	132,268	118,323	112,343	-1.3
20 to 64 years	365,060	384,388	377,603	-0.4
65 years and over	77,510	91,078	106,199	3.9
Median age (years)	37.7	41.5	42.6	0.7
Race and Hispanic Origin				
One race				
White	589,208	598,592	595,181	-0.1
Black	3,063	6,456	7,709	4.5
American Indian and Alaska Native	2,420	2,308	2,356	0.5
Asian	5,217	8,069	9,752	4.9
Native Hawaiian or Other Pacific Islander	141	175	227	6.7
Two or more races	7,335	10,141	11,337	2.8
Hispanic (of any race)	5,504	9,962	11,110	2.8

X = Not applicable.
- = Zero or rounds to zero.
[1]Population figures for 2014 are July 1 estimates. The 2010 estimates are taken from the 2010 Census.

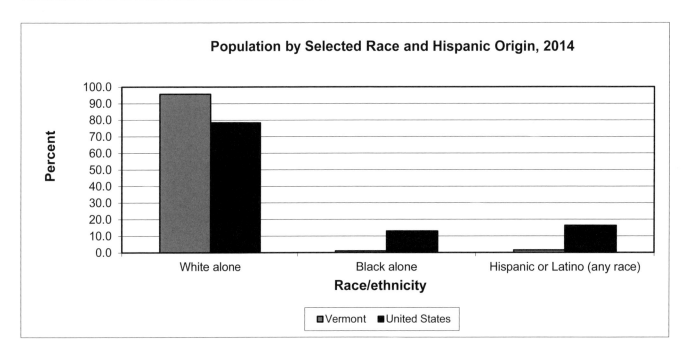

Table VT-2. Marital Status

(Number, percent distribution.)

Sex, age, race, and Hispanic origin	2000	2010	2013
Males, 15 Years and Over	236,517	254,288	256,664
Never married	29.7	34.2	35.8
Now married, except separated	57.1	51.3	49.4
Separated	1.2	1.3	1.3
Widowed	2.4	2.5	2.5
Divorced	9.6	10.7	11.0
Females, 15 Years and Over	251,764	266,860	269,287
Never married	23.9	27.7	28.7
Now married, except separated	53.3	49.7	48.3
Separated	1.4	1.4	1.4
Widowed	10.0	8.2	8.0
Divorced	11.5	13.0	13.6

Table VT-3. Households and Housing Characteristics

(Number, percent, dollars.)

Item	2000	2010	2013	Average annual percent change, 2000–2013
Total Households...	240,634	256,922	253,234	0.4
Family households	157,763	159,846	155,933	-0.1
Married-couple family	126,413	125,678	123,176	-0.2
Other family	31,350	34,168	32,757	0.3
Male householder, no wife present........................	9,078	10,887	9,699	0.5
Female householder, no husband present................	22,272	23,281	23,058	0.3
Nonfamily households	82,871	97,076	97,301	1.2
Householder living alone...................................	63,112	75,243	75,700	1.4
Householder not living alone..............................	19,759	21,833	21,601	0.7
Housing Characteristics				
Total housing units	294,382	322,698	323,936	0.7
Occupied housing units	240,634	256,922	253,234	0.4
Owner occupied	169,784	180,847	179,791	0.4
Renter occupied	70,850	76,075	73,443	0.3
Average household size......................................	2.44	2.34	2.37	-0.2
Financial Characteristics				
Median gross rent of renter-occupied housing	553	823	865	3.5
Median monthly owner costs for housing units with a mortgage	1,021	1,445	1,482	2.9
Median value of owner-occupied housing units............	111,500	216,800	218,300	5.3

Table VT-4. Migration, Origin, and Language

(Number, percent.)

Characteristic	State			U.S.		
	2012	2013	Percent change	2012	2013	Percent change
Residence 1 Year Ago						
Population 1 year and over	620,224	621,256	0.2	310,212,755	312,432,820	0.7
Same house	85.8	87.2	X	85.0	85.0	X
Different house in the U.S.	13.8	12.4	X	14.4	14.4	X
Same county	8.0	6.7	X	9.0	8.9	X
Different county	5.8	5.7	X	5.4	5.5	X
Same state	1.9	2.0	X	3.2	3.2	X
Different state	3.9	3.7	X	2.3	2.3	X
Abroad	0.4	0.4	X	0.6	0.6	X
Place of Birth						
Native born	600,470	599,618	-0.1	273,089,382	274,780,773	0.6
Male	49.7	49.4	X	49.3	49.3	X
Female	50.3	50.6	X	50.7	50.7	X
Foreign born	25,541	27,012	5.8	40,824,658	41,348,066	1.3
Male	43.1	46.9	X	48.7	48.8	X
Female	56.9	53.1	X	51.3	51.2	X
Foreign born; naturalized U.S. citizen...................	15,416	15,904	3.2	18,686,237	19,294,710	3.3
Male	43.3	41.4	X	45.8	45.9	X
Female	56.7	58.6	X	54.2	54.1	X
Foreign born; not a U.S. citizen..........................	10,125	11,108	9.7	22,138,421	22,053,356	-0.4
Male	42.8	54.7	X	51.1	51.3	X
Female	57.2	45.3	X	48.9	48.7	X
Entered 2010 or later	5.7	11.3	X	7.0	9.7	X
Entered 2000 to 2009	29.6	28.1	X	30.4	29.4	X
Entered before 2000...	64.6	60.6	X	62.7	61.0	X
World Region of Birth, Foreign						
Foreign-born population, excluding population born at sea	25,541	27,012	5.8	40,824,553	41,347,945	1.3
Europe	32.9	29.7	X	11.8	11.6	X
Asia..	28.9	28.5	X	29.2	29.5	X
Africa..	8.5	8.7	X	4.2	4.4	X
Oceania	0.6	0.5	X	0.6	0.5	X
Latin America	9.9	11.0	X	52.2	51.9	X
North America	19.1	21.6	X	2.0	2.0	X
Language Spoken at Home and Ability to Speak English						
Population 5 years and over.................................	595,000	596,324	0.2	294,003,714	296,358,760	0.8
English only	94.6	95.0	X	79.0	79.2	X
Language other than English................................	5.4	5.0	X	21.0	20.8	X
Speaks English less than "very well".................	1.4	1.3	X	8.5	8.5	X

NA = Not available.
X = Not applicable.
- = Zero or rounds to zero.

Table VT-5. Median Income and Poverty Status, 2013

(Number, percent, except as noted.)

Characteristic	State		U.S.	
	Number	Percent	Number	Percent
Median Income				
Households (dollars)...	52,578	X	52,250	X
Families (dollars)	68,382	X	64,030	X
Below Poverty Level (All People)	74,058	12.3	48,810,868	15.8
Sex				
Male...	31,641	10.7	21,938,525	14.5
Female	42,417	13.9	26,872,343	17.1
Age				
Under 18 years..	18,697	15.3	16,086,960	22.2
Related children under 18 years.............................	17,731	14.6	15,769,921	21.9
18 to 64 years...	47,447	12.5	28,578,191	14.8
65 years and over	7,914	8.0	4,145,717	9.6

X = Not applicable.

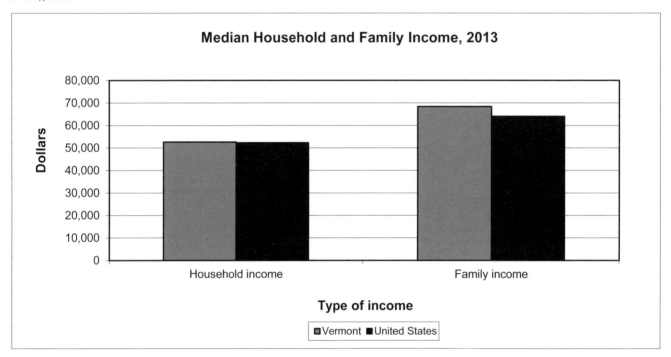

Median Household and Family Income, 2013

■ Vermont ■ United States

Table VT-6. Health Insurance Coverage Status for the Civilian Noninstitutionalized Population and Children Under 18 Years of Age

(Numbers in thousands, percent.)

Item	2005	2006	2007	2008	2009	2010	2011	2012	2013
Civilian Noninstitutionalized Population	622	620	614	615	615	620	620	620	621
Covered by Private or Public Insurance									
Number...	550	557	545	559	562	570	579	580	576
Percent...	88.5	89.8	88.8	90.9	91.4	92.0	93.4	93.5	92.8
Not Covered									
Number...	72	63	69	56	53	50	41	40	45
Percent...	11.5	10.2	11.2	9.1	8.6	8.0	6.6	6.5	7.2
Percent in the U.S. not covered......................	15.3	15.8	15.3	15.1	15.1	15.5	15.1	14.8	14.5
Children Under 18 Years of Age.....................	133	133	129	129	126	130	126	124	124
Covered by Private or Public Insurance									
Number...	126	122	117	124	122	127	123	121	120
Percent...	94.7	92.0	90.6	96.1	96.8	98.0	97.6	97.2	96.9
Not Covered									
Number...	7	11	12	5	4	3	3	3	4
Percent...	5.3	8.0	9.4	3.9	3.2	2.0	2.4	2.8	3.1
Percent in the U.S. not covered......................	10.9	11.7	11.0	9.7	8.6	8.0	7.5	7.2	7.1

Table VT-7. Employment Status by Demographic Group, 2014

(Numbers in thousands, percent.)

Characteristic	Civilian noninstitutional population	Civilian labor force		Employed		Unemployed	
		Number	Percent of population	Number	Percent of population	Number	Percent of population
Total...	514	348	67.6	333	64.8	14	4.2
Sex							
Male...	251	180	71.4	171	68.1	8	4.7
Female..	263	168	64.0	162	61.7	6	3.6
Race, Sex, and Hispanic Origin							
White...	497	336	67.7	322	64.9	14	4.2
Male...	242	173	71.6	165	68.3	8	4.6
Female..	255	163	63.9	157	61.6	6	3.7
Black or African American......................	NA	NA	NA	NA	NA	NA	NA
Male...	NA	NA	NA	NA	NA	NA	NA
Female..	NA	NA	NA	NA	NA	NA	NA
Hispanic or Latino ethnicity[1]..................	NA	NA	NA	NA	NA	NA	NA
Male...	NA	NA	NA	NA	NA	NA	NA
Female..	NA	NA	NA	NA	NA	NA	NA
Age							
16 to 19 years..................................	33	14	43.2	12	36.5	2	15.4
20 to 24 years..................................	39	29	73.2	26	66.7	3	8.8
25 to 34 years..................................	73	63	86.0	60	82.3	3	4.2
35 to 44 years..................................	80	69	86.7	67	84.0	2	3.2
45 to 54 years..................................	85	73	85.2	70	82.5	2	3.2
55 to 64 years..................................	97	75	77.4	74	75.6	2	2.3
65 years and over...............................	106	25	23.2	24	22.4	1	3.3

NOTE: Data in Table 7 are from the Current Population Survey (CPS) and do not match the estimates in Table 8. See notes and definitions for further information.
[1]May be of any race.
NA = Not available.

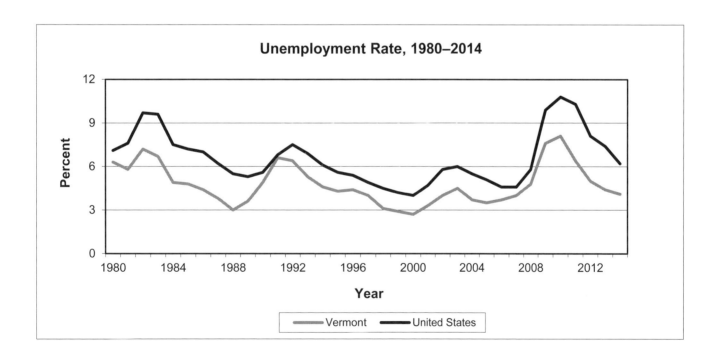

Table VT-8. Employment Status of the Civilian Noninstitutional Population Age 16 Years and Over

(Number, percent.)

Year	Civilian labor force	Civilian participation rate	Employed	Unemployed	Unemployment rate
2006	357,007	71.5	343,865	13,142	3.7
2007	353,739	70.4	339,547	14,192	4.0
2008	354,899	70.3	338,273	16,626	4.7
2009	359,836	71.0	336,104	23,732	6.6
2010	359,402	70.8	337,488	21,914	6.1
2011	358,159	70.2	338,411	19,748	5.5
2012	354,754	69.4	337,120	17,634	5.0
2013	351,209	68.4	335,680	15,529	4.4
2014	348,868	67.8	334,563	14,305	4.1

Table VT-9. Employment and Average Wages by Industry

(Estimates from 2007 through 2010 are based on the 2007 *North American Industry Classification System* [NAICS]. Estimates from 2011 onward are based on the 2012 NAICS.)

Industry	2007	2008	2009	2010	2011	2012	2013
				Number of jobs			
Wage and Salary Employment by Industry	322,306	321,435	311,317	312,230	314,778	317,523	321,355
Farm Wage and Salary Employment	2,163	2,359	2,276	2,282	2,420	2,450	2,903
Nonfarm Wage and Salary Employment	320,143	319,076	309,041	309,948	312,358	315,073	318,452
Private wage and salary employment	263,884	262,280	251,913	252,545	255,425	257,885	259,611
Forestry, fishing, and related activities	796	801	886	903	950	843	858
Mining	834	740	650	594	611	649	621
Utilities	1,738	1,699	1,756	1,801	1,801	1,828	1,790
Construction	17,494	16,221	14,400	14,201	14,835	14,677	14,599
Manufacturing	35,949	34,790	31,153	30,853	30,948	31,908	31,739
Durable goods manufacturing	26,165	25,179	22,088	21,787	21,628	21,695	21,228
Nondurable goods manufacturing	9,784	9,611	9,065	9,066	9,320	10,213	10,511
Wholesale trade	10,602	10,347	9,675	9,634	9,687	9,237	9,258
Retail trade	40,646	40,675	38,854	38,709	38,661	38,017	38,130
Transportation and warehousing	7,173	7,101	6,763	6,896	7,191	7,098	6,997
Information	5,949	5,777	5,510	5,369	4,945	4,675	4,683
Finance and insurance	9,897	9,618	9,373	9,348	9,370	9,299	9,199
Real estate and rental and leasing	3,403	3,388	3,157	3,093	3,066	3,069	3,155
Professional, scientific, and technical services	13,616	13,728	13,450	13,795	13,881	14,189	14,213
Management of companies and enterprises	201	735	778	893	1,417	1,962	1,950
Administrative and waste services	8,811	8,995	8,424	8,867	9,705	10,259	10,498
Educational services	13,886	13,785	13,641	13,683	13,916	14,238	14,438
Health care and social assistance	45,353	46,670	47,664	47,699	47,799	48,977	49,542
Arts, entertainment, and recreation	3,996	3,994	3,866	3,880	3,981	4,050	4,101
Accommodation and food services	29,172	29,080	28,145	28,853	29,023	29,588	30,466
Other services, except public administration	14,368	14,136	13,768	13,474	13,638	13,322	13,374
Government and government enterprises	56,259	56,796	57,128	57,403	56,933	57,188	58,841
				Dollars			
Average Wages and Salaries by Industry	36,405	37,682	38,085	38,735	39,541	40,185	41,099
Average Farm Wages and Salaries	32,749	28,809	28,367	26,723	22,544	24,960	28,702
Average Nonfarm Wages and Salaries	36,429	37,748	38,157	38,823	39,672	40,303	41,212
Average private wages and salaries	35,951	37,110	37,411	38,141	39,048	39,713	40,765
Forestry, fishing, and related activities	26,275	28,313	27,828	28,373	29,278	29,316	30,249
Mining	52,637	53,784	55,386	55,665	54,286	52,570	54,383
Utilities	87,365	88,943	87,929	92,295	92,736	95,723	98,080
Construction	39,984	41,293	41,697	42,705	43,287	43,660	45,447
Manufacturing	49,241	50,530	51,677	53,103	53,784	54,294	54,662
Durable goods manufacturing	53,076	54,343	56,034	57,401	58,356	58,872	59,083
Nondurable goods manufacturing	38,986	40,541	41,061	42,774	43,174	44,568	45,732
Wholesale trade	47,874	50,397	51,531	52,483	54,634	56,334	56,594
Retail trade	24,815	25,291	25,572	25,990	26,772	26,609	27,469
Transportation and warehousing	36,152	36,821	36,804	37,304	37,830	37,944	38,798
Information	42,995	44,230	45,173	45,091	49,309	48,880	51,341
Finance and insurance	61,802	64,673	61,497	62,219	64,123	66,033	67,653
Real estate and rental and leasing	31,269	32,135	32,853	33,356	34,472	36,105	37,800
Professional, scientific, and technical services	57,171	59,530	60,257	63,808	64,562	65,959	68,728
Management of companies and enterprises	53,114	79,751	77,545	78,471	78,258	77,925	81,783
Administrative and waste services	28,559	29,521	30,555	28,779	29,257	31,671	34,511
Educational services	28,677	30,689	31,420	30,674	31,054	30,691	31,759
Health care and social assistance	35,150	36,793	37,601	38,420	39,255	39,929	41,204
Arts, entertainment, and recreation	23,119	22,383	22,841	23,529	23,643	23,858	25,090
Accommodation and food services	20,070	19,587	19,387	19,802	20,710	21,041	21,506
Other services, except public administration	23,678	24,985	25,123	25,701	26,235	26,599	27,512
Government and government enterprises	38,674	40,695	41,444	41,826	42,474	42,962	43,184

Table VT-10. Employment Characteristics by Family Type

(Number, percent.)

Family type and labor force status	2011		2012		2013	
	Total	Families with own children under 18 years	Total	Families with own children under 18 years	Total	Families with own children under 18 years
All Families................................	161,619	66,084	160,878	64,915	155,933	60,395
FAMILY TYPE AND LABOR FORCE STATUS						
Married-Couple Families.........................	128,267	44,516	126,519	44,208	123,176	40,361
Both husband and wife in labor force............	61.4	78.1	59.2	75.9	57.7	75.4
Husband in labor force, wife not in labor force	13.7	16.9	16.1	18.7	15.6	18.1
Wife in labor force, husband not in labor force	8.2	4.1	9.7	4.5	8.3	4.1
Both husband and wife not in labor force.....................	16.7	0.9	15.0	1.0	17.2	1.5
Other Families	33,352	21,568	34,359	20,707	32,757	20,034
Female householder, no husband present........................	66.0	69.1	70.5	72.8	70.4	71.0
In labor force	48.3	54.3	53.4	61.7	50.1	55.0
Not in labor force	17.8	14.9	17.1	11.1	20.3	16.0
Male householder, no wife present...........................	34.0	30.9	29.5	27.2	29.6	29.0
In labor force	27.0	27.5	22.1	22.9	22.5	24.5
Not in labor force	7.0	3.4	7.4	4.4	7.1	4.5

Table VT-11. School Enrollment and Educational Attainment, 2013

(Number, percent.)

Item	State	U.S.
Enrollment		
Total population 3 years and over, enrolled in school	146,569	82,395,254
Enrolled in nursery school or preschool (percent)........................	5.1	6.0
Enrolled in kindergarten (percent).......................................	5.3	5.2
Enrolled in elementary school, grades 1-8 (percent)......................	37.2	40.0
Enrolled in high school, grades 9-12 (percent)...........................	21.6	20.6
Enrolled in college or graduate school (percent)..........................	30.8	28.3
Attainment		
Total population 25 years and over	436,174	210,910,615
Less than ninth grade (percent)	3.2	5.8
9th to 12th grade, no diploma (percent)	5.3	7.6
High school graduate, including equivalency (percent).....................	30.6	27.8
Some college, no degree (percent)	16.9	21.1
Associate's degree (percent)...	8.2	8.1
Bachelor's degree (percent)...	21.4	18.4
Graduate or professional degree (percent)................................	14.3	11.2
High school graduate or higher (percent)	91.5	86.6
Bachelor's degree or higher (percent)....................................	35.7	29.6

Table VT-12. Public School Characteristics and Educational Indicators

(Number, percent; data derived from National Center of Education Statistics.)

Item	State	U.S.
Public Schools, 2012–2013 (except where noted)		
Number of school districts..	361	18,093
Number of schools..	318	98,454
Number of students (in thousands)	90	49,771
Number of teachers (in thousands)	8	3,109
Student-teacher ratio	10.7	16.0
Expenditures per student (dollars), FY 2012.............................	16,651	10,667
Four-year adjusted cohort graduation rate (ACGR)[1,2]	86.6	81.4
Students eligible for free or reduced-price lunch (in thousands)	33	25,188
English language learners (in thousands)	1	4,397
Students age 3 to 21 served under IDEA, part B (in thousands)	14	6,429

Public Schools by Type	Number	Percent of state public schools
Total number of schools..	318	100.0
Regular	302	95.0
Special education..	0	-
Vocational education...	15	4.7
Alternative education	1	0.3

NOTE: Every school is assigned only one school type based on its instructional emphasis.
[1]ACGR data represents a new method of calculating high-school completion rates and may not be comparable to previous years' data for Averaged Freshmen Graduation Rates (AFGR).
[2]The United States 4-year ACGRs were estimated using both the reported 4-year ACGR data from 49 states and the District of Columbia and using imputed data for Idaho. The estimate for American Indian/Alaska Native students also includes imputed data for Virginia.
- = Zero or rounds to zero.

Table VT-13. Reported Voting and Registration of the Voting-Age Population, November 2012

(Numbers in thousands, percent.)

Item	Total population	Total citizen population	Registered			Voted		
			Total registered	Percent registered (total population)	Percent registered (total citizen population)	Total voted	Percent voted (total population)	Percent voted (total citizen population)
U.S. Total	235,248	215,081	153,157	65.1	71.2	132,948	56.5	61.8
State Total	496	487	357	72.0	73.4	308	62.1	63.3
Sex								
Male	241	237	168	69.8	70.7	146	60.6	61.4
Female	255	249	189	74.2	75.9	162	63.5	65.0
Race								
White alone	470	464	341	72.6	73.5	293	62.4	63.2
White, non-Hispanic alone	466	461	339	72.8	73.6	291	62.5	63.2
Black alone	5	5	3	B	B	3	B	B
Asian alone	7	4	4	B	B	3	B	B
Hispanic (of any race)	6	5	3	B	B	3	B	B
White alone or in combination	480	474	348	72.5	73.4	300	62.5	63.2
Black alone or in combination	6	6	3	B	B	3	B	B
Asian alone or in combination	8	5	4	B	B	4	B	B
Age								
18 to 24 years	61	59	30	B	B	23	B	B
25 to 44 years	147	144	94	64.1	65.7	77	52.0	53.3
45 to 64 years	195	193	153	78.8	79.6	133	68.5	69.2
65 to 74 years	49	47	40	B	B	39	B	B
75 years and over	44	44	39	B	B	36	B	B

B = Base is less than 75,000 and therefore too small to show the derived measure.

Table VT-14. Crime

(Number, rate per 100,000. Data are derived from the FBI Uniform Crime Reports.)

Item	State			U.S.[1,2,3,4]		
	2012	2013	Percent change	2012	2013	Percent change
TOTAL POPULATION[5]	625,953	626,630	0.1	313,873,685	316,128,839	0.7
VIOLENT CRIME						
Number	891	720	-19.2	1,217,067	1,163,146	-4.4
Rate	142.3	114.9	-19.3	387.8	367.9	-5.1
Murder and Nonnegligent Manslaughter						
Number	8	10	25.0	14,866	14,196	-4.5
Rate	1.3	1.6	24.9	4.7	4.5	-5.2
Rape[6]						
Number	X	130	X	X	108,612	X
Rate	X	20.7	X	X	34.4	X
Robbery						
Number	114	73	-36.0	355,051	345,031	-2.8
Rate	18.2	11.6	-36.0	113.1	109.1	-3.5
Aggravated Assault						
Number	638	546	-14.4	762,009	724,149	-5.0
Rate	101.9	87.1	-14.5	242.8	229.1	-5.6
PROPERTY CRIME						
Number	15,653	13,875	-11.4	9,001,992	8,632,512	-4.1
Rate	2,500.7	2,214.2	-11.5	2,868.0	2,730.7	-4.8
Burglary						
Number	4,179	3,313	-20.7	2,109,932	1,928,465	-8.6
Rate	667.6	528.7	-20.8	672.2	610.0	-9.3
Larceny-Theft						
Number	11,014	10,228	-7.1	6,168,874	6,004,453	-2.7
Rate	1,759.6	1,632.2	-7.2	1,965.4	1,899.4	-3.4
Motor Vehicle Theft						
Number	460	334	-27.4	723,186	699,594	-3.3
Rate	73.5	53.3	-27.5	230.4	221.3	-4.0

NOTE: Although arson data are included in the trend and clearance tables, sufficient data are not available to estimate totals for this offense. Therefore, no arson data are published in this table.
X = Not applicable.
- = Zero or rounds to zero.
[1]The crime figures have been adjusted.
[2]The data collection methodology for the offense of forcible rape used by the Minnesota state Uniform Crime Reporting (UCR) Program (with the exception of Minneapolis and St. Paul, Minnesota) does not comply with national UCR Program guidelines. Consequently, its figures for forcible rape and violent crime (of which forcible rape is a part) are not published in this table.
[3]Includes offenses reported by the Zoological Police and the Metro Transit Police.
[4]Because of changes in the state's reporting practices, figures are not comparable to previous years' data.
[5]Populations are U.S. Census Bureau provisional estimates as of July 1 of each year.
[6]The figures shown for the offense of rape were estimated using the revised Uniform Crime Reporting (UCR) definition of rape.

Table VT-15. State Government Finances, 2013

(Dollar amounts in thousands, percent distribution.)

Item	Dollars	Percent distribution
Total Revenue	6,295,755	100.0
General revenue	5,635,209	89.5
Intergovernmental revenue	1,872,013	29.7
Taxes	2,878,930	45.7
General sales	347,273	5.5
Selective sales	635,953	10.1
License taxes	106,509	1.7
Individual income tax	663,027	10.5
Corporate income tax	105,635	1.7
Other taxes	1,020,533	16.2
Current charges	527,620	8.4
Miscellaneous general revenue	356,646	5.7
Utility revenue	0	-
Liquor stores revenue	50,950	0.8
Insurance trust revenue[1]	609,596	9.7
Total Expenditure	6,018,247	100.0
Intergovernmental expenditure	1,501,657	25.0
Direct expenditure	4,516,590	75.0
Current operation	3,710,721	61.7
Capital outlay	204,307	3.4
Insurance benefits and repayments	358,256	6.0
Assistance and subsidies	149,104	2.5
Interest on debt	94,202	1.6
Exhibit: Salaries and wages	789,408	13.1
Total Expenditure	6,018,247	100.0
General expenditure	5,607,879	93.2
Intergovernmental expenditure	1,501,657	25.0
Direct expenditure	4,106,222	68.2
General expenditure, by function:		
Education	2,407,364	40.0
Public welfare	1,629,482	27.1
Hospitals	287	0.0
Health	235,775	3.9
Highways	455,461	7.6
Police protection	91,112	1.5
Correction	135,127	2.2
Natural resources	81,883	1.4
Parks and recreation	13,837	0.2
Governmental administration	167,830	2.8
Interest on general debt	94,202	1.6
Other and unallocable	295,519	4.9
Utility expenditure	0	-
Liquor stores expenditure	52,112	0.9
Insurance trust expenditure	358,256	6.0
Debt at End of Fiscal Year	3,330,238	X
Cash and Security Holdings	7,476,113	X

X = Not applicable.
- = Zero or rounds to zero.
[1]Within insurance trust revenue, net earnings of state retirement systems is a calculated statistic (the item code in the data file is X08), and thus can be positive or negative. Net earnings is the sum of earnings on investments plus gains on investments minus losses on investments. The change made in 2002 for asset valuation from book to market value in accordance with Statement 34 of the Governmental Accounting Standards Board is reflected in the calculated statistics.

Table VT-16. State Government Tax Collections, 2014

(Dollars in thousands, percent.)

Item	Dollars	Percent distribution
Total Taxes	2,962,531	100.0
Property taxes	985,478	33.3
Sales and gross receipts	1,014,960	34.3
General sales and gross receipts	354,541	12.0
Selective sales and gross receipts	660,419	22.3
Alcoholic beverages	24,065	0.8
Amusements	0	-
Insurance premiums	60,020	2.0
Motor fuels	103,551	3.5
Pari-mutuels	0	-
Public utilities	21,791	0.7
Tobacco products	71,854	2.4
Other selective sales	379,138	12.8
Licenses	109,996	3.7
Alcoholic beverages	430	-
Amusements	36	-
Corporations in general	3,276	0.1
Hunting and fishing	7,319	0.2
Motor vehicle	70,398	2.4
Motor vehicle operators	7,795	0.3
Public utilities	0	-
Occupation and business, NEC	18,869	0.6
Other licenses	1,873	0.1
Income taxes	781,057	26.4
Individual income	675,240	22.8
Corporation net income	105,817	3.6
Other taxes	71,040	2.4
Death and gift	35,542	1.2
Documentary and stock transfer	30,931	1.0
Severance	X	X
Taxes, NEC	4,567	0.2

X = Not applicable.
- = Zero or rounds to zero.

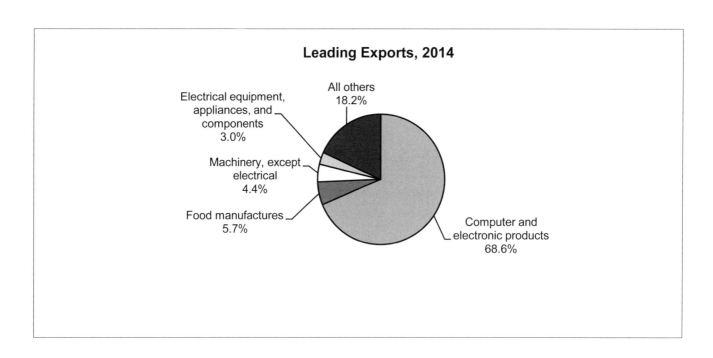

Leading Exports, 2014

- All others 18.2%
- Electrical equipment, appliances, and components 3.0%
- Machinery, except electrical 4.4%
- Food manufactures 5.7%
- Computer and electronic products 68.6%

VIRGINIA

Facts and Figures

Location: Eastern United States; bordered on the N and NE by Maryland and the District of Columbia, on the E by the Atlantic Ocean, on the S by North Carolina and Tennessee, and on the W by Kentucky and West Virginia

Area: 42,774 sq. mi. (110,785 sq. km.); rank—35th

Population: 8,326,289 (2014 est.); rank—12th

Principal Cities: capital—Richmond; largest—Virginia Beach

Statehood: June 25, 1788; 10th state

U.S. Congress: 2 senators, 11 representatives

State Motto: *Sic semper tyrannis* ("Thus always to tyrants")

State Song: "Carry Me Back to Old Virginia"; the Virginia General Assembly (legislature) is in the process of selecting a new state song

State Nickname: The Old Dominion State

Abbreviations: VA; Va.

State Symbols: flower—flowering dogwood; tree—flowering dogwood; bird—cardinal

At a Glance

- With an increase in population of 4.1 percent, Virginia ranked 18th among the states in growth from 2010 to 2014.

- Virginia's violent crime rate (196.2 incidents per 100,000 population) was the third lowest in the country in 2013.

- In 2014, 5.2 percent of Virginians were unemployed, compared to 6.2 percent of the total U.S. population.

- Virginia's median household income in 2013 was $62,666, and 11.7 percent of the population lived below the poverty level.

- In 2013, 12.3 percent of Virginians did not have health insurance, compared to 14.5 percent of the total U.S. population.

Table VA-1. Population by Age, Sex, Race, and Hispanic Origin

(Number, percent, except where noted.)

Sex, age, race, and Hispanic origin	2000	2010	2014[1]	Average annual percent change, 2010–2014
Total Population	7,078,515	8,001,024	8,326,289	1.0
Percent of total U.S. population	2.5	2.6	2.6	X
Sex				
Male	3,471,895	3,925,983	4,095,244	1.1
Female	3,606,620	4,075,041	4,231,045	0.9
Age				
Under 5 years	461,982	509,625	514,893	0.3
5 to 19 years	1,475,104	1,574,060	1,579,096	0.1
20 to 64 years	4,349,096	4,940,402	5,085,414	0.7
65 years and over	79,233	976,937	1,146,886	4.1
Median age (years)	35.7	37.5	37.7	0.1
Race and Hispanic Origin				
One race				
White	5,120,110	5,725,432	5,872,210	0.6
Black	1,390,293	1,579,414	1,638,835	0.9
American Indian and Alaska Native	21,172	41,525	45,725	2.4
Asian	261,025	449,149	526,867	4.1
Native Hawaiian or Other Pacific Islander	3,946	8,201	9,558	3.9
Two or more races	143,069	197,303	233,094	4.3
Hispanic (of any race)	329,540	660,501	737,316	2.8

X = Not applicable.
[1]Population figures for 2014 are July 1 estimates. The 2010 estimates are taken from the 2010 Census.

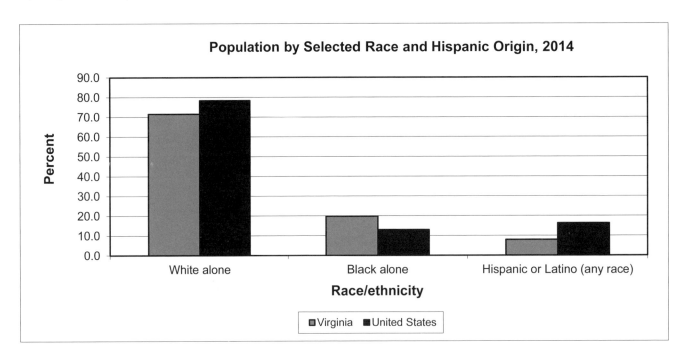

Population by Selected Race and Hispanic Origin, 2014

Table VA-2. Marital Status

(Number, percent distribution.)

Sex, age, race, and Hispanic origin	2000	2010	2013
Males, 15 Years and Over	2,724,334	3,156,115	3,270,177
Never married	29.1	34.2	35.5
Now married, except separated	58.2	52.6	51.3
Separated	2.6	2.3	2.3
Widowed	2.3	2.3	2.2
Divorced	7.9	8.5	8.7
Females, 15 Years and Over	2,899,294	3,331,264	3,437,790
Never married	23.5	28.0	29.0
Now married, except separated	53.4	49.0	47.8
Separated	3.2	2.9	3.0
Widowed	9.9	8.7	8.7
Divorced	10.0	11.4	11.6

Table VA-3. Households and Housing Characteristics

(Number, percent, dollars.)

Item	2000	2010	2013	Average annual percent change, 2000–2013
Total Households	2,699,173	2,992,732	3,055,863	1.0
Family households	1,847,796	2,013,520	2,049,184	0.8
Married-couple family	1,426,044	1,517,627	1,530,934	0.5
Other family	421,752	495,893	518,250	1.6
Male householder, no wife present	101,462	124,273	132,734	2.1
Female householder, no husband present	320,290	371,620	385,516	1.4
Nonfamily households	851,377	979,212	1,006,679	1.3
Householder living alone	676,907	794,535	814,403	1.4
Householder not living alone	174,470	184,677	192,276	0.8
Housing Characteristics				
Total housing units	2,904,192	3,368,674	3,412,577	1.2
Occupied housing units	2,699,173	2,992,732	3,055,863	1.0
Owner occupied	1,837,939	2,025,240	2,005,192	0.7
Renter occupied	861,234	967,492	1,050,671	1.5
Average household size	2.54	2.60	2.62	0.2
Financial Characteristics				
Median gross rent of renter-occupied housing	650	1,019	1,086	4.0
Median monthly owner costs for housing units with a mortgage	1,144	1,728	1,645	2.8
Median value of owner-occupied housing units	125,400	249,100	239,300	5.1

Table VA-4. Migration, Origin, and Language

(Number, percent.)

Characteristic	State			U.S.		
	2012	2013	Percent change	2012	2013	Percent change
Residence 1 Year Ago						
Population 1 year and over	8,085,389	8,163,664	1.0	310,212,755	312,432,820	0.7
Same house	84.8	84.2	X	85.0	85.0	X
Different house in the U.S.	14.4	15.1	X	14.4	14.4	X
Same county	6.6	6.7	X	9.0	8.9	X
Different county	7.8	8.3	X	5.4	5.5	X
Same state	4.7	5.1	X	3.2	3.2	X
Different state	3.1	3.3	X	2.3	2.3	X
Abroad	0.8	0.7	X	0.6	0.6	X
Place of Birth						
Native born	7,238,547	7,311,442		273,089,382	274,780,773	0.6
Male	49.2	49.3	X	49.3	49.3	X
Female	50.8	50.7	X	50.7	50.7	X
Foreign born	947,320	948,963		40,824,658	41,348,066	1.3
Male	48.1	48.1	X	48.7	48.8	X
Female	51.9	51.9	X	51.3	51.2	X
Foreign born; naturalized U.S. citizen	454,617	477,236		18,686,237	19,294,710	3.3
Male	46.9	46.3	X	45.8	45.9	X
Female	53.1	53.7	X	54.2	54.1	X
Foreign born; not a U.S. citizen	492,703	471,727		22,138,421	22,053,356	-0.4
Male	49.2	49.9	X	51.1	51.3	X
Female	50.8	50.1	X	48.9	48.7	X
Entered 2010 or later	9.1	11.3	X	7.0	9.7	X
Entered 2000 to 2009	36.6	34.0	X	30.4	29.4	X
Entered before 2000	54.3	54.7	X	62.7	61.0	X
World Region of Birth, Foreign						
Foreign-born population, excluding population born at sea	947,320	948,963		40,824,553	41,347,945	1.3
Europe	10.6	10.4	X	11.8	11.6	X
Asia	42.1	41.6	X	29.2	29.5	X
Africa	10.0	9.9	X	4.2	4.4	X
Oceania	0.4	0.5	X	0.6	0.5	X
Latin America	35.1	36.1	X	52.2	51.9	X
North America	1.8	1.6	X	2.0	2.0	X
Language Spoken at Home and Ability to Speak English						
Population 5 years and over	7,678,796	7,750,801		294,003,714	296,358,760	0.8
English only	84.5	85.1	X	79.0	79.2	X
Language other than English	15.5	14.9	X	21.0	20.8	X
Speaks English less than "very well"	5.6	5.3	X	8.5	8.5	X

NA = Not available.
X = Not applicable.
- = Zero or rounds to zero.

Table VA-5. Median Income and Poverty Status, 2013

(Number, percent, except as noted.)

Characteristic	State		U.S.	
	Number	Percent	Number	Percent
Median Income				
Households (dollars)...	62,666	X	52,250	X
Families (dollars)	75,524	X	64,030	X
Below Poverty Level (All People)...............................	938,733	11.7	48,810,868	15.8
Sex				
Male..	411,670	10.5	21,938,525	14.5
Female	527,063	12.8	26,872,343	17.1
Age				
Under 18 years..	288,139	15.7	16,086,960	22.2
Related children under 18 years..............................	280,617	15.4	15,769,921	21.9
18 to 64 years...	571,095	11.2	28,578,191	14.8
65 years and over	79,499	7.4	4,145,717	9.6

X = Not applicable.

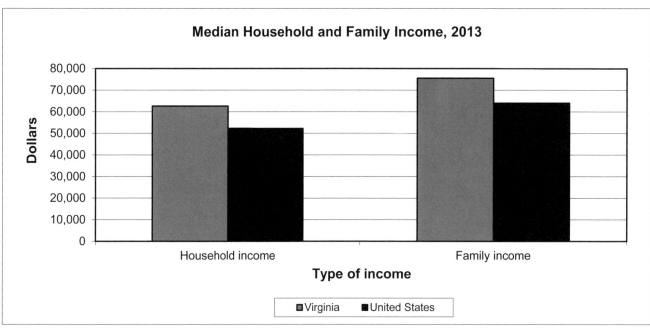

Median Household and Family Income, 2013

Legend: ▨ Virginia   ■ United States

Table VA-6. Health Insurance Coverage Status for the Civilian Noninstitutionalized Population and Children Under 18 Years of Age

(Numbers in thousands, percent.)

Item	2005	2006	2007	2008	2009	2010	2011	2012	2013
Civilian Noninstitutionalized Population.....................	7,454	7,538	7,684	7,520	7,644	7,807	7,887	7,973	8,054
Covered by Private or Public Insurance									
Number..	6,503	6,532	6,548	6,621	6,736	6,787	6,904	6,974	7,064
Percent...	87.2	86.7	85.2	88.0	88.1	86.9	87.5	87.5	87.7
Not Covered									
Number..	951	1,006	1,135	899	908	1,020	983	999	991
Percent...	12.8	13.3	14.8	12.0	11.9	13.1	12.5	12.5	12.3
Percent in the U.S. not covered................................	15.3	15.8	15.3	15.1	15.1	15.5	15.1	14.8	14.5
Children Under 18 Years of Age...............................	1,828	1,827	1,833	1,815	1,843	1,850	1,849	1,852	1,862
Covered by Private or Public Insurance									
Number..	1,672	1,643	1,646	1,677	1,721	1,729	1,741	1,748	1,760
Percent...	91.5	89.9	89.8	92.4	93.4	93.4	94.1	94.4	94.6
Not Covered									
Number..	156	185	187	138	122	121	108	104	101
Percent...	8.5	10.1	10.2	7.6	6.6	6.6	5.9	5.6	5.4
Percent in the U.S. not covered................................	10.9	11.7	11.0	9.7	8.6	8.0	7.5	7.2	7.1

Table VA-7. Employment Status by Demographic Group, 2014

(Numbers in thousands, percent.)

Characteristic	Civilian noninstitutional population	Civilian labor force		Employed		Unemployed	
		Number	Percent of population	Number	Percent of population	Number	Percent of population
Total..	6,451	4,276	66.3	4,055	62.9	221	5.2
Sex							
Male..	3,086	2,248	72.9	2,137	69.2	112	5.0
Female	3,365	2,028	60.3	1,919	57.0	109	5.4
Race, Sex, and Hispanic Origin							
White...	4,684	3,104	66.3	2,963	63.3	141	4.5
Male..	2,272	1,665	73.3	1,591	70.0	73	4.4
Female	2,412	1,440	59.7	1,372	56.9	68	4.7
Black or African American.................	1,216	793	65.3	728	59.9	65	8.2
Male..	551	381	69.0	348	63.2	32	8.5
Female	664	413	62.1	380	57.2	33	8.0
Hispanic or Latino ethnicity[1]	452	339	75.0	318	70.5	21	6.1
Male..	235	195	83.0	186	79.1	9	4.7
Female	217	144	66.4	132	61.1	11	8.0
Age							
16 to 19 years..............................	410	132	32.2	110	26.7	23	17.1
20 to 24 years..............................	528	371	70.2	328	62.2	42	11.4
25 to 34 years..............................	1,135	934	82.3	875	77.1	59	6.3
35 to 44 years..............................	1,070	911	85.1	877	82.0	33	3.7
45 to 54 years..............................	1,164	964	82.8	929	79.8	35	3.6
55 to 64 years..............................	1,042	700	67.1	680	65.2	20	2.9
65 years and over	1,101	265	24.1	256	23.3	9	3.3

NOTE: Data in Table 7 are from the Current Population Survey (CPS) and do not match the estimates in Table 8. See notes and definitions for further information.
[1]May be of any race.

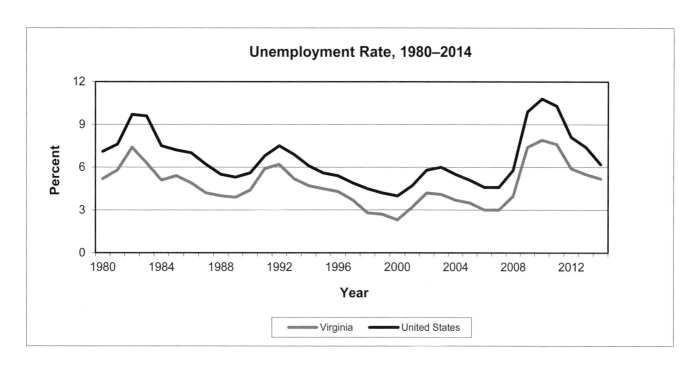

Table VA-8. Employment Status of the Civilian Noninstitutional Population Age 16 Years and Over

(Number, percent.)

Year	Civilian labor force	Civilian participation rate	Employed	Unemployed	Unemployment rate
2006.	3,978,641	68.7	3,855,633	123,008	3.1
2007.	4,036,835	68.9	3,914,087	122,748	3.0
2008.	4,133,443	69.7	3,970,428	163,015	3.9
2009.	4,118,171	68.6	3,842,516	275,655	6.7
2010.	4,157,658	67.7	3,860,386	297,272	7.1
2011.	4,214,262	67.4	3,936,860	277,402	6.6
2012.	4,230,047	66.9	3,974,519	255,528	6.0
2013.	4,245,678	66.4	4,004,513	241,165	5.7
2014.	4,261,175	66.1	4,041,105	220,070	5.2

Table VA-9. Employment and Average Wages by Industry

(Estimates from 2007 through 2010 are based on the 2007 *North American Industry Classification System* [NAICS]. Estimates from 2011 onward are based on the 2012 NAICS.)

Industry	2007	2008	2009	2010	2011	2012	2013
				Number of jobs			
Wage and Salary Employment by Industry	4,009,016	4,006,870	3,882,095	3,874,473	3,909,375	3,930,655	3,952,806
Farm Wage and Salary Employment	9,308	9,264	9,879	13,127	10,085	10,564	11,579
Nonfarm Wage and Salary Employment	3,999,708	3,997,606	3,872,216	3,861,346	3,899,290	3,920,091	3,941,227
Private wage and salary employment	3,141,107	3,125,203	2,998,974	2,987,308	3,027,512	3,047,898	3,072,442
Forestry, fishing, and related activities	5,495	5,452	5,348	5,498	5,694	5,639	5,839
Mining	9,086	9,288	8,489	8,593	9,040	9,019	8,074
Utilities	11,173	11,479	11,448	10,917	10,892	10,640	10,534
Construction	249,949	232,598	199,691	192,176	188,046	182,833	183,581
Manufacturing	276,625	264,666	239,445	230,767	230,872	231,745	231,327
Durable goods manufacturing	161,966	153,764	137,113	132,380	134,413	136,528	136,624
Nondurable goods manufacturing	114,659	110,902	102,332	98,387	96,459	95,217	94,703
Wholesale trade	123,359	121,211	114,278	111,017	113,126	111,914	111,874
Retail trade	433,918	425,957	404,814	404,937	408,642	409,926	414,940
Transportation and warehousing	110,424	109,508	103,624	103,663	104,960	105,996	106,141
Information	91,019	87,883	81,318	76,442	74,404	71,786	71,254
Finance and insurance	135,099	130,268	124,833	124,539	128,440	131,586	134,152
Real estate and rental and leasing	59,896	58,634	56,098	54,237	52,920	52,891	53,451
Professional, scientific, and technical services	365,058	378,425	381,689	387,686	396,367	399,046	397,704
Management of companies and enterprises	78,096	77,465	74,741	73,963	73,355	76,391	76,061
Administrative and waste services	215,152	211,823	193,815	197,862	204,193	207,857	210,765
Educational services	66,153	68,208	68,662	70,827	73,178	73,304	72,864
Health care and social assistance	350,104	364,700	374,283	381,407	389,687	398,241	406,107
Arts, entertainment, and recreation	47,355	48,248	47,108	47,434	48,582	49,245	50,643
Accommodation and food services	302,569	305,294	298,526	298,471	305,160	312,287	318,506
Other services, except public administration	210,577	214,095	210,764	206,872	209,954	207,552	208,625
Government and government enterprises	858,601	872,403	873,242	874,038	871,778	872,193	868,785
				Dollars			
Average Wages and Salaries by Industry	47,221	48,470	49,461	50,948	52,072	53,104	53,267
Average Farm Wages and Salaries	30,939	29,824	25,703	18,648	21,993	23,534	28,909
Average Nonfarm Wages and Salaries	47,259	48,513	49,521	51,057	52,150	53,184	53,338
Average private wages and salaries	46,497	47,667	48,533	50,122	51,372	52,536	52,772
Forestry, fishing, and related activities	26,265	26,746	26,474	27,556	28,453	29,105	30,284
Mining	56,147	60,398	61,570	67,349	70,807	68,916	69,203
Utilities	89,122	91,812	93,856	100,019	100,599	101,588	101,264
Construction	44,536	45,565	46,052	47,559	48,597	49,195	49,701
Manufacturing	48,904	50,193	51,111	53,412	54,527	55,655	56,229
Durable goods manufacturing	50,394	51,970	52,904	55,166	57,091	58,134	58,977
Nondurable goods manufacturing	46,799	47,729	48,710	51,051	50,954	52,100	52,265
Wholesale trade	65,077	66,487	67,121	69,087	72,211	72,613	73,468
Retail trade	25,673	25,823	25,992	26,482	26,853	27,477	27,646
Transportation and warehousing	43,696	45,326	45,935	47,102	48,214	49,578	51,594
Information	76,435	77,818	78,360	80,670	81,724	84,425	87,837
Finance and insurance	73,134	72,672	72,433	75,333	78,514	83,444	83,723
Real estate and rental and leasing	43,703	44,021	43,876	45,192	46,823	48,868	49,558
Professional, scientific, and technical services	84,389	87,808	90,030	93,372	96,059	97,996	97,879
Management of companies and enterprises	100,704	98,278	98,693	103,532	107,867	112,565	113,665
Administrative and waste services	32,391	33,861	35,412	36,980	37,923	38,927	38,529
Educational services	35,833	37,631	39,014	39,727	40,256	38,081	38,747
Health care and social assistance	41,881	43,340	44,110	44,676	45,691	46,533	47,043
Arts, entertainment, and recreation	26,997	26,107	26,084	27,443	26,558	27,184	27,030
Accommodation and food services	18,316	18,100	17,906	18,614	19,030	19,362	19,349
Other services, except public administration	32,301	33,828	34,073	35,211	35,625	36,573	37,139
Government and government enterprises	50,044	51,547	52,916	54,253	54,851	55,448	55,338

Table VA-10. Employment Characteristics by Family Type

(Number, percent.)

Family type and labor force status	2011		2012		2013	
	Total	Families with own children under 18 years	Total	Families with own children under 18 years	Total	Families with own children under 18 years
All Families..	2,010,914	893,805	2,044,422	895,668	2,049,184	887,364
FAMILY TYPE AND LABOR FORCE STATUS						
Married-Couple Families.......................	1,518,944	630,339	1,541,185	632,612	1,530,934	622,543
Both husband and wife in labor force.................	55.3	67.2	55.6	67.9	54.8	67.3
Husband in labor force, wife not in labor force	22.3	28.0	21.8	27.5	21.9	27.9
Wife in labor force, husband not in labor force	7.0	3.1	7.5	3.4	7.3	3.3
Both husband and wife not in labor force.................	15.3	1.7	15.2	1.2	15.6	1.3
Other Families	491,970	263,466	503,237	263,056	518,250	264,821
Female householder, no husband present................	74.3	76.9	74.8	76.2	74.4	77.9
In labor force....................................	54.6	65.2	54.7	64.0	54.1	65.1
Not in labor force	19.7	11.8	20.1	12.2	20.3	12.7
Male householder, no wife present.......................	25.7	23.1	25.2	23.8	25.6	22.1
In labor force....................................	20.5	21.2	20.4	22.1	20.4	20.5
Not in labor force	5.2	1.9	4.8	1.7	5.2	1.7

Table VA-11. School Enrollment and Educational Attainment, 2013

(Number, percent.)

Item	State	U.S.
Enrollment		
Total population 3 years and over, enrolled in school	2,157,510	82,395,254
Enrolled in nursery school or preschool (percent)	5.7	6.0
Enrolled in kindergarten (percent)	5.1	5.2
Enrolled in elementary school, grades 1-8 (percent)............	38.4	40.0
Enrolled in high school, grades 9-12 (percent)................	19.8	20.6
Enrolled in college or graduate school (percent)...............	31.0	28.3
Attainment		
Total population 25 years and over	5,561,224	210,910,615
Less than ninth grade (percent)	4.7	5.8
9th to 12th grade, no diploma (percent)	6.9	7.6
High school graduate, including equivalency (percent).........	24.8	27.8
Some college, no degree (percent)	20.1	21.1
Associate's degree (percent)..............................	7.3	8.1
Bachelor's degree (percent)	21.1	18.4
Graduate or professional degree (percent)..................	15.1	11.2
High school graduate or higher (percent)	88.4	86.6
Bachelor's degree or higher (percent)	36.1	29.6

Table VA-12. Public School Characteristics and Educational Indicators

(Number, percent; data derived from National Center of Education Statistics.)

Item	State	U.S.
Public Schools, 2012–2013 (except where noted)		
Number of school districts..................................	227	18,093
Number of schools...	2,182	98,454
Number of students (in thousands)	1,265	49,771
Number of teachers (in thousands)	89	3,109
Student-teacher ratio......................................	14.2	16.0
Expenditures per student (dollars), FY 2012.................	10,656	10,667
Four-year adjusted cohort graduation rate (ACGR)[1,2]	84.5	81.4
Students eligible for free or reduced-price lunch (in thousands) ...	487	25,188
English language learners (in thousands)	93	4,397
Students age 3 to 21 served under IDEA, part B (in thousands)	161	6,429

Public Schools by Type	Number	Percent of state public schools
Total number of schools....................................	2,182	100.0
Regular	1,874	85.9
Special education......................................	54	2.5
Vocational education...................................	58	2.7
Alternative education	196	9.0

NOTE: Every school is assigned only one school type based on its instructional emphasis.
[1]ACGR data represents a new method of calculating high-school completion rates and may not be comparable to previous years' data for Averaged Freshmen Graduation Rates (AFGR).
[2]The United States 4-year ACGRs were estimated using both the reported 4-year ACGR data from 49 states and the District of Columbia and using imputed data for Idaho. The estimate for American Indian/Alaska Native students also includes imputed data for Virginia.

Table VA-13. Reported Voting and Registration of the Voting-Age Population, November 2012

(Numbers in thousands, percent.)

Item	Total population	Total citizen population	Registered			Voted		
			Total registered	Percent registered (total population)	Percent registered (total citizen population)	Total voted	Percent voted (total population)	Percent voted (total citizen population)
U.S. Total	235,248	215,081	153,157	65.1	71.2	132,948	56.5	61.8
State Total	6,094	5,645	4,210	69.1	74.6	3,778	62.0	66.9
Sex								
Male	2,890	2,648	1,931	66.8	72.9	1,709	59.1	64.5
Female	3,204	2,998	2,279	71.1	76.0	2,069	64.6	69.0
Race								
White alone	4,496	4,245	3,222	71.7	75.9	2,872	63.9	67.6
White, non-Hispanic alone	4,169	4,114	3,118	74.8	75.8	2,778	66.6	67.5
Black alone	1,133	1,063	772	68.1	72.6	715	63.1	67.2
Asian alone	316	223	136	43.1	61.1	118	37.3	53.0
Hispanic (of any race)	375	154	114	30.3	73.6	103	27.5	66.8
White alone or in combination	4,594	4,329	3,278	71.4	75.7	2,925	63.7	67.6
Black alone or in combination	1,206	1,125	810	67.2	72.0	753	62.4	66.9
Asian alone or in combination	332	236	144	43.5	61.2	126	38.0	53.5
Age								
18 to 24 years	695	612	351	50.5	57.4	292	42.0	47.7
25 to 44 years	2,181	1,914	1,415	64.9	73.9	1,239	56.8	64.7
45 to 64 years	2,140	2,050	1,591	74.3	77.6	1,473	68.9	71.9
65 to 74 years	627	625	506	80.7	81.1	468	74.6	74.9
75 years and over	452	444	347	76.8	78.0	306	67.7	68.8

Table VA-14. Crime

(Number, rate per 100,000. Data are derived from the FBI Uniform Crime Reports.)

Item	State			U.S.[1,2,3,4]		
	2012	2013	Percent change	2012	2013	Percent change
TOTAL POPULATION[5]	8,186,628	8,260,405	0.9	313,873,685	316,128,839	0.7
VIOLENT CRIME						
Number	15,676	15,524		1,217,067	1,163,146	-4.4
Rate	191.5	187.9	-1.9	387.8	367.9	-5.1
Murder and Nonnegligent Manslaughter						
Number	322	316	-1.9	14,866	14,196	-4.5
Rate	3.9	3.8	-2.7	4.7	4.5	-5.2
Rape[6]						
Number	X	2,262	X	X	108,612	X
Rate	X	27.4	X	X	34.4	X
Robbery						
Number	4,718	4,565	-3.2	355,051	345,031	-2.8
Rate	57.6	55.3	-4.1	113.1	109.1	-3.5
Aggravated Assault						
Number	9,131	9,062	-0.8	762,009	724,149	-5.0
Rate	111.5	109.7	-1.6	242.8	229.1	-5.6
PROPERTY CRIME						
Number	178,434	170,654	-4.4	9,001,992	8,632,512	-4.1
Rate	2,179.6	2,065.9	-5.2	2,868.0	2,730.7	-4.8
Burglary						
Number	29,651	26,640	-10.2	2,109,932	1,928,465	-8.6
Rate	362.2	322.5	-11.0	672.2	610.0	-9.3
Larceny-Theft						
Number	139,654	135,478	-3.0	6,168,874	6,004,453	-2.7
Rate	1,705.9	1,640.1	-3.9	1,965.4	1,899.4	-3.4
Motor Vehicle Theft						
Number	9,129	8,536	-6.5	723,186	699,594	-3.3
Rate	111.5	103.3	-7.3	230.4	221.3	-4.0

NOTE: Although arson data are included in the trend and clearance tables, sufficient data are not available to estimate totals for this offense. Therefore, no arson data are published in this table.
X = Not applicable.
- = Zero or rounds to zero.
[1]The crime figures have been adjusted.
[2]The data collection methodology for the offense of forcible rape used by the Minnesota state Uniform Crime Reporting (UCR) Program (with the exception of Minneapolis and St. Paul, Minnesota) does not comply with national UCR Program guidelines. Consequently, its figures for forcible rape and violent crime (of which forcible rape is a part) are not published in this table.
[3]Includes offenses reported by the Zoological Police and the Metro Transit Police.
[4]Because of changes in the state's reporting practices, figures are not comparable to previous years' data.
[5]Populations are U.S. Census Bureau provisional estimates as of July 1 of each year.
[6]The figures shown for the offense of rape were estimated using the revised Uniform Crime Reporting (UCR) definition of rape.

Table VA-15. State Government Finances, 2013

(Dollar amounts in thousands, percent distribution.)

Item	Dollars	Percent distribution
Total Revenue	50,851,769	100.0
General revenue	41,140,409	80.9
Intergovernmental revenue	9,959,041	19.6
Taxes	19,186,853	37.7
General sales	3,708,389	7.3
Selective sales	2,484,277	4.9
License taxes	806,572	1.6
Individual income tax	10,900,860	21.4
Corporate income tax	772,001	1.5
Other taxes	514,754	1.0
Current charges	8,138,597	16.0
Miscellaneous general revenue	3,855,918	7.6
Utility revenue	0	-
Liquor stores revenue	636,653	1.3
Insurance trust revenue[1]	9,074,707	17.8
Total Expenditure	47,614,065	100.0
Intergovernmental expenditure	11,255,705	23.6
Direct expenditure	36,358,360	76.4
Current operation	25,953,846	54.5
Capital outlay	3,059,704	6.4
Insurance benefits and repayments	4,570,249	9.6
Assistance and subsidies	1,615,558	3.4
Interest on debt	1,159,003	2.4
Exhibit: Salaries and wages	6,777,430	14.2
Total Expenditure	47,614,065	100.0
General expenditure	42,529,852	89.3
Intergovernmental expenditure	11,255,705	23.6
Direct expenditure	31,274,147	65.7
General expenditure, by function:		
Education	15,214,402	32.0
Public welfare	9,855,058	20.7
Hospitals	3,598,411	7.6
Health	1,343,432	2.8
Highways	3,912,825	8.2
Police protection	559,409	1.2
Correction	1,706,864	3.6
Natural resources	248,919	0.5
Parks and recreation	118,354	0.2
Governmental administration	1,314,461	2.8
Interest on general debt	1,159,003	2.4
Other and unallocable	3,498,714	7.3
Utility expenditure	0	-
Liquor stores expenditure	513,964	1.1
Insurance trust expenditure	4,570,249	9.6
Debt at End of Fiscal Year	28,022,656	X
Cash and Security Holdings	76,702,692	X

X = Not applicable.
- = Zero or rounds to zero.
[1]Within insurance trust revenue, net earnings of state retirement systems is a calculated statistic (the item code in the data file is X08), and thus can be positive or negative. Net earnings is the sum of earnings on investments plus gains on investments minus losses on investments. The change made in 2002 for asset valuation from book to market value in accordance with Statement 34 of the Governmental Accounting Standards Board is reflected in the calculated statistics.

Table VA-16. State Government Tax Collections, 2014

(Dollars in thousands, percent.)

Item	Dollars	Percent distribution
Total Taxes	18,949,272	100.0
Property taxes	35,561	0.2
Sales and gross receipts	6,063,182	32.0
General sales and gross receipts	3,555,745	18.8
Selective sales and gross receipts	2,507,437	13.2
Alcoholic beverages	207,672	1.1
Amusements	70	-
Insurance premiums	459,993	2.4
Motor fuels	694,833	3.7
Pari-mutuels	0	-
Public utilities	107,394	0.6
Tobacco products	180,733	1.0
Other selective sales	856,742	4.5
Licenses	795,515	4.2
Alcoholic beverages	12,756	0.1
Amusements	101	-
Corporations in general	59,245	0.3
Hunting and fishing	27,983	0.1
Motor vehicle	451,215	2.4
Motor vehicle operators	40,370	0.2
Public utilities	0	-
Occupation and business, NEC	199,707	1.1
Other licenses	4,138	-
Income taxes	11,618,200	61.3
Individual income	10,877,689	57.4
Corporation net income	740,511	3.9
Other taxes	436,814	2.3
Death and gift	196	-
Documentary and stock transfer	310,205	1.6
Severance	2,165	-
Taxes, NEC	124,248	0.7

- = Zero or rounds to zero.

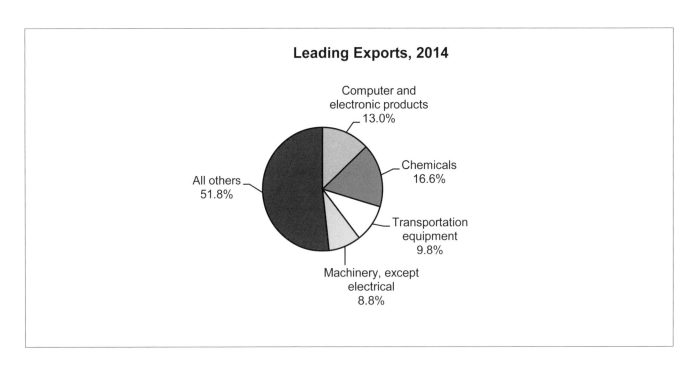

Leading Exports, 2014

Computer and electronic products 13.0%

Chemicals 16.6%

Transportation equipment 9.8%

Machinery, except electrical 8.8%

All others 51.8%

WASHINGTON

Facts and Figures

Location: Northwestern United States; bordered on the N by Canada (British Columbia), on the E by Idaho, on the S by Oregon, and on the W by the Pacific Ocean

Area: 71,300 sq. mi. (184,665 sq. km.); rank—18th

Population: 7,061,530 (2014 est.); rank—13th

Principal Cities: capital—Olympia; largest—Seattle

Statehood: November 11, 1889; 42nd state

U.S. Congress: 2 senators, 10 representatives

State Motto: *Alki* ("By and by")

State Song: "Washington, My Home"

State Nickname: The Evergreen State

Abbreviations: WA; Wash.

State Symbols: flower—coast rhododendron; tree—Western hemlock; bird—willow goldfinch

At a Glance

- With an increase in population of 5.0 percent, Washington ranked 9th among the states in growth from 2010 to 2014.

- Washington's median household income in 2013 was $58,405, and 14.1 percent of the population lived below the poverty level.

- In 2013, 14.0 percent of Washingtonians did not have health insurance, compared to 14.5 percent of the total U.S. population.

- Washington had the second highest property crime rate in the country (3,710.3 incidents per 100,000 population) in 2013.

- Approximately 32.7 percent of Washingtonians had a bachelor's degree or more in 2013, compared to 29.6 percent of all U.S. residents.

Table WA-1. Population by Age, Sex, Race, and Hispanic Origin

(Number, percent, except where noted.)

Sex, age, race, and Hispanic origin	2000	2010	2014[1]	Average annual percent change, 2010–2014
Total Population	5,894,121	6,724,540	7,061,530	1.2
Percent of total U.S. population	2.1	2.2	2.2	X
Sex				
Male	2,934,300	3,349,707	3,529,935	1.3
Female	2,959,821	3,374,833	3,531,595	1.1
Age				
Under 5 years	394,306	439,657	446,570	0.4
5 to 19 years	1,288,713	1,330,238	1,328,009	-
20 to 64 years	3,548,954	4,126,968	4,294,196	1.0
65 years and over	662,148	827,677	992,755	4.7
Median age (years)	35.9	37.3	37.5	0.1
Race and Hispanic Origin				
One race				
White	4,821,823	5,535,262	5,699,754	0.7
Black	190,267	252,333	286,779	3.3
American Indian and Alaska Native	93,301	122,649	132,935	2.0
Asian	322,335	491,685	576,147	4.0
Native Hawaiian or Other Pacific Islander	23,953	43,505	49,986	3.5
Two or more races	213,519	279,106	315,929	3.1
Hispanic (of any race)	441,509	776,539	858,779	2.5

X = Not applicable.
- = Zero or rounds to zero.
[1]Population figures for 2014 are July 1 estimates. The 2010 estimates are taken from the 2010 Census.

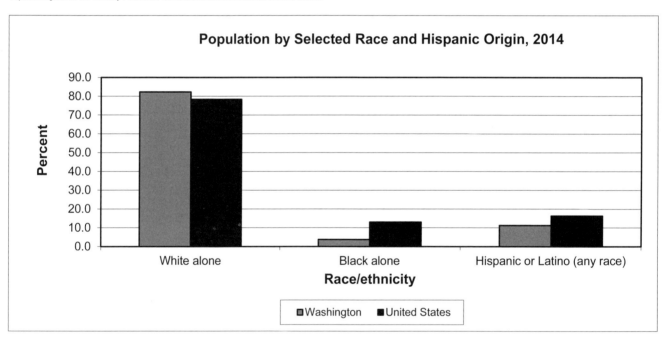

Population by Selected Race and Hispanic Origin, 2014

Table WA-2. Marital Status

(Number, percent distribution.)

Sex, age, race, and Hispanic origin	2000	2010	2013
Males, 15 Years and Over	2,287,431	2,686,801	2,799,219
Never married	29.8	33.8	35.0
Now married, except separated	56.6	52.0	51.0
Separated	1.4	1.6	1.6
Widowed	2.1	2.1	2.1
Divorced	10.1	10.5	10.2
Females, 15 Years and Over	2,352,091	2,746,158	2,840,764
Never married	22.8	26.4	27.2
Now married, except separated	54.1	50.6	49.2
Separated	1.8	2.1	1.8
Widowed	8.6	7.8	7.6
Divorced	12.7	13.2	14.2

Table WA-3. Households and Housing Characteristics

(Number, percent, dollars.)

Item	2000	2010	2013	Average annual percent change, 2000–2013
Total Households	2,271,398	2,606,863	2,644,557	1.2
Family households	1,499,127	1,681,386	1,705,112	1.0
Married-couple family	1,181,995	1,297,240	1,309,075	0.8
Other family	317,132	384,146	396,037	1.7
Male householder, no wife present	92,514	114,187	123,287	2.2
Female householder, no husband present	224,618	269,959	272,750	1.5
Nonfamily households	772,271	925,477	939,445	1.5
Householder living alone	594,325	731,452	728,070	1.6
Householder not living alone	117,946	194,025	211,375	4.6
Housing Characteristics				
Total housing units	2,451,075	2,888,594	2,928,300	1.4
Occupied housing units	2,271,398	2,606,863	2,644,557	1.2
Owner occupied	1,467,009	1,644,939	1,638,028	0.9
Renter occupied	804,389	961,924	1,006,529	1.7
Average household size	2.53	2.53	2.58	0.2
Financial Characteristics				
Median gross rent of renter-occupied housing	663	908	989	3.1
Median monthly owner costs for housing units with a mortgage	1,268	1,736	1,667	2.1
Median value of owner-occupied housing units	168,300	271,800	250,800	3.1

Table WA-4. Migration, Origin, and Language

(Number, percent.)

Characteristic	State			U.S.		
	2012	2013	Percent change	2012	2013	Percent change
Residence 1 Year Ago						
Population 1 year and over	6,815,763	6,888,552	1.1	310,212,755	312,432,820	0.7
Same house	82.9	82.8	X	85.0	85.0	X
Different house in the U.S.	16.4	16.5	X	14.4	14.4	X
Same county	10.5	10.6	X	9.0	8.9	X
Different county	5.9	5.8	X	5.4	5.5	X
Same state	2.7	2.8	X	3.2	3.2	X
Different state	3.2	3.0	X	2.3	2.3	X
Abroad	0.7	0.8	X	0.6	0.6	X
Place of Birth						
Native born	5,980,613	6,027,742		273,089,382	274,780,773	0.6
Male	50.2	50.1	X	49.3	49.3	X
Female	49.8	49.9	X	50.7	50.7	X
Foreign born	916,399	943,664		40,824,658	41,348,066	1.3
Male	48.1	48.1	X	48.7	48.8	X
Female	51.9	51.9	X	51.3	51.2	X
Foreign born; naturalized U.S. citizen	434,688	436,834		18,686,237	19,294,710	3.3
Male	45.1	44.6	X	45.8	45.9	X
Female	54.9	55.4	X	54.2	54.1	X
Foreign born; not a U.S. citizen	481,711	506,830		22,138,421	22,053,356	-0.4
Male	50.9	51.2	X	51.1	51.3	X
Female	49.1	48.8	X	48.9	48.7	X
Entered 2010 or later	7.3	10.8	X	7.0	9.7	X
Entered 2000 to 2009	33.0	30.8	X	30.4	29.4	X
Entered before 2000	59.6	58.4	X	62.7	61.0	X
World Region of Birth, Foreign						
Foreign-born population, excluding population born at sea	916,399	943,664		40,824,553	41,347,945	1.3
Europe	17.2	16.2	X	11.8	11.6	X
Asia	40.0	41.0	X	29.2	29.5	X
Africa	5.5	5.9	X	4.2	4.4	X
Oceania	1.3	1.6	X	0.6	0.5	X
Latin America	31.3	30.5	X	52.2	51.9	X
North America	4.8	4.9	X	2.0	2.0	X
Language Spoken at Home and Ability to Speak English						
Population 5 years and over	6,456,039	6,529,296		294,003,714	296,358,760	0.8
English only	80.7	81.1	X	79.0	79.2	X
Language other than English	19.3	18.9	X	21.0	20.8	X
Speaks English less than "very well"	7.8	7.5	X	8.5	8.5	X

NA = Not available.
X = Not applicable.
- = Zero or rounds to zero.

Table WA-5. Median Income and Poverty Status, 2013

(Number, percent, except as noted.)

Characteristic	State		U.S.	
	Number	Percent	Number	Percent
Median Income				
Households (dollars)...	58,405	X	52,250	X
Families (dollars)	71,371	X	64,030	X
Below Poverty Level (All People)	967,282	14.1	48,810,868	15.8
Sex				
Male..	445,126	13.1	21,938,525	14.5
Female	522,156	15.2	26,872,343	17.1
Age				
Under 18 years..	295,069	18.8	16,086,960	22.2
Related children under 18 years.............................	284,067	18.3	15,769,921	21.9
18 to 64 years..	596,974	13.8	28,578,191	14.8
65 years and over	75,239	8.1	4,145,717	9.6

X = Not applicable.

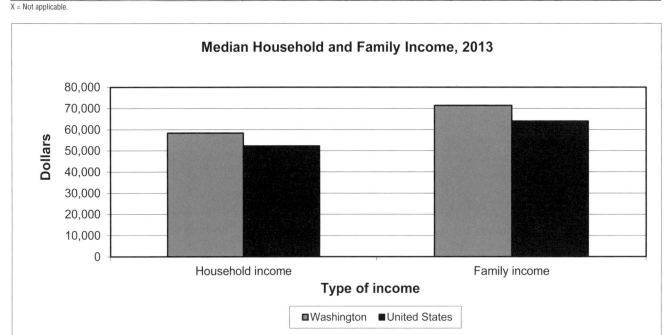

Median Household and Family Income, 2013

Table WA-6. Health Insurance Coverage Status for the Civilian Noninstitutionalized Population and Children Under 18 Years of Age

(Numbers in thousands, percent.)

Item	2005	2006	2007	2008	2009	2010	2011	2012	2013
Civilian Noninstitutionalized Population	6,250	6,318	6,509	6,428	6,546	6,638	6,717	6,793	6,864
Covered by Private or Public Insurance									
Number..	5,422	5,572	5,773	5,586	5,669	5,692	5,764	5,848	5,904
Percent..	86.7	88.2	88.7	86.9	86.6	85.8	85.8	86.1	86.0
Not Covered									
Number..	828	746	737	842	878	946	952	945	960
Percent..	13.3	11.8	11.3	13.1	13.4	14.2	14.2	13.9	14.0
Percent in the U.S. not covered...	15.3	15.8	15.3	15.1	15.1	15.5	15.1	14.8	14.5
Children Under 18 Years of Age...	1,525	1,518	1,558	1,541	1,570	1,583	1,578	1,584	1,595
Covered by Private or Public Insurance									
Number..	1,391	1,413	1,452	1,411	1,462	1,481	1,481	1,493	1,500
Percent..	91.3	93.1	93.2	91.6	93.1	93.6	93.8	94.2	94.1
Not Covered									
Number..	133	105	106	130	108	102	97	91	95
Percent..	8.7	6.9	6.8	8.4	6.9	6.4	6.2	5.8	5.9
Percent in the U.S. not covered...	10.9	11.7	11.0	9.7	8.6	8.0	7.5	7.2	7.1

Table WA-7. Employment Status by Demographic Group, 2014

(Numbers in thousands, percent.)

Characteristic	Civilian noninstitutional population	Civilian labor force		Employed		Unemployed	
		Number	Percent of population	Number	Percent of population	Number	Percent of population
Total...	5,524	3,488	63.1	3,269	59.2	219	6.3
Sex							
Male..	2,717	1,880	69.2	1,744	64.2	136	7.2
Female.......................................	2,808	1,608	57.3	1,525	54.3	83	5.2
Race, Sex, and Hispanic Origin							
White..	4,511	2,834	62.8	2,675	59.3	159	5.6
Male..	2,242	1,533	68.4	1,437	64.1	96	6.3
Female.....................................	2,269	1,301	57.3	1,238	54.6	62	4.8
Black or African American.................	193	125	64.9	108	56.0	17	13.8
Male..	99	74	75.0	65	65.6	9	12.5
Female.....................................	94	51	54.3	43	45.8	8	15.6
Hispanic or Latino ethnicity[1].............	549	387	70.5	352	64.2	35	9.0
Male..	286	230	80.5	210	73.3	20	8.9
Female.....................................	263	157	59.7	143	54.3	14	9.1
Age							
16 to 19 years.............................	339	122	36.1	94	27.7	28	23.2
20 to 24 years.............................	472	343	72.5	294	62.2	49	14.2
25 to 34 years.............................	979	784	80.1	741	75.7	43	5.5
35 to 44 years.............................	915	743	81.3	703	76.9	40	5.4
45 to 54 years.............................	900	726	80.7	699	77.6	28	3.8
55 to 64 years.............................	911	595	65.2	572	62.7	23	3.8
65 years and over..........................	1,008	175	17.4	167	16.5	8	4.8

NOTE: Data in Table 7 are from the Current Population Survey (CPS) and do not match the estimates in Table 8. See notes and definitions for further information.
[1]May be of any race.

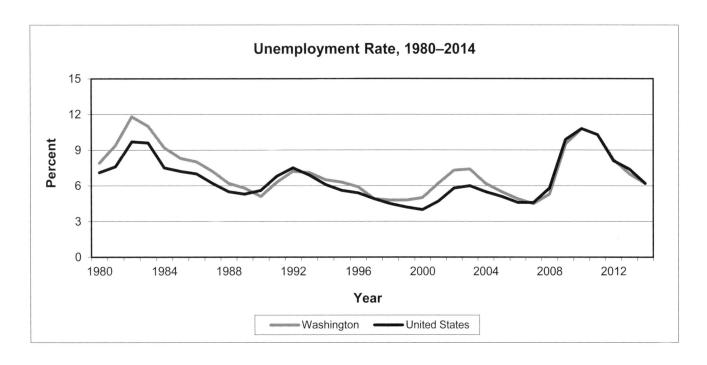

Table WA-8. Employment Status of the Civilian Noninstitutional Population Age 16 Years and Over

(Number, percent.)

Year	Civilian labor force	Civilian participation rate	Employed	Unemployed	Unemployment rate
2006	3,323,938	67.6	3,156,626	167,312	5.0
2007	3,403,163	68.0	3,243,308	159,855	4.7
2008	3,478,577	68.4	3,291,309	187,268	5.4
2009	3,535,200	68.3	3,211,649	323,551	9.2
2010	3,511,326	66.9	3,160,544	350,782	10.0
2011	3,459,200	65.2	3,139,999	319,201	9.2
2012	3,471,158	64.5	3,190,015	281,143	8.1
2013	3,460,038	63.5	3,216,966	243,072	7.0
2014	3,488,183	63.1	3,270,362	217,821	6.2

Table WA-9. Employment and Average Wages by Industry

(Estimates from 2007 through 2010 are based on the 2007 *North American Industry Classification System* [NAICS]. Estimates from 2011 onward are based on the 2012 NAICS.)

Industry	2007	2008	2009	2010	2011	2012	2013
				Number of jobs			
Wage and Salary Employment by Industry	3,154,787	3,190,328	3,055,064	3,017,067	3,050,198	3,089,719	3,202,280
Farm Wage and Salary Employment	40,162	47,160	49,636	48,890	46,644	52,776	50,768
Nonfarm Wage and Salary Employment	3,114,625	3,143,168	3,005,428	2,968,177	3,003,554	3,036,943	3,151,512
Private wage and salary employment	2,504,769	2,516,679	2,374,663	2,336,116	2,378,200	2,412,491	2,529,015
Forestry, fishing, and related activities	26,441	26,002	27,210	26,656	28,470	27,696	30,856
Mining	3,135	2,955	2,367	2,202	2,205	2,158	2,165
Utilities	4,460	4,703	4,767	4,863	4,870	4,913	4,822
Construction	217,517	208,581	166,336	146,762	143,279	143,496	154,574
Manufacturing	293,283	291,067	265,520	257,913	268,681	280,554	286,630
Durable goods manufacturing	211,983	211,250	190,284	183,718	193,063	204,418	209,283
Nondurable goods manufacturing	81,300	79,817	75,236	74,195	75,618	76,136	77,347
Wholesale trade	130,037	130,798	123,355	121,554	123,051	124,363	127,697
Retail trade	330,505	330,081	314,067	313,189	317,476	322,363	332,829
Transportation and warehousing	92,556	92,072	87,026	85,243	87,156	89,301	90,079
Information	102,859	105,724	103,817	102,884	104,202	105,535	106,635
Finance and insurance	106,589	104,081	97,037	93,785	93,779	94,517	96,406
Real estate and rental and leasing	53,185	52,951	49,519	47,356	46,216	45,918	47,623
Professional, scientific, and technical services	161,895	169,754	163,556	164,645	170,210	173,116	177,285
Management of companies and enterprises	34,678	34,783	32,178	31,796	33,282	36,318	38,869
Administrative and waste services	153,566	149,209	132,706	134,751	140,112	143,031	147,868
Educational services	47,336	49,357	49,032	49,908	51,700	52,981	53,463
Health care and social assistance	308,949	321,880	331,044	333,660	337,636	340,181	392,861
Arts, entertainment, and recreation	46,785	48,459	46,577	45,883	46,782	46,452	47,233
Accommodation and food services	237,226	238,717	225,921	224,183	227,794	232,890	242,575
Other services, except public administration	153,767	155,505	152,628	148,883	151,299	146,708	148,545
Government and government enterprises	609,856	626,489	630,765	632,061	625,354	624,452	622,497
				Dollars			
Average Wages and Salaries by Industry	46,223	47,231	48,087	49,282	51,036	52,945	53,334
Average Farm Wages and Salaries	28,025	29,672	27,635	25,520	26,156	24,435	33,317
Average Nonfarm Wages and Salaries	46,458	47,495	48,425	49,673	51,423	53,441	53,656
Average private wages and salaries	46,706	47,552	48,240	49,598	51,602	54,007	54,061
Forestry, fishing, and related activities	33,265	34,826	32,324	33,267	34,648	36,513	35,096
Mining	58,502	55,819	53,328	56,188	59,809	60,970	63,051
Utilities	73,380	76,188	83,464	77,235	81,878	83,778	85,809
Construction	48,308	50,782	52,150	51,817	52,859	53,654	54,405
Manufacturing	60,114	61,573	63,039	65,280	68,479	69,786	71,721
Durable goods manufacturing	64,959	66,644	69,068	72,104	75,748	76,892	79,318
Nondurable goods manufacturing	47,482	48,153	47,792	48,381	49,920	50,710	51,167
Wholesale trade	60,646	62,211	62,367	64,253	66,665	69,501	69,087
Retail trade	30,759	30,791	31,024	31,586	32,647	34,587	36,238
Transportation and warehousing	47,172	47,439	48,340	49,589	51,898	53,205	54,582
Information	106,526	104,789	106,908	111,436	121,621	135,532	136,788
Finance and insurance	70,358	72,858	71,286	70,283	73,173	77,420	79,407
Real estate and rental and leasing	37,537	37,586	37,330	38,878	40,332	42,788	44,139
Professional, scientific, and technical services	72,263	71,567	73,019	76,181	77,882	80,678	82,429
Management of companies and enterprises	90,161	88,966	89,733	100,110	103,999	107,245	106,911
Administrative and waste services	36,604	38,106	39,972	41,923	43,211	43,617	43,529
Educational services	25,625	26,698	27,684	28,562	29,142	29,172	29,883
Health care and social assistance	41,033	42,812	44,377	45,386	46,582	47,828	43,919
Arts, entertainment, and recreation	31,822	29,727	28,123	27,871	27,657	27,881	30,412
Accommodation and food services	18,813	18,723	19,121	20,277	21,311	22,617	22,246
Other services, except public administration	27,969	28,756	28,931	29,844	30,305	33,063	34,255
Government and government enterprises	45,437	47,268	49,121	49,953	50,741	51,253	52,011

Table WA-10. Employment Characteristics by Family Type

(Number, percent.)

Family type and labor force status	2011		2012		2013	
	Total	Families with own children under 18 years	Total	Families with own children under 18 years	Total	Families with own children under 18 years
All Families............................	1,699,851	767,324	1,687,786	752,039	1,705,112	755,115
FAMILY TYPE AND LABOR FORCE STATUS						
Married-Couple Families...................	1,303,418	538,771	1,301,823	530,116	1,309,075	526,959
Both husband and wife in labor force...................	52.5	61.9	51.9	62.4	50.8	62.5
Husband in labor force, wife not in labor force	23.5	32.4	23.7	32.2	23.5	31.8
Wife in labor force, husband not in labor force	7.3	3.8	7.5	3.8	7.7	3.8
Both husband and wife not in labor force...................	16.7	1.8	16.9	1.6	17.4	1.5
Other Families	396,433	228,553	385,963	221,923	396,037	228,156
Female householder, no husband present...................	70.7	72.9	70.0	71.5	68.9	70.4
In labor force...................	51.0	58.9	50.8	57.8	49.2	55.7
Not in labor force	19.7	14.0	19.2	13.7	19.7	14.7
Male householder, no wife present...................	29.3	27.1	30.0	28.5	31.1	29.6
In labor force...................	24.1	24.2	24.6	25.9	25.0	26.2
Not in labor force	5.2	2.9	5.4	2.6	6.1	3.4

Table WA-11. School Enrollment and Educational Attainment, 2013

(Number, percent.)

Item	State	U.S.
Enrollment		
Total population 3 years and over, enrolled in school	1,722,089	82,395,254
Enrolled in nursery school or preschool (percent)	5.5	6.0
Enrolled in kindergarten (percent)	5.0	5.2
Enrolled in elementary school, grades 1-8 (percent)................	41.1	40.0
Enrolled in high school, grades 9-12 (percent)	21.2	20.6
Enrolled in college or graduate school (percent)................	27.1	28.3
Attainment		
Total population 25 years and over	4,706,104	210,910,615
Less than ninth grade (percent)	4.0	5.8
9th to 12th grade, no diploma (percent)	5.9	7.6
High school graduate, including equivalency (percent)	23.3	27.8
Some college, no degree (percent)	24.6	21.1
Associate's degree (percent)	9.5	8.1
Bachelor's degree (percent)	20.9	18.4
Graduate or professional degree (percent)................	11.8	11.2
High school graduate or higher (percent)	90.1	86.6
Bachelor's degree or higher (percent)	32.7	29.6

Table WA-12. Public School Characteristics and Educational Indicators

(Number, percent; data derived from National Center of Education Statistics.)

Item	State	U.S.
Public Schools, 2012–2013 (except where noted)		
Number of school districts................	322	18,093
Number of schools................	2,370	98,454
Number of students (in thousands)	1,052	49,771
Number of teachers (in thousands)	54	3,109
Student-teacher ratio	19.6	16.0
Expenditures per student (dollars), FY 2012................	9,617	10,667
Four-year adjusted cohort graduation rate (ACGR)[1,2]	76.4	81.4
Students eligible for free or reduced-price lunch (in thousands)	475	25,188
English language learners (in thousands)	94	4,397
Students age 3 to 21 served under IDEA, part B (in thousands)	131	6,429

Public Schools by Type	Number	Percent of state public schools
Total number of schools................	2,370	100.0
Regular	1,932	81.5
Special education................	98	4.1
Vocational education................	18	0.8
Alternative education	322	13.6

NOTE: Every school is assigned only one school type based on its instructional emphasis.
[1]ACGR data represents a new method of calculating high-school completion rates and may not be comparable to previous years' data for Averaged Freshmen Graduation Rates (AFGR).
[2]The United States 4-year ACGRs were estimated using both the reported 4-year ACGR data from 49 states and the District of Columbia and using imputed data for Idaho. The estimate for American Indian/Alaska Native students also includes imputed data for Virginia.

Table WA-13. Reported Voting and Registration of the Voting-Age Population, November 2012

(Numbers in thousands, percent.)

Item	Total population	Total citizen population	Registered			Voted		
			Total registered	Percent registered (total population)	Percent registered (total citizen population)	Total voted	Percent voted (total population)	Percent voted (total citizen population)
U.S. Total	235,248	215,081	153,157	65.1	71.2	132,948	56.5	61.8
State Total	5,230	4,832	3,533	67.6	73.1	3,172	60.7	65.6
Sex								
Male	2,546	2,338	1,658	65.1	70.9	1,491	58.5	63.8
Female	2,684	2,495	1,875	69.9	75.2	1,682	62.7	67.4
Race								
White alone	4,301	4,039	2,987	69.4	74.0	2,696	62.7	66.8
White, non-Hispanic alone	3,936	3,829	2,875	73.0	75.1	2,603	66.1	68.0
Black alone	162	149	103	63.8	69.5	72	44.3	48.3
Asian alone	377	255	178	47.2	69.7	169	44.7	66.0
Hispanic (of any race)	460	298	172	37.5	58.0	139	30.2	46.6
White alone or in combination	4,550	4,288	3,171	69.7	73.9	2,868	63.0	66.9
Black alone or in combination	214	201	146	68.2	72.8	115	53.5	57.0
Asian alone or in combination	452	331	236	52.2	71.4	223	49.2	67.3
Age								
18 to 24 years	563	511	275	48.8	53.8	215	38.2	42.1
25 to 44 years	1,933	1,719	1,244	64.4	72.4	1,064	55.1	61.9
45 to 64 years	1,660	1,570	1,183	71.3	75.3	1,101	66.4	70.1
65 to 74 years	625	605	487	77.9	80.4	471	75.5	77.9
75 years and over	449	427	344	76.5	80.5	320	71.3	75.0

Table WA-14. Crime

(Number, rate per 100,000. Data are derived from the FBI Uniform Crime Reports.)

Item	State			U.S.[1,2,3,4]		
	2012	2013	Percent change	2012	2013	Percent change
TOTAL POPULATION[5]	6,895,318	6,971,406	1.1	313,873,685	316,128,839	0.7
VIOLENT CRIME						
Number	20,553	19,377	-5.7	1,217,067	1,163,146	-4.4
Rate	298.1	277.9	-6.8	387.8	367.9	-5.1
Murder and Nonnegligent Manslaughter						
Number	217	160	-26.3	14,866	14,196	-4.5
Rate	3.1	2.3	-27.1	4.7	4.5	-5.2
Rape[6]						
Number	X	2,573	X	X	108,612	X
Rate	X	36.9	X	X	34.4	X
Robbery						
Number	5,801	5,819	0.3	355,051	345,031	-2.8
Rate	84.1	83.5	-0.8	113.1	109.1	-3.5
Aggravated Assault						
Number	12,285	11,601	-5.6	762,009	724,149	-5.0
Rate	178.2	166.4	-6.6	242.8	229.1	-5.6
PROPERTY CRIME						
Number	254,377	258,662	1.7	9,001,992	8,632,512	-4.1
Rate	3,689.1	3,710.3	0.6	2,868.0	2,730.7	-4.8
Burglary						
Number	61,376	58,353	-4.9	2,109,932	1,928,465	-8.6
Rate	890.1	837.0	-6.0	672.2	610.0	-9.3
Larceny-Theft						
Number	166,338	171,910	3.3	6,168,874	6,004,453	-2.7
Rate	2,412.3	2,465.9	2.2	1,965.4	1,899.4	-3.4
Motor Vehicle Theft						
Number	26,663	28,399	6.5	723,186	699,594	-3.3
Rate	386.7	407.4	5.3	230.4	221.3	-4.0

NOTE: Although arson data are included in the trend and clearance tables, sufficient data are not available to estimate totals for this offense. Therefore, no arson data are published in this table.

X = Not applicable.

- = Zero or rounds to zero.

[1]The crime figures have been adjusted.

[2]The data collection methodology for the offense of forcible rape used by the Minnesota state Uniform Crime Reporting (UCR) Program (with the exception of Minneapolis and St. Paul, Minnesota) does not comply with national UCR Program guidelines. Consequently, its figures for forcible rape and violent crime (of which forcible rape is a part) are not published in this table.

[3]Includes offenses reported by the Zoological Police and the Metro Transit Police.

[4]Because of changes in the state's reporting practices, figures are not comparable to previous years' data.

[5]Populations are U.S. Census Bureau provisional estimates as of July 1 of each year.

[6]The figures shown for the offense of rape were estimated using the revised Uniform Crime Reporting (UCR) definition of rape.

Table WA-15. State Government Finances, 2013

(Dollar amounts in thousands, percent distribution.)

Item	Dollars	Percent distribution
Total Revenue	47,862,480	100.0
General revenue	35,669,826	74.5
Intergovernmental revenue	10,030,961	21.0
Taxes	18,667,044	39.0
General sales	11,122,868	23.2
Selective sales	3,524,305	7.4
License taxes	1,359,685	2.8
Individual income tax	0	-
Corporate income tax	0	-
Other taxes	2,660,186	5.6
Current charges	4,719,060	9.9
Miscellaneous general revenue	2,252,761	4.7
Utility revenue	0	-
Liquor stores revenue	612,000	1.3
Insurance trust revenue[1]	11,580,654	24.2
Total Expenditure	45,725,863	100.0
Intergovernmental expenditure	9,777,797	21.4
Direct expenditure	35,948,066	78.6
Current operation	22,335,778	48.8
Capital outlay	3,380,742	7.4
Insurance benefits and repayments	7,344,585	16.1
Assistance and subsidies	1,597,316	3.5
Interest on debt	1,289,645	2.8
Exhibit: Salaries and wages	10,114,009	22.1
Total Expenditure	45,725,863	100.0
General expenditure	37,864,966	82.8
Intergovernmental expenditure	9,777,797	21.4
Direct expenditure	28,087,169	61.4
General expenditure, by function:		
Education	15,582,462	34.1
Public welfare	8,389,040	18.3
Hospitals	2,160,922	4.7
Health	2,185,121	4.8
Highways	3,183,817	7.0
Police protection	356,847	0.8
Correction	954,986	2.1
Natural resources	861,649	1.9
Parks and recreation	124,187	0.3
Governmental administration	747,190	1.6
Interest on general debt	1,289,645	2.8
Other and unallocable	2,029,100	4.4
Utility expenditure	53,312	0.1
Liquor stores expenditure	463,000	1.0
Insurance trust expenditure	7,344,585	16.1
Debt at End of Fiscal Year	30,474,333	X
Cash and Security Holdings	92,193,109	X

X = Not applicable.

- = Zero or rounds to zero.

[1]Within insurance trust revenue, net earnings of state retirement systems is a calculated statistic (the item code in the data file is X08), and thus can be positive or negative. Net earnings is the sum of earnings on investments plus gains on investments minus losses on investments. The change made in 2002 for asset valuation from book to market value in accordance with Statement 34 of the Governmental Accounting Standards Board is reflected in the calculated statistics.

Table WA-16. State Government Tax Collections, 2014

(Dollars in thousands, percent.)

Item	Dollars	Percent distribution
Total Taxes	19,447,899	100.0
Property taxes	1,974,354	10.2
Sales and gross receipts	15,210,264	78.2
General sales and gross receipts	11,767,488	60.5
Selective sales and gross receipts	3,442,776	17.7
Alcoholic beverages	321,412	1.7
Amusements	0	-
Insurance premiums	467,351	2.4
Motor fuels	1,156,242	5.9
Pari-mutuels	1,510	-
Public utilities	497,993	2.6
Tobacco products	443,185	2.3
Other selective sales	555,083	2.9
Licenses	1,414,960	7.3
Alcoholic beverages	153,263	0.8
Amusements	5,699	-
Corporations in general	32,335	0.2
Hunting and fishing	44,906	0.2
Motor vehicle	535,636	2.8
Motor vehicle operators	102,924	0.5
Public utilities	18,689	0.1
Occupation and business, NEC	294,448	1.5
Other licenses	227,060	1.2
Income taxes	0	-
Individual income	X	X
Corporation net income	X	X
Other taxes	848,321	4.4
Death and gift	157,286	0.8
Documentary and stock transfer	649,085	3.3
Severance	41,950	0.2
Taxes, NEC	0	-

X = Not applicable.
- = Zero or rounds to zero.

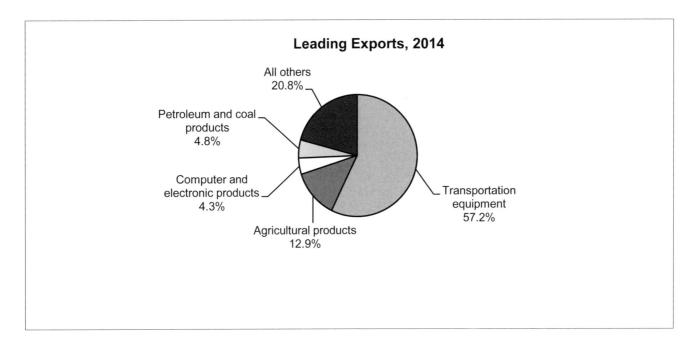

Leading Exports, 2014

All others 20.8%
Petroleum and coal products 4.8%
Computer and electronic products 4.3%
Agricultural products 12.9%
Transportation equipment 57.2%

WEST VIRGINIA

Facts and Figures

Location: East central United States; bordered on the N by Ohio and Pennsylvania, on the E by Pennsylvania, Maryland, and Virginia, on the S by Virginia and Kentucky, and on the W by Kentucky and Ohio

Area: 24,230 sq. mi. (62,755 sq. km.); rank—41st

Population: 1,850,326 (2014 est.); rank—38th

Principal Cities: capital—Charleston; largest—Charleston

Statehood: June 20, 1863; 35th state

U.S. Congress: 2 senators, 3 representatives

State Motto: *Montani semper liberi* (Mountaineers are always free)

State Songs: "West Virginia Hills"; "This Is My West Virginia"; "West Virginia, My Home Sweet Home"

State Nickname: The Mountain State

Abbreviations: WV; W. Va.

State Symbols: flower—rhododendron (great laurel); tree—sugar maple; bird—cardinal

At a Glance

- West Virginia was the only state to experience a population decrease from 2010 to 2014, with its population falling 0.1 percent.

- West Virginia's median household income was $41,253 in 2013, and 18.5 percent of the population lived below the poverty level.

- In 2013, 14.0 percent of West Virginians did not have health insurance, compared to 14.5 percent of the total U.S. population.

- West Virginia had the lowest percent of residents that self-identified as "Hispanic or Latino" in 2014, with 1.2 percent of its population in this category.

- West Virginia had the highest homeownership rate of all the states in 2013 (76.8 percent).

Table WV-1. Population by Age, Sex, Race, and Hispanic Origin

(Number, percent, except where noted.)

Sex, age, race, and Hispanic origin	2000	2010	2014[1]	Average annual percent change, 2010–2014
Total Population	1,808,344	1,852,994	1,850,326	-
Percent of total U.S. population	0.6	0.6	0.6	X
Sex				
Male	879,170	913,586	913,915	-
Female	929,174	939,408	936,411	-0.1
Age				
Under 5 years	101,805	104,060	102,485	-0.4
5 to 19 years	352,910	335,153	323,390	-0.9
20 to 64 years	1,076,734	1,116,377	1,095,839	-0.5
65 years and over	276,895	297,404	328,612	2.5
Median age (years)	38.9	41.3	42.0	0.4
Race and Hispanic Origin				
One race				
White	1,718,777	1,746,513	1,734,220	-0.2
Black	57,232	63,885	67,073	1.2
American Indian and Alaska Native	3,606	3,975	4,441	2.8
Asian	9,434	12,637	14,945	4.3
Native Hawaiian or Other Pacific Islander	400	485	553	3.3
Two or more races	15,788	25,499	29,094	3.4
Hispanic (of any race)	12,279	23,679	26,847	3.2

X = Not applicable.
- = Zero or rounds to zero.
[1]Population figures for 2014 are July 1 estimates. The 2010 estimates are taken from the 2010 Census.

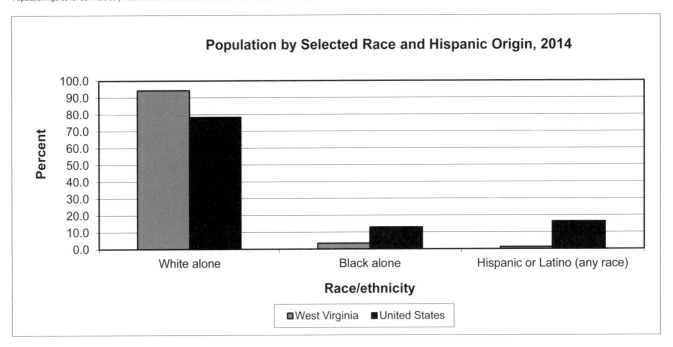

Population by Selected Race and Hispanic Origin, 2014

(Bar chart — Percent vs. Race/ethnicity: White alone, Black alone, Hispanic or Latino (any race). Legend: West Virginia, United States.)

Table WV-2. Marital Status

(Number, percent distribution.)

Sex, age, race, and Hispanic origin	2000	2010	2013
Males, 15 Years and Over	710,443	750,542	754,927
Never married	25.4	30.3	32.0
Now married, except separated	59.9	52.1	50.9
Separated	1.3	1.6	1.4
Widowed	3.2	3.4	3.2
Divorced	10.1	12.6	12.4
Females, 15 Years and Over	768,858	785,182	782,702
Never married	19.1	22.6	24.4
Now married, except separated	54.7	49.7	48.0
Separated	1.6	1.7	1.7
Widowed	13.9	12.8	12.0
Divorced	10.8	13.2	13.9

Table WV-3. Households and Housing Characteristics

(Number, percent, dollars.)

Item	2000	2010	2013	Average annual percent change, 2000–2013
Total Households	736,481	741,940	738,653	-
Family households	504,055	485,652	479,389	-0.4
Married-couple family	397,499	372,301	355,958	-0.8
Other family	106,556	113,351	123,431	1.1
Male householder, no wife present	27,436	28,515	36,884	2.3
Female householder, no husband present	79,120	84,836	86,547	0.7
Nonfamily households	232,426	256,288	259,264	0.8
Householder living alone	199,587	219,848	223,226	0.9
Householder not living alone	32,839	36,440	36,038	0.7
Housing Characteristics				
Total housing units	844,623	882,213	879,424	0.3
Occupied housing units	736,481	741,940	738,653	-
Owner occupied	553,699	553,429	534,266	-0.3
Renter occupied	182,782	188,511	204,387	0.9
Average household size	2.40	2.43	2.44	0.1
Financial Characteristics				
Median gross rent of renter-occupied housing	401	571	620	3.4
Median monthly owner costs for housing units with a mortgage	713	918	939	2.1
Median value of owner-occupied housing units	72,800	95,100	103,200	2.7

- = Zero or rounds to zero

Table WV-4. Migration, Origin, and Language

(Number, percent.)

Characteristic	State			U.S.		
	2012	2013	Percent change	2012	2013	Percent change
Residence 1 Year Ago						
Population 1 year and over	1,837,518	1,837,863	-	310,212,755	312,432,820	0.7
Same house	87.8	88.2	X	85.0	85.0	X
Different house in the U.S.	12.0	11.6	X	14.4	14.4	X
Same county	6.8	6.4	X	9.0	8.9	X
Different county	5.3	5.3	X	5.4	5.5	X
Same state	2.7	2.4	X	3.2	3.2	X
Different state	2.6	2.8	X	2.3	2.3	X
Abroad	0.2	0.2	X	0.6	0.6	X
Place of Birth						
Native born	1,829,567	1,827,983	-0.1	273,089,382	274,780,773	0.6
Male	49.2	49.5	X	49.3	49.3	X
Female	50.8	50.5	X	50.7	50.7	X
Foreign born	25,846	26,321	1.8	40,824,658	41,348,066	1.3
Male	45.1	47.7	X	48.7	48.8	X
Female	54.9	52.3	X	51.3	51.2	X
Foreign born; naturalized U.S. citizen	12,579	13,343	6.1	18,686,237	19,294,710	3.3
Male	40.8	43.2	X	45.8	45.9	X
Female	59.2	56.8	X	54.2	54.1	X
Foreign born; not a U.S. citizen	13,267	12,978	-2.2	22,138,421	22,053,356	-0.4
Male	49.3	52.4	X	51.1	51.3	X
Female	50.7	47.6	X	48.9	48.7	X
Entered 2010 or later	12.0	15.9	X	7.0	9.7	X
Entered 2000 to 2009	37.3	30.4	X	30.4	29.4	X
Entered before 2000	50.7	53.7	X	62.7	61.0	X
World Region of Birth, Foreign						
Foreign-born population, excluding population born at sea	25,846	26,321	1.8	40,824,553	41,347,945	1.3
Europe	20.4	17.9	X	11.8	11.6	X
Asia	43.3	37.7	X	29.2	29.5	X
Africa	6.4	5.1	X	4.2	4.4	X
Oceania	0.4	1.8	X	0.6	0.5	X
Latin America	23.5	32.5	X	52.2	51.9	X
North America	6.0	5.0	X	2.0	2.0	X
Language Spoken at Home and Ability to Speak English						
Population 5 years and over	1,750,150	1,751,468	0.1	294,003,714	296,358,760	0.8
English only	97.6	97.7	X	79.0	79.2	X
Language other than English	2.4	2.3	X	21.0	20.8	X
Speaks English less than "very well"	0.7	0.8	X	8.5	8.5	X

NA = Not available.
X = Not applicable.
- = Zero or rounds to zero.

Table WV-5. Median Income and Poverty Status, 2013

(Number, percent, except as noted.)

Characteristic	State		U.S.	
	Number	Percent	Number	Percent
Median Income				
Households (dollars)...........................	41,253	X	52,250	X
Families (dollars)	51,596	X	64,030	X
Below Poverty Level (All People)...........................	332,347	18.5	48,810,868	15.8
Sex				
Male...........................	147,616	16.7	21,938,525	14.5
Female	184,731	20.2	26,872,343	17.1
Age				
Under 18 years...........................	100,008	27.0	16,086,960	22.2
Related children under 18 years...........................	97,818	26.6	15,769,921	21.9
18 to 64 years...........................	202,992	18.2	28,578,191	14.8
65 years and over	29,347	9.4	4,145,717	9.6

X = Not applicable.

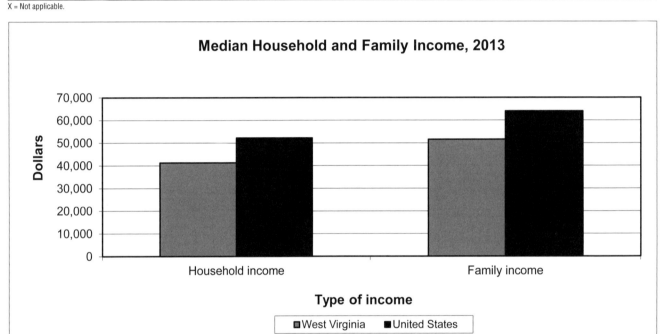

Median Household and Family Income, 2013

West Virginia   United States

Table WV-6. Health Insurance Coverage Status for the Civilian Noninstitutionalized Population and Children Under 18 Years of Age

(Numbers in thousands, percent.)

Item	2005	2006	2007	2008	2009	2010	2011	2012	2013
Civilian Noninstitutionalized Population...........................	1,799	1,814	1,795	1,788	1,793	1,823	1,826	1,827	1,825
Covered by Private or Public Insurance									
Number...........................	1,495	1,570	1,541	1,505	1,539	1,557	1,554	1,563	1,570
Percent...........................	83.1	86.5	85.9	84.2	85.8	85.4	85.1	85.6	86.0
Not Covered									
Number...........................	304	245	254	283	254	266	272	264	255
Percent...........................	16.9	13.5	14.1	15.8	14.2	14.6	14.9	14.4	14.0
Percent in the U.S. not covered...........................	15.3	15.8	15.3	15.1	15.1	15.5	15.1	14.8	14.5
Children Under 18 Years of Age...........................	387	395	394	385	383	385	385	383	381
Covered by Private or Public Insurance									
Number...........................	361	361	376	359	362	367	368	368	361
Percent...........................	93.4	91.5	95.4	93.2	94.5	95.5	95.6	96.1	94.7
Not Covered									
Number...........................	26	34	18	26	21	18	17	15	20
Percent...........................	6.6	8.5	4.6	6.8	5.5	4.5	4.4	3.9	5.3
Percent in the U.S. not covered...........................	10.9	11.7	11.0	9.7	8.6	8.0	7.5	7.2	7.1

Table WV-7. Employment Status by Demographic Group, Preliminary 2013

(Numbers in thousands, percent.)

Characteristic	Civilian noninstitutional population	Civilian labor force		Employed		Unemployed	
		Number	Percent of population	Number	Percent of population	Number	Percent of population
Total.............................	1,485	791	53.3	739	49.8	52	6.6
Sex							
Male..........................	724	419	57.9	387	53.4	33	7.8
Female	761	372	48.9	353	46.3	19	5.2
Race, Sex, and Hispanic Origin							
White	1,403	746	53.2	698	49.8	48	6.4
Male..........................	683	397	58.1	366	53.6	31	7.7
Female	720	349	48.6	332	46.1	17	5.0
Black or African American.................	48	25	52.7	23	47.5	3	9.9
Male..........................	25	12	48.9	11	45.4	1	7.3
Female	23	13	56.8	12	49.8	2.0	12.3
Hispanic or Latino ethnicity[1]	18	12	67	12	65	...	4
Male..........................	NA	NA	NA	NA	NA	NA	NA
Female	NA	NA	NA	NA	NA	NA	NA
Age							
16 to 19 years............	91	26	28.0	20	21.5	6	23.3
20 to 24 years............	119	81	68.1	72	60.6	9	11.0
25 to 34 years............	216	160	74.1	146	67.4	14	9.0
35 to 44 years............	222	166	74.8	156	70.4	10	5.9
45 to 54 years............	252	171	68.0	163	64.7	8	4.9
55 to 64 years............	261	138	52.9	135	51.7	3	2.3
65 years and over	325	50	15.4	49	15.0	1	2.6

NOTE: Data in Table 7 are from the Current Population Survey (CPS) and do not match the estimates in Table 8. See notes and definitions for further information.
[1]May be of any race.
NA = Not available.
... = Fewer than 500 persons.

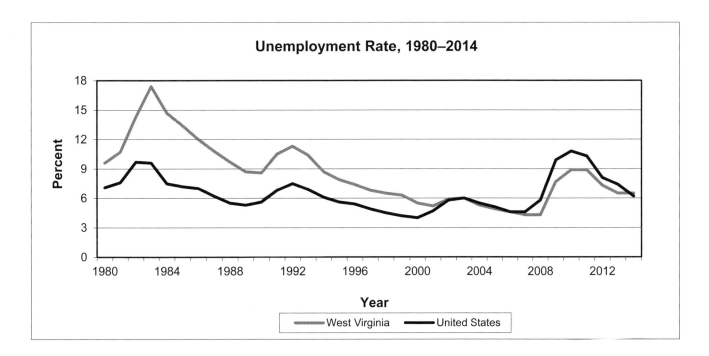

Table WV-8. Employment Status of the Civilian Noninstitutional Population Age 16 Years and Over

(Number, percent.)

Year	Civilian labor force	Civilian participation rate	Employed	Unemployed	Unemployment rate
2006	806,168	56.0	766,399	39,769	4.9
2007	811,160	56.2	773,990	37,170	4.6
2008	812,905	56.1	777,560	35,345	4.3
2009	814,027	56.0	751,165	62,862	7.7
2010	811,125	54.9	740,910	70,215	8.7
2011	807,606	54.4	742,413	65,193	8.1
2012	809,034	54.4	748,359	60,675	7.5
2013	799,630	53.8	745,674	53,956	6.7
2014	790,035	53.2	738,527	51,508	6.5

Table WV-9. Employment and Average Wages by Industry

(Estimates from 2007 through 2010 are based on the 2007 *North American Industry Classification System* [NAICS]. Estimates from 2011 onward are based on the 2012 NAICS.)

Industry	2007	2008	2009	2010	2011	2012	2013
	Number of jobs						
Wage and Salary Employment by Industry	751,719	755,780	737,945	738,582	747,666	752,413	744,520
Farm Wage and Salary Employment	1,492	1,440	1,286	1,308	1,403	1,467	1,404
Nonfarm Wage and Salary Employment	750,227	754,340	736,659	737,274	746,263	750,946	743,116
Private wage and salary employment	595,452	597,771	577,417	575,076	584,884	588,558	584,953
Forestry, fishing, and related activities	1,664	1,549	1,367	1,320	1,254	1,290	1,337
Mining	27,631	30,483	28,947	29,251	32,910	32,741	30,878
Utilities	6,121	6,201	6,194	5,632	5,439	5,307	5,177
Construction	40,543	40,830	35,866	34,324	34,794	36,892	35,621
Manufacturing	58,899	56,586	50,767	49,180	49,560	49,165	48,467
Durable goods manufacturing	37,017	35,426	30,942	29,651	29,944	29,593	29,133
Nondurable goods manufacturing	21,882	21,160	19,825	19,529	19,616	19,572	19,334
Wholesale trade	24,954	24,702	23,555	23,130	23,454	23,605	23,031
Retail trade	92,707	91,213	88,334	88,004	88,367	88,508	88,511
Transportation and warehousing	20,771	20,763	19,485	19,376	19,847	19,428	20,373
Information	11,450	11,175	10,468	10,334	10,369	9,638	9,519
Finance and insurance	22,094	21,846	20,932	20,705	20,429	20,250	19,947
Real estate and rental and leasing	7,727	7,645	7,294	7,259	6,966	6,860	6,848
Professional, scientific, and technical services	24,801	25,182	24,467	24,843	25,421	25,753	26,150
Management of companies and enterprises	4,846	5,116	5,430	5,469	5,699	6,685	6,501
Administrative and waste services	32,024	31,565	30,410	31,060	32,341	32,777	32,804
Educational services	8,598	8,625	8,477	8,835	9,154	9,131	8,714
Health care and social assistance	101,963	104,748	107,358	109,010	110,883	113,399	114,017
Arts, entertainment, and recreation	9,455	9,147	9,305	9,536	7,366	7,656	7,739
Accommodation and food services	63,083	64,562	63,450	63,555	66,294	67,134	67,304
Other services, except public administration	36,121	35,833	35,311	34,253	34,337	32,339	32,015
Government and government enterprises	154,775	156,569	159,242	162,198	161,379	162,388	158,163
	Dollars						
Average Wages and Salaries by Industry	33,632	35,468	36,326	37,098	38,477	39,169	39,651
Average Farm Wages and Salaries	21,531	21,402	22,767	21,144	17,636	18,903	26,912
Average Nonfarm Wages and Salaries	33,656	35,495	36,350	37,126	38,516	39,208	39,675
Average private wages and salaries	33,232	35,073	35,863	36,857	38,463	39,262	39,561
Forestry, fishing, and related activities	23,964	24,680	24,825	26,023	27,258	28,415	28,201
Mining	63,147	69,067	72,252	73,284	78,917	79,266	80,078
Utilities	68,690	71,679	76,112	77,029	80,512	80,685	81,321
Construction	39,977	43,696	44,623	47,229	46,962	50,782	52,022
Manufacturing	45,717	47,564	47,934	49,963	51,693	52,787	53,044
Durable goods manufacturing	42,450	44,552	45,019	46,548	48,386	50,006	49,654
Nondurable goods manufacturing	51,243	52,607	52,484	55,147	56,741	56,992	58,152
Wholesale trade	46,039	48,153	49,287	49,810	51,245	51,727	52,201
Retail trade	21,080	21,891	22,608	23,173	23,729	24,147	24,418
Transportation and warehousing	42,769	45,693	46,467	46,947	49,182	50,032	49,750
Information	40,054	42,125	43,604	46,228	48,520	48,638	47,552
Finance and insurance	38,701	40,220	41,323	42,470	46,743	46,089	47,622
Real estate and rental and leasing	28,180	29,854	31,033	34,849	34,923	20,243	36,490
Professional, scientific, and technical services	43,960	46,393	48,247	50,439	50,623	53,052	53,724
Management of companies and enterprises	65,485	66,177	64,248	67,681	81,738	70,891	69,691
Administrative and waste services	22,619	24,682	25,383	26,618	28,502	29,055	29,569
Educational services	19,995	21,205	22,646	23,274	23,980	24,505	24,905
Health care and social assistance	34,258	35,567	36,934	37,129	37,800	38,773	39,641
Arts, entertainment, and recreation	20,137	19,448	20,694	22,315	19,473	19,333	18,929
Accommodation and food services	14,995	15,104	15,231	15,994	17,304	17,588	17,375
Other services, except public administration	22,518	23,503	24,025	25,163	25,599	26,469	27,351
Government and government enterprises	35,288	37,105	38,118	38,082	38,708	39,013	40,100

Table WV-10. Employment Characteristics by Family Type

(Number, percent.)

Family type and labor force status	2011 Total	2011 Families with own children under 18 years	2012 Total	2012 Families with own children under 18 years	2013 Total	2013 Families with own children under 18 years
All Families	477,809	176,454	471,536	175,829	479,389	177,583
FAMILY TYPE AND LABOR FORCE STATUS						
Married-Couple Families	356,697	115,050	358,666	117,691	355,958	113,167
Both husband and wife in labor force	43.3	59.9	41.0	58.3	41.3	60.9
Husband in labor force, wife not in labor force	21.1	28.9	22.3	30.8	22.5	30.0
Wife in labor force, husband not in labor force	10.6	7.4	10.9	7.3	10.3	5.0
Both husband and wife not in labor force	25.0	3.8	25.8	3.7	25.7	4.1
Other Families	121,112	61,404	112,870	58,138	123,431	64,416
Female householder, no husband present	70.8	73.2	71.8	74.9	70.1	70.3
In labor force	38.4	50.9	41.6	55.3	40.1	49.8
Not in labor force	32.5	22.3	30.2	19.7	30.0	20.5
Male householder, no wife present	29.2	26.8	28.2	25.1	29.9	29.7
In labor force	19.4	23.0	17.8	19.9	20.3	24.0
Not in labor force	9.8	3.8	10.3	5.2	9.6	5.6

Table WV-11. School Enrollment and Educational Attainment, 2013

(Number, percent.)

Item	State	U.S.
Enrollment		
Total population 3 years and over, enrolled in school	414,610	82,395,254
Enrolled in nursery school or preschool (percent)	5.2	6.0
Enrolled in kindergarten (percent)	5.0	5.2
Enrolled in elementary school, grades 1-8 (percent)	41.3	40.0
Enrolled in high school, grades 9-12 (percent)	21.4	20.6
Enrolled in college or graduate school (percent)	27.1	28.3
Attainment		
Total population 25 years and over	1,294,025	210,910,615
Less than ninth grade (percent)	5.4	5.8
9th to 12th grade, no diploma (percent)	10.0	7.6
High school graduate, including equivalency (percent)	40.2	27.8
Some college, no degree (percent)	18.6	21.1
Associate's degree (percent)	6.8	8.1
Bachelor's degree (percent)	11.3	18.4
Graduate or professional degree (percent)	7.6	11.2
High school graduate or higher (percent)	84.6	86.6
Bachelor's degree or higher (percent)	18.9	29.6

Table WV-12. Public School Characteristics and Educational Indicators

(Number, percent; data derived from National Center of Education Statistics.)

Item	State	U.S.
Public Schools, 2012–2013 (except where noted)		
Number of school districts	57	18,093
Number of schools	755	98,454
Number of students (in thousands)	283	49,771
Number of teachers (in thousands)	20	3,109
Student-teacher ratio	14.1	16.0
Expenditures per student (dollars), FY 2012	11,579	10,667
Four-year adjusted cohort graduation rate (ACGR)[1,2]	81.4	81.4
Students eligible for free or reduced-price lunch (in thousands)	148	25,188
English language learners (in thousands)	2	4,397
Students age 3 to 21 served under IDEA, part B (in thousands)	44	6,429

Public Schools by Type	Number	Percent of state public schools
Total number of schools	755	100.0
Regular	692	91.7
Special education	3	0.4
Vocational education	30	4.0
Alternative education	30	4.0

NOTE: Every school is assigned only one school type based on its instructional emphasis.
[1]ACGR data represents a new method of calculating high-school completion rates and may not be comparable to previous years' data for Averaged Freshmen Graduation Rates (AFGR).
[2]The United States 4-year ACGRs were estimated using both the reported 4-year ACGR data from 49 states and the District of Columbia and using imputed data for Idaho. The estimate for American Indian/Alaska Native students also includes imputed data for Virginia.

Table WV-13. Reported Voting and Registration of the Voting-Age Population, November 2012

(Numbers in thousands, percent.)

Item	Total population	Total citizen population	Registered			Voted		
			Total registered	Percent registered (total population)	Percent registered (total citizen population)	Total voted	Percent voted (total population)	Percent voted (total citizen population)
U.S. Total	235,248	215,081	153,157	65.1	71.2	132,948	56.5	61.8
State Total	1,452	1,442	982	67.6	68.1	690	47.5	47.8
Sex								
Male	705	700	474	67.3	67.7	332	47.0	47.4
Female	747	742	508	67.9	68.4	358	47.9	48.2
Race								
White alone..............................	1,391	1,386	948	68.2	68.4	665	47.8	48.0
White, non-Hispanic alone	1,381	1,378	944	68.4	68.6	662	48.0	48.1
Black alone..............................	40	38	23	B	B	19	B	B
Asian alone	7	5	3	B	B	1	B	B
Hispanic (of any race)..................	14	13	8	B	B	4	B	B
White alone or in combination	1,400	1,395	951	68.0	68.2	668	47.7	47.9
Black alone or in combination...........	41	39	24	B	B	20	B	B
Asian alone or in combination..........	7	5	3	B	B	1	B	B
Age								
18 to 24 years..............................	163	162	78	47.8	48.1	37	22.6	22.7
25 to 44 years..............................	450	447	293	65.1	65.6	178	39.5	39.8
45 to 64 years..............................	479	475	326	68.0	68.6	253	52.9	53.3
65 to 74 years..............................	205	204	168	81.7	82.2	134	65.3	65.7
75 years and over	155	155	118	75.8	75.8	88	56.5	56.5

B = Base is less than 75,000 and therefore too small to show the derived measure.

Table WV-14. Crime

(Number, rate per 100,000. Data are derived from the FBI Uniform Crime Reports.)

Item	State			U.S.[1,2,3,4]		
	2012	2013	Percent change	2012	2013	Percent change
TOTAL POPULATION[5]..	1,856,680	1,854,304	-0.1	313,873,685	316,128,839	0.7
VIOLENT CRIME						
Number............................	5,943	5,371	-9.6	1,217,067	1,163,146	-4.4
Rate	320.1	289.7	-9.5	387.8	367.9	-5.1
Murder and Nonnegligent Manslaughter						
Number............................	70	61	-12.9	14,866	14,196	-4.5
Rate	3.8	3.3	-12.7	4.7	4.5	-5.2
Rape[6]						
Number............................	X	653	X	X	108,612	X
Rate	X	35.2	X	X	34.4	X
Robbery						
Number............................	835	651	-22.0	355,051	345,031	-2.8
Rate	45.0	35.1	-21.9	113.1	109.1	-3.5
Aggravated Assault						
Number............................	4,623	4,203	-9.1	762,009	724,149	-5.0
Rate	249.0	226.7	-9.0	242.8	229.1	-5.6
PROPERTY CRIME						
Number............................	44,500	39,013	-12.3	9,001,992	8,632,512	-4.1
Rate	2,396.8	2,103.9	-12.2	2,868.0	2,730.7	-4.8
Burglary						
Number............................	11,466	9,674	-15.6	2,109,932	1,928,465	-8.6
Rate	617.6	521.7	-15.5	672.2	610.0	-9.3
Larceny-Theft						
Number............................	30,800	27,423	-11.0	6,168,874	6,004,453	-2.7
Rate	1,658.9	1,478.9	-10.9	1,965.4	1,899.4	-3.4
Motor Vehicle Theft						
Number............................	2,234	1,916	-14.2	723,186	699,594	-3.3
Rate	120.3	103.3	-14.1	230.4	221.3	-4.0

NOTE: Although arson data are included in the trend and clearance tables, sufficient data are not available to estimate totals for this offense. Therefore, no arson data are published in this table.
X = Not applicable.
- = Zero or rounds to zero.
[1]The crime figures have been adjusted.
[2]The data collection methodology for the offense of forcible rape used by the Minnesota state Uniform Crime Reporting (UCR) Program (with the exception of Minneapolis and St. Paul, Minnesota) does not comply with national UCR Program guidelines. Consequently, its figures for forcible rape and violent crime (of which forcible rape is a part) are not published in this table.
[3]Includes offenses reported by the Zoological Police and the Metro Transit Police.
[4]Because of changes in the state's reporting practices, figures are not comparable to previous years' data.
[5]Populations are U.S. Census Bureau provisional estimates as of July 1 of each year.
[6]The figures shown for the offense of rape were estimated using the revised Uniform Crime Reporting (UCR) definition of rape.

Table WV-15. State Government Finances, 2013

(Dollar amounts in thousands, percent distribution.)

Item	Dollars	Percent distribution
Total Revenue	14,581,453	100.0
General revenue	12,390,766	85.0
Intergovernmental revenue	4,325,052	29.7
Taxes	5,378,122	36.9
General sales	1,255,377	8.6
Selective sales	1,323,634	9.1
License taxes	137,437	0.9
Individual income tax	1,795,947	12.3
Corporate income tax	242,429	1.7
Other taxes	623,298	4.3
Current charges	1,504,885	10.3
Miscellaneous general revenue	1,182,707	8.1
Utility revenue	2,435	-
Liquor stores revenue	90,403	0.6
Insurance trust revenue[1]	2,097,849	14.4
Total Expenditure	13,234,155	100.0
Intergovernmental expenditure	2,469,535	18.7
Direct expenditure	10,764,620	81.3
Current operation	7,755,238	58.6
Capital outlay	1,074,774	8.1
Insurance benefits and repayments	1,446,341	10.9
Assistance and subsidies	234,604	1.8
Interest on debt	253,663	1.9
Exhibit: Salaries and wages	1,868,736	14.1
Total Expenditure	13,234,155	100.0
General expenditure	11,708,850	88.5
Intergovernmental expenditure	2,469,535	18.7
Direct expenditure	9,239,315	69.8
General expenditure, by function:		
Education	4,333,893	32.7
Public welfare	3,526,796	26.6
Hospitals	126,185	1.0
Health	345,537	2.6
Highways	1,102,651	8.3
Police protection	75,101	0.6
Correction	300,693	2.3
Natural resources	225,833	1.7
Parks and recreation	51,269	0.4
Governmental administration	438,545	3.3
Interest on general debt	253,663	1.9
Other and unallocable	928,684	7.0
Utility expenditure	4,854	-
Liquor stores expenditure	74,110	0.6
Insurance trust expenditure	1,446,341	10.9
Debt at End of Fiscal Year	7,355,630	X
Cash and Security Holdings	21,396,404	X

X = Not applicable.
- = Zero or rounds to zero.
[1]Within insurance trust revenue, net earnings of state retirement systems is a calculated statistic (the item code in the data file is X08), and thus can be positive or negative. Net earnings is the sum of earnings on investments plus gains on investments minus losses on investments. The change made in 2002 for asset valuation from book to market value in accordance with Statement 34 of the Governmental Accounting Standards Board is reflected in the calculated statistics.

Table WV-16. State Government Tax Collections, 2014

(Dollars in thousands, percent.)

Item	Dollars	Percent distribution
Total Taxes	5,379,937	100.0
Property taxes	0	-
Sales and gross receipts	2,560,993	47.6
General sales and gross receipts	1,221,966	22.7
Selective sales and gross receipts	1,339,027	24.9
Alcoholic beverages	17,295	0.3
Amusements	50,465	0.9
Insurance premiums	155,021	2.9
Motor fuels	441,096	8.2
Pari-mutuels	2,312	-
Public utilities	153,588	2.9
Tobacco products	101,779	1.9
Other selective sales	417,471	7.8
Licenses	152,754	2.8
Alcoholic beverages	1,380	-
Amusements	3,352	0.1
Corporations in general	5,424	0.1
Hunting and fishing	12,599	0.2
Motor vehicle	2,539	-
Motor vehicle operators	108,409	2.0
Public utilities	369	-
Occupation and business, NEC	11,622	0.2
Other licenses	7,060	0.1
Income taxes	1,973,974	36.7
Individual income	1,770,466	32.9
Corporation net income	203,508	3.8
Other taxes	692,216	12.9
Death and gift	0	-
Documentary and stock transfer	10,392	0.2
Severance	681,824	12.7
Taxes, NEC	0	-

- = Zero or rounds to zero.

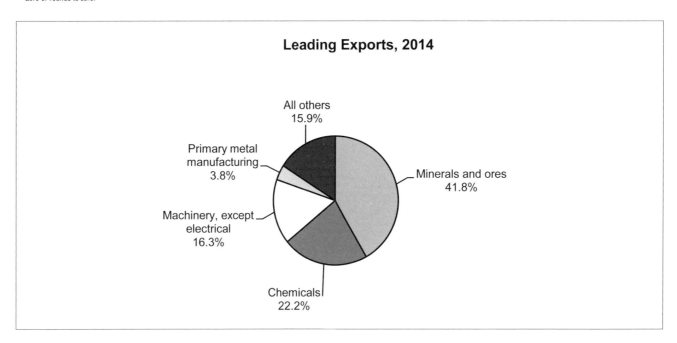

Leading Exports, 2014

- All others 15.9%
- Primary metal manufacturing 3.8%
- Machinery, except electrical 16.3%
- Chemicals 22.2%
- Minerals and ores 41.8%

WISCONSIN

Facts and Figures

Location: North central United States; bordered on the N by Michigan and Lake Superior, on the E by Lake Michigan, on the S by Illinois, and on the W by Iowa and Minnesota

Area: 65,498 sq. mi. (169,639 sq. km.); rank—23rd

Population: 5,757,564 (2014 est.); rank—20th

Principal Cities: capital—Madison; largest—Milwaukee

Statehood: May 29, 1848; 30th state

U.S. Congress: 2 senators, 8 representatives

State Motto: Forward

State Song: "On, Wisconsin!"

State Nickname: The Badger State

Abbreviations: WI; Wis.; Wisc.

State Symbols: flower—wood violet; tree—sugar maple; bird—robin

At a Glance

- With an increase in population of 1.2 percent, Wisconsin ranked 39th among the states in growth from 2010 to 2014.

- Wisconsin's violent crime rate in 2013 was 277.9 per 100,000 population, compared to 367.9 for the entire nation.

- Wisconsin's median household income in 2013 was $51,467, and 13.5 percent of the population lived below the poverty level.

- In 2013, 9.1 percent of Wisconsin residents did not have health insurance, compared to 14.5 percent of the total U.S. population.

- The unemployment rate in Wisconsin in 2014 was 5.5 percent, compared to the national rate of 6.2 percent.

Table WI-1. Population by Age, Sex, Race, and Hispanic Origin

(Number, percent, except where noted.)

Sex, age, race, and Hispanic origin	2000	2010	2014[1]	Average annual percent change, 2010–2014
Total Population	5,363,675	5,686,986	5,757,564	0.3
Percent of total U.S. population	1.9	1.8	1.8	X
Sex				
Male	2,649,041	2,822,400	2,859,507	0.3
Female	2,714,634	2,864,586	2,898,057	0.3
Age				
Under 5 years	342,340	358,443	341,368	-1.2
5 to 19 years	1,189,753	1,143,753	1,116,601	-0.6
20 to 64 years	3,129,029	3,407,476	3,423,727	0.1
65 years and over	702,553	777,314	875,868	3.0
Median age (years)	36.0	38.5	39.2	0.5
Race and Hispanic Origin				
One race				
White	4,769,857	5,036,923	5,057,797	0.1
Black	304,460	367,021	378,526	0.8
American Indian and Alaska Native	47,228	60,100	64,192	1.7
Asian	88,763	131,828	152,512	3.7
Native Hawaiian or Other Pacific Islander	1,630	2,505	2,858	3.4
Two or more races	66,895	88,609	101,679	3.5
Hispanic (of any race)	192,291	349,366	372,248	1.6

X = Not applicable.
[1]Population figures for 2014 are July 1 estimates. The 2010 estimates are taken from the 2010 Census.

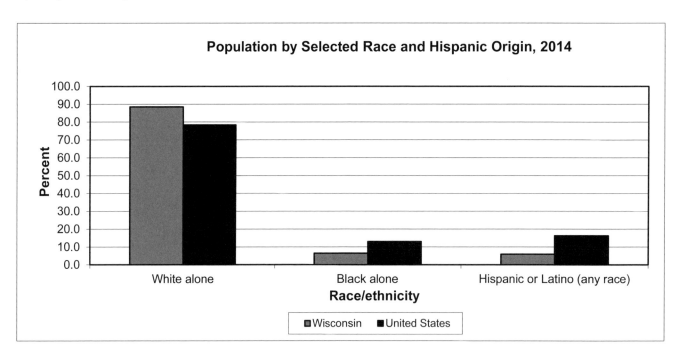

Table WI-2. Marital Status

(Number, percent distribution.)

Sex, age, race, and Hispanic origin	2000	2010	2013
Males, 15 Years and Over	2,072,397	2,261,022	2,300,997
Never married	30.2	34.1	35.1
Now married, except separated	57.9	52.1	51.5
Separated	1.1	1.0	0.9
Widowed	2.4	2.6	2.6
Divorced	8.4	10.2	10.0
Females, 15 Years and Over	2,167,164	2,328,733	2,360,826
Never married	24.3	28.1	29.0
Now married, except separated	54.6	50.1	49.5
Separated	1.3	1.2	1.1
Widowed	10.2	9.2	9.0
Divorced	9.7	11.4	11.4

Table WI-3. Households and Housing Characteristics

(Number, percent, dollars.)

Item	2000	2010	2013	Average annual percent change, 2000–2013
Total Households...	2,084,544	2,279,532	2,289,424	0.7
Family households	1,386,815	1,453,332	1,458,482	0.4
Married-couple family	1,108,597	1,125,314	1,124,707	0.1
Other family	278,218	328,018	333,775	1.4
Male householder, no wife present..............	77,918	96,237	100,615	2.0
Female householder, no husband present........	200,300	231,781	233,160	1.2
Nonfamily households	697,729	826,200	830,942	1.4
Householder living alone...............................	557,875	669,106	667,246	1.4
Householder not living alone..........................	139,854	157,094	163,696	1.2
Housing Characteristics				
Total housing units...	2,321,144	2,625,477	2,633,420	1.0
Occupied housing units	2,084,544	2,279,532	2,289,424	0.7
Owner occupied	1,426,361	1,566,039	1,537,926	0.6
Renter occupied	658,183	713,493	751,498	1.0
Average household size..................................	2.50	2.43	2.44	-0.2
Financial Characteristics				
Median gross rent of renter-occupied housing	540	715	758	2.6
Median monthly owner costs for housing units with a mortgage	1,024	1,404	1,352	2.2
Median value of owner-occupied housing units	112,200	169,400	163,000	2.9

Table WI-4. Migration, Origin, and Language

(Number, percent.)

Characteristic	State			U.S.		
	2012	2013	Percent change	2012	2013	Percent change
Residence 1 Year Ago						
Population 1 year and over	5,660,677	5,681,024	0.4	310,212,755	312,432,820	0.7
Same house..	85.7	85.8	X	85.0	85.0	X
Different house in the U.S.	14.0	13.9	X	14.4	14.4	X
Same county	8.9	8.7	X	9.0	8.9	X
Different county	5.1	5.2	X	5.4	5.5	X
Same state	3.3	3.4	X	3.2	3.2	X
Different state	1.8	1.8	X	2.3	2.3	X
Abroad	0.3	0.3	X	0.6	0.6	X
Place of Birth						
Native born	5,454,389	5,468,026	0.3	273,089,382	274,780,773	0.6
Male	49.6	49.6	X	49.3	49.3	X
Female	50.4	50.4	X	50.7	50.7	X
Foreign born	272,009	274,687	1.0	40,824,658	41,348,066	1.3
Male	51.3	51.4	X	48.7	48.8	X
Female	48.7	48.6	X	51.3	51.2	X
Foreign born; naturalized U.S. citizen.............	115,328	119,720	3.8	18,686,237	19,294,710	3.3
Male	46.9	47.1	X	45.8	45.9	X
Female	53.1	52.9	X	54.2	54.1	X
Foreign born; not a U.S. citizen.......................	156,681	154,967	-1.1	22,138,421	22,053,356	-0.4
Male	54.5	54.7	X	51.1	51.3	X
Female	45.5	45.3	X	48.9	48.7	X
Entered 2010 or later	9.1	11.8	X	7.0	9.7	X
Entered 2000 to 2009	33.6	33.9	X	30.4	29.4	X
Entered before 2000......................................	57.2	54.4	X	62.7	61.0	X
World Region of Birth, Foreign						
Foreign-born population, excluding population born at sea	272,009	274,687	1.0	40,824,553	41,347,945	1.3
Europe	18.8	17.1	X	11.8	11.6	X
Asia..	33.4	34.9	X	29.2	29.5	X
Africa	3.3	3.2	X	4.2	4.4	X
Oceania	0.4	0.5	X	0.6	0.5	X
Latin America	41.6	41.7	X	52.2	51.9	X
North America	2.5	2.6	X	2.0	2.0	X
Language Spoken at Home and Ability to Speak English						
Population 5 years and over.............................	5,375,163	5,401,273	0.5	294,003,714	296,358,760	0.8
English only	91.2	91.3	X	79.0	79.2	X
Language other than English..........................	8.8	8.7	X	21.0	20.8	X
Speaks English less than "very well"...........	3.3	3.2	X	8.5	8.5	X

NA = Not available.
X = Not applicable.
- = Zero or rounds to zero.

Table WI-5. Median Income and Poverty Status, 2013

(Number, percent, except as noted.)

Characteristic	State		U.S.	
	Number	Percent	Number	Percent
Median Income				
Households (dollars)...	51,467	X	52,250	X
Families (dollars)	65,618	X	64,030	X
Below Poverty Level (All People)	755,551	13.5	48,810,868	15.8
Sex				
Male..	337,284	12.2	21,938,525	14.5
Female	418,267	14.8	26,872,343	17.1
Age				
Under 18 years..	236,697	18.4	16,086,960	22.2
Related children under 18 years...........................	229,299	18.0	15,769,921	21.9
18 to 64 years	445,070	12.8	28,578,191	14.8
65 years and over	73,784	9.0	4,145,717	9.6

X = Not applicable.

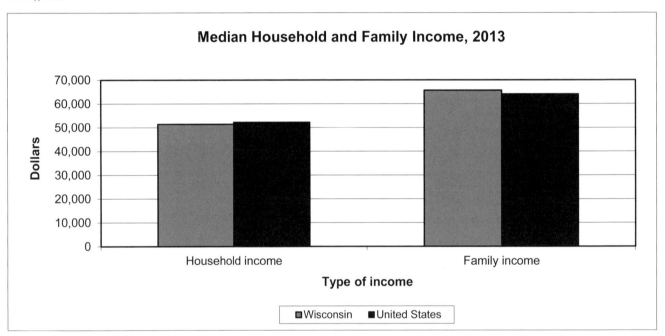

Median Household and Family Income, 2013

Table WI-6. Health Insurance Coverage Status for the Civilian Noninstitutionalized Population and Children Under 18 Years of Age

(Numbers in thousands, percent.)

Item	2005	2006	2007	2008	2009	2010	2011	2012	2013
Civilian Noninstitutionalized Population	5,447	5,476	5,473	5,540	5,566	5,613	5,634	5,652	5,669
Covered by Private or Public Insurance									
Number...	4,938	4,995	5,023	5,034	5,045	5,084	5,127	5,146	5,151
Percent...	90.7	91.2	91.8	90.9	90.6	90.6	91.0	91.0	90.9
Not Covered									
Number...	509	481	451	506	521	529	507	506	518
Percent...	9.3	8.8	8.2	9.1	9.4	9.4	9.0	9.0	9.1
Percent in the U.S. not covered.................................	15.3	15.8	15.3	15.1	15.1	15.5	15.1	14.8	14.5
Children Under 18 Years of Age...................................	1,303	1,290	1,329	1,309	1,303	1,334	1,323	1,315	1,305
Covered by Private or Public Insurance									
Number...	1,212	1,227	1,252	1,241	1,238	1,267	1,265	1,253	1,243
Percent...	93.1	95.1	94.2	94.8	95.0	95.0	95.6	95.3	95.3
Not Covered									
Number...	90	63	77	68	65	67	58	62	61
Percent...	6.9	4.9	5.8	5.2	5.0	5.0	4.4	4.7	4.7
Percent in the U.S. not covered.................................	10.9	11.7	11.0	9.7	8.6	8.0	7.5	7.2	7.1

Table WI-7. Employment Status by Demographic Group, 2014

(Numbers in thousands, percent.)

Characteristic	Civilian noninstitutional population	Civilian labor force		Employed		Unemployed	
		Number	Percent of population	Number	Percent of population	Number	Percent of population
Total..........................	4,534	3,091	68.2	2,918	64.4	174	5.6
Sex							
Male..................................	2,224	1,624	73.1	1,531	68.8	93	5.8
Female	2,310	1,467	63.5	1,387	60.0	80	5.5
Race, Sex, and Hispanic Origin							
White	4,060	2,776	68.4	2,653	65.4	123	4.4
Male..................................	1,996	1,474	73.8	1,405	70.4	68	4.6
Female	2,064	1,303	63.1	1,248	60.5	55	4.2
Black or African American....................................	259	160	61.9	127	49.0	33	20.8
Male..................................	124	78	63.3	63	51.0	15	19.4
Female	135	82	60.6	64	47.2	18	22.2
Hispanic or Latino ethnicity[1]	215	146	67.8	133	61.8	13	8.9
Male..................................	110	81	74.0	74	67.7	7	8.4
Female	106	65	61.4	59	55.6	6	9.4
Age							
16 to 19 years.....................	315	161	51.2	133	42.3	28	17.5
20 to 24 years.....................	349	282	80.8	252	72.1	30	10.8
25 to 34 years.....................	772	679	88.0	640	82.9	39	5.8
35 to 44 years.....................	659	580	88.0	556	84.4	24	4.1
45 to 54 years.....................	801	691	86.2	669	83.5	22	3.2
55 to 64 years.....................	802	567	70.7	541	67.4	26	4.6
65 years and over	835	131	15.7	127	15.2	4	3.0

NOTE: Data in Table 7 are from the Current Population Survey (CPS) and do not match the estimates in Table 8. See notes and definitions for further information.
[1]May be of any race.

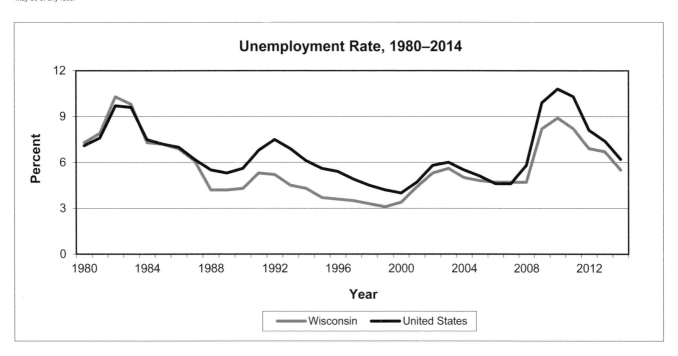

Unemployment Rate, 1980–2014

Table WI-8. Employment Status of the Civilian Noninstitutional Population Age 16 Years and Over

(Number, percent.)

Year	Civilian labor force	Civilian participation rate	Employed	Unemployed	Unemployment rate
2006...............	3,058,935	70.7	2,914,150	144,785	4.7
2007...............	3,087,828	70.9	2,936,452	151,376	4.9
2008...............	3,091,796	70.4	2,940,438	151,358	4.9
2009...............	3,100,348	70.2	2,834,335	266,013	8.6
2010...............	3,081,512	69.5	2,814,393	267,119	8.7
2011...............	3,080,399	69.1	2,841,465	238,934	7.8
2012...............	3,074,255	68.5	2,857,594	216,661	7.0
2013...............	3,084,978	68.4	2,876,712	208,266	6.8
2014...............	3,093,918	68.2	2,923,533	170,385	5.5

Table WI-9. Employment and Average Wages by Industry

(Estimates from 2007 through 2010 are based on the 2007 *North American Industry Classification System* [NAICS]. Estimates from 2011 onward are based on the 2012 NAICS.)

Industry	2007	2008	2009	2010	2011	2012	2013
	Number of jobs						
Wage and Salary Employment by Industry......................	2,940,888	2,932,840	2,803,520	2,795,211	2,824,652	2,840,951	2,874,843
Farm Wage and Salary Employment.............................	23,717	24,483	22,753	23,468	24,791	19,135	25,025
Nonfarm Wage and Salary Employment........................	2,917,171	2,908,357	2,780,767	2,771,743	2,799,861	2,821,816	2,849,818
Private wage and salary employment.................................	2,489,895	2,476,599	2,344,911	2,334,467	2,368,305	2,389,825	2,418,113
Forestry, fishing, and related activities...........................	4,991	5,115	5,250	5,412	5,700	5,541	5,738
Mining...	2,849	2,631	2,308	2,227	2,293	2,754	3,009
Utilities..	11,145	11,319	11,271	11,113	10,920	10,896	10,702
Construction	131,085	123,236	106,731	99,226	97,761	96,783	102,124
Manufacturing...	503,084	494,458	437,035	431,729	445,665	456,493	458,139
Durable goods manufacturing..................................	317,404	310,980	264,048	258,729	270,714	279,741	279,901
Nondurable goods manufacturing..............................	185,680	183,478	172,987	173,000	174,951	176,752	178,238
Wholesale trade	123,475	123,652	116,786	113,855	115,475	117,368	119,634
Retail trade..	320,447	314,818	302,760	299,011	299,853	298,278	301,608
Transportation and warehousing..................................	100,979	97,099	91,549	90,637	91,926	91,951	91,687
Information	50,428	50,426	48,040	46,890	47,056	46,727	47,330
Finance and insurance	134,141	134,603	132,910	130,529	130,186	130,647	129,077
Real estate and rental and leasing................................	28,766	28,348	26,645	26,027	25,295	24,904	25,249
Professional, scientific, and technical services	100,288	102,257	97,654	95,303	97,667	99,466	100,765
Management of companies and enterprises....................	43,534	45,930	46,393	47,130	50,719	53,014	55,750
Administrative and waste services...............................	138,756	138,480	119,381	131,733	139,142	140,960	144,783
Educational services	49,816	51,450	52,492	54,321	55,609	55,365	54,930
Health care and social assistance................................	345,264	353,683	358,739	361,818	364,486	369,115	374,304
Arts, entertainment, and recreation..............................	36,886	36,279	35,227	35,238	35,954	36,251	36,648
Accommodation and food services...............................	228,642	226,511	220,452	219,644	219,657	222,477	226,574
Other services, except public administration..................	135,319	136,304	133,288	132,624	132,941	130,835	130,062
Government and government enterprises........................	427,276	431,758	435,856	437,276	431,556	431,991	431,705
	Dollars						
Average Wages and Salaries by Industry........................	38,588	39,678	39,613	40,479	41,558	42,655	43,403
Average Farm Wages and Salaries	34,611	35,038	35,292	29,335	27,175	32,594	35,830
Average Nonfarm Wages and Salaries...........................	38,621	39,717	39,649	40,573	41,686	42,724	43,470
Average private wages and salaries...............................	38,755	39,814	39,642	40,697	41,876	43,105	43,862
Forestry, fishing, and related activities.........................	27,827	29,241	28,691	29,757	30,923	32,114	33,510
Mining...	50,027	52,482	53,359	56,996	60,382	61,499	61,633
Utilities..	78,590	91,695	93,364	92,701	95,756	97,979	103,692
Construction	48,177	50,503	49,693	50,070	51,149	52,773	54,296
Manufacturing...	48,470	49,672	49,355	51,943	53,093	54,245	54,780
Durable goods manufacturing..................................	49,399	50,813	50,468	53,717	55,081	55,994	56,430
Nondurable goods manufacturing..............................	46,882	47,739	47,657	49,291	50,016	51,478	52,189
Wholesale trade	52,558	54,176	53,362	55,180	57,311	59,207	60,009
Retail trade..	22,823	23,275	23,343	23,834	24,204	24,608	24,910
Transportation and warehousing..................................	39,440	39,976	39,272	39,724	40,815	42,270	43,040
Information	50,649	52,156	52,629	54,155	56,149	58,882	61,128
Finance and insurance	57,028	58,325	57,581	59,821	62,356	65,842	67,204
Real estate and rental and leasing................................	31,992	33,097	33,784	33,071	34,171	35,025	35,665
Professional, scientific, and technical services	57,396	58,692	58,569	59,652	61,676	64,218	64,967
Management of companies and enterprises....................	85,071	80,226	78,337	85,041	87,493	89,815	91,926
Administrative and waste services...............................	25,250	26,110	26,445	26,507	27,239	27,488	28,113
Educational services	30,330	31,454	32,112	33,076	34,023	34,823	35,580
Health care and social assistance................................	40,029	41,594	42,487	42,855	43,680	44,508	45,356
Arts, entertainment, and recreation..............................	26,878	27,523	27,283	28,299	29,215	28,369	29,786
Accommodation and food services...............................	13,455	13,405	13,369	13,956	14,418	14,859	14,888
Other services, except public administration..................	24,869	25,680	25,765	26,596	27,231	27,615	28,361
Government and government enterprises........................	37,840	39,160	39,686	39,910	40,638	40,613	41,273

Table WI-10. Employment Characteristics by Family Type

(Number, percent.)

Family type and labor force status	2011		2012		2013	
	Total	Families with own children under 18 years	Total	Families with own children under 18 years	Total	Families with own children under 18 years
All Families..	1,462,927	633,636	1,461,573	629,141	1,458,482	619,727
FAMILY TYPE AND LABOR FORCE STATUS						
Married-Couple Families................................	1,134,124	429,500	1,126,874	425,308	1,124,707	420,513
Both husband and wife in labor force............................	59.4	75.7	58.5	75.2	58.0	75.4
Husband in labor force, wife not in labor force................	15.9	19.4	16.2	20.3	16.1	19.8
Wife in labor force, husband not in labor force................	8.2	3.6	8.0	3.6	7.9	3.4
Both husband and wife not in labor force........................	16.5	1.3	17.4	0.9	17.6	1.1
Other Families	328,803	204,136	334,699	203,833	333,775	199,214
Female householder, no husband present........................	69.7	71.8	70.0	72.4	69.9	72.5
In labor force	53.1	60.6	52.6	60.7	51.8	61.4
Not in labor force	16.6	11.2	17.3	11.7	18.1	11.1
Male householder, no wife present................................	30.3	28.2	30.0	27.6	30.1	27.5
In labor force..	24.7	25.9	24.1	25.0	24.9	25.0
Not in labor force	5.6	2.3	5.9	2.6	5.3	2.5

Table WI-11. School Enrollment and Educational Attainment, 2013

(Number, percent.)

Item	State	U.S.
Enrollment		
Total population 3 years and over, enrolled in school	1,485,800	82,395,254
Enrolled in nursery school or preschool (percent)	5.0	6.0
Enrolled in kindergarten (percent)..	6.0	5.2
Enrolled in elementary school, grades 1-8 (percent)..	39.5	40.0
Enrolled in high school, grades 9-12 (percent)...	20.6	20.6
Enrolled in college or graduate school (percent)...	28.8	28.3
Attainment		
Total population 25 years and over	3,879,291	210,910,615
Less than ninth grade (percent)	3.1	5.8
9th to 12th grade, no diploma (percent)	6.0	7.6
High school graduate, including equivalency (percent)..	32.0	27.8
Some college, no degree (percent)	21.1	21.1
Associate's degree (percent)...	10.0	8.1
Bachelor's degree (percent)..	18.4	18.4
Graduate or professional degree (percent)...	9.4	11.2
High school graduate or higher (percent)	90.9	86.6
Bachelor's degree or higher (percent)...	27.7	29.6

Table WI-12. Public School Characteristics and Educational Indicators

(Number, percent; data derived from National Center of Education Statistics.)

Item	State	U.S.
Public Schools, 2012–2013 (except where noted)		
Number of school districts...	464	18,093
Number of schools..	2,238	98,454
Number of students (in thousands)	872	49,771
Number of teachers (in thousands)	58	3,109
Student-teacher ratio	15.2	16.0
Expenditures per student (dollars), FY 2012...	11,233	10,667
Four-year adjusted cohort graduation rate (ACGR)[1,2]	88.0	81.4
Students eligible for free or reduced-price lunch (in thousands)	361	25,188
English language learners (in thousands)...	43	4,397
Students age 3 to 21 served under IDEA, part B (in thousands).................................	123	6,429

Public Schools by Type	Number	Percent of state public schools
Total number of schools...	2,238	100.0
Regular	2,125	95.0
Special education...	10	0.4
Vocational education...	5	0.2
Alternative education..	98	4.4

NOTE: Every school is assigned only one school type based on its instructional emphasis.
[1]ACGR data represents a new method of calculating high-school completion rates and may not be comparable to previous years' data for Averaged Freshmen Graduation Rates (AFGR).
[2]The United States 4-year ACGRs were estimated using both the reported 4-year ACGR data from 49 states and the District of Columbia and using imputed data for Idaho. The estimate for American Indian/Alaska Native students also includes imputed data for Virginia.

Table WI-13. Reported Voting and Registration of the Voting-Age Population, November 2012

(Numbers in thousands, percent.)

Item	Total population	Total citizen population	Registered			Voted		
			Total registered	Percent registered (total population)	Percent registered (total citizen population)	Total voted	Percent voted (total population)	Percent voted (total citizen population)
U.S. Total	235,248	215,081	153,157	65.1	71.2	132,948	56.5	61.8
State Total	4,352	4,247	3,318	76.3	78.1	3,127	71.9	73.6
Sex								
Male	2,115	2,058	1,554	73.5	75.5	1,460	69.0	70.9
Female	2,236	2,189	1,764	78.9	80.6	1,667	74.6	76.2
Race								
White alone	3,920	3,856	3,030	77.3	78.6	2,854	72.8	74.0
White, non-Hispanic alone	3,751	3,728	2,968	79.1	79.6	2,797	74.6	75.0
Black alone	242	227	184	76.1	81.0	178	73.7	78.5
Asian alone	35	20	15	B	B	15	B	B
Hispanic (of any race)	214	163	76	35.5	46.8	71	33.3	43.9
White alone or in combination	3,967	3,898	3,061	77.2	78.5	2,885	72.7	74.0
Black alone or in combination	255	241	198	77.3	82.1	192	75.1	79.6
Asian alone or in combination	40	25	17	B	B	17	B	B
Age								
18 to 24 years	539	513	308	57.1	60.1	287	53.3	56.0
25 to 44 years	1,413	1,357	1,024	72.4	75.4	951	67.3	70.1
45 to 64 years	1,552	1,532	1,224	78.9	79.9	1,192	76.8	77.8
65 to 74 years	444	444	398	89.7	89.7	383	86.3	86.3
75 years and over	403	401	364	90.4	90.8	313	77.8	78.1

B = Base is less than 75,000 and therefore too small to show the derived measure.

Table WI-14. Crime

(Number, rate per 100,000. Data are derived from the FBI Uniform Crime Reports.)

Item	State			U.S.[1,2,3,4]		
	2012	2013	Percent change	2012	2013	Percent change
TOTAL POPULATION[5]	5,724,554	5,742,713	0.3	313,873,685	316,128,839	0.7
VIOLENT CRIME						
Number	16,254	15,570	-4.2	1,217,067	1,163,146	-4.4
Rate	283.9	271.1	-4.5	387.8	367.9	-5.1
Murder and Nonnegligent Manslaughter						
Number	169	162	-4.1	14,866	14,196	-4.5
Rate	3.0	2.8	-4.4	4.7	4.5	-5.2
Rape[6]						
Number	X	1,687	X	X	108,612	X
Rate	X	29.4	X	X	34.4	X
Robbery						
Number	4,692	4,834	3.0	355,051	345,031	-2.8
Rate	82.0	84.2	2.7	113.1	109.1	-3.5
Aggravated Assault						
Number	10,165	9,278	-8.7	762,009	724,149	-5.0
Rate	177.6	161.6	-9.0	242.8	229.1	-5.6
PROPERTY CRIME						
Number	140,780	125,688	-10.7	9,001,992	8,632,512	-4.1
Rate	2,459.2	2,188.7	-11.0	2,868.0	2,730.7	-4.8
Burglary						
Number	27,931	24,347	-12.8	2,109,932	1,928,465	-8.6
Rate	487.9	424.0	-13.1	672.2	610.0	-9.3
Larceny-Theft						
Number	104,619	93,953	-10.2	6,168,874	6,004,453	-2.7
Rate	1,827.5	1,636.0	-10.5	1,965.4	1,899.4	-3.4
Motor Vehicle Theft						
Number	8,230	7,388	-10.2	723,186	699,594	-3.3
Rate	143.8	128.6	-10.5	230.4	221.3	-4.0

NOTE: Although arson data are included in the trend and clearance tables, sufficient data are not available to estimate totals for this offense. Therefore, no arson data are published in this table.
X = Not applicable.
- = Zero or rounds to zero.
[1]The crime figures have been adjusted.
[2]The data collection methodology for the offense of forcible rape used by the Minnesota state Uniform Crime Reporting (UCR) Program (with the exception of Minneapolis and St. Paul, Minnesota) does not comply with national UCR Program guidelines. Consequently, its figures for forcible rape and violent crime (of which forcible rape is a part) are not published in this table.
[3]Includes offenses reported by the Zoological Police and the Metro Transit Police.
[4]Because of changes in the state's reporting practices, figures are not comparable to previous years' data.
[5]Populations are U.S. Census Bureau provisional estimates as of July 1 of each year.
[6]The figures shown for the offense of rape were estimated using the revised Uniform Crime Reporting (UCR) definition of rape.

Table WI-15. State Government Finances, 2013

(Dollar amounts in thousands, percent distribution.)

Item	Dollars	Percent distribution
Total Revenue	45,891,806	100.0
General revenue	32,280,837	70.3
Intergovernmental revenue	9,228,907	20.1
Taxes	16,513,692	36.0
General sales	4,410,130	9.6
Selective sales	2,678,281	5.8
License taxes	1,026,823	2.2
Individual income tax	7,227,690	15.7
Corporate income tax	955,752	2.1
Other taxes	215,016	0.5
Current charges	4,011,774	8.7
Miscellaneous general revenue	2,526,464	5.5
Utility revenue	0	-
Liquor stores revenue	0	-
Insurance trust revenue[1]	13,610,969	29.7
Total Expenditure	37,524,804	100.0
Intergovernmental expenditure	9,637,247	25.7
Direct expenditure	27,887,557	74.3
Current operation	18,591,474	49.5
Capital outlay	2,086,899	5.6
Insurance benefits and repayments	5,637,912	15.0
Assistance and subsidies	641,349	1.7
Interest on debt	929,923	2.5
Exhibit: Salaries and wages	4,369,544	11.6
Total Expenditure	37,524,804	100.0
General expenditure	31,878,459	85.0
Intergovernmental expenditure	9,637,247	25.7
Direct expenditure	22,241,212	59.3
General expenditure, by function:		
Education	10,877,543	29.0
Public welfare	8,849,077	23.6
Hospitals	1,422,217	3.8
Health	771,081	2.1
Highways	2,409,285	6.4
Police protection	122,600	0.3
Correction	1,090,920	2.9
Natural resources	664,438	1.8
Parks and recreation	28,419	0.1
Governmental administration	717,793	1.9
Interest on general debt	929,923	2.5
Other and unallocable	3,995,163	10.6
Utility expenditure	8,433	-
Liquor stores expenditure	0	-
Insurance trust expenditure	5,637,912	15.0
Debt at End of Fiscal Year	23,187,772	X
Cash and Security Holdings	87,570,671	X

X = Not applicable.
- = Zero or rounds to zero.
[1]Within insurance trust revenue, net earnings of state retirement systems is a calculated statistic (the item code in the data file is X08), and thus can be positive or negative. Net earnings is the sum of earnings on investments plus gains on investments minus losses on investments. The change made in 2002 for asset valuation from book to market value in accordance with Statement 34 of the Governmental Accounting Standards Board is reflected in the calculated statistics.

Table WI-16. State Government Tax Collections, 2014

(Dollars in thousands, percent.)

Item	Dollars	Percent distribution
Total Taxes	16,410,925	100.0
Property taxes	159,069	1.0
Sales and gross receipts	7,359,539	44.8
General sales and gross receipts	4,628,338	28.2
Selective sales and gross receipts	2,731,201	16.6
Alcoholic beverages	57,958	0.4
Amusements	222	-
Insurance premiums	185,502	1.1
Motor fuels	1,000,595	6.1
Pari-mutuels	0	
Public utilities	379,549	2.3
Tobacco products	640,728	3.9
Other selective sales	466,647	2.8
Licenses	1,040,619	6.3
Alcoholic beverages	1,785	-
Amusements	666	-
Corporations in general	20,628	0.1
Hunting and fishing	66,962	0.4
Motor vehicle	467,502	2.8
Motor vehicle operators	39,691	0.2
Public utilities	72,199	0.4
Occupation and business, NEC	366,526	2.2
Other licenses	4,660	-
Income taxes	7,779,733	47.4
Individual income	6,793,269	41.4
Corporation net income	986,464	6.0
Other taxes	71,965	0.4
Death and gift	0	-
Documentary and stock transfer	51,179	0.3
Severance	8,984	0.1
Taxes, NEC	11,802	0.1

- = Zero or rounds to zero.

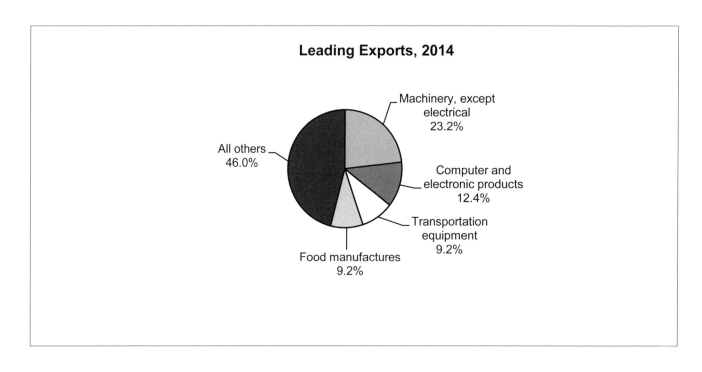

Leading Exports, 2014

Machinery, except electrical 23.2%

Computer and electronic products 12.4%

Transportation equipment 9.2%

Food manufactures 9.2%

All others 46.0%

WYOMING

Facts and Figures

Location: Western United States; bordered on the N by Montana, on the E by South Dakota and Nebraska, on the S by Colorado and Utah, and on the W by Utah and Idaho

Area: 97,814 sq. mi. (253,336 sq. km.); rank—10th

Population: 584,153 (2014 est.); rank—51st

Principal Cities: capital—Cheyenne; largest—Cheyenne

Statehood: July 10, 1890; 44th state

U.S. Congress: 2 senators, 1 representative

State Motto: Equal Rights

State Song: "Wyoming"

State Nicknames: The Equality State; The Cowboy State

Abbreviations: WY; Wyo.

State Symbols: flower—Indian paintbrush; tree—cottonwood; bird—Western meadowlark

At a Glance

- With an increase in population of 3.6 percent, Wyoming ranked 20th among the states in growth from 2010 to 2014.

- Wyoming's violent crime rate in 2013 was 205.1 per 100,000 population, the fourth lowest rate in the country.

- Wyoming residents consumed the most energy in 2013, at 918.1 million Btu per capita.

- Wyoming's median household income in 2013 was $58,752, and 10.9 percent of the population lived below the poverty level.

- In 2013, 13.4 percent of Wyoming residents did not have health insurance, compared to 14.5 of total U.S. residents.

Table WY-1. Population by Age, Sex, Race, and Hispanic Origin

(Number, percent, except where noted.)

Sex, age, race, and Hispanic origin	2000	2010	2014[1]	Average annual percent change, 2010–2014
Total Population	493,782	563,626	584,153	0.9
Percent of total U.S. population	0.2	0.2	0.2	X
Sex				
Male	248,374	287,437	298,042	0.9
Female	245,408	276,189	286,111	0.9
Age				
Under 5 years	30,940	40,203	38,171	-1.3
5 to 19 years	114,406	111,310	114,944	0.8
20 to 64 years	290,743	342,023	349,397	0.5
65 years and over	57,693	70,090	81,641	3.9
Median age (years)	36.2	36.8	36.8	-
Race and Hispanic Origin				
One race				
White	454,670	529,110	541,596	0.6
Black	3,722	5,135	9,112	15.4
American Indian and Alaska Native	11,133	14,457	15,541	1.8
Asian	2,771	4,649	5,821	5.8
Native Hawaiian or Other Pacific Islander	302	521	632	4.9
Two or more races	8,883	9,754	11,451	4.1
Hispanic (of any race)	31,669	52,112	57,065	2.3

X = Not applicable.
- = Zero or rounds to zero.
[1]Population figures for 2014 are July 1 estimates. The 2010 estimates are taken from the 2010 Census.

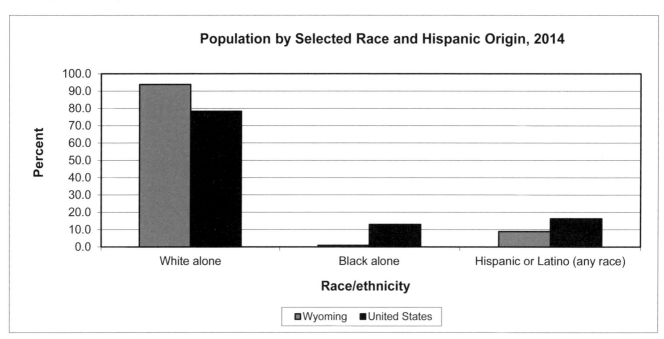

Table WY-2. Marital Status

(Number, percent distribution.)

Sex, age, race, and Hispanic origin	2000	2010	2013
Males, 15 Years and Over	195,412	228,725	235,543
Never married	26.6	29.0	30.2
Now married, except separated	58.8	56.2	54.1
Separated	1.0	1.3	2.2
Widowed	2.3	2.4	2.6
Divorced	11.3	11.2	10.8
Females, 15 Years and Over	195,433	220,169	228,758
Never married	20.0	20.7	23.3
Now married, except separated	57.5	55.1	54.0
Separated	1.3	2.0	1.3
Widowed	9.2	8.6	8.0
Divorced	12.0	13.6	13.4

Table WY-3. Households and Housing Characteristics

(Number, percent, dollars.)

Item	2000	2010	2013	Average annual percent change, 2000–2013
Total Households	193,608	222,803	224,003	1.1
Family households	130,497	147,394	148,556	1.0
Married-couple family	106,179	119,756	118,017	0.8
Other family	24,318	27,638	30,539	1.8
Male householder, no wife present	7,481	7,804	10,300	2.5
Female householder, no husband present	16,837	19,834	20,239	1.4
Nonfamily households	63,111	75,409	75,447	1.4
Householder living alone	50,980	61,775	60,659	1.3
Householder not living alone	12,131	13,634	14,788	1.5
Housing Characteristics				
Total housing units	223,854	262,286	265,471	1.3
Occupied housing units	193,608	222,803	224,003	1.1
Owner occupied	135,514	155,278	154,699	1.0
Renter occupied	58,094	67,525	69,304	1.4
Average household size	2.48	2.47	2.54	0.2
Financial Characteristics				
Median gross rent of renter-occupied housing	437	693	780	4.6
Median monthly owner costs for housing units with a mortgage	825	1,300	1,330	3.7
Median value of owner-occupied housing units	96,600	180,100	195,500	5.6

Table WY-4. Migration, Origin, and Language

(Number, percent.)

Characteristic	State 2012	State 2013	State Percent change	U.S. 2012	U.S. 2013	U.S. Percent change
Residence 1 Year Ago						
Population 1 year and over	569,734	575,933	1.1	310,212,755	312,432,820	0.7
Same house	80.6	81.5	X	85.0	85.0	X
Different house in the U.S.	19.0	18.1	X	14.4	14.4	X
Same county	11.0	9.9	X	9.0	8.9	X
Different county	8.0	8.3	X	5.4	5.5	X
Same state	2.5	3.5	X	3.2	3.2	X
Different state	5.5	4.8	X	2.3	2.3	X
Abroad	0.4	0.3	X	0.6	0.6	X
Place of Birth						
Native born	556,892	564,629	1.4	273,089,382	274,780,773	0.6
Male	51.1	51.2	X	49.3	49.3	X
Female	48.9	48.8	X	50.7	50.7	X
Foreign born	19,520	18,029	-7.6	40,824,658	41,348,066	1.3
Male	40.8	45.9	X	48.7	48.8	X
Female	59.2	54.1	X	51.3	51.2	X
Foreign born; naturalized U.S. citizen	7,318	7,083	-3.2	18,686,237	19,294,710	3.3
Male	33.6	28.1	X	45.8	45.9	X
Female	66.4	71.9	X	54.2	54.1	X
Foreign born; not a U.S. citizen	12,202	10,946	-10.3	22,138,421	22,053,356	-0.4
Male	45.2	57.4	X	51.1	51.3	X
Female	54.8	42.6	X	48.9	48.7	X
Entered 2010 or later	8.7	13.0	X	7.0	9.7	X
Entered 2000 to 2009	41.2	40.5	X	30.4	29.4	X
Entered before 2000	50.2	46.5	X	62.7	61.0	X
World Region of Birth, Foreign						
Foreign-born population, excluding population born at sea	19,520	18,029	-7.6	40,824,553	41,347,945	1.3
Europe	14.0	19.6	X	11.8	11.6	X
Asia	19.9	23.3	X	29.2	29.5	X
Africa	4.6	7.4	X	4.2	4.4	X
Oceania	0.7	2.5	X	0.6	0.5	X
Latin America	53.5	42.8	X	52.2	51.9	X
North America	7.3	4.5	X	2.0	2.0	X
Language Spoken at Home and Ability to Speak English						
Population 5 years and over	538,396	544,279	1.1	294,003,714	296,358,760	0.8
English only	92.4	93.7	X	79.0	79.2	X
Language other than English	7.6	6.3	X	21.0	20.8	X
Speaks English less than "very well"	2.1	1.8	X	8.5	8.5	X

NA = Not available.
X = Not applicable.
- = Zero or rounds to zero.

Table WY-5. Median Income and Poverty Status, 2013

(Number, percent, except as noted.)

Characteristic	State		U.S.	
	Number	Percent	Number	Percent
Median Income				
Households (dollars)...	58,752	X	52,250	X
Families (dollars)	71,446	X	64,030	X
Below Poverty Level (All People)...............................	62,039	10.9	48,810,868	15.8
Sex				
Male..	28,231	9.8	21,938,525	14.5
Female	33,808	12.1	26,872,343	17.1
Age				
Under 18 years..	18,187	13.2	16,086,960	22.2
Related children under 18 years.................................	17,773	12.9	15,769,921	21.9
18 to 64 years..	38,148	10.7	28,578,191	14.8
65 years and over	5,704	7.6	4,145,717	9.6

X = Not applicable.

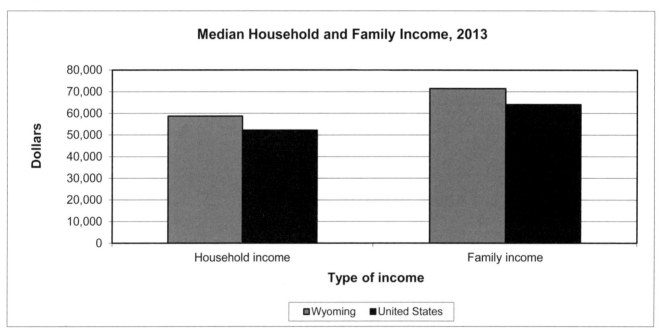

Table WY-6. Health Insurance Coverage Status for the Civilian Noninstitutionalized Population and Children Under 18 Years of Age

(Numbers in thousands, percent.)

Item	2005	2006	2007	2008	2009	2010	2011	2012	2013
Civilian Noninstitutionalized Population	511	516	518	523	534	555	559	567	573
Covered by Private or Public Insurance									
Number..	436	441	447	451	453	472	473	480	496
Percent...	85.4	85.4	86.4	86.2	84.8	85.1	84.6	84.6	86.6
Not Covered									
Number..	75	75	70	72	81	83	86	87	77
Percent...	14.6	14.6	13.6	13.8	15.2	14.9	15.4	15.4	13.4
Percent in the U.S. not covered.......................................	15.3	15.8	15.3	15.1	15.1	15.5	15.1	14.8	14.5
Children Under 18 Years of Age..	118	123	127	127	128	136	135	136	139
Covered by Private or Public Insurance									
Number..	105	113	115	116	117	125	123	123	131
Percent...	89.2	91.8	90.4	91.3	91.0	92.1	91.4	90.7	94.3
Not Covered									
Number..	13	10	12	11	11	11	12	13	8
Percent...	10.8	8.2	9.6	8.7	9.0	7.9	8.6	9.3	5.7
Percent in the U.S. not covered.......................................	10.9	11.7	11.0	9.7	8.6	8.0	7.5	7.2	7.1

Table WY-7. Employment Status by Demographic Group, 2014

(Numbers in thousands, percent.)

Characteristic	Civilian noninstitutional population	Civilian labor force		Employed		Unemployed	
		Number	Percent of population	Number	Percent of population	Number	Percent of population
Total..	451	308	68.2	294	65.2	13	4.4
Sex							
Male..	228	172	75.4	165	72.3	7	4.1
Female	223	136	60.8	130	58.0	6	4.7
Race, Sex, and Hispanic Origin							
White...	423	289	68.3	277	65.5	12	4.1
Male..	212	160	75.5	154	72.6	6	3.8
Female	211	128	61.0	123	58.3	6	4.4
Black or African American....................	7	5	72.2	5	66.7	...	7.7
Male..	NA	NA	NA	NA	NA	NA	NA
Female	NA	NA	NA	NA	NA	NA	NA
Hispanic or Latino ethnicity[1]	34	25	74.8	24	71.9	1	3.9
Male..	18	15	81.1	14	77.1	1	4.9
Female	15	10	67.3	10	65.7	...	2.4
Age							
16 to 19 years......................................	26	13	49.8	11	41.7	2	16.3
20 to 24 years......................................	39	30	77.5	28	71.2	2	8.1
25 to 34 years......................................	83	68	82.2	65	78.6	3	4.4
35 to 44 years......................................	71	62	86.2	59	83.4	2	3.3
45 to 54 years......................................	78	66	84.4	64	82.0	2	2.8
55 to 64 years......................................	76	52	67.8	50	66.1	1	2.5
65 years and over	78	17	22.4	17	21.4	1	4.4

NOTE: Data in Table 7 are from the Current Population Survey (CPS) and do not match the estimates in Table 8. See notes and definitions for further information.
[1]May be of any race.
NA = Not available.
... = Fewer than 500 persons.

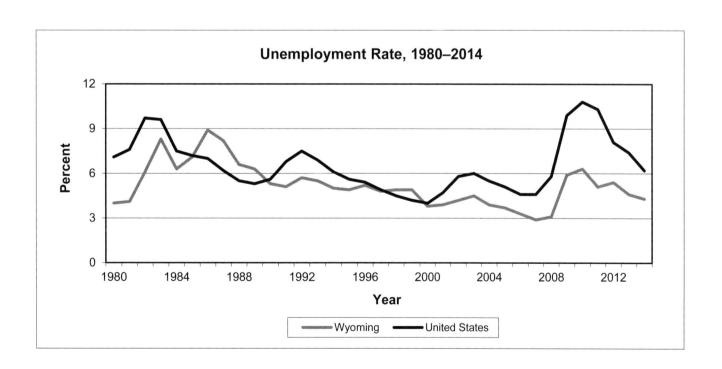

Table WY-8. Employment Status of the Civilian Noninstitutional Population Age 16 Years and Over

(Number, percent.)

Year	Civilian labor force	Civilian participation rate	Employed	Unemployed	Unemployment rate
2006	281,247	71.0	272,336	8,911	3.2
2007	286,560	71.0	278,486	8,074	2.8
2008	293,279	71.4	284,310	8,969	3.1
2009	300,120	71.8	281,150	18,970	6.3
2010	303,297	70.4	283,744	19,553	6.4
2011	306,886	70.2	289,099	17,787	5.8
2012	307,542	69.2	291,177	16,365	5.3
2013	306,767	68.3	292,260	14,507	4.7
2014	306,928	68.1	293,689	13,239	4.3

Table WY-9. Employment and Average Wages by Industry

(Estimates from 2007 through 2010 are based on the 2007 *North American Industry Classification System* [NAICS]. Estimates from 2011 onward are based on the 2012 NAICS.)

Industry	2007	2008	2009	2010	2011	2012	2013
	Number of jobs						
Wage and Salary Employment by Industry	298,916	307,460	295,383	291,969	295,870	298,049	299,516
Farm Wage and Salary Employment	2,837	2,993	2,805	2,878	3,220	3,334	3,432
Nonfarm Wage and Salary Employment	296,079	304,467	292,578	289,091	292,650	294,715	296,084
Private wage and salary employment	225,873	232,960	218,671	214,098	217,690	219,151	220,347
Forestry, fishing, and related activities	887	888	868	902	956	970	1,068
Mining	27,238	29,320	25,344	24,933	27,215	27,556	26,459
Utilities	2,466	2,507	2,493	2,483	2,489	2,471	2,482
Construction	27,602	29,299	25,036	23,470	22,221	22,268	22,629
Manufacturing	10,192	9,964	9,125	8,727	9,185	9,362	9,468
Durable goods manufacturing	5,463	5,209	4,589	4,265	4,617	4,734	4,702
Nondurable goods manufacturing	4,729	4,755	4,536	4,462	4,568	4,628	4,766
Wholesale trade	8,818	9,174	8,809	8,529	8,901	9,196	9,297
Retail trade	32,451	32,605	31,156	29,989	29,639	29,722	30,079
Transportation and warehousing	12,255	12,364	11,668	11,516	12,077	12,307	12,323
Information	4,030	4,011	3,960	3,891	3,850	3,917	3,808
Finance and insurance	7,172	7,441	7,336	7,169	7,108	7,099	7,185
Real estate and rental and leasing	4,543	4,539	4,219	4,101	4,115	4,159	4,445
Professional, scientific, and technical services	9,665	10,064	9,432	9,300	9,236	9,303	9,344
Management of companies and enterprises	845	801	773	857	865	956	1,032
Administrative and waste services	8,143	8,070	7,380	7,332	7,920	7,916	7,920
Educational services	1,748	1,876	1,984	2,101	2,077	2,032	2,114
Health care and social assistance	21,527	22,663	23,587	23,903	24,147	24,184	24,366
Arts, entertainment, and recreation	2,914	2,896	2,798	2,786	2,835	2,857	2,937
Accommodation and food services	30,822	31,931	30,425	30,194	30,561	31,254	31,877
Other services, except public administration	12,555	12,547	12,278	11,915	12,293	11,622	11,514
Government and government enterprises	70,206	71,507	73,907	74,993	74,960	75,564	75,737
	Dollars						
Average Wages and Salaries by Industry	39,985	42,235	41,416	42,587	44,033	45,260	45,751
Average Farm Wages and Salaries	39,030	35,704	42,300	35,817	33,215	27,419	39,899
Average Nonfarm Wages and Salaries	39,995	42,300	41,407	42,655	44,152	45,461	45,818
Average private wages and salaries	40,089	42,439	40,933	42,410	44,204	45,846	46,274
Forestry, fishing, and related activities	21,202	21,499	21,665	22,879	24,353	24,779	25,020
Mining	72,663	76,850	74,342	77,821	80,948	83,511	85,612
Utilities	74,752	76,946	78,796	81,400	84,114	84,567	85,677
Construction	45,291	48,963	46,153	48,298	48,334	50,202	51,190
Manufacturing	46,838	50,023	51,068	52,997	56,101	57,356	58,893
Durable goods manufacturing	41,328	44,921	45,518	47,135	48,502	50,248	50,855
Nondurable goods manufacturing	53,203	55,613	56,682	58,601	63,781	64,627	66,823
Wholesale trade	51,537	55,730	53,876	55,449	57,451	59,062	59,328
Retail trade	24,869	25,637	25,446	25,975	26,736	28,082	27,832
Transportation and warehousing	51,049	53,998	51,566	53,696	56,461	56,305	58,138
Information	37,512	38,495	38,927	39,983	41,812	43,207	44,140
Finance and insurance	47,357	50,883	47,880	49,398	50,982	54,158	55,239
Real estate and rental and leasing	38,507	38,304	36,601	38,757	42,987	45,412	46,571
Professional, scientific, and technical services	48,754	51,820	52,648	53,936	55,925	58,844	59,361
Management of companies and enterprises	93,140	99,074	95,708	103,743	105,391	114,687	113,459
Administrative and waste services	28,132	30,079	29,254	29,052	32,177	32,015	31,878
Educational services	26,368	26,960	27,387	27,683	28,898	29,673	29,246
Health care and social assistance	36,250	38,401	38,435	39,328	40,364	41,861	41,587
Arts, entertainment, and recreation	21,272	20,696	21,594	21,526	21,483	21,325	21,905
Accommodation and food services	18,824	18,401	17,977	18,517	19,058	19,830	20,421
Other services, except public administration	27,452	28,269	28,212	30,297	30,209	32,779	33,344
Government and government enterprises	39,692	41,846	42,811	43,354	44,001	44,345	44,494

Table WY-10. Employment Characteristics by Family Type

(Number, percent.)

Family type and labor force status	2011		2012		2013	
	Total	Families with own children under 18 years	Total	Families with own children under 18 years	Total	Families with own children under 18 years
All Families.................................	142,618	60,196	146,745	63,649	148,556	64,587
FAMILY TYPE AND LABOR FORCE STATUS						
Married-Couple Families...................	114,463	41,491	115,398	43,849	118,017	45,915
Both husband and wife in labor force	56.2	67.9	55.7	67.2	57.6	70.9
Husband in labor force, wife not in labor force	22.0	27.4	22.0	30.0	19.8	25.6
Wife in labor force, husband not in labor force	6.7	3.5	6.9	2.1	7.1	1.9
Both husband and wife not in labor force	15.2	1.2	15.4	0.8	14.9	1.3
Other Families	28,155	18,705	31,347	19,800	30,539	18,672
Female householder, no husband present	69.1	69.3	67.2	66.7	66.3	70.4
In labor force........................	53.5	57.0	51.7	55.6	49.2	60.8
Not in labor force	15.6	12.2	15.5	11.0	17.1	9.7
Male householder, no wife present	30.9	30.7	32.8	33.3	33.7	29.6
In labor force........................	25.9	28.1	28.3	31.6	28.6	28.0
Not in labor force	5.0	2.6	4.5	1.7	5.1	1.5

Table WY-11. School Enrollment and Educational Attainment, 2013

(Number, percent.)

Item	State	U.S.
Enrollment		
Total population 3 years and over, enrolled in school	151,054	82,395,254
Enrolled in nursery school or preschool (percent)	6.7	6.0
Enrolled in kindergarten (percent).................................	5.4	5.2
Enrolled in elementary school, grades 1-8 (percent)............	41.6	40.0
Enrolled in high school, grades 9-12 (percent)	18.3	20.6
Enrolled in college or graduate school (percent).................	28.1	28.3
Attainment		
Total population 25 years and over	383,914	210,910,615
Less than ninth grade (percent)	1.5	5.8
9th to 12th grade, no diploma (percent)	5.0	7.6
High school graduate, including equivalency (percent)...........	28.4	27.8
Some college, no degree (percent)	27.8	21.1
Associate's degree (percent).......................................	10.7	8.1
Bachelor's degree (percent)..	17.8	18.4
Graduate or professional degree (percent)........................	8.8	11.2
High school graduate or higher (percent)	93.5	86.6
Bachelor's degree or higher (percent).............................	26.6	29.6

Table WY-12. Public School Characteristics and Educational Indicators

(Number, percent; data derived from National Center of Education Statistics.)

Item	State	U.S.
Public Schools, 2012–2013 (except where noted)		
Number of school districts...	60	18,093
Number of schools...	364	98,454
Number of students (in thousands)	92	49,771
Number of teachers (in thousands)	7	3,109
Student-teacher ratio	12.5	16.0
Expenditures per student (dollars), FY 2012......................	15,988	10,667
Four-year adjusted cohort graduation rate (ACGR)[1,2]	77.0	81.4
Students eligible for free or reduced-price lunch (in thousands)	35	25,188
English language learners (in thousands)	3	4,397
Students age 3 to 21 served under IDEA, part B (in thousands)	12	6,429

Public Schools by Type	Number	Percent of state public schools
Total number of schools..	364	100.0
Regular	337	92.6
Special education..	3	0.8
Vocational education...	0	-
Alternative education	24	6.6

NOTE: Every school is assigned only one school type based on its instructional emphasis.
[1]ACGR data represents a new method of calculating high-school completion rates and may not be comparable to previous years' data for Averaged Freshmen Graduation Rates (AFGR).
[2]The United States 4-year ACGRs were estimated using both the reported 4-year ACGR data from 49 states and the District of Columbia and using imputed data for Idaho. The estimate for American Indian/Alaska Native students also includes imputed data for Virginia.
- = Zero or rounds to zero.

Table WY-13. Reported Voting and Registration of the Voting-Age Population, November 2012

(Numbers in thousands, percent.)

Item	Total population	Total citizen population	Registered			Voted		
			Total registered	Percent registered (total population)	Percent registered (total citizen population)	Total voted	Percent voted (total population)	Percent voted (total citizen population)
U.S. Total	235,248	215,081	153,157	65.1	71.2	132,948	56.5	61.8
State Total	427	419	268	62.8	63.9	247	57.8	58.9
Sex								
Male	213	209	127	59.6	61.0	118	55.2	56.4
Female	213	211	141	65.9	66.7	129	60.4	61.2
Race								
White alone	403	396	259	64.2	65.3	240	59.4	60.4
White, non-Hispanic alone	373	372	249	66.8	67.0	232	62.1	62.3
Black alone	3	3	1	B	B	1	B	B
Asian alone	2	-	-	B	B	-	B	B
Hispanic (of any race)	32	27	10	B	B	8	B	B
White alone or in combination	409	402	262	64.1	65.2	243	59.4	60.4
Black alone or in combination..........	4	4	2	B	B	2	B	B
Asian alone or in combination..........	4	3	2	B	B	2	B	B
Age								
18 to 24 years	56	55	21	B	B	18	B	B
25 to 44 years	142	137	84	59.4	61.3	75	52.7	54.4
45 to 64 years	155	154	101	65.1	65.8	95	61.1	61.8
65 to 74 years	45	45	38	B	B	36	B	B
75 years and over	29	29	24	B	B	23	B	B

- = Zero or rounds to zero.
B = Base is less than 75,000 and therefore too small to show the derived measure.

Table WY-14. Crime

(Number, rate per 100,000. Data are derived from the FBI Uniform Crime Reports.)

Item	State			U.S.[1,2,3,4]		
	2012	2013	Percent change	2012	2013	Percent change
TOTAL POPULATION[5]	576,626	582,658	1.0	313,873,685	316,128,839	0.7
VIOLENT CRIME						
Number	1,161	1,152	-0.8	1,217,067	1,163,146	-4.4
Rate	201.3	197.7	-1.8	387.8	367.9	-5.1
Murder and Nonnegligent Manslaughter						
Number	14	17	21.4	14,866	14,196	-4.5
Rate	2.4	2.9	20.2	4.7	4.5	-5.2
Rape[6]						
Number	X	187	X	X	108,612	X
Rate	X	32.1	X	X	34.4	X
Robbery						
Number	61	75	23.0	355,051	345,031	-2.8
Rate	10.6	12.9	21.7	113.1	109.1	-3.5
Aggravated Assault						
Number	932	916	-1.7	762,009	724,149	-5.0
Rate	161.6	157.2	-2.7	242.8	229.1	-5.6
PROPERTY CRIME						
Number	13,222	12,809	-3.1	9,001,992	8,632,512	-4.1
Rate	2,293.0	2,198.4	-4.1	2,868.0	2,730.7	-4.8
Burglary						
Number	2,125	1,955	-8.0	2,109,932	1,928,465	-8.6
Rate	368.5	335.5	-9.0	672.2	610.0	-9.3
Larceny-Theft						
Number	10,513	10,276	-2.3	6,168,874	6,004,453	-2.7
Rate	1,823.2	1,763.6	-3.3	1,965.4	1,899.4	-3.4
Motor Vehicle Theft						
Number	584	578		723,186	699,594	-3.3
Rate	101.3	99.2	-2.1	230.4	221.3	-4.0

NOTE: Although arson data are included in the trend and clearance tables, sufficient data are not available to estimate totals for this offense. Therefore, no arson data are published in this table.
X = Not applicable.
- = Zero or rounds to zero.
[1]The crime figures have been adjusted.
[2]The data collection methodology for the offense of forcible rape used by the Minnesota state Uniform Crime Reporting (UCR) Program (with the exception of Minneapolis and St. Paul, Minnesota) does not comply with national UCR Program guidelines. Consequently, its figures for forcible rape and violent crime (of which forcible rape is a part) are not published in this table.
[3]Includes offenses reported by the Zoological Police and the Metro Transit Police.
[4]Because of changes in the state's reporting practices, figures are not comparable to previous years' data.
[5]Populations are U.S. Census Bureau provisional estimates as of July 1 of each year.
[6]The figures shown for the offense of rape were estimated using the revised Uniform Crime Reporting (UCR) definition of rape.

Table WY-15. State Government Finances, 2013

(Dollar amounts in thousands, percent distribution.)

Item	Dollars	Percent distribution
Total Revenue	45,891,806	100.0
General revenue	32,280,837	70.3
Intergovernmental revenue	9,228,907	20.1
Taxes	16,513,692	36.0
General sales	4,410,130	9.6
Selective sales	2,678,281	5.8
License taxes	1,026,823	2.2
Individual income tax	7,227,690	15.7
Corporate income tax	955,752	2.1
Other taxes	215,016	0.5
Current charges	4,011,774	8.7
Miscellaneous general revenue	2,526,464	5.5
Utility revenue	0	-
Liquor stores revenue	0	-
Insurance trust revenue[1]	13,610,969	29.7
Total Expenditure	37,524,804	100.0
Intergovernmental expenditure	9,637,247	25.7
Direct expenditure	27,887,557	74.3
Current operation	18,591,474	49.5
Capital outlay	2,086,899	5.6
Insurance benefits and repayments	5,637,912	15.0
Assistance and subsidies	641,349	1.7
Interest on debt	929,923	2.5
Exhibit: Salaries and wages	4,369,544	11.6
Total Expenditure	37,524,804	100.0
General expenditure	31,878,459	85.0
Intergovernmental expenditure	9,637,247	25.7
Direct expenditure	22,241,212	59.3
General expenditure, by function:		
Education	10,877,543	29.0
Public welfare	8,849,077	23.6
Hospitals	1,422,217	3.8
Health	771,081	2.1
Highways	2,409,285	6.4
Police protection	122,600	0.3
Correction	1,090,920	2.9
Natural resources	664,438	1.8
Parks and recreation	28,419	0.1
Governmental administration	717,793	1.9
Interest on general debt	929,923	2.5
Other and unallocable	3,995,163	10.6
Utility expenditure	8,433	-
Liquor stores expenditure	0	-
Insurance trust expenditure	5,637,912	15.0
Debt at End of Fiscal Year	23,187,772	X
Cash and Security Holdings	87,570,671	X

X = Not applicable.

- = Zero or rounds to zero.

[1]Within insurance trust revenue, net earnings of state retirement systems is a calculated statistic (the item code in the data file is X08), and thus can be positive or negative. Net earnings is the sum of earnings on investments plus gains on investments minus losses on investments. The change made in 2002 for asset valuation from book to market value in accordance with Statement 34 of the Governmental Accounting Standards Board is reflected in the calculated statistics.

Table WY-16. State Government Tax Collections, 2014

(Dollars in thousands, percent.)

Item	Dollars	Percent distribution
Total Taxes	2,263,387	100.0
Property taxes	300,096	13.3
Sales and gross receipts	925,757	40.9
General sales and gross receipts	765,543	33.8
Selective sales and gross receipts	160,214	7.1
Alcoholic beverages	1,828	0.1
Amusements	0	-
Insurance premiums	25,310	1.1
Motor fuels	100,889	4.5
Pari-mutuels	385	-
Public utilities	4,638	0.2
Tobacco products	24,490	1.1
Other selective sales	2,674	0.1
Licenses	148,092	6.5
Alcoholic beverages	0	-
Amusements	0	-
Corporations in general	13,378	0.6
Hunting and fishing	34,371	1.5
Motor vehicle	71,954	3.2
Motor vehicle operators	2,217	0.1
Public utilities	0	-
Occupation and business, NEC	26,172	1.2
Other licenses	0	-
Income taxes	0	-
Individual income	X	X
Corporation net income	X	X
Other taxes	889,442	39.3
Death and gift	0	-
Documentary and stock transfer	0	-
Severance	883,025	39.0
Taxes, NEC	6,417	0.3

X = Not applicable.
- = Zero or rounds to zero.

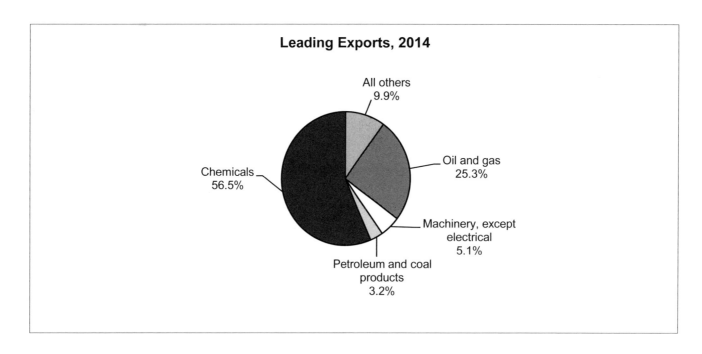

Leading Exports, 2014

All others 9.9%
Oil and gas 25.3%
Machinery, except electrical 5.1%
Petroleum and coal products 3.2%
Chemicals 56.5%

NOTES AND DEFINITIONS

The state chapters in this book follow a standard plan of organization, and the same data sources are used for the tables and figures found in each chapter. These notes describe the standard data sources, which are presented by topic in the order in which they appear in each chapter. Definitions, brief descriptions of methodology, and sources of additional information are also provided.

Symbols used are included in the footnotes of the tables.

Table 1.
Source: U.S. Department of Commerce. U.S Census Bureau. 2000 and 2010 Decennial Census. Census statistics, 2014.
<http://factfinder.census.gov/>.

Population estimates data are accessed through American FactFinder from the U.S. Census Bureau, as well as from the Census Bureau itself. The data for average annual percent change, 2010–2014, were calculated by the editor.

Population estimates and the decennial census. Population data are estimates produced by the Census Bureau. The Bureau's Population Estimates Program (PEP) produces estimates of the population as of July 1 for each year following the most recently published decennial census (the actual physical count of the population made every ten years, which is described below). Existing data on births, deaths, and domestic and international immigration are used to update the decennial census base. PEP estimates are used to set federal funding allocations, update national surveys, and monitor recent demographic changes.

Noncitizens residing in the United States are included, regardless of their immigration status.

Persons temporarily away from their usual residence on Census Day (April 1), for reasons such as vacation or business trips, were counted as being at their usual residence. People who live at more than one residence during the week, month, or year were counted as being at the place in which they lived most of the year. However, people without a usual residence were counted as being where they were staying on Census Day.

Age, sex, race, and ethnicity. While estimates of the age and sex of the population are straightforward, estimates of race and ethnicity are not. Decennial census data on race and ethnicity are based on self-identification by the

respondent, and the same respondent may answer differently on separate occasions. On the 2000 decennial census, respondents could report more than one race; in previous censuses, respondents had to identify themselves as belonging to only one race.

The Census Bureau treats Hispanic or Latino origin as a separate and distinct concept from race. Beginning with the 2000 census, a separate self-identification question was asked regarding Hispanic or Latino origin. Persons of Hispanic or Latino origin are those who classified themselves as belonging to one of the specific categories listed on the questionnaire—Mexican, Puerto Rican, Cuban, or Other Spanish/Hispanic origin (including those whose origins are from Spain, the Spanish-speaking countries of Central and South America, or the Dominican Republic). People who are Hispanic may be of any race, and people in each race group may be Hispanic. The overlap of race and Hispanic origin is a major comparability issue, because Hispanics may be of any race. For a further discussion of this issue, see: U.S. Census Bureau. *U.S. Census Bureau Guidance on the Presentation and Comparison of Race and Hispanic Origin Data.* (June 12, 2003.) <http://www.census.gov/population/www/socdemo/compraceho.html>.

Table 2.
Source: U.S. Department of Commerce. U.S Census Bureau. 2000 Decennial Census. American Community Survey, 2000, 2010, and 2013.
<http://factfinder.census.gov/>.

Data on marital status was tabulated for persons 15 years and over. Marital status was reported for each person as either "now married," "widowed," "divorced," "separated," or "never married." Individuals who were living together (unmarried people, people in commonlaw marriages) reported the marital status which they considered most appropriate.

Now Married, Except Separated. Includes people whose current marriage has not ended through widowhood, divorce, or separation (regardless of previous marital history). The category may also include couples who live together or people in common-law marriages if they consider this category the most appropriate. In certain tabulations, currently married people are further classified as "spouse present" or "spouse absent."

Separated. Refers to people who were not living with their spouse due to marital discord.

Divorced. Indicates people who reported being divorced and had not remarried.

Widowed. Refers to people whose last marriage ended with the death of their spouse and who had not remarried.

Never married. The term applies to those who had never been legally married or people whose only marriage ended in an annulment.

Table 3.
Source: U.S. Department of Commerce. U.S Census Bureau. 2000 Decennial Census. American Community Survey, 2000, 2010, and 2013.
<http://factfinder.census.gov/>.

The annual data were obtained from the Census Bureau. The data for average annual percent change, 2000–2013, were calculated by the editor.

Households. A household comprises one or more persons occupying a single housing unit, such as a house, apartment, or a room occupied as separate living quarters. A household may consist of a person living alone, a single family, two or more families living together, or any other group of unrelated individuals sharing a housing unit.

Householder. The person, or one of the people, in whose name the home is owned, being bought, or rented. If there is no such person present, any household member 15 years old and over can serve as the householder for the purposes of the census.

Two types of householders are distinguished: a family householder and a nonfamily householder. A family householder is a householder living with one or more people related to him or her by birth, marriage, or adoption. The householder and all people in the household related to him are family members. A nonfamily householder is a householder living alone or with nonrelatives only.

Housing unit. A house, an apartment, a mobile home or trailer, a group of rooms, or a single room occupied as separate living quarters, or if vacant, intended for occupancy as separate living quarters.

Median gross rent. The monthly amount of contract rent plus the estimated average monthly cost of utilities (electricity, gas, water, and sewer) and fuels (oil, coal, kerosene, wood, etc.).

Median monthly owner costs for housing units with a mortgage. The sum of payments for mortgages, deeds of trust, contracts to purchase, or similar debts on the property (including payments for the first mortgage, second mortgages, home equity loans, and other junior mortgages); real estate taxes; fire, hazard, and flood insurance on the property; utilities (electricity, gas, water, and sewer); and fuels (oil, coal, kerosene, wood, etc.). It also includes, where appropriate, the monthly condominium fee for condominiums and mobile home costs (installment loan payments, personal property taxes, site rent, registration fees, and license fees). Selected monthly owner costs were tabulated for all owner-occupied units, and usually are shown separately for units "with a mortgage" and for units "not mortgaged."

Median value of owner-occupied housing units. Data for the median value of owner-occupied housing units are respondents' estimates of how much their property would sell for if it was currently on the market.

Table 4.
Source: U.S. Department of Commerce. U.S Census Bureau. American Community Survey, 2012 and 2013.
<http://factfinder.census.gov/>.

The annual data derives from Census estimates. The data for percent change were calculated by the editor.

Residence 1 year ago. The data on residence 1 year ago were derived from answers to Question 15, which were asked of the population 1 year and older. For the American Community Survey, people who had moved from another residence in the United States or Puerto Rico 1 year earlier were asked to report the exact address (number and street name); the name of the city, town, or post office; the name of the U.S. county; and the ZIP Code where they lived 1 year ago. People living outside the United States and Puerto Rico were asked to report the name of the foreign country or U.S. Island Area where they were living 1 year ago.

Native born. The native population includes anyone who was a U.S. citizen or a U.S. national at birth. This includes respondents who indicated they were born in the United States, Puerto Rico, a U.S. Island Area (such as Guam), or abroad of an American (U.S. citizen) parent or parents.

Foreign born. The foreign-born population includes anyone who was not a U.S. citizen or a U.S. national at birth. This includes respondents who indicated they were a U.S. citizen by naturalization or not a U.S. citizen.

Respondent's ability to speak English. Respondents who reported speaking a language other than English were asked to indicate their English-speaking ability based on one of the following categories: "Very well," "Well," "Not well," or "Not at all." Those who answered "Well," "Not well," or "Not at all" are sometimes referred as "Less than 'very well.'" Respondents were not instructed on how to interpret the response categories in this question. Households in which no one 14 and over speaks English only or speaks a language other than English at home and speaks English less than "very well" identifies households that may need English language assistance. This arises when no one 14 and over meets either of two conditions: (1) they speak English at home or (2) even though they speak another language, they also report that they speak English "very well."

Table 5.
Source: U.S. Department of Commerce. U.S. Census Bureau. American Community Survey.
<http://factfinder.census.gov/>.

Median household income. Includes the income of the householder and all other individuals 15 years old and over in the household, whether they are related to the householder or not. Because many households consist of only one person, average household income is usually less than average family income. Total income is the sum of the amounts reported separately for wage or salary income; net self-employment income; interest, dividends, or net rental or royalty income or income from estates and trusts; Social Security or railroad retirement income; Supplemental Security Income (SSI); public assistance or welfare payments; retirement, survivor, or disability pensions; and all other income. Receipts from the following sources are not included as income: capital gains, money received from the sale of property (unless the recipient was engaged in the business of selling such property); the value of income "in kind" from food stamps, public housing subsidies, medical care, employer contributions for individuals, etc.; withdrawal of bank deposits; money borrowed; tax refunds; exchange of money between relatives living in the same household; gifts; and lump-sum inheritances, insurance payments, and other types of lump-sum receipts.

Median family income. The incomes of all members 15 years old and over related to the householder are summed and treated as a single amount.

Poverty. Following the Office of Management and Budget standards that have been in use since the late 1960s, the Census Bureau uses a set of money income thresholds that vary by family size and composition to determine the proportion of Americans in poverty. If a household's total income is less than the threshold for the applicable family size, age of householder, and number of children present in the family under 18 years of age, every individual in that household is considered to be living in poverty.

Table 6.
Source: U.S. Department of Commerce. U.S. Census Bureau. American Community Survey.
<http://factfinder.census.gov/>.

The data on health insurance coverage were derived from answers to Question 16 in the American Community Survey (ACS), which was asked of all respondents. Respondents were instructed to report their current coverage and to mark "yes" or "no" for each of the eight types of private and public insurance listed. Health insurance coverage in the ACS and other Census Bureau surveys define coverage to include plans and programs that provide comprehensive health coverage. Plans that provide insurance for specific conditions or situations such as cancer and long-term care policies are not considered coverage. Likewise, other types of insurance like dental, vision, life, and disability insurance are not considered health insurance coverage.

Private health insurance. Coverage through an employer or union, a plan purchased by an individual from a private company, or TRICARE or other military health care.

Public health insurance. Coverage includes the federal programs Medicare, Medicaid, and VA Health Care (provided through the Department of Veterans Affairs); the Children's Health Insurance Program (CHIP); and individual state health plans.

Table 7.
Source: U.S. Department of Labor. Bureau of Labor Statistics. Current Population Survey.
<http://www.bls.gov/cps/>.

Annual data on the labor force, employment, and unemployment for state and local areas are available from two major sources: the Current Population Survey (CPS) and the Local Area Unemployment Statistics (LAUS) program. In Table 7, the data are obtained from the CPS. The CPS is a monthly survey of approximately 60,000 households conducted by the Census Bureau for the Bureau of Labor Statistics. It provides comprehensive data on topics such as the labor force, employment, unemployment, and persons not in the labor force.

Civilian noninstitutional population included are persons 16 years of age and older residing in the 50 states and the District of Columbia who are not inmates of institutions (for example, penal and mental facilities, homes for the aged), and who are not on active duty in the Armed Forces.

Civilian labor force includes all persons classified as employed or unemployed who are not inmates of institutions (for example, penal and mental facilities, homes for the aged), and who are not on active duty in the Armed Forces. Civilians 16 years of age and over in the noninstitutional population who are not classified as employed or unemployed are defined as not in the labor force.

Employment includes persons 16 years and over in the civilian noninstitutional population who, during the reference week, (a) did any work at all (at least 1 hour) as paid employees; worked in their own business, profession, or on their own farm, or worked 15 hours or more as unpaid workers in an enterprise operated by a member of the family; and (b) all those who were not working but who had jobs or businesses from which they were temporarily absent because of vacation, illness, bad weather, childcare problems, maternity or paternity leave, labor-management dispute, job training, or other family or personal reasons, whether or not they were paid for the time off or were seeking other jobs.

Unemployed persons. All civilians who were not employed (according to the above definition) during the reference week, but who were available for work—except for temporary illness—and who had made specific efforts to find employment sometime during the previous four weeks. Persons who did not look for work because they were on layoff are also counted as unemployed.

Unemployment rate. The number of unemployed as a percentage of the civilian labor force.

Table 8.
Source: U.S. Department of Labor. Bureau of Labor Statistics. Local Area Unemployment Statistics.
<http://www.bls.gov/lau/home.htm>.

The Local Area Unemployment Statistics (LAUS) program is a Federal-State cooperative effort in which monthly estimates of total employment and unemployment are prepared for approximately 7,300 areas.

The concepts and definitions underlying LAUS data come from the Current Population Survey (CPS), the household survey that is the official measure of the labor force for the nation. State monthly model estimates are controlled in "real time" to sum to national monthly labor force estimates from the CPS. These models combine current and historical data from the CPS, the Current Employment Statistics (CES) program, and state unemployment insurance (UI) systems. Estimates for seven large areas and their respective balances of state are also model-based. Estimates for the remainder of the substate labor market areas are produced through a building-block approach

known as the "Handbook method." This procedure also uses data from several sources, including the CPS, the CES program, state UI systems, and the decennial census, to create estimates that are adjusted to the statewide measures of employment and unemployment. Below the labor market area level, estimates are prepared using disaggregation techniques based on inputs from the decennial census, annual population estimates, and current UI data.

Table 9.
Source: U.S. Department of Commerce. Bureau of Economic Analysis.
<http://www.bea.gov/regional>.

In this table, the data by industry reflect the North American Industry Classification System (NAICS), a supply- or production-based system that replaced the Standard Industrial Classification (SIC) system in January 2003. Estimates of state employment and earnings by industry use NAICS. NAICS was adopted to more fully reflect the current composition of U.S. businesses and to establish a standard measure of industry classification throughout the United States, Canada, and Mexico, in accordance with the North American Free Trade Agreement, to enhance cross-border comparisons among these trading partners.

Wage and salary employment, also referred to as wage and salary jobs, measures the average annual number of full-time and part-time jobs in each area by place-of-work. All jobs for which wages and salaries are paid are counted. Full-time and part-time jobs are counted with equal weight. Jury and witness service, as well as paid employment of prisoners, are not counted as wage and salary employment; the payments for these activities are classified as "other labor income" in the personal income measure. Corporate directorships are counted as self-employment. This concept of employment differs from that in the Current Population Survey (CPS), which is the source of the employment data in the table on population and labor force. The CPS is a household survey. It counts each individual only once, no matter how many jobs the person holds, and it includes only civilian employment.

Wages and salaries consist of the monetary remuneration of employees, including corporate officer salaries and bonuses, commissions, pay-in-kind, incentive payments, and tips. It reflects the amount of payments disbursed, but not necessarily earned during the year. Wage and salary disbursements are measured before deductions, such as social security contributions and union dues. In recent years, stock options have become a point of discussion. Wage and salary disbursements include stock options of nonqualified plans at the time that they have been exercised by the individual. Stock options are reported in wage and salary disbursements. The value that is included in wages is the difference between the exercise price and the price that the stock options were granted. Average annual wages and salaries were calculated by the editor by dividing total wages and salaries paid during the year in each sector by total wage and salary employment in that sector.

Table 10.
Source: U.S. Department of Commerce. U.S. Census Bureau. American Community Survey, 2011, 2012, 2013.
<http://factfinder.census.gov/>.

Civilian labor force. (See definition under Table 7.)

Employment. (See definition under Table 7.)

Family. A family consists of a householder and one or more other people living in the same household who are related to the householder by birth, marriage, or adoption. All people in a household who are related to the householder are regarded as members of his or her family. A family household may contain people not related to the householder, but those people are not included as part of the householder's family in tabulations. Thus, the number of family households is equal to the number of families, but family households may include more members than do families. A household can contain only one family for purposes of tabulations. Not all households contain families since a household may be comprised of a group of unrelated people or of one person living alone – these are called nonfamily households. Families are classified by type as either a "married-couple family" or "other family" according to the sex of the householder and the presence of relatives. The data on family type are based on answers to questions on sex and relationship that were asked of all people.

Married-couple family. A family in which the householder and his or her spouse are listed as members of the same household.

Other family:

Male householder, no wife present. A family with a male householder and no spouse of householder present.

Female householder, no husband present. A family with a female householder and no spouse of householder present.

Table 11.
Source: U.S. Department of Commerce. U.S. Census Bureau. American Community Survey, 2013.
<http://www.census.gov/programs-surveys/acs.html>.

Data on school enrollment and educational attainment were derived from a sample of the population. Persons were classified as enrolled in school if they reported attending a "regular" public or private school (or college) during the year. The instructions were to "include only nursery school, kindergarten, elementary school, and schooling which would lead to a high school diploma or a college degree" as regular school. The Census Bureau defines a public school as "any school or college controlled and supported by a local, county, state, or federal government." Schools primarily supported and controlled by religious organizations or other private groups are defined as private schools.

Data on educational attainment are tabulated for the population 25 years old and over. The data were derived from a question that asked respondents for the highest level of school completed or the highest degree received. Persons who had passed a high school equivalency examination were considered high school graduates. Schooling received in foreign schools was to be reported as the equivalent grade or years in the regular American school system.

Vocational and technical training, such as barber school training; business, trade, technical, and vocational schools; or other training for a specific trade are specifically excluded.

High school graduate or more. This category includes persons whose highest degree was a high school diploma or its equivalent, and those who reported any level higher than a high school diploma.

Bachelor's degree or more. This category includes persons who have received bachelor's degrees, master's degrees, professional school degrees (such as law school or medical school degrees), and doctoral degrees.

Graduate degree or more. This category includes persons who have a master's degree, including the traditional MA and MS degrees and field-specific degrees, such as MSW, MEd, MBA, MLS, and MEng., or a professional school degree: medicine, dentistry, chiropractic, optometry, osteopathic medicine, pharmacy, podiatry, veterinary medicine, law, and theology.

Table 12.
Source: U.S. Department of Education, National Center for Education Statistics. *Common Core of Data.*
<http://nces.ed.gov/ccd/>.

The data are from the Common Core of Data (CCD), which is made up of a set of five surveys sent to state education departments. Most of the data are obtained from administrative records maintained by the state education agencies (SEAs). Statistical information is collected annually from approximately 100,000 public elementary and secondary schools and approximately 18,000 public school districts (including supervisory unions and regional education service agencies) in the 50 states, the District of Columbia, Department of Defense Schools, and the outlying areas. The SEAs compile CCD requested data into prescribed formats and transmit the information to NCES.

A **school district** or Local Education Agency (LEA) is the agency at the local level whose primary responsibility is to operate public schools or to contract for public school services.

The primary grades include pre-kindergarten through grade 4. Middle school grades included grades 5 through 8. High school grades include grades 9 through 12. Ungraded students are included in the total but are not separately listed. Some states have no ungraded students.

The **student-teacher ratio** is calculated by dividing the number of students in all schools by the number of full-time equivalent teachers employed by all schools and agencies.

Current expenditures per student are derived by dividing total current expenditures by the fall student membership count from the CCD. Current expenditures are comprised of expenditures for the day-to-day operation of schools and school districts for public elementary and secondary education, including expenditures for staff salaries and benefits, supplies, and purchased services. They exclude expenditures for construction, equipment, property, debt services, and programs outside of public elementary and secondary education, such as adult education and community services. Student membership consists of the count of students enrolled on or about October 1 and is comparable across all states. Data are for FY 2012; please see the NCES Web site for the exact beginning and ending dates of fiscal years for each state.

The 4-year adjusted cohort graduation rate (ACGR) is the number of students who graduate in 4 years with a regular high school diploma divided by the number of students who form the adjusted cohort for the graduating class. From the beginning of 9th grade (or the earliest high school grade), students who are entering that grade for the first time form a cohort that is "adjusted" by adding any students who subsequently transfer into the cohort and subtracting any students who subsequently transfer out, emigrate to another country, or die.

Students are eligible for **free and reduced-price lunch** under the National School Lunch Program, which was established by President Truman in 1946. The program is a federally assisted meal program operated in public and private nonprofit schools and residential child care centers and provides cash subsidies for free or reduced-price meals to students based on family size and income criteria. Participation in the National School Lunch Program depends on income, and eligibility is often used to estimate student needs.

An **English language learner** is an individual who, due to any of the reasons listed below, has enough difficulty speaking, reading, writing, or understanding the English language that it affects their ability to learn in an English-speaking classroom. Such an individual (1) was not born in the United States or has a native language other than English; (2) comes from environments where a language other than English is dominant; or (3) is an American Indian or Alaska Native and comes from environments where a language other than English has had a significant impact on the individual's level of English language proficiency.

Individuals with Disabilities Education Act (IDEA) is a federal law requiring services to children with disabilities throughout the nation. IDEA governs how states and public agencies provide early intervention, special education, and related services to eligible infants, toddlers, children, and youth with disabilities. Infants and toddlers with disabilities (birth–age 2) and their families receive early intervention services under IDEA, Part C. Children and youth (ages 3–21) receive special education and related services under IDEA, Part B.

Public School Types

A **regular school** provides instruction and education services that do not focus primarily on special education, vocational/technical education, or alternative education, or on any of the particular themes associated with magnet/special program emphasis schools.

A **special education school** focuses primarily on special education—including instruction for students with any of the following conditions: autism, deaf-blindness, developmental delay, hearing impairment, mental retardation, multiple disabilities, orthopedic impairment, serious emotional disturbance, specific learning disability, speech or language impairment, traumatic brain injury, visual impairment, and other health impairments—and that adapts curriculum, materials, or instruction for students served.

A **vocational education school** focuses primarily on providing formal preparation for semiskilled, skilled, technical, or professional occupations for high school-age students who have opted to develop or expand their employment opportunities, often in lieu of preparing for college entry.

An **alternative education school** is an elementary/secondary school that (1) addresses needs of students that typically cannot be met in a regular school, (2) provides nontraditional education, (3) serves as an adjunct to a regular school, or (4) falls outside the categories of regular, special education, or vocational education.

Table 13.
Source: U.S. Department of Commerce. U.S. Census Bureau. November Supplement to the Current Population Survey (CPS). *Voting and Registration in the Election of November 2012.*
<http://www.census.gov/hhes/www/socdemo/voting/publications/p20/2012/tables.html>

Voter participation data are obtained from additional questions regarding voting and voter registration, which are added to the Current Population Survey each November. Because these data are from a sample of the noninstitutional population, they differ from the "official" tally of voter participation reported by the Clerk of the U.S. House of Representatives.

Voting, people eligible to register. The population of voting age includes a considerable number of people who meet the age requirement but cannot register and vote. People who are not citizens are not eligible to vote. Among citizens of voting age, some people are not permitted to vote because they have been committed to penal institutions, mental hospitals, or other institutions, or because they fail to meet state and local resident requirements for various reasons. The eligibility to register is governed by state laws, which differ in many respects.

Registration is the act of qualifying to vote by formally enrolling on a list of voters. People who have moved to another election district must take steps to have their names placed on the voting rolls in their new place of residence.

In a few states or parts of states, no formal registration is required. Voters merely present themselves at the polling place on Election Day with proof that they are of age and have met the appropriate residence requirements. Therefore, in these areas people who are citizens and of voting age, and who meet the residence requirement, would be considered as being registered.

Voter, reported participation. Voter participation data are derived from replies to the following question asked of people (excluding noncitizens) of voting age: "In any election some people are not able to vote because they are sick or busy, or have some other reason, and others do not want to vote. Did (this person) vote in the election held on November (date varies)?"

Those of voting age were classified as "voted" or "did not vote." In most tables, this "did not vote" class includes those reported as "did not vote," "do not know," noncitizens, and nonrespondents. Nonrespondents and people who reported that they did not know if they voted were included in the "did not vote" class because of the general over-reporting by respondents in the sample.

Voter, reported registration. The data on registration were obtained by tabulating replies to the following question for those people included in the category "did not vote." "Was (this person) registered to vote in the November (date varies) election?"

All people reported as having voted were assumed to have been registered. Therefore, the total registered population is obtained by combining the number of people who voted and people included in the category "did not vote," but who had registered.

Table 14.
Source: U.S. Department of Justice. Federal Bureau of Investigation. Uniform Crime Reports. *Crime in the United States, 2013.*
<https://www.fbi.gov/about-us/cjis/ucr/crime-in-the-u.s/2013/crime-in-the-u.s.-2013>

The Uniform Crime Reports (UCR) Program, administered by the Federal Bureau of Investigation (FBI), was created in 1929 and collects information on the following crimes reported to law enforcement authorities: murder and nonnegligent manslaughter, rape, robbery, aggravated assault, burglary, larceny-theft, motor vehicle theft, and arson. Law enforcement agencies also report arrest data for 21 additional crime categories.

The UCR Program compiles data from monthly law enforcement reports and from individual crime incident records transmitted directly to the FBI or to centralized state agencies that report to the FBI. The program thoroughly examines each report it receives for reasonableness, accuracy, and deviations that may indicate errors. Large variations in crime levels may indicate modified records procedures, incomplete reporting, or changes in a jurisdiction's boundaries. To identify any unusual fluctuations in an agency's crime counts, the program compares monthly reports to previous submissions of the agency and to those for similar agencies.

The FBI annually publishes its findings in a preliminary release in the spring of the following calendar year, followed by a detailed annual report, *Crime in the United States*, issued in the fall. (The printed copy of *Crime in the United States* is published by Bernan Press.) In addition to crime counts and trends, this report includes data on crimes cleared, persons arrested (age, sex, and race), law enforcement personnel (including the number of sworn officers killed or assaulted), and the characteristics of homicides (including age, sex, and race of victims and offenders; victim-offender relationships; weapons used; and circumstances surrounding the homicides). Other periodic reports are also available from the UCR Program. Any deviations from UCR standard data are noted in the table.

Note for Users

Since crime is a sociological phenomenon influenced by a variety of factors, the FBI discourages data users from ranking agencies and using the data as a measurement of the effectiveness of law enforcement. Until data users examine all the variables that affect crime in a town, city, county, state, region, or college or university, they can make no meaningful comparisons.

Violent crime is composed of four offenses: murder and nonnegligent manslaughter, rape, robbery, and aggravated assault. According to the UCR Program's definition, violent crimes involve force or threat of force.

Murder and nonnegligent manslaughter is the willful (nonnegligent) killing of one human being by another. Deaths caused by negligence, attempts to kill, assaults to kill, suicides, and accidental deaths are excluded. The program classifies justifiable homicides separately and limits the definition to (1) the killing of a felon by a law enforcement officer in the line of duty; or (2) the killing of a felon, during the commission of a felony, by a private citizen.

Rape is defined as: penetration, no matter how slight, of the vagina or anus with any body part or object, or oral penetration by a sex organ of another person, without the consent of the victim. The FBI UCR Program's definition of rape, formerly "forcible rape," was revised in 2013. Attempts or assaults to commit rape are also included; however, statutory rape (no force used—victim is under the age of consent) and incest are excluded. Due to the revised definition, figures for rape in 2013 are not comparable to data from previous years. For comparison, see the FBI's report *Crime in the United States, 2013* for 2013 estimates using the legacy definition of forcible rape.

Robbery is the taking or attempted taking of anything of value from the care, custody, or control of a person or persons by force or threat of force or violence and/or by putting the victim in fear.

Aggravated assault is an unlawful attack by one person upon another for the purpose of inflicting severe or aggravated bodily injury. This type of assault usually is accompanied by the use of a weapon or by means likely to produce death or great bodily harm. Attempted aggravated assaults that involve the display of—or threat to use—a gun, knife, or other weapon is included in this crime category because serious personal injury would likely result if the assault were completed. When aggravated assault and larceny-theft occur together, the offense falls under the category of robbery. Simple assaults are excluded.

Property crime includes the offenses of burglary, larceny-theft, motor vehicle theft, and arson. The object of the theft-type offenses is the taking of money or property, but there is no force or threat of force against the victims. The property crime category includes arson because the offense involves the destruction of property; however, arson victims may be subjected to force.

Burglary (breaking or entering) is the unlawful entry of a structure to commit a felony or a theft. The use of force to gain entry need not have occurred. The Program has three subclassifications for burglary: forcible entry, unlawful entry where no force is used, and attempted forcible entry. The UCR definition of "structure" includes, for example, apartment, barn, house trailer or houseboat when used as a permanent dwelling, office, railroad car (but not automobile), stable, and vessel (i.e., ship).

Larceny-theft (except motor vehicle theft) is the unlawful taking, carrying, leading, or riding away of property from the possession or constructive possession of another. Examples are thefts of bicycles or automobile accessories, shoplifting, pocket-picking, or the stealing of any property or article that is not taken by force and violence or by fraud. Attempted larcenies are included. Embezzlement, confidence games, forgery, worthless checks, and the like, are excluded.

Motor vehicle theft is the theft or attempted theft of a motor vehicle. It includes the stealing of automobiles, trucks, buses, motorcycles, snowmobiles, and the like. The taking of a motor vehicle for temporary use by persons having lawful access is excluded from this definition. A motor vehicle is self-propelled and runs on land surface and not on rails. Motorboats, construction equipment, airplanes, and farming equipment are specifically excluded from this category.

Table 15.
Source: U.S. Department of Commerce. U.S Census Bureau.
<http://www.census.gov/govs/index.html>.

The Census Bureau conducts an annual survey covering a range of government finance activities carried out by all state and local governments in the United States, including revenue, expenditures, debt, and assets. The data in this volume relate to state revenues and expenditures only, with the exception of the District of Columbia, for which local government data was used. Data generally reference state government fiscal year 2013, but data for the District of Columbia is for fiscal year 2012. General revenue comprises all revenue except utilities, liquor store, and insurance trust revenue. Intergovernmental revenue is funds from other governments (mainly the federal government), including general support, grants, shared taxes, and loans or advances. Other data on government finance by state, not shown in this volume, include federal government expenditures, obligations, contract awards, and insurance programs.

Table 16.
Source: U.S. Department of Commerce. U.S. Census Bureau.
<http://www.census.gov/govs/statetax/>.

State tax data include all required taxes taken by government for public purposes, except for employer and employee assessments for Social Security and unemployment compensation. The data are shown in this volume are generally for each state's fiscal year 2014. The Census Bureau does not provide detailed data for the District of Columbia, so there is no Table 16 for D.C.

PROPERTY CRIME
see **CRIME**

R
RACE, POPULATION BY

RANKINGS BY STATE